READING THE MIDDLE AGES

READING THE MIDDLE AGES

SOURCES FROM EUROPE, BYZANTIUM, AND THE ISLAMIC WORLD

EDITED BY BARBARA H. ROSENWEIN

University of Toronto Press

Previously published by Broadview Press © 2006 Barbara H. Rosenwein

Library and Archives Canada Cataloguing in Publication

Reading the Middle Ages : sources from Europe, Byzantium, and the Islamic world / edited by Barbara H. Rosenwein. Includes bibliographical references and index.

ISBN 978-155111-693-8

1. Middle Ages—Sources. 2. Europe—History—476–1492—Sources.
I. Rosenwein, Barbara H.

D113.R415   2006 940.1   C2006-901667-4

We welcome comments and suggestions regarding any aspect of our publications—please feel free to contact us at news@utphighereducation.com or visit our Internet site at www.utphighereducation.com.

North America   UK, Ireland, and continental Europe
5201 Dufferin Street   NBN International
North York, Ontario, Canada, M3H 5T8   Estover Road, Plymouth, PL6 7PY, UK
                                       ORDERS PHONE: 44 (0) 1752 202301
2250 Military Road   ORDERS FAX: 44 (0) 1752 202333
Tonawanda, New York, USA, 14150   ORDERS E-MAIL: enquiries@nbninternational.com

ORDERS PHONE: 1-800-565-9523
ORDERS FAX: 1-800-221-9985
ORDERS E-MAIL: utpbooks@utpress.utoronto.ca

TheUniversity of Toronto Press acknowledges the financial support for its publishing activities of the Government of Canada through the Book Publishing Industry Development Program (BPIDP).

Printed in Canada

To Jess and Frank

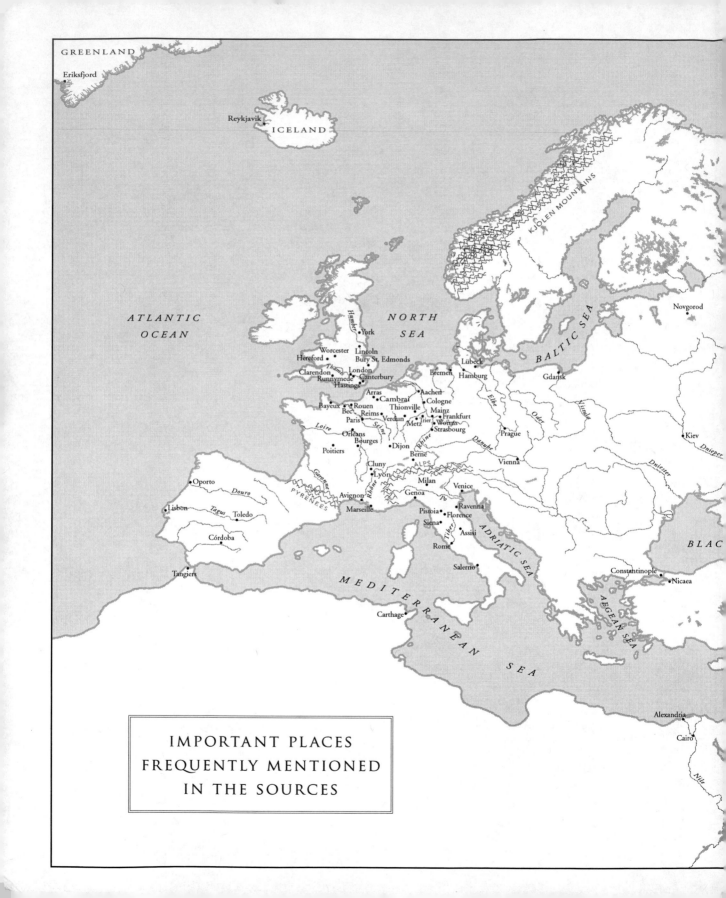

IMPORTANT PLACES
FREQUENTLY MENTIONED
IN THE SOURCES

YET RESEARCH CONTINUES, and it continues to be fruitful, because historians are not passive instruments, and because they read the same old documents with fresh eyes and with new questions in mind.

— Georges Duby, *History Continues*

CONTENTS

Chapter 2. The Emergence of Sibling Cultures (*c.*600-*c.*750)

Chapter 3: Creating New Identities (*c.*750-*c.*900)

Chapter 5: The Expansion of Europe (*c.*1050-*c.*1150)

Chapter 6: Institutionalizing Aspirations (*c*.1150–*c*.1250)

Chapter 7: Discordant Harmonies (*c.*1250-*c.*1350)

Chapter 8: Catastrophe and Creativity (*c.*1350-*c.*1500)

PREFACE

THE MAJOR DIFFERENCE BETWEEN *Reading the Middle Ages* and other medieval history source books is its systematic incorporation of Islamic and Byzantine materials alongside Western readings. The idea is for students and teachers continually to make comparisons and contrasts within and across cultures. I have sometimes provided questions that I hope will aid this process. Although this book may be used independently or alongside any textbook, it is particularly designed to complement *A Short History of the Middle Ages*. The chapters have the same titles and chronological scope; the readings here should help expand, deepen, sharpen, and modify the knowledge gained there.

The sources in *Reading the Middle Ages* are varied: records of sales, poems, histories, and even the tale of Sindbad the Sailor.[1] They are also of many different lengths. Some teachers may wish to assign all the readings in each chapter; others may wish to concentrate on only a few texts from each chapter. It is also possible to use the book thematically: an appendix at the back suggests one way in which sources might be grouped together for this purpose.

The introduction to the first text in this book includes a discussion of how to read a primary source. The same project is repeated in chapter 4, this time with a very different sort of document. It should become clear to users of this book that the sorts of questions one brings to all documents are initially the same, but the answers lead down very different paths that suggest their own new questions and approaches. Each reader's curiosity, personality, and interests become part of the process; this, even more than the discovery of hitherto unknown sources, is the foundation of new historical thought.

This is the place for me to acknowledge—with pleasure and enormous gratitude—the many debts that I have incurred in the preparation of this book. Paul Cobb was in many ways a collaborator in the choice of the Islamic readings, and Dionysios Stathakopoulos was a similarly indispensable consultant for the Byzantine materials. Robert Dankoff, Blake Dutton, Susan Einbinder, Theresa Gross-Diaz, Jacqueline Long, Michael McCormick, Piroska Nagy, Helen Nicholson, Anders Winroth, and Diana Wright provided specially prepared texts, maps, introductions, and/or captions. It has been a great pleasure to work with these patient and learned scholars.

---

1   To make the texts translated from the Greek and Arabic more accessible, I have left out the diacritical marks. Users of this book should, however, keep in mind that Arabic terms like *sura* and names like al-Bukhari should more properly be spelled *sūra* and al-Bukhārī, while Greek terms like *lorikion* and *komes* should more correctly be written *lōrikion* and *komēs*.

I benefitted from the expert criticism of Paul Cobb, Paul Dutton, Maureen C. Miller, Claudia Rapp, Anders Winroth, and many anonymous reviewers of the initial table of contents. Paul Dutton, John Shinners, and Alexander C. Murray kindly allowed me to use their texts. Damien Boquet, Riccardo Cristiani, Steven Epstein, Zouhair Ghazzal, Thomas Head, Jacqueline Long, Graham Loud, Michael Khodarkovsky, Daniel Smail, Sue Sheridan Walker, and Stephen D. White provided unfailingly useful advice.

At Broadview Press, I was sustained at every turn by Mical Moser, Michelle Lobkowicz, and Natalie Fingerhut while Barbara Conolly and Judith Earnshaw, production editors; Jennifer Elsayed, permissions coordinator; Crescent McKeag, permissions freelancer; Martin Boyne, copyeditor; Joan Eadie, indexer; and George Kirkpatrick, designer, were stellar practitioners. At my home institution, Loyola University Chicago, Ursula Scholz, and Jennifer Stegen unstintingly fed my insatiable hunger for Interlibrary Loan books, while Thomas Greene, my graduate student in medieval history, was an able assistant.

I turn now to my family: my daughter, Jess, proofread the entire book and drew on her pedagogical expertise to suggest changes, glosses, and questions. I am grateful as well to my mother, Roz; my sister Oms; my son, Frank; and my husband, Tom. They have sat through more discussions of Averroes and St. Louis than perhaps they care to recall. I thank them all with much love.

ABBREVIATIONS AND SIGNS

AV Authorized Version of the Bible. In *Reading the Middle Ages*, references to the Bible are to the AV version. (Psalms are cited in both AV and Douay versions.) The standard abbreviations for the books of the AV are set out below. The Revised Standard Version of the Bible, which is perhaps the best translation in English, derives from the AV, which is based on the King James version.

b. before a date = born

b. before a name = son of (*ibn, ben*)

B.C.E. before common era. Interchangeable with B.C. See C.E. below.

beg. beginning

bt. daughter of (*bint*)

c. century (used after an ordinal number, e.g. 6th c. means "sixth century")

c. circa (used before a date to indicate that it is approximate)

C.E. common era. Interchangeable with A.D. Both reflect Western dating practices, which begin "our" era with the birth of Christ. In *Reading the Middle Ages*, all dates are C.E. unless otherwise specified or some confusion might arise.

d. date of death

d. dinar = *denarius*, penny

Douay The standard English version of the Vulgate (Latin) version of the Bible. Ordinarily the books are the same as in the AV version (see above). The chief differences are (1) that the Douay version accepts some books considered apocryphal in the AV; and (2) the Psalm numbers sometimes differ. The Douay numbers follow the psalm numbering in the Greek Bible, whereas the AV and other Protestant Bibles follow the numbering of the Hebrew text.

e.g. *exempli gratia*=for example

ff. folios (or pages) following; this means that the reference is to a particular page and those that follow

fl. *floruit* (used—when birth and death dates are not known—to mean that a person "flourished" or was active at the time of the date)

ibid. in the same place, referring to the reference in the preceding note.

i.e. that is (from the Latin *id est*)

£ pound (from the first letter of the Latin word *libra*)

MS manuscript

pl. plural

r. ruled

s. shilling = *solidus*, sous

sing. singular

. . . Ellipses, indicating that words or passages of the original have been left out.

[] Brackets, indicating words or passages that are not in the original but have been added by the editor to aid in the understanding of a passage

Abbreviations for the AV

Old Testament

Genesis	Gen.
Exodus	Exod.
Leviticus	Lev.
Numbers	Num.
Deuteronomy	Deut.
Josue	Josue
Judges	Judges
Ruth	Ruth
1 Samuel	1 Sam.
2 Samuel	2 Sam.
1 Kings	1 Kings
2 Kings	2 Kings
1 Chronicles	1 Chron.
2 Chronicles	2 Chron.
Ezra	Ezra
Nehemiah	Neh.
Esther	Esther
Job	Job
Psalms	Ps.
Proverbs	Prov.
Ecclesiastes	Eccles.
Song of Solomon	Song of Sol. (This is also often called the Song of Songs)
Isaiah	Isa.
Jeremiah	Jer.
Lamentations	Lam.
Ezekiel	Ezek.
Daniel	Dan.
Hosea	Hos.
Joel	Joel
Amos	Amos
Obadiah	Obad.
Jonah	Jon.
Micah	Mic.
Nahum	Nah.
Habakkuk	Hab.
Zephaniah	Zeph.
Haggai	Hag.
Zechariah	Zech.
Malachi	Mal.

Apocrypha

1 Esdras	1 Esd.
2 Esdras	2 Esd.
Tobit	Tob.
Judith	Jth.
The Rest of Esther	Rest of Esther
The Wisdom of Solomon	Wisd. of Sol.
Ecclesiasticus	Ecclus.
Baruch	Bar.
The Song of the Three Holy Children	Song of Three Children
Susanna	Sus.
Bel and the Dragon	Bel and Dragon
Prayer of Manasses	Pr. of Man.
1 Maccabees	1 Macc.
2 Maccabees	2 Macc.

New Testament

Matthew	Matt.
Mark	Mark
Luke	Luke
John	John
Acts of the Apostles	Acts
Romans	Rom.
1 Corinthians	1 Cor.
2 Corinthians	2 Cor.
Galatians	Gal.
Ephesians	Eph.
Philippians	Phil.
Colossians	Col.
1 Thessalonians	1 Thess.
2 Thessalonians	2 Thess.
1 Timothy	1 Tim.
2 Timothy	2 Tim.
Titus	Titus
Philemon	Philem.
Hebrews	Heb.
James	James
1 Peter	1 Pet.
2 Peter	2 Pet.
1 John	1 John
2 John	2 John
3 John	3 John
Jude	Jude
Revelation	Rev.

ONE

PRELUDE: THE ROMAN WORLD TRANSFORMED (*c*.300–*c*.600)

IMPERIAL POLITICS

1.1 Christianity becomes official: *Edict of Milan* (313). Original in Latin.

NO EDICT (AN ORDER ISSUED TO GOVERNORS throughout the empire) was issued at Milan. But Emperors Constantine (r.308-337) and Licinius (r.308-324) met there in 313 and agreed to the provisions of what would be promulgated a few months later—the so-called *Edict of Milan*. It gave notice that Constantine and Licinius agreed to tolerate Christianity along with other religions and that they determined to restore the properties that the Church had lost under Emperor Diocletian (r.284-305). The current owners of the property might be compensated from the emperors' private funds if they applied to their "vicar," an imperial administrator with regional authority.

The *Edict of Milan* is the first source in this collection. Let us use it to begin a discussion of how to read primary sources. Each primary source calls for its own methodology and approach; there is no one way to handle all of them. Moreover, as the epigraph of this book points out, readers should bring their own special insights to old sources. Nevertheless, it is usually helpful to begin by asking a standard series of questions.

Who wrote it and for what audience was it written? Normally this is fairly easy to answer, but often it is not. In this case, it seems that Emperors Constantine and Licinius conceived of the statement, though civil servants in an imperial writing office would have drafted and published it. The immediate recipients were provincial governors, each referred to as "your Excellency" in this document; they were expected to publish—that is, publicize—the contents to the public.

When was it written? Your editor has given the date 313, which is the year in which the document was issued. At this stage in your historical work, you need not worry about how your editor figured out this date. It is more important for you to consider the circumstances and historical events in the context of which this date takes on meaning. In this instance, you should be thinking that the date is pertinent to the history of the Roman empire; that it comes directly after Constantine won a major battle at the Milvian Bridge (312); that he attributed his victory to a sign from the Christian God; that immediately thereafter he took over administration of the western portion of the Roman empire and soon (in 313) allied with Licinius; and that a few months later Licinius became ruler of the eastern half of the empire. Thus you should expect the document to have to do with both imperial authority and religion, which is precisely what you will discover when you read it.

Where was it written? In this case "Milan" is not the right answer. In fact the *Edict* was issued by Licinius at Nicomedia (today Izmit), in the eastern half of the empire. But sometimes you will not know so specific an answer, and you must work with what information you have.

Why was it written? Often you will find a provisional answer to this question right in the text. Ostensibly the *Edict* was written, as it says, "to give both to Christians and to all others free facility to follow the religion which each may desire." But you should go beyond this obvious answer to ask what other motives might have been at work, what sorts of negotiations may have been involved in its writing, and who benefitted.

What is it? In this case, you know that it is *called* an *Edict* but is something a bit different. You might choose to call it an "imperial ordinance," an "official document" or even a "policy statement."

What does it say? This is the most important question of all. To answer it, you need to analyze the document for its various provisions, taking care to understand them fully and seeking further information (if necessary) about its vocabulary.

What are the implications of what it says? This requires you to ask many questions about matters that lie behind the text. Important questions to ask are: *What does the document reveal about such institutions as family, power, social classes and groups, religion, and education and literacy in the world that produced it? What are its underlying assumptions about gender; about human nature, agency, and goals; about the nature of the divine? Does the source apply to men and women in the same way?*

How reliable is it? If the document is authentic—if it really is what it purports to be—then at the very least you can know that it was issued by its writer(s). In this case, you can be sure that Constantine and Licinius did indeed want the *Edict of Milan* promulgated. You may wish to speculate about how much of it was Constantine's idea and how much Licinius's by considering what else you know about their religious convictions and political motives. The document certainly tells you about the ideals and intentions that they wanted the world to believe they had. But it alone cannot tell you whether the provisions were carried out. To know that, you need other documents and evidence about the nature of Roman imperial power at the time. One document that may help here is the *Creed* declared by the Council of Nicaea (p. 19 below), since Constantine presided over that council. *The History of the Church* by Eusebius (below p. 4), written around the same time, may also be useful.

Are there complicating factors? Medieval texts were all handwritten, and they were "published"—in the sense of being made public and distributed—in relatively small numbers. In many cases we do not have them in their original state. The *Edict of Milan* was issued in multiple handwritten copies in Latin. However, none of these has survived. We know its contents because it was incorporated into the writings of two Christian apologists:[1] Lactantius's *On the Deaths of the Persecutors* (written 313-315) and Eusebius's *History of the Church*, which is excerpted on p. 4 below. Eusebius's text of the *Edict*, which he translated and presented in Greek, is not entirely the same as the one given by Lactantius. Scholars think that the one in Lactantius is the original, and that is the one printed here. But you should not be content with that. You should instead ask yourself at least two questions about these intermediary sources: *What motives might lead a later source to reproduce a text? What new meanings does the original source take on when it is embedded in a larger document with its own agenda?* You might also consider the fact that the *Edict* was not considered important enough to be drawn upon by the legal experts who compiled the *Theodosian Code* (438; see below, p. 10) or the later *Codex Justinianus* (529).

You should ask these questions of every source you read. Soon you will see how different the answers are for each document, for every one of them poses special challenges. If you like, look ahead to p. 198 to see this point clearly demonstrated in connection with a very different source, Al-Tabari, *The Defeat of the Zanj Revolt*.

[Source: *Church and State Through the Centuries: A Collection of Historic Documents with Commentaries*, trans. and ed. Sidney Z. Ehler and John B. Morrall (Westminster, MD: Newman Press, 1954), pp. 5-6.]

WE, CONSTANTINE AND Licinius the Emperors, having met in concord at Milan and having set in order everything which pertains to the common good and public security, are of the opinion that among the various things which we perceived would profit men, or which should be set in order first, was to be found the cultivation of religion; we should therefore give both to Christians and to all others free facility to follow the religion which each may desire, so that by this means whatever divinity is enthroned in heaven may be gracious and favorable to us and to all who have been placed under our authority. Therefore we are of the opinion that the following decision is in accordance with sound and true reasoning: that no one who has given his mental assent to the Christian persuasion or to any other which he feels to be suitable to him should be compelled to deny his conviction, so that the Supreme Godhead ("Summa Divinitas"), whose worship we freely observe, can assist us in all things with his usual favor and benevolence. Wherefore it is necessary for your Excellency to know that it is our pleasure that all restrictions which were previously put forward in official pronouncements concerning the sect of the Christians should be removed, and that each one of them who freely and sincerely carries out the purpose of observing the Christian religion may endeavor to practice its precepts without any fear or danger. We believed that these points should be fully brought to your attention, so that you might know that we have given free and absolute permission to practice their religion to the Christians. Now that you perceive what we have granted to them, your Excellency must also learn that for the sake of peace in our time a similar public and free right to practice their religion or cult is granted to others, so that every person may have free opportunity to worship according to his own wish. This has been done by us to avoid any appearance of disfavor to any one religion. We have decided furthermore to decree the following in respect of the Christians: if those places at which they were accustomed in former times to hold their meetings (concerning which a definite procedure

---

1   An "apologist" is someone who justifies or argues in favor of a doctrine or ideology.

was laid down for your guidance in previous communications) have been at any previous time acquired from our treasury or from any other person, let the persons concerned be willing and swift to restore them to the Christians without financial recompense and without trying to ask a price. Let those who have received such property as a gift restore whatever they have acquired to the Christians in similar manner; if those who have bought such property or received it as a gift seek some recompense from our benevolence, let them apply to the vicar, by whom their cases will be referred to our clemency. You are to consider it your duty that all these things shall be handed over to the Christian body immediately and without delay by your intervention. And since the aforesaid Christians are known to have possessed not only those places at which they are accustomed to assemble, but others also pertaining to the law of their body, that is of the churches, not of private individuals, you are to order in accordance with the law which we have described above the return of all those possessions to the aforesaid Christians, that is to their bodies and assemblies without any further hesitation or argument. Our previous statement is to be borne in mind that those who restore this property without price may, as we have said, expect some compensation from our benevolence.

You ought to bring into play your very effective intervention in all these matters concerning the aforesaid Christian body so that there may be a swift fulfilment of our Edict, in which the interests of public quiet have been consulted by our clemency. Let all this be done, so that as we stated above, the divine favor, of which we have experienced so many instances, may continue with us to bless our successors through all time with public well-being. In order that the character of this our perpetual benevolence can reach the knowledge of all, it will be well for you to circulate everywhere, and to bring to the awareness of all, these points which have been written to you as above, so that the enactment of this our benevolence may not be hidden.

1.2 Christian history: Eusebius, *The History of the Church* (c.325). Original in Greek.

EUSEBIUS (c.260-c.340), BISHOP OF Caesarea (in Roman Palestine, just south of present-day Haifa, Israel), experienced the persecutions of Emperor Diocletian (r.284-305) and celebrated the triumph of Emperor Constantine (r.308-337), for whom he was an important propagandist. Before he wrote his *History*, he and others had written accounts of martyrs' passions and brief treatises on parts of Church history, but no one had written about the progress of the Church from the time of Christ to the present. Because it *was* a "progress," the very shape of history changed in Eusebius's hands, from the classical "cycle" that repeated itself (see Procopius below, p. 15) to a "linear" history that pointed to a goal. This notion of history had been first elaborated by Jewish writers, but Eusebius turned it into the triumph of the Church. The movers and shakers of Eusebius's history were above all the apostles and the bishops. But Constantine, too, was a hero, while Emperor Licinius became a villain in Eusebius's treatment. Eusebius's model of historical writing was enormously influential on later historiography, as for example that of Gregory of Tours, *Histories* (below, p. 65).

[Source: Eusebius, *The History of the Church from Christ to Constantine*, trans. G. A. Williamson (Baltimore: Penguin Books, 1965), pp. 380-85, 401, 408-13.]

Book 10: PEACE AND RECOVERY OF THE CHURCH: VIC-
TORY OF CONSTANTINE

The peace bestowed on us by God
1. Thanks be to God, the Almighty, the King of the
universe, for all His mercies; and heartfelt thanks to
the Savior and Redeemer of our souls, Jesus Christ,
through whom we pray that peace from troubles outside and troubles in the heart may be kept for us stable
and unshaken for ever.

Together with my prayers I now add Book 10 of
the *History of the Church* to its predecessors. This I shall
dedicate to you, my most worshipful Paulinus [Bishop
of Tyre], calling on you to set the seal on the entire
work; and it is appropriate that in a perfect number[1] I
should here set out the perfect account in celebration
of the re-establishment of the churches, obeying the
Divine Spirit when He exhorts us thus:

Sing to the Lord a new song, for He has done marvelous things;
His right hand and His holy arm have wrought
salvation for Him.
The Lord has made known His salvation;
In the sight of the heathen He has revealed His
righteousness.[2]

As these inspired lines command me, let me now
obediently sing aloud the new song, because after
those terrifying darksome sights and stories I was now
privileged to see and celebrate such things as in truth
many righteous men and martyrs of God before us
desired to see on earth and did not see, and to hear
and did not hear.[3] But they, hastening with all speed,
attained far better things in the heavens, caught up in
a paradise of divine pleasure;[4] whereas I, acknowledging that even my present lot is better than I deserve,
have been more than amazed at the bountiful grace of
its Author, and am duly filled with wonder, worshiping Him with my whole soul's strength, and testifying
to the truth of the written prophecies which declare:

Come hither and behold the works of the Lord,
What wonders He has wrought in the world,
Making wars cease to the ends of the world:
The bow He will break and will shatter the weapon,
And the shields He will burn up with fire.[5]

Happy that all this has been clearly fulfilled in my own
time let me proceed with the next part of my story.

Destruction, in the way described, had overtaken
the whole brood of God's enemies, and at one stroke
had blotted them out from human sight. Thus yet another inspired saying had been fulfilled:

I saw the wicked high exalted,
And lifted up like the cedars of Lebanon.
And I passed by, and lo, he was not;
And I sought his place, and it was not found.[6]

From that time on a day bright and radiant, with no
cloud overshadowing it, shone down with shafts of
heavenly light on the churches of Christ throughout
the world, nor was there any reluctance to grant even
those outside our community the enjoyment, if not
of equal blessings, at least of the overflow from and a
share in the things that God had bestowed on us.

Re-establishment of the churches
2. Thus all men living were free from oppression by
the tyrants; and released from their former miseries,
they all in their various ways acknowledged as the only
true God the Defender of the godly. Above all for us
who had fixed our hopes on the Christ of God there
was unspeakable happiness, and a divine joy blos-
somed in all hearts as we saw that every place which
a little while before had been reduced to dust by the
tyrants' wickedness was now, as if from a prolonged
and deadly stranglehold, coming back to life; and that
cathedrals were again rising from their foundations
high into the air, and far surpassing in magnificence
those previously destroyed by the enemy.

Emperors too, the most exalted, by a succession of

---

1 I.e., the number 10.
2 See Ps. 98: 1-2; Douay Ps. 97: 1-2.
3 See Matt. 13: 17.
4 See 2 Cor. 12: 3-4.
5 Ps. 46: 8-9; Douay Ps. 45: 9-10.
6 Ps. 37: 35-36; Douay Ps. 36: 35-36.

ordinances in favor of the Christians, confirmed still further and more surely the blessings that God showered upon us; and a stream of personal letters from the emperor reached the bishops, accompanied by honors and gifts of money. I shall take the opportunity at the proper place in my account to inscribe in this book as on a sacred tablet these communications, translated from Latin into Greek, in order that all who come after us may bear them in remembrance.

Dedication ceremonies everywhere

3. The next stage was the spectacle prayed and longed for by us all—dedication festivals in the cities and consecrations of the newly built places of worship, convocations of bishops, gatherings of representatives from far distant lands, friendly intercourse between congregation and congregation, unification of the members of Christ's body conjoint in one harmony. In accordance with a prophet's prediction, which mystically signified beforehand what was to be, there came together bone to bone and joint to joint,[1] and all that in riddling oracles the scripture infallibly foretold. There was one power of the divine Spirit coursing through all the members, one soul in them all,[2] the same enthusiasm for the faith, one hymn of praise on all their lips. Yes, and our leaders performed ceremonies with full pomp, and ordained priests the sacraments and majestic rites of the Church, here with the singing of psalms and intoning of the prayers given us from God, there with the carrying out of divine and mystical ministrations; while over all were the ineffable symbols of the Savior's Passion. And together, the people of every age, male and female alike, with all their powers of mind, rejoicing in heart and soul, gave glory through prayers and thanksgiving to the Author of their happiness, God Himself.

Every one of the dignitaries of the Church present delivered a public oration according to his ability, inspiring the great audience. 4. One of the moderately capable[3] came forward into their midst with a prepared discourse. It was a church assembly, and the many pastors present gave him a quiet and orderly hearing. Addressing himself personally to a single bishop,[4] an admirable man and one dear to God, through whose initiative and enthusiasm the most magnificent cathedral in Phoenicia had been built at Tyre, he delivered the following address.

FESTIVAL ORATION ON THE BUILDING OF THE CHURCHES, ADDRESSED TO PAULINUS, BISHOP OF TYRE

Friends of God, and priests clothed with the sacred vestment and the heavenly crown of glory, the divine unction, and priestly garments of the Holy Spirit; and you, so young yet the pride of the holy temple of God, honored with ripe wisdom from God yet renowned for the precious works and deeds of virtue in its youthful prime, on whom the God who holds the entire universe in His hand has Himself bestowed the supreme honor of building His house upon earth and re-establishing it for Christ, His only begotten and firstborn Word, and for Christ's holy and majestic bride—shall I call you a new Bezalel,[5] the master builder of a divine tabernacle, or a Solomon, king of a new and far nobler Jerusalem, or a new Zerubbabel, who adorned the temple of God with the glory that was far greater than the old?[6] And you too, nurslings of the sacred flock of Christ, home of good words, school of self-discipline, and university of true religion, earnest and dear to God.

Long ago, as the inspired records of miraculous signs from God and the wonders performed by the Lord in the service of men were read aloud in our hearing, we might well send up hymns and songs to God; for we were taught to say:

O God, with our ears have we heard, our fathers
    have told us,
The work which Thou didst in their days, in ancient
    days.[7]

---

1 Ezek. 37: 7. Eusebius has added the word "joint" to make the play upon words—joint and conjoint, which means "joined together."
2 Acts 4: 32.
3 Eusebius himself.
4 I.e., Bishop Paulinus of Tyre.
5 Exod. 35: 30.
6 Hag. 2: 9. All these epithets are for Paulinus.
7 Ps. 44: 1; Douay Ps. 43: 1.

But now it is no longer by hearing the spoken word that men learn of the uplifted arm and the heavenly right hand of our God, All-gracious and King of all; but by deeds, if we may put it so, and with our very eyes we see that the traditions of an earlier age were trustworthy and true. And so we may raise our voices in a second hymn of victory and cry aloud:

As we have heard, so also we have seen
In the city of the Lord of Hosts, in the city of our
   God.[1]

And in what city but this new-made city built by God? It is the Church of the Living God, the pillar and basis of truth,[2] and of it another inspired saying joyously declares:

Glorious things have been spoken of thee,
O city of God.[3]

And since in this city God the All-Gracious has brought us together through the grace of His Only-begotten, let each of the invited guests sing, nay shout,

I was glad when they said to me
"Into the house of the Lord we will go"

and

Lord, I have loved the beauty of Thy house,
And the dwelling-place of Thy glory.[4]

It is not only for each by himself, but for all of us together with one spirit and one soul, to give glory and praise, saying:

Great is the Lord and highly to be praised
In the city of our God, in His holy mountain.[5] ...

Let us now and for all time to come rekindle the memory of these things; and let the Author of the present assembly and of this joyous and most glorious day, the Lord of the festival Himself, be before the eyes of our mind night and day at every hour and, may I say, at every breath. Let us love and reverence Him with all the power of our soul; and let us now stand up and with a loud voice of supplication beseech Him to shelter us in His fold and preserve us to the end, bestowing on us His own unbreakable, unshakable, and everlasting peace in Christ Jesus our Savior, through whom be glory to Him for ever and ever. Amen.

Copies of imperial laws
5. At this point it would be well to reproduce also the imperial ordinances of Constantine and Licinius in translations from the Latin....
[Here Eusebius inserts various documents in favor of the Church, including a version of the *Edict of Milan* (see above, p. 1); a statute to restore the property of the "Catholic Church of the Christians"; an imperial letter calling on bishops to assemble for a council; a letter awarding the bishop of Carthage a large sum in cash; and a letter exempting clergymen from public duties.]

The criminal folly of Licinius, and his calamitous end
8. Such then were the boons conferred on us by the divine, heavenly grace of the manifestation of our Savior; so great was the abundance of good things won for all men through the peace we enjoyed. And thus our new life was inaugurated with festivities and celebrations. But in the eyes of evil-minded envy and of the malignant demon the sight of what was going on was beyond endurance, and in the same way Licinius could not be brought to a sensible frame of mind by the fate of the tyrants already mentioned.[6] He had been honored with sovereign power in time

---

1   Ps. 48: 8; Douay Ps. 47: 8.
2   1 Tim. 3: 15.
3   Ps. 87: 3; Douay Ps. 86: 3.
4   Ps. 122: 1 and 26: 8; Douay Ps. 121: 1 and 25: 8.
5   Ps. 48: 1; Douay Ps. 47: 2.
6   Eusebius here refers to the fates of Emperors Maxentius (d.312) and Maximin (d.313). Maxentius was defeated by Constantine at the Battle of the Milvian Bridge (see above, p. 2), while Maximin, known as a persecutor of Christians, died of a painful disease.

of prosperity; he had ranked next after the great Emperor Constantine, and had become brother-in-law and kinsman of the most exalted person living; yet he turned his back on the examples of good men and emulated the wickedness and criminal folly of the evil tyrants; and he chose to follow the same path as those whose life he had with his own eyes seen ending in calamity, rather than remain on terms of friendship and esteem with his superior. Madly envious of the universal benefactor, he launched an unholy, all-out war against him, paying no respect to natural laws and trampling underfoot solemn pledges, ties of blood, and treaties. For, like the all-gracious emperor that he was, Constantine had given him tokens of real goodwill, not grudging kinship with himself or refusing him the privilege of a brilliant marriage with his sister. Again, he honored him with a share in his ancestral nobility and the imperial blood he had inherited, and conferred on him, as brother-in-law and joint emperor, the privilege of enjoying sovereign power, giving him an equal part of the lands under Roman sway to govern and administer.

But Licinius responded by behaving in the opposite way: he devised scheme after scheme to injure his superior, and invented plan after plan in his efforts to return evil for good. At first he attempted to conceal his intrigues, and posed as a friend, in the hope that by making constant use of trickery and deception he would most easily achieve his purpose. But in God Constantine had a true Friend, Protector, and Guardian, who brought to light the plots devised in darkness and secrecy and frustrated them: so powerful is the great weapon of godliness for the repulse of the enemy and the preservation of its own safety. Thus protected, our Emperor, God's dearly beloved, escaped the plots of this infamous twister. The latter saw that his stealthy intrigue was not going at all according to plan, for God made every trick and fraud manifest to His beloved emperor; so, being unable to remain hidden any longer, he made war openly. Having resolved to fight it out with Constantine, he was already rushing into conflict with the God of the universe too, whom he knew that his rival worshiped. So—quietly and cautiously at first—he planned an attack on the ministers of God among his subjects, though they had never yet shown the least disloyalty to his rule. The motive for this was the terrible blindness forced upon him by his inborn vileness. Thus he failed to keep before his eyes the memory either of those who had persecuted Christians before him, or of those whom he had taken it upon himself to punish and destroy because of their iniquitous activities. But he turned his back on prudence and common sense, lost his sanity altogether, and determined to match his strength against God Himself, as Constantine's Protector, rather than against the person protected.

He began by dismissing every Christian from his household, robbing himself, poor fool, of the supplication to God for him which their fathers had taught them to make for all men.[1]

Next, he ordered the soldiers, city by city, to be picked out and deprived of their rank if they did not choose to sacrifice to demons.

These were mere trifles, judged by comparison with more drastic measures. There is no need to mention one by one the separate acts of this enemy of God, and how laws that were unlawful were invented by this most lawless of men. One actually laid down that where men were languishing in prison no one might give them food as an act of humanity, or pity those who were fettered and starving to death; no one was to show any kind feeling at all, and no kind act was to be done even by those who were compelled by their own nature to show fellow-feeling for their neighbors. Among his laws one was undisguisedly shameless and most cruel, excluding every civilized sentiment: it ordained that those who showed pity should suffer the same punishment as those who aroused it, and that any who performed humane services should be fettered and flung into prison, to share the punishment of those already undergoing it. Such were the orders of Licinius.

Need I enumerate his innovations with regard to marriage, or his startling changes affecting those who departed this life? He had the impudence to rescind the ancient Roman laws, so well and wisely laid down, replacing them with barbarous, uncivilized substitutes, laws unquestionably unlawful and contrary to law. Then there were the innumerable demands that he concocted at the expense of subject peoples, the

---

1 1 Tim. 2: 1.

constant exactions of gold and silver, the revaluations of land, the pocketing of fines imposed on country-dwellers no longer alive but long since departed. In addition, this hater of his fellow-men devised means of banishing persons entirely innocent, and of arresting men of good birth and high reputation, whose lawful wives he removed and handed over to filthy menials to be insulted and humiliated; while he himself, the besotted old dotard, used countless married women and unwedded girls to satisfy his own unbridled lust. But why should I dwell on these things, when the extravagance of his ultimate behavior makes the earlier seem trifling and negligible?

In the later stages of his madness he took action against the bishops. As the servants of the God who is over all, he felt them to be obstacles to his misdeeds; so he began to plot against them, not openly at first, for fear of his superior, but secretly as usual and guilefully; and enlisting the help of the governors he put the most influential of them to death. The way they were murdered was a novel one, till then unheard of. The things done at Amasea and the other Pontic cities[1] outdid the most extravagant cruelty. Some of the churches of God there were again thrown down from roof to foundations; others were locked up, to prevent any of the regular congregation from meeting and giving to God the worship due to Him. And why? Because he did not believe that the prayers were offered on his behalf—the suggestion sprang from his guilty conscience—but was convinced that it was for the Emperor whom God loved that we did everything and made our supplications to Him. That was what brought down his wrath upon our heads. Among the governors were flatterers who—in the conviction that they were doing what the wretched man wanted—subjected some of the bishops to the penalties reserved for criminals, men completely innocent being arrested and executed without pretext as if they were murderers. Others suffered an even more unprecedented form of death: their bodies were hacked with a sword and carved up like butcher's meat; then, after this savage, horrifying spectacle, they were thrown into the depths of the sea to feed the fishes. This led to a new flight of the ministers of God, and once more the fields, once more the deserts, valleys, and hills became the refuge of Christ's servants.

When the evil emperor had achieved his purpose in this way also, he next turned his attention to indiscriminate persecution. His design was in his power, and there was no obstacle to its being carried out, had not the threatened danger been speedily foreseen by God, the defender of the souls that are His, who in the black darkness and utter gloom of night all at once kindled a great beacon light, a savior for them all, with uplifted arm leading His servant Constantine to the spot. 9. On him, as the due reward of his devotion, God bestowed from heaven above the trophies of victory over the wicked; but the guilty one He threw down, with all his counselors and friends, prone beneath Constantine's feet.

Victory of Constantine; the benefits he conferred on his subjects

When Licinius had rushed headlong to the limit of madness, this seemed no longer endurable to the emperor, God's friend, who—reasoning along sound lines and tempering the rigidity of justice with humanity—determined to rescue the tyrant's victims, and by putting a few destroyers out of the way made haste to save the bulk of the human race. He had treated Licinius with nothing but kindness hitherto, and had shown mercy where no sympathy was deserved. But Licinius grew no better: his wickedness continued unabated, and he raged more and more madly against his subject peoples; while for his victims there remained no hope of escape, with a wild beast tyrannizing over them.

And so, his love of goodness blended with a hatred of evil, the champion of the good set out with his son Crispus, that most humane emperor, by his side,[2] holding out a saving hand to all who were perishing. Then, taking God the universal King, and God's Son the Savior of all, as Guide and Ally, father and son together divided their battle array against God's

---

1 The "Pontic cities" were along the southern coast of the Black Sea.
2 Crispus was Constantine's oldest son. He was given the title "Caesar"—a lesser emperor—in 317, and he led the battle against Licinius in 324. But two years later, for reasons that are obscure, Constantine had him executed.

enemies on every side, and easily carried off the victory:[1] every detail of the encounter was made easy for them by God, in fulfilment of His purpose. Suddenly in less time than it takes to say it, those who a day or two before had been breathing death and threats were no more, and even their name was forgotten; their portraits and tributes were swept into merited oblivion; and the very things that Licinius with his own eyes had seen befall the wicked tyrants who preceded him he underwent himself, because he did not allow himself to be disciplined or learn wisdom from the blows that fell on his neighbors; and having pursued the same path of wickedness as they, he deservedly toppled over the identical cliff.[2]

1.3 Imperial legislation: *The Theodosian Code* (438). Original in Latin.

The Theodosian Code, a massive compilation of imperial edicts and letters issued in 438 under Roman Emperor Theodosius II (r.408-450), was meant to serve as an authoritative standard for determining legal cases throughout the empire. Covering topics as diverse as legal procedure, marriage, the army, and the Church, the *Code* was immediately adopted by Roman judicial authorities and was later influential on the laws drawn up in the barbarian successor states (see below, *The Council of Orléans* on p. 60 and *The Visigothic Code* on p. 63). The *Code* divided its topics into "Books," which were further subdivided into "Titles." Under each Title were arranged excerpts from pertinent imperial legislation. These were followed, when the compilers thought necessary, by legal interpretations. The passages below concern two issues: marriage (and divorce) and asylum. The first demonstrates the *Code*'s attempt to control social and moral behavior. The topic of asylum reveals that emperors not only came to recognize the holiness of the altar but also bowed to bishops' desire to allow even criminals the opportunity to do penance.

[Source: *The Theodosian Code and Novels and the Sirmondian Constitutions*, trans. Clyde Pharr (Princeton, NJ: Princeton University Press, 1952), pp. 76-77, 264-66 (slightly modified).]

BOOK 3, TITLE 14: MARRIAGES WITH FOREIGNERS

1. Emperors Valentinian and Valens Augustuses to Theodosius, Master of the Horse. [368–373]

No provincial, of whatever rank or class he may be, shall marry a barbarian wife, nor shall a provincial woman be united with any foreigner. But if there should be any alliances between provincials and foreigners through such marriages and if anything should be disclosed as suspect or criminal among them, it shall be expiated by capital punishment.

INTERPRETATION: No Roman shall presume to have a barbarian wife of any nation whatever, nor shall any Roman woman be united in marriage with a barbarian. But if they should do this, they shall know that they are subject to capital punishment.

TITLE 16: NOTICES OF DIVORCE

1. Emperor Constantine Augustus to Ablavius, Praetorian Prefect. [331]

It is Our[3] pleasure that no woman, on account of her own depraved desires, shall be permitted to send a notice of divorce to her husband on trumped up grounds, as, for instance, that he is a drunkard or a gambler or a philanderer, nor indeed shall a husband be permitted to divorce his wife on every sort of pretext. But

---

1 At Adrianople in July, and at Scutari in September 324.
2 Constantine had him killed.
3 This is the "imperial 'we'"—the emperor refers to himself, as representative of the state, in the plural.

when a woman sends a notice of divorce, the following criminal charges only shall be investigated, that is, if she should prove that her husband is a homicide, a sorcerer, or a destroyer of tombs, so that the wife may thus earn commendation and at length recover her entire dowry. For if she should send a notice of divorce to her husband on grounds other than these three criminal charges, she must leave everything, even to her last hairpin, in her husband's home, and as punishment for her supreme self confidence, she shall be deported to an island. In the case of a man also, if he should send a notice of divorce, inquiry shall be made as to the following three criminal charges, namely, if he wishes to divorce her as an adulteress, a sorceress, or a procuress.[1] For if he should cast off a wife who is innocent of these crimes, he must restore her entire dowry, and he shall not marry another woman. But if he should do this, his former wife shall be given the right to enter and seize his home by force and to transfer to herself the entire dowry of his later wife in recompense for the outrage inflicted upon her.

INTERPRETATION: The right to send notice of divorce is extended to a wife or husband for certain approved reasons and causes; for they are forbidden to dissolve a marriage for a trivial charge. If perchance a woman should say that her husband is either a drunkard or given to licentiousness, she shall not send him notice of divorce on that account. But if perchance she should prove that he is either a homicide, a sorcerer, or a violator of tombs, the husband who is convicted of these crimes appears to be justly divorced, without any fault of the woman; and she may recover her dowry and depart. If the woman should not be able to prove such crimes, she shall be subjected to the following punishment: namely, that she shall forfeit both the dowry which she had given or which had been given on her behalf and the gift[2] which she received, and she shall also be liable to exile by relegation.[3] But if a man should cast off his wife, he also is not permitted to divorce her for a trivial quarrel, as often happens, unless perhaps he should be able to prove that she is guilty of certain crimes, that is, if he is able to prove that she is an adulteress, a sorceress, or a procuress. But if he cannot prove this, he shall restore her dowry to the woman, and he shall not presume to take another wife. But if perchance he should attempt to do so, the woman who was cast off, though innocent, shall have the right to vindicate [claim] for herself her husband's home and all his substance. It is recognized that this is ordained in order that if a woman should be unjustly divorced, she is ordered to acquire the dowry of the second wife also.

2. Emperors Honorius, Theodosius, and Constantius Augustuses to Palladius, Praetorian Prefect. [421]

If a woman should serve notice of divorce upon her husband and separate from him and if she should prove no grounds for divorce, the gifts shall be annulled which she had received when betrothed. She shall also be deprived of her dowry, and she shall be sentenced to the punishment of deportation. We deny her not only the right to a union with a subsequent husband, but even the right of postliminium.[4] But if a woman who has revolted against her marriage should prove merely flaws of character and ordinary faults, she shall lose her dowry and restore to her husband all gifts, and never at all shall she be associated in marriage with any man. In order that she may not defile her unmarried state with wanton debauchery, We grant to the repudiated husband the right to bring an accusation.[5]

1. It remains to say that if a woman who withdraws[6] should prove serious grounds and a conscience involved in great crimes, she shall obtain possession of her dowry and shall also retain the betrothal bounty, and she shall regain the right to marry after a period of five years from the day of the divorce. For then it will appear that she has done this from loathing of her

---

1   I.e., a madam or prostitute.
2   The betrothal and prenuptial gifts.
3   There were two forms of punishment by exile: in the harshest, the exile lost all civil rights. In exile by relegation, he or she retained these rights.
4   The right to return home and resume her former life.
5   On grounds of immorality.
6   From her marriage.

own husband rather than from a desire for another husband.[1]

2(1). Certainly if the husband should be the first to give notice of divorce and if he should charge his wife with a grave crime, he shall prosecute the accused woman in accordance with the law, and when he has obtained his revenge, he shall both get possession of her dowry and recover his bounty [gifts] to her, and he shall acquire the unrestricted right to marry another woman immediately. 3. If it is a fault of character and not of criminality, the husband shall recover his gifts but relinquish the dowry, and he shall have the right to marry another woman after a period of two years. 4. But if the husband should wish to dissolve the marriage because of a mere disagreement and should charge the repudiated woman with no vices or sins, he shall lose both his gifts and the dowry and be compelled to live in perpetual celibacy; he shall suffer punishment for his insolent divorce in the sadness of solitude; and the woman shall be granted the right to marry after the termination of a year. Moreover, We order to be preserved the guarantees of the ancient law in regard to the retentions from dowries, on account of children.

INTERPRETATION: If a woman should be the first to serve a notice of divorce upon her husband and should not prove the statutory grounds for divorce, she shall forfeit the betrothal bounty, and she shall not recover that which she gave her husband as dowry. In addition, she shall also be sent into exile by relegation, and she shall not have the right to marry or to return to her own.[2] Indeed, if she should prove slight faults in her husband, for which she appears to seek a divorce, she shall forfeit her dowry and shall restore the betrothal gifts, and she shall not have the right to marry another man. If, however, after divorcing her husband, she should become involved in adultery, her husband shall have the right to prosecute her even after the divorce. But if a woman who has separated from her husband should prove that he is guilty of grave and definite crimes, she shall both recover her dowry and vindicate that which her husband bestowed upon her as a

betrothal bounty, and she shall have the unrestricted right of marriage after five years.

Indeed, if the husband should be the first to serve notice of divorce, he shall secure his revenge on grounds approved by law, he shall vindicate the dowry of his repudiated wife, shall recover his betrothal gifts, and shall have the right to marry another woman immediately if he wishes. If indeed there were no definite crimes, but, as often happens, the husband is displeased with the frivolity of his wife's character, he shall recover his gifts and shall restore to her immediately anything which he has received from her, and after a period of two years he shall have the right to marry another wife. But if no defect of character should be proved but merely mental discord, the innocent woman who is rejected by her husband shall both vindicate the gifts made to her by the man and shall recover her dowry. But he shall remain alone forever and shall not presume to associate himself in marriage with another woman. The woman, however, is permitted to proceed to another marriage after a year if she should so wish. But for the sake of their common children, if there should be any, the Emperor orders those rules to be observed which have been established in the law concerning retentions according to the number of children, which law Paulus sets forth in his *Book of Responses* under the title, *A Wife's Property*.[3]...

Book 9, TITLE 44: THOSE PERSONS WHO FLEE FOR SANCTUARY TO THE STATUES OF THE EMPERORS

1. Emperors Valentinian, Theodosius, and Arcadius Augustuses to Cynegius, Praetorian Prefect. [386]

We suffer those persons who have taken refuge at the statues of the Emperors, either for the purpose of avoiding danger or of creating ill will, neither to be taken away by anyone before the tenth day nor to go away of their own accord; provided that, if they had definite reasons for which they had to flee to the statues of the Emperors, they shall be protected by law and the statutes. But if they should be revealed

---

1 The husband of another woman?
2 That is, she shall not have the right of postliminium—to return home and resume her normal life.
3 The juridical writings of Julius Paulus (*fl. c.*200) were considered authoritative.

to have wished to create ill will against their enemies by their own artifices, an avenging sentence shall be pronounced against them.

1. Emperors Theodosius, Arcadius, and Honorius Augustuses to Romulus, Count of the Sacred Imperial Largesses. [392]

If public debtors[1] should suppose that they may take refuge in the churches, they shall either be dragged out of their hiding places at once, or payment of their debts shall be exacted of the bishops who are proved to have harbored them. Your Eminent Authority shall know, therefore, that no debtor hereafter shall be defended by clerics, or else the debts shall be paid by the clerics for a debtor who they suppose ought to be defended.

2. Emperors Arcadius and Honorius Augustuses to Archelaus, Augustal Prefect. [397]

If Jews should be harassed by some criminal charge or by debts and should pretend that they wish to be joined to the Christian law,[2] in order that they may be able to avoid criminal charges or the burden of debts by taking refuge in the churches, they shall be driven away, and they shall not be received until they have paid all their debts or have been cleared of criminal charges by proof of their innocence.

3. The same Augustuses to Eutychianus, Praetorian Prefect. [398]

If, in the future, any slave, maidservant, decurion,[3] public debtor, procurator,[4] collector of purple dye fish, or anyone, finally, who is involved in public or private accounts should take refuge in a church, and if he should be either ordained a cleric or defended in any way by clerics and if he should not be returned to his former condition immediately by the issuance of a summons, decurions, indeed, and all others who are called by a customary function to the duty that they owe shall be recalled to their former lot by the energy and wisdom of the judges, as if by forcible seizure. We no longer permit such persons to have the benefit of the law which did not forbid decurions to be clerics after surrender of their patrimonies had ensued. But also those persons who are called stewards, that is, those who customarily manage ecclesiastical accounts shall be compelled without any delay to the repayment of a public or private debt to which it appears that those persons are obligated whom clerics received to be defended and did not suppose should be produced immediately.

4. Emperors Theodosius and Valentinian Augustuses to Antiochus, Praetorian Prefect. [431]

The temples of the Most High God shall be open to those persons who are afraid. Not only do We sanction that the altars and the surrounding oratory of the temple, which encloses the church with a barrier of four walls on the inside, shall be set aside for the protection of those persons who take refuge, but also the space up to the outside doors of the church, which people desiring to pray enter first, We order to be an altar of safety for those who seek Sanctuary. Thus if there should be any intervening space within the circumference of the walls of the temple which We have marked off[5] and within the outer doors of the church behind the public grounds, whether it be in the cells or in the houses, gardens, baths, courtyards, or colonnades, such space shall protect the fugitives just as the interior of the temple does. No one shall attempt to lay sacrilegious hands on them to drag them out, lest a person who dares to do this, when he sees his own peril, may himself also take refuge and seek aid. Moreover, We grant this extent of space for this purpose, namely, that it may not be permitted that any fugitive remain or eat or sleep or spend the night in the very temple of God or on the sacrosanct altars.

---

1 Most of the public debtors were delinquent taxpayers.
2 Become Christians.
3 A decurion was a member of a provincial city senate.
4 In this case, probably an imperial procurator—a fiscal agent or administrator—is meant.
5 By the boundary of walls mentioned above.

The clerics themselves shall forbid this for the sake of reverence for religion, and those who seek sanctuary shall observe it for the sake of piety.

1. We also command that those persons who seek sanctuary shall not have within the churches any arms at all, in the form of any weapon, either of iron or of any other kind. For weapons are barred not only from the temples and divine altars of the Most High God, but also from the cells, houses, gardens, baths, courtyards, and colonnades.

2. Hereafter if any persons should flee without arms to the most holy temple of God or to its sacrosanct altar, either anywhere else in the world or in this fair City, they shall be prevented by the clerics themselves, without any injury to such persons, from sleeping or from taking any food at all within the temple or at the altar. The clerics shall designate spaces within the ecclesiastical enclosures which shall be sufficient for their protection and shall explain that capital punishment has been decreed if anyone should attempt to enter forcibly and seize them. If the fugitive should not agree to these restrictions and should not obey them, reverence for religion must be preferred to humanity, and reckless lawlessness must be driven from these holy places to those that We have mentioned.

3. We warn beforehand those persons who dare to enter the temples with arms that they shall not do this. Then if they should be equipped with weapons in any place in the church, either near the enclosure of the temple or around it or outside it, We command that they be notified immediately and very severely by the clerics alone, under the authority of the bishop, to lay aside their arms, and they shall be given the assurance that they are defended by the name of religion better than by the protection of arms. But if, warned by the voice of the Church and by the declarations of so many and so important persons, the refugees should be unwilling to relinquish their weapons, then the case of Our Clemency and of the bishops is cleared in the sight of God; armed men shall be sent in, if the case so demands, and the refugees shall know that they will be dragged forth, dragged away, and subjected to all kinds of misfortunes. But no armed persons shall be dragged out from the churches without consulting the bishop or without Our order or the order of the judges either in this fair City or anywhere else, lest, if many persons should be generally permitted to do this, confusion may arise.

INTERPRETATION: Churches and places dedicated to God shall so protect accused persons who flee to them, driven by fear, that no one shall presume to bring force and violence to holy places in order to seize accused persons. But We command that whatever space belongs to the church, either in the colonnades, or in the halls, in the houses, or in the courtyards adjacent to the church shall be guarded just as the inner parts of the temple, so that the compulsion of fear may not constrain accused persons to remain around the altars or to defile places to which reverence is due. Certainly, if they should take refuge in holy places, they shall lay aside at once whatever arms they have brought with them, and they shall not suppose that they are defended by the protection of arms more than by reverence for holy places. But if they should be unwilling to lay aside their arms, and if they should not have confidence in the priest or the clerics, they shall know that they will be dragged out by the force of armed men. But if anyone should attempt for any reason to drag out from a holy place any accused person at all, the offender shall know that he will be condemned to capital punishment.

5. The same Augustuses to Hierius, Praetorian Prefect. [432]

We believe that a sanction should be promulgated, which shall be valid forever, concerning those persons who take refuge at the altars of holy religion, to the effect that if the slave of any person, relying only on reverence for the place, should seek refuge in the church or at the altars without any weapon, he shall be sent away after not more than one day in such place; furthermore, notice shall be given by the clerics whom it concerns to his master or to the person for fear of whom the slave appears to have avoided imminent punishment. The master shall grant pardon for his wrongs, and, with no remnants of anger remaining in his heart, in honor of the place and in respect for Him to whose aid the slave has fled, he shall take the slave away.

But if, armed and suspected of this by no one, the slave should rush in suddenly, then he shall he dragged out immediately, or at least notice shall be given at once to his master or to the person from whom such frantic fear has driven the slave, and the opportunity to drag him out at once shall not be denied. But if, relying upon arms and driven by madness, he should conceive the intention of resisting, his master shall be granted the right to drag him out and take him away by whatever means he can effect it. If it should happen that the slave should be killed in the struggle and battle, the master shall incur no blame, nor shall there be an occasion for anyone to originate a criminal action, if a person is killed who has changed from a servile status to the legal condition of a public enemy and a homicide.

If these regulations, so usefully constituted, should be perverted either by negligence or connivance, or in any other manner by those persons who are placed in charge of such matters in accordance with the duties of their office, just punishment will not be lacking, and, under the decision of an episcopal trial, they shall be removed from that place which they could not protect, they shall be cast back into the rank of plebeians,[1] and they shall receive the force of judicial severity.

1.4 The attraction of classical traditions: Procopius, *History of the Wars* (c.550). Original in Greek.

PROCOPIUS (*c*.500–after 562) WAS BORN IN Caesarea and served Belisarius, Justinian's general, as his legal counsel during the wars—Persian, Vandal, and Gothic— that he chronicled. His *History*, like the projects of Emperor Justinian (r.527–565) himself, harked back to ancient models. In the excerpt below Procopius makes clear his debt to Homeric literature—especially Homer's *Iliad*—and to the cyclical notion of history held by classical historians such as Herodotus (d.425 B.C.E.) and Thucydides (d.399 B.C.E.). His war, he claims, is greater than the Trojan. Compare the purposes of and values expressed in Procopius's *History* with Eusebius's *History* on p. 4.

[Source: Procopius, *History of the Wars, Books I and II*, trans. H.B. Dewing, vol. 1, Loeb Classical Library (London: William Heinemann, 1914), pp. 3, 5, 7, 9.]

Book 1.1

Procopius of Caesarea has written the history of the wars which Justinian, Emperor of the Romans, waged against the barbarians of the East and of the West, relating separately the events of each one, to the end that the long course of time may not overwhelm deeds of singular importance through lack of a record, and thus abandon them to oblivion and utterly obliterate them. The memory of these events he deemed would be a great thing and most helpful to men of the present time, and to future generations as well, in case time should ever again place men under a similar stress. For men who purpose to enter upon a war or are preparing themselves for any kind of struggle may derive some benefit from a narrative of a similar situation in history, inasmuch as this discloses the final

result attained by men of an earlier day in a struggle of the same sort, and foreshadows, at least for those who are most prudent in planning, what outcome present events will probably have. Furthermore he had assurance that he was especially competent to write the history of these events, if for no other reason, because it fell to his lot, when appointed adviser to the general Belisarius, to be an eye-witness of practically all the events to be described. It was his conviction that while cleverness is appropriate to rhetoric, and inventiveness to poetry, truth alone is appropriate to history. In accordance with this principle he has not concealed the failures of even his most intimate acquaintances, but has written down with complete accuracy everything which befell those concerned, whether it happened to be done well or ill by them.

It will be evident that no more important or

---

1 This was the lowest class in Roman society. Plebeians had few rights and were subject to taxes and compulsory services.

mightier deeds are to be found in history than those which have been enacted in these wars,—provided one wishes to base his judgment on the truth. For in them more remarkable feats have been performed than in any other wars with which we are acquainted; unless, indeed, any reader of this narrative should give the place of honor to antiquity, and consider contemporary achievements unworthy to be counted remarkable. There are those, for example, who call the soldiers of the present day "bowmen," while to those of the most ancient times they wish to attribute such lofty terms as "hand-to-hand fighters," "shield-men," and other names of that sort; and they think that the valor of those times has by no means survived to the present—an opinion which is at once careless and wholly remote from actual experience of these matters. For the thought has never occurred to them that, as regards the Homeric bowmen who had the misfortune to be ridiculed by this term[1] derived from their art, they were neither carried by horse nor protected by spear or shield.[2] In fact, there was no protection at all for their bodies; they entered battle on foot, and were compelled to conceal themselves, either singling out the shield of some comrade,[3] or seeking safety behind a tombstone on a mound,[4] from which position they could neither save themselves in case of rout, nor fall upon a flying foe. Least of all could they participate in a decisive struggle in the open, but they always seemed to be stealing something

which belonged to the men who were engaged in the struggle. And apart from this they were so indifferent in their practice of archery that they drew the bowstring only to the breast,[5] so that the missile sent forth was naturally impotent and harmless to those whom it hit.[6] Such, it is evident, was the archery of the past. But the bowmen of the present time go into battle wearing corselets and fitted out with greaves[7] which extend up to the knee. From the right side hang their arrows, from the other the sword. And there are some who have a spear also attached to them and, at the shoulders, a sort of small shield without a grip, such as to cover the region of the face and neck. They are expert horsemen, and are able without difficulty to direct their bows to either side while riding at full speed, and to shoot an opponent whether in pursuit or in flight. They draw the bowstring along by the forehead about opposite the right ear, thereby charging the arrow with such an impetus as to kill whoever stands in the way, shield and corselet alike having no power to check its force. Still there are those who take into consideration none of these things, who reverence and worship the ancient times, and give no credit to modern improvements. But no such consideration will prevent the conclusion that most great and notable deeds have been performed in these wars. And the history of them will begin at some distance back, telling of the fortunes in war of the Romans and the Medes [Persians], their reverses and their successes....

---

1 See *Iliad* 11. 385.
2 See *Iliad* 5. 192.
3 See *Iliad* 8. 267; 9. 371.
4 See *Iliad* 4. 113.
5 See *Iliad* 4. 123.
6 See *Iliad* 9. 390.
7 Corselets are armor for the chest, especially breastplates; greaves protect the shins.

1.5 The Donatists: *A Donatist Sermon* (*c*.318). Original in Latin.

EMPEROR CONSTANTINE'S (r.308–337) RECOGNITION and favoring of the Christian church ironically brought numerous tensions within Christianity to the fore. No longer united against a common foe, Christians formed splinter groups that maintained a particular interpretation of doctrine or demanded a certain standard of behavior. In North Africa, the key issue after Constantine's conversion was how to deal with those who had handed over their Bibles, church furnishings, and other emblems of their faith to escape persecution and death. The Donatists scorned the *traditores* (from the Latin verb *tradere*: to hand over), and, when the persecutions were over, they refused to allow such people to pick up their Christian lives again as if nothing had happened. In particular, they denied the pastoral rights of priests and bishops who had been *traditores*, and they were equally wary of anyone even *ordained* by men so compromised. In 311, when Caecilian—whom the Donatists suspected of collaborating with the persecutors—was ordained bishop of Carthage, the Donatists insisted on their own bishop, Majorinus. An appeal by the Catholics to resolve the crisis provoked Constantine to send troops. The resulting bloodshed was interpreted by the Donatists as a new persecution and martyrdom, strengthening their resolve. In this sermon, given a few years later to commemorate the event, the preacher hoped to fire his listeners to remain—or join—with the Donatists. He saw the "Catholics" and the emperor as inspired by the Devil, and he made fun of their epithet "heretic" for what he understood to be the true "Church of Christ."

[Source: *Donatist Martyr Stories: The Church in Conflict in Roman North Africa*, trans. Maureen A. Tilley, Translated Texts for Historians, 24 (Liverpool: Liverpool University Press, 1996), pp. 54–57 (notes modified).]

THE LORD HIMSELF does not wish the death of the one who is perishing but rather that that person should return and live.[1] He was ready to receive the confession of those who were sorry. Knowing this, when the contriver [i.e., the Devil, working largely through his creature, Constantine] came face to face with times of peace, by worldly seduction, he revived those minds he had overcome in battle by fear of torture.[2] He took away their humility, the only way to tame the anger of an indignant God, and he substituted pride, which he knew for certain would gravely offend God. He promoted the idea that the lapsed, the deserters of heavenly sacraments, could illicitly hold ecclesiastical office again.[3]

As much as he recently took pleasure in their weakness of faith, so now he rejoices in this fraud. He is even more secure when they are called "bishops" or "Christians," than when they fell to ruin in their denial of the Christian name. He has these nominal enemies while he remains secure in deception. As we have already said, this is how he holds onto those he deceives by this false use of the Name. Not only does

---

1 See Ezek. 33: 11.

2 Those who were wavering, about to abjure their alliance with the *traditores*, were deterred from repenting of their association with them by the prospect of being persecuted for being Donatists.

3 Donatists did not allow Catholic leaders who joined the Donatist fold to continue to preside over their congregations. They were admitted to the Donatist church as members of the laity. Catholics, on the other hand, recognized pastoral necessity and political prudence in cases where an entire Donatist congregation went over to the Catholic side under the leadership of its priest or bishop. Donatists treated schismatic Donatists returning to their church on a case-by-case basis.

he delight these miserable men with vainglory but he also ensnares the greedy by royal friendship and earthly gifts.[1]

Nevertheless, this rapacious robber was frustrated that he did not control everyone by this ruse. So the enemy of salvation concocted a more subtle conceit to violate the purity of faith. "Christ," he said, "is the lover of unity. Therefore, let there be unity." Those people who were already fawning on him and were deserted by God came to be called "Catholics." By prejudice in favor of the name, those who refused to communicate with them were called "heretics." He sent funds so that he might weaken their faith or provide an occasion for avarice through the publication of the law.[2] But when the course of justice holds firm and inflexible in the face of these seductive temptations, judges are ordered to intervene; the secular powers are forced to use coercion. Homes are encircled with battle standards; at the same time, threats of proscriptions[3] are launched against the rich. Sacraments are profaned; crowds are bedecked with idolatry; holy assemblies are transformed into splendid banquets.

O most faithful brothers and sisters, it is a crime even to publish what was said and done among the banquets of lascivious youths where despicable women were present.

How swiftly and completely did the situation change! The basilica, shameful to say, was turned into a fast-food restaurant. What grief to see such a crime in the house of the Lord, this place accustomed to pious prayers, now profaned by impure deeds and illegitimate incantations! Now I ask you, what person in whatever desperate condition would allow this to be done in their own home? No one would consent except the sort of person who would actually do it. Who denies that such deeds have the children of the Devil as their authors? Who calls the authors of the actions Christians, except the person who wishes to excuse the Devil himself or to disavow Christ the Lord? What diligence by the Serpent! So many evils let loose! How many hatched so that its

family might assume the divine Name and hide itself from that Name, the Name it disgraces by its deeds! O the strength of the divine patience so worthy of praise, bearing up while the villainy of evil is spreading! Divine patience puts up with having the deeds of the crafty enemy imputed to itself or to its Name. Let no one think that something trivial happens when so many schisms and heresies arise. Satan's disguise surely dishonors God and Christ through his wicked ministry and adulterous work.

But lest we wander too far from the main point, let us omit their defilement of holy virgins. I repress any mention of their slaughter of the priests of God. I keep silent about their assaults, their pillaging, their booty. This way even they may know that we deliberately select few things from among many and we expose it quickly and modestly, seeing that we are eager not to exact vengeance on our enemies but to free the souls of these miserable people from the jaws of the ravenous wolf, indeed from the very mouth of the Dragon.[4]

Therefore, the one who corrupts holy discipline could violate the chastity of faith under the by-word of unity, i.e., by compelling unity with himself, not with God. Neither the rulers of this world nor those of darkness arrange things to happen in such a way that what is ordered might reveal the person giving the order. What glorious examples, how many glorious examples of "the Church of God" or "the Church of Christ" issue among them? What signs of Christian confession? What exiles, public tokens of true faith and perfect devotion, might there be? By these deeds truth obviously could not lie hidden unless someone in defiance of conscience determined to place their hope in deceit just as the prophet said.[5]

Let us proceed to the final events. They erupted in open threats and unmistakable fury once their subterfuges failed and their snares wore out. At that time you could have seen bands of soldiers serving the Furies of the traditors. They were brought together to perform a crime, but they were thinking only of pay. They stood

---

1 Eusebius, *The History of The Church* (above, p. 4) quoted the letters documenting such gifts.
2 The author is again referring to imperial gifts.
3 Confiscations of property.
4 Matt. 7: 15; see Ezek. 22: 27.
5 See Jer. 7: 4 and 13: 25.

around with most attentive curiosity lest mercenary cruelty be allowed to do something too gently. The cruel mercenaries asserted that attention to so improper a spectacle was not so much defense of a perverse claim, as the exaction of blood according to some contract.

Although the people of God might have anticipated the coming slaughter and known about it from the arrangements being made, they did not flee out of fear of an imminent death. On the contrary, they flew undaunted to the house of prayer with a desire to suffer. There faith grazed on the sacred readings, and prescribed fasts fed them with continual prayers. When these souls are delivered into the hands of the iniquitous, by their prayers they are actually commended into the hands of God.[1] Behold, in imitation of the Lord's passion, this cohort of soldiers marshaled by latter-day Pharisees sets forth from their camps to the death of Christians. Against innocent hands stretched out to the Lord, their right hands are armed with cudgels.[2] But it may be said that those who are not slaughtered by the sword are less martyrs for having been beaten to death in this impious massacre.[3]

The sword of the tribune had not yet pierced though the honored throat of the holy bishop of Siciliba, but it pricked him and the rage of the devil revealed who his agents were. In the same way the patience of the glorious bishop revealed the Church of Christ. No one else appears as servant of Christ the Lord as much as someone who suffered the same things as the Lord. It says: "No servant is greater than his master; if they persecute me, they will persecute you."[4] This is why these blind "servants of God" who are loved by the world show how the Lord himself was "loved" by the world. If the world does not love even those who are its own, it is necessary for it to hate those whom the Lord Jesus chose from out of the world. It says: "If you were from the world, the world would love what is its own; but because you are not from the world, since I have chosen you from out of the world, for that reason does the world hate you."[5]

Finally, bloodshed marked the end of this hatred. Now the soldiers endorsed the contract and the covenant of crime in no other way than by the seal of blood. Everyone kept their eyes shut tight while each age group and sex was killed, cut down in the midst of the basilica. It is this very basilica, I say, between whose walls so many bodies were cut down and buried. Here, in the inscriptions, memory preserves the name of the persecution as Caecilianist[6] until the end of time, lest after his episcopate the parricide deceive others who were not privy to the things done in his name.

1.6 Orthodoxy's declaration: *The Nicaean Creed* (325). Original in Greek.

A DISPUTE BETWEEN BISHOP Alexander of Alexandria and Arius, an Alexandrian priest, concerning the relationship between the Father and the Son (Jesus Christ) within the Godhead had such far-flung repercussions that Emperor Constantine I (r.307-337) called the Council of Nicaea (325), the first "ecumenical" (universal) council, to adjudicate the matter. We do not know precisely what Arius taught, but he clearly subordinated the Son to the Father. The Council declared that the Son was of the "same substance" (*homousios*) as the Father and thus not subordinate, a formulation that Arius could not accept. Although Arius was excommunicated, some of his supporters remained in high positions. When Constantius II (r.337-361) came to the imperial throne, he favored the position that the Orthodox called "Arian" and supported Wulfilas, whose

---

1 See Luke 23: 46.
2 See Matt. 26: 47.
3 This alludes to the belief that the only true martyrs were those who had actually shed blood. Thus a person beaten to death without the breaking of the skin would be considered less than a martyr. The author obviously repudiates this differentiation among those dying for their faith.
4 John 15: 20.
5 John 15: 19.
6 A reference to Caecilian, appointed bishop of Carthage against Donatist wishes.

missionary work among the Goths led to their adoption of "Arianism." Although—or perhaps because—the Goths were allowed into the empire in 376, the Council of Constantinople, held in 381, affirmed the ban on Arianism, in effect branding as heretics the Goths and other barbarian tribes who adopted the Arian positions.

[Source: J.N.D. Kelly, *Early Christian Doctrines*, 2nd ed. (New York: Harper and Row, 1958), p. 232.]

WE BELIEVE IN ONE God, the Father almighty, maker of all things, visible and invisible;

And in one Lord Jesus Christ, the Son of God, begotten from the Father, only-begotten, that is, from the substance of the Father, God from God, light from light, true God from true God, begotten not made, of one substance [*homousios*] with the Father, through Whom all things came into being, things in heaven and things on earth, Who because of us men and because of our salvation came down and became incarnate, becoming man, suffered and rose again on the third day, ascended to the heavens, and will come to judge the living and the dead;

And in the Holy Spirit.

But as for those who say, There was when He was not, and, Before being born He was not, and that He came into existence out of nothing, or who assert that the Son of God is from a different hypostasis or substance, or is created, or is subject to alteration or change—these the Catholic Church anathematizes.[1]

---

1 I.e., excommunicates.

PATRISTIC THOUGHT

1.7 Relating this world to the next: Augustine, *The City of God* (413-426). Original in Latin.

As A YOUNG MAN, St. Augustine (354-430) wanted to be an orator and teacher—that is, a rhetorician—but his restless quest for life's meaning led him to make a dramatic conversion, chronicled in his *Confessions*. Later, as bishop of Hippo in North Africa (396-430), he became the most influential churchman of his day and for centuries to come. Counted among the Church Fathers, Augustine formulated many of the key themes of Western Christianity until at least the twelfth century. Perhaps the most enduring of his works was *The City of God*, which, by postulating two cities—the City of God and the City of Man—permitted Augustine to explore the mingling of the sacred with the secular realms; the uses of adversity in the world; the vision of Heaven as a place of total peace; and the idea that the life of man on earth is a pilgrimage—a holy trek—from home (the here-and-now) to a longed-for place of succor (the City of God). In spite of these universal and timeless themes, the book was written in response to a very specific historical event, the sack of Rome by the Visigoths under King Alaric in 410.

[Source: Augustine, *Concerning the City of God against the Pagans*, trans. Henry Bettenson (New York: Penguin, 1972), pp. 5-7, 13-17, 858-59, 881, 891-92.]

Book 1

Preface. The Purpose and Argument of this work
Here, my dear Marcellinus,[1] is the fulfilment of my promise, a book in which I have taken upon myself the task of defending the glorious City of God against those who prefer their own gods to the Founder of that City. I treat of it both as it exists in this world of time, a stranger among the ungodly, living by faith,[2] and as it stands in the security of its everlasting seat. This security it now awaits in steadfast patience, until "justice returns to judgment,"[3] but it is to attain it hereafter in virtue of its ascendancy over its enemies,

when the final victory is won and peace established. The task is long and arduous; but God is our helper.[4]

I know how great is the effort needed to convince the proud of the power and excellence of humility, an excellence which makes it soar above all the summits of this world, which sway in their temporal instability, overtopping them all with an eminence not arrogated by human pride, but granted by divine grace. For the King and Founder of this City which is our subject has revealed in the Scripture of his people this statement of the divine Law, "God resists the proud, but he gives grace to the humble."[5] This is God's prerogative; but man's arrogant spirit in its swelling pride has claimed

---

1 Marcellinus was an intimate disciple of St. Augustine sent by the Emperor Honorius to preside over the council summoned at Carthage to settle the dispute between Catholics and Donatists. Marcellinus was anxious to convert Volusianus, proconsul of Africa. Volusianus showed interest, but among his objections to Christianity was the charge that it had undermined the Roman Empire. Marcellinus wrote to ask for help from St. Augustine (who had already corresponded with Volusianus) and this led eventually to the writing of *The City of God*.
2 See Hab. 2: 4; Rom. 1: 17; Gal. 3: 11; Hebr. 10: 38.
3 Ps. 94: 15; Douay Ps. 93: 15.
4 See Ps. 118: 7; Douay Ps. 117: 7.
5 1 Peter 5: 5.

it as its own, and delights to hear this verse quoted in its own praise: "To spare the conquered, and beat down the proud."[1]

Therefore I cannot refrain from speaking about the city of this world, a city which aims at dominion, which holds nations in enslavement, but is itself dominated by that very lust of domination. I must consider this city as far as the scheme of this work demands and as occasion serves.

1. The enemies of Christianity were spared by the barbarians at the sack of Rome, out of respect for Christ

From this world's city there arise enemies against whom the City of God has to be defended, though many of these correct their godless errors and become useful citizens of that City. But many are inflamed with hate against it and feel no gratitude for the benefits offered by its Redeemer. The benefits are unmistakable; those enemies would not today be able to utter a word against the City if, when fleeing from the sword of their enemy, they had not found, in the City's holy places, the safety on which they now congratulate themselves.[2] The barbarians spared them for Christ's sake; and now these Romans assail Christ's name. The sacred places of the martyrs and the basilicas of the apostles bear witness to this, for in the sack of Rome they afforded shelter to fugitives, both Christian and pagan. The bloodthirsty enemy raged thus far, but here the frenzy of butchery was checked; to these refuges the merciful among the enemy conveyed those whom they had spared outside, to save them from encountering foes who had no such pity. Even men who elsewhere raged with all the savagery an enemy can show, arrived at places where practices generally allowed by laws of war were forbidden and their monstrous passion for violence was brought to a sudden halt; their lust for taking captives was subdued.

In this way many escaped who now complain of this Christian era, and hold Christ responsible for the disasters which their city endured. But they do not make Christ responsible for the benefits they received out of respect for Christ, to which they owed their lives. They attribute their deliverance to their own destiny; whereas if they had any right judgment they ought rather to attribute the harsh cruelty they suffered at the hands of their enemies to the providence of God. For God's providence constantly uses war to correct and chasten the corrupt morals of mankind, as it also uses such afflictions to train men in a righteous and laudable way of life, removing to a better state those whose life is approved, or else keeping them in this world for further service.

Moreover, they should give credit to this Christian era for the fact that these savage barbarians showed mercy beyond the custom of war—whether they so acted in general in honor of the name of Christ, or in places specially dedicated to Christ's name, buildings of such size and capacity as to give mercy a wider range. For this clemency our detractors ought rather to give thanks to God; they should have recourse to his name in all sincerity so as to escape the penalty of everlasting fire, seeing that so many of them assumed his name dishonestly, to escape the penalty of immediate destruction. Among those whom you see insulting Christ's servants with such wanton insolence there are very many who came unscathed through that terrible time of massacre only by passing themselves off as Christ's servants. And now with ungrateful pride and impious madness they oppose his name in the perversity of their hearts, so that they may incur the punishment of eternal darkness; but then they took refuge in that name, though with deceitful lips, so that they might continue to enjoy this transitory light....

8. Blessings and disasters often shared by good and bad

No doubt this question will be asked, "Why does the divine mercy extend even to the godless and ungrateful?" The only explanation is that it is the mercy of one "who makes his sun rise on the good and on the bad, and sends rain alike on the righteous and the unrighteous."[3] Some of the wicked are brought to penitence by considering these facts, and amend their impiety, while others, in the words of the Apostle,

---

1 Virgil, *Aeneid* 6. 853.
2 This refers to the clemency of Alaric to those who took sanctuary in Christian shrines, and especially in the basilicas of St. Peter and St. Paul.
3 Matt. 5: 45.

"despise the riches of God's goodness and forbearance, in the hardness and impenitence of their hearts, and lay up for themselves a store of wrath in the day of God's anger and of the revelation of the just judgment of God, who will repay every man according to his actions."[1] Yet the patience of God still invites the wicked to penitence, just as God's chastisement trains the good in patient endurance. God's mercy embraces the good for their cherishing, just as his severity chastens the wicked for their punishment. God, in his providence, decided to prepare future blessings for the righteous, which the unrighteous will not enjoy, and sorrows for the ungodly, with which the good will not be tormented. But he has willed that these temporal goods and temporal evils should befall good and bad alike, so that the good things should not be too eagerly coveted, when it is seen that the wicked also enjoy them, and that the evils should not be discreditably shunned, when it is apparent that the good are often afflicted with them.

The most important question is this: What use is made of the things thought to be blessings, and of the things reputed evil? The good man is not exalted by this world's goods; nor is he overwhelmed by this world's ills. The bad man is punished by misfortune of this kind just because he is corrupted by good fortune.

However, it often happens that God shows more clearly his manner of working in the distribution of good and bad fortune. For if punishment were obviously inflicted on every wrongdoing in this life, it would be supposed that nothing was reserved for the last judgment; on the other hand, if God's power never openly punished any sin in this world, there would be an end to belief in providence. Similarly in respect of good fortune; if God did not grant it to some petitioners with manifest generosity, we should not suppose that these temporal blessings were his concern, while if he bestowed prosperity on all just for the asking we might think that God was to be served merely for the sake of those rewards, and any service of him would prove us not godly but rather greedy and covetous.

This being so, when the good and the wicked suffer alike, the identity of their sufferings does not mean that there is no difference between them. Though the sufferings are the same, the sufferers remain different. Virtue and vice are not the same, even if they undergo the same torment. The fire which makes gold shine makes chaff smoke; the same flail breaks up the straw, and clears the grain; and oil is not mistaken for lees [dregs] because both are forced out by the same press. In the same way, the violence which assails good men to test them, to cleanse and purify them, effects in the wicked their condemnation, ruin, and annihilation. Thus the wicked, under pressure of affliction, execrate God and blaspheme; the good, in the same affliction, offer up prayers and praises. This shows that what matters is the nature of the sufferer, not the nature of the sufferings. Stir a cesspit, and a foul stench arises; stir a perfume, and a delightful fragrance ascends. But the movement is identical.

9. *The reasons why the good and the wicked are equally afflicted*

Thus, in this universal catastrophe, the sufferings of Christians have tended to their moral improvement, because they viewed them with the eyes of faith.

First, they consider in humility the sins which have moved God's indignation so that he has filled the world with dire calamities. And although they are free from criminal and godless wickedness, still they do not regard themselves as so far removed from such wrongdoing as not to deserve to suffer the temporal ills which are the recompense of sin. Everyone of them, however commendable his life, gives way at times to physical desires, and, while avoiding monstrous crimes, the sink of iniquity, and the abomination of godlessness, is yet guilty of some sins, infrequent sins, perhaps, or more frequent because more trivial. Apart from this, it is not easy to find anyone who, when confronted with those whose fearful arrogance, lust, and greed, whose detestable wickedness and impiety, have caused God to give effect to his threats and warnings by bringing destruction on the earth—it is not, I say, easy to find anyone who regards such men as they should be regarded—who, when he meets them, treats them as they should be treated.

We tend culpably to evade our responsibility when we ought to instruct and admonish them, sometimes even with sharp reproof and censure, either because

---

1 Rom. 2: 4-6; "the Apostle" refers always to St. Paul in the works of the early Fathers of the Church.

the task is irksome, or because we are afraid of giving offence; or it may be that we shrink from incurring their enmity, for fear that they may hinder and harm us in worldly matters in respect either of what we eagerly seek to attain, or of what we weakly dread to lose. And so, although the good dislike the way of life of the wicked, and therefore do not fall into the condemnation which is in store for the wicked after this life, nevertheless, because they are tender towards damnable sins of the wicked, and thus fall into sin through fear of such people (pardonable and comparatively trivial though those sins may be), they are justly chastised with afflictions in this world, although they are spared eternal punishment; and they rightly feel this life to be bitter when they are associated with the wicked in the afflictions sent by God. But it was through love of this world's sweetness that they refused to be bitter to those sinners.

If anyone refrains from reproof and correction of ill-doers because he looks for a more suitable occasion, or because he fears that this will make them worse, or fears that they will hinder the instruction of others, who are weak, in a good and godly way of life, and that they will oppress them, and turn them away from the faith, in such a case the action seems to be prompted not by self-interest but by counsels of charity. What is culpable is when those whose life is different and who abhor the deeds of the wicked are nevertheless indulgent to the sins of others, which they ought to reprehend and reprove, because they are concerned to avoid giving offence to them, in case they should harm themselves in respect of things which may be rightly and innocently enjoyed by good men, but which they desire more than is right for those who are strangers in this world and who fix their hope on a heavenly country.

There are the weaker brothers, in the married state, who have children or look to have them, who are masters of houses and households; the Apostle addresses them in the churches, teaching them and warning them how they ought to live, wives with husbands and husbands with wives, children with parents and parents with children, servants with masters and masters with servants.[1] Such men are eager to acquire many of this world's temporal goods, and grieve to lose them, and for that reason they have not the heart to offend men whose lives of shame and crime they detest. But they are not alone.

Even those who have a higher standard of life, who are not entangled in the bonds of marriage, who are content with little food and scanty clothing, are often fearful of attacks by the wicked upon their reputation and their safety, and so refrain from reproaches. They are not so afraid of the wicked as to yield to their villainous threats to the extent of committing crimes like theirs; but though they do not commit them they too often fail to reprehend them, for although they might perhaps convert some by such rebuke they fear that, if the attempt failed, their safety and reputation might be endangered or destroyed. And this is not due to prudence, nor is it because they see their reputation and safety as essential means whereby mankind may receive the benefit of instruction; it is rather due to weakness—because they delight in flattery and popularity and because they dread the judgment of the mob and the torture or death of the body. In fact, they are constrained by self-interest, not by the obligations of charity.

So this seems to me a major reason why the good are chastised along with the evil, when God decides to punish moral corruption with temporal calamities. Good and bad are chastised together, not because both alike live evil lives, but because both alike, though not in the same degree, love this temporal life. But the good ought to have despised it, so that the others might be reformed and corrected and might aim at life eternal; or, if they refused to be partners in this enterprise, so that they might be borne with, and loved as Christians should love their enemies, since in this life it is always uncertain whether or not they are likely to experience a change of heart.

In this matter a uniquely heavy responsibility rests on those to whom this message is given by the prophet: "He indeed will die in his sin, but I will require his blood at the hand of the watchman."[2] For "watchmen," that is, leaders of the people, have been appointed in the churches for this purpose, that they should be unsparing in their condemnation of sin.

---

1 See Col. 3: 18-22.
2 Ezek. 33: 6.

This does not mean that a man is entirely free from blame in this regard if, without being a "watchman," he recognizes, but ignores, opportunities of warning and admonishing those with whom the exigencies of this life force him to associate—if he evades this duty for fear of offending them, because he is concerned for those worldly advantages, which are not in themselves discreditable, but to which he is unduly attached. There is a further reason for the infliction of temporal suffering on the good, as is seen in the case of Job—that the spirit of man may be tested, that he may learn for himself what is the degree of disinterested devotion that he offers to God....

Book 19

5. *Social life; its value and its dangers*

The philosophies hold the view that the life of the wise man should be social; and in this we support them much more heartily. For here we are, with the nineteenth book in hand on the subject of the City of God; and how could that City have made its first start, how could it have advanced along its course, how could it attain its appointed goal, if the life of the saints were not social? And yet, who would be capable of listing the number and the gravity of the ills which abound in human society amid the distresses of our mortal condition? Who would be competent to assess them? Our philosophers should listen to a character in one of their own comedies, voicing a sentiment with which all mankind agrees:

I married a wife; and misery I found!
Children were born; and they increased my cares.[1]

Again, think of the disorders of love, as listed in another quotation from Terence:

Wrongs and suspicions, enmities and war—
Then, peace again.[2]

Have they not everywhere filled up the story of human experience? Are they not of frequent occurrence, even in the honorable love of friends? The story of mankind is full of them at every point; for in that story we are aware of wrongs, suspicions, enmities and war—undoubted evils, these. And even peace is a doubtful good, since we do not know the hearts of those with whom we wish to maintain peace, and even if we could know them today, we should not know what they might be like tomorrow. In fact, who are, in general, more friendly, or at any rate ought to be, than those within the walls of the same home? And yet, is anyone perfectly serene in that situation, when such grievous ills have so often arisen from the secret treachery of people within those walls? And the bitterness of these ills matches the sweetness of the peace that was reckoned genuine, when it was in fact only a very clever pretense.

This explains why some words of Cicero come so close to our hearts that we cannot but sigh when we read:

No treachery is more insidious than that which is hidden under a pretense of loyalty, or under the name of kinship. For against an open adversary you could be on your guard and thus easily avoid him; but this hidden evil, within the house and family, not only arises before you are aware but even overwhelms you before you can catch sight of it and investigate it.[3]

Hence also that inspired utterance, "A man's enemies are those of his own household,"[4] is heard with deep sorrow of heart. For even if anyone is strong enough to bear these ills with equanimity, or watchful enough to guard with foresight and discretion against the contrivances of pretended friendship, nevertheless he cannot but feel grievous anguish, if he himself is a good man, at the wickedness of the traitors, when by experience he knows their utter viciousness, whether they were always evil and their goodness was a sham, or whether they suffered a change from good-nature to the malice that they now display. If, then, safety is not to be found in the home, the common refuge from the evils that befall mankind, what shall we say of the

---

1 Terence, *Adelphi* 5. 4. 13-14.
2 Terence, *Eunuchus* 1. 1. 14-15.
3 Cicero, *Actio in Verrem* 2. 1. 13.
4 Matt. 10: 36.

city? The larger the city, the more is its forum filled with civil lawsuits and criminal trials, even if that city be at peace, free from the alarms or—what is more frequent—the bloodshed, of sedition and civil war. It is true that cities are at times exempt from those occurrences; they are never free from the danger of them....

20. *The fellow-citizens of the saints are in this life made happy by hope*

We see, then, that the Supreme Good, of the City of God is everlasting and perfect peace, which is not the peace through which men pass in their mortality, in their journey from birth, to death, but that peace in which they remain in their immortal state, experiencing no adversity at all. In view of this, can anyone deny that this is the supremely blessed life, or that the present life on earth, however full it may be of the greatest possible blessings of soul and body and of external circumstances, is, in comparison, most miserable? For all that, if anyone accepts the present life in such a spirit that he uses it with the end in view of that other life on which he has set his heart with all his ardor and for which he hopes with all his confidence, such a man may without absurdity be called happy even now, though rather by future hope than in present reality. Present reality without that hope is, to be sure, a false happiness, in fact, an utter misery. For the present does not bring into play the true goods of the mind; since no wisdom is true wisdom if it does not direct its attention, in all its prudent decisions, its resolute actions, its self-control and its just dealings with others, towards that ultimate state in which God will be all in all,[1] in the assurance of eternity and the perfection of peace....

26. ..."Blessed is the people, whose God is the Lord."[2] It follows that a people alienated from that God must be wretched. Yet even such a people loves a peace of its own, which is not to be rejected; but it will not possess it in the end, because it does not make good use of it before the end. Meanwhile, however, it is important for us also that this people should possess this peace in this life, since so long as the two cities are intermingled we also make use of the peace of Babylon—although the People of God is by faith set free from Babylon, so that in the meantime they are only pilgrims in the midst of her. That is why the Apostle instructs the Church to pray for kings of that city and those in high positions, adding these words: "that we may lead a quiet and peaceful life with all devotion and love."[3] And when the prophet Jeremiah predicted to the ancient People of God the coming captivity, and bade them, by God's inspiration, to go obediently to Babylon, serving God even by their patient endurance, he added his own advice that prayers should be offered for Babylon, "because in her peace is your peace"[4]—meaning, of course, the temporal peace of the meantime, which is shared by good and bad alike.

1.8 Biblical exegesis: Pope Gregory the Great, *Moralia in Job* (591). Original in Latin.

POPE GREGORY THE GREAT (r.590-604) was not so much appreciated in his own lifetime or right after his death as he was a century or so later. Because he was instrumental in converting the English, he was much appreciated there (see Bede, *Ecclesiastical History of the English People*, below, p. 97). Eventually his reputation grew in Rome as well. At the same time, his writings became enormously popular. His *Moralia in Job* was the model for biblical exegesis—the critical analysis of the Bible—for centuries, and since the Bible was the foundational text of Christianity, this made his technique exceptionally important. A very long work, the *Moralia* subjected nearly every phrase of every verse of the *Book of Job* to a three-part analysis: historical (or literal), allegorical, and moral. The excerpt here takes up just one simple verse: 1: 2: "And there were

---

1   1 Cor. 15: 28.
2   Ps. 144: 15; Douay Ps. 143: 15.
3   1 Tim. 2: 2.
4   Jer. 29: 7.

born unto him seven sons and three daughters." Gregory first took up the historical explanation of this verse in the context of explaining the first five verses of Chapter 1 of the *Book of Job*. He then backtracked to give the allegorical interpretation for all of these verses. Finally, he provided the moral meaning. To show the different levels clearly, the passages here are concerned with 1:2 only, skipping the other verses.

[Source: Gregory the Great, *Moralia in Iob. Libri I-X*, ed. Marcus Adriaen, Corpus Christianorum. Series Latina 143 (Turnhout: Brepols, 1979), pp. 27, 33-34, 45-46. Translated by Barbara H. Rosenwein.]

[1.4.5] *And there were born unto him seven sons and three daughters.* [Historical interpretation:] Having many children often entices the heart of the parent to avarice, for it is the more inflamed with ambition to acquire an inheritance the more it is fertilized by many children. Blessed Job thus is both called just and said to have been the father of numerous offspring in order to show how holy his mind was. He is the one who, at the beginning of his book, is declared devout in offering sacrifices; later on, he himself reminds us that he was also quick to give alms.[1] Let us then consider what fortitude he showed: all his affection for so many heirs did not induce him to obtain an inheritance for them....

[1.14.18] *And there were born unto him seven sons and three daughters.* [Allegorical interpretation:] What is understood by the number "seven" except the sum total of perfection? For, to say nothing of the arguments of human reason about the number seven—which maintain that it is perfect because it consists of the first even number and the first uneven; because it consists of the first number that can be divided [i.e., 4 can be divided by 2]; and because it consists of the first number that can *not* be divided [namely 3]—we know most certainly that holy Scripture normally uses the number seven to signify perfection. Thus it tells us that on the seventh day the Lord rested from His works. Thus, too, it says that the seventh day was given to human beings to rest on the Sabbath....

[19] *There were born unto him seven sons.* [By this is clearly meant] the Apostles who were powerfully inspired to preach. While they carried out the precepts of perfection, they maintained in their manner of life the fortitude, as it were, of the superior sex. Thus it is that twelve were chosen to be filled with the perfection of the sevenfold grace. From the number seven we rise up to twelve, for when its component parts are multiplied, they make twelve. Whether four is multiplied by three or three by four, seven becomes twelve. Thus the twelve holy Apostles, because they were sent to proclaim the holy Trinity to the four corners of the world, were chosen so that by their very number they might show the perfection which they proclaimed by their lives and their voices.

[20] *And three daughters were born.* What do we understand by the daughters but the weaker people among the faithful who, even if they in no way persevere with tenacious virtue to the perfection of the work, nevertheless steadfastly hold to their approved faith the Trinity? Thus, the order of the preachers is represented by "the seven sons," while the multitude who hear them are "the three daughters." Indeed, it may be that by the "three daughters" are designated the three orders of the faithful. The daughters are named after the sons because, after the outstanding fortitude of the Apostles, there followed three groups of faithful in the life of the Church: the pastors, the continent, and the married. This is why the prophet Ezekiel also says that he had heard of three men who were liberated: Noah, Daniel, and Job. For what is signified by Noah, who guided the ark in the waves, except the order of [Church] leaders who, while they lead the people to the model of life, rule the holy Church amidst the floods of temptation? What is meant by Daniel, whose miraculous abstinence is described, except the life of the continent who, while

---

1 I.e., charity.

they give up all things that have to do with the world, rule over despised Babylon with their high mind? What is signified by Job other than the life of the virtuous married people who, while they do pious deeds with the worldly things that they possess, proceed along the earthly path (as it were) to the heavenly fatherland? Therefore, the three daughters are rightly named after the sons because these three groups of the faithful followed after the holy apostles....

[1.27.38] *And there were born unto him seven sons and three daughters.* [Moral interpretation:] Indeed, seven sons are born to us when, by conceiving good thoughts, the seven virtues of the Holy Spirit are born in us. The prophet enumerates this internal offspring—when the Spirit fertilizes the mind—by saying: "And the spirit of the Lord shall rest upon him: the spirit of wisdom and of understanding, the spirit of counsel and of fortitude, the spirit of knowledge, and of piety. And he shall be filled with the spirit of the fear of the Lord.[1] When, therefore, wisdom, understanding, counsel, fortitude, knowledge, piety, and the fear of the Lord is engendered in each of us by the coming of the Spirit, a sort of abiding posterity is propagated in the mind, which preserves the birth of our heavenly nobility for life the longer it unites with the love of eternity. In addition, without doubt the seven sons have three sisters in us, because whatever virile thing those senses of virtues do, they join to hope, faith, and charity [all feminine nouns in Latin, and therefore "sisters"]. Nor do the seven sons advance to the perfection of the number ten unless all that they do is done in hope, faith, and charity.

1.9 Monasticism: *The Benedictine Rule* (*c.*540). Original in Latin.

ST. BENEDICT (d.*c.*547), FOUNDER OF several monasteries near Rome, wrote the most famous *Rule* for monks. In large measure it is an organized and institutionalized presentation of biblical directives, especially those inspired by the gospels. The key virtue of the monk in Benedict's *Rule* is obedience. The key duty is the Work of God, the hours of daily chant—known as the offices[2]—centered on the psalter, all 150 psalms of which the monks were to complete each week. Within a half century or so, Benedict's *Rule* had been incorporated alongside others in many Western monasteries. Under the Carolingians in the ninth century (see Chapter 3), it was adopted as the official norm for the monasteries of the empire. Compare its notions of human virtue and life on earth with those expressed in Augustine's *City of God*, p. 21 above.

[Source: *The Rule of St. Benedict in Latin and English with Notes*, ed. Timothy Fry (Collegeville, MN: Liturgical Press, 1981), pp. 157, 162, 165, 167, 169, 171, 173, 179, 181, 183, 191, 193, 195, 203, 205, 211, 213, 215, 219, 231, 233, 239, 241, 249, 251, 261, 263, 267, 269, 271, 273, 295, 297 (notes modified).]

PROLOGUE

Listen carefully, my son, to the master's instructions, and attend to them with the ear of your heart. This is advice from a father who loves you; welcome it, and faithfully put it into practice. The labor of obedience will bring you back to him from whom you had drifted through the sloth of disobedience. This message of mine is for you, then, if you are ready to give up your own will, once and for all, and armed with the strong and noble weapons of obedience to do battle for the true King, Christ the Lord....

1 Isa. 11 : 2-3.
2 These are Vigils (the Night Office), Lauds, Prime, Terce, Sext, None, Vespers, and Compline.

The Lord waits for us daily to translate into action, as we should, his holy teachings. Therefore our life span has been lengthened by way of a truce, that we may amend our misdeeds. As the Apostle says: "Do you not know that the patience of God is leading you to repent?"[1] And indeed the Lord assures us in his love: "I do not wish the death of the sinner, but that he turn back to me and live."[2]

Brothers, now that we have asked the Lord who will dwell in his tent, we have heard the instruction for dwelling in it, but only if we fulfill the obligations of those who live there. We must, then, prepare our hearts and bodies for the battle of holy obedience to his instructions. What is not possible to us by nature, let us ask the Lord to supply by the help of his grace. If we wish to reach eternal life, even as we avoid the torments of hell, then—while there is still time, while we are in this body and have time to accomplish all these things by the light of life—we must run and do now what will profit us forever.

Therefore we intend to establish a school for the Lord's service.[3] In drawing up its regulations, we hope to set down nothing harsh, nothing burdensome. The good of all concerned, however, may prompt us to a little strictness in order to amend faults and to safeguard love. Do not be daunted immediately by fear and run away from the road that leads to salvation. It is bound to be narrow at the outset. But as we progress in this way of life and in faith, we shall run on the path of God's commandments, our hearts overflowing with the inexpressible delight of love. Never swerving from his instructions, then, but faithfully observing his teaching in the monastery until death, we shall through patience share in the sufferings of Christ that we may deserve also to share in his kingdom. Amen.

CHAPTER I. THE KINDS OF MONKS

There are clearly four kinds of monks. First, there are the cenobites, that is to say, those who belong to a monastery, where they serve under a rule and an abbot.

Second, there are the anchorites or hermits, who have come through the test of living in a monastery for a long time and have passed beyond the first fervor of monastic life. Thanks to the help and guidance of many, they are now trained to fight against the devil. They have built up their strength and go from the battle line in the ranks of their brothers to the single combat of the desert. Self-reliant now, without the support of another, they are ready with God's help to grapple single-handed with the vices of body and mind.

Third, there are the sarabaites, the most detestable kind of monks, who with no experience to guide them, no rule to try them "as gold is tried in a furnace,"[4] have a character as soft as lead. Still loyal to the world by their actions, they clearly lie to God by their tonsure. Two or three together, or even alone, without a shepherd, they pen themselves up in their own sheep folds, not the Lord's. Their law is what they like to do, whatever strikes their fancy. Anything they believe in and choose, they call holy; anything they dislike, they consider forbidden.

Fourth and finally, there are the monks called gyrovagues, who spend their entire lives drifting from region to region, staying as guests for three or four days in different monasteries. Always on the move, they never settle down and are slaves to their own wills and gross appetites. In every way they are worse than sarabaites.

It is better to keep silent than to speak of all these and their disgraceful way of life. Let us pass them by, then, and with the help of the Lord, proceed to draw up a plan for the strong kind, the cenobites.

CHAPTER 2. QUALITIES OF THE ABBOT

To be worthy of the task of governing a monastery, the abbot must always remember what his title signifies and act as a superior should. He is believed to hold the place of Christ in the monastery, since he is addressed by a title of Christ, as the Apostle indicates: "You have received the spirit of adoption of sons by

---

1   Rom. 2: 4.
2   Ezek. 33: 11.
3   In the Latin of this period, "school" could mean not only a place where instruction was received but the group receiving instruction, as well as, more generally, a vocational corporation (such as a guild) of people devoted to a common craft or service. A similar usage can be seen in the English "school of painters" or "school of porpoises."
4   Prov. 27: 21.

which we exclaim, abba, father."[1] Therefore, the abbot must never teach or decree or command anything that would deviate from the Lord's instructions. On the contrary, everything he teaches and commands should, like the leaven of divine justice, permeate the minds of his disciples. Let the abbot always remember that at the fearful judgment of God, not only his teaching but also his disciples' obedience will come under scrutiny. The abbot must, therefore, be aware that the shepherd will bear the blame wherever the father of the household finds that the sheep have yielded no profit. Still, if he has faithfully shepherded a restive and disobedient flock, always striving to cure their unhealthy ways, it will be otherwise: the shepherd will be acquitted at the Lord's judgment. Then, like the Prophet, he may say to the Lord: "I have not hidden your justice in my heart; I have proclaimed your truth and your salvation,"[2] "but they spurned and rejected me."[3] Then at last the sheep that have rebelled against his care will be punished by the overwhelming power of death....

CHAPTER 3. SUMMONING THE BROTHERS FOR COUNSEL

As often as anything important is to be done in the monastery, the abbot shall call the whole community together and himself explain what the business is; and after hearing the advice of the brothers, let him ponder it and follow what he judges the wiser course. The reason why we have said all should be called for counsel is that the Lord often reveals what is better to the younger. The brothers, for their part, are to express their opinions with all humility, and not presume to defend their own views obstinately. The decision is rather the abbot's to make, so that when he has determined what is more prudent, all may obey. Nevertheless, just as it is proper for disciples to obey their master, so it is becoming for the master on his part to settle everything with foresight and fairness.

Accordingly in every instance, all are to follow the teaching of the rule, and no one shall rashly deviate from it. In the monastery no one is to follow his own heart's desire, nor shall anyone presume to contend with his abbot defiantly, or outside the monastery. Should anyone presume to do so, let him be subjected to the discipline of the rule. Moreover, the abbot himself must fear God and keep the rule in everything he does; he can be sure beyond any doubt that he will have to give an account of all his judgments to God, the most just of judges.

If less important business of the monastery is to be transacted, he shall take counsel with the seniors only, as it is written: "Do everything with counsel and you will not be sorry afterward."[4]

CHAPTER 4. THE TOOLS FOR GOOD WORKS

First of all, "love the Lord God with your whole heart, your whole soul and all your strength, and love your neighbor as yourself."[5] Then the following: "You are not to kill, not to commit adultery; you are not to steal nor to covet; you are not to bear false witness."[6] "You must honor everyone, and never do to another what you do not want done to yourself."[7]

"Renounce yourself in order to follow Christ";[8] "discipline your body";[9] do not pamper yourself, but love fasting. You must relieve the lot of the poor, "clothe the naked, visit the sick,"[10] and bury the dead. Go to help the troubled and console the sorrowing.

Your way of acting should be different from the world's way; the love of Christ must come before all else. You are not to act in anger or nurse a grudge. Rid your heart of all deceit. Never give a hollow greeting of peace or turn away when someone needs your love.

---

1   Rom. 8: 15.
2   Ps. 40: 11; Douay Ps. 39: 11.
3   Isa. 1: 2; Ezek. 20: 27.
4   Ecclus. 32: 24.
5   Matt. 22: 37–39; Mark 12: 30–31; Luke 10: 27.
6   Rom. 13: 9; Matt. 19: 18; Mark 10: 19; Luke 18: 20.
7   1 Pet. 2: 17; Tob. 4: 16; Matt. 7: 12; Luke 6: 31.
8   Matt. 16: 24; Luke 9: 23.
9   1 Cor. 9: 27.
10 Matt. 25: 36.

Bind yourself to no oath lest it prove false, but speak the truth with heart and tongue....

CHAPTER 7. HUMILITY

Brothers, divine Scripture calls to us saying: "Whoever exalts himself shall be humbled, and whoever humbles himself shall be exalted."[1] In saying this, therefore, it shows us that every exaltation is a kind of pride, which the Prophet indicates he has shunned, saying: "O Lord, my heart is not exalted; my eyes are not lifted up and I have not walked in the ways of the great nor gone after marvels beyond me."[2] And why? "If I had not a humble spirit, but were exalted instead, then you would treat me like a weaned child on its mother's lap."[3]

Accordingly, brothers, if we want to reach the highest summit of humility, if we desire to attain speedily that exaltation in heaven to which we climb by the humility of this present life, then by our ascending actions we must set up that ladder on which Jacob in a dream saw "angels descending and ascending."[4] Without doubt, this descent and ascent can signify only that we descend by exaltation and ascend by humility. Now the ladder erected is our life on earth, and if we humble our hearts the Lord will raise it to heaven. We may call our body and soul the sides of this ladder, into which our divine vocation has fitted the various steps of humility and discipline as we ascend.

The first step of humility, then, is that a man keeps the "fear of God" always "before his eyes"[5] and never forgets it. He must constantly remember everything God has commanded, keeping in mind that all who despise God will burn in hell for their sins, and all who fear God have everlasting life awaiting them. While he guards himself at every moment from sins and vices of thought or tongue, of hand or foot, of self-will or bodily desire, let him recall that he is always seen by God in heaven, that his actions every-where are in God's sight and are reported by angels at every hour....

CHAPTER 8. THE DIVINE OFFICE AT NIGHT

During the winter season, that is, from the first of November until Easter, it seems reasonable to arise at the eighth hour of the night. By sleeping until a little past the middle of the night, the brothers can arise with their food fully digested. In the time remaining after Vigils [the Night Office], those who need to learn some of the psalter or readings should study them.

Between Easter and the first of November mentioned above, the time for Vigils should be adjusted so that a very short interval after Vigils will give the monks opportunity to care for nature's needs. Then, at daybreak, Lauds should follow immediately.

CHAPTER 9. THE NUMBER OF PSALMS AT THE NIGHT OFFICE

During the winter season, Vigils begin with the verse: "Lord, open my lips and my mouth shall proclaim your praise."[6] After this has been said three times, the following order is observed: Psalm 3 with "Glory be to the Father"; Psalm 94 with a refrain, or at least chanted; an Ambrosian hymn; then six psalms with refrain.

After the psalmody, a versicle is said and the abbot gives a blessing. When all are seated on the benches, the brothers in turn read three selections from the book on the lectern. After each reading a responsory is sung.[7] "Glory be to the Father" is not sung after the first two responsories, but only after the third reading. As soon as the cantor begins to sing "Glory be to the Father," let all the monks rise from their seats in honor and reverence for the Holy Trinity. Besides the inspired books of the Old and New Testaments, the works read at Vigils should include explanations of Scripture by reputable and orthodox catholic Fathers.

---

1   Luke 14: 11; 18: 14.
2   Ps. 131: 1; Douay Ps. 130: 1.
3   Ps. 131: 2; Douay Ps. 130: 2.
4   Gen. 28: 12.
5   Ps. 36: 2; Douay Ps. 35: 2.
6   Ps. 51: 17; Douay Ps. 50: 17.
7   That is, a chanted response.

When these three readings and their responsories have been finished, the remaining six psalms are sung with an "alleluia" refrain. This ended, there follow a reading from the Apostle recited by heart, a versicle and the litany, that is, "Lord, have mercy." And so Vigils are concluded....

CHAPTER 16. THE CELEBRATION OF THE DIVINE OFFICE DURING THE DAY

The Prophet says: "Seven times a day have I praised you."[1] We will fulfill this sacred number of seven if we satisfy our obligations of service at Lauds, Prime, Terce, Sext, None, Vespers and Compline, for it was of these hours during the day that he said: "Seven times a day have I praised you." Concerning Vigils, the same Prophet says: "At midnight I arose to give you praise."[2] Therefore, we should "praise" our Creator "for his just judgments" at these times: Lauds, Prime, Terce, Sext, None, Vespers and Compline; and "let us arise at night to give Him praise." ...

CHAPTER 18. THE ORDER OF THE PSALMODY

... We urge that if anyone finds this distribution of the psalms unsatisfactory, he should arrange whatever he judges better, provided that the full complement of one hundred and fifty psalms is by all means carefully maintained every week, and that the series begins anew each Sunday at Vigils. For monks who in a week's time say less than the full psalter with the customary canticles betray extreme indolence and lack of devotion in their service. We read, after all, that our holy Fathers, energetic as they were, did all this in a single day. Let us hope that we, lukewarm as we are, can achieve it in a whole week....

CHAPTER 22. THE SLEEPING ARRANGEMENTS OF THE MONKS

The monks are to sleep in separate beds. They receive bedding as provided by the abbot, suitable to monastic life.

If possible, all are to sleep in one place, but should the size of the community preclude this, they will sleep in groups of ten or twenty under the watchful care of seniors. A lamp must be kept burning in the room until morning.

They sleep clothed and girded with belts or cords; but they should remove their knives, lest they accidentally cut themselves in their sleep. Thus the monks will always be ready to arise without delay when the signal is given; each will hasten to arrive at the Work of God before the others, yet with all dignity and decorum. The younger brothers should not have their beds next to each other, but interspersed among those of the seniors. On arising for the Work of God, they will quietly encourage each other, for the sleepy like to make excuses....

CHAPTER 33. MONKS AND PRIVATE OWNERSHIP

Above all, this evil practice must be uprooted and removed from the monastery. We mean that without an order from the abbot, no one may presume to give, receive or retain anything as his own, nothing at all—not a book, writing tablets or stylus [writing implement]—in short, not a single item, especially since monks may not have the free disposal even of their own bodies and wills. For their needs, they are to look to the father of the monastery and are not allowed anything which the abbot has not given or permitted. "All things should be the common possession" of all, as it is written, "so that no one presumes to call anything his own."[3]

But if anyone is caught indulging in this most evil practice, he should be warned a first and a second time. If he does not amend, let him be subjected to punishment.

CHAPTER 34. DISTRIBUTION OF GOODS ACCORDING TO NEED

It is written: "Distribution was made to each one as he had need."[4] By this we do not imply that there should be favoritism—God forbid—but rather con-

---

1   Ps. 119: 164; Douay Ps. 118: 164.
2   Ps. 119: 62; Douay Ps. 118: 62.
3   See Acts 4: 32.
4   Acts 4: 35.

sideration for weaknesses. Whoever needs less should thank God and not be distressed, but whoever needs more should feel humble because of his weakness, not self-important because of the kindness shown him. In this way all the members will be at peace. First and foremost, there must be no word or sign of the evil of grumbling, no manifestation of it for any reason at all. If, however, anyone is caught grumbling, let him undergo more severe discipline....

CHAPTER 39. THE PROPER AMOUNT OF FOOD

For the daily meals, whether at noon or in mid-afternoon, it is enough, we believe, to provide all tables with two kinds of cooked food because of individual weaknesses. In this way, the person who may not be able to eat one kind of food may partake of the other. Two kinds of cooked food, therefore, should suffice for all the brothers, and if fruit or fresh vegetables are available, a third dish may also be added. A generous pound of bread is enough for a day whether for only one meal or for both dinner and supper. In the latter case the cellarer[1] will set aside one third of this pound and give it to the brothers at supper.

Should it happen that the work is heavier than usual, the abbot may decide—and he will have the authority—to grant something additional, provided that it is appropriate, and that above all overindulgence is avoided, lest a monk experience indigestion. For nothing is so inconsistent with the life of any Christian as overindulgence. Our Lord says: "Take care that your hearts are not weighed down with overindulgence."[2]

Young boys should not receive the same amount as their elders, but less, since in all matters frugality is the rule. Let everyone, except the sick who are very weak, abstain entirely from eating the meat of four-footed animals.

CHAPTER 40. THE PROPER AMOUNT OF DRINK

"Everyone has his own gift from God, one this and another that."[3] It is, therefore, with some uneasiness that we specify the amount of food and drink for others. However, with due regard for the infirmities of the sick, we believe that a half bottle of wine a day is sufficient for each. But those to whom God gives the strength to abstain must know that they will earn their own reward.

The superior will determine when local conditions, work or the summer heat indicates the need for a greater amount. He must, in any case, take great care lest excess or drunkenness creep in. We read that monks should not drink wine at all, but since the monks of our day cannot be convinced of this, let us at least agree to drink moderately, and not to the point of excess, for "wine makes even wise men go astray."[4]

However, where local circumstances dictate an amount much less than what is stipulated above, or even none at all, those who live there should bless God and not grumble. Above all else we admonish them to refrain from grumbling....

CHAPTER 48. THE DAILY MANUAL LABOR

Idleness is the enemy of the soul. Therefore, the brothers should have specified periods for manual labor as well as for prayerful reading.

We believe that the times for both may be arranged as follows: From Easter to the first of October, they will spend their mornings after Prime till about the fourth hour at whatever work needs to be done. From the fourth hour until the time of Sext, they will devote themselves to reading. But after Sext and their meal, they may rest on their beds in complete silence; should a brother wish to read privately, let him do so, but without disturbing the others. They should say None a little early, about midway through the eighth hour, and then until Vespers they are to return to whatever work is necessary. They must not become distressed if local conditions or their poverty should force them to do the harvesting themselves. When they live by the labor of their hands, as our fathers and the apostles did, then they are really monks. Yet, all things are to be done with moderation on account of the fainthearted.

---

1   The monk in charge of provisions in the monastery.
2   Luke 21: 34.
3   1 Cor. 7: 7.
4   Ecclus. 19: 2.

From the first of October to the beginning of Lent, the brothers ought to devote themselves to reading until the end of the second hour. At this time Terce is said and they are to work at their assigned tasks until None. At the first signal for the hour of None, all put aside their work to be ready for the second signal. Then after their meal they will devote themselves to their reading or to the psalms....

CHAPTER 55. THE CLOTHING AND FOOTWEAR OF THE BROTHERS

The clothing distributed to the brothers should vary according to local conditions and climate, because more is needed in cold regions and less in warmer. This is left to the abbot's discretion. We believe that for each monk a cowl[1] and tunic will suffice in temperate regions; in winter a woolen cowl is necessary, in summer a thinner or worn one; also a scapular[2] for work, and footwear—both sandals and shoes....

CHAPTER 58. THE PROCEDURE FOR RECEIVING BROTHERS

Do not grant newcomers to the monastic life an easy entry, but, as the Apostle says, "Test the spirits to see if they are from God."[3] Therefore, if someone comes and keeps knocking at the door, and if at the end of four or five days he has shown himself patient in bearing his harsh treatment and difficulty of entry, and has persisted in his request, then he should be allowed to enter and stay in the guest quarters for a few days. After that, he should live in the novitiate, where the novices study, eat, and sleep.

A senior chosen for his skill in winning souls should be appointed to look after them with careful attention. The concern must be whether the novice truly seeks God and whether he shows eagerness for the Work of God, for obedience, and for trials. The novice should be clearly told all the hardships and difficulties that will lead him to God.

If he promises perseverance in his stability, then after two months have elapsed let this rule be read straight through to him, and let him be told: "This is the law under which you are choosing to serve. If you can keep it, come in. If not, feel free to leave." If he still stands firm, he is to be taken back to the novitiate, and again thoroughly tested in all patience. After six months have passed, the rule is to be read to him, so that he may know what he is entering. If once more he stands firm, let four months go by, and then read this rule to him again. If after due reflection he promises to observe everything and to obey every command given him, let him then be received into the community. But he must be well aware that, as the law of the rule establishes, from this day he is no longer free to leave the monastery, nor to shake from his neck the yoke of the rule which, in the course of so prolonged a period of reflection, he was free either to reject or to accept.

When he is to be received, he comes before the whole community in the oratory and promises stability, fidelity to monastic life, and obedience. This is done in the presence of God and his saints to impress on the novice that if he ever acts otherwise, he will surely be condemned by the one he mocks. He states his promise in a document drawn up in the name of the saints whose relics are there, and of the abbot, who is present....

If he has any possessions, he should either give them to the poor beforehand, or make a formal donation of them to the monastery, without keeping back a single thing for himself, well aware that from that day he will not even have his own body at his disposal. Then and there in the oratory, he is to be stripped of everything of his own that he is wearing and clothed in what belongs to the monastery. The clothing taken from him is to be put away and kept safely in the wardrobe, so that, should he ever agree to the devil's suggestion and leave the monastery—which God forbid—he can be stripped of the clothing of the monastery before he is cast out. But that document of his which the abbot took from the altar should not be given back to him but kept in the monastery.

---

1 A hooded robe.
2 A sleeveless outer garment.
3 1 John 4: 1.

CHAPTER 59. THE OFFERING OF SONS BY NOBLES OR BY THE POOR

If a member of the nobility offers his son to God in the monastery, and the boy himself is too young, the parents draw up the document mentioned above; then, at the presentation of the gifts, they wrap the document itself and the boy's hand in the altar cloth. That is how they offer him.

As to their property, they either make a sworn promise in this document that they will never personally, never through an intermediary, nor in any way at all, nor at any time, give the boy anything or afford him the opportunity to possess anything; or else, if they are unwilling to do this and still wish to win their reward for making an offering to the monastery, they make a formal donation of the property that they want to give to the monastery, keeping the revenue for themselves, should they so desire. This ought to leave no way open for the boy to entertain any expectations that could deceive and ruin him. May God forbid this, but we have learned from experience that it can happen.

Poor people do the same, but those who have nothing at all simply write the document and, in the presence of witnesses, offer their son with the gifts....

CHAPTER 73. THIS RULE ONLY A BEGINNING OF PERFECTION

The reason we have written this rule is that, by observing it in monasteries, we can show that we have some degree of virtue and the beginnings of monastic life. But for anyone hastening on to the perfection of monastic life, there are the teachings of the holy Fathers, the observance of which will lead him to the very heights of perfection. What page, what passage of the inspired books of the Old and New Testaments is not the truest of guides for human life? What book of the holy catholic Fathers does not resoundingly summon us along the true way to reach the Creator? Then, besides the *Conferences* of the Fathers, their *Institutes* and their *Lives*, there is also the rule of our holy father Basil.[1] For observant and obedient monks, all these are nothing less than tools for the cultivation of virtues; but as for us, they make us blush for shame at being so slothful, so unobservant, so negligent. Are you hastening toward your heavenly home? Then with Christ's help, keep this little rule that we have written for beginners. After that, you can set out for the loftier summits of the teaching and virtues we mentioned above, and under God's protection you will reach them. Amen.

---

1 The phrase "the *Conferences* of the Fathers, their *Institutes*" almost certainly refers to the works of John Cassian (d.c.435), founder of the monastery of Saint-Victor at Marseille and an enormously influential writer on the ascetic life. The *Lives* are probably a reference to Athanasius, *Life of St. Antony* (see below, p. 36) along with other monastic biographies. The "rule of Basil" was a collection of precepts written by Basil (330-379) in Greek for Byzantine monks, but it was available to Western monks through a Latin translation made by Rufinus of Aquileia in 397.

SAINTS

1.10 The eremetical life: Athanasius, *Life of St. Antony of Egypt* (356–372). Original in Greek.

ATHANASIUS, BISHOP OF ALEXANDRIA (d.373), a ferocious upholder of the anti-Arian view of the Godhead, saw St. Antony (or Anthony, d.356) as the living embodiment of his notion of salvation through Christ. His *Life of St. Antony*, which was translated into Latin in the later fourth century, was the first of what would become an enormously popular genre in the Middle Ages: the saint's biography, or hagiography. The virtues that Athanasius ascribed to Antony—seriousness of vocation even in childhood; resistance to all the temptations of the Devil; application to prayer, vigils, and fasts—were copied in nearly every subsequent saint's Life. This was not mechanical imitation, for Antony's life was meant to be not just the story of one person but the model for all Christians. At the same time, Antony's vocation as a solitary—a monk—became the ideal which even many Christians active in the hurly-burly of worldly life admired and strove to imitate. In what ways might the *Life of St. Antony* have influenced Augustine's ideas in the *City of God*, above, p. 21?

[Source: Athanasius of Alexandria, *Life of St. Antony of Egypt*, trans. David Brakke, in *Medieval Hagiography: An Anthology*, ed. Thomas Head (New York: Garland, 2000), pp. 7–29 (notes modified).]

Letter of Athanasius, Archbishop of Alexandria, to the Monks in Foreign Places Concerning the Life of the Blessed Antony the Great

(Preface.) It is a good competition that you have begun with the monks in Egypt by seeking either to equal or surpass them in your discipline in virtue.[1] For at last there are monasteries among you as well, and the reputation of the [Egyptian] monks is the basis of their organization: therefore, this plan [of yours] deserves praise; may God bring it to completion through your prayers.

Inasmuch as you have asked me about the blessed Antony's way of life and want to learn about how he began the discipline, who he was before this, what the end of his life was like, and if the things that have been said about him are true, so that you might guide yourselves by imitation of him, I have received your charge with great enthusiasm. Indeed, for me as well it is of great profit just to remember Antony, and I know that once you have heard about him, in addition to admiring the man, you too will want to imitate his determination, since monks have in Antony's lifestyle a sufficient pattern for their discipline.

Therefore, do not disbelieve what you have heard from those who have brought reports of him; rather, think that you have heard only a little from them, for even they scarcely can have completely related such great matters. And since I too, urged by you, am telling you what I can by letter, I am sending only a few of the things that I have remembered about him. You for your part should not stop questioning those persons who sail from here, for it is likely that after each person tells what he knows, the account concerning him will still hardly do him justice. Therefore, when I received your letter, I decided to send for certain monks, particularly those who had spent the most time with him, in the hope that I could learn more

---

1 Athanasius presents his biography in the form of a letter to monks in places outside Egypt, most likely in areas of the western Mediterranean, such as North Africa and southern Europe. Many of the sentences in this opening section appear complicated and obscure to us because we do not know the exact situation in which Athanasius writes and because such a style is typical of prefaces to ancient works, in which the writer hopes to impress his readers with his rhetorical skill.

and send you the fullest possible account. But since the sailing season was coming to an end and the letter carrier was ready to go, I hurried to write to your piety what I know—for I saw him often—and what I was able to learn from the man who followed Antony no short period of time and who poured water on his hand.[1] I have in every place kept my mind on the truth, so that no one, having heard too much, would disbelieve it, or, having learned less than necessary, would look down on the man.

(1.) Antony was an Egyptian by birth, and his parents were well-born and possessed considerable wealth. Since they were Christians, he was raised in a Christian manner. As a child, he lived with his parents and was familiar with nothing other than them and their house. When he grew to become a boy and became older, he did not put up with learning letters because he wanted to be removed even from the companionship of children. It was his complete desire, as it is written, to live in his house as an unformed person.[2] He would go to church with his parents. As a boy, he was not lazy, nor did he become rude as he got older. Rather, he was obedient to his parents, and by paying attention to the readings,[3] he preserved in himself what was beneficial in them. Although as a boy he lived in moderate wealth, he did not trouble his parents for diverse and expensive foods, nor did he seek such pleasures. He was happy merely with whatever he found and asked for nothing more.

(2.) After the death of his parents, he was left alone with one small sister; he was about eighteen or twenty, and it was his responsibility to care for the house and his sister. Not six months after his parents' death, he was going to church as usual, and he was thinking to himself and considering all this: how the apostles abandoned everything and followed the Savior;[4] how the people in Acts [of the Apostles] sold their possessions and brought the proceeds and laid them at the feet of the apostles for distribution to the needy;[5] and how such a great hope was stored up for these people in heaven.[6] Considering these things, he entered the church, and it happened that just then the Gospel was being read, and he heard the Lord saying to the rich man, "If you wish to be perfect, go, sell all your possessions, and give the proceeds to the poor, and come, follow me, and you will have treasure in heaven."[7] And Antony, as if the remembrance of the saints had been placed in him by God and as if the readings had been made on his account, left the church immediately and gave to the villagers the possessions he had received from his ancestors—three hundred *arourae* of fertile and very beautiful land—so that they would no longer trouble him and his sister.[8] He sold all their other movable possessions, collecting a sizable sum of money, and gave it to the poor, although he kept a little for his sister's sake.

(3.) But when he again entered the church and heard in the Gospel the Lord saying, "Do not worry about tomorrow,"[9] he could not stay: he went out and gave even that [little money remaining] to the common people. When he had delivered his sister to known and faithful virgins in order to be brought up for virginity, he at last devoted himself to the discipline outside the house, attending to himself and guiding himself with patience. For there were not yet so many monasteries in Egypt, and no monk knew the great desert; rather, each of those who wanted to attend to himself practiced the discipline alone, not far from his own village. Now, at this time there was an old man in the neighboring village who had practiced the solitary life from his youth: when Antony saw him, he imitated him in virtue.[10] At first he too

---

1 See 2 Kings 3: 11.
2 See Gen. 25: 27.
3 See 1 Tim. 4: 13.
4 See Matt. 4: 20; 19: 27.
5 See Acts 4: 35–37.
6 See Col. 1: 5.
7 Matt. 19: 21.
8 Three hundred *arourae* may have been around two hundred acres; thus, Antony is portrayed as very wealthy by the standards of third-century Egypt.
9 Matt. 6: 34.
10 See Gal. 4: 18.

began by remaining in the places around the village; then if he heard of some zealous one somewhere, like the wise bee, he went and sought that person, and he did not return to his own place until he had seen the man and had received from him, so to speak, travel supplies for the road to virtue.

And so, spending time there at first, he strengthened his intention never to return to the things of his parents nor to remember his relatives, but he directed all his desire and all his zeal toward the effort required by the discipline. Therefore, he worked with his hands, since he had heard, "Let not the idle one eat,"[1] and he spent some of the money on bread and some for the needy. He prayed continuously since he knew that it is necessary to pray in secret without ceasing.[2] For indeed he so devoted himself to the reading that nothing of what is written fell from him to the ground,[3] but he retained everything, so that his memory replaced books for him.

(4.) Conducting himself in this way, then, Antony was loved by everyone. He sincerely submitted to the zealous ones whom he visited, and he learned thoroughly the advantage in zeal and discipline that each one possessed in comparison to himself. He contemplated the graciousness of one and the devotion to prayers of another; he observed one's lack of anger and another's love of people; he attended to the one who kept vigils and the other who loved to study; he admired one for his perseverance and another for his fasting and sleeping on the ground; he watched closely the gentle nature of one and the patience of another; but in all he noticed piety toward Christ and love for one another. And when he had been filled in this way, he returned to his own place of discipline, and then he gathered into himself the virtues of each and strove to display them all in himself. Indeed, he was not contentious with those of his own age, except only that he should not appear to be second to them in the better things. And he did this in such a way that he did not hurt anyone's feelings; rather, they rejoiced in him. And so when the people of the village and the lovers of virtue with whom he associated saw that he

was this kind of person, they all called him "Beloved of God"; some welcomed him as a son, others as a brother.

(5.) But the devil, who hates and envies the good, could not bear to see such resolution in a young man, but set out to do against Antony the kinds of things he usually does. First he tried to dissuade him from the discipline by suggesting the memory of possessions, the care of his sister, the intimacy of family, love of money, love of glory, the varied pleasure of food, and the other indulgences of life—and finally the difficulty of virtue and the great effort that it requires. He introduced the weakness of the body and the long duration of time. In short, he raised up a dust cloud of thoughts in Antony's mind, desiring thereby to separate him from his upright intention.

But the enemy saw that he himself was weak in the face of Antony's resolve and saw instead that he was defeated by the other's stubbornness, overthrown by his faith, and falling due to Antony's constant prayers. Then he took confidence in the weapons of the belly's navel[4] and, boasting in these—for they are his primary means of trapping the young—he advanced against the youth, troubling him at night and harassing him by day so that those who watched could sense the struggle that was going on between the two. The one would suggest dirty thoughts, and the other would turn them back with prayers; the one would titillate, and the other, as if seeming to blush, would fortify his body with faith and fasts. And the miserable devil dared at night to dress up like a woman and imitate one in every way merely to deceive Antony. But Antony, by thinking about Christ and the excellence one ought to possess because of him, and by considering the soul's rational faculty, extinguished the ember of the other's deception.

Once again the enemy suggested the ease of pleasure. But Antony, like someone fittingly angry or grieved, thought about the threat of fire and the torment of the worm, and by setting these thoughts against [those of the enemy], he passed through these things unharmed. All this was a source of shame for

---

1 See 2 Thess. 3: 10.
2 See Matt. 6: 6; 1 Thess. 5: 17.
3 See 1 Sam. 3: 19.
4 See Job 40: 16.

the enemy, for he who had considered himself to be like God[1] was now being mocked by a youth, and he who boasted over flesh and blood was being overthrown by a human being who wore flesh. For working with Antony was the Lord, the one who for our sake took flesh and gave to the body the victory over the devil, so that each of those who truly struggle says, "Not I, but the grace of God that is with me."[2]

(6.) At last, when the dragon could not defeat Antony in this way but instead saw himself thrust out of his heart, he gnashed his teeth, as it is written.[3] As if he were beside himself, he finally appeared to Antony in his form just as he is in his mind, as a black boy. And as though he had fallen down, he no longer attacked Antony with thoughts—for the crafty one had been tossed down—but finally he used a human voice and said, "Many people I have deceived, and most I have defeated, but now coming against you and your efforts as I have against others, I have been weakened." Antony asked, "Who are you who say such things to me?" Immediately he answered with a pitiful voice, "It is I who am fornication's lover. It is I who have been entrusted with its ambushes and its titillations against the youth, and I am called the spirit of fornication. How many persons who desired to be prudent I have deceived! How many persons who professed to be so I have persuaded to change by titillating them! It is I on whose account even the prophet blames those who have fallen, saying, "You have been deceived by the spirit of fornication."[4] For it was through me that they were tripped up. It is I who so often troubled you and who as often was overthrown by you." But Antony gave thanks to the Lord and took courage in him, and he said to him, "You are very despicable

then, for you are black in your mind and as weak as a boy. From now on I will have no anxiety about you, 'for the Lord is my helper, and I will look down on my enemies.'"[5] When he heard this, the black one immediately fled, cowering before these words and afraid even to approach the man.[6]

(7.) This was Antony's first struggle against the devil, or rather this was the achievement in Antony of the Savior, "who condemned sin in the flesh so that the righteousness of the Law might be fulfilled in us, who walk not according to the flesh, but according to the spirit."[7] But Antony did not, because the demon had fallen, now become negligent and take no thought of himself, nor did the enemy, because he had been defeated, stop lying in ambush. For the enemy went around again like a lion, looking for some opportunity against him.[8] But Antony, since he had learned from the Scriptures that the wiles of the enemy are numerous,[9] practiced the discipline intensely, figuring that, even if the enemy had been unable to deceive his heart through bodily pleasure, he would attempt to trap him by another method. For the demon is a lover of sin.

Therefore, Antony more and more punished his body and enslaved it,[10] so that, even though he had triumphed in some ways, he would not be overcome in others; he resolved, then, to accustom himself to more severe training measures. Many people were amazed, but he himself endured the labor with ease, for his soul's intention, which had lasted for a long time, created in him a good habit so that, when he received even slight encouragement from others, he would show great enthusiasm for the task. He would keep vigil to such an extent that often he spent the

---

1 See Isa. 14: 14; Ezek. 28: 2.

2 1 Cor. 15: 10.

3 See Ps. 35: 16; 37: 12; 112: 10; Douay Ps. 34: 16; 36: 12; 111: 10.

4 Hos. 4: 12.

5 Ps. 118: 7; Douay 117: 7.

6 The symbolism of this scene is on two levels. First, the appearance of the devil as a boy reflects the homoerotic interest in male adolescents pervasive in the ancient world and condemned by Christian leaders like Athanasius. Second, the devil's black skin illustrates the prejudice based on skin color present in late antique Egypt, which was a multiethnic society. Most Alexandrians like Athanasius were descendants of the Greeks who founded the city in the fourth century B.C.E. and so were of lighter skin color than persons of more sub-Saharan African descent.

7 Rom. 8: 3–4.

8 See 1 Pet. 5: 8.

9 See Eph. 6: 11.

10 See 1 Cor. 9: 27.

entire night without sleep, and when he did this not once but many times, people were amazed. He ate once a day after sunset, but there were times when he went two days and often four days without eating. His food was bread and salt; his drink, only water. Indeed, it is superfluous even to speak about meat and wine, for nothing of the sort was ever found among the other zealous ones. For sleeping he was content with a rush mat, but mostly he lay upon the bare ground. He would not anoint himself with oil, saying that young men ought to pursue the discipline with zeal and should not seek what would pamper the body, rather that they should accustom the body to labors and consider the Apostle's statement, "Whenever I am weak, then I am strong."[1] For at that time he used to say that the soul's intellect grows strong when the body's pleasures are made weak.

He had this truly wonderful thought: that one should not measure progress in virtue or withdrawal made for this purpose by the length of time, but by the desire and intention. Therefore, he himself did not keep track of the time that had gone by; rather, every day, as if he were just starting the discipline, he would make his effort toward advancement greater, constantly saying to himself Paul's statement, "forgetting what lies behind and straining forward to what lies ahead,"[2] and remembering also the voice of the prophet Elijah, saying, "The Lord lives, before whom I stand today."[3] He observed that in saying "today" he was not measuring the time that had gone by, but, as if he were always making a new start, he was zealous every day to show himself to God to be such that one should appear to God: pure in heart and ready to obey his will and nothing else. He would say to himself, "The ascetic ought always to observe his own life in the conduct of the great Elijah as if in a mirror."

(8.) Having constrained himself in this way, Antony departed to the tombs, which happened to lie far outside the village. He commanded one of his acquaintances to bring him bread every several days, and he himself entered one of the tombs; when the other had shut the door, he remained inside by himself. Then, when the enemy could not bear this but was afraid that in a short time Antony would fill the desert with the discipline, he came one night with a crowd of demons and so cut Antony with wounds that he lay on the ground speechless from the tortures. For he used to maintain that the pains were so severe that he would say that blows inflicted by human beings could not have inflicted such torture. But by God's Providence—for the Lord does not neglect those who hope in him—his acquaintance came the next day to bring him the bread. When he opened the door and saw Antony lying on the ground as if dead, he lifted him up, carried him to the village church, and laid him on the ground. Many of his relatives and the villagers sat around Antony as if beside a corpse. But around midnight Antony came to himself and got up; when he saw everyone asleep and only his acquaintance keeping watch, he motioned with his head for him to approach and then asked him to pick him up again and carry him to the tombs without waking anybody.

(9.) And so he was carried back by the man, and as usual, the door was shut, and he was once again inside by himself. He was unable to stand because of the blows from the demons, and so he prayed lying down.[4] After the prayer, he said with a loud voice, "Here I am: Antony! I do not flee from your blows. For even if you do more, nothing shall separate me from the love of Christ."[5] Then he sang, "Though an army encamp against me, my heart shall not fear."[6] This is what the ascetic thought and said.

But the enemy, who hates the good, was amazed that he dared to return after such blows. He called together his dogs and burst out, "See that we have not stopped this one with the spirit of fornication or with blows; rather, he bravely comes against us. Let us attack him in some other way." It is easy for the devil to change forms for his evil purposes, and so at night they raised such a tumult that it seemed as though that entire place was being shaken by an earthquake. The

---

1   2 Cor. 12: 10.
2   Phil. 3: 13.
3   See 1 Kings 17: 1; 18: 15.
4   It was contemporary custom to pray standing with one's arms extended.
5   See Rom. 8: 35–39.
6   Ps. 26: 3; Douay Ps. 25: 3.

demons, as if they had shattered the four walls of the dwelling, seemed to enter through them, transformed into the appearance of beasts and serpents. And the place was immediately filled with the appearances of lions, bears, leopards, bulls, snakes, asps, scorpions, and wolves, and each of them was moving according to his own form. The lion was roaring, wishing to attack; the bull seemed to butt with his horns; the serpent writhed but did not approach; and the wolf rushed forward but was restrained. Altogether the ragings of their apparitions and the sounds of their voices were completely terrifying. Antony, whipped and tortured by them, felt even more severe bodily pain; but his soul was not trembling, and he remained vigilant. He groaned because of his body's pain, but he was sober in his thinking, and as if to mock them, he said, "If you had had the power, it would have been enough for one of you to come alone. But since the Lord has made you weak, you are trying to frighten me by your number. But it is a proof of your weakness that you imitate the shapes of irrational beings." And again he took courage and said, "If you are able and have received authority against me, don't delay, but attack! But if you cannot, why are you harassing me in vain? For faith in our Lord is our seal and wall for safety." And so after many attempts, they gnashed their teeth against him because they were making fools of themselves rather than of him.

(10.) Meanwhile the Lord had not forgotten Antony's struggle, but came to him in assistance. Thus, Antony looked up and saw the roof as if it were being opened[1] and a certain ray of light coming down to him. The demons suddenly vanished; his body's pain immediately stopped; and the building was once again intact. When Antony perceived the assistance, got his breath back, and was relieved of his pains, he asked the vision that appeared to him, "Where were you? Why didn't you appear at the beginning and make my pains stop?" And a voice came to him, "Antony, I was here, but I waited to see your struggle. Because you endured and were not beaten, I will always be your help, and I will make you famous everywhere."

When he heard this, he got up and prayed, and he became so strong that he felt that he had more strength in his body than he had had before. At this time he was around thirty-five years old.

(11.) The next day Antony went out even more enthusiastic about the piety, and when he came to that old man [whom he had imitated earlier],[2] he asked him to live with him in the desert. But when this man declined due to his age and because there was not yet such a custom, immediately he himself set out for the mountain. Yet again the enemy, when he saw his zeal and wanted to impede it, cast in his way an apparition of a large silver disk. But Antony recognized the trick performed by the hater of good; he stood and said to the disk, because he saw the devil in it: "How did a disk end up in the desert? This path is not well-trod, nor is there any trace of people having traveled through here. If it had fallen, it would have been missed thanks to its size; rather, the one who lost it would have turned back, searched, and found it since the place is a desert. This is the devil's work. You will not impede my intention in this way, devil! Indeed, let this go with you into destruction."[3] When Antony had said this, it vanished like smoke from before a fire.[4]

(12.) Next, as he went along, he again saw this time not an apparition, but real gold scattered in the path. He himself has not said nor do we know whether it was the enemy who showed this to him or whether it was some better power who was training the athlete and showing the devil that he truly did not care about money at all, but what appeared really was gold. Antony marveled at the amount, but as if stepping over fire, he passed by it so as not to turn back; rather, he ran so fast that the place became hidden and forgotten.

Having intensified his resolve more and more, he hurried to the mountain. On the other side of the river he found a deserted fort, abandoned for so long that it was full of serpents; he situated himself there and lived in it. The reptiles, as if someone were chasing them, immediately withdrew, but he barricaded

---

1 See Acts 7: 55–56.
2 See p. 37.
3 See Acts 8: 20.
4 See Ps. 68: 2; Douay Ps. 67: 2.

the door, and since he had stored up enough bread for six months—the people of the Thebaid[1] do this, and their bread often stays fresh for a year—and since he had a water supply inside, he descended as if into a shrine, and he remained alone inside the monastic retreat, neither going out himself nor seeing anyone who came. And so in this way he devoted himself to the discipline for a long time, receiving only bread let down from above the house twice each year.

(13.) Those of his acquaintances who came, since he would not allow them to enter, often used to spend days and nights outside, and they would hear what sounded like crowds making a commotion, clamoring, raising up pitiful voices and crying out, "Leave our places! What have you to do with the desert? You cannot endure our attack!" At first those outside thought that there were certain people fighting with him and that these people had gone in to him by ladders. But when they stooped and peeped through a hole and saw no one, then they reckoned that they were demons; they became frightened and called for Antony. He heard them, although he did not give a thought to the demons: coming near to the door, he exhorted the people to withdraw and not to be afraid, for he said, "In this way the demons create apparitions against the cowards. Therefore, seal yourselves [with the sign of the cross] and depart with courage, and let these [demons] make fools of themselves." And so they went away fortified with the sign of the cross, but he stayed behind and was in no way harmed by the demons, nor did he grow weary of fighting them. Indeed, the assistance of the visions that came to his intellect and the weakness of the enemies gave him much rest from his labors and made his intention even greater. For his acquaintances would always come, expecting to find him dead, but instead would hear him singing, "Let God rise up, and let his enemies be scattered; and let those who hate him flee before him. As smoke disappears, let them disappear; as wax melts before fire, let the wicked perish before God."[2] And again: "All nations surrounded me; in the name of the Lord I repelled them."[3]

(14.) For nearly twenty years he continued to discipline himself in this way, not going out himself and being seen by others only rarely. After this, when many eagerly desired to imitate his discipline, and others of his acquaintances came and were pulling down and wrenching out the door by force, Antony emerged, as if from some shrine, initiated into the mysteries and filled with God. Now for the first time he appeared outside the fort to those who had come to him. And they, when they saw him, were amazed to see that his body had its same condition: it was neither fat as if from lack of exercise nor withered as if from fasting and fighting demons, but it was such as they had known it before his withdrawal. The disposition of his soul was pure again, for it was neither contracted from distress, nor dissipated from pleasure, nor constrained by levity or dejection. Indeed, when he saw the crowd, he was not disturbed, nor did he rejoice to be greeted by so many people. Rather, he was wholly balanced, as if he were being navigated by the Word and existing in his natural state.

Therefore, through Antony the Lord healed many of the suffering bodies of those present, and others he cleansed of demons. He gave Antony grace in speaking, and thus he comforted many who were grieved and reconciled into friendship others who were quarreling, exhorting everyone to prefer nothing in the world to the love for Christ. While he discussed and recalled the good things to come and the love for humanity that has come to us from God, "who did not withhold his own son, but gave him up for all of us."[4] he persuaded many to choose the solitary life. And so at last there came to be monasteries even in the mountains, and the desert was made a city of monks, who left their homes and enrolled in the heavenly commonwealth.[5]

---

1   The Egyptian province to which Antony had retreated.
2   Ps. 68: 1–2; Douay Ps. 67: 1-2.
3   Ps. 118: 10; Douay Ps. 117: 10.
4   Rom. 8: 32.
5   See Phil. 3: 20; Heb. 12: 23. Compare with Augustine's idea of the City of God, above, p. 21.

1.11 The active life: Sulpicius Severus, *The Life of St. Martin of Tours* (396). Original in Latin.

SULPICIUS SEVERUS (363–*c*.420), A WELL-TO-DO and well-educated man of Aquitaine (southern Gaul), became a monk later in life. He met St. Martin (d.397) in 393 or 394 and, impressed by the holy man, wrote his *Life* shortly afterwards. It was a great success: St. Martin soon became the subject of a number of supplementary accounts—letters concerning his death; descriptions of his miracles—and was adopted as the patron saint of the Merovingian Kings. Unlike St. Antony, Martin was a bishop, and thus Sulpicius needed to find a way to combine the model of the ascetic monk with that of the active life of a man in the world. Compare the virtues and lifestyles of Antony and Martin. What message did Martin's *Life* have for warriors? What ideals of behavior did it offer to bishops?

[Source: *Medieval Saints: A Reader*, ed. Mary-Ann Stouck (Peterborough, ON: Broadview Press, 1999), pp. 139-42, 144-49 (slightly modified).]

Martin, then, was born at Sabaria in Pannonia [modern Hungary], but was brought up at Ticinum [Pavia] which is situated in Italy. In terms of worldly dignity, his parents were not of the lowest rank, but they were pagans. His father was at first simply a soldier, but afterwards a military tribune. He himself took up a military career while a youth and was enrolled in the imperial guard, first under king Constantine,[1] and then under the Caesar Julian.[2] This, however, was not done of his own free will, for, almost from the earliest years of his holy childhood, this distinguished boy aspired rather to the service of God. For when he was ten years old, against the wish of his parents, he fled to a church and begged to become a catechumen [to begin instruction in Christianity]. Soon afterwards, in a wonderful manner he became completely devoted to the work of God, and when he was twelve years old, he longed for a life in the desert [to become a hermit]; and he would have made the necessary vows if his youthfulness had not been an obstacle. His mind, however, was always intent upon hermitages or the Church, and already meditated in his boyish years on what he later fulfilled as a religious. But since an edict was issued by the rulers of the state that the sons of veterans should be enrolled for military service, his father (who grudged his pious behavior) delivered him up when he was fifteen years old, and he was arrested and put in chains and was bound by the military oath. He was content with only one servant as his attendant, and then, reversing roles, the master waited on the servant to such a degree that, for the most part, it was he who pulled off his [servant's] boots and he who cleaned them with his own hand; and while they took their meals together, it was he who more often served them. For nearly three years before his baptism, he was a professional soldier, but he kept completely free from those vices in which that class of men become too frequently involved. He showed great kindness towards his fellow-soldiers, and wonderful affection, and his patience and humility surpassed what seemed possible to human nature. There is no need to praise the self-denial which he displayed: it was so great that, even at that date, he was regarded not so much as being a soldier as a monk. By all these qualities he had so endeared himself to the whole body of his comrades that they held him in extraordinary affection. Although not yet regenerated in Christ, by his good works he acted the part of a candidate for baptism. This he did, for instance, by aiding those who were in trouble, by giving help to the wretched, by supporting the needy, by clothing the naked, while he reserved nothing for himself from his military pay except what

---

1   Constantine II (r.337-361).
2   Julian "the Apostate" (r.361-363).

was necessary for his daily sustenance. Even then, far from being a senseless hearer of the Gospel, he took no thought for the morrow.[1]

So it happened one day when he had nothing except his weapons and his simple military dress, in the middle of a winter which had been very bitter and more severe than usual, so that the extreme cold had caused the death of many, he chanced to meet at the gate of the city of Amiens a poor naked man. He [the beggar] was entreating the passers-by to have pity on him, but all passed the wretched man without notice, when Martin, that man full of God, recognized that the beggar to whom others showed no pity was reserved for him. But what should he do? He had nothing except the cloak in which he was dressed, for he had already parted with the rest of his garments for similar purposes. Taking, therefore, his sword which he was wearing, he divided his cloak in half, and gave one part to the beggar, and clothed himself again with what was left. At this, some of the bystanders laughed, because he was now an unsightly object in his mutilated clothing. Many, however, who were of sounder understanding, regretted deeply that they themselves had done nothing similar. They especially felt this because, possessing more than Martin, they could have clothed the poor man without reducing themselves to nakedness.

The following night while he slept Martin had a vision of Christ wearing the part of his cloak with which he had clothed the beggar. He was told to regard the Lord with the greatest care, and to recognize [the Lord's] robe as his own. Before long, he heard Jesus saying in a clear voice to the multitude of angels standing round, "Martin, who is still only a catechumen, clothed me with this robe." Truly the Lord remembered his own words, which he had spoken [while on earth]: "Inasmuch as ye have done these things to one of the least of these, ye have done them unto me,"[2] when he declared that he himself had been clothed in that beggar; and he confirmed the testimony he bore to such a good deed by condescending to show himself in that very garment which the beggar had received.

After this vision the sainted man was not puffed up with vainglory, but he acknowledged the goodness of God in his own action, and as he was now twenty years old he rushed off to receive baptism. However, he did not immediately retire from military service, but gave into the entreaties of his tribune, whom he served as one of his private staff. For the tribune promised that, after his term of office had expired, he too would retire from the world. Martin was held back by this expectation, and continued to act the part of a soldier (although only in name) for nearly two years after he had received baptism.

In the meantime, the barbarians were invading the two divisions of Gaul, and the Caesar [Julian] brought an army together at the city of Worms, and began to distribute a donative [bonus] to the soldiers. As the custom was, they were called forward, one by one, until it came to Martin's turn. Then, indeed, thinking it a good time to ask for his discharge—for he did not think it would be proper for him to receive a donative if he did not intend to continue as a soldier—he said to Caesar, "Until now I have served you as a soldier: permit me now to be a soldier for God. Let the man who is to fight for you receive your donative; I am a soldier of Christ: it is not lawful for me to fight." Then the tyrant began to rage at what he said, declaring that [Martin] was withdrawing from military service from fear of the battle which was to take place the next day, and not from any religious motive. But Martin, full of courage, and all the more resolute in the face of this attempt at intimidation, said, "If this is attributed to cowardice and not to faith, tomorrow I will confront the battle-line unarmed, and in the name of the Lord Jesus, protected by the sign of the cross and not by shield or helmet, I will advance unharmed into the ranks of the enemy." Then he was ordered to be thrown back into prison, so that he might keep his promise by exposing himself unarmed to the barbarians. But the next day, the enemy sent ambassadors to negotiate peace, surrendering themselves and everything they possessed. From these circumstances, who can doubt that this victory was indeed due to the saintly man? For it was granted him that he should not be sent unarmed into battle. And although the good Lord could have preserved his own soldier even from the swords and spears of the enemy, yet he

---

1 Matt. 6: 34.
2 Matt. 25: 40.

removed all necessity for fighting so that [Martin's] blessed eyes might not have to witness the death of others. For Christ could not have granted any victory on behalf of his own soldier other than subduing the enemy without bloodshed or the death of anyone.

After leaving military service, [Martin] sought out blessed Hilary [d.387], bishop of the city of Poitiers whose proven faith in the things of God was highly regarded, and he stayed with him for some time.... [Later, Martin left Hilary in order to return home to convert his parents. Hilary, meanwhile, was exiled and lived for a time in Italy. When he was allowed to return to Poitiers, Martin joined him there.]

After he [Martin] had been most joyfully welcomed by him [Hilary], he established for himself a monastery not far from the town [at Ligugé]. At this time he was joined by a certain catechumen who wished to have instruction in the teachings of the most holy man. Only a few days later, however, the catechumen fell suddenly ill, suffering from a high fever. It so happened that Martin was then away from home. He was absent for three days, and on his return he found the lifeless body; and death had been so sudden, that he had left this world without receiving baptism. The body had been laid out in public, and the grieving brethren were visiting it as their sad duty required, when Martin hurried up, weeping and lamenting. But with his soul completely filled with the Holy Spirit, he ordered the others to leave the cell in which the body was lying; and bolting the door, he stretched himself at full length on the dead limbs of the departed brother. After he had stayed lying there for some time in prayer, and had become aware through the Spirit that the power of God was present, he rose up for a short time, and fixing his gaze on the dead man's face he waited with confidence for the result of his prayer and the mercy of the Lord. And after scarcely two hours had passed he saw the dead man begin to move all his limbs little by little, and his eyes trembling and blinking as he recovered his sight. Then indeed he raised a loud voice to the Lord and gave thanks, filling the cell with cries. Hearing the noise, those who had been standing at the door immediately rushed inside. And truly a marvelous spectacle met them, for they beheld the man alive whom they had left for dead.

Thus restored to life, he immediately received baptism and lived for many years afterwards; and he was the first one among us to give both substantial proof of Martin's virtues and to testify to them. He often related that, when he left the body, he was brought before the tribunal of the Judge [God], and had a dismal sentence pronounced on him which relegated him to the dark places among the crowd of common men.[1] Then, however, he added, it was suggested by two angels of the Judge that he was the man for whom Martin was praying; and so the same angels were ordered to lead him back and to give him to Martin, and restore him to his former life. From this time forward, the name of the blessed man became famous, so that he was treated as if he were already a saint by everyone, and was also held to be powerful and a true apostle....

At about the same time, Martin was sought after to be bishop of the church at Tours,[2] but when he could not easily be persuaded to leave his monastery, a certain Rusticius, one of the citizens, pretended that his wife was ill, and by throwing himself down at [Martin's] knees, prevailed on him to leave. A crowd of citizens had previously been posted along the road on which he traveled, and in this way he was escorted to the city as if under guard. In an amazing manner, an incredible number of people not only from that town but also from the neighboring cities had assembled to give their votes. They all had only the same wish, the same desire, the same opinion: that Martin was most worthy of being bishop, and that the Church would be happy with such a priest.

A few impious persons, however, including some of the bishops who had been summoned to appoint the prelate, resisted, asserting strongly that Martin's person was contemptible, that he was unworthy of being a bishop, that he was despicable in appearance, his clothing was shabby and his hair disgusting. This madness of theirs was ridiculed by people of sounder judgment, since even while they attempted to slander him they were proclaiming his extraordinary merits. And in truth, they were not allowed to do anything other than what the people wished for, in accordance with Divine will....

---

1   This is a very early reference to Limbo, the eternal home of the souls of the unbaptized.
2   This happened around 370-372.

And now it is beyond my power to describe completely what Martin was like after he became bishop, and how he distinguished himself. For with the utmost constancy he remained the same as he had been before. There was the same humility in his heart and the same simplicity of clothing. Filled with both authority and courtesy, he kept up the position of a bishop properly, yet in such a way as not to abandon the life and virtues of a monk. For some time he lived in a cell adjacent to the church; but afterwards, when he could not tolerate the disturbance caused by the numbers of visitors, he established a monastery for himself about two miles outside the city.

This spot [Marmoutier] was so hidden and remote that he no longer had to wish for the solitude of a hermit. For on one side it was surrounded by the steep rock of a high mountain, while the rest of the land had been enclosed in a gentle curve of the Loire river; there was only one means of access, and that was very narrow. Here, then, he inhabited a cell built of wood, and a great number of the brothers were housed in the same fashion, but most of them had made themselves shelters by hollowing caves out of the overhanging rock. There were about eighty disciples who were instructed by the example of their holy master. There, no one possessed anything of his own; everything was held in common. No one was allowed either to buy or to sell anything, as is the custom among many monks. No art was practiced there, except that of the scribes, and even this was assigned to the younger brothers while the elder spent their time in prayer. It was rare for any of them to leave his cell, except to gather at the place of prayer. After a period of fasting was over, they all ate their meals together. No one used wine, except when illness compelled them to do so. Most of them wore garments of camel's hair; softer clothing was considered a serious fault there. This must be considered all the more remarkable, because many of them were considered to be of high rank, brought up in a very different fashion, and yet they had forced themselves to accept humility and patience; and we have seen many of these afterwards made bishops. For what city or church would not want a priest from the monastery of Martin?[1]

But let me go on to describe the other virtues which Martin displayed as a bishop....

While Martin was going on a journey he met the body of a pagan that was being carried to the tomb with superstitious funeral rites. Seeing from a distance a crowd approaching, and not knowing what it was about, he stood still for a little while. For there was nearly half a mile between him and the crowd, so that it was difficult to make out what he was seeing. Nevertheless, because he saw it was a group of peasants, when the linen cloths covering the body were blown about by the wind, he believed that some profane sacrificial rites were being performed. For it was the custom among the peasants of Gaul in their wretched madness to carry about through the fields the images of demons covered with a white veil.

Therefore he raised the sign of the cross against them and commanded the crowd not to move from the place where they were and to put down what they were carrying. At this, wonderful to relate, you might have seen the wretched creatures first become as rigid as rocks. Next, when they tried with a great effort to move forward, but were not able to take a step farther, they began to whirl themselves about in the most ridiculous fashion until they were defeated and had to put down the dead body. They were thunderstruck and looked at each other, silently wondering what had happened to them. But when the saintly man discovered that the peasants were simply performing funeral rites, and not sacrifices, with raised hand he gave them back the power of leaving and of lifting up the body. Thus when he wished, he made them stand still, and when he pleased, he let them go.

On another occasion, in a certain village he demolished a very ancient temple, and set about cutting down a pine-tree that stood close to the temple. The chief priest of that place and a crowd of other pagans began to oppose him. And although these people had, at the Lord's command, been quiet while the temple was being destroyed, they could not endure the cutting-down of the tree. Martin carefully impressed upon them that there was nothing sacred in the trunk of a tree, and urged them instead to honor God whom he himself served; the tree had to be cut down because it was dedicated to a demon.

Then one of them who was bolder than the others said, "If you have any trust in your God, whom you

---

1 Compare the standards at Marmoutier with those described in *The Benedictine Rule* (above, p. 28).

say you worship, we ourselves will cut down this tree, and you stand in its path; for if, as you say, your Lord is with you, you will not be hurt." Then Martin, courageously trusting in the Lord, promised to do so. Upon this, all that crowd of pagans agreed to the condition; for they held the loss of their tree a small matter, so long as they got the enemy of their religion buried under its fall. Since that pine-tree was leaning to one side, so that there could be no question as to which way it would fall when it was cut, Martin was bound to the spot where the tree would certainly fall, as the pagans had stipulated.

Then they began to cut down their own tree, with great delight and rejoicing. A wondering crowd stood some distance away. Little by little the pine-tree began to shake, and, on the point of falling, threatened its own ruin. The monks at a distance grew pale and, terrified by the approaching danger, they lost all hope and faith, expecting only Martin's death. But he, trusting in the Lord, waited courageously, even as the falling pine made a cracking noise, even as it was falling and as it rushed down upon him: simply lifting his hand against it, he held up the sign of salvation. Then, indeed—you would have thought it driven back like a spinning top—it swept round to the opposite side, so that it almost crushed the peasants, who had stood in what seemed to be a safe spot.

Then a shout went up to heaven: the pagans were amazed by the miracle while the monks wept for joy, and the name of Christ was proclaimed by them all together. And as it is well known, on that day salvation came to that region. For there was hardly one of that huge crowd of pagans who did not long for the laying-on of hands [to become a catechumen] and, abandoning their impious errors, they believed in the Lord Jesus. Certainly, before Martin's time, very few, indeed hardly any in those regions had received the name of Christ. Through his virtues and example that name has prevailed to such an extent that now there is no region that is not filled either with crowded churches or monasteries. For wherever he destroyed pagan temples, there immediately he used to build either churches or monasteries.

1.12 St. Radegund as ascetic: Venantius Fortunatus, *The Life of St. Radegund* (before *c.*600). Original in Latin.

VENANTIUS FORTUNATUS (*c.*535–*c.*605?) WAS BORN and educated in Italy, where he trained in the late classical rhetorical tradition. He came to Gaul when he was about thirty years old to earn his living by writing poetry for wealthy Merovingian aristocrats, both lay and clerical. A few years later he settled at Poitiers, where he became a priest and a close associate of Queen Radegund (d.587). She had originally been a member of the royal house of Thuringia, a kingdom bordering on Frankish territory. When King Clothar I (r.511–561) invaded Thuringia, Radegund became one of his prizes of war and, eventually, his wife. But following the execution of her brother, probably with Clothar's connivance, Radegund founded—and retired to—a monastery (as medieval nunneries are often called, just like their male counterparts) at Poitiers, known as Holy Cross. Toward the end of his life, around 600, Fortunatus became the bishop of Poitiers. In his *Life* of Radegund, Fortunatus was concerned above all to praise her piety, charity, and asceticism. As we shall see, her community wanted other aspects of her work recognized, and so shortly after Fortunatus wrote his hagiography, another was written by a nun at Holy Cross. How might you compare the virtues of Fortunatus's St. Radegund with those of Athanasius's St. Antony (p. 36 above)? What ideals of queenship does Fortunatus's portrait suggest?

[Source: *Sainted Women of the Dark Ages*, ed. and trans. Jo Ann McNamara and John E. Halborg, with E. Gordon Whatley (Durham, NC: Duke University Press, 1992), pp. 70-81 (slightly modified).]

1. Our Redeemer is so richly and abundantly generous that He wins mighty victories through the female sex and, despite their frail physique, He confers glory and greatness on women through strength of mind. By faith, Christ makes them strong who were born weak so that, when those who appeared to be imbeciles are crowned with their merits by Him who made them, they garner praise for their Creator who hid heavenly treasure in earthen vessels. For Christ the king dwells with his riches in their bowels. Mortifying themselves in the world, despising earthly consort, purified of worldly contamination, trusting not in the transitory, dwelling not in error but seeking to live with God, they are united with the Redeemer's glory in Paradise. One of that company is she whose earthly life we are attempting to present to the public, though in homely style, so that the glorious memory that she, who lives with Christ, has left us will be celebrated in this world. So ends the Prologue.

Here begins the Life.

2. The most blessed Radegund was of the highest earthly rank, born from the seed of the kings of the barbarian nation of Thuringia. Her grandfather was King Bassin, her paternal uncle, Hermanfred and her father, King Bertechar. But she surpassed her lofty origin by even loftier deeds. She had lived with her noble family only a little while when the victorious Franks devastated the region with barbaric turmoil and, like the Israelites, she departed and migrated from her homeland. The royal girl became part of the plunder of these conquerors and they began to quarrel over their captive. If the contest had not ended with an agreement for her disposition, the kings would have taken up arms against one another. Falling to the lot of the illustrious King Clothar,[1] she was taken to Athies in Vermandois, a royal villa, and her upbringing was entrusted to guardians. The maiden was taught letters and other things suitable to her sex, and she would often converse with other children there about her desire to be a martyr if the chance came in her time. Thus, even as an adolescent, she displayed the merits of a mature person. She obtained part of what she sought, for, though the church was flourishing in peace, she endured persecution from her own household. While but a small child, she herself brought the scraps left at table to the gathered children, washing the head of each one, seating them on little chairs and offering water for their hands, and she mingled with the infants herself. She would also carry out what she had planned beforehand with Samuel, a little cleric. Following his lead, carrying a wooden cross they had made, singing psalms, the children would troop into the oratory as somber as adults. Radegund herself would polish the pavement with her dress and, collecting the drifting dust around the altar in a napkin, reverently placed it outside the door rather than sweep it away. When the aforementioned king, having provided the expenses, wished to bring her to Vitry, she escaped by night from Athies through Beralcha[2] with a few companions. When he settled with her that she should be made his queen at Soissons,[3] she avoided the trappings of royalty, so she would not grow great in the world but in Him to Whom she was devoted and she remained unchanged by earthly glory.

3. Therefore, though married to a terrestrial prince, she was not separated from the celestial one and, the more secular power was bestowed upon her, the more humbly she bent her will—more than befitted her royal status. Always subject to God following priestly admonitions, she was more Christ's partner than her husband's companion. We will only attempt to publicize a few of the many things she did during this period of her life. Fearing she would lose status with God as she advanced in worldly rank at the side of a prince, she gave herself energetically to almsgiving. Whenever she received part of the tribute, she gave away a tithe[4] of all that came to her before accepting any for herself. She dispensed what was left to monasteries, sending the gifts to those she could not reach on foot. There was no hermit who could hide from her munificence. So she paid out what she received lest the burden weigh her down. The voice of the needy was not raised in vain for she never turned

---

1 Clothar I (r.511-561) was the third son of Clovis and shared his kingdom with Childebert until the latter's death in 558.
2 Not identified.
3 Soissons was the capital of Clothar's Kingdom.
4 I.e., ten percent.

a deaf ear. Often she gave clothes, believing that the limbs of Christ concealed themselves under the garments of the poor and that whatever she did not give to paupers was truly lost.

4. Turning her mind to further works of mercy, she built a house at Athies where beds were elegantly made up for needy women gathered there. She would wash them herself in warm baths, tending to the putrescence of their diseases. She washed the heads of men, acting like a servant. And before she washed them, she would mix a potion with her own hands to revive those who were weak from sweating. Thus the devout lady, queen by birth and marriage, mistress of the palace, served the poor as a handmaid. Secretly, lest anyone notice, at royal banquets, she fed most deliciously on beans or lentils from the dish of legumes placed before her, in the manner of the three boys.[1] And if the singing of the hours started while she was still eating, she would make her excuses to the king and withdraw from the company to do her duty to God. As she went out, she sang psalms to the Lord and carefully checked what food had been provided to refresh the paupers at the door.

5. At night, when she lay with her prince, she would ask leave to rise and leave the chamber to relieve nature. Then she would prostrate herself in prayer under a hair shirt[2] by the privy so long that the cold pierced her through and through and only her spirit was warm. Her whole flesh prematurely dead, indifferent to her body's torment, she kept her mind intent on Paradise and counted her suffering trivial, if only she might avoid becoming cheap in Christ's eyes. Re-entering the chamber thereafter, she could scarcely get warm either by the hearth or in her bed. Because of this, people said that the King had yoked himself to a *monacha* rather than a queen.[3] Her goodness provoked him to harsher irritation but she either soothed him to the best of her ability or bore her husband's outbursts modestly.

6. Indeed, it will suffice to know how she bore herself during the days of Quadragesima [Lent], a singular penitent in her royal robes. When the time for fasting drew near, she would notify a *monacha* named Pia, who, according to their holy arrangement, would send a hair cloth sealed carefully in linen to Radegund. Draping it over her body through the whole of Quadragesima, the holy woman wore that sweet burden under her royal garment. When the season was over, she returned the hair cloth similarly sealed. Who could believe how she would pour out her heart in prayers when the king was away? How she would cling to the feet of Christ as though He were present with her and satiate her long hunger with tears as though she was gorging on delicacies! She had contempt for the food of the belly, for Christ was her only nourishment and all her hunger was for Christ.

7. With what piety did she care solicitously for the candles made with her own hands that burned all night long in oratories and holy places? When the king asked after her at table during the late hours, he was told that she was delayed, busy about God's affairs. This caused strife with her husband and later on the prince compensated her with gifts for the wrong he did her with his tongue.

8. If she received a report that any of God's servants was on his way to see her, either of his own accord or by invitation, she felt full of celestial joy. Hastening out in the night time with a few intimates, through snow, mud or dust, she herself would wash the feet of the venerable man with water she had heated beforehand and offer the servant of God something to drink in a bowl. There was no resisting her. On the following day, committing the care of the household to her trusted servants, she would occupy herself wholly with the just man's words and his teachings concerning salvation. The business of achieving celestial life fixed her attention throughout the day. And if a bishop should come, she rejoiced to see him, gave him gifts, and was sad to have to let him go home.

9. And how prudently she sought to devote everything possible to her salvation. If the girls attending her when she dressed praised a new veil of coarse linen ornamented with gold and gems in the barbarian fashion as particularly beautiful, she would judge

---

1　See Dan. 1: 12, where Daniel and three other boys at court eat plain food, yet thrive.

2　A hair shirt was a coarse and rough garment, worn by ascetics next to their skin as part of their penitential practices.

3　*Monacha* = female monk.

herself unworthy to be draped in such fabric. Divesting herself of the dress immediately, she would send it to some holy place in the neighborhood where it could be laid as a cloth on the Lord's altar.

10. And if the king, according to custom, condemned a guilty criminal to death, wasn't the most holy queen near dead with torment lest the culprit perish by the sword? How she would rush about among his trusty men, ministers, and nobles, whose blandishments might soothe the prince's temper until the king's anger ceased and the voice of salvation flowed where the sentence of death had issued before!

11. Even while she remained in her worldly palace, the blessed acts which busied her so pleased Divine Clemency that the Lord's generosity worked miracles through her. Once at her villa in Péronne, while that holiest of women was strolling in the garden after her meal, some sequestered criminals loudly cried to her from the prison for help. She asked who it might be. The servants lied that a crowd of beggars was seeking alms. Believing that, she sent to relieve their needs. Meanwhile the fettered prisoners were silenced by a judge. But as night was falling and she was saying her prayers, the chains broke and the freed prisoners ran from the prison to the holy woman. When they witnessed this, those who had lied to the holy one realized that they were the real culprits, while the erstwhile convicts were freed from their bonds.

12. If Divinity fosters it, misfortune often leads to salvation. Thus her innocent brother was killed so that she might come to live in religion. She left the king and went straight to holy [Bishop] Médard at Noyon. She earnestly begged that she might change her garments and be consecrated to God. But mindful of the words of the Apostle: "Art thou bound unto a wife? Seek not to be loosed,"[1] he hesitated to garb the Queen in the robe of a *monacha*. For even then, nobles were harassing the holy man and attempting to drag him brutally through the basilica from the altar to keep him from veiling the king's spouse lest the priest imagine he could take away the king's official queen as though she were only a prostitute. That holiest of women knew this and, sizing up the situation, entered the sacristy, put on a monastic garb and proceeded straight to the altar, saying to the blessed Médard: "If you shrink from consecrating me, and fear man more than God, Pastor, He will require His sheep's soul from your hand." He was thunderstruck by that argument and, laying his hand on her, he consecrated her as a deaconess.[2]

13. Soon she divested herself of the noble costume which she was wont to wear as queen when she walked in procession on the day of a festival with her train of attendants. She laid it on the altar and piled the table of Divine Glory with purple, gems, ornaments and like gifts to honor Him. She gave a heavy girdle of costly gold for the relief of the poor. Similarly, arriving at the cell of St. Jumer one day on which the happy queen decorated herself [with finery] composed of what I would call by the barbarian term "stapio"—blouses, tunics, hair coverings, buckles, all made of gold and some with circlets of gems—she put them on the holy altar for future benefits. Again, proceeding to the venerable Dato's cell one day, spectacularly adorned as she should have been in the world with whatever she could put on, having rewarded the abbot, she gave the whole from her woman's wealth to the community. Likewise going on to the retreat of holy Gundulf, later Bishop of Metz, she exerted herself just as energetically to enrich his monastery.

14. From there her fortunate sails approached Tours. Can any eloquence express how zealous and munificent she showed herself there? How she conducted herself around the courts, shrines, and basilica of Saint Martin, weeping unchecked tears, prostrating herself at each threshold! After mass was said, she heaped the holy altar with the clothing and bright ornaments with which she used to adorn herself in the palace. And when the handmaid of the Lord went from there to the neighborhood of Candes whence the glorious Martin, Christ's senator and confidant, migrated from this world, she gave him no less again, ever profiting in the Lord's grace.

15. From there, in decorous manner, she ap-

---

1 1 Cor. 7: 27.
2 There is no reason to suppose that a deaconess was bound to celibacy; conceivably, Médard had found an ingenious solution to his particular dilemma in consecrating a woman who was still married to the king.

proached the villa of Saix near the aforesaid town in the territory of Poitiers, her journey ever prospering. Who could recount the countless remarkable things she did there or grasp the special quality of each one? At table she secretly chewed rye or barley bread which she had hidden under a cake to escape notice. For from the time she was veiled, consecrated by Saint Médard, even in illness, she ate nothing but legumes and green vegetables: not fruit nor fish nor eggs. And she drank no drink but honeyed water or perry[1] and would touch no undiluted wine nor any decoction of mead[2] or fermented beer.

16. Then, emulating Saint Germanus' custom, she secretly had a millstone brought to her. Throughout the whole of Quadragesima, she ground fresh flour with her own hands. She continuously distributed each offering to local religious communities, in the amount needed for the meal taken every four days. With that holy woman, acts of mercy were no fewer than the crowds who pressed her; as there was no shortage of those who asked, so was there no shortage in what she gave so that, wonderfully, they could all be satisfied. Where did the exile get such wealth? Whence came the pilgrim's riches?

17. How much did she spend daily on relief? Only she who bore it to the beggars ever knew. For beyond the daily meal which she fed to her enrolled paupers, twice a week, on Thursday and Saturday, she prepared a bath. Girding herself with a cloth, she washed the heads of the needy, scrubbing away whatever she found there. Not shrinking from scuff, scabs, lice or pus, she plucked off the worms and scrubbed away the putrid flesh. Then she herself combed the hair on every head she had washed. As in the gospel, she applied oil to their ulcerous sores that had opened when the skin softened or that scratching had irritated, reducing the spread of infection. When women descended into the tub, she washed their limbs with soap from head to foot. When they came out, if she noticed that anyone's clothes were shoddy with age, she would take them away and give them new ones. Thus she spruced up all who came to the feast in rags. When they were gathered around the table and the dinner service laid out, she brought water and napkins for each of them and cleaned the mouth and hands of the invalids herself. Then three trays laden with delicacies would be carried in. Standing like a good hostess before the diners, she cut up the bread and meat and served everyone while fasting herself. Moreover, she never ceased to offer food to the blind and weak with a spoon. In this, two women aided her but she alone served them, busy as a new Martha until the "brothers" were drunk and happily satisfied with their meal.[3] Then, leaving the place to wash her hands, she was completely gratified with her well-served feast. And if anyone protested, she ordered that they sit still until they wished to get up.

18. Summer and winter, on Sundays, she followed a praiseworthy rule. She would provide an undiluted drink of sweet wine to the assembled paupers. First she doled it out herself and then, while she hurried off to Mass, she assigned a maid to serve everyone who remained. Her devotions completed, she would meet the priests invited to her table, for it was her royal custom not to let them return home without a gift.

19. Doesn't this make one shudder, this thing she did so sweetly? When lepers arrived and, sounding a warning,[4] came forward, she directed her assistant to inquire with pious concern whence they came or how many there were. Having learned that, she had a table laid with dishes, spoons, little knives, cups and goblets, and wine and she went in herself secretly that none might see her. Seizing some of the leprous women in her embrace, her heart full of love, she kissed their faces. Then, while they were seated at table, she washed their faces and hands with warm water and treated their sores with fresh ointments and fed each one. When they were leaving, she offered small gifts of gold and clothing. To this there was scarcely a single witness, but the attendant presumed to chide her softly: "Most holy lady, when you have embraced lepers, who will kiss you?" Pleasantly, she answered: "Really, if you won't kiss me, it's no concern of mine."

---

1 Fermented pear juice.
2 A drink made from fermented honey and water.
3 See Luke 10: 40. Martha is customarily presented as the model of the active religious life for women, whereas her sister Mary symbolizes the contemplative life.
4 Lepers wore bells to signal their approach.

20. With God's help, she shone forth in diverse miracles. For example, if anyone was in desperate straits because of pus from a wound, an attendant would bring a vine leaf to the saint speaking with her about what was to be done with it. As soon as the saint made the sign of the cross over it, the attendant would take it to the desperate one, placing it on the wound which would soon be healed. Similarly an invalid or someone with a fever might come and say that he had learned in a dream that to be healed he should hasten to the holy woman and present one of her attendants with a candle. After it had burned through the night his disease would be killed while the invalid was healed. How often when she heard of someone lying bedridden would she sally forth like a pilgrim bearing fruit or something sweet and warm to restore their strength? How quickly would an invalid who had eaten nothing for ten days take food when she served it herself and thus receive both food and health together? And she ordered these things herself lest anyone tell tales.

21. Weren't there such great gatherings of people on the day that the saint determined to seclude herself that those who could not be contained in the streets climbed up to fill the roofs? Anyone who spoke of all the most holy woman had fervently accomplished in fasting, services, humility, charity, suffering and torment, proclaimed her both confessor and martyr. Truly every day except for the most venerable day of the Lord, was a fast day for that most holy woman. Her meal of lentils or green vegetables was virtually a fast in itself for she took no fowl or fish or fruit or eggs to eat. Her bread was made from rye or barley which she concealed under the pudding lest anyone notice what she ate. And to drink she had water and honey or perry and only a little of that was poured out for her, however thirsty she was.

22. The first time she enclosed herself in her cell throughout Quadragesima, she ate no bread, except on Sundays, but only roots of herbs or mallow greens without a drop of oil or salt for dressing. In fact, during the entire fast, she consumed only two *sestaria* [pints] of water. Consequently, she suffered so much from thirst that she could barely chant the psalms through her desiccated throat. She kept her vigils in a shift of hair cloth instead of linen, incessantly chanting the offices. A bed of ashes served her for a couch which she covered with a hair cloth. In this manner, rest itself wearied her but even this was not enough to endure.

23. While all the *monachas* were deep in sleep, she would collect their shoes, restoring them cleaned and oiled to each. On other Quadragesimas, she was more relaxed, eating on Thursday and again on Sundays. The rest of the time when health permitted, except for Easter and other high holy days, she led an austere life in sackcloth and ashes, rising early to be singing psalms when the others awoke. For no monasterial offices pleased her unless she observed them first. She punished herself if anyone else did a good deed before she did. When it was her turn to sweep the pavements around the monastery, she even scoured the nooks and crannies, bundling away whatever nasty things were there, never too disgusted to carry off what others shuddered to look upon. She did not shrink from cleaning the privies but cleaned and carried off the stinking dung. For she believed that she would be diminished if these vile services did not ennoble her. She carried firewood in her arms. She blew on the hearth and stirred the fire with tongs and did not flinch if she hurt herself. She would care for the infirm beyond her assigned week, cooking their food, washing their faces, and bringing them warm water, going the rounds of those she was caring for and returning fasting to her cell.

24. How can anyone describe her excited fervor as she ran into the kitchen, doing her week of chores? None of the *monachas* but she would carry as much wood as was needed in a bundle from the back gate.[1] She drew water from the well and poured it into basins. She scrubbed vegetables and legumes and revived the hearth by blowing so that she might cook the food. While it was busy boiling, she took the vessels from the hearth, washing and laying out the dishes. When the meal was finished, she rinsed the small vessels and scrubbed the kitchen till it shone, free of every speck of dirt. Then she carried out all the sweepings and the nastiest rubbish. Further, she never flagged in supporting the sick and even before she took up the Rule of Arles[2] did her weekly tour of service preparing plenty of warm water for them all.

---

1   Presumably left there by the monks attached to a small service community nearby.
2   This was the strict Rule for nuns written by Caesarius of Arles (d.542).

Humbly washing and kissing their feet, the holy one prostrated herself and begged them all to forgive her for any negligence she might have committed.

25. But I shudder to speak of the pain she inflicted on herself over and above all these labors. Once, throughout Quadragesima, she bound her neck and arms with three broad iron circlets. Inserting three chains in them, she fettered her whole body so tightly that her delicate flesh, swelling up, enclosed the hard iron. After the fast was ended, when she wished to remove the chains locked under her skin, she could not—for the flesh was cut by the circlet through her back and breast over the iron of the chains, so that the flow of blood nearly drained her little body to the last drop.

26. On another occasion, she ordered a brass plate made, shaped in the sign of Christ. She heated it up in her cell and pressed it upon her body most deeply in two spots so that her flesh was roasted through. Thus, with her spirit flaming, she caused her very limbs to burn. One Quadragesima, she devised a still more ter-rible agony to torture herself in addition to the severe hunger and burning thirst of her fast. She forced her tender limbs, already suppurating and scraped raw by the hard bristles of a hair cloth, to carry a water basin full of burning coals. Then, isolated from the rest, though her limbs were quivering, her soul was steeled for the pain. She drew it to herself, so that she might be a martyr though it was not an age of persecution. To cool her fervent soul, she thought to burn her body. She imposed the glowing brass and her burning limbs hissed. Her skin was consumed and a deep furrow remained where the brand had touched her. Silently, she concealed the holes, but the putrefying blood betrayed the pain that her voice did not reveal. Thus did a woman willingly suffer such bitterness for the sweetness of Christ! And in time, miracles told the story that she herself would have kept hidden.

[Fortunatus continues with accounts of Radegund's miracles.]

1.13 St. Radegund as relic collector: Baudonivia, *The Life of St. Radegund* (c.600). Original in Latin.

WE KNOW NOTHING ABOUT Baudonivia except what she tells us in the preface to her *Life* of Radegund. She was a nun at Holy Cross who, around 600, was asked by her abbess and other members of her community to supplement the *Life* written by Fortunatus. As she says, they thought that Fortunatus had not recounted enough of Radegund's miracles. They also must have wanted more discussion of Radegund's interest in relics, since Baudonivia spends much time on this topic. We should not take literally her profession of intellectual inadequacy; this was a *topos*—a commonplace, or customary practice—of ancient and medieval writings, meant to make the reader sympathetic to the author. How would you characterize the different ideals of saint-hood presented in Baudonivia's and Fortunatus's two *Lives*, and how might you account for those differences?

[Source: *Sainted Women of the Dark Ages*, ed. and trans. Jo Ann McNamara and John E. Halborg, with E. Gordon Whatley (Durham, NC: Duke University Press, 1992), pp. 96-87, 94-100 (slightly modified).]

To the holy ladies adorned with the grace of virtuous living, Abbess Dedimia[1] and all Holy Radegund's congregation, from Baudonivia, humblest of all.

I can as easily touch heaven with my fingers as perform the task you have imposed upon me—namely to write something about the life of the holy Lady Radegund, whom you knew best. This task should be assigned to those who have fountains of eloquence

---

1 The abbess was the female counterpart of the abbot in a women's monastery.

within them. For whatever such people are commissioned to write is laid out generously in flowing song. On the contrary, people who are narrow of understanding and lack the full fluency of eloquence to relieve their own sterility and aridity—let alone refresh others—not only have no wish to speak out on their own but become terrified when they are commanded to do so. For in myself, I know that I am weak-minded and have but few intelligent things to say. For good as it is for the learned to speak, it is best for the unlearned to keep silence. For the former know how to produce something great from very little while the latter cannot even make a little from a great deal. Therefore what the learned seek eagerly terrifies the unlearned. I am the smallest of the small ones she nourished familiarly from the cradle as her own child at her feet! So that I may, in obedience to your most gracious wishes, compose, not the full story but a partial account in writing of her famous works, and so that I may offer a public celebration of her glorious life to the ears of her flock, in devout though unworthy language, I pray that you will aid me with your prayers, for I am more devoted than learned. In this book, we will not repeat what the apostolic Bishop Fortunatus[1] recorded of her blessed life but speak of what he omitted in his fear of prolixity, as he explained in his book when he said: "But let this small sample of the blessed one's miracles suffice, lest their very abundance arouse contempt. And even this should in no way be reckoned a small amount, since from these few tales we may recognize in the miracles the greatness with which she lived." Therefore, inspired by the Divine Power whom Radegund strove to please in this world and with Whom she reigns in the next, we will attempt to relate, in rustic rather than refined language, what she did here and to publish a few of her many miracles....

13. While Radegund was still at the villa of Saix, her faithful and devoted mind intent on Christ, she determined, with great devotion, to collect relics of all the saints. At her request, a venerable priest named Magnus brought her relics of Lord Andrew and many others which she placed above the altar. When, at night, she lay prostrate in prayer keeping vigil on her couch, a little sleep came over her while the Lord declared her wish granted, saying: "Know thou, blessed woman, that not only the relics brought by Magnus the priest are here, but all those you gathered together in the villa of Athies are assembled here." When she opened her eyes she saw that a most resplendent man had told her these things and she rejoiced and blessed the Lord.

14. After she had entered into the monastery, she assembled a great multitude of the saints through her most faithful prayers, as the East bears witness and North, South and West acknowledge. For from all sides, she managed to obtain those precious gems which Paradise has and Heaven hoards and as many came freely to her as gifts as came in response to her pleas. In their company, she gave herself up to chanting hymns and psalms continuously in ceaseless meditation. At last, news came to her that the holy limbs of Lord Mammas the Martyr rested at Jerusalem.[2] She drank the information in greedily and thirstily; as the dropsical[3] only increase their thirst by drawing more water, so she, though refreshed by God's dew, was burning up.[4] She sent the venerable priest, Reoval, who was then a secular[5] and still abides in the flesh with us, to the patriarch of Jerusalem to ask Blessed Mammas for a token. The man of God received him benignly and, seeking the will of God, announced his request to the people. Three days later, after celebrating Mass, he approached the blessed martyr's sepulchre with all his people and, full of faith, proclaimed in a loud voice: "I ask you, Confessor and Martyr of Christ, that if the blessed Radegund is truly a handmaid of the Lord, you will make it known to all the nations by your power; permit that faithful soul to receive the relic she asks from you." At the end of the prayer, everyone responded, "Amen." Continually declaring his faith in the Blessed One, he went to the holy sepulchre and touched the limbs in such a way that the most blessed saint might indicate what

---

1   See above, p. 47.
2   A fourth-century martyr particularly venerated in the Eastern church.
3   I.e., those affected by dropsy, or edema, in which fluids accumulate in the tissues.
4   See Horace, *Carmina* 2. 2. 13.
5   The "secular" clergy—priests and bishops—were "in the world," as opposed to the "religious"—the monks.

he would give in response to the Lady Radegund's request. He touched each finger of the right hand and, when he came to the little finger, it came away from the hand it belonged to with a gentle pull. Thus the blessed queen's desire was satisfied and her wish granted. With fitting honors, the apostolic man sent the finger to the blessed Radegund and from Jerusalem even to Poitiers God's praises resounded in her honor. Can you imagine the ardent spirit, the faithful devotion with which she threw herself into abstinence while awaiting the prize, the mighty relic? And then on receiving the heavenly gift, her joy was ecstatic. She devoted herself and all her flock to psalmody, with vigils and fasts for an entire week, blessing the Lord that she had deserved to receive such a reward. For God does not deny the faithful what they ask of Him. Frequently she would say sweetly, in a sort of veiled figure of speech that none could understand: "Anyone who has the care of souls must be sore afraid of universal praise."[1] But no matter how much she wanted to avoid it, the Giver of Virtue labored more and more to display her faith to everyone. Thus, whenever the infirm invoked her, they would be healed of whatever illnesses imprisoned them.

15. The apostolic Bishops Leontius (of Bordeaux) and Eusebius (of Saintes) summoned an illustrious man named Leo to synodal council. While he was on the road, his vision was seriously obscured, clouded by a bloody mist. Without his servants' support, he could hardly see to make his way. He reached the monastery of the blessed one, where, out of devotion to her, he had dedicated his daughters as the Lord's servants, and entered the oratory dedicated in the name of Lady Mary. After a prayer, he prostrated himself, full of faith, on the saint's haircloth, invoking her manfully. For a long time he lay on it, until the pain ceased, the mist dissolved, the blood coagulated, carried away with the help of the vein. He who had come supported by helping hands left with clear eyes, his health restored. From the blessed woman's hair shirt he gained light. Happy and uninjured, he walked to the synod where he had been heading. After that, the whole synod heard his account and he told it to us himself on the way back. Through devotion to her, he laid the foundations for a basilica for Saint Radegund and gave a hundred *solidi*[2] for the construction of the fabric. Who can count how many of the sick were restored to health by invoking her? Who that ever saw her could believe her to be an earthly person? By God in Heaven, I say, truthfully and in good faith, that to every eye her face was always resplendent with the radiance of her soul, so that what appeared outwardly not undeservedly mirrored what occurred inwardly.

16. After having collected many relics of the saints, had it been possible, she would have petitioned the Lord Himself in the seat of His Majesty to dwell here in sight of all. But what she could not see with her carnal eyes, she could contemplate with her spiritual mind sedulously intent on prayer. Since the Lord withholds no good thing from them that walk uprightly,[3] and seek Him with all their hearts, minds and souls as did this blessed woman,[4] He showed His divine clemency in kindness to her in whose breast He lived both day and night. Thus, like Saint Helena, imbued with wisdom, full of the fear of God, glorious with good works, she eagerly sought to salute the wood where the ransom of the world was hung for our salvation that we might be snatched from the power of the devil.[5] When she had found it, she clapped both hands. When she recognized that it was truly the Lord's cross that had raised the dead to life with its touch, she knelt on the ground adoring the Lord and said: "In truth, you are Christ, the Son of God, Who came into the world and with your precious blood you have redeemed your own people, whom you created, from captivity."[6]

---

1 Baudonivia takes every opportunity to emphasize Radegund's pastoral and quasi-priestly activities. Priests were responsible for the "care of souls."
2 *Solidi* (sing., *solidus*) were coins, probably gold in this case.
3 Ps. 84: 11; Douay Ps. 83: 11.
4 Matt. 22: 37.
5 Saint Helena, the mother of Constantine, to whom the discovery of the True Cross was attributed, was much admired as a model of medieval queenship.
6 Baudonivia has borrowed several phrases from the cross legend here, but that legend spoke of *two* discoverers of the cross: Judas Cyriacus and Helena. Baudonivia gives Helena a solo role.

What Helena did in oriental lands, Radegund the blessed did in Gaul! Since she wished to do nothing without counsel while she lived in the world, she sent letters to the most excellent King Sigibert who held this land in his power asking that, for the welfare of the whole fatherland and the stability of his kingdom, he would permit her to ask the emperor for wood from the Lord's cross.[1] Most graciously, he consented to the blessed queen's petition. She who had made herself a pauper for God, full of devotion and inflamed with desire, sent no gifts to the emperor. Instead she sent her messengers bearing nothing but prayers and the support of the saints whom she invoked incessantly. She got what she had prayed for: that she might glory in having the blessed wood of the Lord's cross enshrined in gold and gems and many of the relics of the saints that had been kept in the east living in that one place. At the saint's petition, the emperor sent legates with gospels ornamented in gold and gems. And the wood where once hung the salvation of the world came with a congregation of saints to the city of Poitiers. The bishop of that place should have wished to welcome it devoutly with all the people but the Enemy of humankind, to subject the blessed Radegund to trials and tribulations, worked through his satellites to make the people reject the world's ransom and refuse to receive it in the city. So one and another played the role of the Jews which is not part of our story.[2] But they would see; the Lord knows His own. Her spirit blazing in a fighting mood, she sent again to the benevolent king to say that they did not wish to receive Salvation itself into the city. Until her messengers could return from the lord king, she entrusted the Lord's cross and the tokens of the saints for shelter in a male monastery which the king had founded at Tours for his own salvation, amidst the chanting of priests.

Thus envy inflicted no less injury on the holy cross than on the Lord Himself, who endured every malicious act patiently when He was summoned time and again by the minions of judges and governors so that the people He created might not perish. She cast herself into agonies of fasts and vigils, lamenting and wailing with her whole flock every day until at last the Lord respected his handmaid's humility and moved the heart of the king to do judgment and justice in the midst of the people. Thus the devout king sent word by his trusted man, the famous Count Justin, to the apostolic Bishop, Lord Eufronius of the city of Tours, to deposit the Lord's most glorious cross and the relics of the saints with due honors in the Lady Radegund's monastery. So it was done. The blessed woman exulted in joy with all her cell when Heaven conferred this gift and perfect present on the congregation which she had gathered for God's service, for she had felt in her soul that they might have all too little after her passing. Thus, though she would always be able to help them when she was in glory with the King of Heaven, this best provider, this good shepherdess, would not leave her sheep in disarray. She bequeathed a heavenly gift, the ransom of the world from Christ's relics, which she had searched out from faraway places for the honor of the place and the salvation of the people in her monastery.[3] Thus, with the aid of God's might and heaven's power, the blind receive light for their eyes, the ears of the deaf open, the tongues of the mute resume their office, the lame walk, and demons are put to flight in that place. What more? Anyone who comes in faith, whatever the infirmity that binds them, goes away healed by the virtue of the Holy Cross. Who could attempt to tell the greatness and richness of the gift the blessed woman conferred on this city? For this, all who live by faith do bless her name. And she solemnly called God to witness when she commended her monastery to the most excellent lord king and his most serene lady Queen Brunhild, all of whom she loved with dear affection, and to the sacrosanct churches and their bishops.

17. After receiving this celestial gift, the blessed woman sent the aforementioned priest and other messengers to the emperor with a simple garment as a gift of thanks. On their return, the sea became

---

1   In the partition of Clothar I's lands among his sons, Tours and Poitiers had come to Sigibert (r.561–575). The Byzantine emperor was Justin II, and the date of the mission was 568–569.
2   This is most likely another attempt to parallel Radegund with Helena, whose efforts to find and glorify the True Cross were said to have been resisted by the Jews of Jerusalem.
3   Thereafter the monastery was named Holy Cross.

rough and they suffered many dangers from storms and tempests beyond anything they said they had ever seen before. In the middle of the sea, for forty days and nights, the ship was exposed to these perils. Then despairing of life, with death before their eyes, they made peace among themselves as the sea prepared to swallow them alive. And seeing their great danger, they raised their voices to heaven, crying aloud: "Lady Radegund, help your servants lest we perish by drowning while in your service! Free us from peril of death for now the sea is ready to swallow us alive. You have ever been merciful to those who called on you in good faith. Pity us now. Help your own lest we perish." At these cries, a dove rose from the midst of the sea and circled three times about the ship. As it made its third pass, in the name of the Trinity which the blessed woman ever cherished in her heart, the holy Queen's servant Banissios, reached out, plucked three feathers from its tail and dipped them into the sea. The tempest subsided. When the Blessed Radegund's name was invoked, the dove appeared and returned her servants to life from the jaws of death. Great tranquility descended over the midst of the sea. So they cried out loudly: "You have come, good Lady, full of piety, to rescue your people from captivity lest they drown in the flood." By invoking her name, not only her own folk but all people are set free through the virtues of the Lady Radegund. And those whom she had rescued from death brought the feathers here suitably framed and devoutly made a gift of them to this holy place.

She listens benignly whenever she is invoked. Anyone suffering from fever or smallpox or cast down by infirmity or prevented from reaching her by great distance, can dispel all illness by lighting a candle in her name. Who could venture to express how much she loved her flock? No, though the plectrum swept the strings of my tongue with a hundred tones, it would not suffice to perform the task. She ordained that a lesson would always be read while we were eating, so that we would not only receive food for the jaws but the word of God for the ears. In all that she taught others and all that she did herself, she always fulfilled the word of God. She did nothing and knew nothing carnally, but when she prohibited something or avoided doing something herself it was in her zeal for God alone. Because she did not want any slovenliness to develop in the service of God, she insisted on prayers, reading, almsgiving, and incessant daily preaching so that no one could use ignorance as an excuse to slack off.

18. She had so many gifts in herself through largesse of divine grace that, wherever she went, she followed the Lord in spirit, imitating the teacher of humility who descended to earth from his heavenly throne. After her flock had retired for their rest, she would spend the night in prayer. With her holy right hand, she would protect her monastery with the sign of the cross. Once while the blessed woman was making this sign, one of the sisters saw a thousand thousand demons standing on top of the wall in the form of goats. When the saint raised her blessed right hand in the sign of the cross, this whole multitude of demons fled, never to be seen again.

19. Likewise, one night she stood before her cell, chanting the [Divine] Office as always in her heart and in her mouth—for the perpetual praise of God resounded in the secret places of her hidden heart. Meanwhile, a raucous night bird, hateful to mankind, was breaking the peace from a tree in the middle of the monastery. One of her companions said: "Blessed Lady, if you command, I will expel the bird in your name." To which she replied, "If it troubles you, go and make the sign of the cross over it in the Lord's name." Then she walked over and said to the bird: "In the name of Our Lord Jesus Christ, Lady Radegund orders you to leave this place unless you came at God's behest and presume to sing no more within it." Then, as if the creature had heard the words from God's own mouth, it took flight and was never seen again. She had earned the obedience of birds and beasts, for she had never failed to obey the Lord's commands.

1.14 The conversion of Clovis: Bishop Avitus of Vienne, *Letter to Clovis* (508?). Original in Latin.

THIS LETTER WAS WRITTEN BY the Catholic bishop of Vienne, advisor to the Burgundian kings, to congratulate Clovis, king of the Franks, on his conversion to Catholicism and his baptism. Historians have long been influenced by the *Histories* of Gregory of Tours (for which see an excerpt on p. 65 below), which claimed that Clovis had been a pagan until his miraculous conversion in 496, after which he turned all his energies to fighting the Arians. The letter from Avitus suggests a very different scenario. It begins by pointing out that Clovis had been interested in Arianism (one of the "schisms" that Avitus refers to) until he saw the light. It continues with effusive praise of Clovis, words that could probably not have been uttered by a close associate of Burgundian royalty until after that kingdom became allied with the Franks, in 508. Thus Avitus's letter suggests that Clovis's conversion was in 508. By then it is very likely that the Burgundian kings themselves had already given up Arianism for the Catholic faith. Key to Avitus's letter is the idea, which would be influential only later, that the king should send out missionaries to spread Catholicism to "more distant races."

[Source: *Avitus of Vienne: Letters and Selected Prose*, trans. Danuta Shanzer and Ian Wood, Translated Texts for Historians 38 (Liverpool: Liverpool University Press, 2002), pp. 369-73 (notes modified).]

Avitus the bishop to Clovis the king

The chasers after various schisms,[1] by their opinions, different in nature, many in number, but *all* empty of truth, tried to conceal, under the cover of the name "Christian," the lies that have been uncovered by the keen intelligence of Your Subtlety. While we save such things (i.e., the lies) for eternity, while we reserve for future examination[2] the question of who is right on what, even in our present circumstances a ray of truth has shone through. Divine foresight has found a certain judge for our age. In making a choice for yourself, you judge on behalf of everyone. Your faith is our victory.

Many in this very situation, seeking true belief, if they are moved to the suggestion, encouraged by priests or their friends, usually invoke the custom of their race and the rites of ancestral observance as stumbling-blocks. Thus, to their own detriment, they prefer due reverence to salvation. While they maintain a token respect for their ancestors in continuing to be unbelievers, they demonstrate that they somehow do not know what to choose. Therefore let the dangerous [sense of] shame abandon this excuse after the miracle of your decision! You [alone] among your ancient clan, content with nobility alone,[3] wished whatever could adorn all your lofty ancestry to start from you for the benefit of your race. You have ancestors who did good [deeds], but you wished to be the author of better [ones]. You are the equal of your great-grandfathers in that you reign in the temporal world; for your descendants you have established your rule in heaven.

---

1 By schism here, Avitus means heresy.
2 Presumably the Last Judgment.
3 Avitus hints at the idea of the divine origin of German kings but suggests that Clovis has rightly given up this idea, and the glory reflected upon his descendants will start from his choice.

Therefore let Greece,[1] to be sure, rejoice in having an orthodox ruler, but she is no longer the only one to deserve so great a gift. Now her bright glory adorns *your* part of the world also, and in the West, in the person of a new king, the ray of an age-old light shines forth. It is fitting that it began to shine on the birthday of our Redeemer, so that the vivifying water appropriately gave birth to you in your salvation[2] on the very day when the world received the Lord of Heaven born for its redemption. On the day on which the birthday of our Lord is celebrated, let yours be too—the day on which Christ was born to the world, and you to Christ, the day on which you consecrated your soul to God, your life to those present, and your reputation to posterity.

What can be said about the glorious celebration of your regeneration? Even if I was not present at the rites in the flesh, I was not absent from communion in its joys—above all since divine kindness has added this further cause for thankfulness to our part of the world. Before your baptism a message came to me of the most sublime humility,[3] in which you stated that you were a candidate for baptism. Therefore after this waiting-period, Christmas Eve found me finally sure of you. I was turning things over in my mind and wondering how it would be when a large company of bishops united, striving in the sacred service, would lap the royal limbs in the life-giving waters, when he would bow before the servants of the Lord the head that should be so feared by pagans, when locks grown long beneath a helmet[4] would put on the helmet of the sacred chrism, when his spotless limbs, the breast-plate removed, would shine as white as his baptismal clothes. Have no fear, O most prosperous of Kings! From now on the very softness of that clothing will cause the hardness of your armor to be all the more effective: whatever good luck has offered you in the past, holiness will now provide.

I would like to add some exhortation to my praise of you, were anything escaping either your knowledge or your watchfulness. Certainly I am not going to preach to you the faith that you saw without a preacher *before* your baptism once you have found it. Or should I preach humility perhaps? You had long ago paid it to me by your service, even though only now do you owe it to me through your profession of faith. Or perhaps I should preach the sense of pity that a people, up till recently captive, once released by you, by its joy conveys to the world and by its tears to God?

There is only one thing that I would like to be increased. Because God has made your race completely his own through you, please offer the seeds of faith from the treasure-house of your heart to more distant races too: since they still live in their natural ignorance, no seeds of heresy have corrupted. Do not be ashamed or find it troublesome even to take the step of sending missions for this purpose to build up the party of the God who has raised up yours so greatly. To the extent that whatever foreign pagan peoples there are, ready to serve you for the first time because of the rule of your religion, while they still seem to have some other distinctive quality, let them be distinguished by their race rather than through their ruler ... [Here the text of the letter breaks off.]

---

1 I.e., Byzantium, the eastern half of the Roman Empire.
2 The "vivifying water" is that of Clovis's baptism.
3 The implication seems to have been that Avitus was invited to the ceremony.
4 Long hair was the identifying mark of the Merovingians.

1.15 Church legislation in Gaul: *The Council of Orléans* (511). Original in Latin.

IN 511, THIRTY BISHOPS FROM Gaul (today France) met at Orléans at the request of King Clovis, who was clearly inspired by the imperial model of calling (and sometimes presiding over) Church councils. In turn, the bishops' decisions at Orléans were influenced by imperial legislation. The main provisions of the council concerned strengthening the position of the bishops over other clerics and religious (that is, monks and nuns) in their dioceses (e.g., see canons 7, 14, 17, and 19). But the first three provisions have to do with asylum. How do they compare to the laws of the *Theodosian Code*, p. 10 above? What differences in emphasis do you detect, and how might you explain them?

[Source: *Christianity and Paganism, 350-750: The Conversion of Western Europe*, ed. J.N. Hillgarth (Philadelphia: University of Pennsylvania Press, 1986), pp. 99-103.]

To their Lord, the son of the Catholic Church, the Most Glorious King Clovis, all the bishops whom you have ordered to be present at the Council.

Since so great a care for our glorious Faith excited you to the service of the Catholic religion, that in the zeal of a priestly soul you have commanded the bishops to meet together to treat in common of necessary affairs, we, in conformity with this will and [following the] headings you have given us, have replied by the decisions which seemed to us just. If what we have decided is approved by your judgment, the consent of so great a King and Lord will increase the authority of the resolutions taken by so many prelates.

When, by God's doing, by the summoning of the Most Glorious King Clovis, the Council of high priests was gathered together in the city of Orléans, by discussion in common it was agreed that what they decided by word should be also strengthened by the testimony of writing.

1. Of murderers, adulterers, and thieves, if they fly to a church, we have decided that what the ecclesiastical canons have decreed and the Roman Law has laid down should be observed; it should not be permitted to drag them from the church or the church-house or the bishop's house; they should not be handed over except with oaths sworn on the Gospels that they may be safe from death, from mutilation, and from all nature of punishment, provided that the guilty party agree with him against whom they have acted on the satisfaction [payment] due. If a man is shown to have violated his oath [and harms the man who had sought asylum], as guilty of perjury he shall be separated not only from the communion of the Church and of all clerics but also from the life of Catholics. If the guilty man shall refuse to make composition [compensatory payment] with the man he has wronged and shall, through fear, leave the church, he shall not be sought for by the Church or by clerics.

2. We have decreed that the following is to be done with regard to abductors. If an abductor flees to a church with the girl he has abducted and it appears that the woman has suffered violence, she shall at once be freed from the power of her ravisher, and he, granted impunity from death or serious bodily harm, shall either be subjected to servitude or have freedom to redeem himself. But if she who was abducted has a father and the girl has given her consent to the ravisher, either before or after the abduction, she shall be returned pardoned to the power of her father, and the ravisher shall be obliged to satisfy the father under the aforesaid conditions.

3. The slave who has fled to the church for whatever fault, if he has received oaths from his lord on his confession of fault, shall at once be forced to return to the service of the lord, but if, after these oaths have been sworn by the lord and [the slave] has been handed over, he shall be proved to have suffered some punishment for the fault for which he was pardoned, [the lord], as was stated above [canon 1], for his contempt of the Church and denial of his [sworn] faith, shall be held a stranger to the communion and converse [social interaction] of Catholics. But if in-

deed the slave, defended by the Church, shall, by the insistence of clerics, have received the oaths of his lord for impunity for his fault, and shall refuse to leave [the church], he may be seized by his lord.

4. We have decreed, with regard to the ordination of clerics, that no layman shall presume to the clerical office, unless either by command of the King, or with the consent of the [local] judge, [but] the sons of clerics, that is, the sons, grandsons, and great-grandsons, who are bound to follow the order of their parents, shall be in the power and control of bishops.

5. Of the offerings or lands which our Lord the King has deigned to confer as a gift to the churches, or … may confer by God's inspiration, with the immunity [from taxation] of these lands or of clerics, we have decided it is most just that whatever God shall deign to give as their produce shall be expended in reparation of churches, in alms given to priests and the poor, or in the redemption of captives, and that clerics should be forced to assist the work of the Church. If any bishop shall stand out as less solicitous and devoted to this work he shall be publicly reprimanded by the other bishops of the province. But if he shall not improve even under such a rebuke he shall be held unworthy of the communion of his brethren until he amend his error.

6. If someone believes he has some claim against a bishop, either on behalf of the church or on his own account, if he does not bring forward either insults or calumnies, he may not be removed from the Church's communion simply for bringing the charge.

7. No abbots, presbyters or any clergy or those living in the profession of religion may come to the King without the knowledge and commendation of their bishop to ask for favors. If any one dare to do so, he shall be deprived of the honor of his rank and of communion, until his bishop receive his reparation through full penance.

8. If a slave is ordained either deacon or presbyter in the absence or ignorance of his lord, and the bishop knowing that he is a slave, he shall remain in the clerical office, [but] the bishop shall give his lord double compensation. But if the bishop did not know he was a slave, those who bore testimony, or asked for him to be ordained, shall be bound to [pay] the same recompense.

9. If a presbyter or a deacon shall commit a capital crime he shall at the same time be expelled from office and from communion.

10. We have decreed that this is to be observed regarding heretical clerics, who come to the Catholic Faith in full faith, and the basilicas which the Goths have hitherto held in their perversity. If the clerics are truly converted and entirely accept the Catholic Faith and display a worthy life, they shall receive the office of which the bishop judges them worthy, with the laying on of hands. [Their] churches shall be consecrated by the rite which we use for ours.

11. Those who—having once received penance, forgetful of their religious profession—relapse into lay life shall be suspended from communion and separated from the converse of all Catholics. If, after this interdict, anyone presume to eat with them he also shall be deprived of communion.

12. If a deacon or presbyter, for any offence, shall depart from the altar under the profession of penitence, and if other [ministers] are lacking and the necessity arises, one asking for baptism may be baptized [by the deacons or presbyters doing penance].

13. If any widow of a presbyter or deacon join herself in a second marriage to any man, they shall either be punished and separated, or, if they persist in their criminal intent, they shall both be punished by excommunication.

14. Going through the ancient canons, we thought earlier statutes should be renewed, so that of the offerings of the faithful on the altar [of city churches] the bishop shall claim half for himself and the second rank of clergy shall receive half, all estates remaining in the power of the bishop.

15. … Of the things which any of the faithful offers to parishes, in lands, vines, slaves, and property, all shall be in the power of the bishop; however, of those things offered on the altar [of a country church] a third shall faithfully be handed over to the bishop.

16. The bishop shall distribute, as far as his means allow, clothes and food to the poor or sick, who, because of their weakness, cannot work with their hands.

17. … All basilicas, wherever built or built today, shall be in the power of the bishop in whose territory they are situated.

18. No surviving brother shall marry his brother's

widow; none shall dare to wed his dead wife's sister. If they do this they shall be punished by ecclesiastical penalties.

19. Abbots, because of the humility of religion, shall be under the control of bishops, and if they do something outside their Rule, they shall be corrected by bishops. Every year they shall gather at the bishop's summons in the place he chooses. But monks shall be subject to their abbots in all obedience. If one of them is contumacious [disobedient] or wanders around or presumes to have something of his own, all he may have acquired shall be taken from him by his abbots, according to the Rule, for the profit of his monastery. But those who wander around where they are found, shall be brought, as fugitives, with the bishop's aid, under guard, and the abbot who in future does not discipline such persons with correct punishment, or who receives an alien monk, shall know he is guilty.

20. No monk may use a stole in the monastery or may possess rings with gems.

21. If it is proved that a monk has lived in a monastery or received the habit and later marries a wife, one guilty of such a deception shall never ascend to ecclesiastical office.

22. No monk who has abandoned the monastic congregation, impelled by ambition and vanity, shall presume to build a cell of his own will without permission of his bishop and abbot.

23. If a bishop, out of human kindness, grants small vineyards or plots of land to clerics or monks to cultivate or to hold for a time, even if a long space of years shall elapse, the church shall suffer no prejudice, nor shall the prescription of secular law be opposed to the church, to prevent it [recovering the land].

24. It is decreed … that not fifty but forty days' [fast] be observed before the Feast of Easter.

25. No town dweller may celebrate the Feasts of Easter, the Lord's Nativity, or Pentecost in his villa [country house] unless he is proved to be kept there by illness.

26. When men are gathered to celebrate Mass in God's name, the people are not to leave until the solemnity of Mass is completed and, where a bishop is present, his blessing has been given.

27. Rogations, that is litanies, are to be celebrated by all churches before the Ascension of the Lord, so that the preceding three days' fast shall end in the Lord's Ascension.[1] In these three days slaves and handmaids shall be excused all work, so that the whole people may more easily come together. In these three days let everyone abstain and live on Lenten food.

28. The clerics who neglect to be present at this holy work shall receive discipline according to the will of their bishop.

29. Let bishops, presbyters, and deacons keep the rules of past canons on the [prohibition of] intimacy with women.

30. If any cleric, monk, or layman shall think he should observe divination or auguries or casting the lots,[2] which they lyingly say are "of the Saints," to whomever they should believe they should make them known, they are to be expelled from the Church's communion with those who believed in them.

31. A bishop, unless impeded by infirmity, may not fail to be present on the Lord's Day at the nearest church.

[Subscriptions of thirty-two bishops.]

---

1   Rogation days were apparently invented by the Gallic church. They involved the entire community in processions and psalm-singing.
2   These were considered to be pagan practices.

1.16 Royal legislation in Spain: *The Visigothic Code* (5th–7th c.). Original in Latin.

COMPOSED OF LAWS CONSIDERED "ancient" as well as those promulgated and compiled by Visigothic kings (first in southern Gaul and then in Spain), *The Visigothic Code* remained important in the legal culture of the Iberian Peninsula throughout the Middle Ages. Though taking the *form* of the *Theodosian Code* as its model (see above, p. 10), the *Visigothic Code*—like other barbarian codes—took up many topics not treated there but suited to a rural society. Laws such as those "concerning injuries to trees" and "concerning injuries to animals and other property" were possibly inspired by Roman provincial laws (local laws of the Roman provinces), for which see one example in *The Farmer's Law* below, p. 72. Other provisions, such as those concerning asylum, show the continued influence of the contents of the *Theodosian Code*. How do the laws for asylum compare with those of the near-contemporary *Council of Orléans*? Why might both Church canons and royal laws be concerned with the same topic?

[Source: *The Visigothic Code (Forum Judicum)*, trans. S. P. Scott (Boston: Boston Book Company, 1910), pp. 274-76, 283-85, 331-32.]

Book 8, TITLE 3. CONCERNING INJURIES TO TREES, GARDENS, OR GROWING CROPS OF ANY DESCRIPTION.

Ancient law.

I. Concerning compensation for cutting down trees.
Where anyone, without the knowledge of the owner, cuts down a tree belonging to another; if it is a fruit tree, he shall pay three *solidi* [gold coins]; if it is an olive, five *solidi*; if it is an oak of large size, two *solidi*; if it is an oak of small size, one *solidus*; and for a tree of any other species of considerable size, he shall pay two *solidi*. For such trees, although they do not bear fruit, are useful for many purposes. And this compensation shall be made if the trees should be only cut down; for if they should be cut down and carried away, either similar trees must be given in their stead, or double the above named sums must be paid.

Ancient law.

II. Where anyone destroys the garden of another.
Where anyone destroys the garden of another, he shall, at once, be compelled by the judge to pay to the owner a sum equal to the amount of damage which he has caused. If a slave should be guilty of this offence, he shall, in addition to the payment of said damages. receive a hundred lashes.

Ancient law.

III. Where injury or homicide results from the cutting down of a tree.
If anyone should cut down a tree and any injury should result, or if the tree, in falling, should kill anyone, he who cut it down shall be responsible for the same. If, however, a number of men should be in the neighborhood of said tree and the party should previously notify them that the tree was about to fall; and if, after he gave such notice, anyone should be injured or killed by the falling branches, he who cut down the tree shall incur no liability whatever. But if the fall of the tree should cripple or injure any person who is old, or weak, or asleep, or unable to take care of himself, or any cattle of any description, the guilty party shall give to the master for every quadruped one of equal value; and where a man is killed, he shall be deemed guilty of homicide. In case any person should be mutilated or crippled, he who caused the damage shall be compelled to render satisfaction as prescribed by law, and if anyone should forcibly cut down a tree belonging to another, he shall at once render full compensation therefor. If the owner of a tree should have refused to permit it to be cut down, and any person should be killed while he was cutting it, no responsibility shall attach to anyone on account of his [the cutter's] death....

Book 8, TITLE 4. CONCERNING INJURIES TO ANIMALS, AND OTHER PROPERTY.

Ancient law.

I. Where a horse or any other animal which has been tied up is removed or injured in any way without the consent of the owner.

If any person should free a horse or any other animal belonging to another from its halter or from its hobbles, without the knowledge of the owner, he shall pay him a *solidus*. If said horse or other animal should die, in consequence, said person shall give its owner another of equal value. If he should use said animal to travel or to work with elsewhere without the knowledge of the owner, he shall be compelled to give him another of equal value, provided the owner should find him on that day or on the following one. If said animal should not be found by the third day, the person who took it shall be deemed guilty of theft.

Flavius Recesvintus, King.[1]

II. Where any animal which has been loaned is used against the direction or will of the owner or is abused.

Anyone who, contrary to the wishes or understanding of the owner, abuses an animal which he has borrowed by driving it too fast or too far or by overloading it, shall pay a *solidus* for every ten miles traversed by said animal. If they should have gone less than ten miles, the distance as well as the work shall be estimated, and compensation shall be made accordingly. If said animal should be crippled or killed, it shall belong to him who committed the injury, and he shall give one of equal value to the owner.

Ancient law.

III. Where the mane or tail of a horse, or of any other animal, is cut off by anyone.

Anyone who disfigures the mane of a horse belonging to another, or cuts off its tail, must at once give to the owner of the same another animal of equal value. Should any other animal be mutilated in this manner,

the third part of a *solidus* must be paid for every one so mutilated....

Book 9, Title 3. CONCERNING THOSE WHO SEEK SANCTUARY IN A CHURCH.

I. No one, claiming the privilege of sanctuary in a church, shall be taken from thence by force, unless he defends himself with arms.

No one shall dare to remove, by force, any person who has sought sanctuary in a church unless said person should attempt to defend himself with arms.

II. Where a person seeks sanctuary in a church and is killed while defending himself with arms.

Where anyone takes refuge at the door of a church and does not lay down his arms and is killed, the person who struck him shall be liable to no penalty or reproach therefor.

III. Concerning the penalty for removing a man from a church by force.

Where anyone removes his slave or a debtor from a church or the altar where he sought sanctuary without the consent of a priest or of some other ecclesiastic who has charge of said church, as soon as the fact has been brought to the notice of the judge, if he is a person of high rank, said offender shall be compelled to pay a hundred *solidi* to the church which sustained the injury. A person of inferior station shall pay thirty *solidi*, and if he should not have the means to do so, he shall be arrested by the judge and receive a hundred lashes in public. The master shall then regain possession of his slave, and the debtor shall be surrendered to his creditor.

IV. A debtor or a criminal cannot be forcibly removed from a church and must pay such debts or penalties as are due.

No one shall presume to seize a person who seeks sanctuary in a church or at its doors, but he may petition a priest or a deacon to restore said person to him; and if a debtor or a criminal takes refuge there, and he should not be liable to the penalty of death, the ecclesiastic in charge of the church may interpose his

---

1   This signifies legislation of King Reccesvinth (r.649–672).

good offices and request that said party be pardoned or discharged. If a debtor should take refuge in a church, the church shall have no right to protect him, but the priest or deacon must surrender him without delay, with the admonition that his creditor shall neither injure nor bind him who claimed the right of asylum; and the creditor must state, in the presence of said priest or deacon, within what time he shall expect the payment of the debt. Because the intervention of the church may be invoked for purposes of mercy is no reason why persons should be deprived of their property. The laws relating to homicides and other malefactors are set forth under their respective titles.

1.17 Christian history/personal history: Gregory of Tours, *History* (576-594). Original in Latin.

BISHOP OF TOURS FROM 573 until his death *c*.594, Gregory began his *History* with the Creation itself but soon turned to Gaul and to his own day, which he chronicled in the Augustinian spirit (see *The City of God*, p. 21 above), with both good and bad people and events intermingled. As the successor of St. Martin as bishop of Tours (see *The Life of St. Martin*, above p. 43), Gregory was responsible for the well-being of his flock. But his authority was checked and balanced by that of dukes, counts, and kings. In the excerpt below, in which the former count of Tours, Leudast, accuses Gregory of slandering Chilperic's Queen Fredegund, the role of Merovingian kings in Church affairs and the importance of bishops in royal policy are illuminated. Gregory's trial before King Chilperic at Berny-Rivière was a very dangerous moment for the bishop, who might well have been exiled or even executed for treason. Why, then, was he let off with a token sentence?

[Source: *Gregory of Tours: The Merovingians*, trans. and ed. Alexander Callander Murray (Peterborough, ON: Broadview Press, 2005), pp. 112-20 (slightly modified).]

Book 5

47. [King] Chilperic [r.561-584] heard all about the harm that Leudast [count of Tours] was doing to the churches of Tours and the entire population, and so the king sent Ansovald there. He came on the festival of Saint Martin, and as the choice of count was granted to me on behalf of the people, Eunomius was raised to the comital office.

Leudast, seeing himself set aside, went to Chilperic.

"Most dutiful king," he said, "up to now I have guarded the city of Tours. But now that I have been removed from office, look how it will be guarded. You should know that Bishop Gregory is preparing to surrender it to the son of Sigibert."

"Not at all," said the king on hearing this, "you bring this up only because you have been removed."

"The bishop speaks of even greater matters that concern you," said Leudast; "for he says that your queen [Fredegund] is committing adultery with Bishop Bertram."

At that point the king became angry. He punched and kicked Leudast, ordering him thrown into prison, loaded with chains.

48. Although this book should come to an end, I would like to tell something of Leudast's career. It seems best to begin with his birth, his homeland, and his character.

Gracina is the name of an island off Poitou, where Leudast was born to Leuchadius, a slave of a vine-dresser of the fisc [i.e., royal estates]. From there Leudast was summoned to service and assigned to the royal kitchen. But as his eyes were poor when he was young, and the bitter smoke did not agree with them, he was removed from the pestle and promoted to the baker's basket. Although he pretended to be happy among the fermented dough, he soon ran away and abandoned his service. And when he had been brought back two or three times and could not be prevented from attempting to escape, he was punished by having one of his ears clipped. Then since there was no way for him to conceal the mark imprinted on his body, he fled to Queen Marcovefa, whom King Charibert [r.561-567] loved very much and had admitted to his bed in the place of her sister. She received him willingly, promoted him, and appointed him keeper of her best horses. On this account, now overcome with self-importance and full of arrogance, he canvassed for the office of count of the stables. When he got it, he looked down his nose at everyone, holding them of no account. He was swollen with conceit and undone by the pleasures of the senses; he burned with greed and, as a favorite of his patroness, went here and there on her affairs. After her death, being well-provided with plunder, he tried to maintain with King Charibert his former position by giving gifts.

After this, due to the sinfulness of the people, he was sent as count to Tours, and there the prestige of the high office allowed him to be even more arrogant. He showed himself to be a greedy plunderer, a loud-mouthed brawler, and a filthy adulterer. By sowing dissension and bringing false charges, he there amassed no small fortune.

After Charibert's death, when the city became part of Sigibert's share,[1] he went over to Chilperic, and everything that he had unjustly amassed was seized by the adherents of Sigibert. Then king Chilperic, through his son Theudebert, overran Tours. Since by this time I had arrived in Tours, Theudebert strongly recommended to me that Leudast should hold the office of count, which he had held before. Leudast acted very humbly toward me and was subservient, repeatedly swearing on the tomb of the holy bishop Martin that he would never act unreasonably and that he would be loyal to me in matters affecting my own person as well as in all the needs of the church. For he was afraid that King Sigibert would bring the city back under his authority, as later happened. On Sigibert's death, Chilperic succeeded to his rule and

Leudast again became count. When Merovech came to Tours,[2] he plundered all Leudast's property. During the two years that Sigibert held Tours, Leudast took refuge among the Bretons.

When he assumed the office of count, as we have said, his capriciousness reached the point of his entering the bishop's house wearing body armor and mail, with a bow case slung from a belt, a lance in his hand and a helmet on his head, a man safe from no one because he was the enemy of everyone. If he presided over a trial along with leading members of the clergy and laity and saw someone pursuing justice, he would now immediately go into a rage and belch forth abuse on the citizens; he used to order priests dragged away in fetters and soldiers beaten with staves, and he showed such cruelty as to beggar description.

When Merovech, who had plundered his property, went away, Leudast came forward with false charges against me, claiming that Merovech had followed my advice in taking away his property. But after the injury had been done, he again repeated his oath and offered a covering from the tomb of the blessed Martin as a pledge that he would never be my enemy.

49. But as it is a long story to follow step by step Leudast's perjuries and other crimes, let me come to his attempt to overthrow me by unjust and execrable calumnies and the divine vengeance wreaked upon him, fulfilling the saying, "Everyone who overthrows shall be overthrown,"[3] and again, "Whoever digs a pit shall fall therein."[4]

After the many wrongs Leudast inflicted on me and mine, and after the many seizures of ecclesiastical property, he joined forces with the priest Riculf, a man as twisted as himself, and blurted out the charge that I had accused Queen Fredegund of a criminal act;[5] he claimed that, should my archdeacon Plato or my friend Galien be put to torture, they would certainly convict me of having spoken in this way. It was then, as I have said above, that the king had become angry and, after punching and kicking him and loading him with chains, had him thrown into prison.

---

1 King Sigibert I (r.561-575).
2 Merovech was a rebellious son of King Chilperic.
3 See Jer. 9: 14.
4 See Prov. 26: 27.
5 Note there are two clerics called Riculf to be distinguished in the narrative that follows: the priest Riculf, and the subdeacon Riculf.

Now Leudast said that he had the support of the cleric Riculf, on whose testimony he made these charges. This Riculf was a subdeacon, just as unstable as Leudast. The year before, he had plotted with Leudast on this matter and looked for grounds for going over to him due to my anger. At last he found them and went to him. After preparing all their tricks for four months and having laid their traps, Riculf then came back to me with Leudast and begged me to take him back without penalty. I did it, I confess, and publicly received a secret enemy into my household.

On Leudast's departure, Riculf threw himself at my feet.

"Unless you help me quickly, I am lost," he said. "At the instigation of Leudast, I have said what I should not have said. Send me now to another kingdom; if you do not, I shall be arrested by the king's men and suffer tortures that will kill me."

"If you have said anything that does not correspond to the truth, your words shall be on your own head," I said. "I will not send you to another kingdom in case I fall under suspicion of the king."

After this Leudast came forward as Riculf's accuser, claiming that he had heard the previously mentioned testimony from Riculf the subdeacon. Riculf was bound and put under guard, while Leudast in turn was released. Riculf claimed that Galien and the archdeacon Plato were present on the very day the bishop had uttered his charge.

The priest Riculf, who by this time had been promised the episcopal office by Leudast, was so carried away with himself that his pride was the equal to that of Simon Magus.[1] On the sixth day after Easter [April 26], he who had taken an oath to me three or more times on the tomb of Saint Martin spewed out such abuse that he could scarcely keep his hands off me, confident, of course, in the trap that he had laid.

On the next day, that is, the Sabbath after Easter, Leudast came to the city of Tours pretending to have some business to attend to. He arrested Plato the archdeacon and Galien, tied them up, and ordered them taken to the queen, loaded with chains and stripped of their robes. I heard of this while in my quarters in the bishop's house and, saddened and disturbed, I entered the oratory and took up the Psalms of David so that some consoling verse might be revealed when I opened them. This is what was found: "He led them away in hope and they were not afraid, and the sea covered their enemies."[2]

Meanwhile, as they began crossing the river on a ferry whose deck rested on two skiffs, the boat that was supporting Leudast sank, and if he had not escaped by swimming, he might have perished with his comrades. As for the other boat, which was connected to the first and carried the bound prisoners, it was kept above water by God's help.

Then the prisoners were taken to the king and charges that carried a death sentence were immediately laid against them. But the king, on reflection, freed them from their bonds and kept them under guard, unharmed and unshackled.

At Tours, in the meantime, Duke Berulf and Count Eunomius concocted a tale that King Guntram [r.561-592] wanted to take the city, and for that reason, to prevent anything going wrong, they said, the city must be provided with a guard. They pretended to set watches at the gates to protect the city, but they were really guarding me. They also sent people to advise me to take valuables from the church and make off secretly to Clermont. But I would not take their advice.

Next the king summoned the bishops of his kingdom and ordered the case carefully investigated.

When the cleric Riculf was repeatedly being examined in secret and, as he often did, was uttering many lies against me and my associates, Modestus, a certain carpenter, said to him, "Unlucky man, who so stubbornly has these designs against his bishop, it would be better for you to be quiet, beg pardon from the bishop, and procure his favor."

At this Riculf began to shout out in a loud voice, "Look at this man who bids me be silent and not pursue the truth. He is an enemy of the queen and will not allow the reasons for the charge against her to be investigated."

These words were immediately reported to the queen. Modestus was arrested, tortured, whipped, put in chains, and kept under guard. He was bound to a

---

1 Simon Magus figures in Acts 8: 9-24, where he is a magician who thinks that the power of the Holy Spirit exercised by the apostles is a type of magic that he can buy.

2 See Ps. 78: 53; Douay Ps. 77: 53.

post by chains between two guards, but in the middle of the night, when the guards fell asleep, he prayed for the Lord to be so kind as to exert his power on behalf of a wretched man and to let an innocent prisoner in bonds be freed by the visitation of the bishops Martin and Médard.[1] The bonds were broken, the post shattered, the door opened, and soon he entered the basilica of Saint Médard [in Soissons], where I was keeping vigils.

The bishops then assembled at the villa of Berny and were ordered to meet in one building. Next the king arrived and took his seat, after greeting everyone and receiving their blessing. At that point Bertram, bishop of Bordeaux, against whom, along with the queen, this charge had been brought, explained the case and addressed me, saying that the charge [of adultery] had been brought against him and the queen by me. I denied in truth having uttered these things, saying, I heard others say them, but I had not devised them.

Outside the building there was a lot of talk among people, who said, "Why are these charges made against a bishop of God? Why does the king prosecute such charges? How could a bishop have said such things, even about a slave. Lord God, help your servant."

The king said, "The charge against my wife dishonors me. If therefore it is your judgment that witnesses should be presented against the bishop, here they are. But if it seems that this should not be done, and that the matter should be left to the honor of the bishop, speak up. I will gladly pay heed to your command."

All were amazed at the king's wisdom and forbearance.

At that point, when all the bishops said, "The testimony of an inferior cannot be admitted against a bishop," the case came down to this, that I should say three masses at three altars and clear myself of the alleged charges by taking an oath. And though these conditions were contrary to the canons, still they were fulfilled for the sake of the king. Also I cannot

be silent about the fact that Queen Rigunth,[2] out of sympathy for my suffering, fasted with all her household until a slave reported that I had fulfilled all that had been required of me.

Then the bishops returned to the king.

"All that was imposed upon the bishop has been carried out," they said. "What remains to be done now, king, if not the excommunication of you and Bertram, the accuser of a brother?"

"Oh no," said the king, "I only reported what I had heard."

They asked who had said this, and he answered that he had heard these things from Leudast. He had already fled owing to the weakness of his plan or his resolution. All the bishops then decided that this sower of discord, traducer of the queen, and accuser of a bishop, should be shut out of all churches, because he had withdrawn from the hearing. To the bishops who were not present, they sent a letter to this effect, bearing their signatures. After this, each of them returned to his own see.

When Leudast heard, he took refuge in the church of Saint Peter in Paris. But on hearing the royal edict prohibiting anyone in Chilperic's kingdom from receiving him, and especially since the son whom he had left at home had died, he came to Tours in secret and carried away his more valuable possessions to Bourges. The king's retainers pursued him, but he escaped by flight. They captured his wife, and she was sent into exile in the district of Tournai.

The subdeacon Riculf was sentenced to death. I managed to obtain his life but I could not free him from torture. Nothing, not even metal, could have endured such beating as was given this wretch. With his hands tied behind his back, he was suspended from a tree from the third hour of the day; at the ninth hour, he was taken down, wracked on pulleys, beaten with staves, rods, and doubled thongs, and not by one or two assailants, but by as many as could reach his wretched limbs. Only at the critical point in the torture did he then reveal the truth and make known the

---

1   Bishop Martin was St. Martin (see above, p. 43); Médard (c.470–c.560) was bishop of Vermandois; his body lay at the church at Soissons.
2   Rigunth was the daughter of King Chilperic and Queen Fredegund.

secrets of the plot. This was the explanation he gave for the charge being made against the queen: when she was driven from power, Clovis would obtain the kingdom, once his brothers and father had been killed;[1] Leudast would get a ducal office. As for the priest Riculf, who had been a friend of Clovis from the times of the blessed Bishop Eufronius, he would win appointment to the bishopric of Tours. The sub-deacon Riculf was promised the archdiaconate.

I returned to Tours by God's grace and found the church thrown into a turmoil by the priest Riculf. Now this man had been picked out from among the poor under bishop Eufronius and appointed arch-deacon. Later he was raised to the priesthood and withdrew to his own property. He was always self-important, arrogant, and impudent. For example, while I was still with the king, he brazenly entered the bishop's house as if he were already bishop, in-ventoried the church silver, and brought the rest of the property under his control. He enriched the more important clergy with gifts, granted vineyards, and parceled out meadows; to the lesser clergy, he admin-istered beatings and many blows, even raising his own hand against them.

"Acknowledge your master," he said. "He has gained victory over his enemies, and it is by his de-vices that Tours has been purged of that crew from Clermont."[2]

The wretched man did not know that, with the exception of five bishops, all the others who have held the bishopric of Tours were descendants of my ances-tors. He was accustomed to repeating to his intimates the proverb that no one can expect to trick a wise man without using perjury.

Upon my return, when he continued to hold me in disdain and did not come to greet me as did the other citizens, but rather threatened to kill me, I ordered him taken away to a monastery on the advice of the bishops of my province. While he was closely con-fined, representatives of bishop Felix [of Nantes], who had supported the charge against me, intervened. The abbot was taken in by their perjuries; Riculf slipped away and went to Bishop Felix, who received him warmly, though he should have cursed him.

Leudast meanwhile went to Bourges, taking with him all the treasure that he had plundered from the poor. Not long after, forces from Bourges under their count attacked him and carried off all his gold and sil-ver and whatever else he had brought with him, leav-ing him nothing but what he had on his person; and they would have taken his very life if he had not fled. He regained his strength and in turn led some men from Tours in an attack against his plunderers; killing one of them, he recovered some of his property and returned to the territory of Tours. Duke Berulf heard about this and sent his own retainers outfitted for war to seize him. Leudast realized that he would now be captured, and so he abandoned his property and fled to the church of Saint Hilary in Poitiers.[3] Duke Ber-ulf meanwhile sent the property that he seized to the king.

Leudast would leave the basilica and attack the houses of various people, taking plunder without try-ing to disguise the fact. He was also repeatedly caught in adultery in the holy confines of the very porch of the basilica. For these reasons, the queen, disturbed that a place consecrated to God was being defiled in such a fashion, ordered him to be expelled from the holy basilica. On being expelled, he went again to his supporters in Bourges, begging them to hide him.

50. I should have mentioned my conversation with the blessed Bishop Salvius earlier, but, as it slipped my mind, I do not consider it unwarranted if it is written later.[4]

When I had said farewell to the king after the council that I mentioned [at Berny], and was anxious to return home, I did not want to go without tak-ing leave of Salvius with a kiss. I looked for him and found him in the courtyard of the domain of Berny. I told him that I was about to return home.

1 Clovis was the son of King Chilperic and his first wife.
2 Gregory of Tours's father's family was closely associated with Clermont, and Gregory spent much of his childhood there.
3 How does the description of this particular case of asylum in the Merovingian Kingdom measure up to the legislation about it at *The Council of Orléans*, above, p. 60?
4 Salvius was bishop of Albi *c*.571-584.

We had moved off a little and were speaking of one thing and another when he said to me, "Do you see what I see upon this roof?"

"Why, I see the roof-covering that the king lately had installed," said I.

"Don't you see anything else?"

"I see nothing else." I suspected that he was making some kind of a joke.

"Tell me what more do you see?" I added.

Drawing a deep breath, he said, "I see the sword of divine wrath unsheathed and hanging over this house."

Indeed, the bishop's words were not wrong; for twenty days later died the two sons of the king, whose deaths I have already described.[1]

---

1 In an earlier chapter, Gregory had described the deaths of the two sons of King Chilperic.

TIMELINE FOR CHAPTER ONE

250

300

318 *Donatist Sermon* ———— ———— 313 *Edict of Milan*
325 Eusebius, *History* ———— ———— 325 *Nicaean Creed*

350

356-72 Athanasius, *Life of Antony* ————

396 Sulpicius, *Life of Martin* ———— 400

413-26 Augustine, *City of God* ———— ———— 5th-7th c. *Visigothic Code*

438 *Theodosian Code* ————

450

500

511 *Council of Orléans* ———— ———— 508 Avitus, *Letter to Clovis*

540 *Benedictine Rule* ————
550 Procopius, *History* ———— 550

591 Gregory the Great, *Moralia in Job* ———— ———— 576-94 Gregory of Tours, *History*
600 Fortunatus and Baudonivia, *Lives of St. Radegund* ———— 600

TWO

THE EMERGENCE OF SIBLING CULTURES (*c*.600–*c*.750)

THE RESILIENCE OF BYZANTIUM

2.1 The culture of the small independent farmer: *The Farmer's Law* (8th c.?). Original in Greek.

THIS LAW CODE, ISSUED BY a Byzantine emperor, is difficult to date, though likely from the seventh or eighth century. Regardless of its time of composition, it is important because it reflects the ordinary lives of free peasants in early Byzantine society and because it demonstrates that Byzantine provincial laws were not very different from the so-called barbarian laws of the same or a slightly earlier period. Its 85 articles regulate the relations among free peasants in a village, focusing on such issues as minor crimes, straying animals, and the boundaries between peasant holdings. Compare these laws to the *Visigothic Code*, above, p. 63, and see if you can account for the similarities and differences.

[Source: Walter Ashburner, "The Farmer's Law, II," *The Journal of Hellenic Studies* 32 (1912): 87, 90, 92 (notes modified).]

---

1. The farmer who is working his own field must be just and must not encroach on his neighbor's furrows. If a farmer persists in encroaching and docks a neighboring lot—if he did this in ploughing-time, he loses his ploughing; if it was in sowing-time that he made this encroachment, he loses his seed and his husbandry and his crop—the farmer who encroached.

2. If a farmer without the landowner's cognizance

enters and ploughs or sows, let him not receive either wages for his ploughing or the crop for his sowing—no, not even the seed that has been cast.

3. If two farmers agree one with the other before two or three witnesses to exchange lands and they agreed for all time, let their determination and their exchange remain firm and secure and unassailable.

4. If two farmers, A and B, agree to exchange their lands for the season of sowing and A draws back, then, if the seed was cast, they may not draw back; but if the seed was not cast they may draw back; but if A did not plough while B did, A also shall plough.

5. If two farmers exchange lands either for a season or for all time, and one plot is found deficient as compared with the other, and this was not their agreement, let him who has more give an equivalent in land to him who has less; but if this was their agreement, let them give nothing in addition.

6. If a farmer who has a claim on a field enters against the sower's will and reaps, then, if he had a just claim, let him take nothing from it; but if his claim was baseless, let him provide twice over the crops that were reaped....

27. If a herdsman in the morning receives an ox from a farmer and it happens that it is wounded or blinded, let the herdsman swear that he has not himself played foul, and let him go harmless.

28. If a herdsman on occasion of the loss of an ox or its wounding or blinding makes oath and is afterwards by good evidence proved a perjurer, let his tongue be cut out and let him make good the damage to the owner of the ox.

29. If a herdsman with the stick which he carries injures and wounds an ox or blinds it, he does not go scatheless [without punishment] and let him pay a penalty; but if he did it with a stone he goes scatheless.

30. If a man cuts a bell from an ox or a sheep and is recognized as the thief, let him be whipped; and if the animal disappears, let him make it good who stole the bell.

31. If a tree stands on a lot, if the neighboring lot is

a garden and is overshadowed by the tree, the owner of the garden may trim its branches; but if there is no garden, the branches are not to be trimmed.

32. If a tree is cultivated by some one in an undivided place, and afterwards an allotment took place and it fell to another in his lot, let no one have possession of the tree but him who cultivated it; but if the owner of the place complains "I am injured by the tree," let them give instead of the tree another tree to the man who cultivated it and let them keep it.

33. If a guardian of fruit[1] is found stealing in the place which he guards, let him lose his wages and be well beaten.

34. If a hired shepherd is found milking his flock without the owner's knowledge and selling them,[2] let him be beaten and lose his wages.

35. If a man is found stealing another's straw, he shall restore it twice over....

55. If a man kills a sheepdog and does not make confession but there is an inroad of wild beasts into the sheepfold, and afterwards he who killed the dog is recognized, let him give the whole flock of sheep together with the value of the dog.

56. If a man lights a fire in his own wood or in his field and it happens that the fire spreads and burns houses or cultivated fields, he is not condemned unless he did it in a strong wind.

57. He who burns another's hillside or cuts another's trees is condemned in twice the damage.

58. Let him who burns the fence of a vineyard be beaten and have his hand branded and let him also pay twice the damage done.

59. Let him who cuts another's vines when they are in fruit or who roots them up have his hand cut off and pay the damage.

60. Let those who in harvest-time come into another man's furrow and cut bundles or ears of corn or pulse[3] be whipped and stripped of their shirts.

61. Where people enter another man's vineyard or figyard, if they come to eat, let them go scatheless; if they are there to steal, let them be beaten and stripped of their shirts....

---

1 The guardian may be appointed by the farmer to guard the fruit from thieves; but he may also be appointed by the landlord to ensure an equal division of the fruit between landlord and tenant, where a farm is cultivated on shares.
2 Or "selling the milk."
3 Pod-bearing plants such as peas and beans.

2.2 Byzantine village life and the education of a saint: *The Life of St. Theodore of Sykeon* (7th c.). Original in Greek.

ONE OF ST. PAUL'S LETTERS was written to the Galatians, a Celtic people that settled in north-central Anatolia. By the seventh century, they were thoroughly Christianized, as the anonymous *Life of St. Theodore* makes clear. Although the story is set in the time of Justinian, it probably best reflects the period of its writing, just before the Arab invasions of Anatolia. What evidence do you find that villagers were aware of the imperial court? How many local churches can you count? What sort of schooling was normal in a village?

[Source: *Three Byzantine Saints*: *Contemporary Biographies translated from the Greek*, trans. Elizabeth Dawes and Norman H. Baynes (Crestwood, NY: St. Vladimir's Seminary Press, 1977), pp. 88-96 (notes modified).]

---

(3) In the country of Galatia[1] there is a village called Sykeon under the jurisdiction of the town of Anastasioupolis which belongs to the province of Galatia Prima, namely that of Ancyra. Sykeon lies twelve miles distant from Anastasioupolis.

The public highway of the imperial post ran through this village, and on the road stood an inn kept by a very beautiful girl, Mary, and her mother, Elpidia, and a sister Despoinia. And these women lived in the inn and followed the profession of courtesans.

At that time when Justinian of pious memory was Emperor [r.527-565] certain imperial decrees were being dispatched from the capital, and thus it chanced that a certain well-known man, Cosmas by name, who had become popular in the Hippodrome in the corps of those who performed acrobatic feats on camels, was appointed to carry out the Emperor's orders.

On this man's journey to the East he stayed for some time in the inn, and seeing Mary and how fair she was, he desired her and took her to his bed. From this union she conceived and saw in a dream a very large and brilliant star descending from heaven into her womb. She awoke all trembling with fear and related the vision she had seen in the night to Cosmas, the imperial messenger, and he said to her, "Take good care of yourself, dear, for perchance God will watch over you and give you a son who will be deemed worthy to become a bishop." With these words he left her in the morning and went on his way rejoicing.

(4) Next the woman visited a holy father who could foresee the future who lived six miles off near the village of Balgatia, and related to him what she had seen in her dream. The old man said to her, "I tell you of a truth that the son who shall be born of you will become a great man, not as men hold greatness, but he will be well-pleasing to God. For a brilliant star is held to signify the glory of a king by those who are expert in interpreting visions; but with you it must not be read thus. For it is the brilliant adornment of virtues and graces which God has sent down upon the babe in your womb that you saw in the likeness of a brilliant star; for thus He is wont to consecrate His worthy servants in the womb before they are born." When Theodosius, who had been appointed bishop of the town of Anastasioupolis, heard of her vision, he, too, by God's inspiration gave to her the same interpretation.

(5) When her full time was accomplished, Mary bore the servant of God; and after some days had passed, she carried him, as is the custom among Christians, to the Holy Church of the Orthodox and showed him to the priests who baptized him in the name of the Holy Trinity and named him "Theodore," thus showing by this name that he would be the "gift of God." When the child was about six years old, his mother wanted him to enter the Emperor's service in the capital, so she made ready for him a gold belt and expensive clothes and everything else necessary, and then she prepared herself for the journey. On the night when she intended to start, God's holy

---

1 Galatia was an Anatolian province of Byzantium.

martyr, St. George, appeared to her and said, "What is this plan, lady, which you have made for the boy? Do not labor in vain, for the King in heaven has need of him."[1] And in the morning she arose and related her vision and wept saying, "Assuredly death has drawn near to my boy." After this she abandoned her journey. She wore herself away with increasing care of her son, and when he was eight years old she gave him to a teacher to be taught his letters. By the grace of God he was quicker at learning than all the other boys and made great progress.

He was beloved by all and in his daily life became known to all for his virtues; for when he played with the others he always beat them, but no oath or blasphemy nor any unfitting word ever escaped his lips, nor did he allow the others to use one. And whenever any dispute arose in their games, he at once withdrew and through his actions put an end to it.

(6) Now there lived in the house a God-fearing man called Stephen who used to make skillfully prepared dishes. The women by this time had become quite respectable, for they had abandoned their profession as prostitutes and followed the path of sobriety and godliness. They now relied upon the goodness of the fare when they entertained the many governors and officers who came to the inn, and they congratulated Stephen who had made the food so tasty. Whenever he received any money, either from the women or their guests, he spent it on the churches where he prayed regularly morning and evening. During Lent, although he prepared all the food for the women, he fasted till the evening partaking of nothing except perhaps a little boiled wheat and water.

The women loved him and looked upon him as a father because he was such a true lover of Christ. The boy noticing this abstinence was moved by divine love and desired to copy Stephen's mode of life, according to the words of the apostle who said, "Remember them that have the rule over you who spake unto you the word of God; and consider the issue of their life and imitate their faith ... For it is good that the heart be established by grace; not by meats wherein they

that occupied themselves were not profited."[2] "For meat commends us not to God."[3]

His mother and the other women, unconscious of his heart's desire, compelled him to eat with them when he returned home from school at the dinner-hour; so when school was over he no longer came home for dinner but spent the whole day in the school fasting and in the evening he would come back and go off with the pious man, Stephen, to the holy churches and there pray and partake of the body and blood of Christ. Returning home he would share with Stephen his boiled wheat and water. However much the women and even Stephen himself urged him, he could not be persuaded to do as they wished. Then his mother asked the schoolmaster to send him home at the dinner-hour as she wished to persuade him to eat at least a little vegetable food, because he was getting run down from want of food and from eating only so late in the day. The schoolmaster accordingly sent him away with the other boys, but Theodore did according to the song of David which says: "In the Lord I have trusted; how shall ye say to my soul, Flee as a bird to your mountain?"[4]

(7) When he came out of school he went up the rocky hill which lay near the village. Here there was a shrine dedicated to the martyr St. George. The Saint would guide him to the spot appearing visibly before his eyes in the form of a young man. Entering the shrine, Theodore would sit down and busy himself with the study of the Holy Scriptures, and after midday he went back to the school and returned home in the evening. When his mother inquired why he had not appeared at dinner-time, he tricked her saying either that he had not been able to say his lesson and was therefore kept in, or that he had a pain in his stomach and therefore had no appetite. So she again sent word to the master to send him home with the others, and he replied that since he had received her message he always did send him away with the others. Then she found out that he went up to the shrine and so she sent some of her servants to fetch him, and they brought him down to her. She threatened him and

---

1 St. George (d.303) was martyred in Palestine. He had possibly been a soldier. In any event, he soon became a patron saint of the Byzantine army.
2 Heb. 13: 7, 9.
3 1 Cor. 8: 8.
4 Ps. 11: 1; Douay Ps. 10: 1.

told him to come straight home from school to her, but he continued to act as he had been accustomed to do. His mother was very troubled about him, but in spite of all her threats and advice she was quite unable to make him change his fixed purpose, or to break the rules of abstinence which he had prescribed for himself.

(8) When he was about twelve years old an epidemic of bubonic plague fell upon the village and it attacked him along with the others so that he came near to dying. They took him to the shrine of St. John the Baptist near the village and laid him at the entrance to the sanctuary, and above him where the cross was set there hung an icon of our Savior Jesus Christ. As he was suffering great pain from the plague suddenly drops of dew fell upon him from the icon and immediately by the grace of God, freed from his suffering, he recovered and returned to his home....

(10) The boy had made very good progress in learning to read when one day he went into the church of the holy martyr Gemellus,[1] which was near his home and spent the night there. And he saw himself as though he were in the presence of a king surrounded by a strong bodyguard and a woman clad in purple at his side, and he heard the king say, "Fight the good fight, Theodore, that you may receive full pay in the heavenly army, and on earth I will give you glory and honor in the sight of men." When he had heard this voice, he awoke.

He was twelve years old when his heart was stirred by the message given to him by the King, Christ, in this vision, and in his zeal to follow the path leading to those better things which pertain to salvation he began to shut himself up in one of the cellars of his home from Epiphany to Palm Sunday, and during two weeks in Lent, the first and the middle one, he spoke to no one at all but offered prayers to God alone, and practiced abstinence as he had done before.

(11) Now when the devil, the enemy of truth, saw that Theodore was industriously acquiring the spiritual weapons of virtue against him, he determined to destroy him. Accordingly one day he assumed the appearance of one of Theodore's schoolfellows, Gerontius by name, and took him and led him up to the cliffs of a place called Tzidrama, and, setting him on a lofty crag of the cliffs there, put the temptation to him which was put to our Savior, and said, "If you are willing, master Theodore, to display your powers of conquest, display them here and jump down from this cliff." But Theodore looked at the height which was really great and said to Gerontius, "It is high and I am afraid." The devil said to him, "In the eyes of all the boys you are considered braver than I, and you outshine me, but in this matter I am no coward and will throw myself down." The boy answered him, "Don't do it! You may lame yourself, or even be killed." As the other asserted he could do the feat without any danger, Theodore finally said to him, "If you will, then I will too." So the devil standing with him on the rock jumped down, and alighting on his feet shouted up to the boy Theodore, saying, "See, I have done it! If you dare, come down too, that I may see your bravery: if you can, as in all else, distinguish yourself in this test too." While the boy stood debating within himself full of fear at this utterly useless ordeal, and staggered at the boldness of the supposed Gerontius, who had never previously been so bold, George, the martyr of Christ, suddenly appeared and taking Theodore by the hand, led him away from the place, saying, "Come, follow me, and do not listen to the tempting of him who is seeking your soul; for he is not Gerontius but the enemy of our race." And so saying the holy martyr brought him to his oratory.

(12) One day when Theodore was staying in the chapel of St. George his mother and his mother's mother came up to him and with much coaxing tried to force him to come down home saying that they expected the visit of some important friends. But the boy could not be persuaded by them to go down, for he fulfilled literally the words of holy scripture which says, "The friendship of this world is enmity with God, and whoever would be a friend of the world makes himself an enemy of God,"[2] and "No one can serve God and Mammon."[3] He also regarded the wealth of

---

1 St. Gemellus (d.362) was martyred under Emperor Julian (r.361–363) in Galatia.
2 James 4: 4.
3 Luke 16: 13.

the world as nought, and wishing to get rid of it, he unbuckled his gold belt, took off his necklace and the bracelet from his wrist and threw them down in front of the women saying, "You suspect that these things may get lost and it is because of them you trouble me. Take them then and begone! for I will not leave this place." And the women took them and went, as they could not persuade him. For all his thoughts were towards the Lord Whom he imitated and in Whose footsteps he followed; he fled from his parents and ran to God; he gave up wealth and houses in order to be rewarded a hundredfold and inherit eternal life,[1] as the Lord who has promised this says: "He that wishes to come after me, let him deny himself and take up his cross and follow me!"[2]

For the boy nobly mortified his body, keeping it under and wearing it down, as though it were some alien thing which warred against his soul; and on his forehead he bore the Cross; and just as Peter and James and John and the rest of the apostles "left all and followed Jesus"[3] so this boy likewise believed in the witness of the Scriptures and sought earnestly to mold his life thereon.

(13) Further, he wanted to imitate David in his holy hymn-writing and accordingly began to learn the psalter.[4] With difficulty and much labor he learnt as far as the sixteenth psalm, but he could not manage to get the seventeenth psalm by heart. He was studying it in the chapel of the holy martyr Christopher[5] (which was near the village) and as he could not learn it, he threw himself on his face and besought God to make him quick of learning in his study of the psalms. And the merciful God, Who said, "Ask and it shall be given you,"[6] granted him his request. For as the boy got up from the ground and turned to the icon of our Savior in prayer, he felt a sweetness more pleasant than honey poured into his mouth. He recognized the grace of God, partook of the sweetness and gave thanks to Christ, and from that hour on he memorized the psalter easily and quickly, and had learnt the whole of it by heart in a few days.

And he would wander about to all the churches, "with psalms and hymns and spiritual songs singing and praising the Lord," and wherever a commemorative service in honor of a saint was being held, he attended it with joy. Similarly, on the occasion of the all-night service for the holy martyr Heuretus[7] held in the town of Iopolis, fifteen miles away, he left at the hour of supper and ran fasting to this service and after praying and partaking of the divine mysteries of Christ, he returned and reached his home at midnight. For he was an exceedingly swift runner, so much so that several times for a wager he ran a race of three miles with horses and outstripped them....

2.3 The argument for icons: John of Damascus, *On Holy Images* (c.730). Original in Greek.

ONCE THE OFFICIAL REPRESSION of icons known as "iconoclasm" began in 726, it was dangerous to air the support of images of God and His saints publicly in the Byzantine empire. But Christians in the Islamic world had greater freedom, and soon John of Damascus (c.675-749) became a major spokesman for the iconophile (or iconodule) position—a defender of icons. John was born at Damascus when it was under Umayyad rule; his father, though a Christian, was employed by the caliph, and John succeeded him in the same position. Shortly after composing the

---

1 Luke 18: 29.
2 Matt. 16: 24.
3 Luke 5: 11.
4 The book of the 150 psalms.
5 Nothing is known about St. Christopher, possibly a third-century martyr, except that he died in Anatolia and that a cult grew up around him from a very early period.
6 Matt. 7: 7.
7 St. Heuretus cannot be identified.

treatise in defense of holy images excerpted here, he became a monk at Mar Saba, near Jerusalem, where he spent the rest of his life, practicing the ascetic life while studying, writing, and preaching. His book *The Fount of Knowledge* was a foundational text for Greek Orthodox theology.

[Source: *St. John Damascene on Holy Images*, trans. Mary H. Allies (London: Thomas Baker, 1898), pp. 1, 4–6, 8–17 (slightly modified).]

With the ever-present conviction of my own unworthiness, I ought to have kept silent and confessed my shortcomings before God, but all things are good at the right time. I see the Church which God founded on the Apostles and Prophets, its corner-stone being Christ His Son, tossed on an angry sea, beaten by rushing waves, shaken and troubled by the assaults of evil spirits. I see rents in the seamless robe of Christ, which impious men have sought to part asunder, and His body cut into pieces, that is, the word of God and the ancient tradition of the Church. Therefore I have judged it unreasonable to keep silent and to hold my tongue....

I believe in one God, the source of all things, without beginning, uncreated, immortal, everlasting, incomprehensible, bodiless, invisible, uncircumscribed [i.e., in no one place], without form. I believe in one supersubstantial being, one divine Godhead in three entities, the Father, the Son, and the Holy Ghost, and I adore Him alone with the worship of latreia.[1] I adore one God, one Godhead but three Persons, God the Father, God the Son made flesh, and God the Holy Ghost, one God. I do not adore creation more than the Creator, but I adore the creature created as I am, adopting creation freely and spontaneously that He might elevate our nature and make us partakers of His divine nature. Together with my Lord and King I worship Him clothed in the flesh, not as if it were a garment or He constituted a fourth person of the Trinity—God forbid. That flesh is divine, and endures after its assumption. Human nature was not lost in the Godhead, but just as the Word made flesh remained the Word, so flesh became the Word remaining flesh, becoming, rather, one with the Word through union. Therefore I venture to draw an image of the invisible God, not as invisible, but as having become visible for our sakes through flesh and blood. I do not draw an image of the immortal Godhead. I paint the visible flesh of God, for if it is impossible to represent a spirit, how much more God who gives breath to the spirit.

Now adversaries say: God's commands to Moses the law-giver were, "Thou shalt adore the Lord thy God, and thou shalt worship him alone, and thou shalt not make to thyself a graven thing that is in heaven above, or in the earth beneath."[2] They err truly, not knowing the Scriptures, for the letter kills whilst the spirit quickens—not finding in the letter the hidden meaning....

These injunctions were given to the Jews on account of their proneness to idolatry. Now we, on the contrary, are no longer in toddler harnesses. Speaking theologically, it is given to us to avoid superstitious error, to be with God in the knowledge of the truth, to worship God alone, to enjoy the fulness of His knowledge. We have passed the stage of infancy and reached the perfection of manhood. We receive our habit of mind from God and know what may be imaged and what may not. The Scripture says, "You have not seen the likeness of Him."[3] What wisdom in the law-giver! How depict the invisible? How picture the inconceivable? How give expression to the limitless, the immeasurable, the invisible? How give a form to immensity? How paint immortality? How localize mystery? It is clear that when you contemplate God, who is a pure spirit, becoming man for your sake, you will be able to clothe Him with the human form. When the Invisible One becomes visible to flesh, you may then draw a likeness of His form. When He who is a pure spirit, without form or limit, immeasurable in the boundlessness of His own

---

1   Latreia is the worship due God alone.
2   See Exod. 20: 4–5.
3   Exod. 33: 20.

nature, existing as God, takes upon Himself the form of a servant in substance and in stature, and a body of flesh, then you may draw His likeness, and show it to anyone willing to contemplate it. Depict His ineffable condescension, His virginal birth, His baptism in the Jordan, His transfiguration on Tabor, His all-powerful sufferings, His death and miracles, the proofs of His Godhead, the deeds which He worked in the flesh through divine power, His saving Cross, His Sepulcher, and resurrection, and ascent into heaven. Give to it all the endurance of engraving and color. Have no fear or anxiety; worship is not all of the same kind. Abraham worshiped the sons of Hamor, impious men in ignorance of God, when he bought the double cave for a tomb.[1] Jacob worshiped his brother Esau and the Pharaoh, the Egyptian, but on the point of his staff.[2] He worshiped, he did not adore. Josue and Daniel worshiped an angel of God; they did not adore him.[3] The worship of latreia is one thing, and the worship which is given to merit another. Now, as we are talking of images and worship, let us analyze the exact meaning of each. An image is a likeness of the original with a certain difference, for it is not an exact reproduction of the original. Thus, the Son is the living, substantial, unchangeable Image of the invisible God, bearing in Himself the whole Father, being in all things equal to Him, differing only in being begotten by the Father, who is the Begetter; the Son is begotten. The Father does not proceed from the Son, but the Son from the Father. It is through the Son, though not after Him, that He is what He is, the Father who generates. In God, too, there are representations and images of His future acts—that is to say, His counsel from all eternity, which is ever unchangeable. That which is divine is immutable; there is no change in Him, nor shadow of change.[4] Blessed Denis [i.e., Pseudo-Dionysius][5] who has made divine things in God's presence his study, says that these representations and images are marked out beforehand.

In His counsels, God has noted and settled all that He would do, the unchanging future events before they came to pass. In the same way, a man who wished to build a house, would first make and think out a plan. Again, visible things are images of invisible and intangible things, on which they throw a faint light. Holy Scripture clothes in figure God and the angels, and the same holy man [Blessed Denis] explains why. When sensible things sufficiently render what is beyond sense, and give a form to what is intangible, a medium would be reckoned imperfect according to our standard, if it did not fully represent material vision, or if it required effort of mind. If, therefore, Holy Scripture, providing for our need, ever putting before us what is intangible, clothes it in flesh, does it not make an image of what is thus invested with our nature, and brought to the level of our desires, yet invisible? A certain conception through the senses thus takes place in the brain, which was not there before, and is transmitted to the judicial faculty, and added to the mental store. Gregory, who is so eloquent about God, says that the mind which is set upon getting beyond corporeal things, is incapable of doing it.[6] For the invisible things of God since the creation of the world are made visible through images.[7] We see images in creation which remind us faintly of God, as when, for instance, we speak of the holy and adorable Trinity, imaged by the sun, or light, or burning rays, or by a running fountain, or a full river, or by the mind, speech, or the spirit within us, or by a rose tree, or a sprouting flower, or a sweet fragrance.

Again, an image is expressive of something in the future, mystically shadowing forth what is to happen. For instance, the ark represents the image of Our Lady, Mother of God, as does the staff and the earthen jar. The serpent brings before us Him who vanquished on the Cross the bite of the original serpent; the sea, water, and the cloud [signify] the grace of baptism.[8]

Again, things which have taken place are expressed

---

1 See Gen. 23: 7; Acts 7: 16.
2 See Gen. 33: 3, and 47: 7, 10.
3 See Jos. 5: 14-15.
4 See James 1: 17.
5 Today scholars call the man whom John referred to as Denis "Pseudo-Dionysius." He was a mystical theologian of the late fifth or early sixth century.
6 This may be a reference to Gregory of Nyssa (d. after 385).
7 See Rom 1: 20.
8 See 1 Cor 10: 1.

by images for the remembrance either of a wonder, or an honor, or dishonor, or good or evil, to help those who look upon it later on, so that we may avoid evils and imitate goodness. It is of two kinds, the written image in books, as when God had the law inscribed on tablets, and when He enjoined that the lives of holy men should be recorded and sensible memorials be preserved in remembrance; as, for instance, the earthen jar and the staff in the ark.[1] So now we preserve in writing the images and the good deeds of the past. Either, therefore, take away images altogether and be out of harmony with God who made these regulations, or receive them with the language and in the manner which befits them. In speaking of the manner let us go into the question of worship.

Worship is the symbol of veneration and of honor. Let us understand that there are different degrees of worship. First of all the worship of latreia, which we show to God, who alone by nature is worthy of worship. Then, for the sake of God who is worshipful by nature, we honor His saints and servants, as Josue and Daniel worshiped an angel, and David His holy places, when he says, "Let us go to the place where His feet have stood."[2] Again, in His tabernacles, as when all the people of Israel adored in the tent, and standing round the temple in Jerusalem, fixing their gaze upon it from all sides, and worshiping from that day to this; or in the rulers established by Him, as Jacob rendered homage to Esau, his elder brother, and to Pharaoh, the divinely established ruler....

Of old, God the incorporeal and uncircumscribed was never depicted. Now, however, when God is seen clothed in flesh and conversing with men, I make an image of the God whom I see. I do not worship matter, I worship the God of matter, who became matter for my sake, and deigned to inhabit matter, who worked out my salvation through matter. I will not cease from honoring that matter which works my salvation. I venerate it, though not as God. How could God be born out of lifeless things? And if God's body is God by union, it is immutable. The nature of God remains the same as before, the flesh created in time is quickened by a logical and reasoning soul. I honor all matter besides and venerate it. Through it, filled, as it were, with a divine power and grace, my salvation has come to me. Was not the thrice happy and thrice blessed wood of the Cross matter? Was not the sacred and holy mountain of Calvary matter? What of the life-giving rock, the Holy Sepulchre, the source of our resurrection: was it not matter? Is not the most holy book of the Gospels matter? Is not the blessed table matter which gives us the Bread of Life? Are not gold and silver matter out of which crosses and altar-plate and chalices are made? And before all these things, is not the body and blood of our Lord matter? Either do away with the veneration and worship due to all these things, or submit to the tradition of the Church in the worship of images, honoring God and His friends, and following in this the grace of the Holy Spirit. Do not despise matter, for it is not despicable. Nothing is that which God has made. This is the Manichean heresy.[3] That alone is despicable which does not come from God but is our own invention, the spontaneous choice of will to disregard the natural law—that is to say, sin.

---

1   See Exod. 34: 28 and Heb. 9: 4.
2   Ps. 132: 7; Douay Ps. 131: 7.
3   The Manicheans thought that the world consisted of two entities: evil (matter) and good (spirit).

2.4 The iconoclastic argument: *The Synod of 754.* Original in Greek.

THE BYZANTINE EMPEROR LEO III (r.717-741) launched the period of iconoclasm, but he treated icons as an abuse, not a heresy. His son, Constantine V (r.741-775), took the next step, calling a church council in 754 to declare the veneration of icons a violation of "the fundamental doctrine of our salvation." The synod, whose proceedings survive only because they were included in the account of the later iconodule (pro-icon) synod of 787, compared iconoclasm to the great heresies of Nestorius and Arius, who challenged the orthodox view concerning the nature of the persons of the Trinity. No representation of Christ, the bishops argued, could accurately portray the correct union of His two natures, man and God. The synod included no patriarch or papal representative, but it did involve over 300 bishops—a very large number. What evidence in this document shows that the synod constituted a major triumph for the emperor? How might you argue that iconoclasm was more popular in its day than later iconophile propaganda might suggest?

[Source: *A Select Library of Nicene and Post-Nicene Fathers of the Christian Church,* 2nd ser., ed. Philip Schaff and Henry Wace, vol. 14: *The Seven Ecumenical Councils* (Grand Rapids, MI: Wm. B. Eerdmans, 1971), pp. 543-45 (slightly modified).]

The holy and Ecumenical synod, which by the grace of God and most pious command of the God-beloved and orthodox Emperors, Constantine and Leo[1] now assembled in the imperial residence city, in the temple of the holy and inviolate Mother of God and Virgin Mary, surnamed in Blachernai[2] have decreed as follows.

Satan misguided men, so that they worshiped the creature instead of the Creator. The Mosaic law and the prophets co-operated to undo this ruin; but in order to save mankind thoroughly, God sent his own Son, who turned us away from error and the worshiping of idols and taught us the worshiping of God in spirit and in truth. As messengers of his saving doctrine, he left us his Apostles and disciples, and these adorned the Church, his Bride, with his glorious doctrines. This ornament of the Church the holy Fathers and the six Ecumenical Councils have preserved inviolate. But the before-mentioned demiurgos of wickedness [i.e., Satan] could not endure the sight of this adornment and gradually brought back idolatry under the appearance of Christianity. As then Christ armed his Apostles against the ancient idolatry with the power of the Holy Spirit and sent them out

into all the world, so has he awakened against the new idolatry his servants our faithful Emperors and endowed them with the same wisdom of the Holy Spirit. Impelled by the Holy Spirit they could no longer be witnesses of the Church being laid waste by the deception of demons and summoned the sanctified assembly of the God-beloved bishops, that they might institute at a synod a scriptural examination into the deceitful coloring of the pictures which draws down the spirit of man from the lofty adoration of God to the low and material adoration of the creature, and that they, under divine guidance, might express their view on the subject.

Our holy synod therefore assembled, and we, its 338 members, follow the older synodal decrees and accept and proclaim joyfully the dogmas handed down, principally those of the six holy Ecumenical Synods. In the first place the holy and ecumenical great synod assembled at Nicaea, etc.

After we had carefully examined their decrees under the guidance of the Holy Spirit, we found that the unlawful art of painting living creatures blasphemed the fundamental doctrine of our salvation—namely, the Incarnation of Christ—and contradicted the six

---

1   Constantine (r.741–75); his son Leo was only four years old at the time; he eventually ruled as Leo IV (775–780).
2   The imperial palace at Constantinople.

holy synods. These condemned Nestorius because he divided the one Son and Word of God into two sons, and on the other side, Arius, Dioscorus, Eutyches, and Severus, because they maintained a mingling of the two natures of the one Christ.[1]

Wherefore we thought it right to make clear with all accuracy in our present definition the error of such as make and venerate these, for it is the unanimous doctrine of all the holy Fathers and of the six Ecumenical Synods that no one may imagine any kind of separation or mingling in opposition to the unsearchable, unspeakable, and incomprehensible union of the two natures in the one hypostasis or person. What avails, then, the folly of the painter, who from sinful love of gain depicts that which should not be depicted—that is, with his polluted hands he tries to fashion that which should only be believed in the heart and confessed with the mouth? He makes an image and calls it Christ. The name *Christ* signifies *God and man.* Consequently it is an image of God and man, and consequently he has in his foolish mind, in his representation of the created flesh, depicted the Godhead which cannot be represented and thus mingled what should not be mingled. Thus he is guilty of a double blasphemy—the one in making an image of the Godhead and the other in mingling the Godhead and manhood. Those fall into the same blasphemy who venerate the image, and the same woe rests upon both, because they err with Arius, Dioscorus, and Eutyches, and with the heresy of the Acephali.[2] When, however, they are blamed for undertaking to depict the divine nature of Christ, which should not be depicted, they take refuge in the excuse: We represent only the flesh of Christ which we have seen and handled. But that is a Nestorian error.[3] For it should be considered that that flesh was also the flesh of God the Word, without any separation, perfectly assumed by the divine nature and made wholly divine. How could it now be separated and represented apart? So is it with the human soul of Christ which mediates between the Godhead of the Son and the dullness of the flesh. As the human flesh is at the same time flesh of God the Word, so is the human soul also soul of God the Word, and both at the same time, the soul being deified as well as the body, and the Godhead remained undivided even in the separation of the soul from the body in his voluntary passion. For where the soul of Christ is, there is also his Godhead; and where the body of Christ is, there too is his Godhead. If then in his passion the divinity remained inseparable from these, how do the fools venture to separate the flesh from the Godhead and represent it by itself as the image of a mere man? They fall into the abyss of impiety since they separate the flesh from the Godhead, ascribe to it a subsistence of its own, a personality of its own, which they depict, and thus introduce a fourth person into the Trinity. Moreover, they represent as not being made divine that which has been made divine by being assumed by the Godhead. Whoever, then, makes an image of Christ either depicts the Godhead which cannot be depicted and mingles it with the manhood (like the Monophysites),[4] or he represents the body of Christ as not made divine and separate and as a person apart, like the Nestorians.

The only admissible figure of the humanity of Christ, however, is bread and wine in the holy Supper. This and no other form, this and no other type, has he chosen to represent his incarnation. Bread he ordered to be brought, but not a representation of the human form, so that idolatry might not arise. And as the body of Christ is made divine, so also this figure of the body of Christ, the bread, is made divine by the descent of the Holy Spirit; it becomes the divine body of Christ by the mediation of the priest who, separating the oblation [offering] from that which is common, sanctifies it.

The evil custom of assigning names to the images does not come down from Christ and the Apostles and the holy Fathers; nor have these left behind them any prayer by which an image should be hallowed or made anything else than ordinary matter.

If, however, some say we might be right in regard

---

1   Nestorius, Arius, Dioscorus, Eutyches, and Severus represent the heresiarchs (the originators of the heresies) of early Christianity. Each had a different view of the nature of the persons of the Trinity.

2   The Acephali was another name for the followers of Eutyches.

3   The "error of Nestorius" was to stress the independence of the two natures—divine and human—of Christ.

4   The Monophysites, like the followers of Eutyches, rejected both the Orthodox assertion of the hypostatic (or "underlying") union of the "two natures" of Christ and the Nestorian assertion of a union that was not hypostatic but rather accidental.

to the images of Christ on account of the mysterious union of the two natures, but it is not right for us to forbid also the images of the altogether spotless and ever-glorious Mother of God, or of the prophets, apostles, and martyrs, who were mere men and did not consist of two natures; we may reply, first of all: If those fall away, there is no longer need of these. But we will also consider what may be said against these in particular. Christianity has rejected the *whole* of heathenism, and so not merely heathen sacrifices, but also the heathen worship of images. The Saints live on eternally with God, although they have died. If anyone thinks to call them back again to life by a dead art, discovered by the heathen, he makes himself guilty of blasphemy. Who dares attempt with heathenish art to paint the Mother of God, who is exalted above all heavens and the Saints? It is not permitted to Christians, who have the hope of the resurrection, to imitate the customs of demon-worshipers and to insult the Saints, who shine in so great glory, by common dead matter....

Supported by the Holy Scriptures and the Fathers, we declare unanimously, in the name of the Holy Trinity, that there shall be rejected and removed and cursed out of the Christian Church every likeness which is made out of any material and color whatever by the evil art of painters.

Whoever in future dares to make such a thing, or to venerate it, or set it up in a church, or in a private house, or possesses it in secret, shall, if bishop, presbyter, or deacon, be deposed; if monk or layman, be anathematized[1] and become liable to be tried by the secular laws as an adversary of God and an enemy of the doctrines handed down by the Fathers. At the same time we ordain that no incumbent of a church shall venture, under pretext of destroying the error in regard to images, to lay his hands on the holy vessels in order to have them altered because they are adorned with figures. The same is provided in regard to the vestments of churches, cloths, and all that is dedicated to divine service. If, however, the incumbent of a church wishes to have such church vessels and vestments altered, he must do this only with the assent of the holy Ecumenical patriarch and at the bidding of our pious Emperors. So also no prince or secular official shall rob the churches, as some have done in former times, under the pretext of destroying images. All this we ordain, believing that we speak as does the Apostle, for we also believe that we have the spirit of Christ; and as our predecessors who believed the same thing spoke what they had synodically defined, so we believe and therefore do we speak and set forth a definition of what has seemed good to us following and in accordance with the definitions of our Fathers.

(1) If anyone shall not confess, according to the tradition of the Apostles and Fathers, in the Father, the Son and the Holy Ghost one godhead, nature and substance, will and operation, virtue and dominion, kingdom and power in three subsistences, that is in their most glorious Persons, let him be anathema.[2]

(2) If anyone does not confess that one of the Trinity was made flesh, let him be anathema.

(3) If anyone does not confess that the holy Virgin is truly the Mother of God, etc.

(4) If anyone does not confess one Christ both God and man, etc.

(5) If anyone does not confess that the flesh of the Lord is life-giving because it is the flesh of the Word of God, etc.

(6) If anyone does not confess two natures in Christ, etc.

(7) If anyone does not confess that Christ is seated with God the Father in body and soul, and so will come to judge, and that he will remain God forever without any grossness, etc.

(8) If anyone ventures to represent the divine image of the Word after the Incarnation with material colors, let him be anathema!

(9) If anyone ventures to represent in human figures by means of material colors by reason of the incarnation, the substance or person of the Word, which cannot be depicted, and does not rather confess that even after the Incarnation he [i.e., the Word] cannot be depicted, let him be anathema!

(10) If anyone ventures to represent the hypostatic union of the two natures in a picture and calls it Christ and thus falsely represents a union of the two natures, etc.

---

1 I.e., excommunicated from the Church.
2 I.e., excommunicated from the Church.

(11) If anyone separates the flesh united with the person of the Word from it and endeavors to represent it separately in a picture, etc.

(12) If anyone separates the one Christ into two persons and endeavors to represent Him who was born of the Virgin separately and thus accepts only a relative union of the natures, etc.

(13) If anyone represents in a picture the flesh deified by its union with the Word, and thus separates it from the Godhead, etc.

(14) If anyone endeavors to represent by material colors God the Word as a mere man, who, although bearing the form of God, yet has assumed the form of a servant in his own person, and thus endeavors to separate him from his inseparable Godhead so that he thereby introduces a quaternity into the Holy Trinity, etc.

(15) If anyone shall not confess the holy ever-virgin Mary, truly and properly the Mother of God, to be higher than every creature whether visible or invisible and does not with sincere faith seek her intercessions as of one having confidence in her access to our God, since she bore him, etc.

(16) If anyone shall endeavor to represent the forms of the Saints in lifeless pictures with material colors which are of no value (for this notion is vain and introduced by the devil) and does not rather represent their virtues as living images in himself, etc.

(17) If anyone denies the profit of the invocation of Saints, etc.

(18) If anyone denies the resurrection of the dead and the judgment and the condign [appropriate] retribution to everyone, endless torment and endless bliss, etc.

(19) If anyone does not accept this our Holy and Ecumenical Seventh Synod, let him be anathema from the Father and the Son and the Holy Ghost and from the seven holy Ecumenical Synods!

[At this point the making or teaching of any other faith is prohibited, and the penalties for disobedience are enumerated.]

The divine Kings Constantine and Leo said: Let the holy and ecumenical synod say, if with the consent of all the most holy bishops the definition just read has been set forth.

The holy synod cried out: Thus we all believe, we all are of the same mind. We have all with one voice and voluntarily subscribed. This is the faith of the Apostles. Many years to the Emperors! They are the light of orthodoxy! Many years to the orthodox Emperors! God preserve your Empire! You have now more firmly proclaimed the inseparability of the two natures of Christ! You have banished all idolatry! You have destroyed the heresies of Germanus [of Constantinople], George and Mansur.[1] Anathema to Germanus, the double-minded, and worshiper of wood! Anathema to George, his associate, to the falsifier of the doctrine of the Fathers! Anathema to Mansur, who has an evil name and Saracen opinions![2] To the betrayer of Christ and the enemy of the Empire, to the teacher of impiety, the perverter of Scripture, Mansur, anathema! The Trinity has deposed these three!

---

1 Germanus was the Patriarch of Constantinople 715–732. He opposed iconoclasm and was sent into exile. Mansur ("Victorious") was the Arabic surname of John of Damascus, whose iconodule arguments may be read above on p. 77.

2 Saracen = Arab.

2.5 Vilifying the iconoclasts: *The Chronicle of Theophanes Confessor* (before 818). Original in Greek.

THE BITTER FEELINGS OF THE iconophiles were given free expression in the *Chronicle* of Theophanes Confessor (*c*.760–818), which was in fact written by two men, Theophanes and a high church official named George Synkellus (d. after 810). Both lived during the turbulent period in which iconoclasm was first the norm, then condemned (in 787), and later revived (815–843). It is very likely that the *Chronicle* was written in secret, finished before Theophanes's death in 818, and "published" only after 843. The passage here represents the iconophile take on the Synod of 754.

[Source: *The Chronicle of Theophanes Confessor: Byzantine and Near Eastern History, AD 284-813*, trans. Cyril Mango and Roger Scott (Oxford: Clarendon Press, 1997), pp. 591-92.]

In this year [754] Anastasius, who had held in unholy fashion the episcopal throne of Constantinople, died a spiritual as well as a bodily death of a dreadful disease of the guts after vomiting dung through his mouth, a just punishment for his daring deeds against God and his teacher. In the same year the impious Constantine [V (r.741-775)] convened in the palace of Hiereia an illegal assembly of 338 bishops against the holy and venerable icons under the leadership of Theodosius of Ephesus, son of Apsimarus, and of Pastillas of Perge. These men by themselves decreed whatever came into their heads, though none of the universal sees was represented, namely those of Rome, Alexandria, Antioch, and Jerusalem. Starting on February 10th, they went on until August 8th of the same 7th indiction.[1] On the latter day the enemies of the Theotokos[2] having come to Blachernai [Palace], Constantine ascended the ambo [pulpit] holding the monk Constantine, former bishop of Syllaion, and, after reciting a prayer, said in a loud voice, "Long live Constantine, the ecumenical patriarch!" On the 27th of the same month the emperor went up to the Forum together with the unholy bishop Constantine and the other bishops and they proclaimed their misguided heresy in front of all the people after anathematizing the most holy Germanus, George of Cyprus, and John Damascene [i.e., John of Damascus] of the Golden Stream, son of Mansur, holy men and venerable teachers.

---

1   That is, 754.
2   Theotokos means Mother of God in Greek.

2.6 Pre-Islamic Arabic poetry: Al-A`sha, *Bid Hurayra Farewell* (before 625). Original in Arabic.

AL-A`SHA (WHICH MEANS THE "NEAR-BLIND") was a member of the Bakr tribe—thus related to the caliph Abu-Bakr (r.634-634)—and well known for his satires and songs of wine and women. Like other pre-Islamic poetry, his was written down between the 7th and 11th centuries, and the written version probably, like a piece of jazz, reflects both the original idea and the riffs of subsequent poetry reciters. *Bid Hurayra Farewell* is a parody of a traditional Arabic ode. Like the others, it may be divided into three parts: the remembrance of the beloved, the journey, and the poet's boast. But here the remembrance of the beloved's beauty is overdrawn—"full at the bodice, at the waist sash nil"—and her delicacy over-emphasized—"she braces herself or she'd be thrown back flat." In place of the "journey" is a lover's lament that borders on the ridiculous—"I fell for her by chance. She fell for another who fell for another ..."—and then a depiction of a storm mingled with thoughts about inebriation. "Foretell!" the poet says, and instead of recounting the places that he visits in his "journey," he prophesies where the rain will fall. Then the poet begins the journey, sometimes "barefoot," at other times "wearing boots," combining the normally separate adventures of the shoeless brigand and the well-shod warrior, the accounts of both veiled in a drunken stupor. Then suddenly the poet is serious: "How many a land, like the flat back of a shield ... /Have I cut through." Finally comes the boast "To Yazid of the Bani Shayban," and the poet recalls battles and challenges his enemies to new ones.

[Source: *Desert Tracings: Six Classic Arabian Odes by `Alquama, Shanfara, Labid, `Antara, Al-A`sha, and Dhu al-Rumma*, trans. Michael A. Sells (Middletown, CT: Wesleyan University Press, 1989), pp. 60-66.]

[Remembrance of the beloved]

Bid Hurayra farewell.
The riders are departing.
Can you, man that you are,
bear bidding farewell?
　　Brow aglow, hair flowing,
　a gleam from the side teeth as she smiles,
　　she walks gently as a gazelle,
　tender-hoofed in wet soil,
As if her walk
from the tent of a neighbor
were the gliding of a cloud
neither slow nor hurried.
　　You hear her anklets whisper
　as she turns away
　　like cassia rustling
　suppliant in the breeze.

She's not one of those
whose neighbors hate to see her face.
You won't find her,
ear to their secrets, listening.
　　She braces herself
　or she'd be thrown back flat,
　　when rising to visit a neighbor,
　by languor.
She entertains her companion awhile,
then slackens,
lower back and buttocks
quivering,
　　Full at the bodice,
　at the waist sash nil,
　　a belle, seeming as she comes near
　to divide in two.
How sweet a bedmate
on a cloudy afternoon,

not for some unbathed rude
to lay and take some pleasure,
    Wide-hipped, delicate,
  elbows soft, walk tender,
    as if a thorn were caught
  in the arch of her sandal.
As she rises
a fragrance of musk trails,
her sleeve-cuffs with the scent
of rose jasmine brimming over.
    No meadow of the meadows
  of the roughland plateau,
    luxuriant and green, blessed
  by dark-trailing big-dropped clouds,
Where the sun is teased
by a blossom in full flower,
drenched in color,
mantled deep in rushes and greens,
    Is ever more fragrant,
  more redolent
    than she, or more beautiful
  when evening shadows fall.

—————

[The journey]

Hurayra said
when I came to pay her call
woe to you, woe,
you woesome male!
    I fell for her by chance.
  She fell for another
    who fell for another
  other than her,
For him a girl was falling
he didn't desire,
while a cousin on her father's side
was weakening for her, and dying.
    Then for me there fell another,
  not to my liking,
    love in love on love,
  beside itself, entangled, mad,
Each of us afflicted,
raving to this friend or that,
approaching, backing off,
ensnared, ensnaring.
    Hurayra shut us off,

not speaking,
    ignorance on the part of Umm Khulayd
  of the bond she tied.
Didn't she see a man,
night-blind, wounded
by intimations of death shades
and by time, the demented, the undoing?

—————

    Have you seen it blocking the horizon?
  I passed the night in watch,
    lightning kindled along its edges,
  flickering,
With a dark trail behind it,
its middle full and moving,
girded and held together
by buckets of rain.
    No play diverts me
  from foretelling the rain's direction,
    no pleasure from a cup of wine,
  no languor.
I told them at Durna,
the drinkers, already sodden:
Foretell! But how
can a wine-faced drinker heed?
    Lightning lit up the slopes
  where the rain would fall,
    in Khabiyya, a blackening cloud
  against the horizon.
They said let it pour
on Leopard Streak and Camel Belly,
on Horse Trappings, Tired Man,
and Legland,
    Flowing over the Edgelands,
  then Boar with its tracts
    of rock and sand,
  until the hills and mountains burst,
Until the grouse meadows
and the tree-hedged
soft-curved dunes
take all they can bear,
    A gushing, quenching draught
  for abodes long since desolate,
    off the track
  shunned by horse and camel mare.

—————

You may well find me barefoot,
not a scrap of shoe leather to my name.
Wearing boots or shoeless,
that's the way I am.
    I might well steal upon
  some master of his house
    and catch him unawares. Wary once,
  now he finds no haven.
I might one day lead the reins
of youthful passion,
and it might follow,
a hot-blooded love-talker at my side.
    Many's the time I have set out at dawn
  to the wine shop,
    followed by a bob-skewing, quick-witted,
  path-wise fast-hander,
In a crowd of men like Indian swords
who know that everyone,
barefoot or bootshod,
will perish.
    I rivaled them down for the snip of basil,
  head on elbow, reclining,
    and for a tangy wine
  from a porous, moistened jug of clay.
They don't come to
while there is any of it left,
except to call for more
after a third round or after a second,
    The glass-bearer
  busying here and there,
    shirt bottom tucked up,
  alert, agile.
How many a song—you'd think it sung
to a Persian harp—
when a singing girl in a nightslip
sings it,
    How many a gowned lady,
  trailing silk,
    how many a girl
  with a leather wine flask at her side,
Have I spent my time enjoying,
enduring trial
by amorous talk
and length of pleasure.
    How many a land
  like the flat back of a shield,
    wild, where jinn are overheard

in the corners, rustling,
That no one dares enter,
riding upon the burning heat,
except one who, in what he undertakes,
is unhurried,
    Have I cut through
  on a well-worn, rock-ribbed,
    easy-gaited mare, elbows well apart
  when you show her.
————————

[The boast]

To Yazid of the Bani Shayban
bear this word:
Abu Thubayt,
stop gnawing at your heart!
    Stop carving at the grain
  of our ancient name
    that nothing can harm
  as long as burdened camels groan,
Like a mountain goat
butting against a rock
to split it, the rock unharmed,
the horns weakening.
    I know you well
  when the battle signal calls us,
    when war blazes
  with arms, night raids, and plunder.
You inflame Mas'ud's kin
and his brothers against us,
sowing destruction when we meet,
then drawing away.
    Don't sit alone
  when you've stoked the fire!
    You'll implore refuge one day
  from its burning, praying.
There were among the people of Kahf,
when they fought, and the Jashiriyya,
those who were quick,
those who would take their time.
    You claimed we wouldn't fight you.
  We are—tribe of ours!—
    for the likes of you,
  the killers,
Until the chief of the tribe
lies fallen, head on arm,

protected by child-bereft women's
flailing hands,
    Struck down by an Indian sword
    well aimed toward its target,
      or a supple, well-tempered spear
    from Khatt.
We might well spear the chieftain
in the hollow of his thigh,
and a champion might perish
on our spear tips, unavenged.
    End it!
    Nothing curbs the overbearing
      like a gaping wound
    unstaunched by oil and gauze.
By the life of the one
to whom stamping camels
and long-horned cattle of every kind

are led in offering,
    Kill a chief
who never stood in your way
    and we'll kill one of yours
    like him, one to our choosing.
Try us. You won't find us
after the battle
from the tribe's blood-right
turning away.
    Under the noon sun,
    the day of the Bowbend,
      around Futayma, we were the riders,
    not shirking, not giving way.
They called for a mounted attack.
We said we can do that.
They prepared to fight on foot.
We're a tribe that fights unmounted.

2.7 The sacred text: *Qur'an Suras* 1, 53:1-18, 81, 87, 96, 98 (*c.*610-622). Original in Arabic.

MUHAMMAD (*c.*570-632), BORN IN MECCA, orphaned, raised by an uncle, married to Khadija, heard (*c.*610) what he understood to be revelations from God. He recited them (Qur'an means "recitation"), scribes wrote them down, and they became the foundation of a new religion, Islam. The whole process of recording and arranging the Qur'an did not end until after Muhammad's death. The resulting book begins with a prayer (the *fatiha*, or "Opening"), followed by chapters (suras) that gradually diminish in length. While different from the odes of the pre-Islamic period (see *Bid Hurayra Farewell*, above, p. 86), the verses of the Qur'an are poetry, and they often take up the traditional themes: remembrance of the beloved (who is now God), the journey (turned into a spiritual quest), and the boast (a celebration of God's generosity and justice). The earliest suras generally are found toward the end of the book. Muhammad's first vision is described in Sura 53, "The Star"; his first auditory revelation was probably "Recite in the name of your lord who created ...," which is found in Sura 96. Other suras come from the period after Muhammad made the *hijra*, or emigration, to Medina (622; the year 1 in the Islamic calendar). Most of those presented here are from Muhammad's earliest Meccan period. Note that there is relatively little punctuation (mirroring the Arabic); this is the translator's way of suggesting the open and multiple meanings of the verses.

[Source: *Approaching the Qur'an: The Early Revelations*, trans. Michael Sells (Ashland, OR: White Cloud Press, 1999), pp. 42, 44, 48, 50, 72, 96, 104, 106.]

1: THE OPENING

In the name of God
    the Compassionate the Caring
Praise be to God

lord sustainer of the worlds
the Compassionate the Caring
master of the day of reckoning
To you we turn to worship
    and to you we turn in time of need

5

Guide us along the road straight
the road of those to whom you are giving
   not those with anger upon them
   not those who have lost the way

53: 1–18 THE STAR

In the Name of God the Compassionate the Caring
  By the star as it falls
  Your companion[1] has not lost his way nor is he
    deluded
  He does not speak out of desire
  This is a revelation
5 taught him by one of great power
  and strength that stretched out over
  while on the highest horizon—
  then drew near and came down
  two bows' lengths or nearer
10 He revealed to his servant what he revealed
  The heart did not lie in what it saw
  Will you then dispute with him his vision?

  He saw it descending another time
  at the lote tree of the furthest limit
15 There was the garden of sanctuary
  when something came down over the
    lote tree, enfolding
  His gaze did not turn aside nor go too far
  He had seen the signs of his lord, great signs

81: THE OVERTURNING

In the Name of God the Compassionate the Caring
  When the sun is overturned
  When the stars fall away
  When the mountains are moved
  When the ten-month pregnant camels
    are abandoned
5 When the beasts of the wild are herded together
  When the seas are boiled over
  When the souls are coupled
  When the girl-child buried alive

is asked what she did to deserve murder
When the pages are folded out   10
When the sky is flayed open
When Jahim[2] is set ablaze
When the garden is brought near
Then a soul will know what it has prepared
I swear by the stars that slide,   15
stars streaming, stars that sweep along the sky
By the night as it slips away
By the morning when the fragrant air breathes
This is the word of a messenger ennobled,
empowered, ordained before the lord of the throne, 20
holding sway there, keeping trust
Your friend[3] has not gone mad
He saw him on the horizon clear
He does not hoard for himself the unseen
This is not the word of a satan   25
    struck with stones
Where are you going?
This is a reminder to all beings
For those who wish to walk straight
Your only will is the will of God
    lord of all beings

87: THE MOST HIGH

In the Name of God the Compassionate the Caring
  Holy be the name of your lord most high
  Who created then gave form
  Who determined then gave guidance
  Who made the meadow pasture grow
  then turned it to a darkened flood-swept remnant 5

We will make you recite. You will not forget
  except what the will of God allows
He knows what is declared
  and what lies hidden
He will ease you to the life of ease
So remind them if reminder will succeed[4]
Those who know awe will be brought to remember 10
He who is hard in wrong will turn away
He will be put to the fire

---

1 "Your companion" is ordinarily interpreted as referring to Muhammad.
2 A term for the Day of Reckoning.
3 "Your friend" refers to Muhammad.
4 Muhammad is to "remind" people about God and justice. There is no notion of "original sin" in Islam, but people "forget" the purpose of human life and the Day of Reckoning.

neither dying in it nor living
He who makes himself pure will flourish
15 who remembers the name of his lord and
     performs the prayer

But no. They prefer the lower life
Better is the life ultimate, the life that endures
As is set down in the scrolls of the ancients
the scrolls of Ibrahim and Musa[1]

96: THE EMBRYO

In the Name of God the Compassionate the Caring
Recite in the name of your lord who created—
From an embryo created the human
Recite your lord is all-giving
who taught by the pen
5 Taught the human what he did not know before

The human being is a tyrant
He thinks his possessions make him secure
To your lord is the return of every thing

Did you see the one who stopped a servant
10 from performing his prayer?
Did you see if he was rightly guided
or commanded mindfulness?
Did you see him call lie and turn away?
Did he not know God could see?

15 But no. If he does not change
     we will seize him by the forelock
the lying, wrongful forelock
Let him call out his gang
We will call out the Zabaniya[2]
Do not follow him
     Touch your head to the earth in prayer
     Come near

98: THE TESTAMENT[3]

In the Name of God the Compassionate the Caring

Those who denied the faith—
from the peoples of the book
or the idolators—
could not stop calling it a lie   5
until they received the testament

A messenger of God
reciting pages that are pure

Of scriptures that are sure

Those who were given the book   10
were not divided one against the other
until they received the testament

And all they were commanded
was to worship God sincerely
affirm oneness, perform the prayer   15
and give a share of what they have
That is the religion of the sure

Those who deny the faith—
from the peoples of the book
or the idolators—   20
are in Jahannam's fire,[4]
eternal there
They are the worst of creation

Those who keep the faith
and perform the prayer   25
they are the best of creation

As recompense for them with their lord—
gardens of Eden
waters flowing underground
eternal there forever   30
God be pleased in them
and they in God

That is for those who hold their lord in awe

---

1 Ibrahim is Abraham in the Bible; Musa is Moses.
2 The Zabaniya are probably a species of *jinn*, half-spirit creatures.
3 This sura is from a later period in Muhammad's career, after he experienced the rejection of not only polytheists but also the "peoples of the book"—Christians and Jews—he had expected to join him.
4 The fire of eternal punishment.

2.8 Umayyad diplomacy: *The Treaty of Tudmir* (713). Original in Arabic.

ALTHOUGH THE ISLAMIC conquests seemed to take place with lightning speed, they were at times piecemeal and even non-violent. Five years after Islamic forces entered Spain in 711, almost all of the peninsula was under the rule of the caliph. Yet documents like the Treaty of Tudmir (713) suggest that in some cases the take-over was peaceful, accomplished via agreements with local rulers. In this case 'Abd al-'Aziz, son of Musa (the governor of much of North Africa and a leader in the conquest of Spain), came to an agreement with Theodemir, the local Visigothic commander of the region of Murcia (in the southeast corner of Spain). The Murcians were not to aid any enemies of the Muslims, and they had to pay a modest tax in money and kind. In return, they were offered local autonomy and permission to practice their Christian religion. The Arabic for Theodemir was Tudmir, which for years afterwards was the Arabic name for the region of Murcia.

[Source: *Medieval Iberia: Readings from Christian, Muslim, and Jewish Sources*, ed. Olivia Remie Constable (Philadelphia: University of Pennsylvania Press, 1997), pp. 37-38.]

In the name of God, the merciful and the compassionate.

This is a document [granted] by 'Abd al-'Aziz ibn Musa ibn Nusair to Tudmir, son of Ghabdush, establishing a treaty of peace and the promise and protection of God and his Prophet (may God bless him and grant him peace). We ['Abd al-'Aziz] will not set special conditions for him or for any among his men, nor harass him, nor remove him from power. His followers will not be killed or taken prisoner, nor will they be separated from their women and children. They will not be coerced in matters of religion, their churches will not be burned, nor will sacred objects be taken from the realm, [so long as] he [Tudmir] remains sincere and fulfills the [following] conditions that we have set for him. He has reached a settlement concerning seven towns: Orihuela, Valentilla, Alicante, Mula, Bigastro, Ello, and Lorca. He will not give shelter to fugitives, nor to our enemies, nor encourage any protected person to fear us, nor conceal news of our enemies. He and [each of] his men shall [also] pay one dinar every year, together with four measures of wheat, four measures of barley, four liquid measures of concentrated fruit juice, four liquid measures of vinegar, four of honey, and four of olive oil. Slaves must each pay half of this amount.

[Names of four witnesses follow, and the document is dated from the Muslim month of Rajab, in the year 94 of the Hijra (April 713).]

2.9 Taxation: *A Tax Demand in Egypt* (710). Original in Arabic and Greek.

THE UMAYYADS GENERALLY ADOPTED the administrative apparatus and offices of the regions that they conquered, and often they utilized the indigenous elite to carry out administrative duties. In Egypt, from which we have many papyri attesting to the fiscal system, the Arab governor of Egypt in the early eighth century was Qurra ibn Sharik. In the letter below, he is writing to Basil, *pagarch*—or provincial governor—of Aphrodite, located in the Thebaid just south of Asyut in Upper (that is, southern) Egypt. Basil was neither Arab nor Muslim but rather a local magnate who cooperated with his Islamic overlords. Qurra's letter shows that Basil was in charge of collecting the *jizya*, a money tax imposed on villages. Qurra intended to use the revenue to pay his army.

[Source: *Islam from the Prophet Muhammad to the Capture of Constantinople*, ed. and trans. Bernard Lewis, Vol. 2: *Religion and Society* (New York: Oxford University Press, 1987), p. 130 (slightly modified).]

In the name of God, the Merciful and the Compassionate.

From Qurra ibn Sharik to Basil, *pagarch* of Aphrodite. I praise God, other than Whom there is no God.

As follows: You know how much time has passed, and you still delay the *jizya*, and now the time has come for the pay of the troops and the families and for the departure of the armies on campaign, please God. When this my letter reaches you, take whatever *jizya* is due from your lands, and send whatever you collect, batch by batch. Let me not learn that you have delayed what you have gathered, and let it not be held back, for the people of your land have already completed their sowing. God is their helper in what is due from them to the Commander of the Faithful. Therefore, let there be no deficiency in your affair and no delay or holding back of what you have. Had the money been in my possession, I would have given the troops their pay, please God. Write and inform me what has accumulated with you, of what you have collected of the *jizya*, and how you have done this. Peace be upon those who follow the right guidance.[1]

Written by Jarir in the month of Rabic I of the year 91 [January–February 710].

---

1 A form of greeting used when addressing non-Muslims.

2.10 Civil servants: `Abd al-Hamid, *Letter to the Secretaries* (before 750). Original in Arabic.

CONSIDERED THE FOREMOST LETTER WRITER of the Umayyad period, `Abd al-Hamid (d.*c.*750) produced numerous epistles on topics ranging from advice to rulers, codes of conduct, and hunting, to friendship. He worked in the Umayyad chancery, or writing office, and became the principal secretary of Caliph Marwan II (r.744-750). Much of his work has been lost, but some of it was incorporated into the works of later writers. Such is the case with his *Letter to the Secretaries*, which was quoted—and thus preserved—by the historian and political thinker Ibn Khaldun (1332-1406; see below, p. 552, for one of his own treatises). Note that al-Hamid thought secretaries should be masters not only of writing but of poetry, mathematics, and virtue. How might you compare the ideals of the Umayyad secretary with those of the Western monk (in *The Benedictine Rule*, p. 28 above) and the Byzantine saint (as in the *Life of St. Theodore of Sykeon*, p. 74 above)?

[Source: Ibn Khaldun, *The Muqaddimah: An Introduction to History*, trans. Franz Rosenthal, 3 vols. (New York: Pantheon Books, 1958), 2:29-35.]

And now: May God guard you who practice the craft of secretaryship, and may He keep you and give you success and guidance. There are prophets and messengers and highly honored kings. After them come different kinds of men, all of them made by God. They are of different kinds, even if they are all alike in fact. God occupied them with different kinds of crafts and various sorts of businesses so that they might be able to make a living and earn their sustenance. He gave to you, assembled secretaries, the great opportunity to be men of education and gentlemen, to have knowledge and [good] judgment. You bring out whatever is good in the caliphate and straighten out its affairs. Through your advice, God improves the government for the benefit of human beings and makes their countries civilized. The ruler cannot dispense with you. You alone make him a competent ruler. Your position with regard to rulers is that [you are] the ears through which they hear, the eyes through which they see, the tongues through which they speak, and the hands through which they touch. May God give you, therefore, enjoyment of the excellent craft with which He has distinguished you, and may He not deprive you of the great favors that He has shown unto you.

No craftsman needs more than you to combine all praiseworthy good traits and all memorable and highly regarded excellent qualities, O secretaries, if you aspire to fit the description given of you in this letter. The secretary needs on his own account—and

his master, who trusts him with his important affairs, expects him—to be mild where mildness is needed, to be understanding where judgment is needed, to be enterprising where enterprise is needed, to be hesitant where hesitation is needed. He must prefer modesty, justice, and fairness. He must keep secrets. He must be faithful in difficult circumstances. He must know [beforehand] about the calamities that may come. He must be able to put things in their proper places and misfortunes into their proper categories. He must have studied every branch of learning and know it well, and if he does not know it well, he must at least have acquired an adequate amount of it. By virtue of his natural intelligence, good education, and outstanding experience, he must know what is going to happen to him before it happens, and he must know the result of his actions before action starts. He must make the proper preparations for everything, and he must set up everything in its proper, customary form.

Therefore, assembled secretaries, vie with each other to acquire the different kinds of education and to gain an understanding of religious matters. Start with knowledge of the Book of God and religious duties. Then, study the Arabic language, as that will give you a cultivated form of speech. Then, learn to write well, as that will be an ornament to your letters. Transmit poetry and acquaint yourselves with the rare expressions and ideas that poems contain. Acquaint yourselves also with both Arab and non-Arab political events and with the tales of [both groups] and the biographies describing them, as that will be helpful to you in your endeavors. Do not neglect to study accounting, for it is the mainstay of the land tax register. Detest prejudices with all your heart, lofty ones as well as low ones, and all idle and contemptible things, for they bring humility and are the ruin of secretaryship. Do not let your craft be a low one. Guard against backbiting and calumny and the actions of stupid people. Beware of haughtiness, foolishness, and pride, for they mean acquiring hostility without [even the excuse of] hatred. Love each other in God in your craft. Advise your colleagues to practice it in a way befitting your virtuous, fair, and gifted predecessors.

If times go hard for one of you, be kind to him and console him, until everything be well with him again. Should old age make one of you unable to get around and pursue his livelihood and meet his friends, visit him and honor him and consult him, and profit from his outstanding experience and mature knowledge. Every one of you should be more concerned for his assistants, who may be useful when needed, than for his own children or brothers. Should some praise come [to one of you] in the course of his work, he should ascribe the merit to his colleague; any blame he should bear all by himself. He should beware of mistakes and slips and of being annoyed when conditions change. For you, assembled secretaries, are more prompt to be blamed than Qur'an readers, and blame is more detrimental to you than to them. You know that every one of you has a master, one who gives from his own as much as can be expected, and [every one of you] has the obligation to repay him, since he deserves it, with fidelity, gratefulness, tolerance, patience, good counsel, discretion, and active interest in his affairs, and to show [his good intentions] by his actions whenever his master needs him and his resources. Be conscious of [your obligations]—God give you success—in good and bad circumstances, in privation as in munificence and kindness, in happiness as in misfortune. Any member of this noble craft who has all these qualities has good qualities indeed.

If any one of you be appointed to an office, or if some matter that concerns God's children be turned over to one of you, he should think of God and choose obedience to Him. He should be kind to the weak and fair to those who have been wronged. All crea-

tures are God's children. He loves most those who are kindest to His children. Furthermore, he should judge with justice, he should honor the noble [descendants of Muhammad], augment the booty [gained in wars against infidels], and bring civilization to the country. He should be friendly to the subjects, and refrain from harming them. He should be humble and mild in his office. He should be kind in handling the land tax registers and in calling in outstanding claims.

You should explore the character of him with whom you associate. When his good and bad sides are known, you will be able to help him to do the good things that agree with him and be able to contrive to keep him from the bad things he desires. You must be able to do that in the subtlest and best manner. You know that a person who is in charge of an animal and understands his job endeavors to know the character of the animal. If it is inclined to gallop, he does not goad it when he is riding it. If it is inclined to kick, he takes precautions with its forelegs. If he fears that it will shy, he takes precautions with its head. If it is restive, he gently subdues its desire to go where it wants to go. If it still continues, he pulls it slightly to the side, then has its halter loosened. This description of how to take care of an animal contains good points for those who want to lead human beings and deal with them, serve them, and have intimate contact with them. The secretary, with his excellent education, his noble craft, his subtlety, his frequent dealings with people who confer with him and discuss things with him and learn from him or fear his severity, needs to be kind to his associates, to flatter them, and to supply their wants, even more than the person in charge of an animal which cannot answer, does not know what is right, does not understand what is said to it, and goes only where its master who rides upon it makes it go. Be kind—God show mercy unto you—when you look after things. Use as much reflection and thought as possible. God permitting, you will thus escape harshness, annoyance, and rudeness on the part of your associates. They will be in agreement with you, and you will have their friendship and protection, if God wills.

None of you should have too sumptuous an office or go beyond the proper limits in his dress, his mount, his food, his drink, his house, his servants, or in the other things pertaining to his station, for, despite the nobility of the craft by which God has distinguished you, you are servants who are not permitted to fall short in their service. You are caretakers whom one does not permit to be wasteful or spendthrift. Try to preserve your modesty by planned moderation in all the things I have mentioned and told you. Beware of the wastefulness of prodigality and the bad results of luxury. They engender poverty and bring about humiliation. People who [are prodigal and live in luxury] are put to shame, especially if they be secretaries and men of education.

Things repeat themselves. One thing contains the clue to another. Let yourselves be guided in your future undertakings by your previous experience. Then, choose the method of doing things that is most definite, most accurate, and that promises the best result. You should know that there is something that defeats accomplishment, namely, talking about things. The person who does it is prevented from using his knowledge and his ability to think. Therefore, every one of you, while he is in his office, should endeavor to talk no more than is sufficient; he should be concise in the matters he brings up and in the answers he gives; and he should give thought to all the arguments he advances. His work will profit from that. It will prevent too much preoccupation with other things. He should implore God to grant him success and to support him with His guidance, for he must fear making mistakes that might hurt his body and [cast doubt upon] his intelligence and education. When any one of you says or thinks that the high quality and efficiency of his work is obviously the result of his own cleverness and knowledge of how to do things, he provokes God. God will let him depend upon himself alone, and then he will find that he is not adequate to his task. This is no secret to those who reflect.

None of you should say that he has a better understanding of affairs or knows better how to handle difficult matters than other members of his craft and than those who serve together with him. Of two persons, discerning people consider him the more intelligent who throws off conceit and thinks his colleagues more intelligent and more skillful than he. But at any rate, both parties should acknowledge the excellence of God's favors. No one should let himself be deceived by his own opinions and consider himself free from mistakes. Nor should he strive to outdo his friends, equals, colleagues, or his family. Everybody must give praise to God, in humility in the face of His greatness, in meekness in the face of His might, and in fulfillment of the command to speak of God's favors.

In this letter of mine, let me refer to the old proverb: "He who accepts good advice is successful." This is the essence of this letter and the best that is said in it, after the references to God it contains. Therefore, I have placed it at the end, and I close the letter with it. May God take care of us and of you, assembled students and secretaries, in the same way He takes care of those whom, as He knows in His prescience, He will make happy and guide aright. He can do it. It is in His hand.

Farewell, and God's mercy and blessings upon you.

2.11 Creating a Roman Catholic identity for England: Bede, *The Ecclesiastical History of the English People* (731). Original in Latin.

A CHILD OF THE CLOISTER—he entered the monastery of Wearmouth-Jarrow in the north of England at the age of seven—Bede (*c*.672-753) was among the best-educated men of his day in the Roman, papal tradition and the expertise in Latin that went with it. Because his monastery was extraordinarily well stocked with books—brought back from the Continent (mainly Rome) by Wearmouth and Jarrow's founder, Benedict Biscop—Bede was able to consult a wide range of sources for his numerous writings. These included biblical commentaries, the lives of saints, liturgical works, sermons, scientific texts (his *Computation of Time* was particularly important for calculating the date of Easter and other movable feasts), and histories, including a *History of the Abbots of Wearmouth and Jarrow* and *The Ecclesiastical History*. Although Christianity came to England in a variety of ways, Bede emphasized the Roman contribution. How might you compare the role of Constantine in Eusebius's account of the Christianization of Rome in his *History of the Church* (above, p. 4) with Gregory the Great's role in Bede's story of the Christianization of the English people? How did Bede's writings enhance the reputation of Gregory the Great?

[Source: Bede, *The Ecclesiastical History of the English People*, ed. Judith McClure and Roger Collins (Oxford: Oxford University Press, 1994), pp. 37-41, 55-59, 65-71, 152-59, 370-75, 397 (slightly modified).]

Book 1

CHAPTER 23

In the year of our Lord 582 Maurice,[1] the fifty-fourth from Augustus, became emperor; he ruled for twenty-one years. In the tenth year of his reign, Gregory,[2] a man eminent in learning and in affairs, was elected pontiff of the apostolic see of Rome; he ruled for thirteen years, six months, and ten days. In the fourteenth year[3] of this emperor and about 150 years after the coming of the Angles to Britain, Gregory, prompted by divine inspiration, sent a servant of God named Augustine[4] and several more God-fearing monks with him to preach the word of God to the English race. In obedience to the pope's commands, they undertook this task and had already gone a little way on their journey when they were paralyzed with terror. They began to contemplate returning home rather than going to a barbarous, fierce, and unbelieving nation whose language they did not even understand. They all agreed that this was the safer course; so forthwith they sent home Augustine whom Gregory had intended to have consecrated as their bishop if they were received by the English. Augustine was to beg St. Gregory humbly for permission to give up so dangerous, wearisome, and uncertain a journey. Gregory, however, sent them an encouraging letter in which he persuaded them to persevere with the task of preaching the Word and trust in the help of God. The letter was in these terms:

---

1 Emperor Maurice Tiberius (r.582–602).
2 Pope Gregory the Great (r.590–604).
3 August 595 to August 596.
4 Augustine—who should not be mixed up with St. Augustine (d.430), the bishop of Hippo—had been prior (just below the abbot in administrative status) of the monastery that Gregory founded on his own family property on the Caelian Hill in Rome.

Gregory, servant of the servants of God, to the servants of our Lord.

My dearly beloved sons, it would have been better not to have undertaken a noble task than to turn back deliberately from what you have begun: so it is right that you should carry out with all diligence this good work which you have begun with the help of the Lord. Therefore do not let the toilsome journey nor the tongues of evil speakers deter you. But carry out the task you have begun under the guidance of God with all constancy and fervor. Be sure that, however great your task may be, the glory of your eternal reward will be still greater. When Augustine your prior returns, now, by our appointment, your abbot, humbly obey him in all things, knowing that whatever you do under his direction will be in all respects profitable to your souls. May Almighty God protect you by His grace and grant that I may see the fruit of your labors in our heavenly home. Though I cannot labor with you, yet because I should have been glad indeed to do so, I hope to share in the joy of your reward. May God keep you safe, my dearly loved sons.

Given on July 23, in the fourteenth year of the reign of our most religious emperor Maurice Tiberius, and the thirteenth year after his consulship, and the fourteenth indiction.[1] [July 23, 596]

CHAPTER 24

The venerable pontiff at the same time also sent a letter to Etherius of Arles,[2] asking him to receive Augustine kindly on his return to Britain. This is the text:

To his most reverend and holy brother and fellow bishop Etherius, Gregory, servant of the servants of God.

Although religious men stand in need of no recommendation with those bishops who have that love which is pleasing to God, yet because a suitable occasion for writing presents itself, we think fit to send this letter to you our brother, informing you that we have directed thither the bearer of this document, Augustine, the servant of God, of whose zeal we are assured, together with other servants of God devoted to winning souls with the Lord's help. It is essential that your holiness should assist him with episcopal zeal and hasten to provide him with what he needs. And in order that you may be the more prompt with your help, we have specially enjoined him to tell you of his mission. We are sure that when you know this you will be prepared with all zeal to afford him your help for the Lord's sake as the occasion requires. We also commend to your charity the priest Candidus,[3] a son of both of us, whom we have sent to take charge of a small patrimony of our church. God keep you safe, most reverend brother.

Given on July 23, in the fourteenth year of the reign of our most religious emperor, Maurice Tiberius, and the thirteenth year after his consulship and the fourteenth indiction.
[July 23, 596]

CHAPTER 25

So Augustine, strengthened by the encouragement of St. Gregory, in company with the servants of Christ, returned to the work of preaching the word, and came to Britain. At that time Ethelbert, king of Kent [d.616], was a very powerful monarch. The lands over which he ruled stretched as far as the great river Humber, which divides the northern from the southern Angles. Over against the eastern districts of Kent there is a large island called Thanet which,

---

1 "Indiction" was a regular cycle of fifteen years, used initially for tax-assessment purposes, but which remained a conventional way of dating documents in the late Roman empire.

2 Etherius was actually bishop of Lyon (r.586–562), not of Arles. Bede adopts the term "archbishop" used in the Anglo-Saxon Church, but the Frankish equivalents were called metropolitan bishops. Similar letters were sent to the bishops of Marseille, Arles, and Tours to secure assistance and safe passage for the mission.

3 Candidus was being sent as Rector of the papal Patrimony, to take charge of the running of the estates owned by the Roman Church in southern Gaul.

in English reckoning, is 600 hides[1] in extent. It is divided from the mainland by the river Wantsum, which is about three furlongs wide,[2] can be crossed in two places only, and joins the sea at either end. Here Augustine, the servant of the Lord, landed with his companions, who are said to have been nearly forty in number. They had acquired interpreters from the Frankish race according to the command of Pope St. Gregory. Augustine sent to Ethelbert to say that he had come from Rome bearing the best of news, namely the sure and certain promise of eternal joys in heaven and an endless kingdom with the living and true God to those who received it. On hearing this the king ordered them to remain on the island where they had landed and be provided with all things necessary until he had decided what to do about them. Some knowledge about the Christian religion had already reached him because he had a Christian wife of the Frankish royal family whose name was Bertha.[3] He had received her from her parents on condition that she should be allowed to practice her faith and religion unhindered, with a bishop named Liudhard whom they had provided for her to support her faith.

Some days afterwards the king came to the island and, sitting in the open air, commanded Augustine and his comrades to come there to talk with him. He took care that they should not meet in any building, for he held the traditional superstition that, if they practiced any magic art, they might deceive him and get the better of him as soon as he entered. But they came endowed with divine not devilish power and bearing as their standard a silver cross and the image of our Lord and Savior painted on a panel.[4] They chanted litanies and uttered prayers to the Lord for their own eternal salvation and the salvation of those for whom and to whom they had come. At the king's command they sat down and preached the word of life to himself and all his officials and companions there present. Then he said to them: "The words and the promises you bring are fair enough, but because they are new to us and doubtful, I cannot consent to accept them and forsake those beliefs which I and the whole people of the Angles have held so long. But as you have come on a long pilgrimage and are anxious, I perceive, to share with us things which you believe to be true and good, we do not wish to do you harm; on the contrary, we will receive you hospitably and provide what is necessary for your support; nor do we forbid you to win all you can to your faith and religion by your preaching." So he gave them a dwelling in the city of Canterbury, which was the chief city of all his dominions; and, in accordance with his promise, he granted them provisions and did not refuse them freedom to preach. It is related that as they approached the city in accordance with their custom carrying the holy cross and the image of our great King and Lord, Jesus Christ, they sang this litany in unison: "We beseech Thee, O Lord, in Thy great mercy, that Thy wrath and anger may be turned away from this city and from Thy holy house, for we have sinned. Alleluia."

CHAPTER 26

As soon as they had entered the dwelling-place allotted to them, they began to imitate the way of life of the apostles and of the primitive church. They were constantly engaged in prayers, in vigils and fasts; they preached the word of life to as many as they could; they despised all worldly things as foreign to them; they accepted only the necessaries of life from those whom they taught; in all things they practiced what they preached and kept themselves prepared to endure adversities, even to the point of dying for the truths they proclaimed. To put it briefly, some, marveling at their simple and innocent way of life and the sweetness of their heavenly doctrine, believed and were baptized. There was nearby, on the east of the city, a church built in ancient times in honor of St. Martin,[5] while the Romans were still in Britain, in which the

---

1   The "hide" was theoretically the amount of land that supported one family, its extent varying from place to place.
2   A furlong is 1/8 mile.
3   Bertha was the daughter of the Merovingian king Charibert I (r.561–567), whose short-lived realm had been centered on Paris. As Bede points out, she was a Catholic Christian who brought her own bishop, Liudhard, with her.
4   How might Bede's emphasis on this image be an indirect critique of Byzantine iconoclasm? Bede was writing at the very beginning of that movement.
5   The western section of the chancel (the space around the altar) of the extant church of St. Martin in Canterbury is thought to have formed part of the church of Queen Bertha. This reference, like that to Liudhard, hints at the survival of Christian worship in post-Roman lowland Britain prior to the arrival of Augustine.

queen who, as has been said, was a Christian, used to pray. In this church they first began to meet to chant the psalms, to pray, to say mass, to preach, and to baptize, until, when the king had been converted to the faith, they received greater liberty to preach everywhere and to build or restore churches.

At last the king, as well as others, believed and was baptized, being attracted by the pure life of the saints and by their most precious promises, whose truth they confirmed by performing many miracles. Every day more and more began to flock to hear the Word, to forsake their heathen worship, and, through faith, to join the unity of Christ's holy Church. It is related that the king, although he rejoiced at their conversion and their faith, compelled no one to accept Christianity; though none the less he showed greater affection for believers since they were his fellow citizens in the kingdom of heaven. But he had learned from his teachers and guides in the way of salvation that the service of Christ was voluntary and ought not to be compulsory. It was not long before he granted his teachers a place to settle in, suitable to their rank, in Canterbury, his chief city, and gave them possessions of various kinds for their needs....

CHAPTER 29

Since Bishop Augustine had advised him that the harvest was great and the workers were few, Pope Gregory sent more colleagues and ministers of the word together with his messengers. First and foremost among these were Mellitus, Justus, Paulinus, and Rufinianus; and he sent with them all such things as were generally necessary for the worship and ministry of the Church, such as sacred vessels, altar cloths and church ornaments, vestments for priests and clerks, relics of the holy apostles and martyrs, and very many manuscripts. He also sent a letter in which he announced that he had despatched the pallium[1] to him and at the same time directed how he should organize the bishops in Britain. Here is the text of this letter:

To the most reverend and holy brother Augustine, our fellow-bishop, Gregory, servant of the servants of God.

While it is certain that untold rewards in the eternal kingdom are laid up for those who labor for Almighty God, nevertheless it is necessary that we should bestow rewards and honors upon them so that they may be encouraged by this recognition to toil more abundantly in their spiritual work. And because the new church of the English has been brought into the grace of Almighty God through the bounty of the Lord and by your labors, we grant to you the use of the pallium in the church but only for the performance of the solemn rites of the mass, so that you may ordain twelve bishops in various places who are to be subject to your jurisdiction. However, the bishop of London[2] shall, for the future, always be consecrated by his own synod and receive the honor of the pallium from that holy and apostolic see which, by the guidance of God, I serve. We wish to send as bishop to the city of York one whom you yourself shall decide to consecrate. But if this city together with the neighboring localities should receive the Word of the Lord, he [the bishop of York] is also to consecrate twelve bishops and enjoy the honorable rank of a metropolitan. For it is our intention, God willing, if we live, to give him the pallium too. Nevertheless, brother, we wish him to be subject to your authority. But after your death, he should preside over the bishops he has consecrated, being in no way subject to the authority of the bishop of London. There is, however, to be this distinction in honor, in future, between the bishops of London and York, that he who was first consecrated is to be reckoned senior. But let them agree to do whatever has to be done, taking counsel together and acting out of zeal for Christ. Let them judge rightly and with one mind and so carry out their decisions without disagreement.

---

1 The "pallium" was a thin band of white wool worn by the popes in the performance of the liturgy, the use of which could be conferred on approved metropolitan bishops. It was regularly given to the archbishops of Canterbury.
2 Gregory, relying on the former Roman administrative structures, assumed that London (actually in the kingdom of the East Saxons) would be the seat of the new archbishopric; contemporary political realities had already led to Canterbury's taking this role instead.

You, brother, are to have under your subjection those bishops whom you have consecrated as well as those who shall be consecrated by the bishop of York, and not those only but also all the bishops of Britain, under the guidance of our Lord God, Jesus Christ, so that they may see from the words and actions of your Holiness what true faith and good living are like and so, fulfilling their office in faith and righteousness, may attain to the heavenly kingdom when it shall please the Lord. May God keep you safe, most reverend brother.

Given June 22 in the nineteenth year of the reign of our most religious emperor Maurice Tiberius, the eighteenth year after his consulship and in the fourth indiction. [June 22, 601]

CHAPTER 30

When these messengers had departed, St. Gregory sent after them a letter which is worth recording, in which he plainly showed his eager interest in the salvation of our race. This is what he wrote:

To my most beloved son, Abbot Mellitus, Gregory, servant of the servants of God.

Since the departure of our companions and yourself I have felt much anxiety because we have not happened to hear how your journey has prospered. However, when Almighty God has brought you to our most reverend brother Bishop Augustine, tell him what I have decided after long deliberation about the English people, namely that the idol temples of that race should by no means be destroyed, but only the idols in them. Take holy water and sprinkle it in these shrines, build altars and place relics in them. For if the shrines are well built, it is essential that they should be changed from the worship of devils to the service of the true God. When this people see that their shrines are not destroyed they will be able to banish error from their hearts and be more ready to come to the places they are familiar with, but now recognizing and worshiping the true God. And because they are in the habit of slaughtering much cattle as sacrifices to devils, some solemnity

ought to be given them in exchange for this. So on the day of the dedication or the festivals of the holy martyrs, whose relics are deposited there, let them make themselves huts from the branches of trees around the churches which have been converted out of shrines, and let them celebrate the solemnity with religious feasts. Do not let them sacrifice animals to the devil, but let them slaughter animals for their own food to the praise of God, and let them give thanks to the Giver of all things for His bountiful provision. Thus while some outward rejoicings are preserved, they will be able more easily to share in inward rejoicings. It is doubtless impossible to cut out everything at once from their stubborn minds, just as the man who is attempting to climb to the highest place, rises by steps and degrees and not by leaps. Thus the Lord made Himself known to the Israelites in Egypt, yet he preserved in his own worship the forms of sacrifice which they were accustomed to offer to the devil and commanded them to kill animals when sacrificing to him. So with changed hearts they were to put away one part of the sacrifice and retain the other; even though they were the same animals as they were in the habit of offering, yet since the people were offering them to the true God and not to idols, they were not the same sacrifices. These things then, dearly beloved, you must say to our brother so that in his present position he may carefully consider how he should order all things. May God keep you in safety, most beloved son.

Given July 18 in the nineteenth year of the reign of our most religious emperor Maurice Tiberius, and in the eighteenth year after his consulship and in the fourth indiction. [July 18, 601]

CHAPTER 31

At the same time Pope Gregory heard that Augustine had been performing miracles and sent him a letter on the subject, in which he exhorts Augustine not to incur the danger of being elated by their great number:

I know, most beloved brother, that Almighty God out of love for you has worked great miracles through you for the race which it was his will to have among the chosen. It is therefore necessary that you should rejoice with trembling over this heavenly gift and fear as you rejoice. You will rejoice because the souls of the English are drawn by outward miracles to inward grace: but you will fear lest among these signs which are performed, the weak mind may be raised up by self-esteem and so the very cause by which it is raised to outward honor may lead through vainglory to its inward fall. We ought to remember that when the disciples were returning from their preaching full of joy, they said to their heavenly Master, "Lord, even the devils are subject to us through thy name (Luke 10: 17)." And forthwith they received the reply, "In this rejoice not, but rather rejoice that your names are written in heaven (Luke 10: 20)." They had set their minds on personal and temporal joys when they rejoiced over their own miracles, but they are recalled from private to common joys and from temporal to eternal joys by his words, "Rejoice in this that your names are written in heaven." For not all the elect work miracles, but nevertheless all their names are written in heaven. Therefore those who are true disciples ought not to rejoice except in that good thing which they have in common with all the elect and which they will enjoy for ever. So it remains, most dear brother, that amidst those outward deeds which you perform through the Lord's power you should always judge your inner self carefully and carefully note within yourself what you are and how great is the grace shown to that people for whose conversion you have received the gift of working miracles. And if you remember that you have at any time sinned against your Creator either in word or deed, always call this to mind in order that the memory of your guilt may suppress the vainglory which arises in your heart. And whatever power of working miracles you have received or shall receive, consider that these gifts have been conferred not on you, but on those for whose salvation they have been granted you.

CHAPTER 32

Pope Gregory at the same time also sent a letter to King Ethelbert as well as numerous gifts of every kind. He was anxious to glorify the king with temporal honors, while at the same time he rejoiced to think that Ethelbert had attained to the knowledge of heavenly glory by Gregory's own labor and industry....

Book 2

CHAPTER I

About this time, in the year of our Lord 605,[1] Pope St. Gregory, who had reigned in great glory over the apostolic Roman see for thirteen years, six months, and ten days, died and was taken up to reign for ever in the kingdom of heaven. Well indeed may we, the English nation converted by his efforts from the power of Satan to the faith of Christ, give a somewhat full account of him in this *History*. We can and should by rights call him our apostle, for though he held the most important see in the whole world and was head of Churches which had long been converted to the true faith, yet he made our nation, till then enslaved to idols, into a Church of Christ, so that we may use the apostle's words about him, "If he is not an apostle to others yet at least he is to us, for we are the seal of his apostleship in the Lord (see 1 Cor. 9: 2)."

He was of Roman race, his father's name being Gordianus. He traced his descent from ancestors who were not only noble but also devout. Felix,[2] for example, who was once bishop of the apostolic see and a man of great reputation both in Christ and in the Church, was his forefather. That ancestral tradition of religion he followed with the same religious devotion as his parents and kinsmen, while the noble position which was accounted his, according to the standards of the world, was by God's grace entirely sacrificed to winning glory and honor of a higher kind. He promptly renounced his secular habit and entered a monastery,[3] in which he proceeded to live with such grace and perfection—as he used afterwards to declare with tears—that his soul was then above all transitory

---

1 Gregory died on 12 March 604; otherwise Bede is right about the length of his pontificate. But Bede's facts and dates are not always accurate.
2 Felix IV was pope 526–530.
3 Gregory turned his own family home on the Caelian Hill in Rome into the monastery of St. Andrew.

things, and he soared beyond all things subject to change. He used to think nothing but thoughts of heaven so that, even though still imprisoned in the body, he was able to pass in contemplation beyond the barriers of the flesh. He loved death, which in the eyes of almost everybody is a punishment, because he held it to be the entrance to life and the reward of his labors. He used to relate all this, not boasting over his progress towards moral perfection, but rather bewailing the loss which he seemed to have incurred as the result of his pastoral cares. Once, for instance, when he was talking privately with his deacon Peter and enumerating the former virtues of his soul, he added mournfully that now on account of his pastoral cares he had to trouble himself with the business of men of this world, and after the enjoyment of peace so lovely, he was soiled by the dust of earthly activities. After dissipating his strength on outward things by descending to the affairs of all and sundry, even when he sought the things of the spirit, he inevitably returned to them impaired. "I realize," he said, "what I endure and what I have lost; and when my mind turns to what I have lost, then what I endure becomes so much the more burdensome."

The holy man said all this in a spirit of great humility. We need not believe, however, that he had lost any of his monastic perfection by reason of his pastoral cares. It would appear that he profited more by his efforts over the conversion of many than he had done from the quiet retirement of his earlier way of life. This was largely because, while fulfilling his pontifical duties, he turned his own house into a monastery; and when he was first taken from the monastery and was ordained to the ministry of the altar, having been sent to Constantinople as delegate of the apostolic see, he never ceased from his heavenly manner of life, though he had to live in an earthly palace. He even used some of the brothers from his monastery who had followed him out of brotherly love to the royal city [Constantinople] to protect him in his observance of the Rule. Thus, as he himself writes, through their unremitting example he could bind himself, as it were by an an-

chor cable, to the calm shores of prayer, while he was being tossed about on the ceaseless tide of secular affairs. So his mind, shaken by worldly business, could be strengthened by the encouragement derived from daily reading and contemplation in their company. By their fellowship he was thus not only defended against worldly assaults, but was also encouraged more and more to the activities of the heavenly life.

They urged him to unfold by spiritual interpretation the book of Job, a work which is shrouded in great obscurity. Nor could he refuse the task imposed on him by his loving brethren, seeing that it was likely to be of great use to many. So in thirty-five books[1] of exposition he taught in a marvelous manner the literal meaning of the book, its bearing on the mysteries of Christ and the Church, and the sense in which it applies to each of the faithful. He began this work while he was delegate in the royal city and finished it after he was made pope at Rome. While he was still in the royal city, helped by the grace of the catholic truth, he crushed at its birth a new heresy which arose there concerning our state at the resurrection. Eutychius, the bishop of the city, taught that our body in its resurrection glory, would be impalpable and more subtle than wind or air.[2] When Gregory heard this he proved both by sound reasoning and by the example of our Lord's resurrection that this dogma was contrary in every particular to the orthodox belief. For the catholic faith maintains that our body, while it is indeed exalted by the glory of immortality and made subtle by the effectual working of the spirit, is palpable by the reality of its nature as was our Lord's body, concerning which he said to his disciples, when it had been raised from the dead, "Touch me and see, for a spirit has not flesh and bones as you see me have (Luke 24: 39-40)." The venerable father Gregory strove so earnestly in his declaration of the faith against this newborn heresy and, with the help of the most religious emperor Tiberius Constantine,[3] suppressed it with such resolution, that no one has since been found to resuscitate it.

He composed another remarkable book called

---

1 This was the *Moralia in Job*; see above, p. 26.
2 Eutychius was the Patriarch of Constantinople 552-565.
3 Tiberius Constantine became Caesar and regent in 574, when Justin II (r.565-578) became insane; he was sole emperor from 578 to 582.

the *Pastoral Care*, in which he set forth in the clearest manner what sort of persons should be chosen to rule the Church and how these rulers ought to live; with how much discrimination they should instruct different types of listeners; and how earnestly they ought each day to reflect on their own frailty. He composed forty *Homilies on the Gospel*, which he divided into two volumes of equal size, and made four books of *Dialogues* in which, at the request of Peter his deacon, he collected the virtues of the most famous saints he knew or could learn of in Italy as an example of life to posterity; as in his expository works he taught what virtues men ought to strive after, so, by describing the miracles of the saints, he showed how glorious those virtues are. He also showed in twenty-two homilies how much inner light is to be found within the most obscure sections of the prophet Ezekiel, namely the first part and the last. There is also a useful Synodal book which he composed in collaboration with the bishops of Italy, dealing with some of the Church's vital problems, together with familiar letters to certain individuals, not to mention the book of answers to the questions of St. Augustine, the first bishop of the English race, which I have described above and of which the whole is included in this *History*. It is all the more wonderful that he was able to produce so many books and of such length, since almost continually throughout his early manhood he had been, to use his own words, tortured with frequent pains in the bowels, and every moment of the day he was exhausted by a weakness of the internal organs, and his breathing was affected by a low but unremitting fever. Yet always amid these troubles, when he carefully reflected on the testimony of the scriptures that, "He scourgeth every son whom he receiveth,"[1] the more severely he was oppressed by present evils, the more surely he was refreshed by eternal hope.

This much may be said of his immortal spirit, which could not be quenched by so much bodily pain. Other popes applied themselves to the task of building churches and adorning them with gold and silver, but he devoted himself entirely to winning souls. Whatever money he had he took diligent care to distribute and give to the poor, so that "his righteousness might endure for ever and his horn be exalted with honor,"[2] so that the words of the blessed Job might truly be said of him: "When the ear heard me, then it blessed me and when the eye saw me it gave witness to me because I delivered the poor that cried and the fatherless also that had none to help him. The blessing of him that was ready to perish came upon me and I consoled the widow's heart. I put on righteousness and I clothed myself with my judgment as with a robe and a diadem. I was eyes to the blind and feet was I to the lame. I was a father to the poor and the cause which I knew not, I diligently searched out. I broke the jaws of the wicked and plucked the spoil out of his teeth."[3] And again a little further on he says, "If I have withheld their desire from the poor or have caused the eyes of the widow to fail; if I have eaten my morsel myself alone and the fatherless has not eaten thereof; for from my youth my compassion grew up with me and from my mother's womb it came forth with me."[4]

To his works of piety and justice this also belongs: that he snatched our race from the teeth of the ancient foe and made them partakers of everlasting freedom by sending us preachers. Rejoicing in their faith and commending them with worthy praise he says in his commentary on the blessed Job: "Lo, the mouth of Britain, which once only knew how to gnash its barbarous teeth, has long since learned to sing the praises of God with the alleluia of the Hebrews. See how the proud Ocean has become a servant, lying low now before the feet of the saints, and those barbarous motions, which earthly princes could not subdue with the sword, are now, through the fear of God, repressed with a simple word from the lips of priests; and he who, as an unbeliever, did not flinch before troops of warriors, now, as a believer, fears the words of the humble. For having received the heavenly Word and being enlightened by miracles as well, he is filled with the grace and the knowledge of God. He is restrained by the fear of God so that he dreads to do evil and with all his heart he longs to attain to everlasting grace." In these words St. Gregory also declares that St. Augustine and his companions led the English race

1   Heb. 12: 6.
2   Ps. 112: 9; Douay Ps. 111: 9.
3   Job 29: 11-17.
4   Job 31: 16-18.

to the knowledge of the truth, not only by preaching the Word but also by showing heavenly signs.

Among other things, Pope St. Gregory arranged that masses should be celebrated in the churches of the apostles St. Peter and St. Paul over their bodies. And in the celebration of the mass, he added three quite perfect petitions, "Dispose our days in peace, and command that we be saved from eternal damnation, and that we be numbered among the flock of thine elect."

He ruled the Church during the days of the Emperors Maurice and Phocas.[1] He departed this life in the second year of Phocas and passed to the true life in heaven. His body was buried in the church of St. Peter the Apostle, before the sanctuary, on 12 March; and in that body he will one day rise again in glory together with the other pastors of the Church. His epitaph written on his tomb runs as follows:

Earth, take this corpse—'tis dust of thine own dust:
When God shall give new life, restore thy trust.
Star-bound his soul: for Death's writ does not run
Where grave's but gateway to life new-begun.
A great high-priest this sepulcher inherits,
Who lives for ever by uncounted merits;
Hunger with meat, winter with clothes he ended,
Souls with sound learning from the foe defended;
Whate'er he taught, himself fulfilled in act—
Mystic his words, but his example fact.
Anglia to Christ at piety's dictation
He turned, won thousands from an unknown nation.
Thus that great shepherd labored, thus he wrought;
To increase his Master's flock was all his thought.
Take thy reward in triumph and in joy,
Who in God's council sit'st eternally!

We must not fail to relate the story about St. Gregory which has come down to us as a tradition of our forefathers. It explains the reason why he showed such earnest solicitude for the salvation of our race. It is said that one day, soon after some merchants had arrived in Rome, a quantity of merchandise was exposed for sale in the market-place. Crowds came to buy and Gregory too among them. As well as other merchandise he saw some boys put up for sale, with fair complexions, handsome faces, and lovely hair. On seeing them he asked, so it is said, from what region or land they had been brought. He was told that they came from the island of Britain, whose inhabitants were like that in appearance. He asked again whether those islanders were Christians or still entangled in the errors of heathenism. He was told that they were heathen. Then with a deep-drawn sigh he said, "Alas that the author of darkness should have men so bright of face in his grip, and that minds devoid of inward grace should bear so graceful an outward form." Again he asked for the name of the race. He was told that they were called *Angli*. "Good," he said, "they have the face of angels, and such men should be fellow-heirs of the angels in heaven." "What is the name," he asked, "of the kingdom from which they have been brought?" He was told that the men of the kingdom were called *Deiri*. "*Deiri*," he replied. "*De ira!* [=From anger!] good! snatched from the wrath of Christ and called to his mercy. And what is the name of the king of the land?" He was told that it was Ælle;[2] and playing on the name, he said, "Alleluia! the praise of God the Creator must be sung in those parts." So he went to the bishop of Rome and of the apostolic see, for he himself had not yet been made pope, and asked him to send some ministers of the word to the race of the Angles in Britain to convert them to Christ. He added that he himself was prepared to carry out the task with the help of the Lord provided that the pope was willing. But he was unable to perform this mission, because although the pope was willing to grant his request, the citizens of Rome could not permit him to go so far away from the city. Soon after he had become pope, he fulfilled the task which he had long desired. It is true that he sent other preachers, but he himself helped their preaching to bear fruit by his encouragement and prayers. I have thought it proper to insert this story into this Church *History*, based as it is on the tradition which we have received from our ancestors....

---

1 Emperor Maurice (r.582–602) was overthrown in a military revolt led by Phocas (r.602–610).
2 Ælle was king of the Deirans (in England) c.568–c.598.

Book 3

CHAPTER 25

Meanwhile, after Bishop Aidan's death,[1] Finan succeeded him as bishop,[2] having been consecrated and sent over by the Irish. He constructed a church on the island of Lindisfarne suitable for an episcopal see, building it after the Irish method, not of stone but of hewn oak, thatching it with reeds; later on the most reverend Archbishop Theodore[3] consecrated it in honor of the blessed apostle Peter. It was Eadberht,[4] who was bishop of Lindisfarne, who removed the reed thatch and had the whole of it, both roof and walls, covered with sheets of lead.

In those days there arose a great and active controversy about the keeping of Easter. Those who had come from Kent or Gaul declared that the Irish observance of Easter Sunday was contrary to the custom of the universal church. One most violent defender of the true Easter was Ronan[5] who, though Irish by race, had learned the true rules of the church in Gaul or Italy. In disputing with Finan he put many right or at least encouraged them to make a more strict inquiry into the truth; but he could by no means put Finan right. On the contrary, as he was a man of fierce temper, Ronan made him the more bitter by his reproofs and turned him into an open adversary of the truth. James, once the deacon of the venerable Archbishop Paulinus, as we have already said,[6] kept the true and catholic Easter with all those whom he could instruct in the better way. Queen Eanfleda[7] and her people also observed it as she had seen it done in Kent, having with her a Kentish priest named Romanus who followed the Catholic observance. Hence it is said that in these days it sometimes happened that Easter was celebrated twice in the same year, so that the king had finished the fast and was keeping Easter Sunday, while the queen and her people were still in Lent and observing Palm Sunday. This difference in the observance of Easter was patiently tolerated by all while Aidan was alive, because they had clearly understood that although he could not keep Easter otherwise than according to the manner of those who had sent him, he nevertheless labored diligently to practice the works of faith, piety, and love, which is the mark of all the saints. He was therefore deservedly loved by all, including those who had other views about Easter. Not only was he respected by the ordinary people but also by bishops, such as Honorius of Kent and Felix of East Anglia.

When Finan, Aidan's successor, was dead and Colman,[8] who had also been sent from Ireland, had become bishop, a still more serious controversy arose concerning the observance of Easter as well as about other matters of ecclesiastical discipline. This dispute naturally troubled the minds and hearts of many people who feared that, though they had received the name of Christian, they might have done so in vain. All this came to the ears of the rulers [of Northumbria] themselves, Oswiu [d.670] and his son Alhfrith. Oswiu, who had been educated and baptized by the Irish and was well versed in their language, considered that nothing was better than what they had taught. But Alhfrith had as his instructor in the Christian faith one Wilfrid, a most learned man who had once been to Rome to study church doctrine and had spent much time at Lyon with Dalfinus,[9] archbishop of Gaul, having received there his ecclesiastical tonsure in the form of a crown. So Alhfrith rightly preferred his teaching to all the traditions of the Irish and had

---

1 Aidan (d.642) was the bishop of Lindisfarne (in northern England). He had come from Ireland to teach the Christian faith at the request of Oswald, king of Northumbria (d.642).

2 Finan (d.661).

3 Theodore was archbishop of Canterbury 668–690.

4 Eadberht was bishop of Lindisfarne 687–698.

5 Nothing else is known of Ronan. The church in the south of Ireland had by this time largely adopted Continental practices with respect to the dating of Easter.

6 Paulinus (d.644) was bishop of York and Rochester.

7 Eanfleda (d.c.704) was the daughter of Edwin, king of Deira, and Ethelburg Tata, daughter of Ethelbert and Bertha of Kent. She married Oswin, king of Bernicia (r.642–670).

8 Colman was bishop of Lindisfarne 661–664.

9 Bede confused Dalfinus, who was the prefect (secular ruler) of Lyon, with his brother Aunemundus, the bishop of Lyon (c.650–c.660). Wilfrid (d.709), bishop of York and Hexham, was the chief proponent of the Roman date for Easter.

therefore given him a monastery of forty hides in the place called Ripon. He had presented the site, a short time before, to those who followed Irish ways, but because, when given the choice, they preferred to renounce the site rather than change their customs, he gave it to one who was worthy of the place both by his doctrine and his way of life. At that time there had come to the kingdom of Northumbria Agilbert, bishop of the West Saxons, whom we have mentioned before, a friend of Alhfrith and of Abbot Wilfrid; he stayed some time with them and, at the request of Alhfrith, he ordained Wilfrid priest in his own monastery. Agilbert had with him a priest called Agatho.

When this question of Easter and of the tonsure and other ecclesiastical matters was raised, it was decided to hold a council [in 664] to settle the dispute at a monastery called *Streanæshealh* (Whitby), a name which means the bay of the lighthouse; at this time Hild, a woman devoted to God, was abbess.[1] There came to the council the two kings, both father and son, Bishop Colman with his Irish clergy, and Agilbert with the priests Agatho and Wilfrid. James and Romanus were on their side while the Abbess Hild and her followers were on the side of the Irish; among these also was the venerable Bishop Cedd, who, as has been mentioned, had been consecrated long before by the Irish and who acted as a most careful interpreter for both parties at the council.

First King Oswiu began by declaring that it was fitting that those who served one God should observe one rule of life and not differ in the celebration of the heavenly sacraments, seeing that they all hoped for one kingdom in heaven; they ought therefore to inquire as to which was the truer tradition and then all follow it together. He then ordered his bishop Colman to say first what were the customs which he followed and whence they originated. Colman thereupon said, "The method of keeping Easter which I observe, I received from my superiors who sent me here as bishop; it was in this way that all our fathers, men beloved of God, are known to have celebrated it. Nor should this method seem contemptible and blameworthy seeing that the blessed evangelist John, the disciple whom the Lord specially loved, is said to have celebrated it thus, together with all the churches over which he

presided." When he had said all this and more to the same effect, the king ordered Agilbert to expound the method he observed, its origin, and the authority he had for following it. Agilbert answered, "I request that my disciple, the priest Wilfrid, may speak on my behalf, for we are both in agreement with the other followers of our church tradition who are here present; and he can explain our views in the English tongue better and more clearly than I can through an interpreter." Then Wilfrid, receiving instructions from the king to speak, began thus: "The Easter we keep is the same as we have seen universally celebrated in Rome, where the apostles St. Peter and St. Paul lived, taught, suffered, and were buried. We also found it in use everywhere in Italy and Gaul when we traveled through those countries for the purpose of study and prayer. We learned that it was observed at one and the same time in Africa, Asia, Egypt, Greece, and throughout the whole world, wherever the Church of Christ is scattered, amid various nations and languages. The only exceptions are these men and their accomplices in obstinacy, I mean the Picts and the Britons, who in these, the two remotest islands of the Ocean, and only in some parts of them, foolishly attempt to fight against the whole world."

Colman answered, "I wonder that you are willing to call our efforts foolish, seeing that we follow the example of that apostle who was reckoned worthy to recline on the breast of the Lord; for all the world acknowledges his great wisdom." Wilfrid replied, "Far be it from me to charge John with foolishness: he literally observed the decrees of the Mosaic law when the Church was still Jewish in many respects, at a time when the apostles were unable to bring to a sudden end the entire observance of that law which God ordained in the same way as, for instance, they made it compulsory on all new converts to abandon their idols which are of devilish origin. They feared, of course, that they might make a stumbling-block for the Jewish proselytes dispersed among the Gentiles. This was the reason why Paul circumcised Timothy, why he offered sacrifices in the temple, and why he shaved his head at Corinth in company with Aquila and Priscilla; all this was of no use except to avoid scandalizing the Jews. Hence James said to Paul,

---

1 Under Hild, Whitby was a double monastery with both men and women (in separate quarters). Hild presided over both.

'Thou seest, brother, how many thousands there are among the Jews of them which have believed; and they are all zealous for the law (Acts 21: 20).' But in these days when the light of the Gospel is spreading throughout the world, it is not necessary, it is not even lawful for believers to be circumcised or to offer God sacrifices of flesh and blood. So John, in accordance with the custom of the law, began the celebration of Easter Day in the evening of the fourteenth day of the first month, regardless of whether it fell on the sabbath or any other day. But when Peter preached at Rome, remembering that the Lord rose from the dead and brought to the world the hope of the resurrection on the first day of the week, he realized that Easter ought to be kept as follows: he always waited for the rising of the moon on the evening of the fourteenth day of the first month in accordance with the custom and precepts of the law, just as John did, but when it had risen, if the Lord's Day, which was then called the first day of the week, followed in the morning, he proceeded to celebrate Easter as we are accustomed to do at the present time. But if the Lord's Day was due, not on the morning following the fourteenth day of the moon but on the sixteenth or seventeenth or any other day until the twenty-first, he waited for it, and began the holy Easter ceremonies the night before, that is, on the Saturday evening; so it came about that Easter Sunday was kept only between the fifteenth day of the moon and the twenty-first. So this evangelical and apostolic tradition does not abolish the law but rather fulfils it, by ordering the observance of Easter from the evening of the fourteenth day of the moon in the first month up to the twenty-first of the moon in the same month. All the successors of St. John in Asia since his death and also the whole church throughout the world have followed this observance. That this is the true Easter and that this alone must be celebrated by the faithful was not newly decreed but confirmed afresh by the Council of Nicaea as the history of the Church informs us.[1] So it is plain, Colman, that you neither follow the example of John, as you think, nor of Peter, whose tradition you knowingly contradict; and so, in your observance of Easter, you neither follow the law nor the gospel. For John who kept Easter according to the decrees of the Mosaic law, took no heed of the Sunday; you do not do this, for you celebrate Easter only on a Sunday. Peter celebrated Easter Sunday between the fifteenth and the twenty-first day of the moon; you, on the other hand, celebrate Easter Sunday between the fourteenth and the twentieth day of the moon. Thus you very often begin Easter on the evening of the thirteenth day of the moon, which is never mentioned in the law. This was not the day—it was the fourteenth, in which the Lord, the author and giver of the Gospel, ate the old passover in the evening and instituted the sacraments of the new testament to be celebrated by the church in remembrance of his passion. Besides, in your celebration of Easter you utterly exclude the twenty-first day, which the law of Moses specially ordered to be observed. So, as I have said, in your celebration of the greatest of the festivals you agree neither with John nor Peter, neither with the law nor the Gospel."

Colman replied, "Did Anatolius, a man who was holy and highly spoken of in the history of the Church to which you appeal, judge contrary to the law and the Gospel when he wrote that Easter should be celebrated between the fourteenth and the twentieth day of the moon? Or must we believe that our most reverend father Columba and his successors,[2] men beloved of God, who celebrated Easter in the same way, judged and acted contrary to the holy scriptures, seeing that there were many of them to whose holiness the heavenly signs and the miracles they performed bore witness? And as I have no doubt that they were saints, I shall never cease to follow their way of life, their customs, and their teaching."

Wilfrid replied, "It is true that Anatolius was a most holy and learned man, worthy of all praise; but what have you to do with him since you do not observe his precepts? He followed a correct rule in celebrating Easter, basing it on a cycle of nineteen years, of which you are either unaware or, if you do know of it, you despise it, even though it is observed by the

---

1 This is a reference to the account of the First Council of Nicaea of 325 in Rufinus' translation and in the continuation in Eusebius' *History of the Church*.

2 Columba (d.597) was an Irish monk who left his homeland to found the monastery of Iona (in Scotland), which he used as a base for missionary work. Though he was highly praised in the Irish world, Wilfrid seems to have known very little about him—or, at least, he is presented as knowing little by Bede.

whole Church of Christ. He assigned the fourteenth day of the moon to Easter Sunday, reckoning after the Egyptian manner that the fifteenth day of the moon began on the evening of the fourteenth. So also he assigned the twentieth day to Easter Sunday, reckoning that after evening it was the twenty-first day. But it appears that you are ignorant of this distinction, in that you sometimes clearly keep Easter Day before full moon, that is on the thirteenth day of the moon. So far as your father Columba and his followers are concerned, whose holiness you claim to imitate and whose rule and precepts (confirmed by heavenly signs) you claim to follow, I might perhaps point out that at the judgment, many will say to the Lord that they prophesied in His name and cast out devils and did many wonderful works, but the Lord will answer that He never knew them. Far be it from me to say this about your fathers, for it is much fairer to believe good rather than evil about unknown people. So I will not deny that those who in their rude simplicity loved God with pious intent, were indeed servants of God and beloved by Him. Nor do I think that this observance of Easter did much harm to them while no one had come to show them a more perfect rule to follow. In fact I am sure that if anyone knowing the Catholic rule had come to them they would have followed it, as they are known to have followed all the laws of God as soon as they had learned of them. But, once having heard the decrees of the apostolic see or rather of the universal Church, if you refuse to follow them, confirmed as they are by the holy Scriptures, then without doubt you are committing sin.

For though your fathers were holy men, do you think that a handful of people in one corner of the remotest of islands is to be preferred to the universal Church of Christ which is spread throughout the world? And even if that Columba of yours—yes, and ours too, if he belonged to Christ—was a holy man of mighty works, is he to be preferred to the most blessed chief of the apostles, to whom the Lord said, 'Thou art Peter and upon this rock I will build my Church and the gates of hell shall not prevail against it, and I will give unto thee the keys of the kingdom of heaven.'"?[1]

When Wilfrid had ended, the king said, "Is it true, Colman, that the Lord said these words to Peter?" Colman answered, "It is true, O King." Then the king went on, "Have you anything to show that an equal authority was given to your Columba?" Colman answered, "Nothing." Again the king said, "Do you both agree, without any dispute, that these words were addressed primarily to Peter and that the Lord gave him the keys of the kingdom of heaven?" They both answered, "Yes." Thereupon the king concluded, "Then, I tell you, since he is the doorkeeper I will not contradict him, but I intend to obey his commands in everything to the best of my knowledge and ability. Otherwise, when I come to the gates of the kingdom of heaven, there may be no one to open them, because the one who on your own showing holds the keys has turned his back on me." When the king had spoken, all who were seated there or standing by, both high and low, signified their assent, gave up their imperfect rules, and readily accepted in their place those which they recognized to be better.

2.12 The private penitential tradition: *Penitential of Finnian* (late 6th c.). Original in Latin.

THE PURPOSE OF PENANCE IS TO achieve reconciliation with God after sinning. In early Christian practice, penance was public, dramatic, and humiliating. But within the Celtic, Anglo-Saxon, and Frankish worlds a different sort of penance became popular: the "tariffed," private penance of the penitentials. Drawing on Biblical passages, canons (decisions or laws) of early church councils, monastic practices, and perhaps secular laws, these penitentials listed sins and the penances due for them (the tariffs) as a matter of regular religious discipline. The penitential of Finnian, drawn up in the late sixth century in either Ireland or Brittany, is one of the earliest of these books. Although it was probably created in a monastic context, it was directed mainly to clerics and laymen and -women (i.e., the laity; or laypeople) rather than monks. Since clerics were considered "secular"

---

1 Matt. 16: 18.

(worldly) because of their pastoral duties and laypeople were ordinary men and women—not in orders, not of clerical or monastic status, and normally married—the audience at whom this is aimed is itself evidence of the monastic desire to make an impact on the behavior of those "in the world." Compare the provisions of this penitential with the various conciliar canons and law codes you have read (above, pp. 60, 63, 72) as well as to *The Benedictine Rule*, p. 28.

[Source: *The Irish Penitentials*, ed. Ludwig Bieler (Dublin: Dublin Institute for Advanced Studies, 1963), pp. 75, 77, 79, 81, 87.]

In the name of the Father and of the Son and of the Holy Ghost.

1. If anyone has sinned by thought in his heart and immediately repents, he shall beat his breast and seek pardon from God and make satisfaction, and [so] be whole.

2. But if he frequently entertains [evil] thoughts and hesitates to act on them, whether he has mastered them or been mastered by them, he shall seek help from God by prayer and fasting day and night until the evil thought departs and he is whole.

3. If, however, he has thought evil and intended to do it and has not been able to do it, since opportunity has failed him, it is the same sin but not the same penance; for example, if he intended fornication or murder, he has, by his intention, already committed the sin in his heart which he did not complete by a deed; but if he quickly does penance, he can be helped. His penance is this: half a year he shall do penance on an allowance of bread and water, and he shall abstain from wine and meat for a whole year.

4. If anyone has sinned in word by inadvertence and immediately repented and has not said any such thing of set purpose, he ought to submit to penance, but he shall keep [only] one special fast; but thereafter let him be on his guard throughout his life, lest he commit further sin.

5. If one of the clerics or ministers of God makes strife, he shall do penance for a period of seven days with bread and water and salt, and seek pardon from God and his neighbor, with full confession and humility; and thus can he be reconciled to God and his neighbor.

6. If anyone has decided on a scandalous deed and plotted in his heart to strike or kill his neighbor, if [the offender] is a cleric, he shall do penance for half a year with an allowance of bread and water and for a whole year abstain from wine and meat, and thus he will be reconciled to the altar; 7. but if he is a layman, he shall do penance for a period of seven days; since he is a man of this world, his guilt is lighter in this world and his reward less in the world to come.

8. But if he is a cleric and strikes his brother or his neighbor and sheds blood, it is the same as if he had killed him, but the penance is not the same: he shall do penance with bread and water and salt and be deprived of his clerical office for an entire year, and he must pray with weeping and tears, that he may obtain mercy of God, since Scripture says: "Whosoever hateth his brother is a murderer";[1] how much more he who strikes him. 9. But if he is a layman, he shall do penance forty days and give some money to him whom he has struck, according as some priest or arbiter determines. A cleric, however, ought not to give money to either man or woman.

10. But if one who is a cleric falls miserably through fornication and loses his crown,[2] if it happens once [only] and it is concealed from men but known before God, he shall do penance for an entire year with an allowance of bread and water and for two years abstain from wine and meat, but he shall not lose his clerical office. For, we say, sins can be absolved in secret by penance and by very diligent devotion of heart and body. 11. If, however, they have long been in the habit of sin and it has not come to the notice of men, he shall do penance for three years with bread and water and lose his clerical office, and for three years more he shall abstain from wine and meat, since it is not a

---

1   1 John 3: 15.
2   The crown of virginity.

smaller thing to sin before God than before men.

12. But if one of the clerical order falls to the depths of ruin and begets a son and kills him, great is the crime of fornication with homicide, but it can be expiated through penance and God's mercy. He shall do penance three years with an allowance of bread and water, in weeping and tears and prayers by day and night, and he shall implore the mercy of the Lord to perchance have remission of sins;[1] and he shall abstain for three more years from wine and meat, deprived of his clerical office; and for the forty-day periods[2] in the last three years he shall fast with bread and water; and [he shall] be an exile from his own country, until a period of seven years is completed, and so by the judgment of a bishop or a priest he shall be restored to his office. 13. If, however, he has not killed the child, the sin is less, but the penance is the same.

14. But if one of the clerical order is on familiar terms with any woman and he has himself done no evil with her, neither by cohabiting nor by lascivious embraces, this is his penance: For such time as he has her he shall withdraw from the communion of the altar and do penance for forty days and nights with bread and water and tear out of his heart his fellowship with the woman, and so be restored to the altar.

15. If, however, he is on familiar terms with many women and has given himself to association with them and to their lascivious embraces, but has, as he says, preserved himself from ruin, he shall do penance for half a year with an allowance of bread and water, and for another half year he shall abstain from wine and meat, but he shall not lose his clerical office; and after an entire year of penance, he shall join himself to the altar.[3]

16. If any cleric lusts after a virgin or any woman in his heart but does not speak with his lips, if he sins thus but once he ought to do penance for seven days with an allowance of bread and water. 17. But if he continually lusts and is unable to indulge his desire, since the woman does not admit him or since he is ashamed to speak, still he has committed adultery with her in his heart—yet it is in his heart, and not in his body; it is the same sin whether in the heart or in the body, yet the penance is not the same. This is his penance: let him do penance for forty days with bread and water.

18. If any cleric or woman who practices magic have led astray anyone by their magic, it is a monstrous sin, but it can be expiated by penance. [Such an offender] shall do penance for six years, three years on an allowance of bread and water, and during the remaining three years he shall abstain from wine and meat. 19. If, however, such a person has not led astray anyone but has given [a potion] for the sake of wanton love to someone, he shall do penance for an entire year on an allowance of bread and water.

20. If a woman by her magic destroys the child she has conceived of somebody, she shall do penance for half a year with an allowance of bread and water, and abstain for two years from wine and meat and fast for the six forty-day periods with bread and water.

21. But if, as we have said, she bears a child and her sin is manifest, [she shall do penance] for six years [with bread and water], as is the judgment in the case of a cleric, and in the seventh year she shall be joined to the altar, and then we say her crown can be restored and she may don a white robe and be pronounced a virgin. So a cleric who has fallen ought likewise to receive the clerical office in the seventh year after the labor of penance, as Scripture says: "Seven times a just man falleth and ariseth,"[4] that is, after seven years of penance he who fell can be called "just" and in the eighth year evil shall not lay hold on him, but for the remainder [of his life] let him preserve himself carefully lest he fall, since, as Solomon says, "as a dog returning to his vomit becomes odious, so is he who through his own negligence reverts to his sin."[5] ...

32. We prescribe and urge contributing for the redemption of captives. By the teaching of the Church, money is to be spent fruitfully on the poor and needy.

---

1 "Remission" of sins means "forgiveness" of sins.
2 In the penitentials, three forty-day periods of fasting were prescribed in the course of the Church year: before Easter (Lent), before Christmas, and after Pentecost.
3 Laypeople, too, can be "joined to the altar" (e.g., see § 21 below), and so "he shall join himself to the altar" seems to mean that the person will rejoin the congregation.
4 Prov. 24: 16.
5 See Prov. 26: 11.

33. We are also obliged to serve the churches of the saints and, within our means, have pity on all who are in need; pilgrims are to be received into our houses, as the Lord has commanded; the infirm are to be visited; those who are in chains are to be ministered to; and all commandments of Christ are to be performed, "from the least unto the greatest."[1]

34. If any man or woman is nigh unto death, although he [or she] has been a sinner, and asks for the communion of Christ, we say that it is not to be denied to such a person if that person promise God to take the vow, and do well and be received by Him. If he is restored to this world, let him fulfil that which he has vowed to God; but if he does not fulfil the vow which he has vowed to God, [the consequences] will be on his own head, and we will not refuse what we owe to him: we are not to cease to snatch prey from the mouth of the lion or the dragon, that is of the devil, who ceases not to snatch at the prey of our souls, even though we may have to follow up and strive [for his soul] at the very end of a man's life.

35. If one of the laity is converted from his evil-doing unto the Lord, and if he has wrought every evil deed—by committing fornication, that is, and shedding blood—he shall do penance for three years and go unarmed except for a staff in his hand, and shall not live with his wife, but in the first year he shall fast on an allowance of bread and water and salt and not live with his wife; after a penance of three years he shall give money for the redemption of his soul and the fruit of his penance[2] into the hand of the priest and make a feast for the servants of God, and in the feast [his penance] shall be ended and he shall be received to communion; he may then resume relations with his wife after his entire and complete penance, and if it is so decided he shall be joined to the altar....

2.13 A modern martyr in Francia: *The Passion of Leudegar* (680s). Original in Latin.

THE MARTYRS OF THE PRE-CONSTANTINIAN Church were replaced by heroic ascetics such as St. Antony (see his *Life* above, p. 36) and St. Martin (see his *Life* above, p. 43). Hagiographers of late seventh-century Merovingian Francia created a new generation of martyrs, portraying men and women embroiled in the violent political life of the period as saints. Leudegar (Saint-Léger in French) was one of these. Brother of Gaerin, the count of Paris, and appointed to the bishopric of Autun (which he held *c.*662-*c.*676) by Queen Balthild, regent for her son Clothar III (r.657-673), Leudegar was an important man at court. But he had a falling out with Ebroin, mayor of the palace, who eventually had him executed in *c.*678. His "*Passion,*" which means "suffering" or "martyrdom," was written soon thereafter by an anonymous author who dedicated the work to Hermenar, Leudegar's successor at Autun and originally his rival. The cult of Leudegar was evidently becoming so strong that Hermenar needed to try to claim it, and he appears in the *Passion* as a sympathetic figure. How have the roles and virtues of the bishop changed from the time of St. Martin to that of Leudegar? How might you explain the reasons for these changes?

[Source: *From Roman to Merovingian Gaul: A Reader*, ed. and trans. Alexander Callander Murray (Peterborough, ON: Broadview Press, 2000), pp. 509-18, 524-26 (slightly modified).]

---

[1] Glorious and renowned Leudegar, bishop of the city Autun, has been created a new martyr in Christian times. Just as he was nobly born according to earthly descent, so, accompanied by divine grace and growing in manly strength from an early age, he stood out prominently ahead of others no matter what the office or order in life to which he was promoted. His uncle Dido, bishop of Poitiers,[3] who was provided with a

---

1   Heb. 8: 11.
2   "The fruit of his penance" refers to the savings that accrue from fasting.
3   Bishop Dido of Poitiers died in 667.

notable abundance of prudence and wealth beyond that of his neighbors, took great pains to raise him; and so, thoroughly polished in all respects by the file of instruction in the various studies that the powerful of the world are accustomed to undertake, Leudegar was chosen to assume the burden of the archdiaconate of the same city.

His courage and wisdom became so conspicuous that he appeared to have no equal among his predecessors. Especially because he was not unacquainted with the penalties of the temporal law, he was a terrifying judge of secular matters. And since he was filled with the doctrines of the church canons, he emerged as a distinguished teacher of clerics. He was also spirited in the punishment of offenders and never tried to be lenient with excesses of the flesh. He was vigilant, keenly concerned with the duties of church personnel, energetic in keeping accounts, prudent in giving advice, and glowing with eloquence.

[2] Meanwhile it became necessary to ordain him bishop of the city of Autun. For lately a dispute between two candidates for the episcopal office of that city had erupted and had reached the point of bloodshed. When one of the candidates lay dead on the spot and the other had been exiled for committing the crime, Balthild, who with her son Clothar [III] was in charge of the palace of the Franks, at that point, inspired, I believe, by divine counsel, sent this energetic man to that city to be its bishop. The church which, as if widowed, had already been left to the uncertainties of the world for almost two years, would now be protected by his direction and strength and defended against those who were attacking it.

How much more should be said? All the enemies of the church and the town, as well as those who endlessly disputed among themselves with hateful acts and killings, were so afraid on his arrival that they did not want to hear the outrage that had taken place recalled. Those whom his preaching could not persuade to accept peace, the terror of justice forced to do so.

Now that he was in office by God's will, he lav-ished such concern on giving alms to the poor that it would take too long to recount it in detail. But if we are silent, his works are a witness: the station for poor relief that he established stands at the doors of the church; the beauty of the precious objects which glow with the flash of gold in the service of the church; and also the decorations of the baptistry made with marvelous workmanship. The tomb of Saint Symphorian and the translation of his body reveals to those who remain silent the extent to which he was devoted to the love of the martyrs.[1] Moreover the pavement and the golden awning of the church, the construction of a new atrium, the repair of the town walls, the restoration of buildings and his reconstruction of whatever had deteriorated through great age, suggest as visible reminders to onlookers the extent of his energy.

Let these few special examples among many suffice. We turn in our account to the time the champion of Christ first took up the fight against the devil....

[4] In those days Ebroin was, as we say, mayor of the palace. He ran the palace at that time under King Clothar [III, r.657–673], for the queen whom we mentioned above was now living in the monastery which she had previously prepared for herself.[2] Moreover, envious men came to Ebroin and roused his anger against Leudegar the man of God, and whereas they found no charge to lay that was true, they made up a false one that, while everyone obeyed Ebroin's commands, only Bishop Leudegar defied his orders.

The aforesaid Ebroin was so inflamed by the torch of gain and so captive to the desire for money that only those who brought more money had their cause judged to be just by him. As some out of fear, and others to purchase justice, lavished immense sums of gold and silver on him, for this reason the hearts of certain people were roused against him, distressed at being robbed but especially because he not only trafficked in plunder but even shed the innocent blood of many nobles for a minor offense. And so Ebroin continued to be suspicious of Bishop Leudegar; for Ebroin could not conquer him by words, and Leudegar, unlike

---

1 Symphorian was martyred at Autun c.200. A monastery was dedicated to him there while, as we see here, his tomb was in the cathedral church. The "translation of his body" refers to the ritual in which his body was moved from one place to another.

2 Queen Balthild was "eased" out of court and went to live at Chelles, a monastery for women that she had founded and endowed.

others, did not pay court to him with flattery. Ebroin recognized that Leudegar always remained firm in the face of all his threats.

At the time, Ebroin had issued a tyrant's edict that no one should presume to come to the palace from Burgundy without receiving his authorization. Out of fear, all the leading men were now suspicious that he was contemplating adding to his crime by condemning certain people to lose their heads or by inflicting losses of property on them.

[5] While the matter remained unresolved, King Clothar, called by God, passed away [673]. But although Ebroin ought to have called the magnates together and, as is customary, solemnly raised to the kingship the king's brother, Theuderic [III, r.673, 675–691] by name, he was puffed up with pride and decided not to call them from this time onwards. They became more afraid because as long as he kept control of the king, whom he should have raised up in public for the glory of the homeland, he would be able fearlessly to inflict evil on anyone he desired in the king's name. A host of nobles were hastening to meet the new king when Ebroin sent a command for them to give up their journey. They took counsel among themselves, abandoned the king, and all sought out Childeric [II, d.675], the king's younger brother who had been allotted the kingship in Austrasia. Whoever did not want to accept this decision either escaped by flight or agreed against his will under threat of death by burning.

[6] When, out of fear of the tyrant Ebroin, they had all brought Childeric into the kingdom of Neustria as well as that of Burgundy, the tyrant recognized that it was his own villainy that brought this about and took refuge at the altar of the church; his treasure was at once broken into many pieces and what the wicked man had gathered together wrongly for so long was immediately well dispersed. They did not kill him because certain bishops stepped in between them, and especially because the bishop Leudegar intervened;

but they sent him to the monastery of Luxeuil in exile so that, through penance, he might escape the consequences of the crimes he had committed. But since the eyes of his heart were blinded by the dust of earthly desire, spiritual wisdom did not prevail in his spiteful soul.

Childeric ordered his brother, against whom he had been asked to come, brought into his presence so he could speak with him. That is when certain leaders in the kingdom who wanted to dissuade Childeric from bloodshed through flattery had the audacity to order the hair of their lord cut and took pains to deliver him before his brother in this condition.[1] But when Theuderic was asked by his brother what he wished done to him, he declared only that he was awaiting the swift judgment of God because he had been unjustly degraded from his position as king. Then orders were given that Theuderic live in the monastery of the holy martyr Dionysius;[2] and he was kept safe there until such time as he grew back the hair they cut off. And the God of heaven, whom he had declared as his judge, happily allowed him to reign afterwards.

[7] Meanwhile everyone asked King Childeric to issue throughout the three kingdoms he had acquired[3] edicts to the following effect. Judges must, as in antiquity, preserve the law and custom of each of the homelands. Officials (rectores) must not pass from one province into another. And one person must not be allowed to usurp power in the fashion of Ebroin and then, like him, hold his peers in disdain; as long as it was recognized that advancement to the top offices would take place by turns, no one would dare set himself before another. Although the king granted the requests freely, he was corrupted by foolish, almost heathen, counselors—for the superficiality of youth got the better of him—and immediately opposed what he had authorized with the advice of wise men.

[8] The king kept holy Leudegar constantly by his side in the palace because he had seen that the bishop out-

---

1   "The audacity to order the hair of their lord cut" means that they tonsured him—the sign of the monk. He could not reign until his hair grew back.
2   This was Saint-Denis, near Paris.
3   I.e., Austrasia, Neustria, and Burgundy—the whole of the Frankish Kingdom. Childeric had become king of Austrasia in 662; now, 673-675, he ruled over all of them.

shone everyone in wisdom. For this reason the envy of evil men revived and grew. Again they looked for grounds for making accusations against him, so that whatever the king did, whatever just or unjust decision he made, they accused Leudegar of doing it. Had the king complied with Leudegar's advice, he would have acted with divine authority. But by now the sentence laid down by heaven had overtaken him, so that his heart could not comprehend the teachings of justice; instead he deserved that a swift sentence carry out the judgment that Theuderic declared he was awaiting from God.

When the man of God saw the envy of the devil heat up once more against him, following the apostle, he took up the armor of faith, the helmet of salvation, and the sword of the Spirit, which is the word of God, and went into single combat with the ancient enemy. And since priestly integrity knows not how to fear the threats of a king, Leudegar censured him for suddenly altering the customs of the kingdoms after he had ordered them to be preserved; and likewise, it is said, he told him that the queen [Bilichild], his wife, was the daughter of his uncle [Sigibert III]; and, if he did not emend these deeds as well as other transgressions, he should know truly that divine vengeance would immediately be at hand.

Indeed, at first the king began to listen willingly, but the advice of his followers got the better of him. At the same time as he should have been using Leudegar's words to reform himself, the king began to look for pretexts for bringing about the bishop's death. This was on the advice of those who wanted to overturn justice and, disorderly themselves, were in favor of the king acting in an immature fashion, as well as of those who enticed the king into breaking his own decree. All of them, and others like them living amidst the desires of the world, feared their works would be destroyed by the man of God, for by now they knew that he marched a straight course along the path of justice. The old world, weighed down by vices, could not withstand the manly power of the heavenly citizen.

[9] There was in those days a certain nobleman called Hector, who had taken up the fasces of office over the patriciate of Marseille.[1] He was endowed beyond others with nobility of birth and worldly wisdom, being descended from a famous lineage. He had come to see King Childeric about a certain legal case and hoped to gain what he was seeking through the intercession of the man of God. The holy man of God had welcomed Hector to his city and provided him with lodging, waiting for the time when he could recommend Hector to the king and speak on his behalf, as Hector had requested. For Leudegar had asked Childeric to come to the church of his city[2] during the celebration of Easter. The envious ones found this the pretext by which they might fill the king's heart to the full with the vileness they had lately been pouring into it. They brought the then mayor of the palace, who was called Wulfoald, into their subterfuge and made up a lying story that Leudegar and Hector had joined together to overthrow royal authority and usurp for themselves the reins of power.

[10] There was also at the time in the monastery of Saint Symphorian a certain man in the garb of a religious by the name of Marcolinus, a recluse in body but not in mind and, as was publicly revealed afterwards, rather too eager to seek human praise and honors through the false appearance of religion. Of his way of life I think it better to be silent than to speak, especially since it was revealed to everyone. The king, therefore, mistook this fellow for a prophet of God in all matters because Marcolinus flattered his desire to be favored above all else with accusations against the man of God.

And so on the night when the holy vigils of Easter were celebrated in the city, the king, by now suspicious, refused to come there, but with a few flatterers sought the advice of the aforesaid hypocrite; and since the king bore ill feelings towards the servant of God, he had no qualms about receiving the Easter sacrifice at the right time where he was.

But afterwards, shamefully drunk on wine, he en-

---

1 The patriciate of Marseille was the major governmental authority in the city. "Fasces of office": rods bound together with an ax were carried before ancient Roman magistrates, and although this had for centuries ceased to be the case, it remained a literary image of authority.

2 That is, Autun.

tered the church while others, fasting, were awaiting the holy services. He looked for Leudegar, shouting out his name, trying to put him to flight; all the while he terrified those who now relayed messages, threatening to strike them with the sword. Frequently calling for Leudegar, the king learned that he was in the baptistery, and when he entered it, stood amazed at the brightness of the light and the aroma of the chrism that was used by those conducting baptisms there to give blessings. But although Leudegar answered the shouting by saying, "I am here,"[1] the king completely failed to see him. He crossed the baptistery and took up quarters in the bishop's mansion of the church, which had been made ready.

The other bishops who were celebrating the vigils with the man of God returned to their quarters. But when Leudegar finished the holy office, showing no sign of fear, he approached the angry king and gently asked him why he had not come before the vigils and why he stayed so angry through the celebrations of such a holy night. Disturbed, the king could only answer the ineffable wisdom of Leudegar by saying that he had suspicions about him concerning a certain matter.

[11] Leudegar the man of God saw that the king had not changed his mind. The king, at the urging of his followers, would inflict death on him and Hector, just as he had resolved; or Hector, with no place to turn, would rise up against the despised king, just as the king's men feared. Leudegar was not concerned for his own life but for those who had come to him for protection, and looking for safety, chose for the time being to find refuge in flight rather than offer a pretext for the church to be bloodied by his martyrdom or to be ravaged during the celebrations of Christ's resurrection, or for those who had turned to him to lose their lives without any consideration. For surely there is no one who thinks that he was afraid even of martyrdom.

In fact, when earlier he got word of his own destruction through a monk by the name of Berthar on the day of the Lord's supper, the next day, that of the passion of the Lord, he went to the king's palace, and, bursting in uninvited, tried to offer his blood to Christ on the very day that Christ poured forth his own blood for the salvation of the world. On the same day the king even tried to strike him with his own hand, but, because of the respect due the day, was prevented from doing so by the wise advice of certain magnates. One must believe without doubt that he was saved at that moment by heaven so that the furnace of lengthy persecution would purify any impurity he might have acquired from living a human life, which cannot be led without fault. And placed like pure gold in the crown of his own king, he would afterward shine like gleaming jewels by the power of miracle.

Those who were waiting to exploit this opportunity thereupon mounted a swift pursuit of him. Hector was killed on the spot; and since he manfully tried to defend himself, as was God's will, it took large numbers to overcome him and some of those accompanying him. And it is believed to be not impossible that indulgence can be obtained from God through the merits of the holy martyr for those souls who along with him tried innocently to ward off the storm of persecution.

[12] As soon as Leudegar, the servant of God, had been taken into custody by certain of his pursuers, they immediately sent word to Childeric that the deed was done; he who had successfully arrested Leudegar thought that he would enjoy the utmost favor of the king. On the advice of the magnates and bishops, orders were given for Leudegar to be taken to the monastery of Luxeuil until such time as they could deliberate together as to what to do with a man of such rank.

In the meantime, Childeric inquired of all the chief officials of the palace together what judgment they would determine for this saint of God, and they answered unanimously that, if the king granted him his life, he should order Leudegar to remain in perpetual exile in Luxeuil. The king immediately authorized the judgment decreed against him. Some bishops and priests, for their part, agreed to it to free Leudegar for the moment from the anger of the king.

For, led astray by the advice of the wicked, the king had given orders for him to be taken from Luxeuil and placed at the disposal of his accusers as an object

---

1 See 1 Sam. 3: 4.

of mockery for them to have killed as they wished, as formerly Herod had intended the Jews to do to Peter.[1] Now there was present a venerable abbot of the church of Saint Symphorian by the name of Hermenar—it was to him that the king assigned the city at the request of the people after the death of the man of God—and he repeatedly threw himself at the feet of the king begging him over and over again to allow Leudegar to remain in Luxeuil and not to have him led into the waiting arms of cruel men whose anger the devil had inflamed against him. Because of entreaties of this kind, Leudegar was at that time at last saved from death. But some were of the false belief that Hermenar often visited the lodging of the king to be first among Leudegar's accusers and thereby more readily get permission to hold the bishopric. At length the truth emerged, and because the eye of the flesh does not see spiritual love, the deeds of that man afterwards bore witness, for as long as Leudegar was still alive he tended to his needs with devout charity as best he could.

[13] In those days Ebroin was still lodged as an exile in Luxeuil, tonsured and in a monk's garb, pretending to act with the peaceable intention that as long as both he and Leudegar were serving the same but separate sentences of exile they would lead their lives in harmony.

In the meantime, after these events had taken place, divine vengeance did not refrain long from imposing its judgment on Childeric. For his loose behavior among the palace magnates grew worse. Then one of them, who found this more troubling than the others, gave him his death wound as he was hunting in safety in the forest.

[14] But before that happened, while a certain two dukes to whom the orders had been given to remove Leudegar from Luxeuil were waiting to do that, one of their servants agreed to put Leudegar to the sword if he saw him outside Luxeuil. When the time came to do it, an unbearable trembling so engulfed the man's heart that he not only said in a public confession that he was contemplating such a momentous deed but also told why. Trembling, he threw himself

at Leudegar's feet begging to be forgiven by him for this wickedness.

[15] As soon as Childeric's death was suddenly announced, certain of those who had been sentenced to exile at his command returned without fear, like poisonous snakes after wintertime that come forth from their caves in the spring. Their wild rage caused a huge disturbance in the homeland, so that it was openly believed that the approach of the Antichrist was at hand.[2] As for those who should have been in charge of the regions, they rose against each other, and those who should have kept the bonds of peace together began to provoke each other with hateful deeds. And as long as the king was not established on top, each one did what seemed right according to his own desires, without fear of punishment. Indeed we recognized at that time that the anger of God became manifest, so that even a star that the astrologers call a comet was seen in the sky [August 676]: on its rising, they say, the land is thrown into confusion by famine, by the succession of kings, and by disturbance among the nations, and destruction by the sword is imminent. It is certain that all these events plainly happened after that. But as it is written that the foolish cannot be corrected by words, much less by portents, they returned from exile with evil intent. They made the claim that whatever they had suffered for their crimes was the fault of Leudegar's supporters.

[16] In these days the man of God was held in custody by the aforementioned dukes for safety's sake and had by now recently been taken by them from Luxeuil. At that very moment divine grace had granted its servant a venerable honor whereby those same dukes, their wives, all their servants and their households, and also the common people in those districts, were joined together in such love of him that, if the need had arisen, they would not have hesitated to sacrifice themselves on his behalf. When those who were holding the servant of God in their custody informed the other authorities round about that they could see that divine grace was upon the servant of God, they now came together in pious Christian love to support

---

1 See Acts 12: 3-4.
2 The false Christ who was expected to rule as an antagonist to Christ before the Second Coming—and triumph—of Christ himself.

him. Reaching an agreement among themselves, they affirmed that, as long as the disorderly confusion that had arisen prevailed in those districts, holy Leudegar would be protected with their help should anyone try to do harm to him before they had also raised Theuderic to the kingship.

In those days Ebroin also came forth from Luxeuil, like Julian [the Apostate] who pretended to live the life of a monk.[1] And since he was immediately mobbed by a swarm of friends as well as servants, the aforesaid exiles, who were seeking to serve him—and an evil service it was, tacked together from their own claim of injustice—made him leader. This way they could use Ebroin's help and advice to take vengeance on the man of God all together. Ebroin himself raised his venomous head, and like a viper restoring its poison, he pretended to be a follower of Theuderic, hurrying to his side for that reason as quickly as possible.

[17] As the man of God was traveling quickly along the same road with his above-mentioned allies, it happened that, when they were less than a day's journey from the city of Autun, Ebroin, forgetting the pledge of friendship he had once made and at the urging of his associates, would have seized him at that point, had he not been prevented by the advice of Genesius, metropolitan of Lyon, or been frightened by the strong band accompanying Leudegar. Again Ebroin feigned friendship, and joining forces they reached the city together.

The church rejoiced at the restored presence of its shepherd, the streets were strewn with fresh boughs, the deacons prepared candles, the clergy celebrated with singing, the whole city rejoiced at the advent of its bishop after the storm of persecution. And not undeservedly was the display of praise offered to him, for in the presence of God he rushed toward the crown of martyrdom, and there, as part of the advent of their pastor, they made ready pleasures for his enemies.

The next day Leudegar and Ebroin moved on together so that they might arrive at a meeting with Theuderic united.

[18] The journey begun, they went to meet the king, but in the meantime, almost in the middle of the trip, the tyrant Ebroin abandoned their company and pressed straight on to his own people, tossing aside his clerical status and returning to his wife behind the holy veil [i.e., she was now a nun] "as a dog returns to its vomit."[2] He who could not serve in the camp of Christ took up the weapons of the world with his enemies. And whereas he had now abandoned faith and God, he showed himself an open enemy of his earthly lord.

Now Theuderic had already recovered the kingdom and was staying safely at the time at the villa of Nogent-les-Vierges when Ebroin attacked swiftly with Austrasians. Who can recount fully the plundering that then took place of the royal treasury and of the vessels of the church that previous Catholic princes had devoutly conferred on the Lord's sanctuary out of Christian love, and who can recount the killing of Theuderic's mayor of the palace?

[19] The reason Ebroin committed this evil was that he was furnished with advice by diabolical and envious men. Their complaint was that they had been brought down by the punishment they deserved. Since they saw that the whole realm had faithfully taken Theuderic's side, that he was now established in the kingship, and that Leudegar the servant of God was living in his own city with the king's favor, envious, they began to be tormented by spite again. For as long as the just were standing tall, the wicked would be unable to make a comeback. Under the influence of the devil, who stripped them of faith, and now blinded, they could devise no truthful strategy for bringing about the ruin of the man of God; and so they resorted to greater destruction by inventing a lie: with this they introduced into the kingdom great evil and devastating slaughter in persecuting many people....

[Ebroin and his faction controlled the kingdom in the name of a "certain young lad," Clovis, who was said to be the son of Clothar III and rightful king. They now carried through the plan to get rid of Leudegar by bringing him to trial at the palace.]

[33] ... When Leudegar had been brought forward into the midst of the assembly [of bishops], they tried

---

1 Emperor Julian (r.361–363), called "the Apostate," was vilified by Christians. He was never a monk.
2 Prov. 26: 11.

to get from him a confession that he had been privy to the killing of Childeric. Then realizing that again conflict threatened him because of a diabolical fiction, Leudegar said that, just as he did not absolve himself from human wrongdoing, so too he had never advised this deed, but declared that God knew this rather than man. They interrogated him for some time but could not get anything else out of him. So they tore apart his tunic from top to bottom, and the impious tyrant gave orders for him to be handed over to a certain Chrodobert, who was count of the palace at the time, and for his life in this world to be taken from him by a stroke of the sword.

The martyr of God found joy in all his suffering, for he could sense the approach of the martyr's crown that was due to him as a reward from God. Now Chrodobert took him to his own residence. And he obtained such a heavenly blessing on his arrival that, when all those living there saw this plainly, they abandoned their own sins by confessing and eagerly took refuge in the healing medicine of penance. God had adorned his servant with this gift so that whenever he was handed over as an exile to be treated badly, those who received him, on the contrary, all paid him the reverence due from servants.

[34] At last arrived the day of death on which his persecution came to an end. At that time the results of a judicial decision were issued by the palace that Leudegar must live no longer. The impious Ebroin, fearing that faithful Christians would pay Leudegar the respect of a martyr, gave orders for a well to be found deep in the woods and his mutilated corpse to be sunk in it so that, once the mouth of the well was filled in with earth and stones, people would not know where he was buried.

Meanwhile Leudegar, by his preaching to Chrodobert, had already begun to some extent to bring about the latter's conversion. Because Chrodobert could not bear to look at the death of the man of God, he charged two of his servants to carry out the orders he had been given. When this news reached his house, his wife began to weep in bitter distress because such a cruel and shameful act had become the duty of her husband.

[35] When the man of God saw that his end was now at hand, he began to comfort the weeping woman, saying, "Please do not weep over my passing. No demand for vengeance will ever be made against you for my death, but rather a blessing will be given by God from heaven if you devoutly bury my body in its grave."

And when he had spoken these words, he said goodbye at the urging of the servants and was taken to the woods for them to carry out the sentence of the order.

Now they had previously found a well where they could hide his body as they had been told; but they never found it again. While looking for the well, they wandered hopelessly about and on this account put off killing him. In the meantime the martyr of God was allowed to prostrate himself in prayer and to entrust his passing to God. To both of his killers, who were looming over him, he began to predict the future through the spirit of prophecy. One of them, sparked by the ancient enemy, was quite anxious to carry out the deed. But the other, who was a gentle man, tremblingly begged him not to take vengeance on Leudegar.

Leudegar addressed the two of them.

"You, who follow orders against your will," he said, "confess your previous sins immediately to a priest and by doing penance you shall also escape the consequences of this deed."

To the other he said, "And as for you, if you do not do the same, you shall have to be delivered up immediately to God for swift vengeance."

Again, prostrating himself in prayer, he confidently entrusted his soul to Christ the lord. And getting up, he extended his neck and bade the executioner do what he had been ordered to do. And when the man we mentioned above suddenly cut off his head, a chorus of angels, rejoicing, conducted the spirit of the blessed martyr to heaven to be presented to the Lord so he might reign in heaven with all the saints. There in joyful company of the saints is our lord Jesus Christ, who with the Father and holy Spirit lives and reigns through the course of the ages …

2.14 The settlement of disputes: *Judgment of Childebert III* (709 or 710). Original in Latin.

IN THE MEROVINGIAN period, as today, most disputes were probably settled out of court. Nevertheless, some did lead to formal action in assemblies or meetings. Normally a document was drawn up, called a *placitum*, reporting on the proceedings and the outcome. These were kept by the institution that won the case. In the judgment presented below, King Childebert presided over an assembly at which Abbot Dalfinus of the monastery of Saint-Denis (near Paris) litigated against Grimoald, mayor of the palace. Dalfinus claimed for his monastery all the tolls collected from merchants at the annual fair held at Saint-Denis. While most such disputes were real, this one seems to have been "fictive"—a way for the abbot of Saint-Denis to get public reaffirmation of rights that had long been granted to his monastery. As in real cases, the proceedings included the testimony of witnesses and the production of written documents, in this case "the directives" of former kings who had issued such grants to Saint-Denis against the interest of the "fisc"—the king's own treasury. What factors might lead you to argue that the fair at Saint-Denis generated a lot of income? What might lead you to conclude the opposite—that these revenues were negligible? What might be the uses of a fictive dispute for the abbot—or even for the mayor of the palace?

[Source: *From Roman to Merovingian Gaul: A Reader*, ed. and trans. Alexander Callander Murray (Peterborough, ON: Broadview Press, 2000), pp. 585-87.]

Childebert [III], king of the Franks, to those of illustrious rank.

Representatives of the venerable Dalfinus, abbot of the basilica of our own special patron Saint Dionysius [i.e., Saint-Denis], wherein lies the precious body of this lord, came before us and our leading men in our palace at Montmacq. They claimed in opposition to the representatives of the illustrious Grimoald, mayor of our palace, that over a long period of time our grandfather the late Clovis [II], and after him our uncle Childeric [II] and our father Theuderic [III], as well as our brother Clothar [III, IV, Clovis III?] had issued directives granting to that basilica of Saint Dionysius the entire toll collected from all merchants, whether of Saxon or other nationality, who attend the fair held on the holy feast of Lord Dionysius [9 October]; as a consequence of the grant, they said, the fisc was precluded at that time [of Clovis II] and later from exacting or collecting on its own behalf tolls from those merchants either there, at the fair, or within the district of Paris or within the city of Paris; the basilica of Saint Dionysius, they said, had been granted and awarded this right in its entirety for all time.

They then produced the directives of the aforesaid princes to that effect for the court to read. Those directives were deposited and examined, and it was determined that such a grant in its entirety had been made to that house of God by those princes.

Then the representatives of Dalfinus said that the representatives of Grimoald, mayor of our palace as well as count of the district of Paris, collected half the toll from them, removing its benefits from the basilica.

The representatives of the mayor of our palace Grimoald replied on the contrary that for a long time it had been customary for the house of Saint Dionysius to receive one half the toll and the count the other on behalf of the fisc.

The representatives of Saint Dionysius contended in reply that Gaerin, [Gaerin was the brother of Leudegar; see above, p. 112] the late count of Paris, introduced this custom by force and at times collected half the toll from them; but those representatives informed the palace of this and, they said, always renewed their royal directives without diminution of the grant.

Again an examination was undertaken of numerous people and of the directives that the aforesaid princes had granted originally and had subsequently confirmed without diminution of the grant.

And so, with Grimoald's agreement and that of many other loyal followers of the king, a determination was made and judgment given that the representatives of Grimoald were on behalf of our fisc to invest that toll in its entirety once again upon the agents of the abbot by means of a pledge. And so they did.

Whereas it is known that the suit has been brought forward and settled, investigated and adjudicated, in just such a fashion as the illustrious count of our palace Rigofred has reported, it is our command, now that the previous directives granted to the monastery have been examined, that for all time the aforesaid monastery of Saint Dionysius, wherein that most precious lord's body rests, and abbot Dalfinus and his successors have successfully sued for and laid claim to that entire toll collected at the feast of Saint Dionysius, both that which arises on the lands of the basilica and later in Paris.

In earlier times, the market was moved on account of a catastrophe from the site of Saint Dionysius and was established in the city of Paris between the basilicas of Saints Martin and Laurence. The abbey received directives from the aforesaid princes to the effect that the aforesaid basilica of Saint Dionysius should get the toll in its entirety either there or wherever it set up to conduct business and commerce on the occasion of that feast. In view of these circumstances, if it happens that on account of some catastrophe or interruption the fair should be moved somewhere else, let that aforesaid toll, because of our devotion to that holy place, in present and future times, remain granted to and bestowed upon that house of God to offset the cost of lighting. And between our fisc and the representatives of Saint Dionysius, may all dispute and contention be laid to rest.

Actulius has been ordered to certify this.

Given, under auspicious signs, in December, on the thirteenth day, in the sixteenth year of our reign at Montmacq.

2.15 Reforming the Continental Church: *Letters to Boniface* (723-726). Original in Latin.

BORN IN WESSEX, ENGLAND, Boniface (c.672-754) entered a monastery at the age of seven, where he received an excellent education. In 716 he undertook the first of his missionary efforts, going to Frisia, where he followed in the footsteps of earlier English evangelists. In 717 he traveled to Rome—where he changed his name from the Anglo-Saxon "Winfrith" to the Latinate "Boniface"—and received a commission from Pope Gregory II (r.715-731) to evangelize the people living east of the Rhine—in Bavaria and Thuringia. In fact, these regions had already been Christianized, and Boniface spent most of his time reforming churches already established rather than preaching the Word to pagans. In all of his work he was avidly supported by Charles Martel (d.741), the powerful mayor of the palace in Francia (as we may now call Gaul). After Charles's death, Boniface focused on reforming the Frankish church itself, which he did through a series of Church councils that he called between 742 and 744. A year later he became archbishop of Mainz, but not long thereafter he returned to Frisia, which had not yet been Christianized, and there suffered a martyr's death in 754. The letters below come from Boniface's earliest period in Germany. In the first, Charles Martel offers him protection. In the second, Gregory II commends him to the Thuringians, whose Christianization he does not recognize. In the third, the pope instructs Boniface on particular matters of Christian practice. Why did Gregory II support Boniface's work? In what ways did the model of Pope Gregory the Great's missionary work in England (see the letters in Bede, pp. 98-102) inspire Gregory II? What might explain Charles Martel's support of Boniface?

[Source: *The Letters of Saint Boniface*, trans. Ephraim Emerton (New York: W.W. Norton, 1940), pp. 47, 52-56.]

[Charles Martel commends Boniface to all Frankish officials, 723]

To the holy and apostolic bishops, our fathers in Christ, and to the dukes, counts, vicars, palace officials, all our lower agents, our circuit judges [*missi*] and all who are our friends, the noble Charles, mayor of the palace, your well-wisher, sends greeting.

Be it known to you that the apostolic man in Christ, Father Boniface, a man of apostolic character and a bishop, came to us with the request that we should take him under our guardianship and protection. Know that we have acquiesced with pleasure and, hence, have granted his petition before witnesses and commanded that this written order signed by our own hand be given him, that wheresoever he may choose to go, he is to be left in peace and protected as a man under our guardianship and protection to the end that he may render and receive justice. If he shall be in any need or distress which cannot be remedied according to law, let him and those dependent upon him come in peace and safety before our presence, so that no person may hinder or do him injury, but that he may rest at all times in peace and safety under our guardianship and protection.

And that this may the more surely be given credit, I have signed it with my own hand and sealed it with our ring.

[Pope Gregory II commends Boniface to the Thuringians, December 724]

Gregory, servant of the servants of God, to all the people of the Thuringians.

The Lord Jesus Christ, Son of God and very God, descended from Heaven, was made man, deigned to suffer and be crucified for us, was buried, rose from the dead on the third day, and ascended into Heaven. To His holy Apostles and disciples He said: "Go forth and teach all peoples, baptizing them in the name of the Father, the Son, and the Holy Spirit (Matt. 28:19)"; and He promised those who believed in Him eternal life.

We, therefore, desiring that you may rejoice with us forever where there is no ending, neither sorrow nor any bitterness, but eternal glory, have sent to you our most holy brother, Bishop Boniface, that he may baptize you and teach you the doctrine of Christ and lead you out of error into the way of safety, that you may win salvation and life eternal. But do you be obedient unto him in all things, honor him as your father, and incline your hearts to his instruction, for we have sent him to you, not for any temporal gain, but for the profit of your souls. Therefore love God and receive baptism in his name, for the Lord our God has prepared for those who love him things which the eye of man hath not seen, and which have never entered into the heart of man. Depart from evil doing, and do what is right. Worship not idols, neither sacrifice offerings of flesh to them, for God does not accept such things, but observe and do as our brother Boniface shall direct, and you and your children shall be in safety forever.

Build also a house where this your father and bishop may live and churches where you may offer up your prayers, that God may forgive your sins and grant you eternal life.

[Replies of Pope Gregory II to questions of Boniface, November 22, 726]

Gregory, servant of the servants of God, to his most reverend and holy brother and fellow bishop Boniface.

Your messenger, the pious priest Denuald, has brought us the welcome news that you are well and prospering, with the help of God, in the service for which you were sent. He also brought a letter from you showing that the field of the Lord which had been lying fallow, bristling with the thorns of unbelief, has received the plowshare of your instruction, plowing in the seed of the word, and is bringing forth an abundant harvest of true belief.

In this same letter you inserted several paragraphs of inquiries as to the faith and teaching of this Holy and Apostolic Roman Church. And this was well done; for the blessed apostle Peter stands as the fountainhead of the apostolate and the episcopate. And to you who consult us about ecclesiastical matters we show what decision you have to take according to the teaching of apostolic tradition, and we do this not as if by our own personal authority, but by the grace of Him who opens the mouth of the dumb and makes eloquent the tongues of infants.

You ask first within what degrees of relationship marriage may take place. We reply: strictly speaking, in so far as the parties know themselves to be related they ought not to be joined together. But since moderation is better than strictness of discipline, especially toward so uncivilized a people, they may contract marriage after the fourth degree.

As to your question, what a man is to do if his wife is unable, on account of disease, to fulfill her wifely duty: it would be well if he could remain in a state of continence. But, since this is a matter of great difficulty, it is better for him who cannot refrain to take a wife. He may not, however, withdraw his support from the one who was prevented by disease, provided she be not involved in any grievous fault.

In regard to a priest or any cleric accused by the people: unless the evidence of the witnesses to the charge against him is positive, let him take oath before the assembly, calling as witness of his innocence Him to whom all things are plain and open; and so let him keep his proper standing.

In the case of one confirmed by a bishop, a repetition of this rite is prohibited.

In the celebration of the Mass, the form is to be observed which our Lord Jesus Christ used with his disciples. He took the cup and gave it to them, saying: "This cup is the new testament in my blood; this do ye as oft as ye take it." Wherefore it is not fitting that two or three cups should be placed on the altar when the ceremony of the Mass is performed.

As to sacrificial foods: You ask whether, if a believer makes the life-giving sign of the cross above them, it is permitted to eat them or not. A sufficient answer is given in the words of the blessed apostle Paul: "If any man say unto you, This is offered in sacrifice unto idols, eat not for his sake who showed it, and for conscience' sake."[1]

You ask further, if a father or mother shall have placed a young son or daughter in a cloister under the discipline of a rule, whether it is lawful for the child after reaching the years of discretion to leave the cloister and enter into marriage. This we absolutely forbid, since it is an impious thing that the restraints of desire should be relaxed for children offered to God by their parents.

You mention also that some have been baptized by adulterous and unworthy priests without being questioned whether they believe, as it is in the ritual. In such cases you are to follow the ancient custom of the Church. He who has been baptized in the name of the Father, Son, and Holy Spirit may on no account be baptized again; for he has received the gift of His grace not in the name of the one who baptizes, but in the name of the Trinity. Let the word of the Apostle be observed: "One God, one faith, one baptism."[2] We require you to convey spiritual instruction to such persons with especial zeal.

As to young children taken from their parents and not knowing whether they have been baptized or not, reason requires you to baptize them, unless there be someone who can give evidence in the case.

Lepers, if they are believing Christians, may receive the body and blood of the Lord, but they may not take food together with persons in health.

You ask whether, in the case of a contagious disease or plague in a church or monastery, those who are not yet attacked may escape danger by flight. We declare this to be the height of folly; for no one can escape from the hand of God.

Finally, your letter states that certain priests and bishops are so involved in vices of many sorts that their lives are a blot upon the priesthood and you ask whether it is lawful for you to eat with or to speak with them, supposing them not to be heretics. We answer, that you by apostolic authority are to admonish and persuade them and so bring them back to the purity of church discipline. If they obey, you will save their souls and win reward for yourself. You are not to avoid conversation or eating at the same table with them. It often happens that those who are slow in coming to a perception of the truth under strict discipline may be led into the paths of righteousness by the influence of their table companions and by gentle admonition. You ought also to follow this same rule in dealing with those chieftains who are helpful to you.

This, my dear brother, is all that need be said with the authority of the Apostolic See. For the rest we im-

---

1 I Cor. 10: 28.
2 Eph. 4: 5.

plore the mercy of God, that He who has sent you into that region in our stead and with apostolic authority and has caused the light of truth to shine into that dark forest by means of your words may mercifully grant the increase, so that you may reap the reward of your labors and we may find remission for our sins.

God keep you in safety, most reverend brother.

Given on the tenth day before the Kalends of December, in the tenth year of our most pious and august Lord Leo, by God crowned emperor, in the tenth year of his consulship and the seventh of the Emperor Constantine his son, in the tenth indiction.[1]

2.16 The papacy: *The Life of Gregory II* in *The Book of the Pontiffs* (c.730). Original in Latin.

The Book of the Pontiffs (Liber Pontificalis) is a collection of biographies of the popes, starting with St. Peter and ending with Pius II (d.1464), but its first version was begun in the sixth century and continued until the end of the ninth. The biography of Gregory II (r.715-731) allows us to glimpse from a different angle the pope who supported Boniface (see his letters above, pp. 122-24), who dealt with the start of iconoclasm, and whose difficult relations with the Lombards—the rulers of much of Italy—and friction with the Byzantines would eventually lead (after Gregory's death) to the pope's decision to abandon the Byzantine emperor and seek protection from the West. In what ways does this document suggest that events involving the Muslims contributed to this crucial shift in loyalties towards the West?

[Source: *The Lives of the Eighth-Century Popes (Liber Pontificalis)*, trans. Raymond Davis (Liverpool: Liverpool University Press, 1992), pp. 3-14 (somewhat modified).]

Gregory of Roman origin, son of Marcellus, held the see 15 years 8 months 24 days. From early youth he was brought up in the patriarchate, he was made subdeacon.[2] Next he was advanced to the order of the diaconate and set out with the holy pontiff Constantine for the imperial city.[3] He was chaste, learned in divine Scripture, eloquent and of resolute mind, a defender of the church establishment and a strenuous adversary of its assailants.

2. In his time John, bishop of Constantinople, sent his synodic letter, and the pontiff adopted the same terms in his reply.[4]

At St. Paul's [at Rome] he replaced the roof beams which had broken through age, and he roofed the greater part of the basilica which had fallen down, and

rebuilt the altar and the silver canopy which had been broken by the collapse. He also repaired St. Laurence's outside the walls, which with its roof beams broken was near to collapse, and he restored the long-failed water supply to the same church by joining up the pipes. He renewed various basilicas which were collapsing, which would take too long to list.

3. Through bishop Boniface he preached the message of salvation in Germany [see the *Letters of Boniface* above, p. 122], and by teaching light to a people that sat in darkness he converted them to Christ, and he bathed the greater part of that people with the water of holy baptism.

The holy pope renewed the deserted monasteries alongside St. Paul's, and by installing monks as God's

---

1 The letter is thus dated by the reign of Byzantine Emperor Leo III (r.717–741) and his son Constantine, for whom see *The Synod of 754* (above, p. 81) and the *Chronicle of Theophanes* (above, p. 85).

2 The "patriarchate" refers to the episcopal living quarters, which may at this time have doubled as a school. Gregory was the first Roman to be elected after a succession of seven Greek or Syrian popes.

3 The "imperial city" refers to Constantinople. Constantine was pope 708–715.

4 A "synodic letter" was a letter containing a profession of faith and sent out by a new pope or patriarch. John VI was Patriarch of Constantinople 712–715.

servants he established the long failed community, so that three times by day and night they should recite Matins.[1]

He also established the old people's home close to the church of God's holy mother *ad praesepe*[2] and restored the nearby monastery of St. Andrew's called Barbara's, which had both been abandoned without a single monk; he admitted monks and arranged for them to perform Terce, Sext, None and Matins on weekdays in the church of God's holy mother and his pious arrangement survives even now.[3]

4. Then on this great man's advice and reproof King Liutprand confirmed the restoration of the patrimony of the Cottian Alps; king Aribert had made this donation and he had repeated it.[4]

In his time there occurred a sign in the moon: it was bloody until midnight.

Theodo, duke of the Bavarian people, with others of his people was the first of that people to come and pray at the home of St. Peter.

5. In his time the Emperor Anastasius [II; r.713-715] made ready a fleet of ships and sent them to the districts of Alexandria against the Agareni[5] (whom God destroy!). But before they arrived at their intended destination, they changed their plan and in mid journey returned to the imperial city; seeking out the orthodox Theodosius [III; r.715-717], they elected him emperor and after compelling him to accept the imperial throne they confirmed him as such. So Anastasius made his way to the fortified city of Nicaea with those citizens and such of the army as he could; there he battled with the fleet on board which the emperor Theodosius had been, and about 7,000 of the army were cut down. Anastasius' faction was defeated and asked for a safe-conduct, and when he had been given

it on oath, he was made a cleric and consecrated as a priest. The moment Theodosius entered the imperial city, he set up on its original monument and place the venerable image on which the six holy synods were depicted and which had been taken down by the unspeakable Philippicus.[6] So it was that by the fervor of his faith all dispute in the church ended.

6. The river called Tiber then left its channel and spread itself over the plains; it swelled in spate and entered the Gate called Flaminia. Meanwhile in some places it even lapped over the walls, and it extended itself through the streets beyond St. Mark's basilica, so that on the Via Lata the river water rose up to one and a half times a man's height. The waters dispersed themselves from St. Peter's Gate to the Milvian Bridge, and the force of the river took it as far as near the Remissa.[7] It overturned houses and desolated fields, uprooting trees and crops and sweeping them away. At that time the greater part of the Romans could not even sow, which meant that great trouble was in store. For seven days the water held Rome in its grip. So litanies were held repeatedly by the lord pope, and when he continued in prayer and litanies, on the eighth day God showed his mercy and removed the water, and the river returned to its own channel [716/7].

7. At that time too the Lombards, though pretending peace, seized the castrum [fortification] of Cumae; at this news all were utterly dismayed at the loss of the castrum.[8] The holy pontiff urged and advised the Lombards to return it—he declared in his writings that if they would not do so their treachery would incur God's wrath. He was even willing to give them many gifts to get them to restore it. But in their haughtiness they would endure neither to hear his ad-

---

1   Matins (or Vigils) was one of the offices of prayer chanted by monks; see *The Benedictine Rule* above, pp. 31-32.

2   "God's holy mother *ad praesepe*" refers to the church of Santa Maria Maggiore. "*Ad praesepe*" means "at the manger" and refers to relics brought there from the Bethlehem manger.

3   Like Matins, Terce, Sext, and None refer to the hours of prayer service that formed the monastic liturgy.

4   Liutprand was king of the Lombards 712–744; Aribert II, Liutprand's predecessor, had been king 701–712. The Cottian Alps is a segment of the West Alps which today follows the border of France and Italy.

5   The "Agareni" refers to the Muslims.

6   Emperor Philippicus Bardanes (r.711–713), a monothelete (that is, maintaining a non-orthodox view of the nature of Christ), had taken down the image that symbolized the anti-monothelite 6th Ecumenical Council of 681. Theodosius restored it.

7   Probably near St. Peter's square.

8   This refers to the Lombards in the Duchy of Benevento, to Rome's south. Led by Duke Romuald, they captured the defensive stronghold (*castrum*) at Cumae, in the duchy of Rome.

vice nor to return it. This made the holy pontiff smart greatly. He entrusted himself to his hope in God and supplied leadership by devoting himself to advising the duke and people of Naples, writing to them every day how they were to act. Obeying his instruction they adopted a plan and entered the walls of that castrum by force in the quiet of the night—that is to say, the duke John, with Theodimus the subdeacon and rector, and the army. They killed about 300 Lombards including their gastald, and they captured more than 500 and took them to Naples. In this way they managed to get the Castrum back. Even so the holy pope paid the 70 £ of gold he had promised for its ransom.[1]

8. The holy Jerusalem church[2] had for a long time been roofless and all the porticos around were broken through age. He brought roof beams and roofed and repaired it. In the same church he provided a marble ambo [pulpit], and enriched it with various linens and services.

11.[3] Then the unspeakable race of the Agareni crossed the strait from the place called Ceuta, entered Spain, and slaughtered most of it along with their king.[4] They subdued all the rest with their property and in this way occupied that province for 10 years. But in the eleventh year [721] a general campaign of the Franks against the Saracens [Muslims] surrounded them and cut them down. The letter of the Franks to the pontiff mentioned that 375,000 were killed on one day; they said that only 1,500 Franks had died in the war. As for the three sponges, the pontiff had sent them as a blessing the previous year from those provided for use on his own table; at the time the war was beginning Eudes, prince of Aquitania, had given them to his people to consume in small amounts, and of those who had shared in them not one had been injured or killed.

9. He instituted that on the Thursdays in Lent there should be a celebration of mass in churches; this used not to occur.

He built a new oratory indeed in the patriarchate in the name of St. Peter and adorned it with various metals.

12. Meanwhile in that same period the unspeakable Saracens besieged Constantinople for two years, but God was against them and the greater number there were cut down by famine and war, and they fell back in confusion, Leo then being emperor. It is said that of that city's population 300,000 of all ages were destroyed by scarcity and plague.

10. After his mother's death he reconstructed his own house in honor of Christ's martyr St. Agatha from the ground up, inserting chambers and all that was needed for a monastery; and there he presented city and country estates for the monks' needs; and in this church of St. Agatha he built anew a canopy.

13. Then the Lombards seized the Castrum of Narni.[5] Liutprand king of the Lombards [r.712-744] in a general campaign proceeded to Ravenna and besieged it for some days, and seizing the Castrum of Classe they took many captives and removed untold wealth.[6]

14. Some time later the duke Basil, the cartularius [army commander] Jordanes, and the subdeacon John surnamed Lurion, adopted a plan to kill the pontiff.[7] Marinus the imperial spatharius [duke] who held the duchy of Rome—he had been sent from the imperial city with the emperor's order for this—gave them his consent, but they could find no opportunity. By God's judgment he was weakened by arthritis and so withdrew from Rome. 15. Afterwards Paul the patrician was sent to Italy as exarch [Byzantium's chief official in Italy], and again they were thinking of carrying out the crime. But their plan was made clear to

---

1   John was duke of Naples; Theodimus was a Roman church official. The *gastald* refers to an important local Lombard leader, just under the duke. The 70 pounds of gold was no doubt paid to Romuald, the Lombard duke.

2   This refers to Santa Croce in Gerusalemme, a church in Rome.

3   The chapters are out of order because of an error by an early editor of this text.

4   Compare this account of the Muslim conquest of Spain with the evidence from the *Treaty of Tudmir*, above, p. 92.

5   In this sentence, the "Lombards" were those of the Duchy of Spoleto. Under Duke Faraold, they took the defensive stronghold at Narni, which belonged to the Duchy of Rome but was near the border of the Duchy of Spoleto.

6   Ravenna and nearby Classe belonged to the Exarchate, Byzantine territory.

7   Basil, Jordanes, and John Lurion were local officials—thus their titles "duke" and "cartularius"—working for Byzantium. They and Marinus were probably reacting to the pope's refusal to pay the taxes that Emperor Leo III imposed in 722 or 723. Leo wanted Italy to contribute more money to its own defense. Gregory's resistance to the taxes was tantamount to political rebellion.

the Romans. They killed Jordanes and John Lurion, while Basil was made a monk and his life came to an end in confinement somewhere. 16. In those days on the order of the emperors, Paul the patrician, who had been exarch, was attempting to kill the pontiff for the reason that he was preventing the imposition of tax in the province. [He wanted to] strip the churches of their wealth as had been done elsewhere and ordain someone else in [the pope's] place.

After him another spatharius [duke] was sent with mandates to remove the pontiff from his see; again, Paul the patrician sent from Ravenna some men he was able to pervert, along with his count and some men from the castra [fortifications], to carry out this crime. But the Romans rose up, and the Lombards on every side—the Spoletines and the dukes of the Lombards from all areas surrounding the borders of the Romans—came to defend the pontiff at the Milvian Bridge and prevented it.

17. In the mandates he later sent, the emperor had decreed that no image of any saint, martyr or angel should be kept, as he declared them all accursed;[1] if the pontiff would agree he would have the emperor's favor; if he prevented this being carried out as well he would be degraded from his office. So the man [Gregory] despised the prince's profane mandate, and now he armed himself against the emperor as against an enemy, denouncing his heresy and writing that Christians everywhere must guard against the impiety that had arisen. So all the Pentapolitans and the armies of the Venetiae rose in resistance to the emperor's mandate—never would they stoop to killing this pontiff; rather they would manfully strive to defend him and to subject Paul the exarch, the one who had sent him [i.e., Emperor Leo], and his adherents to an anathema.[2] Throughout Italy, scorning the exarch's arrangement, they all elected their own dukes, and in this way they all tried to achieve freedom for the pontiff and themselves. Once the emperor's wickedness was known, the whole of Italy adopted a plan: they would elect themselves an emperor and take him to Constantinople; but the pontiff restrained this plan

as he hoped for the prince's conversion.

18. In this same period the duke Exhilaratus, taken in and prompted by the devil, was, along with his son Hadrian, holding the districts of Campania; they were leading the people astray to obey the emperor and kill the pontiff. Then all the Romans pursued, caught, and killed him with his son saying they had written to the emperor against the pontiff; and after him they also blinded the duke Peter.[3]

There was dispute in the districts of Ravenna. Some agreed with the emperor's iniquity, others sided with the pontiff and those who kept the faith. There was strife between them, and they killed Paul the patrician. The castra in Emilia—Ferronianum, Monteveglio and Verabulum, with their towns Buxum and Persiceto—and in the Pentapolis the city of Osimo, surrendered to the Lombards.

19. Some time after, the emperor sent Eutychius the patrician and eunuch to Naples to achieve what the exarch Paul, the spatharii [Byzantine dukes], and the other schemers of evil could not do. But even so, it was God's bidding that the miserable treachery did not remain secret: the appalling plan was evident to everyone: that they were attempting to violate Christ's churches, put everyone to death, and lay waste everybody's property. When he sent his own man to Rome with his written instructions for the death of the pontiff and the chief men in Rome, and when his cruel madness became known, they straightaway wanted to kill this envoy of the patrician. Only the pontiff's vigorous defense prevented this. But they anathematized the exarch Eutychius: great and small, they bound themselves under oath never to permit a pontiff who was a zealot for the Christian faith and a defender of the churches to be harmed or removed; instead they were all ready to die for his safety. Then the patrician used his envoys to promise numerous gifts to the dukes of the Lombards in all areas and to the king, to persuade them to give up helping the pontiff. They wrote back scorning the man's detestable treachery; and Romans and Lombards bound themselves together like brothers in the tie of faith, all of them willing to undergo a glorious death

---

1 This was Leo III's first iconoclastic edict.
2 The "Pentapolitans and the armies of the Venetiae" refers to the people living in the territories in Italy under Byzantine rule.
3 Peter was the duke of Rome at the time.

in the pontiff's defense—they would not tolerate his having to endure any vexation as he fought for the true faith and the safety of Christians. 20. In this situation the father [Gregory] chose as a greater safeguard to distribute whatever he could find to the poor with a bountiful hand. He devoted himself to prayers and fasting and implored God in litanies every day; he always continued to rely more on this hope than on men, though he thanked the people for their goodwill and intention. In persuasive language he asked them all to gain credit with God by good works and be steadfast in the faith, but he urged them not to abandon their love for and loyalty to the Roman empire. In this way he soothed everyone's hearts and lessened their unremitting suffering.

TIMELINE FOR CHAPTER TWO

late 6th c. *Penitential of Finnian*

600

610-22 *Qur'an Suras*

bef. 625 Al-A`sha, *Bid Hurayra Farewell*

650

7th c. *St. Theodore of Sykeon*

680s *Passion of Leudegar*

700

8th c. *Farmer's Law*

710 *Tax Demand in Egypt*

709-10 *Judgment of Childebert III*

713 *Treaty of Tudmir*

723-26 *Letters to Boniface*

730 John of Damascus, *On Holy Images*

730 *The Life of Gregory II*

731 Bede *Ecclesiastical History*

bef. 750 `Abd al-Hamid, *Letter to the Secretaries*

750

754 Iconoclastic synod

800

bef. 818 *Chronicle of Theophanes Confessor*

THREE

CREATING NEW IDENTITIES (*c.*750–*c.*900)

THE MATERIAL BASIS OF SOCIETY

3.1 Manors in the West: *Polyptyque of the Church of Saint Mary of Marseille* (814–815). Original in Latin.

IN THE VERY YEAR THAT Charlemagne died (814), an enterprising official began to make an inventory of 13 of the estates (*villae*; sing.: *villa*) held by the cathedral of Marseille—Saint Mary, the seat of the bishop—and the monastery of Saint-Vincent of Marseille. Since the properties of Saint-Vincent were administered by the bishop of Marseille, there tended to be some overlap. The resulting register, called a *polyptyque*, provides a partial snapshot of some peasant households and the products and taxes that they owed. Each villa consisted of tenements, or small landholdings. In this polyptyque they are called *colonicae* (sing. *colonica*); in other regions they were called *mansi* (sing. *mansus*).

The entries (which are labeled A, B, and so on) follow a predicable pattern. First the villa is named. Then there are entries for each holding (*colonica*). First comes the holding's location. Next come the name and status of the male tenant (*colonus, mancipium*), the name of his wife and children, the age of the children (if under 14 or 15) or indication that the child is grown (here translated as "adult"). Sometimes the entry indicates which of the children are in school (precious evidence of village schooling in the period) and which are in holy orders, that is, ordained as priests, deacons, and so on. The adult children's husbands and wives are sometimes named, and sometimes we learn whether they were "foreigners"—that is, from outside the village. Dues are mentioned occasionally, but sometimes not. How does this document compare with a modern census? What evidence does it provide for the size and composition of peasant households in early-ninth-century Provence? In the welter of names, can you discover any family naming patterns?

[Source: *Carolingian Civilization: A Reader*, ed. Paul Edward Dutton, 2nd ed. (Peterborough, ON: Broadview Press, 2004), pp. 214–18 (slightly modified).]

B: Description of the Dependents of Saint Mary of Marseille from the Villa Domado of that Third Part, Made in the Time of the lord bishop Waldus [r.814–818], from the seventh indiction [814]

1. Holding [colonica] at Nemphas. Martinus, colonus. Wife Dominica. Bertemarus, an adult son. Desideria, an adult daughter. It pays the tax: 1 pig, 1 suckling [pig]; 2 fattened hens; 10 chickens; 40 eggs. Savarildis, an adult woman. Olisirga, a daughter 10 years old. Rica, a daughter 9 years old.
2. Holding of a colonus in vineyards. Ingoaldus, a dependent [mancipium]. Wife Unuldis. Martinus, a son; wife Magna. Onoria, a daughter, with a foreign husband. Deda, a daughter. Danobertus, an adult son. Ingolbertus, an adult son. Arubertus, an adult son.
3. Holding at Code: 1 lot without tenant.
4. Holding at Ruinolas: 1 lot without tenant.
5. In total these make 4 holdings.
6. Holding at Ursiniangas: 1 lot without tenant.

C. Description of the Dependents of Saint Mary of Marseille from the Villa of Lambisco,[1] Made in the Time of the lord bishop Waldus, from the seventh indiction

1. Holding in Siverianis. Valerius, colonus. Wife Dominica. Ducsana, a daughter 5 years old. An infant at the breast. It pays in tax: 1 pig; 1 suckling [pig]; 2 fattened hens; 10 chickens; 20 eggs.
2. In Siverianis. Valerianus, a colonus. Wife Desiderada. Anastasia, a daughter 5 years old. Stephanus, a son 4 years old. Martinus, a son 3 years old. An infant at the breast. It pays the same taxes.
3. Holding in Marte. Adjutor, a colonus. Wife Natalia. Justa, a daughter 1 year old. [It pays:] 1 pig; 1 fattened hen; 5 chickens; 20 eggs.
4. Holding in the Campo Miliario. The colonus Sidonius. Wife Lia. It pays tax similarly; [plus] 1 castrated ram.
5. Holding in Roveredo: 1 lot without tenant.
6. Holding in Dominicio. Guntardus with his infants: information required.
7. Holding in Siverianis. Mercorinus, a colonus. Wife Vina, with their infants: information required. It pays tax similarly; [plus] 1 castrated ram.
8. Holding in Rovereto: 1 lot without tenant.
9. Holding in Burbuliana: 1 lot without tenant.
10. Holding in Campo Macuni: 1 lot without tenant.
11. Holding in Plama. Maria, a female [serf]. Maria, a widow. Anastasia, an adult daughter. Eligia, a daughter 5 years old. An infant at the breast.
12. Holding in Maurisca: 1 lot without tenant.
13. Holding at Marcella, which Landefredus holds for 1 solidus.
14. In the same place, a holding [at Marcella]: 1 lot without tenant.
15. In Argentia: 1 lot without tenant.
16. Holding in Valle Quinana: 1 lot without tenant.
17. Holding in Armellaria: 1 lot without tenant.
18. Likewise the holding in Burbuliana: 1 lot without tenant.
19. Holdings in Seucia: 5 lots without tenants.
20. In total there are 22 holdings.
21. Juvinus and wife, with their infants; information required.
22. The wife of Julianus, with their infants; information required.

F. Description of the Dependents of Saint Mary of Marseille from the Villa of Betorrida,[2] Made in the Time of the lord bishop Waldus, from the seventh indiction

1. Holding in Cenazello. Dructaldus, tenant (*accola*); with his foreign wife. Dructomus, a son. Dutberta, an adult daughter. Drueterigus, a son at school. Sinderaldus, a son at school. Joannis. For pasturage: 1 denarius.[3]
2. Holding in Albiosco. Teodorus, colonus. Wife

---

1 Today this is Lambesc, near Aix-en-Provence.
2 Today Bezaudun, near Grasse.
3 A denarius (pl.: denarii) was a silver penny.

Eugenia. Marius, a deacon. Teobaldus, an adult son. Teodericus, a cleric. Ing … dus, a son 7 years old. Teodesia, a daughter 7 years old. For pasturage: 1 denarius.

3. Therein a holding: 1 lot without tenant. 2 denarii.[1]

4. Holding in Asaler. Candidus, colonus. Wife Dominica. Celsus, a son: information required. Mariberta, an adult daughter. Regitrudis, an adult daughter. Gennarius, a son, shepherd. Saviniana, a daughter: information required. It pays in tax: 1 pig, 1 sucking [pig]; 2 fattened hens; 10 chickens; 40 eggs; for pasturage: 1 castrated ram; in tribute: 1 denarius.

5. Holding without tenant in Nonticlo, which Bertarius, priest, holds in benefice. It pays tax and tribute similarly: [plus] a castrated ram.

6. Holding in the same place: 1 lot without tenant. Paulus and Valeriana, with their infants: information required. It pays tax and tribute similarly; for pasturage: 1 castrated ram.

7. Holding in Albiosco: information required.

8. Holding in Curia. Calumniosus, colonus, with a foreign wife. It pays tax: 1 denarius and similarly in tribute. Saumo, with his infants: information required.

9. Holding in the same place. Colonus Martinus. Wife Primovera. Felicis, an adult son. Deidonus, an adult son. Leobertga, an adult daughter. Martina, a daughter 6 years old. An infant at the breast. It pays tax and tribute similarly; for pasturage: 1 denarius.

10. Holding [in] Cusanulas, which Nectardus holds in benefice. It pays tax and tribute similarly.

11. Holding in Carmillo Sancto Promacio, held by the priest of the local church. It pays for pasturage: 1 denarius.

12. Holding in Cumbis: 1 lot without tenant, which Dructebertus has. For pasturage: 2 denarii.

13. Holding in Massimana. Donaldus, dependent. Wife Dominica. Domnildis, daughter. Bertarius, an adult son. Bertulfus, an adult son. Bertelaicus, an adult son. Saisa, an adult daughter. It pays for pasturage: 2 denarii.

14. Holding in Asinarius: 1 lot without tenant. For pasturage: 1 castrated ram.

15. Holding in Terciago, which Martinus holds in benefice. For pasturage: 2 denarii.

16. Holdings in Cenazellis: 2 lots without tenants. For pasturage: 1 castrated ram.

17. Holding in Tullo: 1 lot without tenant. For pasturage: 1 castrated ram. Vuarmetrudis, with her infants: information required.

18. Holding in Galiana. Cannidus, colonus. Wife Inguildis. An infant at the breast. Domecianus, a cleric. Laurada, a daughter 8 years old. It pays tax and tribute similarly. For pasturage: 2 denarii.

19. Holding in Cleo. Aquilo, an equitarius [a serf performing messenger duty on horseback]. Wife Vumiberga. Candidus, a son 6 years old. An infant at the breast. For pasturage: 1 denarius.

20. Holding in Gencianicus. Ursius, cleric. The dependent Lubus, son, with foreign wife, who ought to manage that holding.… Gencuonca, an adult daughter. Teodo, an adult son.

21. Holding in Nidis: 1 lot without tenant. Bernarius, cotidianus [owing daily service to the lord]. Wife Dominica. Magnildis, daughter: information required. Dominico, son. Bernardus, son. Teodranus, son: information required. In tribute: 1 denarius. Montigla, a female [serf], with foreign husband. Cenazello, son: information required.

22. Holding in Vencione. Ildebertus, a dependent. Wife Luborfolia. It pays tax: 2 denarii.

23. Holding in Cumbis: 1 lot without tenant. It pays for pasturage: 2 denarii.

24. Holding in Tasseriolas: 1 lot without tenant. For pasturage: 1 denarius.

25. Holding in Massimiana Sancto Promacio: belonging to the office of the local priest. Donobertus, Babilda: information required.

26. Holding in Camarjas, which Bertaldus, priest, holds.

27. We have a holding in Sugnone, a third part of that small village, and there are 10 holdings [there].

28. Holding in Camarja: 1 lot without tenant.

29. We have in Salo a third part of that small village, and there are three holdings without tenants.

---

1 Presumably this means that it pays 2 denarii when occupied by a tenant.

30. Holding in Puncianicus: 1 lot without tenant.
31. Holding in Campellis: 1 lot without tenant.
32. Holding in Rosolanis: 1 lot without tenant.
33. Holding in Speluca: 1 lot without tenant.

34. Vualdebertus, Guirbertus, Ragnebertus: information required.
35. In total that makes 49 holdings.

3.2 Commerce in the Islamic world: Abu `Uthman Al-Jahiz, *Avarice and the Avaricious* (850s?). Original in Arabic.

AL-JAHIZ (776-*c*.869) WAS BORN IN Basra and obtained an excellent education despite his family's apparent poverty. Spending much of his life in Baghdad and Samarra, he wrote on a wide variety of topics, including the satire on thrift excerpted here. His short, pointed tales in *Avarice and the Avaricious* make clear that there was a thriving money economy in Iraq under the early Abbasid caliphs. What luxuries are mentioned in this piece? What examples does it give of people squeezing out the last bit of value from their possessions? How do women participate in this "avaricious" society?

[Source: *Avarice and the Avaricious (kitâb al-bukhalâ')*, trans. Jim Colville (London: Kegan Paul International, 1999), pp. 30-33, 205.]

"Did you hear about the death of Assiduous Miriam?" a sheikh asked his colleagues. "She was a thrifty old soul, bent on improvement."

"Tell us more."

"Many were her works and long is her story but I will tell one tale to give you an idea."

"Get on with it."

"She married off her daughter when the girl was twelve, dressing her in silver and gold jewelry, satin and silk and a gown of embroidered Marwi cloth. She hung the walls with saffron-yellow drapes and prepared her own incense and perfume. This greatly enhanced her status with her own family as well as in the eyes of the in-laws.

"Where did you get all the money for this, Miriam?" her husband asked.

"From God."

"Leave out the generalities and let's have the detail! You never had any money before and you've not come into an inheritance of late. You are not dishonest and you don't pinch from me. Perhaps it's treasure you've discovered! But however you managed it, you have saved me from a full-scale, financial disaster."

"From the day that she was born," Miriam told him, "until the day of her engagement, I set aside a handful of flour every time I baked—and you know how I bake daily—and when I'd made up half a pound, I sold it."

"God has been your guiding hand and given you a judgment truly sound!" exclaimed her husband. "And He has blessed and graced the man who is your confidant and partner. When the Prophet said, 'With a few from here and a few from there, an entire camel herd is acquired,' he had this sort of thing in mind. I hope and pray your children will grow up to be like you and conduct themselves so splendidly. My joy at what you have done is surpassed only by my happiness in knowing that, through you, God may guide them, too, along the path of righteousness."

The group rose as a man to attend her funeral. They prayed for her, then turned to her husband to offer their condolences at his loss and share with him his sadness.

★

"Do not undervalue little things," announced a member of the group [Mosque loungers at Basra], "because everything big starts out small. If God wants to turn something little into something big, He makes it big. If He chooses to multiply the few and make them many, He multiplies them. What are treasuries but one *dirham* upon another, multiplied? Are their reserves not amassed by taking one *dirham* from here and one *dirham* from there? And is a *dirham* not simply one *qirat* beside other *qirats*?[1] Are the sands of the desert and the waters of the sea not exactly the same?

I know of a pedlar who acquired the rights to one hundred acres of Arab land and yet I have seen that same man selling pepper for half a *qirat* and chick-peas for a *qirat* and the only profit he made was a *habba* or two on the stalks. Nevertheless, he built up these small sums into a lot, until he had saved enough to buy one hundred acres."

"There was once a time when bronchitis had been giving me pain in my chest for days," he continued. "Some folk recommended barley sugar and others advised a syrup of almond oil, cornstarch, sugar and the like but, grudging the expense, I preferred simply to look forward to recovery. I struggled on as best as I could until, one day, a man on whom fortune had shone suggested I try sipping hot bran water. Well, I did and delicious it was, too. It dulled my appetite so much that I didn't feel hungry at all that day until noon. By the time lunch was over and I'd washed my hands, it was almost mid-afternoon and, being then so close to supper-time, I was able to pass on an evening meal. I had hit upon a canny plan of action. I proposed to the wife that she cook bran for the family's lunch every day.

'Bran water clears the chest and is a nourishing and satisfying food,' I told her. 'Allow the bran to dry out afterwards and return to its original state then, when you've collected enough, sell it for the same price you paid. Our profit will be what we take out in between.'

'I hope this bronchitis of yours will inspire other golden opportunities like the bran,' said she, 'with its benefit to your health and its saving on your pocket.'"

"I am convinced," the man concluded, "that the advice I received was divine inspiration."

"You are absolutely right," his audience concurred. "Something like that is beyond the grasp of reason. It must have been a revelation!"

★

"Tinder and flints once gave me no end of trouble," declared another. "I mean, when the edges get worn down and become rounded and blunt, the flint will not strike properly. It clicks but doesn't spark. This is a nuisance when it's raining or drizzling and you're in a hurry. Besides, the flint wears down the edges of the fire steel, leaving it in the shape of a bow. The price of a new flint is steep and the cost of a fire steel is painful. Then there's the nuisance of preparing the tinder and treating the cotton, and the smell is awful. You can't use dirty or dyed or worn cloth and linen is no use. All in all, tinder was costing me a fortune. Then, a few days ago, we were discussing the ways of the Bedouin and how they use the wood of the *markh* and *'afar* trees for kindling. Our good friend Thawri who is, as you know, a rightly guided fellow, claimed that date stalks make an excellent substitute and showed me how to use them. Well, they cost me nothing since I get them from my own land for free and, nowadays, that's all the maid uses for kindling."

"We have heard lots of helpful, money-saving hints today," said the group, "which confirms the saying of the sages of old that 'the counsel of men acts as pollen to their understanding.'"

★

"I have never known anyone as good as Mu'adha 'Anbariya at finding uses for things and putting everything in its proper place," announced a sheikh.

"What's this Mu'adha's story, then?" asked the group.

"Earlier this year, a cousin of hers brought her a sheep for sacrifice. Seeing her looking downcast, thoughtful and worried, he asked her what the matter was.

'I am a widow,' she replied, 'with no one to support me and no one to use up the meat. Those who once did have gone and I'm worried that some of this sheep will be wasted simply because I do not know what to do with it all. I do know that every part of a sheep—and of everything else, too—has been created by God for a purpose, but what can an old woman do?

---

1   The *dirham* was a silver coin weighing just under 3 grams; 1 *dirham* = 6 *daniq* = 12 *qirat* = 24 *tasouj* = 48 *habba* = 96 *fils*. The *dinar* was a gold coin weighing 4.25 grams (although silver *dinars* also existed). The *dinar* / *dirham* rate was variable but approximately 1 *dinar* = 10 or 12 *dirhams*.

What worries me is that the waste of a little will be the prelude to the waste of a lot.'

'It is obvious what to do with the horns,' she continued. 'They will get nailed to a roof beam, as hooks to hang baskets and bags on and anything else that I don't want the ants, cats, mice, cockroaches, and snakes to get into. The guts can become strings for a carding machine, which is something much needed right now. Once all the meat's been removed, the skull, the jawbone, and the rest of the bones will be boiled and the grease skimmed off to be used as lamp fuel, dripping, and in porridge. When dry, the bones can be used for fuel. Dry bones make a bright and clean-burning fuel and, because they're almost smokeless, food cooks in rapid time. The hide can be made into a satchel, while the wool has too many uses to count. When dry, the contents of the stomach and intestines make an excellent substitute for firewood. Now there's just the problem of what to do with the blood. It's only the consumption of spilt blood that religion forbids us, you know. It must have some permissible uses but I have no idea what these might be. And until I can work out what to do, it will remain a constant, nagging worry, like grit in my eyes and a branding iron in my heart.'

Suddenly I saw her relax and smile to herself.

'You must have realized what to do with the blood.'

'I've just remembered that there are some brand-new Syrian cooking pots at home. Folk say that nothing brings up the shine or strengthens them like a good wiping with warm, greasy blood. Now everything has fallen into place and I can relax.'

I met her again six months later and asked how she was enjoying the mutton she had salted and dried.

'Good Lord, it's not time for that yet! I've still got the fat, the tail, the ribs, the bones and more, to go. To everything, its proper time!'"

3.3 Byzantine guilds: *The Book of the Prefect* (912). Original in Greek.

CONSTANTINOPLE TEEMED WITH MERCHANTS, craftsmen, and notaries (the ancient version of lawyers). Organized as collective professional organizations, that is, guilds, these groups were regulated by the chief official of the city, the Prefect. The *Book of the Prefect*, an imperial edict issued in 911 or 912 by Emperor Leo VI (886-912), shows how tightly the economy of the capital was controlled—or supposed to be controlled—by the state. What evidence does this document provide for arguing that the early tenth-century economy of Constantinople was well-organized and vibrant? What evidence does it offer for the contrary argument: that the economy of the capital was stifled by rules and regulations?

[Source: A.E.R. Boak, "Notes and Documents: The Book of the Prefect," *Journal of Economic and Business History* 1 (1929): 600-02, 604-10 (slightly modified).]

PREFACE

God, after having created all things that are and given order and harmony to the universe, with his own finger engraved the Law on the tables and published it openly so that men, being well directed thereby, should not shamelessly trample upon one another and the stronger should not do violence to the weaker but that all things should be apportioned with just measure. Therefore it has seemed good for Our Serenity also to lay down the following ordinances based on the statutes in order that the human race may be governed fittingly and no person may injure his fellow.

I. THE NOTARIES

1. Whoever wishes to be appointed a notary must be elected by a vote and decision both of the *primicerius*[1]

---

1 The chief of the guild of the notaries.

and the notaries acting with him to ensure that he has a knowledge and understanding of the laws, that he excels in handwriting, that he is not garrulous or insolent, and that he does not lead a corrupt life, but on the contrary is serious in his habits, guileless in his thoughts, eloquent, intelligent, a polished reader, and accurate in his diction, to guard against his being easily led to give a false meaning in places to what he writes or to insert deceptive clauses. And if at any time a notary is found to be doing something contrary to the law and the authorized written regulations, those who have acted as his witnesses shall be responsible.

2. The candidate must know by heart the forty titles of the *Manual of Law*[1] and must also know the sixty books of the Basilika.[2] He shall also have received a general education so that he may not make mistakes in formulating his documents and be guilty of errors in his reading. He shall also have abundant time to give proof of his ability both mental and physical. Let him prepare a handwritten document in a meeting of the guild, so that he may not later commit unforeseen errors; but if he should then be detected in any, let him be expelled from the order.

3. The election of the candidate shall be carried out as follows. After the hearing of the witnesses and the examination he shall present himself wearing a cloak before the most glorious Prefect of the City accompanied by the guild of the notaries and the *primicerius*. These shall swear before God and by the safety of the emperors that he is being enrolled in the order not through any favor, influence, family connection, or friendship, but by reason of his good conduct, knowledge, ability, and general fitness. After the oaths have been taken, by means of a sign the Prefect in office shall elect him in the prefectural bureau, and he shall be enrolled in the guild and numbered among the notaries. Then he shall go to the church nearest his residence, while all the notaries wear their cloaks, and doffing his cloak and donning a white surplice shall be consecrated by a prayer of the priest. He shall be escorted on his way by all the notaries clad in their cloaks, while the *primicerius* himself holds a censer[3] and directs the fumes towards the newly elect, who carries the Bible openly before him. This signifies that his ways shall be made straight as the incense ascending before the face of God. In this glorious fashion he shall proceed to the seat to which he has been allotted and then return home with the same pomp, there to feast and rejoice with his associates.

4. Any notary who intends to absent himself from a royal procession or ceremony in the hippodrome or a meeting or assembly summoned by the most glorious Prefect or from any other gathering of this sort shall pay four *keratia*[4] to the officers of the Prefect and an equal sum to the members of the guild. But if he shows a clear and reasonable ground for his absence, which is not for his own profit, he shall be excused from the penalty if the *primicerius* approves.

5. If a notary has been summoned by the *primicerius* for a necessary purpose and has failed to come once, twice, or thrice, he shall pay on the first occasion two *keratia*, on the second, four, and on the third, six. But if he does this out of bravado and a spirit of contempt, he shall be punished by whipping at the Prefect's order.

6. If a notary should be summoned to draw up a contract, and afterwards another should be called in, let them both do the work and share the fee equally. But if one should come uninvited, let him not only be chased out without pay but also be punished by whipping. And if one of the two should leave voluntarily while the work is being completed, he shall not receive any part of the fee.

7. If a notary who is called in to draw up a contract wishes to leave for some adequate reason and calls in another, the one thus summoned shall receive two-thirds of the fee, while the one first called in shall get a third.

8. If a notary has been called in and has completed the agreement, and then another has been summoned and has both completed the agreement and finished the work, the latter shall receive the whole fee if he

---

1 A brief compilation of laws in forty titles published by Basil I between 870 and 878.
2 The great codification of Byzantine Law begun under Basil I and completed and published by Leo VI (r.886–912).
3 A vessel for burning incense.
4 The Byzantine coins mentioned in the Edict are the following: the *nomisma* (pl.: *nomismata*), a gold coin; the *miliarision* (pl.: *miliarisia*), a silver coin equal to $1/12$ of a *nomisma*; the *keration* (pl.: *keratia*) also of silver, equal to $1/2$ of a *miliarision* or $1/24$ of a *nomisma*; the copper *follis* or *obol* worth about $1/12$ of a *keration*.

is ignorant that it had previously been completed by the other. But if he came with knowledge of this, he shall receive one third, while the former received two thirds. And if two have been called in together, the junior shall yield to his senior in rank, but they shall share the fee equally.

9. If a notary approaches the seat of another and the latter does not greet him respectfully, or if one seats himself at table without regard to precedence, or if one is convicted of having verbally abused another, the guilty one shall in each case pay six *keratia*. But if one also lays violent hands upon another, he shall be punished by the Prefect....

II. THE JEWELERS

1. We ordain that the jewelers may, if any one invites them, buy the things that pertain to them, such as gold, silver, pearls, or precious stones; but not bronze and woven linens or any other materials which others should purchase rather than they. However, they are not hereby prevented from buying anything they wish for private use.

2. They must not depreciate or increase the price of things for sale to the detriment of the vendors, but shall appraise them at their just value. If anyone acts deceitfully in this, he shall forfeit the appraised value of the things to the vendor.

3. Following the old custom, on the regular market days the jewelers shall take their seats in their shops along with their statores or attendants in charge of their sales tables. Their money is to be counted out in *miliarisia* so that if anyone tries to sell some jewelers' ware they may purchase it.

4. If a jeweler discovers a woman offering for sale objects of gold or silver, or pearls, or precious stones, he shall inform the Prefect of these things to prevent their being exported to foreign peoples.

5. If anyone adulterates uncoined metal and manufactures things for sale from it, he shall have his hand cut off.

6. If any foreigner sells gold or silver in a worked or unworked state, he is to be questioned as to its origin and to be reported to the chief of the guild, in order that stolen goods may be detected.

7. If any jeweler is found to have bought a sacred object, whether damaged or intact, without having shown it to the Prefect, both he and the seller shall suffer confiscation.

8. We command that no goldsmith, whether slave or free, shall purchase for his work more than a single pound of unminted gold, be it unwrought or wrought.

9. And if one does take from somebody more than a pound of uncoined gold for his work, and does not declare it at once to the chief of the goldsmiths, if he is a slave he shall be confiscated by the state, but if a freeman he shall be whipped and subjected to a fine of a pound of gold.

10. A slave who is going to be set up in a jeweler's shop shall be sponsored by his own master if the latter is a man of means. But a freeman shall be vouched for by five persons, who shall assume the same risk as he whom they have nominated.

11. We order that no goldsmith shall have the right to work gold or silver in his home, but only in the shops on the Mese.[1] Also that no one shall be nominated as a goldsmith without the knowledge of the Prefect.

12. The jewelers shall not undertake any work of evaluation without the knowledge of the Prefect, nor shall they when making appraisals stir up strife with one another. If they are caught doing any of these things, they shall be whipped; shorn;[2] and removed from the roll of their guild....

IV. THE SILK-GARMENT MERCHANTS[3]

1. The silk-garment merchants shall buy silk garments but not any other merchandise except something for their personal needs which they may not sell to others. They shall not give foreigners any of the prohibited articles, such as red or purple silk goods of large size, so that these may not be transported to strange peoples. Whoever violates these regulations shall be flogged and suffer confiscation of goods.

---

1 The Middle Street, the main industrial and commercial thoroughfare of Constantinople.
2 That is, their hair and beard cut off.
3 *Vestiopratai*: dealers in manufactured articles of clothing and the like as opposed to raw or spun silk.

2. Silk-garment merchants, whether slaves or free persons, when purchasing garments valued at ten *nomismata* from persons of any sort whatsoever, even from princes or silk weavers, shall declare this to the Prefect so that he may know where they are to be sold. Those who fail to do so are liable to the aforesaid punishment.

3. Whoever fails to declare to the Prefect cloaks or robes of a blue color or purple two-thirds red, shall be liable to punishment.

4. Whoever fails to show to the Prefect goods that are to be exported to foreign peoples so that they may receive his seal, shall suffer punishment.

5. Whoever is to be enrolled in the craft of the silk-garment merchants shall first be declared by five persons of the same guild in the presence of the Prefect to be worthy to be in this trade. He shall then be entered on the roll, shall open a shop, and engage in trade. He shall also pay to the corporation six *nomismata*.

6. Whoever wishes to become the owner of a silk-garment shop, shall pay ten *nomismata*. He must also have the approval of the Prefect.

7. One who is both a silk-garment merchant and a silk weaver shall be allowed to choose one of these trades but must give up the other. If he dares to practice both, he shall come under the punishment mentioned above [i.e., flogging and confiscation of goods].

8. Strangers who reside in the inns of the city must be carefully prevented from purchasing either prohibited articles of clothing or those woven in a single piece, except something for personal use and that prepared in the imperial city. Upon their departure they shall declare such articles to the Prefect so that he may know the goods that they have bought. Whoever helps them to conceal such things shall be flogged and suffer confiscation of goods.

9. Any silk-garment merchant who secretly or openly seeks to raise the rental of another, shall be flogged, shorn, and suffer confiscation of goods....

VI. THE DEALERS IN RAW SILK

1. The dealers in raw silk shall not practice another trade but shall exercise their own openly in the place assigned to them. Those who do not do so shall be flogged, shorn, and banished.

2. The dealer in raw silk who employs a hired helper shall not enter into a contract with him for more than a month, nor shall he give him pay for more than thirty days' work, which pay the employee is to earn by working the full month. If anyone gives pay for more than the appointed period, he shall forfeit this [privilege].

3. A dealer in raw silk shall not hire the employee of another until that employee has given full service for the pay which he has received. Whoever does so shall be fined the amount of the unearned pay which the employee has received.

4. The raw-silk dealers shall pay their chiefs one *keration* on each hundred pounds of raw silk. All of them who possess scales or weights not marked with the seal of the Prefect, shall be flogged and shorn.

5. Those who come to the inns with raw silk from foreign peoples shall not pay the sales tax but only the costs of their lodging and sojourn. Likewise, those who buy from them shall be exempt from the sales tax.

6. A candidate for admission to the guild of the raw-silk dealers must have the testimony of some estimable and honest men as to his good repute. Thereafter he shall be enrolled upon giving two *nomismata* to the corporation.

7. If a raw-silk dealer wishes to set his own slave to carry on this trade in his place, he shall go surety for him and subject himself to the same risks as the slave if the latter does anything wrong.

8. At the time of the market all the members of the guild shall make deposits, each according to his means. And the division of the material shall follow in proportion to the contribution of each.

9. If a rich dealer in raw silk happens to have bought a quantity from foreigners, he shall sell it to his poorer colleagues at a profit of one ounce on the *nomisma*.[1]

10. If any dealer imports raw silk under his own name but for some influential or wealthy person or even for a silk weaver for pay, he shall be flogged, shorn, and expelled from the guild.

11. Whoever accepts a deposit on a sale of raw silk and then deceitfully raises the price, shall be fined the amount of the deposit.

---

1 The ounce here is equivalent to a twelfth part, i.e., a *miliarision*. Therefore the profit allowed is 8½ per cent.

12. If a dealer is caught going abroad for the purpose of selling raw silk, he shall be expelled from the guild.

13. Dealers must not sell the unworked raw silk in their homes, but only in the marketplace so that it may not be shipped secretly to those who are forbidden to purchase it. Anyone who sells it at home shall pay the guild fifteen *nomismata*.

14. The dealers shall not enjoy the right of spinning raw silk, but only that of buying and selling it. Any one of them discovered violating this restriction shall suffer the penalty of being whipped and shorn.

15. The so-called *melathrarioi*[1] shall not purchase clean raw silk either in secret or openly. If they disobey, they shall be liable to the punishment aforesaid.

16. The dealers in raw silk shall not sell it to Hebrews [Jews] or to traders for resale outside the city. Those who do so shall be flogged and shorn....

VIII. THE SILK WEAVERS

1. The silk weavers are forbidden to manufacture the prohibited cloaks, namely, large-sized outer cloaks of a single color and large-sized inner cloaks of purple alternating with light yellow or purple and deep green. However, they may make cloaks of deep blue of many shades and ordinary Slav turbans with scarlet bands. But they must declare to the Prefect the deep blue cloaks and the small cloaks of two palms, and also robes valued at more than ten *nomismata*, even if they are multicolored.[2]

2. We forbid any prince or private person to make a purple robe of six or eight widths, but they may make ones of ten or twelve widths, provided they are true purple and of light quality, and are not in the class of those which have to be restricted by the Prefect for the use of the imperial house. They are also pro-

hibited from making the robes with rounded bottoms reserved for the emperor, except those of medium size forming folds on the tunic and of many colors and having at least ten widths.[3] If anyone is caught manufacturing these prohibited garments, his goods shall be confiscated and he shall be made to give up his trade.

3. Whoever prevents an inspector of seals or looms from entering his workshops, and whoever sells a robe valued at more than ten *nomismata* to foreigners, shall be beaten and shorn.

4. Whoever dyes raw silk with the juice of the murex or makes from it cloaks of two or three colors or two-thirds red shall have his hand cut off.

5. Anyone who sells material to foreigners without the knowledge of the Prefect shall suffer confiscation of goods.

6. Anyone who happens to be both a silk weaver and a silk-garment merchant has the right to choose one of the trades but must give up the other.

7. Whoever sells a slave, a hired worker, or an overseer to persons outside the city or to foreigners shall have his hand cut off.

8. The silk weavers shall buy their raw silk from the dealers. If they are caught buying it from strangers, they shall be beaten, shorn, and ousted from the business.

9. Robes found rolled in storerooms without the seals of the Prefect shall be confiscated, and the storekeepers who receive them shall be punished in like manner.

10. Any weaver who knowingly takes into his service the employee of another, before the employee has done full work for the pay he has received, shall be fined the amount of pay remaining unearned.

11. Anyone who places goods made abroad in the imperial storeroom shall be beaten and shorn.

---

1   Ordinary raw-silk dealers (*metaxopratai*) purchased only pure, clean, silk, but the *melathrarioi* were restricted to buying soiled and damaged silk.
2   The explanation of these restrictions imposed upon the silk weavers lies in the existence of an imperial monopoly of the use of purple dyes and of purple-colored garments. The dyeing was carried out in the imperial dye-works by imperial workmen, who received the natural silk yarn from the spinners. From the dyed yarn the imperial weavers prepared the garments for the exclusive use of the imperial household and the court. But the members of the weavers' guild also procured colored yarn from the imperial dye-works, and from it they manufactured the colored materials which they were permitted to sell to the silk-garment merchants who in turn disposed of them to the public. The meaning of the measure of "two palms" is uncertain.
3   The "widths" are apparently the pieces sewn together to make up the garment. The fewer the widths, the more valuable the garment.

12. If a weaver brings a hired worker into his workshops, he shall not make a contract with him for longer than a month and shall not give him pay for more than thirty days but only so much as he can earn by working a full month. Anyone who advances pay for more than the authorized period shall lose this.

13. If anyone wishes to set up a workshop, he must be vouched for by five persons if he is a freeman, but if he is a slave, by his own master, provided that the latter is a person of means. The sponsors shall assume the same risks as the one whom they nominate. The newly enrolled member shall pay the corporation three *nomismata*.

[Further sections include regulations for the linen merchants, perfume dealers, candle makers, grocers, leather cutters, butchers (except pork), pork dealers, fishmongers, bakers, tavern keepers, and contractors (such as joiners, plasterers, locksmiths, and painters).]

Map 3.1 *Major European Slave Exports* (700-900).

Coin hoard evidence suggests that Islamic—and, to a lesser extent, Byzantine—money came into Europe in considerable abundance during the period 700-900. What did the Europeans provide in return? Swords is one answer; slaves is another, as this map demonstrates. It shows where European slaves were captured and the places to which they were transported. Some remained in Europe (as *A Contract of Sale*, below, p. 142 attests); many others were traded to the Islamic world. Note the convergence of many routes at Córdoba. As you read through the other documents in this book, take note of how often slaves are mentioned. How differently were they treated from free men and women?

[Based on Michael McCormick, *Origins of the European Economy: Communications and Commerce A.D. 300-900* (Cambridge: Cambridge University Press, 2001), p. 562, Map 25.1, modified by, and with many thanks to, Michael McCormick.]

MAP 3.1 MAJOR EUROPEAN SLAVE EXPORTS (700-900)   141

3.4 The sale of a slave in Italy: *A Contract of Sale* (724). Original in Latin.

THIS IS AN ABSOLUTELY ORDINARY record of a sale, much like many others drawn up at the same time in the Lombard kingdom of Italy for land and animals. In this case, however, the item sold was a boy. What does this transaction add to the information presented in the map of *Major European Slave Exports* on p. 141?

[Source: *Medieval Trade in the Mediterranean World*, trans. and ed. Robert S. Lopez and Irving W. Raymond (New York: Columbia University Press, 2001), pp. 45-46 (slightly modified).]

Milan, June 6, 725

In the thirteenth year of the reign of our lord, most excellent man, King Liutprand,[1] on the eighth day before the Ides of June, eighth indiction; good fortune. I, Faustino, notary by royal authority, wrote this document of sale, invited by Ermedruda, honorable woman, daughter of Lorenzo, acting jointly with consent and will of that parent of hers, and being the seller. And she acknowledges that she has received, as indeed she at the present time is receiving from Totone, most distinguished man, 12 new gold solidi [coins] as the full price for a boy of the Gallic people named Satrelano, or by whatever other name the boy may be called. And she declared that it[2] had come to her from her father's patrimony. And she, acting jointly with her aforesaid father, promises from this day to protect that boy against all men on behalf of the buyer. And if the boy is injured or taken away and they [Ermedruda and Lorenzo] are in any way unable to protect it against all men, they shall return the solidi in the double to the buyer, [including all] improvements in the object.[3] Done in Milan, in the day, reign, and in the eighth indiction mentioned above.

The sign[4] of the hand of Ermedruda, honorable woman, seller, who declared that she sold the aforesaid Frankish boy of her own good will with the consent of her parent; and she asked this sale to be made.

The sign of the hand of Lorenzo, honorable man, her father, consenting to this sale.

The sign of the hand of Theoperto, honorable man, maker of cuirasses, son of the late Giovannace, relative of the same seller, in whose presence she proclaimed that she was under no constraint, giving consent.

The sign of the hand of Ratchis, honorable man, Frank, witness.

Antonino, devout man, invited by Ermedruda, honorable woman, and by her father giving his consent, undersigned as a witness to this record of sale.

I, the above Faustino, writer of this [record] of sale, after delivery gave [this record].

---

1 Liutprand, King of the Lombards 712-744, ruled over much of northern Italy.

2 A slave in Lombard as well as in Roman law was not considered as a person but as a thing (*res*); hence the document uses the neuter pronoun when referring to the boy.

3 Again, the boy is considered as a thing. He may learn some skill and hence become more valuable.

4 Ermedruda could not write her name, but she indicated her assent to the terms of the contract with a cross or other sign, recorded by the notary as her "sign." He himself supplied her name.

3.5 The post-iconoclastic Church: Photius, *Letter to the Bulgar Khan* (864-867?). Original in Greek.

PHOTIUS (820-*c*.897) WAS A SCHOLAR, courtier, and twice patriarch of Constantinople (in 858-867 and 877-886). During the first period of his patriarchate he was responsible for sending Constantine and Methodius to Moravia (see their *Prologue to the Gospel* below, on p. 146) as well as working to convert the Bulgars, who were much nearer to Byzantium. He had success in 864, when the Bulgar Khan, Boris, converted to Christianity and took the baptismal name of Michael, after Emperor Michael III (r.856-867). In the letter below, Photius writes a "mirror of princes"—a guide for rulers—to the Bulgar Khan. Subtly he maintains the Byzantine form of the Creed in which the Holy Spirit proceeds from the Father alone; the West maintained that the Holy Spirit proceeded from the father *and the son* (expressed in Latin by the word *filioque*: "and the son"). The argument over this Creed was one of the factors leading to the later schism between the eastern and western churches. Above all, in this excerpt Photius gives a sense of the relief and triumph of the post-iconoclast Byzantine Church.

[Source: *The Patriarch and the Prince: The Letter of Patriarch Photios of Constantinople to Khan Boris of Bulgaria*, trans. Despina Stratoudaki White and Joseph R. Berrigan, Jr. (Brookline, MA: Holy Cross Orthodox Press, 1982), pp. 39-41, 50-53.]

The Task of a Ruler

1. Some gifts, my most illustrious and beloved son, confer small and fleeting advantages upon their subjects, but those that better the soul, as they cleanse it from error and suffering and shine with the radiance and glory of virtue and truth, are gifts in the truest of senses. They confer great and eternal blessings upon an eternal and godlike object, the soul, and gain for it imperishable, heavenly riches. The most noble and supreme of gifts is the sure and saving introduction to divinity, if one has been granted the one and only instruction in the pure and blameless faith of us Christians and initiation into it.

2. For this instruction frees man from manifold error, cleanses the eyes of the mind from the murkiness of this world, and allows him to gaze purely upon the pure loveliness of worship with the pure intelligence of his soul. By it we are brought to that being beyond our minds, the cause and creator of everything and, insofar as it is humanly possible, we glimpse at the Holy Trinity in its unity and absolute divinity. Since we have found your prudent soul worthy of so great a grace and gift (for we are convinced that you love virtue and piety), we extend to you this beloved and extraordinary gift. In it we have arranged the sacred and divine instruction of our spotless and undefiled faith; in a clear and concise presentation we have added a discussion of the seven holy ecumenical synods, which are a kind of bulwark of the divine orthodox teaching. Nor shall we be altogether silent on matters that guide our life and testify to the correctness of our faith. For just as it would be foolish to try to deal with everything from the very beginning, so it would be dishonorable to say nothing.

3. The other virtues must be arranged alongside faith; the godly man must be equipped with both. Correctness of belief ensures good citizenship, purity of conduct proclaims the divinity of faith. Either one without the other usually becomes wild and exorbitant, since it cannot reside by itself in the souls of men. But of this later. Now we set before you the sacred and divine teaching of our holy religion.

4. I believe in one God, the Father almighty, the maker of heaven and earth, of all that is seen and unseen.

And in one Lord Jesus Christ, the only begotten Son of God, born of the Father before all ages, light of light, true God of true God, begotten, not made, of one substance with the Father, by whom all things were made.

For us men and for our salvation he came down from Heaven, was made flesh by the Holy Spirit and the Virgin Mary, and was made man.

And he was crucified for us under Pontius Pilate, suffered and was buried.

And he arose on the third day according to the Scriptures.

And he ascended to Heaven and sits at the right hand of the Father.

And he will come again in glory to judge the living and the dead. Of his kingdom there will be no end.

And in the Holy Spirit, the Lord, the giver of life, who proceeds from the Father, who with the Father and the Son is adored and glorified, who spoke through the Prophets.

And in one, holy, catholic and apostolic Church.

I confess one baptism for the remission of sins.

I expect the resurrection of the dead,

And the life of the world to come. Amen.

5. Such should be your thoughts and beliefs in accord with the tradition of the holy, catholic and apostolic Church of God, O great glory of my efforts. Now you shall ponder upon the seven holy ecumenical synods, some of which will be the champions of piety. By them all innovation, all heresy is driven away. The pure and traditional teaching of Orthodoxy guides the souls of the pious to the safe haven of religious veneration. I will offer an explanation of the synods and provide a sketch of the site, the number in attendance, the leaders in each synod, for the sake of clarity, along with the actions taken in each one....

[Photius describes the first six ecumenical councils, paying particular attention to the heresies that they condemned. He then turns to the seventh.]

17. The Seventh holy and Ecumenical Synod was held in Nicaea, the capital of Bithynia [in 787]. Of old it had determined the truth of doctrines; now it provided a touchstone of piety. Some 368 men of God were in attendance. The leaders and principal figures of this great and sacred assembly included Tarasius,[1] renowned among the bishops of God; he was a pious and altogether excellent man, worthy, if any other man ever was, to direct the patriarchal affairs of the imperial city. There was also the most prudent Peter, the first priest of the holy Roman Church, and another Peter, also a priest, the abbot of the monastery of St. Sabbas there in Rome. They were allotted the place of the apostolic see, since they represented Pope Adrian.[2] Along with them there were John and Thomas, men illustrious for their monastic life, and those who shone with episcopal glory, those who represented the entire area of Anatolia, rich in apostolic sees, and those who embodied the dignity of patriarchs. I mean Apollinarios, Theodoretos, and Elias, the one of Alexandria, the second of Antioch, the last of Jerusalem.[3] Each ruled his see wisely and well. At that time Constantine and Irene, crowned with the chaplet of the true faith, were garbed in the imperial purple of Roman majesty.[4] This great and holy synod considered the recent and barbarous heresy, introduced by impious and dreadful men.[5] The synod condemned it with a divine and unanimous decision and placed its contrivers and champions under the same judgment. These wretches did not dare to blaspheme Christ, our true God, with their words, but by their deeds they contrived all manner of outrages, blasphemies, and impieties. They did not dare to defame him directly and without any disguise, but through His sacred image they fulfilled the whole desire of those who war against Christ. They condemned the sacred image of Christ (O the discordance of a daring and godless mind and tongue!) as an idol, that image by which the error of idols is routed. They subjected it to all kinds of indignity; through the streets and squares they kicked it

---

1   Tarasius was the patriarch of Constantinople 784–806.
2   Pope Adrian I (r.772–795).
3   John and Thomas were sent to the synod to represent the patriarchs of Alexandria, Antioch, and Jerusalem who, being in Islamic territory, did not even know about the meeting.
4   Constantine was Constantine VI (r.780–797); Irene was his mother and regent.
5   The "heresy" that Photius refers to is iconoclasm.

with their feet, they ridiculed it, they threw it into the fire. A pitiful sight for Christians and fit only for those pagans who were at war with Christ. They did the same sort of thing to the other sacred images as, swift to shed blood, they mistreated them with their feet, with their murderous hands, and their profane lips, nor were these accursed men ever satisfied with this wild madness. In their hatred for the sacred symbols and images of Christians, they felt a loathing for them that was not less, but in fact more than their loathing for the idols of the Greeks [pagans]. Thereby they declared an unquenchable war against Christ and his saints; the fight was bitter and all-out. For everyone sees that the honor paid to images produces honor to those who are imaged forth, even as dishonor to the former affects those who are imaged forth. But these men, freshly sprung from the Jews who warred with Christ, as they insulted the sacred image of Christ and his saints, made good the deficiency of their ancestors; they tried to outdo the Jews, their progenitors, in the excess of their zeal. But since, in the presence of Christians, they did not dare to deny Christ with their lips, right there they proved that they had tempered the Jewish zeal of their ancestors; they showed that their imitation was a spurious thing, and they kept no one position. But as though they had their heads bowed with evil, they called themselves Christians, but were insolent towards Christ. They did not call themselves Jews, but they rivaled their combat against Christ in their iconoclasm; in fact they surpassed them. Not only that, but shunning the very name of idolatry, they made charges against Christians and the holy and undefiled mysteries of Christianity that were no more tolerable than those made by idolaters. Therefore, as many of them as were unwilling to flee the meanness of this adultery, of this luxuriant and well-kneaded belief, were condemned by this sacred ecumenical synod as illegitimate, as foreign to the genuine character of believers; it subjected them to the unbreakable bonds of anathema. But the image of Christ, who is truly our God, in accordance with traditions handed down from the Apostles and Fathers as well as by divine revelation, should be reverenced and honored out of respect and veneration for the person who is imaged forth: this was the unanimous decision ratified by the synod. Such respect and veneration should be paid in the same manner in which we do reverence to the other sacred images and symbols of our most holy religion. We do not fix our respect and veneration on them nor do we limit our respect and veneration to them, nor are we divided into different and diverse ends. Through the palpably different and divided service and veneration we pay them we are led aloft, in a sacred and indivisible manner, to that undivided, simple, and unifying deity.

18. Thus we venerate the holy cross, upon which our Lord's body was stretched, from which his blood, as an expiation for the universe, gushed forth. The nature of that wood was watered by those streams and bloomed with eternal life rather than death. Thus we reverence the image of the cross, by which legions of devils are routed and strange maladies cured. Grace and power were infused once and for all in that first cross and continue to be active in all other crosses. Each of them, then, I mean the image of Christ, the cross itself, and the representation of the cross, we judge worthy of honor and veneration, but we do not limit or prescribe the reverence and honor given to them. Rather we refer and elevate this veneration to the One who became man for us out of his ineffable, abundant love for man and willingly endured a most shameful death on our behalf. So we reverence in faith the churches of the saints, their graves, and their relics, which produce cures for the faithful, as we glorify and extol Christ our God, who honored them. And if there is something similar to them in our sacred mysteries, e.g., their active grace and good works, we acknowledge and acclaim the source as responsible. Therefore that divine and sacred assemblage of blessed and holy men confirmed through its decisions that not only should the image of Christ be honored and reverenced, as we have said, but also that of our spotless and ever-virgin lady, the Mother of God, and those of all the saints in keeping with the abundant holiness of their prototypes. By them we are brought to a simple and unifying contemplation. These were wise and inspired decrees, which drove out that whole heretical disease and all the ugliness of that rational herd. The Church was shown resuming her proper beauty and raiment. Like a bride, not bedecked with golden ornaments, but with sacred images, she was placed on the right of her bridegroom Christ, a sight for happy and joyful eyes, a delight for the entire body of believers....

3.6 The conversion of the Slavs: Constantine/Cyril, *Prologue to the Gospel* (863–867). Original in Old Church Slavonic.

IN 864 THE BROTHERS Constantine and Methodius arrived in Moravia at the behest of Photius and the invitation of Ratislav, the Moravian ruler. They stayed about four years, translating the Scriptures into the Slavic dialect they had learned in Macedonia, which was not the language of Moravia but was nevertheless comprehensible to the people living there. They used a new alphabet, the Glagolitic, which, after the failure of their mission, was replaced by the Cyrillic alphabet, still in use today. In the prologue to his translation of the Gospels, Constantine speaks of the importance of literacy: "The soul lacking letters/ Grows dead in human beings." How does this view reflect the importance of the written word at Byzantium in the period, as seen, for example, in the *Book of the Prefect* (above, p. 135) and Photius's *Letter to the Bulgar Khan* (above, p. 143)?

[Source: Roman Jakobson, "St. Constantine's Prologue to the Gospel," *St. Vladimir's Seminary Quarterly* 7 (1963): 16–19.]

I am the Prologue to the Holy Gospels:
As the prophets prophesied of old—
"Christ comes to gather the nations and tongues,
Since He is the light of the world"[1]—
So it has come to pass in this seventh millennium.
Since they have said, "The blind shall see,
The deaf shall hear the Word of the Book,
For it is proper that God be known."[2]
Therefore hearken, all ye Slavs!
For this gift is given by God,
The gift on God's right hand,
The incorruptible gift to souls,
To those souls that will accept it.
Matthew, Mark, Luke, and John
Teach all the people, saying:
"If you see and love the beauty of your souls,
And hence are striving
To dispel the darkness of sin,
And to repel the corruptness of this world,
Thus to win paradise life
And to escape the flaming fire,
Then hear now with your own mind,
Since you have learned to hear, Slavic people,
Hear the Word, for it came from God,
The Word nourishing human souls,
The Word strengthening heart and mind,
The Word preparing all to know God."

As without light there can be no joy—
For while the eye sees all of God's creation,
Still what is seen without light lacks beauty—
So it is with every soul lacking letters,
Ignorant of God's law,
The sacred law of the Scriptures,
The law that reveals God's paradise.
For what ear not hearing
The sound of thunder, can fear God?
Or how can nostrils which smell no flower
Sense the Divine miracle?
And the mouth which tastes no sweetness
Makes man like stone;
Even more, the soul lacking letters
Grows dead in human beings.
Thus, considering all this, brethren,
We speak fitting counsel
Which will divide men
From brutish existence and desire,
So that you will not have intellect without intelligence,
Hearing the Word in a foreign tongue,
As if you heard only the voice of a copper bell.
Therefore St. Paul has taught:
"In offering my prayer to God,
I had rather speak five words
That all the brethren will understand

---

1   See Isa. 66: 8 and John 8: 12.
2   See Isa. 29: 18.

Than ten thousand words which are
    incomprehensible."[1]
What man will not understand this?
Who will not apply the wise parable,
Interpreting to us the true message?
As corruption threatens the flesh,
Decaying and rotting everything worse than pus
If there is no fit nourishment,
So each soul no longer lives
Deprived of Divine Life,
Hearing not the Divine Word.
Let another very wise parable
Be told, ye men that love each other
And wish to grow toward God!
Who does not know this true doctrine?
As the seed falls on the field,
So it is upon human hearts
Craving the divine shower of letters
That the fruit of God may increase.
What man can tell all the parables
Denouncing nations without their own books
And who do not preach in an intelligible tongue?
Even one potent in all tongues
Lacks power to tell their impotence.
Let me add my own parable
Condensing much sense into few words:
Naked indeed are all nations without their own
    books
Who being without arms cannot fight
The Adversary of our souls

And are ripe for the dungeon of eternal torments.
Therefore, ye nations whose love is not for the
    Enemy
And who truly mean to fight him:
Open eagerly the doors of your intelligence—
You who have now taken up the sturdy arms
That are forged through the Lord's Books,
And who mightily crush the head of the Enemy.
Whoever accepts these letters,
To him Christ speaks wisdom,
Feeds and strengthens your souls,
And so do the Apostles with all the Prophets.
Whoever speak their words
Will be fit to slay the Foe,
Bringing God good victory,
Escaping the suppurant corruption of flesh—
Flesh that lives as in a sleep;
These will not fall but hold fast,
And come forth before God as men of valor,
Standing on the right hand of God's throne,
When He judges the nations with fire,
And rejoicing throughout the ages with the angels,
Eternally praising God the merciful,
Always with songs from the holy books,
Singing to God who loves man:
To Him befits all glory,
To the Son of God, honor and praise forever,
With the Father and the Holy Ghost,
Unto the ages of ages, from all creatures!

---

1   See 1 Cor. 14:19.

THE ABBASID RECONFIGURATION

3.7 An early view of the Prophet: Muhammad ibn Ishaq, *Life of Muhammad* (754-767). Original in Arabic.

WRITING UNDER THE PATRONAGE of the Abbasid Caliph al-Mansur, Ibn Ishaq (*c.*704-767), who was born in Medina, wrote the first extant life of Muhammad. It was soon attacked for including spurious poetry and for lacking sufficient *isnad*—the chains of named sources that were, by the end of the eighth century, considered essential to prove the authenticity of any narrative about the Prophet (hadith). (For hadith considered authoritative, see Al-Bukhari, *On Fasting*, below, p. 152). Ibn Ishaq was also accused of Shi`ite sympathies. It is thus not surprising that his original work is lost. The version that we have today is an edition by Ibn Hisham (d.834), a Arabic scholar who, though somewhat critical of the original, also considered it of great value. Throughout, Ibn Ishaq calls Muhammad "the apostle of God" and emphasizes how fully he fulfilled the Christian and Jewish prophecies. In what ways were the mission, virtues, and lifestyle of Muhammad in Ibn Ishaq's account similar to—and different from—those of saints in Christian hagiography, such as the *Life of St. Antony*, above, p. 36?

[Source: *The Life of Muhammad: A Translation of Ishaq's* Sirat Rasul Allah, trans. and ed. A. Guillaume (London: Oxford University Press, 1955), pp. 81-83, 104-07 (slightly modified).]

The apostle of God grew up, God protecting him and keeping him from the vileness of heathenism because he wished to honor him with apostleship, until he grew up to be the finest of his people in manliness, the best in character, most noble in lineage, the best neighbor, the most kind, truthful, reliable, the furthest removed from filthiness and corrupt morals through loftiness and nobility, so that he was known among his people as "The trustworthy" because of the good qualities which God had implanted in him. The apostle, so I was told, used to tell how God protected him in his childhood during the period of heathenism, saying, "I found myself among the boys of Quraysh[1] carrying stones such as boys play with; we had all uncovered ourselves, each taking his shirt and putting it round his neck as he carried the stones. I was going to and fro in the same way, when an unseen figure slapped me most painfully saying, 'Put your shirt on'; so I took it and fastened it on me and then began to carry the stones upon my neck wearing my shirt alone among my fellows." …

THE APOSTLE OF GOD MARRIES KHADIJA

Khadija was a merchant woman of dignity and wealth. She used to hire men to carry merchandise outside the country on a profit-sharing basis, for Quraysh were a people given to commerce. Now when she heard about the prophet's truthfulness, trustworthiness, and honorable character, she sent for him and proposed that he should take her goods to Syria and trade with them, while she would pay him more than she paid others. He was to take a lad of hers called Maysara. The apostle of God accepted the proposal, and the two set forth until they came to Syria.

The apostle stopped in the shade of a tree near a monk's cell, when the monk came up to Maysara and asked who the man was who was resting beneath the tree. He told him that he was of Quraysh, the people who held the sanctuary; and the monk exclaimed: "None but a prophet ever sat beneath this tree."

Then the prophet sold the goods he had brought and bought what he wanted to buy and began the return journey to Mecca. The story goes that at the

---

1 The tribe at Mecca to which Muhammad also belonged.

height of noon, when the heat was intense as he rode his beast, Maysara saw two angels shading the apostle from the sun's rays. When he brought Khadija her property she sold it and it amounted to double or thereabouts. Maysara for his part told her about the two angels who shaded him and of the monk's words. Now Khadija was a determined, noble, and intelligent woman possessing the properties with which God willed to honor her. So when Maysara told her these things, she sent to the apostle of God and—so the story goes—said: "O son of my uncle I like you because of our relationship and your high reputation among your people, your trustworthiness and good character and truthfulness." Then she proposed marriage. Now Khadija at that time was the best born woman in Quraysh, of the greatest dignity and, too, the richest. All her people were eager to get possession of her wealth if it were possible.

Khadija was the daughter of Khuwaylid b. Asad b. 'Abdu'l-'Uzza b. Qusayy b. Kilab b. Murra b. Ka'b b. Lu'ayy b. Ghalib b. Fihr.[1] Her mother was Fatima bt. Za'ida b. al-Asamm b. Rawaha b. Hajar b. 'Abd b. Malis b. 'Amir b. Lu'ayy b. Ghalib b. Fihr. Her mother was Hala bt. 'Abd Manaf b. al-Harith b. 'Amr b. Munqidh b. 'Amr b. Ma'is b. 'Amir b. Lu'ayy b. Ghalib b. Fihr. Hala's mother was Qilaba bt. Su'ayd b. Sa'd b. Sahm b. 'Amr b. Husays b. Ka'b b. Lu'ayy b. Ghalib b. Fihr.

The apostle of God told his uncles of Khadija's proposal, and his uncle Hamza b. 'Abdu'l-Muttalib went with him to Khuwaylid b. Asad and asked for her hand and he married her.

She was the mother of all the apostle's children except Ibrahim, namely al-Qasim (whereby he was known as Abu'l-Qasim); al-Tahir, al-Tayyib, Zaynab, Ruqayya, Umm Kulthum, and Fatima.

Al-Qasim, al-Tayyib, and al-Tahir died in paganism. All his daughters lived into Islam, embraced it, and migrated with him to Medina.

Khadija had told Waraqa b. Naufal b. Asad b. 'Abdu'l-'Uzza, who was her cousin and a Christian who had studied the scriptures and was a scholar, what her slave Maysara had told her that the monk had said and how he had seen the two angels shading him. He said, "If this is true, Khadija, then truly Muhammad is the prophet of this people. I knew that a prophet of this people was to be expected. His time has come," or words to that effect. Waraqa was finding the time of waiting wearisome and used to say "How long?" Some lines of his on the theme are:

I persevered and was persistent in remembering
An anxiety which often evoked tears. And
Confirmatory evidence kept coming from Khadija.
Long have I had to wait, O Khadija,
In the vale of Mecca in spite of my hope
That I might see the outcome of thy words.
I could not bear that the words of the monk
You told me of should prove false
That Muhammad should rule over us
Overcoming those who would oppose him.
And that a glorious light should appear in the land
To preserve men from disorders.
His enemies shall meet disaster
And his friends shall be victorious.
Would that I might be there then to see,
For I should be the first of his supporters,
Joining in that which Quraysh hate
However loud they shout in that Mecca of theirs.
I hope to ascend through him whom they all dislike
To the Lord of the Throne though they are cast
    down.
Is it folly not to disbelieve in Him
Who chose him Who raised the starry heights?
If they and I live, things will be done
Which will throw the unbelievers into confusion.
And if I die, 'tis but the fate of mortals
To suffer death and dissolution....

THE PROPHET'S MISSION

When Muhammad the apostle of God reached the age of forty, God sent him in compassion to mankind, "as an evangelist to all men."[2] Now God had made a covenant with every prophet whom he had sent before him that

---

1 The abbreviation b. means "ibn," son of, while bt. means "bint," daughter of. Through this string of names, the author is authenticating Khadija's lineage. Compare Matt. 1: 1–11.

2 Sura 34: 27.

he should believe in him, testify to his truth, and help him against his adversaries. He required His prophets to transmit that to everyone who believed in them, and they carried out their obligations in that respect. God said to Muhammad, "When God made a covenant with the prophets, [He said], 'This is the scripture and wisdom which I have given you; afterwards an apostle will come confirming what you know that you may believe in him and help him.' He said, 'Do you accept this and take up my burden?' i.e., the burden of my agreement which I have laid upon you. They said, 'We accept it.' He answered, 'Then bear witness and I am a witness with you.'"[1] Thus God made a covenant with all the prophets that they should testify to his truth and help him against his adversaries, and they transmitted that obligation to those who believed in them among the two monotheistic religions.

Al-Zuhri related from 'Urwa b. Zybayr that 'A'isha[2] told him that when Allah desired to honor Muhammad and have mercy on His servants by means of him, the first sign of prophethood granted to the apostle was true visions, resembling the brightness of daybreak, which were shown to him in his sleep. And Allah, she said, made him love solitude so that he liked nothing better than to be alone.

'Abdu'l-Malik b. 'Ubaydullah b. Abu Sufyan b. al-'Ala' b. Jariya the Thaqafite, who had a retentive memory, related to me from a certain scholar that the apostle at the time when Allah willed to bestow His grace upon him and endow him with prophethood would go forth for his affair and journey far afield until he reached the glens of Mecca and the beds of its valleys where no house was in sight; and there was no stone or tree that he passed that didn't say, "Peace unto thee, O apostle of Allah." And the apostle would turn to his right and left and look behind him and he would see nothing but trees and stones. Thus he stayed seeing and hearing so long as it pleased Allah that he should stay. Then Gabriel came to him with the gift of God's grace while he was on Hira'[3] in the month of Ramadan.

Wahb b. Kaisan, a client of the family of al-Zubayr, told me: I heard 'Abdullah b. al-Zubayr say to 'Ubayd b. 'Umayr b. Qatada the Laythite, "O 'Ubayd tell us how began the prophethood which was first bestowed on the apostle when Gabriel came to him." And 'Ubayd in my presence related to 'Abdullah and those with him as follows: The apostle would pray in seclusion on Hira' every year for a month to practice *tahannuth* as was the custom of Quraysh in heathen days. *Tahannuth* is religious devotion. Abu Talib said:

By Thaur and him who made Thabir firm in its place
And by those going up to ascend Hira' and coming
  down[4]

Wahb b. Kaisan told me that 'Ubayd said to him: Every year during that month the apostle would pray in seclusion and give food to the poor that came to him. And when he completed the month and returned from his seclusion, first of all before entering his house he would go to the Ka'ba[5] and walk round it seven times or as often as it pleased God; then he would go back to his house until, in the year when God sent him, in the month of Ramadan in which God willed concerning him what He willed of His grace, the apostle set forth to Hira' as was his custom, and his family with him. When it was the night on which God honored him with his mission and showed mercy on His servants thereby, Gabriel brought him the command of God. "He came to me," said the apostle of God, "while I was asleep, with a coverlet of brocade whereon was some writing, and said, 'Read!' I said, 'What shall I read?' He pressed me with it so tightly that I thought it was death; then he let me go and said, 'Read!' I said, 'What shall I read?' He pressed me with it again so that I thought it was death; then he let me go and said 'Read!' I said, 'What shall I read?' He pressed me with it the third time so that I thought it was death and said 'Read!' I said, 'What then shall I read?'—and this I said only to deliver myself from him, lest he should do the same to me again. He said:

---

1 Sura 3: 75.
2 One of Muhammad's wives.
3 A nearby mountain.
4 Thaur and Thabir are mountains near Mecca.
5 This was Mecca's holy site. At this time, before Mecca became Muslim, it was filled with images of many gods.

Read in the name of thy Lord who created,
Who created man of blood coagulated.
Read! Thy Lord is the most beneficent,
Who taught by the pen,
Taught that which they knew not unto men.[1]

So I read it, and he departed from me. And I awoke from my sleep, and it was as though these words were written on my heart. When I was midway on the mountain, I heard a voice from heaven saying, 'O Muhammad! thou art the apostle of God and I am Gabriel.' I raised my head towards heaven to see (who was speaking), and lo, [there was] Gabriel in the form of a man with feet astride the horizon, saying, 'O Muhammad! thou art the apostle of God and I am Gabriel.' I stood gazing at him, moving neither forward nor backward; then I began to turn my face away from him, but towards whatever region of the sky I looked, I saw him as before. And I continued standing there, neither advancing nor turning back, until Khadija sent her messengers in search of me and they gained the high ground above Mecca and returned to her while I was standing in the same place; then he parted from me and I from him, returning to my family. And I came to Khadija and sat by her thigh and drew close to her. She said, 'O Abu'l-Qasim,[2] where have you been? By God, I sent my messengers in search of you, and they reached the high ground above Mecca and returned to me.' Then I told her of what I had seen; and she said, 'Rejoice, O son of my uncle, and be of good heart. Truly, by Him in whose hand is Khadija's soul, I have hope that you will be the prophet of this people.'" Then she rose and gathered her garments about her and set forth to her cousin Waraqa b. Naufal b. Asad b. 'Abdu'l-'Uzza b. Qusayy, who had become a Christian and read the scriptures and learned from those that follow the Torah and the Gospel. And when she related to him what the apostle of God told her he had seen and heard, Waraqa cried, "Holy! Holy! Truly, by Him in whose hand is Waraqa's soul, if you have spoken the truth to me, O Khadija, then the greatest Namus [i.e., Gabriel], who came to Moses in the past, has come to him [Muhammed], and lo, he is the prophet of this people. Bid him be of good heart." So Khadija returned to the apostle of God and told him what Waraqa had said. And when the apostle of God had finished his period of seclusion and returned [to Mecca], in the first place he performed the circum-ambulation of the Ka'ba, as was his custom. While he was doing it, Waraqa met him and said, "O son of my brother, tell me what you have seen and heard." The apostle told him, and Waraqa said, "Surely, by Him in whose hand is Waraqa's soul, you are the prophet of this people. Unto you has come the greatest Namus, who came unto Moses. You will be called a liar, and they will use you spitefully and cast you out and fight against you. Truly, if I live to see that day, I will help God in such ways as He knows." Then he brought his head near to him and kissed his forehead; and the apostle went to his own house.

Isma'il b. Abu Hakim, a freedman[3] of the family of al-Zubayr, told me on Khadija's authority that she said to the apostle of God, "O son of my uncle, are you able to tell me about your visitor, when he comes to you?" He replied that he could, and she asked him to tell her when he came. So when Gabriel came to him, as he was wont, the apostle said to Khadija, "This is Gabriel who has just come to me." "Get up, O son of my uncle," she said, "and sit by my left thigh." The apostle did so, and she said, "Can you see him?" "Yes," he said. She said, "Then turn round and sit on my right thigh." He did so, and she said, "Can you see him?" When he said that he could she asked him to move and sit in her lap. When he had done this she again asked if he could see him, and when he said yes, she disclosed her form and cast aside her veil while the apostle was sitting in her lap. Then she said, "Can you see him?" And he replied, "No." She said, "O son of my uncle, rejoice and be of good heart, by God he is an angel and not a satan."

I told 'Abdullah b. Hasan this story and he said, "I heard my mother Fatima, daughter of Husayn, talking about this tradition from Khadija, but as I heard it she made the apostle of God come inside her shift, and thereupon Gabriel departed, and she said to the apostle of God, 'This truly is an angel and not a satan.'"…

---

1 Sura 96: 1–5. For a different translation, see "The Embryo" above, p. 91.
2 The *kunya* or 'name of honor' of Muhammad.
3 I.e., a former slave who has been freed.

3.8 The "New Poetry": Abu Nuwas, *Youth and I* (*c*.800). Original in Arabic.

UMAYYAD POETRY LARGELY FOLLOWED the forms, subject matter, and style of pre-Islamic poetry. The Abbasid revolution changed all that. Poets experimented with structure and vocabulary. They wrote satirical and obscene works as well as delicate and tender ones. Abu Nuwas (*c*.750-*c*.810), one of Harun al-Rashid's boon companions, mingles thoughts of the "tents" with praises of wine.

[Source: *Translations of Eastern Poetry and Prose*, trans. R.A. Nicholson (New York: Greenwood Press, 1969), p. 30.]

Youth and I, we ran
    a headlong race of pleasure,
No recorded sin
    but soon I took its measure.
Of the gifts of Time
    there's none to heaven nigher
Than when music wakes
    the string of lute and lyre.
O the girl whose song—
    I had it for the asking—
Oft at Dhi Tuluh
    rose where our tents were basking!
Make the most of Youth,
    it stayeth not for ever;
Let the wine flow round
    from eve to morn—one river!

Pour into thy cup
    a sparking ruddy vintage
That will melt to ruth
    the miser's hardest mintage,
Sought and chosen out
    of old for Persia's ruler,
Dower'd with twin delights
    of fragrancy and color.
Seest not thou that I
    have pawned my soul for liquor,
Kissed the mouth of fair
    gazelle and foaming beaker?
'Tis because I know,
    full well I know and fear it,
Far apart shall be
    my body and my spirit.

3.9 Hadith: Al-Bukhari, *On Fasting* (9th c.). Original in Arabic.

THE HADITH ARE THE traditions about the prophet handed down by authoritative transmission. There are two parts to every hadith: the first consists of the chain of oral transmitters (*isnad*), with the most recent one listed first; the second part consists of the text of the tradition, which is always about the Prophet, his family, and his close associates. (Shi`ite hadith also include traditions about the imams—those few leaders who contained the "Muhammadan light.") Numerous questions occurred to Muslims after the time of Muhammad; they attempted to answer them by recourse to "what the Prophet would do in such-and-such situation," for that was the guide to "right behavior" (*sunna*). By the early Abbasid period, numerous, sometimes conflicting, answers to these questions were circulating. Al-Bukhari and other ninth-century scholars who followed him attempted in their collections (though not entirely successfully) to include only the "authentic" hadith. The *isnad*—which should be unbroken and come from reliable sources close to Muhammad—were an important element in their winnowing process. The section below, on fasting, illustrates their attempt to account for every possible situation.

[Source: *A Reader on Islam: Passages from Standard Arabic Writings Illustrative of the Beliefs and Practices of Muslims*, ed. Arthur Jeffery ('S-Gravenhage: Mouton & Co., 1962), pp. 88-90, 92-94, 98-101.]

1. *On the necessity of the Fast of Ramadan, and on the verse (II, 183/179): "O you who have believed, fasting is prescribed for you, just as it was prescribed for those who were before you. Maybe you will show piety."*

Qutaiba related to us, saying: Isma'il b. Ja'far related to us from[1] Abu Suhail, from his father, from Talha b. 'Ubaidallah, that a nomad Arab came to the Apostle of Allah—on whom be Allah's blessing and peace—with dishevelled head, saying: "O Apostle of Allah, inform me of what Allah has laid on me as incumbent duty in the matter of saying prayers." He answered: "The five prayer-services, unless you would voluntarily add thereto." Then [the Arab] said: "O Apostle of Allah, inform me of what Allah has laid on me as incumbent duty in the matter of fasting." He answered: "The month of Ramadan, unless you would voluntarily add thereto." Said [the Arab]: "Inform me of what Allah has laid on me as incumbent duty in that matter of alms." So the Apostle of Allah informed him of the legal prescriptions of Islam [with regard to alms (charity)]. Said he: "By Him who has honored you with the truth, I will not voluntarily add anything, but neither will I come short of what Allah has prescribed as incumbent duties for me." Then the Apostle of Allah—upon whom be Allah's blessing and peace—said: "He will be one of the fortunate ones, if he means that." Or [according to another version, he said]: "He will be brought into Paradise, if he means that."

Musaddad related to us, saying: Isma'il related to us from Ayyub, from Nafi', from Ibn 'Umar, who said: "The Prophet—upon whom be Allah's blessing and peace—fasted 'Ashura'[2] and bade it be kept as a fast, but when Ramadan was made an incumbent duty [on the Muslims], it was abandoned. 'Abdallah[3] used not to fast therein save when it happened to coincide with his [voluntary] fasts."

Qutaiba b. Sa'id said: al-Laith has related to us from Yazid b. Abi Habib, that 'Irak b. Malik related to him that 'Urwa informed him from 'A'isha[4] that the Quraish[5] used to fast the Day of "Ashura" in the pre-Islamic days, and then the Apostle of Allah—upon whom be Allah's blessing and peace—bade it be kept as a fast, [which it was] till Ramadan was made an incumbent duty. Said the Apostle of Allah—upon whom be Allah's blessing and peace—: "If anyone so wishes, let him still keep it as a fast, but if anyone so wishes, let him eat thereon."

2. *On the Merits of the Fast*

'Abdallah b. Maslama related to us from Malik, from Abu'z-Zinad, from al-A'raj, from Abu Huraira, that the Apostle of Allah—upon whom be Allah's blessing and peace—said: "Fasting is a protective covering [from the fires of Hell], so let there be no unseemly speech, no foolish acting [during it]. If a man is attacked or vilified [during it], let him say twice: 'I am fasting;' for by Him in whose hand is my soul, the odor from the mouth of him who fasts is sweeter to Allah than the perfume of musk. [Allah says to Himself]: 'He is giving up his food and his drink and his body lusts for My sake when he is fasting unto Me, so I shall reward him, and for each good deed [that he does] grant him the merit of ten.'"

3. *On Fasting as an Expiation*

'Ali b. 'Abdallah related to us, saying: Sufyan related to us, saying: several have related to us from Abu Wa'il, from Hudhaifa, who said: "Umar once asked: 'Who is there who has memorized a Tradition from

---

1 The particle *'an* used in these *isnad*s really means "on the authority of," but as the transmission of the Tradition was "from" one authority to another, it is translated throughout by "from" for brevity's sake. The b. in names means "son of."

2 A fast said to have been observed by the Jews and some of the Arabs in the pre-Islamic days as commemoration of their deliverance from their enemies.

3 Probably the companion of the Prophet 'Abdallah ibn 'Abbas.

4 The Prophet's youngest wife, who is quoted as the source for a vast number of Traditions.

5 The ruling Arab tribe in Mecca in the days of the Prophet.

the Prophet—upon whom be Allah's blessing and peace—about discord?' Hudhaifa answered: 'I heard him say that discord arises for a man from [three sources: from] his family, from his property, and from his neighbor; but prayer, fasting and gifts of charity may be its expiation.' Said ['Umar]: 'I am not asking about this [general matter of discord arising among men], but about that [which will come at the Last Days] billowing like the billows of the sea.' 'Facing that,' said [Hudhaifa], 'there is a gate shut.' 'Will it be opened,' asked ['Umar], 'or broken down?' 'It will be broken down,' answered [Hudhaifa]. 'Then,' said he, 'it is not likely to be shut again until the Day of Resurrection.'" We said to Masruq: "Ask him if 'Umar knew who the 'Gate' would be?"[1] So he asked him, and he answered: "Yes, [he knew that] just as he knew that night is before morning." ...

8. *On him who does not give up saying false words and doing false deeds during Ramadan*

Adam b. Abi Iyas related to us, saying: Ibn Abi Dhi'b related to us, saying: Sa'id al-Maqburi related to us from his father, from Abu Huraira, who said: Said the Prophet—upon whom be Allah's blessing and peace—: "If one does not give up saying false words and doing false deeds in Ramadan, his giving up eating and drinking means nothing to Allah."

9. *On whether, if one is reviled, he should say: "I am fasting"*

Ibrahim b. Musa related to us, saying: Hisham b. Yusuf informed us from Ibn Juraij, who said: 'Ata' informed me from Abu Salih az-Zayyat, that he heard Abu Huraira say: The Apostle of Allah—upon whom be Allah's blessing and peace—said: "Allah, mighty and majestic is He, has said: 'Every deed of a child of Adam is his [and will be recorded and rewarded in due measure] save fasting, which is Mine, and which I will reward [in My own measure].' Fasting is a protective covering, so when the day comes for anyone of you to fast, let there be no unseemly speech, no clamoring. If anyone reviles such a person, or attacks him, let him say: 'I am fasting.' By Him in whose hand is my soul, the odor from the mouth of him who fasts is sweeter to Allah than the perfume of musk. He who fasts has two occasions of rejoicing. He will have joy when he breaks his fast, and when he meets his Lord he will have joy because of his fasting."

10. *On Fasting [as a help] for one who fears [the temptations of one who remains] celibate*

'Ubdan related to us from Abu Hamza, from al-A'mash, from Ibrahim, from 'Alqama, [who said]: While I was walking with 'Abdallah he said: "I was once with the Prophet—upon whom be Allah's blessing and peace—when he said: 'Let him who is able to marry take a wife, for it is the best way of averting lascivious glances and of providing chaste enjoyment, but let him who is not able [to marry] fast, for it will be a remover [of unseemly passions] for him.'"

11. *On the saying of the Prophet—upon whom be Allah's blessing and peace—: "When you see the new moon, fast, and when you see it, break your fast."*

Sila quoted from 'Ammar: "Whosoever fasts on a doubtful day is disobeying Abu'l-Qasim,[2]—upon whom be Allah's blessing and peace.

'Abdallah b. Maslama related to us from Malik, from Nafi', from 'Abdallah b. 'Umar, that the Apostle of Allah—upon whom be Allah's blessing and peace—mentioned Ramadan, and said: "Do not fast until you see the new moon, and do not break the fast until you see it, and if it is cloudy make a computation for it."

'Abdallah b. Maslama related to us, saying: Malik related to us from 'Abdallah b. Dinar, from 'Abdallah b. 'Umar, that the Apostle of Allah—upon whom be Allah's blessing and peace—said: "The month is twenty-nine nights, so do not fast till you see it (i.e., the new moon), and if it is cloudy then compute the number to thirty."

Abu'l-Walid related to us, saying: Shu'ba related

---

1   The technical word in this Tradition is *fitna*, "dissension," "discord," and in Muslim accounts of the events of the Last Days preceding the great Day of Judgment there are innumerable stories about the dissensions which will arise among the people. The "gate" (*bab*) is the individual who will usher in any particular dissension.

2   Abu'l-Qasim means "Father of Qasim," and Muhammad was familiarly so called because Qasim was the name of his first-born son.

to us from Jabala b. Suhaim, who said: "I heard Ibn 'Umar say that the Prophet—upon whom be Allah's blessing and peace—said: 'The month is so-and-so,' and he tucked in [his] thumb the third time."

Adam related to us, saying: Shu'ba related to us, saying: Muhammad b. Ziyad related to us, saying: I heard Abu Huraira say that the Prophet—upon whom be Allah's blessing and peace—said:—or maybe he said: Abu'l-Qasim, upon whom be, etc. said:—"Fast when it (i.e., the moon) becomes seeable, and break your fast when it becomes seeable, and if it is cloudy then complete the number of Sha'ban,[1] [i.e.,] thirty."

Abu 'Asim related to us from Ibn Juraij, from Yahya b. 'Abdallah b. Saifi, from 'Ikrima b. 'Abd al-Rahman from Umm Salama, that the Prophet—upon whom be Allah's blessing and peace—took an oath to abstain from his women for a month. When twenty-nine days had elapsed he came in the morning—or maybe it was in the evening—[to 'A'isha]. Someone objected, "But you swore that you would not enter for a month," and he replied: "A month has twenty-nine days."

'Abd al-'Aziz b. 'Abdallah related to us, saying: Sulaiman b. Bilal related to us from Humaid, from Anas, who said: "The Apostle of Allah—upon whom be Allah's blessing and peace—took an oath to abstain from his women. As his foot was injured he stayed in an upper chamber for twenty-nine nights. Then he came down, but they said: 'O Apostle of Allah, you took an oath for a month', whereat he said: 'The month is twenty-nine [days].'"

12. *On how the two months of festival may not be curtailed*
Musaddad has related to us, saying: Mu'tamir related to us, saying: I heard Ishaq b. Suwaid [quoting] from 'Abd al-Rahman b. Abi Bakra, from his father, from the Prophet—upon whom be Allah's blessing and peace—[or according to another *isnad*], Musaddad related to me, saying: Mu'tamir related to us from Khalid al-Hadhdha', who said: 'Abd al-Rahman b. Abi Bakra related to me from his father, from the Prophet—upon whom be Allah's blessing and

peace—who said: "There are two months which may not be curtailed, the two months of festival, Ramadan and Dhu'l-Hijja."[2] Said Abu 'Abdallah: "Ishaq said: 'Twenty-nine complete days.' Ahmed b. Jundub said: 'If Ramadan is curtailed, complete Dhu'l-Hijja, and if Dhu'l-Hijja is curtailed, complete Ramadan.' Abu'l-Hasan said: 'Ishaq b. Rahuwaih used to say, 'Let neither be curtailed in [their] meritoriousness, whether it is twenty-nine or thirty [days].'" …

22. *On the faster who awakes in the morning in a state of sexual pollution*
'Abdallah b. Maslama related to us from Malik, from Sumayy, a client of Abu Bakr b. 'Abd al-Rahman b. al-Harith b. Hisham b. al-Mughira, that he heard Abu Bakr b. 'Abd al-Rahman say: "I was with my father when we entered to 'A'isha and Umm Salama," [or as another *isnad* has it], Abu'l-Yaman related to us, saying: Shu'aib informed us from al-Zuhri, who said: Abu Bakr b. 'Abd al-Rahman b. al-Harith b. Hisham informed me that his father 'Abd al-Rahman informed Marwan that 'A'isha and Umm Salama had both informed him, that the Apostle of Allah—upon whom be Allah's blessing and peace—would be overtaken by the dawn while he was still in a state of pollution from [sexual contact with] his wives, but he would bathe and then fast. Marwan said to 'Abd al-Rahman b. al-Harith; "I swear by Allah you shall surely [go and] disturb Abu Huraira by that [information]." Marwan was at that time [Governor] over Medina. Said Abu Bakr: "'Abd al-Rahman, however, disliked [the idea of doing] that, so it was decided among us that we would gather together at Dhu'l-Hulaifa, where Abu Huraira had some land. Then 'Abd al-Rahman said to Abu Huraira: 'I am about to mention to you a matter that I should never have mentioned to you had not Marwan sworn that I should.' Then he mentioned what 'A'isha and Umm Salama had said. Said [Abu Huraira]: 'That is so. Al-Fadl b. 'Abbas related [it] to me, and no one would know better than him.'" Said Hammam and Ibn 'Abdallah b. 'Umar [quoting] from Abu Huraira: "The Prophet—upon whom be Allah's blessing and peace—used to order [in such a case that]

---

1   Sha'ban is the month which precedes the fasting month of Ramadan.
2   Ramadan, the month of fasting, is the ninth month in the Islamic calendar, and Dhu'l-Hijja is the twelfth month, the month during which takes place the annual pilgrimage to Mecca—the *hajj*.

the fast be broken," but the first [version] has the better *isnad*.

23. *On the [restrictions of] sex relations for one who is fasting.*

'A'isha said: "It is her vulva which is forbidden to him."

Sulaiman b. Harb related to us from Shu'ba, from al-Hakam, from Ibrahim, from al-Aswad, from 'A'isha, who said: "The Prophet—upon whom be Allah's blessing and peace—used to kiss and handle [his wives] while he was fasting, but he had more control over his *irb* than any of you." [As to this word *irb*], Ibn 'Abbas said that [the derivative from it] *ma'arib* means "need," and Tawus used to use the phrase "one who possesses no *irba*" for a defective who has no need of women. Jabir b. Zaid said: "If one looks [at a woman] and has an emission let him go on with his fast."

24. *On the [legitimacy of] kissing for one who is fasting*

Muhammad b. al-Muthanna related to us, saying: Yahya related to us from Hisham, who said: My father informed me from 'A'isha—with whom may Allah be pleased—from the Prophet—upon whom be Allah's blessing and peace—[or by another *isnad*], 'Abdallah b. Maslama related to us from Malik, from Hisham, from his father, from 'A'isha—with whom may Allah be pleased—who said: "There were times when the Apostle of Allah—upon whom be Allah's blessing and peace—would kiss certain of his wives while he was fasting." Then she laughed.

Musaddad related to us, saying: Yahya related to us from Hisham b. Abi 'Abdallah, who said: Yahya b. Abi Kathir related to us from Abu Salama, from Zainab daughter of Umm Salama, from her mother,[1] who said: "While I was with the Prophet—upon whom be Allah's blessing and peace—in bed, my menses started, so I slipped out and put on my menstrual clothes. He asked: 'What is the matter with you? has your period come on?' 'Yes,' I replied, and I entered the bed with him again." Now she and the Apostle of Allah—upon whom be Allah's blessing and peace—used both to bathe at the same [water] vessel, and he used to kiss her when he was fasting.

25. *On the bathing of one who is fasting*

Ibn 'Umar soiled his garment with urine but put it on him while he was fasting. Ash-Sha'bi entered the [public] baths while he was fasting. Ibn Abbas said: "There is no harm in tasting [what is in] the cooking pot [while fasting] or [any other] thing." Al-Hasan said: "There is no harm in the faster gargling or cooling himself off" (i.e., provided he does not drink the water). Ibn Mas'ud said: "When the day comes around for any one of you to fast he may, as he rises in the morning, use oil and comb." Anas said: "I had a copper wash-basin in which I used to plunge even while I was fasting, and Ibn 'Umar used to brush his teeth at the beginning and at the end of the day [while he was fasting]." Ibn Sirin said: "There is no harm in the use of the tooth-brush if it is fresh." The objection was raised: "But it has taste," and [he replied]: "and so does the water have taste when you gargle with it, [yet that is not considered to be breaking the fast]. Anas, al-Hasan and Ibrahim also saw no harm in the faster making use of kohl [for the eyes].

Ahmad b. Salih related to us, saying: Ibn Wahb related to us, saying: Yunus related to us, from Ibn Shihab, from 'Urwa and Abu Bakr, who said: 'A'isha—with whom may Allah be pleased—said: "The dawn used to overtake the Prophet in Ramadan when he was polluted—and not from an [erotic] dream—but he would bathe and [then commence the] fast."

Isma'il related to us, saying: Malik related to me from Sumayy, a client of Abu Bakr b. 'Abd al-Rahman b. al-Harith b. Hisham b. al-Mughira, that he heard Abu Bakr b. 'Abd al-Rahman say: "I was with my father and went along with him till we entered to 'A'isha—with whom may Allah be pleased—who said: 'I bear witness of the Apostle of Allah—upon whom be Allah's blessing and peace—that he used to wake up in the morning polluted [by sperm] from intercourse, not from dreaming, and then he would fast [that day].' Then we entered to Umm Salama, who said the same thing."

26. *On the faster who eats and drinks from forgetfulness*

'Ata' said: "If one snuffs up water and some of it enters the throat so that one is not able to reject it, no harm

---

1 Her mother was one of the Prophet's wives.

is done [thereby to one's fast]." Also al-Hasan said: "If a fly should get into one's throat, that is nothing," and al-Hasan and Mujahid both said: "If one should have sexual intercourse forgetfully, that is nothing."

'Abdan related to us [saying], Yazid b. Zurai' informed us, saying, Hisham related to us, saying: Ibn Sirin related to us from Abu Huraira, from the Prophet—upon whom be blessing and peace—that he said: "If anyone forgets and eats or drinks, let him complete his fast, for it was Allah who caused him thus to eat or drink."

27. *On the fresh and the dry tooth-brush for him who is fasting*

It is reported from 'Amir b. Rabi'a, who said: "I have seen the Prophet—upon whom be Allah's blessing and peace—using the tooth-brush while he was fasting more times than I can reckon or count." 'A'isha said, quoting the Prophet—upon whom be Allah's blessing and peace—: "The tooth-brush is a purifier for the mouth and a thing well-pleasing to the Lord." 'Ata' and Qatada said: "One may swallow one's saliva [without thereby breaking one's fast]." Abu Huraira said, quoting the Prophet—upon whom be Allah's blessing and peace—: "Were it not that I might be causing distress to my community I should bid them use the tooth-brush at every ablution." The like of this Tradition is transmitted from Jabir and Zaid b. Khalid from the Prophet—upon whom be Allah's blessing and peace—who [in this matter] did not particularize the one fasting from anyone else.

'Abdan related to us, saying: 'Abdallah informed us, saying: Ma'mar informed us, saying: al-Zuhri related to us from 'Ata' b. Yazid, from Humran, who said: "I saw 'Uthman [i.e., the third Caliph] performing ablutions. He poured [the water out] over his hands three times. Then he gargled and snuffed up [the water]. Then he washed his face three times. Then he washed his right arm up to the elbow three times. Then he washed his left arm up to the elbow three times. Then he rubbed his head [with his moist hands]. Then he washed his right foot three times. Then he washed his left foot three times. Then he said: 'I have seen the Apostle of Allah—upon whom be Allah's blessing and peace—performing ablution just like this ablution of mine, after which he [i.e., the Prophet] said: Whosoever performs [his] ablutions as I have done here, and prays a two-bow prayer, not allowing anything to distract him during them, will have all his past sins forgiven him.'"

3.10 Law: Abu Dawud al-Sijistani, *Compilation of the Jurisprudential Responses of Ahmad ibn Hanbal* (before 888). Original in Arabic.

ABU DAWUD AL-SIJISTANI (d.888) WAS A disciple of Ahmad ibn Hanbal (d.855), a teacher of theology, hadith, and jurisprudence (*fiqh*) at Baghdad. Al-Sijistani was one of a number of scholars to collect ibn Hanbal's responses to legal questions and publish them in a long compilation from which the passages below are taken. In some cases he reported what he heard ibn Hanbal say to others; in other cases he recorded the answers given to questions that he himself posed. By the time that ibn Hanbal was teaching there was already a tradition of questions and opinions pertaining to the law derived from passages in the Qur'an and opinions about them. Ibn Hanbal drew on these for his pronouncements, while also from time to time turning directly to the hadith and the Qur'an for guidance. The passages below concern marriage.

[Source: *Chapters on Marriage and Divorce: Responses of Ibn Hanbal and Ibn Rahwayh*, trans. Susan A. Spectorsky (Austin: University of Texas Press, 1993), pp. 61-62, 65.]

Chapter on Marrying *Dhimmi* Women[1]

§9 I heard Ahmad asked whether a Muslim should marry Jewish and Christian women.
He said, "There is no harm in it if they are free, but if they are slaves, no."

§10 I heard Ahmad say, "Free Jewish and Christian wives are treated the same as a man's Muslim wives with regard to his dividing his time between them and providing maintenance for them."

Chapter on Marrying a Slave Woman in Addition to a Free One

§11 I heard Ahmad asked whether a man who is already married to a free woman can marry a female slave as well.
He said, "Most scholars find it reprehensible."

§12 I heard Ahmad asked about marrying female slaves [in general].
He said, "The strongest opinion related concerning this matter is on the authority of Ibn 'Abbas."[2]

§13 I heard Ahmad asked about a man who manumits a female slave and makes her manumission her dower.[3]
He said, "He does not need a *wali*,[4] but his marriage must be witnessed."

§14 I said to Ahmad, "What does he say [if he wants to marry her]?"
He said, "He says, 'I hereby make your manumission your dower,' and if he says, 'I hereby manumit you and make your manumission your dower,' this is valid, [because] it is connected

speech, unless he has manumitted her [previously], then wishes to marry her. [In that case a dower] is due to her."

§15 I heard Ahmad asked about a man who manumits his female slave making her manumission her dower and then divorces her before having intercourse with her.
He said, "She returns to him half her price [i.e., the price at which she would have been sold before her manumission]."[5]

§16 Someone said to Ahmad, "[What if] she does not have it?"
He said, "Then she is in debt for it."

§17 I heard Ahmad asked what the minimum prerequisites were for a marriage contract.
He said, "A suitor, someone to give the bride in marriage, and two witnesses."

Chapter on *Tafwid*[6]

§35 I heard Ahmad asked about a woman's *wali*s who give her in marriage for less than her fair dower.
He said, "If she consents, then it is a valid marriage."

§36 Someone said to Ahmad, "Then [the validity of] the marriage does not depend on her dower being a fair one?"
He said, "No, not if she has consented [to be married for less than her fair dower]."

§37 I heard Ahmad asked about a woman's fair dower.
He said, "It is the dower given to the women in her family."

§38 Someone said to Ahmad, "Ishaq b. Ibrahim, that is al-Marwazi, says five hundred dirhams [is a

---

1 *Dhimmi* refers to a "protected subject," normally a Christian or Jew—people "of the book"—who lived in Islamic territory.

2 The two conditions usually given that necessitate marriage with a slave rather than a free woman are a man's inability to afford a free wife's dower (the gift, usually of money or property, that a husband gives his wife) and fear that if he remains single he will commit an act of fornication.

3 Here the owner of a slave frees her and gives her price to her as a dower.

4 A *wali* is a guardian, usually a girl's father. He is also normally a witness to the marriage. In this instance, a slave girl's father is presumably not around, but the marriage nevertheless needs to be witnessed.

5 Normally a woman retains the dower in case of divorce, but if she is divorced before intercourse, she is to return half the dower. In this case the price of the slave's freedom is her dower, but since she is divorced before intercourse, she must return half of it.

6 A *tafwid* marriage is one in which the dower is not specified or is unusual in some way.

fair dower]."[1] But Ahmad found that objection-able.

§39 I heard him say, "If a woman says, 'Give me in marriage for one thousand dirhams,' and he (i.e., her guardian) says, 'I give you in marriage for five hundred,' and her fair dower is ten thousand, she should receive one thousand, because she made her body available [for that sum] and was content [with it]."

§40 I said to Ahmad, "[What about] the *hadith* of Ma'qil b. Yasar—the story of Barwa' bt. Washiq?"[2] [I asked whether] he followed it. He said, "Yes."

3.11 Fiction: *Sindbad the Sailor* (9th c.). Original in Arabic.

A SERIES OF LEGENDARY STORIES from Persia, India, and Greece, *The Thousand and One Nights* underwent many transformations. In the eighth century two Arabic versions translated from Persian were circulating. In the ninth century various stories were added, including *Sindbad the Sailor*, which depicts the caliphate of Harun al-Rashid (r.786–809) as a period of opulence and commercial expansion. A later version from the twelfth century reflects Egyptian influence, while a still later version includes stories that reflect the Crusading and Mongol periods. The gaze of the author of *Sindbad*, excerpted here, is on the gulf of Basra and the lands that could be reached from the Arabian Sea.

[Source: *The Thousand and One Nights: The Hunchback, Sindbad, and Other Tales*, trans. N. J. Dawood (Harmondsworth: Penguin Books, 1954), pp. 110–20, 158–66.]

Once upon a time, in the reign of the Caliph Harun al-Rashid, there lived in the city of Baghdad a poor man who earned his living by carrying burdens upon his head. He was called Sindbad the Porter.

One day, as he was staggering under a heavy load in the sweltering heat of the summer sun, he passed by a merchant's house that stood in a pleasant, shaded spot on the roadside. The ground before it was well swept and watered; and Sindbad, seeing a broad wooden bench just outside the gates, put down his load and sat there to rest awhile and to wipe away the sweat which trickled down his forehead. A cool and fragrant breeze blew through the doorway, and from within came the melodious strains of the lute and voices singing. They mingled with the choirs of birds warbling hymns to Allah in various tongues and tunes: curlews and pigeons, merles and bulbuls and turtle-doves.

Moved with great joy, he went up to the door and, looking within, saw in the center of the noble court-yard a beautiful garden, around which stood numerous slaves and eunuchs, and such an array of attendants as can be found only in the courts of illustrious kings. And all about the place floated the aroma of the choicest meats and wines.

Still marvelling at the splendor of what he saw, Sindbad lifted up his burden and was about to go his way when there came from within a handsome and well-dressed little page, who took him by the hand, saying: "Pray come in; my master wishes to speak with you."

The porter politely declined; but the lad would take no refusal. So Sindbad left his burden in the vestibule with the door-keeper and followed the page into the house.

He was conducted into a magnificent and spa-

---

1 Al-Marwazi was a scholar living at about the same time as Ibn Hanbal.
2 Barwa' bt. Washiq's husband died before determining her dower and before having intercourse with her. The *hadiths* about her are somewhat different in different collections, so it is not clear what ibn Hanbal's view is. The bt. means "bint," daughter of.

cious hall, where an impressive company of nobles and mighty sheikhs were seated according to rank at tables spread with the daintiest meats and richest wines, and gaily decked with flowers and fruit. On one side of the hall sat beautiful slave-girls who sang and made music; and to the fore reclined the host, a venerable old man whose beard was touched with silver. Bewildered at the grandeur and majesty of all that he beheld, the porter thought to himself: "By Allah, this must either be a corner of Paradise or the palace of some mighty king!"

Sindbad courteously greeted the distinguished assembly and, kissing the ground before them, wished them joy and prosperity. He then stood in silence with eyes cast down.

The master of the house welcomed him kindly and bade him draw near and be seated. He ordered his slaves to set before the porter a choice of delicate foods and pressed him to eat. After pronouncing the blessing Sindbad fell to, and when he had eaten his fill washed his hands and thanked the old sheikh for his hospitality.

"You are welcome to this house, my friend," said the host, "and may this day bring you joy. We would gladly know your name and calling."

"My name is Sindbad," he answered, "by trade a porter."

"How strange a chance!" smiled the old man. "For my name, too, is Sindbad. They call me Sindbad the Sailor, and marvel at my strange history. Presently, my brother, you shall hear the tale of my fortunes and all the hardships that I suffered before I rose to my present state and became the lord of this mansion where we are now assembled. For only after long toil, fearful ordeals, and dire peril did I achieve this fame. Seven voyages I made in all, each a story of such marvel as confounds the reason and fills the soul with wonder. All that befell me had been pre-ordained; and that which the moving hand of Fate has written no mortal power can revoke."

The First Voyage of Sindbad the Sailor

Know, my friends, that my father was the chief merchant of this city and one of its richest men. He died while I was still a child, leaving me great wealth and many estates and farm-lands. As soon as I came of age

and had control of my inheritance, I took to extravagant living. I clad myself in the costliest robes, ate and drank sumptuously, and consorted with reckless prodigals of my own age, thinking that this mode of life would endure for ever.

It was not long before I awoke from my heedless folly to find that I had frittered away my entire fortune. I was stricken with horror and dismay at the gravity of my plight, and bethought myself of a proverb of our master Solomon son of David (may peace be upon them both!) which my father often used to cite: "The day of death is better than the day of birth, a live dog is better than a dead lion, and the grave is better than poverty." I sold the remainder of my lands and my household chattels for the sum of three thousand dirhams, and, fortifying myself with hope and courage, resolved to travel abroad and trade in foreign lands.

I bought a large quantity of merchandise and made preparations for a long voyage. Then I set sail together with a company of merchants in a river-ship bound for Basra. There we put to sea and, voyaging many days and nights from isle to isle and from shore to shore, buying and selling and bartering wherever the ship anchored, we came at length to a little island as fair as the Garden of Eden. Here the captain of our ship cast anchor and put out the landing-planks.

The passengers went ashore and set to work to light a fire. Some busied themselves with cooking and washing, some fell to eating and drinking and making merry, while others, like myself, set out to explore the island. While we were thus engaged we suddenly heard the captain cry out to us from the ship: "All aboard, quickly! Abandon everything and run for your lives! The mercy of Allah be upon you, for this is no island but a gigantic whale floating on the bosom of the sea, on whose back the sands have settled and trees have grown since the world was young! When you lit the fire it felt the heat and stirred. Make haste, I say; or soon the whale will plunge into the sea and you will all be lost!"

Hearing the captain's cries, the passengers made for the ship in panic-stricken flight, leaving behind their cooking-pots and other belongings. Some reached the ship in safety, but others did not; for suddenly the island shook beneath our feet and, submerged by mountainous waves, sank with all that stood upon it to the bottom of the roaring ocean.

Together with my unfortunate companions I was engulfed by the merciless tide; but Providence came to my aid, casting in my way a great wooden trough which had been used by the ship's company for washing. Impelled by that instinct which makes all mortals cling to life, I held fast to the trough and, bestriding it firmly, paddled away with my feet as the waves tossed and buffeted me on every side. Meanwhile the captain hoisted sail and set off with the other passengers. I followed the ship with my eyes until it vanished from sight, and I resigned myself to certain death.

Darkness soon closed in upon the ocean. All that night and throughout the following day I drifted on, lashed by the wind and the waves, until the trough brought me to the steep shores of a densely wooded island, where trees hung over the sea.

I caught hold of one of the branches, and with its aid managed to clamber ashore after fighting so long for my life. Finding myself again on dry land, I realized that I had lost the use of my legs, and my feet began to smart with the bites of fish.

Worn out by anguish and exertion, I sank into a death-like slumber; and it was not until the following morning when the sun rose that I came to my senses. But my feet were so sore and swollen that I could move about only by crawling on my knees. By good fortune, however, the island had an abundance of fruit trees, which provided me with sustenance, and many springs of fresh water; so that after a few days my body was restored to strength and my spirit revived. I cut myself a staff from the branch of a tree, and with its aid set out to explore the island and to admire the many goodly things which Allah had planted on its soil.

One day, as I was roaming about the beach in an unfamiliar part of the island, I caught sight of a strange object in the distance which appeared to be some wild beast or sea-monster. As I drew nearer and looked more closely at it, I saw that it was a noble mare of an uncommonly high stature haltered to a tree. On seeing me the mare gave an ear-splitting neigh which made me take to my heels in terror. Presently there emerged from the ground a man, who pursued me, shouting: "Who are you and whence have you come? What are you doing here?"

"Sir," I replied, "I am a luckless voyager, aban-doned in the middle of the sea; but it was Allah's will that I should be rescued from the fury of the waves and cast upon this island."

The stranger took me by the hand and bade me follow him. He led me to a subterranean cavern, and, after asking me to be seated, he placed some food before me and invited me to eat. When I had eaten my fill he questioned me about the fortunes of my voyage, and I related to him all that had befallen me from first to last.

"But, pray tell me, sir," I inquired, as my host marvelled at my adventure, "what is the reason of your vigil here and for what purpose is this mare tethered on the beach?"

"Know," he replied, "that I am one of the many grooms of King Mahrajan. We have charge of all his horses and are stationed in different parts of this island. Each month, on the night of the full moon, we tether all the virgin mares on the beach and hide in shelters near by. Presently the sea-horses scent the mares and, emerging from the water, leap upon the beasts and cover them. Then they try to drag them away into the sea. But this they fail to do, as the mares are securely roped. With angry cries the sea-horses attack the mares and kick them with their hind legs. At this point we rush from our hiding-places and drive the sea-horses back into the water. The mares then conceive and bear colts and fillies of inestimable worth. To-night," he added, "when we have completed our task, I shall take you to our King and show you our city. Allah be praised for this happy encounter; for had you not chanced to meet us you would have surely come to grief in the solitude of these wild regions."

I thanked him with all my heart and called down blessings upon him. While we were thus engaged in conversation we heard a dreadful cry in the distance. The groom quickly snatched up his sword and buckler and rushed out, shouting aloud and banging his sword on his shield. Thereupon several other grooms came out from their hiding-places, brandishing their spears and yelling at the top of their voices. The sea-horse, who had just covered the mare, took fright at this tumult and plunged, like a buffalo, headlong into the sea, where he disappeared beneath the water.

As we sat on the ground to recover our breath, the other grooms, each leading a mare, approached us. My companion explained to them the circumstances of my presence, and, after exchanging greetings, we rode to the city of King Mahrajan.

As soon as the King was informed of my arrival he summoned me to his presence. He marvelled at my story, saying: "By Allah, my son, your preservation has been truly miraculous. Praise be to the Highest for your deliverance!"

Thenceforth I rose rapidly in the King's favor and soon became a trusted courtier. He vested me with robes of honor and appointed me Comptroller of Shipping at the port of his kingdom. And during my sojourn in that realm I earned the gratitude of the poor and the humble for my readiness to intercede for them with the King.

There I witnessed many prodigies and met travellers from different foreign lands. One day I entered the King's chamber and found him entertaining a company of Indians. I exchanged greetings with them and questioned them about their country. In the course of conversation I was astonished to learn that there were no fewer than seventy-two different castes in India. The noblest of these castes is known as Shakiriyah, and its members are renowned for piety and fair dealing. Another caste are the Brahmins. They are skilled breeders of camels, horses, and cattle, and though they abstain from wine, they are a merry and pleasure-loving people.

Not far from the King's dominions there is a little island where at night is heard a mysterious beating of drums and clash of tambourines. Travellers and men from neighboring isles told me that its inhabitants were a shrewd and diligent race.

In those distant seas I once saw a fish two hundred cubits in length, and another with a head that resembled an owl's. This I saw with my own eyes, and many other things no less strange and wondrous.

Whenever I walked along the quay I talked with the sailors and travellers from far countries, inquiring whether any of them had heard tell of the city of Baghdad and how far off it lay; for I never lost hope that I should one day find my way back to my native land. But there was none who knew of that city; and as the days dragged by, my longing for home weighed heavy upon my heart.

One day, however, as I stood on the wharf, leaning upon my staff and gazing out to sea, a ship bearing a large company of merchants came sailing into the harbor. As soon as it was moored, the sails were furled and landing-planks put out. The crew began to unload the cargo, and I stood by entering up the merchandise in my register. When they had done, I asked the captain if all the goods had now been brought ashore.

"Sir," he replied, "in the ship's hold I still have a few bales which belonged to a merchant who was drowned at an early stage of our voyage. We shall put them up for sale and take the money to his kinsmen in Baghdad, the City of Peace."

"What was the merchant's name?" I demanded.

"Sindbad," he answered.

I looked more closely into his face, and, recognizing him at once, uttered a joyful cry.

"Why!" I exclaimed, "I am Sindbad, the self-same owner of these goods, who was left to drown with many others when the great whale plunged into the sea. But through the grace of Allah I was cast by the waves onto the shores of this island, where I found favor with the King and became Comptroller at this port. I am the true owner of these goods, which are my only possessions in this world."

"By Allah," cried the captain, "is there no longer any faith or honesty in man? I have but to mention a dead man's goods and you claim them for your own! Why, we saw Sindbad drown before our very eyes. Dare you lay claim to his property?"

"I pray you, captain," I rejoined, "listen to my story and you shall soon learn the whole truth." I then recounted to him all the details of the voyage from the day we set sail from Basra till we cast anchor off the treacherous island and reminded him of a certain matter that had passed between us.

The captain and the passengers now recognized me, and all congratulated me on my escape, saying: "Allah has granted you a fresh span of life!"

At once my goods were brought ashore and I rejoiced to find the bales intact and sealed as I had left them. I selected some of the choicest and most precious articles as presents for King Mahrajan, and had them carried by the sailors to the royal palace, where I laid them at his feet. I informed the King of the unexpected arrival of my ship and the happy recovery of all my goods. He marvelled greatly at this chance, and, in return for my presents, bestowed upon me priceless treasures.

I sold my wares at a substantial profit and re-equipped myself with the finest produce of that island. When all was ready for the homeward voyage I presented myself at the King's court, and, thanking him for the many favors he had shown me, begged leave to return to my land and people.

Then we set sail, trusting in Allah and propitious Fortune; and after voyaging many days and nights we at length safely arrived in Basra.

I spent but a few days in that town and then, loaded with treasure, set out for Baghdad, the City of Peace. I was overjoyed to be back in my native city, and hastening to my old street entered my own house, where by and by all my friends and kinsmen came to greet me.

I bought fine houses and rich farm-lands, concubines and eunuchs and black slaves, and became richer than I had ever been before. I kept open house for my old companions, and, soon forgetting the hardships of my voyage, resumed with new zest my former mode of living.

That is the story of the first of my adventures. Tomorrow, if Allah wills, I shall relate to you the tale of my second voyage.

The day was drawing to its close, and Sindbad the Sailor invited Sindbad the Porter to join the guests in the evening meal. When the feast was finished he gave him a hundred pieces of gold, saying: "You have delighted us with your company this day."

The porter thanked him for his generous gift and departed, pondering over the vicissitudes of fortune and marvelling at all that he had heard.

Next morning he went again to the house of his benefactor, who received him courteously and seated him by his side. Presently the other guests arrived, and when they had feasted and made merry, Sindbad the Sailor began: ...

[Feeling "an irresistible longing to travel again about the world and visit distant cities and islands in quest of profit and adventure," Sindbad took off on five more voyages. Each involved monsters and miseries, yet Sindbad survived them all, returning home a rich man every time. One day after another, Sindbad told one adventure, and when he finished he gave one hundred pieces of gold to Sindbad the Porter and told him to return the next day. Then came the moment to tell of his seventh and final voyage. When all were assembled, Sindbad the Sailor began the story.]

The Last Voyage of Sindbad the Sailor

For many years after my return I lived joyfully in Baghdad, feasting and carousing with my boon companions and revelling away the riches which my far-flung travels had earned me. But though I was now past the prime of life, my untamed spirit rebelled against my declining years, and I once again longed to see the world and travel in the lands of men. I made preparations for a long voyage and, boarding a good ship in company with some eminent merchants, set sail from Basra with a fair wind and a rich cargo.

We voyaged peacefully for many weeks, but one day, whilst we were sailing in the China Sea, a violent tempest struck our ship, drenching us with torrents of rain. We hastily covered our bales with canvas to protect them from the wet, and fervently prayed to Allah to save us from the fury of the sea; while the captain, rolling up his sleeves and tucking the skirts of his robes into his belt, climbed the mast and from the top scanned the horizon in all directions. Presently he climbed down again, all in a tremble with terror, and, staring at us with an expression of blank despair, beat his face and plucked the hairs of his beard.

"Pray to Allah," he cried, "that He may save us from the peril into which we have fallen! Weep and say your farewells, for the treacherous wind has got the better of us and driven our ship into the world's farthermost ocean!"

Thereupon the captain opened one of his cabin chests and took from it a small cotton bag filled with an ash-like powder. He sprinkled some water over the powder and, after waiting a little, inhaled it into his nostrils; then, opening a little book, he intoned aloud some strange incantations and at length turned to us, crying: "Know that we are now approaching the Realm of Kings, the very land where our master Solomon son of David (may peace be upon him) lies buried. Serpents of prodigious size swarm about that coast, and the sea is filled with giant whales which can swallow vessels whole. Farewell, my friends; and may Allah have mercy upon us all!"

Scarcely had the captain uttered these words when suddenly the ship was tossed high up in the air and then flung down into the sea, while an ear-splitting cry, more terrible than thunder, boomed through the swelling ocean. Terror seized our hearts as we saw a gigantic whale, as massive as a mountain, rushing swiftly towards us, followed by another no less huge, and a third greater than the two put together. This last monster bounded from the surging billows and, opening wide its enormous mouth, seized in its jaws the ship with all that was in it. I hastily ran to the edge of the tilting deck and, casting off my clothes, leapt into the sea just before the whale swallowed up the ship and disappeared beneath the foam with its two companions.

With Allah's help I clung to a piece of timber which had fallen from the lost vessel and, contending with the mighty waves for two days and nights, was at length cast on an island covered with fruit trees and watered by many streams. After refreshing myself I wandered aimlessly about, and soon came to a fast-flowing river which rolled its waters towards the interior of the island. As I stood upon the bank I hit upon the idea of building a raft and allowing myself to be carried down by the current, as I had done in my last voyage. "If I succeed in saving myself this time," I said, "all will be well with me and I solemnly vow never in all my life to let the mere thought of voyaging cross my mind again. If I fail, I shall at last find rest from all the toils and tribulations which my incorrigible folly has earned me."

I cut down several branches from an exotic tree which I had never seen before and bound them together into a raft with the stems of some creeping plants. I loaded the raft with a large quantity of fruit, and, commending myself to Allah, pushed off down the river.

For three days and nights I was hurried swiftly along by the current, until, overcome by dizziness, I sank into a dead faint. When I recovered consciousness I found myself heading towards a fearful precipice, down which the waters of the river were tumbling in a mighty cataract. I clung with all my strength to the branches of the raft and, resigning myself to my fate, prayed silently for a merciful end. When I had reached the very edge of the precipice, however, I suddenly felt the raft halted upon the water and found myself caught in a net which a crowd of men had thrown from the bank. My raft was quickly hauled to land, and I was released from the net half dead with terror and exhaustion.

As I lay upon the mud, I gradually became aware of a venerable old man who was bending over me. He wrapped me in warm garments and greeted me kindly; and when my strength had returned a little he helped me to rise and led me slowly to the baths of the city, where I was washed with perfumed water. Then the old man took me to his own house. He regaled me sumptuously with excellent meats and wines, and when the feast was ended, his slaves washed my hands and wiped them with napkins of the rarest silk. After this my host conducted me to a noble chamber and left me alone after assigning several of his slaves to my service.

The kind old man entertained me in this fashion for three days. When I had completely recovered, he visited me in my chamber and sat conversing with me for an hour. Just before leaving my room, however, he turned to me and said: "If you wish to sell your merchandise, my friend, I will gladly come down with you to the market-place."

I was greatly puzzled at these words and did not know what to answer, as I had been cast utterly naked in that city.

"Do not be troubled over your goods, my son," went on the old man. "If we receive a good offer, we will sell them outright; if not, I will keep them for you in my own storehouse until they fetch a better price."

Concealing my perplexity, I replied: "I am willing to do whatever you advise." With this I rose and went out with him to the market-place.

There I saw an excited crowd admiring an object on the ground with exclamations of enthusiastic praise. Pushing my way among the gesticulating merchants, I was astonished to find the center of attention to be no other than the raft aboard which I had sailed down the river. And presently the old man ordered a broker to begin the auction.

"Who will make the first bid for this rare sandalwood?" began the broker.

"A hundred dinars!" cried one of the merchants.

"A thousand!" shouted another.

"Eleven hundred!" exclaimed my host.

"Agreed!" I cried.

Upon this the old man ordered his slaves to carry the wood to his store and walked back with me to his house, where he paid me eleven hundred pieces of gold locked in an iron coffer.

One day, as we sat conversing together, the old man said: "My son, pray grant me a favor."

"With all my heart," I replied.

"I am a very old man, and have not been blessed with a son," went on my benefactor. "Yet I have a young and beautiful daughter, who on my death will be sole mistress of my fortune. If you will have her for your wife, you will inherit my wealth and become chief of the merchants of this city."

I readily consented to the sheikh's proposal. A sumptuous feast was held, a cadi [judge] and witnesses were called in, and I was married to the old man's daughter amidst great rejoicings. When the wedding guests had departed I was conducted to the bridal chamber, where I was allowed to see my wife for the first time. I found her incomparably beautiful, and rejoiced to see her decked with the rarest pearls and jewels.

My wife and I grew to love each other dearly, and we lived together in happiness and contentment. Not long afterwards my wife's father died, and I inherited all his possessions. His slaves became my slaves and his goods my goods, and the merchants of the city appointed me their chief in his place.

One day, however, I discovered that every year the people of that land experienced a wondrous change in their bodies. All the men grew wings upon their shoulders and for a whole day flew high up in the air, leaving their wives and children behind. Amazed at this prodigy, I importuned one of my friends to allow me to cling to him when he next took his flight, and at length prevailed on him to let me try this novel adventure. When the long-awaited day arrived, I took tight hold of my friend's waist and was at once carried up swiftly in the air. We climbed higher and higher into the void until I could hear the angels in their choirs singing hymns to Allah under the vault of heaven. Moved with awe, I cried: "Glory and praise eternal be to Allah, King of the Universe!"

Scarcely had I uttered these words when my winged carrier dropped headlong through the air and finally alighted on the top of a high mountain. There he threw me off his back and took to the air again, calling down curses on my head. Abandoned upon this desolate mountain, I lifted my hands in despair and cried: "There is no strength nor help save in Allah! Every time I escape from one ordeal I find myself in another as grievous. Surely I deserve all that befalls me!"

While I was thus reflecting upon my plight, I saw two youths coming up towards me. Their faces shone with an unearthly beauty, and each held a staff of red gold in his hand. I at once rose to my feet, and, walking towards them, wished them peace. They returned my greeting courteously, and I inquired: "Who are you, pray, and what object has brought you to this barren mountain?"

"We are worshippers of the True God," they replied. With this, one of the youths pointed to a certain path upon the mountain and, handing me his staff, walked away with his companion.

Bewildered at these words, I set off in the direction he had indicated, leaning upon my gold staff as I walked. I had not gone far when I saw coming towards me the flyer who had so unceremoniously set me down upon the mountain. Determined to learn the reason of his displeasure, I went up to him and said gently: "Is this how friends behave to friends?"

The winged man, who was now no longer angry, replied: "Know that my fall was caused by your unfortunate mention of your god. The word has this effect upon us all, and this is why we never utter it."

I assured my friend that I had meant no harm and promised to commit no such transgression in future. Then I begged him to carry me back to the city. He took me upon his shoulders and in a few moments set me down before my own house.

My wife was overjoyed at my return, and when I told her of my adventure, she said: "We must no longer stay among these people. Know that they are the brothers of Satan and have no knowledge of the True God."

"How then did your father dwell among them?" I asked.

"My father was of an alien race," she replied. "He shared none of their creeds, and he did not lead their life. As he is now dead, let us sell our possessions and leave this blasphemous city."

Thereupon I resolved to return home. We sold our houses and other property, and hiring a vessel set sail with a rich cargo.

Aided by a favouring wind, we voyaged many days and nights and at length came to Basra and thence to Baghdad, the City of Peace. I conveyed to my stores the valuables I had brought with me and, taking my wife to my own house in my old street, rejoiced to meet my kinsfolk and my old companions. They told me that this voyage had kept me abroad for nearly twenty-seven years and marvelled exceedingly at all that had befallen me.

I rendered deep thanks to Allah for bringing me safely back to my friends and kinsfolk and solemnly vowed never to travel again by sea or land. Such, dear guests, was the last and longest of my voyages.

When the evening feast was ended, Sindbad the Sailor gave Sindbad the Porter a hundred pieces of gold, which he took with thanks and blessings and departed, marvelling at all he had heard.

The porter remained a constant visitor at the house of his illustrious friend, and the two lived in amity and peace until there came to them the Spoiler of worldly mansions, the Dark Steward of the graveyard; the Shadow which dissolves the bonds of friendship and ends alike all joys and all sorrows.

AL-ANDALUS

3.12 The minority—that is, Christian—view: *Chronicle of Albelda* (*c*.883). Original in Latin.

The *Chronicle of Albelda* is generally considered to be the earliest of the surviving Asturian histories, the bulk of it apparently dating from 881 with an additional section that we know was completed in November 883. Its author(s) and place of composition are unknown, but given that the work promoted the legitimacy of the Asturian monarchy we can safely assume its author was connected in some way to the Asturian court.

The *Chronicle of Albelda* has come down to us as part of a broader historical mélange containing geographical information, genealogies, lists of bishops, and curious prophetic materials. The chronicle proper begins with a chronological summary of the reigns of Roman rulers from Romulus to Tiberius III (r.698–704), followed by a similar outline of the reigns of the Visigothic kings. It ends with entries describing Pelayo and his descendants, the rulers of Asturias. We begin here with the entry for Ordoño I.

[Source: *Medieval Iberia: Readings from Christian, Muslim, and Jewish Sources*, ed. Olivia Remie Constable (Philadelphia: University of Pennsylvania Press, 1997), pp. 56-60. Translated and introduced by Kenneth B. Wolf.]

[Ordoño I: 850–866]

Ordoño, the son of Ramiro, ruled for seventeen years. He increased the kingdom of the Christians with the help of God. He populated León and Astorga as well as Tuy and Amaya and he garrisoned many other fortresses. Many times he emerged victorious over the Saracens.[1] He took the city of Talamanca in battle and he permitted its king, Mozeror, whom he captured there, to go freely to Peña Santa with his wife, Balkaiz. He likewise stormed the strong city of Albelda. He ambushed its exceedingly powerful king Musa[2] at Mt. Laturce and weakened [Musa's] army with the sword. Musa himself was wounded with a lance, but was saved by a certain friend—who was known to have been one of our [men]—and was carried to a safe place by this friend on horseback. In Ordoño's time, the Northmen came again to the shores of Galicia, where they were killed by a count named Peter. The Moors,[3] coming in their ships, were also defeated on the coasts of Galicia. Such gentleness of soul and mercy [was attributed] to this prince, being so pious to everyone, that he was worthy of being called a father to his people. He died a peaceful death in Oviedo on the sixth day before the Kalends of June [May 27], in the era 904 [866].

[Alfonso III: 866–910]

Alfonso, the son of Ordoño, assumed the kingship in his eighteenth year. In the first flower of his adolescence—in the first year of his kingship and the eighteenth since his birth—he was deprived of his rule as the result of a rebellion by the apostate count of Galicia, Fruela. The king left for Castile. After a short time, this same rebel and unfortunate king, Fruela, was killed by those faithful to our prince [Alfonso] in Oviedo, and the glorious young man was brought back from Castile. He rejoiced, ruling happily from

---

1 *Sarraceni* is the most common Latin designation for "Arabs." It is somewhat misleading in the context of Spanish history since the bulk of the original invading force was made up not of Arabs but of Berbers from Morocco.
2 Musa ibn Musa, one of the leaders of the Banu Qasi, a clan of *muwallads* (converts to Islam) that controlled much of the Ebro region in the ninth century.
3 Berbers.

the throne of his father. From the outset of his reign he always enjoyed victory over his enemies. Twice he humiliated and overcame the fierceness of the Basques with his army. During his reign, in a year long past, the Ishmaelite host advanced toward León under the command of Almundar, son of King Abd al-Rahman [II][1] and brother of King Muhammad [I][2] of Córdoba. No sooner had Almundar arrived than he was impeded [from achieving his goal], for after losing many of his soldiers there, the rest of the army left in flight. Another army approached Bierzo at that time and was completely annihilated. This happened in many regions controlled by the enemy. [Alfonso] took the fortress Deza and then acquired Atienza peacefully. He depopulated Coimbra, which was held by the enemy, and afterward peopled it with Galicians. He subjected many more fortresses to his rule. In his time the church grew and his kingdom increased in size. The cities of Braga, Oporto, Orense, Eminio, Viseo, and Lamego were populated with Christians. By means of yet another victory, he depopulated and destroyed Coria, Idanha, and the rest of the territory of Lusitania[3] all the way to Mérida and the sea, consuming it with the sword as well as hunger. Shortly before that, in the era 915 [877], Abuhalit, the consul of Spain and counselor to King Muhammad, was captured in battle in the territory of Galicia and was taken to our king in Oviedo. Afterward he redeemed himself, handing over his two brothers, his son, and his nephew [to be held as hostages], until he paid the king 100,000 gold *solidi*. During that same time in the era 916 [878], Almundar, son of King Muhammad,[4] came from Córdoba to Astorga and León with the general Ibn Ganim and an army of Saracens. One contingent of the enemy forces, following opposite the army—a force of 13,000 from Toledo, Talamanca, Guadalajara

and other fortresses—was destroyed by our prince in Polvorosa at the river Orbigo. The [king] knew that Almundar wanted to press on to the fortress of Sublancio because of what happened in Polvorosa. Once Almundar learned that our king was waiting with his entire army to do battle with him in the fortress of Sublancio, he fearfully fled before the light of dawn. At the instigation of Abuhalit, there was a three-year truce between the two kings. Afterward our king, waging war against the Saracens, mobilized his army and entered [Muslim] Spain, in the era 919 [881]. After plundering the castle of Nefza, Alfonso pressed on through the province of Lusitania and, after crossing the Tagus River, advanced to the territory of Mérida. Ten miles outside of Mérida, he crossed the Guadiana River and came to Mt. Oxiferio, which no one before him had ever tried to approach.[5] There he triumphed over enemies with a glorious victory: for more than 15,000 others are known to have been killed at the same mountain. Thus our prince returned to his royal throne in victory. All of the churches of the Lord were restored by this prince and a city was built in Oviedo with a royal palace. He was brilliant in his knowledge and placid in his appearance, dress, and stature. The Lord always inclined [Alfonso's] soul to rule his people piously. After his long rule, he passed from his earthly kingdom to his heavenly one. Amen.

[Continuation]

While this king [Alfonso] was ruling, in the era 920 [882], the above-mentioned Almundar, son of King Muhammad, set out from Córdoba to Zaragoza, accompanied by the general Abuhalit and an army from [Muslim] Spain numbering 80,000. [This was because] Ismail ibn Musa[6] of Zaragoza had become

---

1 Emir of Córdoba (r.822–852). The "Ishmaelite host" refers to the Islamic army.
2 Emir of Córdoba (r.852–886).
3 The old Roman province that corresponds more or less with modern-day Portugal but which also included the cities of Mérida and Salamanca.
4 It is not clear whether this is a different Almundar from the brother (of the same name) of Muhammad mentioned above or simply an error on the part of the chronicler.
5 The success of this long-distance raid in particular seems to have been regarded by the chronicler (and presumably his royal patrons) as a sign that the days of Muslim rule in Spain were numbered. Hence the flurry of self-promoting historical literature produced in Asturias in the 880s.
6 Son of Musa ibn Musa (a member of the Banu Qasi).

an enemy of the Cordobans. When the army arrived at Zaragoza, it fought there for twenty-two days but won no victory. From there it advanced to Tudela and attacked a fortress held by Fortun ibn Musa,[1] but accomplished nothing. Then Ababdella—also known as Muhammad ibn Lope,[2] who had always been, like his father, a friend to us—made peace with the Cordobans and sent the strongest of his [men] to their army out of envy for his uncles to whom the king [Alfonso] had entrusted his son Ordoño to be reared. Thus the army of the Chaldeans,[3] entering the confines of our kingdom, first attacked the fortress at Cellorigo but accomplished nothing except to lose many of their own men. Vigila Jimenez was the count in Alava at that time. This same army, coming to the frontier of Castile, attacked the fortress called Poncorbo for three days, but won no victory and lost many of its own [men] to the avenging sword. Diego, son of Roderic, was the count in Castile [at that time]. Munio, son of Nuño, left the fortress of Castrojeriz deserted on account of the advance of the Saracens, because it was not yet heavily fortified. Our king, formidably garrisoned in the city of León with his army, waited for the enemy forces so that he might fight them in the suburbs of the city. But when the [Saracen] forces learned that our king was eagerly and daily anticipating their approach to the city, they, on the advice of Abuhalit, who had spied the king's men [in the city], crossed the river Esla fifteen miles from the city and burned a number of garrisoned fortresses. From the plains of Alcoba, [Abuhalit] sent envoys to the Orbigo River to meet our king, asking for the release of his son Abulkazim, whom the king had been holding [as a hostage] up to that time. So Abuhalit sent [as a hostage], for the sake of peace, the son of Ismail ibn Musa, who had been sent to his father from Córdoba, along with Fortun ibn Alazela, whom they had captured by trickery in Tudela. And so, entreating [King Alfonso] and giving him many gifts, [Abuhalit] received his son and made his way across the river Orbigo to Cea. Then he returned to Córdoba. They arrived in Córdoba, whence they had set out the previous March, in

September. Later our king handed over the [hostages] from the Banu Qasi—whom he had received from Abuhalit in exchange for his son—to their friends without ransom. The above-mentioned Ababdella, the son of Lope, turned in hate against his uncles and cousins on account of his friendship with the Cordobans, and the question of war arose between them. That winter, on account of the insolence of Ababdella, his uncle Ismail ibn Musa and his cousin Ismail ibn Fortun moved their armies about seven miles wanting to do battle against Ababdella. Ababdella waited for them in rough terrain. Both Ismails, with light escorts, came to the same rugged mountain where they knew him to be, and ascended it with a few men and servants. Ababdella rushed toward them at full speed and, as they broke into flight, Ismail ibn Fortun fell from his horse and was immediately captured. Likewise Ismail ibn Musa was captured as he tried to seize his nephew. Many of the nobles of the Banu Qasi were also captured. The rest of the army, which had been waiting in the plain, escaped in flight. Having won a victory, Ababdella transported those whom he had captured, bound in chains, to his fortress called Viguera. From there he proceeded to Zaragoza, and took it in the name of peace without resorting to the sword, thus subjecting it to his authority. He sent messengers to Córdoba at once, acting as if he had done all of this for the sake of the king, so as to appear faithful in all things. But when the Cordoban king requested the city of Zaragoza itself along with the others that Ababdella had captured, and Ababdella would by no means consent to do this, the Cordobans were moved to anger. As a result, [Ababdella and his kinsmen] were reconciled. He released his uncle and received the fortress of Valtierra from him. Likewise Ababdella released his cousin and on account of this received Tudela and the fortress of St. Stephan from him. Ababdella retained (and still holds) Zaragoza, which he had taken before. During this same period, Ababdella sustained many raids and attacks from the counts of Castile and Alava, Diego and Vigila. When he saw that he was hard pressed by them, he immedi-

---

1 Another son of Musa ibn Musa.
2 A grandson of Musa ibn Musa.
3 Yet another synonym for Saracens, this one emphasizing the biblical role of the "scourge" that Christians often invoked when trying to make sense out of their defeat at the hands of Muslims.

ately sent legates to our king [Alfonso] for the sake of peace and indeed he still sends them, but as yet he has not received any firm peace from the prince. Still he remains friendly toward us and wants to remain that way even if our king does not consent [to a formal peace].

3.13 An Islamic Andalusian voice: Ibn 'Abd Rabbihi, *I Have Never Seen* (before 940). Original in Arabic.

ARABIC POETRY IN AL-ANDALUS, as in the rest of the Arabic world, became newly experimental and free when the Umayyad caliphate fell. Having lost regular contact with the eastern half of the Islamic world, Andalusian poets abandoned the imagery of the desert, concentrating on urban life and metaphors of leisure and opulence. Ibn 'Abd Rabbihi (858-940) was a Cordoban poet of great renown, and his poetry is exemplary for its simplicity. Compare it with Abu Nuwas, *Youth and I*, above p. 152.

[Source: *Poems of Arab Andalusia*, trans. Cola Franzen from the Spanish versions of Emilio Garcia Gómez (San Francisco: City Lights Books, 1989), pp. 3-4.]

WHITE SKIN

I have never seen
nor heard of such a thing

her modesty turns
pearl into carnelian.

Her face is so clear
that when you gaze
on its perfections

you see your own face
reflected.

3.14 A Jewish poet in al-Andalus: Dunash ben Labrat, *There Came a Voice* (mid-10th c.). Original in Hebrew.

BORN IN FEZ (TODAY MOROCCO), Dunash ben Labrat (*fl.* mid-10th c.) became a rabbi in Spain (perhaps at Córdoba). He was one of many scholars and writers to flourish under the patronage of Hasdai ibn Shaprut, the first Jew to be an important figure at the Islamic Spanish court. Under these favorable conditions, ben Labrat and others debated Hebrew grammar, compiled Hebrew dictionaries, and created a new, secular form of Hebrew poetry. Mastering the traditions of Arabic poetic meter and rhyme, ben Labrat took up many of the same themes as the Arabic poets while invoking a very specific Jewish identity.

[Source: *Wine, Women, & Death: Medieval Hebrew Poems on the Good Life*, trans. and ed. Raymond P. Scheindlin (Oxford: Oxford University Press, 1986), pp. 41-42.]

There came a voice: "Awake!
Drink wine at morning's break.
'Mid rose and camphor make
A feast of all your hours,

'Mid pomegranate trees
And low anemones,
Where vines extend their leaves
And the palm tree skyward towers,

Where lilting singers hum
To the throbbing of the drum,
Where gentle viols thrum
To the plash of fountains' showers.

On every lofty tree
The fruit hangs gracefully.
And all the birds in glee
Sing among the bowers.

The cooing of the dove
Sounds like a song of love.
Her mate calls from above—
Those trilling, fluting fowls.

We'll drink on garden beds
With roses round our heads.
To banish woes and dreads
We'll frolic and carouse.

Dainty food we'll eat.
We'll drink our liquor neat,
Like giants at their meat,
With appetite aroused.

When morning's first rays shine
I'll slaughter of the kine

Some fatlings; we shall dine
On rams and calves and cows.

Scented with rich perfumes,
Amid thick incense plumes,
Let us await our dooms,
Spending in joy our hours."

I chided him: "Be still!
How can you drink your fill
When lost is Zion hill[1]
To the uncircumcised.

You've spoken like a fool!
Sloth you've made your rule.
In God's last judgment you'll
For folly be chastised.

The Torah, God's delight
Is little in your sight,
While wrecked is Zion's height,
By foxes vandalized.

How can we be carefree
Or raise our cups in glee,
When by all men are we
Rejected and despised?"

---

1   A reference to the land of Israel, "lost" to the Jews of the diaspora.

3.15 The imperial claims of the papacy: *The Donation of Constantine* (760s). Original in Latin.

The Donation of Constantine was a forgery. Purporting to be an edict issued by Emperor Constantine in 317, it was in fact confected in the eighth century. (For the uncovering of the forgery in the fifteenth century, see Lorenzo Valla, *Discourse on the Forgery of the Alleged Donation of Constantine*, below, p. 539.) The myth had a long history. Already in the fourth century *The Book of the Pontiffs (Liber Pontificalis)* claimed that Constantine was cured of leprosy when he was baptized by Pope Sylvester.[1] The *Liber Pontificalis* went on to list the many gifts—churches, revenues, ornaments—that Constantine gave to Rome. However, the *Donation of Constantine* added a new dimension to Constantine's gratitude, claiming that he gave the pope "imperial power" in the West. Thus, although this is a forgery when considered as a fourth-century document, it is an authentic creation of the eighth century. It allows us to glimpse the mentality of at least some members of the papal court at the crucial moment when the Lombard Kings, rulers of northern Italy, were threatening the papal states, and the Carolingians, a Frankish family on the rise, were engineering with the pope's connivance the downfall of the Merovingians—the royal dynasty that had ruled Francia for about 250 years.

[Source: *Carolingian Civilization: A Reader*, ed. Paul Edward Dutton, 2nd ed. (Peterborough, ON: Broadview Press, 2004), pp.14-22.]

---

1. In the name of the holy and indivisible Trinity of the Father, Son, and Holy Spirit. The emperor Caesar Flavius Constantine in Christ Jesus, the Lord God our Savior—one of that same holy Trinity—faithful, merciful, supreme, beneficent ruler of the Alemannians, Goths, Sarmatians, Germans, Britains, Huns, pious, fortunate, victorious, triumphant, and always august: to the most holy and blessed father of fathers Sylvester, bishop of the city of Rome and pope, and to all his successors, the pontiffs who are about to sit upon the chair of Saint Peter until the end of time, and to all the most reverend and beloved catholic bishops, subjected by this our imperial decree throughout the whole world to this same holy Roman church, who have been established now and in all previous times. May grace, peace, charity, rejoicing, and long suffering mercy be with you all from God the Father almighty and from Jesus Christ his Son and from the Holy Ghost.

2. Our most gracious serenity desires, in clear discourse, through the page of this our imperial decree, to bring to the knowledge of all the people in the whole world what things our Savior and Redeemer the Lord Jesus Christ, the Son of the most high Father, has most wonderfully seen fit to bring about through the intervention of his holy apostles Peter and Paul and through our father Sylvester, the highest pontiff and universal pope. First, indeed, putting forth, with the inmost confession of our heart, for the purpose of instructing the mind of all of you, our creed which we have learned from the aforesaid most blessed father and our confessor, Sylvester the universal pontiff; and then at length announcing the mercy of God which has been poured upon us.

3. For we wish you to know, as we have signified through our former sacred imperial decree, that we have departed from the worship of idols, from mute and deaf images made by hand, from devilish con-

---

1 For a brief discussion of the *Liber Pontificalis*, see the Introduction to the *Life of Gregory II* above, p. 124.

trivances, and from all the pompous displays of Satan; and have arrived at the pure faith of the Christians, which is the true light and everlasting life. We believe what that revered supreme father and teacher, the pontiff Sylvester has taught us: in God the Father, the almighty maker of heaven and earth, of all things visible and invisible; and in Jesus Christ, his only Son, our Lord God, through whom all things are created. And we believe in the Holy Spirit, in such a way that, in the perfect Trinity, there shall also be a fullness of divinity and a unity of power. The Father is God, the Son is God, and the Holy Spirit is God, and these three are one in Jesus Christ.

4. There are, therefore, three forms but one power. For God, wise in all previous time, gave forth from himself the word through which all future ages were to be born; and when, by that sole word of his wisdom, he formed the whole creation from nothing, he was with it, arranging all things in his mysterious secret place.

Therefore, the virtues of the heavens and all the material parts of the earth having been perfected, by the wise nod of his wisdom first creating man from the clay of the earth in his own image and likeness, he places him in a paradise of delight. Him the ancient serpent and envious enemy, the Devil, through the most bitter taste of the forbidden tree, made an exile from these joys; and, he [the Devil] being expelled, did not cease in many ways to cast his poisonous darts; in order that, turning the human race from the way of truth to the worship of idols, he might persuade it, namely, to worship the creature and not the creator; so that, through them [the idols], he might cause those whom he might be able to entrap in his snares to be burned with him in eternal punishment. But our Lord, pitying his creature, sending ahead his holy prophets, announcing through them the light of the future life—the coming, that is, of his Son our Lord and Savior Jesus Christ—sent that same only begotten Son and Word of wisdom: in him descending from heaven on account of our salvation, being born of the Holy Spirit and of the Virgin Mary, the word was made flesh and dwelt among us. He did not cease to be what he had been, but began to be what he had not been, perfect God and perfect man: as God, performing miracles; as man, sustaining human sufferings. We so learned Him to be very man and very God by the preaching of our father Sylvester, the supreme pontiff, that we can in no way doubt that He was truly God and truly man. And, having chosen twelve apostles, he shone with miracles before them and before an innumerable multitude of people. We confess that this same Lord Jesus Christ fulfilled the law and the prophets; that he suffered, was crucified, on the third day arose from the dead according to the Scriptures; was received into heaven, and sitteth on the right hand of the Father. Whence he shall come to judge the quick and the dead, whose kingdom shall have no end.

5. For this is our orthodox creed, placed before us by our most blessed father Sylvester the supreme pontiff. We exhort, therefore, all people, and all the different nations, to hold, cherish and preach this faith; and, in the name of the Holy Trinity, to obtain the grace of baptism; and, with devout heart, to adore the lord Jesus Christ our Savior, who, with the Father and the Holy Spirit, lives and reigns through infinite ages; whom Sylvester our father, the universal pontiff, preaches.

6. For he himself, our Lord God, having pity on me a sinner, sent his holy apostles to visit us, and caused the light of his splendor to shine upon us. And do rejoice that I, having been withdrawn from the shadow, have come to the true light and to the knowledge of truth. For, at that time a mighty and foul leprosy had invaded my entire body. Though I was tended by many physicians who collected by my side, not one of them was able to cure me. Then the priests of the Capitol gathered, saying to me that a font should be made on the Capitol, and that I should fill this with the blood of innocent infants; and that, if I bathed in it while it was warm, I might be cleansed. And many innocent infants were rounded up in response to their words, whom the sacrilegious priests of the pagans intended to slaughter in order to fill the font with their blood. Our serenity, however, perceived the tears of their mothers, and I was at once shocked by the demanded deed. Pitying the mothers, I ordered their sons to be restored to them; and, giving them vehicles and gifts, I sent them off rejoicing to their homes.

7. When that day had passed and the silence of the night and sleep had come upon us, the apostles Peter and Paul appeared, saying to me: "Since you have put an end to your vices, and have rejected the shedding of innocent blood, we have been sent by Christ the Lord

our God, to give to you a plan for restoring your health. Hear, therefore, our warning, and do what we tell you. Sylvester, the bishop of the city of Rome, is on Monte Soratte, fleeing your persecutions; there he clings in caves to the darkness with his clergy. This one, when you have called him to yourself, will show you a pool of piety. Once he has immersed you in it for the third time, the power of that leprosy will disappear. When this has been done, make this promise to your Savior, that by your order churches may be restored throughout the whole world. Purify yourself, moreover, in this way, so that, leaving behind all superstitious belief in idols, you may adore and cherish the living and true God, who stands alone and true, and that you may commit yourself to carrying out his will."

8. Rising, therefore, from my sleep, I immediately did what I had been advised to do by the holy apostles; and, having summoned that excellent and benignant father and our enlightener—Sylvester, the universal pope—I told him all the words that had been taught to me by the holy apostles; and asked him who were those gods Peter and Paul. But he said that they were not really called gods, but apostles of our Savior the Lord God Jesus Christ. And again we began to ask that same most blessed pope whether he had some clear image [a painting] of those apostles, so that, from that likeness, we might learn if they were those whom the revelation had shown to us. Then that same venerable father ordered the images of those apostles to be shown to us by his deacon. And, when I had looked at them, and recognized in those images the images of those whom I had seen in my dream, with a great noise, before all my satraps,[1] I confessed that those were the very faces that I had seen in my dream.

9. Hereupon, that same most blessed Sylvester our father, bishop of the city of Rome, imposed upon us a time of penance to be served in our Lateran Palace, in the chapel, in a hair garment, so that I might obtain pardon from our Lord God Jesus Christ our Savior by vigils, fasts, tears and prayers, for all the things that I had impiously done and unjustly ordered. Then through the imposition of the hands of the clergy, I came to

the bishop himself, and there, renouncing the pomps of Satan and his works and all idols made by hands, of my own will before all the people I confessed: that I believed in God the Father almighty, maker of heaven and earth, and of all things visible and invisible; and that I believed in Jesus Christ, his only Son our Lord, who was born of the Holy Spirit and of the virgin Mary. And, the font having been blessed, the wave of salvation purified me there with a triple immersion. For there I, being placed at the bottom of the font, saw with my own eyes a hand from heaven touching me. You should know that once I rose up clean from the font I was cleansed entirely of the squalor of leprosy. Rising from that venerable font and putting on white raiment, the pope administered to me the sign of the sevenfold holy Spirit, the unction of the holy oil, and he traced the sign of the holy cross upon my brow, saying: "God seals you with the seal of his faith in the name of the Father, the Son, and the Holy Spirit, to symbolize your faith." All the clergy replied: "Amen." The bishop added, "peace be with you."

10. And so, on the first day after receiving the mystery of the holy baptism, and after the cure of my body from the squalor of the leprosy, I recognized that there was no other God save the Father, Son, and Holy Spirit—whom the most blessed Sylvester the pope preaches about—a trinity in one, a unity in three. All the gods of the nations, whom I have worshiped up to this time, are proved to be demons; they are works made by the hand of men. That same venerable father told us most clearly how much power in heaven and on earth our Savior conferred on his apostle Saint Peter, when discovering how faithful he was after questioning him, the Lord said: "Thou art Peter, and upon this rock I shall build my church, and the gates of hell shall not prevail against it." Listen you powerful ones, and bend the inner ear of your hearts towards that which the good Lord and Master said to his disciple: "I will give you the keys of the kingdom of heaven, and whatever you shall bind on earth shall be bound also in heaven, and whatever you shall loose on earth shall be loosed also in heaven."[2] This is very

---

1   To the forger of the donation, *satrap* was a perfectly good, if fairly rare, word for "vassal." But as Valla pointed out in his debunking of the document, the word was not used in the time of Constantine. See below, p. 543. How is this passage a response to iconoclasm?

2   Matt. 16: 18-19. This so-called "power of the keys" to bind and loose referred to Peter's ministry to impose penance (bind) and to forgive sins (loose). This ministry was thought to have been transmitted to all of Peter's successors, the popes.

wonderful and glorious, to bind and loose on earth and to have it bound and loosed in heaven.

11. And with the blessed Sylvester preaching these things, I perceived them and learned that by the kindness of Saint Peter himself I had been entirely restored to health: I and all my satraps and the whole senate and the nobles [*optimates*] and all the Roman people, who are subject to the glory of our rule, considered it advisable that, as on earth he [Peter] is seen to have been constituted vicar of the Son of God, so the pontiffs, who are the representatives of that same chief of the apostles, should obtain from us and our empire greater power of supremacy than the earthly goodness of our imperial serenity is seen to have. We choose that same prince of the apostles, or his vicars, to be our constant intercessors with God. And, to the extent of our earthly imperial power, we decree that his holy Roman church shall be honored with veneration. And that the most sacred seat of Saint Peter shall be more gloriously exalted than our empire and earthly throne, we give to it imperial power, the dignity of glory, vigor and honor.

12. And we ordain and decree that he [the pope] shall have the supremacy as well over the four chief seats—Antioch, Alexandria, Constantinople and Jerusalem—as also over all the churches of God in the whole world. And he who for the time being shall be pontiff of that holy Roman church shall be more exalted than, and chief over, all the priests of the whole world; and everything which is to be provided for the service of God or the stability of the faith of the Christians is to be administered according to his judgment. It is, indeed, just, that there the holy law should have the seat of its rule where the founder of holy laws, our Savior, told Saint Peter to take the chair of the apostleship; where also, sustaining the cross, he blissfully took the cup of death and appeared as imitator of his Lord and Master; and that there the people should bend their necks in confession at Christ's name, where their teacher, Saint Paul the apostle, extending his neck for Christ, was crowned with martyrdom. There, until the end, let them seek a teacher, where the holy body of the teacher lies; and there, prone and humiliated, let them perform the service of the heavenly king, God our Savior Jesus Christ, where the proud were accustomed to serve under the rule of an earthly king.

13. Meanwhile we wish all the people, of all races and nations throughout the whole world, to know that we have constructed within our Lateran Palace, to the same Savior our Lord God Jesus Christ, a church with a baptistery. And know that we have carried on our own shoulders, from its foundations, twelve baskets weighted with earth, according to the number of the holy apostles. Which holy church we command to be spoken of, cherished, venerated and preached of, as the head and summit of all the churches in the whole world, as we have commanded through our other imperial decrees. We have also constructed the churches of Saints Peter and Paul, the chief apostles, which we have enriched with gold and silver; where also, placing their most sacred bodies with great honor, we have constructed their caskets of electrum, against which no force of the elements prevails. And we have placed a cross of purest gold on each of their caskets, and fastened them with golden keys. And on these churches, in order to provide light, we have conferred estates, and have enriched them with different objects; and, through our sacred imperial decrees, we have granted them our gift of land in the east as well as in the west; and even on the northern and southern coast: namely in Judea, Greece, Asia, Thrace, Africa, Italy, and various islands. All shall be administered by the hand of our most blessed father the pontiff Sylvester and his successors.

14. Let all the peoples and nations of the whole world rejoice with us. We exhort all of you to give unbounded thanks, together with us, to our Lord and Savior Jesus Christ. For he is God in Heaven above and on earth below, who, visiting us through his holy apostles, made us worthy to receive the holy sacrament of baptism and health of body. In return for which, to those same holy apostles, my masters, Peter and Paul, and through them also to Saint Sylvester, our father and the chief pontiff and universal pope of the city of Rome, and to all the succeeding pontiffs, who until the end of the world shall sit on the seat of Saint Peter, we concede and, by this present, do confer, our imperial Lateran Palace, which is preferred to, and ranks above, all the palaces in the whole world; then a diadem, that is, the crown of our head, and at the same time the tiara; and, also, the shoulder band, that is, the collar that usually surrounds our imperial neck; and also the purple mantle, and crimson tunic, and

all the imperial raiment; and the same rank as those presiding over the imperial cavalry; conferring also the imperial scepters, and, at the same time, the spears and standards; also the banners and different imperial ornaments, and all the advantages of our high imperial position, and the glory of our power.

15. And we decree, as to those most reverend men, the clergy who serve, in different orders, the holy Roman church, that they shall have the same advantages, distinctions, powers and excellence by the glory of which our most illustrious senate is adorned; that is, that they shall be made patricians and consuls. We also command that they be decorated with the other imperial dignities. And even as the imperial soldiery, so, we decree, shall the clergy of the holy Roman church be adorned. And even as the imperial power is adorned by different offices—by the distinction, that is, of chamberlains, and door keepers, and all the guards—so we wish the holy Roman church to be adorned. And, in order that the pontifical glory may shine forth more fully, we decree this also: that the clergy of this same holy Roman church may use saddle cloths of linen of the whitest color, namely that their horses may be adorned and so be ridden, and that, as our senate uses shoes with goats' hair, so they may be distinguished by gleaming linen, in order that, as the celestial beings, so the terrestrial may be adorned to the glory of God. Above all things, moreover, we give permission to that same most holy one, our father Sylvester, bishop of the city of Rome and pope, and to all the most blessed pontiffs who shall come after him and succeed him in all future times—for the honor and glory of Jesus Christ our Lord—to receive into that great catholic and apostolic church of God, even into the number of the monastic clergy, any one from the whole assembly of our nobles, who, in free choice and of his own accord, may wish to become a cleric. No one should presume for this reason to act in a haughty manner.

16. We also decreed that this same venerable one, our father Sylvester, the supreme pontiff, and all his successors might use and bear upon their heads—to the praise of God and for the honor of Saint Peter—the diadem, that is, the crown of purest gold and precious gems, which we have granted him from our own head. But he, the most holy pope, did not at all allow that crown of gold to be used over the clerical crown which he wears to the glory of Saint Peter; but we placed upon his most holy head, with our own hands, a tiara of gleaming splendor representing the glorious resurrection of our Lord. And, holding the bridle of his horse, out of reverence for Saint Peter we performed for him the duty of groom, decreeing that all the pontiffs, his successors, and they alone, may use that tiara in processions.

17. Behold that, in imitation of our own power, so that the supreme pontificate might not deteriorate, but rather be adorned with even more power and glory than the dignity of an earthly government, we are handing over to that blessed pontiff, our father Sylvester, the universal pope, our palace, the city of Rome and all the provinces, districts and cities of Italy or of the western regions. We are relinquishing them, by our inviolable gift, to the power and sway of himself and his successors. We do decree this by our sacred charter and imperial constitution, that it shall be so arranged, and do concede that these [properties and rights] shall lawfully remain with the holy Roman church.

18. Wherefore we have perceived it to be fitting that our empire and the power of our kingdom should be transferred and changed to the regions of the east, and that, in the province of Byzantium, in a most fitting place, a city should be built in our name; and that our empire should there be established. For, where the supremacy of priests and the head of the Christian religion has been established by a heavenly ruler, it is not just that there an earthly ruler should have jurisdiction.

19. We decree, moreover, that all these things which, through this our imperial charter and through other godlike commands, we have established and confirmed, shall remain uninjured and unshaken until the end of the world. Wherefore, before the living God, who commanded us to reign, and in the face of his terrible judgments we conjure, through this our imperial decree, all the emperors, our successors, and all our nobles, the satraps also, and the most glorious senate, and all the people in the whole world now and in all times previously subject to our rule, that no one of them, in any way, allow himself to oppose or disregard, or in any way seize, these things which, by our imperial sanction, have been conceded to the holy Roman church and to all its pontiffs. If any one,

moreover—which we cannot believe—should prove a scorner or despiser in this matter, he shall be subject and bound over to eternal damnation, and shall feel that the holy chiefs of the apostles of God, Peter and Paul, will be opposed to him in the present and in the future life. And, being burned in the nethermost hell, he shall perish with the Devil and all the impious.

20. This page of our imperial decree, we, confirming it with our own hands, did place above the venerable body of Saint Peter, chief of the apostles. There we promised to that same apostle of God that we would preserve inviolably all its provisions, and would leave directions for all our successors to pre-serve them. Thus did we hand it over, to be enduringly and happily possessed, to our most blessed father Sylvester, the supreme pontiff and universal pope, and, through him, to all the pontiffs, his successors, with the consent of God, Our Lord and our Savior Jesus Christ.

And the imperial subscription: may God preserve you for many years, you most holy and blessed fathers.

Given at Rome on the third day before the Kalends of April, our master the august Flavius Constantine, for the fourth time, and Gallicanus, being consuls and illustrious men.

3.16 Charlemagne as the light of the world: Anonymous, *Once Again my Burdened Anchor* (early 9th c.). Original in Latin.

THE COURTIERS AROUND CHARLEMAGNE were as busy churning out propaganda as the papal curia of the time, but in this case they wrote on behalf of the emperor. The excerpt below from a fragmentary epic poem possibly written by Einhard (d.840), a key person at the Carolingian court of Charlemagne and his son Louis the Pious, proclaims that the "lighthouse"—Charlemagne himself—casts "the light of his great name all the way to the stars." While the king sits "on his high throne/ Giving laws to his many lands, and confirming royal treaties," the pope arrives, mutilated and grateful. How might you compare the image projected here of Charlemagne's relationship to the pope with that of Constantine and Sylvester in the *Donation of Constantine*, above, p. 172?

[Source: *Carolingian Civilization: A Reader*, ed. Paul Edward Dutton, 2nd ed. (Peterborough, ON: Broadview Press, 2004), pp. 62-65.]

Once again my burdened anchor wishes me to get moving,
To set sail in unpredictable winds on an unknown course.
My feeble limbs have survived two storms [the two previous books]
Only to repair now their exhausted muscles for this new strain,
To ready my accomplished hands to row with these heavy oars
Out to where the gentle breezes call; where ships test a still
And flat sea with soft winds blowing behind them.

I would sail rapidly over the seas to unknown lands
And on my voyage even risk ramming into rocky promontories.
Now the gentle east wind, with powerful puffs, sets me sailing,
And forces me swiftly on my difficult way
Towards Europe where a lighthouse with a brilliant light flashes forth.
King Charles [Charlemagne] casts the light of his great name all the way to the stars.
Just as the sun illumines with its rays, so this David[1]
Lights up the world with the great light of his kindness....

---

1 A reference to the king of Israel, who was also thought to be the author of the psalms.

[There follows after this opening of the third book a long panegyric (a poem of praise), full of the imagery of light and radiance, on Charlemagne's many accomplishments and his perfection. Next the poet imagines Charlemagne ordering the construction of a new Rome, with a forum and senate, in Aachen, and then, in the company of his assembled family, preparing for a great hunt. After his exertions, the king lies down to sleep.]

While the sun falls and night shadows and locks up
    the light,
His tired limbs long for quiet sleep.
But in his dreams the king sadly sees an awful
And horrifying sight, for there stands Leo,
The supreme pontiff of the city of Rome, shedding
    sad tears,
His eyes are wounded, his face covered with blood,
His tongue is mutilated and he bears many frighten-
    ing wounds.[1]
A cold fear now steals over the restless limbs of the
    emperor.
[Awaking] he orders three agents to travel rapidly to
    Rome,
To learn if Leo, the good pastor of his flock, were
    indeed well.…

[The agents of the king discovered that there had, in fact, been an attempt upon the pope's life, but that he had somehow survived. They accompanied the pope to Paderborn in the summer of 799 where he was royally received by Charles.]

Charles, [having heard of the pope's actual fate]
    recalled his dreams,
And recognizing from their account the vestiges of
    his vision,
Did not doubt that this had happened, that he had
    seen,
In his dream, the pope shed sad tears.
Hence, without delay, he ordered [his son] Pepin to
    go out
To meet the pope, conveying wishes of peace and
    well-being.

Carrying out the orders of his father, Pepin readied
    to go;
He gladly went out with a great throng of troops.
King Charles, ever just, sat on his high throne
Giving laws to his many lands, and confirming royal
    treaties.
On a huge wide field, the apostolic pastor sees noble
    Pepin
And his great crowd of men come towards him;
He stretches both his hands to the sky
And prays from his heart for the [Frankish] people.
The entire army prostrates itself three times before
    the pope,
And the suppliant throng three times pays its re-
    spects.
Pope Leo with generous and open heart welcomes
    Pepin,
Embracing him with his holy arms,
And in this embrace, the pope kisses Pepin [in
    welcome].
Prince Pepin walks and talks with the pope,
Discussing a number of different problems.
Meanwhile kind King Charles, [our] great hero,
Raises himself up on his throne and addresses the
    people:
"O you warriors, rouse yourselves and put on your
    weapons.
You are to go [as if] to war, to tempt harsh contests,
And to be confident in bloody battles.
We shall soon in a speedy manner meet the good
    pontiff."
Scarcely does [our] hero say this, when the crowd
    breaks out in a clamor;
The throng assembles with its javelins, leather
    breastplates,
Broad shields, helmets, and arrows.
Bronze shields rattle; the cavalry seems ready to
    charge;
Clouds of dust darken the sky;
And horns from a hill blast the troops below.
Battle signals sound; the fields are covered with troops;
The whole army, plumed, marvelously shines.
Javelins sparkle in the light, standards flutter in the
    wind,

---

1   A reference to Pope Leo III (r.795-816), whose troubles led Charlemagne to make the trip to Rome that culminated in his imperial coronation.

Armed young men are afire [with passion] and
  confident youth
Rejoices on horseback; a firm ardor grows as they
  listen [to their king.]
Charles at the front and center of his troops shines in
  joy:
A golden plume encircles his brow and, outfitted in
  arms,
He stands out, the best general astride an immense
  horse.
Before the camp stand lines of priests divided into
  three choirs;
They are dressed in long vestments
And hold up the sacred standards of the holy cross.
The priests and the joyful people await the pope's
  advent.
Now father Charles sees his troops arrayed on the
  wide field;
He knows that Pepin and the highest pastor are fast
  approaching;
He orders his people to wait for them.
He divides his troops into a ring-like shape,
In the center of which, he himself, that blessed one,
  stands,
Awaiting the advent of the pope, but higher up than
  his comrades
On the summit of the ring; he rises above the as-
  sembled [Franks].
Now Pope Leo approaches and crosses the front line
  of the ring.
He marvels at the many peoples from many lands
  whom he sees,
At their differences, their strange tongues, dress, and
  weapons.
At once Charles hastens to pay his reverent respects,
Embraces the great pontiff, and kisses him.
The two men join hands and walk together, speaking
  as they go.

The entire army prostrates itself three times before
  the pope,
And the suppliant throng three times pays its re-
  spects.
The pope prays from his heart for the people three
  times.
The king, the father of Europe, and Leo, the world's
  highest pastor,
Walk together and exchange views,
Charles inquiring as to the pope's case and his
  troubles.
He is shocked to learn of the wicked deeds of the
  [Roman] people.
He is amazed by the pope's eyes which had been
  blinded,
But to which sight had now returned,
And he marveled that a tongue mutilated with tongs
  now spoke …
When the church service was over,
Charles invited Leo to his great palace.
His gorgeous court-hall shines inside with colorful
  tapestries,
And its chairs are covered in purple and gold.
The joyful company sits down at table and enjoys a
  variety of delights.
In the middle of the high hall they celebrate a great
  banquet.
Golden bowls overflow with Falernian wine.
King Charles and Leo, the highest prelate in the
  world,
Dine together and quaff sparkling wine from their
  bowls.
After the joyful repast and much drinking,
Kind [King] Charles gives many gifts to great Leo.
Then the king returns to his private chambers in the
  palace
And the pope retires to his own quarters.

3.17 Modeling the state on Old Testament Israel: *The Admonitio Generalis* (789). Original in Latin.

ELEVEN YEARS BEFORE HE was crowned emperor, King Charles drew up a set of general instructions, *The Admonitio Generalis*, for the great men of his realm, both lay and ecclesiastical, "to lead the people of God to the pastures of eternal life." He took as his model the biblical King Josais, who discovered a copy of "the book of the law," realized how badly his people deviated from what was written therein, and immediately took steps to reform his kingdom (see 2 Kings 22-23). In effect, the many laws set forth by *The Admonitio Generalis*, only some of which are excerpted here, were Charlemagne's attempts to govern his kingdom according to the laws of God.

[Source: *Christianity Through the Thirteenth Century*, ed. Marshall W. Baldwin (New York: Harper and Row, 1970), pp. 115-19.]

Our Lord Jesus Christ ruling forever.

I, Charles by the grace of God and the gift of His mercy, king and ruler of the kingdom of the Franks, devout defender and humble supporter of holy church, give greetings of lasting peace and beatitude to all grades of the ecclesiastical order and to all ranks of the secular power, in Christ our Lord, eternal God.

Reflecting with dutiful and calm consideration, along with our priests and councilors, on the abundant mercy of Christ the King toward us and our people, we have considered how necessary it is not only with our whole heart and voice to offer thanks for His goodness unceasingly, but also to persist in the continuous exercise of good works in His praise so that He who has given our kingdom such honors may deign to preserve and protect us and our kingdom forever. Accordingly it has pleased us to solicit your efforts, O pastors of the churches of Christ and leaders of His flock and distinguished luminaries of the world, to strive to lead the people of God to the pastures of eternal life by watchful care and urgent advice and stir yourselves to bring back the wandering sheep within the walls of ecclesiastical constancy on the shoulders of good example or exhortation, lest the wolf, plotting against anyone who transgresses the canonical laws or evades the fatherly traditions of the ecumenical councils—which God forbid!—find him and devour him. Thus they must be admonished, urged, and even forced by the great zeal of piety, to restrain themselves within the bonds of paternal sanctions with staunch faith and unrelenting constancy.

Therefore, we have sent our *missi* who by the authority of our name are to correct along with you what should be corrected. And we append herewith certain chapters from canonical ordinances which seem to us to be particularly necessary.

Let no one judge this admonition to piety, by which we endeavor to correct errors, remove superfluous matter, and condense those things which are right, to be presumptuous. I entreat him rather to accept it with a benevolent spirit of charity. For we read in the book of Kings how the holy Josias, traveling around the kingdom bestowed on him by God, correcting and admonishing, labored to recall it to the worship of the true God: not that I hold myself equal to his holiness, but because the examples of the saints are always to be followed by us, and we must bring together whomsoever we can to a devotion to the good life in the praise and glory of our Lord Jesus Christ....

CHAPTER 70, TO THE CLERGY

Bishops should carefully see to it that throughout their dioceses (*parochiae*) the priests observe their Catholic faith and baptism and understand well the prayers of the mass; and that the psalms are chanted properly according to the divisions of the verses and that they understand the Lord's Prayer and preach that it is to be understood by all, so that each person may know what he is asking of God; and that the "Glory be to the Father" be sung with all dignity by everyone and that the priest himself with the holy angels and all the people of God with one voice intone the "Holy, Holy,

Holy." And it should in every way be made clear to priests and deacons that they should not bear arms but trust in the protection of God rather than in arms.

CHAPTER 71, SOMETHING TO THE PRIEST, SOMETHING TO PEOPLE

It is likewise our will to urge your reverences that each throughout his diocese see that the church of God is held in His honor and the altars venerated with suitable dignity, and that the house of God is not used as a pathway for dogs and that the vessels consecrated to God are kept with great care or used with honor; and that secular or mundane affairs are not transacted in churches because the house of God must be a house of prayer and not a den of thieves;[1] and that the people when they come to the solemnities of the mass are attentive and do not leave before the completion of the priest's blessing.

CHAPTER 72, TO THE CLERGY

And we also demand of your holiness that the ministers of the altar of God shall adorn their ministry by good manners, and likewise the other orders who observe a rule and the congregations of monks. We implore them to lead a just and fitting life, just as God himself commanded in the Gospel. "Let your light so shine before men that they may see your good works and glorify your Father which is in heaven,"[2] so that by their example many may be led to serve God; and let them join and associate to themselves not only children of servile condition, but also sons of free men. And let schools be established in which boys may learn to read. Correct carefully the Psalms, the signs in writing (*notas*), the songs, the calendar, the grammar in each monastery or bishopric, and the catholic books; because often some desire to pray to God properly, but they pray badly because of the incorrect books. And do not permit your boys to corrupt them in reading or writing. If there is need of writing the Gospel, Psalter, and Missal, let men of mature age do the writing with all diligence.

CHAPTER 73, TO THE CLERGY

We have likewise taken pains to ask that all, wherever they are, who have bound themselves by the vow of a monastic life live in every way regularly in a monastic manner according to that vow. For it is written, "Render your vows to the Lord God";[3] and again, "it is better not to vow than not to fulfil."[4] And let those coming to monasteries according to the regular manner be first tested in the examination room and so accepted. And let those who come to the monastery from the secular life not be sent immediately on monastic tasks outside before they are well educated within. And monks are not to seek worldly pleasures. Likewise, those who are admitted to that clerical state which we call the canonical life, we desire that they live such a life canonically and in every way according to its rule; and the bishop should govern their life as the abbot does the monks.

CHAPTER 74, TO ALL

Let all have equal and correct weights and just and equal measures, whether in the towns or in the monasteries, whether in giving in them or in receiving, as we have the command in the law of the Lord,[5] and likewise in Solomon, when the Lord says, "[Different] weight and [different] measure, my soul abhors."[6] …

CHAPTER 80, TO ALL THE CLERGY

Let them teach fully the Roman chant and let the office be followed according to the direction of the nocturnal or gradual as our father Pepin, of blessed memory, ordered done when he suppressed the Gallican use for the sake of unity with the apostolic see and the peaceful harmony of the holy church of God.[7]

---

1 See Matt. 21: 13.
2 Matt. 5: 16.
3 Deut. 23: 21.
4 Eccles. 5: 4.
5 See Lev. 19: 35–36.
6 Prov. 20: 10.
7 The "Gallican use" refers to the words and melodies used in Church liturgy in Francia under the Merovingians. Although Charlemagne here attributes the suppression of this liturgy to his father, Pippin III (d.768), in fact it was Charlemagne himself who was most instrumental in reforming the chants used in his kingdom along Roman models.

CHAPTER 81, TO ALL

And we also decree, according to what the Lord ordained in the law,[1] that there be no servile work on Sundays, as my father, of good memory, ordered in the edicts of his synods, that is: that men do no farm work, either in plowing fields or in tending vineyards, in sowing grain or planting hedges, in clearing in the woods or in cutting trees, in working with stone or in building houses, or in working in the garden; nor are they to gather for games or go hunting. Three tasks with wagons may be performed on Sunday, the arms' cart or the food wagon, or if it is necessary to bear someone's body to the grave.

Likewise, women are not to work with cloth nor cut out clothes, nor sew or embroider; nor is it permissible to comb wool or crush flax or wash clothes in public, or shear sheep, to the end that the honor and quiet of the Lord's day be kept. But let people come together from all places to the church for the solemnities of the mass and praise God on that day for all the good things He has done for us.

CHAPTER 82, TO ALL

And you are to see to it, O chosen and venerable pastors and rulers of the church of God, that the priests whom you send through your dioceses (*parochiae*) for ruling and preaching in the churches to the people serving God, that they rightly and justly preach; and you are not to allow any of them to invent and preach to the people new and unlawful things according to their own judgment and not according to Holy Scripture. And you too are to preach those things which are just and right and lead to eternal life, and instruct others that they are to preach these same things.

3.18 Imperial administration: *Double Capitulary of Thionville for the* missi (805). Original in Latin.

FROM THIONVILLE (GERMAN: DIEDENHOFEN), where Charlemagne had an important residence, the emperor and his counselors issued a set of instructions—a capitulary—for reforming the realm. The *missi* were the king's "overseers"—there were two for each district, a bishop and an important layman—who were expected to correct local abuses and hear complaints, working closely with the regional "governors," the counts. As with all of Charlemagne's capitularies, the provisions given here are brief summaries or reminders, sometimes consisting of only a word; fuller instructions to the *missi* would have been given orally. The first part of this capitulary concerns Church affairs; the second half turns to everything else. Compare the notions of good rulership expressed here with those in the earlier *Admonitio Generalis* above, p. 180. In what ways did Charlemagne's methods and goals change after he became emperor?

[Source: *The Reign of Charlemagne: Documents on Carolingian Government and Administration*, ed. H. R. Loyn and John Percival (New York: St. Martin's Press, 1975), pp. 87–91 (notes added).]

WITHIN THE CHURCH

1. Readings.
2. Singing.
3. Scribes, that they should not write badly.
4. Notaries.
5. Other disciplines.
6. Calculation.
7. The art of medicine.
8. Concerning churches that are left without land and without appointments or lighting; and concerning those people who exact tithes and do not take proper care of the churches; and concerning altars, that there should not be an overabundance of them in the churches.
9. Concerning laymen recently converted, that

---

1 See Exod. 20: 8–10.

they should not be sent out on other business before they have learned their law fully by living according to it.

10. Concerning those who withdraw from the world rather than perform some service for their lord, and then do neither: let them choose one of two courses—either they must live fully in accordance with the canons[1] or they must follow the monastic rule.

11. Concerning male and female slaves belonging to the king, that they should not receive the tonsure or the veil except in moderation, and only where there are enough of them and the estates will not be deserted.

12. Concerning excessively large gatherings, that they should in no circumstances take place; only so many people should be gathered together as can take proper counsel.

13. Concerning those who have not been submitted to probation according to the [monastic] rule, that they should straightway make amends and be submitted as the rule directs.

14. That young girls of the age of infancy should not take the veil before they know how to choose what they want, so preserving the authority of the canons.[2]

15. That laymen should not be put in charge of monks within the monasteries, nor be made archdeacons.

16. Concerning incestuous persons, that they should be examined according to the canons, nor through anyone's friendship should some be let off lightly and others punished.

TO ALL AND SUNDRY

1. Concerning the peace, that all who as the result of some crime are rebels against it should be brought to justice.

2. Concerning the administration of justice in cases affecting God's churches, widows, orphans and minors, that they should not be looked down upon when they appear as plaintiffs in the public courts, but should be given a careful hearing.

3. Concerning the administration of the royal justice, that it be fully inquired into.

4. Concerning the occasions when famine occurs, or plague, or pestilence, or unseasonable weather, or any such tribulation, that men should not wait for our edict but should straightway pray to God for his mercy. As to the scarcity of food in this present year, let each man help his own people as best he can, and not sell his grain at too high a price; and let no foodstuffs be sold outside our empire.

5. Concerning arms, and the prohibition on carrying them within the country—that is, shields and lances and coats of mail. And if there is a private feud, an inquiry is to be made as to which of the two parties is in the wrong, with a view to pacifying them, even if it means doing so against their will; and if there is no other way of pacifying them, let them be brought to our presence. And if, after they are appeased, one of them should kill the other, he must make a payment for him and must lose the hand by which he was forsworn, and in addition pay the royal fine.

6. Concerning the provision of arms for the army, the arrangements which we commended in an earlier capitulary are to be observed, and in addition every man with 12 manses[3] is to have a coat of mail; anyone who has a coat of mail and does not bring it with him is to lose all his benefice along with it.

7. Concerning traders who travel in the territories of the Slavs and Avars, and how far they ought to go on their business; in the region of Saxony as far as Bardowiek, where Hredi is to be in charge; to Schesel, where Madelgaudus is to be in charge; to Magdeburg, with Aito in charge; to Erfurt, with Madelgaudus; to Halazstadt, with Madelgaudus again; to Forcheim, to Pfreimt and to Regensburg, with Audulfus; and to Lorsch,

---

1 Under the Carolingians, there were two rules for "those who withdraw from the world." One was for canons (priests who lived together) and the other—the *Benedictine Rule* (for which see above, p. 28)—was for monks.
2 Here "the canons" refers to Church law in general.
3 A manse was a farming unit. A person with 12 manses had a handsome estate.

with Warnarius. They must not take arms and coats of mail with them to sell; and if they are caught while carrying them their entire stock is to be confiscated, one half being given to the palace, the other being divided between the *missi* already mentioned and the man who discovered them.

8. Concerning plaintiffs and counsel who will neither submit to the judgment of the magistrates[1] nor make a formal renunciation of it, the old custom is to be observed, that is, they are to be kept in custody until they do one thing or the other. And if they appeal to the palace concerning the matter and bring letters they are not to be believed, but they should not be put in prison; rather, they should be sent to our palace together with their guard and the letters themselves, so that they can be examined there as is fitting.

9. Concerning the swearing of oaths, that fealty should not be sworn to anyone except to us, and by each man to his [own] lord with a view to our interest and that of the lord himself; excepted from this are those oaths which are rightly owed by one man to another in accordance with the law. Infants, who were formerly unable to swear because of their tender age, should now swear fealty to us.

10. Concerning conspiracies, those who dare to undertake them and who seal any conspiracy with an oath are to be judged in one of three ways. First, whenever any harm has been done as a result of it, the authors of the deed are to be put to death, and their helpers are to be flogged by one another and made to cut off one another's noses. Where no harm has been done, they are again to be flogged by one another, and must take turns to shave one another's hair. If a conspiracy has been sealed by the clasping of hands, those responsible, if they are free men, are to swear before suitable witnesses that they had no evil intention in so doing, or, if they cannot

swear this, are to compound according to their law; if they are slaves they are to be flogged. And for the future let there be no conspiracy of this kind in our kingdom, with or without the swearing of oaths.

11. Concerning perjuries, that they should be guarded against, and that witnesses should not be brought to oath before they have been examined; and if they cannot be examined otherwise they should be separated and questioned individually. And it should not be allowed for the accuser alone to choose witnesses in the absence of his opponent. And under no circumstances should anyone who has not fasted be brought to oath or allowed to give testimony. And if anyone is brought to give testimony and is refuted, let him who would refute him and prove him wrong say why he refuses to accept his word. And witnesses should be chosen from the district in question and not from another one, lest it become necessary to inquire into the case too far outside the county. And if anyone is convicted of perjury he must lose his hand or else make payment to redeem it.

12. Concerning advocates: that is, that corrupt advocates, and bad *vicedomini*, *vicarii* and *centenarii* should be removed from office, and only those chosen who are both able and willing to examine and deal with cases justly.[2] And if a bad count is discovered he is to be reported to us.

13. Concerning tolls, it is our wish that the old established and lawful tolls should be exacted from traders on bridges, on water crossings and on sales; and that the new and unlawful ones— when ropes are slung across or when people go under bridges in boats or for similar situations, in which no assistance is being provided for the traveller—are not to be exacted; nor should they be exacted from people who are moving their property for reasons other than trade, from one of their houses to another or to the palace or to

---

1 The Latin term for these magistrates was *scabini*. There were seven in each county court, appointed by the local count to sit as permanent judges.

2 The advocates (*advocati*) along with the *vicedomini*, *vicarii*, and *centenarii* were officials who served as justices in matters involving church lands.

the army. If any doubtful case should arise it is to be looked into at the next court hearing which we are due to hold along with our *missi*.

14. Concerning runaway clerks or laymen, and also women, the instructions which we have given in another capitulary are to be observed.

15. Concerning free men who wish to devote themselves to the service of God, that they should not do so before they have asked permission of us. The reason for this is that we have heard that some of them do so not so much from devotion as from a desire to escape the army or some other royal service, while others do so because of someone's greed, when they are at the mercy of people who want to acquire their property; it is for these reasons that we have made the restriction.

16. Concerning the oppression of poor free men, that they should not be unjustly oppressed by men more powerful than themselves for any evil purpose, to the point of being compelled to sell or hand over their property. The reason for our previous statements about free men, and for this present one, is that their relatives should not be unjustly dispossessed so that their service to the king is lessened, and that their heirs should not, as a result of their poverty, be reduced to beggars or robbers or criminals. Also, poor men should not be summoned too often to court, and our instructions in an earlier capitulary to this effect are to be observed.

17. Concerning churches, and saints which have been recently adopted without authority, that they should not be venerated without the bishop's approval: in this, and in all the churches, canonical authority is to be maintained.

18. Concerning false mints, because they are appearing unlawfully and against our edict in many places it is our wish that the only place for a mint

shall be in our palace, unless other instructions are given by us; however, those pennies which have now been minted are to be used, provided they are of good weight and pure metal.

19. Concerning the payment for the host [army], it is our wish that our *missi* should this year exact it faithfully, without showing favor to anyone or succumbing to blandishments or threats, in accordance with our orders; that is, from a man who owns six pounds worth of gold, silver, coats of mail, bronze vessels, clothes, horses, oxen, cows or other livestock (and the wives and children are not to be deprived of their garments for this purpose) they are to take the lawful payment, that is, three pounds. From those who own no more than three pounds worth of the above-mentioned items 30 shillings are to be exacted; from anyone who has not more than two pounds worth, 10 shillings; and if he has one pound they are to take five shillings, so that he can prepare himself again for the service of God and for employment by us. And our *missi* should take care and make diligent inquiry, that they do not with any ill intent subvert our justice by giving it or commending it to another.

20. It is our wish that the royal *census*[1] should be paid wherever it has been lawfully due, whether on a man's own person or on his property.

21. Concerning robbers, our instructions in an earlier capitulary are to hold good.

22. Concerning free men who have married wives belonging to the royal fisc,[2] and women who have husbands of similar status, that they should not as a result of this be debarred from inheriting of their parents, from pleading their case, or from giving testimony; rather, the same honor should be shown to us in this matter as we know was shown to our ancestors, whether kings or emperors.

---

1 The term "royal *census*" was used for various customary taxes due to the state.
2 The fisc consisted of the estates—including the people living on them—and revenues belonging to the monarchy.

3.19 Ideals of family and fidelity: Dhuoda, *Handbook for her Son* (841-843). Original in Latin.

A PRECIOUS DOCUMENT FOR the values of the Carolingian laity—or, more precisely, for aristocratic lay women of the time—Dhuoda's *Handbook for her Son* was written in the time of crisis just before the Treaty of Verdun (843). Her husband, Bernard, count of the Spanish March (Septimania), had once been an important courtier under Louis the Pious, but, accused of adultery with the queen, he was expelled from the court by Louis's sons. Her son William, to whom she wrote, was being held hostage at the court of Charles the Bald, partly to guarantee his father's "good behavior" and partly to ensure William's own advancement at court. Dhuoda herself was in the south of the Frankish kingdom, attempting, as she put it, "to defend the interests of my lord and master Bernard." She had just given birth to another son, whom Bernard had "brought to him in Aquitaine." In her *Handbook*, motherhood, politics, and religion mingle as she tries to define a righteous and honorable rule of conduct for this life and the next. Just as Carolingian—and Byzantine (see above, p. 143)—court scholars wrote "Mirrors of Princes" for kings to model themselves upon, so Dhuoda wrote a "mirror" for her son in which he could "contemplate the health" of his soul, measuring it against the mirror's standard. We have no idea how William responded to Dhuoda's advice. Bernard was executed by the king shortly after she wrote, and William was executed in 850. Dhuoda may have died before she knew about these sad events; she was certainly contemplating death as she wrote her *Handbook*'s near-final section (Book 10). Compare the sources of conduct and the ideals of behavior that Dhuoda presents to William with those in *The Benedictine Rule* (p. 28 above). What evidence can you find in Dhuoda's writings to suggest that the Carolingian laity was influenced by the norms of monasticism? What evidence is there for other—and divergent—ideals, and where might they have come from? What does Dhuoda's writing suggest about the nature of lay aristocratic education in the Carolingian empire?

[Source: *Handbook for William: A Carolingian Woman's Counsel for Her Son*, trans. Carol Neel (Washington, DC: Catholic University of America Press, 1991), pp.1, 5-6, 21-27, 33, 95-102, 113, 115-16, 121-23, 125-26, 144-45 (notes slightly modified).]

The little book before you branches out in three directions. Read it through and, by the end, you will understand what I mean. I would like it to be called three things at once, as befits its contents—rule, model, and handbook.[1] These terms all mirror each other. The rule comes from me, the model is for you, and the handbook is as much from me as for you—composed by me, received by you....

Here begins the prologue.
Things that are obvious to many people often escape me. Those who are like me lack understanding and

have dim insight, but I am even less capable than they.[2] Yet always there is he at my side who "opened the mouths of the dumb, and made the tongues of infants eloquent."[3] I, Dhuoda, despite my weakness of mind, unworthy as I am among worthy women—I am still your mother, my son William, and it is to you that I now address the words of my handbook. From time to time children are fascinated by dice more than all the other games that they enjoy. And sometimes women are absorbed in examining their faces in mirrors, in order then to cover their blemishes and be more beautiful for the worldly intention

---

1   Dhuoda begins by describing her own work as threefold, reflecting the trinity of the one Christian God—Father, Son, and Holy Spirit. In doing so, she affirms her adherence to this central element in Catholic doctrine.
2   See 2 Cor. 11: 23.
3   Wisd. of Sol. 10: 21.

of pleasing their husbands. I hope that you may bring the same care, burdened though you may be by the world's pressures, to reading this little book addressed to you by me. For my sake, attend to it—according to my jest—as children do to their dice or women to their mirrors.

Even if you eventually have many more books, read this little work of mine often. May you, with God's help, be able to understand it to your own profit. You will find in it all you may wish to know in compact form. You will find in it a mirror in which you can without hesitation contemplate the health of your soul, so that you may be pleasing not only in this world, but to him who formed you out of dust.[1] What is essential, my son William, is that you show yourself to be such a man on both levels that you are both effective in this world and pleasing to God in every way.

My great concern, my son William, is to offer you helpful words. My burning, watchful heart especially desires that you may have in this little volume what I have longed to be written down for you, about how you were born through God's grace. I shall best begin there.

Preface.

In the eleventh year of the imperial rule of our lord Louis, who then reigned by Christ's favor—on the twenty-ninth of June 824—I was given in marriage at the palace of Aachen to my lord Bernard, your father, to be his legitimate wife.[2] It was still in that reign, in its thirteenth year on the twenty-ninth of November,[3] that with God's help, as I believe, you were born into this world, my firstborn and much-desired son.

Afterward, as the wretchedness of this world grew and worsened, in the midst of the many struggles and disruptions in the kingdom, that emperor followed the path common to all men. For in the twenty-eighth year of his reign, he paid the debt of his earthly existence before his time.[4] In the year after his death, your brother was born on the twenty-second of March in the city of Uzès.[5] This child, born after you, was the second to come forth from my body by God's mercy. He was still tiny and had not yet received the grace of baptism when Bernard, my lord and the father of you both, had the baby brought to him in Aquitaine in the company of Elefantus, bishop of Uzès, and others of his retainers.

Now I have been away from you for a long time, for my lord [Bernard] constrains me to remain in this city. Nonetheless I applaud his success. But, moved by longing for both of you, I have undertaken to have this little book—a work on the scale of my small understanding—copied down and sent to you. Although I am besieged by many troubles, may this one thing be God's will, if it please him—that I might see you again with my own eyes. I would think it certain that I would, if God were to grant me some virtue. But since salvation is far from me, sinful woman that I am,[6] I only wish it, and my heart grows weak in this desire.[7]

As for you, I have heard that your father, Bernard, has given you as a hostage to the lord king Charles.[8] I hope that you acquit yourself of this worthy duty with perfect good will. Meanwhile, as Scripture says, "Seek ye therefore the kingdom of God … and all these things shall be added unto you,"[9] that is all that is necessary for the enjoyment of your soul and your body.

So the preface comes to an end.

---

1 See Gen. 1: 7.
2 The marriage of Bernard and Dhuoda at the Carolingian capital, Aachen, suggests that they were children of families of great importance.
3 The year was 826.
4 Louis the Pious died in 840, late in his sixties, so Dhuoda's comment is polite.
5 The year was 841. It is possible, given the long period between the births of Dhuoda's two sons, that she saw little of her husband in the interim. Bernard was heavily involved in politics and warfare across the Frankish dominions throughout their marriage.
6 See Ps. 119: 155; Douay Ps.118: 155.
7 See Job 30: 16.
8 William had been entrusted to Charles the Bald after the battle of Fontenoy in 841.
9 Matt. 6: 33.

[In Book One, Dhuoda expounds on William's primary task: to love God. In Book Two, she discusses the Trinity, the trinity of virtues (faith, hope, and charity), and the importance of prayer.]

Book Three

1. *On the reverence you should show your father throughout your life.*

Now I must do my best to guide you in how you should fear, love, and be faithful to your lord and father, Bernard, in all things, both when you are with him and when you are apart from him. In this Solomon is your teacher and your wisest authority. He chastises you, my son, and says to you in warning, "For God hath made the father" who flourishes in his children "honorable."[1] And likewise: "He that honoreth his father shall have joy in his own children"[2] and "shall enjoy a long life. He that obeyeth the father shall be a comfort to his mother."[3] "As one that layeth up good things,"[4] so is he who honors his father. "He that feareth the Lord, honoreth his parents."[5] "So honor thy father," my son, and pray for him devotedly, "that thou mayest be longlived upon the land,"[6] with a full term of earthly existence. "Remember that thou hadst not been born" but through him.[7] In every matter be obedient to your father's interest and heed his judgment.[8] If by God's help you come to this, "support the old age of thy father and grieve him not in his life."[9] "Despise him not when thou art in thy strength."[10]

May you never do this last, and may the earth cover my body before such a thing might happen. But I do not believe that it will. I mention it not because I fear it but rather so that you may avoid it so completely that such a crime never comes to your mind, as I have heard that it indeed has done among many who are not like you.[11] Do not forget the dangers that befell Elias's sons, who disobediently scorned the commands of their father and for this met with a bitter death.[12] Nor should I fail to mention the tree of Absalom, who rebelled against his father and whom a base death brought to a sudden fall. Hung from an oak and pierced by lances, he ended his earthly life in the flower of his youth, with a groan of anguish. Lacking as he did an earthly kingdom, he never reached that highest of kingdoms promised to him.[13]

What of the many more who behave as he did? Their path is perilous. May those who perpetrate such evil suffer accordingly. It is not I who condemn them, but Scripture that promises their condemnation, threatening them terribly and saying, "Cursed is he that honoreth not his father."[14] And again, "He who curseth his father, dying let him die"[15] basely and uselessly. If such is the punishment for harsh, evil words alone, what do you think will happen to those who inflict real injury upon their parents and insult the dignity of their fathers? We hear of many in our times who, thinking their present circumstances unjust, consider such crimes without taking into account the past. On them and on those like them fall hatred, jealousy, disaster, and calamity, and "nourishment to their envy."[16] They lose rather than keep those goods of others that they seek, and they are scarcely able even to keep their own property. I say these things not because I have seen them happen, but because I

---

1 Ecclus. 3: 3. Dhuoda here assumes a traditional attribution of this Old Testament book to David's son Solomon.
2 Ecclus. 3: 6.
3 Ecclus. 3: 7.
4 Ecclus. 3: 5.
5 Ecclus. 3: 8.
6 Exod. 20: 12.
7 Ecclus. 7: 30.
8 See Ecclus. 3: 2.
9 Ecclus. 3: 14.
10 Ecclus. 3: 15.
11 Dhuoda here clearly alludes to the conflict among Louis the Pious and his sons.
12 1 Sam. 4: 11.
13 See 2 Sam 18: 15.
14 Deut. 27: 16.
15 Lev. 20: 9.
16 Gen. 37: 8.

have read about such matters in books. I have heard of them in the past, you hear about them yourself, and I am hearing them even now. Consider what will happen in the future to those who treat others in this fashion. But God has the power to bring even these people—if there are such—to lament their evil ways and, in their conversion, to do penance and be worthy of salvation. May anyone who behaves so ill stay away from you, and may God give him understanding.

Everyone, whoever he may be, should consider this, my son: if the time comes that God finds him worthy to give him children of his own, he will not wish them to be rebellious or proud or full of greed, but humble and quiet and full of obedience, so that he rejoices to see them. He who was a son before, small and obedient to his father, may then be fortunate in his own fatherhood. May he who thinks on these things in the hope that they will happen consider too what I have said above. Then "all his limbs" will work "in concert, peacefully."[1]

Hear me as I direct you, my son William, and "listen carefully," follow the "instructions ... of a father."[2] Heed the words of the holy Fathers, and "bind them in thy heart"[3] by frequent reading so that "years of life may be multiplied to thee"[4] as you grow continually in goodness. For "they that wait upon"[5] God, blessing him, obeying the Fathers and complying freely with their precepts—such men "shall inherit the land."[6] If you listen to what I say above and if you put it into worthy practice, not only will you have success here on this earth, but also you will be found worthy to possess with the saints what the Psalmist describes: "I believe to see the good things of the Lord in the land of the living."[7] So that this other land may be your inheritance, my son, I pray that he who lives eternally may deign to prepare you to dwell there.

2. *On the same topic, on reverence for your father.*
In the human understanding of things, royal and imperial appearance and power seem preeminent in the world, and the custom of men is to account those men's actions and their names ahead of all others, as though these things were worthy of veneration and as though worldly power were the highest honor. This attitude is testified in the words of him who said, "whether it be to the king as excelling, or to the governors."[8] But despite all this, my wish is as follows, my son. In the smallness of my understanding—but also according to God's will—I caution you to render first to him whose son you are special, faithful, steadfast loyalty as long as you shall live. For it is a fixed and unchangeable truth that no one, unless his rank comes to him from his father, can have access to another person at the height of power.

So I urge you again, most beloved son William, that first of all you love God as I have written above. Then love, fear, and cherish your father. Keep in mind that your worldly estate proceeds from his. Recognize that from the most ancient times, men who have loved their fathers and have been truthfully obedient to them have been found worthy to receive God's benediction from those fathers' hands.

3. *On the examples of the early Fathers.*
We read that Sem, the son of Noah, reached heaven because he loved his father, and so did his brother Japheth. Their father said over their heads as he blessed them: may God bless Sem and Japheth, and may he dwell in their tents;[9] may they prosper, may they flourish, and may they be enriched in all good things. What shall I say about Cham and others like him?[10] Is it not necessary for you to know? For it is very useful to discern the meaning of these examples. Let us

---

1 See *The Benedictine Rule*, chap. 34, p. 33 above: "all the members will be at peace." See as well 1 Cor. 12: 12–30.
2 Here Dhuoda recalls the opening words of *The Benedictine Rule*. See above, p. 28.
3 Prov. 16: 21.
4 Prov. 4: 10.
5 Ps. 37: 9; Douay Ps. 36: 9.
6 Ibid.
7 Ps. 27: 13; Douay Ps. 26: 13.
8 1 Pet. 2: 13–14.
9 See Gen. 9: 26–27.
10 See Gen. 9: 22. Dhuoda quickly passes over Noah's third son, who saw his father drunken and naked and did not cover him.

think upon them always, turning toward those who have been good.

In obeying his father, Isaac was found worthy to share with his wife and descendants many goods in this world, for he received that father's benediction. Isaac is also called "laughter"[1] in holy Scripture, or "rejoicing," and "rejoicing" is a fitting name for one such as he, just as "mourning" is rightly applied to an idle, confused, and profligate man. So too Jacob, because he loved and obeyed his father, was found worthy to be snatched away from many tribulations and pressing difficulties. He received double and triple benediction from God and from his earthly father, and also from his mother and an angel. It was said to him, "I will bless thee, and I will multiply your name as the stars of heaven."[2] You will be blessed and you will be called Israel,[3] "for if thou hast been strong against God, how much more shalt thou prevail against men?"[4]

Consider, my son, how strong those are in the secular world who are worthy of God's blessing because of their parents' merits and because of their own filial obedience. If such was the case for Jacob, then you too should fight, seek, struggle, and strive manfully in all situations that you too may be worthy to receive at least that blessing from him who is called God and to receive your inheritance along with Jacob. For it is according to Jacob's model that faults are washed away and vices overcome; all his enemies submitted to the weight of his gentleness as if they wore yokes in his service.[5] The creator of the world gave Jacob a wife, children, and much material wealth. We read of him that he was always satisfied and rich in this world and that he pleased God in every way.

And what shall I say of Joseph, Jacob's son, who was so loving and obedient to his father that he would have been willing to die for him if God and that father's merits had not protected him? Joseph was betrayed and accused because of his obedience to his father; he was sent to his brothers, and they sold him. But he feared and avoided fornication with women, maintaining chastity of the mind for God's sake and of the body for his earthly lord's sake. Thus he was worthy to be loved more than all the other servants of his lord. He was imprisoned, he was beaten, and he suffered greatly—all these things for his father's sake, and throughout he gave thanks to God. Finally he was set free of this swarm of troubles and hardships. He became the greatest of counselors and interpreters of dreams; he was raised to great authority and crowned with the highest power. In the royal hall, when he shone forth as the second in command on account of his merits, he was higher in rank than all the rest.

He was called "Joseph ... a growing son, a growing son,"[6] and the Egyptians changed his name to ruler of the world and savior because of the goodness of his great love. Beautiful in demeanor, beautiful in spirit, beautiful in appearance, he was still more beautiful in understanding, chaste in body and humble in heart. And what else shall I say? Eminent and rich in this world, he was pleasing in everything to God and man alike. Ruling his father and his brothers, governing all of Egypt, he ended his earthly life in peace. Walking "from virtue to virtue,"[7] he was found worthy in his humility, chastity, and obedience to be joined to God, shining forth in heaven and ruling with the saints in glory. And all this because of his devotion to his father.

Many others who have been obedient to God and mindful of the commands of a devoted father have been honored and respected in the secular world and have safely reached that heavenly reward for which they struggled. May what happened to them happen also for you if the good Lord grants you children. But what else shall I write for you about that humble respect I have described above? I beseech and I caution you that you act worthily toward deserving individuals. Always do good works. And always grow and increase in him who is called God, the maker of heaven and earth, about whom it is written: and he was subject to his parents.[8] May the redeemer of the human race cause you to grow, to progress, and to be

---

1 Gen. 21: 6.
2 Gen. 22: 17. In fact, Dhuoda here quotes God's blessing on Jacob's grandfather Abraham.
3 See Gen. 35: 10.
4 Gen. 32: 28.
5 See Jer. 27: 12.
6 Gen. 49: 22.
7 Ps. 84: 8; Douay Ps. 83: 8.
8 See Luke 2: 51.

enlarged in age and wisdom before God and men.[1] May Jesus Christ, our Lord in whom all good things are possible and who reigns eternally, deign to grant these things to you. Amen.

4. *Direction on your comportment toward your lord.*

You have Charles[2] as your lord; you have him as lord because, as I believe, God and your father, Bernard, have chosen him for you to serve at the beginning of your career, in the flower of your youth. Remember that he comes from a great and noble lineage on both sides of his family.[3] Serve him not only so that you please him in obvious ways, but also as one clearheaded in matters of both body and soul. Be steadfastly and completely loyal to him in all things.

Think on that excellent servant of the patriarch Abraham. He traveled a great distance to bring back a wife for his master's son.[4] Because of the confidence of him who gave the command and the wise trustworthiness of him who followed it, the task was fulfilled. The wife found great blessing and great riches in her many descendants. What shall I say of the attitude of Joab, of Abner, and of many others toward the king David?[5] Facing dangers on their king's behalf in many places, they desired with all their might to please their lord more than themselves. And what of those many others in holy Scripture who faithfully obeyed their lords' commands? Because of their watchful strength they were found worthy to flourish in this world. For we know that, as Scripture tells, all honor and authority are given by God. Therefore we should serve our lords faithfully, without ill will, without reluctance, and without sluggishness. As we read, "there is no power but from God: and he … that resisteth the power, resisteth the ordinance of God."[6]

That is why, my son, I urge you to keep this loyalty as long as you live, in your body and in your mind.

For the advancement that it brings you will be of great value both to you and to those who in turn serve you. May the madness of treachery never, not once, make you offer an angry insult. May it never give rise in your heart to the idea of being disloyal to your lord. There is harsh and shameful talk about men who act in this fashion. I do not think that such will befall you or those who fight alongside you because such an attitude has never shown itself among your ancestors. It has not been seen among them, it is not seen now, and it will not be seen in the future.[7]

Be truthful to your lord, my son William, child of their lineage. Be vigilant, energetic, and offer him ready assistance as I have said here. In every matter of importance to royal power take care to show yourself a man of good judgment—in your own thoughts and in public—to the extent that God gives you strength. Read the sayings and the lives of the holy Fathers who have gone before us. You will there discover how you may serve your lord and be faithful to him in all things. When you understand this, devote yourself to the faithful execution of your lord's commands. Look around as well and observe those who fight for him loyally and constantly. Learn from them how you may serve him. Then, informed by their example, with the help and support of God, you will easily reach the celestial goal I have mentioned above. And may your heavenly Lord God be generous and benevolent toward you. May he keep you safe, be your kind leader and your protector. May he deign to assist you in all your actions and be your constant defender. "As it shall be the will of God in heaven so be it done."[8] Amen.…

9. *Regarding the magnates*[9]

As for the magnates and their counselors—and all those like them who serve faithfully—show them

---

1 See Luke 2: 52.
2 William served Charles, later known as "the Bald."
3 Charles's father was Emperor Louis the Pious. He was only slightly older than William.
4 Gen. 24.
5 See 1 Kings 2.
6 Rom. 13: 1–2.
7 Dhuoda says this in spite of the fact that Bernard, the boy's father, was clearly under suspicion of disloyalty at the time—as he had been for much of his career.
8 1 Macc. 3: 60.
9 The "magnates" refer to the courtiers, nobles, and other important men.

your love, affection, and service often. Do so to them together and individually, to whomever is important at court. Learn attentively from the model of their distinction and adhere to it firmly. For in a house as great as the king's there are, there have been, and there will be, if the good Lord so commands, many conversations. There, one who wishes can learn from others humility, charity, chastity, patience, gentleness, modesty, sobriety, discretion, and other virtues, as well as the desire to do good.

So, my son, while you are a young boy still growing,[1] learn from those elders whose understanding is rich whatever good you can with the Father's help so you may be pleasing to God before all else and then be useful to man. I urge you to strive to act among your associates, peers, and faithful friends so that your life may hold to a good course, marked with no shame of disloyalty to your lords but with eagerness for good action, in a laudable fashion, worthy and proper. May that God who makes the tongues of infants speak in his praise—as it is written, "out of the mouths of infants"[2]—himself cause you, filled with the eloquence of worthy, noble men who fear the Lord, to climb to the ranks of heaven....

[In Books Four through Nine, Dhuoda takes up in turn the moral life; sin, punishment, and God's justice; the beatitudes; the two deaths of man (of body and spirit); prayer; and biblical and numerical metaphors.]

Book Ten

1. *On the age you have attained.*

1 You have now reached four times four years.
 If my second son too were of this age,
  I would have another copy of this little book made
   for him.

2 And if in twice as many years and half again
 I were to see your image,
  I would write to you of more difficult things, and in
   more words.

But because the time of my parting hastens,   3
And the suffering of pains everywhere wears my
  body down,
 I have in haste gathered this book for your benefit
  and your brother's.

Knowing that I cannot reach that time I have   4
  mentioned,
 I urge you to taste this as if it were the food of your
  mouth,
Like a sweetened drink mixed with grain.

For the time at which I came to your father,   5
Or when you were born of us into this earthly
  world—
 All this is known to us according to the dates of the
  months.

From the first line of this little book   6
To its last syllable, know that
 All this is written for your salvation.

To find what is included here,   7
Read the chapter headings
 So that you may easily take up what follows.

All the verses here—above and below, with all the   8
  rest—
 I have dictated for the good of your spirit and your
  body.
 I never cease directing you to read them aloud and
  keep them in your heart.

2. *On the verses I have begun with the letters of your name.*[3]

So that you may flourish and be strong, best of   1
  children,
Do not hesitate to read the things I have spoken,
Written down, and addressed to you.
  There you will easily find what is pleasing for you.

---

1 See Gen. 49: 22.
2 Ps. 9: 3; Douay Ps. 8: 3.
3 The first letters of the following stanzas spell VERSI AD VVILHELMUM F[ILIUM], or "verses to William, my son." These verses form a synopsis of the preceding text.

2 God's word is living.[1] Seek it out.
Diligently study its sacred learning.
For your mind will be filled with great joy
        Throughout all time.

3 May that great and strong king, the good, bright
        Lord,
Deign to nurture your mind through all that befalls
        you,
My young son. May he protect you and defend you
        In every hour.

4 May you be humble of mind and chaste
Of body, ready to do good service,
So that you can readily accommodate yourself to all,
        Both great and small.

5 Foremost, fear and love the Lord God
With all your mind and heart, and all your strength,
And then honor your father
        In every way.[2]

6 As for that bountiful descendant of a line,
Scion of his race and lineage,
Him who shines in his great deeds—
        Never hesitate to serve him constantly.[3]

7 Love the great magnates; esteem
Those who are first in the court, and act as the equal
        of those of low degree.
Join yourself to those of good will, and take care
        Not to yield to the proud and the evil.

8 Always hold in honor the rightly constituted minis-
        ters of the divine rites,
Those who are worthy of the prelate's status.
With simple sincerity, commend yourself always with
        outstretched hands
        To those who keep the altars.

9 Help widows and orphans often,
And be generous to pilgrims with food and drink,

Prepare lodgings for them, and extend your hand
        with
        Clothing for the naked.

Be a strong and fair judge in legal matters,   10
Never take a bribe from anyone,
Nor oppress anyone. For he who has been your
        benefactor
        Will repay you.

Generous in gift giving, always watchful and   11
        prudent,
Agreeable to all, with a winning manner,
Profoundly joyful—such a countenance
        Will always be yours.

There is one who weighs out, who gives out in one   12
        direction or another.
He returns for the merits of all what their deeds
        deserve,
Granting the greatest reward, the stars of heaven,[4]
        For words and works.

And so, my noble son, seek diligently.   13
Take care to hasten to receive
Such great rewards, and turn away your eyes
        From the fires of blackened wood.

Although you count to your flourishing youth   14
Only four times four years' growth,
Your tender limbs grow older
        As you travel your course.

It seems very far from me,   15
Wishing as I do to see the shape of your face—
If strength were given me, still my merits
        Are not enough to win it.

May you live for him who made you   16
With a clear mind, and join the worthy company of
        his servants,
So that you may rise again in joy

---

1 See Heb. 4: 12.
2 See Mark 12: 33.
3 Dhuoda here refers to Charles the Bald.
4 Compare Rev. 2: 28.

After your course is ended.

17 Although my mind is wrapped in shadows,
    Nevertheless I urge this, that you constantly read
    The pages of this little book written out above,
        And that you fix them in your mind.

18 With God's help these verses end,
    Now that eight years have twice gone by,
    At the beginning of December, feast of St. Andrew,
        The season of the coming of the Word.

    The verses end.

3. *A postscript on public life.*

Here the words of this little book conclude. I have dictated them with an eager mind and have had them copied down for your benefit, as a model for you.

For I wish and urge that, when with God's help you have grown to manhood, you may arrange your household well, in appropriate order. As is written of another man who lived in this fashion, a man "like the most tender little worm of the wood,"[1] perform all the duties of your public life with loyalty, in a well-ordered fashion.

As for whether I survive to that time when I may see this with my own eyes, I am uncertain—uncertain in my own merits, uncertain in my strength, battered as I am among the waves in my frail toil. Although such is what I am, all things are possible for the Almighty. It is not in man's power to do his own will; rather whatever men accomplish is according to God's will. In the words of Scripture, "it is not of him that willeth, nor of him that runneth, but of God that showeth mercy."[2] Now, trusting in him, I say nothing else but "as it shall be the will of God in heaven so it be done."[3] Amen.

4. *Returning to myself, I grieve.*

The sweetness of my great love for you and my desire for your beauty have made me all but forget my own situation. I wish now, "the doors being shut,"[4] to return to my own self. But because I am not worthy to be numbered among those who are mentioned above,[5] I still ask that you—among the innumerable people who may do so—pray without ceasing for the remedy of my soul on account of your special feeling for me, which can be measured.

You know how much, because of my continual illnesses and other circumstances, I have suffered all these things and others like them in my fragile body—according to the saying of a certain man, "in perils from my own nation, in perils from the Gentiles"[6]—because of my pitiful merits. With God's help and because of your father, Bernard, I have at last confidently escaped these dangers, but my mind still turns back to that rescue. In the past I have often been lax in the praise of God, and instead of doing what I should in the seven hours of the divine office, I have been slothful seven times seven ways.[7] That is why, with a humble heart and with all my strength, I pray that I may take my pleasure in continually beseeching God for my sins and my transgressions. May he deign to raise even me into heaven, shattered and heavy though I am.

And since you see me as I live in the world, strive with watchful heart—not only in vigils and prayer but also in alms to the poor—that I may be found worthy, once I am liberated from the flesh and from the bonds of my sins, to be freely received by the good Lord who judges us.

Your frequent prayer and that of others is necessary to me now. It will be more and more so in time to come if, as I believe, my moment is upon me. In my great fear and grief about what the future may bring me, my mind casts about in every direction. And I am unsure how, on the basis of my merits, I may be able to be set free in the end. Why? Because I have sinned in thought and in speech. Ill words themselves lead to evil deeds. Nevertheless I will not despair of the

---

1 2 Sam 23: 8.
2 Rom. 9: 16.
3 1 Macc. 3: 60.
4 John 20: 26.
5 Dhuoda may mean William's deceased ancestors, for whom he should pray; or she may mean the great men of the past.
6 2 Cor. 11: 26.
7 See Gen. 7: 2.

mercy of God. I do not despair now and I will never despair. I leave no other such as you to survive me, noble boy, to struggle on my behalf as you do and as many may do for me because of you, so that I may finally come to salvation.

I acknowledge that, to defend the interests of my lord and master Bernard, and so that my service to him might not weaken in the March and elsewhere[1]—so that he not abandon you and me, as some men do—I know that I have gone greatly into debt. To respond to great necessities, I have frequently borrowed great sums, not only from Christians but also from Jews. To the extent that I have been able, I have repaid them. To the extent that I can in the future, I will always do so. But if there is still something to pay after I die, I ask and I beg you to take care in seeking out my creditors. When you find them, make sure that everything is paid off either from my own resources, if any remain, or from your assets—what you have now or what you eventually acquire through just means, with God's help.

What more shall I say? As for your little brother, I have above directed you time and again concerning what you should do for him. What I ask now is that he too, if he reaches the age of manhood, deign to pray for me. I direct both of you, as if you were together here before me, to have the offering of the sacrifice and the presentation of the host made often on my behalf.

Then, when my redeemer commands that I depart this world, he will see fit to prepare refreshment for me. And if this transpires through your prayers and the worthy prayers of others, he who is called God will bring me into heaven in the company of his saints.

This handbook ends here. Amen. Thanks be to God.

5. *Names of the dead.*

Here, briefly, are the names of those persons whom I failed to mention above. They are William, Cunigund, Gerberge, Witburgis, Theoderic, Gotzhelm, Guarnarius, Rothlindis.[2]

Other members of your lineage still flourish in this world with God's help. It is entirely at the will of him who made them to summon them too. Son, what should you do in regard to them but say with the Psalmist, "we that live bless the Lord: from this time now and for ever"?[3]

When a member of your family passes on, this does not befall except through God's power. When the Lord so commands, as in the case of your uncle the lord Aribert, you who survive must effect that his name be written down among the others, and you must pray for him.

6. *I ask that you write this epitaph on my grave.*[4]

When I too have reached the end of my days, see to it that my name as well be written down among the names of those dead persons. What I wish and what I yearn for with all my might, as though it were happening now, is that you order the following verses to be cut in the stone of the place where I am buried, on the slab that hides my body. Then those who see this epitaph on my burial place may pour out worthy prayers to God for my unworthy self.

And as for any other who may someday read the handbook you now peruse, may he too ponder the words that follow here so that he may commend me to God's salvation as if I were buried beneath these words.

Find here, reader, the verses of my epitaph:[5]

† D † M †[6]
Formed of earth, in this tomb
Lies the earthly body of Dhuoda.

---

1 Dhuoda refers to her support for Bernard's position as count of the Spanish March.
2 The names here seem to refer to members of Bernard's family, not Dhuoda's, and thus contribute to the mother's emphasis on William's obligation to his patrilineage. Dhuoda surely does not wish her son to ignore his spiritual duty toward the other side of his family, however, for she argues that prayer on her behalf is among his primary responsibilities.
3 Ps. 115: 18; Douay Ps. 113: 18.
4 Other Carolingian authors, such as Alcuin, likewise composed their own epitaphs.
5 Dhuoda here offers another acrostic. The initial letters of the following verses spell DHUODANE, perhaps an alternate Latin spelling of her name or an adjectival form.
6 Dhuoda abbreviates *dis manibus*, "into the hands of God."

Great king, receive her.

The surrounding earth has received in its depths
The flimsy filth of which she was made.
        Kind king, grant her favor.

The darkness of the tomb, bathed with her sorrow,
Is all that remains to her.
        You, king, absolve her failings.

You, man or woman, old or young, who walk back
   and forth
In this place, I ask you, say this:
        Holy one, great one, release her chains.

Bound in the dark tomb by bitter death,
Closed in, she has finished life in earth's filth.
        You, king, spare her sins.

So that the dark serpent
Not carry away her soul, say in prayer:
        Merciful God, come to her aid.

Let no one walk away without reading this.
I beseech all that they pray, saying:
        Give her peace, gentle father,

And, merciful one, command that she at least be
   enriched
With your saints by your perpetual light.
        Let her receive your amen after her death.

α † ω[1]

[In the final book, Eleven, Dhuoda copies a work by
Alcuin on how to read and use the psalms.]

---

1   Dhuoda uses the Greek letters alpha and omega to invoke Christ. See Rev. 1: 8.

TIMELINE FOR CHAPTER THREE

700

724   *Sale of a slave in Italy* ————

760s   *Donation of Constantine* ———— 750

754-67   Ibn Ishaq, *Life of Muhammad* ————

789   *Admonitio generalis* ————
800   Abu Nuwas, *Youth and I* ————
805   *Capitulary of Thionville* ———— 800
early 9th c.   *Once again my Burdened Anchor...* ————   ———— 9th c.   *Sindbad the Sailor*
9th c.   Al-Bukhari, *On Fasting* ————
814-5   *Polyptyque of the Church of Saint Mary of Marseille* ————

841-3   Dhuoda, *Handbook* ————
850s   Al-Jahiz, *Avarice and the Avaricious* ———— 850

864-7   Photius, *Letter to the Khan* ————   ———— 863-7   Constantine/Cyril, *Prologue to the Gospel*

883   *Chronicle of Albelda* ————

bef. 888   Al-Sijistani, *Compilation of the Jurisprudential Responses* ————

900

912   *Book of the Prefect* ————

mid 10th   Dunash ben Labrat, *There Came a Voice* ————   ———— bef. 940   Ibn `Abd Rabbihi, *I Have Never Seen*

FOUR

POLITICAL COMMUNITIES REORDERED (*c*.900-*c*.1050)

REGIONALISM: ITS ADVANTAGES AND ITS DISCONTENTS

4.1 Fragmentation in the Islamic world: Al-Tabari, *The Defeat of the Zanj Revolt* (*c*.915). Original in Arabic.

AL-TABARI (839-923) WAS BORN IN Amul, on the southern shore of the Caspian Sea. His education took him to Baghdad, Basra, and Egypt before he returned to Baghdad (*c*.870) to write and teach. He was a prolific author, producing works on jurisprudence, the Qur'an, and history. His universal history, from which comes the excerpt below, began with Creation and continued to 915. He modestly called this extremely long work *The Short Work on the History of Messengers, Kings, and Caliphs.* The section printed here covers the last part of the reign of Caliph al-Mu`tamid (r.870-892), a period through which al-Tabari lived himself. Key to the events of this period was the revolt of the Zanj, black slaves who were put to work removing the salt from the marshes formed by the Tigris and Euphrates rivers. Led by `Ali b. Muhammad, whom al-Tabari calls "the abominable" and "the traitor," the Zanj pillaged the cities around Basra and incited some local groups to challenge the caliph's authority. In response, al-Mu`tamid called on his brother al-Muwaffaq Abu Ahmad and Abu Ahmad's son Abu al-Abbas (later Caliph al-Mu`tadid) to wage war against the Zanj. The passage here begins in 880 with a victory by Abu al-Abbas. Although ruthlessly killing all the captives in this instance, father and son also offered amnesty and "robes of honor" to those who deserted the Zanj cause, severely dividing and weakening the opposition. They ultimately won the war against the Zanj in 883, but al-Tabari hints of other local defections from the caliphate, presaging its eventual decline.

Let us use this document to discuss once again how to read a primary source. Al-Tabari's account of the Zanj revolt is very different from *The Edict of Milan* on p. 1. Nevertheless, it should be subjected to the same series of questions. The answers lead to new questions that work just for al-Tabari (and perhaps a small cluster of similar documents), in the same way as the answers to the questions about *The Edict of Milan* led to questions largely pertinent to it alone.

Who wrote it, and for what audience was it written? In this case, the answer is quite simple: the author was al-Tabari, and you know a bit about his career from the introductory note of your editor. You can easily guess that his audience was meant to be his students and other educated readers in the Islamic world.

When was it written? Your editor has given you the date *c*.915. At this point in your studies, you need not worry much about how this date was arrived at. It is more important to consider the circumstances and historical events in the context of which a date like 915 takes on meaning. You should be considering how, even as the caliphate was weakening, the Islamic world was open to wandering students and supported scholarly work.

Where was it written? The answer is, no doubt, Baghdad. But you should not be content with that. You should consider its significance at the time. Was it still the capital of the Islamic world? If not, why do you suppose that al-Tabari settled there?

Why was it written?. Al-Tabari begins this voluminous history with an extended passage in praise of God. He then says that he intends to begin with the Creation of the world and to continue by chronicling all the kings, messengers, and caliphs that he has heard about. But the first topic that he addresses in some detail is philosophical: "What is Time?" Thus, although al-Tabari does not say precisely why he wrote, he clearly wished to produce both a comprehensive chronicle about the powerful men in the world and a reflective work on the nature of history itself. But you should go beyond this answer to ask what other motives might have been at work. For example, might al-Tabari have thought that there were moral, practical, and religious—even doctrinal—lessons to be learned from history? Might he have been interested in legitimizing the Abbasids or other caliphs?

What is it? Clearly it was a history; the word was in the title. But what sort of history? Al-Tabari was careful to document many of his facts by citing the chain of sources (*isnad*) that attested to them. This technique was important both in religious studies (see above, p. 152) and legal studies (see above, p. 157). Al-Tabari's work thus assimilated history with the scholarly traditions of other disciplines. Moreover his history might be called "universal," given its huge time frame. On the other hand, it is not a history of everything but rather of certain key figures.

What does it say? This is the most important question of all. To answer it, you need to analyze the text (or, here, the excerpt) carefully, taking care to understand what the author is describing and seeking further information (if necessary) about the institutions that he takes for granted.

What are the implications of what it says? This requires you to ask many questions about matters that lie behind the text. Important questions to ask are: *What does the document reveal about such institutions as family, power, social classes and groups, religion, and education and literacy in the world that produced it? What are its underlying assumptions about gender; about human nature, agency, and goals; about the nature of the divine?*

How reliable is it? Certainly al-Tabari's citations of his sources suggest that he was interested in reliability. On the other hand, you may ask if al-Tabari included everything that he knew, or if he had a certain "slant" on the events.

Are there complicating factors? In the Middle Ages authors often dictated their thoughts and then reworked them over time. Al-Tabari apparently finished lecturing on his *History* in about 915, but he continued to rework it. After his death, the work was copied numerous times—by hand. Paper was prevalent in the Islamic world, and it was cheaper and more abundant than parchment, which the West and the Byzantine Empire relied on. Nevertheless today we have no complete manuscript of al-Tabari's history, and scholars have had to reconstruct the full text from the various parts that are extant.

If you compare the questions and answers here with those introducing the *Edict of Milan*, you should be convinced that reading primary sources is both complex and fascinating.

[Source: *The History of Al-Tabari*, vol. 27: *The 'Abbasid Recovery*, trans. Philip M. Fields, annotated Jacob Lassner (Albany: State University of New York Press, 1987), pp. 24-27, 65-66, 132-36.]

Abu Ahmad remained in al-Firk for several days to permit his troops, and any others who wanted to proceed with him, to join on. He had prepared the barges, galleys, ferries and boats. Then, on Tuesday, the second of Rabi' I [October 11, 880], he and his clients, pages, cavalry and infantry reportedly left al-Firk, bound for Rumiyat al-Mada'in. From there they journeyed on, stopping at al-Sib, Dayr al-'Aqul, Jarja-raya, Qunna, Jabbul, al-Silh and a place one *farsakh* [about four miles] from Wasit.[1] He remained at the latter for one day and one night and was met by his son Abu al-'Abbas and a squadron of cavalry including his leading officers and men. Abu Ahmad inquired about the state of his men, and getting from his son a picture of their gallantry and devotion in fighting, he ordered that robes of honor be bestowed upon them and Abu al-'Abbas. Thereupon, the son returned to his camp at al-'Umr where he remained throughout the day. In the early morning of the next day, Abu Ahmad took to the water where he was met by his son, Abu al-'Abbas, and all his troops in military formation, as fully equipped as they would be when confronting the traitor's forces. Abu Ahmad sailed on until he reached his camp on the waterway called Shirzad, where he stopped. On Thursday, the twenty-eighth of Rabi' I [November 6, 880], he departed from there

and stopped at the canal called Nahr Sindad, opposite the village called 'Ab-dallah. He instructed his son Abu al-'Abbas to halt on the eastern side of the Tigris, opposite the mouth of the Barduda, and put him in charge of the vanguard. Then he allotted the soldiers' allowances and paid them. Following that, he instructed his son to advance in front of him with the equipment that he had in his possession, toward the mouth of the Bar Musawir Canal.

Abu al-'Abbas set out with the best of his officers and troops, including Zirak al-Turki, the commander of his vanguard, and Nusayr Abu Hamzah, the commander of the barges and galleys. After this it was Abu Ahmad who set out with his selected cavalry and infantry, leaving the bulk of his army and many of his horsemen and foot soldiers behind in his place of encampment.

His son Abu al-'Abbas met him with a show of captives, heads and bodies of slain enemies from among the troops of al-Sha'rani. For, on that same day, before the arrival of his father Abu Ahmad, Abu al-'Abbas had been attacked by al-Sha'rani who came upon the former's camp. Abu al-'Abbas dealt him a severe blow, killing a great many of his men and taking captives. Abu Ahmad ordered that the captives be beheaded, which was done. Then Abu Ahmad descended to the

---

1   The places mentioned in this document are in or near Iraq.

mouth of the Bar Musawir, where he stayed for two days. From there, on Tuesday, the eighth of Rabi' II [November 17, 880], he departed from Suq al-Khamis with all his men and equipment bound for the city which the leader of the Zanj had named al-Mani'ah bi-Suq al-Khamis. He proceeded with his ships along the Bar Musawir while the cavalry marched before him along the eastern side of the waterway until they reached the waterway called Baratiq, which led to Madinat al-Sha'rani. Abu Ahmad preferred to begin fighting against Musa al-Sha'rani before he fought Sulayman b. Jami' because he feared that al-Sha'rani, who was to his rear, might attack and thus divert him from the adversary in front of him. That is why he set out against al-Sha'rani. He ordered the cavalry to cross the canal and proceed along both banks of the Baratiq. Abu Ahmad also instructed his son Abu al-'Abbas to advance with a flotilla of barges and galleys, and he himself followed with barges along with the bulk of his army.

When Sulayman, his Zanj troops and others noticed the cavalry and infantry proceeding on both banks of the canal and the ships advancing along the waterway—this was after Abu al-'Abbas had met them and engaged them in a skirmish—they fled and scattered. The troops of Abu al-'Abbas climbed the walls killing those who opposed them. When the Zanj and their supporters scattered, Abu al-'Abbas and his forces entered the city, killed a great many of its people, took many prisoners and laid hold of whatever was there. Al-Sha'rani and the others who escaped with him fled; they were pursued by Abu Ahmad's men up to the marshes where many drowned. The rest saved themselves by fleeing into the thickets.

Thereupon, Abu Ahmad instructed his troops to return to their camp before sunset of that Tuesday, and he withdrew. About five thousand Muslim women and some Zanj women, who were taken in Suq al-Khamis, were saved. Abu Ahmad gave instructions to take care of all the women, to transfer them to Wasit and return them to their families.

Abu Ahmad spent that night opposite the Baratiq Canal and in the early morning of the next day, he entered the city and gave the people permission to take all the Zanj possessions there. Everything in the city was seized. Abu Ahmad ordered the walls razed, the trenches filled, and the remaining ships burned. He left for his camp at Bar Musawir with booty taken in the districts and villages previously possessed by al-Sha'rani and his men; this included crops of wheat, barley and rice. He ordered that the crops be sold and the money realized from the sale be spent to pay his mawla's pages,[1] the troops of his regular army, and other people of his camp.

Sulayman al-Sha'rani escaped with his two brothers and others, but he lost his children and possessions. Upon reaching al-Madhar he reported to the traitor [that is, the leader of the Zanj] what had befallen him and that he had taken refuge in al-Madhar.

According to Muhammad b. al-Hasan—Muhammad b. Hisham, known as Abu Wathilah al-Kirmani: I was in the presence of the traitor—he was having a discussion—when the letter from Sulayman al-Sha'rani arrived with the news of the battle and his flight to al-Madhar. As soon as he had the letter unsealed and his eye fell on the passage describing the defeat, his bowel muscles loosened and he got up to relieve himself, then he returned. As his Assembly came to order, he took the letter and began reading it again, and when he reached the passage which had disturbed him the first time, he left once more. This repeated itself several times. There remained no doubt that the calamity was great, and I refrained from asking him questions. After some time had elapsed, I ventured to say, "Isn't this the letter from Sulayman b. Musa?" He replied, "Yes, and a piece of heartbreaking news, too. Indeed, those who fell upon him dealt him a crushing blow 'that will not spare nor leave unburned.' He has written this letter from al-Madhar, and he has barely saved his own skin."

I deemed this news momentous and only God knows what a joy filled my heart, but I concealed it and refrained from rejoicing at the prospect of the approaching relief. However, the traitor regained self-control in face of vicissitude, and showed firmness. He wrote to Sulayman b. Jami', cautioning him against al-Sha'rani's fate and instructing him to be vigilant and watchful concerning what might lie before him....

On Tuesday, the first day of al-Muharram [August

---

1 A mawla could mean either master or servant. Here it undoubtedly refers to a servant or dependent.

12, 881], Ja'far b. al-Ibrahim, who was known as al-Sajjan, sought safe-conduct from Abu Ahmad al-Muwaffaq. It is mentioned that the reason for this was Abu Ahmad's battle at the end of Dhu al-Hijjah 267 [July 3–31, 881], to which we have referred above, as well as the flight of Rayhan b. Salih al-Maghribi and his men from the camp of the deviate, and their linking up with Abu Ahmad. The abominable one became completely discouraged at this; al-Sajjan was, reportedly, one of his trustworthy associates.

Abu Ahmad conferred on this al-Sajjan robes of honor, various gifts, as well as a military allotment, and a place of lodging. Al-Sajjan was assigned to Abu al-'Abbas, who was ordered to transport him in a barge to a position in front of the abominable one's fortress so his [former] compatriots could see him. Al-Sajjan addressed them and told them that they were misled by the abominable one; he informed them what he had experienced because of the latter's lies and immoral behavior. The same day that al-Sajjan was placed in front of the abominable one's camp, a great many Zanj officers and others sought guarantees of safety; all of them were treated kindly. One after another the enemy sought safety and abandoned the abominable one.

After that battle which I have mentioned as having taken place on the last day of Dhu al-Hijjah of the year 267 [July 31, 881], Abu Ahmad did not cross over to fight the abominable one, thus giving his troops a respite until the month of Rabi' II [November 9–December 7, 881].

In this year, 'Amr b. al-Layth went to Fars to fight Muhammad b. al-Layth, his own governor in this province. 'Amr routed Muhammad b. al-Layth and auctioned off the spoils of his camp; the latter escaped with a small group of his men. 'Amr entered Istakhr, which was looted by his troops, and then sent a force to chase after Muhammad b. al-Layth. They seized him, and then delivered him to 'Amr as a prisoner. Thereupon, 'Amr went to Shiraz where he remained....

Now [August, 883] Abu Ahmad was sure of victory, for he saw its signs, and all the people rejoiced at what God had granted—namely, the rout of the profligate and his men. They rejoiced as well at God's having made it possible to expel the enemy from their city, and seize everything in it, and distribute what had been taken as booty—that is the money,

treasures and weapons. Finally there was the rescue of all the captives held by the rebels. But Abu Ahmad was angry at his men because they disobeyed orders and abandoned the positions in which he had placed them. He ordered that the commanders of his mawlas and pages and the leading men among them be gathered together. When they were assembled for him, he scolded them for what they had done, judging them weak and castigating them in harsh language. Then they made excuses; they supposed that he had returned, and they had not known about his advance against the profligate, nor about his having pressed so far into the rebel's camp. Had they known this, they would have rushed toward him. They did not leave their places until they had taken a solemn oath and covenant that, when sent against the abominable one, none of them would withdraw before God had delivered him into their hands; and should they fail, they would not budge from their positions until God had passed judgment between them and him. They requested of al-Muwaffaq that, after they had left al-Muwaffaqiyyah to fight, he order the ships transporting them to return and, thus, eliminate any temptation to those who might seek to leave the battle against the profligate.

Abu Ahmad accepted their apologies for their wrongdoing and again took them into his favor. Then he ordered them to prepare for crossing and to forewarn their troops just as they themselves had been forewarned. Abu Ahmad spent Tuesday, Wednesday, Thursday and Friday preparing whatever he would need. When this was completed, he sent word to his entourage and the officers of his pages and mawlas, instructing them as to their tasks when crossing [into combat]. Friday evening he sent word to Abu al-'Abbas and the officers of his pages and mawlas to set out for places which he, that is, Abu Ahmad, had specified.

Al-Muwaffaq instructed Abu al-'Abbas and his troops to set a course for a place known as 'Askar Rayhan, which lay between the canal known as Nahr al-Sufyani and the spot where the rebel sought refuge. He and his army were to follow the route along the canal known as Nahr al-Mughirah, so that they would exit where the canal intersects the Abu al-Khasib and reach 'Askar Rayhan from this direction. He forwarded instructions to an officer of his black pages to reach the Nahr al-Amir and cross at its center. At the same time, he ordered the rest of his officers and pages to pass the night on the eastern side of the Tigris, opposite the profligate's camp, and be prepared to attack him in the early morning.

During Friday night, al-Muwaffaq made the rounds among the officers and men in his barge. He divided amongst them key positions and locations which he had arranged for them in the profligate's camp. According to the assigned plan, they were to march towards these places in the morning. Early Saturday morning, on the second of Safar, 270 [August 11, 883], al-Muwaffaq reached the Abu al-Khasib Canal in his barge. He remained there until all his men had crossed [the waterway] and disembarked from their vessels, and the cavalry and infantry had assumed their positions. Then, after giving instructions for the vessels and ferries to return to the eastern side, he gave the troops the go-ahead to march against the profligate. He himself preceded them until he reached the spot where he estimated the profligates would make a stand in an attempt to repel the government army. Meanwhile, on Monday, after the army had withdrawn, the traitor and his men returned to the city and stayed there, hoping to prolong their defense and repel the attack.

Al-Muwaffaq found that the fastest of his cavalry and infantry among the pages had preceded the main force of the army and had attacked the rebel and his companions, dislodging them from their positions. The enemy force fled and dispersed without paying attention to one another, and the government army pursued them, killing and capturing whomever they managed to catch. The profligate, with a group of his fighting men, was cut off from [the rest] of his officers and troops—among them was al-Muhallabi. Ankalay, the rebel's son, had abandoned him, as had Sulayman b. Jami'. Moving against each of the contingents which we have named was a large force of al-Muwaffaq's mawlas, and cavalry and infantry drawn from his pages. Abu al-'Abbas's troops, assigned by al-Muwaffaq to the place known as 'Askar Rayhan, met the rebel's fleeing men and put them to the sword. The officer assigned to the Amir Canal also arrived there, and having blocked the rebels' path he attacked them. Encountering Sulayman b. Jami', he took the fight to him, killing many of his men and seizing Sulayman.

He made Sulayman a captive and delivered him to al-Muwaffaq without conditions. The people were glad to learn of Sulayman's capture, and there were many cries of "God is Great!" and great clamor. They felt certain of victory, since Sulayman was known to be the most able of the rebel's companions. After him, Ibrahim b. Ja'far al-Hamdani, one of the field commanders of the rebel's army, was taken captive; then Nadir al-Aswad, the one known as al-Haffar, one of the earliest companions of the rebel, was captured.

Upon al-Muwaffaq's order, precautionary measures were taken, and the captives were transferred in barges to Abu al-'Abbas.

Following this, those Zanj who had separated from the main body, together with the profligate, assaulted the government force, dislodging them from their positions and causing them to lose the initiative. Al-Muwaffaq noticed the loss of initiative, but he pressed on with the search for the abominable one, advancing quickly in the Abu al-Khasib Canal. This bolstered his mawlas and pages, who hastened to pursue (the enemy) with him. As al-Muwaffaq reached the Abu al-Khasib Canal, a herald arrived with the good news of the rebel's death; before long another herald arrived carrying a hand, and claimed that this was the hand of the rebel. This seemed to lend credence to the report of the rebel's demise. Finally a page from Lu'lu''s troops arrived, galloping on a horse and carrying the head of the abominable one. Al-Muwaffaq had the head brought closer, and then showed it to a group of former enemy officers who were in his presence. They identified it, and al-Muwaffaq prostrated himself in adoration to God for both the hardships and bounties He had conferred upon him. Abu al-'Abbas, the mawlas and the officers of al-Muwaffaq's pages then prostrated themselves, offering much thanks to God, and praising and exalting Him. Al-Muwaffaq ordered the head of the rebel raised on a spear and displayed in front of him. The people saw it and thus knew that the news of the rebel's death was true. At this, they raised their voices in praise to God.

It is reported that al-Muwaffaq's troops surrounded the abominable one after all his field commanders had abandoned him save al-Muhallabi; the latter now turned away from him and fled, thus betraying the rebel. The rebel then set off for the canal known as Nahr al-Amir and plunged into the water, seeking safety. Even before that, Ankalay, the son of the abominable one, had split off from his father and fled in the direction of the canal known as Nahr al-Dinari, where he entrenched himself in the swampy terrain.

Al-Muwaffaq retired, with the head of the abominable one displayed on a spear mounted in front of him on a barge. The vessel moved along the Abu al-Khasib Canal, with the people on both sides of the waterway observing it. When he reached the Tigris, he took his course along the river and gave the order to return the vessels, with which he had crossed to the western side of the Tigris at daylight, to the eastern side of the river. They were returned to ferry the troops [back] across the river.

Then al-Muwaffaq continued his trip, with the abominable one's head on the spear before him, while Sulayman b. Jami' and al-Hamdani were mounted for display. When he arrived at his fortress in al-Muwaffaqiyyah, he ordered Abu al-'Abbas to sail the barge, keeping the rebel's head and Sulayman b. Jami' and al-Hamdani in place, and to take his course to the Jatta Canal where the camp of al-Muwaffaq began. He was to do this so that all the people of the camp could have a look at them. Abu al-'Abbas did this, and then returned to his father, Abu Ahmad, whereupon the latter imprisoned Sulayman b. Jami' and al-Hamdani and ordered that the rebel's head be properly prepared and cleaned.

4.2 The powerful in the Byzantine countryside: Romanus Lecapenus, *Novel* (934). Original in Greek.

IN BYZANTINE LEGAL TERMS, a "novel" is a "new law." Emperor Romanus Lecapenus (r.920-944) issued one such law on behalf of the poor in the countryside in 934. Newly powerful provincial landowners, collectively known as *dynatoi*, were taking advantage of a recent famine to buy up whole villages, enhancing both their economic and social position. Romanus tried to set back the clock—he wanted the land to stay in the hands of the original peasant families or at least in the hands of their village neighbors. He insisted that the powerful "return [the land] without refund to the owners." What reasons can you give for Romanus's opposition to the powerful?

[Source: *The Land Legislation of the Macedonian Emperors*, trans. and ed. Eric McGeer (Toronto: Pontifical Institute of Mediaeval Studies, 2000), pp. 53-56, 59-60 (notes modified).]

NOVEL OF THE LORD EMPEROR ROMANUS THE ELDER

PROLOGUE

To dispose the soul in imitation of the Creator is the desire and ardent endeavor of those for whom it is a great and blessed thing to regard and to call themselves the work of the all-creating hand. As for those by whom this has not been accounted great and holy, they have the task of denying the Creation and the reckoning of Judgment, and, as with persons wholly content with life on earth and who choose to live their lives upon the earth alone, the display of their choice has been left in their wake.[1] Hence the great confusion of affairs, hence the great tide of injustices, hence the great and widespread oppression of the poor, and the great sighing of the needy, for whose sake the Lord rose from the dead. For He says, "For the oppression of the poor, for the sighing of the needy, now will I arise, saith the Lord."[2] If God, our Creator and Savior, Who made us emperor, rises in

---

1   The general sense seems to be this: people who see themselves as part of God's Creation try to act in accordance with God's ways, while people who do not venerate the Creation will have to reckon with the Last Judgment; such people have left ample evidence behind them of their choice to ignore divine justice and to lead their lives in pursuit of earthly, not eternal, rewards.
2   Ps. 12: 5; Douay Ps. 11: 6.

retribution, how will the poor man, who awaits only the eyes of the emperor for intercession, be neglected and altogether forgotten by us? Therefore, not only upon examination of the actions taken against them in the recent past or attempts to make amends, but also administering a common and lasting remedy to the matter, we have issued the present law to avenge them, having prepared this as a purgative and a cleansing of the predilection of greed. We have considered it advantageous that now no longer will anyone be deprived of his own properties, nor will a poor man suffer oppression, and that this advantage is beneficial to the common good, acceptable to God, profitable to the treasury, and useful to the state. Careful attention to this subject, for the sake of which decrees and judgments restraining the wickedness of the will and curtailing the reach of the grasping hand have streamed down to all the officials under our authority, has not been long neglected, nor has [our concern] arisen inappropriately. But since evil is versatile and multifarious, and all evils—not least greed, if indeed not even more so—contrive to evade the grip of laws and edicts and to regard the inescapable eye of divine justice as of no account, these measures, ejecting and excising the crafty workings of the will of the evildoers, have as a result now warranted more secure and rigorous codification.

1.1. We ordain therefore that those living in every land and district, where after God our rule extends, are to keep the domicile which has come down to them free and undisturbed. If time continues to preserve this arrangement, let the subsequent acquisition by the offspring or relatives through testamentary disposition, or the intention of the owner's preference, be fulfilled. If, though, given the course of human life and the ebb and flow of time, the pressure of necessity or even the prompting of the will alone, be it as it may, the owner embarks on the alienation of his own lands either in part or in whole, the purchase must first be set before the inhabitants of the same or adjacent fields

or villages. We do not introduce this legislation out of animosity or malice towards the powerful; but we issue these rulings out of benevolence and protection for the poor and for public welfare. Whereas those persons who have received authority from God, those risen above the many in honor and wealth, should consider the care of the poor an important task, these powerful persons who regard the poor as prey are vexed because they do not acquire these things more quickly. Even if such impious conduct is not true of all, let adherence to the law be common to all, lest the tare [weeds] brought in with the wheat escape notice.[1]

1.2. As a result, no longer shall any one of the illustrious *magistroi*[2] or *patrikioi*,[3] nor any of the persons honored with offices, governorships, or civil or military dignities, nor anyone at all enumerated in the Senate,[4] nor officials or ex-officials of the themes nor metropolitans most devoted to God, archbishops, bishops, *higoumenoi* [abbots], ecclesiastical officials, or supervisors and heads of pious or imperial houses,[5] whether as a private individual or in the name of an imperial or ecclesiastical property, dare either on their own or through an intermediary to intrude into a village or hamlet for the sake of a sale, gift, or inheritance—either whole or partial—or on any other pretext whatsoever. As this sort of acquisition has been ruled invalid, the acquired properties, along with the improvements since added, are to return without refund to the owners or, if they or their relatives are no longer alive, to the inhabitants of the villages or hamlets. For the domination of these persons has increased the great hardship of the poor, bringing upheavals, persecutions, coercion, and other concomitant afflictions and difficulties through the multitude of their servants, hirelings or other attendants and followers, and, to those able to see it, will cause no little harm to the commonwealth unless the present legislation puts an end to it first. For the settlement[6] of the population demonstrates the great benefit of its function—the

---

1 Echoing the parable of the wheat and the tares related in Matt. 13: 24–30; 36–43.
2 Those holding the highest possible dignity conferred on non-imperial family members.
3 Those who hold a high dignity conferred on governors of themes (military districts) or military leaders.
4 The Byzantine Senate was an advisory body whose members were high civil officials and dignitaries.
5 Philanthropic foundations administered by crown officials.
6 The Greek word for "settlement" also embraces the notions of stability and prosperity among the rural populace.

contribution of taxes and the fulfillment of military obligations—which will be completely lost should the common people disappear. Those concerned with the stability of the state must eliminate the cause of disturbance, expel what is harmful, and support the common good.

II.I. Let time hereafter maintain these measures for the common benefit and settled order of our subjects; but it is necessary to apply the approved remedy not only to the future, but also to the past. For many people seized upon the indigence of the poor—which time bringer of all things brought, or rather, which the multitude of our sins, driving out divine charity, caused—as the opportunity for business instead of charity, compassion, or kindness; and when they saw the poor oppressed by famine, they bought up the possessions of the unfortunate poor at a very low price, some with silver, some with gold, and others with grain or other forms of payment. Harsher than the duress at hand, in those times which followed they were like a pestilential attack of disease to the miserable inhabitants of the villages, having entered like gangrene into the body of the villages and causing total destruction....

EPILOGUE It is our desire that these regulations remain in force for the safety of our subjects for whose sake great and constant care is our concern. For if we have expended so much care for those under our authority, so as to spare nothing that contributes to freedom, on account of which lands, towns, and cities have, with the help of God, come into our hands from the enemy, some as the result of war, while others have passed over to us by the example [of the conquered towns] or through fear of capture and were taken before the trumpet's call to battle; and if we have striven, with the help of God, to provide our subjects with such great freedom from enemy attack, setting this as the goal of our prayers and exertions, how will we, after accomplishing so much against the onslaught of external enemies, not rid ourselves of our own enemies within, enemies of the natural order, of the Creation, and of justice, by reviling and repressing insatiety [endless desire], by excising the greedy disposition, and by liberating our subjects from the yoke of the tyrannical, oppressive hand and mind with the righteous intention to free them with the cutting sword of the present legislation? Let each of those to whom judicial authority has fallen see to it that these provisions remain in force in perpetuity [forever], for the service of God and for the common benefit and advantage of our empire received from Him.

In the Month of September of the eighth indiction in the year 6443 from the creation of the world, Romanus, Constantine, Stephanus, and Constantine, emperors of the Byzantines and faithful to God.

4.3 Donating to Cluny: Cluny's *Foundation Charter* (910) and various charters of donation (10th-11th c.). Originals in Latin.

WILLIAM, DUKE OF AQUITAINE, and his wife Ingelberga, anxious to ensure their eternal salvation, founded the monastery of Cluny on family property in the region of Mâcon (Burgundy, France). Soon the monastery gained an astonishing reputation for piety, and the prayers of its monks were praised for sending souls to heaven (see the remarks of one of its abbots, Peter the Venerable, on p. 331 below). Local donors, ranging from small peasants to rich aristocrats, gave land to Cluny in order to associate themselves with the monks' redemptive work. The donations were recorded in charters. The charters below consist, first, of the original donation, made by William and Ingelberga, and then of a group of charters drawn up for one family, later known as the Grossi. The family relationships were as follows:

(The Majolus of this family was *not* the same person as the Majolus who was abbot of Cluny 954–994.)

What reasons did people give for donating to the monastery of Cluny? What roles did women have in supporting the monastery? How do these charters show the conflicting tugs of family ties and charitable desires?

[Source: *Readings in Medieval History*, 3rd ed., ed. Patrick J. Geary (Peterborough, ON: Broadview Press, 2003), pp. 321-27 (slightly modified).]

[The Foundation Charter of Cluny: *Charter # 112* (September 11, 910)]

To all right thinkers it is clear that the providence of God has so provided for certain rich men that, by means of their transitory possessions, if they use them well, they may be able to merit everlasting rewards. As to which thing, indeed, the divine word, showing it to be possible and altogether advising it, says: "The riches of a man are the redemption of his soul."[1] I, William, count and duke by the grace of God, diligently pondering this, and desiring to provide for my own salvation while I am still able, have considered it advisable—nay, most necessary, that from the temporal goods which have been conferred upon me I should give some little portion for the gain of my soul. I do this, indeed, in order that I who have thus increased in wealth may not, perchance, at the last be accused of having spent all in caring for my body, but rather may rejoice, when fate at last shall snatch all things away, in having reserved something for myself. Which end, indeed, seems attainable by no more suitable means than that, following the precept of Christ: "I will make his poor my friends"[2] and making the act not a temporary but a lasting one, I should support at my own expense a congregation of monks. And this is my trust, this my hope, indeed, that although I myself am unable to despise all things, nevertheless, by receiving despisers of the world, whom I believe to be righteous, I may receive the reward of the righ-

---

1 See Prov. 13: 8.
2 Luke 16: 9.

teous. Therefore be it known to all who live in the unity of the faith and who await the mercy of Christ, and to those who shall succeed them and who shall continue to exist until the end of the world, that, for the love of God and of our Savior Jesus Christ, I hand over from my own rule to the holy apostles, Peter, namely, and Paul, the possessions over which I hold sway, the villa[1] of Cluny, namely, with the court and demesne *mansus*,[2] and the chapel in honor of St. Mary the mother of God and of St. Peter the prince of the apostles, together with all the things pertaining to it, the villas, indeed, the chapels, the serfs of both sexes, the vines, the fields, the meadows, the woods, the waters and their outlets, the mills, the incomes and revenues, what is cultivated and what is not, all in their entirety. Which things are situated in or about the county of Mâcon, each one surrounded by its own bounds. I give, moreover, all these things to the aforesaid apostles—I, William, and my wife Ingelberga—first for the love of God; then for the soul of my lord king Odo;[3] of my father and my mother; for myself and my wife—for the salvation, namely, of our souls and bodies;—and not least for that of Ava who left me these things in her will;[4] for the souls also of our brothers and sisters and nephews, and of all our relatives of both sexes; for our faithful ones who adhere to our service; for the advancement, also, and integrity of the catholic religion. Finally, since all of us Christians are held together by one bond of love and faith, let this donation be for all,—for the orthodox, namely, of past, present or future times.

I give these things, moreover, with this understanding, that at Cluny a regular monastery shall be constructed in honor of the holy apostles Peter and Paul, and that there the monks shall congregate and live according to the rule of St. Benedict,[5] and that they shall possess, hold, have and order these same things unto all time, provided that the venerable house of prayer which is there shall be faithfully filled with vows and supplications, and that celestial converse shall be sought and striven after with all desire and with the deepest ardor; and also that there shall be diligently directed to God prayers, beseechings and exhortations both for me and for all, according to the order in which mention has been made of them above. And let the monks themselves, together with all the aforesaid possessions, be under the power and dominion of the abbot Berno, who, as long as he shall live, shall preside over them according to the Rule and consistent with his knowledge and ability. But after his death, those same monks shall have power and permission to elect any one of their order whom they please as abbot and rector, following the will of God and the rule promulgated by St. Benedict,—in such a way that neither by the intervention of our own or of any other power may they be impeded from making a purely canonical election. Every five years, moreover, the aforesaid monks shall pay to the church of the apostles at Rome ten *solidi*[6] to supply them with lights; and they shall have the protection of those same apostles and the defense of the Roman pontiff; and those monks may, with their whole heart and soul, according to their ability and knowledge, build up the aforesaid place. We will, further, that in our times and in those of our successors, according as the opportunities and possibilities of that place shall allow, daily, works of mercy towards the poor, the needy, strangers, and pilgrims will be performed with the greatest zeal. It has pleased us also to insert in this document that, from this day, those same monks there congregated shall be subject neither to our yoke, nor to that of our relatives, nor to the sway of any earthly power. And, through God and all his saints, and by the awful day of judgment, I warn and abjure that no one of the secular princes, no count, no bishop whatever, not the pontiff of the aforesaid Roman see,

---

1 In this instance, the word *villa* means an estate, which included an enclosed area (the "court"), land, waste, meadow and various other appurtenances. In many of the other charters of Cluny, however, the word *villa* refers to a small district in which many landowners held land.

2 A *mansus* (pl. *mansi*) was a farming unit. A "demesne *mansus*" was an outsize farming unit belonging to the lord (in this case William, and soon the monastery of Cluny), which included the *mansi* of dependent peasants.

3 Odo, related to the later Capetians, was king of the west Franks 888-898.

4 Ava was a sister of the donor.

5 For *The Benedictine Rule* see above, p. 28.

6 A *solidus* was a coin, in this case silver.

shall invade the property of these servants of God, or alienate it, or diminish it, or exchange it, or give it as a benefice to any one, or constitute any prelate over them against their will. And that such unhallowed act may be more strictly prohibited to all rash and wicked men, I subjoin the following, giving force to the warning. I adjure you, oh holy apostles and glorious princes of the world, Peter and Paul, and you, oh supreme pontiff of the apostolic see, that, through the canonical and apostolic authority which you have received from God, you remove from participation in the holy church and in eternal life, the robbers and invaders and alienators of these possessions which I do give to you with joyful heart and ready will; and be protectors and defenders of the aforementioned place of Cluny and of the servants of God abiding there, and of all these possessions—on account of the clemency and mercy of the most holy Redeemer. If any one—which Heaven forbid, and which, through the mercy of the God and the protection of the apostles I do not think will happen—whether he be a neighbor or a stranger, no matter what his condition or power, should, through any kind of wild attempt to do any act of violence contrary to this deed of gift which we have ordered to be drawn up for the love of almighty God and for reverence of the chief apostles Peter and Paul; first, indeed, let him incur the wrath of almighty God, and let God remove him from the land of the living and wipe out his name from the book of life, and let his portion be with those who said to the Lord God: Depart from us; and, with Dathan and Abiron whom the earth, opening its jaws, swallowed up, and hell absorbed while still alive, let him incur everlasting damnation.[1] And being made a companion of Judas let him be kept thrust down there with eternal tortures, and, lest it seem to human eyes that he pass through the present world with impunity, let him experience in his own body, indeed, the torments of future damnation, sharing the double disaster with Heliodorus and Antiochus, of whom one being coerced with sharp blows and scarcely escaped alive; and the other, struck down by the divine will, his members putrefying and swarming with worms, perished most miserably.[2] And let him be a partaker with other sacrilegious persons who presume to plunder the treasure of the house of God; and let him, unless he come to his senses, have as enemy and as the one who will refuse him entrance into the blessed paradise, the key-bearer of the whole hierarchy of the church,[3] and, joined with the latter, St. Paul; both of whom, if he had wished, he might have had as most holy mediators for him. But as far as the worldly law is concerned, he shall be required, the judicial power compelling him, to pay a hundred pounds of gold to those whom he has harmed; and his attempted attack, being frustrated, shall have no effect at all. But the validity of this deed of gift, endowed with all authority, shall always remain inviolate and unshaken, together with the stipulation subjoined. Done publicly in the city of Bourges. I, William, commanded this act to be made and drawn up, and confirmed it with my own hand.

[Here follow the names of Ingelberga and 42 other people, mainly bishops, nobles, and members of William's family.]

[Charters of the Grossi Family: *Charter # 802* (March, 951)]

To all who consider the matter reasonably, it is clear that the dispensation of God is so designed that if riches are used well, these transitory things can be transformed into eternal rewards. The Divine word showed that this was possible, saying "Wealth for a man is the redemption of his soul," and again, "Give alms and all things will be clean unto you."[4]

We, that is, I, Doda, a woman, and my son Letbald

---

1   For Dathan and Abiron, Hebrews who challenged Moses in the desert and were swiftly swallowed up by the earth, see Num. 16: 12-15, 25-34.
2   Judas is the betrayer of Christ. In 2 Macc. 3: 7-27, Heliodorus, minister of King Seleusis of Syria, is sent to plunder the Temple at Jerusalem but is beaten up by mysterious persons sent by divine will. In 2 Macc. 9: 7-9, King Antiochus of Syria falls from a chariot and suffers horribly thereafter.
3   The "key-bearer of the whole hierarchy of the church" is St. Peter.
4   Prov. 13: 8 and Luke 11: 41.

[II], carefully considering this fact, think it necessary that we share some of the things that were conferred on us, Christ granting, for the benefit of our souls. We do this to make Christ's poor our friends, in accordance with Christ's precept and so that He may receive us, in the end, in the eternal tabernacle.

Therefore, let it be known to all the faithful that we—Doda and my son Letbald—give some of our possessions, with the consent of lord Aquin [I], my husband, for love of God and his holy Apostles, Peter and Paul,[1] to the monastery of Cluny, to support the brothers [i.e., monks] there who ceaselessly serve God and His apostles. [We give] an allod[2] that is located in the *pagus*[3] of Mâcon, called Nouville.[4] The serfs [*servi*] that live there are: Sicbradus and his wife, Robert, Eldefred and his wife and children, Roman and his wife and children, Raynard and his wife and children, Teutbert and his wife and children, Dominic and his wife and children, Nadalis with her children, John with his wife and children, Benedict with his wife and children, Maynard with his wife and children, another Benedict with his wife and children, and a woman too …[5] with her children.

And we give [land in] another *villa*[6] called Colonge and the serfs living there: Teotgrim and his wife and children, Benedict and his wife and children, Martin and his children, Adalgerius and his wife and children, [and] Sicbradus.

And [we give] a *mansus*[7] in Culey and the serfs there: Andrald and his wife and children, Eurald and his wife and children. And [we give] whatever we have at Chazeux along with the serf Landrad who lives there. We also give a little harbor on the Aar river and the serfs living there: Agrimbald and Gerald with their wives and children.

In addition, we give an allod in the *pagus* of Autun, in the *villa* called Beaumont and the serfs living there, John, Symphorian, Adalard and their wives and children, in order that [the monks] may, for the love of Christ, receive our nephew, Adalgysus, into their society.[8]

[We give] all the things named above with everything that borders on them: vineyards, fields, buildings, serfs of every sex and age, ingress and egress, with all mobile and immobile property already acquired or to be acquired, wholly and completely. We give all this to God omnipotent and His apostles for the salvation of our souls and for the soul of Letbald [I], the father of my son, and for the salvation of Aquin [I], my husband, and of all our relatives and finally for all the faithful in Christ, living and dead.

Moreover, I, the aforesaid Letbald, uncinch the belt of war, cut off the hair of my head and beard for divine love, and with the help of God prepare to receive the monastic habit in the monastery [of Cluny]. Therefore, the property that ought to come to me by paternal inheritance I now give [to Cluny] because of the generosity of my mother and brothers. [I do so] in such a way that while [my mother and brothers] live, they hold and possess it. I give a *mansus* in Fragnes, along with the serf Ermenfred and his wife and children, to [my brother] Theoderic, *clericus*,[9] and after his death let it revert to [Cluny]. And I give another *mansus* at Verzé with the serf Girbald and his wife and children to my brother Hugo. In the *pagus* of Autun I give to [my brother] Aquin [II] the allod that is called Dompierre-les-Ormes, and the serf Benedict and his wife and their son and daughter. [I give Aquin also] another allod in Vaux, and the serfs Teutbald and his wife and children and Adalgarius. [I give all this] on condition that, if these brothers of mine [Hugh and Aquin], who are laymen, die without legitimate offspring, all these properties will go to the monastery as general alms.

If anyone (which we do not believe will happen)

---

1 As William's foundation charter stipulated, Cluny had been handed over to the Apostles Saints Peter and Paul.

2 An allod in this region was land that was owned outright, in contrast to land held in fief, for example.

3 A *pagus* was a Roman administrative subdivision.

4 Almost all the places mentioned in these charters are within about ten miles of the monastery of Cluny.

5 Effaced in the manuscript.

6 Here the word *villa* refers to a district.

7 The reference here is no doubt to a demesne *mansus*.

8 Possibly Adalgysus is to become a monk; but it is more likely that he is to become a special "friend" of the monastery for whom prayers will be said.

9 I.e., a priest.

either we ourselves (let it not happen!) or any other person, should be tempted to bring a claim in bad faith against this charter of donation, let him first incur the wrath of God, and let him suffer the fate of Dathan and Abiron and of Judas, the traitor of the Lord. And unless he repents, let him have the apostles [Peter and Paul] bar him from the celestial kingdom. Moreover, in accordance with earthly law, let him be forced to pay ten pounds. But let this donation be made firm by us, with the stipulation added. S[ignum][1] of Doda and her son Letbald, who asked that it be done and confirmed. S. of Aquin, who consents. S. of Hugo. S. of Evrard. S. of Walo. S. of Warembert. S. of Maingaud. S. of Giboin. S. of Leotald. S. of Widald. S. of Hemard. S. of Raimbald. Dated in the month of March in the 15th year of the reign of King Louis.[2] I, brother Andreas, *levite*,[3] undersign at the place for the secretary.

[*Charter # 1460* (November 12, 978–November 11, 979)][4]

I, Majolus, humble abbot [of Cluny] by the will of God, and the whole congregation of brothers of the monastery of Cluny. We have decided to grant something from the property of our church to a certain cleric, named Letbald [III] for use during his lifetime, and we have done so, fulfilling his request.

The properties that we grant him are located in the *pagus* of Mâcon, in the *ager*[5] of Grevilly, in a *villa* called Collonge: *mansi*, vineyards, land, meadows, woods, water, and serfs of both sexes and whatever else we have in that place, which came to us from Raculf.[6] And we grant two *mansi* at Boye and whatever we have there. And in Massy, one *mansus*. And in "Ayrodia" [not identified], in a place called Rocca, we give *mansi* with vineyards, land, woods, water, and serfs of every sex and age; and we grant all the property of

Chassigny [a place near Lugny that has disappeared]: vineyards, land, meadows, woods, water, mills and serfs and slaves. And at "Bussiacus" [near Saint-Huruge], similarly [we grant] *mansi*, vineyards, lands, meadows, and woods. And at "Ponciacus" [not id.] [we give] *mansi*, vineyards, and land. Just as Raculf gave these things to us in his testament, so we grant them to [Letbald] on the condition that he hold them while he lives and after his death these things pass to Cluny. And let him pay 12 dinars every year to mark his taking possession.

We also grant to him other property that came from lord Letbald [I], his uncle: a *mansus* at La Verzé and another at Bassy and another at Les Légères, and again another in Fragnes and another in Chazeux. And again a *mansus* in the *pagus* of Autun, at Dompierre-les-Ormes and another in Vaux and the serfs and slaves of both sexes that belong to those *mansi*. Let him hold and possess these properties as listed in this *precaria*[7] for as long as he lives. And when his mortality prevails—something no man can avoid—let this property fall to [Cluny] completely and without delay. [Meanwhile] let him pay 12 dinars every year, on the feast day of Apostles Peter and Paul.

I have confirmed this decree with my own hand and have ordered the brethren to corroborate it, so that it will have force throughout his lifetime. S. of lord Majolus, abbot. S. of Balduin, monk. S. of Vivian. S. of John. S. of Arnulf. S. of Costantinus. S. of Tedbald. S. of Joslen. S. of Grimald. S. of Hugo. S. of Rothard. S. of Ingelbald. S. of Achedeus. S. of Vuitbert. S. of Ingelman. Dated by the hand of Rothard, in the 25th year of the reign of King Lothar.

[*Charter # 1577* (Nov. 12, 981–Nov. 11, 982)]

To this holy place, accessible to our prayers [et cetera].[8]

---

1 Usually laypeople did not sign charters; rather they made a mark or sign (their *signum*) which was indicated by the scribe in front of their name. The S refers to this sign.

2 This was King Louis D'Outremer, one of the last of the Carolingians, who reigned from 936 to 954.

3 A *levite* was a deacon.

4 This charter has this range of dates because the scribe dated it in the 25th year of the reign of King Lothar, the son of King Louis, whose rule began on November 12, 954.

5 The *pagus* of Mâcon was divided into subdivisions called *agri* (sing.: *ager*). There were perhaps ten or more *villae* in each *ager*.

6 Raculf was probably a member of the Grossi family.

7 This document is a "precarial" donation. A *precaria* was a conditional grant of land *by* a monastery to someone outside of the monastery for his or her lifetime.

8 This charter began with a formula considered so commonplace that it did not need to be fully written out.

I, Rotrudis, and [my husband] Josseran, and my sons, all of us give to God and his holy Apostles, Peter and Paul and at the place Cluny, half of a church[1] that is located in the *pagus* of Mâcon, named in honor of St. Peter, with everything that belongs to it, wholly and completely, and [property in] the *villa* that is called Curtil-sous-Buffières. There [we give] a field and a meadow that go together and have the name *ad Salas*. This land borders at the east on a *via publica*[2] and a man-made wall; at the south on a meadow; at the west on a *via publica*, and similarly at the north. [I make this gift] for the salvation of the soul of my husband Josseran, and [for the soul of my son] Bernard. Done at Cluny. Witnesses: Rotrudis, Josseran, Bernard, Israel, Erleus, Hugo, Odo, Raimbert, Umbert. Ingelbald wrote this in the 28th year of the reign of King Lothar.

[Charter # 1845 (990–991)]

By the clemency of the Savior a remedy was conceded to the faithful: that they could realize eternal returns on His gifts if they distributed them justly. Wherefore, I, Majolus,[3] in the name of God, give to God and his holy apostles Peter and Paul and at the place Cluny some of my property which is located in the county of Lyon, in the *villa* "Mons" [not id.]. It consists of a demesne *mansus* with a serf named Durannus and his wife, named Aldegard, and their children, and whatever belongs or appears to belong to this *mansus*, namely fields, vineyards, meadows, woods, pasture-lands, water and water courses, that is already acquired or will be acquired, whole and complete. I make this donation first for my soul and for my burial [in Cluny's cemetery] and for the soul of my father Josseran and of my mother Rotrudis and of my brothers, and for

the souls of my *parentes*[4] and for the salvation of all the departed faithful, so that all may profit in common. [I give it] on the condition that I may hold and possess it while I live, and that every year I will pay a tax of 12 dinars on the feast day of the Prince of the Apostles [i.e., St. Peter]. After my death, let [the property] go to Cluny without delay.

But if anyone wants to bring any bad-faith claim against this donation, let him first incur the wrath of the Omnipotent and all His saints; and unless he returns to his senses, let him be thrust into Hell with the devil. As in the past, let this donation remain firm and stable, with the stipulation added. Done publicly at Cluny. S. of Majolus, who asks that it be done and confirmed. S. of Bernard, S. of Israel, S. of Arleius, S. of Bernard, S. of Hubert. Aldebard, *levita*, wrote this in the 4th year of the reign of Hugh [Capet].

[Charter # 2508 (994–1030?)][5]

Notice of a quitclaim[6] that took place at Cluny in the presence of lord Rainald, venerable prior at that place; and of other monks who were there, namely Walter, Aymo, Amizon, Warner, Lanfred, Locerius, Giso; and of noblemen: Witbert, Robert, Ildinus, Gislebert, Bernard, and Hugo. In the first place, let all, present and future, know that a long and very protracted quarrel between the monks of Cluny and Majolus[7] finally, by God's mercy, came to this end result: first that he [Majolus] quit his claim to the land which Oddo and Teza [Oddo's] daughter[8] destined for us and handed over by charter: the woods in *Grandi Monte* with its borders [as follows]: on the east [it borders on] its own inheritance [namely] passing between mountains and through wasteland and across

---

1 Churches could be given in whole or in part—since the revenues could be divided—and with or without their tithes (which often belonged not to the holder of the church but to the local bishop).
2 In this region, a *via publica* was a dirt road. There was a very extensive network of roads in the area around Cluny, left over from the Roman period.
3 Not the Cluniac abbot but rather a member of the Grossi family.
4 The *parentes* were much broader than the nuclear family but perhaps not quite as large as a clan.
5 The scribe did not give a date. But we know that Rainald was prior at Cluny beginning in 994 and that Majolus died *c.*1030. These give us, respectively, the *terminus post quem* [time after which] and the *terminus ante quem* [the time before which] the document must have been drawn up.
6 That is, this gives notice that a claim has been dropped ("quit").
7 The donor from the Grossi family.
8 Oddo and Teza were probably relatives of Majolus.

the castle of Teodoric; on the south [it borders on] *terra francorum*;[1] on the west and north [it borders on] land of St. Peter. [Majolus] draws up this notice at this time so that he may reunite himself with the favor of St. Peter and the brothers, and so that he may persevere in future as a faithful servant in the service of St. Peter. S. Hugo, S. Witbert, S. Robert, S. Ildinus, S. Gislebert, S. Bernard.

[*Charter # 2946* (1018–1030?)][2]

In the name of the incarnate Word. I, Raimodis, formerly the wife of the lord Wichard, now dead, and now joined in matrimony to lord Ansedeus, my husband; with the consent and good will [of Ansedeus], I give or rather give again some land which is called Chazeux to St. Peter and Cluny. [I give it] for the soul of my husband Wichard. This land once belonged to St. Peter and Cluny. But the abbot and monks gave it as a precarial gift to lord Letbald [III], a certain cleric who afterwards became bishop of Mâcon. Letbald, acting wrongly, alienated [the land] from St. Peter and gave it to Gauzeran to make amends for killing Gauzeran's relative, Berengar.

Therefore I give it again to St. Peter for the soul of my husband Wichard, and for Gauzeran, Wichard's father. I also give a slave named Adalgarda and her children, and [I give] the whole inheritance for the soul of my husband Wichard, and of my daughter Wiceline, and for my own soul.

If anyone wants to bring false claim against this donation, let him not prevail, but let him pay a pound of gold into the public treasury. S. of Raimodis, who asked that this charter be done and confirmed. S. of Ansedeus. S. of another Ansedeus. S. of Achard. S. of Walter. S. of Costabulus. S. of Ugo.

4.4 Love and complaints in Angoulême: *Agreements between Count William of the Aquitanians and Hugh of Lusignan* (1028). Original in Latin.

THIS DOCUMENT OF A series of disputes and their eventual settlement is written from the point of view of Hugh, who was the castellan (the lord of a castle and its garrison) of Lusignan, although he here calls himself Chiliarch—"leader of one thousand." The events described may be dated between about 1022 and 1028. The chief protagonists of Hugh's drama are Hugh himself and William, whom he calls "count of the Aquitainians" but who was, more importantly, count of Poitou (he ruled from *c.*995–1030). The center of his county was Poitiers, which included Lusignan (about 15 miles southwest of Poitiers) and many of the other locations mentioned in this document. Other characters who appear are mainly laymen, laywomen, and a few bishops. The *Agreements* presents an admittedly one-sided picture of the activities of the Poitevin aristocracy in the early eleventh century, a representation of relationships that may well also have inspired epic poems of the period, such as *Raoul de Cambrai* (see below, p. 384). As you read this document, consider what it meant to be the "man" of a lord. In what ways were legal and quasi-legal proceedings essential institutions in the Poitou? What were the meanings of "love," "anger," and "sorrow" in early eleventh-century Poitou? Try writing an account of the agreements between Hugh and the count from the *count's* point of view.

[Source: Jane Martindale, "Conventum inter Guillelmum Aquitanorum comitem et Hugonem Chiliarchum," in *Status, Authority and Regional Power: Aquitaine and France, 9th to 12th Centuries* (Aldershot: Variorum, 1997), Paper VIIb, pp. 541-52. Translated by Thomas Greene and

---

1 This probably refers to land of free peasants.
2 This date, which is quite uncertain, is suggested on the basis of other charters that tell us at what date Raimodis, the donor in this charter, became a widow.

Barbara H. Rosenwein from the Latin text, in consultation with translations by George Beech, "Hugh of Lusignan: Agreement between Lord and Vassal," in *Readings in Medieval History*, ed. Patrick J. Geary, 3rd ed., (Peterborough, ON: Broadview Press, 2003), pp. 387–92; Martindale, "Conventum," pp. 542a–552; and Paul Hyams, "The Agreements between Duke William V and Hugh IV, Lord of Lusignan" at http://www.lancs.ac.uk/depts/history/course-sites/hist213/seminars/lusignan.htm]

William, called count of the Aquitainians, had an agreement with Hugh the Chiliarch that when Viscount Boso died, William would give Boso's honor in commendation to Hugh.[1] Bishop Roho saw and heard this and kissed the arm of the count.[2] But Viscount Savary seized from Hugh land which Hugh held from Count William.[3] When the viscount died the count promised Hugh that he would make no agreement or accord with Ralph, the brother of the dead viscount, until the land had been restored. He said this in the presence of all, but afterwards he secretly gave the land to Ralph. For that land itself, or for a larger one, or for other things, Hugh had an agreement with Viscount Ralph that he would accept Ralph's daughter as his wife. When the count heard this he was greatly angered and he went humbly to Hugh and said to him, "Don't marry Ralph's daughter. I will give to you whatever you ask of me, and you will be my friend before all others except my son." Hugh did what the count ordered, and out of love and fidelity for the count he secretly rejected the woman.

At that time it happened that Joscelin of Parthenay castle died.[4] The count said that he would give Joscelin's honor and wife to Hugh, and if Hugh refused to accept them, he would no longer have confidence in him. Hugh did not entreat or request this from the count, either for himself or for anyone else. Thinking it over, he said to the count, "I will do all that you have ordered." The count, however, after holding a public meeting with Count Fulk,[5] promised to give Fulk something from his own benefices, and Fulk promised that he would give Hugh what belonged to him. At the meeting, the count called for Viscount Ralph and said to him: "Hugh will not keep the agreement he has with you because I forbid him to. But Fulk and I have an agreement that we will give to Hugh the honor and wife of Joscelin. We do this to mess up your life, because you are not faithful to me." When he heard this Ralph was very hurt and he said to the count, "For God's sake do not do that." So the count said, "Pledge to me that you will not give Hugh your daughter, nor keep your agreement with him, and in turn I will arrange that he not possess the honor and wife of Joscelin." And they so acted that Hugh got neither the one nor the other. Ralph went to Count William, who was at Montreuil castle, sending a message to Hugh that they should talk together. That was done. And Ralph said to Hugh, "I tell you this in confidence so that you will not give me away. Pledge to me that you will help me against Count William, and I will keep your agreement for you and will aid you against all men." But Hugh refused all of this out of his love for Count William. Hugh and Ralph parted unhappily. Then Ralph began to prosecute a public dispute with Count William, while Hugh, out of love for the count, started one with Ralph. And Hugh suffered great harm.

---

1   Boso (d. by 1033) was Viscount of Chatellerault, 20 miles northeast of Poitiers. An "honor" was property. "Chiliarch" means "leader of a thousand," a rather grandiose title that adds to the likelihood that Hugh was the person who had this document drawn up.

2   Roho was Bishop of Angoulême *c.*1020–*c.*1030. Formal agreements were often concluded by a kiss of peace; sometimes witnesses participated in this gesture of concord and, as here, the kiss might function as well as a sign of deference.

3   Savary was viscount of Thouars.

4   The "castles" that this document refers to were not luxurious chateaux but rather strongholds or fortresses. Some of them were thrown up haphazardly and minimally fortified; others were built more solidly and sometimes included a stone tower. Armed garrisons of horsemen guarded the castles and were important players—as victims, as hostages, as guarantors—in the disputes and negotiations between regional lords. Included in the notion of the castle was the surrounding district that it dominated.

5   Fulk was count of Anjou 987–1040.

When Ralph died, Hugh asked the count to restore to him the land which Ralph had seized from him. Moreover the count said to Hugh, "I will not make an agreement with Viscount Josfred, the nephew of Ralph, nor with the men of Thouars castle, until I return your land." Yet none of this was done, and the count went and made an agreement with Viscount Josfred and with the men of Thouars castle. He never made an agreement with Hugh, and Hugh did not get his land. And because of the misdeeds which Hugh committed on the count's behalf, Josfred got into a dispute with Hugh, and he burned Mouzeuil castle and captured Hugh's horsemen and cut off their hands and did many other things. The count did not help Hugh at all nor did he broker a good agreement between Josfred and Hugh, but Hugh even now has lost his land, and for the sake of the count he has lost still other land that he was holding peacefully. And when Hugh saw that he was not going to get his land he took forty-three of the best horsemen of Thouars. He could have had peace and his land and justice for the wrongdoing; and if he had been willing to accept a ransom he could have had 40,000 *solidi*.[1]

When the count heard this he should have been glad, but he was sad and sent for Hugh, saying to him, "Give me back the men." Hugh answered him, "Why do you ask these things of me, Lord? I am a loser only because of my loyalty to you." Then the count said, "I do not ask this of you to hurt you, but in fact because you are mine to do my will. And as all will know by our agreement, I will take over those men on condition that I make a settlement with you that your lands will be secured and the wrongdoing compensated, or I will return the men to you. Do this without doubting my credibility and good faith, and if anything should turn out badly for you, you can be sure that I will hand them over to you." Hugh put his trust in God and the count and handed the men over to the

count according to this agreement. Later on Hugh got neither the men nor justice, and he lost his land.

The count of the Poitevins[2] and Bishop Gilbert[3] had an agreement among themselves with Joscelin, Hugh's uncle.[4] It was about the castle at Vivonne, and it said that after the death of Bishop Gilbert it was to be Joscelin's castle. During his lifetime, the bishop made the men of that castle commend themselves to Joscelin, and he gave Joscelin the tower. And after the death of both men, the count made an agreement between Hugh and Bishop Isembert[5] that Hugh would get half of the castle and half of the demesne and two shares of the vassals' fiefs.[6] Then the count made Hugh commend himself to Bishop Isembert—but now he has taken the better estate from them.

A certain official named Aimery seized the castle called Civray from Bernard, his lord, but this castle was rightly Hugh's, as it had been his father's. Because of his anger at Aimery, Count William urged Hugh to become the man[7] of Bernard for the part of the castle that had belonged to his father, so that together they might wage a dispute with Aimery. But it seemed wrong to Hugh that he become Bernard's man, and he did not want to do it. The count persisted in this admonition for a year, and the more he got angry, the more he urged Hugh to become the man of Bernard. After a year passed, the count came to Hugh as if in anger and said to him, "Why don't you make an agreement with Bernard? You owe so much to me that if I should tell you to make a peasant into a lord you should do it. Do what I say, and if it should turn out badly for you, come and see me about it." Hugh believed him and became the man of Bernard for the fourth part of Civray castle. But Bernard made the count a guarantor to Hugh, as well as four hostages. The count said to Hugh, "Commend those hostages to me under such conditions that if Bernard does not faithfully keep your agreements, I will turn them over

---

1 A *solidus* (pl. *solidi*) is here a silver coin.
2 That is, Count William.
3 Gilbert was Bishop of Poitiers *c*.1018–*c*.1028.
4 This is presumably a different Joscelin from the one of Parthenay.
5 Isembert was Gilbert's successor as Bishop of Poitiers.
6 It was possible to have "half a castle" because what was at stake were the revenues due the castle, not the stronghold itself. See below, Text 4.6, p. 221 for some of the resources a castellan might command. The "demesne" was land belonging to the fortress directly; other land pertaining to it was granted out in fief.
7 The word used here is *homo*, which may be translated as "man" or "vassal," depending on your view of the relations among these aristocrats and the implications of these words.

to your custody and I will faithfully aid you." How strongly the count promised this to Hugh he himself knows very well. Hugh trusted in his lord and began a fierce dispute on account of Civray castle and suffered great losses in men and many other things. The count started to build a castle which he called Couhé, but he did not finish it for Hugh. Instead, he talked it over with Aimery, abandoned the castle, and in no way aided Hugh.

Afterwards the count grew even more unhappy with Aimery on account of the castle called Chizé, which Aimery had seized, and Hugh and the count joined together in a dispute against Aimery. The count besieged the castle called Mallevault because of the injuries which Aimery had done to him and captured it, and Hugh aided him as best he could. Before Hugh left the count, the count promised him—just as a lord ought rightly to promise to his man—that he would make no agreement or alliance with Aimery without Hugh, and that Mallevault would not be rebuilt without his advice. But the count did make an agreement with Aimery and allowed him to rebuild Mallevault without the advice of Hugh. As long as Aimery lived, none of the property mentioned above came to Hugh.

After the death of Aimery a great dispute began between his son Aimery and Hugh. At the same time Hugh went to the count and said to him, "Things are going badly for me now, my Lord, because I have none of the property which you acquired for me." The count answered him, "I am going to hold a public hearing with them so that if they act well, good; if not, I will turn over to you the castle which I started." And the castle was constructed on the advice of Bernard, who thus far had helped Hugh in the dispute. When they saw the heavy demands Hugh was making on them, the men of Civray were not able to hold out, and they made an agreement with Bernard and returned the castle to him. He received it without the advice of Hugh. Now both Bernard and Aimery were in dispute with Hugh, and he was alone against them. Coming to the count, Hugh said to him, "Lord, I am doing very badly because the lord whom I got upon your advice has just taken away my property. I beg and urge you by the faith which a lord owes to aid his man: either let me have a proper public hearing or my property, just as you pledged to me; or return to me

the hostages which I commended to you; and above all help me as you pledged to me." The count, however, neither aided him, nor made an agreement with him, nor returned the hostages but released them and gave them back to Bernard. And after that the dispute between Bernard and Aimery and Hugh increased.

And since Hugh saw that the count aided him in no way, he went to seek the advice of Gerald, the bishop of Limoges. Gerald and Hugh went together into La Marche against Bernard and built a castle. But the count, who ought to have aided Hugh, seized the castle from him and burned it. And the count and his son ordered all their men not to help Hugh unless they wished to die. Then Bernard accepted the council of his men that they should do harm to Hugh on the advice of the count, and they appointed a deadline fifteen days away. During those fifteen days the count arranged a truce between Bernard and Hugh. Three days into the truce the count took Hugh along with his army to Apremont castle, and a meeting was held in his castle. From there the count went to Blaye, where he was to have a meeting with Count Sancho, and he told Hugh that he should come along. And Hugh responded, "Lord, why do you ask me to go with you? You yourself know how short the truce is which I have with Bernard, and he himself is threatening to do me harm." The count said to him: "Do not fear that they will do anything to you as long as you are with me." And the count took Hugh with him by force and against Hugh's will.

While they were staying at the meeting place, Hugh's men heard that Bernard was coming against him; they sent a message to Hugh to come. Then Hugh said to the count, "Bernard is attacking me." And the count said, "Don't be afraid that they will dare attack you; and, besides, you need them to attack so that I can destroy them and aid you." In that same hour the count sent orders through his men, and he told Hugh to go on ahead, and he followed him. When Hugh reached Lusignan, Bernard was at Confolens castle. He had captured the suburb and the outskirts and burned everything; he had taken spoils, captured men, and done plenty of other evil deeds. A messenger ran up to Hugh and said to him, "Bernard has your wife besieged in the old castle which survived the fire." Hugh came to the count and said to him: "My lord, help me now, because my wife is now being besieged." But the count gave him no aid or advice at all. And Bernard turned back, and he and his men did so much harm to Hugh and his men that 50,000 *solidi* would not have paid for it. And Hugh suffered this damage during the truce which the count offered to him at Blaye.

Not long after this Hugh went to Gençay castle and burned it and seized the men and women and took everything with him. Hastening to the count, he said to him, "Lord, give me permission to build the castle which I burned." And the count said to him, "You are the man of Fulk, how can you build the castle? Fulk will demand it of you, and you will not be strong enough to keep it from him." Hugh said, "Lord, when I became Fulk's man I told him that his men were seizing what was my right and that if I was able to regain possession of them, I would do it, but I would only hold it in his fealty, which is what I want to do. And Fulk said to me, 'If you take anything from them, don't take from me.'" When the count heard that Fulk and Hugh had such an agreement, he was pleased. And the count said to Hugh: "Build the castle under such an agreement that if I am able to negotiate with Count Fulk about my price and yours, one part will be mine and the other yours."

And Hugh built the castle. Then Fulk asked the count for it. The count responded to him, "Ask Hugh for it." And Fulk did that. Hugh answered him, "When I became your man, I said to you that if I would be strong enough to take castles from my enemies, I should take them and hold them in your fealty, and I wanted to do that because the castle which you are demanding belonged to my relatives, and I have a better right to it than those who were holding it." But Fulk said, "You who are mine, how can you hold against my will something I didn't give to you?" And Hugh sought advice from the count. The count told him, "If he is willing to give you guarantees that your enemies will not have the castle, then you cannot keep it. If not, keep it, because he will not be able to accuse you of anything." Hugh asked that Fulk give hostages to him, and Fulk gave him nothing, but said, "I will make my demands known to the count and give hostages to him and he will give you some of his own." Then the meeting turned angry. Fulk demanded Hugh's castle from the count. Hugh said,

"I will not give it up without assurances." The count said to him, "I will give an assurance, and he has told me what sort to give." Hugh said, "Take what you want from Count Fulk and give me what I'm asking for. Give me the man who has custody of the tower at Melle, so that if Aimery should get the castle without my advice, and harm should befall me, that man will turn the tower over to me." The count said to him, "I will not do this, because I cannot." Hugh said, "If you don't want to do this with Melle, make the same agreement with regard to Chizé." But the count didn't want to do either.

It seemed to Hugh and his men that the count was treating him badly. And they parted in anger. Then Hugh sent all kinds of necessities into the castle and intended to hold it against all comers if they would not give him assurances. The count came out of the city,[1] asked Hugh to come to him, and commanded through Count William of Angoulême that he submit himself to the mercy of the count, because the count could not change the fact that he had to aid Fulk; and he was afraid to lose either Fulk or Hugh. Then Hugh committed himself to the trust and friendship of the count his lord, and he did this out of love for him because he was assured that he would not suffer harm at Fulk's hands. And the count said: "Let Hugh do this for me and I will keep the faith with him that a lord ought to keep with his man. If he suffers harm, he will know that I have betrayed him, and he will never trust me again." And Hugh said, "My lord has spoken similarly to me about many things by which he has deceived me." And not a single one of Hugh's men would advise him to trust the count. But the count reminded Hugh of all the good things which he had done for him, and Hugh, holding back the count by his love and entreaties—that is by their common oath—said to the count, "I will put all my trust in you, but watch out that you do not do me wrong, for if you do, I will not be faithful to you nor will I serve you, nor will I render fidelity to you. But, on account of the fact that I will be separated from you and you are not able to give me guarantees, I want you to give me my fief as a pledge that then I will no longer serve you, and release me from the oath which I have made to you." The count answered, "Gladly."

---

1 Presumably Poitiers.

Hugh returned the castle to the count, against the wishes of his men, on condition that Aimery would not have it without Hugh's advice and that Hugh would suffer no harm. On account of hearing those lies, Hugh accepted his fief as a pledge, and the count gave it to him on condition that if he should suffer harm because of the agreement about Gençay, Hugh would never again serve him. And the count released him from his oaths, so that he would no longer do anything for the count on account of them, but not out of ill will. [But] the count handed over Gençay without the advice of Hugh and got money and some demesne land. It went very badly for Hugh, with men killed, houses burned, booty taken, land seized and many other things which in truth cannot be enumerated. When this had ended the count gave Hugh a respite and promised that he would give him a benefice either of something which was his by right or something which would be pleasing to him. But when this period passed the count did nothing for Hugh. He sent an order to him: "Don't wait, because I am not going to do anything for you. Even if the whole world were mine I would not give you as much as a finger could lift with regard to this matter."

When Hugh heard this he went to the court of the count and made the case for his rights, but it did him no good. This saddened Hugh, and in the hearing of all he renounced his fealty[1] to the count, except what he owed for the city [of Poitiers] and his own person. Before either Hugh or his men did any harm, the men of the count seized a benefice from Hugh's men in the name of war. When Hugh saw this he went to Chizé castle, which had been his uncle's but which Peter[2] was holding unjustly, and from which much harm was being done to Hugh. He seized the tower and threw out Peter's men. Hugh did this because he thought he had the right—because it had belonged to his father or others of his relatives—which he was losing. When the count heard of this he was greatly saddened and sent an order to Hugh that he turn over the tower that he had taken away from Peter. Hugh demanded that the count return the honor of his father and the other

things which belonged to his relatives and to which he had right, and he would surrender the tower and all the things that he had taken within it, and in addition the entire honor which had belonged to Joscelin[3] and which the count had given him. The count thought this over and they arranged for a hearing. And the count said to Hugh, "I will not give you those honors which you ask of me, but I will give you that honor which was your uncle's—the castle, the tower and the entire honor—on condition that you no longer demand of me that honor which was your father's, or others of your relatives, nor anything which you claim as your right."

When he heard this Hugh greatly mistrusted the count, because through evil trickery in the past the count had deceived Hugh in many things. He said to the count, "I don't dare do this, because I fear that you will threaten me with harm, as you have done with regard to many other things." The count said to Hugh, "I will give such assurances to you that you will no longer distrust me." Hugh said to him, "What kind of assurances?" The count said, "I will produce a serf who will undergo an ordeal for you so that you will not doubt that the agreement which we make among ourselves will be good and firm. And with regard to all the affairs of the past, no harm will ever again be done to you, but the agreement will be kept firmly without any evil trickery." When Hugh heard what the count was saying in this way, he said, "You are my lord. I will not take a guarantee from you, but I will simply rely on the mercy of the Lord and yourself." The count said to Hugh, "Give up all those claims that you have demanded from me in the past and swear fidelity to me and my son, and I will give you your uncle's honor or something else of equal value in exchange for it." And Hugh said, "Lord, I beg you by God and this blessed crucifix which is made in the figure of Christ that you do not make me do this if in future you and your son intend to threaten me with evil trickery." The count said, "My son and I will do this in faith and without evil trickery." Hugh said, "And when I have sworn fidelity to you, you will

---

1   The Latin word here is *defidavit*, which means defied. The root of the word is "faith"; a man declares his faith (*fides*=fidelity) to his lord, but if he formally renounces that fealty, as here, he "defies"—"de-fealties"—him.

2   Peter has not been identified.

3   This Joscelin was Hugh's uncle, mentioned above on p. 215, n. 4.

ask me for Chizé castle, and if I should not turn it over to you, you will say that it is not right that I deny you the castle which I hold from you; but if I should turn it over to you, you and your son will take it away from me because you will have given me no guarantee except the mercy of God and yourself." The count said, "We will not do that, but if we should demand it of you, don't turn it over to us."

They received Hugh as their man in faith and trust under the terms of the agreement as it was finally pronounced: that the count and his son should bear faith to Hugh without evil trickery. And they made Hugh give up everything which he claimed from the past. And he swore fidelity to them, and they gave him the honor of his uncle Joscelin, just as Joscelin held it one year before he died.

Here end the agreements between the count and Hugh.

4.5 The Peace of God at Bourges: Andrew of Fleury, *The Miracles of St. Benedict* (1040–1043). Original in Latin.

THE PEACE OF GOD was a movement initiated by bishops and eventually declared by kings as well to protect unarmed people and property from armed predators. At church synods, laypeople and churchmen alike met to proclaim the Peace. Those who fought (the "bellatores" or "milites": the knights) swore oaths not to violate the Peace. In the late 1030s, at one such synod, Aimon, the archbishop of Bourges organized a militia consisting of clergy, peasants, and a few nobles which succeeded in forcing most of the nobility of the region to take the oath. The militia even enforced the Peace by going to war against breakers of the oath. But it ran into opposition from one holdout, Odo, lord of Déols, who defeated it soundly. Andrew, a monk at the monastery of Fleury, recounted the incident in the course of his work on the *Miracles of St. Benedict*, written 1040–43. He praised the militia's initial promise but berated it for its "ambition" and confidence in its own power rather than God's. From this document, consider what might have been the interest of common people in the Peace of God. How might the sorts of disputes described in *The Agreements between Count William and Hugh* have contributed to the Peace of God movement?

[Source: *The Peace of God: Social Violence and Religious Response in France around the Year 1000*, ed. Thomas Head and Richard Landes (Ithaca, NY: Cornell University Press, 1992), pp. 339–42.]

5.1 In the 1038th year after the incarnation of the Lord, on the eighth day of August, in the middle of the day, the sun was darkened and hid the rays of its splendors for a space of almost two hours. Again the following morning it remained under the same appearance for the entire day and unremittingly gave off bloody flames.

5.2. At this very same time, Archbishop Aimon of Bourges wished to impose peace in his diocese through the swearing of an oath. After he had summoned the fellow bishops of his province and had sought advice from these suffragans, he bound all men of fifteen years of age and over by the following law: that they would come forth with one heart as opponents of any violation of the oath they had sworn, that they would in no way withdraw secretly from the pact even if they should lose their property, and that, what is more, if necessity should demand it, they would go after those who had repudiated the oath with arms. Nor were ministers of the sacraments excepted, but they often took banners from the sanctuary of the Lord and attacked the violators of the sworn peace with the rest of the crowd of laypeople. In this way they many times routed the faithless and brought their castles down to the ground. With the help of God they so terrified the rebels that, as the coming of the faithful was proclaimed far and wide by rumor among the populace, the rebels scattered. Leaving the gates of their towns open, they sought safety in flight, harried by divinely inspired terror. You would have seen [the faithful] raging against the multitude of those who ignore God, as if they were some other people of Israel. Presently they trampled [the rebels] underfoot so that they forced them to return to the laws of the pact which they had ignored.

We thought it fitting to insert in writing that which was agreed to in the pact which the archbishop himself, along with various fellow bishops, promised under oath in the following way: "I Aimon, by the gift of God archbishop of Bourges, promise with my whole heart and mouth to God and to his saints that I shall discharge with my whole spirit and without any guile or dissimulation everything that follows. That is, I will wholeheartedly attack those who steal ecclesiastical property, those who provoke pillage, those who oppress monks, nuns, and clerics, and those who fight against holy mother church, until they repent. I will not be beguiled by the enticement of gifts, or moved by any reason of bonds of kinship or neighborliness, or in any way deviate from the path of righteousness. I promise to move with all my troops against those who dare in any manner to transgress the decrees and not to cease in any way until the purpose of the traitor has been overcome."

He swore this over the relics of Stephen, the first martyr for Christ, and urged the other [bishops] to do likewise. Obeying with one heart, his fellow bishops made among everyone age fifteen or older (as we already said) in their separate dioceses subscribe [the pact] with the same promise. Fear and trembling then struck the hearts of the unfaithful so that they feared the multitude of the unarmed peasantry as if it were a battle line of armored men. Their hearts fell so that, forgetting their status as knights and abandoning their fortified places, they fled from the humble peasants as from the cohorts of very powerful kings. The prayer of David fitted the situation most aptly: "For thou dost deliver a humble people, but the haughty eyes thou dost bring down, for who is God but the Lord?"[1] ... Odo of Déols remained alone among the whole multitude [of rebels], reserved by the judgment of God for the punishment of evil doers.

5.3. When by the will of God they had, trusting in the help of divine strength, established peace in every direction, ambition (the root and aid of all evil) began to seep along the stalks of such good works. They forgot that God is the strength and rampart of his people and ascribed the power of God to their apostate power.... Thus the aforementioned bishop was touched by the sting of mammon[2] and raged around and around in blind ambition. Unmindful of his episcopal dignity, he attacked Beneciacum, the castle of one Stephen, along with a multitude of the people of Bourges. He reproached Stephen for the fault of having ignored the peace, he tried to burn the castle with flames and ordered it to be leveled to the ground, as if he were exacting the vengeance of God upon it. They burned the castle, which was hemmed in on all sides by the siege, with more than one thousand four hundred people of both sexes inside. Stephen alone of that great number escaped, although his brothers, wife, and sons were all consumed by the fire, and he placed the laurel wreath of his great victory on their wretched heads. The inhabitants of that region for a radius of fourteen miles had fled to this castle and, since they feared the theft of their possessions, they had brought them along. The cruel victors were hardly moved by the laments of the dying, they did not take pity on women beating their breasts; the crowd of infants clinging to their mothers' breasts did not touch any vein of mercy.... And so the just bore responsibility for the crime of the iniquitous and the just perished in place of the impious. Having been granted this great triumph, the people returned to their homes dancing with a pitiable joy. Stephen was placed under guard in a prison in Bourges.

5.4. Almighty God wished to avenge the blood of his servants and, not long after this, set the aforesaid bishop against Odo, the sole rebel. The bishop sought to force Odo to join in the pact common to all, but he would not delay in making an armed attack. Discovering that Odo's spirit remained inflexible, as was God's will, Aimon began—while the blood of the innocents was not yet dry—to collect allies together from all

---

1 Ps. 18: 27, 31; Douay, Ps. 17: 28, 32.
2 The false god personifying riches and avarice.

sides, including a large contingent of God's ministers. Confiding in lesser things, he directed his battleline against the enemy. When both armies stood almost at grips, a sound was made heavenward [indicating that Aimon's forces should] retreat, since they no longer had the Lord with them as a leader. When they made no sign of following this advice, an enormous globe of flashing light fell in their midst. Thus it came to pass, as it is said, "Flash forth the lightning and scatter them, send out the arrows and rout them!"[1] Then the people perceived that they were much inferior to their adversaries, since those exceeded in number the sands of the sea. They decided that some foot soldiers should be mounted on various animals and mixed into the cohorts of mounted warriors [*milites*] so that they would be judged mounted warriors by their opponents, more because of the appearance of their being mounted than because of the setting of their weapons. Without delay up to two thousand of the plebeian rabble were mounted on asses and arrayed as knights among the order of knights. But these men were terrified and they took flight along the banks of the Cher. They were killed in such numbers that they blocked the river in such a way that they made a bridge out of the bodies of the dying over which their enemies proceeded. More fell by their own swords than by those of their pursuers.... The number of the dying could not be comprehended: in one valley seven hundred clerics fell. Thus the most tempered judgment of God made those people—who had refused obedience to any requests for mercy, and had not been moved by the smell of their brothers' being burned, and had rejoiced more than was just to have their hands in an unfortunate victory—lost their lives along with that victory.

4.6 A castellan's revenues and properties in Catalonia: *Charter of Guillem Guifred* (1041-1075). Original in Latin.

SOME TIME BETWEEN 1041 and 1075 Bishop Guillem Guifred had a memorandum drawn up of the dues, properties, and services that were owed him as one of the lords of Sanahuja, a castle in Catalonia (today Spain). Although other castellans, such as Hugh of Lusignan (see above, p. 213), could not claim precisely the same mix that Guillem commanded, this list provides a good example of the sort of resources which holders of fortifications might count on. Compare it with the revenues that the bishop of Marseille could command in the Carolingian period, as evidenced by the *Polyptyque of the church of Saint Mary of Marseille*, above, p. 130.

[Source: Pierre Bonnassie, "The Banal Seigneury and the 'Reconditioning' of the Free Peasantry," in *Debating the Middle Ages: Issues and Readings*, ed. Lester K. Little and Barbara H. Rosenwein (Oxford: Basil Blackwell, 1988), pp. 114-15.]

This is a brief reminder of what the bishop ought to have in his castellany of Sanahuja, by use and by right.

In the first place, half of the revenue of the courts without deceit. From the market, half of what comes to the lords, by justice and by right, that is to say of the fines, with the exception of rights on the udders of the cows, which belong to the castle. Of the oven, half. Of rights on minting, half.

And the bishop agrees with the lords of Sanahuja that they should bring before him the men [of the castellany], and that he should levy on them, every year, the *queste* [a tax] of bread and meat. The bailiff of the lord should go with the bailiff of the bishop to the cellars of Sanahuja, and they should judge the barrels together for levying the *compra* [a tax] of the bishop. And that the bailiffs of the lords should assess the service of those who owe army service with donkeys and

---

1 Ps.144: 6; Douay Ps. 143: 6.

other equipment, that it should be estimated under oath, and when it has been estimated, the revenue should be shared by the lord and the *castlà* [the head of the garrison that guards the castle], and the *castlà* should give the bishop his part....

In the houses of Sanahuja, the bishop has the use of the wood, cabbages, chard, cheese, ewes, except in the houses of the priests, the *cabalers* [horsemen] and the bailiffs of the lords; and all this he may use in all the other houses of Sanahuja.... And the peasants of Sanahuja who work with a team should give the bishop a *sextarius* [a unit of measure] of oats and a sheaf, those who share a team with several others should give a *hemina* [another unit of measure] of oats, and a sheaf.

And if an animal enters into the bishop's *dominicatura* [demesne—the land belonging to the lord] in Sanahuja, and is retaken there, his master should buy him back for as many pennies as the animal has feet. And the bishop's woods enjoy a franchise [a privilege] such that no man may hunt within a stone's throw of it ... and a man of Sanahuja who catches a rabbit in the woods must give an ox, a pig, and nine pairs of live rabbits to the bishop in reparation.

And all the men of Sanahuja must work for the bishop on the construction of his houses and owe him transport services on the back of their beasts, with the exception of priests, *cabalers*, the lords' bailiffs, and merchants.

And no lord may award any franchise at Sanahuja without the consent of the bishop.

And the men of Sanahuja must carry the bishop's bulls and messages at his command, to any place he may desire....

And in all the mills in the territory of Sanahuja already constructed, or those to be constructed, the bishop should have the quarter [of the revenues?], and in all the use of *destre mugar* [free use of the mill for his grain], under compulsion....

This was enacted by Guillem Guifred, bishop.

BYZANTINE EXPANSION

4.7 Military life: Constantine VII Porphyrogenitus, *Military Advice to His Son* (950–958). Original in Greek.

EMPEROR CONSTANTINE VII PORPHYROGENITUS (r.913–959) was a major force behind the revival of art and learning at Byzantium known as the Macedonian Renaissance. Likely the author of a famous book on the ceremonies of the court, he also wrote other treatises including the shorter work on military expeditions excerpted here, intended for his son but never finished. Here, as in his book on ceremonies, he concentrated on the formal aspects of the job: the requisitioning of materiel, the opportunities for gift-giving, the triumphal return, and the officials involved in all of these events. What would Dhuoda (p. 186 above) say about Constantine's advice to his son? What would Constantine say about Dhuoda's?

[Source: *Constantine Porphyrogenitus: Three Treatises on Imperial Military Expeditions*, ed. and trans. John F. Haldon (Vienna: Österreichischen Akademie der Wissenschaften, 1997), pp. 95, 97, 99, 101, 107, 109, 123, 141, 143, 145 (slightly modified).]

CONSTANTINE, EMPEROR OF THE ROMANS IN CHRIST THE ETERNAL KING, SON OF LEO THE MOST WISE EMPEROR OF BLESSED MEMORY, DESCENDANT OF BASIL THE MOST COURAGEOUS AND MOST BRAVE EMPEROR, TO ROMANUS, GOD-CROWNED EMPEROR, HIS SON

WHAT SHOULD BE OBSERVED WHEN THE GREAT AND HIGH EMPEROR OF THE ROMANS GOES ON CAMPAIGN

Listen, son, to the words of your father, Solomon exhorts you. For you will hear about duties from many, but you will not reap the lessons of virtue by nature alone unless you hear the best things from your father. For when you have accepted his words as genuinely truthful, you will have what amounts to a paternal legacy, always promoting your salvation. For the words of others, spoken for favors, often lack truth; whereas those from a father's heart, being honest, bestow upon their sons perpetual advantage. Listen, therefore, son, to your father, whose advice it is not good to ignore; for if ignorance is bad, it is clear that a knowledge of practical matters is good, and most especially of those things touching upon the affairs of the state, to which much care has been devoted. For what could be more important than courage in warfare and the ancient discipline of our forefathers, the order of things to which they held formerly in imperial wartime expeditions? …

When the great and high emperor is about to go on an expedition and to mobilize arms and troops against the enemy, he orders first of all that a *lorikion*[1] and a sword and shield should be hung up on the Chalke, outside the gates.[2] From this, the preparation of an imperial expedition is made clear to all, and from this moment each officer and soldier begins to prepare his weapons and such things as are necessary and required of a soldier. Then, after this has taken place, he orders the *logothetes* of the herds that a fair distribution and rationing (of baggage animals) from the *mitata*[3] of Asia and Phrygia, and according to the strength and capacity of each *mitaton*, should be carried out in the fear of God and in all truth and piety. For each of the

---

1 A *lorikion* was a suit of mail. Special clothing was often displayed to signal a special event.
2 The Chalke was the bronze gate of the imperial palace in Constantinople.
3 *Logothetes* was a bureaucrat of high position. The logothete of the herd was the man in charge of the farms (*mitata* [sing: *mitaton*]) that supplied horses and pack animals for military expeditions.

above-mentioned *mitata* has a specific number of animals due from it according to its status, which is set down clearly for all: from Asia and Phrygia 200 mules at 15 *nomismata*, 200 pack-horses at 12 *nomismata*, in total 5,424 *nomismata*, which is 76 lbs. gold.[1]

On the customary dues of the officers of the imperial stables, both in the City and in the provincial stables:

From the *komes* of the stable, 4 mules and 4 pack-horses; from the *chartoularios* and the *epeiktes* 4 mules and 4 pack-horses; from the provincial *chartoularios* 2 mules and 2 pack-horses; from the commissariat 1 mule and 1 pack-horse; from the 4 *komites* 1 mule.[2] Altogether from the officers, 322 *nomismata*, which is 4 lbs. 26 *nomismata*. In sum, 80 lbs. 26 *nomismata*.

The *logothetes* of the herds brings the 200 mules and likewise the 200 pack-horses down to Malagina, and the *komes* of the stable and the inner *chartoularios* of the stable select five-, six- and seven-year old animals, with no blemishes on their flanks. These 400 are then branded with the imperial seal on both sides of the forequarters. The same requisition and branding takes place furthermore in the following year. All the pack-horses are castrated and thus become geldings, and serve as a supplement for the expedition's needs. The *logothetes* brings the 200 pack-animals fully harnessed, with felt coverings over their saddle-cloths, carrying ropes for the loads, equipped with leggings, horse-shoes and with their halters....

From the metropolitans and archbishops:

Fifty-two fully-harnessed mules from the metropolitans; 52 mules from the fifty-two archbishops. These 104 fully harnessed mules, with their loads, are also to be shoed. The *komes* of the stable, together with the *chartoularios* of the inner stable takes them, and brands them with the rest of the baggage train, in all 104 mules. And the grand total from both sources, the *mitata* of the *logothetes* of the herds, and the (animals provided as) gifts, 585 mules.

From the pious monasteries:

One hundred complementary horses, led before the emperor to left and right. They should be castrated and gelded; but they are not branded, since when the emperor orders a gift to be made, it is from among these that animals are presented wherever he commands. Likewise from the animals brought as gifts to the emperor during the course of the expedition. The *komes* of the stable, along with the *chartoularios* of the stable takes 3 lbs. of gold from the *eidikon* for expenses.[3] ...

For the personal imperial vestiarion and for those seconded by the bedchamber for the baggage of the same imperial vestiarion, 30 pack-animals:[4]

All the imperial clothing and the remaining regalia in vessels encased in purple leather and burnished iron chains and straps likewise burnished, so that they can be carried by the pack-animals; eight silver coolers with covers, for scented wine, rose-water, and water: of these, one small cooler for white wine, two large ones for rosewater, and four large ones for water. Two silver pails for water; various water-skins, large and small; four other coolers, large, of burnished copper, like earthenware pots, for water; two burnished copper pails; and sacred vessels for the chapel, which the *minsourator* transports.[5]

Books: the liturgy of the Church, military manuals, books on mechanics, including siege machinery and the production of missiles and other information relevant to the enterprise, that is to say, to wars and sieges; historical books, especially those of Polyainos and Syrianos;[6]

---

1 *Nomismata* were Byzantine gold coins.
2 The *komes* (pl. *komites*), or "count," of the stable was the chief officer of the imperial stable, who purchased the animals from the *mitata* at a set price. The *chartoularios* and *epeiktes* were the titles of other officials of the stable. The "inner chartoularios," referred to in the next paragraph, is, by contrast with the "provincial chartoularios," in charge of the office in the capital.
3 The *eidikon* was an imperial office for fiscal matters.
4 The *vestiarion*, also part of fiscal administration, was in charge of cloth production as well as metals and bullion.
5 The *minsourator* was responsible for the imperial tent.
6 Polyainos (*fl.* 2nd c. C.E.) wrote a book on military strategy for the Roman emperors which was highly prized later at Constantinople. Syrianos was a later (perhaps 9th c.) writer on the same topic.

an oneirocritical book;[1] a book of chances and occurrences; a book dealing with good and bad weather and storms, rain and lightning and thunder and the vehemence of the winds; and in addition to these a treatise on thunder and a treatise on earthquakes, and other books, such as those to which sailors are wont to refer. Note that such a book was researched and compiled from many books by myself, Constantine emperor of the Romans in Christ the eternal King.

Tufted rugs for reclining, so that guests may rest; … theriac, serapium juice, other antidotes, both mixed and unmixed, for those who have been poisoned; receptacles with all kinds of oils and remedies; and diverse salves and unguents and ointments and other medical substances, herbs and whatever else is necessary for the curing of men and beasts. Small silver pails and sprinklers with covers for the emperor, and others of polished bronze for officers and distinguished refugees; thick and thin double-bordered cushions for the emperor to recline upon; two chairs for the cortège [procession], chairs for the chamber-pot, of metal gilded with beaten gold, with covers, and with other covers above concealing the space for the latrine; and for the distinguished refugees two other, similar, seats, bound in silver; imperial chalices for the guests invited to dine with the emperor; two imperial swords, one ceremonial, one for the campaign; one sabre; ointments, various perfumes; incense, mastic, frankincense, sachar, saffron, musk, amber, bitter aloes, moist and dry, pure ground cinnamon of first and second quality, cinnamon wood, and other perfumes. Silken sheets, rough linen blankets, linen towels, sheets, "western" patchwork covers, "western" towels.

From the untailored cloths despatched to foreigners as gifts:

Skaramaggia of different colors and patterns:[2] all-white, all-yellow and all-blue *skaramaggia;* tunics of high value, produced in the imperial workshops; under-garments of middling value produced in the imperial workshops; undergarments of lower value produced in the imperial workshops; undergarments of lower value of varying colors and patterns produced in the imperial workshops; off-white coats, two-tone silk garments of white and violet; triple-warped striped garments of violet, of purple and a selection of different hues. Note that all these are carried in containers encased in purple leather and burnished chains, with straps similarly burnished.…

Once the emperor has passed into the *themata*, he is welcomed by each *thema*, when the *thema* is drawn up in parade order, of course.[3] When the emperor approaches, the *strategos* and the *protonotarios* of the *thema* and the *tourmarchai* and the *drouggarokomites* and the *merarches* and the *komes* of the tent and the *chartoularios* and the *domestikos* of the *thema* dismount from their horses while the emperor is still some distance from reaching them, and form a reception party.[4] And when the emperor passes through, all the aforementioned fall to the ground, paying homage to the emperor; but the soldiers all remain mounted. After the *strategoi* and the officers referred to have paid homage to the emperor, the latter makes a short detour from the road, saying to them: "Well met!" Then he asks them: "How are you, my children? How are your wives, my daughters-in-law, and the children?" And they reply, that "In the life of your Majesty, so we, your servants, are well." And again, the emperor responds: "Thanks be to Holy God who keeps us in health." When all have acclaimed the emperor, he commands the *strategos* and all the above-mentioned officers to mount up, and to leave with their army for their own ordained position.…

The victorious return of the Christ-loving Emperor Basil [I] from campaign in the regions of Tephrike and Germanikeia[5]

When the emperor returned victorious from the war against Tephrike and Germanikeia, he passed via

---

1 I.e., a book that interprets dreams.
2 *Skaramaggia* were silk tunics decorated with embroidery. They might be worn or used as altar cloths or banners.
3 The *themata* (sing. *thema*) are the themes.
4 The *strategos* (pl. *strategoi*) and the *protonotarios* were the chief military officers of the theme, while the other officials named here were their subordinates.
5 The emperor that Constantine is referring to here is Basil I the Macedonian (867-886). The "regions of Tephrike and Germanikeia" were in southeastern Anatolia.

Hiereia to the Hebdomon, where citizens of every age met him, with crowns prepared from flowers and roses.[1] Likewise the whole senate then in the City received him there also, and the emperor greeted them verbally. And when he had entered and prayed in the Church of the Baptist in the Hebdomon, and lit candles, he went out; and donning a triple-bordered *skaramaggion*, and riding together with his son Constantine, they came to the Church of the All-Holy Virgin of the Abramites, with the whole senate going ahead with the people of the City, and with processional banners. Dismounting from their horses, they entered the Church of the Virgin; and having prayed and lit candles, they sat for a short time.

In the meantime, the Eparch of the City had prepared the City in advance, garlanding the route from the Golden Gate as far as the Chalke with laurel and rosemary and myrtle and roses and other flowers, also with a variety of *skaramaggia* and silk hangings and candelabra; he similarly strewed the ground, which was completely covered in flowers.[2] …

On the meadow outside the Golden Gate, tents were set up, and they brought over the noble and important Hagarene prisoners[3] together with the best of the booty of war, banners, and weapons. When it had been deposited in the tents, this was divided up and paraded triumphally along the Mese from the Golden Gate to the Chalke of the palace, for the central, great Golden Gate was then opened.

After the booty had been paraded, the emperors rose and, changing out of their *skaramaggia*, the autocrat and great emperor donned a gold-embroidered breastplate-tunic covered in pearls set in a criss-cross pattern, and with perfect pearls along the hems; girding himself also with a belted sword, bearing upon his head a Caesar's diadem.… His son Constantine wore a gold *klibanion*[4] and a belted sword, golden greaves, and in his hand a gilded spear decorated with pearls. On his head he wore a low turban with a circlet of white embroidered with gold, having on the forehead a likeness of a gold-embroidered crown. Both rode mounted on white horses equipped with gem-encrusted caparisons. While mounted, they received the demarchs and the two factions, wearing deme tunics and segmented diadems on their heads, with other garlands made from roses and flowers around their necks, carrying kerchiefs in their hands.[5] The demarchs wore their triumphal mantles, and their officials tunics and ordinary mantles. The acclamations were to begin with as follows: "Glory to God, who returns our own Lords to us victorious! Glory to God, who exalts you, autocrats of the Romans! Glory to you, All-Holy Trinity, that we see our own Lords victorious! Welcome as conquerors, most courageous Lords!" Then other acclamations in praise of victory were made, and processional military hymns were sung, as the two factions processed before (the emperor).

When they had come from the Church of the Abramites to the Golden Gate, as we said, which was open to them, they stood before the entry to it, and were similarly acclaimed. They received then the Eparch of the City and the emperor's representative who, falling to the ground, paid homage, and presented to the emperor a golden crown, after the old custom, along with other crowns of laurel, as symbols of victory. And they then received from the emperor coin to the value and above of the golden crown. When the demes had completed their acclamations, the emperors went in procession through the great Golden Gate.…

---

1   The Hebdomon palace complex was outside the walls of Constantinople on the Sea of Marmara, by the route to the Golden Gate.
2   The Mese, the main boulevard from the Golden Gate, led to the Chalke. The Eparch of Constantinople was in effect the "mayor" of the city.
3   The "Hagarene prisoners" were the Muslims who were captured in the wars.
4   A *klibanion* was sleeveless body armor, in this case of gold, covering the chest to the waist. At this point in the procession, the emperor and his son were still outside the Golden Gate.
5   The demarchs were the leaders of the two traditional hippodrome factions—the chariot-racing teams and their supporters (the demes)—at Constantinople, the Blues and the Greens.

4.8 Imperial rule: Michael Psellus, *Portrait of Basil II* (c.1063). Original in Greek.

MICHAEL PSELLUS (1018–c.1092) WAS BORN and educated in Constantinople and served at the courts of many of the emperors and empresses of the second half of the eleventh century. Among his many writings was the *Chronographia*, a book containing the biographies of the very Byzantine emperors and empresses whom he had known personally. Its first subject, however, was Basil II the Bulgar-Slayer, whose rule (963-1025) just barely overlapped Psellus's birth. In his account, Psellus suggested that Basil's military successes and autocratic attitude went hand in hand. How might you put this document together with Constantine's description of the military activities of the emperor in the treatise above, p. 223 to help explain Byzantium's extraordinary expansion in the early 11th century?

[Source: *Fourteen Byzantine Rulers: The* Chronographia *of Michael Psellus*, trans. E.R.A. Sewter (New York: Penguin Books, 1966), pp. 28-30, 43-48.]

Once invested with supreme power over the Romans, Basil was unwilling to share his designs with anyone else; he refused advice on the conduct of public affairs. On the other hand, having had no previous experience of military matters or of good civil administration, he discovered that to rely on his own unaided judgment was impossible. He was compelled to turn for help to the *parakoimomenus* (Lord Chamberlain).[1] This man, called Basil, happened at that time to be the most remarkable person in the Roman Empire, outstanding in intellect, bodily stature, and regal appearance. Although he was born of the same father as the father of Basil and Constantine, on his mother's side he came of different stock. In early infancy he had suffered castration—a natural precaution against a concubine's offspring, for as a eunuch he could never hope to usurp the throne from a legitimate heir. Actually he was resigned to his fate and was genuinely attached to the Imperial house—after all, it was his own family. He was particularly devoted to his nephew Basil, embracing the young man in the most affectionate manner and watching over his progress like some kindly foster-parent. One should not be surprised, then, that Basil placed on this man's shoulders the burden of Empire. The older man's serious nature, too, had its influence on the emperor's character. The *parakoimomenus*, in fact, was like an athlete competing at the games while Basil watched him as a spectator—not a spectator present merely to cheer on the victor, but rather one who trained himself in the running and took part in the contests himself, following in the other's footsteps and imitating his style. So the *parakoimomenus* had the whole world at his feet. It was to him that the civilian population looked, to him that the army turned, and he was responsible, indeed solely responsible, for the administration of public finance and the direction of government. In this task he was constantly assisted by the emperor both in word and in deed, for Basil not only backed up his minister's measures, but confirmed them in writing.

To most men of our generation who saw the Emperor Basil he seemed austere and abrupt in manner, an irascible person who did not quickly change his mind, sober in his daily habits and averse to all effeminacy, but if I am to believe the historians of that period who wrote about him, he was not at all like that when his reign began. A change took place in his character after he acceded to the throne, and instead of leading his former dissolute, voluptuous sort of life, he became a man of great energy. The complete metamorphosis was brought about by the pressure of events. His character stiffened, so to speak. Feebleness gave way to strength and the old slackness disappeared before a new fixity of purpose. In his early days he used to feast quite openly and frequently indulged in the pleasures of love; his main concern was with his banqueting and a life spent in the gay, indolent atmosphere of the court. The combination of youth

---

1 Son of Emperor Romanus I Lecapenus (r.920–944), he was promoted by Emperor Nicephorus Phocas (r.963–969).

and unlimited power gave him opportunities for self-indulgence, and he enjoyed them to the full. The change in his mode of living dates from the attempted revolutions of the notorious Sclerus[1] and of Phocas.[2] Sclerus twice raised the standard of revolt, and there were other aspirants to the throne, with two parties in opposition to the emperor. From that time onward, Basil's carefree existence was forgotten and he wholeheartedly applied himself to serious objects. Once the first blow had been struck against those members of his family who had seized power, he set himself resolutely to compass their utter destruction.

[Psellus discusses the rebellion of Phocas, the two rebellions of Sclerus, and downfall of the eunuch Basil, the Lord Chamberlain. He then turns to Basil II's reconciliation with Sclerus.]

As soon as he saw Sclerus enter, Basil rose and they embraced one another. Then they held converse, the one excusing his revolt and explaining the reason why he had plotted and carried it out, the other quietly accepting the apology and attributing to bad luck what had occurred. When they shared a common drinking-bowl, the emperor first put to his own lips the cup offered to Sclerus and took a moderate sip of its contents before handing it back to his guest. Thus he relieved him of any suspicion of poison, and at the same time proved the sanctity of their agreement. After this Basil questioned him, as a man accustomed to command, about his Empire. How could it be preserved free from dissension? Sclerus had an answer to this, although it was not the sort of advice one would expect from a general; in fact, it sounded more like a diabolical plot. "Cut down the governors who become over-proud," he said. "Let no generals on campaign have too many resources. Exhaust them with unjust exactions, to keep them busied with their own affairs. Admit no woman to the imperial councils. Be accessible to no one. Share with few your most intimate plans."

On this note their conversation came to an end. Sclerus went off to the country estate which had been apportioned him, and soon afterwards he died. We will leave him and return to the emperor. In his dealings with his subjects, Basil behaved with extraordinary circumspection. It is perfectly true that the great reputation he built up as a ruler was founded rather on terror than on loyalty, for as he grew older and became more experienced, he relied less on the judgment of men wiser than himself. He alone introduced new measures, he alone disposed his military forces. As for the civil administration, he governed, not in accordance with the written laws, but following the unwritten dictates of his own intuition, which was most excellently equipped by nature for the purpose. Consequently he paid no attention to men of learning; on the contrary, he affected utter scorn—towards the learned folk, I mean. It seems to me a wonderful thing, therefore, that while the emperor so despised literary culture, no small crop of orators and philosophers sprang up in those times. One solution of the paradox, I fancy, is this: the men of those days did not devote themselves to the study of letters for any ulterior purpose—they cultivated literature for its own sake and as an end in itself, whereas the majority nowadays do not approach the subject of education in this spirit, but consider personal profit to be the first reason for study. Perhaps I should add that though gain is the object of their zeal for literature, if they do not immediately achieve this goal, then they desist from their studies at once. Shame on them!

However, we must return to the emperor. Having purged the Empire of the barbarians, he dealt with his own subjects and completely subjugated them too—I think "subjugate" is the right word to describe it. He decided to abandon his former policy, and after the great families had been humiliated and put on an equal footing with the rest, Basil found himself playing the game of power-politics with considerable success. He surrounded himself with favorites who were neither remarkable for brilliance of intellect, nor of noble lineage, nor too learned. To them were entrusted the imperial rescripts,[3] and with them he

---

1   Bardas Sclerus had been brother-in-law of Emperor John Tzimisces (r.969–976), who had married his sister Maria. He had expected to succeed John, for he had been promised the throne by the emperor on his deathbed.
2   The Phocas family came from Cappadocia and for several generations had enjoyed high repute as soldiers. Bardas Phocas's uncle was Emperor Nicephorus.
3   Laws written in response to particular cases.

was accustomed to share the secrets of State. However, since at that time the emperor's comments on memoranda or requests for favors were never varied, but only plain, straightforward statements (for Basil, whether writing or speaking, avoided all elegance of composition), he used to dictate to his secretaries just as the words came to his tongue, stringing them all together, one after the other. There was no subtlety, nothing superfluous in his speech.

By humbling the pride or jealousy of his people, Basil made his own road to power an easy one. He was careful, moreover, to close the exit-doors on the monies contributed to the treasury. So a huge sum was built up, partly by the exercise of strict economy, partly by fresh additions from abroad. Actually the sum accumulated in the imperial treasury reached the grand total of 200,000 talents. As for the rest of his gains, it would indeed be hard to find words adequately to describe them. All the treasures amassed in Iberia and Arabia, all the riches found among the Celts or contained in the land of the Scyths[1]—in brief, all the wealth of the barbarians who surround our borders—all were gathered together in one place and deposited in the emperor's coffers. In addition to this, he carried off to his treasure-chambers, and sequestrated there, all the money of those who rebelled against him and were afterwards subdued. And since the vaults of the buildings made for this purpose were not big enough, he had spiral galleries dug underground, after the Egyptian style, and there he kept safe a considerable proportion of his treasures. He himself took no pleasure in any of it; quite the reverse, indeed, for the majority of the precious stones, both the white ones (which we call pearls) and the colored brilliants, far from being inlaid in diadems or collars, were hidden away in his underground vaults. Meanwhile Basil took part in his processions and gave audience to his governors clad merely in a robe of purple, not the very bright purple, but simply purple of a dark hue, with a handful of gems as a mark of distinction. As he spent the greater part of his reign serving as a soldier on guard at our frontiers and keeping the barbarian marauders at bay, not only did he draw nothing from his reserves of wealth, but even multiplied his riches many times over.

On his expedition against the barbarians, Basil did not follow the customary procedure of other emperors, setting out at the middle of spring and returning home at the end of summer. For him the time to return was when the task in hand was accomplished. He endured the rigors of winter and the heat of summer with equal indifference. He disciplined himself against thirst. In fact, all his natural desires were kept under stern control, and the man was as hard as steel. He had an accurate knowledge of the details of army life, and by that I do not mean the general acquaintance with the composition of his army, the relative functions of individual units in the whole body, or the various groupings and deployments suited to the different formations. His experience of army matters went further than that: the duties of the *protostate*, the duties of the *hemilochites*,[2] the tasks proper to the rank immediately junior to them—all these were no mysteries to Basil, and the knowledge stood him in good stead in his wars. Accordingly, jobs appropriate to these ranks were not devolved on others, and the emperor, being personally conversant with the character and combat duties of each individual, knowing to what each man was fitted either by temperament or by training, used him in this capacity and made him serve there.

Moreover, he knew the various formations suited to his men. Some he had read of in books, others he devised himself during the operations of war, the result of his own intuition. He professed to conduct his wars and draw up the troops in line of battle, himself planning each campaign, but he preferred not to engage in combat personally. A sudden retreat might otherwise prove embarrassing. Consequently, for the most part he kept his troops immobile. He would construct machines of war and skirmish at a distance, while the maneuvering was left to the light-armed soldiers. Once he had made contact with the enemy, a regular military liaison was established between the different formations of the Roman army. The whole force was drawn up like a solid tower, headquarters being in touch with the cavalry squadrons, who were themselves kept in communica-

---

1   Iberia was an eastern theme of the Byzantine empire. The "riches of the Celts" refers to the riches of western states. The Slavs were called "Scyths" by classicizing authors like Psellus.

2   Military ranks, junior officers.

tion with the light infantry, and these again with the various units of heavy-armed foot [soldiers]. When all was ready, strict orders were given that no soldier should advance in front of the line or break rank under any circumstances. If these orders were disobeyed, and if some of the most valiant or daring soldiers did ride out well in front of the rest, even in cases where they engaged the enemy successfully, they could expect no medals or rewards of valor when they returned. On the contrary, Basil promptly discharged them from the army, and they were punished on the same level as common criminals. The decisive factor in the achievement of victory was, in his opinion, the massing of troops in one coherent body, and for this reason alone he believed the Roman armies to be invincible. The careful inspections he made before battle used to aggravate the soldiers and they abused him openly, but the emperor met their scorn with common sense. He would listen quietly, and then with a gay smile point out that if he neglected these precautions, their battles would go on for ever.

Basil's character was two-fold, for he readily adapted himself no less to the crises of war than to the calm of peace. Really, if the truth be told, he was more of a villain in wartime, more of an emperor in time of peace. Outbursts of wrath he controlled, and like the proverbial "fire under the ashes" kept anger hidden in his heart, but, if his orders were disobeyed in war, on returning to his palace he would kindle his wrath and reveal it. Terrible then was the vengeance he took on the miscreant. Generally he persisted in his opinions, but there were occasions when he did change his mind. In many cases, too, he traced crimes back to their original causes, and the final links in the chain were exonerated. So most defaulters obtained forgiveness, either through his sympathetic understanding, or because he showed some other interest in their affairs. He was slow to adopt any course of action, but never would he willingly alter the decision once it was taken. Consequently his attitude to friends was unvaried, unless perchance he was compelled by necessity to revise his estimate of them. Similarly, where he had burst out in anger against someone, he did not quickly moderate his indignation. Whatever estimate he formed, indeed, was to him an irrevocable and divinely-inspired judgment.

4.9 Political theory: Al-Farabi, *The Perfect State* (c.940–942). Original in Arabic.

ABU NASR AL-FARABI (c.870–c.950) WAS BORN in Turkestan, spent most of his adulthood in Baghdad, where he made a very modest living as a philosopher and writer, and joined the court of the emir of Aleppo in Syria toward the end of his life. His *Perfect State* engaged a long tradition of Greek thought on a great variety of spiritual, biological, and social topics; al-Farabi wanted to show their importance for a Muslim audience. His work thus began with God, angels, the heavens, the "bodies below the heavens," and so on, leading to the chapters below, which deal with human societies and their different degrees of excellence. How does al-Farabi's view of the "excellent and ignorant cities" compare with Augustine's notion of the "cities of God and Man" in *The City of God*, above, p. 21?

[Source: *Al-Farabi on the Perfect State*, ed. and trans. Richard Walzer (Oxford: Clarendon Press, 1985), pp. 231, 235, 239, 241, 253, 255, 257, 259.]

Chapter 15

Perfect Associations and Perfect Ruler; Faulty Associations

... §3. The most excellent good and the utmost perfection is, in the first instance, attained in a city, not in a society which is less complete than it. But since good in its real sense is such as to be attainable through choice and will and evils are also due to will and choice only, a city may be established to enable its people to cooperate in attaining some aims that are evil. Hence felicity is not attainable in every city. The city, then, in which people aim through association at cooperating for the things by which felicity in its real and true sense can be attained, is the excellent city, and the society in which there is a cooperation to acquire felicity is the excellent society; and the nation in which all of its cities cooperate for those things through which felicity is attained is the excellent nation. In the same way, the excellent universal state will arise only when all the nations in it cooperate for the purpose of reaching felicity.

§4. The excellent city resembles the perfect and healthy body, all of whose limbs cooperate to make the life of the animal perfect and to preserve it in this state. Now the limbs and organs of the body are different and their natural endowments and faculties are unequal in excellence, there being among them one ruling organ, namely the heart, and organs which are close in rank to that ruling organ, each having been given by nature a faculty by which it performs its proper function in conformity with the natural aim. So, too, the parts of the city are by nature provided with endowments unequal in excellence which enable them to do one thing and not another. But they are not parts of the city by their inborn nature alone but rather by the voluntary habits which they acquire such as the arts and their likes; to the natural faculties which exist in the organs and limbs of the body correspond the voluntary habits and dispositions in the parts of the city.

§5. The ruling organ in the body is by nature the most perfect and most complete of the organs in itself and in its specific qualification, and it also has the best of everything of which another organ has a share as well; beneath it, in turn, are other organs which rule over organs inferior to them, their rule being lower in rank than the rule of the first and indeed subordinate to the rule of the first; they rule and are ruled. In the same way, the ruler of the city is the most perfect part of the city in his specific qualification and has the best of everything which anybody else shares with him; beneath him are people who are ruled by him and rule others.

The heart comes to be first and becomes then the

cause of the existence of the other organs and limbs of the body, and the cause of the existence of their faculties in them and of their arrangement in the ranks proper to them, and when one of its organs is out of order, it is the heart which provides the means to remove that disorder. In the same way the ruler of this city must come to be in the first instance, and will subsequently be the cause of the rise of the city and its parts and the cause of the presence of the voluntary habits of its parts and of their arrangement in the ranks proper to them; and when one part is out of order he provides it with the means to remove its disorder.

The parts of the body close to the ruling organ perform of the natural functions, in agreement—by nature—with the aim of the ruler, the most noble ones; the organs beneath them perform those functions which are less noble, and eventually the organs are reached which perform the meanest functions. In the same way the parts of the city which are close in authority to the ruler of the city perform the most noble voluntary actions, and those below them less noble actions, until eventually the parts are reached which perform the most ignoble actions. The inferiority of such actions is sometimes due to the inferiority of their matter, although they may be extremely useful—like the action of the bladder and the action of the lower intestine in the body; sometimes it is due to their being of little use; at other times it is due to their being very easy to perform. This applies equally to the city and equally to every whole which is composed by nature of well ordered coherent parts: they have a ruler whose relation to the other parts is like the one just described.

§6. This applies also to all existents.[1] For the relation of the First Cause to the other existents is like the relation of the king of the excellent city to its other parts.[2] For the ranks of the immaterial existents are close to the First [Cause]. Beneath them are the heavenly bodies, and beneath the heavenly bodies the material bodies. All these existents act in conformity with the First Cause, follow it, take it as their guide and imitate it; but each existent does that according to its capacity, choosing its aim precisely on the strength of its established rank in the universe: that is to say the

last follows the aim of that which is slightly above it in rank, equally the second existent, in turn, follows what is above itself in rank, and in the same way the third existent has an aim which is above it. Eventually existents are reached which are linked with the First Cause without any intermediary whatsoever. In accordance with this order of rank all the existents permanently follow the aim of the First Cause. Those which are from the very outset provided with all the essentials of their existence are made to imitate the First [Cause] and its aim from their very outset, and hence enjoy eternal bliss and hold the highest ranks; but those which are not provided from the outset with all the essentials of their existence, are provided with a faculty by which they move towards the expected attainment of those essentials and will then be able to follow the aim of the First [Cause]. The excellent city ought to be arranged in the same way: all its parts ought to imitate in their actions the aim of their first ruler according to their rank.

§7. The ruler of the excellent city cannot just be any man, because rulership requires two conditions: (a) he should be predisposed for it by his inborn nature, (b) he should have acquired the attitude and habit of will for rulership which will develop in a man whose inborn nature is predisposed for it. Nor is every art suitable for rulership, most of the arts, indeed, are rather suited for service within the city, just as most men are by their very nature born to serve. Some of the arts rule certain [other] arts while serving others at the same time, whereas there are other arts which, not ruling anything at all, only serve. Therefore the art of ruling the excellent city cannot just be any chance art, nor due to any chance habit whatever. For just as the first ruler in a genus cannot be ruled by anything in that genus—for instance the ruler of the limbs cannot be ruled by any other limb, and this holds good for any ruler of any composite whole—so the art of the ruler in the excellent city of necessity cannot be a serving art at all and cannot be ruled by any other art, but his art must be an art towards the aim of which all the other arts tend, and for which they strive in all the actions of the excellent city....

---

1   That which exists, whether thing, action, or quality.
2   The First Cause is God. The term itself comes from Aristotle, but the hierarchy of Being that al-Farabi describes here is neo-Platonic.

[Al-Farabi now explores the qualities of the ruler of the excellent city: his Passive Intellect (the only sort of intellect that human beings have) learns all the intelligibles—all that can be understood by the intellect alone—from the Active Intellect, which is God.]

§15. In opposition to the excellent city are the "ignorant" city, the wicked city, the city which has deliberately changed its character and the city which has missed the right path through faulty judgment. In opposition to it are also the individuals who make up the common people in the various cities.

§16. The "ignorant" city is the city whose inhabitants do not know true felicity, the thought of it never having occurred to them. Even if they were rightly guided to it they would either not understand it or not believe in it. The only good things they recognize are some of those which are superficially thought of as good among the things which are considered to be the aims in life such as bodily health, wealth, enjoyment of pleasures, freedom to follow one's desires, and being held in honor and esteem. According to the citizens of the ignorant city each of these is a kind of felicity, and the greatest and perfect felicity is the sum total of all of them. Things contrary to these goods are misery such as deficiency of the body, poverty, no enjoyment of pleasures, no freedom to follow one's desires, and not being held in honor.

§17. The ignorant city is divided into a number of cities. One of them is the city of necessity, that is the city whose people strive for no more food, drink, clothes, housing and sexual intercourse than is necessary for sustaining their bodies, and they cooperate to attain this. Another is the city of meanness; the aim of its people is to cooperate in the acquisition of wealth and riches, not in order to enjoy something else which can be got through wealth, but because they regard wealth as the sole aim in life. Another is the city of depravity and baseness; the aim of its people is the enjoyment of the pleasure connected with food and drink and sexual intercourse, and in general of the pleasures of the senses and of the imagination, and to give preference to entertainment and idle play in every form and in every way. Another is the city of honor; the aim of its people is to cooperate to attain honor and distinction and fame among the nations, to

be extolled and treated with respect by word and deed, and to attain glory and splendor either in the eyes of other people or among themselves, each according to the extent of his love of such distinction or according to the amount of it which he is able to reach. Another is the city of power; the aim of its people is to prevail over others and to prevent others from prevailing over them, their only purpose in life being the enjoyment which they get from power. Another is the "democratic" city: the aim of its people is to be free, each of them doing what he wishes without restraining his passions in the least.

§18. There are as many kings of ignorant cities as there are cities of this kind, each of them governing the city over which he has authority so that he can indulge in his passion and design.

We have herewith enumerated the designs which may be set up as aims for ignorant cities.

§19. The wicked city is a city whose views are those of the excellent city; it knows felicity, God Almighty, the existents of the second order, the Active Intellect and everything which as such is to be known and believed in by the people of the excellent city; but the actions of its people are the actions of the people of the ignorant cities.

The city which has deliberately changed is a city whose views and actions were previously the views and actions of the people of the excellent city, but they have been changed and different views have taken their place, and its actions have turned into different actions.

The city which misses the right path [the "erring" city] is the city which aims at felicity after this life, and holds about God Almighty, the existents of the second order, and the Active Intellect pernicious and useless beliefs, even if they are taken as symbols and representations of true felicity. Its first ruler was a man who falsely pretended to be receiving "revelation"; he produced this wrong impression through falsifications, cheating and deceptions.

§20. The kings of these cities are contrary to the kings of the excellent cities: their ways of governing are contrary to the excellent ways of governing. The same applies to all the other people who live in these cities.

4.10 Logic: Ibn Sina (Avicenna), *Treatise on Logic* (1020s or 1030s). Original in Persian.

THE STUDY OF LOGIC as a discipline was the original achievement of the ancient Greek philosopher Aristotle (384-322 B.C.E.) His treatises on the topic, later grouped together under the title *Organon*, dealt with what would remain the classic issues of the topic: the relationship of words to reality, the valid forms by which we may derive new truths from what is already known, and the criteria by which we may make and judge inferences. Aristotelian logic was a topic of keen interest in the pre-Christian world and remained important even into the Christian era, with the commentaries of Boethius (*c.*480-524 C.E.). After that, its study continued in the Islamic world, beginning in the ninth century and gaining real momentum in the tenth. The Muslim Persian scholar Ibn Sina (980-1037), known as Avicenna in the West, was one of the most important scholars in this tradition. He was able to draw on translations of Aristotle, made from their original Greek mainly by Christians living in Muslim societies. In the excerpt below he talks about the importance of logic for attaining a particularly high-grade form of knowledge that he calls "science," and he argues that such knowledge is concerned with universals such as "human being" rather than with singulars such as "Mohammed" or "Zid." For Ibn Sina, logic—and philosophy more generally—was essential for understanding Islam itself. Compare the conception and role of logic in the text of al-Farabi above, p. 231, with Ibn Sina's view.

[Source: *Avicenna's Treatise on Logic*, ed. and trans. Farhang Zabeeh (The Hague: Martinus Nijhoff, 1971), pp. 13-17 (slightly modified).]

The Purpose and Use of Logic

There are two kinds of cognition: One is called intuitive or perceptive or apprehensive. For example, if someone says, "Man," or "Fairy," or "Angel," or the like, you will understand, conceive, and grasp what he means by the expression. The other kind of cognition is judgment. As for example, when you acknowledge that angels exist or human beings are under surveillance and the like.

Cognition can again be analyzed into two kinds. One is the kind that may be known through Intellect; it is known necessarily by reasoning through itself. For example, there are the intuitive cognitions of the whatness of the soul, and judgments about what is grasped by intuitive cognition, such as, the soul is eternal.

The other kind of cognition is one that is known by intuition. Judgments about these intuitions, however, are made, not by Intellect, or by reason but by the First Principle.[1] For example, it is known that if two things are equal to the same thing then those things are equal to each other. Then there is the kind of cognition known by the senses, such as, the knowledge that the sun is bright. Also, there is the knowledge that is received from authority such as those received from sages and prophets. And the kind that is obtained from the general opinion and those we are brought by it, for example, that it is wrong to lie and injustice ought not to be done. And still other kinds—which may be named later.

Whatever is known by Intellect, whether it is simple intuitive cognition, or judgment about intuitive cognition, or cognitive judgment, should be based on something which is known prior to the thing.

An example of an intuitive or perceptual cognition is this: If we don't know what "man" means, and someone tells us that man is an animal who talks, we first have to know the meaning of "animal" and "talking," and we must have intuitive cognition of these things before we can learn something we didn't know before about man.

An example of a judgment acquired by Intellect is this: If we don't know the meaning of "the world was

---

1 The First Principle, as defined by Aristotle, was that which was self-evident.

created," and someone tells us that the world possesses color, and whatever possesses color is created; then, and only then, can we know what we didn't know before about the world.

Thus, whatever is not known but desired to be known, can be known through what is known before. But it is not the case that whatever is known can be a ground for knowing what is unknown. Because for everything that is unknown there is a proper class of known things that can be used for knowing the unknown.

There is a method by which one can discover the unknown from what is known. It is the science of logic. Through it one may know how to obtain the unknown from the known. This science is also concerned with the different kinds of valid, invalid, and near valid inferences.

The science of logic is the science of scales. Other sciences are practical, they can give direction in life. The salvation of men lies in their purity of soul. This purity of soul is attainable by contemplating the pure form and avoiding this-worldly inclinations. And the way to these two is through science. And no science which cannot be examined by the balance of logic is certain and exact. Thus, without the acquisition of logic, nothing can be truly called science. Therefore, there is no way except learning the science of logic. It is characteristic of the ancient sciences that the student, at the beginning of his study, is unable to see the use or application of the sciences. This is so, because only after a thorough study of the whole body of science will the real value of his endeavor become apparent. Thus I pray that the reader of this book will not grow impatient in reading things which do not appear of use upon first sight.

The Beginning of the Science of Logic, and a Discussion of What is Called Simple Expressions and Simple Meanings

It should be known that there are two kinds of expressions: One is simple, the other compound.[1] A simple expression is one which has no part signifying a part of the meaning of the expression, e.g., "Zid," "Mohammed," "Man," and "Wise." A compound expression is one which has some part of it denoting some part of the meaning of the expression, such as when you say, "Human beings are wise," or "The wise people." An inquiry into the nature of compound expressions first requires a discussion of the nature of simple expressions.

A Discussion of Simple and Compound Expressions

Every simple expression is either universal or individual. A universal expression is one whose meaning applies to many entities. For example, "man" signifies the same meaning when applied to Zid, Omar and Mohammed. However, even if a universal expression applies to only one entity it can be used in such a way as to indicate many entities, since it is possible to imagine, by understanding the meaning of that term, many other entities. For example, by knowing the meaning of "sun" and "moon," you can imagine many suns and moons.

An individual expression is one which signifies a single entity. It is such that it cannot be imagined that the same expression could be applied to many entities. When you say "Zid," "Zid" signifies only Zid. If you call some other entities "Zid" you are giving the term another meaning. The business of the scientist is not to deal with individual expressions and their meanings, but to investigate the nature of universals. No doubt, each universal has many particular instances.

A Discussion of Essential and Accidental Universals

The universal contains its particulars either (a) essentially or (b) accidentally. The Essential Universal and its Particulars are apprehended if, at least, three conditions are fulfilled:

(1) The particular has meaning. Thus, if you know the meaning of "animal," "man," "number," and "number four," you cannot help knowing the meaning of the expressions, "man is an animal" and "four is a number." But if you add "exists" or "is white" to the word "animal" and "number," you will not understand the meaning of the resulting expressions "man exists," "number four exists," or "man is not white" or "man is white."

(2) The existence of the Essential Universal is

---

1 The topic of simple and complex expression and universal or individual or common name and proper name corresponds to Aristotle's statements in the *Categories*.

prerequisite for the existence of its Particular. For example, there should first be animal in order that animal be man, and first there should be number in order that number be four, and first there should be human being in order that human being be Zid.

(3) Nothing gives meaning to a particular; rather its meaning is derived from its essence. For example, nothing makes human being animal, and nothing makes four number, except its essence. For if it were otherwise, if the essence of a thing did not exist, there could be a man which is not animal, and there could be four, but no number; but this is impossible.

To further elaborate what has been said, take the saying "something may make some other thing." Its meaning is this: a thing can not be in its essence another thing, but only could be that other thing by means of something else which is accidental to it. If it is impossible for a thing to be what another thing is, nothing could make it that thing. That thing which makes man, man, makes animal, animal. But it does not make man, animal, since man in itself is animal, and four in itself is number. But this relation does not exist between whiteness and man. Hence, there should be something which makes man, white.

Thus, when every meaning has the above three characteristics it is essential. Whatever does not have all these characteristics is accidental. Accidental quali-ties are those which can never arise from the essence of a thing, not even by imagination. Therefore, they are unlike kinds of deduction that are made in the case of number thousand which is an even number or in the case of a triangle, the sum total of whose angles is equal to two right angles. An example of an accidental quality is laughter, an attribute of men. This problem will be discussed later on.

And I should have mentioned also that a human being has two characteristics: essential and accidental. His essential characteristic may be exemplified by his ability to speak, because this property is the essence of his soul. An accidental quality of his is laughter, because it is the character of man, on seeing or hearing a strange and unfamiliar thing, (unless hindered by instinct or habit), to perchance laugh. But before there be wonder and laughter there must be a soul for a man, in order that this soul be united with a body and man becomes a man. First, there should be a soul in order that there be a man; not first, there should be laughter in order that there be a soul. Thus, the characteristic which comes first is essential, and whatever does not come from a man is not essential, but accidental. When you say, "Zid is seated," "Zid slept," "Zid is old," and "Zid is young," these characteristics, without doubt, are accidental, no matter what their temporal sequence be.

KINGS, QUEENS, AND PRINCES

4.11 Kievan Rus: *The Russian Primary Chronicle* (*c*.1113, incorporating earlier materials). Original in Russian.

The Russian Primary Chronicle is one of the earliest sources that we have for Russian history. Composed *c*.1113 by an anonymous monk of the Crypt Monastery near Kiev, it was clearly tied to the history of the princes of Kiev. In the excerpt below, Kievan Prince Yaroslav the Wise (r.1019-1054) is portrayed as following the model of the Christian ruler, especially the Byzantine emperor, even to the point of naming the church that he founded "St. Sophia," after the church built by Justinian at Constantinople. The passage says that Yaroslav not only patronized monks but had the learned among them copy books to be distributed in turn to new monasteries. Russian dates, which counted the years from the time of the Creation, followed the Byzantine dating system. In parentheses are the corresponding dates C.E. How does the *Chronicle*'s description of the model Christian ruler compare with Psellus's *Portrait of Basil II*, p. 227 above?

[Source: *The Russian Primary Chronicle: Laurentian Text*, trans. and ed. Samuel Hazzard Cross and Olgerd P. Sherbowitz-Wetzor (Cambridge, MA: Medieval Academy of America, 1953), pp. 136-38 (slightly modified).]

6544 (1036) Thereafter Yaroslav assumed the entire sovereignty, and was the sole ruler in the land of Rus. Yaroslav went to Novgorod, where he set up his son Vladimir as prince, and appointed Zhidyata bishop.[1] At this time, a son was born to Yaroslav, and he named him Vyacheslav. While Yaroslav was still at Novgorod, news came to him that the Pechenegs were besieging Kiev.[2] He then collected a large army of Varangians[3] and Slavs, returned to Kiev, and entered his city. The Pechenegs were innumerable. Yaroslav made a sally from the city and marshaled his forces, placing the Varangians in the center, the men of Kiev on the right flank, and the men of Novgorod on the left. When they had taken position before the city, the Pechenegs advanced, and they met on the spot where the metropolitan church of St. Sophia now stands. At that time, as a matter of fact, there were fields outside the city. The combat was fierce, but toward evening Yaroslav with difficulty won the upper hand. The Pechenegs fled in various directions, but as they did not know in what quarter to flee, they were drowned, some in the Setoml',[4] some in other streams, while the remnant of them disappeared from that day to this. In the same year, Yaroslav imprisoned his brother Sudislav in Pskov because he had been slanderously accused.

6545 (1037). Yaroslav built the great citadel at Kiev, near which stands the Golden Gate. He founded also the metropolitan Church of St. Sophia, the Church of the Annunciation over the Golden Gate, and also the Monastery of St. George and the convent of St. Irene. During his reign, the Christian faith was fruitful and multiplied, while the number of monks increased, and new monasteries came into being. Yaroslav loved religious establishments and was devoted to priests, especially to monks. He applied himself to books, and read them continually day and night. He assembled

---

1 The first bishop of Novgorod died in 1030 after designating his successor. Yaroslav, however, insisted on Luka Zhidyata, who presided over the see from 1036 to 1055.
2 The Pechenegs were a Turkic nomadic people who in the tenth century occupied the region between the Don and the Danube but, squeezed by other nomadic groups and the expanding Byzantines and Rus, raided into Rus only to be repulsed by Yaroslav.
3 The Varangians were the Scandinavian settlers of Rus.
4 The Setoml' was a small stream in Kiev.

many scribes, and translated from Greek into Slavic. He wrote and collected many books through which true believers are instructed and enjoy religious education. For as one man plows the land, and another sows, and still others reap and eat food in abundance, so did this prince. His father Vladimir[1] plowed and harrowed the soil when he enlightened Rus through baptism, while this prince sowed the hearts of the faithful with the written word, and we in turn reap the harvest by receiving the teaching of books. For great is the profit from book-learning.

Through the medium of books, we are shown and taught the way of repentance, for we gain wisdom and continence from the written word. Books are like rivers that water the whole earth; they are the springs of wisdom. For books have an immeasurable depth; by them we are consoled in sorrow. They are the bridle of self-restraint. For great is wisdom. As Solomon said in its praise, "I (wisdom) have inculcated counsel; I have summoned reason and prudence. The fear of the Lord is the beginning of wisdom. Mine are counsel, wisdom, constancy, and strength. Through me kings rule, and the mighty decree justice. Through me are princes magnified and the oppressors possess the earth. I love them that love me, and they who seek me shall find grace."[2] If you seek wisdom attentively in books, you obtain great profit for your spirit. He who reads books often converses with God or with holy men. If one possesses the words of the prophets, the teachings of the evangelists and the apostles, and the lives of the holy fathers, his soul will derive great profit therefrom. Thus Yaroslav, as we have said, was a lover of books, and as he wrote many, he deposited them in the Church of St. Sophia which he himself had founded. He adorned it with gold and silver and churchly vessels, and in it the usual hymns are raised to God at the customary seasons. He founded other churches in the cities and districts, appointing priests and paying them out of his personal fortune. He bade them teach the people, since that is the duty which God has prescribed them, and to go often into the churches. Priests and Christian laymen thus increased in number. Yaroslav rejoiced to see the multitude of his churches and of his Christian subjects, but the devil was afflicted, since he was now conquered by this new Christian nation.

6546 (1038). Yaroslav attacked the Yatvingians.[3]

6547 (1039). The Church of the Blessed Virgin which had been founded by Vladimir, Yaroslav's father, was consecrated by the Metropolitan Theopemptos.

6548 (1040). Yaroslav attacked Lithuania.

6549 (1041). Yaroslav attacked the Mazovians by boat.

4.12 Hungary: King Stephen, *Laws* (1000–1038). Original in Latin.

ONCE HUNGARY BECAME A PART OF Christian Europe, with the conversion and coronation of King Stephen *c.*1000, it adopted many of the institutions of the post-Roman successor states, including written laws. Those excerpted below are from the oldest of the laws promulgated by Stephen, probably at the beginning of his reign. The selection below begins with the 6th chapter because the five chapters before it were probably added after Stephen's death. This code was clearly concerned above all with moral and religious issues and should be compared with Charlemagne's *Admonitio generalis* (above, p. 180) and the near-contemporary Anglo-Saxon legislation of King Æthelred (below, p. 262).

---

1   St. Vladimir I (r.978–1015) converted to Christianity under the influence of Byzantine Emperor Basil II, took the baptismal name of Basil, and married Basil's sister.
2   Prov. 8: 12, 13, 14–17.
3   The Yatvingians were a Lithuanian people. Attacks on them and on Lithuania and the Mazovians (below) were evidently designed both to protect Rus's northwest flank and to keep open access to eastern Poland, on which Yaroslav made claim.

[Source: *The Laws of the Medieval Kingdom of Hungary*, vol 1: *1000-1301*, trans. and ed. János M. Bak, György Bónis, and James Ross Sweeney (Bakersfield, CA: Charles Schlacks, Jr. Publisher, 1989), pp. 1, 3-8, 80-83 (slightly modified).]

Preface to the royal law

The work of the royal office subject to the rule of divine mercy is by custom greater and more complete when nourished in the Catholic faith than any other office. Since every people use their own law, we, governing our monarchy by the will of God and emulating both ancient and modern caesars, and after reflecting upon the law, decree for our people too the way they should lead an upright and blameless life. Just as they are enriched by divine laws, so may they similarly be strengthened by secular ones, in order that as the good shall be made many by these divine laws so shall the criminals incur punishment. Thus we set out below in the following sentences what we have decreed....

6. Royal concessions of free disposition of goods.

We, by our royal authority have decreed that anyone shall be free to divide his property, to assign it to his wife, his sons and daughters, his relatives, or to the church;[1] and no one should dare to change this after his death.

7. The preservation of royal goods.

It is our will that just as we have given others the opportunity to master their own possessions, so equally the goods, warriors,[2] bondmen,[3] and whatever else belongs to our royal dignity should remain permanent, and no one should plunder or remove them, nor should anyone dare to obtain any advantage from them.

8. The observance of the Lord's day.

If a priest or *ispán* [local lord], or any faithful person find anyone working on Sunday with oxen, the ox shall be confiscated and given to the men of the castle to be eaten;[4] if a horse is used, however, it shall be confiscated, but the owner, if he wishes, may redeem it with an ox which should be eaten as has been said. If anyone uses other equipment, this tool and his clothing shall be taken, and he may redeem them, if he wishes, with a flogging.

9. More on the same.

Priests and *ispánok* shall enjoin village reeves[5] to command everyone both great and small, men and women, with the exception of those who guard the fire, to gather on Sundays in the church. If someone remains at home through their negligence let them be beaten and shorn.

10. The observance of Ember days.[6]

If someone breaks the fast known to all on the Ember day, he shall fast in prison for a week.

11. The observance of Friday.

If someone eats meat on Friday, a day observed by all Christianity, he shall fast incarcerated during the day for a week.

---

1   The king seems to have wanted to transform the undivided property of clans into the personal property of freemen and nobles, as was the case in western European societies of the time. But he was not successful.

2   The Latin word used here was *milites*, (sing.: *miles*), the same word for "fighters" or "warriors" that was used in the Peace Movement (see *The Miracles of St. Benedict* above, p. 221). In the *Laws of Hungary* the *milites* seem to have been armed servants of the king and magnates.

3   The Latin word used here was *servi*, (sing.: *servus*), which could mean either "slave" or "serf." Since the meaning here is not clear, the neutral term "bondmen" is used.

4   The "men of the castle" (*cives* in Latin) were dependent men attached to the castles of the royal *ispánok* (the plural of *ispán*) for their defense and maintenance, much like the garrisons that guarded the castles in the document about Hugh of Lusignan and his lord (above, p. 213).

5   In this period the reeves (*villici* in Latin) were free peasants in charge of enforcing some laws.

6   The observance of three days' fast during the weeks following Ash Wednesday, Pentecost, the Exaltation of the Holy Cross, and the feast of St. Lucy was widespread in the Carolingian realm and, as we see here, adopted in Hungary.

12. Those who die without confession.

If someone has such a hardened heart—God forbid it to any Christian—that he does not want to confess his faults according to the counsel of a priest, he shall lie without any divine service and alms like an infidel. If his relatives and neighbors fail to summon the priest, and therefore he should die unconfessed, prayers and alms should be offered, but his relatives shall wash away their negligence by fasting in accordance with the judgment of the priests. Those who die a sudden death shall be buried with all ecclesiastical honor, for divine judgment is hidden from us and unknown.

13. The observances of Christianity.

If someone neglects a Christian observance and takes pleasure in the stupidity of his negligence, he shall be judged by the bishops according to the nature of the offense and the discipline of the canons.[1] If he rebelliously objects to suffer the punishment with equanimity, he shall be subject to the same judgment seven times over. If, after all this, he continues to resist and remains obdurate, he shall be handed over for royal judgment, namely to the defender of Christianity.[2]

14. On homicide.

If someone driven by anger and arrogance, willfully commits a homicide, he should know that according to the decrees of our [royal] council he is obliged to pay one hundred ten gold *pensae*,[3] from which fifty will go to the royal treasury, another fifty will be given to relatives, and ten will be paid to arbiters and mediators. The killer himself shall fast according to the rules of the canons.[4]

More on the same.

If someone kills a person by chance, he shall pay twelve *pensae* and fast as the canons command.

The killing of slaves.

If someone's slave kills another's slave, the payment shall be a slave for a slave, or he may be redeemed and do penance as has been said.

More on the same.

If a freeman kills the slave of another, he shall replace him with another slave or pay his price, and fast according to the canons.

15. Those who kill their wives.

If an *ispán* with a hardened heart and a disregard for his soul—may such remain far from the hearts of the faithful—defiles himself by killing his wife, he shall make his peace with fifty steers[5] to the kindred of the woman, according to the decree of the royal council, and fast according to the commands of the canons. And if a warrior or a man of wealth commits the same crime he shall pay according to that same council ten steers and fast, as has been said. And if a commoner has committed the same crime, he shall make his peace with five steers to the kindred and fast.

16. Drawing the sword.

In order that peace should remain firm and unsullied among the greater and the lesser of whatever station, we forbid anyone to draw the sword with the aim of injury. If anyone in his audacity should put this prohibition to the test, let him be killed by the same sword.

17. On perjury.

If a powerful man of stained faith and defiled heart be found guilty of breaking his oath by perjury, he shall atone for the perjury with the loss of his hand; or he may redeem it with fifty steers. If a commoner commits perjury, he shall be punished with the loss of his hand or may redeem it by twelve steers and fast, as the canons command.

18. On manumission.

If anyone, prompted by mercy, should set his male and female slaves free in front of witnesses, we decree that no one out of ill will shall reduce them to servitude after his death. If, however, he promised them

---

1   This chapter in fact authorizes the introduction of canon law into Hungary.
2   The "defender of Christianity" was Stephen himself.
3   The *pensa auri* was a coin equivalent to the contemporary Byzantine gold *solidus*.
4   In this provision, Stephen's law code is much like a penitential. See *The Penitential of Finnian*, above, p. 109.
5   Steers were valued at one gold *pensa* each; hence fifty oxen, that is fifty *pensa*, here reflect the cost of legal compensaton for the death of a woman by a man of the *ispán* class.

freedom but died intestate, his widow and sons shall have the power to bear witness to this same manumission and to render *agape*[1] for the redemption of the husband's soul, if they wish.

19. Gathering at church and those who mutter or chatter during mass.

If some persons, upon coming to church to hear the divine service mutter among themselves and disturb others by relating idle tales during the celebration of mass and by being inattentive to Holy Scripture with its ecclesiastical nourishment, they shall be expelled from the church in disgrace if they are older, and if they are younger and common folk they shall be bound in the narthex of the church[2] in view of everyone and punished by whipping and by the shearing off of their hair.

20. Inadmissibility of accusations and testimony of bondmen or bondwomen against their masters or mistresses.

In order that the people of this kingdom may be far removed and remain free from the affronts and accusations of bondmen and bondwomen, it is wholly forbidden by decree of the royal council that any servile person be accepted in accusation or testimony against their masters or mistresses in any criminal case.

21. Those who procure liberty for bondmen of others.

If anyone thoughtlessly brings the bondman of another, without the knowledge of his master, before the king or before persons of higher birth and dignity in order to procure for him the benefits of liberty after he has been released from the yoke of servitude, he should know that if he is rich, he shall pay fifty steers of which forty are owed to the king and ten to the master of the bondman, but if he is poor and of low rank, he shall pay twelve steers of which ten are due to the king and two to the master of the bondman.

22. Those who enslave freemen.

Because it is worthy of God and best for men that everyone should conduct his life in the vigor of liberty, it is established by royal decree that henceforth no *ispán* or warrior should dare to reduce a freeman to servitude. If, however, compelled by his own rashness he should presume to do this, he should know that he shall pay from his own possessions the same composition, which shall be properly divided between the king and the *ispánok*, as in the other decree above.

Similarly on the same.

But if someone who was once held in servitude lives freely after having submitted to a judicial procedure[3] held to consider his liberty, he shall be content with enjoying his freedom, and the man who held him in servitude shall pay nothing.

23. Those who take the warriors of another for themselves.

We wish that each lord have his own warriors and no one shall try to persuade a warrior to leave his longtime lord and come to him, since this is the origin of quarrels.

24. Those who take guests of another for themselves.[4]

If someone receives a guest with benevolence and decently provides him with support, the guest shall not leave his protector as long as he receives support according to their agreement, nor should he transfer his service to any other.

25. Those who are beaten while looking for their own.

If a warrior or a bondman flees to another and he whose warrior or man has run away sends his agent to bring him back, and that agent is beaten and whipped by anyone, we decree in agreement with our magnates that he who gave the beating shall pay ten steers.

---

1 The *agape* was a memorial meal shared by the manumitted (those released from slavery) or an offering made in memory of the dead.

2 The entrance hall or porch.

3 The "judicial procedure" refers to the ordeal by hot iron: the subject (in this case a person claiming to be free) must carry a hot iron for a few paces, then put it down. His hand is bandaged. After three days the wound is inspected. If "clean," he is judged to have told the truth (or, in criminal cases, he is judged not guilty); if discolored or infected, he is judged to have lied.

4 The "guests" were foreigners, most of whom were Western clerics and knights.

26. Widows and orphans.

We also wish widows and orphans to be partakers of our law in the sense that if a widow, left with her sons and daughters, promises to support them and to remain with them as long as she lives, she shall have the right from us to do so, and no one should force her to marry. If she has a change of heart and wants to marry and leave the orphans, she shall have nothing from the goods of the orphans except her own clothing.[1]

More about widows.

If a widow without a child promises to remain unmarried in her widowhood, she shall have the right to all her goods and may do with them what she wishes. But after her death her goods shall go to the kin of her husband, if she has any, and if not, the king is the heir.

27. The abduction of girls.

If any warrior debased by lewdness abducts a girl to be his wife without the consent of her parents, we decree that the girl should be returned to her parents, even if he raped her, and the abductor shall pay ten steers for the abduction, although he may afterwards have made peace with the girl's parents. If a poor man who is a commoner should attempt this, he shall compensate for the abduction with five steers.

28. Those who fornicate with bondwomen of another.

In order that freemen preserve their liberty undefiled, we wish to warn them. Any transgressor who fornicates with a bondwoman of another, should know that he has committed a crime, and he is to be whipped for the first offense. If he fornicates with her a second time, he should be whipped and shorn; but if he does it a third time, he shall become a slave together with the woman, or he may redeem himself. If, however, the bondwoman should conceive by him and not be able to bear but dies in childbirth, he shall make compensation for her with another bondwoman.

The fornication of bondmen.

If a bondman of one master fornicates with the bondwoman of another, he should be whipped and shorn, and if the woman should conceive by him and dies in childbirth, the man shall be sold and half of his price shall be given to the master of the bondwoman, the other half shall be kept by the master of the bondman.

29. Those who desire bondwomen as wives.

In order that no one who is recognized to be a freeman should dare commit this offense, we set forth what has been decreed in this royal council as a source of terror and caution so that if any freeman should choose to marry a bondwoman of another with her master's consent, he shall lose the enjoyment of his liberty and become a slave forever.

30. Those who flee their wives by leaving the country.

In order that people of both sexes may remain and flourish under fixed law and free from injury, we establish in this royal decree that if anyone in his impudence should flee the country out of loathing for his wife, she shall possess everything which her husband rightfully possessed, so long as she is willing to wait for her husband, and no one shall force her into another marriage. If she voluntarily wishes to marry, she may take her own clothing leaving behind other goods, and marry again. If her husband, hearing this, should return, he is not allowed to replace her with anyone else, except with the permission of the bishop.

31. Theft committed by women.

Because it is terrible and loathsome to all to find men committing theft, and even more so for women, it is ordained by the royal council, that if a married woman commits theft, she shall be redeemed by her husband, and if she commits the same offense a second time, she shall be redeemed again; but if she does it a third time, she shall be sold.

32. Arson of houses.

If anyone sets a building belonging to another on fire out of enmity, we order that he replace the building

---

1 Here women apparently did not have a right to their dower—the gift that a husband gave his new wife—after the death of their husbands, though in later laws that right was recognized.

and whatever household furnishings were destroyed by the fire, and also pay sixteen steers which are worth forty *solidi*.[1]

33. On witches.
If a witch is found, she shall be led, in accordance with the law of judgment into the church and handed over to the priest for fasting and instruction in the faith. After the fast she may return home. If she is discovered in the same crime a second time, she shall fast and after the fast she shall be branded with the keys of the church in the form of a cross on her bosom, forehead, and between the shoulders. If she is discovered on a third occasion, she shall be handed over to the judge [of the secular court].

34. On sorcerers.
So that the creatures of God may remain far from all injury caused by evil ones and may not be exposed to any harm from them—unless it be by the will of God who may even increase it—we establish by decree of the council a most terrible warning to magicians and sorcerers that no person should dare to subvert the mind of any man or to kill him by means of sorcery and magic. Yet in the future if a man or a woman dare to do this he or she shall be handed over to the person hurt by sorcery or to his kindred, to be judged according to their will. If, however, they are found practicing divination as they do in ashes or similar things, they shall be corrected with whips by the bishop.

35. The invasion of houses.
We wish that peace and unanimity prevail between great and small according to the Apostle: Be ye all of one accord, etc.,[2] and let no one dare attack another. For if there be any *ispán* so contumacious that after the decree of this common council he should seek out another at home in order to destroy him and his goods, and if the lord of the house is there and fights with him and is killed, the *ispán* shall be punished according to the law about drawing the sword.[3] If, however, the *ispán* shall fall, he shall lie without compensation. If he did not go in person but sent his warriors, he shall pay compensation for the invasion with one hundred steers. If, moreover, a warrior invades the courtyard and house of another warrior, he shall pay compensation for the invasion with ten steers. If a commoner invades the huts of those of similar station, he shall pay for the invasion with five steers.

4.13 An Ottonian queen: *The "Older Life" of Queen Mathilda* (973–974). Original in Latin.

THE *Older Life* OF QUEEN MATHILDA was written 973–974 by an anonymous author, quite possibly a well-educated nun or abbess from the female monastery of Nordhausen. As befitted a work of the Ottonian Renaissance, the *Life* was filled with echoes and quotations from numerous sources. Many of these were classical (such as quotations from Virgil and Terence), but the author also drew extensively from the sixth-century writer Venantius Fortunatus, whose *Life of Radegund* (p. 47 above) seems to have served as a particularly important model for Mathilda's biography. Making careful comparison of the two texts (the notes will guide you), consider the techniques of borrowing and the purposes of innovation in medieval hagiography. In light of this *Life*, what would you say were the ways in which queens were important in Ottonian politics?

[Source: *Queenship and Sanctity: The* Lives *of Mathilda and the* Epitaph *of Adelheid*, trans. Sean Gilsdorf (Washington, DC: Catholic University of America Press, 2004), pp. 72–84, 86–87, 173–81 (slightly modified).]

---

1 In this particular case, Bavarian silver *solidi* are meant, of which 25 were equal to a Byzantine gold *solidus*.
2 See Phil. 2: 2–4.
3 See chapter 16 of this same law code, above.

1. At the time when Conrad was king of the Franks, the duke of all Germany was a prince named Otto, a man whose family was exceedingly noble (insofar as this is measured by worldly distinction).[1] He was possessed of great wealth, esteemed above all others on account of the virtues with which he was endowed, and had for his wife Hadwig, a venerable matron with a character like his own. They produced daughters as well as three sons, all of them brought up according to their parents' noble standards. But divine providence, which "oversees all things and directs them towards the good,"[2] raised up one of these, named Henry, on account of his greater excellence, for although he was the youngest, his upright character made him shine brighter than the others. From his early youth, as soon as he was free to do those things in life which reveal one's own inclinations, he lived wisely. He was accommodating to everyone, loved whomever he was with, opposed no one, and placed himself ahead of none, consoling those who suffered and helping those in need; he earned praise while avoiding envy, and found friends who were his equals.[3] While he deserved the honor afforded him, he was nonetheless particularly beloved by all, and honored even more on account of his kindness and humility.

When he had left boyhood behind and attained manly vigor, his kinfolk sought out a bride for him who was suitably well-born and upright in character.[4] Meanwhile it came to their attention that there was a most beautiful girl named Mathilda in the monastery at Herford,[5] one well-trained in literary studies (the source of both the active and the contemplative life)[6] and whose noble birth was almost the equal of her future husband's. She traced her ancestry to the lineage of Duke Widukind of Saxony, who once had been ensnared in demonic error and who, because there was no one to preach to him, had worshiped idols and ceaselessly persecuted the Christians. In those days, Charles the Great wielded imperial power, a most Christian man who was mighty in combat, learned in the law, committed to the catholic faith, and benevolent and devout towards those who worshiped God. He led his forces into battle against this Widukind, as he did against all pagans, in order to defend the faith. When the sides had confronted one another, both leaders decided to meet in single combat; whoever happened to emerge victorious would be followed without question by the entire army. They fell upon one another and battled long and hard until the Lord, smitten by the tears of the Christian people, finally allowed his faithful warrior to triumph over the enemy, rewarding him for his faith. Then the stubborn Widukind underwent such a change of heart that he willingly subjected himself, his household, and the entire pagan army to the king's power as well as the catholic faith. The emperor kindly received him and had him baptized by the blessed Bishop Boniface, raising him from the holy font himself.[7] Widukind, now that he had set aside error in favor of true belief, penitently sought to know the truth,[8] and he who once had been the church's persecutor and unyielding destroyer now became a most Christian supporter of churches and of God.[9] He zealously devoted himself to the construction of small chapels, which when finished housed many saints' relics and performed other useful functions. One of these, known to many, is still standing in a place called Enger, and many of those relics which I mentioned remain there today.[10]

---

1 Conrad, Duke of Franconia, became East Frankish king upon the death of Louis the Child in 911. Otto (c.830/40-912) became Duke of Saxony around 900.

2 This is from Boethius, *Consolation of Philosophy* 4. 6. 96-97.

3 This description of Henry is based upon that of Pamphilus in Terence's *Andria (The Lady of Andros)*, lines 52-53.

4 Henry had in fact been married earlier to Hatheburg, the widowed daughter and heir of a wealthy Saxon count.

5 The Westfalian convent of Herford was founded around 800.

6 In Luke 10: 38-42, Christ enters a household in which one sister, Martha, is busy serving, while the other, Mary, listens to Christ teach. Mary thus became associated with the "contemplative life," Martha with the "active life."

7 In fact, Boniface (see his *Letters* above, p. 121) died in 754, while Widukind's baptism took place at Attigny in 785.

8 See 1 Tim. 2: 4.

9 The author may mean to draw a parallel here between Widukind and St. Paul, who also "persecuted the church of God" (1 Cor. 15: 9) before becoming an apostle.

10 Enger, in northeastern Westfalia, was the site of a monastery founded by Mathilda sometime between 936 and the summer of 947. Widukind's role in Enger's early history is uncertain.

Among his descendants, after their submission to the Christian religion, was Mathilda's father Dietrich, whose wife was Reinhild, a most noble woman of Frisian and Danish stock. The maiden, who entered the monastery of Herford not in order to become a nun, but to receive literary training as well as instruction in handicrafts, grew in nobility and virtue in the company of her father's mother, who after becoming a widow had performed so many good works there that she was made ruler and abbess over the nuns. The beauty of Mathilda's father and grandfather were revealed in her as well, and with her lovely face, adorable behavior as a child, dedication to her labors, modest disposition, humility, and generosity, she earned so much praise for a child of her age, with God's benevolent support,[1] that none could surpass her.

2. When Duke Otto learned of this, he sent Count Thietmar, the young Henry's tutor, to see whether the maiden was as beautiful and praiseworthy as he had been told. When Thietmar saw that she was well-suited for a noble marriage and was the future hope of the people, he returned and reported all that he had learned. Upon hearing this, Henry's father ordered his son together with Thietmar and other military retainers to set out for the monastery. Upon their arrival, a few men disguised themselves as common folk and came into the chapel, where they spied a maiden with a face both modest and fair.[2] They left the town, returned in royal garb, and entered "with an ample throng in tow,"[3] before approaching the abbess and begging her to bring out the maiden for whom they had come. She appeared before them, her snowy cheeks touched with ruddy fire; like white lilies woven with blushing roses were the hues which her face revealed.[4]

As soon as Henry saw her and understood the situation completely, he "fastened his gaze upon the maiden"[5] and so burned with love for her that he would brook no delay in their betrothal. Early the next morning, unbeknownst to any of her relatives save for her grandmother, who was the abbess there, and secretly, without the joyful sounds of the cymbal and the pipe,[6] she was conveyed in honor to Henry's homeland by a select company of princes. At Wallhausen a wedding feast was prepared, one befitting persons of such noble and eventually royal status.[7] There at last they enjoyed a lawful love,[8] and Henry gave her as her dower the town and all that belonged to it.

Duke Otto, Henry's father, died three years later.[9] The leading men of the kingdom took counsel together and discussed who should assume this heroic position. Mindful of the services which he had rendered before, they chose Otto's son as duke, for he was the most accomplished warrior among all the Saxons. His unusually deep love of charity so pleased the people and bound them to him that they hoped he might become king. Not long afterwards, it happened that King Conrad of the Franks[10] passed away (whether in time of war or of peace, we do not know), and Henry received his scepter and all the resources of the kingdom.[11]

3. After all of the events which we have described, the Saxons now were blessed with a king and received great honor on account of the rule of men whose like they had never experienced. O Germany, once bowed

---

1 "God's benevolent support" was a very common phrase in official royal and imperial acts of the time.
2 See Terence, *Andria*, lines 119-20.
3 Virgil, *Aeneid* 2. 40.
4 Ibid., 12. 65-69.
5 Ibid., 12. 70.
6 See Ps. 150: 4-5.
7 Wallhausen, in the valley of the Helme river approximately 50 miles west of Leipzig, was a Frankish settlement since Merovingian times and became an important base for the Saxon dukes in the ninth century.
8 A wry adaptation of Virgil, *Aeneid* 8. 468.
9 Duke Otto died at Wallhausen on November 30, 912; Henry and Mathilda's marriage thus took place in 909.
10 This is a reference to Conrad's Franconian origins.
11 Conrad I died on December 23, 918. Henry I was king 919 to 936.

under the yoke of other peoples but now raised up in imperial splendor, love your king by faithfully serving him, and to the best of your abilities strive to help him; do not stop hoping that his posterity will abound in princes, lest you be stripped of every trapping of honor and return to your former servility! The afore-mentioned Henry, who had received the kingdom, now ascended ever higher, using his martial prowess to overpower the great peoples around him—Slavs, Danes, Bavarians, and Bohemians—which never had been under Saxon rule. Is it any wonder that he defeated every enemy and attained this glorious vic-tory, since he offered constant thanks to the greatest of victors and heavenly king, spending large sums for the repair of churches? He was generous to the poor, protected widows and the oppressed, paid his soldiers their due, and ruled over the rest piously, peaceably, and temperately.

Now although Mathilda was happily married to an earthly ruler and had acquired temporal power, she sought after obedience to God rather than the exalta-tion that comes with worldly glory. Submissive at all times to God and heedful of priestly advice, she was Christ's partner more than her husband's companion.[1] During the night, she would find some way to leave the king's side and sneak off to the church, for she loved prayer more than her husband's bed.[2] Who would believe how she poured herself out in prayer while the king was away, or how she would cling to Christ's feet as though he were there with her,[3] from the cock's first crow until dawn's first light on the 'morrow?[4] She loved Christ not only in her words but in her deeds as well. If, as often happened, someone was brought to trial for committing a crime and was condemned to death by the king, the most holy queen would take pity upon his suffering, softening the

prince's heart with flattering words until the king's wrath, which had produced a sentence of death, was won over by the voice of salvation.[5]

4. Let us not leave aside her outstanding offspring, both women and men, who all attained honor and the highest renown. Otto was the eldest, named af-ter his grandfather; milder than the others and more modest in character, he was warmly embraced by the people, assuming kingdom and crown after the death of his father. He took a royal wife named Edith from among the Anglo-Saxons, one both beautiful and of outstanding virtue.[6] Henry, the second-born, was set over the Bavarians as their splendid leader.[7] It befell Brun, who although the youngest was a wise, dignified, and priestly man, to be appointed arch-bishop of Cologne.[8] Their sister Gerberga was given in marriage to Giselbert, the prince of the Belgians.[9] The king and his most worthy wife became ever more fervent in their love of God; they looked after Christ's servants, and every year that they lived, they made countless gifts to every monastery on their itinerary, and sent generous sums of money to those they did not visit. Besides their dedication to such efforts, they also heeded divine counsel and devoted themselves to the construction of monasteries. When they spoke with the leaders of the army about their wishes in this regard, the latter immediately sug-gested to the king that he could transfer to Quedlin-burg nuns who were cloistered at Wendhausen, since there were daughters from leading families living there whose kinfolk were unhappy to have them remain amidst so much poverty.

After this conversation, the king went on his usual hunting excursion to Botfeld, and there was afflicted with a serious illness. When his condition grew more

---

1 See Venantius Fortunatus, *Life of Radegund* 3, above, p. 48.
2 Ibid., 5, above, p. 49.
3 Ibid., 6, above, p. 49.
4 A passage reminiscent of Virgil, *Aeneid* 4.118-19.
5 See Fortunatus, *Life of Radegund* 10, above, p. 50.
6 Edith (Eadgifu) was the daughter of King Edward the Elder (r.899-924) of Wessex, and sister of Kings Æthelstan and Edmund. Her marriage to Otto took place in 929.
7 Henry was born in 919. He received the duchy of Bavaria in November 947, after the death of Duke Berthold.
8 Brun was born in 925 and became archbishop in 953.
9 Gerberga was Henry and Mathilda's second child, born sometime between 913 and 917. In 929, she married Duke Giselbert of Lotharingia, and after his death in 939, became the wife of Louis IV D'Outremer, king of the West Franks (r.936-954).

dire and he realized that death was imminent, he went on to Erfurt, and after ordering all those subject to his rule to join him there, he convened an assembly to address the condition of the kingdom. The abbess of the aforesaid convent[1] also came by command of the king. He and his partner had not forgotten their earlier wishes, and asked the abbess to have God's aforementioned handmaidens transferred to Quedlinburg. She graciously listened to their request and, persuaded by many of the leading men, agreed that things should be done as the king decreed. When the assembly was over and the people had returned home, the king traveled to Memleben with a few companions, and at God's command departed this present life. A vast crowd gathered for his funeral, and with great lamentation followed his body on its way to Quedlinburg, where it was buried with due honor. Then the queen, unswayed in her desire to see her wishes carried out, urged that the girls be brought there. At first, the abbess steadfastly refused to allow this. But what more do we need to say? The queen, with the aid of her son King Otto and the other leading men, fulfilled her vow and established the monastery, devoting her every thought to how its needs might best be met.[2]

5. After the death of the venerable King Henry, when his eldest son Otto occupied the royal throne, the queen proved to be such a virtuous widow that few members of either sex could hope to imitate her. She was wise in her counsel, exceedingly gentle to the good and harsh to the arrogant, generous in her almsgiving, single-minded in her prayers, pious to all the needy, and mild in her speech; her love for God and neighbor as well as her chastity remained unsullied. Nonetheless, the instigator of all evil, the jealous enemy, appeared to some of the leading men and spurred them to tell the king and her other sons that she possessed more riches than was fitting. In accordance with the demands of insatiable greed, which does not spare even its own,[3] they pressed her to hand over the hidden heaps of treasure which she used to support churches and paupers in Christ's name. Carefully hunting hither and yon, they ordered search parties to scour mountains and valleys, forests and glades for those places through which, so they claimed, the queen sent her wealth to monasteries. If they found her servants bearing some precious item (since God's beloved secretly strove to place whatever remained to her in Christ's hands), they heaped abuse upon them, forcibly seized what they were carrying, and left them empty handed.

By means of these as well as other, more serious affronts, they drove her to abandon that portion of the kingdom which belonged to her dower, enter a monastery, and take up the sacred veil. Yet even as she was beset with such great afflictions, she never forgot the holy scripture which teaches that "it is through many tribulations that we must enter the kingdom of God";[4] thus she relinquished the towns given to her in marriage,[5] returned to her patrimony, and entered the monastery of Enger in the lands to the west. There she continued, no less than before, in her customary good works. Many blows rained down upon King Otto in retribution for what had happened to his mother, as his triumphant victories turned into defeats and his other affairs suffered in turn. The grace of the Holy Spirit truly dwelt in the king's mother, Mathilda, and she possessed abundant love in Christ.

6. Now when the king saw that the good fortune of earlier days was no more, he was greatly saddened and became deathly afraid. Queen Edith, of blessed memory, came in to see him and said, "Do not mourn, my lord king! You have been scourged by God for driving your esteemed mother from the kingdom as if she were a stranger. Therefore, this most holy woman must be asked back and, as is only fitting, she must occupy the first place in the kingdom." When the prince heard this, he was at first stunned and then filled with the utmost joy. He dispatched his bishops, magnates, and other distinguished followers to bring back his

---

1 I.e., Wendhausen.
2 The convent of St. Servatius at Quedlinburg was founded in 936, within the fortified hilltop complex build by Henry I. One of Otto I's first acts as king was to place it under royal protection and grant it immunity from outside secular or ecclesiastical interference, as well as place the convent of Wendhausen under Quedlinburg's control.
3 See Prudentius, *Psychomachia*, lines 478-79.
4 Acts 14: 22.
5 Henry had given Mathilda, as part of her dower, the royal estates of Pöhlde, Quedlinburg, and Nordhausen.

most worthy mother, dedicating himself and every-thing he possessed to this end, and declaring that he would gladly accept any conditions she imposed, so long as he ultimately regained her favor. His mother accepted his demands joyfully, as if she had forgotten all that had taken place, and quickly made her way back to Grone.[1] There the king together with his wife met her, prostrated himself at her feet, and promised to change his ways however she pleased. With tears glistening upon her lovely cheeks,[2] however, she em-braced her son, kissed him, and assured him that her sins were to blame for all that had happened. Apolo-gies accepted, he immediately returned the portion of the kingdom given to her in marriage, so that peace might be restored. While these loving bonds were enduring ones, it came to pass that the pious Queen Edith departed this present life for an everlasting one.[3] The king, who now was advanced in years,[4] joined his mother in the construction of churches and monas-teries, maintaining peace, judging with fairness, and imitating his father's piety in every way.

7. Meanwhile, news reached King Otto's ears that Louis, the renowned king of the Latins, had died, and that Queen Adelheid, his most noble wife, was suffering mightily on account of a certain Berengar's attempt to seize the kingdom and take Italy for him-self by force. King Otto, swayed by the advice of his leading men, put his affairs in order and gathered his comrades for an expedition into Latium, where he snatched up the queen after a triumphant victory and brought her back in honor to his homeland.[5] They were joined in lawful matrimony and ruled over the kingdom, and produced splendid children of both sexes. The king committed his daughter Mathilda, named after her grandmother, to the nuns at the convent of Quedlinburg, thus fulfilling his excellent mother's wishes.[6] While he was still quite young, and his father had many more years to live, Otto, who was named for his father, was preordained to become king, just as the blessed Mathilda had prophesied.[7] For whenever a royal child was born and news of it reached her ears, she would say, "Thanks be to God." But when the messenger told her of this boy's birth, she knelt down, called together all those who served God in that place, and ordered them to sing hymns of praise to God and ring the church bells. She then commended the newborn boy to the heavenly king and prayed that his life would be a prosperous one, saying, "This one will do remarkable things, and will be more illustrious than any of his forebears."

8. Let us now return to Mathilda's good deeds, which would require us to produce an immense volume if we tried to recount them all; yet, while all cannot be included here, we also cannot allow all to remain hidden.[8] As her life became ever more dedicated to God, and she progressed "from virtue to virtue,"[9] she established a community of canons at Pöhlde, thus in-creasing the number of monasteries.[10] After that, with

---

1 In the valley of the Leine, approximately three miles west of modern-day Göttingen.
2 See Virgil, *Aeneid* 12. 64-65.
3 Edith died on January 16, 946 and was buried in the cathedral church at Magdeburg, an establishment which she had pa-tronized and which was founded on land that was part of her dower.
4 Otto was 33 years old at Edith's death.
5 Adelheid's husband was actually Lothar, son and co-ruler over Italy with Hugh of Provence. Berengar II (d.964) was the margrave of Ivrea, in what is now northwestern Italy. Long opposed to Hugh, he gained the support of Otto I in the 940s and invaded Hugh's kingdom in 945, eventually seizing the throne after Lothar's death in 950. Otto I, already hostile to Berengar's seizure of the Italian throne, responded to appeals by Adelheid and her supporters and descended with an army into Italy in 951. By October of that year, he and Adelheid were married, and he was crowned king of Italy with the ap-proval of the local magnates before returning to Germany with his new wife in the spring of 952. Later that year, Berengar was allowed to regain his crown after acknowledging Otto's overlordship.
6 Mathilda was born early in 955 and became abbess of Quedlinburg in 966.
7 This was Otto II, born late in 955. He was made co-ruler with his father in a ceremony at Aachen in 961.
8 See Sulpicius Severus, *Letter to Eusebius*.
9 Ps. 84: 7; Douay Ps. 83: 7.
10 Pöhlde, one of the estates given to Mathilda by Henry, was in the valley of the Oder River, on the southwestern edge of the Harz mountains.

her support another congregation of brothers arose in the valley at Quedlinburg,[1] as well as a convent on the hill there and another convent nearby at Gernrode.[2] In addition, while she built many monasteries, she devoutly aided not only those who served God in the cloisters, but also all those who were in need. For besides the twice-daily meal for the gathered multitude of the poor, on whom she bestowed royal refreshment, she made sure to provide pilgrims and paupers with baths every Saturday. She would wash each woman's limbs, sometimes doing so herself, while at other times sending her followers when she wished to avoid the crowd. She then would give each person not only the customary ration of food, but also a gift of clothing as they departed.[3] Indeed, her merciful acts were always equal to the needs of the throng before her: while there always were people seeking her aid, she always had something to give them.[4] When she was about to sit down to one of her three daily meals, and delicacies of every kind had been brought to the table, if she was visiting a monastery she would not eat until everything had been shared with Christ's servants there. If she was not at a monastery, however, she would prolong her fast until the same had been done for her sickly guests and servants.[5]

9. We should not forget to mention that wherever she was, she always kept fires burning throughout the night, not only indoors but also in the open air, for the benefit of all those present.[6] The holy woman also was in the habit of carrying candles with her on every trip, whether it was a short or a lengthy one, so that she might distribute them to each chapel on her way; likewise, she kept a supply of food in her carriage, so that she might feed the sick and needy along the way.

When sleep crept over her as she rode in the carriage (for she was wont to spend sleepless nights in prayerful vigils), if she crossed paths with some unfortunate soul, and the nun sitting across from her named Ricburg—first among all those who served her—failed either through inattention, or because she was asleep, or because she was poring over a book, to care for the pauper and to wake her mistress, the queen immediately would awaken, chide her beloved servant with salubrious words, order the carriage to stop, and attend to the pauper whom she had passed by. What more needs to be said? On account of such good deeds she nearly acquired the virgin's distinction, save only for the trappings of worldly splendor with which she was covered.[7] Never indeed was there a day, not even an hour, which found her idle in relaxation, uninvolved in good works. Even on feast days when she was free not to read, she occupied herself either by reading or by listening to others do the same. On weekdays, when work is permitted, she would perform handiwork while engaged in prayer or singing psalms, which she always did. If she was occupied all day long with her numerous public dealings—as happens to those who oversee the earthly kingdom—she would at least stand before the table at mealtime and perform some task before eating, reflecting upon it and saying, "Whoever does not wish to work should not eat."[8]

10. Engaged in these blessed activities, the queen made such progress, by divine favor, that God allowed her to shine with the light of miracles.[9] One day in the town of Quedlinburg, while standing on top of the hill, she saw a crowd of poor people eating in the valley below. She asked her servant if bread had

---

1   This refers to the canonry of Saints Wigbert and James, which occupied the site of Henry I's first fortified settlement at Quedlinburg.
2   Gernrode, about four miles south of Quedlinburg, at the edge of the Harz mountains, was in fact founded by the east Saxon margrave Gero. Its first abbess, Gero's recently widowed daughter-in-law, Hadwig, was Mathilda's niece.
3   See Fortunatus, *Life of Radegund* 17, above, p. 51.
4   Ibid., 16, above, p. 51.
5   Ibid., 17, above, p. 51.
6   Ibid., 7, above, p. 49.
7   The point here seems to be that Mathilda's good works likened her, although a married woman and mother, to a consecrated virgin.
8   2 Thess. 3: 10.
9   See Fortunatus, *Life of Radegund* 11, above, p. 50.

been provided for them along with the other food, to which he responded, "Not at all." At this, as though angry at her almsgiver, she snatched up a loaf of bread, made the sign of the cross on it with her hand, called upon the Lord's name (as she always did), and threw the bread from the peak. Tumbling over the boulders and thickets it landed, unbroken, in the lap of one of the paupers below. Those who were there and saw this marvelled, declaring that this had come to pass through divine power.[1]

She also illuminated the same city with another miracle. When she had made her offering to God in the church, a certain faithful pet deer which lived within the cloister sneaked up and swallowed a small wine bottle of the sort normally found in monasteries. The stunned bystanders tried to retrieve the bottle from the beast, beating it, threatening it, and clapping their hands, but all in vain. Finally God's worthy queen held out her hand to the beast's mouth and said, in a soothing voice, "Give back what you took—it's ours." As soon as she spoke the deer vomited up the bottle which it had swallowed. Who can doubt that on account of her merits the heavenly overlord gave human understanding to an animal?[2] Indeed, the Lord did many things through her which, if each of them could be described here, would appear wondrous. Nevertheless, the virtues within her shone brighter than the signs and wonders without.

11. Meanwhile, after the pope had called King Otto to Rome to accept the imperial crown (which, we believe, was divinely ordained), he set out to acquire Italy, which Queen Adelheid previously had owned as her bridal portion.[3] Therefore, after committing the kingdom to his son Otto, he gathered together stout-hearted men and departed together with his wife.[4] With Christ leading him, this most outstanding victor attacked Latium, by force of arms captured Berengar, who had usurped the kingdom of the Latins, and ordered him and his entire family to be sent off to Bavaria. The emperor then was crowned with his wife at the cathedral of St. Peter, took possession of the Roman empire, and ruled with absolute power over the "cities of Ausonia."[5]

It is certain, during those days when the king first ventured into Italy, that his mother, seized by hope as well as fear, offered up constant prayers to God on her son's behalf, a singular sacrifice meant to please the greatest of warriors[6] and assure victory for her child. After careful consideration she resolved[7] to build a monastery in Nordhausen, and with the consent of her grandson, the younger Otto, she gathered a congregation of sisters there to ensure her own well-being and that of those close to her, both in body and in soul. She built it from the ground up, and like a mother always lavished the greatest care upon it, providing whatever was needed there as long as she remained on this earth.[8]

Now, when the emperor's conquest of Latium was complete, he returned to his homeland and proceeded to Cologne, where his brother Brun ruled as archbishop. He ordered that his mother be brought to him there, together with his son the king and the lovely maiden.[9] Queen Gerberga, his sister, also came, as did

---

1 The author's model here is Gregory the Great's account in his *Dialogues* of a similar miracle (involving oil rather than bread) performed by St. Benedict.

2 See Sulpicius Severus, *Dialogues* 1:14, the story of a wolf which steals bread from a hermit before returning to seek his forgiveness.

3 The pope was John XII (r.955-64). Otto left for Italy in 961. When the author speaks of acquiring "Italy," he is referring to the northern and central regions of modern-day Italy, which had long been under Carolingian rule.

4 As Otto II was only six years old, affairs in Germany were in fact entrusted to William, Otto I's illegitimate son and archbishop of Mainz from 954 to 968.

5 Virgil, *Aeneid* 7. 104-5. The chronology here is confused. Otto and Adelheid's imperial coronation took place in February 962, while it was not until late in 963 that Berengar and his wife Willa were defeated and sent into captivity at Bamberg, where Berengar died in 966.

6 Josh. 10: 2; but here the phrase is applied to God.

7 An echo of Virgil, *Aeneid* 11. 551.

8 Nordhausen, in northern Thuringia at the edge of the Harz mountains, was one of the properties given to Mathilda by Henry I as her dower.

9 I.e., Otto II and his sister Mathilda.

all of the royal progeny of both sexes, who we believe were brought together through God's benevolence so that they might gaze with love upon one another. Indeed, after this meeting they never saw each other again in this life.[1] But the esteemed mother and queen, Mathilda, pleased with the great leaders she had borne, was received in honor first by the emperor, then by all of her offspring. She joyfully embraced and looked upon each of her grandchildren,[2] rejoicing and offering special thanks to God that her son the emperor had arrived safely and in such glory. She then explained to him in detail what she had done concerning the monastery, and how afraid she was of leaving incomplete the work which she had begun, afraid that she would leave the congregation which she had joined late in life alone and abandoned after her death, and that she would not be able to see to other monasteries which she had already finished. At this the king, burning with love for God and his neighbor, acknowledged gratefully that his victories were due to her merits, and soothed his mother's mind, asking that "she not fashion such fears for him."[3] He swore that he and his posterity would never cease to support the monastery, and with these words he soothed the *domina* [lordly lady]. After traveling through Saxony, they arrived at the town of Nordhausen and the monastery there;[4] whatever the mother or his son the king[5] had given before, he now increased, and he granted the monastery its possessions in lasting perpetuity with a charter subscribed by his own hand. Afterwards he remained for a time in those parts, traveling through the other towns and ruling over his people, until at last he set out for Rome accompanied by his son....

[The narrative continues with an account of Mathilda's preparations for death: she distributed her wealth and gave counsel to her granddaughter, the abbess of Quedlinburg.]

15. After her death, messengers carrying letters entered Italy, where her son the emperor Otto ruled over public affairs in Latium, "a man whose whole life would have deserved praise, if only he could have refused a crown offered to him amidst military turmoil rather than through legitimate means, or could have refrained from the use of armed force. But without armed force, one cannot hold onto a great empire."[6] Yet "neither the wealth of the kingdom, nor imperial glory, nor the crown, nor purple vestments" could tear him away from service to Christ.[7] The legates, as we have said, entered the king's palace where he sat upon his lofty throne. When "leave to speak was granted them,"[8] they opened their letters and announced that his mother had died. Upon hearing these words he was deeply shaken; his face grew pale and "flowed with tears as he wept mightily,"[9] driven by the love which he had for his mother. He then confirmed that he would do everything that his mother had asked. Indeed, he fulfilled this promise immediately, handing over to Nordhausen both that part of his mother's bridal portion lying in the western regions, as well as the privilege given by the Roman pontiff, just as the *domina* herself had requested. He remained for a time in Ausonia [Italy], until his son Otto the younger had been given a wife from Greece, a princess from the imperial palace with the noble name of Theophanu, along with countless amounts of treasure.[10] And once he had had both adorned with the imperial title,[11] he returned to his Saxon homeland together with his spouse, accompanied by his son and the latter's wife.

---

1 This is a reference to Brun's death in October of the same year.
2 This is an echo of Virgil's description of Cybele embracing her divine offspring: *Aeneid* 6. 784–86.
3 See Virgil, *Aeneid* 7. 438.
4 The chronology here is misleading. The visit to Nordhausen took place a year later.
5 "His son the king" refers to Otto II.
6 Sulpicius Severus, *Dialogues* 2. 6.
7 Ibid. This curious juxtaposition of passages from Sulpicius, describing, respectively, the Western Roman emperor Maximus (imperial usurper, 383–388) and his wife, likely was meant to criticize Otto's violent Italian campaign of 966–967 while still praising him as a personally pious ruler.
8 Virgil, *Aeneid* 1. 520.
9 Sulpicius Severus, *Letter to Aurelius*.
10 Theophanu was the niece of Emperor John Tzimisces.
11 In fact, Otto II had already been made co-emperor with his father in 967.

16. At Eastertide he arrived in Quedlinburg, where his father and mother were buried. He was received with honor by the people who lined his route, and remained there during those most holy days. After his departure he was taken ill, and travelled to Memleben. During his stay there he was brought into the chapel, and as he listened to the divine praises at Vespers (for he always loved the churches as well as service to God), he released his spirit into the care of the angels.[1] Therefore, after his death his most excellent son, the younger Otto, took possession of the kingdom of the Latins and the Saxons. We believe that he will equal his father and grandfather in virtue and strength, with the help of our Lord Jesus Christ, who lives and reigns for ever and ever. Amen.

4.14 An Ottonian king: Thietmar of Merseberg, *The Accession of Henry II* (1013-1018). Original in Latin.

THIETMAR OF MERSEBERG (975-1018) came from a prominent Saxon family. Educated in the classics (especially Virgil) and Christian texts at Magdeburg, Thietmar was a learned product of the Ottonian Renaissance, groomed to serve the king as well as to preside in high church office. In 1009, he became bishop of Merseberg, a key bishopric created by the Ottonian house to strengthen its control of its eastern border. Thietmar was an eyewitness to many of the events he recounted in his *Chronicon*, and, as the excerpt below on the accession of Henry II (r.1002-1024) demonstrates, members of his family were closely connected to the plots and plans that led to the crowning of the new king. How did the Ottonian court compare with the Byzantine around this time, as revealed by Michael Psellus in his account of Basil II (above, p. 227)? How have the conditions and ideals of Western rulership changed since the time of Charlemagne (as in the poem *Once Again my Burdened Anchor*, above, p. 177)?

[Source: *Ottonian Germany: The Chronicon of Thietmar of Merseburg*, trans. David A. Warner (Manchester: Manchester University Press, 2001), pp. 205-11, 213 (slightly modified).]

Book five

PROLOGUE

After conquering infancy, Henry,
sprung from a lineage of kings, ascended the heights
    of valor.
Duke Henry was his father and his mother was Gisela
who added to her good qualities the imprint of a king,
namely her father, Conrad, who held the Burgundian
    realms.
The brilliant pupil was nourished by Bishop
    Wolfgang[2]
who followed the Lord Christ with every effort.
After the death of his father, he succeeded him as
    duke and as his heir.
At a distance, he also contemplated the government
    of the empire.
The greater part of the realm, wasted by the cruel
    Slav,[3]
rejoiced exceedingly because, by his peace and
    justice,
he made himself master of the desired seats,[4]
with high-born bandits thoroughly repulsed and
    restrained by a harsh law.

---

1 Otto died on May 7, 973. His body was later taken to Magdeburg (notably, the resting place of his first wife) and buried there.

2 Bishop Wolfgang of Regensburg (r.972–94). Educated at Reichenau and Würzburg, Wolfgang had been head of the school at Trier and Einsiedeln prior to his appointment as bishop. His pupils included various members of the Bavarian ducal house, including Henry II's brother Bruno and sister Gisela.

3 A reference to Slavic raids into Germany.

4 Virgil, *Aeneid* 6. 203, a reference to the place where Aeneas found the golden bough.

He crushed every enemy who rose against him
while soothing all his allies with agreeable talk.
If he lacked moderation in anything, he immediately
   recovered
and saw to the wounds of the flesh with worthy
   fruits.
Helpful to the church, he was compassionate to all,
   everywhere.
Merseburg, if you knew his pious vows,
you would long for the arrival of such a great
   ruler,
praising the renowned gifts of Christ
and bestowing worthy rewards.

CHAPTER ONE

The stream of divine grace, overflowing to human needs by the free gift of God's compassion and not by our own merit, inspires the hearts of the faithful to offer loving praise and thanks to him. It also compels me, slow-witted by nature, clumsy in speech, and both negligent and overly hasty in all things, to imitate good people in this. God is great, as David testified, and very praiseworthy; no one can discover the extent of his wisdom which created everything out of nothing and also formed man.[1] Whoever, unmindful, does not reflect on such things is justly called an animal rotting in its own waste. But whoever well retains the word *gnoti seaucton*, written in ancient times on the lintels of the temple,[2] and troubles himself to fulfil all things which in words or deeds are to be done in the name of the Lord, as St Paul advises: he is the one who was chosen by God the Father for the Son, receiving his payment for the day although he had arrived late.[3] Considering these things, because I can scarcely respond to the Holy Trinity and the indivisible unity with a worthy repayment, I, a supplicant, implore the intercession of John the Baptist that in body and heart I might be worthy to offer this.[4]

CHAPTER TWO

With a happier mind and a more expansive pen I will write about the time in which God looked upon our church and deigned to remove its shame and I will disclose the piety of Duke Henry who was elected king according to the divine will. Concerning that, after the death of Otto III, a certain venerable father had a revelation from heaven. A voice said to him: "Do you recall, brother, how the people sang, 'Duke Henry wants to rule, but God is unwilling'?[5] Now, however, Henry must provide for the care of the kingdom by the divine will." Everything pertaining to divine or human matters promoted him to the kingdom before others contemporary with him, whether they were willing or not. I will describe with a few words those who opposed him from our region. Then, I will relate the iniquitous presumption of the West which neither by council, nor prudence, nor strength could prevail against God.[6]

CHAPTER THREE [1002]

Herman, Duke of Swabia and Alsace, was a God-fearing and humble man. Seduced by many who were pleased by his mildness, he armed himself against Henry,[7] Duke Dietrich of Lotharingia, a wise man experienced in warfare, to whom the larger and better part of the people would incline, waited confidently.[8] Meanwhile my father's brother, whom I mentioned above, traveled secretly to Bamberg with his uncle Rikbert. Otto III had deposed Rikbert from his countship, which he then gave to Liudger, a *miles*[9] of Bishop Arnulf. With his nephew Henry's help, he received the duke's favor and the hope of retaining and

---

1   Ps. 96: 4; Douay Ps. 95: 4; 2 Macc. 7: 28.
2   I.e., 'gnotis eaucton,' or "know thyself" (Macrobius, *Saturnalia* 1. 6. 6). Thietmar divided the two words in the wrong place because he didn't know Greek.
3   Col. 3: 17; Matt. 20: 1–16.
4   John the Baptist was patron of the first church at Merseburg.
5   Reference to the efforts of Henry the Quarrelsome, the father of Henry II, to seize the throne from the infant Otto III.
6   Prov. 21: 30.
7   Thietmar consistently attributes greater legitimacy to Duke Henry, emphasizing his regal qualities, especially his lineage, and noting the unkingly qualities of his rivals Ekkehard and Herman.
8   Duke Dietrich of Upper Lotharingia (r.978–1026/27).
9   See the comments on the translation of this word (warrior, knight, vassal) above, p. 239, n. 2.

increasing his benefice. Nevertheless, he preserved his oath by not doing homage.[1] On Liuthar's advice, the duke dispatched a certain *miles* to Werla where his nieces, the sisters Sophia and Adelheid, and all the great men of the realm had convened.[2] He revealed his commission to the whole assembly and promised many good things to those who helped his lord obtain the throne. The majority immediately responded with one voice: Henry should rule with the aid of Christ and by hereditary right, and they were prepared to be supportive in all that he asked of them. They affirmed this with their right hands raised.

CHAPTER FOUR [1002]

Along with his following, Ekkehard was not present but subsequently pretended to be in agreement because, as it is written, whatever sin is committed by many is unpunished.[3] Nevertheless, in the evening, when benches decorated with hangings and a table filled with various dishes had been prepared in the palace for the already-mentioned ladies, Ekkehard commandeered it and dined with Bishop Arnulf and Duke Bernhard.[4] Before the fall the heart will be exalted and before the glory it will be humiliated.[5] Ekkehard's actions greatly agitated the two sisters, who were already sorrowful, and many others who were present. Likewise, the long-concealed animosity towards the margrave was renewed and, alas, would quickly find an end.[6] For then, seeing that everything had turned out differently from what was expected,

he thought it wiser to resort to the western regions where he could speak to Duke Herman and other leading men regarding the realm and its welfare. The next day, he bade farewell to his friends, carefully noted his enemies, and accompanied Bishop Bernward to Hildesheim where he was received as king and treated with honor.

CHAPTER FIVE [1002]

Then, coming to Paderborn, he found the doors closed. After being admitted by order of Bishop Rethar, he first went to the church to pray, and then went to the episcopal residence where the bishop was dining, and was kindly received.[7] There, he was informed that the meeting in Duisburg, which had been the reason for his coming, would not take place. Moreover, he noticed that much of his unsuitable plan displeased the bishop. Leaving because of this, he journeyed to Northeim, a *curtis* [an estate] belonging to Count Siegfried, where he was warmly received and invited to stay the night. The Countess Ethelind secretly informed him that Sigifrith and Benno, her husband's sons, were plotting with the brothers Henry and Udo and other conspirators to ambush and kill him. She humbly beseeched him to remain there until the next day or else go in another direction. The margrave accepted this news in a kindly manner but responded that he neither could nor wished to interrupt the course of his journey. Setting out from there, he watched his companions the whole day through and, as he was the best of warriors,

---

1   Thietmar refers to the oath which Thietmar's uncle and other Saxon lords had sworn at Frohse, namely that they would not give allegiance to any candidate for the throne prior to meeting together at Werla.

2   Thietmar refers to the daughters of Otto II. Adelheid (b.977) was abbess at Quedlinburg (999–1045), at Gernrode and Vreden (from 1014), and at Gandersheim (from 1039). Sophia (b.978) was abbess at Gandersheim (1002–1039) and Essen (from 1011).

3   Augustine, *Letter* no. 137.

4   The absence of a male heir made the princesses the most visible representatives of the Ottonian house. It has been suggested that Ekkehard's provocative actions were intended to demonstrate that direct descent from the traditional ruling house was no longer a prerequisite for the throne.

5   Prov. 18: 12.

6   The reference to a "long-concealed hatred" is somewhat unclear but probably should be associated with incidents such as Ekkehard's reneging on an agreement to marry his daughter to the son of Margrave Liuthar and his feud with Archbishop Giselher of Magdeburg. It may well have been Ekkehard's arrogant behavior towards his peers (or towards those who believed that they were such) that prevented his being elected king in 1002.

7   Bishop Rethar of Paderborn (983–1009). Rethar was closely allied with Archbishop Willigis of Mainz, one of Henry II's strongest supporters. In limiting Ekkehard's reception essentially to what was due by general right of hospitality he made it plain that he opposed Ekkehard's plan. The regal reception accorded him by Bernward of Hildesheim clearly sent the opposite message.

admonished them not to be frightened. The enemy observed this at a distance, from their concealed ambushes. Because the circumstances appeared unfavorable, they decided to postpone their attack, confirming with raised hands that they would carry out the plot on the following night.

CHAPTER SIX [1002]

The count arrived at Pöhlde, his intended destination.[1] In the evening, he ate and bedded down with a few companions in a wooden sleeping chamber. Others, indeed just as many, slept near by in a loft. After the exhausted men fell asleep, the hostile band attacked, falling on the unwary. The excited clamor caused the count to quickly rise from his bed. With his own undergarments and whatever else he could find, he built up the fire and broke the windows. As he could not foresee, this worked more to his injury than his defense, because he thereby revealed an entry to his enemies. At once, the *miles* Herman was killed in front of the door, as was Athulf, who was outside, as he ran to help his lord. Each was brave and faithful unto death. Also, Erminold, Otto III's chamberlain, was wounded. Now Ekkehard, a man praiseworthy in both domestic and military matters, fought alone. With a strongly thrown javelin, Siegfried hit him in the neck and forced him to the ground. As soon as they realized that Ekkehard had fallen, all eagerly attacked, cutting off his head and, even more wretched, plundering his corpse. This was done on April 30th. Having carried out their savage crime, the attackers returned, happy and uninjured. Those cowards who were on the balcony neither helped their besieged lord nor attempted to avenge his death. Alfger, the abbot of the place, visited the corpse and commended Ekkehard's soul to God with the greatest devotion.

CHAPTER SEVEN [1002]

I cannot truly explain what persuaded them to undertake such a shameful deed. Some say that Henry had been flogged by the emperor at the count's instigation and that he often thought about this. Others say, as I have already suggested, that they did this because of the insult inflicted on the sisters at Werla whom they were glad to serve. Thus the plot was undertaken in response to the meal and to threats publicly uttered by Ekkehard. I know only this, he was the glory of the realm, the solace of the fatherland, the hope of subjects, and the terror of enemies, indeed he would have been perfect in all things if only he had wished to remain humble. The course of Ekkehard's life was so worthy that his lord allowed him to hold the greater part of his benefice as personal property. He forced the free-born Milzeni under the yoke of servitude. With flattery and threats, he won Duke Boleslav [III] of Bohemia, called "the Red," for his military service and turned the other Boleslav into a personal ally.[2] He acquired the office of duke over all of Thuringia by the election of the whole populace. With only a few exceptions, he reckoned on the support of the eastern counts and therefore of the duchy [of Saxony]. All of this came to such a miserable end....

CHAPTER ELEVEN [1002]

... At the beginning of June, Henry came to Worms with the leaders of the Bavarians and the eastern Franks with the intention of crossing the Rhine and proceeding to Mainz for his consecration. Duke Herman tried to prevent this and, with the Rhine favoring, offered him no entry. After consulting with his supporters, Henry went to [the monastery of] Lorsch where St. Nazarius rests, acting as if he had given up the idea of crossing the river and planned to return to Bavaria. And then, quickly going to Mainz, he crossed the Rhine in safety. At Mainz, on 6 June, Henry was unanimously elected king. Following his anointment, he was crowned by Willigis, archbishop of that see, with his suffragans [subordinate bishops] assisting and all in attendance praising God.[3] Then, the great men of the Franks [i.e., of Franconia] and the region of the Mosel commended themselves to the king and received his favor.

---

1 Location of a much visited royal residence and a monastic community in the region of the Harz mountains.
2 Boleslav III of Bohemia (r.999–1003, d.1037) and "the other Boleslav," Boleslav Chrobry of Poland.
3 It is important to note that these acts chiefly affected the aristocracies of Franconia and Upper Lotharingia. Henry still had to secure the acceptance of their counterparts in Lower Lotharingia, Thuringia, Saxony, and Swabia.

4.15 Literacy: King Alfred, *Prefaces* to Gregory the Great's *Pastoral Care* (*c.*890) Original in Old English.

ALFRED THE GREAT (r.871–899), THE king of Wessex, energetically beat back Viking invaders, promulgated a code of law that drew from all the others in England—thus establishing a "common" law—and undertook a program to translate major works of Latin into the vernacular, Anglo-Saxon (also known as Old English), so that everyone could understand them. The text below presents Alfred's twin prefaces to his translation of Gregory the Great's *Pastoral Care* (590), a handbook for bishops. What commonalities do you find in Alfred's attitudes towards books and those of Yaroslav the Wise as depicted in the *Russian Primary Chronicle* (p. 237 above)?

[Source: *Alfred the Great: Asser's* Life of King Alfred *and Other Contemporary Sources*, trans. Simon Keynes and Michael Lapidge (New York: Penguin Books, 1983), pp. 124–27, 294–96 (slightly modified).]

Prose Preface

King Alfred sends words of greeting lovingly and amicably to [...].[1]

And I would have it known that very often it has come to my mind what men of learning there were formerly throughout England, both in religious and secular orders; and how there were happy times then throughout England; and how the kings, who had authority over this people, obeyed God and his messengers; and how they not only maintained their peace, morality and authority at home but also extended their territory outside; and how they succeeded both in warfare and in wisdom; and also how eager were the religious orders both in teaching and in learning as well as in all the holy services which it was their duty to perform for God; and how people from abroad sought wisdom and instruction in this country; and how nowadays, if we wished to acquire these things, we would have to seek them outside.[2] Learning had declined so thoroughly in England that there were very few men on this side of the Humber who could understand their divine services in English, or even translate a single letter from Latin into English: and I suppose that there were not many beyond the Humber either. There were so few of them that I cannot recollect even a single one south of the Thames when I succeeded to the kingdom. Thanks be to God Almighty that we now have any supply of teachers at all! Therefore I beseech you to do as I believe you *are* willing to do: as often as you can, free yourself from worldly affairs so that you may apply that wisdom which God gave you wherever you can. Remember what punishments befell us in this world when we ourselves did not cherish learning nor transmit it to other men.[3] We were Christians in name alone, and very few of us possessed Christian virtues.

When I reflected on all this, I recollected how—before everything was ransacked and burned—the

---

1 It is probable that in Alfred's original, no name was given at this point, but that the name of the bishop to whom a particular copy was to be sent would be added as the copy was being made. If each bishop in Alfred's kingdom of Wessex were to receive a copy, at least ten would have been needed; and we may assume that other important monastic centers would have been sent copies as well.

2 Alfred is here alluding to his own activities in the 880s, when it was necessary to seek learned men from outside the kingdom of Wessex—from Mercia (to the north), Francia (across the English Channel), and Wales (to the west).

3 This is presumably a reference to the Viking invasions of the central decades of the ninth century; in common with many Christian authors before and after him, Alfred regarded the invasion of hostile peoples as a form of divine punishment for decadence and decay.

churches throughout England stood filled with treasures and books. Similarly, there was a great multitude of those serving God. And they derived very little benefit from those books, because they could understand nothing of them, since they were not written in their own language.[1] It is as if they had said: "Our ancestors, who formerly maintained these places, loved wisdom, and through it they obtained wealth and passed it on to us. Here one can still see their track, but we cannot follow it." Therefore we have now lost the wealth as well as the wisdom, because we did not wish to set our minds to the track.

When I reflected on all this, I wondered exceedingly why the good, wise men who were formerly found throughout England and had thoroughly studied all those books, did not wish to translate any part of them into their own language. But I immediately answered myself, and said: "They did not think that men would ever become so careless and that learning would decay like this; they refrained from doing it through this resolve, namely they wished that the more languages we knew, the greater would be the wisdom in this land." Then I recalled how the Law was first composed in the Hebrew language, and thereafter, when the Greeks learned it, they translated it all into their own language, and all other books as well. And so too the Romans, after they had mastered them, translated them all through learned interpreters into their own language. Similarly all the other Christian peoples turned some part of them into their own language.[2] Therefore it seems better to me—if it seems so to you—that we too should turn into the language that we can all understand certain books which are the most necessary for all men to know, and accomplish this, as with God's help we may very easily do provided we have peace enough, so that all the free-born young men now in England who have the means to apply themselves to it, may be set to learning (as long as they are not useful for some other employment) until the time that they can read English writings properly. Thereafter one may instruct in Latin those whom one wishes to teach further and wishes to advance to holy orders.

When I recalled how knowledge of Latin had previously decayed throughout England, and yet many could still read things written in English, I then began, amidst the various and multifarious afflictions of this kingdom, to translate into English the book which in Latin is called *Pastoralis*, in English "Shepherd-book,"[3] sometimes word for word, sometimes sense for sense, as I learnt it from Plegmund my archbishop, and from Asser my bishop, and from Grimbald my mass-priest and from John my mass-priest. After I had mastered it, I translated it into English as best I understood it and as I could most meaningfully render it; I intend to send a copy to each bishopric in my kingdom; and in each copy there will be an *Æstel* worth fifty mancuses.[4] And in God's name I command that no one shall take that *Æstel* from the book, nor the book from the church. It is not known how long there shall be such learned bishops as, thanks be to God, there are now nearly everywhere. Therefore I would wish that they [the book and the *Æstel*] always remain in place, unless the bishop wishes to have the book with him, or it is on loan somewhere, or someone is copying it.

Verse Preface
Augustine brought this work from the south over the salt sea to the island-dwellers, exactly as the Lord's champion, the pope of Rome, had previously set it out. The wise Gregory was well versed in many doctrines through his mind's intelligence, his hoard of ingenuity. Accordingly, he won over most of mankind to the guardian of the heavens, this greatest of Romans, most gifted of men, most celebrated for his glorious deeds.

---

1 The books were written in Latin.
2 There is no certainty about what translations Alfred is referring to here. The Bible was translated into Gothic by Ulfilas in the fourth century, but Alfred is unlikely to have known of this work. It is more likely that he knew of one of the translations made in Germany during the ninth century: a prose translation of the gospel story in East Franconian made at the monastery of Fulda *c*.830; a metrical version of the same gospel story in Old Saxon made during the decade 830-840, known as the *Heliand*; and a metrical version of the gospels in Rhenish Franconian made by the monk Otfrid of Weissenburg sometime between 863 and 871.
3 Today in English it is ordinarily known as *Pastoral Care*.
4 An *æstel* was a "book-mark." A *mancus* (pl.: *mancuses*) was a coin or a unit of value equal to 30 pennies.

King Alfred subsequently translated every word of me into English and sent me south and north to his scribes;[1] he commanded them to produce more such copies from the exemplar, so that he could send them to his bishops, because some of them who least knew Latin had need thereof.

4.16 Literature: *Battle of Maldon* (not long after 991). Original in Anglo-Saxon.

ONE OF THE REASONS WHY Alfred could imagine translating great works of literature into the vernacular—the common language of the people—was that Anglo-Saxon was already a written and highly literary language. However, it was a language of poetry; indeed, one of Alfred's achievements was to turn it into a language of prose as well. Many of the earliest surviving poems—such as *Beowulf* and *Deor*—were heroic epics that drew from a mythical past. Others, such as *The Wanderer*, were elegies. Christian elements were often woven into these early poems, but there were also some with fully Christian themes, such as the *Dream of the Rood*, which claimed to be the voice of the cross on which Christ was crucified. The *Battle of Maldon*, also known as *Byrhtnoth's Death*, was written not long after the historical event itself, a battle between the Danes and a local leader, Byrhtnoth, that took place at Maldon in 991. A less heroic account of the event would point out that the leader died, some men deserted, and the battle was lost. But the poet has a different story to tell. He has Byrhtnoth—proclaiming himself the defender of king and country—reject the Danes' offer to be bought off and rally his men to glorious battle. Due to a fire, the very beginning and end of the poem is lost; the rest is printed here (in translation) in full.

[Source: *The Battle of Maldon and Other Old English Poems*, trans. Kevin Crossley-Holland, ed. Bruce Mitchell (London: Macmillan/New York: St. Martin's Press, 1966), pp. 29-38.]

... it was shattered.
Then Byrhtnoth ordered every warrior to dismount,
Let loose his horse and go forward into battle
With faith in his own skills and bravery.
Thus Offa's young son could see for himself
That the earl was no man to suffer slackness.
He sent his best falcon flying from his wrist
To the safety of the forest and strode into the fight;
The boy's behavior was a testament
That he would not be weak in the turmoil of battle.
Eadric too was firmly resolved to follow his leader
Into the fight. At once he hurried forward
With his spear. He feared no foe
For as long as he could lift his shield
And wield a sword: he kept his word
That he would pierce and parry before his prince.

Then Byrhtnoth began to martial his men.
He rode about, issuing instructions
As to how they should stand firm, not yielding an
    inch,
And how they should tightly grip their shields
Forgetting their qualms and pangs of fear.
And when he had arrayed the warriors' ranks
He dismounted with his escort at a carefully chosen
    place
Where his finest troops stood prepared for the fight.
Then a spokesman for the Vikings stood on the river
    bank
And aggressively shouted
A message from the seafarers
To Byrhtnoth, the earl, on the opposite bank.
"The brave seafarers have sent me to say to you
That they will be so good as to let you give gold rings
In return for peace. It is better for you
To buy off our raid with gold
Than that we, renowned for cruelty, should cut you
    down in battle.

---

1   In Old English poetry, it is a common convention to have the book speak in the first person.

Why destroy one another? If you're good for a certain sum,
We'll settle for peace in exchange for gold.
If you, most powerful over there, agree to this
And wisely decide to disband your men,
Giving gold to the seafarers on their own terms
In return for a truce,
We'll take to the sea with the tribute you pay
And keep our promise of peace."

Then Byrhtnoth spoke. He grasped his shield
And brandished his slender ashen spear,
Resentful and resolute he shouted his reply:
"Can you hear, you pirate, what these people say?
They will pay you a tribute of whistling spears,
Of deadly darts and proven swords,
Weapons to pay you, pierce, slit and slay you in
    storming battle.
Listen, messenger! Take back this reply:
Tell your people the unpleasant tidings
That over here there stands a noble earl with his
    troop—
Guardians of the people and of the country,
The home of Æthelred, my prince—who'll defend
    this land
To the last ditch. We'll sever the heathens' heads
From their shoulders. It would be much to our shame
If you took our tribute and embarked without battle
Since you've intruded so far
And so rudely into this country.
No! You'll not get your treasure so easily.
The spear's point and the sword's edge, savage battle-
    play,
Must teach us first that we have to yield tribute."
Then Byrhtnoth gave word that all his warriors
    should walk
With their shields to the river bank.
The troops on either side could not get at one
    another,
For there the flood flowed after the turn of the tide;
The water streams ran together. Waiting seemed like
    passing years,
Waiting to cross and clash their spears.
The East-Saxons and the Ship-army
Stood beside the River Panta in proud array.
But no warrior could work harm on another
Except by the flight of a feathered arrow.

The tide ebbed; the pirates stood prepared,
Many bold Vikings ready for battle.
Then Byrhtnoth, brave protector of his men, ordered
A warrior, Wulfstan by name, to defend the ford.
He was Ceola's son, outstanding for his courage
    amongst courageous men.
He struck the first seafarer with his spear
Who fearlessly stepped onto the ford.
Two experienced warriors stood with Wulfstan,
Ælfere and Maccus, both brave men.
Nothing could have made them take flight at the
    ford.
They would have defended it
For as long as they could wield their weapons.
But as it was, the Danes found the dauntless guard-
    ians
Of the ford too fierce for their liking.…
The hateful strangers began to use guile
And asked if they could cross,
Leading their warriors over the water.
Then, in foolhardy pride, the earl permitted
Those hateful strangers to have access to the ford.
The son of Byrhthelm began to call out
Across the cold water (the warriors listened):
"Now the way is clear for you. Come over to us
    quickly,
Come to the slaughter. God alone can say
Who of us that fight today will live to fight again."

Then the wolvish Vikings, avid for slaughter,
Waded to the west across the River Panta;
The seafarers hoisted their shields on high
And carried them over the gleaming water.
Byrhtnoth and his warriors awaited them,
Ready for battle: he ordered his men
To form a phalanx with their shields, and to stand
    firm
Against the onslaught of the enemy. Then was the
    battle,
With its chance of glory, about to begin. The time
    had come
For all the doomed men to fall in the fight.
The clamor began; the ravens wheeled and the eagle
Circled overhead, craving for carrion; there was
    shouting on earth.
They hurled their spears, hard as files,
And sent sharp darts flying from their hands.

Bow strings were busy, shield parried point,
Bitter was the battle. Brave men fell
On both sides, youths choking in the dust.
Byrhtnoth's sister's son, Wulfmær, was wounded;
Slashed by the sword, he decided
To sleep on the bed of death.
This was violently requited, the Vikings were repaid
    in kind.
I was told that Eadweard swung his sword
So savagely—a full-blooded blow—
That a fated warrior fell lifeless at his feet.
Byrhtnoth shouted out his thanks to him,
His chamberlain, as soon as he had a chance to do so.
The brave men stood resolute, rock firm.
Each of them eagerly hunted for a way
To be first in with his spear,
Winning with his weapons the life
Of a doomed warrior; the dead sank down to the
    earth.
But the rest stood unshaken and Byrhtnoth spurred
    them on,
Inciting each man to fight ferociously
Who wished to gain glory against the Danes.
Then a brave seafarer raised up his spear,
Gripped his shield and advanced towards Byrhtnoth.
The resolute earl advanced towards the churl;
Each had evil designs on the other.
The Viking was the quicker—he hurled his foreign
    spear
Wounding the lord of the warriors.
Byrhtnoth broke the shaft with the edge of his shield;
The imbedded spear-head sprang out of his wound.
Then he flung his spear in fury
At the proud Viking who dared inflict such pain.
His aim was skilful. The spear
Slit open the warrior's neck.
Thus Byrhtnoth put paid to his enemy's life.
Then, for safety's sake, he swiftly hurled another
Which burst the Viking's breastplate, cruelly wound-
    ing him
In the chest; the deadly spear pierced his heart.
The brave earl, Byrhtnoth, delighted at this;
He laughed out loud and gave thanks to the Lord
That such good fortune had been granted to him.
But one of the seafarers sent a sharp javelin
Speeding from his hand

That pierced Byrhtnoth's body, the noble thane of
    Æthelred.
By his side stood a young warrior,
Wulfmær by name, Wulfstan's son,
Who without a moment's hesitation
Drew out the blood-red javelin from Byrhtnoth's side
And hurled it back as hard as he could
At the man who had grievously injured his prince.
The sharp point struck home; the Viking sagged, and
    sank into the dust.
Another seafarer advanced on the earl, meaning to
    make
Short work of him and snatch away his treasures—
His armor and his rings and his ornamented sword.

Byrhtnoth drew out his sword from its sheath,
Broad-faced and gleaming, and made to slash at the
    seafarer's corselet,
But his enemy stopped him all too soon,
Savagely striking Byrhtnoth's arm.
The golden-hilted sword dropped from his hand.
He could hold it no longer
Nor wield a weapon of any kind. Then the old
    warrior
Raised his men's morale with bold words,
Called on his brave companions to do battle again.
He no longer stood firmly on his feet
But swayed, and raised his eyes to heaven:
"O Guardian of the people, let me praise and thank
    you
For all the real joys I received in this world.
Now, gracious Lord, as never before,
I need Your grace,
That my soul may set out on its journey to You,
O Prince of Angels, that my soul may depart
Into Your power in peace. I pray
That the devils may never destroy it."
Then the heathens hewed him down
And the two men who stood there supporting him;
Ælfnoth and Wulfmær fell to the dust,
Both gave their lives in defense of their lord.
Then certain cowards beat a hasty retreat:
The sons of Odda were the first to take flight;
Godric fled from the battle, forsaking Byrhtnoth.
Forgetting that his lord had given him often the gift
    of a horse,

He leapt into the saddle
Of his lord's own horse, most unlawfully,
And both his brothers, Godwine and Godwig,
Galloped beside him; forgetting their duty
They fled from the fight
And saved their lives in the silent wood.
And more men followed than was at all fitting
Had they remembered the former rewards
That the prince had given them, generous presents.
It was just as Offa once said to Byrhtnoth
At an open council in the meeting place,
That many spoke proudly of their prowess
Who would prove unworthy of their words under
    battle-stress.

So Æthelred's earl, the prince of those people,
Fell; all his hearth-companions
Could see for themselves that their lord lay low.
Then the proud thanes, with the utmost bravery,
Threw themselves once more into the thick of the
    battle.
They all, without exception, strove to one of two
    ends—
To avenge their lord or to leave this world.
Ælfwine the son of Ælfric, still a young man,
Shouted encouragement, urging them on.
He rallied them with valiant words:
"Think of all the times we boasted
At the mead-bench, heroes in the hall
Predicting our own bravery in battle.
Now we shall see who meant what he said.
Let me announce my ancestry to one and all:
I come from a mighty family of Mercian stock;
My grandfather was Ealhelm,
A wise ealdorman, well endowed with worldly riches.
No thane shall ever have reason to reproach me
With any desire to desert this troop
And hurry home, now that my prince has been hewn
    down
In battle. This is the most bitter sorrow of all.
He was my kinsman and my lord."
Then he went forward into the fight
And pierced a pirate's body with his spear.
The man keeled over, dead,
Killed by Ælfwine's weapon. Again he urged
His friends and companions

To follow him into the fray.
Then Offa spoke and brandished his ash-spear:
"Ælfwine, you've encouraged all the thanes
At exactly the right time. Now that our prince
Is slain, the earl on the earth,
We must all encourage each other
To fight, for as long as we can wield
Our weapons, pierce with our spears,
And lunge and parry with our swords.
Godric, the cowardly son of Odda, has betrayed us
    all.
When he hurried off toward the woods on our lord's
    fine horse
He misled many men into believing it was Byrhtnoth
    himself;
And so they followed him, and here on the field
The phalanx was broken: may fortune frown on him
Whose cowardice has caused this catastrophe."
Then Leofsunu spoke. He raised his shield
For protection, and replied to Offa:
"I give you my word that I will not retreat
One inch; I shall forge on
And avenge my lord in battle.
Now that he has fallen in the fight
No loyal warrior living at Sturmere
Need reproach me for returning home lordless
In unworthy retreat, for the weapon shall take me,
The iron sword." He strode forward angrily,
Fighting furiously; he spurned escape.
Then Dunnere spoke and shook his spear;
A lowly churl, he cried out loud
And asked every man to avenge Byrhtnoth's death:
"Whoever intends to avenge our prince
Must not flinch, nor care for his own life."
Then they hurried forward, heedless of their lives;
The brave followers, fiercely carrying spears,
Fought with great courage, and prayed to God
That they should be allowed to avenge their lord
By killing all his enemies.
The hostage helped them with all his might—
His name was Æscferth, the son of Ecglaf;
He came from a family renowned in Northumbria.
In the fire of battle he did not flinch,
Notching arrow after arrow as quick as he could.
Sometimes he hit a shield, sometimes he pierced a
    man,

Again and again he inflicted wounds
For as long as he could hold a bow in his hands.
Eadweard the tall, eager and impetuous,
Did not stray from the line of battle. He boasted that
    he
Would not shrink so much as a footstep,
Or seek safety by flight, now that his lord lay dead.
He smashed the wall of shields, and attacked the
    seafarers
Worthily avenging his ring-giver's death.
He sold his life dearly in the storm of battle.
And so too did Ætheric, a stalwart companion....
He grappled aggressively and without delay.
The brother of Sibyrht, both he and many others
Split the hollow shields and warded off the seafarers.
The corner of the shield broke and the corselet sang
A terrible song. Then in the turmoil
Offa struck a seafarer; he fell dead at his feet.
But the kinsman of Gadd was killed there too,
Offa was quickly brought down in the battle.
Yet he had kept his promise to his prince;
He fulfilled his former boast to Byrhtnoth, the
    ring-giver,
That they should either return unhurt, riding to the
    stronghold
In victory together, or together surrender their lives,
Bleeding from wounds on the battlefield.
He lay near his lord as befits a thane.
Then shields were shattered; the seafarers surged
    forward,
Embittered by bloodshed. Often a spear
Sank into the body of a fated warrior. Then Wistan
    advanced,

The son of Thurstan; he fought with the Vikings,
Slew three in the struggling throng
Before he, Wigelm's brave son, was himself brought
    down.
That was a savage fight; the warriors stood firm
In the struggle. Strong men fell,
Utterly worn out by wounds; the dead dropped to
    the earth.
The brothers Oswold and Eadweard
Continuously encouraged the companions;
They urged their kinsmen to use
Their weapons without slackening
And endure the stress to the best of their strength.
Byrhtwold grasped his shield and spoke.
He was an old companion. He brandished his ash-
    spear
And with wonderful courage exhorted the warriors:
"Mind must be the firmer, heart the more fierce,
Courage the greater, as our strength diminishes.
Here lies our leader, dead,
An heroic man in the dust.
He who now longs to escape will lament for ever.
I am old. I will not go from here,
But I mean to lie by the side of my lord,
Lie in the dust with the man I loved so dearly."
Godric, too, the son of Æthelgar, gave them
    courage
To continue the fight. Often he let fly his spear,
His deadly javelin, at the Vikings
As he advanced at the head of the host.
He humbled and hewed down until at last he fell
    himself....

4.17 Law: King Æthelred, *Law Code* (1008). Original in Old English.

LAW CODES, SO IMPORTANT A PART of the identity of the early barbarian kingdoms (see, for example, *The Visigothic Code*, p. 63 above), continued to be issued, as is evident from this code from Æthelred II the Unready (r.978-1016) and from the law code of King Stephen of Hungary (see above, p. 238). Although all were drawn up to seem timeless, they were very much products of local conditions and circumstances. Æthelred the Unready's reign was beset by Viking invasions—the Battle of Maldon, about which the poem above was sung, which took place during his reign, and which mentions him several times—was only one example of the warfare of his period. The nickname "Unready" came from the Anglo-Saxon word *unræd*, meaning "no-counsel"—even though Æthelred's code says that it was issued with the approval of his "ecclesiastical and lay councillors." In fact, one of those councillors was the most distinguished churchman of his age, Archbishop Wulfstan of York (r.1002-1023), whose handwriting may be detected in several of the entries in the manuscripts of this code. What evidence can you find in this code of military crisis?

[Source: *English Historical Documents*, Vol. 1: *c. 300-1042*, ed. Dorothy Whitelock, 2nd ed. (London: Routledge, 1979), pp. 442-46 (slightly modified).]

PROLOGUE. This is the ordinance which the king of the English and both ecclesiastical and lay councillors have approved and decreed.

1. First, namely, that we all shall love and honor one God and zealously hold one Christian faith and entirely cast off every heathen practice; and we all have confirmed both with word and with pledge that we will hold one Christian faith under the rule of one king.

1.1. And it is the decree of our lord and his councillors that just practices be established and all illegal practices abolished, and that every man is to be permitted the benefit of law;

1.2. and that peace and friendship are to be rightly maintained in both religious and secular concerns within this country.

2. And it is the decree of our lord and his councillors that no Christian and innocent men are to be sold out of the country, and especially not among the heathen people, but care is earnestly to be taken that those souls be not destroyed which God bought with his own life.

3. And it is the decree of our lord and his councillors that Christian men are not to be condemned to death for all too small offences.

3.1. But otherwise life-sparing punishments are to be devised for the benefit of the people, and God's handiwork and his own purchase which he paid for so dearly is not to be destroyed for small offences.

4. And it is the decree of our lord and his councillors that men of every order are each to submit willingly to that duty which befits them both in religious and secular concerns.

4.1 And especially God's servants—bishops and abbots, monks and nuns, priests and women dedicated to God—are to submit to their duty and to live according to their rule and to intercede zealously for all Christian people.

5. And it is the decree of our lord and his councillors that every monk who is out of his monastery and not heeding his rule, is to do what behooves him: return readily into the monastery with all humility, and cease from evil-doing and atone very zealously for what he has done amiss; let him consider the word and pledge which he gave to God.

6. And that monk who has no monastery is to come to the bishop of the diocese, and pledge himself to God and men that from that time on he will at least observe three things, namely his chastity, and monastic garb, and serve his Lord as well as ever he can.

6.1. And if he keeps that, he is then entitled to the greater respect, no matter where he dwell.

7. And canons,[1] where there is property such that they can have a refectory and dormitory, are to hold their minster [church] with right observance and with chastity, as their rule directs; otherwise it is right that he who will not do that shall forfeit the property.

8. And we pray and instruct all mass-priests to protect themselves from God's anger.

9. They know full well that they may not rightly have sexual intercourse with a woman.

9.1. And whoever will abstain from this and preserve chastity, may he have God's mercy and in addition as a secular dignity, that he shall be entitled to a

---

1 Canons here refer to priests who live together in common.

thegn's wergild and a thegn's rights, in life as well as in the grave.[1]

9.2. And he who will not do what belongs to his order, may his dignity be diminished both in religious and secular concerns.

10. And also every Christian man is zealously to avoid illegal intercourse, and duly keep the laws of the Church.[2]

10.1. And every church is to be under the protection of God and of the king and of all Christian people.

10.2. And no man henceforth is to bring a church under subjection, nor illegally to traffic with a church,[3] nor to expel a minister of the church without the bishop's consent.

11. And God's dues are to be readily paid every year.

11.1. Namely, plough-alms 15 days after Easter, and the tithe of young animals by Pentecost, and of the fruits of the earth by All Saints' day, and "Rome-money" by St. Peter's day and light-dues three times a year.[4]

12. And it is best that payment for the soul be always paid at the open grave.

12.1. And if any body is buried elsewhere, outside the proper parish, the payment for the soul is nevertheless to be paid to the minster to which it belonged.

12.2. And all God's dues are to be furthered zealously, as is needful.

12.3. And festivals and fasts are to be properly observed.

13. The Sunday festival is to be diligently observed, as befits it.

13.1. And one is readily to abstain from markets and public meetings on the holy day.

14. And all the festivals of St. Mary are to be diligently observed, first with a fast and afterwards with a festival.

14.1. And at the festival of every Apostle there is to be fasting and festivity, except that we enjoin no fast for the festival of St. Philip and St. James, because of the Easter festival.

15. Otherwise other festivals and fasts are to be kept diligently just as those kept them who kept them best.

16. And the councillors have decreed that St. Edward's festival is to be celebrated over all England on March 18th.[5]

17. And there is to be a fast every Friday, except when it is a feast day.

18. And ordeals and oaths are forbidden on feast days and the legal Ember days, and from the Advent of the Lord until the octave of Epiphany, and from Septuagesima [Lent] until 15 days after Easter.

19. And at these holy seasons, as it is right, there is to be peace and unity among all Christian men, and every suit is to be laid aside.

20. And if anyone owes another a debt or compensation concerning secular matters, he is to pay it readily before or after [these seasons].

21. And every widow who conducts herself rightly is to be under the protection of God and the king.

21.1. And each [widow] is to remain unmarried for twelve months; she is afterwards to choose what she herself will.

22. And every Christian man is to do what is needful for him, heed zealously his Christian duties, form the

---

1 The wergild was the price of compensation, which varied with the status of the victim. Thegns were noblemen, and they had the high wergild of 1200 shillings.
2 This provision involves not marrying within six degrees of relationship, or with the widow of so near a kinsman, or a close relative of a previous wife, or a nun, or anyone related by spiritual affinity, or a deserted woman.
3 This refers to buying a church office or bartering a church.
4 "Rome money" refers to Peter's Pence, dues sent to Rome to support the papacy. "Light-dues" were revenues to pay for church candles.
5 St. Edward was the martyred King Edward (r.975-978), the brother of Æthelred.

habit of frequent confession, and freely confess his sins and willingly atone for them as he is directed.

22.1. And everyone is to prepare himself often and frequently for going to communion;

22.2. and to order words and deeds rightly and keep carefully oath and pledge.

23. And every injustice is to be zealously cast out from this country, as far as it can be done.

24. And deceitful deeds and hateful abuses are to be strictly shunned, namely, false weights and wrong measures, and lying witnesses and shameful frauds,

25. and horrible perjuries and devilish deeds of murder and manslaughter, of stealing and spoliation, of avarice and greed, of over-eating and over-drinking, of deceits and various breaches of law, of injuries to the clergy and of breaches of the marriage law, and of evil deeds of many kinds.

26. But God's law henceforth is to be eagerly loved by word and deed; then God will at once become gracious to this nation.

26.1. And people are to be zealous about the improvement of the peace, and about the improvement of the coinage everywhere in the country, and about the repair of boroughs in every province and also about military service,[1] according to what is decreed, whenever it is necessary,

27. and about the supplying of ships, as zealously as possible, so that each may be equipped immediately after Easter every year.

28. And if anyone deserts without leave from an army which the king himself is with, it is to be at the peril of his life and all his property.

28.1. And he who otherwise deserts from the army is to forfeit 120 shillings.

29. And if any excommunicated man—unless it be a suppliant for protection—remain anywhere in the king's neighborhood before he has submitted readily to ecclesiastical penance, it is to be at the peril of his life and all his possessions.

30. And if anyone plots against the king's life, he is to forfeit his life; and if he wishes to clear himself, he is to do it by [an oath of the value of] the king's wergild or by the three-fold ordeal in [the area under] English law.[2]

31. And if anyone commit obstruction or open resistance anywhere against the law of Christ or the king, he is to pay either wergild or fine or *lahslit*,[3] ever in proportion to the deed.

31.1. And if he illegally offers resistance with assault, and so brings it about that he is killed, no wergild is to be paid to any of his friends.

32. And ever henceforth the abuses are to cease which hitherto have been too common far and wide.

33. And every abuse is to be zealously suppressed.

33.1. For [only] as a result of suppressing wrong and loving righteousness will there be improvement at all in the country in religious and secular concerns.

34. We must all love and honor one God and entirely cast out every heathen practice.

35. And let us loyally support one royal lord, and all together defend our lives and our land, as well as ever we can, and pray Almighty God from our inmost heart for his help.

---

1   Boroughs, or burhs, were fortifications.
2   In the "three-fold" ordeal, the hot iron weighed three times more than its usual weight. For the ordeal, see above, p. 241, n. 3.
3   *Lahslit* meant "breach of the law"; it was the term given in the Danelaw (the law in the eastern region of England heavily settled by the Danes) to a fine varying with the rank of the offender, 10 half-marks for the king's thegn, 6 half-marks for other landowners, 12 ores (there were 8 ores to the mark) for the ordinary freeman.

Plate 4.1 Christianity comes to Denmark: *The Jelling Monument* (960s)

THE JELLING MONUMENT IS A LARGE boulder with writing and carvings on it. It is important for understanding how Christianity became incorporated into the networks of power and prestige in Scandinavia.

Powerful people with great resources had long lived in Jelling, close to what is today Vejle, on the Jutland peninsula. During the Bronze age, before 500 B.C.E., they built an earthen mound, and, just south of the mound, they lined up several large standing stones to suggest the outline of a ship.

In 958 the Viking King Gorm died at Jelling. His son Harald Bluetooth buried his father in the old mound, adding more soil to make it taller. He also constructed another mound a short distance to the south, in the process destroying the "ship." The construction of mounds was a newly resuscitated custom in the tenth century. It was a self-conscious appeal to old traditions in the face of Christian customs spreading from Denmark's southern neighbors, the Germans. Accompanying Gorm in his tomb was a horse, riding gear, an elegant silver cup, a chest, a small wooden cross, and other artifacts. A powerful man or woman was not to arrive in the afterlife without suitable equipment. This was entirely the opposite of Christian customs, which by the tenth century prohibited burying goods with bodies: the Christian afterlife was supposed to be immaterial.

Harald took over his father Gorm's kingdom. Then, in the 960s, he became a Christian. The reminders in Jelling of his pagan past, including his father, became an embarrassment. Harald built a large wooden church close to the northern mound. He dug up the body of his father and moved him to an honored place in the middle of the church, thus posthumously Christianizing Gorm. The centerpiece of the new Christian compound was a piece of art, a large granite boulder situated exactly at the midpoint between the two mounds—the "Jelling Monument." Harald had the boulder inscribed on three sides with large pictures and a text in runic characters, a special alphabet. When they were new, the pictures and the text would have been painted in bright colors. The stone proudly proclaimed that this was a Christian site. One side depicts a great rampant animal (a dragon? a lion?) entwined by a snake. Another side (see photo) portrays Christ crucified. Remarkably, the cross itself is lacking. Instead, interlacing bands surround Christ.

The inscription reads: "King Harald had this monument made in memory of his father Gorm and in memory of his mother Thyre; that Harald who won for himself all of Denmark and Norway and made the Danes Christian." The last words are visible on the photo under the figure of Christ.

Thousands of runestones still dot the landscape of Scandinavia, most put up in the eleventh century, when most of the population had converted to Christianity. The text of these runestones was usually along the lines of the formula of Jelling: "X had this stone made/raised in memory of Y, his/her mother/father/brother/companion-at-arms." Many stones added "God save his (or her) soul," and others had crosses.

These inscriptions may appear to be selfless acts of remembrance of loved ones, but they served at least as much to remind all who passed of the power and wealth of the sponsor of the inscription, the person who was able to afford such a great monument. Certainly Harald did not hide behind any false humility; he forthrightly included his name twice to drive the point home. Harald, no one else, was the powerful conqueror and the religious benefactor of those he conquered. In this he appeared both as a traditional warlord and as a good Christian ruler.

The Jelling compound was part of Harald's efforts to consolidate his power, which also included the construction of forts all over his kingdom. It did not help. His son Svein Forkbeard

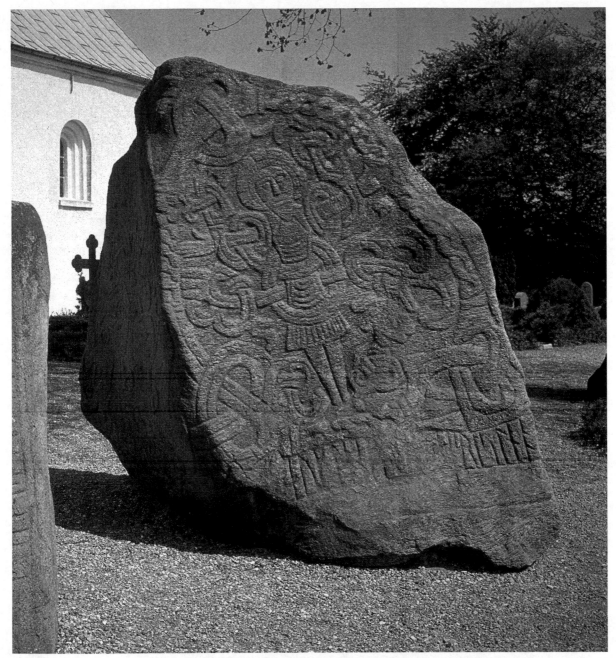

rebelled against him in 986 or 987. Harald had to go into exile, where he soon died. The tomb that he had reserved for himself in the church next to his father Gorm is still empty. Taking this monument together with Bede's account of the Christianization of England, above, p. 97, consider how the new religion was—and was not—compatible with pre-Christian forms of kingship. Why do you suppose that interlace was used in place of the Cross?

[Source: Denmark, Nationalmuseet. Caption by Anders Winroth.]

PLATE 4.1 CHRISTIANITY COMES TO DENMARK: THE JELLING MONUMENT (960S)   267

4.18 The making of Iceland: Ari Thorgilsson, *The Book of the Icelanders* (*c.*1125). Original in Icelandic.

SOME MONKS FROM THE British Isles already inhabited Iceland when it was discovered and settled, mainly by Norwegian nobles and their slaves, in the last half of the ninth century. By the mid-tenth century, the Icelanders were a mainly agrarian community led by "chieftains"; they had a roughly representative government (whose major institution was the high court, the Althing); and they cultivated a tradition of poetic expression. Originally practicing polytheism, Icelanders converted to Christianity *c.*1000 under pressure from the King of Norway. A bishop was set in place—and by the end of the century a second one—and the Althing granted tithes to the Church. Ari Thorgilsson (*c.*1067-1148), born and educated in Iceland, wrote, in the vernacular, the first history of the country. His *The Book of the Icelanders* spends considerable time on genealogy, establishing the origins of the lines and settlements of his contemporaries, both male and female. He relied on oral sources for most of his information. How does his account of the conversion of Iceland compare both in content and style with Bede's account of the conversion of the English (above, p. 97)?

[Source: Ari Thorgilsson, *The Book of the Icelanders*, ed. and trans. Halldór Hermannsson (Ithaca, NY: Cornell University Library, 1930; rpt. New York: Kraus Reprint Corporation, 1966), pp. 60-67 (slightly modified).]

HERE BEGINS THE BOOK OF THE ICELANDERS

CHAPTER I: Of the Settlement of Iceland
Iceland was first settled from Norway in the days of Harald the Fairhaired,[1] son of Halfdan the Black, at the time—according to the opinion and calculation of Teit my foster-father, the wisest man I have known, son of Bishop Isleif, and of my paternal uncle Thorkel Gellisson who remembered far back, and of Thurid daughter of Snorri Godi who was both learned in many things and trustworthy—when Ivar, son of Ragnar Lodbrok, caused Edmund the Saint, king of the English, to be slain; and that was 870 years after the birth of Christ.[2]

A Norwegian called Ingolf, it is told for certain, first went from there to Iceland when Harald the Fairhaired was sixteen winters old, and for the second time a few winters later. He settled south in Reykjavik. Ingolf's Head, east of Munthakseyri, is the name given to the place where he first landed, but Ingolf's Fell, west of Ölfus River, is where he afterwards took possession of land.

At that time Iceland was covered with forests between mountains and seashore. Then Christian men whom the Norsemen call Popes were here; but afterwards they went away, because they did not wish to live here together with heathen men, and they left behind Irish books, bells, and crooks. From this could be seen that they were Irishmen.

And then a very great emigration started out hither from Norway until King Harald forbade it, because he thought that the country would be laid waste. Then they came to this agreement that every man who was not exempted and who went from there hither should pay the king five ounces. And it is said that Harald was king seventy winters and became an octogenarian. These are the origins of that tax which is now called land-ounces; it was sometimes higher and sometimes lower until Olaf the Stout[3] declared that every man who went between Norway and Iceland should pay

---

1 Harald the Fairhaired (9th to 10th c.) was the first king to rule all of Norway.
2 Edmund the Saint was king of East Anglia before 865 until his death in 869. He was martyred by the Vikings, and his body was buried at Bury St. Edmunds, later a monastery.
3 Olaf the Stout, or Olaf II Haraldsson, was king of Norway 1015-1030.

the king half a mark, except women and those men whom he exempted. Thus Thorkel Gellisson told us.

CHAPTER II: Of the Settlers and Legislation
Hrollaug, son of Earl Rögnvald of Mœri, settled in the east in Sida; thence the Men of Sida are descended.

Ketilbjörn Ketilsson, a Norwegian, settled in the south at Upper Mosfell; from there the Men of Mosfell are descended.

Aud, daughter of Ketil Flatnose, a Norwegian lord, settled in the west in Breidafjord; thence the Men of Breidafjord are descended.

Helgi the Lean, a Norwegian, son of Eyvind the Eastman, settled in the north in Eyjafjord; thence the Men of Eyjafjord are descended.

And when Iceland had become widely settled, a Norwegian called Ulfljot (so Teit told us) brought for the first time hither from Norway law, and this was then called Ulfljot's Law. He was the father of Gunnar from whom the Men of Djupadal in Eyjafjord are descended. But this law was chiefly modeled upon the Gulathing [Norwegian] Law of that time, additions, omissions, or different provisions being made therein upon the advice of Thorleif the Wise, son of Hörda-Kari. Ulflot lived east in Lón; and it is told that Grim Goat-beard was his foster-brother, the man who, at his instance, explored all Iceland before the Althing was established. And every man in this land gave him a penny for this, but afterwards he presented that money to the temples.

CHAPTER III: The Establishment of the Althing
The Althing was established by the counsel of Ulfljot and all the people of the land where it now is. There was before, however, a moot at Kjalarness which Thorstein, son of Ingolf the settler and the father of Thorkel Moon the lawspeaker, held there [along with] those chieftains who joined it.[1] But a man who owned the land in Bláskógar [Bluewoods] had been found guilty of the murder of a slave or freedman. His name was Thorir Crop-beard, and his daughter's son was called Thorwald Crop-beard who later went to the Eastfjords and burnt his brother Gunnar to death in his house. So Hall Orækjuson told us. But Kol was the name of the man who was murdered; after him is called that cleft which since is named Kol's Cleft, where the corpse was found. That land afterwards became public property, and the people set it apart for the use of the Althing. Therefore there is free cutting of wood for the Althing in the forests, and on the heath there is pasture for the keeping of horses. This Ulfhedin told us.

Wise men have also told that Iceland was fully settled in sixty winters so that there was no further settlement made afterwards. About that time Hrafn, son of Hæng the settler, assumed the lawspeakership next after Ulfljot and held it twenty summers [930–949]. He was from the Rang River district. That was sixty winters after the slaying of King Edmund, a winter or two before Harald the Fairhaired died, according to the reckoning of wise men. Thorarin Raga-brother, son of Oleif Hjalti, assumed the lawspeakership next after Hrafn and held it another twenty summers [950–969]. He was from Borgarfjord....

CHAPTER V: Of the Division into Quarters
A great law suit came to pass at the moot between Thord Gellir, son of Oleif Feilan from Breidafjord, and Odd who was called Odd of Tunga; he was from Borgarfjord. His son Thorvald was with Hen-Thorir at the burning of Thorkel Blund-Ketilsson in Örnolfsdal. But Thord Gellir became the chief plaintiff in the case, because Herstein son of Thorkel son of Blund-Ketil was married to Thora, his sister's daughter. She was the daughter of Helga and Gunnar and sister of Jofrid, wife of Thorstein Egilsson. They were first prosecuted at the moot which was held in Borgarfjord at that place which since is called Thingness. Then it was the law that suits for slaughter must be brought before the moot which was nearest to the place where the slaughter had been committed. But they fought there, and the moot could not be carried on by law. There Thorolf Fox, brother of Alf of Dalir, of Thord Gellir's party, fell. Thereafter the case was brought

---

1 A "moot" is a formal meeting, often a law court, and is treated here as a precedent for the Althing. The "lawspeaker" was elected for a three-year term. His job was to know and recite the law, both to anyone who asked and to the Althing. As the law was unwritten, this required a prodigious memory.

before the Althing, and there they fought again. Then men fell of Odd's party and besides Hen-Thorir was found guilty and was afterwards killed, as were others who had been at the burning.

Then Thord Gellir delivered a speech at the Law Rock concerning how badly it suited men to go to strange moots in suing for slaughter or injuries, and he told what had happened to him before he could bring this case to law, and said that many in their turn would experience difficulties if that was not remedied. Then the country was divided into Quarters, so that there were three moots in each Quarter, where moot-mates should bring their own lawsuits; only in the Northern Quarter there were four moots, because they could not reach any other agreement; those living north of Eyjafjord were not willing to attend the moot there, nor that of Skagafjord those who lived there to the west. Yet the appointment of judges and the constitution of the Lögrétta should be the same from that Quarter as from any of the others. Afterwards, however, the Quarter-moots were established. So Ulfhedin Gunnarsson the lawspeaker told us.

Thorkel Moon, son of Thorstein, son of Ingolf, assumed the lawspeakership after Thorarin Ragabrother, and held it fifteen summers [970–984]. Thereupon Thorgeir Thorkelsson of Ljósavatn had it for seventeen summers [985–1001].

CHAPTER VI: Of the Settlement of Greenland
The country which is called Greenland was discovered and settled from Iceland. Erik the Red was the name of a man from Breidafjord who went from here thither and took possession of land at the place which since has been called Eriksfjord.[1] He gave a name to the country and called it Greenland, and said that people would desire to go thither, if the country had a good name. Both east and west in the country they found human habitations, fragments of skin boats and stone implements from which it was evident that the same kind of people had been there as inhabited Wineland[2] and whom the Greenlanders called Skrellings. He began colonizing the country fourteen or fifteen winters before Christianity came to Iceland [985 or 986] according to what a man who himself had gone thither with Erik the Red told Thorkel Gellisson in Greenland.

CHAPTER VII: Of how Christianity came to Iceland
King Olaf, son of Tryggvi, son of Olaf, son of Harald the Fairhaired, brought Christianity into Norway and into Iceland.[3] He sent to this country a priest by the name of Thangbrand who taught Christianity to people here and baptized all those who embraced the faith. Hall Thorsteinsson of Sida let himself be baptized early and so did Hjalti Skeggjason of Thjorsardal and Gizur the White, son of Teit, son of Ketilbjörn of Mosfell, and many other chieftains; yet those were more numerous who opposed and refused it. And when he had been here a winter or two he went away, having at that time slain here two or three men who had libelled him. And when he came east [to Norway] he told King Olaf all that had befallen him here, and said that it was beyond hope that Christianity yet would be received here. The king grew very angry at this, and because of it designed to kill or maim all our countrymen who were there in the east. But that same summer Gizur and Hjalti came out thither from here and persuaded the king to let those men off, promising him to use their good offices for a new trial that Christianity might still be received here, and they expressed a firm hope that this would meet with success.

The next summer after that they went from the east [Norway] and with them a priest called Thormod, and they landed in the Westman Isles when ten weeks of the summer were past, and they had a good voyage. Teit said he had been told so by a man who had himself been there. Now it had been made law the summer before that people should come to the Althing when ten weeks of summer were past, but until then they had met one week earlier. Gizur and his men went immediately to the mainland, and afterwards to the Althing; and they prevailed on Hjalti that he with eleven men stay behind in Laugardal

---

1   Erik the Red (*fl.* late 10th c.) founded the first Scandinavian settlement in Greenland in 985.
2   Also known as Vinland, this was the portion of the North American coast discovered by Erik's son Leif Ericsson *c.*1000.
3   Olaf I Tryggvesson, king of Norway 995–999, was largely responsible for the conversion of Iceland.

because the preceding summer he had been sentenced to the lesser outlawry for blasphemy. And the reason for that was that he had recited at the Law Rock the following ditty:—

Barking gods I disesteem,
And a bitch I Freya deem.[1]

Gizur and his followers proceeded until they came to a place by Ölfus Lake called Vellankatla and sent word from there to the Althing that all their supporters should come to meet them, because they had heard that their adversaries were going to keep them from the moot-field by force of arms. But before they broke up from there Hjalti came riding thither and those who had stayed behind with him. And then they rode to the moot, having before been joined by their kinsmen and friends as they had requested. The heathen men, however, gathered together fully armed, and whether it would come to a fight hung upon the slenderest thread. On the second day Gizur and Hjalti went to the Law Rock and made known their message;[2] and it is reported that it was striking how well they spoke. But the consequence was that one man after the other called witnesses, the Christians and the heathen, each declaring themselves out of law with the other, and then they went away from the Law Rock.

Then the Christians asked Hall of Sida to proclaim their law in conformity with Christianity, but he disengaged himself from that by bargaining with Thorgeir the lawspeaker that he should declare the law though he was still a heathen. And afterwards when men had gone to their booths Thorgeir lay down and spread his cloak over himself, and rested all that day and the next night, nor did he speak a word. But the next morning he rose and sent word that men should go to the Law Rock.

And when men gathered there he began his speech, saying that he thought that the people would be in a sorry plight if men in this land were not all to have the same law; and he remonstrated with them in various ways that they should not let this come to pass, saying that it would lead to disturbance, and certainly it was to be expected that there would occur such fights between men that the land would be laid waste thereby. He related how the kings of Denmark and Norway had carried on war and battles against one another for a long time until the people of those countries made peace between them although they did not wish it; and that counsel turned out so well that within a short while they were exchanging precious gifts, and that peace lasted also so long as they both lived. "And now it seems advisable to me," he said, "that we do not let their will prevail who are most strongly opposed to one another, but so compromise between them that each side may win part of its case, and let us all have one law and one faith. It will prove true that if we sunder the law we will also sunder the peace." And so he concluded his speech that both parties agreed that all would keep the law which he should declare.

Then it was made law that all people should be Christian and those be baptized who still were unbaptized in this land; but as to infanticide the old law should stand, and also as to eating of horse flesh. People might sacrifice to the heathen gods secretly, if they wished, but under the penalty of the lesser outlawry if this was proved by witnesses. But a few winters later this heathendom was abolished like the rest. In this way it was, Teit told us, that Christianity came into Iceland. And King Olaf Tryggvesson fell the same summer according to the account of Sæmund the priest. At that time he fought against Svein Haraldson, king of the Danes, and Olaf the Swedish, son of Erik king of the Swedes at Uppsala, and Erik Hakonsson who afterwards was earl of Norway. That was 130 winters after the slaying of Edmund, and 1000 after the birth of Christ according to the general count.

---

1 Freya was an important Norse goddess.
2 The Law Rock was the place at the Althing where lawsuits were formally announced and where the lawspeaker recited the law. Gizur and Hjalti were using it to proclaim Christian law.

TIMELINE FOR CHAPTER FOUR

890 King Alfred, *Prefaces*

900

915 Al-Tabari, *Defeat of the Zanj*

934 Lekapenus, *Novel*
940-2 Al-Farabi *The Perfect State*

950-8 Porphyrogenitus, *Military Advice*

950

960s *Jelling Monument*

910 thru 11th c. *Charters of Cluny*

973-4 *Life of Mathilda*

after 991 *Battle of Maldon*

1008 Æthelred, *Law Code*

1000

1000-38 Stephen, *Laws*

1013-18 Thietmar, *Henry II*
1020s or 30s Ibn Sina (Avicenna), *Treatise on Logic*

1028 *Agreements of William and Hugh*

1040-3 Andrew of Fleury, *Miracles of Benedict*

1041-75 *Charter of the bishop of Urgel*

1050

1063 Psellus, *Basil II*

1100

1113 *Russian Primary Chronicle*

1125 Ari Thorgilsson, *Book of the Icelanders*

FIVE

THE EXPANSION OF EUROPE (*c*.1050–*c*.1150)

MAPS

Plate 5.1 The West: *T-O Map* (12th c.).

WESTERN ARMIES KNEW PERFECTLY WELL how to get to Jerusalem. But their sophisticated working knowledge of geography had little to do with maps. Based on theories of the divine order, medieval maps were ordinarily conceptual rather than practical. This plate shows the simplest sort, a T-O map. The earth is round (this was never a question in the Middle Ages) and divided into three major land masses: in this instance (but not on all T-O maps), Africa is at the top (south), while dividing the bottom are Europe (west) and Asia (east). The whole is surrounded by the ocean. The reason that Africa receives such emphasis here is because the map illustrates a manuscript page of Sallust's *Jugurthine War*, the story of Rome's struggle with a North African leader.

[Source: Paris, BNF lat. 5751, fol. 18r, detail.]

PLATE 5.1 THE WEST: T-O MAP (12TH C.)   273

Plate 5.2 The West: *The Image of the World* (late 12th c.).

FAR MORE COMPLEX than the T–O map, this one, drawn in a manuscript of Honorius Augustodunensis (d.1156) called *Imago Mundi* (*The Image of the World*), implies that a sacred history is at stake. At the top (east) is paradise. At the upper left-hand side, an angel is pointing to a fortress holding Gog and Magog (as the label says), a reference to the scourge prophesied in Rev. 20: 7: "And when the thousand years shall be finished, Satan shall be loosed out of his prison, and shall go forth, and seduce the nations ... Gog and Magog, and shall gather them together to battle." Find "hispania" (Spain), "britannia insula" (Britain), and "hibernia" (Ireland) on the western edge of this map.

[Source: Parker Library, MS 66, p. 2, Corpus Christi College, Cambridge.]

Plate 5.3 The Islamic world: *Directions to Mecca* (12th c.).

MECCA WAS THE GEOGRAPHICAL focus of Islam, since each believer was to turn in prayer toward Mecca, and each was to make a pilgrimage to Mecca at least once in his or her lifetime during the proper period (the *hajj*). This emphasis on Mecca gave rise to maps showing that city's location in relation to the parts of the Islamic world. In this diagrammatic map, drawn for a treatise by al-Dimyati, a twelfth-century Egyptian scholar, the square on the upper left signifies the perimeter of the Ka'ba at Mecca. (The map is oriented with south at the top.) The four straight lines that radiate from the Ka'ba mark off abstract sectors. The semi-circular wavy lines are pilgrimage routes. Major cities are named: for example, to the left of the third sector line (starting from the left) are the cities of Aleppo, Damascus, and Jerusalem. The main purpose of the map is for the viewer—or the builder of a mosque—to know the direction of Mecca (the *qiblah*) and how to face the proper segment of the Ka'ba from his or her part of the world.

[Source: Oxford Bodleian Library Marsh 592, fol. 88v.]

PLATE 5.3 THE ISLAMIC WORLD: DIRECTIONS TO MECCA (12TH C.) 275

Plate 5.4 Byzantium: *The Inhabited World*, from a copy of Ptolemy's *Geography* (13th c.).

BYZANTINE SCHOLARS PRODUCED almost no maps whatever until the end of the thirteenth century, when, in a great spurt of intellectual activity, Maximus Planudes and others not only rediscovered the ancient *Geography* of Ptolemy (*fl.* 2nd c. C.E.) but also began copying or making maps to accompany this work. Ptolemy had used a roughly accurate system of latitude and longitude, and he had elaborated a series of projections so that map makers could depict the spherical earth on a flat surface. However, it is not entirely clear that Ptolemy himself drew any maps for his work. The Byzantine copyists of Ptolemy, by contrast, most certainly included numerous maps, many regional and also one—as depicted here—of the "inhabited world." In this late thirteenth-century Byzantine map, from one of the earliest copies of Ptolemy's *Geography* extant, the coastline of the European countries on the Mediterranean Sea (roughly, the middle line of the F formed by the seas to the west [on the left]) is not entirely unlike that of maps drawn today. This was a map with scientific, rather than symbolic or religious, purpose. Compare it with the portolan chart of a later period (Plate 8.1 below, p. 556).

[Source: Rome, Biblioteca Apostolica Vaticana Urbinas Graecus 82, fols. 60v–61r.]

COMMERCIAL TAKE OFF

5.1 Cultivating new lands: *Frederick of Hamburg's Agreement with Colonists from Holland* (1106). Original in Latin.

THE COMMERCIAL REVOLUTION TOOK place in both town and countryside. In the countryside it depended on the enterprise of peasants and the support of people in power. In this charter the archbishop of Hamburg-Bremen, Frederick (r.1105-1123), granted swamp land in his diocese to colonists from Holland willing to undertake the backbreaking, collective work of drainage. (They were used to this sort of work; much of Holland itself was swampland.) The bishop required payments in return, not only for the produce of the land but also for the right of the colonists to hear their own court cases. His call to settlers was part of a wider movement. Hamburg-Bremen was on the Slavic frontier. Bringing Christians to settle it was one way that German leaders meant to subdue the polytheistic natives. For a contemporary account of a later phase of this development, see Helmold, *Chronicle of the Slavs*, below, p. 342.

[Source: *Ausgewählte Urkunden zur Erläuterung der Verfassungsgeschichte Deutschlands im Mittelalter*, ed. Wilhelm Altmann and Ernst Bernheim, 5th ed. (Berlin: Weidmannsche Buchhandlung, 1920), pp. 161-62, no. 80. Translated by Barbara H. Rosenwein.]

[1] In the name of the holy and individual Trinity, Frederick, bishop of the church of Hamburg by grace of God, [gives] to all the faithful in Christ, present and future, perpetual benediction. We wish to notify all of a certain agreement which certain people living on this side of the Rhine, who are called Hollanders, made with us.

[2] The aforementioned men came to Our Majesty resolutely asking us to concede to them territory for them to cultivate. This land is situated in our bishopric and has hitherto been uncultivated, marshy, and useless to our locals. And so, having taken counsel with our vassals (*fideles*), and thinking it would be beneficial for us and our successors not to refuse their petition, we gave [our] assent.

[3] Moreover, the agreement of their petition was that they give to us a single denar [a silver coin] each year for every manse of this land.[1] We have thought it necessary to write down here the dimensions of a manse, lest there be a dispute later on among the people: a manse is 720 royal rods long and 30 wide, including the streams which flow through the land, which we grant in similar manner.

[4] Finally, they promised to give us a tithe according to our decree, that is, the eleventh part of the fruit of the earth, the tenth of the lambs, similarly of pigs, similarly of goats, the same of geese, and also they will give in the same way a tenth of the amount of honey and flax. They will render a dinar for each foal on the feast of St. Martin [November 11], and an obol [a coin worth less than a dinar] for each calf.

[5] They promised that they would obey us always in all matters pertaining to ecclesiastical law according to the decrees of the holy fathers, canon law, and the customs of the church of Utrecht [the home diocese of the colonists].

[6] With regard to judgments and court hearings involving secular law, they affirm that they will pay 2 marks [a gold or silver coin worth a substantial amount] each year for every 100 manses so that they may try all disputes themselves, lest they suffer from the prejudice of foreign [judges]. If they are unable to

---

1 A manse (*mansus*) was a farming unit: it often included a house, waste, meadow, a garden, and, of course, land for crops. Here its dimensions are standardized and declared because the land is considered "virgin" and ready to be parceled out at will.

settle the more serious hearings or judgments, they shall refer them to the tribunal of the bishop. If they bring him with them to decide the case, for however long he remains [with them] they shall provide for him at their own expense in this manner: they shall keep two thirds of the court fees and give the last third to the bishop.

[7] We have allowed them to construct churches on said territory wherever it seems appropriate to them. We have offered to each church, for the express use of the priests serving God there, a tithe from our tithes of those parish churches. They confirm that the parishioners of each church will give no less than one manse to each church as an endowment for the use of the priest.

[8] The names of the men who came together to make and confirm this agreement are: Heinricus, the priest, to whom we have granted the aforesaid churches for life, and other laymen: Helikinus, Arnol-

dus, Hiko, Fordoltus, and Referic. To them and their heirs after them we concede the said land according to the secular laws and abovementioned agreement.

[9] The affirmation of this agreement was made in the year of our Lord's incarnation 1106, in the sixth indiction, in the reign of Lord Henry IV, Emperor Augustus of the Romans. To confirm this document with our affirmation, it pleases us that the charter be affixed with the impression of our seal. If anyone says anything against it, let him be anathema.

[10] In confirmation of this document, I, Bishop (*prepositus*) Wernherus was present and signed. I, Bishop Marquardus. I, Bishop Hasoko. I, Bishop Hujo. I, Adelbero. I, Thieto was present and signed. I, Gerungus, *advocatus* [a lay protector of a church] was present and witnessed. I, Hericus, was present. I, Thidericus. I, Willo, was present. I, Erpo, was present and witnessed. I, Adelbertus. I, Gerwardus. I, Ermbertus. I, Reinwardus. I, Ecelinus.

5.2 Local markets: Ibn Jubayr, *A Market near Aleppo* (1184). Original in Arabic.

IBN JUBAYR, an Islamic merchant from Spain, wrote a diary about his travels throughout the Mediterranean. In the passage below he describes a rural market at Dunaysar, near Aleppo in northern Syria, which he visited in 1184. Such weekly markets were characteristic not only of the Islamic world but of the Byzantine and western regions as well.

[Source: *Medieval Trade in the Mediterranean World*, ed. and trans. Robert S. Lopez and Irving W. Raymond (New York: Columbia University Press, 2001), pp. 76–77 (slightly modified).]

Dunaysar, June 13–15 [1184]

Next morning, Wednesday, 2 Rabi' al-awwal [June 13], we left with a large caravan of mules and donkeys, together with men from Harran and Aleppo and others from the Bilad Bakr and the neighboring countries.... We kept on the lookout for an attack from the Kurds infesting these regions from Mosul to Nisibin and the town of Dunaysar and raiding the roads and trying to bring disorder into the land. They live among inaccessible mountains in the neighborhood of these countries, the sultans of which have never been assisted by God in subduing them.... There is

nobody who can drive them out and keep them away but God, the Great and Powerful....

[Dunaysar] lies in a broad plain and is surrounded by fragrant plants and irrigated vegetable gardens. It is rather agrarian in aspect and has no walls; it is crowded with people; it has well-attended and well-supplied markets; and it is the supply center of the people of Syria and Diyarbakr, of the countries of the Romans subject to Emir Mas'ud,[1] and of the neighboring countries. It has broad fields and abundant foodstuffs. We camped outside the city with the caravan and in the morning of Thursday, 3 Rabi' al-awwal, we rested in the city.... We remained in Dunaysar until after

---

1 This was the Seljuk ruler Quilij Arslan II (r.1156–1192). The "Romans" in this passage refers to the Byzantines.

prayer on Friday, 4 Rabi' al-awwal. The caravan postponed its departure from this locality in order to be present at the market, because on Thursdays, Fridays, Saturdays, and the following Sundays they hold here a well-attended market. In it congregate the peoples of the neighboring places and of the nearby villages, since the entire road to the right and to the left is an unbroken series of villages and inns. This market, to which people come from various places, they call the bazaar. All these markets are held on fixed days.

5.3 The role of royal patronage: Henry I, *Privileges for the Citizens of London* (1130-1133). Original in Latin.

TOWNS WERE PERMANENT COMMERCIAL CENTERS, and their citizens often demanded and received special privileges that gave them considerable autonomy. In this charter, Henry I, King of England (r.1100-1135), grants privileges to the citizens of London *c.*1130, basing them on grants handed out by previous kings. The Londoners have the right to the "farm" or revenues of their own borough, Middlesex, holding it, as a vassal might hold a fief, of the king and his heirs. The citizens are also allowed to have their own courts and freedom from various duties and tolls (called "customs" here). The reference to "sokes" in this text means "jurisdictions," which, among other things, were sources of revenues. Compare the freedoms granted by King Henry to those granted by Bishop Frederick in his *Agreement with Colonists*, p. 277 above.

[Source: *English Historical Documents*, vol. 2: *1042-1189*, ed. David C. Douglas and George W. Greenaway, 2nd ed. (London: Routledge, 1981), pp. 1012-13 (slightly modified).]

Henry, by the grace of God, king of the English, to the archbishop of Canterbury, and to the bishops and abbots, and earls and barons and justices and sheriffs, and to all his liegemen, both French and English, of the whole of England, greeting. Know that I have granted to my citizens of London that they shall hold Middlesex at "farm" for 300 pounds "by tale" for themselves and their heirs from me and my heirs, so that the citizens shall appoint as sheriff from themselves whomsoever they may choose, and shall appoint from among themselves as justice whomsoever they choose to look after the pleas of my crown and the pleadings which arise in connection with them. No other shall be justice over the men of London. And the citizens shall not plead outside the walls of the city in respect of any plea; and they shall be quit of scot and of Danegeld and the murder-fine.[1] Nor shall any of them be compelled to offer trial by battle.[2] And if any one of the citizens shall be impleaded [sued] in respect of the pleas of the crown, let him prove himself to be a man of London by an oath which shall be judged in the city. Let no one be billeted within the walls of the city, either of my household, or by the force of anyone else. And let all the men of London and their property be quit and free from toll and passage and lestage and from all other customs throughout all England and at the seaports. And let the churches and barons and citizens hold and have well and in peace their sokes, with all their customs, so that those who dwell in these sokes shall pay no customs except to him who possesses the soke, or to the steward whom he has placed there. And a man of London shall not be fined at mercy[3] except accord-

---

1 The "murder-fine" (*murdrum*) penalized an entire community for the death of any Norman. It dated from the period after the Norman conquest, when feelings ran high against the invaders. The Londoners are here exempt from paying this.
2 This was a duel to determine which party was in the right; the tradesmen of London preferred other forms of trial.
3 "Fined at mercy" means fined at discretion, and to an unlimited amount.

ing to his "were",[1] that is to say, up to 100 shillings: this applies to an offence which can be punished by a fine. And there shall no longer be "miskenning"[2] in the hustings court, nor in the folk-moot,[3] nor in other pleas within the city. And the hustings court shall sit once a week, to wit, on Monday. I will cause my citizens to have their lands and pledges and debts within the city and outside it. And in respect of the lands about which they make claim to me, I will do them right according to the law of the city. And if anyone has taken toll or custom from the citizens of London, then the citizens of London may take from the borough or village where toll or custom has been levied as much as the man of London gave for toll, and more also may be taken for a penalty. And let all debtors to the citizens of London discharge their debts, or prove in London that they do not owe them; and if they refuse either to pay or to come and make such proof, then the citizens to whom the debts are due may take pledges within the city either from the borough or from the village or from the county in which the debtor lives. And the citizens shall have their hunting chases, as well and fully as had their predecessors, namely, in Chiltern and Middlesex and Surrey. Witness: the bishop of Winchester; Robert, son of Richer; Hugh Bigot; Alfred of Totnes; William of Aubigny; Hubert the king's chamberlain; William of Montfiquet; Hagulf "de Tani"; John Belet; Robert, son of Siward. Given at Westminster.

---

1 The "were" was the wergild, the price a murderer had to pay as compensation to the kin of his victim. In this case, the price of 100 shillings is slightly higher than the "were" of a commoner but lower than that of a thegn. Compare the discussion in Æthelred's *Law Code* above, p. 264, n. 1.

2 A "miskenning" was a verbal error in reciting the formal oaths protesting innocence; this entailed the loss of the case.

3 The "hustings court" and the "folk-moot" were both judicial assemblies, but the folk-moot was slightly larger.

CHURCH REFORM

5.4 The royal view: Henry IV, *Letter to Gregory VII* (1075). Original in Latin.

THE MOVEMENT FOR CHURCH reform was initially supported by both popes and emperors. But as the issue of church leadership came to the fore, the two powers inevitably clashed. When, in 1075, Emperor Henry IV (r.1056-1106) "invested"—put into office— his episcopal candidate at Milan, Pope Gregory VII (r.1073-1085) complained. Henry reacted vigorously. He met with his bishops at Worms, and the assembly denounced Gregory (called by his old name, Hildebrand) as a usurper of the papal throne. The letter below, which was circulated within Germany, charges Gregory with throwing the church into chaos and calls upon him to resign. A milder version was sent to the pope himself.

[Source: *Imperial Lives and Letters*, ed. Robert L. Benson; trans. Theodor E. Mommsen and Karl F. Morrison (New York: Columbia University Press, 2000), pp. 150-51.]

Henry, King not by usurpation, but by the pious ordination of God,[1] to Hildebrand, now not Pope, but false monk:

You have deserved such a salutation as this because of the confusion you have wrought; for you left untouched no order of the Church which you could make a sharer of confusion instead of honor, of malediction instead of benediction.

For to discuss a few outstanding points among many: Not only have you dared to touch the rectors of the holy Church—the archbishops, the bishops, and the priests, anointed of the Lord as they are[2]—but you have trodden them under foot like slaves who know not what their lord may do.[3] In crushing them you have gained for yourself acclaim from the mouth of the rabble. You have judged that all these know nothing, while you alone know everything. In any case, you have sedulously used this knowledge not for edification, but for destruction,[4] so greatly that we may believe Saint Gregory, whose name you have arrogated to yourself, rightly made this prophesy of you when he said: "From the abundance of his subjects, the mind of the prelate is often exalted, and he thinks that he has more knowledge than anyone else, since he sees that he has more power than anyone else."[5]

And we, indeed, bore with all these abuses, since we were eager to preserve the honor of the Apostolic See. But you construed our humility as fear, and so you were emboldened to rise up even against the royal power itself, granted to us by God. You dared to threaten to take the kingship away from us—as though we had received the kingship from you, as though kingship and empire were in your hand and not in the hand of God.

Our Lord, Jesus Christ, has called us to kingship, but has not called you to the priesthood. For you have risen by these steps: namely, by cunning, which the monastic profession abhors, to money; by money to favor; by favor to the sword. By the sword you have come to the throne of peace, and from the throne of peace you have destroyed the peace. You have armed subjects against their prelates; you who have not been called by God have taught that our bishops who have been called by God are to be spurned; you have usurped for laymen the bishops' ministry over priests, with the result that these laymen depose and condemn the very men whom the laymen themselves received as teachers from the hand of God, through

---

1 Rom. 13: 2.
2 Ps. 105: 15; Douay Ps. 104: 15; 2 Sam. 1: 14.
3 See John 15: 15.
4 See 2 Cor. 10: 8, 13: 10.
5 Gregory I, *Pastoral Care* 2. 6.

the imposition of the hands of bishops.

You have also touched me, one who, though unworthy, has been anointed to kingship among the anointed. This wrong you have done to me, although as the tradition of the holy Fathers has taught, I am to be judged by God alone and am not to be deposed for any crime unless—may it never happen—I should deviate from the Faith. For the prudence of the holy bishops entrusted the judgment and the deposition even of Julian the Apostate not to themselves, but to God alone. The true pope Saint Peter also exclaims, "Fear God, honor the king."[1] You, however, since you do not fear God, dishonor me, ordained of Him.

Wherefore, when Saint Paul gave no quarter to an angel from heaven if the angel should preach heterodoxy,[2] he did not except you who are now teaching heterodoxy throughout the earth. For he says, "If anyone, either I or an angel from heaven, preach any other gospel unto you than that which we have preached unto you, let him be accursed."[3] Descend, therefore, condemned by this anathema and by the common judgment of all our bishops and of ourself. Relinquish the Apostolic See which you have arrogated. Let another mount the throne of Saint Peter, another who will not cloak violence with religion but who will teach the pure doctrine of Saint Peter.

I, Henry, King by the grace of God, together with all our bishops, say to you: Descend! Descend!

5.5 The papal view: Gregory VII, *Letter to Hermann of Metz* (1076). Original in Latin.

SOON AFTER RECEIVING Henry's letter, the pope met with *his* bishops and excommunicated Henry. Many of Henry's supporters abandoned the king, and Bishop Hermann of Metz, one of a handful of bishops at Worms who had opposed the condemnation of Gregory, was important in fomenting the resulting war. Yet Hermann needed arguments to back up the actions of the pope and convince others to separate themselves from the excommunicated king. Gregory supplied some reasons in this letter, downgrading the dignity of kingship and maintaining that the act of excommunicating a king had a long and illustrious history.

[Source: H.E.J. Cowdrey, *The Register of Pope Gregory VII, 1073-1085: An English Translation* (Oxford: Oxford University Press, 2002), pp. 208-11 (notes modified).]

Gregory, bishop, servant of the servants of God, to Hermann, bishop of Metz, greeting and apostolic blessing.

By your questioning you are seeking many things of me who am exceedingly busy, and you send a messenger who presses me too much at his own pleasure. Accordingly, if I do not reply sufficiently, I ask you to bear it with patience.

Therefore how I am in my bodily health, or how the Romans and the Normans[4] who are proving themselves to be with regard to me, the bearer of this letter may tell you. But as regards the other matters about which you have questioned me, would that blessed Peter[5] might answer through me, for he is often honored or suffers injury in me, his servant such as I am.

Now, who the excommunicated bishops, priests, or laymen are there is no need that you should inquire of me, for undoubtedly they are those who are known to have held communion with the excommunicated

---

1   1 Pet. 2: 17.
2   That is, doctrine that diverges from correct belief.
3   Gal. 1: 18.
4   When Gregory spoke of the Romans, he meant the people—and above all the nobles—of Rome. By the Normans he meant the rulers of Southern Italy, with whom the papacy had been allied since 1059.
5   This refers to St. Peter, whose "servant" but also spokesman Gregory considered himself.

King Henry, if it is right that he should be called king. For they do not scruple to set human favor or fear before the precept of the eternal King, nor do they fear by their support to drive their king towards the wrath of Almighty God. He, however, by communicating with his own courtiers who were excommunicated for the simoniac heresy[1] has not feared to incur excommunication, and has not been ashamed to draw others to be excommunicated by communicating with him. Concerning such men, what else is there that we might think except what we have learnt in the Psalms: "The fool has said in his heart, 'There is no God,'" and again, "All have together been made unprofitable" in their intentions?[2]

Now, as for those who say, "it is not right that the king should be excommunicated," although in view of their great folly we have no need so much as to answer them, yet lest we seem to pass impatiently over their foolishness we direct them to the words or deeds of the holy fathers, in order that we may call them back to sound teaching. Let them, therefore, read what blessed Peter commanded to the Christian people at the ordination of St. Clement about him whom they knew not to have the favor of the pontiff.[3] Let them learn why the Apostle says, "Ready to avenge every act of disobedience,"[4] and of whom he says, "With such a man not even to take food."[5] Let them ponder why Pope Zacharias deposed the king of the Franks and absolved all the Frankish people from the bond of the oath that they had taken to him.[6] Let them also learn in the Register of blessed Gregory that in privileges that he drew up for certain churches he not only excommunicated kings and dukes who contravened

his words but also adjudged that they should forfeit their office.[7] Nor let them overlook that blessed Ambrose not only excommunicated Theodosius—not only a king but indeed an emperor in habitual conduct and power, but even debarred him from remaining in church in the place of the priests.[8]

But perhaps these men wish to have it thought that, when God three times committed his church to blessed Peter saying, "Feed my sheep,"[9] he made an exception of kings. Why do they not take notice, or rather shamefacedly confess, that, when God gave principally to blessed Peter the power of binding and loosing in heaven and upon earth,[10] he excepted nobody and withheld nothing from his power. For when a man denies that he can be bound by the chain of the church, it remains that he must deny that he can be loosed by its power; and whoever brazenly denies this altogether separates himself from Christ. And if the holy apostolic see, deciding through the pre-eminent power that is divinely conferred upon it, settles spiritual matters, why not also secular matters? In truth, as for the kings and princes of this world who place their own honor and temporal gains before the righteousness of God, and who by neglecting his honor seek their own, whose members they are or to whom they cleave your charity is not in ignorance. For just as those who set God before their own entire will and obey his command rather than men[11] are members of Christ,[12] so also those of whom we have been speaking above are members of Antichrist. If, then, spiritual men are judged when it is necessary, why are not secular ones the more under constraint concerning their wicked deeds?

---

1 Gregory called the purchasing of church offices "simony" or the "simoniac heresy" after Simon Magus, who in Acts 8: 18-24 offered money to Peter and John if they would give him the power to confer the Holy Spirit.
2 Ps. 14: 1-3; Douay Ps. 13: 1-3.
3 *Epistola Clementis prior*, chap. 18.
4 2 Cor. 10: 6.
5 1 Cor. 5: 11.
6 In 751, Pope Zacharias (r.741-752) sanctioned the deposition of Childeric III (r.743-c.751), the last of the Merovingian kings.
7 This refers to the letters of Pope Gregory the Great (r.590-604).
8 The reference is to St. Ambrose's measures against the Emperor Theodosius I (r.379-395) after the emperor responded to a revolt at Thessalonica by massacring its inhabitants.
9 John 21: 15-17.
10 See Matt. 16: 19. The power of binding and loosing, as interpreted by the papacy, was the priestly power to impose penance and to administer absolution.
11 See Acts 5: 29.
12 See 1 Cor. 6: 15.

But perhaps they think that the royal dignity excels the episcopal. From their origins they can gather how greatly they each differ from the other. For human pride has instituted the former; divine mercy has instituted the latter. The former ceaselessly snatches at vain glory; the latter always aspires to the heavenly life. And let them learn what the blessed Pope Anastasius wrote to the Emperor Anastasius about these dignities,[1] and how blessed Ambrose distinguished between these dignities in his pastoral letter: "The episcopal honor and excellence," he said, "if you compare them with the splendor of kings and the diadem of emperors, leave them much more inferior than if you compare the metal of lead with the splendor of gold."[2] Being not unaware of these things, the Emperor Constantine the Great chose not the principal but the least place to sit amongst the bishops; for he knew that "God resists the proud, but he gives favor to the humble."[3]

Meanwhile, brother, we are letting you know that, having received letters from certain of our brother bishops and dukes, by the authority of the apostolic see we have given licence to these bishops to absolve those excommunicated by us who are not afraid to keep themselves from communion with the king. As regards the king himself, [Henry IV] we have absolutely forbidden that anyone should venture to absolve him until his assured penitence and sincere satisfaction shall have been reported to us by trustworthy witnesses, so that we may at the same time ascertain how, if divine mercy shall look upon him, we may absolve him to the honor of God and to his own salvation. For it is not hidden from us that there are some of you who, seizing any pretext that might seem to come from us, would be led astray by fear or human favor and presume to absolve him if we were not to forbid, and to add wound to wound in place of medicine. If any who are bishops in truth should forbid them, they would conclude that they were not defending righteousness but pursuing enmities.

Now, as for the ordination and consecration of bishops who venture to communicate with the excommunicated king, as blessed Gregory testifies, before God they become an execration.[4] For when they proudly resist to obey the apostolic see, as Samuel is witness, they fall into the crime of idolatry.[5] For if he is said to be of God who is stirred up by the zeal of divine love to destroy vices, he assuredly denies that he is of God who refuses, so far as he is able, to reprove the life of carnal men. And if he is accursed who withholds his sword from blood,[6] that is, the word of preaching from the slaying of carnal life, how much more is he accursed who from fear or favor drives the soul of his brother to eternal perdition [damnation]? In sum, that the accursed and excommunicated can bless and bestow upon anyone the divine grace that they do not fear to deny by their own works, can be discovered in no ruling of the holy fathers.

Meantime, we order you to have a word with the venerable archbishop of Trier,[7] our brother that is, who is to forbid the bishop of Toul[8] from intruding into the affairs of the abbess of the monastery of Remiremont,[9] and who, in concert with you, is to annul whatever he has decided against her. Now, as regards Matilda,[10] the daughter of us both and the faithful handmaid of blessed Peter, what you wish, I wish. But in what state of life she should continue under God's direction, I do not yet grasp for certain. But of Godfrey her late husband,[11] you may know for a certainty that I, although a sinner, frequently make memorial before God; for neither

---

1   This refers to a letter from Pope Anastasius II (r.496-498) to the Emperor Anastasius I (r.491-518).
2   We now know that the work in question was not written by St. Ambrose.
3   James 4: 6. The reference is to Emperor Constantine I (r.308-337) at the Council of Nicaea (325).
4   This is a reference to a letter of Gregory the Great.
5   See 1 Sam. 15: 23.
6   See Jer. 48: 10.
7   Bishop Udo.
8   Bishop Pibo.
9   Gisela.
10   Matilda was countess of Tuscany and a staunch supporter of Gregory.
11   Godfrey, duke of Lorraine, was killed on February 26, 1076.

his enmity nor any vain consideration holds me back and, moved by your own brotherly love and Matilda's pleading, I long for his salvation.

May Almighty God, by the intercession of the queen of heaven, Mary ever-virgin, and by the authority of the blessed apostles Peter and Paul which is granted by him to them, absolve from all sins both you and all our brothers in whatever order who are defending the Christian religion and the dignity of the apostolic see; and, giving to you the increase of faith, hope, and charity, may he make you strong in the defence of his law, so that you may deserve to attain to eternal salvation. Given at Tivoli on August 25th, in the fourteenth indiction.

THE CRUSADES AND RECONQUISTA

5.6 Martyrs in the Rhineland: Rabbi Eliezer b. Nathan ("Raban"), *O God, Insolent Men* (early-to-mid-12th c.). Original in Hebrew.

IN THE SPRING OF 1096, IRREGULAR crusader armies passed through the Rhine valley. They were responding to Pope Urban II's call to regain the Holy Land from the Muslim "infidels" who ruled it, but they also decided to attack the "infidels in their midst"—the Jews. Confronting their persecutors with a new and unprecedented religious fervor, the Jews actively sought martyrdom rather than submit to the enemy's demand that they convert. Indeed, not only did hundreds of Jews meet their death at the hands of the crusaders, but many preferred to kill themselves and their children rather than be defiled by the crusaders' swords. These suicide-martyrdoms became a rallying image for northern European Jews over the next century. Three short chronicles dramatized the resistance and martyrdom of the Rhineland Jews in 1096. In addition, dozens of liturgical poems—including *O God, Insolent Men* by Rabbi Eliezer b. Nathan (*c.*1090-1170), known as the "Raban"—described the martyrdoms of 1096 and those of subsequent persecutions.

Poems such as R. Eliezer's, excerpted here, were written as hymns and often performed in commemorative liturgies that were rich in symbolic display. The texts were written for a highly literate audience, men deeply immersed in the study of Jewish texts and trained to recognize the shorthand allusions to them in the verses. *O God, Insolent Men* taps all the motifs of the new genre of Hebrew martyrological verse: it is polemical, including a number of insulting comments about Christianity; it is eschatological, interpreting historical catastrophe as a prelude to messianic redemption and overlaying images of violence with biblical images of revelation and covenant; and it offers consolation, particularly in its call for vengeance. Formally, the poem is an alphabetic acrostic; it is extremely controlled, as if to reassure its listeners that order prevails over seeming chaos.

[Source: A. Habermann, *Sefer gezerot ashkenaz vetzarfat* (Jerusalem: 1945, repr. 1971), pp. 84-87. Introduced and translated by Susan L. Einbinder.]

1 O God, insolent men have risen against me[1]
They have sorely afflicted us from our youth[2]
They have devoured and destroyed us in their wrath
    against us[3]
Saying, let us take [their] inheritance for ourselves.[4]
...

Their hearts were turned to plotting evil and
    trouble.[5]
They went to seek pollution far away:[6]
The crucified one, buried and placed in a deep pit
20 in the depths of hell.[7]

And the insolent ones, alien idolators, plotted.
They stubbornly sought deceit and treachery[8]
And put their hand to leaving the House of Jacob in
    ruins,[9]
Saying, God will not see.

"O abandoned ones, why do you hope for relief and   25
    healing?[10]
Your King has abandoned you to the nations to be
    devoured
Do this and live: worship the icon!"[11]
Remember this, O Lord, how the enemy scoffs![12]

"Heaven forbid," cried the innocent ones.
"It would be shameful to abandon Him," they   30
    proclaimed from the bare heights.[13]
"We live by His favor, and his anger is but a moment
    to the weak,[14]
The Lord is merciful and compassionate and long-
    suffering."[15]

When the impure ones heard this, they were filled
    with poison.
They slaughtered them, they wrung their necks. No
    household was spared.[16]

---

1 Ps. 86: 14. The Douay version will not be cited for R. Eliezer's text. R. stands for Rabbi in the notes here.
2 Ps. 124: 3; Ps. 129: 1-2.
3 The first half of the verse echoes Jer. 10: 25, which begins with the vengeful "pour out thy wrath upon the nations," echoed in Psalm 79 (evoked below). The end of Raban's verse is from Ps. 124: 3.
4 Ps. 83: 12.
5 Isa. 59: 7 (see also Isa. 55: 7 and Mic. 2: 1); 1 Sam. 25: 31.
6 The tone is contemptuous. The speaker inverts the crusaders' mission, in its sense of a pilgrimage to the site of Jesus' life and death, to a journey toward impurity. By Jewish law, contact with a corpse, or with anything that has come into contact with a corpse or other unclean thing, is a source of pollution (See Lev. 11 and 21). Thus the crusaders, by returning to the site of Jesus' crucifixion, seek their own contamination.
7 This verse cannot be translated literally. It is clipped from Prov. 30: 16, where it is already corrupt and caused the commentators great trouble. The great northern French commentator, R. Solomon b. Isaac ("Rashi," d.1105) referred to an exegetical tradition according to which the expression refers to Sheol, or Gehenna, i.e., hell. R. Eliezer would have known this tradition.
8 See Num. 25: 18; Ps. 78: 57.
9 See Isa. 24: 12.
10 See Jer. 33: 6.
11 The polemical literature of medieval Jews often represented Christians as worshiping "icons" or "idols." As with the case of biblical critiques of the use of idols, the writers probably understood that the image was not the actual object of worship but a representation of something immaterial. However, it served their purposes to emphasize the stupidity of those who would worship pieces of wood and stone. Here, too, R. Eliezer puts in the Christian speech the type of argument Jews must have actually heard: God's covenant with the Jews had been superseded by a new covenant with the Christians, and the flourishing of Christendom, like the abasement of the Jews, proved this.
12 Ps. 74: 18.
13 Perhaps an allusion to Jer. 3: 21, "a voice on the bare heights is heard, the weeping and pleading of Israel's sons...."
14 Rearranging the language of the Hebrew version of Ps. 30: 5 ("his anger is but for a moment, [but] his favor is for a lifetime"). The Hebrew word for "weak" may echo a passage in the Talmud, B.Hullin 3b, where it refers to a weakness in the hands before the slaughter of sacrificial animals.
15 A common tribute to God: see, e.g., Exod. 34: 6.
16 Literally, the verse says "according to the number of persons, they were counted," which is an allusion to Exod. 12: 4. The cryptic formulation makes sense when its biblical context is recalled. In Exod. 12, God orders the enslaved Israelites

35 They piled together infants and women, young and old.[1]

The prideful ones concealed [their] trap for me, and spread their snares.[2]

Together, with a full heart, the remnant came forth willingly.[3]

They went out to perform their worship and fulfilled it energetically.

Their lips moved as they made their peace with Heaven:[4]

40 "There is a God who judges the earth."[5]

Brides and grooms behaved identically[6]

As one they were determined to sanctify You, O Awesome and Dreadful One.

Our eyes failed [watching] them day after day[7]

For we are killed for You every day.[8]

Tender children said sweetly to their mothers, 45

"Make us whole offerings! We are desired in Heaven."

Weep for all this, weep, O daughters of Israel.

Teach your daughters mourning; let each woman teach her companion laments.[9]

Youths like saplings pleaded with their fathers:

"Hurry! Hasten to do our Maker's Will! 50

The One God is our portion and destiny

Our days are over, our end has come."[10]

"Bound on Mt. Moriah, [Isaac's] father tied him

so he would not kick and ruin his slaughter.[11]

In our love for God, we will be slaughtered without 55 being tied

Our souls will rejoice in the Lord and be glad for His salvation."[12]

---

to slaughter a lamb per household and mark their doorposts with its blood. If "a household is too small for a lamb," two neighboring households may combine their number ("according to the number of persons") and so "make the count" for the lamb. By analogy, the medieval Jews are slaughtered "per household," meaning that no household is spared.

1 References to the mingled blood of male and female, young and old, etc., are a common motif in 1096 poetry, including this example. The demographic variety of the martyrs is equalized in death. In the next century, this equality will disappear in the literature to emphasize the martyrdom of elite, scholarly, men.

2 See Ps. 140: 5; Prov. 29: 5.

3 See 1 Chron. 29: 9, but evoking also Exod. 35: 21, 29. Notice how this section switches its allusions to Exodus and its tale of collective revelation and covenant. Thus the martyrological lament becomes a polemical response to the dreadful possibility voiced in Exod. 25-28. God has not abandoned the Jews but is with them and renewing his covenant precisely at this moment of suffering.

4 Alternatively, it is possible to read this line as "they reconciled themselves in vigor" or, possibly, "they reconciled themselves in fear."

5 Ps. 58: 11.

6 Literally, brides and grooms "did not divide their twin-ness." The verse alludes to the allegorical readings of the Song of Songs, interpreted as the "twinned" marriage of Israel and God.

7 Ps. 69: 3, 119: 82.

8 Or, all day long. See Ps. 44: 22.

9 See Jer. 9: 20. A number of Hebrew martyrological poems include a call to women to make lament, perhaps an allusion to professional keeners or to the prominence of women among public mourners.

10 See Lam. 4: 18.

11 This legend would be familiar to most medieval Jews. The ancient rabbis determined by adding and subtracting their way through the first chapters of Genesis that Isaac must have been a grown man (37!) at the time Abraham was ordered to "offer him up" in Gen. 22. How could it be that he would not have resisted? The rabbis concluded that Isaac knew very well what Abraham intended, and asked his father to tie him down tightly so as not to mar the sacrifice (comparing himself to the ritual offerings of the Temple cult). Here, R. Eliezer claims that the Jewish children slaughtered by their fathers also undertook to die willingly; moreover, their courage and piety exceeded that of the biblical Isaac because they did not flinch or require restraint. The idea of the exemplary piety of the Ashkenaz (German) communities and in particular of their martyrs is found throughout this poetry. It is a hallmark of the Ashkenazic "self-image," and undoubtedly contributed to the resistance of the communities to conversion.

12 See Ps. 35: 9.

The fathers were glad when they heard these pleasing words.
They hastened to lay hands upon the pure lambs[1]
They trilled: "God is One!" They cried out in consolation:[2]
60 "My witness is in Heaven, my witness is above!"[3]

They took their stations and slaughtered them while weeping
Free-will offerings as if on God's altars
Mothers swooned, naked, upon their children[4]
For this I weep.[5]
….

Their blood spatters on [God's] purple robe[6]
In exchange for silver, I bring gold.[7]
For these the Almighty's pious ones, no ransom has been set.[8]   95
I will avenge their blood, and I will not clear the guilty.[9]

[So] cry and call out to Your Creator always
Demand the blood of Your servants from those who shed it[10]
Give them, O Lord, what their evil deeds deserve.[11]
Give them broken hearts, let Your curse be upon them.[12]   100

---

1 Again, comparing the young victims to the sacrificial lambs of the Temple cult.
2 Deut. 6: 4. This is the "battle-cry" of the Jewish martyr. According to tradition, these were the last words of the famous first-century Jewish martyr, R. Akiba, who was executed by the Romans. The stories of the so-called "Ten Martyrs" of the Roman period were well-known to medieval Jews and recited annually on Yom Kippur (the Day of Atonement). Two versions of the "Ten Martyrs" were current, one in the Babylonian Talmud, Avodah Zara 18ab, and one in the long poem known as "Eleh ezkerah" ("These I shall remember").
3 See Job 16: 19.
4 They have been stripped by the crusaders. See Mic. 1: 11, but also the description in Ezek. 16 of God as a lover who finds Israel naked and covered in blood, pledges his love for her, and makes his covenant with her. Like the allusion to the paschal lambs in v.34, this passage would be associated with the Jewish holiday of Passover, as it is included in the Haggadah—the service book for that holiday. For medieval Jews, however, the Passover liturgy and imagery were messianic, i.e., they enacted a dramatic, sacred, narrative in which God's intervention in history and redemption of his people was an event to be anticipated as much as recalled.
5 Lam. 1: 16.
6 R. Eliezer alludes here to an ancient legend, which underwent a powerful revival in medieval martyrological laments. According to rabbinic legend, God would not step into history to avenge the deaths of the innocent until his coat was sufficiently saturated with their blood (hence, the "purple" coat). In the writings of the 1096 survivors and their followers, this ancient legend came to justify the suicide-martyrdoms of medieval Ashkenaz: if God's coat was not yet saturated with the blood of the martyrs, the innocent Jews who killed themselves and their families were adding to it, hoping to prod God into action. This motif is eschatological as well as a call for vengeance.
7 Here again, as in the preceding line, R. Eliezer is "speaking in shorthand" for a complex theological argument. It was possible that Jewish communities would interpret their persecution as a deserved punishment for wrongdoing. Many did, but not in Ashkenaz (Germany). On the contrary, the rabbis would argue, the Jewish communities of Ashkenaz and their holy martyrs were exemplars of piety. Precisely because of their unimpeachable goodness, God had waited to exact from them the cost of earlier transgressions, most notably the biblical sale of Joseph by his brothers for twenty pieces of silver. In exchange for this "silver," therefore, the Rhineland Jews offer the "gold" of their own meritorious lives.
8 It is critical that the survivors believe that repentance and prayer can atone for sin. In the case of the holy martyrs, however, there was no "ransom" (this word can also be translated as "redemption," as in the redemption of slaves) because their exemplary piety had pre-determined that their lives would pay for the sins of earlier generations.
9 Joel 3: 21.
10 Echoing the call for vengeance in Ps. 79: 10, "Let the avenging of the outpoured blood of thy servants be known among the nations…." This psalm, too, is a familiar element of the Passover liturgy.
11 Ps. 28: 4.
12 See Lam. 3: 65, which the Revised Standard Version of the Bible translates as "dullness of heart." Rashi notes this as a secondary meaning, and perhaps then the sense would be numbness, rather than broken-ness, of heart. His first gloss is "broken-hearted."

5.7 The Greek experience: Anna Comnena, *The Alexiad* (*c.*1148). Original in Greek.

AT CONSTANTINOPLE, ANNA COMNENA (1083-1148), daughter of the Byzantine Emperor Alexius Comnenus (r.1081-1118), watched the crusaders arrive. Her *Alexiad*, written thirty years after her retirement to a monastery in 1118, portrays her father as a hero worthy of comparison with Odysseus in the *Iliad*. In the passage below, Anna depicts Alexius trying to convince the crusader armies to cross the Bosporus and enter Asia Minor before they could do too much damage to Byzantine soil, and she tells how he exacted an oath from the crusade leaders, never honored, that they would return all former Byzantine territory to the emperor. Looking down her nose at the intruders, Anna called the crusaders indifferently "Latins," "Franks," and "Celts," while she referred to the Byzantines as "Romans." Does her *Alexiad* suggest that an unbridgeable gulf had grown up between the Christian East and West?

[Source: *The Alexiad of Anna Comnena*, trans. E.R.A. Sewter (Harmondsworth: Penguin, 1969), pp. 318-25 (slightly modified).]

It was at this time that Count Godfrey [of Bouillon][1] made the crossing with some other counts and an army of 10,000 horsemen and 70,000 infantry. When he reached the capital he quartered his men in the vicinity of the Propontis,[2] from the bridge nearest the Kosmidion[3] as far as the Church of St. Phocas. But when the emperor urged him to go over to the far side of the Propontis he put off the decision from day to day; the crossing was deferred with a series of excuses. In fact, of course, he was waiting for Bohemond[4] and the rest of the counts to arrive. Peter[5] had in the beginning undertaken his great journey to worship at the Holy Sepulcher, but the others (and in particular Bohemond) cherished their old grudge against Alexius and sought a good opportunity to avenge the glorious victory which the emperor had won at Larissa.[6] They were all of one mind, and in order to fulfil their dream of taking Constantinople they adopted a common policy. I have often referred to that already: to all appearances they were on pilgrimage to Jerusalem; in reality they planned to dethrone Alexius and seize the capital. Unfortunately for them, he was aware of their perfidy from long experience. He gave written orders to move the auxiliary forces with their officers from Athyra to Philea *en masse* (Philea is a place on the coast of the Black Sea). They were to lie in wait for envoys from Godfrey on their way to Bohemond and the other counts coming behind him, or *vice versa*; all communications were thus to be intercepted. Meanwhile the following incident took place. Some of the counts who accompanied Godfrey were invited by the emperor to meet him. He intended to give them advice: they should urge Godfrey to take the oath of allegiance. The Latins, however, wasted time with their usual verbosity and love of long speeches, so that a false rumor reached the Franks that their counts had been arrested by Alexius. Immediately they marched in serried ranks on Byzantium, starting with the palaces near the Silver Lake; they demolished them completely. An assault was also made on the city walls, not with helepoleis (because they had none),[7] but trusting in their

---

1 Godfrey of Bouillon (d.1110), duke of Lower Lorraine, led one of the chief armies of the First Crusade.
2 The Propontis was the Greek term for the Sea of Marmara.
3 The Kosmidion refers to the monastery of St. Kosmas.
4 Bohemond of Taranto (d.1111) and his nephew Tancred led an important contingent of southern Italian Normans on the crusade.
5 Peter the Hermit, who led the so-called "Peasants' Crusade."
6 Bohemond and his father, Robert Guiscard, had attacked Byzantium in the 1080s, but they were defeated by Alexius.
7 Helepoleis were assault towers.

great numbers they had the effrontery to try to set fire to the gate below the palace,[1] near the sanctuary of St. Nicolas. The vulgar mob of Byzantines, who were utterly craven, with no experience of war, were not the only ones to weep and wail and beat their breasts in impotent fear when they saw the Latin ranks; even more alarmed were the emperor's loyal adherents. Recalling the Thursday on which the city was captured,[2] they were afraid that on that day,[3] (because of what had occurred then) vengeance might be taken on them. All the trained soldiers hurried to the palace in disorder, but the emperor remained calm: there was no attempt to arm, no buckling on of scaled cuirass, no shield, no spear in hand, no girding on of his sword. He sat firmly on the imperial throne, gazing cheerfully on them, encouraging and inspiring the hearts of all with confidence, while he took counsel with his kinsmen and generals about future action. In the first place he insisted that no one whatever should leave the ramparts to attack the Latins, for two reasons: because of the sacred character of the day (it was the Thursday of Holy Week, the supreme week of the year, in which the Savior suffered an ignominious death on behalf of the whole world); and secondly because he wished to avoid bloodshed between Christians. On several occasions he sent envoys to the Latins advising them to desist from such an undertaking. "Have reverence," he said, "for God on this day was sacrificed for us all, refusing neither the Cross, nor the Nails, nor the Spear—proper instruments of punishment for evil-doers—to save us. If you must fight, we too shall be ready, but after the day of the Savior's resurrection." They, far from listening to his words, rather reinforced their ranks, and so thick were the showers of their arrows that even one of the emperor's retinue, standing near the throne, was struck in the chest. Most of the others ranged on either side of the emperor, when they saw this, began to withdraw, but he remained seated and unruffled, comforting them and rebuking them in a gentle way—to the wonder of all. However, as he saw the Latins brazenly approaching the walls and rejecting sound advice, he took active steps for the first time. His son-in-law Nicephorus (my Caesar)[4] was summoned. He was ordered to pick out the best fighters, expert archers, and post them on the ramparts; they were to fire volleys of arrows at the Latins, but without taking aim and mostly off-target, so as to terrify the enemy by the weight of the attack, but at all costs to avoid killing them. As I have remarked, he was fearful of desecrating that day and he wished to prevent fratricide. Other picked men, most of them carrying bows, but some wielding long spears, he ordered to throw open the gate of St. Romanus and make a show of force with a violent charge against the enemy; they were to be drawn up in such a way that each lancer had two peltasts[5] to protect him on either side. In this formation they would advance at a walking pace, but send on ahead a few skilled archers to shoot at the Celts from a distance and alter direction, right or left, from time to time; when they saw that the space between the two armies had been reduced to a narrow gap, then the officers were to signal the archers accompanying them to fire thick volleys of arrows at the horses, not at the riders, and gallop at full speed against the enemy. The idea was partly to break the full force of the Celtic attack by wounding their mounts (they would not find it easy to ride in this condition) and partly (this was more important) to avoid the killing of Christians. The emperor's instructions were gladly followed. The gates were flung open; now the horses were given their head, now reined in. Many Celts were slain, but few of the Romans on that day were wounded. We will leave them and return to the Caesar, my lord. Having taken his practiced bowmen, he set them on the towers and fired at the barbarians. Every man had a bow that was accurate and far-shooting. They were all young, as skilled as Homer's Teucer in archery. The Caesar's bow was truly worthy of Apollo. Unlike the famous Greeks of Homer he did not "pull the bow-string

1   The Blachernae Palace.
2   This refers to the revolt of the Comneni, when Alexius took the imperial office.
3   April 2, 1097, also a Thursday.
4   "My Caesar"—a reference to Anna's husband.
5   "Peltasts" were shield-bearing soldiers.

until it touched his breast and draw back the arrow so that the iron tip was near the bow";[1] he was making no demonstration of the hunter's skill, like them. But like a second Hercules he shot deadly arrows from deathless bows and hit the target at will. At other times, when he took part in a shooting contest or in a battle, he never missed his aim: at whatever part of a man's body he shot, he invariably and immediately inflicted a wound there. With such strength did he bend his bow and so swiftly did he let loose his arrows that even Teucer and the two Ajaxes were not his equal in archery.[2] Yet, despite his skill, on this occasion he respected the holiness of the day and kept in mind the emperor's instructions, so that when he saw the Franks recklessly and foolishly coming near the walls, protected by shield and helmet, he bent his bow and put the arrow to the bow-string, but purposely shot wide, shooting sometimes beyond the target, sometimes falling short. Although, for the day's sake, he refrained from shooting straight at the Latins, yet whenever one of them in his foolhardiness and arrogance not only fired at the defenders on the ramparts, but seemingly poured forth a volley of insults in his own language as well, the Caesar did bend his bow. "Nor did the dart fly in vain from his hand,"[3] but pierced the long shield and cleft its way through the corselet of mail, so that arm and side were pinned together. "Straightway he fell speechless to the ground," as the poet says, and a cry went up to heaven as the Romans cheered their Caesar and the Latins bewailed their fallen warrior. The battle broke out afresh, their cavalry and our men on the walls both fighting with courage; it was a grim, dour struggle on both sides. However, when the emperor threw in his guards, the Latin ranks turned in flight. On the next day Hugh advised Godfrey to yield to the emperor's wish, unless he wanted to learn a second time how experienced a general Alexius was.[4] He should take an oath, he said, to bear his true allegiance. But Godfrey rebuked him sternly. "You left your own country as a king," he said, "with all that wealth and a strong army; now

from the heights you've brought yourself to the level of a slave. And then, as if you had won some great success, you come here and tell me to do the same." "We ought to have stayed in our own countries and kept our hands off other peoples," replied Hugh. "But since we've come thus far and need the emperor's protection, no good will come of it unless we obey his orders." Hugh was sent away with nothing achieved. Because of this and reliable information that the counts coming after Godfrey were already near, the emperor sent some of his best officers with their troops to advise him once more, even to compel him to cross the straits. No sooner were they in sight when the Latins, without a moment's hesitation, not even waiting to ask them what they wanted, launched an attack and began to fight them. In this fierce engagement many on both sides fell and all the emperor's men who had attacked with such recklessness were wounded. As the Romans showed greater spirit the Latins gave way. Thus Godfrey not long after submitted; he came to the emperor and swore on oath as he was directed that whatever cities, countries or forts he might in future subdue, which had in the first place belonged to the Roman Empire, he would hand over to the officer appointed by the emperor for this very purpose. Having taken the oath he received generous largess, was invited to share Alexius' hearth and table, and was entertained at a magnificent banquet, after which he crossed over to Pelekanum and there pitched camp. The emperor then gave orders that plentiful supplies should be made available for his men.

In the wake of Godfrey came Count Raoul,[5] with 15,000 cavalry and foot-soldiers. He encamped with his attendant counts by the Propontis near the Patriarch's Monastery; the rest he quartered as far as Sosthenion along the shore. Following Godfrey's example he procrastinated, waiting for the arrival of those coming after him, and the emperor who dreaded it (guessing what was likely to happen) used every means, physical and psychological, to hurry them into crossing the straits. For instance, Opus was summoned—a man

---

1   Homer, *Iliad* 4. 123.
2   Teucer and the two Ajaxes appear in Homer's *Iliad*.
3   See Homer, *Iliad* 5. 18
4   Hugh of Vermandois (d.1102) was the brother of King Philip I of France and count of Vermandois.
5   Count Raoul was one of a number of petty lords, many of them vassals of Godfrey, who had taken a route through Italy.

of noble character, unsurpassed in his knowledge of things military—and when he presented himself before the emperor he was despatched overland with other brave men to Raoul. His instructions were to force the Frank to leave for the Asian side. When it was clear that Raoul had no intention of going, but in fact adopted an insolent and quite arrogant attitude to the emperor, Opus armed himself and set his men in battle order, maybe to scare the barbarian. He thought this might persuade him to set sail. But the Celtic reaction was immediate: with his available men he accepted the challenge, "like a lion who rejoices when he has found a huge prey." There and then he started a violent battle. At this moment Pegasios arrived by sea to transport them to the other side and when he saw the fight on land and the Celts throwing themselves headlong at the Roman ranks, he disembarked and himself joined in the conflict, attacking the enemy from the rear. In this fight many men were killed, but a far greater number were wounded. The survivors, under the circumstances, asked to be taken over the straits; reflecting that if they joined Godfrey and told him of their misfortunes he might be stirred to action against the Romans, the emperor prudently granted their request; he gladly put them on ships and had them transported to the Savior's tomb, especially since they themselves wanted this. Friendly messages, offering great expectations, were also sent to the counts whom they were awaiting. Consequently, when they arrived, they willingly carried out his instructions. So much for Count Raoul. After him came another great contingent, a numberless heterogeneous host gathered together from almost all the Celtic lands with their leaders (kings and dukes and counts and even bishops). The emperor sent envoys to greet them as a mark of friendship and forwarded politic letters. It was typical of Alexius: he had an uncanny prevision and knew how to seize a point of vantage before his rivals. Officers appointed for this particular task were ordered to provide victuals on the journey—the pilgrims must have no excuse for complaint for any reason whatever. Meanwhile they were eagerly pressing on to the capital. One might have compared them for number to the stars of heaven or the grains of sand poured out over the shore; as they hurried towards Constantinople they were indeed "numerous as the leaves and flowers of spring" (to quote Homer).[1] For all my desire to name their leaders, I prefer not to do so. The words fail me, partly through my inability to make the barbaric sounds—they are so unpronounceable—and partly because I recoil before their great numbers.

5.8 A Westerner in the Holy Land: Stephen of Blois, *Letter to His Wife* (March 1098). Original in Latin.

THEIR SELF-CONFIDENCE AT LEAST EQUAL TO Anna Comnena's, the crusaders had moderate success in their war against the Muslims. During the long siege of Antioch, which began in October 1097 and was not over until July 1098, one of the crusade leaders, Count Stephen of Blois (d.1102), dictated a letter to his wife, Adela. Full of love, bravado, false claims (for example, that he was the leader of the "whole expedition"), and pious sentiments, the letter betrays little sign that Stephen was about to desert the army and return home. The letter is a good illustration of what a crusader was supposed to think about the enterprise, whether he did or not.

[Source: *The Crusades: A Reader*, ed. S.J. Allen and Emilie Amt (Peterborough, ON: Broadview Press, 2003), pp. 63-66, revised from *Translations and Reprints from the Original Sources of European History*, ed. Dana C. Munro, Ser. 1, Vol. 1 (Philadelphia: University of Pennsylvania Department of History, 1895), no. 4, pp. 5-8.]

---

1 Homer, *Iliad* 2. 468; *Odyssey* 9. 51.

Count Stephen to Adela, his sweetest and most amiable wife, to his dear children, and to all his vassals of all ranks—his greeting and blessing.

You may be very sure, dearest, that the messenger whom I sent to give you pleasure, left me before Antioch safe and unharmed, and through God's grace in the greatest prosperity. And already at that time, together with all the chosen army of Christ, endowed with great valor by him, we had been continuously advancing for twenty-three weeks toward the home of our Lord Jesus. You may know for certain, my beloved, that of gold, silver and many other kind of riches I now have twice as much as your love had assigned to me when I left you. For all our princes, with the common consent of the whole army, against my own wishes, have made me up to the present time the leader, chief and director of their whole expedition.

You have certainly heard that after the capture of the city of Nicaea we fought a great battle with the perfidious Turks and by God's aid conquered them. Next we conquered for the Lord all Romania[1] and afterwards Cappadocia. And we learned that there was a certain Turkish prince Assam, dwelling in Cappadocia; thither we directed our course. All his castles we conquered by force and compelled him to flee to a certain very strong castle situated on a high rock. We also gave the land of that Assam to one of our chiefs and in order that he might conquer the above-mentioned Assam, we left there with him many soldiers of Christ. Thence, continually following the wicked Turks, we drove them through the midst of Armenia, as far as the great river Euphrates. Having left all their baggage and beasts of burden on the bank, they fled across the river into Arabia.

The bolder of the Turkish soldiers, indeed, entering Syria, hastened by forced marches night and day, in order to be able to enter the royal city of Antioch before our approach. The whole army of God, learning this, gave due praise and thanks to the omnipotent Lord. Hastening with great joy to the aforesaid chief city of Antioch, we besieged it and very often had many conflicts there with the Turks; and seven times with the citizens of Antioch and with the innumerable troops coming to its aid, whom we rushed to meet, we fought with the fiercest courage, under the leadership of Christ. And in all these seven battles, by the aid of the Lord God, we conquered and most assuredly killed an innumerable host of them. In those battles, indeed, and in very many attacks made upon the city, many of our brethren and followers were killed and their souls were borne to the joys of paradise.

We found the city of Antioch very extensive, fortified with incredible strength and almost impregnable. In addition, more than 5,000 bold Turkish soldiers had entered the city, not counting the Saracens, Publicans, Arabs, Turcopolitans, Syrians, Armenians and other different races of whom an infinite multitude had gathered together there. In fighting against these enemies of God and of our own we have, by God's grace, endured many sufferings and innumerable evils up to the present time. Many also have already exhausted all their resources in this very holy passion. Very many of our Franks, indeed, would have met a temporal death from starvation, if the clemency of God and our money had not succored them. Before the above-mentioned city of Antioch indeed, throughout the whole winter we suffered for our Lord Christ from excessive cold and enormous torrents of rain. What some say about the impossibility of bearing the heat of the sun throughout Syria is untrue, for the winter there is very similar to our winter in the west.

When truly Caspian,[2] the emir of Antioch—that is, prince and lord—perceived that he was hard pressed by us, he sent his son Sensodolo[3] by name, to the prince who holds Jerusalem, and to the prince of Calep, Rodoam[4] and to Docap prince of Damascus.[5] He also sent into Arabia for Bolianuth[6] and to Carathania for Hamelnuth.[7] These five emirs with

---

1 "Romania" here refers to the Byzantine Empire; at the time Stephen was writing, much of Anatolia had been taken by the Seljuk Turks.
2 This was Yaghi Siyan, appointed emir in 1087.
3 Shams ad-Daulah.
4 This was Ridwan of Aleppo.
5 Docap was Duqaq, Seljuk ruler of Damascus 1095–1104.
6 This was Kerbogha, the Turkish governor of Mosul (d.1102).
7 Carathania refers to Khorasan, today in Iran.

12,000 picked Turkish horsemen suddenly came to aid the inhabitants of Antioch. We, indeed, ignorant of all this, had sent many of our soldiers away to the cities and fortresses. For there are 165 cities and fortresses throughout Syria which are in our power. But a little before they reached the city, we attacked them at three leagues' distance with 700 soldiers, on a certain plain near the "Iron Bridge."[1] God, however, fought for us, his faithful, against them. For on that day, fighting in the strength that God gives, we conquered them and killed an innumerable multitude—God continually fighting for us—and we also carried back to the army more than two hundred of their heads, in order that the people might rejoice on that account. The emperor of Babylon also sent Saracen messengers to our army with letters, and through these he established peace and concord with us.[2]

I love to tell you, dearest, what happened to us during Lent. Our princes had caused a fortress to be built before a certain gate which was between our camp and the sea. For the Turks, daily issuing from this gate, killed some of our men on their way to the sea. The city of Antioch is about five leagues' distance from the sea. For this reason they sent the excellent Bohemond[3] and Raymond, count of St. Gilles,[4] to the sea with only sixty horsemen, in order that they might bring mariners to aid in this work. When, however, they were returning to us with those mariners, the Turks collected an army, fell suddenly upon our two leaders and forced them to a perilous flight. In that unexpected flight we lost more than 500 of our footsoldiers—to the glory of God. Of our horsemen, however, we lost only two, for certain.

On that same day truly, in order to receive our brethren with joy, and ignorant of their misfortunes, we went out to meet them. When, however, we approached the above-mentioned gate of the city, a mob of horsemen and footsoldiers from Antioch, elated by the victory which they had won, rushed upon us in the same manner. Seeing these, our leaders sent to the camp of the Christians to order all to be ready to follow us into battle. In the meantime our men gathered together and the scattered leaders, namely, Bohemond and Raymond, with the remainder of their army came up and narrated the great misfortune which they had suffered.

Our men, full of fury at these most evil tidings, prepared to die for Christ and, deeply grieved for their brethren, rushed upon the sacrilegious Turks. They, the enemies of God and of us, hastily fled before us and attempted to enter their city. But by God's grace the affair turned out very differently; for, when they wanted to cross a bridge built over the great river Moscholum,[5] we followed them as closely as possible, killed many before they reached the bridge, forced many into the river, all of whom were killed, and we also slew many upon the bridge and very many at the narrow entrance to the gate. I am telling you the truth, my beloved, and you may be very certain that in this battle we killed thirty emirs, that is princes, and, three hundred other Turkish nobles, not counting the remaining Turks and pagans. Indeed, the number of Turks and Saracens killed is reckoned at 1,230, but of ours we did not lose a single man.

While on the following day (Easter) my chaplain Alexander was writing this letter in great haste, a party of our men, lying in wait for the Turks, fought a successful battle with them and killed sixty horsemen, whose heads they brought to the army.

These which I write to you are only a few things, dearest, of the many which we have done, and because I am not able to tell you, dearest, what is in my mind, I charge you to do right, to carefully watch over your land, to do your duty as you ought to your children and your vassals. You will certainly see me just as soon as I can possibly return to you. Farewell.

---

1   The "Iron Bridge" crossed the Orontes River, about 7 miles north of Antioch.
2   A reference to an offer of neutrality by the Fatimid caliph of Egypt, who was Shi'a, and thus hostile to the Sunni Turks.
3   Bohemond of Taranto (d.1111), leader of the Norman contingent.
4   Raymond of St. Gilles (d.1109) was the count of Toulouse and an important crusade leader.
5   The Orontes River; this was another battle at the Iron Bridge.

5.9 The Muslim reaction: Ibn al-Athir, *The First Crusade* (13th c.). Original in Arabic.

FROM THE MUSLIM POINT OF VIEW, the conquests "for the Lord" that Stephen of Blois spoke about were, to the contrary, entirely ungodly. In the writings of ibn al-Athir (1160-1233), the key events of the First Crusade—the siege and conquest of Antioch, the capture of Jerusalem—are told with some dispassion, for al-Athir, while drawing on earlier sources, was writing over a century after the events. His inclusion of a poem by al-Abiwardi shows that, just as a new Hebrew literature of martyrdom emerged after the massacre of the Jews, so too an Arabic literature of lamentation accompanied the Muslim experience of the First Crusade. How would you compare his account of the siege of Antioch with that of Stephen of Blois in his letter home, above, p. 293? How would you compare the sentiments in the poem of al-Abiwardi here with those of Raban in his poem above, p. 286?

[Source: *Arab Historians of the Crusades*, ed. and trans. (from Arabic) Francesco Gabrieli, trans. (from Italian) E. J. Costello (Berkeley: University of California Press, 1969), pp. 3-12 (slightly modified).]

THE FRANKS SEIZE ANTIOCH

The power of the Franks first became apparent when in the year 478 [1085–86][1] they invaded the territories of Islam and took Toledo and other parts of Andalusia, as was mentioned earlier. Then in 484 [1091] they attacked and conquered the island of Sicily[2] and turned their attention to the African coast. Certain of their conquests there were won back again but they had other successes, as you will see.

In 490 [1097] the Franks attacked Syria. This is how it all began: Baldwin, their King,[3] a kinsman of Roger the Frank who had conquered Sicily,[4] assembled a great army and sent word to Roger saying: "I have assembled a great army and now I am on my way to you, to use your bases for my conquest of the African coast. Thus you and I shall become neighbors."

Roger called together his companions and consulted them about these proposals. "This will be a fine thing both for them and for us!" they declared, "for by this means these lands will be converted to the Faith!" At this Roger raised one leg and farted loudly, and swore that it was of more use than their advice. "Why?" "Be-cause if this army comes here it will need quantities of provisions and fleets of ships to transport it to Africa, as well as reinforcements from my own troops. Then, if the Franks succeed in conquering this territory they will take it over and will need provisioning from Sicily. This will cost me my annual profit from the harvest. If they fail they will return here and be an embarrassment to me here in my own domain. As well as all this Tamim[5] will say that I have broken faith with him and violated our treaty, and friendly relations and communications between us will be disrupted. As far as we are concerned, Africa is always there. When we are strong enough we will take it."

He summoned Baldwin's messenger and said to him: "If you have decided to make war on the Muslims your best course will be to free Jerusalem from their rule and thereby win great honor. I am bound by certain promises and treaties of allegiance with the rulers of Africa." So the Franks made ready and set out to attack Syria.

Another story is that the Fatimids of Egypt were afraid when they saw the Seljuks extending their

---

1 The first date is the Islamic one, the *anno Hejirae* (A.H.), named after the *hijra* or emigration of Muhammad to Medina; the second date is C.E. The year 1 A.H. is equal to 622 C.E.
2 This date clearly refers to the end of the Norman conquest of Sicily.
3 No "King Baldwin" led the First Crusade, but several Baldwins were involved in it, and later one of them, Baldwin of Boulogne (d.1118) was crowned King of Jerusalem.
4 Roger Guiscard (d.1101).
5 Tamim was the Zirid emir of Tunisia.

empire through Syria as far as Gaza, until they reached the Egyptian border and Atsiz[1] invaded Egypt itself. They therefore sent to invite the Franks to invade Syria and so protect Egypt from the Muslims.[2] But God knows best.

When the Franks decided to attack Syria they marched east to Constantinople, so that they could cross the straits and advance into Muslim territory by the easier, land route. When they reached Constantinople, the Emperor of the East refused them permission to pass through his domains.[3] He said: "Unless you first promise me Antioch, I shall not allow you to cross into the Muslim empire." His real intention was to incite them to attack the Muslims, for he was convinced that the Turks, whose invincible control over Asia Minor he had observed, would exterminate every one of them. They accepted his conditions and in 490 [1097] they crossed the Bosphorus at Constantinople. Iconium and the rest of the area into which they now advanced belonged to Qilij Arslan ibn Sulaiman ibn Qutlumísh, who barred their way with his troops. They broke through in rajab 490 [July 1097], crossed Cilicia, and finally reached Antioch, which they besieged.

When Yaghi Siyan, the ruler of Antioch, heard of their approach, he was not sure how the Christian people of the city would react, so he made the Muslims go outside the city on their own to dig trenches and the next day sent the Christians out alone to continue the task. When they were ready to return home at the end of the day he refused to allow them. "Antioch is yours," he said, "but you will have to leave it to me until I see what happens between us and the Franks." "Who will protect our children and our wives?" they said. "I shall look after them for you." So they resigned themselves to their fate, and lived in the Frankish camp for nine months, while the city was under siege.

Yaghi Siyan showed unparalleled courage and wisdom, strength and judgment. If all the Franks who died had survived they would have overrun all the lands of Islam. He protected the families of the Christians in Antioch and would not allow a hair of their heads to be touched.

After the siege had been going on for a long time the Franks made a deal with one of the men who were responsible for the towers. He was a breast-plate maker called Ruzbih whom they bribed with a fortune in money and lands. He worked in the tower that stood over the riverbed, where the river flowed out of the city into the valley. The Franks sealed their pact with the breast-plate maker, God damn him! and made their way to the water-gate. They opened it and entered the city. Another gang of them climbed the tower with ropes. At dawn, when more than 500 of them were in the city and the defenders were worn out after the night watch, they sounded their trumpets. Yaghi Siyan woke up and asked what the noise meant. He was told that trumpets had sounded from the citadel and that it must have been taken. In fact the sound came not from the citadel but from the tower. Panic seized Yaghi Siyan and he opened the city gates and fled in terror, with an escort of thirty pages. His army commander arrived, but when he discovered on enquiry that Yaghi Siyan had fled, he made his escape by another gate. This was of great help to the Franks, for if he had stood firm for an hour, they would have been wiped out. They entered the city by the gates and sacked it, slaughtering all the Muslims they found there. This happened in jumada I [491; April/May 1098].[4] As for Yaghi Siyan, when the sun rose he recovered his self control and realized that his flight had taken him several *farsakh*[5] from the city. He asked his companions where he was, and on hearing that he was four *farsakh* from Antioch he repented of having rushed to safety instead of staying to fight to the death. He began to groan and weep for his desertion of his household and children. Overcome by the violence of his grief he fell fainting from his horse. His companions tried to lift him back into the saddle, but they could not get him to sit up, and so left him for dead while they escaped. He was at his last gasp

---

1 Atsiz ibn Uwaq, a Seljuk general.
2 The Fatimid rulers of Egypt were Shi'ite Muslims.
3 The "Emperor of the East" refers to Byzantine Emperor Alexius (d.1118).
4 June 3rd, according to European sources.
5 One *farsakh* is about four miles.

when an Armenian shepherd came past, killed him, cut off his head and took it to the Franks at Antioch.

The Franks had written to the rulers of Aleppo and Damascus to say that they had no interest in any cities but those that had once belonged to Byzantium. This was a piece of deceit calculated to dissuade these rulers from going to the help of Antioch.

THE MUSLIM ATTACK ON THE FRANKS, AND ITS RESULTS

When Qawam ad-Daula Kerbuqa[1] heard that the Franks had taken Antioch he mustered his army and advanced into Syria, where he camped at Marj Dabiq. All the Turkish and Arab forces in Syria rallied to him except for the army from Aleppo. Among his supporters were Duqaq ibn Tutush,[2] the Ata-beg Tughtikin, Janah ad-Daula of Hims, Arslan Tash of Sanjar, Sulaiman ibn Artuq and other less important emirs. When the Franks heard of this they were alarmed and afraid, for their troops were weak and short of food. The Muslims advanced and came face to face with the Franks in front of Antioch. Kerbuqa, thinking that the present crisis would force the Muslims to remain loyal to him, alienated them by his pride and ill-treatment of them. They plotted in secret anger to betray him and desert him in the heat of battle.

After taking Antioch the Franks camped there for twelve days without food. The wealthy ate their horses and the poor ate carrion and leaves from the trees. Their leaders, faced with this situation, wrote to Kerbuqa to ask for safe-conduct through his territory but he refused, saying "You will have to fight your way out." Among the Frankish leaders were Baldwin, Saint-Gilles, Godfrey of Bouillon, the future Count of Edessa, and their leader Bohemond of Antioch. There was also a holy man who had great influence over them, a man of low cunning, who proclaimed that the Messiah had a lance buried in the Qusyan, a great building in Antioch:[3] "And if you find it you will be victorious and if you fail you will surely die." Before saying this he had buried a lance in a certain spot and concealed all trace of it. He exhorted them to fast and repent for three days, and on the fourth day he led them all to the spot with their soldiers and workmen, who dug everywhere and found the lance as he had told them.[4] Whereupon he cried "Rejoice! For victory is secure." So on the fifth day they left the city in groups of five or six. The Muslims said to Kerbuqa: "You should go up to the city and kill them one by one as they come out; it is easy to pick them off now that they have split up." He replied: "No, wait until they have all come out and then we will kill them." He would not allow them to attack the enemy, and when some Muslims killed a group of Franks, he went himself to forbid such behaviour and prevent its recurrence. When all the Franks had come out and not one was left in Antioch, they began to attack strongly, and the Muslims turned and fled. This was Kerbuqa's fault, first because he had treated the Muslims with such contempt and scorn, and second because he had prevented their killing the Franks. The Muslims were completely routed without striking a single blow or firing a single arrow. The last to flee were Suqman ibn Artuq and Janah ad-Daula, who had been sent to set an ambush. Kerbuqa escaped with them. When the Franks saw this they were afraid that a trap was being set for them, for there had not even been any fighting to flee from, so they dared not follow them. The only Muslims to stand firm were a detachment of warriors from the Holy Land, who fought to acquire merit in God's eyes and to seek martyrdom. The Franks killed them by the thousand and stripped their camp of food and possessions, equipment, horses and arms, with which they re-equipped themselves.

THE FRANKS TAKE MA'ARRAT AN-NU'MAN

After dealing this blow to the Muslims the Franks marched on Ma'arrat an-Nu'man and besieged it. The inhabitants valiantly defended their city. When the Franks realized the fierce determination and devotion of the defenders they built a wooden tower as high as the city wall and fought from the top of it, but failed to do the Muslims any serious harm. One night a few Muslims were seized with panic and in their demoral-

---

1 This was Kerbogha, the Turkish governor of Mosul (d.1102).
2 Duqaq was Seljuk ruler of Damascus 1095-1104.
3 This is a reference to the church of St. Peter in Antioch.
4 The finding of the Sacred Lance at the instigation of Peter Bartholomew was a major turning point for the crusade armies. Western sources do not accuse Peter of burying it.

ized state thought that if they barricaded themselves into one of the town's largest buildings they would be in a better position to defend themselves, so they climbed down from the wall and abandoned the position they were defending. Others saw them and followed their example, leaving another stretch of wall undefended, and gradually, as one group followed another, the whole wall was left unprotected and the Franks scaled it with ladders. Their appearance in the city terrified the Muslims, who shut themselves up in their houses. For three days the slaughter never stopped; the Franks killed more than 100,000 men and took innumerable prisoners. After taking the town the Franks spent six weeks shut up there, then sent an expedition to 'Arqa, which they besieged for four months. Although they breached the wall in many places they failed to storm it. Munqidh, the ruler of Shaizar, made a treaty with them about 'Arqa and they left it to pass on to Hims. Here too the ruler Janah ad-Daula made a treaty with them, and they advanced to Acre by way of an-Nawaqir. However they did not succeed in taking Acre.

THE FRANKS CONQUER JERUSALEM

Taj ad-Daula Tutush was the Lord of Jerusalem but had given it as a fief to the emir Suqman ibn Artuq the Turcoman. When the Franks defeated the Turks at Antioch the massacre demoralized them, and the Egyptians, who saw that the Turkish armies were being weakened by desertion, besieged Jerusalem under the command of al-Afdal ibn Badr al-Jamali. Inside the city were Artuq's sons, Suqman and Ilghazi, their cousin Sunij and their nephew Yaquti. The Egyptians brought more than forty siege engines to attack Jerusalem and broke down the walls at several points. The inhabitants put up a defence, and the siege and fighting went on for more than six weeks. In the end the Egyptians forced the city to capitulate, in sha'ban 489 [August 1096].[1] Suqman, Ilghazi and their friends were well treated by al-Afdal, who gave them large gifts of money and let them go free. They made for

Damascus and then crossed the Euphrates. Suqman settled in Edessa and Ilghazi went on into Iraq. The Egyptian governor of Jerusalem was a certain Iftikhar ad-Daula, who was still there at the time of which we are speaking.[2]

After their vain attempt to take Acre by siege, the Franks moved on to Jerusalem and besieged it for more than six weeks. They built two towers, one of which, near Sion, the Muslims burnt down, killing everyone inside it. It had scarcely ceased to burn before a messenger arrived to ask for help and to bring the news that the other side of the city had fallen. In fact Jerusalem was taken from the north on the morning of Friday 22 sha'ban 492 [15 July 1099]. The population was put to the sword by the Franks, who pillaged the area for a week. A band of Muslims barricaded themselves into the Oratory of David[3] and fought on for several days. They were granted their lives in return for surrendering. The Franks honored their word, and the group left by night for Ascalon. In the Masjid al-Aqsa the Franks slaughtered more than 70,000 people, among them a large number of Imams and Muslim scholars, devout and ascetic men who had left their homelands to live lives of pious seclusion in the Holy Place. The Franks stripped the Dome of the Rock[4] of more than forty silver candelabra, each of them weighing 3,600 drams, and a great silver lamp weighing forty-four Syrian pounds, as well as a hundred and fifty smaller silver candelabra and more than twenty gold ones, and a great deal more booty. Refugees from Syria reached Baghdad in ramadan, among them the qadi Abu Sa'd al-Harawi. They told the Caliph's ministers a story that wrung their hearts and brought tears to their eyes. On Friday they went to the Cathedral Mosque and begged for help, weeping so that their hearers wept with them as they described the sufferings of the Muslims in that Holy City: the men killed, the women and children taken prisoner, the homes pillaged. Because of the terrible hardships they had suffered, they were allowed to break the fast....

---

1   In fact, the Fatimids took Jerusalem in August 1098.
2   The crusaders' attack on Jerusalem began in June 1099.
3   Known as the Tower of David in European sources, it was in the citadel at Jerusalem (and is not to be confused with the small sanctuary of the same name in the Temple precinct).
4   The rock from which, Muslims believe, Muhammad ascended into heaven. Over it was built the "Mosque of 'Umar," the chief Islamic monument in Jerusalem.

It was the discord between the Muslim princes, as we shall describe, that enabled the Franks to overrun the country. Abu l-Muzaffar al-Abiwardi[1] composed several poems on this subject, in one of which he says:

We have mingled blood with flowing tears, and there is no room left in us for pity.
To shed tears is a man's worst weapon when the swords stir up the embers of war.
Sons of Islam, behind you are battles in which heads rolled at your feet.
Dare you slumber in the blessed shade of safety, where life is as soft as an orchard flower?
How can the eye sleep between the lids at a time of disasters that would waken any sleeper?
While your Syrian brothers can only sleep on the backs of their chargers, or in vultures' bellies!
Must the foreigners feed on our ignominy, while you trail behind you the train of a pleasant life, like men whose world is at peace?
When blood has been spilt, when sweet girls must for shame hide their lovely faces in their hands!
When the white swords' points are red with blood, and the iron of the brown lances is stained with gore!
At the sound of sword hammering on lance young children's hair turns white.
This is war, and the man who shuns the whirlpool to save his life shall grind his teeth in penitence.
This is war, and the infidel's sword is naked in his hand, ready to be sheathed again in men's necks and skulls.
This is war, and he who lies in the tomb at Medina seems to raise his voice and cry: "O sons of Hashim![2]
I see my people slow to raise the lance against the enemy: I see the Faith resting on feeble pillars.
For fear of death the Muslims are evading the fire of battle, refusing to believe that death will surely strike them."
Must the Arab champions then suffer with resignation, while the gallant Persians shut their eyes to their dishonor?

5.10 The crusade in Spain and Portugal: *The Conquest of Lisbon* (1147–1148). Original in Latin.

MANY EUROPEAN CATHOLICS CONSIDERED the *Reconquista* of the Iberian Peninsula another theater of the crusade. In fact, one group of crusaders left for the Second Crusade by way of the North Sea and England. They arrived in Spain in 1147 and were immediately put to work conquering the Muslims at Lisbon. The anonymous author of *The Conquest of Lisbon*, evidently an Anglo-French priest with high connections in both England and Spain, personally participated in the siege. In the excerpt below he records a speech given by Peter, bishop of Oporto, who rallied the army to undertake the assault. Peter's rhetoric was precisely that of the popes and other preachers who had inspired armies for the First and now Second Crusade. The siege was, Peter said, a sacrifice, a pious pilgrimage, and a righteous use of force against robbers and murderers. Although the warriors were on their way to Jerusalem, they could do no better than pause to do God's good work in Spain first. In this text the term "Moors" refers to the first Islamic invaders of Spain, who had by 1147 been settled there for about 400 years, while the "Moabites" are the Almoravids, more recent arrivals from the Maghreb. The passage below begins as the crusaders' ships pulled into the port of Oporto on their way to the Holy Land. What justifications does

---

1 An Iraqi poet, writing after the fall of Jerusalem.
2 The image here is of the Prophet who, from the tomb, raises his voice to rebuke his descendants (the sons of Hashim), that is, the unworthy caliphs whose opposition to the crusades is only half-hearted.

Peter give for the attack on Lisbon? Compare the way Peter and Rabbi Eliezer (in the poem above, p. 286) use passages from the Bible to make their points.

[Source: *De expugnatione Lyxbonensi: The Conquest of Lisbon*, trans. Charles Wendell David (New York: Columbia University Press, 2001), pp. 69, 71, 73, 77, 79, 81.]

Early next morning we all gathered from all the ships before the bishop on a hilltop in the cathedral churchyard, for our numbers were so great that the church would not hold us. When silence had been proclaimed of all, the bishop delivered a sermon in Latin, so that it might be made known to everyone in his own language through interpreters. Thus it begins:

"'Blessed is the nation whose God is the Lord, and the people whom he hath chosen for his own inheritance.'[1] And assuredly are they blessed on whom God has by some inestimable privilege conferred both understanding and riches: understanding, in order that they should know the ways of discipline; and riches, in order that they should be able to accomplish that which they piously desire. And truly fortunate is your country which rears such sons, and in such numbers, and unites them in such a unanimous association in the bosom of the mother church. And deservedly is the truth of that highest beatitude accomplished in you, in which it is said, 'Blessed are they that have not seen me and yet have believed.'[2]

"Christ, the mediator between God and men, when he came in person into the world, found very few who were followers of this way and of pure religion; hence, when a certain young man who said that he had fulfilled and kept the law asked him how he could be perfect, he answered, 'Go and sell all,' etc. Weigh carefully what follows: 'He was sad, for he had great possessions.'[3] Oh how great is the righteousness and mercy of our Creator! Oh how great the blindness and the hardness of the human mind! The young man spoke with Truth and about truth, and the voice of Truth was in his ears, and yet, since the hardness of his callous mind was not softened by the word of Truth, it is not to be wondered at if, when his mind had been emptied of the joy of sincerity, sadness entered in. And what shall we say to all this? How many there are among you here who are richer in possessions than this young man! How many who are higher in the rank of honors! How many who are more fortunate in a prolific stock and a numerous offspring! Yet it is a fact that they have exchanged all their honors and dignities for a blessed pilgrimage in order to obtain from God an eternal reward. The alluring affection of wives, the tender kisses of sucking infants at the breast, the even more delightful pledges of grown-up children, the much desired consolation of relatives and friends—all these they have left behind to follow Christ, retaining only the sweet but torturing memory of their native land. Oh, marvelous are the works of the Savior! Without the urging of any preacher, with the zeal of the law of God in their hearts, led by the impulse of the [Holy] Spirit, they have left all and come hither to us, the sons of the primitive church, through so many perils of lands and seas and bearing the expenses of a long journey. They are the most recent proof of the mysterious power of the cross. Oh, how great is the joy of all those who present a more cheerful face to hardships and pain than we do, we who, alas, are vegetating here in slothful idleness. Verily, 'this is the Lord's doing, and it is marvelous in our eyes.'[4] Verily, dear brothers, you have gone forth without the camp bearing the reproach of the cross;[5] you are seeking God while he may be found,[6] in order that you may lay hold on him. For it seems not strange that men should go unto God, since for the

---

1 Ps. 33: 12; Douay Ps. 32: 12.
2 John 20: 29.
3 Compare Matt. 19: 16-22; Mark 10: 17-22; Luke 18: 18-23.
4 Ps. 118: 23; Douay Ps. 117: 23.
5 See Heb. 13: 13.
6 See Isa. 55: 6.

sake of man God also came among men. Even now unto you at the ends of the earth hath the seed of the word of God been borne, for 'a sower went out to sow his seed.' 'The seed is the word of God.'[1] The word of God is God. If it ascend the throne of your mind, your mind is accordingly good, but not without it. These divine seeds have been sown in your bodies, and, if you receive them as good husbandmen, they must needs produce fruit like unto its source and the counterpart of that from which it sprang; but, if you prove bad husbandmen, the result can only be that sterile and swampy ground will destroy the seeds, and afterwards it will bring forth trash instead of fruit. And may the good God 'increase the fruits of your righteousness.'[2]

"Verily, dear sons, reborn of a new baptism of repentance, you have put on Christ once more, you have received again the garment of innocence to keep it stainless. Take care lest you wander away again after your own lusts....

"We believe it has already become well enough known in the countries from which you come that through the presence of the Moors and Moabites divine vengeance has smitten all Spain with the edge of the sword,[3] and that but few Christians, resident in but a few cities, have been left in it, [and these] under the yoke of a grievous servitude. But these matters, of which a knowledge was brought to you by fame only, now most certainly lie open to your view more clear than day. Alas, that in all Galicia and the kingdom of Aragon and in Numantia, of the numberless cities, castles, villages, and shrines of the saints there should now remain hardly anything to be seen but the signs of ruin and marks of the destruction which has been wrought! Even this city of ours which you see, once among the populous, now reduced to the semblance of an insignificant village, has within our memory repeatedly been despoiled by the Moors. Indeed, but seven years ago it was so oppressed by them that from the church of the blessed Virgin Mary, which according to my poor talents by God's grace I serve, they car-ried away the insignia, the vestments, the vessels, and all the ecclesiastical ornaments, after they had slain the clergy or made them captive. And from among the citizens and from the surrounding territory as far as the church of St. James the Apostle, they bore away with them into their own country almost innumerable captives, though not without bloodshed on the part of our nobles; and everything that remained they destroyed with fire and sword. Indeed, what does the coast of Spain offer to your view but a kind of memorial of its desolation and the marks of its ruin? How many cities and churches have you discovered to be in ruins upon it, either through your own observation or through information given you by the inhabitants? To you the mother church, as it were with her arms cut off and her face disfigured, appeals for help; she seeks vengeance at your hands for the blood of her sons. She calls to you, verily, she cries aloud. 'Execute vengeance upon the heathen and punishments upon the people.'[4] Therefore, be not seduced by the desire to press on with the journey which you have begun; for the praiseworthy thing is not to have been to Jerusalem, but to have lived a good life while on the way; for you cannot arrive there except through the performance of His works. Verily, it is through good work that anyone deserves to come to a glorious end. Therefore, as worthy rivals [strive together] to raise up the fallen and prostrate church of Spain; reclothe her soiled and disfigured form with the garments of joy and gladness. As worthy sons, look not on the shame of a father nor say to a mother, 'It is a gift by whatsoever thou mightest be profited by me.'[5] Weigh not lightly your duty to your fellow men; for, as St. Ambrose says, 'He who does not ward off an injury from his comrades and brothers, if he can, is as much at fault as he who does the injury.'[6]

"Now, as worthy sons of the mother church, repel force and injury; for in law it happens that whatever anyone does in self-defense he is held to have done lawfully. Brothers, you have laid aside the arms [of violence] by which the property of others is laid

---

1   Luke 8: 5, 11.
2   2 Cor. 9: 10.
3   Compare 2 Kings 10: 25.
4   Ps. 149: 7.
5   Matt. 15: 5.
6   Ambrose, *De officiis* 1.36.

waste—concerning which it is said, 'He that strikes with the sword shall perish with the sword,'[1] that is, he who, without the command or consent of any higher or legitimate power, takes up arms against the life of his brothers—but now by God's inspiration you are bearing the arms [of righteousness] by means of which murderers and robbers are condemned, thefts are prevented, acts of adultery are punished, the impious perish from the earth, and parricides are not permitted to live nor sons to act unfilially. Therefore, brothers, take courage with these arms, courage, that is to say, either to defend the fatherland in war against barbarians or to ward off enemies at home, or to defend comrades from robbers; for such courage is full of righteousness. Indeed, such works of vengeance are duties which righteous men perform with a good conscience."

---

1 See Matt. 26: 52.

5.11 The pro-Norman position: William of Jumièges, *The Deeds of the Dukes of the Normans* (c.1070). Original in Latin.

CELEBRATING DUKE WILLIAM OF Normandy's victory at Hastings and justifying his anointment as king of England was William, a monk of Jumièges, a monastery near Rouen founded and supported by the Norman ducal family. William's account was enormously popular, surviving in many manuscripts and inspiring numerous other chroniclers, so that his became the predominant voice in depicting the events of 1066. In the passage below, Duke Harold is the man who was crowned king of England after the death of Edward the Confessor. William of Jumièges portrays this as a usurpation. Note that the Norman Conquest was taking place at the same time as the Investiture Conflict: compare notions of kingship and royal rights in the letter of Henry IV to Gregory VII (above, p. 281), the letter of Gregory VII to Hermann of Metz (above, p. 282), and this account by William of Jumièges.

[Source: *The Norman Conquest*, ed. and trans. R. Allen Brown (London: Edward Arnold, 1984), pp. 13-15 (slightly modified).]

---

23 Edward, king of the English,[1] by Divine disposition lacking an heir, had formerly sent Robert [of Jumièges] archbishop of Canterbury to the duke[2] to nominate him as the heir to the kingdom which God had given him. Furthermore he afterward sent to the duke Harold,[3] the greatest of all the earls of his dominions in riches, honor and power, that he should swear fealty to him[4] concerning Edward's crown and confirm it with Christian oaths. Harold, hastening to fulfil this mission, crossed the narrow seas and landed in Ponthieu, where he fell into the hands of Guy, count of Abbeville, who at once took him and his companions prisoner. When the duke heard of this he sent envoys and angrily caused them to be released. Harold remained with the duke for some time, and swore fealty concerning the kingdom with many oaths, before being sent back to the king laden with gifts.

At length king Edward, having completed the term of his fortunate life, departed this world in the year of Our Lord 1066. Whereupon Harold immediately usurped his kingdom, perjured in the fealty which he had sworn to the duke. The duke at once sent envoys to him, exhorting him to withdraw from this madness and keep the faith which he had sworn. But he not only would not listen but caused the whole English people also to be faithless to the duke. Then there appeared in the heavens a comet which, with three long rays, lit up a great part of the southern hemisphere for 15 nights together, foretelling, as many said, a change in a kingdom.

24 Duke William therefore, who himself by right should have been crowned with the royal diadem, seeing Harold daily grow in strength, quickly caused a fleet of 3,000 vessels to be built and anchored at St. Valery (sur-Somme) in Ponthieu, loaded both with splendid horses and the finest warriors, with hauberks[5] and with helmets. Thence with a following wind, sails spread aloft, he crossed the sea and landed at Pevensey, where he at once raised a strongly entrenched castle. Leaving a force of warriors in that, he hastened on to Hastings where he quickly raised another. Harold, hastening to take him by surprise, raised an immense

---

1 Edward the Confessor, king 1042-1066.
2 I.e., Duke William of Normandy. Throughout this document he is the man known as the "duke."
3 Harold, son of the powerful Earl Godwine of Wessex, and thus known as Harold Godwineson.
4 I.e., Duke William.
5 A hauberk is a long tunic made out of chain mail.

army of English and, riding through the night, appeared at the place of battle in the morning.

25 The duke however, in case of night attack, ordered his army to stand to arms from dusk to dawn. At daybreak he marshalled the squadrons of his warriors in three divisions and fearlessly advanced against the dread foe. He engaged the enemy at the third hour (9 a.m.) and the carnage continued until nightfall. Harold himself fell in the first shock of battle,[1] pierced with lethal wounds. The English, learning that their king had met his death, despairing of their lives, with night approaching, turned about and sought safety in flight.

26 The victorious duke returned to the battlefield from the pursuit and slaughter of his enemies in the middle of the night. Early next morning, the loot having been collected up from the fallen foe and the corpses of his own cherished men buried, he began his march towards London. It is said that in this battle many thousands of English lost their lives, Christ in them exacting retribution for the violent and unlawful death

meted out to Alfred, brother of king Edward [the Confessor]. At length the fortunate war-leader, who was no less protected by good counsel, leaving the highroad, turned away from the city at Wallingford, where he crossed the river and ordered camp to be pitched. Moving on from there he came to London, where an advance-party of warriors on entering the city found a large force of rebels determined to make a vigorous resistance. At once engaging them, the warriors inflicted much sorrow upon London by the death of many of her sons and citizens. At length the Londoners, seeing that they could resist no longer, gave hostages and submitted themselves and all they had to their noble conqueror and hereditary lord. And thus his triumph duly completed in spite of so many perils, our illustrious duke, to whom our inadequate words do not begin to do justice, on Christmas Day, was chosen king by all the magnates both Norman and English, anointed with holy oil by the bishops of the kingdom and crowned with the royal diadem, in the year of Our Lord 1066.

5.12 The native position: "Florence of Worcester," *Chronicle of Chronicles* (early 12th c.). Original in Latin.

NOT EVERYONE AGREED THAT William ruled "by right." Members of the Anglo-Saxon lay and ecclesiastical aristocracy bitterly resented their displacement by William's followers. Monks, too, were unhappy, as William imposed a new regime on English monastic life closely modeled on the elaborate round of collective prayer at Cluny. Submerged opposition may be seen in the *Chronicle of Chronicles*, produced in the early twelfth century by a monk at Worcester who was for a long time thought to be "Florence" but is now thought to have been a different monk, named John. The source is still generally known as "Florence of Worcester." In the passage below the author gives the Anglo-Saxon view of William (whom he calls "count" of Normandy) and the events of 1066. Note that Wulfstan, bishop of Worcester (d.1095), is mentioned in the text as among the few Anglo-Saxon prelates to swear fealty to William. At the same time, Wulfstan was almost certainly the person who commissioned "Florence of Worcester" to write. After analyzing the accounts of "Florence of Worcester" and William of Jumièges (p. 304 above), consider who had the better argument and explain why.

[Source: *English Historical Documents*, vol. 2: *1042-1189*, ed. David C. Douglas and George W. Greenaway, 2nd ed. (London: Routledge, 1981), pp. 225-28 (slightly modified).]

1066 On Thursday the vigil of our Lord's Epiphany, in the Fourth Indiction, the pride of the English, the pacific king, Edward, son of King Æthelred, died at London, having reigned over the English twenty-three years six months and seven days. The next day he was buried in kingly style amid the bitter lamenta-

---

1   This is unlikely; Harold seems to have fallen at the end of the battle, not at the start.

tions of all present. After his burial the under-king, Harold, son of Earl Godwine, whom the king had nominated as his succesor, was chosen king by the chief magnates of all England; and on the same day Harold was crowned with great ceremony by Aldred, archbishop of York. On taking the helm of the kingdom Harold immediately began to abolish unjust laws and to make good ones; to patronise churches and monasteries; to pay particular reverence to bishops, abbots, monks and clerks; and to show himself pious, humble and affable to all good men. But he treated malefactors with great severity, and gave general orders to his earls, ealdormen, sheriffs and thegns to imprison all thieves, robbers and disturbers of the kingdom. He labored in his own person by sea and by land for the protection of his realm. On April 24th in this year a comet was seen not only in England but, it is said, all over the world, and it shone for seven days with an exceeding brightness. Shortly afterwards Earl Tosti[1] returned from Flanders and landed in the Isle of Wight. After making the islanders pay tribute he departed and went pillaging along the sea-coast until he came to Sandwich. As soon as King Harold who was then at London heard this, he assembled a large fleet and a contingent of horsemen, and prepared himself to go to Sandwich. Tosti, learning of this, took some of the shipmen of that place (whether willing or unwilling) and set his course towards Lindsey, where he burnt many villages and put many men to death. Thereupon Edwin, earl of the Mercians, and Morcar, earl of the Northumbrians, hastened up with an army and expelled them from that part of the country. Afterwards he went to Malcolm, king of Scots, and remained with him during the whole of the summer. Meanwhile, King Harold arrived at Sandwich and waited there for his fleet. When it was assembled, he crossed over with it to the Isle of Wight, and, inasmuch as William, count of the Normans, was preparing to invade England with an army, he watched all the summer and autumn for his coming. In addition he distributed a land force at suitable points along the sea coast. But about the feast of the Nativity of St. Mary[2] provisions fell short so that the naval and land forces returned home. After this Harald Hardraada, king of the Norwegians and brother of St. Olaf, the king, suddenly arrived at the mouth of the river Tyne with a powerful fleet of more than five hundred large ships. Earl Tosti, according to previous arrangement, joined him with his fleet. Hastening, they entered the Humber and, sailing up the Ouse against the stream, landed at Riccall. On hearing this, King Harold marched with speed towards Northumbria. But before his arrival the two brother earls, Edwin and Morcar, at the head of a large army fought a battle with the Norwegians on the northern bank of the river Ouse near York on Wednesday[3] which was the vigil of the feast of St. Matthew the Apostle. They fought so bravely at the onset that many of the enemy were overthrown; but after a long contest the English were unable to withstand the attacks of the Norwegians and fled with great loss. More were drowned in the river than slain on the field.[4] The Norwegians remained masters of the place of carnage, and having taken one hundred and fifty hostages from York and left there the same number of their own men as hostages they went to their ships. Five days after this, namely on Monday, September 25th, as Harold, king of the English, was coming to York with many thousand well-armed fighting men, he fell in with the Norwegians at a place called Stamford Bridge. He slew King Harald and Earl Tosti with the greater part of their army and gained a complete victory. Nevertheless the battle was stoutly contested. Harold, king of the English, permitted Olaf, the son of the Norwegian king, and Paul, earl of Orkney, who had been sent off with a portion of the army to guard the ships, to return home unmolested with twenty ships and the survivors, but only after they had sworn oaths of submission and had given hostages. In the midst of these things, and when the king might have thought that all his enemies were subdued, it was told him that William, count of the Normans, had arrived with a

---

1 Earl Tosti was King Harold's brother. He sided with the Norwegian claimant to the English throne, Harald Hardraada, and the two were killed at the battle of Stamford Bridge on September 25, 1066.
2 September 8, 1066.
3 September 20, 1066.
4 This was the battle of Fulford.

countless host of horsemen, slingers, archers and foot-soldiers, and had brought with him also powerful help from all parts of Gaul. It was reported that he had landed at Pevensey. Thereupon the king at once, and in great haste, marched with his army to London. Although he well knew that some of the bravest Englishmen had fallen in the two former battles, and that one-half of his army had not yet arrived, he did not hesitate to advance with all speed into Sussex against his enemies. On Saturday, October 22nd,[1] before a third of his army was in order for fighting, he joined battle with them nine miles from Hastings, where his foes had erected a castle. But inasmuch as the English were drawn up in a narrow place, many retired from the ranks, and very few remained true to him. Nevertheless from the third hour of the day until dusk he bravely withstood the enemy, and fought so valiantly and stubbornly in his own defence that the enemy's forces could make hardly any impression. At last, after great slaughter on both sides, about twilight the king, alas, fell. There were slain also Earl Gyrth, and his brother, Earl Leofwine, and nearly all the magnates of England. Then Count William returned with his men to Hastings. Harold reigned nine months and as many days. On hearing of his death earls Edwin and Morcar, who had withdrawn themselves from the conflict, went to London and sent their sister, Queen Edith,[2] to Chester. But Aldred, archbishop of York, and the said earls, with the citizens of London and the shipmen planned to elevate to the throne Prince Edgar, nephew of Edmund Ironside, and promised they would renew the contest under his command.[3] But while many were preparing to go to the fight, the earls withdrew their assistance and returned home with their army. Meanwhile Count William was laying waste Sussex, Kent, Hampshire, Surrey, Middlesex and Hertfordshire, burning villages and slaying their inhabitants until he came to Berkhamsted. There Archbishop Aldred, Wulfstan, bishop of Worcester, Walter, bishop of Hereford, Prince Edgar, the earls Edwin and Morcar, the chief men of London, and many others came to him, and giving hostages they surrendered and swore fealty to him. So he entered into a pact with them, but none the less permitted his men to burn villages and keep on pillaging. But when Christmas day drew near, he went to London with his whole army in order that he might be made king. And because Stigand, the primate of all England, was accused by the pope of having obtained the *pallium* in an uncanonical manner, William was anointed king by Aldred, archbishop of York.[4] This was done on Christmas day with great ceremony. Before this (since the archbishop made it a condition), the king had sworn at the altar of St. Peter the Apostle,[5] and in the presence of the clergy and people, that he would defend the holy churches of God and their ministers, that he would rule justly and with kingly care the whole people placed under him, that he would make and keep right law, and that he would utterly prohibit all spoliation and unrighteous judgments.

---

1 This is an error; the battle of Hastings was fought on St. Calixtus's day, Saturday, October 14, 1066.

2 She had married King Harold.

3 Edmund Ironside was a son of King Æthelred II the Unready of England. For Æthelred, see the introduction to his *Law Code* above, p. 262.

4 A "pallium" was a thin band of white wool worn by the popes in the performance of the liturgy, the use of which could be conferred on approved metropolitan bishops. It was regularly given to the archbishops of Canterbury.

5 This was Westminster Abbey.

Plate 5.5 The Conquest depicted: *The Bayeux Tapestry* (end of the 11th c.).

NOT A TAPESTRY AT ALL BUT rather an embroidery, this long (120 feet) and narrow (20 inches) piece of linen tells in uninterrupted pictures, comic-strip style, the story that we have already seen in William of Jumièges (above, p. 304). It covers Harold's early fealty to Duke William, his usurpation of the crown, and his defeat at the Battle of Hastings. The pictures are flanked by borders at top and bottom, while embroidered labels in Latin identify important people and briefly explain the action. Probably commissioned by Odo of Bayeux, Duke William's half brother and a key figure in the story, the Tapestry is a work of propaganda. The portion shown here depicts Harold taking an oath before William. On the left is Duke William, sitting in authority upon a throne. Behind him are two Norman witnesses. Each of Harold's hands touches a reliquary as he swears the oath, recognizing his dependency on William. To his right, pointing a finger at him, is an English witness. His going back on this oath—his perjury—justifies the invasion of England. Might William's conquest have been a dress rehearsal for the First Crusade? What does the visual evidence suggest?

[Source: Musée de la Tapisserie de Bayeux.]

5.13 Exploiting the Conquest: *Domesday Book* (1087). Original in Latin.

IN 1085 WILLIAM ORDERED THE SURVEY of England's counties (or shires) that came to be called "Domesday." The result, which dates from 1087, when the king died, consists of two books. The first and longer is a well-digested and abbreviated account of the commissioners' reports for all except three counties. The second contains less reworked reports for the remaining counties. The excerpt below, from the first volume, is part of the survey of Huntingdonshire. The excerpt begins with the landholders—the king and his tenants-in-chief—in the shire. There follows an itemization of the properties of each of these landholders along with the geld, or tax, they yielded in the "time of King Edward" (=*tempore Regis Edwardi*, abbreviated TRE). For example, in the time of Edward, the lands at Cotton (see p. 310) were assessed at 2 hides when a geld (a tax) was collected. "There is land for 3 ploughs" was a way to express the acreage: "1 plough" was the theoretical amount of land that could be ploughed each year by a team of 8 oxen. The "demesne" was the lord's share of the land. The villans (sometimes spelled villains or villeins) were fairly well-off peasants, at least in comparison with bordars, who represented the poorest peasants. The whole manor at Cotton was worth 40 shillings, both in 1066 and in 1086, when the royal commissioners were asking their questions. While the tenant-in-chief holding Cotton was the bishop of Lincoln, he gave it to Tursin to "hold," probably in return for knight's service. Compare this document with the *Polyptyque of the Church of Saint Mary of Marseille*, above, p. 130, with regard to their purposes and the things they inventory.

[Source: *Domesday Book: A Complete Translation*, ed. Ann Williams and G. H. Martin (New York: Penguin, 2002), pp. 551-53 (slightly modified).]

HUNTINGDONSHIRE

Here Are Entered the Holders of Lands in Huntingdonshire

I KING WILLIAM
II The Bishop of Lincoln
III The Bishop of Coutances
IIII The Abbey of Ely
V The Abbey of Crowland
VI The Abbey of Ramsey
VII The Abbey of Thorney
VIII The Abbey of Peterborough
IX Count Eustace
X The Count of Eu
XI Earl Hugh
XII Walter Giffard
XIII William de Warenne
XIIII Hugh de Bolbec
XV Eudo fitzHubert
XVI Swein of Essex
XVII Roger d'Ivry

XVIII Ernulf de Hesdin
XIX Eustace the sheriff
XX Countess Judith
XXI Gilbert de Ghent
XXII Aubrey de Vere
XXIII William fitzAnsculf
XXIIII Ranulph, Ilger's brother
XXV Robert Fafiton
XXVI William Engaine
XXVII Ralph fitzOsmund
XXVIII Rohais, Richard's wife
XXIX The king's thegns

I. The land of the King

HURSTINGSTONE HUNDRED

IN HARTFORD King EDWARD had 15 hides of land to the geld. [There is] land for 17 ploughs. Ranulph, Ilger's brother, has custody of it now. There are now 4 ploughs in demesne; and 30 villans and 3 bordars have 8 ploughs. There is a priest and 2 churches, and 2 mills [rendering] £4, and 40 acres of meadow, [and] woodland pasture 1 league long and half a league broad. TRE worth £24; now £15.

NORMANCROSS HUNDRED

In BOTOLPH BRIDGE [in Peterborough] King Edward had 5 hides to the geld. [There is] land for 8 ploughs. There the king now has 1 plough in demesne; and 15 villans having 5 ploughs. There is a priest and a church, and 60 acres of meadow, and 12 acres of woodland pasture in Northamptonshire. TRE worth 100s;[1] now £8 Ranulph has custody of it. In this manor of the king and in other manors the sluice of the Abbot of Thorney has flooded 300 acres of meadow.

In Stilton the king's sokemen [dependents, rather freer than villans] of Normancross [Hundred] have 3 virgates of land to the geld. [There is] land for 2 ploughs, and 5 oxen ploughing.

In Orton Waterville [in Peterborough] the king has soke [jurisdictional rights, which brought in revenue] over 3½ hides of land in the land of the Abbot of Peterborough which was Godwine's.

TOSELAND HUNDRED

In GREAT GRANSDEN Earl Ælfgar had 8 hides of land to the geld. [There is] land for 15 ploughs. There are now 7 ploughs in demesne; and 24 villans and 8 bordars having 8 ploughs. There is a priest and a church, and 50 acres of meadow and 12 acres of scrubland. From the pasture come 5s4d [5 shillings, 4 pennies]. TRE worth £40; now £30. Ranulph has custody of it.

LEIGHTONSTONE HUNDRED

In ALCONBURY and Great Gidding, a BEREWICK,[2] there were 10 hides to the geld. [There is] land for 20 ploughs. There are now 5 ploughs belonging to the hall, on 2 hides of this land; and 35 villans have 13 ploughs there, and 8 acres of meadow. TRE worth £12; now the same. Ranulph, Ilger's brother, has custody of it.

In KEYSTON King Edward had 4 hides of land to the geld. [There is] land for 12 ploughs. There are now

2 ploughs in demesne; and 24 villans and 8 bordars have 10 ploughs, and [there are] 86 acres of meadow. [There is] woodland, pasture in places, 5 furlongs long and 1½ furlongs broad. TRE, as now, worth £10. Ranulph, Ilger's brother, has custody of it.

In BRAMPTON King Edward had 15 hides to the geld. [There is] land for 15 ploughs. There are now 3 ploughs, and 36 villans and 2 bordars have 14 ploughs. There is a church and a priest and 100 acres of meadow, woodland pasture half a league long and 2 furlongs broad, and 2 mills rendering 100s. TRE, as now, worth £20. Ranulph, Ilger's brother, has custody of it.

In Grafham are 5 hides to the geld. [There is] land for 8 ploughs. The SOKE[3] [is] in "Leightonstone" Hundred. There 7 sokeman and 17 villans now have 6 ploughs, and 6 acres of meadow. [There is] woodland pasture 1 league long and broad. TRE worth £5: now 10s less.

In GODMANCHESTER King Edward had 14 hides to the geld. [There is] land for 57 ploughs. There are 2 ploughs now in the king's demesne, on 2 hides of this land; and 80 villans and 16 bordars have 24 ploughs. There is a priest and a church, and 3 mills [rendering] 100s, and 160 acres of meadow and 50 acres of woodland pasture. From the pasture 20s. From the meadows 70s. TRE worth £40: now the same, by tale [counting rather than weighing].

II. The land of the Bishop of Lincoln

TOSELAND HUNDRED

In COTTON the Bishop of Lincoln had 2 hides to the geld. [There is] land for 3 ploughs. There are now 2 ploughs in demesne; and 3 villans having 2 oxen, and [there are] 20 acres of meadow. TRE, as now, worth 40s. Turstin holds it of the bishop.

In GREAT STAUGHTON the Bishop of Lincoln had 6 hides to the geld. [There is] land for 15 ploughs. There are now 2½ ploughs in demesne: and 16 villans and

---

1 "100s" means 100 shillings, or *solidi*.
2 Berewick = an outlying estate.
3 Right of jurisdiction.

4 bordars having 8 ploughs. There is a priest and a church, and 24 acres of meadow and 100 acres of woodland pasture. TRE, as now, worth £10. Eustace holds it of the bishop. The Abbot of Ramsey claims this manor against the bishop.

In DIDDINGTON the Bishop of Lincoln had 2½ hides to the geld. [There is] land for 2 ploughs. There are now 2 ploughs in demesne; and 5 villans having 2 ploughs. There is a church, and 18 acres of meadow, [and] woodland pasture half a league long and a half broad. TRE worth 60s; now 70s. William holds it of the bishop.

In BUCKDEN the Bishop of Lincoln had 20 hides to the geld. [There is] land for 20 ploughs. There are now 5 ploughs in demesne; and 37 villans and 20 bordars having 14 ploughs. There is a church and a priest and 1 mill [rendering] 30s, and 84 acres of meadow, [and] woodland pasture 1 league long and 1 league broad. TRE worth £20; now £16.10s.

NORMANCROSS HUNDRED
In DENTON Godric had 5 hides to the geld. [There is] land for 2 ploughs. There is now 1 plough in demesne; and 10 villans and 2 bordars have 5 ploughs. There is a church and a priest, and 24 acres of meadow and 24 acres of scrubland. TRE worth 100s; now £4. Turstin holds it of the bishop.

In ORTON WATERVILLE [in Peterborough] Leofric had 3 hides and 1 virgate of land to the geld. [There is] land for 2 ploughs and 1 ox. There is now 1 plough in demesne, and 2 villans, and 9 acres of meadow. TRE worth 20s; now 10s. John holds it of the bishop. The king claims the soke of this land.

In STILTON Tovi had 2 hides to the geld. [There is] land for 2 ploughs and 7 oxen. There is now 1 plough in demesne; and 6 villans with 3 ploughs, and 16 acres of meadow and 5 acres of scrubland. TRE, as now, worth 40s. John holds it of the bishop. This land was given to Bishop Wulfwine TRE.

LEIGHTONSTONE HUNDRED
In LEIGHTON BROMSWOLD Thorkil the Dane had 15 hides to the geld. [There is] land for 17 ploughs. There are now 6 ploughs in demesne; and 33 villans and 3 bordars having 10 ploughs, and 1 mill [rendering] 3s. 3 knights hold 3 hides, less 1 virgate, of this land. There they have 3 ploughs, and 3 villans with half a plough. There are 30 acres of meadow and 10 acres of scrubland. TRE, as now, the bishop's demesne was worth £20; the land of the knights, 60s. Earl Waltheof gave this manor in alms to ST. MARY of Lincoln.

In Pertenhall Alwine had 1 virgate of land to the geld. [There is] land for half a plough. This land is situated in Bedfordshire but renders geld and service in Huntingdonshire. The king's servants claim this [land] for his use. TRE, as now, worth 5s. William holds it of Bishop Remigius and ploughs it there with his own demesne.

III. The land of the Bishop of Coutances

In HARGRAVE [Northants] Sæmær had 1 virgate of land to the geld. [There is] land for 2 oxen. The SOKE [is] in Leightonstone [Hundred]. The same man himself holds it now of the Bishop of Coutances, and ploughs there with 2 oxen, and has 2 acres of meadow. TRE worth 5s; now the same.

IIII. The land of the Abbey of Ely

[HURSTINGSTONE HUNDRED]
In COLNE the Abbot of Ely had 6 hides to the geld. [There is] land for 6 ploughs, and in demesne [he had] land for 2 ploughs apart from the 6 hides. There are now 2 ploughs in demesne; and 13 villans and 5 bordars having 5 ploughs; and 10 acres of meadow. [There is] woodland pasture a league long and a half broad, and as much marsh. TRE worth £6; now 100s.

In BLUNTISHAM the Abbot of Ely had 6½ hides to the geld. [There is] land for 8 ploughs and, apart from these hides, [he had] land for 2 ploughs in demesne. There are now 2 ploughs in demesne; and 10 villans and 3 bordars with 3 ploughs. There is a priest and a church, and 20 acres of meadow, [and] woodland pasture 1 league long and 4 furlongs broad. TRE, as now, worth 100s.

In SOMERSHAM the Abbot of Ely had 8 hides to the geld. [There is] land for 12 ploughs and, apart from these hides, [he had] land for 2 ploughs in demesne. There are now 2 ploughs in demesne; and 32 villans and 9 bordars having 9 ploughs. There are 3 fishponds [rendering] 8s. and 20 acres of meadow, [and] woodland pasture 1 league long and 7 furlongs broad. TRE worth £7; now £8.

In SPALDWICK the Abbot of Ely had 15 hides to the geld. [There is] land for 15 ploughs. There are now 4 ploughs in demesne, on 5 hides of this land; and 50 villans and 10 bordars having 25 ploughs. There is 1 mill [rendering] 2s, and 160 acres of meadow and 60 acres of woodland pasture. TRE worth £16; now £22.

In Little Catworth, a BEREWICK of Spaldwick, [there are] 4 hides to the geld. [There is] land for 4 ploughs. There 7 villans have 2 ploughs now.

5.14 Logic: Abelard, *Glosses on Porphyry* (*c.*1100). Original in Latin.

WHILE AVICENNA (SEE ABOVE, p. 234) could draw directly on the works of Aristotle, only a small sample of those writings was available in the West when the philosopher Abelard (1079-1142) was fired up to use logic as a tool to arrive at truth. Abelard could draw on only a few of Aristotle's works on logic. He had, in addition, a treatise that the Greek neo-Platonist Porphyry (d.*c.*300) had written as an introduction to Aristotle's *Categories*; it had been commented on and translated into Latin by the late Roman philosopher Boethius (d.525). Like Avicenna, whose writings at the time were, however, unknown in the West, Abelard was interested in using and developing logic. He concentrated particularly on understanding the kind of reality possessed by "universals"—the "genera and species" that Aristotle spoke of in his writings on logic. Confronting William of Champeaux (d.1121), a scholar of Abelard's day who believed that universals existed outside the mind as common entities, Abelard formulated a set of arguments against this possibility. In his view, every real being outside the mind was entirely singular and in no way common. So-called universals, he concluded, were nothing more than names. They were common not because they possessed any kind of common being but simply because they could be predicated of many different subjects. We can say, for example, that Peter is human; Paul is human; Mary is human; and so on for countless others. As 'human' is thus predicable of many, it is accordingly a universal. In the selection below, we see some of Abelard's arguments against William's view, which has come to be known as realism. These arguments were apparently so successful that, much to Abelard's delight, they forced William to modify his position.

[Source: *Basic Issues in Medieval Philosophy*, ed. Richard N. Bosley and Martin Tweedale (Peterborough, ON: Broadview Press, 1997), pp. 382-83. Introduced by Blake Dutton.]

It remains now to object to those who say that each individual in that it agrees with others is universal and who allow that the same items are predicated of many, not in that many are essentially them, but because many agree with them. But if to be predicated of many is the same as agreeing with many, how is it that we say an individual is predicated of only one, since there is nothing which agrees with only one thing? Also how does being predicated of many constitute a difference between universal and singular, since Socrates agrees with many in exactly the same way as a human being agrees with many? Certainly a human being insofar as he is a human being and Socrates insofar as he is a human being agrees with others. But neither a human being insofar as he is Socrates nor Socrates insofar as he is Socrates agrees with others. Therefore, whatever a human being has Socrates also has, and in the same way.

Besides, since human being which is in Socrates and Socrates himself are conceded to be completely the same things, there is no difference of the latter from the former. For no thing is diverse from itself at one and the same time, because whatever it has in itself it has and in entirely the same way. Thus Socrates while white and literate is not in virtue of these diverse from himself, although he has diverse things in himself, for he has both these and in entirely the same way. He is not in one way of himself literate and another way white, just as it is not one thing which of itself is white and another literate.

Also when they say that Socrates and Plato agree in human being, how is that to be understood when it is agreed that all humans differ from each other both in matter and in form? For if Socrates agrees with Plato in the thing which is human being, but no thing is human being other than Socrates himself or some other human being, he will have to agree with Plato either in himself or in someone else. But in himself he is diverse from Plato and likewise in another since he is not the other.

There are those who understand agreeing in human being negatively as if it were said: Socrates does not differ from Plato in human being. But we could also say that he does not differ from Plato in stone since neither is a stone. Then we note no greater agreement between them in human being than in stone, unless perhaps there is an earlier proposition, as though we said: They are human being because they do not differ in human being. But this cannot be since it is altogether false that they do not differ in human being. For if Socrates does not differ from Plato in the thing which is human being, neither does he in himself. For if he differs in himself from Plato, since he is the thing which is human being, certainly he will differ from Plato in the thing which is human being.

Now that we have given the arguments why things either individually or collectively cannot be called universal, i.e. said to be predicated of many, it remains to ascribe universality to utterances alone. So just as grammarians call some nouns common and others proper, so dialecticians call some simple expressions universal, some particular, i.e. singular. A word is universal when it is apt to be predicated of many individually on account of its establishment, like the noun "human being" which is conjoinable to particular names of humans in virtue of the nature of the subject things to which it is applied. A singular word is one which is predicable of only one, like "Socrates," since it is taken to be a name of only one.

Plate 5.6: Gilbert of Poitiers, *Gloss on Psalm 101 (c.1117)*.

THE BOOK OF PSALMS WAS AS important a text for secular scholars as it was for monks. In the schools—whether the early cathedral schools or the later universities—the prophetic, liturgical, pastoral, and even literary aspects of the psalms were taught using commentaries (continuously written) and glosses (short notes). The teacher would read aloud and explain passages of the text, prompted by these glosses or commentaries, which themselves were based on Patristic and Carolingian writing on the psalms. This approach both preserved earlier traditions and encouraged adaptation and innovation.

Gilbert of Poitiers (or "de la Porrée") (d.1154) was both a teacher and a bishop. In this selection from his commentary on Psalm 101, his pedagogical interests are as much in evidence as his theological and pastoral concerns. The visual features of the manuscript, many of which he invented, are striking. On the page (or folio) shown here on p. 315, we note first the unique index symbols (1). The roman numerals above and below each symbol tell us that this is the fifth "penitential psalm" (the next of which is 129) and the fourth "prayer" (with psalm 141 being the next). In this way groups of thematically related psalms could be taught together, typical of the scholastic desire to organize subject matter. Next (2), the psalm itself is provided with its number, so that the index system would work smoothly (numbering psalms in the manuscripts was rare before this time; verses would not be numbered for another century). In the column reserved for the psalm text, red letters (3) set off the title of the psalm; in this case the scribe forgot to leave room for the title, so the rubricator—the scribe who wrote the titles in red ink—had to squeeze it in above the lines. The title provides Gilbert with the key to the spiritual meaning of the psalm, which he explains in his introduction. The unique format, with the text of the psalm (4) alongside the commentary (5), was created for greater convenience in the classroom. On this folio, the commentary only reaches to verse 4, while the psalm continues to verse 6; they catch up to each other eventually. In the commentary column, the words of the psalm are lightly underlined (6) to differentiate them from Gilbert's words. The underlining also helps alert the reader to multiple explanations—spiritual, moral, and literal—of the same verse (see Gregory the Great's

comments on *The Moralia in Job*, above, p.26 for these levels of interpretation). Since the words of the psalm are already written in the other column, these underlined quotations are extremely abbreviated. Gilbert provides a final visual aid with his "footnotes": in the margins, the initials (7) Au (for Augustine) twice indicate the source for his comments on that section. Elsewhere in the commentary Gilbert indicates his use of the Church Fathers Cassiodorus and Jerome, the Carolingian thinkers Remigius and Haimo of Auxerre, and others.

The commentary itself represents Gilbert's blend of biblical references and other commentaries. This dense "hypertext" of allusions makes the commentary difficult to render into English. Below is a translation of Gilbert's comments to verses 1 through 4. He begins by following Augustine, but just as we leave folio 157v (the page shown here) he turns to Cassiodorus in order to introduce another interpretation for verse 4.

[Source: Troyes, Bibliothèque Municipale 988, f. 157v. Caption by Theresa Gross-Diaz.]

5.15 Biblical scholarship: Gilbert of Poitiers, *Gloss on Psalm 101 (c.*1117). Original in Latin.

THE TEXT THAT FOLLOWS HERE IS a translation of Gilbert's commentary—a transcription, but in English, of the folio (page) that appears in Plate 5.6 above. As in the manuscript, the words of the psalm are underlined. Gilbert's citation of other biblical passages, unmarked in the manuscript, are here in quotation marks; others he paraphrases.

[Source: Troyes, Bibliothèque Municipale MS 988, f. 157v. Translated by Theresa Gross-Diaz and Jacqueline Long.]

Psalm 101[1]
<u>Hear, O Lord</u>. Title:[2] <u>The prayer of the poor man, when he was anxious, and poured out his supplication before the Lord</u>. This psalm is the fifth penitential psalm, and the fourth of those which are called prayers.[3] [Augustine:] Christ is the rich one,[4] who was the Word of God, in the beginning, with God;[5] yet through God, by whom all things were made, he became a pauper, putting on the form of a servant.[6] And yet it was not the sort of poverty of which he might say, "I did eat bread like ashes."[7] Therefore, so that such heights might be reconciled to such depths,[8] he added poverty to poverty, transfiguring us in himself; so that just as the head and members[9] (among whom

---

1   Vulgate (Douay) numbering; the medieval Latin Bible followed the Greek (Septuagint) numbering rather than the Hebrew numbering. In some "modern" Bibles (like the King James and the Revised Standard Version) this is Psalm 102. All psalm references for this text refer to the Vulgate (Douay) version.

2   These titles seem to have been added by Greek-speaking Jews around the 4th century C.E., and could include what was believed to be the author of a particular psalm, or a tune to which the psalm was sung. Translated into Latin, these extra-scriptural "titles" were interpreted allegorically as early as the time of Augustine (d.430). Here, the "poor man" is identified with the poor/rich Christ in Paul's Second Letter to the Corinthians, and the commentary unfolds from there.

3   These designations Gilbert takes from Cassiodorus; the index symbols are his own invention. The rest of this selection is essentially from Augustine, as Gilbert's marginal reference, here in brackets, shows.

4   See 2 Cor. 8: 9.

5   See John 1: 1.

6   See Phil. 2:7.

7   This psalm, verse 10.

8   That is, the heights were the omnipotent Creator and the depths were the lowly creature, Man; Gilbert's interest in the theological and philosophical question of the two natures of Christ (divine and human) spanned his career and permeates this commentary.

9   I.e., Christ (head) and the "body" (limbs, members) of the faithful on earth; see 1 Cor. 12: 12, 27.

are even the penitent) are "two in one flesh,"[1] so also may they be in one voice.[2] For this reason in Isaiah he [Christ] calls himself bridegroom and bride, thus: "as a bridegroom he hath decked me with a crown, and as a bride adorned me with jewels."[3] As "head" he calls himself the bridegroom, and as "members," the bride. Thus Christ is poor in us and with us; and for our sakes, he prays in this psalm both as head and as members, as one person, for the miseries of this world, into which he was cast down by the just judgment of God because of the sin of the first parent.[4] Therefore he says: when he was anxious; and because he knows that he could not be freed unless by the Lord, he poured out his supplication before the Lord. First is an opening which attracts the goodwill of the listener;[5] in which neither is his deed defended, nor the soul of the doer excused. Second is a tearful narration where he expounds what poverty he suffers, thus: For my days are vanished [v.4]. Third is a more confident address,[6] thus: But Thou,O Lord [v.13]. In the fourth part, comparing his [human] brevity to divine eternity: the former shall pass, but the latter shall remain, thus: He answered [v.24]. And in the fifth part he concludes by inhabiting that eternity, thus: The children of the servants [v.29]. With this intention[7] he warns all to recognize their misery, and to beg for mercy by which they might be restored. According to the rule of penitents, he will be finishing in joy what he begins in tears,[8] thus: O Lord hear my prayer and let my cry come to thee, that is, let not clouds of sin stand in the way; about which Jeremias said, "Thou hast set a cloud before, that our prayer may not pass through it."[9] He adds a cry to his prayer, so that you will know by the repetition that the emotion of the penitent has increased.[10] Next, Turn not away thy face from me, penitent; as if to say: you who reject the offerings of sinners—as Isaiah said, "I desire not the blood of calves"[11] —receive the gift of the penitent. You who "despise not a sad heart,"[12] to me, humble, incline thy ear, in whatsoever day I am in trouble. He says "in whatsoever day" because he suffered tribulation not just one day but at all times. In everything and at all times he prays. Wherefore he adds: In whatever day I call upon thee, hear me, and speedily at that, because now I ask not for the earth but for heaven. You promised that you would be speedily present to one who is desiring heaven; proclaiming: "Even as you are speaking, I will say, 'Here I am.'"[13] Note in these

---

1 Gen. 2: 24.

2 I.e., the "voice" or speaker of this psalm. Gilbert, like most medieval exegetes, believed all the psalms to have been written by David; but since they were prophecies, Christ spoke through them and thus the prophetic voice was generally either Christ himself or the Church. David and other characters could be the "voice" for the literal, historical, or moral sense of a psalm.

3 Isa. 61: 10. There was a long exegetical tradition of comparing Christ and the Church, or Christ and the soul, to a bridegroom and bride (not only in Isaiah and the psalms, but also in the Song of Songs). Speaking as he does in this psalm as both head and members, Christ is here both the bridegroom and the bride. The metaphorical gender-bending occasioned by this tradition is much studied today.

4 I.e., Christ "was cast down" onto earth; original sin was understood as the reason for God becoming man (the Incarnation).

5 Gilbert is treating the psalm as if it were a classical work. In classical oratory, for example, the speaker first tried to gain the goodwill of his—very rarely her—audience. This was called the *captatio benevolentiae*.

6 The "confident address" (*impetrandi certitudo*), like the preceding tearful entreaty, is another rhetorical device.

7 The intention (*intentio*) was one of the formal parts of the "introduction to the authors" (*accessus ad auctores*), a scholarly introduction to a literary work that discussed, among other things, the authorship, genre, and intention of the work at hand before the commentator turned to the content. Gilbert may have been the first commentator to apply this academic tool to the Bible.

8 Though the majority of this section is an extremely terse adaptation of Augustine, this line is almost verbatim from Cassiodorus, who was writing expressly for monks.

9 Lam. 3: 44.

10 Augustine used *petentis* (supplicant) here when he commented on this psalm because he was highlighting its rhetorical character. However, in a somewhat similar discussion of this verse Cassiodorus used *penitens* (a penitent), and Gilbert borrowed this word because of its more pastoral focus.

11 Isa. 1: 11; the "I" here is God speaking.

12 Consider "God does not reject the contrite heart" ("cor contritum ... Deus non spernit") of Ps. 50: 19. This particular manuscript, however, has *tritum* (sad or beaten down) instead of the more usual *contritum* (contrite).

13 Isa. 58: 9.

three verses the figure of speech called "epinome," which is the frequent repetition of an idea.

For my days have vanished. Second part. From where he would cry out, he explains what poverty and tribulation are to him, because his misery will move the pious judge. As if to say, Hear, and it is necessary, because my days are vanished like smoke. He says "day," not in the sense of daylight, but rather as the times that vanish like smoke because of the puffing up of Adam's pride. What is puffed up, falls. He adds, And my bones are dry like fuel for the fire, or fried as in a pan.[1] As bones support the flesh, so in the body of Christ, the strong support the weak, whose scandals are the "frying pan" of the strong. On this the apostle says, "Who is weak, and I am not weak? Who is scandalized, and I do not burn?"[2] Love, which abounds in the bones, does this. The good man is burned by the danger to any person, in proportion to how much he loves that person.[3] [Going on to folio 158:] Or [Cassiodorus:] bones, he says, are the strength of the soul, as Solomon says in Proverbs: "A good name makes the bones fat."[4]

Plate 5.7 The "standard gloss": *Glossa Ordinaria on Psalm 101* (1130s).

THOUGH BEGUN BY Gilbert's teacher Anselm of Laon (d.1117), the complete set of marginal and interlinear glosses on all the books of the Bible, called the *Glossa Ordinaria*, the Ordinary (or "usual") Gloss, was not completed for generations. The Ordinary Gloss on the Psalms was based on a teaching gloss created by Anselm, but it first appeared in Paris in the 1130s when Gilbert was teaching there. The format is similar to Gilbert's, in that the entire text of the psalm is present on the page. The difference is that the glosses are chopped up: some short comments are written between the lines; the rest are set in the margins. The abbreviated comments are often mere phrases and, without expert handling by the master, could easily be taken out of context. References to the original sources help to offset that danger, but they do not appear in all manuscripts. Only a few passages are here translated: compare them to Gilbert's comments on those verses. Sometimes they are closer to the original sources; at other times they reflect Gilbert's wording. In spite of the apparent difficulty in reading such a confusing page, the *Glossa Ordinaria* was popular throughout the entire Middle Ages, and was set in type as soon as the printing press was invented.

Here is a translation, taken from the Douay version of the text, of the first six verses of Psalm 101, which are written in large letters with generous spaces between lines on these manuscript folios. The verses are not numbered in manuscripts of the period.

1. The prayer of the poor man, when he was anxious, and poured out his supplication before the Lord. 2. Hear, O Lord, my prayer: and let my cry come to thee. 3. Turn not away thy face from me: in the day when I am in trouble, incline thy ear to me. In what day soever I shall call upon thee, hear me speedily. 4. For my days are vanished like smoke: and my bones are grown dry like fuel for the fire. 5. I am smitten as grass, and my heart is withered: because I forgot to eat my bread. 6. Through the voice of my groaning, my bone hath cleaved to my flesh.

---

1 The Gallican Psalter, the version most familiar in Gilbert's day, has "like fuel for the fire"; but he includes the alternate translation "fried as in a pan," which was known to Augustine and Cassiodorus.

2 2 Cor. 11: 29; "the apostle" for Gilbert is always Paul.

3 This passage is more obscure than usual; the key is the citation from Paul. The sense is that good people (Paul, or as in this passage, Christ) suffer for the sins or "scandals" of a sinner in proportion to how much they love that person.

4 Prov. 15: 30; Here Gilbert turns to Cassiodorus for an interpretation not found in Augustine. The sign Ca is found in the margin of the next page, not pictured here.

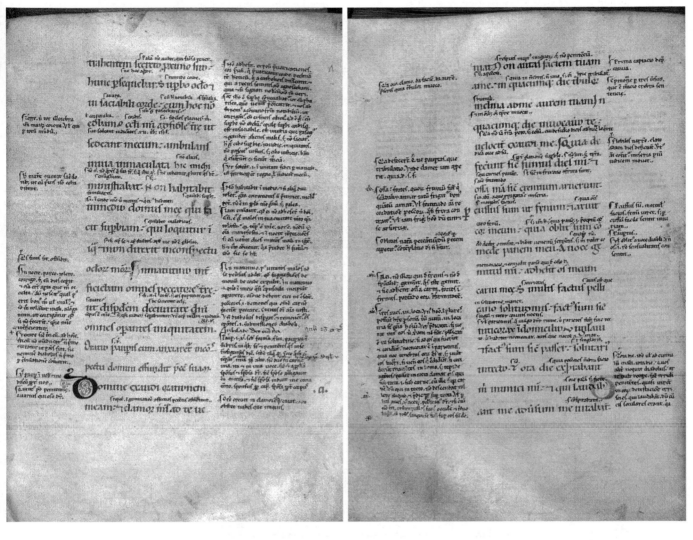

At the very bottom of the left-hand folio (fol. 136) you can see in the middle column the first words of Psalm 101, "Domine exaudi." (The D of Domine is like an upside-down Q.) The psalm and its glosses continue on the following page (fol. 136v). Here are some of the interlinear glosses—that is, the glosses written "between the lines" of the psalm (here printed between brackets).

Between the lines on fol. 136:

[at "The prayer of the poor man"] Christ.

[at "hear my cry"] Repetition; in duplication he shows the emotion of the petitioner.

Between the lines on fol. 136v:

[at "Turn not away"] You reject the gift of the wicked, but not the penitence of the devout.

[at "speedily"] Because now I ask not the earth but heaven; to which desire you said, "Even as you are speaking, I will say, 'Here I am.'"

[at "my bones have grown dry"] Or, fried in a pan.

Here are some of the marginal glosses. Their sources (given in brackets here) are not indicated in this manuscript. On the left-hand side of fol. 136:

[Augustine] Christ, poor in us and with us and for us.

[Cassiodorus] The fifth psalm of penitence; the fourth of which is called a "prayer."

On the right-hand side of fol. 136v:

[Cassiodorus] The first part, the opening to attract the benevolence of the listener.

[Cassiodorus] Epinome for three verses, that is, frequent repetition of the meaning.

[Source: Bibliothèque Mazarine MS 89, fols. 136 and 136v. Caption by Theresa Gross-Diaz.]

5.16 Rethinking the religious life: Heloise, *Letter* (1130s). Original in Latin.

AFTER AN ILLICIT LOVE affair, Heloise (*c.*1100–*c.*1163) and Abelard, the great twelfth-century philosopher whose work on logic is excerpted above, p. 313, were secretly married. But Heloise's guardian, suspecting foul play, had Abelard castrated. Thereafter, probably in 1118, both entered monasteries at Abelard's bidding. Many years later, *c.*1132, Abelard wrote about the trials of his life in a "letter of consolation to a friend," and Heloise, reacting to it, wrote a letter to Abelard that initiated a steady correspondence between the two. In one of these letters, excerpted below, Heloise, who by the time of its writing was abbess of the monastery of the Paraclete, founded by Abelard, asks Abelard to provide a Rule appropriate for women. How would you characterize Heloise's view of women and why do you suppose she expresses such a view? What are her criticisms of *The Benedictine Rule* (above, p. 28)? How does Heloise draw on her knowledge of biblical and classical texts to make her points?

[Source: *The Letters of Abelard and Heloise*, trans. Betty Radice (New York: Penguin Books, pp. 159-66, 178-79 (notes modified).]

We handmaids of Christ, who are your daughters in Christ, come as suppliants to demand of your paternal interest two things which we see to be very necessary for ourselves. One is that you will teach us how the order of nuns began and what authority there is for our profession. The other, that you will prescribe some Rule for us and write it down, a Rule which shall be suitable for women, and also describe fully the manner and habit of our way of life, which we find was never done by the holy Fathers. Through lack and need of this it is the practice today for men and women alike to be received into monasteries to profess the same Rule, and the same yoke of monastic ordinance is laid on the weaker sex as on the stronger.

At present the one Rule of St. Benedict is professed in the Latin Church by women equally with men, although, as it was clearly written for men alone, it can only be fully obeyed by men, whether subordinates or superiors. Leaving aside for the moment the other articles of the Rule: how can women be concerned with what is written there about cowls, drawers or scapulars?[1] Or indeed, with tunics or woollen garments worn next to the skin, when the monthly purging of their superfluous humors must avoid such things? How are they affected by the ruling for the abbot,[2] that he shall read aloud the Gospel himself and afterwards start the hymn? What about the abbot's table, set apart for him with pilgrims and guests?

---

1 *The Benedictine Rule* ch. 55; see above, p. 34.
2 Ibid., ch. 11.

Which is more fitting for our religious life: for an abbess never to offer hospitality to men, or for her to eat with men she has allowed in? It is all too easy for the souls of men and women to be destroyed if they live together in one place, and especially at table, where gluttony and drunkenness are rife, and wine which leads to lechery[1] is drunk with enjoyment. St. Jerome warns us of this when he writes to remind a mother and daughter that "It is difficult to preserve modesty at table."[2] And the poet himself, that master of sensuality and shame, in his book called *The Art of Love* describes in detail what an opportunity for fornication is provided especially by banquets:[3]

When wine has sprinkled Cupid's thirsty wings
He stays and stands weighed down in his chosen
　　place ...
Then laughter comes, then even the poor find plenty,
Then sorrow and care and wrinkles leave the brow ...
That is the time when girls bewitch men's hearts,
And Venus in the wine adds fire to fire.

And even if they admit to their table only women to whom they have given hospitality, is there no lurking danger there? Surely nothing is so conducive to a woman's seduction as woman's flattery, nor does a woman pass on the foulness of a corrupted mind so readily to any but another woman; which is why St. Jerome particularly exhorts women of a sacred calling to avoid contact with women of the world.[4] Finally, if we exclude men from our hospitality and admit women only, it is obvious that we shall offend and annoy the men whose services are needed by a convent of the weaker sex, especially if little or no return seems to be made to those from whom most is received.

But if we cannot observe the tenor of this Rule, I am afraid that the words of the apostle James may be quoted to condemn us also: "For if a man keeps the whole law but for one single point, he is guilty of breaking all of it."[5] That is to say, although he carries out much of the law he is held guilty simply because he fails to carry out all of it, and he is turned into a law-breaker by the one thing he did not keep unless he fulfilled all the law's precepts. The apostle is careful to explain this at once by adding: "For the One who said 'Thou shalt not commit adultery' said also 'Thou shalt not commit murder.' You may not be an adulterer, but if you commit murder you are a law-breaker all the same."[6] Here he says openly that a man becomes guilty by breaking any one of the law's commandments, for the Lord himself who laid down one also laid down the other, and whatever commandment of the law is violated, it shows disregard of him who laid down the law in all its commandments, not in one alone.

However, to pass over those provisions of the Rule which we are unable to observe in every detail, or cannot observe without danger to ourselves: what about gathering in the harvest—has it ever been the custom for convents of nuns to go out to do this, or to tackle the work of the fields? Again, are we to test the constancy of the women we receive during the space of a single year, and instruct them by three readings of the Rule, as it says there?[7] What could be so foolish as to set out on an unknown path, not yet defined, or so presumptuous as to choose and profess a way of life of which you know nothing, or to take a vow you are not capable of keeping? And since discretion is the mother of all the virtues and reason the mediator of all that is good, who will judge anything virtuous or good which is seen to conflict with discretion and reason? For the virtues which exceed all bounds and measure are, as Jerome says,[8] to be counted among vices. It is clearly contrary to reason and discretion if burdens are imposed without previous investigation into the strength of those who are to bear them, to ensure that human industry may depend on natural constitution. No one would lay on an ass a burden suitable for an elephant, or expect the same from children and old people as

---

1　Eph. 5: 18.
2　Jerome, *Letters* 116.6.
3　Ovid, *Art of Love* 1.233-34, 239-40, 243-44.
4　Jerome, *Letters* 22.16.
5　James 2: 10.
6　James 2: 11.
7　*The Benedictine Rule* ch. 58; see above, p. 34.
8　Jerome, *Letters* 130.11.

from men, the same, that is, from the weak as from the strong, from the sick as from the healthy, from women, the weaker sex, as from men, the stronger one. The Pope St. Gregory was careful to make this distinction as regards both admonition and precept in the twenty-fourth chapter of his *Pastoral Care*: "Therefore men are to be admonished in one way, women in another; for heavy burdens may be laid on men and great matters exercise them, but lighter burdens on women, who should be gently converted by less exacting means."

Certainly those who laid down rules for monks were not only completely silent about women but also prescribed regulations which they knew to be quite unsuitable for them, and this showed plainly enough that the necks of bullock and heifer should in no sense be brought under the same yoke of a common Rule, since those whom nature created unequal cannot properly be made equal in labor. St. Benedict, who is imbued with the spirit of justice in everything, has this discretion in mind when he moderates everything in the Rule according to the quality of men or the times, so that, as he says himself at one point,[1] all may be done in moderation. And so first of all, starting with the abbot himself, he lays down that he shall preside over his subordinates in such a way that (he says)

> he will accommodate and adapt himself to them all in accordance with the disposition and intelligence of each individual. In this way he will suffer no loss in the flock entrusted to him but will even rejoice to see a good flock increase … At the same time he must always be conscious of his own frailty and remember that the "bruised reed must not be broken."[2] … He must also be prudent and considerate, bearing in mind the good sense of holy Jacob when he said "If I drive my herds too hard on the road they will all die in a single day."[3]

Acting on this, and on other examples of discretion, the mother of the virtues, he must arrange everything so that there is always what the strong desire and the weak do not shrink from.[4]

Such modification of regulations is the basis of the concessions granted to children, and the old and the weak in general, of the feeding of the lector or weekly server in the kitchen before the rest, and in the monastery itself, the provision of food and drink in quality or quantity is adapted to the diversity of the people there.[5] All these matters are precisely set out in the Rule. He also relaxes the set times for fasting according to the season or the amount of work to be done, to meet the needs of natural infirmity. What, I wonder, when he adapts everything to the quality of men and seasons, so that all his regulations can be carried out by everyone without complaint—what provision would he make for women if he laid down a Rule for them like that for men? For if in certain respects he is obliged to modify the strictness of the Rule for the young, the old and weak, according to their natural frailty or infirmity, what would he provide for the weaker sex whose frailty and infirmity is generally known?

Consider then how far removed it is from all reason and good sense if both women and men are bound by profession of a common Rule, and the same burden is laid on the weak as on the strong. I think it should be sufficient for our infirmity if the virtue of continence[6] and also of abstinence makes us the equals of the rulers of the Church themselves and of the clergy who are confirmed in holy orders, especially when the Truth says: "Everyone will be fully trained if he reaches his teacher's level."[7] It would also be thought a great thing if we could equal religious laymen; for what is judged unimportant in the strong is admired in the weak. In the words of the Apostle: "Power comes to its full strength in weakness."[8] But lest we should underestimate the religion of the laity, of men like Abraham, David and Job, although they had wives, Chrysostom reminds us in his seventh sermon on the Letter to the Hebrews:

---

1 *The Benedictine Rule* ch. 48; see above, p. 33.
2 See Isa. 42: 3.
3 Gen. 33: 13.
4 *The Benedictine Rule* ch. 2 (see above, p. 29) and ch. 64.
5 See *The Benedictine Rule* ch. 35-41.
6 I.e., self-restraint.
7 Luke 6: 40.
8 2 Cor. 12: 9.

There are many ways whereby a man may struggle to charm that beast. What are they? Toil, study, vigils. "But what concern are they of ours, when we are not monks?" Do you ask me that? Rather, ask Paul, when he says "Be watchful in all tribulation and persevere in prayer" and "Give no more thought to satisfying the bodily appetites."[1] For he wrote these things not only for monks but for all who were in the cities, and the layman should not have greater freedom than the monk, apart from sleeping with his wife. He has permission for this, but not for other things; and in everything he must conduct himself like a monk. The Beatitudes too,[2] which are the actual words of Christ, were not addressed to monks alone, otherwise the whole world must perish ... and he would have confined the things which belong to virtue within narrow limits. And how can marriage be honorable[3] when it weighs so heavily on us?

From these words it can easily be inferred that anyone who adds the virtue of continence to the precepts of the Gospel will achieve monastic perfection. Would that our religion could rise to this height—to carry out the Gospel, not to go beyond it, lest we attempt to be more than Christians! Surely this is the reason (if I am not mistaken) why the holy Fathers decided not to lay down a general Rule for us as for men, like a new law, nor to burden our weakness with a great number of vows; they looked to the words of the Apostle: "Because law can bring only retribution; but where there is no law there can be no breach of law." And again, "Law intruded to multiply law-breaking."[4] The same great preacher of continence also shows great consideration for our weakness and appears to urge the younger widows to a second marriage, when he says "It is my wish, therefore, that young widows shall marry again, have children and preside over a home. Then they will give no opponent occasion for slander."[5] St. Jerome also believes this to be salutary advice, and tells Eustochium of the rash vows taken by women in these words: "But if those who are virgins are still not saved, because of other faults, what will become of those who have prostituted the members of Christ and turned the temple of the Holy Spirit into a brothel? It were better for a man to have entered matrimony and walked on the level than to strain after the heights and fall into the depths of hell."[6] St. Augustine too has women's rashness in taking vows in mind when he writes to Julian in his book *On the Continence of Widows*: "Let her who has not begun, think it over, and her who has made a start, continue. No opportunity must be given to the enemy, no offering taken from Christ."[7]

Consequently, canon law has taken our weakness into account, and laid down that deaconesses must not be ordained before the age of forty,[8] and only then after thorough probation, while deacons may be promoted from the age of twenty. And in the monasteries there are those called the Canons Regular of St. Augustine who claim to profess a certain rule and think themselves in no way inferior to monks although we see them eating meat and wearing linen. If our weakness can match their virtue, it should be considered no small thing. And Nature herself has made provision for our being safely granted a mild indulgence in any kind of food, for our sex is protected by greater sobriety. It is well known that women can be sustained on less nourishment and at less cost than men, and medicine teaches that they are not so easily intoxicated. And so Macrobius Theodosius in the seventh book of his *Saturnalia* notes that:

> Aristotle says that women are rarely intoxicated, but old men often. Woman has an extremely humid body, as can be known from her smooth and glossy skin, and especially from her regular purgations which rid the body of superfluous moisture. So when wine is drunk and merged with so general a humidity, it loses its power and

1 See Eph. 6: 18; Rom. 13: 14.
2 The Beatitudes are the portions of Christ's Sermon on the Mount in which he names all who are to be blessed.
3 See Heb. 13: 4.
4 Rom. 4: 15, 5: 20.
5 1 Tim. 5: 14.
6 Jerome, *Letters* 22.
7 Augustine, *On the Continence of Widows* 9.12.
8 This is taken from the canons of the Council of Chalcedon (451).

does not easily strike the seat of the brain when its strength is extinguished.

Again:

A woman's body which is destined for frequent purgations is pierced with several holes, so that it opens into channels and provides outlets for the moisture draining away to be dispersed. Through these holes the fumes of wine are quickly released. By contrast, in old men the body is dry, as is shown by their rough and wrinkled skin.[1]

From this it can be inferred how much more safely and properly our nature and weakness can be allowed any sort of food and drink; in fact we cannot easily fall victims to gluttony and drunkenness, seeing that our moderation in food protects us from the one and the nature of the female body as described from the other. It should be sufficient for our infirmity, and indeed, a high tribute to it, if we live continently and without possessions, wholly occupied by service of God, and in doing so equal the leaders of the Church themselves in our way of life or religious laymen or even those who are called Canons Regular and profess especially

to follow the apostolic life....

[Heloise continues with the argument that people of both sexes enter monastic life too lightly, unaware of its rigors. She then turns, once again, to the evils of wine, "so contrary to the religious life and peace of the monastery," but as for meat, she wishes that concessions might be made, since it falls "between good and evil." Christ's apostles were allowed to eat anything, and the whole issue, Heloise argues, is "external," while true virtues have to do with the "inner" person. Thus she asks Abelard to "modify your instructions ... to suit our weak nature, so that we can be free to devote ourselves to the offices of praising God."]

It is for you then, master, while you live, to lay down for us what Rule we are to follow for all time, for after God you are the founder of this place, through God you are the creator of our community, with God you should be the director of our religious life. After you we may perhaps have another to guide us, one who will build something upon another's foundation, and so, we fear, he may be less likely to feel concern for us, or be less readily heard by us; or indeed, he may be no less willing, but less able. Speak to us then, and we shall hear. Farewell.

5.17 Medicine: *The Trotula* (*c*.1250, based on 12th-c. sources). Original in Latin.

MEDICINE, LIKE LOGIC AND LAW, was a passion of twelfth-century scholars. In the West, Latin translators first worked on Arabic treatises on medicine, later turning to those in Greek. In twelfth-century Salerno (southern Italy) medical theory from such books was combined with the traditions of local healers. Before the thirteenth century, when the study of medicine came to be confined largely to the universities and a predominately male pursuit, women as well as men were practitioners; at the same time, women's health was an important subject. *The Trotula* was a compendium of three twelfth-century treatises on women's health. The book from which the passage below is taken was written *c*.1250; the passage itself, however, comes from a twelfth-century text called the *Book on the Conditions of Women*. Enormously popular, *The Trotula* remained the medical handbook for the treatment of women through the fifteenth century.

[Source: *The Trotula. A Medieval Compendium of Women's Medicine*, ed. and trans. Monica H. Green (Philadelphia: University of Pennsylvania Press, 2001), pp. 95, 97, 99 (notes added).]

---

1 *Saturnalia* 7. 6. 16–18.

On Impediment to Conception

[74] There are some women who are useless for conception, either because they are too lean and thin, or because they are too fat and the flesh surrounding the orifice of the womb constricts it, and it does not permit the seed of the man to enter into [the womb]. Some women have a womb so slippery and smooth that the seed, once it has been received, is not able to be retained inside. Sometimes this also happens by fault of the man who has excessively thin seed which, poured into the womb, because of its liquidity slips outside. Some men, indeed, have extremely cold and dry testicles. These men rarely or never generate because their seed is useless for generation.

[75] Treatment. If a woman remains barren by fault of the man or herself, it will be perceived in this manner. Take two pots and in each one place wheat bran and put some of the man's urine in one of them with the bran, and in the other [put] some urine of the woman [with the rest of the bran], and let the pots sit for nine or ten days. If the infertility is the fault of the woman, you will find many worms in her pot and the bran will stink. [You will find the same thing] in the other [pot] if it is the man's fault. And if you find this in neither, then in neither is there any defect and they are able to be aided by the benefit of medicine so that they might conceive.

[76] If she wishes to conceive a male, let her husband take the womb and the vagina of a hare and let him dry them, and let him mix the powder with wine and drink it. Similarly, let the woman do the same thing with the testicles of a hare, and at the end of her period let her lie with her husband and then she will conceive a male.

[77] In another fashion, let the woman take the liver and testicles of a small pig which is the only one a sow has borne, and let these be dried and reduced to a powder, and let it be given in a potion to a male who is not able to generate and he will generate, or to a woman and she will conceive.

[78] In another fashion, let the woman take damp wool dipped in ass's milk and let her tie it upon her navel and let it stay there until she has intercourse.

On the Regimen of Pregnant Women

[79] Note that when a woman is in the beginning of her pregnancy, care ought to be taken that nothing is named in front of her which she is not able to have, because if she sets her mind on it and it is not given to her, this occasions miscarriage. If, however, she desires clay or chalk or coals, let beans cooked with sugar be given to her. When the time of birth comes, let her be bathed often, let her belly be anointed with olive oil or with oil of violets, and let her eat light and readily digestible foods.

[80] If her feet swell up, let them be rubbed with rose oil and vinegar, and after the remaining foods let her eat poultry, quince, and pomegranate.

[81] If her belly is distended from windiness, take three drams[1] each of wild celery, mint, and cowbane, three drams each of mastic, cloves, watercress, and madder root, five drams of sugar, two drams each of castoreum,[2] zedoary,[3] and gladden.[4] Let there be made a very fine powder, and let it be prepared with honey, and let three scruples[5] of it be given to her with wine. This medicine takes away windiness and [danger of] miscarriage if it is taken as it should be needed.

A Proven Procedure for Becoming Pregnant

[82] If a woman wishes to become pregnant, take the testicles of an uncastrated male pig or a wild boar and dry them and let a powder be made, and let her drink this with wine after the purgation of the menses. Then let her cohabit with her husband and she will conceive.

On Women Who Ought Not Have Sexual Relations with Men

[83] Galen says that women who have narrow vaginas and constricted wombs ought not have sexual

---

1 A "dram" is a unit of weight equal to 1/16 of an ounce or 1.77 grams.
2 Castoreum is an odorous secretion of the beaver.
3 Zedoary is also known as turmeric.
4 Gladden is also known as stinking iris.
5 A "scruple" is a unit of apothecary weight equal to about 1.3 grams.

relations with men lest they conceive and die.[1] But all such women are not able to abstain, and so they need our assistance.

On Those Who Do Not Wish to Conceive

[84] If a woman does not wish to conceive, let her carry against her nude flesh the womb of a goat which has never had offspring.

[85] Or there is found a certain stone, [called] "gagates," which if it is held by the woman or even tasted prohibits conception.

[86] In another fashion, take a male weasel and let its testicles be removed and let it be released alive. Let the woman carry these testicles with her in her bosom and let her tie them in goose skin or in another skin, and she will not conceive.

[87] If she has been badly torn in birth and afterward for fear of death does not wish to conceive any more, let her put into the afterbirth as many grains of caper spurge[2] or barley as the number of years she wishes to remain barren. And if she wishes to remain barren forever, let her put in a handful.

On Preservation of the Fetus

[88] Galen reports that the fetus is attached to the womb just like fruit to a tree, which when it proceeds from the flower is extremely delicate and is destroyed by any sort of accident. But when it has grown and become a little mature and adheres firmly to the tree, it will not be destroyed by any minor accident. And when it is thoroughly mature it will not be destroyed by any mishap at all. So it is when at first the infant is brought out from the conceived seed, for its ligaments, with which it is tied to the womb, are thin and not solid, and from a slight [accident] it is ejected through miscarriage. Whence a woman on account of coughing and diarrhea or dysentery or excessive motion or anger or bloodletting can loose the fetus. But when the soul is infused into the child, it adheres a little more firmly and does not slip out so quickly. But when the child has matured, it is led out quickly by the function of Nature. Whence Hippocrates[3] says that if a woman needs purging or bloodletting [during pregnancy], she ought not be purged or let blood before the fourth month.[4] But in the fifth or sixth month, she can be purged or let blood, but nevertheless gently and carefully with a medicine that purges bile or a decoction, and only as much as the strength of the patient is able to tolerate. But beyond this [i.e., what her strength can endure] and before this time purgation is dangerous.

[89] When the time of birth has arrived, the child moves itself vehemently and it exerts itself toward its egress when, in its own time, Nature makes the vagina open so that the fetus finds liberty of its exit. And so the fetus is expelled from its bed, that is to say the afterbirth, by the force of Nature.

---

1   Galen (130?-200? C.E.) was the ancient physician whose theories informed medical thought throughout the Middle Ages.
2   "Caper spurge" has oily seeds that were used in medicines.
3   Hippocrates (460?-377? B.C.E.), known as the "Father of Medicine" was a Greek physician whose teaching laid the foundations of medical theory and practice.
4   The theory of the humors, elaborated by Galen and adhered to by Trotula and other medieval physicians, held that the proper balance of the four "humors" of the body—blood, yellow bile (choler), black bile, and phlegm—was essential to good health. One way to bring them into balance was to "let" or draw out some of the humor that was disordered.

5.18 The Cistercian view: St. Bernard, *Apologia* (1125). Original in Latin.

AN *apologia* is a defense, not an apology. This one emerged from the growing tension between the competing claims of holiness of the Cistercians and the traditional Benedictines, the "black monks," particularly Cluny. Bernard's *Apologia*, written in the guise of a letter to William of Saint-Thierry, the reform-minded abbot of a Cluniac-style house, is modeled on classical rhetorical practice: first you belittle your own side and then you turn to demolish your opponent. The passage below begins at the end of Bernard's criticism of his own order, the Cistercians, which, he says, ought not to be overly proud of its own style of life. Then he turns to "certain monks of yours"—he means the black monks in general and the Cluniacs in particular—offering a bit of "friendly" advice. What follows is a scathing satire on what Bernard took to be the excess, luxury, and laxity of the Cluniacs. Putting together Bernard's critique of the monastic practices of his day and Heloise's call for a new Rule for the "weak" (see her letter above, p. 320), how would you characterize the nature of the monastic reforming impulse of the twelfth century?

[Source: *The Cistercian World: Monastic Writings of the Twelfth Century*, trans. and ed. Pauline Matarasso (New York: Penguin Press, 1993), pp. 47-51, 55-58 (notes modified).]

---

15 If this is to be a letter, it is time I finished it. I have taken up the pen and rebuked as vigorously as I could those monks of ours whom you, Father, complained of as having criticized your Order,[1] and have cleared myself at the same time, as it behoved me, of any unfounded suspicion on this count. However, I feel bound to add a few remarks. Because I give our own men no quarter, I might seem to condone the behavior of certain monks of yours—conduct which I know you disapprove of, and which all good monks must necessarily avoid. I refer to abuses that, if they exist in the Order, God forbid should ever be a part of it. Certainly no order can contain an element of disorder, for disorder and order are incompatible. So long, therefore, as I attack in the men I censure not the Order they belong to but their vices, I shall be seen as arguing for the Order and not against it. In doing this I have no fear of offending those who love the Order. On the contrary they will surely thank me for hunting down what they themselves detest. Any who might be displeased would prove by their refusal to condemn the vices that corrupt it that they did not have the Order's good at heart. To them I make the Gregorian rejoinder: better that scandal erupt than that the truth be abandoned.[2]

AGAINST SUPERFLUITY

VIII, 16 It is said, and quite rightly, that the Cluniac way of life was instituted by holy Fathers; anxious that more might find salvation through it, they tempered the Rule to the weak without weakening the Rule. Far be it from me to believe that they recommended or allowed such an array of vanities or superfluities as I see in many religious houses. I wonder indeed how such intemperance in food and drink, in clothing and bedding, in horses and buildings can implant itself among monks. And it is the houses that pursue this course with thoroughgoing zeal, with full-blown

---

1 Throughout the following passage Bernard plays on the meaning of "order," which can refer to the general and abstract notion of order; the monks of the Benedictine Order—that is, those who adhere to the *Benedictine Rule*—and finally, the monks of the Order of Cluny—that is, those who were juridically under the abbot of Cluny, whether at Cluny or not, or, more loosely, those who belonged to a "Cluniac-style" monastery.

2 Gregory the Great, *Homilies on Ezechiel* 1.7.5.

lavishness, that are reputed the most pious and the most observant. They go so far as to count frugality avarice, and sobriety austerity, while silence is reputed gloom. Conversely, slackness is called discretion, extravagance liberality, chattering becomes affability, guffawing cheerfulness, soft clothing and rich caparisons are the requirements of simple decency, luxurious bedding is a matter of hygiene, and lavishing these things on one another goes by the name of charity. By such charity is charity destroyed, and this discretion mocks the very word. It is a cruel mercy that kills the soul while cherishing the body. And what sort of charity is it that cares for the flesh and neglects the spirit? What kind of discretion that gives all to the body and nothing to the soul? What kind of mercy that restores the servant and destroys the mistress? Let no one who has shown that sort of mercy hope to obtain the mercy promised in the Gospel by him who is the truth: "Blessed are the merciful, for they shall receive mercy."[1] On the contrary, he can expect the sure and certain punishment which holy Job invoked with the full force of prophecy on those whom I call "cruelly kind": "Let him be no longer remembered, but let him be broken like a sterile tree." The cause—and a sufficient cause for that most proper retribution—follows at once: "He feeds the barren, childless woman and does no good to the widow."[2]

17 Such kindness is obviously disordered and irrational. It is that of the barren and unfruitful flesh, which the Lord tells us profits nothing[3] and Paul says will not inherit the kingdom of God.[4] Intent on satisfying our every whim it pays no heed to the Sage's wise and warning words: "Have mercy on your own soul and you will please God."[5] That is indeed true mercy, and must perforce win mercy, since one pleases God by exercising it. Conversely it is, as I said, not kindness but cruelty, not love but malevolence, not discretion but confusion to feed the barren woman and do no good to the widow—in other words, to

pander to the desires of the profitless flesh while giving the soul no help in cultivating the virtues. For the soul is indeed bereaved in this life of her heavenly Bridegroom.[6] Yet she never ceases to conceive by the Holy Spirit and bring forth immortal offspring, which, provided they are nurtured with diligent care, will rightfully be heirs to an incorruptible and heavenly inheritance.[7]

18 Nowadays, however, these abuses are so widespread and so generally accepted that almost everyone acquiesces in them without incurring censure or even blame, though motives differ. Some use material things with such detachment as to incur little or no guilt. Others are moved by simple-mindedness, by charity or by constraint. The first, who do as they are bidden in all simplicity, would be ready to act differently if the bidding were different. The second kind, afraid of dissension in the community, are led, not by their own pleasure, but by their desire to keep the peace. Lastly there are those who are unable to stand out against a hostile majority that vociferously defends such practices as pertaining to the Order and moves swiftly and forcibly to block whatever judicious restrictions or changes the former try to bring in.

IX, 19 Who would have dreamed, in the far beginnings of the monastic order, that monks would have slid into such slackness? What a way we have come from the monks who lived in Anthony's day![8] When one of them paid on occasion a brotherly call on another, both were so avid for the spiritual nourishment they gained from the encounter that they forgot their physical hunger and would commonly pass the whole day with empty stomachs but with minds replete. And this was the right order of precedence—to give priority to what is nobler in man's make-up; this was real discretion—making greater provision for the more important part; this indeed true charity—to tend with loving care the souls for love of whom Christ died.

---

1 Matt. 5: 7.
2 Job 24: 20-21.
3 John 6: 64.
4 1 Cor. 15: 50.
5 Ecclus. 30: 24; the "Sage" is the author of Ecclesiasticus, Jesus son of Sirach.
6 The "heavenly Bridegroom" is Christ.
7 See 1 Pet. 1:4.
8 A reference to St. Antony, for whose life see above, p. 36.

As for us, when we come together, to use the Apostle's words, it is not to eat the Lord's supper.[1] There is none who asks for heavenly bread and none who offers it. Never a word about Scripture or salvation. Flippancy, laughter and words on the wind are all we hear. At table our ears are as full of gossip as our mouths of festive fare, and all intent on the former we quite forget to restrain our appetite.

ON MEALS

20 Meanwhile course after course is brought in. To offset the lack of meat—the only abstinence—the laden fish dishes are doubled. The first selection may have been more than enough for you, but you have only to start on the second to think you have never tasted fish before. Such are the skill and art with which the cooks prepare it all that one can down four or five courses without the first spoiling one's enjoyment of the last, or fullness blunting the appetite. Tickle the palate with unaccustomed seasonings and the familiar start to pall, but exotic relishes will restore it even to its preprandial sharpness; and since variety takes away the sense of surfeit, one is not aware that one's stomach is overburdened. Foodstuffs in their pure and unadulterated state have no appeal, so we mix ingredients pell-mell, scorning the natural nutriments God gave us, and use outlandish savors to stimulate our appetite. That way we can eat far more than we need and still enjoy it.

To give but one example: who could itemize all the ways in which eggs are maltreated? Or describe the pains that are taken to toss them and turn them, soften and harden them, botch them and scotch them, and, finally serve them up fried, baked and stuffed by turns, in conjunction with other foods or on their own? What is the purpose of all this unless it be to titillate a jaded palate? Attention is also lavished on the outward appearance of a dish, which must please the eye as much as it gratifies the taste buds, for though a belching stomach may announce that it has had enough, curiosity is never sated. Poor stomach! the eyes feast on color, the palate on flavor, yet the wretched stomach, indifferent to both but forced to accept the lot, is more often oppressed than refreshed as a result.

ON DRINK

21 What can I say about the drinking of water when even watering one's wine is inadmissible? Naturally all of us, as monks, suffer from a weak stomach, which is why we pay good heed to Paul's advice to use a little wine.[2] It is just that the word *little* gets overlooked, I can't think why. And if only we were content with drinking it plain, albeit undiluted. There are things it is embarrassing to say, though it should be more embarrassing still to do them. If hearing about them brings a blush, it will cost you none to put them right. The fact is that three or four times during the same meal you might see a half-filled cup brought in, so that different wines may be not drunk or drained so much as carried to the nose and lips. The expert palate is quick to discriminate between them and pick out the most potent. And what of the monasteries—and there are said to be some—which regularly serve spiced and honeyed wine in the refectory on major feasts? We are surely not going to say that this is done to nurse weak stomachs? The only reason for it that I can see is to allow deeper drinking, or keener pleasure. But once the wine is flowing through the veins and the whole head is throbbing with it, what else can they do when they get up from table but go and sleep it off? And if you force a monk to get up for vigils before he has digested, you will set him groaning rather than intoning. Having got to bed, it's not the sin of drunkenness they regret if questioned, but not being able to face their food....

ON MOUNTING ONE'S HIGH HORSE

Leaving the rest aside, what evidence is there of humility when one solitary abbot travels with a parade of horseflesh and a retinue of lay-servants that would do honor to two bishops? I swear I have seen an abbot with sixty horses and more in his train. If you saw them passing, you would take them for lords with dominion over castles and counties, not for fathers of monks and shepherds of souls. Moreover, napery, cups, dishes and candlesticks have to be taken along, together with packs stuffed full, not with ordinary

---

1 1 Cor. 11: 20.
2 1 Tim. 5:35.

bedding, but with ornate quilts. A man cannot go a dozen miles from home without transporting all his household goods, as though he were going on campaign or crossing the desert where the basic necessities were unobtainable. Surely water for washing one's hands and wine for drinking can be poured from the same jug? Do you think that your lamp will fail to burn and shine[1] unless it stands in your very own candlestick, and a gold or silver one at that? Can you really not sleep except on a chequered blanket and under an imported coverlet? And is a single servant not capable of loading the packhorse, serving the food and making up the bed? And lastly, if we must travel with these retinues of men and beasts, can we not mitigate the evil by taking the necessary provisions instead of battening on[2] our hosts?

ON THE PLACE OF PICTURES, SCULPTURE, GOLD AND SILVER IN MONASTERIES

XII, 28 But these are minor points. I am coming to the major abuses, so common nowadays as to seem of lesser moment. I pass over the vertiginous height of churches, their extravagant length, their inordinate width and costly finishings. As for the elaborate images that catch the eye and check the devotion of those at prayer within, they put me more in mind of the Jewish rite of old. But let this be: it is all done for the glory of God. But as a monk I ask my fellow monks the question a pagan poet put to pagans: "Tell me, O priests, why is there gold in the holy place?"[3] "Tell me, O poor men," say I—for it is the meaning, not the measure that concerns me—"tell me, O poor men, if poor you are, what is gold doing in the holy place?" It is one thing for bishops but quite another for monks. Bishops are under an obligation both to the wise and the foolish. Where people remain impervious to a purely spiritual stimulus, they use material ornamentation to inspire devotion. But we who have separated ourselves from the mass, who have relinquished for Christ's sake all the world's beauty and all that it holds precious, we who, to win Christ, count

as dung[4] every delight of sight and sound, of smell and taste and touch, whose devotion do we seek to excite with this appeal to the senses? What are we angling for, I should like to know: the admiration of fools, or the offerings of the simple? Or have we perhaps, through mixing with the Gentiles, learned their ways and taken to worshipping their idols?

To put it plainly: suppose that all this is the work of cupidity,[5] which is a form of idol-worship; suppose that the real objective is not yield but takings. You want me to explain? It's an amazing process: the art of scattering money about that it may breed. You spend to gain, and what you pour out returns as a flood-tide. A costly and dazzling show of vanities disposes to giving rather than to praying. Thus riches elicit riches, and money brings money in its train, because for some unknown reason the richer a place is seen to be the more freely the offerings pour in. When eyes open wide at gold-cased relics, purses do the same. A beautiful image of a saint is on show: the brighter the colors the holier he or she will be considered. Those who hasten to kiss the image are invited to leave a gift, and wonder more at the beauty than at the holiness they should be venerating.

Instead of crowns one sees in churches nowadays great jewelled wheels bearing a circle of lamps, themselves as good as outshone by the inset gems. Massive tree-like structures, exquisitely wrought, replace the simple candlestick. Here too the precious stones glimmer as brightly as the flames above.

What is this show of splendor intended to produce? Tears of contrition or gasps of admiration? O vanity of vanities,[6] but above all insanity! The walls of the church are ablaze with light and color, while the poor of the Church go hungry. The Church revets its stones in gold and leaves its children naked. The money for feeding the destitute goes to feast the eyes of the rich. The curious find plenty to relish and the starving nothing to eat. As for reverence, what respect do we show for the images of the saints that pattern the floor we tread beneath our feet? People often spit

---

1   See John 5: 35.
2   Thriving at someone else's expense.
3   Persius, *Satires* 2.69.
4   See Phil. 3: 8.
5   I.e., greed.
6   Eccles. 1: 2.

on angels' faces, and their tramping feet pummel the features of the saints. If we care little for the sacred, why not save at least the lovely colors? Why decorate what is soon to be defaced? Why paint what is bound to be trodden on? What good are beautiful pictures where they receive a constant coating of grime? And lastly, what possible bearing can this have on the life of monks, who are poor men and spiritual? And yet perhaps the poet's well-known line can be countered by the Prophet's words: "Lord, I have loved the beauty of your house and the place where your glory dwells."[1] Very well, we will tolerate such doings in our churches on the grounds that they harm only the foolish and the grasping and not the simple-hearted and devout.

29 But what can justify that array of grotesques in the cloister where the brothers do their reading, a fantastic conglomeration of beauty misbegotten and ugliness transmogrified? What place have obscene monkeys, savage lions, unnatural centaurs, manticores, striped tigers, battling knights or hunters sounding their horns? You can see a head with many bodies and a multi-bodied head. Here is a quadruped with a dragon's tail, there an animal's head stuck on a fish. That beast combines the forehand of a horse with the rear half of a goat, this one has the horns in front and the horse's quarters aft. With such a bewildering array of shapes and forms on show, one would sooner read the sculptures than the books, and spend the whole day gawking at this wonderland rather than meditating on the law of God. Ah, Lord! if the folly of it all does not shame us, surely the expense might stick in our throats?

30 This is a rich vein, and there is plenty more to be quarried, but I am prevented from carrying on by my own demanding duties and your imminent departure, Brother Oger.[2] Since I cannot persuade you to stay, and you do not want to leave without this latest little book, I am falling in with your wishes: I am letting you go and shortening my discourse, particularly since a few words spoken in a spirit of conciliation do more good than many that are a cause of scandal. And would to heaven that these few lines do not occasion scandal! I am well aware that in rooting out vices I shall have offended those involved. However, God willing, those I fear I may have exasperated may end up grateful for my strictures if they desist from their evil ways—that is to say, if the rigorists stop carping and the lax prune back their excesses, and if both sides act in conscience according to their own beliefs, without judging the others who hold different views. Those who are able to live austerer lives should neither despise nor copy those who cannot. As for the latter, they should not be led by admiration for their stricter brethren to imitate them injudiciously: just as there is a danger of apostasy when those who have taken a more exacting vow slip into easier ways, not everyone can safely scale the heights.

5.19 The Cluniac view: Peter the Venerable, *Miracles* (mid 1130s–mid 1150s). Original in Latin.

PETER THE VENERABLE (c.1093-1156) was born into a well-to-do land-owning family. When he became abbot of Cluny in 1122, he inherited a troubled institution, weakened by a revolt against a former abbot and struggling to find a way to deal with hundreds of monasteries which, in one way or another, were dependent on Cluny. After he read Bernard's *Apology*, Peter responded to it in a long letter, rebutting each point. But he also answered the Cistercian critique by regulating the Cluniac lifestyle in his *Statutes* and by praising Cluny in his *Miracles*. Written over the course of the last twenty years of his life, the *Miracles*, which contained mainly stories having to do with

---

1   Ps. 26: 8; Douay Ps. 25: 8.
2   Oger was Bernard's friend and a canon at Mont-Saint-Éloi, in the very north of France. The idea that Oger was a sort of messenger, on the point of taking the letter to William of Saint-Thierry, is a literary conceit. In fact, Bernard revised and polished the *Apologia* over the course of many months.

Cluny, had one major purpose: to praise Cluniac monks. For Peter, Cluny was the embodiment of Christian virtue on earth, the "refuge" of sinners, and the model of monastic life. In the passage below he prefaces a discussion of miraculous visions of the dead with thoughts about Cluny's particular excellence. How did his emphasis on Cluny's function as the "asylum of all Christians" implicitly belittle the Cistercians?

[Source: Peter the Venerable, *De miraculis* 1.9, ed. Denise Bouthillier (Turnhout: Brepols, 1988), pp. 35-36. Translated by Barbara H. Rosenwein.]

The monastery of Cluny is the best known in just about the entire world for its religion, the severity of its discipline, the number of its monks, and its complete observance of the monastic rule. It is the individual and collective place of refuge for sinners by means of which much harm has been inflicted on Hell and a great many profits have been gained by the Heavenly Kingdom. There [at Cluny] innumerable multitudes of men, casting off the heavy burdens of the world from their shoulders, have submitted their necks to the sweet yoke of Christ.[1] There the men of every profession, dignity, and order have changed secular arrogance and luxury into the humble and poor life of monks. There the venerable fathers of these churches [i.e., bishops], fleeing the burdens of church affairs, have chosen to live more safely and more quietly and to obey rather than to command. There the unending and turbulent struggle against spiritual evils offers daily palms of victory to the soldiers of Christ. For the inhabitants of this place, who subject their flesh to the spirit by a continuous effort, the Apostle speaks truly: "To live is Christ, and to die is gain."[2]

By the balm of spiritual virtues that is diffused from this place, the whole house of the world has been filled with the odor of ointment,[3] while the ardor of monastic religion, which at one time had grown cold, grew warm again by the example and zeal of these men. Gaul, Germany, and even Britain across the sea bear witness to this; Spain, Italy, and all of Europe acknowledge it. All of them are full of monasteries either newly founded by them or restored from their earlier decline. There [at these Cluniac houses] colleges of monks, like the celestial troops that surround God in their proper orders, with other armies of holy power, apply themselves day and night to divine praises, so that the saying of the prophet may be understood to also be about them: "Blessed are they that dwell in thy house, O Lord: they shall praise thee for ever and ever."[4] But why do I list other parts of the world, since Cluny's fame has reached from our westernmost regions all the way to the East and has not been hidden from even a corner of the Christian world? For Cluny is the vineyard, and its monks are the branches which, truly clinging to the vine, Christ, and pruned by the Father, the gardener, bear much fruit according to the words of the Evangelist.[5] We read about this vineyard in the Psalms: "It stretched forth its branches unto the sea, and its boughs unto the river."[6] Although this was said about the synagogue of the Jews brought out of Egypt, and above all about the present Church, nevertheless nothing prevents us from understanding it also about this Cluniac Church, which is not the least member of the Universal Church.

---

1 See Matt. 11: 28-30.
2 Phil. 1: 21.
3 See John 12: 3.
4 Ps. 84: 4; Douay Ps. 83: 5.
5 See John 15: 1-17.
6 Ps. 80: 11; Douay Ps. 79: 12.

TIMELINE FOR CHAPTER FIVE

1070 William of Jumièges, *Deeds of the Dukes*

1076 Gregory VII, *Letter to Hermann of Metz*

1075 Henry IV, *Letter to Gregory VII*

1087 *Domesday*

1098 Stephen of Bois, *Letter to His Wife*

end 11th c. *Bayeux Tapestry*

1100 Abelard, *Glosses on Porphyry*

1100

1106 *Agreement with Colonists*

early 12th c. "Florence of Worcester"

12th c. *Trotula*

1100-50 Rabbi Eliezer, *O God, Insolent Men*

12th c. T-O Map

1117 Gilbert of Poitiers, *Gloss on Psalm 101*

1125 St. Bernard, *Apologia*

1130s *Glossa Ordinaria*

1130s Heloise, *Letter*

1130-3 Henry I, *London Privileges*

1148 Anna Comnena, *Alexiad*

1150

1130s-50s Peter the Venerable, *Miracles*

1147-8 *Conquest of Lisbon*

1184 Ibn Jubayr,. *Market near Aleppo*

late 12th c., *Directions to Mecca* (map)

late 12th c., *Image of the World* (map)

1200

13th c. Ptolemy's *Geography* (map)

13th c. Ibn al-Athir, *First Crusade*

SIX

INSTITUTIONALIZING ASPIRATIONS (*c.*1150-*c.*1250)

NEW HEROES IN THE EAST

6.1 Saladin: Ibn Shaddad, *The Rare and Excellent History of Saladin* (1198-1216). Original in Arabic.

IN 1187, AFTER ROUTING THE Christian forces at the battle of Hattin, Saladin (r.1171-1193), the Kurdish sultan of Egypt and Syria, entered Jerusalem in triumph, reducing the crusader states to a few tiny outposts. His victory was, as his biographer Ibn Shaddad (1145-1234) put it, "a blessing for the Muslims." Ibn Shaddad was a scholar and diplomat who worked closely with Saladin as both a friend and administrator. After Saladin's death he continued to serve the sultan's successors. He built a school (madrasa) of law and wrote several treatises; one called *The Virtues of Jihad* first brought him to Saladin's attention. He may have written the *History of Saladin* to inspire the sultan's son to similarly virtuous jihad.

[Source: *The Rare and Excellent History of Saladin*, trans. D. S. Richards (Aldershot: Ashgate, 2001), pp. 72-78 (slightly modified).]

ACCOUNT OF THE BATTLE OF HATTIN, A BLESSING FOR THE MUSLIMS

It took place on Saturday 24 Rabi' II 583 [July 4, 1187]. The sultan perceived that his gratitude for God's favor towards him, evidenced by his strong grasp on sovereignty, his God-given control over the lands and the people's willing obedience, could only be demonstrated by his endeavoring to exert himself to the utmost and to strive to fulfil the precept of Jihad. He sent to summon all his forces, which gathered on the date given at 'Ashtara.[1] He reviewed them and made his dispositions, then set forth into the God-forsaken enemy's lands at midday on Friday 17 Rabi' II [June 26]. He always sought out Fridays for his battles, especially the times of Friday prayer, to gain the blessing of the preachers' prayers on the pulpits, for they were perhaps more likely to be answered.

As he marched out at that time in battle array, he heard that the enemy, when they learnt that he had concentrated his armies, gathered in full on the plain of Saffuriyya in the territory of Acre and intended to come to battle. The same day, the sultan camped at Lake Tiberias near a village called Sannabra. He then moved and camped west of Tiberias on the top of the mountain, in battle formation and expecting that the Franks, when they heard that, would come against him. However, they did not move from their encampment. He took up this position on Wednesday 21 Rabi' II [July 1], and having seen that they were not moving, he descended upon Tiberias with a light force, leaving the main divisions in position facing the direction in which the enemy were. He attacked Tiberias and took it within one hour after a direct assault. Eager hands then turned to plundering, taking captives, burning and killing. The citadel alone held out.

Learning what had happened to Tiberias, the enemy could not bear not to give into their impulsive zeal, but set out at once and marched to defend Tiberias. The Muslim scouts told the emirs that the Franks were on the move, and they sent people to inform the sultan. He left men in Tiberias to watch the citadel and then he and his force joined the main army. The two armies encountered one another on the slopes of the mountain of Tiberias, to the west of the town, late on Thursday 22 Rabi' II [July 2].

Nightfall separated the two sides and both spent the night at battle stations, bristling with weapons, until the morning of Friday 23rd [July 3]. Both armies mounted and clashed together. The vanguard was in operation, then the main divisions moved forward and battle was joined and became very intense. This was around a village called Lubiya. They were closely beset as in a noose, while still marching on as though being driven to a death that they could see before them, convinced of their doom and destruction and themselves aware that the following day they would be visiting their graves.

The conflict continued at close quarters, each horseman clashing with his opponent, until victory [for the Muslims] and for the infidels the onset of disaster were imminent, but night and its darkness intervened. That day there occurred mighty deeds and momentous doings, such as have not been related of past generations. Each party spent the night in arms, expecting his adversary at every moment, though too weak through tiredness to stand up and unable through fatigue to crawl, let alone run.

Eventually, there came the Saturday morning, on which the blessing was vouchsafed. Both sides sought their positions and each realized that whichever was broken would be driven off and eliminated. The Muslims were well aware that behind them was the Jordan and before them enemy territory and that there was nothing to save them but God Almighty.

God had already ordained and prepared the believers' victory, and he duly brought it about according to what he had predestined. The Muslim divisions charged on the wings and in the center. They let out a shout as one man, at which God cast terror into the hearts of the unbelievers. "It was right for Us to give aid to the believers."[2]

The Count [Raymond] was a clever and shrewd leader of theirs. He saw that the signs of defeat were already upon his co-religionists and no notion of aiding his fellows stopped him thinking of himself, so he fled at the beginning of the engagement before it grew fierce and made his way towards Tyre, pursued by a group of Muslims. He alone was saved, but Islam became safe from his wiles.

The forces of Islam surrounded the forces of unbelief and impiety on all sides, loosed volleys of arrows at them and engaged them hand to hand. One group fled and was pursued by our Muslim heroes. Not one of them survived. Another group took refuge on a hill called the Hill of Hattin, the latter being a village near which is the tomb of Shu'ayb[3] (on him and on the rest of the

---

1   A town in Syria.
2   Sura 30: 47.
3   The Arabic name for Jethro, father-in-law of Moses.

prophets be blessings and peace). The Muslims pressed hard upon them on that hill and lit fires around them. Their thirst was killing and their situation became very difficult, so that they began to give themselves up as prisoners for fear of being slain. Their commanders were taken captive but the rest were either killed or taken prisoner, and among those who lived were their leader, King Guy,[1] Prince Reynald, the brother of the king, the prince who was lord of Shawbak, the son of Humfrey, the son of the Lady of Tiberias, the Master of the Templars, the lord of Jubayl and the Master of the Hospitallers.[2] The rest of the commanders were killed, and the lowly soldiers were divided up, either to be slain or made captive. Everyone not killed was made prisoner. Some nobles amongst them willingly surrendered in fear for their lives. Someone I trust told me that in the Hawran he met a single person holding a tent-rope with which all by himself he was pulling along thirty odd prisoners because of the desperate defeat that had befallen them.

As for their leaders that survived, we shall recount their fate. The count who fled arrived at Tripoli and was taken ill with pleurisy,[3] and thus God brought about his death. As for the officers of the Hospitallers and the Templars, the sultan chose to put them to death and killed them all without exception. The sultan had vowed to kill Prince Reynald if he got him in his power. This was because a caravan from Egypt had passed through his land at Shawbak during the state of truce. They halted there under safe conduct, but he treacherously killed them. The sultan heard of this and religion and his zeal encouraged him to swear that, if he seized his person, he would kill him. After God had bestowed the great victory on him, the sultan sat in the entrance lobby of his tent, for it had not been fully erected, while people were offering him prisoners and any commanders they had found. The [main] tent was then erected and he sat there in great delight, expressing his gratitude for the favor that God had shown him. Then he summoned King Guy, his brother and Prince Reynald. He handed the king a drink of iced julep, from which he drank, being dreadfully thirsty, and he then passed some of it

to Prince Reynald. The sultan said to the interpreter, "Tell the King, 'You are the one giving him a drink. I have not given him any drink.'" According to the fine custom of the Arabs and their noble ways, if a prisoner took food or a drink of water from whoever had captured him, his life was safe. His intention was to follow these noble ways.

He ordered them to proceed to a place assigned for their lodging. They did so and ate something. Then the sultan summoned them again, now having with him none but a few servants. He gave the king a seat in the vestibule and, having summoned Prince Reynald, confronted him as he had said. He said to him, "Here I am having asked for victory through Muhammad, and God has given me victory over you." He offered him Islam but he refused. The sultan then drew his scimitar and struck him, severing his arm at his shoulder. Those present finished him off and God speedily sent his soul to Hell-fire. His body was taken and thrown down at the door of the tent. The king, when he saw him brought out in this manner, was convinced that he would be next. The sultan called him in and reassured him, saying, "It has not been customary for princes to kill princes, but this man transgressed his limits, so he has suffered what he suffered." That night was spent by our people in the most complete joy and perfect delight, raising their voices in praise of God and gratitude towards him, with cries of "God is great" and "There is no god but God," until daybreak on Sunday.

THE TAKING OF THE CITADEL OF TIBERIAS
On Sunday 25 Rabi' II [July 5] the sultan camped at Tiberias and during the remainder of that day received the surrender of the citadel. He remained there until the Tuesday [July 7].

ACCOUNT OF THE TAKING OF ACRE
Saladin then departed for Acre, where he arrived on Wednesday, the last day of Rabi' II [July 8]. He attacked on the morning of Thursday 1 Jumada I [July 9] and took the city, delivering the Muslim prisoners there, who were about 4,000 souls. He seized the

---

1 Guy of Lusignan, king of Jerusalem (r.1186-1192).
2 The Templars and the Hospitallers were both military and monastic orders, a hybrid product of the crusades.
3 Inflammation of the membrane around the lungs.

money, stores, goods and commodities it contained, for it was renowned as a trading emporium. The troops dispersed throughout the coastal lands, taking forts, castles and fortified places. They took Nablus, Haifa, Caesarea, Saffuriya and Nazareth. That was because they were empty of men, who had been either killed or captured. When the administration of Acre had been settled and those due booty had received their share of wealth and captives, the sultan set out for Tibnin.

[80] THE TAKING OF TIBNIN

Tibnin, a strong fortress, was besieged on Sunday 11 Jumada I [July 19]. The sultan set up trebuchets[1] and pressed hard with assaults and a blockade. It was held by courageous men, strong in their religion. The Muslims required an extreme effort, but God gave Saladin the victory and he took the place by assault on Sunday the 18th [July 26] and made prisoners of those who had escaped death. He moved away to the city of Sidon, which he attacked and took control of after one day, that is, on Wednesday 21 Jumada I [July 29].

HIS TAKING OF BEIRUT

The sultan remained at Sidon long enough to arrange its administration and then he marched to Beirut. He attacked it on Thursday 22 Jumada I [July 30], carried out assaults and pressed hard on the city, eventually taking it on Thursday 29 Jumada I [August 6]. While he was attacking Beirut, his men gained possession of Jubayl.

When his mind was easy concerning these parts, he decided to go to Ascalon as, after he had camped before Tyre and made a trial assault at this time, he determined not to occupy himself with it because his troops had scattered throughout the coast. Every man had gone to take something for himself, tired of fighting and constant campaigning. Every Frankish survivor on the coast had flocked to Tyre. Thus he decided to attack Ascalon because it was an easier objective.

THE CAPTURE OF ASCALON

Saladin came to camp before the city on Sunday 16 Jumada II [August 23], having taken many places on his way there, such as Ramla, Yubna,[2] and Darum. He set up trebuchets and made fierce attacks. The city fell to him on Saturday 29 Jumada II [September 5], and he remained there while his men took over Gaza, Bayt Jibrin and Latrun without meeting any resistance.

Between the recovery of Ascalon and the Franks' taking it from the Muslims thirty-five years had passed, for the enemy gained control of it on 27 Jumada II 548 [September 19, 1153].

THE CONQUEST OF JERUSALEM THE BLESSED, THE NOBLE

Having gained Ascalon and the places surrounding Jerusalem, the sultan buckled down to the task and supreme effort of attacking the latter place. The forces which had scattered throughout the coast rejoined him after satisfying their desire for plunder and pillage. He then marched towards it, relying on God and entrusting his cause to Him, to take the opportunity to open the door to success which one is urged to grasp when it opens, in the words of Muhammad (upon him be peace), "If a door to some advantage is opened for anyone, then let him grasp it, for he knows not when it may be closed against him."[3]

He descended on the city on Sunday 15 Rajab 583 [September 20, 1187]. He took up position on the western side. It was crammed with fighting men, both mounted and foot soldiers. Experienced sources estimated the number of soldiers who were there at more than 60,000, apart from women and children. Then, because of an advantage he saw, he transferred to the north side, which move took place on Friday 20 Rajab [September 25]. He set up trebuchets and pressed hard on the city with assaults and a hail of missiles. Eventually, he undermined the city wall on the side next to the Valley of Gehenna in the northern angle. The enemy saw the indefensible position they had fallen into and the signs were clear to them that our true religion would overcome the false. Their hearts were downcast on account of the killing and imprisonment that had befallen their knights and men-at-arms and

---

1 A siege engine used to hurl heavy stones.
2 Known to the crusaders as Ibelin, about 13 miles south of Jaffa.
3 Not found in any of the canonical hadith.

the fall and conquest of their fortresses. They realized that their lot was ineluctable and that they would be killed by the sword that had killed their brethren. Humbled, they inclined towards seeking terms. An agreement was reached through an exchange of messages between the two sides.

The sultan received the surrender on Friday 27 Rajab [October 2]. The eve had been the [date of the] Prophetic Ascension which is written about in the Noble Qur'an. Observe this remarkable coincidence, how God facilitated its restoration to Muslim hands on the anniversary of their Prophet's Night-Journey. This is a sign that God had accepted this proffered obedience. It was a great victory, witnessed by a vast crowd of men of religion, Sufis[1] and mystics. The reason for this was that, when people heard of the conquest of the coastal lands that God had effected at Saladin's hand and his intention to move against Jerusalem became widely known, the ulema[2] from Egypt and Syria made their way to him, so much so that no-one of any note failed to be present. Voices were raised in shouts and prayers, with cries of "There is no god but God" and "God is great." On the Friday of the conquest the khutbah[3] was delivered and Friday prayers held in Jerusalem. The cross of vast size, which was over the Dome of the Rock, was lowered. God gave victory to Islam by His might and strength.

The basic provision in the treaty was that they would pay ransoms, for every man ten Tyrian dinars, for every woman five dinars and for every child, male or female, a dinar. All who produced the ransom would secure their freedom, otherwise they would be made captive. God freed those Muslims who were prisoners, a large multitude of about 3,000 souls.

The sultan remained there, collecting money and distributing it to the emirs and the ulema, and also conveying all who payed their ransom to their place of safety, namely Tyre. I have heard that the sultan departed from Jerusalem without keeping any of that money, which amounted to 220,000 dinars. He left on Friday 25 Sha'ban 583 [October 30, 1187].

6.2 The lone Byzantine warrior: *Digenis Akritis* (12th c.). Original in Greek.

DIGENIS MEANS "TWIN-BLOODED," while Akritis means "military frontiersman." The epic poem about *Digenis Akritis*—unlike Saladin, an entirely mythical being—tells of a warrior hero who is the son of an emir (originally Muslim, but later converted to Christianity) and a Byzantine girl. He lives on Byzantium's frontier in peace with his Arab neighbors and at war with monsters, bandits, and Byzantine "guerrillas" (in this case, huntsmen out looking for girls). He acts independently, without the emperor's interference (indeed, in one version of the poem, the emperor visits to praise him). The original poem either reflects the heroic fantasies of the south-eastern Byzantine border in Anatolia before the Seljuk incursion in the eleventh century or, alternatively, looks back upon that era with nostalgia. The excerpt below is from the earliest of the *Digenis* manuscripts now extant, which dates from around 1300. Compare the attributes of the hero in this poem with those of Psellus's hero, Basil II, described above, p. 227; what do you think explains the differences?

[Source: *Digenis Akritis: The Grottaferrata and Escorial versions*, ed. and trans. Elizabeth Jeffreys (Cambridge: Cambridge University Press, 1998), pp. 153, 155, 157, 159, 161 (slightly modified).]

---

1   Sufis practiced an ascetic and mystical Islamic piety.
2   Those learned in Islamic law.
3   The Friday sermon, which contained prayers for the ruler.

Book six
The present sixth book of many valiant deeds
will narrate the marvellous actions of Digenis
    Akritis, the Frontiersman of Double Descent,
as he himself related them to his own friends.
    "If any one should wish to choose an emperor
      of the months,
5 May would reign over them all.
He is the whole earth's most delightful adornment,
the budding eye of all plants and the brightness of
    flowers,
flashing forth the blushing and the beauty of the
    meadows;
he breathes out passions marvelously and brings on
    Aphrodite,
10 he makes the earth ready to mimic heaven,
decorating it with flowers, both roses and narcissus.
    In this marvelous, most sweet month
I wished to move away on my own with my lovely
    girl,
the beautiful daughter of the general Doukas.[1]

15 And after we had arrived at a marvelous meadow,
I put up the tent there and my own couch,
setting all sorts of plants around it.
Reeds grew there, reaching upwards,
cold water bubbled up in the middle of the meadow
20 and flowed out all over the ground there.
Several kinds of birds lived in the grove—
tame peacocks, parrots and swans;
the parrots hung on the branches and sang,
the swans browsed for food in the water,
25 the peacocks paraded their wings among the flowers
and reflected the flowers' colors in their wings;
the rest, having won freedom for their wings,
played as they perched on the branches of the trees.
And the brightly flashing beauty of the high-born
    girl
30 outshone the peacocks and all the plants.
For her face mimicked the narcissus' color,
her cheeks burgeoned like a blooming rose,
her lips resembled a newly opened rose
when it begins to burst out of its bud.

Curls floating just above her brows   35
sent out rays of golden delight,
and over all there was an ineffable joy.
Around the bed were burning spices of all kinds,
musk, nard and ambergris, camphor and cassia,
and great was the pleasure and the scent of joys.   40
Such were the delights this garden offered.
    At the hour of noon I turned to sleep,
while the high-born girl sprinkled rose-water over
    me
and the nightingales and other birds sang.
The girl was thirsty and went to the spring,   45
and as she was enjoying herself there, wetting her
    feet,
a serpent, who had transformed himself into a good-
    looking boy,
came up to her, wishing to seduce her.
She, not at all unaware who he was, said:
'Serpent, abandon your scheme, I am not taken in.   50
He who loves me has been keeping watch and has
    just gone to sleep
(for she said to herself: "This is a serpent,
I have never before seen a sight like this");
if he wakes up and finds you, he will do you harm.'
    But he jumped up and shamelessly tried   55
    to violate her,
and the girl immediately let out a shriek, calling for
    me;
'Wake up, my lord, and rescue your dearest.'
The shriek rang in my heart,
and I promptly sat up and saw the intruder
(for the spring was straight in front of me on pur-   60
    pose);
I drew my sword and found myself at the spring,
for my feet ran swiftly like wings.
    As I reached him he revealed a hideous
    apparition to me,
huge and terrifying to human eyes—
three gigantic heads, completely engulfed in fire;   65
from each it gushed out flame like lightning flashes;
as it changed its position it let out a thunderclap,
so that the earth and all the trees seemed to shake.
Thickening its body and drawing its heads into one,

---

1   The "beautiful daughter of the general Doukas" is Digenis' wife, who is Greek, while Digenis himself is "twin-blooded,"
    i.e., Greek and Muslim.

70 growing thin behind and making a sharp tail,
at one moment coiling itself and then unfolding
   again,
it launched its whole attack against me.
But I, reckoning this spectacle as nothing,
stretched my sword up high with all my might
75 and brought it down on the ferocious beast's heads,
and cut them all off at once. It collapsed on the
   ground,
twitching its tail up and down in its last spasms.
I wiped my sword and replaced it in its scabbard,
summoned my boys who were some way off
80 and ordered that the serpent be removed at once.
When this had been done at indescribable speed,
the boys ran back to their own tents,
while I went back to my couch to sleep once more,
for the sweet sleep I had been enjoying drew me back
   again
85 as I had not yet had my fill of it when I was first
   woken.
   The girl was moved to unbounded laughter
as she remembered the serpent's apparitions
and the huge monster's sudden death,
and she went towards a tree so as not to wake me
90 and to pull herself together a little after her fright.
And, look, a fearsome lion came out of the wood
and also began to attack the girl.
She let out a shriek, calling me to help.
I heard her and got up from my bed with all speed;
95 when I saw the lion I promptly leaped forward,
brandishing my stick in my hand, and charged at it
   immediately,
striking it on the head. It died on the spot.
When the lion, and the serpent too, had been flung
   far away,
my girl swore upon her life, saying,
100 'Listen to me, my lord, if you would give me pleasure,
take your kithara, play it for a while
and distract my soul from fear of the wild beast.'
As I could not disobey the girl,
I immediately began to play it, and she began to sing:
105 'I offer thanks to Eros who gives me my delectable
   sweetheart,
and I rejoice as an empress, fearing nobody;
he is a flourishing lily, a perfumed apple,
and like a fragrant rose he enchants my heart.'

As the girl spoke of the rose while she sang,
I thought she held a rose between her lips,   110
for they truly seemed like a freshly opened bloom.
The notes of the kithara and the voice of the girl
gave out a delightful sound as the hills re-echoed,
so that even people far distant heard the melody.
   And we realized it from this sign.   115
By chance, at that hour, soldiers were
passing along the road called Trosis,
where it had happened that many had been badly
   wounded,
as is clear from the name that the place had acquired.
They were—as I learnt from them later—   120
Ioannikis, the marvellous young guerrilla,
old Philopappous and Kinnamos, the third.
And, as they were travelling along the road, they
   heard the songs
whilst they were a mile distant from us, as far as I can
   tell;
they left the road and came near us.   125
When they saw that the renowned girl was on her
   own,
they were wounded in their souls by her beauty, as if
   by an arrow,
and they were all moved to boundless passion,
all forty-five of them.
Seeing that I was on my own, they hoped to wound   130
   me with words.
'Leave the girl,' they said, 'and save yourself.
If you do not, you will win death for your
   disobedience.'
   They still had no idea who I was.
The sun-born girl, suddenly glimpsing
all these armed men astride their horses,   135
believed their words and was utterly terrified;
she covered her face with her veil
and ran to the tent, overwhelmed by fear.
I said to her, 'Why do you not speak, dearest?'
'Because,' she said, 'my voice has died before my soul. 140
For look, we are being separated and I don't want to
   go on living.'
'My soul,' I said, 'stop thinking such things.
Those whom God has joined, men shall not separate.'
   Immediately I picked up my stick and my hand-
   shield,
attacking them like an eagle swooping on partridges 145
   from above,

and in those my stick managed to touch
no remnant of life whatever was left.
Many wanted to get away, but I caught up with them
(for no horse has ever got the better of me in run-
        ning,
150 and I am stating this not to glorify myself
    but so that you can appreciate the gifts of the
        Creator).

Some got away from me by hiding in the marshes,
and just before I had put all to death,
I captured one on his own alive, from whom I learnt
        who
these senseless and witless people were.   155
And boiling over with fury, I spared none.
Then I threw down my sword and my hand-shield,
shook off my sleeve-guard and went to the girl."

6.3 The Northern Crusade: Helmold, *The Chronicle of the Slavs* (1167–1168). Original in Latin.

HELMOLD (*c*.1125–after 1177?) WAS A PRIEST at Bosau, a small town about 25 miles north of Lübeck. Equipped with an adequate education and a zeal to praise the Church by writing about the conversion of the Slavs, he became a major chronicler of the Northern Crusades. The excerpt here begins with his account—some of it prejudiced—of the religious practices of the Slavs. This helped to justify the deflection of part of the Second Crusade to the north.

[Source: Helmold, Priest of Bosau, *The Chronicle of the Slavs*, trans. Francis Joseph Tschan (New York: Columbia University Press, 1935), pp. 158–60, 168–69, 180–81 (notes modified).]

52. THE RITES OF THE SLAVS

After the death of Cnut, surnamed Laward, the king of the Abodrites, there succeeded to his place Pribislav and Niclot.[1] They divided the principate into two parts so that one governed the country of the Wagiri and the Polabi, the other, that of the Abodrites.[2] These two men were truculent beasts, intensely hostile to the Christians. In those days a variety of idolatrous cults and superstitious aberrations grew strong again throughout all Slavia.[3]

Besides the groves and the household gods in which the country and towns abound, the first and foremost deities are Prove, the god of the land of Old-enburg; Siva, the goddess of the Polabi; Redigast, the god of the land of the Abodrites.[4] To these gods are dedicated priests, sacrificial libations, and a variety of religious rites. When the priest declares, according to the decision of the lot, what solemnities are to be celebrated in honor of the gods, the men, women, and children come together and offer to their deities sacri-fices of oxen and sheep, often, also, of Christians with whose blood they say their gods are delighted. After the victim is felled the priest drinks of its blood in or-der to render himself more potent in the receiving of oracles. For it is the opinion of many that demons are very easily conjured with blood. After the sacrifices have been consummated according to custom, the populace turns to feasting and entertainment.

The Slavs, too, have a strange delusion. At their feasts and carousals they pass about a bowl over which they utter words, I should not say of consecration but of execration, in the name of the gods—of the good one, as well as of the bad one—professing that all pro-pitious fortune is arranged by the good god, adverse, by the bad god. Hence, also, in their language they call the bad god Diabol, or Zcerneboch, that is, the black god. Among the multiform divinities of the Slavs, however, Svantowit, the god of the land of the Rugiani, stands out as the most distinguished: he is so much more effective in his oracular responses that out of regard for him they think of the others as demi-gods. On this account they also are accustomed every year to select by lot a Christian whom they sacrifice in his especial honor. To his shrine are sent fixed sums from all the provinces of the Slavs toward defraying the cost of sacrifices. The people are, moreover, actu-ated by an extraordinary regard for the service of the fane [temple], for they neither lightly indulge in oaths

---

1 Here the term "Abodrites," which were strictly speaking one Slavic group, refers to the Slavs as a whole. The "king of the Abodrites" was the man given the title by the emperor in Germany; Cnut Laward, whose father had been king of Denmark, gained it in *c*.1128 and ruled for four years. Pribislav and Niclot were native Slavs, heirs of an earlier ruling dynasty.
2 The Abodrites, Wagiri and Polabi were various Slavic groups. The Lutici, mentioned below, was another.
3 By Cnut's time, the Slavs in the region had been both evangelized and ruled by Christians, but the Slavs revolted politically and religiously from time to time, as here, upon Cnut's death.
4 These are Helmold's names, but perhaps "Prove" corresponds to the Slavic diety Perun, the god of weather and fertility.

nor suffer the vicinity of the temple to be desecrated even in the face of an enemy. Besides, there has been inborn in the Slavic race a cruelty that knows no satiety, a restlessness that harries the countries lying about them by land and sea. It is hard to tell how many kinds of death they have inflicted on the followers of Christ. They have even torn out the bowels of some and wound them about a stake and have affixed others to crosses in ridicule of the sign of our redemption. It is said that they crucify their most infamous criminals. Those, too, whom they hold for ransom they afflict with such tortures and fetter so tightly that one who does not know their ways would hardly believe....

57. THE BUILDING OF THE CITY OF LÜBECK

Matters having been arranged in this manner, Adolph began to rebuild the fortress at Segeberg and girded it with a wall.[1] As the land was without inhabitants, he sent messengers into all parts, namely, to Flanders and Holland, to Utrecht, Westphalia, and Frisia, proclaiming that whosoever were in straits for lack of fields should come with their families and receive a very good land,—a spacious land, rich in crops, abounding in fish and flesh and exceeding good pasturage. To the Holzatians and Sturmarians[2] he said:

> Have you not subjugated the land of the Slavs and bought it with the blood of your brothers and fathers? Why, then, are you the last to enter into possession of it? Be the first to go over into a delectable land and inhabit it and partake of its delights, for the best of it is due you who have wrested it from the hands of the enemy.

An innumerable multitude of different peoples rose up at this call and they came with their families and their goods into the land of Wagria to Count Adolph that they might possess the country which he had promised them. First of all the Holzatians received abodes in the safest places to the west in the region of Segeberg along the River Trave, also the Born-höved open and everything extending from the River Schwale as far as Agrimesov[3] and the Plöner-See. The Westphalians settled in the region of Dargune, the Hollanders around Eutin, and the Frisians around Süssel. The country about Plön, however, was still uninhabited. Oldenburg and Lütjenburg and the rest of the lands bordering on the sea he gave to the Slavs to live in, and they became tributary to him.

Count Adolph came later to a place called Bucu and found there the wall of an abandoned fortress which Cruto, the tyrant of God, had built, and a very large island, encircled by two rivers. The Trave flows by on one side, the Wakenitz on the other. Each of these streams has swampy and pathless banks. On the side, however, on which the land road runs there is a little hill surmounted by the wall of the fort. When, therefore, the circumspect man saw the advantages of the site and beheld the noble harbor, he began to build there a city. He called it Lübeck, because it was not far from the old port and city which Prince Henry had at one time constructed.[4] He sent messengers to Niclot, prince of the Abodrites, to make friends with him, and by means of gifts drew to himself all men of consequence, to the end that they would all strive to accommodate themselves to him and to bring peace upon his land. Thus the deserted places of the land of Wagria began to be occupied and the number of its inhabitants was multiplied. Vicelin, the priest, too, on the invitation as well as with the assistance of the count, got back the properties about the fortress of Segeberg which the emperor Lothar had in times past given him for the construction of a monastery and for the support of servants of God....

[Helmold turns to the activities of crusade armies: the first went through Hungary to Greece; the second fought the battle of Lisbon (see above, p. 300); a third was directed against the Slavs.]

65. THE SIEGE OF DEMMIN

In the meantime the news spread through all Saxony and Westphalia that the Slavs had broken forth and

---

1   Adolph II, count of Holstein (r.1131-1164) was granted some Slavic territory by Emperor Lothar; these are the "arrangements" that Helmold refers to.
2   These were Christian natives of Saxony, and thus neighbors of the Slavs. For an earlier precedent to this sort of colonization, see Frederick of Hamburg's *Agreement with Colonists from Holland*, above, p. 277.
3   Today Grimmelsberg near Tensebeck, east of Bornhöved.
4   Prince Henry was a Slavic ruler.

had been the first to engage in war. All that army, signed with the sign of the cross,[1] hastened to descend upon the land of the Slavs and to punish their iniquity. They divided the army and invested two fortresses, Dobin and Demmin, and they "made many engines of war against" them.[2] There came also an army of Danes, and it joined those who were investing Dobin, and the siege waxed. One day, however, those who were shut up noticed that the army of the Danes acted dilatorily—for they are pugnacious at home, unwarlike abroad. Making a sudden sally, they slew many of the Danes and laid them as a thickness for the ground. The Danes, also, could not be aided on account of intervening water. Moved to anger by this, the army pressed the siege more obstinately. The vassals of our duke and of the margrave Albert, however, said to one another: "Is not the land we are devastating our land, and the people we are fighting our people? Why are we, then, found to be our own enemies and the destroyers of our own incomes? Does not this loss fall back on our lords?"

From that day, then, uncertainty of purpose began to seize the army and repeated truces to lighten the investment. As often as the Slavs were beaten in an engagement, the army was held back from pursuing the fugitives and from seizing the stronghold. Finally, when our men were weary, an agreement was made to the effect that the Slavs were to embrace Christianity and to release the Danes whom they held in captivity. Many of them, therefore, falsely received baptism, and they released from captivity all the Danes that were old or not serviceable, retaining the others whom more robust years fitted for work. Thus, that grand expedition broke up with slight gain. The Slavs immediately afterward became worse: they neither respected their baptism nor kept their hands from ravaging the Danes....

6.4 The Fourth Crusade: Nicetas Choniates, *O City of Byzantium* (c.1215). Original in Greek.

INNOCENT III (r.1198-1216) CALLED A NEW crusade in the first year of his reign. But the Fourth Crusade that resulted was deflected from its course; its chief "triumph" was the conquest of Constantinople. Nicetas Choniates (c.1150-1215), an official at the imperial court, wrote a long lament about the event. The excerpt below begins on February 2, 1204, when the crusaders' armies went on a foraging expedition to Philea, on the Black Sea, and on their return encountered the imperial troops. Taking together the various crusade documents presented here—Raban's poem about Jewish martyrdom, above, p. 286; Anna Comnena's history above, p. 290; the letter home of Stephen of Blois, above, p. 293; Ibn al-Athir's account of the First Crusade on p. 296; *The Conquest of Lisbon*, p. 300; Ibn Shaddad's praise of Saladin, above, p. 334; Helmold's *Chronicle*, p. 342; and this lamentation by Choniates—consider the origins, motivations, and results of the Crusade movement as a whole.

[Source: *O City of Byzantium, Annals of Niketas Choniatēs*, trans. Harry J. Magoulias (Detroit: Wayne State University Press, 1984), pp. 312-17 (slightly modified).]

When Baldwin, count of Flanders, ravaged the lands around Philea and collected tribute thence, the emperor marched against him.[3] As the Romans were moving out and the enemy troops returning from their battle array, they met in close combat.[4] The Romans were paralyzed by fear and took to impetuous

---

1   I.e., wearing the symbols of the crusaders.
2   1 Macc. 11: 20.
3   Count Baldwin of Flanders became the first Latin Emperor at Constantinople in 1204. It was in fact his brother who led the expedition to Philea. The emperor, who had just been crowned, was Alexius V Ducas Murtzuphlus.
4   The "Romans" are the Byzantines.

flight; the emperor, left all alone, very nearly perished, and the icon of the Mother of God, which the Roman emperors reckon as their fellow general, was taken by the enemy.

Not only were these events dreadful, but those that followed were much worse than expected and most calamitous. In the larger ships frightful scaling ladders were once again fabricated and all manner of siege engines were constructed. Banners were flown on top, and huge rewards were offered those who would ascend to give battle.

A measure of the horrors was about to begin, others were already under way, and still others were to follow; the deliberations on amity were disregarded, wholly ignored. Certain wicked Telchines[1] frequently confounded the negotiations. The doge of Venice, Enrico Dandolo, electing to discuss peace terms with the emperor, boarded a trireme and put in at Kosmidion. As soon as the emperor arrived there on horseback, they exchanged views on the peace, paying no heed to anyone else. The demands made by the doge and the remaining chiefs were for the immediate payment of five thousand pounds of gold and certain other conditions which were both galling and unacceptable to those who have tasted freedom and are accustomed to give, not take, commands.[2] These demands were deemed to be heavy Laconian lashes[3] to those for whom the danger of captivity was imminent and universal destruction had erupted, while the doge loudly again declared what had been stated earlier, that the conditions were quite tolerable and not at all burdensome. As the conditions for peace were being negotiated, Latin cavalry forces, suddenly appearing from above, gave free rein to their horses and charged the emperor, who wheeled his horse around, barely escaping the danger, while some of his companions were taken captive. Their inordinate hatred for us and our excessive disagreement with them allowed for no humane feeling between us.

Thereupon [April 8, 1204], the enemy's largest ships, carrying the scaling ladders that had been readied and as many of the siege engines as had been prepared, moved out from the shore, and, like the tilting beam of a scale's balance, they sailed over to the walls to take up positions at sufficient intervals from one another. They occupied the region extending in a line from the Monastery of Evergetes to the palace in Blachernai, which had been set on fire, the buildings within razed to the ground, thus stripping it of every pleasant spectacle. Observing these maneuvers, Ducas[4] prepared to resist the enemy. He issued instructions for the imperial pavilion to be set up on the hill of the Pantepoptes monastery whence the warships were visible and the actions of those on board were in full view.

As dawn broke on the ninth day of the month of April in the seventh indiction of the year 6712 [April 9, 1204], the warships and dromons[5] approached the walls, and certain courageous warriors climbed the scaling ladders and discharged all manner of missiles against the towers' defenders. All through the day, a battle fraught with groans was waged. The Romans had the upper hand: both the ships carrying the scaling ladders and the dromons transporting the horses were repulsed from the walls they had attacked without success, and many were killed by the stones thrown from the City's engines.

The enemy ceased all hostilities through the next day and the day after, which was the Lord's day [Sunday, April 10-11, 1204]; on the third day, the twelfth day of the month of April, Monday of the sixth week of the Great Lent, they again sailed towards the City and put in along the shore. By midday our forces prevailed, even though the fighting was more intense and furious than on the preceding Friday. Since it was necessary for the queen of cities to put on the slave's yoke, God allowed our jaws to be constrained with bit and curb[6] because all of us, both priest and people,

---

1 The Telchines were spiteful sorcerers with webbed fingers and feet.
2 The crusaders, and particularly Doge Enrico Dandolo, had negotiated with Alexius IV Angelus, the rival emperor, to help him and his father, Isaac II Angelus, regain the imperial throne at Constantinople in return for various favors, including nearly 200,000 marks of silver. The crusaders were here asking for about half of that from Murtzuphlus.
3 A reference to practices at Sparta as recorded in Xenophon, *Republica Lacedaemoniorum* 2. 2.
4 The emperor.
5 A sailing galley.
6 See Ps. 32: 9; Douay Ps. 31: 9.

had turned away from him like a stiff-necked and un-bridled horse. Two men on one of the scaling ladders nearest the Petria Gate, which was raised with great difficulty opposite the emperor, trusting themselves to fortune, were the first from among their comrades to leap down onto the tower facing them. When they drove off in alarm the Roman auxiliaries on watch, they waved their hands from above as a sign of joy and courage to embolden their countrymen. While they were jumping onto the tower, a knight by the name of Peter entered through the gate situated there. He was deemed most capable of driving in rout all the battalions,[1] for he was nearly nine fathoms tall[2] and wore on his head a helmet fashioned in the shape of a towered city. The noblemen about the emperor and the rest of the troops were unable to gaze upon the front of the helm of a single knight so terrible in form and spectacular in size and took to their customary flight as the efficacious medicine of salvation. Thus, by uniting and fusing into one craven soul, the cowardly thousands, who had the advantage of a high hill, were chased by one man from the fortifications they were meant to defend. When they reached the Golden Gate of the Land walls, they pulled down the new-built wall there, ran forth, and dispersed, deservedly taking the road to perdition and utter destruction. The enemy, now that there was no one to raise a hand against them, ran everywhere and drew the sword against every age and sex. Each did not join with the next man to form a coherent battle array, but all poured out and scattered, since everyone was terrified of them.

That evening the enemy set fire to the eastern sections of the City not far from the Monastery of Evergetes; from there the flames spread to those areas that slope down to the sea and terminate in the vicinity of the Droungarios Gate. After despoiling the emperor's pavilion and taking the palace in Blachernai by assault without difficulty, they set up their general headquarters at the Pantepoptes monastery. The emperor went hither and yon through the City's narrow streets, attempting to rally and mobilize the populace who wandered aimlessly about. Neither were they convinced by his exhortations nor did they yield to his blandishments, but the fiercely shaken aegis filled all with despair.[3]

To continue with the remaining portions of my narrative, the day waned and night came on, and each and every citizen busied himself with removing and burying his possessions. Some chose to leave the City, and whoever was able hastened to save himself.

When Ducas saw that he was gaining nothing,[4] he was fearful lest he be apprehended and put into the jaws of the Latins as their dinner or dessert, and he entered the Great Palace. He put on board a small fishing boat the Empress Euphrosyne, Emperor Alexius's wife, and her daughters, one of whom he loved passionately [Eudocia] (for he had frequently engaged in sexual intercourse from the first appearance of hair on his cheek, and he was a proven lecher in bed, having put away two wedded wives[5]) and sailed away from the City [night of April 12-13, 1204], having reigned two months and sixteen days.

When the emperor had fled in this manner, a pair of youths sober and most skillful in matters of warfare, these being Ducas[6] and Lascaris,[7] bearing the same name as the first emperor of our faith [Constantine], contested the captaincy of a tempest-tossed ship, for they viewed the great and celebrated Roman empire as Fortune's prize, depending upon the chance move of a chessman. They entered the Great Church,[8] evenly matched, competing against each other and being compared one with the other, neither one having more or less to offer than the other, and they were deemed equal in the balance because there was no one to examine them and pass judgment.

---

1 The imagery is from Homer, *Iliad* 5. 93. 96. This was Peter of Amiens, who led a party of ten knights and sixty sergeants.
2 The image is from Homer, *Odyssey* 11. 312.
3 See Homer, *Iliad* 15. 229-230. The aegis was the shield or breastplate of Zeus and Athena.
4 See Matt. 27: 24.
5 See Homer, *Iliad* 1. 114.
6 This Constantine Ducas was probably the son of John Angelus Ducas, the uncle of Isaac II and Alexius III.
7 Constantine Lascaris was the brother of the future emperor of Nicaea, Theodore I Lascaris.
8 The Great Church was Hagia Sophia, built by Justinian.

Receiving the supreme office by lot, Lascaris refused the imperial insignia; escorted by the patriarch to the Milion, he continuously exhorted the assembled populace, cajoling them to put up a resistance. He pressed those who lift from the shoulder and brandish the deadly iron ax, sending them off to the imminent struggle, reminding them that they should not fear destruction any less than the Romans should the Roman empire fall to another nation: no longer would they be paid the ample wages of mercenaries or receive the far-famed gifts of honor of the imperial guard, and their pay in the future would be counted at a hair's worth.[1] Thus did Lascaris, but not a single person from the populace responded to his blandishments. The ax-bearers agreed to fight for wages, deceitfully and cunningly exploiting the height of the danger for monetary gain, and when the Latin battalions clad in full armor made their appearance, they took flight to save themselves [early morning of April 13, 1204].

The enemy, who had expected otherwise, found no one openly venturing into battle or taking up arms to resist; they saw that the way was open before them and everything there for the taking. The narrow streets were clear and the crossroads unobstructed, safe from attack, and advantageous to the enemy. The populace, moved by the hope of propitiating them, had turned out to greet them with crosses and venerable icons of Christ as was customary during festivals of solemn processions. But their disposition was not at all affected by what they saw, nor did their lips break into the slightest smile, nor did the unexpected spectacle transform their grim and frenzied glance and fury into a semblance of cheerfulness. Instead, they plundered with impunity and stripped their victims shamelessly, beginning with their carts. Not only did they rob them of their substance but also the articles consecrated to God; the rest fortified themselves all around with defensive weapons as their horses were roused at the sound of the war trumpet.

What then should I recount first and what last of those things dared at that time by these murderous men? O, the shameful dashing to earth of the venerable icons and the flinging of the relics of the saints, who had suffered for Christ's sake, into defiled places! How horrible it was to see the Divine Body and Blood of Christ poured out and thrown to the ground! These forerunners of Antichrist, chief agents and harbingers of his anticipated ungodly deeds, seized as plunder the precious chalices and patens; some they smashed, taking possession of the ornaments embellishing them, and they set the remaining vessels on their tables to serve as bread dishes and wine goblets. Just as happened long ago, Christ was now disrobed and mocked, his garments were parted, and lots were cast for them by this race; and although his side was not pierced by the lance, yet once more streams of Divine Blood poured to the earth.[2]

The report of the impious acts perpetrated in the Great Church are unwelcome to the ears. The table of sacrifice,[3] fashioned from every kind of precious material and fused by fire into one whole—blended together into a perfection of one multicolored thing of beauty, truly extraordinary and admired by all nations—was broken into pieces and divided among the despoilers, as was the lot of all the sacred church treasures, countless in number and unsurpassed in beauty. They found it fitting to bring out as so much booty the all-hallowed vessels and furnishings which had been wrought with incomparable elegance and craftsmanship from rare materials. In addition, in order to remove the pure silver which overlay the railing of the bema,[4] the wondrous pulpit and the gates, as well as that which covered a great many other adornments, all of which were plated with gold, they led to the very sanctuary of the temple itself mules and asses with packsaddles; some of these, unable to keep their feet on the smoothly polished marble floors, slipped and were pierced by knives so that the excrement from the bowels and the spilled blood defiled the sacred floor. Moreover, a certain silly woman laden with sins, an attendant of the Erinyes, the handmaid of demons, the workshop of unspeakable spells and reprehensible charms, waxing wanton against Christ,

---

1 Homer, *Iliad* 9. 378.
2 See John 19: 1-4, 23-24, 34.
3 I.e., the altar.
4 In the Greek Church the area in which the altar is placed is called the bema, or sanctuary.

sat upon the synthronon and intoned a song, and then whirled about and kicked up her heels in dance.[1]

It was not that these crimes were committed in this fashion while others were not, or that some acts were more heinous than others, but that the most wicked and impious deeds were perpetrated by all with one accord. Did these madmen, raging thus against the sacred, spare pious matrons and girls of marriageable age or those maidens who, having chosen a life of chastity, were consecrated to God? Above all, it was a difficult and arduous task to mollify the barbarians with entreaties and to dispose them kindly towards us, as they were highly irascible and bilious and unwilling to listen to anything. Everything incited their anger, and they were thought fools and became a laughing-stock. He who spoke freely and openly was rebuked, and often the dagger would be drawn against him who expressed a small difference of opinion or who hesitated to carry out their wishes.

The whole head was in pain.[2] There were lamentations and cries of woe and weeping in the narrow ways, wailing at the crossroads, moaning in the temples, outcries of men, screams of women, the taking of captives, and the dragging about, tearing in pieces, and raping of bodies heretofore sound and whole. They who were bashful of their sex were led about naked, they who were venerable in their old age uttered plaintive cries, and the wealthy were despoiled of their riches. Thus it was in the squares, thus it was on the corners, thus it was in the temples, thus it was in the hiding places; for there was no place that could escape detection or that could offer asylum to those who came streaming in.

O Christ our Emperor, what tribulation and distress of men at that time! The roaring of the sea, the darkening and dimming of the sun, the turning of the moon into blood, the displacement of the stars—did they not foretell in this way the last evils?[3] Indeed, we have seen the abomination of desolation stand in the holy place,[4]

rounding off meretricious and petty speeches and other things which were moving definitely, if not altogether, contrariwise to those things deemed by Christians as holy and ennobling the word of faith.

Such then, to make a long story short, were the outrageous crimes committed by the Western armies against the inheritance of Christ. Without showing any feelings of humanity whatsoever, they exacted from all their money and chattel, dwellings and clothing, leaving to them nothing of all their goods. Thus behaved the brazen neck, the haughty spirit, the high brow, the ever-shaved and youthful cheek, the bloodthirsty right hand, the wrathful nostril, the disdainful eye, the insatiable jaw, the hateful heart, the piercing and running speech practically dancing over the lips. More to blame were the learned and wise among men, they who were faithful to their oaths, who loved the truth and hated evil, who were both more pious and just and scrupulous in keeping the commandments of Christ than we "Greeks."[5] Even more culpable were those who had raised the cross to their shoulders, who had time and again sworn by it and the sayings of the Lord to cross over Christian lands without bloodletting, neither turning aside to the right nor inclining to the left, and to take up arms against the Saracens and to stain red their swords in their blood; they who had sacked Jerusalem, and had taken an oath not to marry or to have sexual intercourse with women as long as they carried the cross on their shoulders, and who were consecrated to God and commissioned to follow in his footsteps.

In truth, they were exposed as frauds. Seeking to avenge the Holy Sepulcher, they raged openly against Christ and sinned by overturning the Cross with the cross they bore on their backs, not even shuddering to trample on it for the sake of a little gold and silver. By grasping pearls, they rejected Christ, the pearl of great price, scattering among the most accursed of brutes the All-Hallowed One.[6] The sons of Ismael did not

---

1 The Erinyes were the Furies of mythology. The synthronon were the thrones of the bishop and the clergy behind the altar in the sanctuary. The words "waxing wanton against Christ" echoes 1 Tim. 5: 11.

2 See Isa. 1: 5.

3 See Matt. 24: 29; Mark 13: 24; Luke 21: 25; Rev. 6: 12.

4 Matt. 24:15.

5 This sentence is meant to be sarcastic, as is shown by the use of the term *Graikoi*, the Latin term of derision for the Byzantines.

6 See Matt. 13: 45 and 7: 6.

behave in this way, for when the Latins overpowered Sion the Latins showed no compassion or kindness to their race. Neither did the Ismaelites neigh after Latin women,[1] nor did they turn the cenotaph[2] of Christ into a common burial place of the fallen, nor did they transform the entranceway of the life-bringing tomb into a passageway leading down into Hades, nor did they replace the Resurrection with the Fall. Rather, they allowed everyone to depart in exchange for the payment of a few gold coins; they took only the ransom money and left to the people all their possessions, even though these numbered more than the grains of sand.[3] Thus the enemies of Christ dealt magnanimously with the Latin infidels, inflicting upon them neither sword, nor fire, nor hunger, nor persecution, nor nakedness, nor bruises, nor constraints. How differently, as we have briefly recounted, the Latins treated us who love Christ and are their fellow believers, guiltless of any wrong against them.

O City, City, eye of all cities, universal boast, supramundane wonder, wet nurse of churches, leader of the faith, guide of Orthodoxy, beloved topic of orations, the abode of every good thing! O City, that hast drunk at the hand of the Lord the cup of his fury![4] O City, consumed by a fire far more drastic than the fire which of old fell upon the Pentapolis![5] "What shall I testify to thee? What shall I compare to thee? The cup of thy destruction is magnified," says Jeremias, who was given to tears as he lamented over ancient Sion.[6] What malevolent powers have desired to have you and taken you to be sifted?[7] What jealous and relentless avenging demons have made a riotous assault upon you in wild revel? If these implacable and crazed suitors neither fashioned a bridal chamber for thee, nor lit a nuptial torch for thee, did they not, however, ignite the coals of destruction?

---

1 See Jer. 5: 8. The "sons of Ismael" refers to the Muslims.
2 I.e., tomb.
3 This passage refers to the Muslim retaking of Jerusalem in 1187.
4 See Isa. 51: 17.
5 See Wisd. of Sol. 10: 6 and Gen. 19: 24; the Pentapolis refers to the five cities that united to defeat King Chedorlaomer (Gen. 14: 1)—Sodom, Gomorrha, Segor, Adama, and Seboim—only one of which was not destroyed by God.
6 See Lam. 2: 13.
7 See Luke 22: 31.

6.5 English common law: *The Assize of Clarendon* (1166). Original in Latin.

THE ASSIZE OF CLARENDON reflected the decisions of a meeting at Clarendon in which King Henry II (r.1154-1189) and his leading men determined to reform the English legal system. Building on administrative institutions already in place, they fortified and regularized them, so that royal law would pervade every county and hundred (English local districts). The Assize provided for a regular system of itinerant (traveling) judges with important police powers. Encroaching on older methods of keeping law and order, it called for the widespread use of sworn inquests to bring criminal cases to the attention of royal justices.

[Source: *English Historical Documents*, vol. 2: *1042-1189*, ed. David C. Douglas and George W. Greenaway, 2nd ed. (London and New York: Routledge, 1981), pp. 440-43 (notes modified).]

Here begins the assize of Clarendon made by King Henry II with the assent of the archbishops, bishops, abbots, earls and barons of all England.

1. In the first place the aforesaid King Henry, on the advice of all his barons, for the preservation of peace, and for the maintenance of justice, has decreed that inquiry shall be made throughout the several counties and throughout the several hundreds[1] through twelve of the more lawful men of the hundred and through four of the more lawful men of each vill upon oath that they will speak the truth, whether there be in their hundred or vill any man accused or notoriously suspect of being a robber or murderer or thief, or any who is a receiver of robbers or murderers or thieves, since the lord king has been king.[2] And let the justices inquire into this among themselves and the sheriffs among themselves.[3]

2. And let anyone, who shall be found, on the oath of the aforesaid, accused or notoriously suspect of having been a robber or murderer or thief, or a receiver of them, since the lord king has been king, be taken and put to the ordeal of water,[4] and let him swear that he has not been a robber or murderer or thief, or receiver of them, since the lord king has been king, to the value of 5 shillings, so far as he knows.

3. And if the lord of the man, who has been arrested, or his steward or his vassals shall claim him by pledge within the third day following his capture, let him be released on bail with his chattels[5] until he himself shall stand his trial.

4. And when a robber or murderer or thief or receiver of them has been arrested through the aforesaid oath, if the justices are not about to come speedily enough into the county where they have been taken, let the sheriffs send word to the nearest justice by some well-informed person that they have arrested such men, and the justices shall send back word to the sheriffs informing them where they desire the men to be brought before them; and let the sheriffs bring them before the justices. And together with them let the sheriffs bring from the hundred and the vill, where

---

1   The inquiries were to be made by the visitation of itinerant justices, also called "justices in eyre."

2   These "lawful men" on oath are the ancestors of the modern jury. The "vill"—or village—was smaller than the "hundred," hence the jury was smaller. The jury—technically termed a jury of presentment—was asked to "speak the truth" about criminals or suspected criminals in the locality. Here Henry was regularizing an institution (the frankpledge) already in place. See n. 4 on p. 351 below.

3   I.e., the sheriff was left with certain powers of criminal jurisdiction beyond the powers of the justices.

4   Ordeals were meant to show guilt or innocence through "tests," the outcome of which were determined by God's judgment. In the case of the ordeal of water, the accused was immersed in a pool or stream. If she immediately rose to the surface, she was guilty; if he sank, he was innocent.

5   I.e., movable property.

they have been arrested, two lawful men to bear the record of the county and of the hundred as to why they have been taken, and there before the justice let them stand trial.

5. And in the case of those who have been arrested through the aforesaid oath of this assize, let no man have court or justice or chattels save the lord king in his court in the presence of his justices; and the lord king shall have all their chattels.[1] But in the case of those who have been arrested otherwise than by this oath let it be as is customary and due.

6. And let the sheriffs, who have arrested them, bring them before the justice without any other summons than that they have from him. And when robbers or murderers or thieves, or receivers of them, who have been arrested through the oath or otherwise, are handed over to the sheriffs, let them receive them immediately and without delay.

7. And in the several counties where there are no gaols,[2] let such be made in a borough or some castle of the king at the king's expense and from his wood, if one shall be near, or from some neighboring wood at the oversight of the king's servants, to the end that in them the sheriffs may be able to guard those who shall be arrested by the officials accustomed to do this, or by their servants.

8. Moreover, the lord king wills that all shall come to the county courts to take this oath, so that none shall remain behind on account of any franchise which he has, or any court or soke,[3] which he may have, but that they shall come to take this oath.

9. And let there be no one within his castle or without, nor even in the honor of Wallingford, who shall forbid the sheriffs to enter into his court or his land to take the view of frankpledge and to see that all are under pledges; and let them be sent before the sheriffs under free pledge.[4]

10. And in cities or boroughs let no one hold men or receive them into his house or on his land or in his soke, whom he will not take in hand to produce before the justice, should they be required; or else let them be in frankpledge.

11. And let there be none in a city or a borough or a castle or without it, nor even in the honor of Wallingford, who shall forbid the sheriffs to enter into their land or their soke to arrest those who have been accused or are notoriously suspect of being robbers or murderers or thieves or receivers of them, or outlaws, or persons charged concerning the forest;[5] but the king commands that they shall aid the sheriffs to capture them.

12. And if anyone shall be taken in possession of the spoils of robbery or theft, if he be of evil repute and bears an evil testimony from the public and has no warrant, let him have no law.[6] And if he has not been notoriously suspect on account of the goods in his possession, let him go to the ordeal of water.

13. And if anyone shall confess to robbery or murder or theft, or to harboring those who have committed them, in the presence of the lawful men or in the hundred court, and afterwards he wish to deny it, let him not have his law.[7]

14. Moreover, the lord king wills that those who shall be tried by the law and absolved by the law, if

---

1 "Court or justice or chattels" refers to the fees generated by the case. By this provision the king claimed the sole rights to the profits of jurisdiction in this new procedure. But, as the next sentence makes clear, profits arising from arrests according to the older system were to be distributed in the old way.

2 I.e., jails.

3 Franchises, courts, and sokes were private jurisdictions, often granted by privilege or charter. This clause was aimed at limiting the powers of private courts.

4 This clause overrode guarantees of privilege—often granted by kings—against the entry of public officials into private jurisdictions. The frankpledge was a group of men pledged not to commit any offenses and to produce any of their number who did so. (Another name for this group was a "tithing.") Most ordinary freemen were part of one. The "view of frankpledge" was customarily taken twice a year by the sheriff to verify membership in the frankpledge and to hear of any of its members' criminal activities.

5 The king claimed special jurisdiction over forests.

6 I.e., criminals taken red-handed and without "warrant" (or surety)—namely, a person to guarantee their court appearance—were to be punished without trial.

7 I.e., the case was not to be tried after the accused had pleaded guilty to the offense. In all these clauses the particular importance attached both to the past record of the accused and to local opinion concerning him should be noted.

they have been of ill repute and openly and disgracefully spoken of by the testimony of many and that of the lawful men, shall abjure the king's lands, so that within eight days they shall cross the sea, unless the wind detains them; and with the first wind they shall have afterwards they shall cross the sea, and they shall not return to England again except by the mercy of the lord king; and both now, and if they return, let them be outlawed; and on their return let them be seized as outlaws.[1]

15. And the lord king forbids that any vagabond, that is, a wanderer or unknown person, shall be given shelter anywhere except in a borough, and even there he shall not be given shelter longer than one night, unless he become sick there, or his horse, so that he can show an evident excuse.

16. And if he shall remain there longer than one night, let him be arrested and held until his lord shall come to give surety for him, or until he himself shall procure safe pledges; and let him likewise be arrested who gave him shelter.[2]

17. And if any sheriff shall send word to another sheriff that men have fled from his county into another county, on account of robbery or murder or theft or the harboring of them, or on account of outlawry or of a charge concerning the king's forest, let him (the second sheriff) arrest them; and even if he knows of himself or through others that such men have fled into his county, let him arrest them and guard them until he has taken safe pledges for them.

18. And let all the sheriffs cause a record to be made of all fugitives who have fled from their counties; and let them do this before the county courts and carry the names of those written therein before the justices, when next they come to them, so that these men may be sought throughout England, and their chattels may be seized for the needs of the king.

19. And the lord king wills that from the time the sheriffs shall receive the summons of the itinerant justices to present themselves before them, together with the men of the county, they shall assemble them and make inquiry for all who have newly come into their counties since this assize; and they shall send them away under pledge to attend before the justices, or they shall keep them in custody until the justices come to them, and then they shall present them before the justices.

20. Moreover, the lord king forbids monks or canons or any religious house to receive any men of the lower orders as a monk or a canon or a brother, until it be known of what reputation he is, unless he shall be sick unto death.

21. Moreover, the lord king forbids anyone in all England to receive in his land or his soke or in a house under him any one of that sect of renegades who were branded and excommunicated at Oxford.[3] And if anyone shall so receive them, he himself shall be at the mercy of the lord king, and the house in which they have dwelt shall be carried outside the village and burnt. And each sheriff shall swear an oath that he will observe this, and shall cause all his officers to swear this, and also the stewards of the barons and all knights and freeholders of the counties.

22. And the lord king wills that this assize shall be kept in his realm so long as it shall please him.

---

1 This is a new feature in criminal law administration: even those who have been acquitted on a particular indictment are not regarded as free and lawful persons if their past record is shady, and they are to suffer exile.
2 Sureties and "safe pledges" are all ways to insure that the person will appear in court if allowed to go free.
3 A reference to the Cathars.

6.6 English litigation on the ground: *The Costs of Richard of Anstey's Law Suit* (1158–1163). Original in Latin.

THE COMPLEXITY AND EXPENSE OF litigating in twelfth-century England is well illustrated by the account of Richard of Anstey's suit to recover lands bequeathed to him by his uncle, William "de Secqueville." The lands were being held by Mabel "de Francheville," William's daughter by a second marriage. That marriage had been condemned as "null and void" by the papacy, a verdict that was pronounced in an ecclesiastical court in London. Richard's claim to the land was based on that decision. Nevertheless, as the following account makes clear, he had to travel to many places in order to obtain various writs (orders), attend many hearings, and spend a lot of money before his case was decided.

[Source: *English Historical Documents*, vol. 2: *1042–1189*, ed. David C. Douglas and George W. Greenaway, 2nd ed. (London and New York: Routledge, 1981), pp. 488–90 (notes modified).]

These are the expenses which I, Richard of Anstey, incurred in gaining possession of the land of my uncle. First of all I sent one of my men to Normandy to obtain the king's writ to put my adversaries on trial. This man spent half a mark on the journey. When my messenger had brought me the writ I took it to Salisbury that it might be sent back sealed with the queen's seal; in this journey I spent 2 silver marks.

On my return thence, hearing that Ralph Brito[1] was obliged to cross the Channel, I followed him as far as Southampton to speak with him and to ask him to convey the king's writ to the archbishop for me, because I knew that the suit ought to be transferred to the archbishop's court. In that journey I spent 22 shillings 7 pence, and lost a palfrey,[2] which I had bought for 15 shillings. Returning thence with the queen's writ, I went to Ongar and handed the writ to Richard of Lucé.[3] And when he had given me audience, he appointed a day, the eve of St. Andrew,[4] for my suit to be heard at Northampton. Before that day arrived, I sent Nicholas, my clerk, for Geoffrey of Troisgots and Alfreda, his sister, because she was my uncle's widow. Them he found at Burnham in Norfolk. This journey cost me 15 shillings and the loss of a packhorse, which I had bought for 9 shillings.

On my return I went with my friends and helpers to Northampton to plead my case, and on that journey I spent 54 shillings. There another day was appointed me at Southampton a fortnight later; on that journey I spent 57 shillings and lost a packhorse worth 12 shillings. After this came Ralph Brito from Normandy bringing me the king's writ transferring the suit to the archbishop's court. This writ I took to Archbishop Theobald, whom I found at Winchester, and on that journey I spent 25 shillings 4 pence. Then the archbishop appointed me the feast of St. Vincent, and the case was heard at Lambeth. There the case was adjourned until St. Valentine's day.[5] On this journey I spent 8 shillings 6 pence, and the case was heard at Maidstone.

Here the feast of Saints Perpetua and Felicitas[6] was appointed me. But before that day arrived I went to the bishop of Winchester to ask him to bear witness to the decree of nullity which had been previously decreed in a synod at London.[7] This journey cost me a silver mark. The bishop having agreed to testify, I

---

1   Ralph Brito was one of Henry II's barons.
2   I.e., a saddle horse.
3   Richard of Lucé was the king's justiciar. At this point in time, the justiciar was the king's chief justice minister, but very soon, in the 1170s, he would take on greater powers, becoming a kind of substitute king when the king was not present.
4   November 29, 1158.
5   February 14, 1159.
6   March 7, 1159.
7   This was the declaration of nullity of his uncle's second marriage.

went on the appointed day all prepared to plead my case at Lambeth. There I spent 37 shillings 6 pence, and the case was adjourned till the Monday following *Laetare Jerusalem*.[1] Before this I went for Master Ambrose, who was then with the abbot of St. Albans in Norfolk; on that journey I spent 9 shillings 4 pence. I sent also Samson, my chaplain, for Master Peter "de Mileto" at Buckingham. On this journey he lost his palfrey for which I recompensed him with a silver mark; he had spent there 7 shillings.

Having obtained the services of these clerks, I came with my counsel at the appointed day to London, spending on the journey 5 silver marks. Here the day *Quasi modo geniti*[2] was set for me, before which I sent my brother, John, overseas to the king's court, since it was told me that my adversaries had secured a writ from the king giving them leave not to plead until the king should return to England. For this cause I sent my brother for another writ, lest my suit should be held over on account of my adversaries' writ. In this journey my brother spent 3 silver marks. Meanwhile I myself went to Chichester to speak with Bishop Hilary and to get him to witness to the decree of nullity made in his presence by the bishop of Winchester in the synod at London. This I received in letters sent by him to the archbishop testifying to the decree. On that journey I spent 14 shillings 4 pence. So I came to London on the appointed day with my clerks, my witnesses and my counsel. There I remained four days, pleading my suit

each day. This journey cost me 103 shillings.

Then the case was adjourned till Rogationtide.[3] And when I appeared at Canterbury on the appointed day, my adversaries declared they would not plead because of the summons to the king's army for the war of Toulouse. On that journey I spent 8 shillings and I returned thence without a day being fixed for further hearing....

[Finally after many further delays and fruitless journeys and two appeals to Rome, the plaintiff obtained a writ summoning the case before the king's court.]

We came then to the king at Woodstock, where we remained eight days; and *at length* by grace of the lord king and by the judgment of his court my uncle's land was adjudged to me. There I spent 7 pounds 10 shillings and 6 pence.

These are the presents which I gave to my counsel and to the clerks, who assisted me in the archbishop's court, namely 11 silver marks. In the court of the bishop of Winchester 14 silver marks, to Master Peter "de Mileto" 10 marks and a gold ring worth half a silver mark. To Master Robert "de Chimay" 1 mark. In the king's court I have spent in gifts, in gold and silver and in horses, 17½ marks. To Master Peter of Littlebury I gave 40 shillings. To the other counsel from among my friends, who had come regularly to the hearings of my suit, I gave in silver and in horses 12½ marks.

6.7 The legislation of a Spanish king: *The Laws of Cuenca* (1189–1193). Original in Latin.

THE TOWN OF CUENCA, originally founded by Muslims in al-Andalus, was conquered by King Alfonso VIII of Castile (r.1158–1214) in 1177. Soon thereafter he issued a set of laws (*fueros*) for the citizens. Unlike English laws, those of Cuenca were to be enforced by local—not royal—officials (*alcaldi; iudices*), though there were provisions for appealing the most serious cases to the king. The code makes clear that a few Muslims still lived in the town and that Jews and Christians regularly interacted there. Woman and children had numerous rights, and the laws paid particular attention to what today would be called "family law." What might explain this fact?

[Source: *The Code of Cuenca: Municipal Law on the Twelfth-Century Castilian Frontier*, trans. James

---

1   The fourth Sunday in Lent.
2   The first Sunday after Easter.
3   The Sunday and three days preceding Ascension Day, which is the 40th day after Easter.

F. Powers (Philadelphia: University of Pennsylvania Press, 2000), pp. 28-29, 66-69, 92, 160-65 (slightly modified, and notes making use of the Glossary on pp. 229-32).]

Prologue

... The memory of men is fragile and insufficient for a multitude of things, and for this reason one has proceeded with the sagacity to put the laws of legal statute and civil rights in writing. After meditative selection [these laws] sprouted from royal authority to calm the discord between citizens and inhabitants; thus some could crush villains by the greatest possible cunning, since they are protected by royal guarantee, and cannot subsequently be weakened by fraudulent subterfuge.

For this consideration, then, I, Alfonso, proclaimed king by the grace of God, the most powerful of the Hispanic kings, notice of whose immense greatness and concordant fame resonated far and wide, from the rising of the sun to the bounds of the earth, under whose domain the kings are happy to be subjected, under whose government the laws are pleased to be administered; I, the guide of those who take pride in the Hispanic kingdoms, codified the summation of the judicial institutions in behalf of safeguarding peace and the rights of justice between clergy and laity, between townsmen and peasants, among the needy and the poor; and I codified it, ordered it written with much care so that any question or discussion, as much in the petition as in the judicial action (as much for the cause as for the accusation), which occurs between the citizens and the inhabitants, removing all appeal, except those which later on excluded the laws, and having torn the veil of the sham, could determine under the judgment of the justice, once imputed and discerned, the cause of both parties to the tenor of the written laws and the use of the custom "in which rests the right and the norm of the language,"[1] the reason of each part having been expressed and versed, so let the law be defined under the supervision of the knighthood.

Thus, [this is] a king of such renowned authority, that from sea to sea the kings [who are] enemies of the name of Christ fear his name only, since they have experienced his power and have been crushed by him many times; [of such renowned authority that] Christian princes serve him as the first [lord], and from whom Don Conrado, illustrious descendant of the Roman Emperor, and Don Alfonso, king of León, are happy to have received the weapons of combat and his backing, a reminder of his goodness and of having kissed his hand.

After laying siege and after many tasks, tormented by numerous difficulties and distressed by the enemies within, nine months having passed, he made his entry into the city of Cuenca, preferring it to the others; since he chose Cuenca as Alphonsipolis, he preferred it for his residence, and he adopted its citizens as his favorite people in order to strengthen its prosperity, freedom, and distinction among the others he had liberated from the captivity of Babylon and from the yoke of the Pharaoh with the weapons of his royal power, once he suppressed the filth of its idolatry.[2]

Therefore, so that so great a prerogative of dignity should be known, he conceded high rank to the inhabitants and settlers of Cuenca, as much to those already there as those to come; by this code of freedom, the tenor of which concerns matters of public affairs and its sentences, which are examined in justice with meditating decision and granted by royal agreement, he confirmed it forever with the seal of the royal effigy.

Happy is that marriage certainly when Law and Justice join in uniform alliance, so that when the Law instructs that one should be cleared, he is cleared by the Law, and that which it determines should be condemned, is condemned by Justice, which sufficiently favors definition by both. Thus Law is that which permits the honest and prohibits the opposite; Justice, on the other hand, is the virtue that concedes each one his rights, punishes the culprit, and acquits the innocent.

Disposing these things continually for the honor

---

1 Horace, *Epistulae* 2. 3. 71-72.
2 Alfonso likens his capture of Cuenca from the Muslims to the liberation of the Jews from Babylon and Egypt.

of Holy Mother Church and for the increase of the Catholic faith, which in the district of Cuenca remained overwhelmed in an extraordinary way, for God Living and True, to whom to serve is to rule and whose yoke is soft and his load light, they serve in freedom, and just as they obey the Commandments of a single God, they also obey the orders of a single king and prince.

Therefore, I, Alfonso, king by the grace of God, together with Leonor my wife the queen, and our serene son Fernando, whose birth distinguished the above city with serene and pleased look, grant to all the inhabitants of Cuenca and to their successors this summary of dignity and prerogative of freedom; and so that for posterity it could not be broken, I confirm it with the guarantee of our seal and with our royal protection....

CHAPTER X
The Right of Succession of Children and Parents

1. THE RIGHT OF SUCCESSION OF CHILDREN AND PARENTS

Any child should inherit the goods of his father and mother, movable goods as well as real estate. The father and mother [should inherit] the movable goods of the children. The father, however, should not have to inherit the real estate of his child which comes to the latter through inheritance. Regarding the other real estate which the parents acquire jointly, the one who survives, father or mother, should inherit this for lifetime use only, by right of inheritance through their child, if he lives at least nine days. After the death of the father or mother, the real estate returns to the estate.

For this reason I command that, although the surviving parent has to inherit this real estate for lifetime use, and the real estate has to revert to the estate, the survivor should provide bondsmen who will guard the real estate from harm. The real estate that belongs to the child through his estate should revert to that estate the day the survivor dies.

2. THE NEAREST RELATIVES OF A DEAD PERSON ARE HIS HEIRS

The relatives who are nearest [in blood] and also citizens should inherit the goods of their deceased relative. If someone comes forward as a closer relative than these others, this person should inherit the goods of the deceased but first should provide bondsmen who establish that this person should have been an inhabitant of Cuenca for at least ten years. Those who do not do this should not inherit.

3. THOSE WHO ENTER A MONASTIC ORDER

Whoever enters a monastic order should take with him only a fifth portion of his movable property, and the rest, joined with the entirety of his real estate, should remain for his heirs. It will be seen as unjust and inequitable that someone should disinherit his children by donating their movable property and real estate to the monks, because it is established in the code that nobody should disinherit their children.

4. CHILDREN ARE UNDER THE POWER OF THEIR PARENTS

Children should be under the power of their parents and are family members until they should contract marriage. And until that moment, everything the children acquire or obtain should belong entirely to their parents; the children holding nothing against their parents' will.

5. PARENTS RESPOND FOR THE CRIMES OF THEIR CHILDREN

Parents should respond for the crimes of their children, whether or not the latter should be sound in judgment.[1] If someone enters the home of another and commits any crime, whether or not they should be a hireling of the house, the owner of the house should not respond with a surety for them unless he defends them. If he defends them, he should respond for them or bring them to give juridical satisfaction. But if they do not return to the house of their *señor*, or the *señor* does not go forth in their defense, no one should

---

1 "Respond for" means be legally responsible for.

respond for them but their parents.[1] Nevertheless, if a child commits a homicide, even though he should be in the pay of another, no one should respond for him except his parents, because they should pay the pecuniary penalties; however, the parents should not depart as enemies unless they are blamed for the homicide. Then, if they are accused and convicted of homicide, they are obligated also to depart from our city as enemies. If the child is bereft of one of his parents, the one who acts as his guardian should respond for him until the child is given the portion of goods that belongs to him. After the partition of goods, the guardian does not have to respond.

6. PARENTS DO NOT RESPOND FOR THE DEBTS OF THEIR CHILDREN

Parents should not respond for the loans or debts of their children.

7. THE DISTURBED CHILD

If a father or mother has a disturbed child and is concerned for paying the pecuniary penalties of the crimes that he might commit, he should hold the child captive or bound until he calms down or is treated, while he remains deranged, so that the child does not cause damage. The parents have to respond for any damage that he causes, even if they have renounced him in front of the council or have disinherited him. This precept is established so that none may say that their child is insane or disturbed and renounce him before the council and then, with concealment and deception, cause him to kill someone or start a fire or do any other harm.

8. SEPARATION OF THE WIFE AND THE HUSBAND

When husband and wife, for any reason and by common agreement, want to separate, only those things they have acquired together should be distributed equally and nothing else; they should also distribute equally the works that both have completed on their property. And after one of those who has been separated in life dies, the survivor should receive nothing from the other's goods, but rather the heirs of the dead person should be those to receive all his or her goods, and these should be divided among themselves.

9. THE PARTITION OF GOODS OF PARENTS AND CHILDREN

All partitions of goods that are done in the presence of three citizens and recorded should hold as firm, so that the partition or the names of the witnesses are written in the public record, because, if some or all of the witnesses have died, he who holds the document should swear with two citizens that this is authentic, and he should be believed, in case some of the heirs deny the partition. Likewise, the division and the partition are firm and sound that the parents, whether healthy or sick, had made for their heirs, being all present without exception and in agreement; because the partition done in another way by the father or the mother is not legal. The donation should also be accepted and sound that the father and mother confirm only by oath.

10. THE DOCUMENT OF PARTITION

The document of partition should have this formulation: "All should know absolutely, those present as well as those to come, that I, *N.*, desiring the end of all flesh, which one is born for, so that before a man should die he should pay the debts of nature, allot and concede to my heirs and successors that, by right of patrimony after my death, according to hereditary right, they should possess my things, all that I have acquired with my sweat and my service up to the present day, as much in movable property as in real estate, and in this manner: to *G.*, my firstborn son, the vineyard that is within the district of Cuenca, near the river, with the orchard that lies within it; I leave you also all the houses that I built or bought in the locale *N.*; to *R.*, my younger son, the field *N.* or the vineyard with the portion [of land] that belongs to it. Witnessed by those whose names appear below: *F.P.D.J.* Era one

---

1 The *señor* was the male head of a family or household or, as in this case, an owner, employer, or master. Apparently at Cuenca many children did not live in the homes of their parents but rather were sent to other homes to work as maids, servants, or apprentices. The parents remained responsible for them if they committed a crime but not, as the next law makes clear, if they defaulted on a loan.

thousand two hundred.[1] N., being king. N., being *iudex*. N., being *merino*. N., being *sagio*."[2]

11. ALSO REGARDING THE PARTITION

If the spouses have children and are not separated in life, and neither of the two has other children, when one of them dies, having settled all the common debts that they have contracted jointly, and having paid also the share of the dead for alms for their soul[3] and their shroud, their children or heirs should distribute all the goods of the dead among each other, both goods and real estate. If a child dies, the surviving parent should inherit his goods, as has already been said. But if the child has a descendant, the latter should succeed him [the child] and not the father or the mother....

CHAPTER XIII
No One Should Respond for Counseling

1. NO ONE SHOULD RESPOND FOR GIVING ADVICE

I command that no one should respond or pay any fine for giving advice. However, he should respond if he advises the selling of a Christian. I also command that each one should pay the same fine, even if he should go in assistance of another and the fight should be another's fight.

2. WHOEVER TAKES PART IN A GANG SHOULD PAY, EXCEPT THEIR WIVES

Whoever takes part in a gang in order to lend aid to someone should pay double the pecuniary fine for the crime that they have committed, even though he should be that one's son or his blood kin, except for his wife; if the wife takes part in the gang of her husband, or if the latter is in the gang of his wife, the couple do not have to pay double [fines] for this, since it is a single fine for both.

3. HE WHO HOLDS ANOTHER'S WIFE

If someone holds another's wife, he should pay three hundred *solidi* and should be considered an enemy.[4]

4. HE WHO SELLS FOOD TO THE MUSLIMS

Whoever sells or gives weapons or food to the Muslims let him be hurled from the city cliffs, if it can be proved; but if not, he should clear himself with twelve citizens and should be believed; or he should swear alone and respond to the challenge by judicial combat,[5] the one which pleases the council more. We call food bread, cheese, and everything which one can eat, except for living livestock.

5. THE SERVANT WHO KILLS OR INJURES A CHRISTIAN

If someone's servant or Moor[6] hurts or kills a Christian, his master should pay the fine for the crime that he has committed or he should put the injurer in the hands of the plaintiff, the servant's master choosing that which pleases him more....

CHAPTER XXIX
Cases Between Christians and Jews

1. CASES BETWEEN CHRISTIANS AND JEWS

If a Jew and a Christian litigate for something, two citizen *alcaldi*[7] should be designated, one of whom should be Christian and the other Jewish. If one of the litigants is not pleased by the judgment, he should appeal to four citizen *alcaldi*, two of whom should be Christian and two Jewish. These four should have fi-

---

1   The date of the Era was 38 years ahead of the Year of Our Lord, so the date C.E. would be 1162. This chapter provides a form that must be filled out according to the facts and names of each case.

2   The *iudex* was the chief elected civil official of the town; the *merino* was the royal territorial administrator who received the king's rents from the town council; the *sagio* was the bailiff, town crier, and executioner. Naming these officials, along with the reigning king, was a way to authenticate the document and its date.

3   "Alms for their soul" refers to the distribution of money to the poor on behalf of the soul of the departed.

4   A *solidus* (pl.: *solidi*) was a silver coin worth 1/20th of a silver pound.

5   "Judicial combat" was an ordeal by duel. It might be on foot or on horseback. Care was taken to choose combatants well matched in size, strength, and skill.

6   A "Moor" was a Muslim living in Spain; in this case he was the slave or servant of a Christian.

7   The *alcaldi* (sing.: *alcaldus*) were elected officials who served as aldermen and judges in the parish; the word was derived from the Arabic *al-qadi*.

nal judgment. Whoever appeals the judgment of these four should know that he will lose the case. These *alcaldi* should guard against judging anything else than what the Code of Cuenca prescribes.

2. WITNESSES BETWEEN A JEW AND A CHRISTIAN

The witnesses between a Christian and a Jew should be two citizens, one Christian and the other Jewish, and all the things denied by the testimony of these [two] should be confirmed and believed. Anyone who ought to testify should swear with double the sureties or on his feet, according to the Code of Cuenca. If it is the Christian who places his foot and is defeated in the case, the *iudex* should imprison him in the jail of the king until he pays.[1]

3. THE JEW WHO TESTIFIES THAT HIS DEBTOR WAS OUTSIDE JAIL

If the Jew testifies that the prisoner is outside jail, the *iudex* should put him in the power of the Jew until he pays. Moreover, if it is the Jew who places his foot and is defeated in the case, the *albedí* [Jewish *iudex*, chancery official] should imprison him in the jail of the king.

4. THE CHRISTIAN WHO TESTIFIES THAT HIS DEBTOR IS OUTSIDE JAIL

If it is the Christian who attests that the prisoner is outside jail, the *albedí* should place him in the prison of the Christians, from whence he should not leave until he pays.

5. THE TESTIMONY FOR DELIVERY OF SURETIES

Be it known concerning witnesses, whether a Christian or a Jew, [if] he delivers double the sureties and he does not redeem them within the term of nine days, he should lose them completely.

6. IF THE ALBEDÍ DOES NOT WANT TO DO JUSTICE

If the *albedí* does not do justice, he should pay ten *aurei*[2] to the *iudex* and, furthermore, the plaintiff should take as sureties with impunity what he can seize of the things of the Jews outside of the *alcacería* [district of shops Jews rented from the king]. The *iudex* should divide the above-mentioned ten *aurei* with the plaintiff.

7. THE IUDEX WHO DOES NOT WANT TO DO JUSTICE

If it is the *iudex* who does not do justice for a Jew, he should pay ten *aurei* to the *albedí* and, furthermore, the Jew should take as sureties all that he can seize of the things of the Christian....

16. THE PLACE AND TIME OF JUDGMENTS

The cases between Jews and Christians should be before the gate of the *alcacería* and not at the synagogue. The time of the meetings of the court should be from the completion of matins in the cathedral church until terce.[3] When they sound terce, they should conclude the judgments. He who does not present himself before the court should lose the case.

17. THE OATH OF THE JEW AND OF THE CHRISTIAN

For all claims, should they be Christian, should they be Jewish, up to a value of four *menkales*,[4] the Christian should swear without the cross and the Jew without the Torah. If the claim is worth four *menkales* or more, the Christian should swear on the cross and the Jew on the Torah. And if the Jew or the Christian does not want to swear, he should lose the case.

---

1 The expressions "on his feet" and "places his foot" probably mean to undertake judicial combat. "Double the sureties" means double the payment—or goods equal to the payment—that was required to cover the penalty of the crime.

2 The *aureus* (pl.: *aurei*) was a gold coin.

3 The timing of the judgments is here regulated by the canonical hours of the church: matins often began at sunrise; terce was the third hour.

4 A *menkal* (pl.: *menkales*) was a coin of copper or copper and silver mixed, valued at about 1/4 of an *aureus*.

LOCAL LAWS AND ARRANGEMENTS

6.8 A manorial court: *Proceedings for the Abbey of Bec* (1246). Original in Latin.

THE ENGLISH ROYAL COURTS were not only places where verdicts were handed down but also writing offices that carefully recorded cases and outcomes. In the thirteenth century, the proceedings of local manorial courts—*not* controlled by the king but rather by local lords—began to be recorded. The monastery of Bec, in Normandy, had numerous estates in England; on these manors its officials held court at various times during the year. The cases covered numerous petty offenses, whether against the lord of the manor or against royal law. The documents, as the excerpt below makes clear, consisted largely of lists of fines, for the proceedings were written up for lords (in this case the monastery of Bec) whose main interest lay in the income that the courts produced. What crimes were tried in manorial counts, and how much revenue did they produce?

[Source: *Select Pleas in Manorial and Other Seignorial Courts, Reigns of Henry III. and Edward I.*, ed. F.W. Maitland (London: Bernard Quaritch, 1889), pp. 7, 8, 9 (new notes and some modifications of original notes).]

TOOTING [SURREY]. SUNDAY AFTER ASCENSION DAY.[1]

The court presented that the following had encroached on the lord's land, to wit, William Cobbler, Maud Robin's widow (fined 12 d.), John Shepherd (fined 12 d.), Walter Reeve (fined 2 s.), William of Moreville (fined 12 d.), Hamo of Hageldon (fined 12 d.), Mabel Spendlove's widow (fined 6 d.). Therefore they are in mercy.[2]

Godwin is in mercy for contemning to do what was bidden him on the lord's behalf. Fine, 12 d.

Roger Rede in mercy for detention of rent. Pledge, John of Streatham.[3] Fine, 6 d.

One acre which Sarah the widow held of the land of William Roce is seised into the lord's hand until she produces her warrantor.[4]

William of Streatham is in mercy for not producing what he was pledged to produce. Fine, 12 d.

RUISLIP [MIDDLESEX]. TUESDAY AFTER ASCENSION DAY.

The court presents that Nicholas Brakespeare is not in a tithing and holds land. Therefore let him be distrained.[5]

Breakers of the assize:[6] Alice Salvage's widow (fined 12 d.), Agnotta the Shepherd's mistress, Roger Canon (fined 6 d.), the wife of Richard Chayham, the widow of Peter Beyondgrove, the wife of Ralph Coke (fined 6 d.), Ailwin (fined 6 d.), John Shepherd (fined 6 d.), Geoffrey Carpenter, Roise the Miller's wife (fined 6 d.), William White, John Carpenter, John Bradif.

---

1 Tooting [Surrey] is the name of the manor. The court was held on Sunday after Ascension, 1246.
2 "In mercy" means that they are liable to a fine. A fine of 1 d. is one penny; a fine of 1 s. is one "solidus," or shilling; there were 12 pennies to a shilling.
3 John of Streatham serves as "pledge," or guarantor, of Roger Rede's fine.
4 "Seisin" is possession, and thus "seised into the lord's hand" means that the lord gains possession of the land; Sarah must produce a warrantor (someone to give assurances as to her right to hold the acre of land).
5 "Not in a tithing": most freeholders (non servile) men of a village were in a "tithing," that is a group pledged to one another to keep the peace and to produce anyone who committed a crime. Nicholas Brakespeare is not in a tithing, so he must be dealt with in another way: by seizing his land and forcing him thereby to do something or accept some punishment.
6 This probably refers to the assize of beer, which was a court that regulated the price of beer. Note how many women were involved in its brewing.

Roger Hamo's son gives 20s. to have seisin of the land which was his father's and to have an inquest of twelve as to a certain croft which Gilbert Bisuthe holds.[1] Pledges, Gilbert Lamb, William John's son and Robert King.

Isabella Peter's widow is in mercy for a trespass which her son John had committed in the lord's wood. Fine, 18 d. Pledges, Gilbert Bisuthe and Richard Robin.

Richard Maleville is at his law[2] against the lord [to prove] that he did not take from the lord's servants goods taken in distress to the damage and dishonor of his lord [to the extent of] 20 s. Pledges, Gilbert Bisuthe and Richard Hubert.

Hugh Tree in mercy for his beasts caught in the lord's garden. Pledges, Walter Hill and William Slipper. Fine, 6 d.

[The] twelve jurors say that Hugh Cross has right in the bank and hedge about which there was a dispute between him and William White. Therefore let him hold in peace and let William be distrained for his many trespasses. (Afterwards he made fine for 12 d.) They say also that the hedge which is between the Widow Druet and William Slipper so far as the bank extends should be divided along the middle of the bank, so that the crest of the bank should be the boundary between them, for the crest was thrown up along the ancient boundary.

6.9 Doing business: A Genoese *societas* (1253). Original in Latin.

MEDIEVAL BUSINESS ARRANGEMENTS called for numerous kinds of contracts, i.e., documents with legal force in court. The cities of the Mediterranean abounded in such documents, normally drawn up by notaries. One such arrangement was a *societas*, a partnership in which the partners normally pooled their money and labor and reaped equal profits or losses. All the members were liable for the others; there was no concept (yet) of limited liability. The *societas* contract recorded below was a bit unusual: two of the partners (Consolino and Friedrich) contributed their skill (in this case in metallurgy) but no money, while another, Orlando Paglia, gave money but no labor. The rest of the partners promised both money and work. The profits, too, were shared unequally.

[Source: *Medieval Trade in the Mediterranean World: Illustrative Documents*, trans. Robert S. Lopez and Irving W. Raymond (New York: Columbia University Press, 2001), pp. 194-95.]

Genoa, September 7, 1253

In the name of the Lord, amen. Orlando Paglia; Giovanni Puliti; Ranieri of Verona; Giacomo Migliorati; Consolino, son of the late Konrad, German; and Friedrich, German, acknowledge that they have jointly made among themselves a *societas* to last forever for the purpose of buying mines, furnaces, or veins for the production of silver in Sardinia or wherever God may guide them more [wisely]. In this *societas* said Orlando invested £ 100 Genoese; Giovanni Puliti, £ 50; Ranieri of Verona, £ 15; Giacomo Migliorati, £ 25;

waiving the exception that the money has not been had or received in cash. According to [the conditions of] this *societas* all are to go to Sardinia or wherever God may guide them more [wisely] to do said work, except Orlando, who is not himself going at present but may go whenever he likes and [may send] whatever messenger he wishes. And they are to share the expenses of said *societas* in food and drink and chartering of boats and renting of houses, both in sickness and in health, while engaged in said work; and they are to buy with [the capital of] said *societas* the equipment needed to do that work. And Consolino

---

1   "An inquest of twelve as to a certain croft": a croft is a piece of arable land; Roger Hamo's son has paid to have a jury of twelve men of the neighborhood inquire into Gilbert's rights in this croft.
2   "At his law": Richard proposes to clear himself with compurgators—men who will swear to his innocence.

and Friedrich are to be in said *societas* with the above-mentioned [investors] and to labor in good faith and without fraud, and to preserve and to protect said *societas*, and to give aid and counsel for the increase of said *societas*. They promise one another to make an accounting of the profit which God may grant to said *societas* every fourth month. And said Consolino and Friedrich are to have for their labor the sixth share of the profit which God may grant in that *societas*. And of the rest, [after deduction] of said sixth share, Orlando is to have a third share, Giovanni Puliti a third share, Ranieri and Giacomo another third share. And Consolino and Friedrich promised to the aforesaid not to forsake that *societas* in any way nor to leave it unless for the purpose of going to Tuscany. And if they, or one of them, should leave for said cause, they promised to return to said *societas* within two or three months from the day they left. They all swore, placing their hands on the sacred and holy Gospels of God, to undertake, to complete, and to observe each and all [of the aforesaid conditions] and not to violate [them] in any [way] under penalty of £ 100 Genoese, the pact remaining as settled among them [as] mutually stipulated and solemnly promised and under pledge of their goods, [the penalty] being given by the one who does not observe to those who do observe [it]. And we may be sued, wherever any of us and any of our goods [may be], waiving the privilege of [choosing] the tribunal. Done in Genoa in the house where said Orlando lives. Witnesses: Giacomo of Parma, son of the late Marina, and Obertino of Reggio [Emilia]. 1253, tenth indiction, on the seventh day of September, between terce and nones.

Only one [instrument] was made.[1]

6.10 Women's work: *Guild Regulations of the Parisian Silk Fabric Makers* (13th c.). Original in French.

CRAFTSPEOPLE DREW UP THEIR OWN LAWS to regulate themselves and guarantee the integrity and uniformity of their products. At Paris there were perhaps a dozen such trades in the time of King Philip Augustus (r.1180-1223), but the number had swelled to over a hundred by the time of Louis IX (r.1226-1270), as we know from the collection of regulations published in 1268 by Etienne de Boileau, Louis's appointee as Provost of Paris from *c*.1261 to 1270. The regulations for the makers of silk fabrics in Boileau's book, given below, shows that women as well as men were involved in important trades.

[Source: *Women's Lives in Medieval Europe: A Sourcebook*, ed. Emilie Amt (New York and London: Routledge, 1993), pp. 194-99 (notes added).]

THE CRAFT OF SILK FABRIC

1. No journeywoman[2] maker of silk fabric may be a mistress of the craft until she has practiced it for a year and a day, after she has done her apprenticeship, because she will be more competent to practice her craft and observe the regulations.

2. No mistress of this craft may take an apprentice for fewer than six years with a fee of four livres [pounds], or for eight years with forty sous, or for ten years with no fee; and she may have no more than two apprentices at the same time, and she may not take another until their apprenticeships are completed.

3. No mistress or journeywoman may work at night or on a feast day observed by the whole town.

4. No mistress of the craft may weave thread with silk, or foil with silk, because the work is false and bad; and it should be burned if it is found.[3]

5. No mistress or journeywoman of the craft may

---

1 This is an annotation of the notary, meaning that only one copy of the document was drafted for the parties.
2 A journeywoman or journeyman was a day laborer; the job normally came after a long apprenticeship. Few laborers attained the status of mistress or master of the craft, who dominated the offices and policies of the guild.
3 Presumably, weaving thread or foil with the silk would contaminate its purity.

make a false hem or border, either of thread or of foil, nor may she do raised work of thread or foil. And if such work is found, it should be burned, because it is false and bad.

6. No mistress or journeywoman of the craft, after she has done her apprenticeship, may hire anyone who is not a mistress of the craft, but she may take work to do from whomever she likes.

7. It is ordered that all the mistresses of the said craft who send their work outside the town to be done must show it to those who are designated to watch over the craft, along with the work of their own house, to make sure that it is up to standard.

8. And anyone who infringes on any of the above regulations must pay eight Parisian sous, each time she is found at fault; of which the king will have five sous, and the craft guild twelve deniers, and the masters who oversee the craft two sous for their pains and for the work they do in overseeing the craft.

9. To safeguard this craft in the manner described above, there should be established three masters and three mistresses, who will swear by the Saints that they will make known to the provost of Paris[1] or to his representative all the infringements of the regulations of the said craft, to the best of their ability.

6.11 Men's work: *Guild Regulations of the Shearers of Arras* (1236). Original in French.

WOOL, BOTH RAISED DOMESTICALLY AND IMPORTED from England, was the underpinning of the Flemish textile industry, the region's major export. Specialized labor was involved, all under the oversight of the drapers, who in turn were supervised by the merchants who sold the goods on the international market. First lowly spinners turned the wool into thread. Then the weavers created the cloth on great looms, often worked by two men. The dyers, prestigious owners of great vats, gave the cloth its color; alternatively, the thread itself was dyed before the weaving process. The fullers beat the cloth to shrink it and make it heavier. Finally the shearers cropped the nap of the cloth with great scissors to make it smooth. At Arras the regulations for the shearers were mainly concerned with the fees that the workers had to pay, mainly to the Fraternity—i.e., the guild. What provisions in this document demonstrate the close alliance between the town government and the guild?

[Source: *A Source Book for Medieval Economic History*, ed. Roy C. Cave and Herbert H. Coulson (New York: Bruce Publishing Co., 1936), pp. 250-52 (notes added).]

Here is the Shearers' Charter, on which they were first founded.

This is the first ordinance of the shearers, who were founded in the name of the Fraternity of God and St. Julien,[2] with the agreement and consent of those who were at the time mayor and aldermen.[3]

1. Whoever would engage in the trade of a shearer shall be in the Confraternity of St. Julien, and shall pay all the dues, and observe the decrees made by the brethren.

2. That is to say: first, that whoever is a master shearer shall pay 14 solidi to the Fraternity.[4] And there may not be more than one master shearer working in a house. And he shall be a master shearer all the year, and have arms for the need of the town.

3. And a journeyman shall pay 5 solidi to the Fraternity.

4. And whoever wishes to learn the trade shall be

---

1 The provost of Paris was the city's chief public magistrate.
2 Guilds were religious and charitable as well as trade organizations.
3 The mayor and aldermen were the chief magistrates of the town.
4 Solidi (sing.: solidus) were silver coins.

the son of a burgess[1] or he shall live in the town for a year and a day; and he shall serve three years to learn this trade.

5. And he shall give to his master *3 muids* for his bed and board;[2] and he ought to bring the first *muid* to his master at the beginning of his apprenticeship, and another *muid* a year from that day, and a third *muid* at the beginning of the third year.

6. And no one may be a master of this trade of shearer if he has not lived a year and a day in the town, in order that it may be known whether or not he comes from a good place.

8. And if masters, or journeymen, or apprentices, stay in the town to do their work they owe 40 solidi, if they have done this without the permission of the aldermen of Arras.

9. And whoever does work on Saturday afternoon, or on the Eve of the Feast of Our Lady, or after Vespers on the Eve of the Feast of St. Julien, and completes the day by working, shall pay, if he be a master, 12 denarii, and if he be a journeyman, 6 denarii. And whoever works in the four days of Christmas, or in the eight days of Easter, or in the eight days of Pentecost, owes 5 solidi.

11. And an apprentice owes to the Fraternity for his apprenticeship 5 solidi.

12. And whoever puts the cloth of another in pledge shall pay 10 solidi to the Fraternity, and he shall not work at the trade for a year and a day.

13. And whoever does work in defiance of the mayor and aldermen shall pay 5 solidi.

14. And if a master flee outside the town with another's cloth and a journeyman aids him to flee, if he does not tell the mayor and aldermen, the master shall pay 20 solidi to the Fraternity and the journeyman 10 solidi: and they shall not work at the trade for a year and a day.

16. And those who are fed at the expense of the city shall be put to work first. And he who slights them for strangers owes 5 solidi: but if the stranger be put to work he cannot be removed as long as the master wishes to keep him.... And when a master does not work hard he pays 5 solidi, and a journeyman 2 solidi.

18. And after the half year the mayor and aldermen shall fix such wages as he ought to have.

19. And whatever journeyman shall carry off from his master, or from his fellow man, or from a burgess of the town, anything for which complaint is made, shall pay 5 solidi.

20. And whoever maligns the mayor and aldermen, that is while on the business of the Fraternity, shall pay 5 solidi.

22. And no one who is not a shearer may be a master, in order that the work may be done in the best way, and no draper may cut cloth in his house, if it be not his own work, except he be a shearer, because drapers cannot be masters.

23. And if a draper or a merchant has work to do in his house, he may take such workmen as he wishes into his house, so long as the work be done in his house. And he who infringes this shall give 5 solidi to the Fraternity.

25. And each master ought to have his arms when he is summoned. And if he has not he should pay 20 solidi.

26–30. [Other army regulations.]

31. And whatever brother has finished cloth in his house and does not inform the mayor and aldermen, and it be found in his house, whatever he may say, shall forfeit 10 solidi to the Fraternity.

32. And if a master does not give a journeyman such wage as is his due, then he shall pay 5 solidi.

33. And he who overlooks the forfeits of this Fraternity, if he does not wish to pay them when the mayor and aldermen summon him either for the army or the district, then he owes 10 solidi, and he shall not work at the trade until he has paid. Every forfeit of 5 solidi, and the fines which the mayor and aldermen command, shall be written down. All the fines of the Fraternity ought to go for the purchase of arms and for the needs of the Fraternity.

34. And whatever brother of this Fraternity shall betray his confrère for others shall not work at the trade for a year and a day.

35. And whatever brother of this Fraternity perjures himself shall not work at the trade for forty days. And if he does so he shall pay 10 solidi if he be a mas-

---

1 I.e., a citizen of the town.
2 A *muid* was a unit of capacity, like a bushel.

ter, but if he be a journeyman let him pay 5 solidi.

36. And should a master of this Fraternity die and leave a male heir he may learn the trade anywhere where there is no apprentice.

37. And no apprentice shall cut to the selvage for half a year, and this is to obtain good work.[1] And no master or journeyman may cut by himself because no one can measure cloth well alone. And whoever infringes this rule shall pay 5 solidi to the Fraternity for each offense.

38. Any brother whatsoever who lays hands on, or does wrong to, the mayor and aldermen of this Fraternity, as long as they work for the city and the Fraternity, shall not work at his trade in the city for a year and a day.

And if he should do so, let him be banished from the town for a year and a day, saving the appeal to Monseigneur the King and his Castellan.[2]

39. And the brethren of this Fraternity, and the mayor and aldermen shall not forbid any brother to give law and do right and justice to all when it is demanded of them, or when some one claims from them. And he who infringes this shall not have the help of the aldermen at all.

---

1 The selvage is the woven edge of a fabric; apprentices were not to cut to the fabric's end until he (or possibly she) had some experience in shearing.
2 The king of France at the time was St. Louis (Louis IX, r.1226-1270).

6.12 The growth of papal business: Innocent III, *Letters* (1200-1202). Original in Latin.

IN THE WAKE OF THE Gregorian Reform the papacy reorganized itself as a major court for all sorts of church matters—disputed elections, appeals from individual churches regarding their rights, decisions about canonical marriages, and many other issues. By the time of Innocent III (r.1198-1216), the pope was involved in many local church affairs. The three letters here illustrate this point for England. The first shows Innocent intervening in a case involving a priest who resigned his post; the second has him determining the fitness of a priest to continue his work; and the third shows him interceding in a property dispute. How do all these interests explain the rapid expansion of the papal bureaucracy?

[Source: *Selected Letters of Pope Innocent III concerning England (1198-1216)*, ed. C.R. Cheney and W.H. Semple (London: Thomas Nelson and Sons, 1953), pp. 15, 23, 33-34 (notes modified).]

[Letter 1, February 5, 1200]
To the bishop, dean, and subdean of Lincoln.[1]

It has come to our hearing, on information from our beloved son Master Elias de Chieveley,[2] that having canonically obtained the church of Chieveley on the authority of the Apostolic See, and having had peaceful possession for some time, he was at length compelled, through his very great fear of the king, to promise on oath to resign it, and has in fact resigned it into the hands of the appropriate persons.[3] But because actions done under duress or through fear ought not to have binding force, by apostolic letter we command you that, if it be established to your satisfaction that Master Elias was forced to resign by such fear, as could and should affect a man of courage, then notwithstanding the aforesaid oath (by which he was bound only to resign, but not precluded from seeking reinstatement) by ecclesiastical censure you will cause the aforesaid church to be restored to him without appeal.

No letter prejudicial to truth and justice etc. If you cannot all etc., then let two of you etc.[4]

The Lateran, the 5th of February.

[Letter 2, November 8, 1200]
To the bishop of Lincoln.[5]

Our beloved son A., a priest, appearing in our presence, by his own confession disclosed to us that, being so badly troubled by a certain physical ailment that desire for sleep and food seemed to have left him, with the idea of wakening some slight appetite for a meal he mounted a horse he had bred. The horse not being completely obedient to the reins, but prancing and leaping contrary to the rider's will, he pulled hard on the bridle and pricked with the spurs in order to curb its impetuosity. But the rein snapped, and the horse, as left to its own caprice, bolted at a gallop—when a woman, approaching from the side and carrying a baby, met it. The horse collided with her, threw its rider to a distance, and crushed the child. The priest himself, as a result of his sudden fall, was brought almost to the gates of death: ultimately he recovered, but has not since presumed to celebrate mass. As the foregoing account is uncorroborated, by apostolic letter we command you carefully to enquire into the truth and, if you find the occurrence

---

1 Bishop Hugh I (St. Hugh of Avallon), r.1186-1200; the dean was Roger de Rolveston, 1195-1223; the subdean was either Richard Kentensis or William de Bramfeld.

2 Master Elias of Chieveley, Berkshire had obtained the church there by order of Pope Celestine III (r.1191-1198).

3 I.e., to his ecclesiastical superiors. The king in question was John (r.1199-1216), who at the time was quarreling with the Church.

4 These are formulas so common as to allow abbreviation, rather like A.S.A.P.

5 There was no bishop, in fact; Hugh died in 1200 and no successor was appointed until 1203.

to have happened as stated, not to debar the priest from celebrating the divine offices, since he will have committed homicide neither by will nor act, nor have deliberately attempted anything unlawful.

The Lateran, the 8th of November.

[Letter 3, March 6, 1202]

Innocent, bishop, servant of the servants of God, to his beloved sons the priors of St. Oswald and of Pontefract and Roger dean of Ledsham in the diocese of York, greeting and apostolic benediction.[1]

The petition of our beloved son William de Midelton has been read to us: it set forth that his father once pledged a piece of land at Ecclefechan to Ivo de Crossby of the diocese of York as security for a certain sum of money, and that, though the said Ivo in his lifetime and his son Richard after his death gained from that property the capital and more, nevertheless the said Richard, to the peril of his salvation, still holds it and refuses to return it. Therefore by apostolic letter we command you that, if the case is as stated, you should compel, without appeal, the said Richard to content himself with his capital, and to restore to the complainant the said land and any takings in excess of the capital sum, on threat of the penalty published in the Lateran Council against usurers.[2] If any witnesses cited have withdrawn through favor, hatred, or fear, you are to compel them, by ecclesiastical censure without appeal, to give evidence establishing the truth.

But if you cannot all take part in discharging this business, let two of you discharge it, notwithstanding.

The Lateran, the 6th of March, in the fifth year of our Pontificate.

6.13 Petitioning the papacy: *Register of Thomas of Hereford* (1281). Original in Latin.

THIS DOCUMENT IS FROM THE Episcopal Register of Thomas Cantilupe, bishop of Hereford (r.1275-1282). Episcopal Registries, which came to be drawn up in the thirteenth century in England and elsewhere, were official record books, each put together by a scribe working for a bishop. They covered the gamut of episcopal activities, including visitations to monasteries (during which monks were interviewed and problems attended to), ordinations of priests, presentations of church benefices, excommunications, and, as here, appeals to the papal court. In this document, Bishop Thomas writes to his "proctors"—his agents—at the papal curia. All bishops depended largely on their manors to generate the income that they needed; when Thomas complains about the "poverty of the bishopric," he means that he can ill afford the costs of litigation. He has to go into debt to Italian bankers, whom he calls the "merchants of Pistoia." One case that Thomas is litigating has to do with "the cause against St. Asaph." This refers to his dispute with Anian II, bishop of St. Asaph, in Wales, who claimed the right to some of the same parishes that Thomas claimed. The pope referred the dispute to John Peckham, the archbishop of Canterbury (r.1279-1292), but Thomas, who was already disputing Peckham's jurisdiction over Hereford, appealed to the pope—at considerable cost.

[Source: *English Historical Documents*, vol. 3: *1189-1327*, ed. Harry Rothwell (London: Routledge, 1975), pp. 763-65 (notes modified).]

---

1   St. Oswald in Yorkshire was a priory of Austin canons—that is a community organized much like a monastery but made up of priests following the Rule of St. Augustine rather than of St. Benedict. The prior was Ralph (r.1199-1208). Pontefract, also in Yorkshire, was a Cluniac priory; its prior was Hugh (r.c.1184-c.1203). Roger of Ledsham, rural dean of Pontefract between 1191 and 1203, may be the third person addressed here.

2   This was a reference to the decrees of the Third Lateran Council (1179).

To our proctors staying at the Roman court. To masters William Brun and John de Bitterley greeting. Although word has passed between us before and an account by letter followed afterwards upon the same matter, i.e. of "visiting"[1] every one of the cardinals, we think after deliberation that the burden of debt and the poverty of the bishopric do not permit this; yet, because we understand, know indeed, that affairs in the curia are not advanced at all unless there are visits general and particular, we send you on that account for the expediting of our affairs by letters of merchants of Pistoia one hundred pounds sterling to be received in sterling or *gros* of Tours. Which sum of money, though it seems little, can nevertheless be useful if carefully distributed, which in the judgment of some can be done in this way: viz [clearly], that sir Hugh, the English cardinal, should have thirty marks, sir Gerard, cardinal, our auditor,[2] ten pounds, and his household five marks. Sir Matthew Ruffus, cardinal, ten marks, sir Jordan, cardinal, ten marks, the vice-chancellor, fifteen pounds, the auditor of objections, ten marks, B. de Neapoli and another notary who is particularly outstanding and particularly intimate with the lord pope, twenty marks in equal portions; the chamberlain of the lord pope ten marks, the usher of the lord pope, forty shillings sterling.

To others it seems that five marks can be deducted from the sum set aside for the vice-chancellor, so that he has ten marks only; from the two notaries and the chamberlain of the pope they can subtract seven and a half marks so that each of them has as much as the other. And so of the hundred pounds there will remain 33½ marks.[3]

To others it seems that it would be a good thing to bear in mind the pope, with whom the archbishop (from whom appeal is being made) is on familiar terms, to the extent of forty or fifty marks, first taking out of the list as many people as would together receive that amount of money. But to us it seems that the middle way is more profitable and honorable, though if necessity compels it, let the pope be considered in some way which will please him on whom it is recognized all favor depends. This however which we write about the pope we have no mind for, unless for lack of its being done our cause against St. Asaph and our other affairs were to be manifestly in danger. For which reason we should very much like you to present forty or fifty marks, or jewels to that amount, to the said lord rather by raising a new loan than that you should subtract any part of the aforementioned sum. For contracting which loan we are not sending you our signet because we do not believe that it is necessary for us to do this this time. The merchants of Pistoia, we believe, will, to oblige us, lend us on any sort of bond of ours that amount of money. But if it is not possible to provide for our needs through them or our other friends, then you may take out of the hundred pounds for the lord's use[4] as much as you consider expedient, distributing what is left of the said money amongst the others as shall seem expedient for advancing our cause and our other affairs. In the cause against St. Asaph let us hold in the main to the rule of the defendant, whose instinct is to drag out the cause as long as possible. In the aforementioned cause, however, in which we have an acceptance lately drawn up in legal form of the appeal from [the decision of] the lord archbishop of Canterbury, we do not wish to hunt for shameful and doubtful subterfuges with which to sway the mind of the judge or such things as might render us suspect in his eyes or by which danger might threaten us if we are sent back to the former judge: a thing which perhaps might be preferred by our adversary. We wish instead to avoid the manifold dangers while the cause is at the aforesaid court; so long as our expenses incurred in sending a modest mission to obtain a decision are first refunded to us, or at least claimed with sufficient force, before he from whose decision we are appealing defers to our appeal; on account of that, as in this method of distribution, with which as we have stated above we are in more agreement, there are 33½ marks left over for distribution, we very much wish our lord the Spanish cardinal (to whom we are writing) to have ten marks and sir Benedict, cardinal, and sir James, cardinal, or William, the French cardinal, whichever of these at the time of distribution is friendlier with the

---

1   That is, "giving gifts."
2   I.e., the judge delegated to hear the bishop's cause.
3   The arithmetic is faulty, but could be corrected by assuming a copyist's error and reading fifteen marks (instead of pounds) for the vice-chancellor in the first scheme.
4   *Ad opus Domini*—in the context, this is probably the lord pope.

lord pope and in the promotion of our affairs is able to exert more influence for us, to have ten marks, indeed eleven marks. What is left over after these we leave you to deal with jointly, for one or more other visits or for other necessary expenditure.

After the distribution, though, we should like our envoys to return to us with the utmost speed, with your letters recounting what has been done and the attitude of the recipients, along with other news worth mentioning.

Because we are (praised be the Most High) so restored spiritually and improved bodily that our body suffices these days for the labors, troubles and duties of our office, we propose to return home about the feast of St. Michael if the Lord allows, especially because the lord king has now written twice to us about this since Easter. And if you send back one of our envoys or someone else to us to tell us the exact state of our cause we shall be able to send back to you our pleasure in writing before our return by him or another from Fontaine, where we shall then be. Indeed we do not want you to retain even one of our envoys for too long, since messengers sufficiently reliable and faithful return from the curia every day, by whom you will be able to tell us what you have to say and we thank you

for having reported the state of affairs at the curia to us by such hitherto.

We are indeed sending you the contents of the letters in which we write as you ask, and in the light of them you will be able to speak more circumspectly with them. Mr. Adam de Fileby, according to what we have heard, will arrive at the curia soon. In what frame of mind he is, though, towards us we do not know at all.[1] If in addition to the amounts distributed and necessary expenses four marks can be paid to Mr. E. de Warefelde as salary, then by all means let it be done; that too among other things you might tell us about. And because in addition to the ten marks which you have received from us and which you have expended on difficult business of ours, you have spent eight shillings sterling and three shillings and one penny of *gros* of Tours, as we understand from a certain schedule of yours sent to us, we very much want you to recompense yourselves from the money sent to you, if it can be done conveniently for us.

If you can distribute the said money to better advantage than is set out in any of the ways mentioned, then in the name of the Lord do as will be most useful to us, provided there is agreement about what is done. Farewell. Given at Brynum on 16 June, A.D. 1281.

6.14 Mocking the papal bureaucracy: *The Gospel according to the Marks of Silver* (c.1200). Original in Latin.

The sorts of experiences Thomas of Hereford had at the papal curia and recorded in his *Register*, above, p. 367, especially the tips and other expenses he had to pay, led some people to mock the papacy and to interpret its need for revenues as simple greed. *The Gospel according to the Marks of Silver* satirizes the curia in the cadences of the Gospel of St. Mark 1:1: "The beginning of the gospel of Jesus Christ, the Son of God."

[Source: *The Medieval Record: Sources of Medieval History*, ed. Alfred J. Andrea (Boston: Houghton Mifflin, 1997), p. 296.]

Here begins the Gospel according to the marks of silver. In that time, the pope said unto the Romans: "When the Son of Man comes to the seat of Our majesty,[2] first say unto him, 'Friend, wherefore art thou come?'[3] But if he should persevere in his knocking and give thee nothing,[4] cast him forth into the outer

---

1 Relations were strained.
2 Matt. 25: 31.
3 Matt. 26: 50.
4 Luke 11: 5–13 and Matt. 7: 7–11.

darkness."[1] And it came to pass that a certain poor cleric came to the lord pope's court and cried out, saying: "Have mercy even unto me, ye doorkeepers of the pope, because the hand of poverty has touched me.[2] For I am needy and poor, and I beg thee to relieve my calamitous misery."[3] They, however, upon hearing this were right indignant and said: "Friend, thy poverty go with thee to damnation.[4] Get thee behind me, Satan, because ye taste not of the things that savor of money.[5] Amen, Amen, I say unto thee, thou shalt not enter into the joy of thy Lord, until thou hast given the very last penny."[6] And the pauper went away and sold his cloak and tunic and everything that he owned, and he gave to the cardinals, and the doorkeepers, and the chamberlains.[7] But they said: "And this, what is it among so much?" And they cast him out before the gates,[8] and he going forth wept bitterly[9] and could not be consoled.

Thereafter there came to the court a certain rich, fat, well-fed,[10] and bloated cleric, who had committed murder while engaging in a riot.[11] He first gave to the doorkeeper, in the second place to the chamberlain, and in the third place to the cardinals.[12] And they took counsel among themselves as to who of them should have received the most.[13] But the lord pope, hearing that his cardinals and ministers had received so many gifts from the cleric, took ill well unto death.[14] Then the rich cleric sent unto him a sweet elixir of gold and silver, and straightway he was recovered.[15] Then the lord pope called unto himself his cardinals and ministers and said unto them: "Brothers, be watchful lest anyone seduce thee with empty words.[16] For I give unto you an example that even as much as I take, ye also should take."[17]

---

1   Matt. 25: 30.
2   Matt. 15: 22.
3   Job 19: 21.
4   Acts 8: 20.
5   Mark 8: 33.
6   Matt. 5: 26.
7   Matt. 13: 44–46.
8   Matt. 22: 13.
9   Matt. 26: 75.
10 Deut. 32: 15.
11 Mark 15: 7.
12 Matt. 25: 14–15.
13 Matt. 20: 10.
14 Phil. 2: 27.
15 John 5: 9.
16 Eph. 5: 6.
17 John 13: 15.

CONFRONTATIONS

6.15 Henry II and Becket: *Constitutions of Clarendon* (1164). Original in Latin.

As PART OF HIS REFORM of the English legal system, Henry II (r.1154-1189) expected "criminous clerks"—that is, clerics who were suspected of committed a crime—to come before his courts. "Clerks" included numerous members of the minor Church orders and thus a large proportion of the free male population. Archbishop Thomas Becket (r.1162-1170) wanted church courts to have jurisdiction over all clerical cases. Pressed by the pope as well as by numerous cardinals and bishops to give in to Henry, Becket reluctantly agreed in 1164. The king insisted on a public assent, and the *Constitutions of Clarendon* was the result. It cast the issue as a matter of tradition, claiming to record the "customs, liberties and privileges" that prevailed in the time of Henry I (r.1100-1135). The *Constitutions* did not end the dispute between Henry and Becket, however. Becket escaped to France, from where he hurled excommunications against bishops and great laymen in England who, in his view, infringed his rights. Henry II famously (but perhaps apocryphally) let slip the words, "Will no one rid me of this turbulent priest?" Four knights in the royal entourage took to the road and murdered Becket in his cathedral at Canterbury (in 1170), turning him into an instant martyr. In the end most of the provisions of the *Constitutions* stood, regulating the relationship between royal courts and criminous clerks.

[Source: *English Historical Documents*, vol. 2: *1042-1189*, ed. David C. Douglas and George W. Greenaway, 2nd ed. (London: Routledge, 1981), pp. 766-70 (notes modified).]

In the year 1164 from our Lord's Incarnation, being the fourth of the pontificate of Alexander,[1] and the tenth of Henry II, most illustrious king of the English, in the presence of the said king was made this record and declaration of a certain part of the customs, liberties and privileges of his ancestors, that is, of King Henry, his grandfather, and of other things which ought to be observed and maintained in the realm. And by reason of the dissensions and discords which had arisen between the clergy and the justices of the lord king and the barons of the realm concerning the customs and privileges of the realm, this declaration was made in the presence of the archbishops, bishops and clergy, and of the earls, barons and magnates of the realm. And these same customs were acknowledged by the archbishops and bishops, and the earls, barons, nobles and elders of the realm, Thomas, archbishop of Canterbury; and Roger, archbishop of York; Gilbert, bishop of London; Henry, bishop of Winchester....[2]

Now of the acknowledged customs and privileges of the realm a certain part is contained in the present document, of which part these are the heads:

1. If a dispute shall arise between laymen, or between clerks and laymen, or between clerks, concerning advowson and presentation to churches, let it be treated and concluded in the court of the lord king.[3]

2. Churches within the fief of the lord king cannot

---

1 Alexander III (r.1159-1181).

2 Here numerous bishops are named and said to have "agreed, and by word of mouth steadfastly promised on the word of truth to the lord king and his heirs, that these customs should be kept and observed in good faith and without evil intent." After that come the names of numerous "magnates and nobles of the realm."

3 "Advowson and presentation" had to do with rights over churches. The Church claimed that suits arising out of such disputes had to do with spiritual matters, while the king regarded them as questions of property.

be granted in perpetuity without his consent and concession.[1]

3. Clerks cited and accused of any matter shall, when summoned by the king's justice, come before the king's court to answer there concerning matters which shall seem to the king's court to be answerable there, and before the ecclesiastical court for what shall seem to be answerable there, but in such a way that the justice of the king shall send to the court of holy Church to see how the case is there tried. And if the clerk shall be convicted or shall confess, the Church ought no longer to protect him.[2]

4. It is not lawful for archbishops, bishops and beneficed clergy of the realm to depart from the kingdom without the lord king's leave. And if they do so depart, they shall, if the king so please, give security that neither in going, nor in tarrying, nor in returning will they contrive evil or injury against the king or the kingdom.[3]

5. Excommunicates ought not to give pledges of security for future good behavior nor take oaths, but only to give sufficient pledge of security to abide by the judgment of the Church in order to obtain absolution.

6. Laymen ought not to be accused save by accredited and lawful accusers and witnesses in the presence of the bishop, in such a way, however, that the archdeacon may not lose his right nor anything due to him thereby. And if the accused persons be such that no one either wishes or dares to prefer a charge against them, the sheriff, when requested by the bishop, shall cause twelve lawful men of the neighborhood or township to swear before the bishop that they will manifest the truth of the matter to the best of their knowledge.

7. No one who holds of the king in chief nor any of the officials of his demesne[4] shall be excommunicated, nor the lands of any of them placed under interdict, unless application shall first be made to the lord king, if he be in the realm, or to his chief justice, if he be abroad, that right may be done him; in such wise that matters pertaining to the royal court shall be concluded there, and matters pertaining to the ecclesiastical court shall be sent thither to be dealt with.

8. With regard to appeals, if they should arise, they should proceed from the archdeacon to the bishop, and from the bishop to the archbishop. And if the archbishop should fail to do justice, the case must finally be brought to the lord king, in order that by his command the dispute may be determined in the archbishop's court, in such a way that it proceed no further without the assent of the lord king.[5]

9. If a dispute shall arise between a clerk and a layman, or between a layman and a clerk, in respect of any holding which the clerk desires to treat as free alms, but the layman as lay fee, it shall be determined by the recognition of twelve lawful men through the deliberation, and in the presence of the king's chief justice, *whether* the holding pertains to free alms or to lay fee.[6] And if it be judged to pertain to free alms, the plea shall be heard in the ecclesiastical court; but if to lay fee, it shall be heard in the king's court, unless both of them shall claim from the same bishop or baron. But if each of them appeal concerning this fief to the same bishop or baron, the plea shall be heard in the latter's court, in such a way that he who was originally in possession shall not lose possession by reason of the recognition that has been made, until the matter has been settled by the plea.

---

1 I.e., the ownership of churches on royal estates was not to be transferred without the king's consent. The object of this clause was to preserve all the rights and services due the king. Becket raised no objection to this clause.

2 I.e., a clerk accused of a grave offense, murder and the like, was to answer before the king's justice for the breach of the king's peace committed by the felony. He was then to be sent on the church court to answer there, as a clerk, to the homicide. If convicted, he would be "degraded," and the "Church ought no longer to protect him." He was then to be brought back to the king's court as a layman, to be sentenced to the penalties any other layman would suffer—that is, either death or mutilation. The provision that the "justice of the king shall send to the court of holy Church to see how the case is there tried" was meant to ensure that the offender would not escape.

3 This clause was an attempt to prevent appeals to Rome.

4 This clause protected the royal tenants-in-chief, i.e., those who held fiefs directly from the king.

5 I.e., no appeals might proceed to Rome without the king's consent.

6 "Free alms" versus "lay fee" refer to the terms by which land was held. Land was held in "free alms" when it was held in exchange for prayers or other charitable activity; it was held in "lay fee" when it owed feudal obligations.

10. If any one of a city or castle or borough or demesne manor of the lord king be cited by archdeacon or bishop for any offence for which he is obliged to make answer to them, and he refuse to give satisfaction at their citations, it is highly proper to place him under interdict;[1] but he ought not to be excommunicated until application has been made to the chief officer of the lord king in that town, in order that it may be adjudged proper for him to make satisfaction. But if the king's officer fails to act in this, he himself shall be at the mercy[2] of the lord king, and thereafter the bishop shall be allowed to coerce the accused by ecclesiastical justice.

11. Archbishops, bishops and all beneficed clergy of the realm, who hold of the king in chief, have their possessions from the lord king by barony and are answerable for them to the king's justices and officers; they observe and perform all royal rights and customs and, like other barons, ought to be present at the judgments of the king's court together with the barons,[3] until a case shall arise involving a judgment concerning mutilation or death.[4]

12. When an archbishopric or bishopric is vacant, or any abbey or priory of the king's demesne, it ought to be in the king's hand, and he shall receive from it all revenues and profits as part of his demesne. And when the time shall come to provide for the church, the lord king ought to summon the more important of the beneficed clergy of the church, and the election ought to take place in the lord king's chapel with the assent of the lord king and the advice of the clergy of the realm whom he shall summon for this purpose. And the clerk elected shall there do homage and fealty to the lord king as his liege lord for his life and limbs and his earthly honor, saving his order, before he is consecrated.[5]

13. If any of the magnates of the realm should forcibly prevent an archbishop or bishop or archdeacon from doing justice to himself or to his people, the lord king ought to bring him to justice. And if perchance anyone should forcibly dispossess the lord king of his right, the archbishops, bishops and archdeacons ought to bring him to justice, so that he may make satisfaction to the lord king.

14. The chattels of those who are under forfeiture to the king may not be retained by any church or cemetery against the king's justice, because they belong to the king, whether they be found within the churches or without.[6]

15. Pleas of debt due under pledge of faith, or even without pledge of faith, are to lie in the justice of the king.[7]

16. Sons of villeins ought not to be ordained without the consent of the lord on whose land they are known to have been born.[8]

This record of the aforesaid customs and privileges of the crown was drawn up by the archbishops, bishops, earls, barons, nobles and elders of the realm at Clarendon on the fourth day previous to the Purification of the Blessed Virgin Mary[9] in the presence of the lord Henry,[10] and of his father, the lord king. There are, moreover, many other great customs and

---

1 "Interdict" refers to the ecclesiastical punishment of denying a person participation in most sacraments and burial in consecrated ground.

2 "At the mercy of the lord king," i.e., liable to a royal fine.

3 I.e., ecclesiastical tenants-in-chief of the crown were to hold their fiefs by ordinary feudal tenures and were bound by feudal laws and customs, including being present at court to give the king counsel.

4 By canon law no churchman could be present at, or take part in, the "shedding of blood"; hence the ecclesiastical tenants-in-chief of the king were to leave the court when sentences of this nature were pronounced.

5 King Henry I and his archbishop, Anselm, fought their own "Investiture Conflict" in the early twelfth century, and the outcome, which was a precedent for the Concordat of Worms, is here placed on record: the king had a role in the election of bishops—but did not appoint them outright—and the cleric, before consecration, did "homage and fealty" to the king for his "life and limbs and earthly honor"—that is, his temporal possessions.

6 This clause asserted the king's right over the chattels—i.e., the movable property—left by those who had been condemned for treason or felony and had fled the country. Such possessions were often stored within ecclesiastical precincts, where they enjoyed the privilege of sanctuary. The king regarded this as an abuse of his rights.

7 I.e., under the king's jurisdiction.

8 A clause aimed at preventing the loss of villein (also spelled villan and villain) services to the lords.

9 January 29, 1164.

10 This was the son of Henry II, who died in 1183.

privileges pertaining to holy mother-church and to the lord king and the barons of the realm which are not contained in this document. Let them be safe for holy Church and for our lord, the king and his heirs and the barons of the realm. And let them be inviolably observed for ever and ever.

6.16 Emperor and pope: *Diet of Besançon* (1157). Original in Latin.

IN GERMANY, THE ELECTION of Frederick I Barbarossa (r.1154-1190) brought peace after years of civil war. But the emperor's claim to overlordship in Italy—and in Rome—threatened the papacy's autonomy. The contest between ruler and pope in the empire was not about jurisdiction over criminous clerics, as it was in England; rather it was about how to understand the relationship between the institutions of empire and papacy. At Besançon the pope's emissaries reminded the emperor of the "dignity and honor" as well as the "emblem of the imperial crown" that the church at Rome had "conferred" on him—as if the symbol of empire had been the pope's to give. Adding insult to injury, the emissaries spoke of these gifts as "beneficia," a Latin word that meant both the neutral "benefits" and the potentially explosive "fiefs." Translated for the assembly by its more potent meaning, *beneficia* launched a diplomatic crisis. Ultimately the pope wrote a conciliatory letter to Frederick explaining that by *beneficia* he had meant only "good deeds," and the emergency subsided. But the struggle between emperor and pope to define themselves with respect to each other continued.

[Source: *The Deeds of Frederick Barbarossa by Otto of Freising and his Continuator, Rahewin*, trans. Charles Christopher Mierow (New York: Columbia University Press, 1953), pp. 180-86 (slightly modified).]

8. ... In the middle of the month of October [1157] the emperor set out for Burgundy to hold a diet [meeting] at Besançon. Now Besançon is the metropolis of one of the three parts into which the renowned Charles the Great divided his empire for distribution among his three sons, all enjoying the royal title.[1] It is situated on the river Doubs. In this city practically all the chief men of that land had assembled, and also many ambassadors from foreign lands, namely, Romans, Apulians [i.e., from Apulia, in Italy], Tuscans, Venetians, Franks, English, and Spaniards, awaited the emperor's arrival. He was received with the most festive display and solemn acclaim. For the whole world recognized him as the most powerful and most merciful ruler, and undertook, with mingled love and fear, to honor him with new tokens of respect, to extol him with new praises.

But before our pen addresses itself to an account of the affairs of this province and its management, we must speak of the ambassadors of the Roman pontiff, Adrian [IV, r.1154-1159]—why they came and how they departed—because the authority of this delegation was very great and their errand very serious. No one will complain at the prolixity of this account who considers carefully the importance of the matter and the length of time that this tempest has raged and still rages. The personnel of the embassy consisted of Roland, cardinal priest of the title of St. Mark and chancellor of the Holy Roman Church,[2] and Bernard, cardinal priest of the title of St. Clement, both distinguished for their wealth, their maturity of view, and their influence, and surpassing in prestige almost all others in the Roman Church.

Now the cause of their coming seemed to have an air of sincerity; but it was afterward clearly discerned that unrest and an occasion for mischief lay beneath

---

1 After the death of Charlemagne and his son Louis the Pious, the empire was divided among Louis's three sons. Besançon was in the portion that went to Lothar.

2 Roland Bandinelli, later Pope Alexander III (r.1159-1181).

the surface. One day, upon the prince's retiring from the uproar and tumult of the people, the aforesaid messengers were conducted into his presence in the more secluded retreat of a certain oratory and—as was fitting—were received with honor and kindness, claiming (as they did) to be the bearers of good tidings.

But the beginning of their speech appeared notable at the very outset. It is said to have been as follows: "Our most blessed father, Pope Adrian, salutes you, and the College of Cardinals of the Holy Roman Church, he as father, they as brethren." After a brief interval they produced the letter that they bore. Copies of this and other letters which passed back and forth in this time of confusion, I have taken pains to insert in this work that any reader who may wish to judge, attracted and summoned not by my words or assertions but by the actual writings of the parties themselves, may choose freely the side to which he desires to lend his favor. Now the content of the letter was as follows:

9. "Bishop Adrian, the servant of the servants of God, to his beloved son Frederick, the illustrious emperor of the Romans, greeting and apostolic benediction.

"We recollect having written, a few days since, to the Imperial Majesty, of that dreadful and accursed deed, an offense calling for atonement, committed in our time, and hitherto, we believe, never attempted in the German lands. In recalling it to Your Excellency, we cannot conceal our great amazement that even now you have permitted so pernicious a deed to go unpunished with the severity it deserves. For how our venerable brother E[skil], archbishop of Lund, while returning from the apostolic see, was taken captive in those parts by certain godless and infamous men—a thing we cannot mention without great and heartfelt sorrow—and is still held in confinement;[1] how in taking him captive, as previously mentioned, those men of impiety, a seed of evildoers, children that are corrupters,[2] drew their swords and violently assaulted him and his companions, and how basely and shamefully they treated them, stripping them of all they had, Your Most Serene Highness knows, and the report of so great a crime has already spread abroad to the most distant and remote regions. To avenge this deed of exceptional violence, you, as a man to whom we believe good deeds are pleasing but evil works displeasing, ought with great determination to arise and bring down heavily upon the necks of the wicked the sword which was entrusted by divine providence to you 'for the punishment of evildoers and for the praise of them that do well,'[3] and should most severely punish the presumptuous. But you are reported so to have ignored and indeed been indifferent to this deed, that there is no reason why those men should be repentant at having incurred guilt, because they have long since perceived that they have secured immunity for the sacrilege which they have committed.

"Of the reason for this indifference and negligence we are absolutely ignorant, because no scruple of conscience accuses our heart of having in any way offended the glory of Your Serenity. Rather have we always loved, with sincere affection, and treated with an attitude of due kindness, your person as that of our most dear and specially beloved son and most Christian prince, who, we doubt not, is by the grace of God grounded on the rock of the apostolic confession.

"For you should recall, O most glorious son, before the eyes of your mind, how willingly and how gladly your mother, the Holy Roman Church, received you in another year, with what affection of heart she treated you, what great dignity and honor she bestowed upon you, and with how much pleasure she conferred the emblem of the imperial crown, zealous to cherish in her most kindly bosom the height of Your Sublimity, and doing nothing at all that she knew was in the least at variance with the royal will.

"Nor do we regret that we fulfilled in all respects the ardent desires of your heart; but if Your Excellency had received still greater benefits[4] at our hand

---

1 Eskil (r.c.1100-1182) was archbishop of Lund (today Sweden but in Eskil's day part of Denmark). His efforts to free his church from the jurisdiction of the archbishop of Hamburg-Bremen may well have led to the "captivity" recorded here.

2 See Isa. 1: 4.

3 1 Pet. 2: 14.

4 The word used was *beneficia*, which could mean "benefices" (i.e., fiefs) as well as benefits. The emperor and his attendants understood the first meaning, and they concluded that the pope claimed overlordship of the empire.

(had that been possible), in consideration of the great increase and advantage that might through you accrue to the Church of God and to us, we would have rejoiced, not without reason.

"But now, because you seem to ignore and hide so heinous a crime, which is indeed known to have been committed as an affront to the Church universal and to your empire, we both suspect and fear that perhaps your thoughts were directed toward this indifference and neglect on this account: that at the suggestion of an evil man, sowing tares,[1] you have conceived against your most gracious mother the Holy Roman Church and against ourselves—God forbid!—some displeasure or grievance.

"On this account, therefore, and because of all the other matters of business which we know to impend, we have thought best to dispatch at this time from our side to Your Serenity two of the best and dearest of those whom we have about us, namely, our beloved sons, Bernard, cardinal priest of St. Clement's, and Roland, cardinal priest of St. Mark's and our chancellor, men very notable for piety and wisdom and honor. We very earnestly beseech Your Excellency that you receive them with as much respect as kindness, treat them with all honor, and that whatever they themselves set forth before Your Imperial Dignity on our behalf concerning this and concerning other matters to the honor of God and of the Holy Roman Church, and pertaining also to the glory and exaltation of the empire, you accept without any hesitation as though proceeding from our mouth. Give credence to their words, as if we were uttering them." [September 20, 1157.]

10. When this letter had been read and carefully set forth by Chancellor Rainald[2] in a faithful interpretation, the princes who were present were moved to great indignation, because the entire content of the letter appeared to have no little sharpness and to offer even at the very outset an occasion for future trouble. But what had particularly aroused them all was the fact that in the aforesaid letter it had been stated, among other things, that the fullness of dignity and honor had been bestowed upon the emperor by the Roman pontiff, that the emperor had received from his hand the imperial crown, and that he would not have regretted conferring even greater benefits (*beneficia*) upon him, in consideration of the great gain and advantage that might through him accrue to the Roman Church. And the hearers were led to accept the literal meaning of these words and to put credence in the aforesaid explanation because they knew that the assertion was rashly made by some Romans that hitherto our kings had possessed the imperial power over the City,[3] and the kingdom of Italy, by gift of the popes, and that they made such representations and handed them down to posterity not only orally but also in writing and in pictures. Hence it is written concerning Emperor Lothar, over a picture of this sort in the Lateran palace:

Coming before our gates, the king vows to safeguard
    the City,
Then, liegeman to the Pope, by him he is granted the
    crown.

Since such a picture and such an inscription, reported to him by those faithful to the empire, had greatly displeased the prince when he had been near the City in a previous year [1155], he is said to have received from Pope Adrian, after a friendly remonstrance, the assurance that both the inscription and the picture would be removed, lest so trifling a matter might afford the greatest men in the world an occasion for dispute and discord.

When all these matters were fully considered, and a great tumult and uproar arose from the princes of the realm at so insolent a message, it is said that one of the ambassadors, as though adding sword to flame,[4] inquired: "From whom then does he have the empire, if not from our lord the pope?" Because of this remark, anger reached such a pitch that one of them, namely, Otto, count palatine of Bavaria (it was said), threatened the ambassador with his sword. But Frederick, using his authority to quell the tumult, commanded that the ambassadors, being granted safe-conduct, be led to their quarters and that early

---

1 Matt. 13: 25.
2 Rainald of Dassel, archbishop of Cologne and imperial chancellor.
3 Throughout this document, "the City" refers to Rome.
4 See Horace, *Satires* 2. 3. 276.

in the morning they should set forth on their way; he ordered also that they were not to pause in the territories of the bishops and abbots, but to return to the City by the direct road, turning neither to the right nor to the left. And so they returned without having accomplished their purpose, and what had been done by the emperor was published throughout the realm in the following letter [October 1157]:

11. "Whereas the Divine Sovereignty, from which is derived all power in heaven and on earth, has entrusted unto us, His anointed, the kingdom and the empire to rule over, and has ordained that the peace of the churches is to be maintained by the imperial arms, not without the greatest distress of heart are we compelled to complain to Your Benevolence that from the head of the Holy Church, on which Christ has set the imprint of his peace and love, there seem to be emanating causes of dissensions and evils, like a poison, by which, unless God avert it, we fear the body of the Church will be stained, its unity shattered, and a schism created between the temporal and spiritual realms.

"For when we were recently at the diet in Besançon and were dealing with the honor of the empire and the security of the Church with all due solicitude, apostolic legates arrived asserting that they bore to Our Majesty such tidings that the honor of the empire should receive no small increase. After we had honorably received them on the first day of their arrival, and on the second, as is customary, had seated ourself with our princes to hear their tidings, they, as though inspired by the Mammon of unrighteousness,[1] by lofty pride, by arrogant disdain, by execrable haughtiness, presented a message in the form of a letter from the pope, the content of which was to the effect that we ought always to remember the fact that the lord pope had bestowed upon us the imperial crown and would not even regret it if Our Excellency had received greater benefits (*beneficia*) from him.

"This was the message of fatherly kindness, which was to foster the unity of Church and empire, which was to bind them together in the bonds of peace, which was to bring the hearts of its hearers to harmony with both and obedience to both! Certain it is that at that impious message, devoid of all truth, not only did Our Imperial Majesty conceive a righteous indignation, but all the princes who were present were filled with so great fury and wrath that they would undoubtedly have condemned those two wicked priests to death, had not our presence averted this.

"Moreover, because many copies of this letter were found in their possession, and blank parchments with seals affixed that were still to be written on at their discretion, whereby—as has been their practice hitherto—they were endeavoring to scatter the venom of their iniquity throughout the churches of the Teutonic realm, to denude the altars, to carry off the vessels of the house of God,[2] to strip crosses of their coverings, we obliged them to return to the City by the way they had come, lest an opportunity be afforded them of proceeding further.

"And since, through election by the princes, the kingdom and the empire are ours from God alone, Who at the time of the passion of His Son Christ subjected the world to dominion by the two swords,[3] and since the apostle Peter taught the world this doctrine: 'Fear God, honor the king,'[4] whosoever says that we received the imperial crown as a benefice (*pro beneficio*) from the lord pope contradicts the divine ordinance and the doctrine of Peter and is guilty of a lie. But because we have hitherto striven to snatch from the hand of the Egyptians[5] the honor and freedom of the churches, so long oppressed by the yoke of undeserved slavery, and are intent on preserving to them all their rights and dignities, we ask Your University[6] to grieve at so great an insult to us and to the empire, hoping that your unwavering loyalty will not permit the honor of the empire, which has stood, glorious and undiminished, from the founding

---

1 Luke 16: 9.
2 Dan. 1: 2. The "Teutonic realm" is Germany.
3 Luke 22: 38. Because Christ said of two swords, "It is enough," the passage was used as a justification for the equal power of the Church and the State.
4 1 Pet. 2: 17.
5 See Ex. 18: 9; 1 Sam. 10: 18.
6 I.e., the Pope as the Universal Pope.

of the City and the establishment of the Christian religion even down to your days, to be disparaged by so unheard-of a novelty, such presumptuous arrogance, knowing that—all ambiguity aside—we would prefer to encounter the risk of death rather than to endure in our time the reproach of so great a disorder."

12. Having dealt thus with this matter, Frederick turned his attention to ordering the affairs of the empire in the kingdom of Burgundy.

6.17 King and nobles: *Magna Carta* (1215). Original in Latin.

AFTER KING JOHN'S SOUND DEFEAT by the king of France at the Battle of Bouvines (1214), the barons of England, angry about losing their French possessions and chafing under the taxes and other indignities they had suffered at John's hands in his quest for revenues, rebelled. At Runnymede in 1215 they forced the king to give his assent to a charter which has come to be known as Magna Carta. In the version published below, the starred clauses indicate those which were not repeated when Magna Carta was reissued in 1225. What were the enduring provisions of this document, and whom did they benefit?

[Source: *English Historical Documents*, vol. 3: *1189-1327*, ed. Harry Rothwell (London and New York: Routledge, 1975), pp. 316-24 (notes added).]

John, by the grace of God, king of England, lord of Ireland, duke of Normandy and Aquitaine, and count of Anjou, to the archbishops, bishops, abbots, earls, barons, justiciars, foresters, sheriffs, stewards, servants, and to all his bailiffs and faithful subjects, greeting. Know that we, out of reverence for God and for the salvation of our soul and those of all our ancestors and heirs, for the honor of God and the exaltation of holy church, and for the reform of our realm, on the advice of our venerable fathers, Stephen, archbishop of Canterbury, primate of all England and cardinal of the holy Roman church, Henry archbishop of Dublin, William of London, Peter of Winchester, Jocelyn of Bath and Glastonbury, Hugh of Lincoln, ... [The names of numerous churchmen and barons follow.]

[1] In the first place have granted to God, and by this our present charter confirmed for us and our heirs for ever that the English church shall be free, and shall have its rights undiminished and its liberties unimpaired; and it is our will that it be thus observed; which is evident from the fact that, before the quarrel between us and our barons began, we willingly and spontaneously granted and by our charter confirmed the freedom of elections which is reckoned most important and very essential to the English church, and obtained confirmation of it from the lord pope Innocent III,[1] which we will observe and we wish our heirs to observe it in good faith for ever. We have also granted to all free men of our kingdom, for ourselves and our heirs for ever, all the liberties written below, to be had and held by them and their heirs of us and our heirs.

[2] If any of our earls or barons or others holding of us in chief by knight service dies, and at his death his heir be of full age and owe relief[2] he shall have his inheritance on payment of the old relief, namely the heir or heirs of an earl £100 for a whole earl's barony, the heir or heirs of a baron £100 for a whole barony, the heir or heirs of a knight 100s, at most, for a whole knight's fee; and he who owes less shall give less according to the ancient usage of fiefs.

[3] If, however, the heir of any such be under age

---

1 Innocent III (r.1198-1216).
2 "Relief" was the payment that the heir of a vassal made to the lord upon inheriting the fief.

and a ward, he shall have his inheritance when he comes of age without paying relief and without making fine.

[4] The guardian of the land of such an heir who is under age shall take from the land of the heir no more than reasonable revenues, reasonable customary dues and reasonable services, and that without destruction and waste of men or goods;[1] and if we commit the wardship of the land of any such to a sheriff, or to any other who is answerable to us for its revenues, and he destroys or wastes what he has wardship of, we will take compensation from him and the land shall be committed to two lawful and discreet men of that fief, who shall be answerable for the revenues to us or to him to whom we have assigned them; and if we give or sell to anyone the wardship of any such land and he causes destruction or waste therein, he shall lose that wardship, and it shall be transferred to two lawful and discreet men of that fief, who shall similarly be answerable to us as is aforesaid.

[5] Moreover, so long as he has the wardship of the land, the guardian shall keep in repair the houses, parks, preserves, ponds, mills and other things pertaining to the land out of the revenues from it; and he shall restore to the heir when he comes of age his land fully stocked with ploughs and the means of husbandry according to what the season of husbandry requires and the revenues of the land can reasonably bear.

[6] Heirs shall be married without disparagement,[2] yet so that before the marriage is contracted those nearest in blood to the heir shall have notice.

[7] A widow shall have her marriage portion and inheritance forthwith and without difficulty after the death of her husband; nor shall she pay anything to have her dower or her marriage portion or the inheritance which she and her husband held on the day of her husband's death; and she may remain in her husband's house for forty days after his death, within which time her dower shall be assigned to her.[3]

[8] No widow shall be forced to marry so long as she wishes to live without a husband provided that she gives security not to marry without our consent if she holds of us or without the consent of her lord of whom she holds, if she holds of another.[4]

[9] Neither we nor our bailiffs will seize for any debt any land or rent, so long as the chattels of the debtor are sufficient to repay the debt....

*[10] If anyone who has borrowed from the Jews any sum, great or small, dies before it is repaid, the debt shall not bear interest as long as the heir is under age, of whomsoever he holds; and if the debt falls into our hands, we will not take anything except the principal mentioned in the bond.

*[11] And if anyone dies indebted to the Jews, his wife shall have her dower and pay nothing of that debt; and if the dead man leaves children who are under age, they shall be provided with necessaries befitting the holding of the deceased; and the debt shall be paid out of the residue, reserving, however, service due to lords of the land; debts owing to others than Jews shall be dealt with in like manner.[5]

*[12] No scutage or aid shall be imposed in our kingdom unless by common counsel of our kingdom, except for ransoming our person, for making our eldest son a knight, and for once marrying our eldest daughter; and for these only a reasonable aid shall be levied.[6] Be it done in like manner concerning aids from the city of London.

---

1   The king had previously sold wardships to men who cut down the trees and otherwise exploited the property, leaving little for the wards when they came into their inheritance.
2   The king had previously made money by forcing heirs to marry beneath them ("with disparagement"). In effect, he sold off diseased or disfigured widows and wards.
3   The dower was the gift the husband gave his new wife, which remained her property upon his death.
4   The king had previously been marrying widows to the highest bidder.
5   The Jews were the property of the king, who shared in their gains. Limiting the amounts that Jews might charge also affected the king.
6   Scutage was a money payment in lieu of military service, and it was much favored by the king, who could then hire warriors rather than make do with vassals who owed only 40 days' service. By denying the king the right to demand scutages without their consent (here and in clause 14) the barons were in effect denying the king's right to an effective army. Aids were customary payments from a vassal to his lord, but the king had been requiring these aids much more frequently, and for many more occasions, than was traditional.

[13] And the city of London shall have all its ancient liberties and free customs as well by land as by water. Furthermore, we will and grant that all other cities, boroughs, towns, and ports shall have all their liberties and free customs.[1]

*[14] And to obtain the common counsel of the kingdom about the assessing of an aid (except in the three cases aforesaid) or of a scutage, we will cause to be summoned the archbishops, bishops, abbots, earls and greater barons, individually by our letters—and, in addition, we will cause to be summoned generally through our sheriffs and bailiffs all those holding of us in chief—for a fixed date, namely, after the expiry of at least forty days, and to a fixed place; and in all letters of such summons we will specify the reason for the summons. And when the summons has thus been made, the business shall proceed on the day appointed, according to the counsel of those present, though not all have come who were summoned.

*[15] We will not in future grant any one the right to take an aid from his free men, except for ransoming his person, for making his eldest son a knight and for once marrying his eldest daughter, and for these only a reasonable aid shall be levied.

[16] No one shall be compelled to do greater service for a knight's fee or for any other free holding than is due from it.

[17] Common pleas shall not follow our court, but shall be held in some fixed place.[2]

[18] Recognitions of *novel disseisin*, of *mort d'ancester*, and of *darrein presentment*, shall not be held elsewhere than in the counties to which they relate,[3] and in this manner—we, or, if we should be out of the realm, our chief justiciar,[4] will send two justices through each county four times a year, who, with four knights of each county chosen by the county, shall hold the said assizes in the county and on the day and in the place of meeting of the county court....

[20] A free man shall not be amerced [fined] for a trivial offence except in accordance with the degree of the offence, and for a grave offence he shall be amerced in accordance with its gravity, yet saving his way of living;[5] and a merchant in the same way, saving his stock-in-trade; and a villein shall be amerced in the same way, saving his means of livelihood—if they have fallen into our mercy:[6] and none of the aforesaid amercements shall be imposed except by the oath of good men of the neighborhood.

[21] Earls and barons shall not be amerced except by their peers, and only in accordance with the degree of the offence.

[22] No clerk shall be amerced in respect of his lay holding except after the manner of the others aforesaid and not according to the amount of his ecclesiastical benefice.

[23] No vill or individual shall be compelled to make bridges at river banks, except those who from of old are legally bound to do so.[7]

[24] No sheriff, constable, coroners, or others of our bailiffs, shall hold pleas of our crown.[8]

*[25] All counties, hundreds, wapentakes and trithings[9] shall be at the old rents without any additional payment, except our demesne manors....

*[27] If any free man dies without leaving a will,

---

1 For an example of such liberties see *Privileges for the Citizens of London* (above, p. 279).

2 For an example of the expenses involved in following the king's court around in order to pursue a suit, see *The Costs of Richard of Anstey's Law Suit*, p. 353 above. In John's day the establishment of a permanent court at Westminster was in fact underway.

3 *Novel disseisin, mort d'ancester,* and *darrein presentment* were the names of royal writs. By purchasing one of these, suitors could bring disputes involving property into the royal courts, where they would be heard locally by the king's justices, deciding on the basis of the sworn testimony of 12 jurors.

4 The king's justiciar was by this time the king's representative in all matters.

5 "Saving his way of living," that is, allowing him and his dependents enough to live on.

6 "Fallen into our mercy," that is, liable to our—the king's—fines. Amercements are fines.

7 The king claimed the right to compel the local population to repair bridges so that royal hunts could take place. John had ordered the repair of numerous bridges in order to impose heavy fines on those who did not comply.

8 I.e., all criminal trials were to be held under the auspices of the king's justices. For the origins of this practice, see the *Assize of Clarendon*, p. 350 above.

9 "Hundreds, wapentakes and trithings" were subdivisions of the county. The rents were collected by the sheriff, who gave a fixed portion to the royal treasury and kept the rest for himself.

his chattels [movable goods] shall be distributed by his nearest kinsfolk and friends under the supervision of the church, saving to every one the debts which the deceased owed him.

[28] No constable or other bailiff of ours shall take anyone's corn [grain] or other chattels unless he pays on the spot in cash for them or can delay payment by arrangement with the seller.

[29] No constable shall compel any knight to give money instead of castle-guard if he is willing to do the guard himself or through another good man, if for some good reason he cannot do it himself; and if we lead or send him on military service, he shall be excused guard in proportion to the time that because of us he has been on service.

[30] No sheriff, or bailiff of ours, or anyone else shall take the horses or carts of any free man for transport work save with the agreement of that freeman.

[31] Neither we nor our bailiffs will take, for castles or other works of ours, timber which is not ours, except with the agreement of him whose timber it is.

[32] We will not hold for more than a year and a day the lands of those convicted of felony, and then the lands shall be handed over to the lords of the fiefs.

[33] Henceforth all fish-weirs [traps] shall be cleared completely from the Thames and the Medway and throughout all England, except along the sea coast.

[34] The writ called *Praecipe* shall not in future be issued to anyone in respect of any holding whereby a free man may lose his court.[1]

[35] Let there be one measure for wine throughout our kingdom, and one measure for ale, and one measure for corn, namely "the London quarter"; and one width for cloths whether dyed, russet or halberget, namely two ells within the selvedges. Let it be the same with weights as with measures.

[36] Nothing shall be given or taken in future for the writ of inquisition of life or limbs: instead it shall be granted free of charge and not refused.[2] …

[39] No free man shall be arrested or imprisoned or disseised or outlawed or exiled or in any way victimized, neither will we attack him or send anyone to attack him, except by the lawful judgment of his peers or by the law of the land.[3]

[40] To no one will we sell, to no one will we refuse or delay right or justice.

[41] All merchants shall be able to go out of and come into England safely and securely and stay and travel throughout England, as well by land as by water, for buying and selling by the ancient and right customs free from all evil tolls, except in time of war and if they are of the land that is at war with us. And if such are found in our land at the beginning of a war, they shall be attached,[4] without injury to their persons or goods, until we, or our chief justiciar, know how merchants of our land are treated who were found in the land at war with us when war broke out; and if ours are safe there, the others shall be safe in our land.…

*[47] All forests that have been made forest in our time shall be immediately dis-afforested; and so be it done with river banks that have been made preserves[5] by us in our time.

*[48] All evil customs connected with forests and warrens, foresters and warreners, sheriffs and their officials, river-banks and their wardens shall immediately be inquired into in each county by twelve sworn knights of the same county who are to be chosen by good men of the same county, and within forty days of the completion of the inquiry shall be utterly

---

1 The royal writ *Praecipe* took a case out of local courts and put it under royal jurisdiction. The barons who demanded Magna Carta wanted to preserve their customary courts. Reading *Proceedings for the Abbey of Bec*, p. 360 above, may help to explain why.

2 Anyone accused of homicide and subject to trial by combat could claim that his accuser had brought charges "out of spite and hate" and buy a "writ of inquisition of life or limbs" that would require a local jury to determine whether trial by combat was lawful. This clause made the writ free.

3 This, the most famous clause of Magna Carta, was not a guarantee of trial by jury but was a privilege granted all free men (a minority of the population, consisting of barons, nobles, and some particularly substantial peasants who held free, rather than a servile, land) that they be judged according to established procedures by members of their own class. To be "disseised" meant to be dispossessed of one's property.

4 I.e., seized.

5 The king had claimed the right to "afforest" whole districts, turning open land into forests, so that he might hunt there, and he had set apart river banks so that he might shoot the birds flying there.

abolished by them so as never to be restored, provided that we, or our justiciar if we are not in England, know of it first....

*[51] As soon as peace is restored, we will remove from the kingdom all foreign knights, cross-bow-men, serjeants, and mercenaries, who have come with horses and arms to the detriment of the kingdom.

*[52] If anyone has been disseised [dispossessed] of or kept out of his lands, castles, franchises or his right by us without the legal judgment of his peers, we will immediately restore them to him: and if a dispute arises over this, then let it be decided by the judgment of the twenty-five barons who are mentioned below in the clause for securing the peace:[1] for all the things, however, which anyone has been disseised or kept out of without the lawful judgment of his peers by king Henry, our father, or by king Richard, our brother, which we have in our hand or are held by others, to whom we are bound to warrant them, we will have the usual period of respite of crusaders,[2] excepting those things about which a plea was started or an inquest made by our command before we took the cross; when however we return from our pilgrimage, or if by any chance we do not go on it, we will at once do full justice therein....

[54] No one shall be arrested or imprisoned upon the appeal of a woman for the death of anyone except her husband.[3] ...

*[56] If we have disseised or kept out Welshmen from lands or liberties or other things without the legal judgment of their peers in England or in Wales, they shall be immediately restored to them; and if a dispute arises over this, then let it be decided in the March[4] by the judgment of their peers—for holdings in England according to the law of England, for holdings in Wales according to the law of Wales, and for holdings in the March according to the law of the March. Welshmen shall do the same to us and ours....

*[59] We will act toward Alexander, king of the Scots, concerning the return of his sisters and hostages and concerning his franchises and his right in the same manner in which we act towards our other barons of England, unless it ought to be otherwise by the charters which we have from William his father, formerly king of the Scots, and this shall be determined by the judgment of his peers in our court.

[60] All these aforesaid customs and liberties which we have granted to be observed in our kingdom as far as it pertains to us towards our men, all of our kingdom, clerks as well as laymen, shall observe as far as it pertains to them towards their men.

*[61] Since, moreover, for God and the betterment of our kingdom and for the better allaying of the discord that has arisen between us and our barons we have granted all these things aforesaid, wishing them to enjoy the use of them unimpaired and unshaken for ever, we give and grant them the under-written security, namely, that the barons shall choose any twenty-five barons of the kingdom they wish, who must with all their might observe, hold and cause to be observed, the peace and liberties which we have granted and confirmed to them by this present charter of ours, so that if we, or our justiciar, or our bailiffs or any one of our servants offend in any way against anyone or transgress any of the articles of the peace or the security and the offence be notified to four of the aforesaid twenty-five barons, those four barons shall come to us, or to our justiciar if we are out of the kingdom, and, laying the transgression before us, shall petition us to have that transgression corrected without delay. And if we do not correct the transgressions or if we are out of the kingdom, if our justiciar does not correct it, within forty days, reckoning from the time it was brought to our notice or to that of our justiciar if we were out of the kingdom, the aforesaid four barons shall refer that case to the rest of the twenty-five barons and those twenty-five barons together with the community of the whole land shall distrain and distress us in every way they can, namely, by seizing castles, lands, possessions, and in such other ways as they can, saving our person and the persons of our queen and our children, until, in their

---

1   See clause 61.
2   The "respite for crusaders" was three years' immunity from all litigation and payment of debts.
3   A woman could choose her own champion in a trial by combat, and thus she was thought to have an unfair advantage in bringing a charge.
4   The March was the border region between England and Wales.

opinion, amends have been made; and when amends have been made, they shall obey us as they did before. And let anyone in the land who wishes take an oath to obey the orders of the said twenty-five barons for the execution of all the aforesaid matters, and with them to distress us as much as he can, and we publicly and freely give anyone leave to take the oath who wishes to take it and we will never prohibit anyone from taking it. Indeed, all those in the land who are unwilling of themselves and of their own accord to take an oath to the twenty-five barons to help them to distrain and distress us, we will make them take the oath as aforesaid at our command. And if any of the twenty-five barons dies or leaves the country or is in any other way prevented from carrying out the things aforesaid, the rest of the aforesaid twenty-five barons shall choose as they think fit another one in his place, and he shall take the oath like the rest. In all matters the execution of which is committed to these twenty-five barons, if it should happen that these twenty-five are present yet disagree among themselves about anything, or if some of those summoned will not or cannot be present, that shall be held as fixed and established which the majority of those present ordained or commanded, exactly as if all the twenty-five had consented to it; and the said twenty-five shall swear that they will faithfully observe all the things aforesaid and will do all they can to get them observed. And we will procure nothing from anyone, either personally or through anyone else, whereby any of these concessions and liberties might be revoked or diminished; and if any such thing is procured, let it be void and null, and we will never use it either personally or through another.

*[62] And we have fully remitted and pardoned to everyone all the ill-will, indignation and rancor that have arisen between us and our men, clergy and laity, from the time of the quarrel. Furthermore, we have fully remitted to all, clergy and laity, and as far as pertains to us have completely forgiven, all trespasses occasioned by the same quarrel between Easter in the sixteenth year of our reign and the restoration of peace. And, besides, we have caused to be made for them letters testimonial patent of the lord Stephen archbishop of Canterbury, of the lord Henry archbishop of Dublin and of the aforementioned bishops and of master Pandulf about this security and the aforementioned concessions.

*[63] Wherefore we wish and firmly enjoin that the English church shall be free, and that the men in our kingdom shall have and hold all the aforesaid liberties, rights and concessions well and peacefully, freely and quietly, fully and completely, for themselves and their heirs from us and our heirs, in all matters and in all places for ever, as is aforesaid. An oath, moreover, has been taken, as well on our part as on the part of the barons, that all these things aforesaid shall be observed in good faith and without evil disposition. Witness the above-mentioned and many others. Given by our hand in the meadow which is called Runnymede between Windsor and Staines on the fifteenth day of June, in the seventeenth year of our reign.

VERNACULAR LITERATURE

6.18 Epic poetry: *Raoul de Cambrai* (1180-1223). Original in French.

AT THE HEART OF THE anonymous epic poem *Raoul de Cambrai* is the dissatisfied, violent, and prideful Raoul, whose quest for a fief leads to tragedy. Dating from the age of King Philip Augustus (r.1180-1123), but set in the mythical past of a "King Louis," the poem reflects the French aristocracy's struggle with changing notions of inheritance, marriage, fidelity, and the roles of kings and vassals, women and men. Compare Raoul's dilemma with that of Hugh of Lusignan in the text above, p. 213.

[Source: *Raoul de Cambrai*, ed. and trans. Sarah Kay (Oxford: Clarendon Press, 1992), pp. 3, 57, 59, 61, 63, 65, 67, 79, 81, 83, 85, 87, 89, 91, 93, 95, 97.]

I

Listen to a song of exuberance and celebration! Very many of you have heard, and other *jongleurs* have sung, a song which is new, but the best of all has been left out, about the great baronial family who were so brave: it is the song of Raoul, who held the fief of Cambrai—he was called Taillefer, on account of his warlike character. This Taillefer had a son who was a splendid warrior; Raoul was his name, a man of extraordinary strength. He fought a series of grim battles against the sons of Herbert [of Vermandois], but then met a sorry death at the hands of young Bernier....

[Raoul was son of Lady Alice and Raoul, lord of Cambrai. His father died before he was born, and he was sent to be brought up at the court of Emperor (or King) Louis, who was his uncle as well. Since Cambrai had been the fief of his father, Raoul would normally expect to be invested with it when he came of age, but Louis gave the fief to another man. Nevertheless, Raoul was one of Louis's favorites at court. He was knighted by the king and promised a fief. Looking out for him was his uncle, Guerri the Red, and constantly at his side was his vassal Bernier, another young man at court. When grown, Raoul demanded a fief from Louis. In desperation, Louis granted him Vermandois, the fief of Count Herbert, who had just died—but only if he could take it. This was a very dangerous grant, since the heirs to Vermandois were alive. In addition, Bernier's inheritance was in Vermandois, and his mother, Marsent, was a nun there. The passage below begins when the King gives his

"glove as pledge" for Vermandois, but refuses to help Raoul fight for it.]

XLIII

With a heavy heart the king speaks. "Raoul my nephew," he said, "step forward. I hereby give you my glove as pledge, on condition that neither I nor my vassals will act as guarantors." And Raoul said: "I ask for nothing better." Hearing this, Bernier rises to his feet; now he will speak out loud for all to hear. "Herbert's sons are valiant knights, rich in possessions and with so many allies that they will never lose so much as a bezant through you." Several of the Frenchmen in the great hall are talking about it; one says to another, high and low alike: "That boy Raoul has the sense of a grown man; he is making a substantial claim in return for his father's fief and the king is unleashing war on such a scale that many ladies' hearts will mourn."

XLIV

Noble-hearted Bernier speaks so loudly [now] that everyone could easily hear. "For St. Simon's sake, rightful emperor, consider now, is this justice? Herbert's sons are guilty of no crime, and judgment should not go against them in your court. Why do you lightly give away their land? May the Lord God never forgive them if they don't defend it against Baron Raoul." "I agree," the king promptly replied. "Since he has accepted the gift against my will, I'll never fasten on my gonfalon on his account."

XLV

Bernier addresses himself to Raoul of Cambrai. "I am your vassal, I'll not deny it, but for my part I don't advise you to take their lands for I know very well that Ernaut of Douai has fifty men—I never saw such barons anywhere. Accept a settlement rather than harm them; if they have harmed you, I will make amends for them and for love of you I will give them safe conduct here." "Indeed," said Raoul, "I will not think of it. The gift is made, I won't give it up for any consideration." And Bernier said, "My lord, I shall keep silence for the time being, until I see what force they bring to their defense."

XLVI

When Raoul sees that his affairs have gone so well that the gift has been made to him in the high court and that Louis will not rescind it, then Bernier almost tears his hair. Count Raoul returns to his lodging; mounting his horse, he has his departure sounded, and leaves Paris without any further disturbance.

XLVII

Raoul spurs away and quickly reaches Cambrai; and the barons dismount at their lodgings. Young Bernier's head was bowed: he had made the mistake of quarreling with Raoul; now he will sleep before he drinks anything or shows his face in the great hall or the keep, for he does not want to start a quarrel with his lady. Count Raoul dismounted at the block. The lovely Lady Alice kissed her son on the mouth and chin.

XLVIII

Lady Alice, whose figure was handsome and distinguished, kissed and welcomed her noble son Raoul, who took her by the hand. Together they went up into the ancestral hall. She addresses him in the hearing of many barons, saying: "My son, I see you are tall and well built. You are seneschal of France, thanks be to God. I am much astonished at mighty King Louis: you have served him for a long time now, and he has not rewarded your service in the slightest. It's now time he showed favor to you and gave you back all bold Taillefer's lands—your dear father who was my husband—for the Mansel has had the use of them too

long. I am amazed that you have borne it for such a long time, without killing or dishonoring him long ago." Hearing this, Raoul's heart was filled with bitterness. "Deal kindly with me, lady, for the sake of God who never lets you down. Louis has rewarded all my service: Herbert is dead, I promise you, and I have been given his vast estate." Hearing this, the lady replied with a sigh: "My son," she said, "I spent a long time bringing you up. Whoever granted you Péronne and Origny, Saint-Quentin, Nesle and Flavy, and Ham and Roie and the town of Cléry, invested you, my son, with sudden death. Leave their land, in God's name I implore you! Raoul your father, who sired you, and Count Herbert were always friends. Together they fought many great battles; there was never any enmity or strife between them. If you believe me, by the saints of Ponthieu, his sons will have none with you either." But Raoul said, "I will not let it go at that, for all the world would regard me as a failure and my heirs would be disgraced."

XLIX

"Raoul, my son," said the lovely Alice, "I fed you with milk from my own breast. Why do you strike pain deep in my heart? Whoever granted you Péronne and Péronnelle and Ham and Roie and the town of Nesle invested you, my son, with sudden death. One would need rich harness and saddlery, and trusty barons, to go to war against such a force. As for me, I know that I would rather be a servant girl or take the veil and live in a convent [than see you go]. All my land will go up in flames." Jutting his jaw in his hand, Raoul swears by God who was born of a virgin that he would not leave off for all the gold of Tudela. He would rather see people disemboweled, and the brains dashed from many heads, than give it up....

LIX

Raoul of Cambrésis makes his adieux and leaves his fair-featured mother Alice. He rides through the Arrouaise, which is his territory. Together with him goes Guerri the Red; they are well armed on their splendid horses. On the far side they cross over into the Vermandois, and seize the livestock, reducing countless men to ruin. They set fire to the land—the farms are ablaze—plunging young Bernier into gloom and despondency. When he sees his father's and relatives' lands burning in this way, Bernier is almost beside himself with rage. Wherever Raoul and Guerri might go, Bernier would always stay behind: he was in no hurry to put his armor on.

LX

Count Raoul called Manecier, Count Droon and his brother Gautier. "Quickly take up arms without delay: there are to be 400 of you, each on a good horse, and you must reach Origny by nightfall. Pitch my tent in the middle of the church and my packhorses will stand in its porches; prepare my food in the crypts, my sparrow-hawks can perch on the gold crosses, and prepare a magnificent bed for me to sleep on in front of the altar; I will use the crucifix as a back rest and my squires can make free with the nuns. I want to destroy the place utterly, because it is well loved by Herbert's sons." "We cannot ignore your orders," they reply. Quickly the noble warriors go to arm themselves and mount their horses—not one of them is without a steel sword, shield, lance, and double hauberk. They began to advance on Origny. The bells rang out high in the principal church; remembering God the Father of justice, even the craziest of them felt compelled to show reverence: they had no wish to desecrate the holy relic[s]. [And so] they pitched their tent out here in the fields, and slept in it all night until daybreak. They set about installing themselves as well as if they were due to spend a whole year here.

LXI

Below Origny there was an attractive patch of woodland; there the brave knights camped until daybreak the next morning. Raoul arrived at about the hour of prime, and angrily reprimanded his men. "You sons of whores, you treacherous, low-born villains! How base and wrong-headed can you be, ever to disobey my orders!" "Do not be hard on us, lord, for God the Redeemer's sake! We are not Jews or executioners, to destroy holy relics."

LXII

Count Raoul cast all moderation aside. "You sons of whores!"—these were the madman's words—"I ordered my tent to be in the church, pitched right inside it, complete with gilded top. Whose idea was it to put it somewhere else?" "Indeed," said Guerri, "you are getting above yourself! It's scarcely any time since you were knighted. If God takes against you, you won't last long. This place is venerated by men of good standing; the holy relics should not be brought into dishonor. See how fresh and pleasant the grass is in the meadows, and the river alongside is clear; there you could settle your vanguard and your vassals so that you will not be surprised or harmed." And Raoul replied, "Just as you say. I'll let it go at that since you wish it." They spread the rugs on the green grass, and Raoul lay down there, leaning on his elbow. He brought ten knights with him: they took counsel together, with terrible results.

LXIII

Raoul shouts, "To arms, knights! Let's go quickly and break Origny into little pieces! Anyone who stays behind loses my friendship for ever!" The barons mount, for they dare not disobey—there were more than 3,000 all told—and they start their advance on Origny. They attack the town, and begin hurling missiles; those inside defend themselves in their hour of need. Then Raoul's troops begin to draw closer: they are hacking down the trees in front of the town, and the nuns, ladies of noble birth, each one with her psalter, file out of the church, reciting the holy office. Marsent, Bernier's mother, was among them. "Have pity, Raoul, by God our judge! You are committing a grave sin if you allow us to be slaughtered; we are an easy prey for you."

LXIV

Young Bernier's mother's name was Marsent: she was holding a book from the time of Solomon and reciting a prayer to the Lord God. She seized Raoul by his mail hauberk. "For God and his holy name's sake, Sir," she said "where is Bernier, the noble baron's son?" "In God's name, lady, in the chief tent, where he is amusing himself with many good companions. There is not a knight to equal him from here to Nero's Field.[1] He has prompted me to go to war with Herbert's sons, and indeed he has said may he never

---

1 Nero's Field was the name given to the site of St. Peter's in Rome.

put on spurs again if I leave them so much as a button." "God!" said the lady, "what a treacherous heart he must have! They are his uncles, everybody knows that. If they lose what is theirs, ill betide whoever comes up against them.

LXV

"Sir Raoul, would prayer persuade you to withdraw a little? We are nuns, by the saints of Bavaria, and will never hold lance or standard, or cause anyone ever be laid to rest through force of ours." "Indeed," said Raoul, "you are a deceiving woman. I have no dealings with a slag of a chambermaid who's been a tart and whore, a common slut for all takers. I knew you as Count Ybert's prostitute; your flesh was never too expensive—if anyone wanted some, by St. Peter, you could be hauled off for next to nothing!" "God!" said the lady, "what fierce words I hear! What strange insults I hear heaped upon me! I was never a prostitute or a whore. If a noble man made me his mistress, I had a son by him of whom I am still very proud. With God's grace, I do not hold myself the worse for it: God turns his face towards those who serve him well.

LXVI

"Sir Raoul," said Bernier's mother, "we are not able to handle weapons. You can easily slaughter and destroy us. I tell you truly, you will not see us wield lance or shield in our defense. We have to derive all our livelihood and all our sustenance from this altar, and we get all our food from within this town. Men of position value this place highly and so they send us silver and fine gold. Spare our hearth and church, and go and make yourself at home in our meadows. We will provide for you and your knights, if you will accept it, and the squires shall receive supplies—plenty of hay and oats for fodder." And Raoul said, "By St. Riquier! For love of you, since you request it of me, you shall have the truce, whoever may be annoyed by it." "That deserves my thanks," replied the lady. Raoul leaves on his fast horse, and Bernier—that admirable man—came to see his mother, proud-faced Marsent. He had a great need to speak with her.

LXVII

Raoul departs, quickening his pace; and Bernier, dressed in a rich suit of clothing, arrived to see his mother and dismounted. She kisses him and takes him in her arms—she embraces him three times, there was nothing faint-hearted about the way she did it. "You have received your arms, my son," she said. "I wish the count well through whom you have got them so quickly, and you better still if you have deserved them. But be frank with me about one thing: why should you make war on your father's fief? He has no other heirs, you cannot fail to inherit it—you will gain it by your valor and your good sense." "By St. Thomas!" Bernier replied, "I would rather not do it for all the wealth of Baghdad. Raoul my overlord is more villainous than Judas: [yet] he is my overlord, he gives me horses and clothing and arms and oriental silks. I wouldn't fail him, not [even] for the fief of Damascus, until such time as all can declare: 'Bernier, you are in the right!'" "Son," said his mother "by my faith, you *are* right: serve your overlord, and God be your reward."

LXVIII

The large and spacious town of Origny—Herbert's sons cared deeply for the place—had a dense palisade which they had erected around it, but it was worthless for purposes of defense. There was an exceedingly large field below the town where people used to joust. The ford belonged to the nuns of the convent, and by it they pasture their oxen which they need for ploughing. There is no one under heaven who would dare harm it. Count Raoul has his tent pitched there; all the tent poles are of silver and pure gold, and 400 men could lodge inside it. Three low-born scoundrels steal away from the army, and do not stop spurring until they reach the town. They covet the wealth there, they can't bear to leave it alone; [but] it brought grief to those whom it was supposed to help, for ten men rush at them, each bearing a crowbar. They kill two with their fierce onslaught, and the third escapes on his horse. From here back to the camp nothing would induce him to stop. Then he dismounts on to the sandy ground, and goes to kiss his overlord's shoe. Tearfully he began to appeal to him for mercy, crying out loud: "May God never come to your aid if you don't take revenge on these townspeople who are so rich and haughty and fierce. They don't give twopence for you or any man; instead they are threatening to slice your head off: if they can catch you and have you in their power, not all the gold of Montpellier would save you. I saw my brother killed and cut to bits, and my nephew butchered and brought down. They would have killed me, by St. Riquier, but I escaped on my horse here." When Raoul heard this, he was beside himself. "To the attack, noble knights!" he cries. "I mean to go and break Origny into little pieces! Since they provoke me to war, so help me God, they shall pay dearly for it!" When they hear the order they go and quickly arm themselves, for they dare not disregard it. They are a good 10,000 strong—that's how many I heard them reckoned at. They spur out towards Origny; they rush across the moats in pursuit of their purpose; they hack down the palisade with blows from their steel blades and bring it down underfoot; now they are crossing the moat beside the fishpond—there is no hanging back till they reach the walls. That was a day of anguish for the townspeople, when they could get no protection from the palisade.

LXIX

The townspeople see that they have lost the palisade: the bravest of them were dismayed. They have withdrawn to the fortified sections of the walls, and are hurling stones and quantities of great pointed staves—they have laid low many of Raoul's force. Not a single man remained in the town but came to the defense of the ramparts, and they swear by God and his power, ill betide Raoul if they catch him. Let young and old defend themselves well! The sight of this filled Raoul's heart with anger—he doesn't reckon himself worth a straw if they are not all slaughtered and strung up. At the top of his voice he calls out, "Barons, start the fire!" And when they heard him they did so, for they came eager for looting. How badly Raoul kept the agreement he made with the abbess; how dreadfully he greeted them that day, when his men burned the town—there was nothing left of it. Young Bernier was filled with grief when he saw Origny destroyed in this way.

LXX

Count Raoul was heartily angry with the townspeople for crossing him. He swore by God and his mercy that not for the diocese of Reims would he hold off from burning every one of them by nightfall. He shouted the order for fire—and [now] the squires have lit it. Rooms are burning here and floors collapsing there,

barrels are catching fire, their hoops split, and children are burning to death in horrible agony. Count Raoul has behaved atrociously: the day before he had given his word to Marsent that they wouldn't lose so much as a folded cloth—and today he burns them to death, that's how crazy he was! They flee to the church, but that doesn't do them any good: if they had stood up to him they wouldn't have set foot there.

LXXI

In the great spacious town of Origny—Herbert's sons loved the place dearly, establishing Marsent there who was Bernier's mother, and 100 nuns to pray to God—fierce-hearted Raoul had all the streets set ablaze. All the homes are burning and the floors give way, the wines spill and the cellars are awash with it, sides of bacon burn and larders collapse. The bacon fat makes the great fire fiercer: it spreads to the towers and the highest steeple—the roofs were brought crashing down. Within the two walls the blaze was so intense that the nuns are burned to death, it was such a furnace. All hundred of them are burning in that great disaster—Marsent, Bernier's mother, is burning to death, and Clamados, Duke Renier's daughter. Amid the conflagration the smell was inescapable and the bold knights shed tears of pity. When young Bernier sees this catastrophic turn of events he is so appalled that he is quite beside himself. You should have seen him grip his shield! With drawn sword he runs to the church to find the flames pouring out of the doors—no one could get within a javelin's throw of the fire. Alongside a precious marble monument Bernier looks and sees his mother lying outstretched, her sweet face [consumed by fire?]. On her breast, he saw her psalter in flames. "I am wasting my time in foolishness," the boy said then. "Assistance will never be any use to her again. Sweet mother, you kissed me yesterday! But I am no good as a son to you: I cannot save or help you. May God rest your soul, who will judge the world! And Raoul, you scoundrel, may God bring disaster on you! I no longer want to be your vassal, and if I can't avenge this outrage, I shan't think myself worth a penny." He is so grief-stricken the steel blade falls from his hand—he faints three times on his horse's neck. He turned to Guerri the Red for advice, but advice couldn't mend matters now....

6.19 A troubadour poem of love: Jaufré Rudel, *When Days are Long in May* (c.1125-1150). Original in Occitan.

THE TROUBADOURS WERE POETS and singers who generally worked for courtly patrons. They might themselves be of the petty nobility, like Jaufré Rudel (*fl.* 1125-1150), who was the lord of Blaye and a crusader. We have six of his poems, four of them with music. To appreciate their artistry, it is good to know how they were constructed in Occitan (or Provençal). This one, for example, begins:

> Lanquan li jorn son lonc en may
> m'es belhs dous chans d'auzelhs de lonh,
> e quan mi suy partitz de lay
> remembra·m d'un' amor de lonh: …

Clearly *lonh* (far away) is the key word here, and it becomes even more important as it is repeated over and over. In fact, *lonh* ends the second and fourth line of every verse except the final one, when the poet realizes that it is not just distance that keeps him from his love.

[Source: *Lyrics of the Troubadours and Trouvères*, trans. Frederick Goldin (Garden City, NY: Anchor Books, 1973), pp. 105-07.]

When days are long in May,
I enjoy the sweet song of the birds far away,
and when I am parted from their song,
the parting reminds me of a love far away:
5 I go bent with desire, head bowed down;
then neither the song nor the hawthorn's flower
pleases me more than the winter's ice,

I shall consider him my lord, in truth, the man
who lets me see this love far away;
10 but for one good thing that falls to me,
I get two evils, for this love is far away.
Ai! I wish I were a pilgrim there,
my staff and my cloak
reflected in her beautiful eyes.

15 My joy will come forth, when I entreat her
for the love of God, the love far away,
and, if it pleases her, I shall lodge
close to her, though now I am far away.
Then what fine conferring will come forth,
20 when the lover come from afar will be so close
I shall know the comfort of her sweet words.

Sad and rejoicing I shall part from her,
when I have seen this love far away:
but when I shall see her I do not know,
our lands are very far away: 25
there are many ways and roads,
and I am no prophet …
but as it pleases God!

I shall have no pleasure in love
if it is not the pleasure of this love far away,   30
for I do not know a gentler or a better one
anywhere, not close by, not far away:
her worth is true, and perfect, so
that there, in the kingdom of the Saracens,
I wish I were a prisoner for her.   35

God, who made everything that comes and goes
and formed this love far away,
give me the power—for I have the heart—
to see this love far away
face to face, in such pleasant dwellings   40
that the chamber and the garden
would all the while be a palace to my eyes.

He speaks the truth who says I crave
and go desiring this love far away,
45 for no other joy pleases me more
than the rich enjoyment of this love far away.
But the path is blocked to my desire,

for my godfather gave me this fate:
I must love and not be loved.

But the path is blocked to my desire,   50
a great curse on this godfather
who doomed me to be unloved.

6.20 A poem of war: Bertran de Born, *I Love the Joyful Time* (12th c.). Original in Occitan.

BERTRAN DE BORN (*c.*1140–bef. 1215) WAS THE LORD of Hautefort in the Périgord region of France. Much like Hugh of Lusignan (see above, p. 213), Bertran was almost constantly at war—in his case with his brother and with Henry II of England (Bertran was on the side of Henry's first son, "young Henry"). We have forty songs written by him.

[Source: *Lyrics of the Troubadours and Trouvères*, trans. Frederick Goldin (Garden City, NY: Anchor Books, 1973), pp. 243, 245, 247.]

I love the joyful time of Easter,
that makes the leaves and flowers come forth,
and it pleases me to hear the mirth
of the birds, who make their song
5 resound through the woods,
and it pleases me to see upon the meadows
tents and pavilions planted,
and I feel a great joy
when I see ranged along the field
10 knights and horses armed for war.

And it pleases me when the skirmishers
make the people and their baggage run away,
and it pleases me when I see behind them coming
a great mass of armed men together,
15 and I have pleasure in my heart
when I see strong castles besieged,
the broken ramparts caving in,
and I see the host on the water's edge,
closed in all around by ditches,
20 with palisades, strong stakes close together.

And I am as well pleased by a lord
when he is first in the attack,
armed, upon his horse, unafraid,
so he makes his men take heart
25 by his own brave lordliness.

And when the armies mix in battle,
each man should be poised
to follow him, smiling,
for no man is worth a thing
till he has given and gotten blow on blow.   30

Maces and swords and painted helms,
the useless shields cut through,
we shall see as the fighting starts,
and many vassals together striking,
and wandering wildly,   35
the unreined horses of the wounded and dead.
And once entered into battle
let every man proud of his birth
think only of breaking arms and heads,
for a man is worth more dead than alive and beaten.   40

I tell you there is not so much savor
in eating or drinking or sleeping,
as when I hear them scream, "There they are! Let's
    get them!"
on both sides, and I hear riderless
horses in the shadows, neighing,   45
and I hear them scream, "Help! Help!"
and I see them fall among the ditches,
little men and great men on the grass,
and I see fixed in the flanks of the corpses
stumps of lances with silken streamers.   50

Barons, pawn your castles,
and your villages, and your cities
before you stop making war on one another.

Papiols, gladly go
fast to my Lord Yes-and-No[1]
and tell him he has lived in peace too long.

6.21 Song of a *trobairitz*: Comtessa de Dia, *I've Been in Great Anguish* (*c*.1200?). Original in Occitan.

A *trobairitz*, i.e., a female troubadour, the Comtessa de Dia was a poet of *fin'amor*—courtly, refined love. We know almost nothing about her except that she has left to us several songs, one with music. Taking all of these poems together (*When Days are Long in May*, p. 389, *I Love the Joyful Time*, p. 390, and this one by the Comtessa de Dia) discuss the themes that are most important in troubadour poetry.

[Source: *The Writings of Medieval Women*, trans. Marcelle Thiébaux (New York: Garland Publishing, 1987), p. 188.]

I've been in great anguish
over a noble soldier I once had,
and I want everyone to know, for all time,
that I loved him—too much!
Now I see I'm betrayed
because I didn't yield my love to him.
For that I've suffered greatly,
both in my bed and fully clad.

How I'd yearn to have my soldier
naked in my arms for one night!
He would feel a frenzy of delight
to have only me for his pillow.

I'm more in love with him
than Blancheflor ever was with Floris.[2]
To him I'd give my heart, my love,
my mind, my eyes, my life.

Beautiful, gracious, sweet friend,
when shall I hold you in my power?
If I could lie with you for one night,
and give you a kiss of love,
you can be sure I would desire greatly
to grant you a husband's place,
so long as you promised
to do everything I wished!

6.22 Fabliaux: *Browny, the Priest's Cow* and *The Priest Who Peeked* (13th c.). Original in Old French.

ORIGINATING IN NORTHERN FRANCE and performed by jongleurs (who were also acrobats, dancers, and jugglers), fabliaux were popular entertainment for all classes, though today only about 150 are extant in manuscripts. Short, humorous poems, fabliaux were meant to make people laugh; they highlighted human foibles and poked fun at peasants, women, and—especially—priests. The priest in *The Priest who Peeked* is one of the few clergymen who succeeds in his amorous intentions in a fabliau; the poet (Guerin) wants to show how the husband is tricked. But in *Browny, the Priest's Cow* (which is by the most famous fablior of all, Jean Bodel, 1165?-1210), the priest (a different priest) gets his comeuppance for his greed. Although rough and bawdy,

---

1 Richard I the Lion-Heart (d.1199), the duke of Aquitaine (in southern France) as well as king of England.
2 Blancheflor and Floire (or Floris) were famous lovers in a French Romance poem.

fabliaux were quite sophisticated poems, each written in rhyming couplets. For example, *Browny* begins:

> D'un vilain conte et de sa fame,
> c'un jor de feste Nostre Dame
> Aloient ourer à l'yglise,
> Li prestres, devant le servise,

Here *fame* rhymes with *Dame*, *l'yglise* with *servise*; and—as with all fabliaux—all of the lines contain exactly eight syllables. How do these poems pick up some themes of troubadour poetry while at the same time parodying courtly ideals?

[Source: *Cuckolds, Clerics, & Countrymen: Medieval French Fabliaux*, trans. John Du Val, ed. Raymond Eichmann (Fayetteville: University of Arkansas Press, 1982), pp. 31-32, 45-46.]

Browny, the Priest's Cow

Once, on blessed Mary's day,
A peasant took his wife to pray
And celebrate the mass in town.
4   Before the office, the priest came down
And turned to the people to deliver
His sermon: Blessed be the giver
Who gives for love of God in heaven.
8   God will return what has been given
Double to him whose heart is true.
"My wife!" the peasant said, "Did you
Hear what the parson up there said?
12   Whoever gives for God will get
The gift returned and multiplied?
What better use could we decide
For our cow, Berny, than to give her
16   To God through the priest? Besides, she never
Did give much milk. She's not much good."
"Well," said the wife, "I guess we should,
Since that's a fact. Let's take that cow
20   And give her to the parson now."
They rose at once and left together.
When they got home, the farmer tethered
His cow and led her from the shed
24   And took her back to town and said
To the priest, whose name was Constant, "Sir,
Here's my cow Berny. I'm giving her
To you because I love the Lord."
28   He handed him the tether cord

And swore that she was all he had.
"That's wise indeed," the parson said,
Who night and day kept careful watch
For any handout he could catch.   32
"Well done, my son. In peace depart.
If all my parish were as smart
And sensible as you, there'd be
Plenty of animals for me."   36
    The farmer left and made his journey
Home to his wife. The priest gave Berny
To one of his clerks to be secured
To *his* cow, Browny, till they were sure   40
She felt at home. The clerk pulled hard
And brought the cow to the backyard
And got the priest's fat cow and tied
Berny and Browny side by side,   44
Then turned around and left the cows.
The parson's cow preferred to browse,
And bent her head to keep on chewing,
But Berny balked: no, nothing doing.   48
She pulled the tether good and hard,
Dragging her out of the priest's yard,
Past houses and hemp fields, over bridges,
Through meadows and hedges, hills and ditches   52
Till home she came to her own backyard.
The parson's cow, who held back hard
The whole long way, came dragging after.
The farmer looked outside, and laughter   56
Filled his heart. He gave a cheer.
"Hey!" he shouted, "Look, my dear!

See how the good Lord multiplies.
60 Here's Berny back and Berny twice—
Only the second's brown, and bigger!
That's two for one the way I figure.
And now our barn's not big enough."

64   My lords, this fabliau is proof
It's foolish not to give all you own.
The good things come from God alone.
They are not buried in the ground.
68 Nothing ventured, nothing found,
And nothing multiplied. That's how
God blessed the man who risked his cow:
Two for the peasant, none for the priest,
72 And those who have the most, get least.

The Priest Who Peeked

If you will kindly listen well
To my next tale, I'd like to tell
A short and courtly fabliau
4 As Guerin has it. Long ago
There lived a peasant who had wed
A maiden courteous, well bred,
Wise, beautiful, of goodly birth.
8 He cherished her for all his worth
And did his best to keep her pleased.
The lady loved the parish priest,
Who was her only heart's desire.
12 The priest himself was so afire
With love for her that he decided
To tell his love and not to hide it.
So off he started, running hard.
16 As he came running through their yard,
The peasant and his wife were sitting
Together at the table eating.
    The priest neither called their name nor knocked.
20 He tried the door. The door was locked
And bolted tight. He looked around
And up and down until he found
A hole to spy through and was able
24 To see the peasant at the table,
Eating and drinking as she served.
The priest indignantly observed
The way the peasant led his life,
28 Taking no pleasure of his wife.
And when he'd had enough of spying,

He pounded at the doorway, crying,
"Hey there, good people! You inside!
What are you doing?" The man replied, 32
"Faith, Sir, we're eating. Why not come
In here to join us and have some?"
—"Eating? What a lie! I'm looking
Straight through this hole at you. You're fucking." 36
—"Hush!" said the peasant, "Believe me,
We're eating, Sir, as you can see."
—"If you are," said the priest, "I'll eat my hat.
You're fucking, Sir. I can see that! 40
Don't try to talk me out of it.
Why not let me go in and sit?
You stand out here and do the spying,
And let me know if I've been lying 44
About the sight I'm looking at."

The peasant leapt from where he sat, 48
Unlocked the door and hurried out.
The priest came in, turned about,
Shut and latched and bolted the door.
However hard the peasant bore 52
The sight of it, the parson sped
To the peasant's wife. He caught her head,
Tripped her up and laid her down.
Up to her chest he pulled her gown 56
And did of all good deeds the one
That women everywhere want done.
He bumped and battered with such force
The peasant's wife had no recourse 60
But let him get what he was seeking.
And there the other man was, peeking
At the little hole, through which he spied
His lovely wife's exposed backside 64
And the priest, riding on top of her.
"May God Almighty help you, Sir,"
The peasant called, "Is this a joke?"
The parson turned his head and spoke: 68
"No, I'm not joking. What's the matter?
Don't you see: I have your platter.
I'm eating supper at your table."
"Lord, this is like a dream or fable. 72
If I weren't hearing it from you,
I never would believe it true
That you aren't fucking with my wife."
"I'm not, Sir! Hush! As God's my life, 76

That's what I thought I saw you do."
The peasant said, "I guess that's true."
   That's how the peasant got confused,
80 Bewitched, befuddled, and confused,
By the priest and by his own weak brain

And didn't even feel the pain.
Because of the door, it still is said,
"Many a fool by God is fed."   84
Here ends the fabliau of the priest.

The End: Amen.

6.23 Disciplining and purifying Christendom: *Decrees of Lateran IV* (1215). Original in Latin.

CALLED BY POPE INNOCENT III (r.1198-1216), the Fourth Lateran Council was a turning point in the history of the Church. It codified many doctrines, policies, and practices that had hitherto been informal, local, or fuzzy. It meant to purify Christendom of the contaminating presence of heretics and Jews while determining the religious behavior and beliefs of those within the fold. How did it define a "Christian"? Comparing this document with the provisions of the sixth-century *Council of Orléans*, above, p. 60, how might you characterize the changes in the scope and character of church law over time?

[Source: *Decrees of the Ecumenical Councils*, ed. Norman P. Tanner, vol. 1: *Nicaea I to Lateran V* (London and Washington, DC: Sheed & Ward and Georgetown University Press, 1990), pp. *230-31, * 233-36, *245, *257-58, *265-67 (notes modified).]

CONSTITUTIONS

1. On the catholic faith

We firmly believe and simply confess that there is only one true God, eternal and immeasurable, almighty, unchangeable, incomprehensible and ineffable, Father, Son and holy Spirit, three persons but one absolutely simple essence, substance or nature. The Father is from none, the Son from the Father alone, and the holy Spirit from both equally, eternally without beginning or end; the Father generating, the Son being born, and the holy Spirit proceeding; consubstantial and coequal, co-omnipotent and coeternal; one principle of all things, creator of all things invisible and visible, spiritual and corporeal; who by his almighty power at the beginning of time created from nothing both spiritual and corporeal creatures, that is to say angelic and earthly, and then created human beings composed as it were of both spirit and body in common. The devil and other demons were created by God naturally good, but they became evil by their own doing. Man, however, sinned at the prompting of the devil.

This holy Trinity, which is undivided according to its common essence but distinct according to the properties of its persons, gave the teaching of salvation to the human race through Moses and the holy prophets and his other servants, according to the most appropriate disposition of the times. Finally the only-begotten Son of God, Jesus Christ, who became incarnate by the action of the whole Trinity in common and was conceived from the ever virgin Mary through the cooperation of the holy Spirit, having become true man, composed of a rational soul and human flesh, one person in two natures, showed more clearly the way of life. Although he is immortal and unable to suffer according to his divinity, he was made capable of suffering and dying according to his humanity. Indeed, having suffered and died on the wood of the cross for the salvation of the human race, he descended to the underworld, rose from the dead and ascended into heaven. He descended in the soul, rose in the flesh, and ascended in both. He will come at the end of time to judge the living and the dead, to render to every person according to his works, both to the reprobate and to the elect. All of them will rise with their own bodies, which they now wear, so as to receive according to their desserts, whether these be good or bad; for the latter perpetual punishment with the devil, for the former eternal glory with Christ.

There is indeed one universal church of the faithful, outside of which nobody at all is saved, in which Jesus Christ is both priest and sacrifice. His body and blood are truly contained in the sacrament of the altar under the forms of bread and wine, the bread and wine having been changed in substance, by God's power, into his body and blood, so that in order to achieve this mystery of unity we receive from God what he received from us. Nobody can effect this sacrament except a priest who has been properly ordained according to the church's keys, which Jesus Christ himself gave to the apostles and their successors. But the sacrament of baptism is consecrated in water at the invocation of the undivided Trinity—namely Father, Son and holy Spirit—and brings salvation to both children and adults when it is correctly carried out by anyone in the form laid down by the church. If someone falls into sin after having received baptism, he or she can always be restored through true penitence. For not only virgins and the continent but also married persons find favor with God by right faith and good actions and deserve to attain to eternal blessedness.…

3. On heretics

We excommunicate and anathematize every heresy raising itself up against this holy, orthodox and catholic faith which we have expounded above. We condemn all heretics, whatever names they may go under. They have different faces indeed but their tails are tied together inasmuch as they are alike in their pride. Let those condemned be handed over to the secular authorities present, or to their bailiffs, for due punishment. Clerics are first to be degraded from their orders. The goods of the condemned are to be confiscated, if they are lay persons, and if clerics they are to be applied to the churches from which they received their stipends. Those who are only found suspect of heresy are to be struck with the sword of anathema, unless they prove their innocence by an appropriate purgation, having regard to the reasons for suspicion and the character of the person. Let such persons be avoided by all until they have made adequate satisfaction. If they persist in the excommunication for a year, they are to be condemned as heretics. Let secular authorities, whatever offices they may be discharging, be advised and urged and if necessary be compelled by ecclesiastical censure, if they wish to be reputed and held to be faithful, to take publicly an oath for the defense of the faith to the effect that they will seek, in so far as they can, to expel from the lands subject to their jurisdiction all heretics designated by the church in good faith. Thus whenever anyone is promoted to spiritual or temporal authority, he shall be obliged to confirm this article with an oath. If however a tem-

poral lord, required and instructed by the church, neglects to cleanse his territory of this heretical filth, he shall be bound with the bond of excommunication by the metropolitan and other bishops of the province. If he refuses to give satisfaction within a year, this shall be reported to the supreme pontiff so that he may then declare his vassals absolved from their fealty to him and make the land available for occupation by Catholics so that these may, after they have expelled the heretics, possess it unopposed and preserve it in the purity of the faith—saving the right of the suzerain [ruler] provided that he makes no difficulty in the matter and puts no impediment in the way. The same law is to be observed no less as regards those who do not have a suzerain.

Catholics who take the cross and gird themselves up for the expulsion of heretics shall enjoy the same indulgence, and be strengthened by the same holy privilege, as is granted to those who go to the aid of the holy Land. Moreover, we determine to subject to excommunication believers who receive, defend or support heretics. We strictly ordain that if any such person, after he has been designated as excommunicated, refuses to render satisfaction within a year, then by the law itself he shall be branded as infamous and not be admitted to public offices or councils or to elect others to the same or to give testimony. He shall be intestable, that is he shall not have the freedom to make a will, nor shall he succeed to an inheritance. Moreover nobody shall be compelled to answer to him on any business whatever, but he may be compelled to answer to them. If he is a judge, sentences pronounced by him shall have no force and cases may not be brought before him; if an advocate, he may not be allowed to defend anyone; if a notary, documents drawn up by him shall be worthless and condemned along with their condemned author; and in similar matters we order the same to be observed. If however he is a cleric, let him be deposed from every office and benefice, so that the greater the fault the greater be the punishment. If any refuse to avoid such persons after they have been pointed out by the church, let them be punished with the sentence of excommunication until they make suitable satisfaction. Clerics should not, of course, give the sacraments of the church to such pestilent people nor give them a Christian burial nor accept alms or offerings from them; if they do, let them be deprived of their office and not restored to it without a special indult [privilege] of the apostolic see. Similarly with regulars,[1] let them be punished with losing their privileges in the diocese in which they presume to commit such excesses.

There are some who "holding to the form of religion but denying its power"(as the Apostle says),[2] claim for themselves the authority to preach, whereas the same Apostle says, "How shall they preach unless they are sent?"[3] Let therefore all those who have been forbidden or not sent to preach, and yet dare publicly or privately to usurp the office of preaching without having received the authority of the apostolic see or the catholic bishop of the place, be bound with the bond of excommunication and, unless they repent very quickly, be punished by another suitable penalty. We add further that each archbishop or bishop, either in person or through his archdeacon or through suitable honest persons, should visit twice or at least once in the year any parish of his in which heretics are said to live. There he should compel three or more men of good repute, or even if it seems expedient the whole neighborhood, to swear that if anyone knows of heretics there or of any persons who hold secret conventicles or who differ in their life and habits from the normal way of living of the faithful, then he will take care to point them out to the bishop. The bishop himself should summon the accused to his presence, and they should be punished canonically [according to canon law] if they are unable to clear themselves of the charge or if after compurgation[4] they relapse into their former errors of faith. If however any of them with damnable obstinacy refuse to honor an oath and so will not take it, let them by this very fact be regarded as heretics. We therefore will and command and, in virtue of obedience, strictly command that bishops see carefully to the effective execution of these things throughout their dioceses, if they wish to avoid canonical penalties. If any bishop is negligent or remiss in cleansing his diocese of the ferment of heresy, then when this shows itself by unmistakable signs he shall be deposed from his office as bishop and there shall be put in his place a suitable person who both wishes and is able to overthrow the evil of heresy.

4. On the pride of Greeks towards Latins

Although we would wish to cherish and honor the Greeks who in our days are returning to the obedience of the apostolic see, by preserving their customs and rites as much as we can in the Lord, nevertheless we neither want nor ought to defer to them in matters which bring danger to souls and detract from the church's honor. For, after the Greek church together with certain associates and supporters withdrew from the obedience of the apostolic see, the Greeks began to detest the Latins so much that, among other wicked things which they committed out of contempt for them, when Latin priests celebrated on their altars they would not offer sacrifice on them until they had washed them, as if the altars had been defiled thereby. The Greeks even had the temerity to rebaptize those baptized by the Latins; and some, as we are told, still do not fear to do this. Wishing therefore to remove such a great scandal from God's church, we strictly order, on the advice of this sacred council, that henceforth they do not presume to do such things but rather conform themselves like obedient sons to the holy Roman church, their mother, so that there may be "one flock and one shepherd."[5] If anyone however does dare to do such a thing, let him be struck with the sword of excommunication and be deprived of every ecclesiastical office and benefice....

21. On confession being made, and not revealed by the priest, and on communicating at least at Easter

All the faithful of either sex, after they have reached the age of discernment, should individually confess all their sins in a faithful manner to their own priest at least once a year, and let them take care to do what they can to perform the penance imposed on them. Let them reverently receive the sacrament of the Eucharist at least at Easter unless they think, for a good

---

1 I.e., monks.
2 2 Tim 3: 5.
3 Rom. 10: 15.
4 A procedure whereby witnesses swear to the innocence of the accused.
5 John 10: 16.

reason and on the advice of their own priest, that they should abstain from receiving it for a time. Otherwise they shall be barred from entering a church during their lifetime and they shall be denied a Christian burial at death. Let this salutary decree be frequently published in churches, so that nobody may find the pretense of an excuse in the blindness of ignorance. If any persons wish, for good reasons, to confess their sins to another priest let them first ask and obtain the permission of their own priest; for otherwise the other priest will not have the power to absolve or to bind them.[1] The priest shall be discerning and prudent, so that like a skilled doctor he may pour wine and oil[2] over the wounds of the injured one. Let him carefully inquire about the circumstances of both the sinner and the sin, so that he may prudently discern what sort of advice he ought to give and what remedy to apply, using various means to heal the sick person. Let him take the utmost care, however, not to betray the sinner at all by word or sign or in any other way. If the priest needs wise advice, let him seek it cautiously without any mention of the person concerned. For if anyone presumes to reveal a sin disclosed to him in confession, we decree that he is not only to be deposed from his priestly office but also to be confined to a strict monastery to do perpetual penance....

50. *On the restriction of prohibitions to matrimony*

It should not be judged reprehensible if human decrees are sometimes changed according to changing circumstances, especially when urgent necessity or evident advantage demands it, since God himself changed in the New Testament some of the things which he had commanded in the Old Testament. Since the prohibitions against contracting marriage in the second and third degree of affinity, and against uniting the offspring of a second marriage with the kindred of the first husband, often lead to difficulty and sometimes endanger souls, we therefore, in order that when the prohibition ceases the effect may also cease, revoke with the approval of this sacred council the constitutions published on this subject[3] and we

decree, by this present constitution, that henceforth contracting parties connected in these ways may freely be joined together. Moreover the prohibition against marriage shall not in future go beyond the fourth degree of consanguinity and of affinity, since the prohibition cannot now generally be observed to further degrees without grave harm. The number four agrees well with the prohibition concerning bodily union about which the Apostle says, that "the husband does not rule over his body, but the wife does; and the wife does not rule over her body, but the husband does";[4] for there are four humors in the body, which is composed of the four elements. Although the prohibition of marriage is now restricted to the fourth degree, we wish the prohibition to be perpetual, notwithstanding earlier decrees on this subject issued either by others or by us. If any persons dare to marry contrary to this prohibition, they shall not be protected by length of years, since the passage of time does not diminish sin but increases it, and the longer that faults hold the unfortunate soul in bondage the graver they are.

51. *On the punishment of those who contract clandestine marriages*

Since the prohibition against marriage in the three remotest degrees has been revoked, we wish it to be strictly observed in the other degrees. Following in the footsteps of our predecessors, we altogether forbid clandestine marriages and we forbid any priest to presume to be present at such a marriage. Extending the special custom of certain regions to other regions generally, we decree that when marriages are to be contracted they shall be publicly announced in the churches by priests, with a suitable time being fixed beforehand within which whoever wishes and is able to may adduce a lawful impediment. The priests themselves shall also investigate whether there is any impediment. When there appears a credible reason why the marriage should not be contracted, the contract shall be expressly forbidden until there has been established from clear documents what ought to be done in the matter. If any persons presume to enter

---

1 The power to "bind and loose"—that is to impose penance and to absolve—is based on Matt. 16: 19 and 18: 18.
2 See Luke 10: 34.
3 The reference is to decisions of earlier councils.
4 1 Cor. 7: 4.

into clandestine marriages of this kind, or forbidden marriages within a prohibited degree, even if done in ignorance, the offspring of the union shall be deemed illegitimate....

67. On the usury of Jews

The more the Christian religion is restrained from usurious practices, so much the more does the perfidy of the Jews grow in these matters, so that within a short time they are exhausting the resources of Christians. Wishing therefore to see that Christians are not savagely oppressed by Jews in this matter, we ordain by this synodal decree that if Jews in future, on any pretext, extort oppressive and excessive interest from Christians, then they are to be removed from contact with Christians until they have made adequate satisfaction for the immoderate burden. Christians too, if need be, shall be compelled by ecclesiastical censure, without the possibility of an appeal, to abstain from commerce with them. We enjoin upon princes not to be hostile to Christians on this account, but rather to be zealous in restraining Jews from so great oppression. We decree, under the same penalty, that Jews shall be compelled to make satisfaction to churches for tithes and offerings due to the churches, which the churches were accustomed to receive from Christians for houses and other possessions, before they passed by whatever title to the Jews, so that the churches may thus be preserved from loss.

68. That Jews should be distinguished from Christians in their dress

A difference of dress distinguishes Jews or Saracens from Christians in some provinces, but in others a certain confusion has developed so that they are indistinguishable. Whence it sometimes happens that by mistake Christians join with Jewish or Saracen women, and Jews or Saracens with Christian women. In order that the offence of such a damnable mixing may not spread further, under the excuse of a mistake of this kind, we decree that such persons of either sex, in every Christian province and at all times, are to be distinguished in public from other people by the character of their dress—seeing moreover that this was enjoined upon them by Moses himself, as we read.[1] They shall not appear in public at all on the days of lamentation and on passion Sunday; because some of them on such days, as we have heard, do not blush to parade in very ornate dress and are not afraid to mock Christians who are presenting a memorial of the most sacred passion and are displaying signs of grief. What we most strictly forbid, however, is that they dare in any way to break out in derision of the Redeemer. We order secular princes to restrain with condign [appropriate] punishment those who do so presume, lest they dare to blaspheme in any way him who was crucified for us, since we ought not to ignore insults against him who blotted out our wrongdoings.

69. That Jews are not to hold public offices

It would be too absurd for a blasphemer of Christ to exercise power over Christians. We therefore renew in this canon, on account of the boldness of the offenders, what the council of Toledo[2] providently decreed in this matter: we forbid Jews to be appointed to public offices, since under cover of them they are very hostile to Christians. If, however, anyone does commit such an office to them let him, after an admonition, be curbed by the provincial council, which we order to be held annually, by means of an appropriate sanction. Any official so appointed shall be denied commerce with Christians in business and in other matters until he has converted to the use of poor Christians, in accordance with the directions of the diocesan bishop, whatever he has obtained from Christians by reason of his office so acquired, and he shall surrender with shame the office which he irreverently assumed. We extend the same thing to pagans.

70. That converts to the faith among the Jews may not retain their old rite

Certain people who have come voluntarily to the waters of sacred baptism, as we learnt, do not wholly cast off the old person in order to put on the new more perfectly.[3]

---

1 See Lev. 19: 19; Deut. 22: 5 and 22: 11.
2 A reference to the Council of Toledo of 589, canon 14.
3 See Col. 3: 9.

For, in keeping remnants of their former rite, they upset the decorum of the Christian religion by such a mixing. Since it is written, cursed is he who enters the land by two paths,[1] and a garment that is woven from linen and wool together should not be put on,[2] we therefore decree that such people shall be wholly prevented by the prelates of churches from observing their old rite, so that those who freely offered themselves to the Christian religion may be kept to its observance by a salutary and necessary coercion. For it is a lesser evil not to know the Lord's way than to go back on it after having known it.

[71.] Expedition for the recovery of the holy Land
It is our ardent desire to liberate the holy Land from infidel hands. We therefore declare, with the approval of this sacred council and on the advice of prudent men who are fully aware of the circumstances of time and place, that crusaders are to make themselves ready so that all who have arranged to go by sea shall assemble in the kingdom of Sicily on June 1st after next: some as necessary and fitting at Brindisi and others at Messina and places neighboring it on either side, where we too have arranged to be in person at that time, God willing, so that with our advice and help the Christian army may be in good order to set out with divine and apostolic blessing. Those who have decided to go by land should also take care to be ready by the same date. They shall notify us meanwhile so that we may grant them a suitable legate *a latere*[3] for advice and help. Priests and other clerics who will be in the Christian army, both those under authority and prelates, shall diligently devote themselves to prayer and exhortation, teaching the crusaders by word and example to have the fear and love of God always before their eyes, so that they say or do nothing that might offend the divine majesty. If they ever fall into sin, let them quickly rise up again through true penitence. Let them be humble in heart and in body, keeping to moderation both in food and in dress, avoiding altogether dissensions and rivalries, and putting aside entirely any bitterness or envy, so that thus armed with spiritual and material weapons they may the more fearlessly fight against the enemies of the faith, relying not on their own power but rather trusting in the strength of God. We grant to these clerics that they may receive the fruits of their benefices in full for three years, as if they were resident in the churches, and if necessary they may leave them in pledge for the same time.

6.24 Art and architecture as religious devotion: Suger, *On What was Done under his Administration* (1148-1149). Original in Latin.

SUGER (*c.*1080-1151) WAS A CHILD of Saint-Denis; he was given to the monastery as an oblate (offering) when he was ten years old. It was a royal house, the burial place of the Capetian kings, and Suger was involved in politics even before Louis VI (r.1108-1137) came to the throne. Those two men, however, were especially close, evidenced by the admiring biography Suger wrote of Louis, known in English as *The Deeds of Louis the Fat* but originally called simply *The Life of King Louis*. At the same time, Suger was a passionate advocate for his monastery, and when he became abbot there in 1122 he began to raise funds to enlarge the monastery's church, especially the east end—where various chapels and relics could be viewed by the faithful— and the west end, where the faithful could make a grand entrance. Suger's remodeled Saint-Denis was at the cutting edge of religious architecture, making particularly remarkable use of open walls pierced by stained glass. Suger understood the effect not as allowing in natural light but as permitting God's own "enlightenment" to enter the minds of the worshipers. The whole idea was animated by Suger's conviction—shared by his monks—that the saint to whom Saint-Denis was dedicated was none

---

1   See Ecclus. 2: 14 and 3: 28.
2   See Deut. 22: 11.
3   "*A latere*" means "from the side [of the pope]." The pope is here saying that a papal legate is necessary.

other than Dionysius (=Denis) the Areopagite (mentioned in Acts 17: 34) who in turn was thought to have written the mystical works now known to have been composed by an anonymous Syrian (known to historians as Pseudo-Dionysius) *fl. c.500*. Pseudo-Dionysius had written that God was a kind of light, and this tract, available at Suger's monastery, helped inspire him to build a church that would serve as a model of Gothic architecture for centuries to come.

[Source: *Abbot Suger: On the Abbey Church of St.-Denis and its Art Treasures*, ed. and trans. Erwin Panofsky, 2nd ed., Gerda Panofsky-Soergel (Princeton, NJ: Princeton University Press, 1979), pp. 41, 43, 45, 47, 49, 51 (slightly modified).]

I

In the twenty-third year of our administration, when we sat on a certain day in the general chapter, conferring with our brethren about matters both common and private, these very beloved brethren and sons began strenuously to beseech me *in charity*[1] that I might not allow the fruits of our so great labors to be passed over in silence; and rather to save for the memory of posterity, in pen and ink, those increments which the generous munificence of Almighty God had bestowed upon this church, in the time of our prelacy, in the acquisition of new assets as well as in the recovery of lost ones, in the multiplication of improved possessions, in the construction of buildings, and in the accumulation of gold, silver, most precious gems, and very good textiles. For this one thing they promised us two in return: by such a record we would deserve the continual fervor of all succeeding brethren in their prayers for the salvation of our soul; and we would rouse, through this example, their zealous solicitude for the good care of the church of God. We thus devoutly complied with their devoted and reasonable requests, not with any desire for empty glory nor with any claim to the reward of human praise and transitory compensation; and lest, after our demise, the church be diminished in its revenue by any or anyone's roguery and the ample increments which the generous munificence of God has bestowed in the time of our administration be tacitly lost under bad successors, we have deemed it worthy and useful, just as we thought fitting to begin, in its proper place, our tale about the construction of the buildings and the increase of the treasures with the body of the church of

the most blessed Martyrs Denis, Rusticus, and Eleutherius (which [church] has most tenderly fostered us from mother's milk to old age),[2] so to inform present and future readers about the increase of the revenue [by starting] from his own little town, that is to say, his first resting-place, and its vicinity on all sides....

XXIV: *Of the Church's Decoration*

Having assigned these increases of the revenue in this manner, we turned our hand to the memorable construction of buildings, so that by this thanks might be given to Almighty God by us as well as by our successors; and that by good example their ardor might be roused to the continuation and, if necessary, to the completion of this [work]. For neither any want nor any hindrance by any power will have to be feared if, for the love of the Holy Martyrs, one takes safely care of oneself by one's own resources. The first work on this church which we began under the inspiration of God [was this]: because of the age of the old walls and their impending ruin in some places, we summoned the best painters I could find from different regions, and reverently caused these [walls] to be repaired and becomingly painted with gold and precious colors. I completed this all the more gladly because I had wished to do it, if ever I should have an opportunity, even while I was a pupil in school.

XXV: *Of the First Addition to the Church*

However, even while this was being completed at great expense, I found myself, under the inspiration of the Divine Will and because of that inadequacy which

---

1 See, e.g., 1 Cor. 4: 21.
2 The church of Saint-Denis, where Suger had been raised from boyhood and was now abbot, was dedicated to Saints Denis, Rusticus, and Eleutherius.

we often saw and felt on feast days, namely the Feast of the blessed Denis, the Fair,[1] and very many others (for the narrowness of the place forced the women to run toward the altar upon the heads of the men as upon a pavement with much anguish and noisy confusion), encouraged by the counsel of wise men and by the prayers of many monks (lest it displease God and the Holy Martyrs) to enlarge and amplify the noble church consecrated by the Hand Divine; and I set out at once to begin this very thing. In our chapter as well as in church I implored Divine mercy that He Who is the One, *the beginning and the ending, Alpha and Omega,*[2] might join a good end to a good beginning by a safe middle; that He might not repel from the building of the temple a *bloody man*[3] who desired this very thing, with his whole heart, more than to obtain the treasures of Constantinople. Thus we began work at the former entrance with the doors. We tore down a certain addition asserted to have been made by Charlemagne on a very honorable occasion (for his father, the Emperor Pepin, had commanded that he be buried, for the sins of his father Charles Martel, outside at the entrance with the doors, face downward and not recumbent); and we set our hand to this part. As is evident we exerted ourselves incessantly with the enlargement of the body of the church as well as with the trebling of the entrance and the doors, and with the erection of high and noble towers.

XXVI: *Of the Dedication*

We brought about that the chapel of St. Romanus be dedicated to the service of God and His Holy Angels by the venerable man Archbishop Hugues of Rouen and very many other bishops. How secluded this place is, how hallowed, how convenient for those celebrating the divine rites has come to be known to those who serve God there as though they were already dwelling, in a degree, in Heaven while they sacrifice. At the same solemn dedication ceremony, there were dedicated in the lower nave of the church two chapels, one on either side (on one side that of St. Hippolytus and his Companions, and on the other that of St. Nicholas), by the venerable men Manasseh, Bishop of Meaux, and Peter, Bishop of Senlis. The one glorious procession of these three men went out through the doorway of St. Eustace; it passed in front of the principal doors with a huge throng of chanting clergy and exulting people, the bishops walking in front and performing the holy consecration; and, thirdly, they reentered through the single door of the cemetery which had been transferred from the old building to the new. When this festive work had been completed in the honor of Almighty God, and when we were girding ourselves to officiate in the upper part, [the visiting bishops] invigorated us, as we were a little tired, and most graciously exhorted us not to be discouraged by the fear of labor or of any want.

XXVII: *Of the Cast and Gilded Doors*

Bronze casters having been summoned and sculptors chosen, we set up the main doors on which are represented the Passion of the Savior and His Resurrection, or rather Ascension, with great cost and much expenditure for their gilding as was fitting for the noble porch. Also [we set up] others, new ones on the right side and the old ones on the left beneath the mosaic which, though contrary to modern custom, we ordered to be executed there and to be affixed to the tympanum of the portal. We also committed ourselves richly to elaborate the tower[s] and the upper crenelations of the front, both for the beauty of the church and, should circumstances require it, for practical purposes. Further we ordered the year of the consecration, lest it be forgotten, to be inscribed in copper-gilt letters in the following manner:

For the splendor of the church that has fostered and
    exalted him,
Suger has labored for the splendor of the church.
Giving thee a share of what is thine, O Martyr Denis,
He prays to thee to pray that he may obtain a share of
    Paradise.
The year was the One Thousand, One Hundred, and
    Fortieth
Year of the Word when [this structure] was
    consecrated.

---

1 The fairs of Saint-Denis were celebrated events drawing even long-distance merchants.
2 Rev. 21: 6.
3 2 Kings 16: 7.

The verses on the door, further, are these:

Whoever thou art, if thou seekest to extol the glory
  of these doors,
Marvel not at the gold and the expense but at the
  craftsmanship of the work.
Bright is the noble work; but, being nobly bright, the
  work
Should brighten the minds, so that they may travel,
  through the true lights,
To the True Light where Christ is the true door.
In what manner it be inherent in this world the
  golden door defines:
The dull mind rises to truth through that which is
  material
And, in seeing this light, is resurrected from its
  former submersion.

And on the lintel:

Receive, O stern Judge, the prayers of Thy Suger;
Grant that I be mercifully numbered among Thy
  own sheep.

XXVIII: *Of the Enlargement of the Upper Choir*

In the same year, cheered by so holy and so auspicious
a work, we hurried to begin the chamber of divine
atonement in the upper choir where the continual and
frequent Victim of our redemption should be sacrificed in secret without disturbance by the crowds.
And, as is found in [our] treatise about the consecration of this upper structure, we were mercifully
deemed worthy—God helping and prospering us and
our concerns—to bring so holy, so glorious, and so
famous a structure to a good end, together with our
brethren and fellow servants; we felt all the more indebted to God and the Holy Martyrs as He, by so long
a postponement, had reserved what had to be done
for our lifetime and labors. *For who am I, or what is my
father's house,*[1] that I should have presumed to begin so
noble and pleasing an edifice, or should have hoped
to finish it, had I not, relying upon the help of Divine mercy and the Holy Martyrs, devoted my whole
self, both with mind and body, to this very task? But

He Who gave the will also gave the power; because
the good work was in the will therefore it stood in
perfection by the help of God. How much the Hand
Divine Which operates in such matters has protected
this glorious work is also surely proven by the fact
that It allowed that whole magnificent building [to
be completed] in three years and three months, from
the crypt below to the summit of the vaults above,
elaborated with the variety of so many arches and columns, including even the consummation of the roof.
Therefore the inscription of the earlier consecration
also defines, with only one word eliminated, the year
of completion of this one, thus:

The year was the One Thousand, One Hundred,
  Forty and
Fourth of the Word when [this structure] was
  consecrated.

To these verses of the inscription we choose the following ones to be added:

Once the new rear part is joined to the part in front,
The church shines with its middle part brightened.
For bright is that which is brightly coupled with the
  bright,
And bright is the noble edifice which is pervaded by
  the new light;
Which stands enlarged in our time,
I, who was Suger, being the leader while it was being
  accomplished.

  Eager to press on my success, since I wished nothing more under heaven than to seek the honor of my
mother church which with maternal affection had
suckled me as a child, had held me upright as a stum-
bling youth, had mightily strengthened me as a mature man, and had solemnly *set me among the princes*[2]
of the Church and the realm, we devoted ourselves
to the completion of the work and strove to raise and
to enlarge the transept wings of the church [so as to
correspond] to the form of the earlier and later work
that had to be joined [by them].

---

1 See 1 Kings 18: 18.
2 See 1 Kings 2: 8.

6.25 Devotion through poverty: *Peter Waldo in the Chronicle of Laon* (1173-1178). Original in Latin.

PETER WALDO (d. bef. 1218), A WEALTHY merchant at Lyon, was inspired, like many people of his time, by the *Acts of the Apostles*. Some time in the 1170s, he rid himself of his material possessions and began to preach to his neighbors "to place your hopes in God and not in wealth." He and his followers (called the Poor, or the Poor Men) were initially embraced by the papacy but forbidden to preach. However, they continued to preach and were declared heretics in 1184. Their continued association with heresy may be seen in Jacques Fournier's *Episcopal Register*, p. 435 below. In the account printed here, written by an anonymous chronicler who was not entirely hostile to the movement, Peter is called Valdès, the original form of his name.

[Source: *The Birth of Popular Heresy*, ed. and trans. R.I. Moore (New York: St. Martin's Press, 1975), pp. 111-13 (slightly modified).]

At about this time, in 1173, there was a citizen of Lyons named Valdès, who had made a great deal of money by the evil means of usury. One Sunday he lingered by a crowd that had gathered round a *jongleur*,[1] and was much struck by his words. He took him home with him, and listened carefully to his story of how St. Alexis had died a holy death in his father's house. Next morning Valdès hastened to the schools of theology to seek advice about his soul. When he had been told of the many ways of coming to God he asked the master whether any of them was more sure and reliable than the rest. The master quoted to him the words of the Lord, "If thou wilt be perfect go sell what thou hast and give to the poor and thou shalt have treasure in heaven. And come follow me."[2]

Valdès returned to his wife and gave her the choice between having all his movable wealth or his property in land and water, woods, meadows, fields, houses, rents, vineyards, mills and ovens. She was very upset at having to do this and chose the property. From his movable wealth he returned what he had acquired wrongly, conferred a large portion on his two daughters, whom he placed in the order of Fontevrault[3] without his wife's knowledge, and gave a still larger amount to the poor. At this time a terrible famine was raging through Gaul and Germany. For three days a week, from Whitsun to St Peter-in-chains [May 27–August 1] Valdès generously distributed bread, soup and meat to anyone who came to him. On the Assumption of the Virgin [August 15] he scattered money among the poor in the streets saying, "You cannot serve two masters, God and Mammon."[4] The people around thought that he had gone out of his senses. Then he stood up on a piece of high ground and said, "Friends and fellow-citizens, I am not out of my mind, as you think. I have avenged myself on the enemies who enslaved me when I cared more for money than for God and served the creature more faithfully than the creator. I know that many of you disapprove of my having acted so publicly. I have done so both for my own sake and for yours: for my sake, because anybody who sees me with money in future will be able to say that I am crazy; for your sake, so that you may learn to place your hopes in God and not in wealth."

Next day as he was coming out of church Valdès begged a certain citizen, formerly a friend of his, for God's sake to give him something to eat. The man took him home, and said, "As long as I live I will provide you with the necessities of life." When his wife heard this story she was very upset, and rushed dis-

---

1 A *jongleur* was an entertainer.
2 Matt. 19: 21.
3 Fontevrault was a monastery founded by Robert of Arbrissel (*c*.1045-1116). It consisted of two houses, one for men and the other for women, both of which were presided over by the same female prioress.
4 Matt. 6: 24; Luke 16: 13.

traught to complain to the archbishop that Valdès had begged his bread from someone other than herself. This moved everybody who was with the archbishop to tears. The archbishop requested the citizen to bring his guest before him. The wife seized her husband by his tattered clothes, and said, "Is it not better, my man, for me to redeem my sins by giving you alms than a stranger?" After this, by the archbishop's command, he was not allowed to accept alms from anybody in the city except his wife.

1177 Valdès, the citizen of Lyon whom we have already mentioned, who had vowed to God that he would possess neither gold nor silver, and take no thought for the morrow, began to make converts to his opinions. Following his example they gave all they had to the poor and willingly devoted themselves to poverty. Gradually, both in public and in private, they began to inveigh against both their own sins and those of others.

1178 Pope Alexander III[1] held a council at the Lateran palace.... The council condemned heresy and all those who fostered and defended heretics. The pope embraced Valdès, and applauded the vows of voluntary poverty which he had taken, but forbade him and his companions to assume the office of preaching except at the request of the priests. They obeyed this instruction for a time, but later they disobeyed, and affronted many, bringing ruin on themselves.

6.26 Devotion through mysticism: Jacques de Vitry, *The Life of Mary of Oignies* (1213). Original in Latin.

JACQUES DE VITRY (d.1240) LEARNED about Mary of Oignies while he was a regular canon (much like a monk but living according to the Rule of St. Augustine rather than Benedict) at Oignies, today in the north of France. Mary (1177-1213) led a nearby house of Beguines—a community in which women took no formal vows but nevertheless dedicated themselves to lives of piety. Jacques's support for the Beguines helped legitimize them: his biography made Mary into a kind of saint, while his direct appeal to the papacy in 1216 resulted in the Beguines' official recognition. Although they spent their days at simple tasks—caring for the sick, spinning, weaving—Beguines like Mary lived passionate lives, weeping cascades of tears as they contemplated the Lord. Comparing this account of a female saint with the early seventh-century lives of St. Radegund (above, pp. 47-57), how might you characterize the transformations that occurred in medieval conceptions of female piety?

[Source: *Medieval Women's Visionary Literature*, ed. Elizabeth Alvilda Petroff, trans. Margot King (New York: Oxford University Press, 1986), pp. 179-81 (a few notes added).]

BOOK I, Chapter 16
The beginning of her conversion to you, O Lord, the first fruits of her love, was your Cross and Passion. She heard you hearing and was afraid,[2] she considered your works and feared. One day when she was reflecting on the blessings you had sent and visited upon her and which you had graciously shown forth in the flesh to mankind, and while she was considering your torment upon the Cross, she found such grace of compunction and wept so abundantly that the tears which flowed so copiously from her eyes fell on the floor of the church and plainly showed where she had been walking. For a long time after this visitation, she could not look at an image of the Cross, nor could she speak of the

---

1 Alexander III was pope 1159 to 1181.
2 Hab. 3: 2.

Passion of Christ, nor hear other people speaking of it without falling into ecstasy by reason of her enfeebled heart. She therefore would sometimes moderate her sorrow and restrain the flood of her tears and, leaving behind His humanity, would raise her mind so that she might find some consolation in His unchangeableness. The more, however, she tried to restrain the vehemence of the flood, the more wondrously did her ardor increase it. When she considered how great was He who had allowed Himself to be so humiliated for us her sorrow was redoubled and her soul renewed with sweet compunction and fresh tears.

Chapter 17

Once, just before Holy Thursday when the Passion of Christ was approaching, she began to offer herself up as a sacrifice to the Lord with an even greater flood of tears, sighs, and sobs. One of the priests of the church exhorted her with honey-tongued rebukes to pray in silence and to restrain her tears. Although she had always been bashful and would, with dove-like simplicity, make an effort to obey in all things, yet she knew that she could not restrain these tears. She therefore slipped quietly out of the church and hid herself in a secret place far from everyone, and she tearfully begged the Lord that he show this priest that it is not in man to restrain the impulse of tears when the waters flow with the vehemence of the blowing wind.[1]

On that very day while the priest was celebrating Mass, it happened that "the Lord opened and none shut"[2] and "He sent forth waters and they overturned the earth."[3] His spirit was drowned with such a flood of tears that he almost suffocated. The harder he tried to restrain this force, the more drenched he became and the more soaked did the book and the altar become. What could he do, he who had been so lacking in foresight, he who had rebuked the handmaid of Christ? With shame and through personal experience he was taught what he previously had not learned through humility and compassion. Sobbing frequently and with disordered and broken speech,

he barely avoided total collapse, which one of his acquaintances has testified. After Mass was finished, the handmaid of Christ returned to the church and told the priest everything that had happened, as if she herself had been present. "Now," she said, "you have learned through personal experience that man cannot restrain the impulse of the spirit 'when the south wind blows.'"[4]

Chapter 18

When a constant outburst of tears gushed forth from her eyes both day and night and ran down her cheeks and made the church floor all muddy, she would catch the tears in the linen cloth with which she covered her head. She went through many veils in this way since she had to change them frequently and put a dry one on in place of the wet one she had discarded.

In my love for her I suffered with her in her long fasts and frequent vigils and while she was enduring many such deluges of tears. I therefore asked her whether she felt any pain or discomfort as one is accustomed to experience in such a state of exhaustion. "These tears," she said, "are my refreshment. Night and day they are my bread. They do not impair my head but rather feed my mind. They do not torment me with pain but, on the contrary, they rejoice my soul with a kind of serenity. They do not empty the brain but fill the soul to satiety and soften it with a sweet anointing. They are not violently wrenched out but are freely given by the Lord."

Chapter 22

Having once tasted the spirit, she held as nothing all sensual delights until one day she remembered the time when she had been gravely ill and had been forced, from necessity, to eat meat and drink a little wine for a short time. From the horror she felt at her previous carnal pleasure, she began to afflict herself and she found no rest in spirit until, by means of extraordinary bodily chastisements, she had made up for all the pleasures she had experienced in the past. In vehemence of spirit, almost as if she were inebriated,

---

1   See Ps. 147: 18 and Exod. 14: 21.
2   Isa. 22: 22.
3   Job 12: 15.
4   See Acts 28: 13.

she began to loathe her body when she compared it to the sweetness of the Paschal Lamb[1] and, with a knife, in error cut out a large piece of her flesh which, from embarrassment, she buried in the earth. Inflamed as she was, however, by the intense fire of love, she did not feel the pain of her wound and, in ecstasy of mind, she saw one of the seraphim standing close by her. Much later when women were washing her corpse, they were amazed when they found the places of the wounds but those to whom she had made her confession knew what they were. Why do those who marvel at the worms which swarmed from the wounds of Simeon [Stylites] and are awe-struck at the fire with which Antony burnt his feet[2] not wonder at such strength in the frail sex of a woman who, wounded by charity and invigorated by the wounds of Christ, neglected the wounds of her own body?

Chapter 38

The prudent woman knew that after the sin of the first parents, the Lord enjoined penance through them to their sons, that is to say "you will earn your bread by the sweat of your brow."[3] This is the reason why she worked with her own hands as often as she could. In this way she mortified her body with penance, furnished the necessities of life to the poor, and acquired food and clothing for herself—that is, all the things she had given up for Christ. The Lord bestowed on her such strength in labor that she far exceeded her companions and was able to obtain for herself and for one companion the fruit of her hands and she gave heed to the words of the Apostle "Whoever will not work, will not eat."[4] She considered all exertion and labor sweet when she considered that the only begotten Son of the High King of heaven "who opens his hand and fills with blessing every living creature,"[5]

was nourished by Joseph's manual labor and by the work of the poor little Virgin. In quiet and silence she followed the injunction of the Apostle and by the labor of her hands she ate her bread, for her strength was in silence and hope. She so loved quiet and silence that she fled noisy crowds and once barely said a word from the Feast of the Holy Cross[6] until Easter. The Holy Spirit revealed to her that the Lord had accepted this silence and that especially because of it she had obtained from the Lord that she would fly up to heaven without going to Purgatory.[7]

BOOK II, Chapter 72

It frequently occurred that when the priest raised the Host, she saw between his hands the corporeal form of a beautiful boy and an army of the heavenly host descending with a great light. When the priest received the Host after the general confession, she saw in the spirit the Lord remain in the soul of the priest illuminating him with a wondrous brightness. If, on the other hand, he received it unworthily, she saw the Lord withdraw with displeasure and the soul of the wretched man would remain empty and dark. Even when she was not present in the church but remained in her cell, she prayed with her eyes covered with a white veil, as was her habit, and when Christ descended to the altar at the utterance of the sacred words, then, wondrously transformed, she felt His coming. If she was present at the reception of the sacrament of Extreme Unction by invalids,[8] she felt the presence of Christ when, with a multitude of saints, He tenderly strengthened the sick person, expelled demons, and purged the soul and, as it were, transfused Himself in light throughout the whole body of the invalid while the different limbs were being anointed.

---

1 The Pascal Lamb, that is, the sacrificial lamb of the Jewish Passover, was understood to be a prefiguration of Christ.
2 A reference to the temptations of Antony, as depicted in *The Life of Antony*, above, p. 36. Simeon Stylites was another saint whose ascetic practices—particularly his long endurance on a pillar—were well known.
3 Gen. 3: 19.
4 2 Thess. 3: 10.
5 Ps. 145: 16; Douay Ps. 144: 16.
6 Celebrated on September 14.
7 The doctrine of Purgatory, which was becoming increasingly important and precise in the thirteenth century, held that souls had to endure a period of purification in a place—Purgatory—for their venial (minor, forgivable) sins before they might enter heaven.
8 Extreme Unction is the sacrament of anointing the sick and the dying.

Chapter 88

Sometimes it seemed to her that for three or more days she held Him close to her so that He nestled between her breasts like a baby, and she hid Him there lest He be seen by others. Sometimes she kissed him as though He were a little child and sometimes she held Him on her lap as if He were a gentle lamb. At other times the Holy Son of the Virgin manifested Himself in the form of a dove for the consolation of His daughter or He would walk around the church as if He were a ram with a bright star in the middle of his forehead and, as it seemed to her, He would visit His faithful ones.

6.27 The mendicant movement: St. Francis, *The Canticle to Brother Sun* (1225). Original in Umbrian dialect.

SAINT FRANCIS (*c.*1182-1226) HAD AN EXTRAORDINARY impact on late medieval religious life. Born into a wealthy merchant family in Assisi, Francis, like Peter Waldo, had a conversion experience in his mid-twenties that led him to strip himself of all belongings and take up the lifestyle of a poor person—a mendicant—who preached and begged for his daily bread and lodging. The effect in the cities of Italy was electric: Francis gained numerous followers (called "friars" from the Latin term for brothers). Women too were drawn to his example, among them Clare, who formed the Order of the Sisters of Saint Francis. Francis, who wrote the poem printed here in his native dialect, loved simple language and poetry. In this *Canticle* he praised all of God's creation as part of his family. According to one of Francis's biographers, the verse beginning "Praised be You, my Lord, through those who give pardon for Your love," was written in order to reconcile disputants at Assisi (it was successful!); while the verse "Praised be You, my Lord, through our Sister Bodily Death," was sung by Francis himself on his deathbed. How might you compare the sensibilities of Peter Waldo, Mary of Oignies, and Francis to arrive at a composite picture of the idea of "following Christ" at the turn of the thirteenth century?

[Source: *Francis and Clare: The Complete Works*, trans. Regis J. Armstrong and Ignatius C. Brady (New York: Paulist Press, 1982), pp. 38-39 (notes modified).]

1. Most High, all-powerful, good Lord,
   Yours are the praises, the glory, the honor, and all blessing.[1]
2. To You alone, Most High, do they belong,
   and no man is worthy to mention Your name.
3. Praised be You, my Lord, with all your creatures,
   especially Sir Brother Sun,
   Who is the day and through whom You give us light.
4. And he is beautiful and radiant with great splendor;
   and bears a likeness of You, Most High One.
5. Praised be You, my Lord, through Sister Moon and the stars,
   in heaven You formed them clear and precious and beautiful.
6. Praised be You, my Lord, through Brother Wind,
   and through the air, cloudy and serene, and every kind of weather
   through which You give sustenance to Your creatures.
7. Praised be You, my Lord, through Sister Water,
   which is very useful and humble and precious and chaste.
8. Praised be You, my Lord, through Brother Fire,
   through whom You light the night
   and he is beautiful and playful and robust and strong.

---

1 See Rev. 4: 9, 11.

9. Praised be You, my Lord, through our Sister Mother Earth,
who sustains and governs us,
and who produces varied fruits with colored flowers and herbs.

10. Praised be You, my Lord, through those who give pardon for Your love
and bear infirmity and tribulation.[1]

11. Blessed are those who endure in peace
for by You, Most High, they shall be crowned.

12. Praised be You, my Lord, through our Sister Bodily Death,
from whom no living man can escape.

13. Woe to those who die in mortal sin.
Blessed are those whom death will find in Your most holy will,
for the second death shall do them no harm.[2]

14. Praise and bless my Lord and give Him thanks
and serve Him with great humility.

---

1 Here Francis evokes Jesus, who bore "infirmity and tribulation."
2 See Rev. 2: 11 and 20: 6.

6.28 The expulsion of the Jews from Bury St. Edmunds: Jocelin of Brakelond, *Chronicle* (1190-1202). Original in Latin.

IN THE COURSE OF his life as monk at the monastery of Bury St. Edmunds in England, Jocelin (*fl.* late 12th c.) wrote a *Chronicle* of the things he had "seen and heard." It was a lively record of the doings of the abbots, especially Abbot Samson (d.1211), the pursuits of the monastery, and the activities of the town of Bury St. Edmunds, which belonged to the monastery. In the course of praising Samson, Jocelin brought up quite casually three good things that the abbot had done for the monastery: he had gained the manor of Mildenhall at a very cheap price, he had founded a new hospital, and he had expelled all the Jews from the town. Taking this account together with the *Laws of Cuenca*, p. 354 above, and the *Decrees of Lateran IV*, p. 395 above, how might you describe the spectrum of attitudes and policies toward the Jews in the thirteenth century?

[Source: *The Chronicle of Jocelin of Brakelond concerning the Acts of Samson, Abbot of the Monastery of St. Edmund*, trans. H.E. Butler (London: Thomas Nelson and Sons, 1949), pp. 45-46 (slightly modified).]

The recovery of the manor of Mildenhall for eleven hundred paltry marks of silver, and the expulsion of the Jews from the town of St. Edmund, and the foundation of the new hospital of Babwell are all proofs of the Abbot's excellence.

The lord Abbot petitioned the King that he might have letters for the expulsion of the Jews from the town of St. Edmund, alleging that everything that is in the town of St. Edmund or within its liberties belongs of right to St. Edmund: therefore the Jews must either be St. Edmund's men or be expelled from the town. Leave was therefore given him to expel them, but on this condition, that they should keep all their chattels [movable property] and have the value of their houses and lands as well. And when they had been sent forth and conducted under armed escort to other towns, the Abbot ordered that all those who from that time forth should receive Jews or harbor them in the town of St. Edmund should be solemnly excommunicated in every church and at every altar. Nevertheless afterwards the King's justices ordained that, if Jews came to the Abbot's great pleas[1] to exact the money owed them from their debtors, they should under those circumstances have leave to be lodged in the town for two nights and two days, and on the third day should depart in freedom.

---

1 The great pleas were held at the central court of St. Edmund's jurisdiction, at Cateshill, which was about 2 miles east of Bury. The abbot himself presided in place of the sheriff.

6.29 Burning heretics in Germany: *Chronicle of Trier* (1231). Original in Latin.

BEGINNING IN THE TWELFTH century, the monks of the monastery of St. Matthias, just outside Trier, began keeping a *Gesta* or *Chronicle* of their city and its saints and religious institutions. For the year 1231 they recorded the burning of heretics "throughout the whole of Germany."

[Source: *Heresies of the High Middle Ages*, ed. and trans. Walter L. Wakefield and Austin P. Evans (New York: Columbia University Press, 1969), pp. 267-69 (slightly modified).]

In the year of our Lord 1231 began a persecution of heretics throughout the whole of Germany, and over a period of three years many were burned. The guiding genius of this persecution was Master Conrad of Marburg;[1] his agents were a certain Conrad, surnamed Tors, and John, who had lost an eye and a hand. Both of these were said to have been converted heretics.[2] It is this Master Conrad who, renowned for active preaching, especially in behalf of the crusades, had built up a great following among the people; who interfered in the visitation of clergy and nuns and sought to constrain them to strict observance and continence;[3] and who, supported by apostolic authority and endowed with firmness of purpose, became so bold that he feared no one—not even a king or a bishop, who rated no higher with him than a poor layman. Throughout various cities the Preaching Friars [Dominicans] cooperated with him and with his afore-mentioned lieutenants; so great was the zeal of all that from no one, even though merely under suspicion, would any excuse or counterplea be accepted, no exception or testimony be admitted, no opportunity for defense be afforded, nor even a recess for deliberation be allowed. Forthwith, he must confess himself guilty and have his head shaved as a sign of penance, or deny his crime and be burned.

Furthermore, one who has thus been shaved must make known his associates, otherwise he again risks the penalty of death by burning. Whence it is thought that some innocents have been burned, for many, because of love of earthly existence or out of affection for their heirs, confessed themselves to have been what they were not and, constrained to make accusation, brought charges of which they were ignorant against those to whom they wished ill. Indeed, it was finally discovered that heretics instigated some of their number to permit themselves to be shaved in penance and thus to accuse Catholics and the innocent. Of such three were taken at Mainz; thereafter there was no one so pure of conscience as not to fear meeting a calamity of this sort. For no one dared, I will not say to intercede for the accused, but even to make the mildest observation in their behalf, for he would immediately be considered a defender of heretics. And, indeed, in accordance with the decision pronounced by the lord pope,[4] he [Conrad] proceeded against defenders and receivers of heretics exactly as against heretics themselves. Furthermore, if anyone had once abjured this impiety and was reported to have relapsed, he was apprehended and without any reconsideration was burned.

Nor was the diocese of Trier free from this infection. For in the city of Trier itself three groups of heretics were uncovered. There was burned a certain Leuchard, who was reputed to have been of a most saintly life, but who bewailed with dreadful laments the unjust banishment from heaven of Lucifer, whom she wished again restored to heaven. Nor was it surprising that such occurrences happened in other cities, since in Rome itself, according to a letter from the pope, not a few had been thus infected. There were a large number in this sect. Many of them were versed in the Holy Scriptures,

---

1   Conrad of Marburg (d.1233) was a papal inquisitor in Germany.
2   Conrad Tors was a Dominican; John a layman.
3   I.e., self-control; discipline.
4   Gregory IX (r.1227-1241).

which they had in German translation. Some, indeed, performed a second baptism; some did not believe in the sacrament of the Lord's body; some held that the body of the Lord could not be consecrated by evil priests; some said that the body of the Lord could be consecrated with salver and chalice in any place whatsoever, equally well by a man or a woman, whether ordained or not; some judged confirmation and extreme unction to be superfluous; some scorned the supreme pontiff, the clergy, and the monastic life; some denied the value of prayers of the Church for the souls of the dead; some took their own mothers in marriage, making amends for the consanguinity that existed by the payment of eighteen pence; some kissed a pallid man or even a cat, and performed still worse acts; some, believing all days to be the same, refused to keep holidays or fasts, and thus worked on feast days and ate meat on Good Friday. Let this suffice as a catalogue of their errors, not that we have listed them all but only noted the most outstanding.

At that time the archbishop of Trier convened a synod in which he publicly announced that the heretics in his diocese had a bishop, to whom they had given his own name, Theodoric, and that others did the same elsewhere after the bishops of other places; and he also announced that they shared in common a pope, whom they called Gregory after the bishop of the Church Universal, so that, should they be questioned about the faith, they could say that they had the same faith as did Pope Gregory and bishop so-and-so (giving the name of the bishop), naming our bishop and meaning theirs.

Three heretics were cited before this synod, of whom two were released and one burned.

TIMELINE FOR CHAPTER SIX

12th c. *Digenis Akritis*

12th c. Bertran de Born, *I Love the Joyful Time*

1125-50 Jaufré Rudel, *When Days are Long*

1148-9 Suger, *On What was Done*

1150

1157 *Diet of Besançon*

1158-63 *Anstey's Law Suit*

1164 *Constitutions of Clarendon*   1166 *Assize of Clarendon*

1167-8 Helmold, *Chronicle of the Slavs*

1173-8 *Chronicle of Laon*

1180-1223 *Raoul de Cambrai*

1189-93 *Laws of Cuenca*   1190-1202 Jocelin of Brakelond, *Chronicle*

1198-1216 Ibn Shaddad, *History of Saladin*   1200 Comtessa de Dia, *I've been in Great Anguish*

1200 *Gospel according to the Marks of Silver*   1200

1200-2 Innocent III, *Letters*   13th c. *Parisian Silk Guild Regulations*

13th c. *Browny* and *The Priest Who Peeked*

1213 Jacques de Vitry, *Life of Mary of Oignies*

1215 Choniates, *O City of Byzantium*

1215 *Lateran IV*   1215 *Magna Carta*

1225 St. Francis, *Canticle to Brother Sun*

1231 *Chronicle of Trier*

1236 *Shearers' Guild Regulations*

1246 *Bec Manorial Proceedings*

1250

1253 A Genoese *societas*

1281 *Register of Thomas of Hereford*

1300

SEVEN

DISCORDANT HARMONIES (*c.*1250-*c.*1350)

THE MONGOLS

7.1 The Mongols speak: *The Secret History of the Mongols* (first half of the 13th c.). Original in Mongolian.

ALTHOUGH NOT, STRICTLY SPEAKING, "secret," the text known by that name was probably written for an exclusive group among the Mongols, perhaps limited to the royal family of the Khans itself. Celebrating the rise to power of Chingis Khan (r.1206-1227)[1] and his son Ogodei (r.1227-1241), the *Secret History* begins with the origins of the Mongols and their warlike relations with other clans and tribes, such as the Tatars. It continues (in the excerpt below) with the clan leader Temujin's election as Khan and his new identity as Chingis Khan. As the Mongols absorb the Tatars and other groups, according to the *Secret History*, they become the supreme military power of the region. In subsequent sections of the *Secret History*, Chingis's hegemony widens as he takes over all of Central Asia; soon his son Ogodei moves into southern Russia, the Middle East, and Eastern Europe.

[Source: *The Secret History of the Mongols: The Origin of Chinghis Khan*, trans. Francis Woodman Cleaves, adapted by Paul Kahn (San Francisco: North Point Press, 1984), pp. 48-51, 71-74.]

Then they moved the whole camp
to the shores of Blue Lake in the Gurelgu Mountains.
Altan, Khuchar, and Sacha Beki conferred with each
   other there,
and then said to Temujin:
"We want you to be khan.
Temujin, if you'll be our khan
we'll search through the spoils

for the beautiful women and virgins,
for the great palace tents,
for the young virgins and loveliest women,
for the finest geldings and mares.
We'll gather all these and bring them to you.
When we go off to hunt for wild game
we'll go out first to drive them together for you to
   kill.

---

1 In older books he is Ghengis Khan.

We'll drive the wild animals of the steppe together
so that their bellies are touching.
We'll drive the wild game of the mountains together
so that they stand leg to leg.
If we disobey your command during battle
take away our possessions, our children, and wives.
Leave us behind in the dust,
cutting off our heads where we stand and letting
    them fall to the ground.
If we disobey your counsel in peacetime
take away our tents and our goods, our wives, and
    our children.
Leave us behind when you move,
abandoned in the desert without a protector."
Having given their word,
having taken this oath,
they proclaimed Temujin khan of the Mongol
and gave him the name Chingis Khan.

Once Chingis had been elected
Ogele Cherbi, Bogorchu's young kinsman,
was named as his archer.
Soyiketu Cherbi promised him:
"I'll see to it
you'll never miss your morning drink,
you'll never miss your evening meal,"
and he became head cook.
Degei promised him:
"I'll see to it
that a lamb is brought in for the morning broth,
that another's brought in for the evening.
I'll herd the speckled sheep
and see that your carts are filled with their wool.
I'll herd the yellow sheep
and see that your flocks are filled with their number,"
and he became head shepherd.
Then his younger brother, Guchugur, promised:
"I'll see to it
that the lynch-pins are always tight on the wheels of
    your carts,
that the axletree doesn't break when the carts are on
    the road.
I'll be in charge of the tent carts."
Dodai Cherbi promised:
"I'll be in charge of the men and women who serve
    in your tents."
Then Chingis appointed three men,

along with his brother Khasar,
to be his personal swordsmen, saying:
"Anyone who thinks they are stronger,
you'll strike off their heads.
Anyone who thinks they're more courageous,
you'll cut them in two.
My brother Belgutei will bring the geldings in from
    the pasture.
He will be in charge of the horses.
Mulkhalkhu will be in charge of the cattle.
Arkhai Khasar, Taghai, Sukegei, and Chakhurkhan,
these four warriors will be like my arrows,
like the arrows I shoot near and far."
Then Subetai the Brave promised him:
"I'll be like a rat and gather up others,
I'll be like a black crow and gather great flocks.
Like the felt blanket that covers a horse,
I'll gather up soldiers to cover you.
Like the felt blanket that guards a tent from the wind,
I'll assemble great armies to shelter your tent."
Then Chingis Khan turned to Bogorchu and Jelme,
    and said:
"You two,
from the time when there was no one to fight beside
    me but my own shadow,
you were my shadow and gave my mind rest.
That will always be in my thoughts.
From the time when there was nothing to whip my
    horses with but their own tails,
you were their tails and gave my heart peace.
That will always be in my heart.
Since you were the first two who came to my side
you'll be chiefs over all the rest of the people."
Then Chingis Khan spoke to the people, saying:
"If Heaven and Earth grant me their protection so
    that my powers increase,
then each of you elders of the clans
who've chosen to leave Anda Jamugha and follow me
will be happy with the choice that you've made.
I'll give you each your position and office." …

At the end of that winter
in the autumn of the Year of the Dog,
Chingis Khan assembled his army at Seventy Felt
    Cloaks
to go to war with the four Tatar clans.
Before the battle began

Chingis Khan spoke with his soldiers and set down
     these rules:
"If we overcome their soldiers
no one will stop to gather their spoils.
When they're beaten and the fighting is over
then there'll be time for that.
We'll divide their possessions equally among us.
If we're forced to retreat by their charge
every man will ride back to the place where we
     started our attack.
Any man who doesn't return to his place for a
     counterattack will be killed."
Chingis Khan met the Tatar at Seventy Felt Cloaks
and made them retreat.
He surrounded them
and drove them back into their camp at Ulkhui
     Shilugeljid.
But as they destroyed the army of the four Tatar clans
Altan, Khuchar and Daritai ignored the orders
     Chingis had set down
and they stopped with their men to gather the spoils.
When Chingis Khan heard this, he said:
"They've broken their word,"
and he sent Jebe and Khubilai to punish them.
They took away from them everything they had
     gathered
and left them with nothing at all.
Having destroyed the Tatar army and taken their
     spoils,
a council was called to decide what to do with the
     captives.
Chingis Khan presided over the great council
in a tent set away from the rest of the camp.
They said to each other:
"Since the old days
the Tatar have fought our fathers and grandfathers.
Now to get our revenge for all the defeats,
to get satisfaction for the deaths of our grandfathers
     and fathers,
we'll kill every Tatar man taller than the linch-pin
     on the wheel of a cart.
We'll kill them until they're destroyed as a tribe.
The rest we'll make into slaves and disperse them
     among us."
That being what they decided to do,
they filed out of the tent.
As they came out the door of the council tent

the Tatar chief, Yeke Cheren, asked Belgutei:
"What have you decided?"
Belgutei told him:
"We've decided to kill every man taller than the
     linch-pin on the wheel of a cart."
Hearing that, Yeke Cheren warned all the Tatar
     survivors
and they threw up a fort to fight us off.
We had to storm this fort
and many of our soldiers were killed.
Then after we'd finally forced the Tatar to surrender
     their fort
and were measuring them against the height of a
     linch-pin and executing them,
they saw there was no way to escape death.
They said to each other:
"Every man place a knife in his sleeve.
When the Mongol come to kill you,
take that man as your pillow."
And we lost many more of our soldiers.
When all of the Tatar men taller than the height of a
     linch-pin were dead,
Chingis Khan made this decree:
"Because Belgutei revealed the decision we'd reached
     in the great council
many of our soldiers have died.
From now on Belgutei won't be allowed to take part
     in such councils.
He'll be in charge outside the council tent until it is
     over.
Let him judge the fights in the camp
and the men accused of lying and theft.
After the council is over and we've all drunk the holy
     wine
only then will Belgutei and Daritai be allowed to
     enter the tent."

From among all the Tatar women
Chingis Khan took Yeke Cheren's daughter, Yesugen
     Khatun,
to be one of his wives.
After she'd become Chingis Khan's wife she said to
     him:
"If the Khan loves me and wants to care for me,
if he thinks I'm good enough to be his wife,
then I have something to ask him.
I have an older sister named Yesui

who is a much better woman than I am
and would make you a much better wife.
But she was married to another man a short time ago
and now since your attack on our camp
who knows where she's gone?"
Hearing this, Chingis Khan said to her:
"If your older sister is such a fine woman then I'll
   find her.
And when I do will you give her your place?"
And Yesugen Khatun answered him:
"If the Khan will search for Yesui,
just for the pleasure of seeing her again
I'd be happy to give her my place."
Chingis ordered his soldiers to search for Yesugen's
   sister,

and they found her travelling through the woods
   with her husband.
When the soldiers approached them he ran away,
and our men brought Yesui Khatun back to our camp.
When Yesugen Khatun saw her elder sister again
she remembered her promise.
She stood up and gave her place to her sister,
then sat down below her in the line of the wives.
This older sister was a beautiful woman
just as Yesugen had said,
and Chingis Khan loved her as well.
He married Yesui Khatun
and gave her a place in the line of his wives.

7.2 A Mongol reply to the pope: Guyuk Khan, *Letter to Pope Innocent IV* (1246). Original in Persian.

IN THE WEST THE MONGOLS were often called Tatars or Tartars. In 1245, Pope Innocent IV (r.1243-1254) wrote two letters to "the emperor of the Tartars" to school him in the essentials of the Christian religion, informing him that the pope held "the keys of the kingdom of heaven," expressing amazement that the "emperor"—that is, the Great Khan (*khagan*)—would invade "many countries belonging both to Christians and to others," and asking him to do penance. The letters were delivered by two Franciscan friars, Lawrence of Portugal and John of Plano Carpini, who reached their destination just as Guyuk Khan (r.c.1246-c.1248), oldest son and successor of Ogodei, was being installed as Great Khan. Guyuk's reply, printed below, shows him as firm in his own beliefs and certain of his self-righteousness as the pope; his conquests, he said, were God-given: "How could anybody seize or kill by his own power contrary to the command of God?"

[Source: *The Mongol Mission: Narratives and Letters of the Franciscan Missionaries in Mongolia and China in the Thirteenth and Fourteenth Centuries*, ed. Christopher Dawson (New York: Sheed and Ward, 1955), pp. 85-86 (language modernized and some notes added).]

We, by the power of the eternal heaven,
Khan of the great Ulus[1]
Our command:—

This is a version sent to the great Pope, that he may know and understand in the [Persian] tongue, what has been written. The petition of the as-sembly held in the lands of the Emperor [for our support], has been heard from your emissaries.

If he reaches [you] with his own report, you who are the great Pope, together with all the Princes, come in person to serve us. At that time I shall make known all the commands of the *Yasa*.[2]

---

1   Ulus is a large or small social group, here consisting of all the peoples under the supreme ruler as a community.
2   The *Yasa* refers to the customs and laws of the Mongols.

You have also said that supplication and prayer have been offered by you, that I might find a good entry into baptism. This prayer of yours I have not understood. Other words which you have sent me: "I am surprised that you have seized all the lands of the Magyar and the Christians. Tell us what their fault is." These words of yours I have also not understood. The eternal God has slain and annihilated these lands and peoples because they have neither adhered to Chingis Khan, nor to the Khagan,[1] both of whom have been sent to make known God's command, nor to the command of God. Like your words, they also were impudent; they were proud and they slew our messenger-emissaries. How could anybody seize or kill by his own power contrary to the command of God?

Though you also say that I should become a trembling Nestorian Christian, worship God, and be an ascetic, how do you know whom God absolves in truth, to whom He shows mercy? How do you know that such words as you speak are with God's sanction? From the rising of the sun to its setting, all the lands have been made subject to me. Who could do this contrary to the command of God?

Now you should say with a sincere heart: "I will submit and serve you." You yourself, at the head of all the Princes, come at once to serve and wait upon us! At that time I shall recognize your submission.

If you do not observe God's command, and if you ignore my command, I shall know you as my enemy. Likewise I shall make you understand. If you do otherwise, God knows what I know.

At the end of Jumada the second in the year 644.[2] The Seal

We, by the power of the eternal Tengri,[3] universal Khan of the great Mongol Ulus—our command. If this reaches peoples who have made their submission, let them respect and stand in awe of it.

7.3 Accommodations: Mengu-Temir Khan, *Charter to Protect the Russian Church* (1308). Original lost; reconstructed from Russian versions.

THE MONGOLS TOOK THE city of Kiev in 1240 and, making the mouth of the Volga River their center, became the dominant power in Russia for about two hundred years. Called the "Golden Horde" (golden, for the color of their leader's tent, horde, from the Turkish word for camp), the Mongols of Russia adopted much of the local governmental apparatus and native institutions. The Russian princes were left in place if they did homage and paid tribute to the khan. In addition, as the document below attests, the Russian Church was exempted from taxes.

[Source: *A Source Book for Russian History from Early Times to 1917*, vol. 1: *Early Times to the Late Seventeenth Century*, ed. George Vernadsky (New Haven, CT, and London: Yale University Press, 1972), p. 49.]

And this third *iarlyk* [charter] Tsar [Khan] Mengu-Temir gave to Metropolitan Peter, in the year 6816 [1308].

... Tsar [Khan] Chingis [ordered] that in the future: [in exacting] tribute [*dan'*] or subsistence for officials [*korm*], do not touch [the clergy]; may they pray to God with righteous hearts for us and for our tribe, and give us their blessing.... And past tsars [khans] have granted [privileges] to priests and monks by the same custom.... And we who pray to God have not altered their charters and, in keeping with the former custom, say thus: let no one, whoever it may be, demand tribute, or tax on land [*popluzhnoe*], or transport [*podvoda*], or korm; or seize what belongs

---

1 Khagan is the supreme ruler.
2 I.e., 1246 C.E.
3 The Mongolian great god.

to the church: land, water, orchards, vineyards, windmills ...; and if anything has been taken, it shall be returned; and let no one, whoever he may be, take under his protection what belongs to the church: craftsmen, falconers, huntsmen; or seize, take, tear, or destroy what belongs to their faith: books, or anything else; and if anyone insults their faith, that man shall be accused and put to death. Those who eat the same bread and live in the same house with a priest—be it a brother, be it a son—they shall likewise be granted [privileges] by the same custom, so long as they do not leave them; if they should leave them, they shall give tribute, and everything else. And you priests, to whom we granted our previous charter, keep on praying to God and giving us your blessing! And if you do not pray to God for us with a righteous heart, that sin shall be upon you.... Saying thus, we have given the charter to this metropolitan; having seen and heard this charter, the *baskaki* [tax inspectors], princes, scribes, land-tax collectors, and customs collectors shall not demand or take tribute, or anything else from the priests and from the monks; and if they should take anything, they shall be accused and put to death for this great crime.

7.4 The Hungarian king bewails the Mongol invasions. Béla IV, *Letter to Pope Innocent IV* (*c.*1250). Original in Latin.

IT WAS PROBABLY IN 1250 that King Béla IV of Hungary (r.1235-1270) wrote a letter to Pope Innocent IV (r.1243-1254) on the situation in his country. It was, he said, threatened by the Mongols (or "Tartars"), who had already invaded Hungary in 1241-1242 and were thought to be preparing a second, definitive conquest of the West (which, however, never occurred). The letter described the difficulties that Hungary—and all of Europe—would face in case of this second assault. Above all, the king explained the general peril of his country, which was on the eastern frontier of Christendom: on one side, to be sure, were Christians, but on the other side were heretics and pagans. Traditionally understood as a complaint to the Pope and as a desperate demand for help from the great powers of Christendom, the letter may also be interpreted as Béla's attempt to use Hungary's frontier to create an ideology in the service of royal power. Hungary has always been situated on the eastern frontier of western Christendom; although strongly tied to the Christian side, it was bound to negotiate as well with its non-Christian neighbors when necessary.

[Source: Archivio Segreto Vaticano, AA Arm. I-XVIII-605; Augustin Theiner, *Vetera monumenta historica Hungariam sacram illustrantia*, vol.1: *1216-1352* (Rome, 1859), pp. 230-32. Translated and introduced by Piroska Nagy.]

To the most holy father in Christ and Lord Innocent, by divine providence Supreme pontiff of the Holy Roman and Universal Church, Béla, king of Hungary by the same grace, with the respect both due and devoted. Most of the kingdom of Hungary has been reduced to a desert by the scourge of the Tartars, and it is surrounded like a sheepfold by different infidel peoples like the Ruthenians and the Brodniks[1] on the eastern side and the Bulgarians and Bosnian heretics against whom we have been fighting until now with our armies on the southern side. On the western and northern side there are Germans, from whom, because of our common faith, our kingdom should gain the fruit of some aid. However, it is not any fruit, but rather the thorns of war that our land is forced to endure as they snatch away the wealth of the country by unexpected plundering. For this reason—and especially because of the Tartars, whom the experience

---

1 Steppe peoples with which Hungary had to contend.

of war has taught us to fear in the same way as all the other nations that they have passed through have learned—after having asked for advice from the prelates and princes of our kingdom, we hasten to flee to the worthy vicar of Christ [the pope] and to his brethren, as to the sole and very last true protector of Christian faith in our ultimate need, so that what we all fear will not happen to us, or rather, through us, to you and to the rest of Christendom. Day after day news of the Tartars come to us: that they have unified their forces—and not only against us, with whom they are the most enraged, because we refuse to submit to them even after all that injury, while all the other nations that they put to the test became their tributaries, especially the regions which are at the east of our kingdom, such as Russia, the countries of the Cumans and the Brodniks, and Bulgaria, which in large part had once belonged to our dominion. It is rather against the whole of Christendom that their forces are unified, and, insofar as it is deemed certain by several trustworthy people, they have firmly decided to send their countless troops against the whole of Europe soon. Thus we are afraid that, if their people arrive, our subjects will be unable or even unwilling to withstand the cruelty of the Tartar ferocity in battle and, against our will, guided by fear, they will end up by submitting to their yoke, just as the above-mentioned neighbors have already done, unless by its careful consideration the farsighted Apostolic see securely and powerfully fortifies our kingdom in order to comfort the peoples living in it.

Indeed we write this letter principally for two reasons: not to be accused of having shirked what is possible, and not to be considered negligent. As far as what is possible is concerned, we say that we can conclude after our experience that we did whatever was possible when we exposed ourselves and all we had to the heretofore unknown men and capabilities of the Tartars. As for negligence, we can by no means be accused of it. For, while the Tartars were still fighting against us in our country, we turned to the three principal courts of Christendom seeking

help in this affair, namely yours, which is believed and held by Christians to be the highest and master of all the courts; [and we turned to the court] of the emperor,[1] to whom we even declared that we would be ready to submit ourselves if, during the time of the above-mentioned scourge he would have given us valid assistance and help; and we also turned for help to the court of the Franks.[2] But from all of them we received neither encouragement nor support, only words. In fact, we had recourse to all that was ours and, for the profit of Christendom, we humiliated our royal majesty and gave two of our daughters in marriage to two Ruthenian dukes and the third one to a Polish duke, aiming to learn through them and other friends of ours in the Eastern parts all the secret news about Tartars, so that this way we might face them and resist in a more suitable way their intentions and fraudulent schemes. We even received the Cumans into our kingdom, and—for shame!—today we defend our kingdom with pagans and put down the infidels of the Church with the help of pagans. Moreover, in order to defend the Christian faith, we have joined by marriage our first born son to a Cuman woman, in order to avoid the worst, and to have the possibility to create some occasion to bring them to the baptismal font—as we have already done more than once. So for all these and other reasons we very much hope that it is clear to the Sanctity of your Supreme pontiff, that in these oppressive times we have received no useful aid from any prince or people of the whole Christian Europe, with the exception of the knights Hospitaller in Jerusalem, whose brothers at our request have recently taken up arms against the pagans and the schismatics in defense of our kingdom and the Christian faith.[3] We have already placed part of them in a very dangerous spot, namely in the neighborhood of the Cumans and the Bulgars beyond the Danube, in the area through which the Tartar army found its way to us at the time of the invasion of our kingdom. Regarding that region, we hope and intend that, if God helps our acts and those of the above-mentioned Hospitallers, the Apostolic See may find them sufficiently worthy

---

1   Emperor Frederick II (r.1220-1250).
2   The French king at this time was St. Louis (r.1226-1270).
3   The Knights Hospitaller was a crusading order of warrior-monks. While originally formed to defend the Crusader States, it was also involved in numerous other military ventures.

to grant them its favor. Just as the Danube stretches to the sea of Constantinople, so we can succeed through them to propagate progeny of the Catholic faith, and thus they may bring useful aid to the Roman empire and also to the Holy Land. We have installed another part of them in the middle of our country, to defend the castles that we are constructing around the Danube, because our peoples are not accustomed to do this. For, after more than one discussion, our council decided that it would be more beneficial to us and to the whole of Europe to safeguard the Danube by fortifications: the Danube is the water of resistance.[1] It was here that Heraclius met Chosroes when he defended the Roman empire,[2] and it was here that we resisted—entirely unprepared, and thus badly injured—the Tartars for ten months, while our kingdom was still almost completely lacking fortifications and defenders. Because if—God forbid!— this territory were possessed by the Tartars, the door would be open for them to [invade] the other regions of the Catholic faith. This is in part because there is no sea to hamper their passage from here to other Christians, and in part it is because they can settle their families and animals—in which they abound—marvelously well here, better than elsewhere. Attila[3] may serve as an example of someone who, coming from the East to subdue the West, established the center of his authority in the middle of the kingdom of Hungary. On the other hand the emperors, who came fighting from the West in order to subdue the East, laid down their frontiers inside our country, however much they did for the organization of the army. May your pontifical Sanctity, pondering all this, find us worthy to procure a medicine before the wound rots. Indeed the multitude of wise people is very surprised that, in the present state of affairs, your Paternity permitted the departure of the king of France, such a noble member of the Church, from the frontiers of Europe.[4]

The multitude is wondering and cannot cease to be amazed at the fact that your Apostolic Clemency offers substantial help to the empire of Constantinople and regions overseas, which, if they were lost—God forbid!—would not harm the inhabitants of Europe as much as if our kingdom alone passed into the possession of the Tartars. We take God and man as our witness that our necessity and the gravity of our situation are so great that, if the various dangers of the roads did not prevent us, we would send not only messengers, as we have done so far, but would personally come as a servant and fall down at your feet to proclaim before the face of the whole Church—so that we may be justified and excused—that, if your fatherly sanctity does not send us help and the need becomes overwhelming, against our will, we may reach an arrangement with the Tartars. So we humbly beseech you that the Holy Mother Church consider, if not ours, at least the merits of our predecessors, the holy kings who, full of devotion and reverence submitted themselves and their people, preaching to them the orthodox faith, and serving you with purity of faith and in obedience. That is why the Apostolic see promised to them and to their successors all grace and favor if any necessity threatened, at a moment when they did not even ask for it, as the course of things was prosperous for them. Alas, now this heavy constraint seems to be imminent. Thus open your fatherly heart, and in this time of persecution, extend your hand with the necessary support for the defense of the faith and for the public utility. Otherwise, if our petition—which is so necessary and so universally favorable for the faithful of the Roman Church—suffers a refusal (which we cannot believe) then we should be obliged by necessity, not like sons but like step-sons, excluded from the flock of the father, to beg for aid elsewhere. Dated in Patak the day of the bishop and confessor Saint Martin, III of the ides of November.

---

1 "Water of resistance": i.e., the Danube is the watery frontier that will keep out the Tartars.
2 A reference to the wars between Byzantine Emperor Heraclius (r.610-641) and the Persian King Chosroes II (r.591-628).
3 The original contains the name Totila, as Béla confused Totila, king of the Ostrogoths (d.552), with Attila, king of the Huns (d.453).
4 St. Louis left for the Seventh Crusade in 1248.

NICCOLO AND HIS BROTHER Matteo Polo, merchants of Venice, had already traveled to China when they decided to take Niccolo's son Marco Polo (1254-1324) with them on a return trip. They chose an arduous overland route, arriving in 1275 at the Khan's court. A quarter century later and after many adventures, Marco, held as a prisoner by the Genoese, told his adventures to a fellow captive, Rustichello, a writer of French romances. The result was *The Travels*, which records Polo's tales with elements of a chivalric romance (for an example of such a romance, see *Sir Gawain and the Green Knight* below, p. 473). The passage here begins with Marco's trip to the city of Kinsai (today Hangzhou) on the east coast of southern China. How and why did Marco's view of the Mongols differ from that of Béla IV (above, p. 419)?

[Source: *The Travels of Marco Polo*, trans. Ronald Latham (New York: Penguin Books, 1958), pp. 213-23 (slightly modified).]

For three days' journey from Changan the traveler passes through a fine country full of thriving towns and villages, living by commerce and industry. The people are idolaters, using paper money and subject to the Great Khan, and amply provided with all the means of life. Then he reaches the splendid city of Kinsai, whose name means "City of Heaven." It well merits a description, because it is without doubt the finest and most splendid city in the world. I will follow the account of it sent in writing by the queen of the realm to Bayan,[1] the conqueror of the province, when he was besieging it. This was for him to pass on to the Great Khan, so that, learning of its magnificence, he might not let it be sacked or laid waste. I will recount the contents of her letter in due order; and it is all true, as I, Marco Polo, later saw clearly with my own eyes.

First, then, it was stated that the city of Kinsai is about 100 miles in circumference, because its streets and watercourses are wide and spacious. Then there are market-places, which because of the multitudes that throng them must be very large and spacious. The layout of the city is as follows. On one side is a lake of fresh water, very clear. On the other is a huge river, which entering by many channels, diffused throughout the city, carries away all its filth and then flows into the lake, from which it flows out towards the Ocean. This makes the air very wholesome. And through every part of the city it is possible to travel either by land or by these streams. The streets and the watercourses alike are very wide, so that carts and boats can readily pass along them to carry provisions for the inhabitants. There are said to be 12,000 bridges, mostly of stone, though some are of wood. Those over the main channels and the chief thoroughfare are built with such lofty arches and so well designed that big ships can pass under them without a mast, and yet over them pass carts and horses; so well are the street-levels adjusted to the height. Under the other bridges smaller craft can pass. No one need be surprised that there are so many bridges. For the whole city lies in water and surrounded by water, so that many bridges are needed to let people go all over the town.

On the other side the city is confined by a moat, some forty miles long and very wide and deep, which flows out of the river. This was made by the ancient kings of the province, so as to draw off flood-water whenever the river rises above its banks. It serves also to fortify the city. And the earth dug from it was heaped on the inner side, forming a low mound that encircles the city.

There are ten principal market-places, not to speak of innumerable local ones. These are square, being half a mile each way. In front of them lies a main thoroughfare, forty paces wide, which runs straight from one end of the city to the other. It is crossed by many bridges, carefully designed to avoid sharp inclines. And every four miles there is one of these

---

1 Bayan Ching-siang, "Hundred Eyes," a Mongol general.

squares, with a circumference, as stated, of two miles. Correspondingly there is a very wide canal, which runs along the side of the squares opposite to the thoroughfare. On the nearer bank of this are constructed large stone buildings, in which all the merchants who come from India and elsewhere store their wares and merchandise, so that they may be near and handy to the market squares. And in each of these squares, three days in the week, there is a gathering of forty to fifty thousand people, who come to market bringing everything that could be desired to sustain life. There is always abundance of victuals, both wild game, such as roebuck, stags, harts, hares, and rabbits, and of fowls, such as partridges, pheasants, francolins, quails, hens, capons, and as many ducks and geese as can be told; for so many are reared in the lake that for a silver groat of Venice you may have a brace of geese or two brace of ducks. Then there are the shambles, where they slaughter the bigger animals, such as calves, oxen, kids, and lambs, whose flesh is eaten by the rich and the upper classes. The others, the lower orders, do not scruple to eat all sorts of unclean flesh.

Among the articles regularly on sale in these squares are all sorts of vegetables and fruits, above all huge pears, weighing 10 lb. apiece, white as dough inside and very fragrant, and peaches in season, yellow and white, which are great delicacies. Grapes and wine are not produced locally; but raisins of excellent quality are imported from other ports and so too is wine, though the inhabitants do not set much store by this, being accustomed to the wine made of rice and spices. Every day a vast quantity of fish is brought upstream from the ocean, a distance of twenty-five miles. There is also abundance of lake fish, varying in kind according to the season, which affords constant employment for fishermen who have no other occupation. Thanks to the refuse from the city, these fish are plump and tasty. Seeing the quantity on sale, you would imagine they could never be disposed of. But in a few hours the whole lot has been cleared away—so vast are the numbers of those accustomed to dainty living, to the point of eating fish and meat at one meal. All the ten squares are surrounded by high buildings, and below these are shops in which every sort of craft is practiced and every sort of luxury is on sale, including spices, gems, and pearls. In some shops nothing is sold but spiced rice wine, which is being made all the time, fresh and

very cheap. There are many streets giving on to these squares. In some of these are many baths of cold water, well supplied with attendants, male and female, to look after the men and ladies who go there for a bath; for these people, from childhood upwards, are used to taking cold baths all the time, a habit which they declare to be most conducive to good health. They also maintain in these bath-houses some rooms with hot water for the benefit of foreigners who, not being accustomed to the cold, cannot readily endure it. It is their custom to wash every day, and they will not sit down to a meal without first washing.

Other streets are occupied by women of the town, whose number is such that I do not venture to state it. These are not confined to the neighborhood of the squares—the quarter usually assigned to them—but are to be found throughout the city, attired with great magnificence, heavily perfumed, attended by many handmaids and lodged in richly ornamented apartments. These ladies are highly proficient and accomplished in the uses of endearments and caresses, with words suited and adapted to every sort of person, so that foreigners who have once enjoyed them remain utterly beside themselves and so captivated by their sweetness and charm that they can never forget them. So it comes about that, when they return home, they say they have been in "Kinsai," that is to say in the city of Heaven, and can scarcely wait for the time when they may go back there.

In other streets are established the doctors and astrologers, who also teach reading and writing; and countless other crafts have their allotted places round the squares. Fronting on each of these squares are two palatial buildings, one at either end, in which are the offices of the magistrates appointed by the king to impose a summary settlement if any dispute arises among the traders or among the inhabitants of these quarters. It is the task of these magistrates to check every day whether the guards that are stationed on the neighboring bridges, as will be explained below, are duly posted or have failed in their duty, and to punish any negligence at their discretion.

Along both sides of the main street, which runs, as we have said, from one end of the city to the other, are stately mansions with their gardens, and beside them the residences of artisans who work in their shops. Here at every hour of the day are crowds of people going to and fro on their own business, so that anyone seeing such a multitude would believe it a stark impossibility that food could be found to fill so many mouths. Nevertheless, every market day all these squares are thronged with a press of customers and traders bringing in supplies by cart and by boat, and the whole business is accomplished. Let me quote as an illustration the amount of pepper consumed in this city so that from this you may be able to infer the quantities of provisions—meat, wine, and groceries—that are required to meet the total consumption. According to the figures ascertained by Messer Marco from an official of the Great Khan's customs, the pepper consumed daily in the city of Kinsai for its own use amounts to 43 cartloads, each cart-load consisting of 223 lb.

It was further stated in the report that the city was organized in twelve main guilds, one for each craft, not to speak of the many lesser ones. Each of these twelve guilds had 12,000 establishments, that is to say 12,000 workshops, each employing at least ten men and some as many as forty. I do not mean that they were all masters, but men working under the command of masters. All this work is needed because this city supplies many others of the province. As for the merchants, they are so many and so rich and handle such quantities of merchandise that no one could give a true account of the matter; it is so utterly beyond reckoning. And I assure you that the great men and their wives, and all the heads of the workshops of which I have spoken, never soil their hands with work at all, but live a life of as much refinement as if they were kings. And their wives too are most refined and angelic creatures, and so adorned with silks and jewelry that the value of their finery is past compute. It was decreed by their king, in the days of his rule, that every man must follow his father's craft: if he possessed 100,000 bezants, he could still practice no other craft than his father had done before him. Not, of course, that he was obliged to labor at it with his own hands, but rather, as I have said above, to employ men to work at it. But this rule is by no means enforced by the Great Khan. Nowadays, if a craftsman has attained to such riches that he is able and desirous to abandon his craft, he is no longer constrained by anyone to practice it. For the Great Khan reasons thus: if a man practices a craft because he is poor and could not get a living without it, and then in process of time so

prospers in his fortunes that he can lead an honorable life without the practice of his craft, why should he be compelled against his will to go on practicing it? For it would seem unfitting and unjust, if the gods were generous to him, that men should oppose their will.

Let me tell you further that on the southern side of the city is a lake, some thirty miles in circuit. And all round it are stately palaces and mansions, of such workmanship that nothing better or more splendid could be devised or executed. These are the abodes of the nobles and magnates. There are also abbeys and monasteries of the idolaters in very great numbers. Furthermore in the middle of the lake there are two islands, in each of which is a marvelous and magnificent palace, with so many rooms and apartments as to pass belief, and so sumptuously constructed and adorned that it seems like the palace of an emperor. When anyone wishes to celebrate a wedding or hold a party, he goes to this palace. Here their wedding parties and feasts are held, and here they find all that is needful for such an occasion in the way of crockery, napery, and plate, and everything else, all kept in stock in the palaces for this purpose for the use of the citizenry; for it was they who had made it all. On occasion the need may arise to cater for a hundred clients at once, some ordering banquets, others wedding feasts; and yet they will all be accommodated in different rooms and pavilions so efficiently that one does not get in the way of another. Besides this, the lake is provided with a great number of boats or barges, big and small, in which the people take pleasure trips for the sake of recreation. These will hold ten, fifteen, twenty, or more persons, as they range from fifteen to twenty paces in length and are flat-bottomed and broad in the beam, so as to float without rocking. Anyone who likes to enjoy himself with female society or with his boon companions hires one of these barges, which are kept continually furnished with fine seats and tables and all the other requisites for a party. They are roofed over with decks on which stand men with poles which they thrust into the bottom of the lake (for it is not more than two paces in depth) and thus propel the barges where they are bidden. The deck is painted inside with various colors and designs and so is the whole barge, and all round it are windows that can be shut or opened so that the banqueters ranged along the sides can look this way and that and feast their eyes on the diversity and beauty of the scenes through which they are passing. And indeed a voyage on this lake offers more refreshment and delectation than any other experience on earth. On one side it skirts the city, so that the barge commands a distant view of all its grandeur and loveliness, its temples, palaces, monasteries, and gardens with their towering trees, running down to the water's edge. On the lake itself is the endless procession of barges thronged with pleasure-seekers. For the people of this city think of nothing else, once they have done the work of their craft or their trade, but to spend a part of the day with their womenfolk or with hired women in enjoying themselves either in these barges or in riding about the city in carriages—another pleasure in which, as I ought to mention, these people indulge in the same way as they do in boat trips. For their minds and thoughts are intent upon nothing but bodily pleasure and the delights of society.

Here and there throughout the city there are big stone towers in which the townsfolk deposit all their valuables when a fire breaks out. You must understand that such outbreaks are very frequent, because many of the houses are made of wood. The houses in general are very solidly built and richly decorated. The inhabitants take such delight in ornaments, paintings, and elaborations that the amount spent on them is something staggering. The natives of Kinsai are men of peace, through being so cosseted and pampered by their kings, who were of the same temper. They have no skill in handling arms and do not keep any in their houses. There is prevalent among them a dislike and distaste for strife or any sort of disagreement. They pursue their trades and handicrafts with great diligence and honesty. They love one another so devotedly that a whole district might seem, from the friendly and neighborly spirit that rules among men and women, to be a single household. This affection is not accompanied by any jealousy or suspicion of their wives, for whom they have the utmost respect. A man who ventured to address an unseemly remark to any married woman would be looked upon as a thorough blackguard. They are no less kind to foreigners who come to their city for trade. They entertain them in their houses with cordial hospitality and are generous of help and advice in the business they have to do. On the other hand, they cannot bear the sight of a soldier or of the Great Khan's guards, believing that it is through them that they have been deprived of their own natural kings and lords.

The people of Kinsai are idolaters, subject to the Great Khan and using paper money. Men as well as women are fair-skinned and good-looking. Most of them wear silk all the time, since it is produced in great abundance in all the surrounding territory, not to speak of the great quantity continually imported by traders from other provinces. They eat all sorts of flesh, including that of dogs and other brute beasts and animals of every kind which Christians would not touch for anything in the world.

Let me tell you further that each of the 12,000 bridges is guarded by ten men, five by day and five by night, who are stationed under cover. These are to protect the city from malefactors and check any attempt at rebellion. In every guardhouse there is a big wooden drum with a big gong and a clock by which they tell the hours of the night and also of the day. At the beginning of every night, when the first hour has passed, one of the guards strikes a single blow on the drum and the gong, so that the whole neighborhood knows that it is one o'clock. At the second hour they strike two blows; and so on, hour by hour, increasing the number of strokes. They never sleep, but are always on the alert. In the morning after sunrise they strike first one hour, as they did after nightfall, and so from hour to hour. A detachment of them patrols the district to see if anyone has a light or a fire burning beyond the authorized hours. When they find an offending house, they put a mark on the door; and in the morning the owner is summoned to appear before the magistrates and, unless he can offer a legitimate excuse, he is punished. If they find anyone abroad at night after the approved hours, they arrest him, and in the morning they bring him before the magistrates. Again, if they come across some poor man by day, who is unable to work on account of illness, they have him taken to one of the hospitals, of which there are great numbers throughout the city, built by the ancient kings and lavishly endowed. And when he is cured, he is compelled to practice some trade. As soon as the guards see that fire has broken out in some house, they give warning of it by beating the drum, and the guards from other bridges come running up to extinguish it and rescue the goods of the merchants, or whoever it may be, by stowing them in the towers of which I have spoken or by loading them on barges and taking them out to the islands in the lake. For no resident in the city would venture to leave his house during the night, even to go to the fire, except the owners of the goods and these guards who come to help, of whom there cannot be less than one or two thousand.

Let me tell you also that at one point in the city there stands a hill crowned by a tower inside which is a big wooden drum, which a man beats from within with a mallet, so as to be heard at a great distance. This is beaten as a danger signal in case of a conflagration or a civil disturbance.

The reason why the Great Khan has such a careful watch kept in this city and by so many guards is because it is the capital of the whole province of Manzi,[1] a great repository of his treasure, and the source of such immense revenue that one who hears of it can scarcely credit it. So he is at special pains to guard against rebellion here, and to this end he keeps huge forces of infantry and cavalry in the city and its environs, and especially of his leading barons and most trusted henchmen.

You may take it for a fact that all the streets of this city are paved with stone and brick. So too are all the high roads and causeways of the province of Manzi, so that it is possible to ride or to walk dry-shod through the length and breadth of the land. But since the Great Khan's couriers could not ride post-haste on horseback over paved roads, one strip of road at the side is left unpaved for their benefit. The main street, which we have already described as running from one end of the city to the other, is likewise paved with stones and bricks for a width of ten paces on either side. But the strip down the middle is filled with fine gravel, with vaulted sewers leading from it to drain off the rain water into the neighboring canals so that it keeps permanently dry. Along this street you may see passing to and fro a continuous procession of long carriages, decked with awnings and cushions of silk, which seat six persons. These are hired by the day by gentlemen and ladies bent on taking pleasure trips. Countless numbers of these carriages are to be seen at all hours of the day passing along the middle of this street on their way to the gardens, where they are welcomed by the garden keepers under arbors specially designed for the purpose. Here they stay all day long enjoying a good time with their womenfolk; and then in the evening they return home in these carriages.

Let me tell you further that in this city there are fully 3,000 public baths, to which men resort for their pleasure several times a month; for they believe in keeping their bodies very clean. I assure you that they are the finest baths and the best and biggest in the world—indeed they are big enough to accommodate a hundred men or a hundred women at once.

I would also have you know that twenty-five miles distant from this city, between north-east and east, lies the Ocean. There stands a city called Kan-p'u,[2] at which there is a very fine port frequented by great quantities of shipping with valuable merchandise from India and elsewhere. Between the city and the port runs a big river by which ships can come as far as the city. The course of the river also extends much farther afield than this city.

I should add that the province of Manzi has been split up by the Great Khan into nine parts—that is to say, he has put it under the rule of nine great kings, each with a great kingdom of his own. But you must understand that these kings govern on behalf of the Great Khan, and on such terms that they render a yearly account of their several kingdoms to his agents for the revenue and everything else, and they are changed every three years like all the other officials. This city is the residence of one of these nine kings, whose rule extends over more than 140 large and wealthy cities. In the whole province of Manzi, incredible as it may seem, there are fully 1,200 cities, and each one of them has a garrison of the Khan's troops on the following scale. You may take it for a fact that no city has a garrison of less than 1,000 men, and some are manned by 10,000, some by 20,000 and some (including Kinsai) by 30,000, so that the total number is almost beyond reckoning. You must not suppose that these troops are all Tartars.[3] The Tartars

---

1 I.e., south China.
2 This is the port of Hangzhou.
3 I.e., Mongols.

are horsemen and are stationed only near those cities that do not stand on watery sites but on firm, dry ground, where they can exercise themselves on horseback. In the cities on watery sites he stations Cathayans[1] or such of the men of Manzi as are accustomed to arms. Out of all his subjects he has a yearly levy made of those who devote themselves to arms for enrolment in his forces, and all these are counted as his soldiers. The men who are recruited from the province of Manzi are not set to guard their own cities but are posted to others twenty days' journey away, where they stay four or five years. They then return home and others are sent in their place. This arrangement applies both to the Cathayans and to the men of Manzi. The greater part of the revenue of these cities that is paid into the Great Khan's treasury is devoted to the maintenance of these garrisons of soldiers. And if ever it happens that some city rebels—for there are times when the men in a sudden access of madness or intoxication massacre their rulers—then as soon as the news is known the neighboring cities send a sufficient detachment of these troops to crush the erring cities; for any attempt to bring up a force from another province of Cathay would be a long operation, involving a lapse of two months.

To sum up, I can tell you in all truthfulness that the business of the province of Manzi—its riches, its revenue and the profit derived from it by the Great Khan—is on such a stupendous scale that no one who hears tell of it without seeing it for himself can possibly credit it. Indeed it is scarcely possible to set down in writing the magnificence of this province. So I will hold my peace on the subject.

---

1   That is, people from northern China.

TRANSFORMATIONS IN THE CITIES

7.6 The *popolo* gains power: *The Ghibelline Annals of Piacenza* (1250). Original in Latin.

IN THE TWELFTH CENTURY, nobles dominated the towns of northern Italy, making their power concretely visible by building lofty town towers reminiscent of castles. In the thirteenth century, the nobles were challenged by the *popolo*—a group composed mainly of artisans and shopkeepers but also often joined by interested or opportunistic nobles—who formed local armed bands, tried to oust the nobles, and demanded a role in communal government. In many cities the commune and the *popolo* ended in a sort of stalemate, each having their own officials and laws, and eventually representatives of the *popolo* were integrated in some way alongside the head of the commune, the podestà. At Piacenza an initial revolt of the *popolo* in the 1220s was led by the nobleman Guglielmo Landi, but he was expelled in 1235. In 1250, according to the so-called *Ghibelline Annals of Piacenza* (from which the excerpt here is taken), the *popolo* rose up again during a period of grain shortage. Originally led by a man named Antolino Saviagata, the *popolo* later named Uberto de Iniquitate, from a noble family rival to the Landi family, to lead it. Soon factions within the *popolo* emerged, as different groups supported or opposed Uberto's policies.

[Source: *The Towns of Italy in the Later Middle Ages*, ed. and trans. Trevor Dean (Manchester and New York: Manchester University Press, 2000), pp. 158-60 (slightly modified).]

At the beginning of June, the Milanese army rode into the territory of Lodi with a great quantity of corn [grain] which they were sending to Parma, where there was a great shortage. They transported the corn as far as the Po [River] and then handed it over to the Piacentines ...

In 1250 the common people of Piacenza saw that they were being badly treated regarding foodstuffs: first, because all the corn that had been sent from Milan, as well as other corn in Piacenza, was being taken to Parma, with farm laborers being forced to transport it without payment; second, because the Parmesans were touring Piacentine territory buying corn from the threshing floors and fields, which seemed very serious to the Piacentines. The Parmesans could do this in safety because Matteo da Correggio, a citizen of Parma, was podestà of Piacenza, and supported them as much as he could in having corn taken to Parma. Knowing about all this, on Friday July 27th early in the morning, Antolino Saviagata, at the instigation of the Scotti family, because he was their neighbor, and of others, gathered twenty or thirty leaders (consuls) of the popular societies of Piacenza in the church of

San Pietro, with the purpose of going to the podestà and telling him to oppose this export of Piacentine corn to Parma. In the church they all swore to support each other if anything was said to them on account of this meeting. It was then maliciously reported to the podestà that Antolino Saviagata and others had gathered to cause damage and harm to the city of Piacenza. The podestà sent one of his judges ... to the church; he arrested Antolino, but let the others leave. The podestà immediately held a general council and so maligned Antolino and his assembly that it was immediately decreed that no more than three people could assemble in the city, that the podestà had full power to inquire into Antolino's actions, and to put him to death if he deserved it. Some of those who had been at Antolino's gathering, fearing death, convened their own societies and told them they had done nothing wrong in the assembly; and the societies decided to support their consuls within the law. Meanwhile, the podestà held Antolino in his home, not doing him any harm. The *populares*, inflamed by what had happened and by what was going on ... took up arms and banners, rang their bells, gathered together and came to the podestà. The podestà, in fact, wanted to release Antolino on surety, more out of fear than love, but Antolino refused ... His father was pressing him to let himself be bound over, and there were many magnates willing to stand surety for him, including Pietro Malvicini, Filippo Visdomini, Giacomo Visconti and Uberto de Iniquitate, but he refused them. The podestà, seeing the crowd coming towards him and hearing the bells ring, let Antolino go. Antolino was badly dressed, with shoes on his feet but nothing covering his legs. On his release, Antolino did not go home at once, but wishing to accomplish his desires, went well-supported to a certain well, where he found a great crowd of men armed for battle, and he addressed them, provoking and inducing them to do what he desired, reminding them of the great harms that had been done to the *popolo* over the past fifteen years, how they had been killed, condemned and expelled from one city to another, and that they would rather die than suffer any more ... [The men of each of the six city districts] elected two consuls of the people ...

On the following Saturday, all the consuls, with a great number of the *popolo*, came to the communal council. Antolino excused their presence, arguing and explaining that what had been done by the *popolo* was not done as an affront to the podestà, but to his honor and that of the Roman church, of the commune of Milan and their friends ... The consuls of the *popolo* then assembled at Santa Maria del Tempio and resolved to issue statutes and to hold a council of the people. The statutes were passed, and on Sunday morning the council met in the church of San Pietro. There was such a press of people that they could not stay there, so they moved to the church of San Sisto. Among the first clauses [of the statutes] ... was one about electing a rector of the *popolo*. Many men believed themselves to be leaders of the *popolo*, namely Fredenzio da Fontana, Filippo Visdomini, Uberto Zanardi, Guelfo Stricto ... and when this clause was read out, great division arose among the *popolo*: some wanted one man, some another, and there was great clamor. Then [one man] said "Why do you not accept Uberto de Iniquitate, for he has already suffered many injuries and losses on your behalf?" And so he was elected by acclamation. Those who had betrayed the *popolo* and Guglielmo Landi—and there were many of them among both the consuls and the others present—complained loudly and wanted to leave the church to raise uproar, but some of those who had been unable to enter the church closed the doors so that they could not leave. They regarded lord Uberto as an excessively "imperial" man.[1] Once things had calmed down, however, they resumed their seats and took part in the election of consuls of the people: one or two from each society, according to its standing, with other men from each district of the city. Unanimously these elected Uberto de Iniquitate as podestà and rector of the *popolo* for one year. Envoys were sent to his home, and he came immediately and gladly took the oath of office, without consulting any of his relatives or friends. All of the *popolo* then accompanied him home with great rejoicing and honor. As he had been poorly dressed before, he later held a great meeting in the piazza San Pietro, dressed in scarlet with squirrel fur. This was attended by a huge crowd of men of the *popolo*, at the news of which many knights and commoners were scared to death because of the harm they had done him and the *popolo* in the past. And from that day on, he began to lead the *popolo*. After a short interval, he held another council in San Sisto, saying what some of his friends had said to him, that "a vassal of one year brings little profit and little loss," and so he was elected podestà of the *popolo* for five years, and after him his son Giannone. Men of the *popolo* who had relatives and friends among the Piacentine exiles began to tell them "Come, come back, brothers, exiles from Piacenza"; others though ... strongly opposed this. However, such was the number of the former that the latter could do nothing: people today delight in upsetting things. And at last, Uberto de Iniquitate and his advisors were content to let the exiled *populares* return, but leaving the Landi ... and other knights outside. Meanwhile, Antolino Saviagata ... went to Milan as an envoy ... on some business. There, either because he was offered money, or because he regretted what he had done, and fearing the return of the exiles whom he had persecuted and

---

1   That is, he supported the imperial, rather than the papal, party.

expelled, he sought to disobey and harm the *popolo*. Conspiring with others … he sought to return the city to its previous regime. When this was discovered by the podestà of the *popolo*, Antolino was captured and greatly tortured. But, because what he had done pleased Uberto de Iniquitate, who did not want the Landi and others to return, Uberto let him go unpunished, expelling him from the city. And thus faction arose among the *popolo*.

7.7 The Hanseatic League: *Decrees of the League* (1260-1264). Original in Latin.

THE WORD "HANSA" PROBABLY originally meant "armed convoy," but it came to be used of associations of merchants and, most especially, of the merchants of the cities along the North and Baltic Seas. Lübeck provided the hinge between the two seas, and its decrees from 1260-1264, printed below, reveal that its legislation touched the other member cities as well. To what degree did the interests of the merchants override the interests of the various princes under whom the various cities were technically subject?

[Source: *A Source Book for Mediaeval History*, ed. Oliver J. Thatcher and Edgar Holmes McNeal (New York: Charles Scribner's, 1905), pp. 611-12 (slightly modified).]

We wish to inform you of the action taken in support of all merchants who are governed by the law of Lübeck.

(1) Each city shall, to the best of her ability, keep the sea clear of pirates, so that merchants may freely carry on their business by sea. (2) Whoever is expelled from one city because of a crime shall not be received in another. (3) If a citizen is seized [by pirates, robbers, or bandits] he shall not be ransomed, but his sword-belt and knife shall be sent to him [as a threat to his captors]. (4) Any merchant ransoming him shall lose all his possessions in all the cities which have the law of Lübeck. (5) Whoever is proscribed[1] in one city for robbery or theft shall be proscribed in all. (6) If a lord besieges a city, no one shall aid him in any way to the detriment of the besieged city, unless the besieger is his lord. (7) If there is a war in the country, no city shall on that account injure a citizen from the other cities, either in his person or goods, but shall give him protection. (8) If any man marries a woman in one city, and another woman from some other city comes and proves that he is her lawful husband, he shall be beheaded. (9) If a citizen gives his daughter or niece in marriage to a man [from another city], and another man comes and says that she is his lawful wife, but cannot prove it, he shall be beheaded.

This law shall be binding for a year, and after that the cities shall inform each other by letter of what decisions they make.

7.8 Hospitals: *Charters for Bury St. Edmunds* (1248-1272). Originals in Latin.

FIVE OF THE SIX medieval hospitals founded in or near the town of Bury St. Edmunds were established by the monastery there. (See the *Chronicle* of Jocelin of Brakelond above, p. 410 for less charitable activities by the same monastery.) The hospital of St. John's, also known as the *domus Dei* [house of God], was built between 1248 and 1272 to care for the temporary ills of the able-bodied poor. As these donation charters make clear, all sorts of properties were given to the

---

1   I.e., declared an outlaw.

hospital, including land and a butcher's stall. The charters also show that the prior of the monastery—the monk whose office was just under that of the abbot—gave payments in return for most of the donations. The documents printed below are close summaries—rather than word-for-word translations—of the originals. Consider the earlier *Charters of Donation* to the monastery of Cluny (p. 207 above) alongside these to see if there are any important changes in donor networks, things given, and motives for charity from one period to the other.

[Source: *Charters of the Medieval Hospitals of Bury St. Edmunds*, ed. and summarized Christopher Harper-Bill (Woodbridge: Boydell Press, 1994), pp. 30, 35, 41 (modified).]

1. [1248–1252: First foundation of the hospital by Abbot Edmund, Prior Richard and the convent.]

Mandate by Abbot Edmund and the convent to all those who shall hold the office of almoner[1] of St. Edmunds that they shall faithfully allow to the new *domus Dei*, established in Bury St. Edmunds to shelter and restore Christ's poor, all movable and immoveable goods which have been or shall be granted to or purchased for the said *domus Dei*, which shall in perpetuity remain a hospital. No monk or layman in the abbey's jurisdiction shall venture to destroy the hospital or curtail the benefits of hospitality therein. By their common consent the abbot and convent have ordained that only the begging poor shall be sheltered and recuperated there, according to the resources of the house. If any should fall seriously ill while there, they should be maintained according to the hospital's means, but when recovered they should depart and set out on Christ's path wheresoever they may wish. If by God's grace the hospital's resources should expand, greater benefits may be rendered not only to the poor housed there who have fallen ill, but in the reception of other poor people who are frail or diseased. Brethren and sisters [i.e., monks and nuns] shall not be admitted for any reason, as in some other such houses, except for two wardens, men of wisdom, discretion and good reputation, who under the almoner's supervision shall procure the necessities for Christ's poor. When these wardens become incapacitated by illness or old age, two others shall be chosen in their place by the almoner, who shall present them to the abbot and convent in chapter, where they shall take an oath to execute faithfully their office. Such discharged wardens shall be maintained for their lifetime in the hospital. Fidelity and obedience to the abbot and convent are stipulated, and the liberties and privileges of the church of St. Edmunds reserved. Mass shall not be celebrated in the *domus Dei*, nor shall an altar be set up there, but those sheltered there shall devote themselves only to private prayer. To all benefactors of the hospital is granted full participation in all the spiritual benefits of the church of St. Edmunds.

2. [1248–1252] Notification by Ralph son of Benedict the mercer [textile merchant] of the old market in the town of St. Edmunds that he has granted, conceded and by this charter confirmed to God and to the hospital established for the reception of the poor, both ignorant and instructed, both healthy and sick, for 5 marks of silver given to him by Richard prior of St. Edmunds, an acre and a rood[2] of land, be there more or less, lying between the land of the parson of Rushbrooke of the fee of the church[3] and the land of William the priest, son of Fulton, abutting at the east on the land of Stephen the alderman and at the west on that of Edith the widow; also an acre lying between the land of Baldwin of Shimpling and that of Edith the widow, abutting at the west on the land of Beatrice the widow of Rushbrooke and at the east on "Rugeweie"; to have and to hold of the capital lords of the fee freely, quit, wholly and peacefully, rendering annually in two instalments at Easter and Michaelmas

---

1 The monk responsible for the charitable activities of the monastery.
2 A rood is equal to 1/4 acre.
3 I.e., held as a fief from the church.

for a rood and an acre to Godfrey son of Benedict Cook (Cok) 2d, and for the other acre to Thomas son of Beatrice of Rushbrooke 4d, for all service, exaction and demand. Warranty is granted in perpetuity against all men and women.

By these witnesses: Stephen, alderman of St. Edmunds; Martin et Thomas, bailiffs of St. Edmunds; Simon, son of Paganus; John, son of Luca; Ada Wudard; Simone Pottare; Thomas, clerk of the bailiffs; John de Pikenham; Ada Fraunceys; Simone Portar'; and many others.

3. [Mid-thirteenth century, before 1271] Notification by Simon Sparrowhawk of St. Edmunds that he has conceded and granted and by this charter confirmed to John of Wattisham, his heirs and to whomsoever to whom he may wish to grant, sell, assign or at the end of his life bequeath it, and to their heirs, for their homage and service, a stall in the town of St. Edmunds set up in Butchers' Street between the stall of Richard son of Robert the butcher on both sides, to hold and to have of him and his heirs freely, quit and wholly, peacefully, well and in peace, in fee and heredity, rendering annually to the grantor and his heirs 1d a year in two instalments, at Michaelmas [September 29] and Easter, and rendering the annual service due therefrom to the capital lords of the fee, that is, to the *domus Dei* of the town of St. Edmunds 2s at the said terms, and saving the stallage [rent for the stall] due to the office of bailiff of St. Edmunds

for all services, aids, customs and demands. Warranty is granted in perpetuity against all persons. Sealed in corroboration.

By these witnesses: John, son of Luca the alderman; William de Feretro; Richard de Pulham, bailiff; Richard de Wlepet; Walter de Westle; Ada, his child; Radulf Cuterun; William, his son; John in Cizor; Robert Herbeiur; Walter Smeresmoker; William son of Clement; Simon Coco; Huge de Barw', clerk; et others.

4. [1257–1272] Notification by John Framlingham and Marsilia his wife and Matilda, his wife's sister, that they have conceded, granted and by this present charter confirmed to the lord Simon, abbot of St. Edmunds, and the convent, for the use of the *domus Dei* sited outside the south gate of Bury St. Edmunds, a parcel of land with all that belongs to it lying between the *domus Dei* and the toft [homestead] of Alan the glover to the south, to have and to hold, well and in peace, wholly and quit, in free, pure and perpetual alms. Warranty is granted against all. Sealed in corroboration.

By these witnesses: Galfrid, son of Robert, at the time alderman of St. Edmunds; Richard de Polham and William de Northwode, at the time bailiffs; Luca, son of John; William, son of Bartholomew; Henry, goldsmith; John, his son; Galfrid de Hoylond; Thomas de Wolferston; Daniel de Beccles; Ada de Ysingham; and others.

7.9 Famine at Constantinople: Athanasius I, Patriarch of Constantinople, *Letter* (1306-1307). Original in Greek.

WHILE MANY WESTERN CITIES had secured a measure of self-government and economic independence by the thirteenth century, Constantinople remained tightly controlled by the Byzantine emperor himself. When grain became scarce at the capital at the beginning of the fourteenth century, the patriarch, Athanasius I (r.1289-1293 and again 1303-1309) wrote to the emperor, Andronicus II Palaeologus (r.1281-1328), to solve the problem. He exhorted him with quotes from the Bible not to "yield to bribes" or to "drive the grain we yearn for out of the city." The issues were complex. The city was crowded with impoverished refugees from Anatolia, and middlemen who controlled the grain supplies kept prices high. Meanwhile, Catalans and Turks were raiding the Byzantine countryside and living off its grain, so the emperor ordered that no crops be grown near Constantinople. Compounding the problem, Venetian and Genoese merchants who brought grain to the city from the Black Sea region exported much of it to Italy, producing a "grain drain." Andronicus had probably taken bribes to allow them to do so. One way that the emperor eventually addressed the problem was by making peace with the ruler of Bulgaria and importing grain from there.

[Source: *The Correspondence of Athanasius I Patriarch of Constantinople: Letters to the Emperor Andronicus II, Members of the Imperial Family, and Officials*, ed. and trans. Alice-Mary Maffry Talbot (Washington, DC: Dumbarton Oaks, 1975), pp. 179, 181, 183.]

To the emperor concerning the famine which is afflicting the people

Formerly when I walked through the streets, one poor person would ask me for one thing, another for another, but now they complain as if with one voice about the grain, and almost everyone entreats me piteously that it not leave the capital, and bind me with oaths to put before any other request to your divine majesty a petition about the grain. I myself share their sorrow and suffering, and am persuaded of the plight of these people, and am able to estimate the distress which will befall my brethren and fellow poor, on account of the scarcity of food. And again as I estimate the suffering which such an evil will cause to the survivors of the threat to the Christians which has occurred on account of my sins, I entreat your divine majesty to heed and register in your mind my and their pleas for grain; and do not yield to bribes, either through the disease of greed or simply of friendship, preferring gold to God Who ordered the bread to be distributed among the hungry,[1] but not that one should kill the people of God because of one's love of gold. "For what shall it profit them, if they shall gain the whole world" (which is impossible), "but will lose their soul?"[2] For it is impossible for someone to gain the whole world, but it is possible for everyone to lose his own soul, if he wishes. Very few people are unaware of the shame and blame which results from betraying a possible good for an evil which cannot be obtained anyhow. For they should keep in mind the words, "If wealth should flow in, set not your heart upon it,"[3] and "wealth unjustly collected shall be vomited up,"[4] and "they that will be rich fall into the temptation and snare of the devil,"[5] and "he who raises the price of grain is cursed by the people; but blessing be on the head of him that gives it."[6]

I make this request of your divine majesty: either let them be taught or rebuked, and do not have "faith in uncertain riches, but in the living God, who giveth us richly all things to enjoy."[7] Because it is terrible and worse than terrible for me and my brethren, my fellow poor and beggars, to fall at your feet and entreat you, a great and most pious king who is right-thinking and a lover of Christ, who is exceedingly merciful and is swayed by the sympathy and goodness of his own soul, and by the sorrow and affliction of his subjects, while a few gifts and bribes triumph over such good qualities, and drive the grain we yearn for out of the city as should not happen. In addition let the rich realize the incurable disease and affliction which is about to befall us needy people, and that "the spoils of the poor are in their houses,"[8] as, of their own accord, they close their ears so as not to hear about the man mocked by the Lord, because in his misplaced eagerness he "tore down his barns" in order to build "greater ones."[9]

---

1   See Isa. 58: 7.
2   Mark 8: 36.
3   Ps. 62: 10; Douay Ps. 61: 11.
4   Job 20: 15.
5   1 Tim. 6: 9.
6   Prov. 11: 26.
7   1 Tim. 6: 17.
8   Isa. 3: 14.
9   Luke 12: 18.

The cure for this disease will be found neither by ruler nor priest nor Levite, but only by your divine majesty together with a certain Samaritan [i.e., God] who did not pass by with loathing the man wounded by thieves.[1] For He gave your divine majesty the two pence, piety and empire, and cries out, "Inasmuch as ye have done it unto one of the least of these, ye have done it unto me."[2] And on His return He will give you the kingdom which He came to receive, even if the people of that time weren't willing to give to Him that which He had as God, and which He also has as man made God and ruler of heaven and earth; and He has decreed that He will arise again on account of the groans and misery of the poor; to Him be glory for ever and ever, Amen.

---

1 For the priest and the Levite who did not help a robbery victim, and the Samaritan who did, see Luke 10: 31-32.
2 Matt. 25: 40.

7.10 Inquisition: Jacques Fournier, *Episcopal Register* (1318-1325). Original in Latin.

JACQUES FOURNIER WAS POPE BENEDICT XII (r.1334-1342), the third pope at Avignon, and responsible for building the papal palace there. But before that, between 1317 and 1327, he was bishop of his native city of Pamiers, in southern France. Officials under his jurisdiction there took meticulous care to record and preserve the inquests into and confessions of 114 villagers suspected of heresy between 1318 and 1325. (Compare this use of an Episcopal Register with that of the one drawn up for Thomas of Hereford, above, p. 367.) Most were accused of the dualist heresy of the Manichaeans—people who were also called Cathars, Albigensians, and, among themselves, Christ's Poor. The original proceedings were in Occitan, the vernacular language of the region, but they were translated into Latin for the record. The result, as may be seen from the materials printed here regarding Guillaume Austatz—a wealthy peasant farmer and also the king's *baille*, or legal and fiscal authority—is a portrait of village life revealing friendships, enmities, gossip, and class tensions. Why might Guillaume's fellow villagers have testified against him? What leads you to think that Guillaume was innocent—or guilty?

[Source: *Medieval Popular Religion, 1000-1500: A Reader*, ed. John Shinners, 2nd ed. (Peterborough, ON: Broadview Press, 2006). Translated by John Shinners.]

WITNESSES AGAINST GUILLAUME AUSTATZ OF ORNOLAC FOR THE CRIME OF HERESY

In the year of the Lord 1320, May 11, Gaillarde, wife of Bernard Ros of Ornolac (sworn as a witness and questioned because the said Guillaume Austatz had spoken certain heretical words) said that about four years ago she was in her house at Ornolac, and Alazaïs, the wife of Pierre Mounié of the same place, was there with her. The said Guillaume arrived along with some other people whose names she says she does not recall. When they had gathered around the hearth in the house, they started talking about God and about the General Resurrection. Among other things, they said that God really needed to be great in power and strength since each human soul would return to its own body at the General Resurrection. Hearing this, Guillaume said, "And do you believe that God made as many human souls as there are men and women? Surely not! For when at death souls exit the human bodies they have been in, they steal into the bodies of children who have just been born; as they leave one body, they enter into another one." For, as he said, if

each human soul were to reclaim the very same body it had been in, since the world has lasted for many years, the whole world would be filled up with souls— so much so, as he said, that they couldn't be contained in the area between Toulouse and the Mérens Pass. For although souls are quite small, so many people have existed that their souls could not be contained within that space. When she heard these words, Alazaïs took the witness in her arms and held her closely. And when, after a while, Guillaume left the witness's house, Alazaïs said to her, "O godmother, these are evil words that Guillaume spoke," and the witness said that they were strong words.

Asked why she had concealed these words for such a long time, she said that she had not believed they were as serious as they are, but, goaded by her conscience, she had revealed them this year to the priest Bernard Petron, who was staying at Ornolac, so that he could counsel her what to do about them. And this priest, so she said, advised her to reveal the words to the lord bishop of Pamiers. So, led by her conscience, as she said, she reported these words to the bishop.

Asked if she had seen Guillaume take communion

or doing the other things which good and faithful Christians are accustomed to do, she responded that for the past twelve years she had lived in the village of Ornolac and she had never seen Guillaume take communion, not even when he was sick or on the feast days when people usually receive communion, though she had seen him going into the church. And she should know since, as she said, his mother-in-law is her sister. She said moreover that Guillaume, while he lived at Lordat where he was born, used to practice usury; but after he moved to Ornolac, he practiced no usury that she knew of.

Asked if she deposed the previous testimony out of hate, love, fear, or bad will, instructed, or suborned, she said no, but because it is the truth, as she said above.

In the same year on May 26, the said Gaillarde, wife of the said Bernard Ros, cited on the same day, appeared before the lord bishop in the episcopal see at Pamiers and was received by the lord bishop as a witness against Guillaume Austatz concerning some matters touching on the Catholic faith. Swearing an oath as a witness, she said and deposed that this year, around the feast of the nativity of St. John the Baptist [June 24], some money and some other things had been stolen from her which she had kept in a certain chest that had been broken into. The witness went to the said Guillaume (who was then and is now the *baille* [royal official] of Ornolac) and requested him to carry out his office, search for the thief, and to do what needed to be done for her to get her stolen things back. When he was unwilling to listen to her about her case, weeping and wailing she went to the church of Our Lady of Montgauzy to get a miracle from her to recover her money and property. In order to better get the miracle, she girded the candle on Blessed Mary's altar [probably by tying a string around it which she would later use to make a wick for another candle to be offered at the altar]. When she got back to Ornolac, she again asked Guillaume to investigate the theft, but he did not want to bother himself with it. The witness told him he should search for the money and things stolen from her just as he had searched for grain stolen from him that year. He told her that he had looked for the grain because he

would have recognized it had he found it, but he wouldn't recognize her stolen money and property, as she said. And she said, "I put my trust in Blessed Mary of Montgauzy. I visited her and asked her to restore my stolen money and property; and I asked her to take revenge against those who stole from me if they don't restore them." Then Guillaume told the witness in the presence of some other people whose names she does not recall (except for Julien de Ornolac from Ornolac), that Blessed Mary did not have the power to restore the witness's money and things. When she said that yes she did, and that what he had said was bad, and also that the Blessed Mary would avenge her, Guillaume said Blessed Mary did not kill people or commit murders....

The same year, July 25, the said Alazaïs, wife of Pierre Mounié, again appeared and offered testimony after she had been told to swear to tell the truth as a witness. She said that about two years ago she had lost her four sons one after the other and was terribly sad and depressed over this. One day when Guillaume had come back from his fields, he saw her standing in the doorway of her house looking quite depressed, and he asked her why she was so sad. She told him it was because she had so suddenly lost her four handsome boys. Guillaume told her not to be sad about this, for she would get her four dead sons back. And when she told Guillaume that she believed she would see her dead sons and get them back in paradise but not in this world, Guillaume told her that, on the contrary, she would get them back in this very world. For when she got pregnant the souls of her four dead sons would be reincarnated in the sons she conceived and carried in her womb; and in that way she would recover her dead sons in this world. Asked about those present, she said she did not recall that anyone was present except herself and Guillaume. Asked about the time and place, she answered as above.

Also she said that this year, on what day she did not recall, but after the [Waldensian] heretics Raymond de la Côte and the woman Agnes had been burned,[1] she and Guillaume were standing near the door of his house and Guillaume said that the bishop of Pamiers was a proud and harsh man. She said that a man who had great power could do much. And then Guillaume

---

1   For the Waldensians in an earlier period, as depicted in the *Chronicle of Laon*, see above p. 404.

said that if Raymond and Agnes had been listened to and had had an audience, just as the bishop did, the bishop would be worthier of burning than Raymond and Agnes. And when the witness said that it was not theirs to judge this, Guillaume quickly went inside his house....

The year as above, July 27, Pierre de Bordas of Ornolac was sworn as a witness and asked to tell the truth plainly and fully about the above matters and others touching on the Catholic faith against Guillaume Austatz. He said that this year, after the heretic Raymond de la Côte was burned by the lord bishop of Pamiers and the inquisitor of Carcassone, when the news reached Ornolac, the witness; his wife, Alazaïs; Barchinona, the wife of the late Bernard de Bordas; and Guillaume Austatz were sitting at the table eating when Guillaume said that the heretic Raymond who had been burned was a good cleric, one of the better people in all Christendom. And it would have been better for [the region of] Sabarthès if the bishop of Pamiers had been burned instead of Raymond. Asked whether he heard Guillaume saying that this heretic was a good Christian and a holy man, and that, if he had been treated justly, he would not have been burned, he said that he does not recall. Asked if, when Guillaume said these words—that it would have been better for Sabarthès for the lord bishop to have been burned than the heretic—he agreed or disagreed with him or chastised him for these words, he responded that he said nothing to him, though it seemed to him that he had spoken badly, so he said....

THE CONFESSION OF THE CONVERTED HERETIC GUILLAUME AUSTATZ

In the year of the Lord 1320, July 15, it came to the attention of the reverend father in Christ, Lord Jacques [Fournier], by God's grace bishop of Pamiers, that Guillaume Austatz of Ornolac in the diocese of Pamiers, had said and asserted before many people: that each human soul does not have its own body, but when it exits from one body, it steals into another body; and that even at the resurrection not every soul will resume its own body. He also said that each soul will not be rewarded or punished in the body it dwelled in, and that he personally did not trust that his soul would be saved or damned. He also

said that, if each soul had its own body and was not reincarnated into another body, even though souls were very small, still the land of Sabarthès would be filled up from Toulouse all the way to the Mérens Pass—giving to understand through this that souls are corporeal. He also said that Raymond de la Côte, the heretic condemned this year by the lord bishop and the inquisitor of Carcassone, was a good Christian, and that what he taught was true. He also said that the church was not able to compel anyone to offer any specific thing at mass, but that it sufficed to offer a straw to the priest. Through these things it was apparent that he was a believer, favorer, and harborer of the Manichaean heretics and a member of their sect. The lord bishop informed himself about these matters and, wishing to question this man about them and other things pertaining to the Catholic faith, about which he was vehemently suspect, he cited him by his letters to appear on this day. Guillaume, appearing before the lord bishop and Frère Gaillard de Pomiès (the lord inquisitor of Carcassone's deputy), was asked by the same simply and not under oath if he had said, taught, or believed the aforesaid heretical words. He responded no.

The same lord bishop, wishing to lead him back to faith and free him from danger, gave him some time (until early tomorrow evening) to think about the aforesaid; and because Guillaume said that his enemies made these denunciations, the lord bishop asked him who he thought his enemies were, and Guillaume answered that the priest and assistant priest of Ornolac were, and no one else.

The next day at early evening the said Guillaume appeared before the lord bishop in his episcopal chambers, assisted by Frère Gaillard de Pomiès, and made a physical oath that he would tell the truth plain and simple without any falsehoods intermixed about the aforesaid heretical articles and other matters pertaining to the Catholic faith, both insofar as they concerned him as the defendant and others, living or dead, as witnesses. After the articles contained in the preceding were explained to him again in the vernacular, he responded to the first article that he had never said nor did he believe that each human soul does not possess its own body.

To the second article he said he had not said or believed that the human soul, when it exits from its body, enters at that point or later into another body.

To the third article he said he believes that the human soul will rise and resume the flesh and bones it occupied in this life, and he never said or believed otherwise, so he said.

To the fourth article he said that at the General Judgment, a soul will be punished or rewarded in the body it occupied in this life, and he had never said or believed otherwise, so he said.

To the fifth article he said he had never said that if each human being who ever was, is, or will be had his own soul, then the land between Toulouse and the Mérens Pass would be filled up with the souls of the people of Sabarthès, past and present.

To the sixth article he said that he had never said that Raymond de la Côte was a good Christian.

To the seventh article he said that, repeating a statement he heard from a man from Chateauverdun (who was repeating a statement of the Romans), he had indeed said that the church could not compel anyone to make a specific offering, but that it sufficed to offer anything, no matter how small. But the man had not said that he believed this or was trying to discourage anyone from making agreeable or proper offerings. Asked the name of the man from Chateauverdun, he said that he did not know. Asked when he heard the man say these words, he said this year. Asked who else was present, he said he did not remember. Asked if he had seen heretics, believed in them, harbored them, or favored them, he said no.

Since the above information made it clear that the said Guillaume had neither told the truth about nor confessed the aforesaid heretical articles, the lord bishop arrested him and ordered him to be incarcerated immediately at Alemanns by his deputies, ordering him not to leave the castle without the lord bishop's permission.

The same year as above, August 11, Guillaume Austatz standing for judgment at the residence of the episcopal see of Pamiers before the lord bishop assisted by Frère Gaillard de Pomiès, said and confessed that three or four years ago—he did not really remember the time or day—he was in his house at Ornolac, and [either] Bartholomette, the wife of Arnaud d'Urs of Vicdessos, who was then staying at his house, or Alazaïs, wife of Pierre de Bordas, had lost a son whom she had discovered lying dead next to her in bed. But

he did not remember, so he said, which of the two women had lost her son. And when this woman wept and wailed over the death of her son, and he saw and heard her, he said to the woman that she should not weep or wail because God would give that dead son's soul to the next child, boy or girl, that she conceived and bore, or else his soul will be in a good place in the next world. Asked what he understood it to mean when he said God would return the dead son's soul to whatever boy or girl the woman conceived or bore in the future, he said that he understood through these words that amends would be made to the woman with another child, and, so he said, though these words meant nothing, he said them anyway just as they came to his head. Asked if he had heard anyone saying that souls exiting human bodies reenter other human bodies, or if he had ever believed this or believed it still, he said he had never heard it from anyone, nor had he believed it, nor did he believe it now. Asked if he had ever said the same words or words to that effect to any person or persons except to Bartholomette or Alazaïs, he said he did not recall saying such words or words to that effect.

Also he said that around a year and a half ago he was in the village common of Ornolac and with him there, as he recalled, were Raymond de Ornolac, Pierre Doumenc, Pons Barrau, Guillaume de Aspira, Pierre de Gathlep, Bertrand de Ville, Raymond Benet the Younger, and some others he did not recall, so he said. Someone from among them, he did not remember who, started talking about the location of the souls of the dead, asking what place could hold as many souls as there were people who had died every day. Guillaume replied that they were received into paradise. And when those standing around asked him if paradise was so huge a place that it could hold every soul, he said that it was huge—so huge that if a house were made that occupied the whole area between Toulouse and Mérens, paradise would still be a bigger place and could hold many souls in it.

The same year as above, August 28, standing for judgment at the episcopal see of Pamiers before the lord bishop assisted by the said Frère Gaillard de Pomiès (the deputy of the lord inquisitor of Carcassone), Guillaume Austatz said and confessed that two and a half years ago or so, on the day that the said lord bishop first visited Sabarthès and the church of St. Martin of

Ussat, the son of Alazaïs Mounié of Ornolac and also some other boy were burned by a fire that they had [accidentally] set in the house of Bernard Mounié. And when the said Alazaïs was crying over the loss of her son, Guillaume came over and visited Alazaïs at her house to console her about her son's death. While comforting her he said, "Godmother, don't weep and wail, for you can still get back the souls of your dead children." Alazaïs said that yes, she would get them back in paradise. He told her that in fact she would get them back in some son or daughter whom she would conceive and bear, for she was still young; and if she didn't get them back in a son or daughter, she would regain them in paradise.

The same year as above, August 29, standing for judgment at the aforesaid see before the said bishop assisted by the said Frère Gaillard de Pomiès, Guillaume Austatz said and confessed that eight years ago or so, as he recalled, his mother, Guillemette de Austatz, was cited for the crime of heresy by the lord inquisitor of Carcassone. When he heard this, he went on a market day to Lordat to be with his mother who had to go to Carcassone. And in his mother's house at Lordat they sat alone together by the fire and, as he said, he asked his mother if she thought she was guilty of heresy since she had been cited by the lord inquisitor. She said yes. And then he said to her, "How? Have you met heretics?" And she said yes: Pierre Authié and Prades Tavernier at Arnaud de Albiès's house in Lordat. And when he asked her why and how she had gone to that house to see these heretics, she said that late one evening she was standing at the door of her house, and Guillemette (the wife of the surgeon Arnaud Teisseire of Lordat and the daughter of the heretic Pierre Authié) arrived with Raymond Sabatié of Lordat. Then Raymond said to Guillaume's mother, "Come join Guillemette de Teisseire." She said "Gladly," so they went together (namely his mother, Guillemette, and Raymond) and went inside Albiès's house to a room where the heretics were. When they were at the door to the room, Raymond asked Guillaume's mother if she would like to see some holy men, and, quickly opening the door, they entered and found there the heretics Pierre Authié and Prades Tavernier, whom first Guillemette and next Raymond reverenced in a heretical fashion. When these two had greeted the heretics, they told Guillaume's mother she should

adore them in the same way they had. Guillemette told her that this master [i.e., Pierre] was her [i.e., Guillemette's] father, and they taught her how she should adore them. And so his mother, after they had instructed her, reverenced the heretics. After this adoration, they stayed there with the heretics, and Pierre Authié preached to them. This heretic told them among other things that when children's souls exit after their death, they enter by stealth into the bodies of children who were generated and conceived after the death of the first children. This happens after the mother of the dead children conceives and bears other children....

On August 30, standing for judgment at the episcopal see of Pamiers before the lord bishop assisted by the said Frère Gaillard de Pomiès (the deputy of the lord inquisitor of Carcassone), Guillaume Austatz said and confessed that this year, after the heretic Raymond de la Côte was burned in the village of Alemanns, one Sunday the men of Ornolac (namely Pons Barrau, Guillaume de Aspira, Pierre Doumenc, Bernard de Ville, Guillaume Forsac, Raymond de Ornolac, all of them from Ornolac) were in the village common next to the elm tree there, and they were talking about the burning of the heretic. Guillaume arrived and said, "I'll tell you this for a fact: this fellow they burned was a good cleric—there was none better in these parts except the bishop of Pamiers. He constantly argued with the bishop and he disagreed with him, but he believed in God, Blessed Mary, and all the saints, and in the seven [sic] articles of faith, and he was a good Christian. And since he believed all these things, it was a great injustice to burn him." The men asked him why he was burned considering he was a good cleric and a good Christian, and he replied it was because he said the pope could not absolve sins and he denied purgatory—that is why he was burned.

Also he said that before he said these words in the village common of Ornolac, Raymond de Nan, who was staying with Pierre Mir, the canon of Foix, came to his house at Ornolac and told him, in the hearing of Pierre Bordas, Arnaud Pere, and Guillaume Garaud of Chateauverdun, that a man had been burned at the village of Allemans by the bishop of Pamiers. People said he was a good cleric, and that he had disagreed with the bishop but believed in God, Blessed Mary, all the saints, and the seven articles of faith, and was a good Christian, and it was a great injustice to burn him. When Guillaume heard this, he suggested that "it would have been better for Sabarthès if the bishop of Pamiers had been burned instead of this man, for afterwards he wouldn't make us spend our money." By this he understood not that the bishop was a heretic, but that the bishop demanded a tithe on sheep called *carnelages* from the people of Sabarthès. This was why he said it would have been better for the lord bishop to be burned than the heretic. Asked if he then believed or still believes it would have been better for Sabarthès if the bishop had been burned instead of the heretic Raymond de la Côte, he said he believed it then when he spoke these words, and he held that opinion for fifteen days; but after fifteen days he did not believe it nor does he now. He was asked—when he believed it was better for Sabarthès to burn the lord bishop of Pamiers instead of the heretic since the bishop exacted the tithe of sheep from Sabarthès—whether he believed or still believes the bishop can justly demand the tithe. He said he thought the bishop could justly demand the tithe. He was asked, since he believed the bishop could justly demand the tithe, whether he believed the people of Sabarthès acted justly in refusing to pay the tithe. He said that although the bishop exacted the tithe according to law, the people of Sabarthès also justly refused to pay the tithe according to their customs. Asked why he believed it was better to burn the bishop than the heretic, since, when he said this, he thought the lord bishop justly demanded the tithe from the people of Sabarthès, he responded that he said this because of the expenses the lord bishop cost the people of Sabarthès....

He was asked if, when he said the heretic Raymond de la Côte was a good Christian and was unjustly burned, he knew that he had been condemned by the lord bishop and the inquisitor of Carcassone as a heretic and had been judged a heretic. He said he did indeed know that Raymond had been condemned as a heretic by the bishop and the inquisitor; still, it did not seem to him or to others with whom he spoke that he was a heretic since he believed in God, Blessed Mary, all the saints, and the seven articles of faith. This was why it seemed to him that Raymond was a good Christian and had been unjustly condemned. But later, when they considered that the lord bishop and

the inquisitor would not have burdened themselves with so great a sin as killing a man unless it was just, it seemed to them that—although to some small degree they had unjustly condemned him—still, in some measure they had acted justly. He was asked whether, after he had heard it said—as he confessed—that Raymond had been condemned as a heretic since he did not believe the pope could absolve sins and he denied that purgatory existed, he then believed and still believes that Raymond had been justly condemned as a heretic for denying these two articles. He said that at the time he spoke these words, he did not believe that the heretic should have been condemned for not believing the two articles; but before then and after then he believed and still believes he was justly condemned as a heretic for denying the two articles. However, for fifteen days he remained convinced that he had been unjustly condemned for denying the articles. He was asked whether, at the time he believed Raymond had been unjustly condemned as a heretic for denying the two articles, he thought that to say the pope could not absolve sins and to deny that purgatory existed in the next world were heresies. He said that for those fifteen days he did not believe it was heresy to say the pope could not absolve sins and that purgatory did not exist. But before and after those fifteen days, he believed and still believes that to deny these two articles is heresy, and also that someone denying these articles should be justly condemned as a heretic.

The year as above, September 1, the said Guillaume Austatz appeared for judgment at the episcopal see before the lord bishop assisted by Frère Gaillard de Pomiès, the deputy of the lord inquisitor of Carcassone. He said and confessed that about five years ago he was at home, and Pierre Bordas and his wife Alazaïs and Barchinona Bordas were there. They started talking about the salvation of souls. He said that, if it were true what the priests say—namely that if someone wanted to be saved, it was necessary for him to confess all his sins, and, if he could, to restore or return everything he had taken from other people against their will—not ten out a hundred people will be saved. Better yet, not ten out of a thousand. For people do not confess their sins very well, either because they have forgotten them or because they are embarrassed to confess them; and they take lots of things from other people. So only a few out of many will be saved, if what the priests say is true. Asked if he then believed and still believes that when priests say these two things they are telling the truth, he said yes. Asked whether he believed he would be damned for eternity if he died and had not wanted to confess that he had knowingly committed simple fornication or loaned money at interest or had failed to return interest that he had received if he could, he said that he did.

Also, he had said he believed that if each soul had its own body, the world could scarcely hold these souls since, though they were very small, there were so many of them that they would fill up the world. From this it appeared that he believed souls were material. He was asked if he thought human souls were material and had physical parts: hands, feet, and other parts. He said that at the time he had said this, he believed human souls had the physical shape of a man or woman and parts resembling the human body. But now he believed human souls were spirits without parts resembling the human body.

He was asked whether he believed the saints dwelling in paradise could help people living in this world; he said yes. He was asked whether he had ever said otherwise. He said that this year around Pentecost, when Gaillarde Ros had lost five sous stolen from a chest, she complained to him that since he was the local *baille*, and since he had not immediately discovered who had committed the theft, she had asked Blessed Mary of Montgauzy to expose the thief. He said to Gaillarde, "And don't you think Blessed Mary would commit a greater sin if she revealed the person who stole the four [*sic*] sous from you? For wouldn't the thief be thrown into confusion and brought to justice [with the risk of capital punishment] by this than if Blessed Mary didn't return the four sous to you?" But he said this, so he said, as a joke, not really believing Blessed Mary would sin if she revealed the thief. He also did not think it would be a sin if she revealed the wrongdoer, or even if he were sentenced to death or killed by order of his superior.

He was asked if he had ever confessed the aforesaid heresies to a priest or in any other way. He said no, because he had not believed he had sinned by believ-

ing them and persisting in that belief. But now he realized that he had been gravely at fault for believing these errors, and he humbly begged absolution for the sentence of excommunication he incurred for believing them. He said he was prepared to perform any penance and suffer any penalty the lord bishop and the inquisitors enjoined on him for these things. But he was obliged that if he later recalls any other crime beyond that which he had confessed, or also if he remembers that someone else living or dead had committed this crime, as quickly as he can he will reveal this to the bishop, his successors, or the lord inquisitor of Carcassone. And the lord bishop, seeing his humility and contrition, absolved him in the church's due form from the sentence of excommunication he incurred for believing these heresies, provided that he fully confessed them and that he now and forevermore believes what the Roman Church preaches and teaches. But before granting him this absolution, he received from him an abjuration and oath as follows:

There Guillaume Austatz abjured all heresy, belief in, support of, defense of, harboring of, approval of the sect, life, or faith of, agreement with, and every other kind of participation with Manichaeans or Waldensians, etc… otherwise his absolution is not valid.

This was done in the presence of the said lord bishop, Frère Gaillard, Frère Arnaud de Caslar (both of the Order of Preachers at Pamiers),[1] and Master Guillaume Pierre Barthe, the lord bishop's notary, who recorded and wrote the preceding. And I, Rainaud, faithfully corrected all of it against the original copy.

The year as above, September 3, standing for judgment at the episcopal see of Pamiers before the lord bishop assisted by the said Frère Gaillard de Pomiès (deputy of the lord inquisitor of Carcassone), Guillaume Austatz heard the bishop read to him in the vernacular everything he confessed above. Asked whether everything he confessed against himself and against others in the above confession was true, he said yes. He said he wished and wishes to stand firm in this confession, seeking mercy that he be not judged upon the above matters; and he finished his business, and sought to be given a sentence and mercy for the above matters….

On the Sunday assigned to the said Guillaume

---

1 The Order of Preachers refers to the Dominicans.

Austatz, he appeared in the cemetery of St. John the Martyr and sentence was rendered to him by the lord bishop and the lord inquisitor in this manner: "May all know, etc...." Look for this sentence in the Sentence Book of the inquisition of heretical depravity, which sentence was issued against the said Guillaume Austatz on Sunday, March 2 in the said cemetery.

And I, the aforesaid Rainaud, faithfully corrected all of this against the original copy.

[We do not know whether Guillaume was punished or was allowed to return home.]

7.11 Procedures for isolating lepers: *Sarum manual* (based on materials from *c.*1360s). Original in Latin.

LEPROSY WAS A PUBLIC DISEASE: a disfigurement of the skin, easily seen by all. Today we identify leprosy with the illness caused by one bacillus, *mycobacterium leprae*, but in the Middle Ages people with many sorts of skin diseases were considered lepers. From at least the fourth century on, kissing lepers was an admirable attribute of many saints. For example, Fortunatus wrote of St. Radegund that "seizing some of the leprous women in her embrace, her heart full of love, she kissed their faces" (see above, p. 51). But lepers were also despised, and by the twelfth century their illness was understood to be the outward manifestation of a diseased and sinful soul. Leper hospitals were built, often just outside the walls of towns; they were provided with alms-boxes so that travelers entering the city might give a contribution to these most abject and marginal of human beings. Lepers were segregated: they were not allowed to live among or attend church with the healthy, and procedures for expelling lepers from their normal communities were written up. The one here comes from a fifteenth-century edition of the so-called *Sarum manual*, a book of rites used initially in the diocese of Salisbury and then adopted throughout much of England. It was probably taken verbatim from the expulsion ritual used in some southern French dioceses in the 1360s, and it reflects the normal practice in western Europe.

[Source: Rotha Mary Clay, *The Medieval Hospitals of England* (Frank Cass: London, 1909), Appendix A, pp. 273-76, revised by John Shinners, ed., *Medieval Popular Religion, 1000-1500: A Reader* (Peterborough, ON: Broadview Press, 1997), pp. 279-81.]

Method for casting out or separating those who are sick with leprosy from the healthy.

First of all the sick man or leper clad in a cloak and in his usual dress, being in his house, ought to have notice of the coming of the priest who is on his way to the house to lead him to the church, and must in that guise wait for him. For the priest vested in surplice and stole, with the cross preceding him, makes his way to the sick man's house and addresses him with comforting words, pointing out and proving that if he blesses and praises God, and bears his sickness patiently, he may have a sure hope that though he be sick in body he may be whole in his soul, and may obtain the gift of everlasting health. And let him offer other words suitable to the occasion. When he has sprinkled him with holy water, let the priest lead the leper to the church, the cross leading the procession, the priest following, and then the leper. Within the church let a black cloth, if it is available, be set upon two trestles at some distance apart before the altar, and let the sick man take his place on bended knees beneath it between the trestles, after the manner of a dead man, although by the grace of God he yet lives in body and spirit, and in this posture let him devoutly hear mass. When this is finished, and he has been sprinkled with holy water, he must be led by the priest with the cross to the place where he will live. When they have arrived there, the priest shall counsel him with the words of holy scripture: "Remember thy last end, and thou shalt never sin"[1] Whence Augustine says, "He readily rejects all things, who ever bears in mind that he will die." Then the priest with a spade casts earth on both of his feet, saying "Be dead to the world, but live again with God." And he comforts him and strengthens his patience with the words of Isaiah spoken concerning our Lord Jesus Christ: "Truly he hath borne our infirmities and carried our sorrows, and we have thought him as it were a leper, and as one struck by God and afflicted."[2] Let him say also: "If in bodily weakness by means of suffering you become like Christ, you may surely hope that you will rejoice in spirit with God. May the Most High grant this to you, numbering you among his faithful ones in the book of life. Amen."

It is to be noted that the priest must lead him to the church and from the church to his house as a dead man, chanting the Responsory *Libera me domine*.[3] Thus, the sick man should be covered with a black cloth. And the mass celebrated at his exclusion may be chosen either by the priest or by the sick man, but it is customary to say the following:

Introit: "They have surrounded me."[4] See Septuagesima Sunday. *Collect*: "Almighty and ever-eternal God, give everlasting salvation to those believing in you." *Epistle*: "Beloved, is any one of you sad?"[5] *Response*: "Have mercy on me." *Verse*: "For my bones are troubled."[6] Alleluia *Verse*: "He who heals." If during Lent, *Tract*: "Thou hast moved the earth."[7] *Gospel*: "Jesus entered Capharnaum."[8] *Offertory*: "Lord, hear me."[9] *Secret and Post-communion*: "Deliver Israel, O God, from all his tribulations."[10]

When leaving the church after mass the priest ought to stand at the door and sprinkle him with holy water. And he ought to commend him to the care of the people. Before mass the sick man ought to make

his confession in the church but never again there. In leading him forth the priest again begins the Responsory *Libera me domine* with the other versicles. Then when he has come into the open fields he does as is aforesaid; and he ends by imposing prohibitions upon him in the following manner:

"I forbid you ever again to enter churches, or to go to a market, a mill, a bakehouse, or gatherings of people.

Also I forbid you ever to wash your hands or even any of your belongings in a spring or stream of water of any kind; and if you are thirsty you must drink water from your pot or some other vessel.

Also I forbid you ever henceforth to go out without your leper's dress, that you may be recognized by others; and you must not go outside your house unshod.

Also I forbid you, wherever you may be, to touch anything which you wish to buy other than with a rod or staff to show what you want.

Also I forbid you ever henceforth to enter taverns or other houses if you wish to buy wine; and have what they give you put into your cask.

Also I forbid you to have intercourse with any woman except your wife.

Also I command you when you are on a journey not to answer anyone who questions you until you have moved to the side of the road downwind from him so that he may not be harmed by you; and that you never go down a narrow lane lest you should meet someone.

Also I charge you that if you need to pass across some toll bridge over water or elsewhere you touch no posts or structures on the path where you cross until you have first put on your gloves.

Also I forbid you to touch infants or young folk, whoever they might be, or to give to them or to any others any of your possessions.

Also I forbid you henceforth to eat or drink in any

---

1   Ecclus. 7: 40.
2   Isa. 53: 4.
3   "Free me, O Lord."
4   Ps. 17: 11; Douay Ps. 16: 11. These quotations represent the initial verses of the various parts of the mass.
5   James 5: 13.
6   Ps. 6: 2; Douay Ps. 6: 3.
7   Ps. 60: 2; Douay Ps. 59: 4.
8   Luke 7: 1.
9   Ps. 17: 1; Douay Ps. 16: 1.
10 Ps. 25: 22; Douay Ps. 24: 22.

company except that of lepers. And know that when you die you will be buried in your own house, unless you received permission beforehand to be buried in a church."

And note that before he enters his house, he ought to have a coat and shoes of fur, his own plain shoes, a clapper as his signal, a hood and a cloak, two pairs of sheets, a pot, a funnel, a belt, a small knife, and a bowl. His house ought to be small, with a cistern, a bed furnished with sheets, a pillow, a chest, a table and chair, a lamp, a shovel, a cup, and other necessities.

When all is complete the priest must point out to him the ten rules which he has made for him; and let him live on earth in peace with his neighbor. Next, in the presence of the people the priest must point out to him the Ten Commandments of God, that he may live in heaven with the blessed. And let the priest also point out to him that every day each faithful Christian is bound to say devoutly the Our Father, Hail Mary, and the Creed, and to protect himself with the sign of the cross, saying often *Benedicite*. The priest departs from him saying: "Worship God and give thanks to God. Have patience and the Lord will be with you. Amen."

7.12 Jews in England: *Statute of the Jewry* (1275) and *Petition of the "Commonalty" of the Jews* (shortly after 1275). Originals in Latin and French, respectively.

THE ENDLESS NEED OF King Henry III (r.1216-1272) for revenues hit the Jews of England hard. Numerous taxes, fines, and confiscations left many bankrupt. Some left the country. Meanwhile stories of Jewish ritual killings circulated, touching off mass executions. In 1231 the Jews of Leicester were expelled, the first such expulsion since the one at Bury St. Edmunds, recounted in Jocelin of Brakelond's *Chronicle*, above, p. 410. Between 1234 and 1243, numerous cities and even whole counties of England shut their doors to Jews. When Edward I (r.1272-1307) came to the throne, he compounded the problem. Reacting to church canons against the "sin of usury," he issued the *Statute of the Jewry* in 1275, prohibiting Jews from charging interest and insisting that all current debts to Jews be settled quickly for less than was owed. In effect the statute deprived the Jews of their livelihood. To compensate, it allowed Jews to become merchants, artisans, or farmers (though only for a short term). But, as the Jews pointed out in their *Petition of the "Commonalty,"* Jews could not be merchants or artisans, for they could not travel safely, and they would never be able to extend credit (since they were unlikely ever to be paid). Under such circumstances, they could not compete with Christians. In fact the *Statute* was an utter failure, and Edward ended by expelling all the Jews from England in 1291.

[Source: *English Historical Documents*, vol. 3: *1189-1327*, ed. Harry Rothwell (London and New York: Routledge, 1975), pp. 411-13 (notes added).]

[The Statute of the Jewry, 1275]

Because the king has seen that many evils and instances of the disinheriting of good men of his land have happened as a result of the usuries which the Jews have made in the past, and that many sins have followed thereupon, the king, though he and his ancestors have always received great benefit from the Jewish people in the past, has nevertheless for the honor of God and the common benefit of the people, ordained and es-

tablished that from now on no Jew shall lend anything at usury, either on land or rent or anything else, and that usuries shall not continue beyond the feast of St. Edward [October 13] last. Agreements made before that shall be kept, save that the usuries shall cease. All those who owe debts to Jews on pledges of movables are to clear them between now and Easter; if not the pledges shall be forfeited. And if any Jew shall lend at usury contrary to what the king has established the king will not concern himself either personally or through his officials to get him recovery of his loan, but will punish him at his discretion for the offence and will do justice to the Christian that he may recover his pledge.

And so that distresses for debts due to Jews shall not henceforth be so grievous, a half of the lands and chattels of Christians is to be kept for their sustenance,[1] and no distress for a debt owing to a Jew is to be made upon the heir of the debtor named in the Jew's deed or other person holding the land that was the debtor's before the debt is proved and acknowledged in court.

And if a sheriff or other bailiff has by the king's command to give a Jew, or a number of Jews, for a debt due to them seisin[2] of chattels or land to the value of the debt, the chattels are to be valued by the oaths of good men and be delivered to the Jew or Jews or to their agent to the amount of the debt, and if the chattels do not suffice, the lands shall be extended by the same oath before seisin is given to the Jew or Jews, to each one according to what is due to him, so that it may be known for certain that the debt is paid and the Christian may have his land again, saving always to the Christian half of his land and chattels for his sustenance as aforesaid, and the chief dwelling.

And if any movables be found hereafter in the seisin of a Jew and any one wishes to sue him, the Jew shall have his warranty if he is entitled to it, and if not, let him answer: so that in future he is not in this matter to be otherwise privileged than a Christian.

And that all Jews shall dwell in the king's own cities and boroughs, where the chirograph chests of the Jews are wont to be:[3] and that each Jew after he is seven years old shall wear a distinguishing mark on his outer garment, that is to say in the form of two Tables joined, of yellow felt of the length of six inches and of the breadth of three inches. And that each one after he is twelve years old shall yearly at Easter pay to the king, whose serf he is, a tax of three pence, and

this be understood to hold as well for a woman as for a man.

And that no Jew have power to enfeoff[4] another, Jew or Christian, with houses, rents or tenements that he now has, or to alienate them in any other manner, or to acquit any Christian of his debt without special permission of the king, until the king shall have otherwise ordained thereon.

And as it is the will and sufferance of holy church that they may live and be preserved, the king takes them into his protection and grants them his peace; and wills that they may be safely preserved and defended by his sheriffs and his other bailiffs and faithful; and commands that none shall do them harm or damage or wrong in their bodies or in their goods movable or immovable and that they shall neither plead nor be impleaded in any court, nor be challenged or troubled in any court, save in the court of the king, whose bondmen they are. And that none shall owe obedience or service or rent save to the king or to his bailiffs in his name, unless it be for their dwellings which they now hold by paying rent, saving the right of holy church.

And the king grants them that they may live by lawful trade and by their labor and that they may have intercourse with Christians in order to carry on lawful trade by selling and buying. But that no Christian for this cause or any other shall dwell among them. And the king wills that they shall not by reason of their trading be put to scot and lot or tallaged,[5] with those of the cities and boroughs where they live because they are liable for tallage to the king as his serfs and to no one other than the king.

Moreover the king grants them that they may buy houses and curtilages[6] in the cities and boroughs where they live, so that they hold them in chief of the king, saving to the lords of the fee[7] their services due and accustomed. And they may take and buy

---

1 As a legal term, "distress" means holding someone's property against the payment of a debt. Chattels are movable property, as opposed to land, which cannot be moved.
2 I.e., legal possession.
3 The "chirograph chests" were the boxes in which the records of debts were held. A chirograph was a document written in duplicate and cut such that the two parts would fit only with one another.
4 I.e., to give a fief to.
5 "Scot and lot" and tallage were taxes.
6 Yards or courtyards.
7 "Fee" is equivalent to fief.

farms or land for the term of ten years or less, without taking homages or fealties[1] or such sort of obedience from Christians, and without having advowsons[2] of churches, that they may be able to gain their living in the world if they have not the means of trading or cannot labor. And this power of taking lands at farm shall be open to them only for fifteen years from this time forward.

[*Petition of the "Commonalty" of the Jews* (shortly after 1275)]

To our lord the king and to his council the commonalty of the Jews ask the favor of their assent and discretion on the things written below.

Because the new statutes will that the Jews should have seisin of half only of lands and rents pledged to them, leaving the other half of the lands and rents and the chief messuage[3] for the sustenance of the Christian who is the debtor of the Jew, this is their enquiry: if the debtor of the Jew dies without heir of his body and without wife and the lands and rents fall to a rich man or to someone who has enough of his own to live on without these lands and rents that are pledged to the Jew, in such circumstances shall the Jew have possession of the whole of the pledged property until the debt is paid, or not?

Besides this, our question is about a Christian who has borrowed money from Jews which is the king's money and this Christian has no lands, rents or chattels save a large house which he occupies worth 100 shillings or 10 marks a year and if it were sold would fetch 100 marks or £100, what seisin will the Jew have of his pledge for the recovery of the debt seeing that this Christian has nothing save this house.

Further, the commonalty of the Jews beseech our lord the king that the poor Jews, who have nothing whereby to live or trade, may have leave to sell their houses and their rents to other Jews richer than themselves: it would be worth as much to our lord the king for the one lot of Jews to have the rents and houses as the other, and he could not lose by it. That if they have not leave to sell their houses they will have to demolish them and sell the stone and timber to various people.

Furthermore, the commonalty of the Jews demonstrate that they would be compelled if they were to trade at all to buy dearer than a Christian and to sell dearer, for Christian merchants sell their merchandise on credit and if the Jew sold on credit he would never be paid a single penny. And Christian merchants can carry their merchandise far and near but if the Jew carried his beyond the ...[4] he would be ... and robbed. And they beseech our lord the king and his council that ... such counsel in the Jewry that they can live in his time with his ... as in the time of his ancestors since the Conquest.

---

1   Lords normally received homage and fealty from their vassals, but such relations were not permitted between Jews and Christians.
2   The advowson was the right to an ecclesiastical benefice.
3   Messuage is a house and the land and buildings attached to it.
4   Here and elsewhere in this and the next sentence the writing is defaced and can no longer be read.

RULERS AND RULED

7.13 A charismatic ruler: Joinville, *The Life of St. Louis* (1272). Original in French.

LIKE IBN SHADDAD, WHO wrote about Saladin in his *Rare and Excellent History* (above, p. 334), Jean de Joinville (1225-1317) was a friend and confidant of the ruler he praised. In this case, the ruler was Louis IX (r.1226-1270), who would be canonized as St. Louis in 1297. Joinville met Louis on the Seventh Crusade in 1248 and remained in active service to the king thereafter. He began the first part of his *Life*, excerpted here, in 1272; he added a second part between 1298 and 1309. What did he admire most about the king? Did he have any criticisms? Compare the virtues that Joinville saw in St. Louis with the characteristics that ibn Shaddad prized in Saladin.

[Source: Joinville and Villehardouin, *Chronicles of the Crusades*, trans. M.R.B. Shaw (New York: Penguin Books, 1963), pp. 163-79 (slightly modified).]

PART ONE

CHAPTER I: *The Servant of God*

In the name of God Almighty, I, Jean, Lord of Joinville, Seneschal[1] of Champagne, dictate the life of our good King, Saint Louis, in which I shall record what I saw and heard both in the course of the six years in which I was on pilgrimage in his company overseas, and after we returned to France. But before I speak to you of his great deeds and his outstanding valor, I will tell you what I myself observed of his good teaching and his saintly conduct, so that it may be set down in due order for the edification of those to whom this book is read.

This saintly man loved our Lord with all his heart, and in all his actions followed His example. This is apparent from the fact that as our Lord died for the love he bore His people, even so King Louis put his own life in danger, and that several times, for the very same reason. It was danger too that he might well have avoided, as I shall show you later.

The great love King Louis bore his people is shown by what he said, as he lay dangerously ill at Fontainebleau, to his eldest son, my Lord Louis. "My dear son," he said, "I earnestly beg you to make yourself loved by all your people. For I would rather have a Scot come from Scotland to govern the people of this kingdom well and justly than that you should govern them ill in the sight of all the world." This upright king, moreover, loved truth so well that, as I shall show you later, he would never consent to lie to the Saracens[2] with regard to any covenant he made with them.

He was so temperate in his appetite that I never heard him, on any day of my life, order a special dish for himself, as many men of wealth and standing do. On the contrary, he would always eat with good grace whatever his cooks had prepared to set before him. He was equally temperate in his speech. I never, on any single occasion, heard him speak evil of any man; nor did I ever hear him utter the name of the Devil—a name in very common use throughout the kingdom—which practice, so I believe, is not pleasing to God.

He used to add water to his wine, but did so reasonably, according as the strength of the wine allowed it. While we were in Cyprus he asked me why I did not mix my wine with water. I replied that this was on the advice of my doctors, who had told me that I had a strong head and a cold stomach, so that I could not get drunk. He answered that they had deceived

---

1   Technically a senechal was a royal officer. But Joinville inherited the title from his father, and in his case it was largely an honorific.
2   The Saracens, i.e., the Muslims.

me; for if I did not learn to mix my wine with water while I was still young, and wished to do so in my old age, gout and stomach troubles would take hold on me, and I should never be in good health. Moreover, if I went on drinking undiluted wine when I was old, I should get drunk every night, and it was too revolting a thing for any brave man to be in such a state.

The king once asked me if I wished to be honored in this world, and to enter paradise when I died. I told him I did. "If so," said he, "you should avoid deliberately saying or doing anything which, if it became generally known, you would be ashamed to acknowledge by saying 'I did this,' or 'I said that.'" He also told me not to contradict or call in question anything said in my presence—unless indeed silence would imply approval of something wrong, or damaging to myself, because harsh words often lead to quarrelling, which has ended in the death of countless numbers of men.

He often said that people ought to clothe and arm themselves in such a way that men of riper age would never say they had spent too much on dress, or young men say they had spent too little. I repeated this remark to our present king when speaking of the elaborately embroidered tabards that are in vogue today.[1] I told him that, during the whole of our voyage overseas, I had never seen such embroidered tabards, either on the king or on any one else. He said to me that he had several such garments, with his own arms embroidered on them, and they had cost him eight hundred *livres parisis*. I told him that he would have put his money to better use if he had given it to God, and had his clothes made of good plain taffeta bearing his arms, as his father had done.

King Louis once sent for me and said: "You have such a shrewd and subtle mind that I hardly dare speak to you of things concerning God. So I have summoned these two monks to come here, because I want to ask you a question." Then he said: "Tell me, seneschal, what is your idea of God?" "Your Majesty," I replied, "He is something so good that there cannot be anything better." "Indeed," said he, "you've given me a very good answer; for it's precisely the same as the definition given in this book I have here in my hand."

"Now I ask you," he continued, "which you would prefer: to be a leper or to have committed some mortal sin?" And I, who had never lied to him, replied that I would rather have committed thirty mortal sins than become a leper. The next day, when the monks were no longer there, he called me to him, and making me sit at his feet said to me: "Why did you say that to me yesterday?" I told him I would still say it. "You spoke without thinking, and like a fool," he said. "You ought to know there is no leprosy so foul as being in a state of mortal sin; for the soul in that condition is like the Devil; therefore no leprosy can be so vile. Besides, when a man dies his body is healed of its leprosy; but if he dies after committing a mortal sin, he can never be sure that, during his lifetime, he has repented of it sufficiently for God to forgive him. In consequence, he must be greatly afraid lest that leprosy of sin should last as long as God dwells in paradise. So I beg you," he added, "as earnestly as I can, for the love of God, and for love of me, to train your heart to prefer any evil that can happen to the body, whether it be leprosy or any other disease, rather than let mortal sin take possession of your soul."

At another time King Louis asked me if I washed the feet of the poor on Maundy Thursday.[2] "Your Majesty," I exclaimed, "what a terrible idea! I will never wash the feet of such low fellows." "Really," said he, "that is a very wrong thing to say; for you should never scorn to do what our Lord Himself did as an example for us. So I beg you, first for the love of God and then for love of me, to accustom yourself to washing the feet of the poor."

This good king so loved all manner of people who believed in God and loved Him that he appointed Gilles le Brun, who was not a native of his realm, as High Constable of France, because he was held in such high repute for his faith in God and devotion to His service. For my part, I believe he well deserved that reputation. Another man, Master Robert de Sorbon,[3]

---

1 A tabard was a tunic worn over armor and embroidered with a coat of arms. "Our present king" was Louis's grandson Philip IV "The Fair," king of France 1285-1314.

2 This is also known as Holy Thursday, the Thursday before Easter Sunday.

3 Robert de Sorbon was Louis's chaplain and founder (in 1257) of the college of the Sorbonne, today the University of Paris. He had the title of Master because he was qualified, by his university training, to teach Theology.

who was famed for his goodness and his learning, was invited, on that account, to dine at the royal table.

It happened one day that this worthy priest was sitting beside me at dinner, and we were talking to each other rather quietly. The king reproved us and said: "Speak up, or your companions may think you are speaking ill of them. If at table you talk of things that may give us pleasure, say them aloud, or else be silent."

When the king was feeling in a mood for fun, he would fire questions at me, as for instance: "Seneschal, can you give me reasons why a wise and upright layman is better than a friar?" Thereupon a discussion would begin between Master Robert and myself. When we had disputed for some length of time the king would pronounce judgement. "Master Robert," he would say, "I would willingly be known as a wise and upright man, provided I were so in reality—and you can have all the rest. For wisdom and goodness are such fine qualities that even to name them leaves a pleasant taste in the mouth."

On the other hand, he always said that it was a wicked thing to take other people's property. "To 'restore,'" he would say, "is such a hard thing to do that even in speaking of it the word itself rasps one's throat because of the *r*'s that are in it. These *r*'s are, so to speak, like the rakes of the Devil, with which he would draw to himself all those who wish to 'restore' what they have taken from others. The Devil, moreover, does this very subtly; for he works on great usurers and great robbers in such a way that they give to God what they ought to *restore* to men."

On one occasion the king gave me a message to take to King Thibaut,[1] in which he warned his son-in-law to beware lest he should lay too heavy a burden on his soul by spending an excessive amount of money on the house he was building for the Predicants[2] of Provins. "Wise men," said the king, "deal with their possessions as executors ought to do. Now the first thing a good executor does is to settle all debts incurred by the deceased and restore any property belonging to others, and only then is he free to apply what money remains to charitable purposes."

One Pentecost the saintly king happened to be at Corbeil, where all the knights had assembled. He had come down after dinner into the court below the chapel, and was standing at the doorway talking to the Count of Brittany, the father of the present count—may God preserve him!—when Master Robert de Sorbon came to look for me, and taking hold of the hem of my mantle led me towards the king. So I said to Master Robert: "My good sir, what do you want with me?" He replied: "I wish to ask you whether, if the king were seated in this court and you went and sat down on his bench, at a higher place than he, you ought to be severely blamed for doing so?" I told him I ought to be. "Then," he said "you certainly deserve a reprimand for being more richly dressed than the king, since you are wearing a fur-trimmed mantle of fine green cloth, and he wears no such thing." "Master Robert," I answered, "I am, if you'll allow me to say so, doing nothing worthy of blame in wearing green cloth and fur, for I inherited the right to such dress from my father and mother. But you, on the other hand, are much to blame, for though both your parents were commoners, you have abandoned their style of dress, and are now wearing finer woollen cloth than the king himself." Then I took hold of the skirt of his surcoat and of the surcoat worn by the king, and said to Master Robert: "See if I'm not speaking the truth." At this the king began to take Master Robert's part, and say all in his power to defend him.

A little later on the king beckoned to his son, the Prince Philip—the father of our present king—and to King Thibaut. Then, seating himself at the entrance to his oratory, he patted the ground and said to the two young men: "Sit down here, quite close to me, so that we won't be overheard." "But, my lord," they protested, "we should not dare to sit so close to you." Then the king said to me, "Seneschal, you sit here." I obeyed, and sat down so close to him that my clothes were touching his. He made the two others sit down next, and said to them: "You have acted very wrongly, seeing you are my sons, in not doing as I commanded the moment I told you. I beg you to see this does not happen again." They assured him it would not.

---

1 Thibaut (1201-1253) was count of Champagne and, starting in 1234, king of Navarre. He was a *trouvère*, that is a troubadour who wrote in French rather than Occitan, the language of southern France.

2 Predicants was another word for the Dominicans.

Then the king said to me that he had called us to-gether to confess that he had wrongly defended Mas-ter Robert against me. "But," said he, "I saw he was so taken aback that he greatly needed my help. All the same you must not attach too great importance to anything I may have said in his defence. As the seneschal rightly says, you ought to dress well, and in a manner suited to your condition, so that your wives will love you all the more and your men have more respect for you. For, as a wise philosopher has said, our clothing and our armor ought to be of such a kind that men of mature experience will not say that we have spent too much on them, nor younger men say we have spent too little."

I will tell you here of one of the lessons King Louis taught me on our voyage back from the land over-seas.[1] It so happened that our ship was driven on to the rocks off the island of Cyprus by a wind known as the *garbino*, which is not one of the four great winds. At the shock our ship received the sailors were so frantic with despair that they rent their clothes and tore their beards. The king sprang out of bed barefoot—for it was night—and with nothing on but his tunic went and lay with arms outstretched to form a cross before the body of Our Lord on the altar, as one who ex-pected nothing but death.

The day after this alarming event, the king called me aside to talk with him alone, and said to me: "Sen-eschal, God has just shown us a glimpse of His great power; for one of these little winds, so little indeed that it scarcely deserves a name, came near to drown-ing the King of France, his children, his wife, and his men. Now Saint Anselm says that such things are warnings from our Lord, as if God meant to say to us: 'See how easily I could have brought about your death if that had been My will.' ' Lord God,' says the saint, 'why do You thus threaten us? For when you do, it is not for Your own profit, nor for Your ad-vantage—seeing that if You had caused us all to be lost You would be none the poorer, nor any the richer either if You had caused us to be saved. Therefore, the warning You send us is not for Your own benefit, but for ours, if we know how to profit by it.'

"Let us therefore," said the king, "take this warn-ing God has sent us in such a way that if we feel there is anything in our hearts or our bodies that is displeas-ing to Him, we shall get rid of it without delay. If, on the other hand, we can think of anything that will please Him, we ought to see about doing it with equal speed. If we act thus our Lord will give us blessings in this world, and in the next greater bliss than we can tell. But if we do not act as we ought, He will deal with us as a good lord deals with his unfaithful ser-vant. For if the latter will not amend his ways after he has been given warning, then his lord punishes him with death, or with penalties even harder to bear."

So I, Jean de Joinville, say: "Let the king who now reigns over us beware; for he has escaped from per-ils as great as those to which we were then exposed, or even greater. Therefore, let him turn from doing wrong, and in such a way that God will not smite him cruelly, either in himself or in his possessions."

In the conversations he had with me, this saintly king did every thing in his power to give me a firm belief in the principles of Christianity as given us by God. He used to say that we ought to have such an unshaken belief in all the articles of faith that neither fear of death nor of any harm that might happen to our bodies should make us willing to go against them in word or deed. "The Enemy,"[2] he would add, "works so subtly that when people are at the point of death he tries all he can to make them die with some doubt in their minds on certain points of our religion. For this cunning adversary is well aware that he cannot take away the merit of any good works a man has done; and he also knows that a man's soul is lost to him if he dies in the true faith.

"Therefore," the king would say. "it is our duty so to defend and guard ourselves against this snare as to say to the Enemy, when he sends us such a temptation: 'Go away! You shall not lure me from my steadfast be-lief in the articles of my faith. Even if you had all my limbs cut off, I would still live and die a true believer.' Whoever acts thus overcomes the Devil with the very same weapons with which this enemy of mankind had proposed to destroy him."

---

1 Louis went overseas on two crusades. This refers to his first, the Seventh Crusade, which, like the next one, was a failure. Louis died in the course of his second crusade.
2 "The Enemy" is the devil.

King Louis would also say that the Christian religion as defined in the creed was something in which we ought to believe implicitly, even though our belief in it might be founded on hearsay. On this point he asked me what was my father's name. I told him it was Simon. So he asked me how I knew it, and I replied that I thought I was certain of it, and believed it without question, because I had my mother's word for it. "Then," said he, "you ought to have a sure belief in all the articles of our faith on the word of the Apostles, which you hear sung of a Sunday in the Creed."

On one occasion the king repeated to me what Guillaume, Bishop of Paris, had told him about a certain eminent theologian who had come to see him. This man told the bishop that he wished to speak with him. "Speak as freely as you like, sir," said the bishop. However, when the theologian tried to speak to him he only burst into tears. So the bishop said: "Say what you have to say, sir; don't be disheartened; no one can be such a sinner that God can no longer forgive him." "Indeed, my lord," said the theologian, "I cannot control my tears. For I fear I must be an apostate, since I cannot compel my heart to believe in the sacrament of the altar, in the way that Holy Church teaches. Yet I know very well that this is a temptation of the Enemy."

"Pray tell me, sir," said the bishop, "do you feel any pleasure when the Enemy exposes you to this temptation?" "On the contrary, my lord," said the theologian, "it worries me as much as anything can." "Now," said the bishop, "I will ask you whether you would accept any gold or silver if it were offered you on condition you allowed your mouth to utter anything derogatory to the sacrament of the altar, or the other sacraments of Holy Church?" "My lord," said the other, "I can assure you that nothing in the world would induce me to do so. I would rather have one of my limbs torn from my body than consent to say such a thing."

"I will now," said the bishop, "take a different approach. You know that the King of France is at war with the King of England; you also know that the castle nearest the boundary-line between their two domains is the castle of Rochelle in Poitou. So I will ask you a question: Suppose the king had set you to guard the castle of Rochelle, and had put me in charge of the castle of Montlhéri, which is in the very center of France, where the land is at peace, to which of us do you think the king would feel most indebted at the end of the war—to you who had guarded La Rochelle without loss, or to me who had remained in safety at Montlhéri?" "Why, in God's name, my lord," cried the theologian, "to me, who had guarded La Rochelle, and not lost it to the enemy."

"Sir," said the bishop, "my heart is like the castle of Montlhéri; for I have neither temptation nor doubts concerning the sacrament of the altar. For this reason I tell you that if God owes me any grace because my faith is secure and untroubled, He owes four times as much to you, who have kept your heart from defeat when beset by tribulations, and have moreover such good-will towards Him that neither worldly advantage, nor fear of any harm that might be done to your body, could tempt you to renounce Him. So I tell you to be comforted; for your state is more pleasing to Our Lord than mine." When the theologian heard this, he knelt before the bishop, at peace with himself, and well satisfied.

The king once told me how several men from among the Albigenses[1] had gone to the count of Montfort, who at the time was guarding their land for his Majesty, and asked him to come and look at the body of our Lord, which had become flesh and blood in the hands of the priest. The count had answered: "Go and see it for yourselves, you who do not believe it. As for me, I believe it firmly, in accordance with Holy Church's teaching on the sacrament of the altar. And do you know," he added, "what I shall gain for having, in this mortal life, believed what Holy Church teaches us? I shall have a crown in heaven, and a finer one than the angels, for they see God face to face and consequently cannot but believe."

King Louis also spoke to me of a great assembly of clergy and Jews which had taken place at the monastery of Cluny. There was a poor knight there at the time to whom the abbot had often given bread for the

---

1 The "Albigenses" (or Albigensians), like the Cathars and Manichaeans, was another name for those who called themselves "Christ's Poor." For a document from the inquisition of an accused member of this group by the bishop of Pamiers, see above, p. 435.

love of God. This knight asked the abbot if he could speak first, and his request was granted, though somewhat grudgingly. So he rose to his feet, and leaning on his crutch, asked to have the most important and most learned rabbi among the Jews brought before him. As soon as the Jew had come, the knight asked him a question. "May I know, sir," he said, "if you believe that the Virgin Mary, who bore our Lord in her body and cradled Him in her arms, was a virgin at the time of His birth, and is in truth the Mother of God?"

The Jew replied that he had no belief in any of those things. Thereupon the knight told the Jew that he had acted like a fool when—neither believing in the Virgin, nor loving her—he had set foot in that monastery which was her house. "And by heaven," exclaimed the knight, "I'll make you pay for it!" So he lifted his crutch and struck the Jew such a blow with it near the ear that he knocked him down. Then all the Jews took to flight, and carried their sorely wounded rabbi away with them. Thus the conference ended.

The abbot went up to the knight and told him he had acted most unwisely. The knight retorted that the abbot had been guilty of even greater folly in calling people together for such a conference, because there were many good Christians there who, before the discussion ended, would have gone away with doubts about their own religion through not fully understanding the Jews. "So I tell you," said the king, "that no one, unless he is an expert theologian, should venture to argue with these people. But a layman, whenever he hears the Christian religion abused, should not attempt to defend its tenets, except with his sword, and that he should thrust into the scoundrel's belly, and as far as it will enter."

CHAPTER 2: *The Servant of his People*
In the midst of attending to the affairs of his realm King Louis so arranged his day that he had time to hear the Hours[1] sung by a full choir and a Requiem mass without music. In addition, if it was convenient, he would hear low mass for the day, or high mass on Saints' days. Every day after dinner he rested on his bed, and when he had slept and was refreshed, he and one of his chaplains would say the Office for the Dead privately in his room. Later in the day he attended vespers, and compline at night.

A Franciscan friar once came to see him at the castle of Hyères, where we had disembarked on our return to France. In his sermon, intended for the king's instruction, he said that in his reading of the Bible and other books that speak of non-Christian princes he had never found, in the history of either heathen or Christian peoples, that a kingdom had been lost or had changed its ruler, except where justice had been ignored. "Therefore," said he, "let the king who is now returning to France[2] take good care to see that he administers justice well and promptly to his people, so that our Lord may allow him to rule his kingdom in peace to the end of his days." I have been told that the worthy man who taught the king this lesson lies buried at Marseille, where our Lord, for his sake, still performs many a fine miracle. He would never consent to remain with the king for more than a single day, however strongly his Majesty pressed him to stay. All the same, the king never forgot the good friar's teaching, but governed his kingdom well and faithfully according to God's law.

In dealing with each day's business, the king's usual plan was to send for Jean de Nesles, the good count of Soissons, and the rest of us, as soon as we had heard mass, and tell us to go and hear the pleadings at the gate of the city which is now called the Gate of Requests.

After he had returned from church the king would send for us, and sitting at the foot of his bed would make us all sit round him, and ask us if there were any cases that could not be settled except by his personal intervention. After we had told him which they were, he would send for the interested parties and ask them: "Why did you not accept what our people offer?" "Your Majesty," they would reply, "because they offer us too little." Then he would say: "You would do well to accept whatever they are willing to give you." Our saintly king would thus do his utmost to bring them round to a right and reasonable way of thinking.

In summer, after hearing mass, the king often went to the wood of Vincennes, where he would sit down

---

1 The Hours refers to the daily offices of prayer.
2 "France" refers to the Ile-de-France. Hyères was (and is) in Provence. Joinville is again referring to the king's return from the Seventh Crusade.

with his back against an oak, and make us all sit round him. Those who had any suit to present could come to speak to him without hindrance from an usher or any other person. The king would address them directly, and ask: "Is there anyone here who has a case to be settled?" Those who had one would stand up. Then he would say: "Keep silent all of you, and you shall be heard in turn, one after the other." Then he would call Peter de Fontaines and Geoffry de Villette, and say to one or other of them: "Settle this case for me." If he saw anything needing correction in what was said by those who spoke on his behalf or on behalf of any other person, he would himself intervene to make the necessary adjustment.

I have sometimes seen him, in summer, go to administer justice to his people in the public gardens in Paris, dressed in a plain woollen tunic, a sleeveless surcoat of linsey-woolsey,[1] and a black taffeta cape round his shoulders, with his hair neatly combed, but no cap to cover it, and only a hat of white peacock's feathers on his head. He would have a carpet laid down so that we might sit round him, while all those who had any case to bring before him stood round about. Then he would pass judgement on each case, as I have told you he often used to do in the wood of Vincennes.

I saw the king on another occasion, at a time when all the French prelates had said they wished to speak with him, and he had gone to his palace to hear what they had to say. Bishop Guy of Auxerre, the son of William de Mello, was among those present, and he addressed the king on behalf of all the prelates. "Your Majesty," he said, "the Lords Spiritual of this realm here present, have directed me to tell you that the cause of Christianity, which it is your duty to guard and defend, is being ruined in your hands." On hearing these words the king crossed himself and said: "Pray tell me how that may be."

"Your Majesty," said the bishop, "it is because at the present time excommunications are so lightly regarded that people think nothing of dying without seeking absolution, and refuse to make their peace with the Church. The Lords Spiritual[2] require you therefore, for the love of God and because it is your duty, to command your provosts and your bailiffs[3] to seek out all those who allow themselves to remain under the ban of the Church[4] for a year and a day, and compel them, by seizure of their possessions, to get themselves absolved."

The king replied that he would willingly give such orders provided he himself could be shown without any doubt that the persons concerned were in the wrong. The bishop told him that the prelates would not on any account accept this condition, since they questioned his right to adjudicate in their affairs. The king replied that he would not do anything other than he had said; for it would be against God and contrary to right and justice if he compelled any man to seek absolution when the clergy were doing him wrong.

"As an example of this," he continued, "I will quote the case of the Count of Brittany, who for seven whole years, while under sentence of excommunication, pleaded his cause against the bishops of his province, and carried his case so far that in the end the Pope condemned all his adversaries. Now, if at the end of the first year I had forced the count to seek absolution, I should have sinned against God and against the man himself." So the prelates resigned themselves to accepting things as they were; and I have never heard tell that any further demand was made in relation to this matter.

In making peace with the King of England, King Louis acted against the advice of his council, who had said to him: "It seems to us that Your Majesty is needlessly throwing away the land you are giving to the King of England; for he has no right to it, since it was justly taken from his father." To this the king replied that he was well aware that the King of England had no right to the land, but there was a reason why he felt bound to give it to him. "You see," said he, "our wives are sisters and consequently our children are first cousins. That is why it is most important for us to be at peace with each other. Besides, I gain increased honor for myself through the peace I have made with

---

1   A coarse woven fabric made of wool and linen.
2   I.e., the bishops.
3   Provosts and bailiffs were royal officers (Guillaume Austatz, the man accused of heresy by the bishop of Pamiers [p. 435 above], was a bailiff).
4   "The ban of the church," was excommunication.

the King of England, for he is now my vassal, which he has never been before."

The king's love for fair and open dealing may be gathered from his behaviour in the case of a certain Renaud de Trit. This man had brought the king a charter stating that he had granted the county of Dammartin in Gouelle to the heirs of the late countess of Boulogne. However, the seal of the charter was broken, so that nothing remained of it except half the legs of the figure representing the king, and the stool on which his feet were resting. The king showed the seal to all of us who were members of his council, and asked us to help him come to a decision. We all unanimously expressed the opinion that he was not bound to put the charter into effect. Then he told Jean Sarrasin, his chamberlain, to hand him a charter he had asked him to get. As soon as this was in his hands the king said to us: "My lords, here is the seal I used before I went overseas, and you can clearly tell from looking at it that the impression on the broken seal corresponds exactly with that of the one that is whole. Therefore I could not, with a clear conscience, keep back this land." So the king sent for Renaud de Trit and said to him: "I restore your county to you."

7.14 The commons participate: *Summons of Representatives of Shires and Towns to Parliament (1295). Original in Latin.*

IN 1264, THE ENGLISH REBEL Simon de Montfort called members of the commons in both town and country to a meeting of parliament. It became a precedent for subsequent assemblies. When King Edward I (r.1272-1307) issued summonses to a parliament of 1295, he sent out letters individually to the members of the higher clergy and his barons. At the same time, as the document printed below shows, he sent letters to the sheriffs of the realm to summon representatives of "the knights, citizens, and burgesses"—the commons.

[Source: *Translations and Reprints from the Original Sources of European History,* vol. 1, no. 6, *English Constitutional Documents,* ed. Edward Potts Cheyney (Philadelphia: Department of History of the University of Pennsylvania, 1902), p. 35.]

The king to the sheriff of Northamptonshire.

Since we intend to have a consultation and meeting with the earls, barons and other principal men of our kingdom with regard to providing remedies against the dangers which are in these days threatening the same kingdom, and on that account have commanded them to be with us on the Lord's day next after the feast of St. Martin,[1] in the approaching winter, at Westminster, to consider, ordain, and do as may be necessary for the avoidance of these dangers, we strictly require you to cause two knights from the aforesaid county, two citizens from each city in the same county, and two burgesses from each borough, of those who are especially discreet and capable of laboring, to be elected without delay, and to cause them to come to us at the aforesaid time and place.

Moreover, the said knights are to have full and sufficient power for themselves and for the community of the aforesaid county, and the said citizens and burgesses for themselves and the communities of the aforesaid cities and boroughs separately, then and there for doing what shall then be ordained according to the common counsel in the premises, so that the aforesaid business shall not remain unfinished in any way for defect of this power. And you shall have there the names of the knights, citizens and burgesses and this writ.

Witness the king at Canterbury, on the third day of October.

[Identical summonses were sent to the sheriffs of each county.]

---

1   I.e., the first Sunday after November 11.

The pope throws down the gauntlet: Boniface VIII, *Clericis Laicos* (1296). Original in Latin.

PREPARING FOR WAR AGAINST ONE another, Kings Philip IV of France and Edward I of England taxed their clergy along with everyone else. But Pope Boniface VIII (r.1294-1303) vehemently objected, arguing in his bull *Clericis Laicos* that laymen, even rulers, had "no control over the clergy," calling on clerics not to give in to royal demands, and threatening excommunication of all who ignored his prescriptions. In response, Philip prohibited any gold or silver from leaving France, thus depriving the pope of a major revenue source. For his part, Edward declared the English clergy "outlaw"—that is, outside the protection of the law. Boniface backed down. Looking back at Gregory VII's *Letter to Hermann of Metz* on p. 282, how new would you consider Boniface's complaints about secular rulers and his notions of papal powers and rights?

[Source: *Translations and Reprints from the Original Sources of European History,* vol. 3, no. 6, *The Pre-Reformation Period,* ed. James Harvey Robinson (Philadelphia: Department of History of the University of Pennsylvania, 1907), pp. 23-25.]

Bishop Boniface, servant of the servants of God, in perpetual memory of this matter. Antiquity shows us that the laity has always been exceeding hostile to the clergy; and this the experience of the present time clearly demonstrates, since, not content with their limitations, the laity strive for forbidden things and give free reign to the pursuit of illicit gain.

They do not prudently observe that all control over the clergy, as well as over all ecclesiastical persons and their possessions, is denied them, but impose heavy burdens upon the prelates of the churches, upon the churches themselves, and upon ecclesiastical persons both regular and secular, exacting tallages[1] and other contributions from them. From such persons they require and extort the payment of a half, a tenth, a twentieth or some other quota of their property or income, and strive in many other ways to subject the churchmen to slavery and bring them under their control.

And (with grief do we declare it) certain prelates of the churches and ecclesiastical persons, fearing where they ought not to fear, and seeking a temporary peace, dreading to offend a temporal more than the eternal majesty, do, without having received the permission or sanction of the Apostolic See, acquiesce in such abuses, not so much from recklessness, as want of foresight. We, therefore, desiring to check these iniquitous practices, by the council of our brothers, do, of our apostolic authority, decree that whatever prelates and ecclesiastical persons, whether monastic or secular, whatever their order, condition or status, shall pay, or promise or agree to pay to laymen, any contributions or tallages, tenths, twentieths, or hundredths of their own, or their churches' revenues or possessions, or shall pay any sum, portion or part of their revenues or goods, or of their estimated or actual value, in the form of an aid, loan, subvention, subsidy or gift, or upon any other pretense or fiction whatsoever, without authority from this same Apostolic See,—likewise emperors, kings and princes, dukes, counts, barons, podestà, captains, officers, rectors, whatever their title, of cities, castles or other places wherever situated, or any other persons, whatever their rank, condition or status, who shall impose, exact or receive such payments, or who shall presume to lay hands upon, seize or occupy the possessions of churches or the goods of ecclesiastical persons deposited in the sacred edifices, or who shall order such to be seized or occupied, or shall receive such things as shall be seized or occupied,—likewise all who shall consciously lend aid, council or support in such undertakings, either publicly or privately,—shall, by the very act, incur the sentence of excommunication; corporations, moreover, which shall show themselves

---

1 I.e., taxes.

guilty in these matters, we place under the interdict.[1]

We strictly command all prelates and ecclesiastical persons above mentioned, in virtue of their obedience, and under penalty of deposition, that they shall not hereafter acquiesce in any such demands, without the express permission of the aforesaid Chair.[2] Nor shall they pay anything under pretext of any obligation, promise or declaration made in the past, or which may be made before this notice, prohibition or order shall be brought to their attention. Nor shall the above-mentioned laymen in any way receive any such payments. And if the former pay or the latter receive anything, they shall incur, by the act itself, the sentence of excommunication. No one, moreover, shall be freed from the above mentioned sentences of excommunication or of the interdict, except in the article of death, without the authority and special per-

mission of the Apostolic See, since it is our intention to make no kind of compromise with such a horrible abuse of the secular power; and this notwithstanding any privileges, whatever their tenor, form or wording, conceded to emperors, kings or other persons above mentioned, for we will that such concessions as are in conflict with the preceding prohibitions shall avail no individual person or persons. Let no man at all, therefore, violate the page of this our decree, prohibition or order, or with rash assumption, contravene it. Whoever shall presume to attempt this, let him know that he shall incur the indignation of omnipotent God and of the blessed Peter and Paul, His apostles.

Given at Rome, at Saint Peter's, on the sixth day before the Kalends of March, in the second year of our Pontificate.

7.16 The pope reacts again: Boniface VIII, *Unam Sanctam* (1302). Original in Latin.

IN 1301, KING PHILIP IV OF France arrested—on charges of treason—the bishop of Pamiers, Bernard Saisset, whom Boniface had named to the post without royal approval. Like Becket some 130 years before in England, Boniface demanded that the bishop be tried in a church court. In *Unam Sanctam* he affirmed the superior power of the pope. Soon thereafter, he excommunicated Philip. How might you compare his claims for papal power in this bull with his assertions in *Clericis Laicos*, above, p. 455?

[Source: *Translations and Reprints from the Original Sources of European History,* vol. 3, no. 6, *The Pre-Reformation Period,* ed. James Harvey Robinson (Philadelphia: Department of History of the University of Pennsylvania, 1907), pp. 20-23 (notes added).]

That there is one Holy Catholic and Apostolic Church we are impelled by our faith to believe and to hold—this we do firmly believe and openly confess—and outside of this there is neither salvation or remission of sins, as the bridegroom proclaims in Canticles, "My dove, my undefiled is but one; she is the only one of her mother; she is the choice one of her that bare her."[3] The Church represents one mystic body and of this body Christ is the head; of Christ, indeed, God is the head. In it is one Lord, and one faith, and one baptism. In the time of

the flood, there was one ark of Noah, pre-figuring the one Church, finished in one cubit, having one Noah as steersman and commander. Outside of this, all things upon the face of the earth were, as we read, destroyed. This Church we venerate and this alone, the Lord saying through his prophets, "Deliver my soul, O God, from the sword; my darling from the power of the dog."[4] He prays thus for the soul, that is for Himself, as head, and also for the body which He calls one, namely, the Church on account of the unity of the bridegroom,

---

1 The interdict deprived people in a particular area or district of the benefit of many of the sacraments.
2 I.e., the Apostolic See.
3 See Song of Sol. 5: 2 and 6: 8.
4 Ps. 22: 20; Douay Ps. 21: 21.

of the faith, of the sacraments, and of the charity of the Church. It is that seamless coat of the Lord, which was not rent, but fell by lot.[1] Therefore, in this one and only Church, there is one body and one head,—not two heads as if it were a monster—namely, Christ and Christ's Vicar, Peter and Peter's successor, for the Lord said to Peter himself, "Feed my sheep:"[2] *my* sheep, he said, using a general term and not designating these or those sheep, so that we must believe that all the sheep were committed to him. If, then, the Greeks, or others, shall say that they were not entrusted to Peter and his successors, they must perforce admit that they are not of Christ's sheep, as the lord says in John, "there is one fold, and one shepherd."[3]

In this Church and in its power are two swords, to wit, a spiritual and a temporal, and this we are taught by the words of the Gospel, for when the Apostles said, "Behold, here are two swords"[4] (in the Church, namely, since the Apostles were speaking), the Lord did not reply that it was too many, but enough. And surely he who claims that the temporal sword is not in the power of Peter has but ill understood the word of our Lord when he said, "Put up thy sword in its scabbard."[5] Both, therefore, the spiritual and the material swords, are in the power of the Church, the latter indeed to be used for the Church, the former by the Church, the one by the priest, the other by the hand of kings and soldiers, but by the will and sufferance of the priest. It is fitting, moreover, that one sword should be under the other, and the temporal authority subject to the spiritual power. For when the Apostle said, "there is no power but of God and the powers that are of God are ordained," they would not be disposed in an orderly manner unless one sword were guided by the performance of the most exalted deeds. For, according to the Holy Dionysius,[6] the law of divinity is to lead the lowest through the intermediate to the highest. Therefore, according to the law of the universe, things are not reduced to order directly, and upon the same footing, but the lowest through the intermediate, and the inferior through the superior. It behooves us, therefore, the more freely to confess that the spiritual power excels in dignity and nobility any form whatsoever of earthly power, as spiritual interests exceed the temporal in importance. All this we see fairly from the giving of tithes, from the benediction and sanctification, from the recognition of this power and the control of these same things. For the truth bearing witness, it is for the spiritual power to establish the earthly power and judge it, if it be not good. Thus, in the case of the Church and the power of the Church, the prophecy of Jeremiah is fulfilled: "See, I have this day set thee over the nations and over the kingdoms"[7]—and so forth. Therefore, if the earthly power shall err, it shall be judged by the spiritual power; if the lesser spiritual power err, it shall be judged by the higher. But if the supreme power err, it can be judged by God alone and not by man, the apostles bearing witness saying, the spiritual man judges all things but he himself is judged by no one. Hence this power, although given to man and exercised by man, is not human, but rather a divine power, given by the divine lips to Peter, and founded on a rock for Him and his successors in Him [Christ] whom he confessed, the Lord saying to Peter himself, "Whatsoever thou shalt bind," etc.[8] Whoever, therefore, shall resist this power, ordained by God, resists the ordination of God, unless there should be two beginnings, as the Manichaean imagines. But this we judge to be false and heretical, since, by the testimony of Moses, not in the *beginnings*, but in the *beginning*, God created the heaven and the earth. We, moreover, proclaim, declare and pronounce that it is altogether necessary to salvation for every human being to be subject to the Roman Pontiff.

Given at the Lateran the twelfth day before the Kalends of December, in our eighth year, as a perpetual memorial of this matter.

---

1   See John 19: 23-24.
2   John 21: 15-17.
3   John 10: 16.
4   Luke 22: 38.
5   John 18: 11.
6   Now known as Pseudo-Dionysius, this is the same Syrian thinker (*fl. c.*500) whose ideas inspired Suger's rebuilding of Saint-Denis; see *On What was Done under his Administration* above, p. 401.
7   Jer. 1: 10.
8   A reference to Matt. 16: 18-19, where Jesus refers to Peter as the "rock" upon which he will build his church. The papacy quoted this as a foundational text: compare its use in Gregory VII's *Letter to Hermann of Metz*, above, p. 283.

7.17 The French king responds to Boniface: William of Plaisians, *Charges of Heresy against Boniface VIII* (1303). Original in Latin.

IN THE WAKE OF *Unam Sanctam*, William of Plaisians—a councillor to King Philip IV well trained in the law—claimed that Boniface was a heretic and drew up a bill of particulars that he presented at a great assembly of high churchmen and nobles at Paris. There was indeed some question about Boniface's election as pope, but mainly the charges were invented—pure propaganda aimed at arousing public opinion. In that they were successful. Taking *Clericis Laicos* and *Unam Sanctam* into account, and considering how Guillaume Austatz defended himself against charges of heresy (above, p. 435), write what you think might be Boniface's replies to these charges.

[Source: *Philip the Fair and Boniface VIII: State vs. Papacy*, ed. Charles T. Wood, 2nd ed. (New York: Holt, Rinehart and Winston, 1967), pp. 64-65 (notes added).]

I, William of Plaisians, say, advance, and affirm that Boniface, who now occupies the Holy See, will be found a perfect heretic, according to the heresies, prodigious facts, and perverse doctrines hereafter mentioned:

1. He does not believe in the immortality or incorruptibility of the rational soul, but believes that the rational soul is corrupted along with the body.

2. He does not believe in the life eternal, ... and he has not been ashamed to assert that he would rather be a dog, ass, or any other brute than a Frenchman, which he would not say if he believed that a Frenchman had a soul....

4. He does not faithfully believe that, because of the words instituted by Christ, spoken by a faithful and ordained priest over a Host in the way set by the Church, it becomes the true body of Christ....

6. He is reported to claim that fornication is no more a sin than is rubbing one's hands together: and this he has said loudly and publicly.

7. He has often said that if nothing else could be done to humble the king and the French, he would ruin himself, the whole world, and the whole Church....

9. To perpetuate his most damnable memory he has had silver statues of himself erected in churches, in this way leading men into idolatry.

10. He has a private demon whose advice he follows in all things. Whence he has once said that if all the men in the world were on one side and he on the other, they could not deceive him, either in law or in deed, which is impossible unless he employs the demonic art. And all this is publicly known.

11. He is a soothsayer who consults diviners and oracles. And all this is publicly known.

12. He has publicly preached that the Roman pontiff cannot commit simony,[1] which is heretical to say....

14. Like a confirmed heretic, who claims the true faith as his alone, he has termed the French, notoriously a most Christian people, heretics....

15. He is a Sodomite and keeps concubines. And this is publicly and commonly known.

16. He has had many clerks killed in his presence, rejoicing in their deaths....

17. When he condemned a certain noble to prison, despite the latter's penitent pleas he forbade anyone to minister the sacrament of penance at the hour of death; from which it seems he believes that the sacrament of penance is not necessary for salvation.

18. He has compelled priests to violate the secrets of the confessional and, without the assent of those who confessed, has made their confessions public to their confusion and shame....

---

1 Simony was the purchasing of church offices; its name derived from Simon Magus, who in Acts 8: 18-24 offered money to Peter and John if they would give him the power to confer the Holy Spirit.

19. He fasts neither on fast days nor in Lent....

20. He has lowered and debased the status and rank of the cardinals, the black and white monks, and the Friars Minor and Preacher, often repeating that the world was being ruined by them, that they were false hypocrites, and that nothing good would happen to anyone who confessed to them....

21. Seeking to destroy the faith, he has long harbored an aversion against the king of France, in hatred of the faith, because in France there is and ever was the splendor of the faith, the grand support and example of Christendom....

23. It is notorious that the Holy Land has been lost as a result of his sins....

24. He is openly termed a simonist, indeed the font and source of simony, selling benefices to the highest bidder, imposing on the Church and bishops both serfdom and the *taille*,[1] so that he may enrich his family and friends with the patrimony of the Crucified and make them marquises, counts, and barons....

25. It is notorious that he has dissolved many legitimately consummated marriages against the precept of the Lord and to the hurt and scandal of many; and he raised to the cardinalate his married nephew, a man wholly unworthy and inexperienced, one who led and leads a notoriously dissolute life, while his wife was alive.... And all this is publicly known.[2]

26. It is notorious that he treated his predecessor Celestine inhumanely, a man of holy memory who led a holy life;[3] and that, because Celestine could not resign and because, therefore, Boniface could not legitimately succeed to the Holy See, the latter threw him in prison and had him quickly and secretly killed. And all this is widely and publicly known by the whole world....

29. It is notorious that he seeks not the salvation of souls, but their perdition.

7.18 Assembly of the Estates General in Paris: *Grand Chronicles of France* (1314). Original in French.

THE ESTATES GENERAL OF France was roughly comparable to the English parliament, though it was not called so regularly, and it originated later. It was an assembly of the "estates" or "orders": the higher clergy, the nobles, and—sometimes—the non-noble laymen from the towns. The king called it together when he thought it would be in his interest: the first meeting was in 1302, when Philip the Fair and Boniface were in dispute. In fact, William of Plaisians's charges of heresy against Boniface VIII (see above, p. 458) were presented to one of the earliest such assemblies, held in Paris in 1303. That one did not include non-noble laity. But in 1314 the king called another meeting to get revenue, and this time he summoned the third estate as well. The meeting was described in the so-called *Grand Chronicles of France*, an ongoing, semi-official history written at Saint-Denis close to the time of the events it described.

[Source: *Medieval Representative Institutions: Their Origins and Nature*, ed. Thomas N. Bisson (Hinsdale, IL: The Dryden Press, 1973), p. 79 (slightly modified).]

In this year [1314], on the feast of St. Peter, August 1st, Philip the Fair, king of France, assembled numerous barons and bishops at Paris; and in addition he caused burghers of each city of the kingdom to be summoned. When they were assembled in the palace of Paris on the day aforesaid, Enguerran de Marigny,

---

1 *Taille* was a tax.
2 Francesco Caetani, Cardinal of Santa Maria in Cosmedin (r.1295-1317), was Boniface's nephew.
3 Pope Celestine V (r.1294) had been a hermit and the founder of the Celestines. Almost as soon as he was elected pope, he wanted to abdicate, and his advisor, Benedetto Caetani, later Boniface VIII, encouraged him in this. Once out of office,

knight, chamberlain[1] to King Philip of France and governor of the whole kingdom, mounted a platform, at the king's order, with the king and the prelates and the barons who were sitting there on the said platform, where he was manifest to all, and preached to the people there before the platform as well as to the prelates aforesaid, making known the king's need and why he had caused them to come and convene.

[There follows Marigny's speech on the troubles with Flanders.]

Wherefore the said Enguerran on behalf of the king told the burghers of the communes assembled there that he wanted to know which of them would give him aid, or not, to mount an army against the Flemings in Flanders. And as Enguerran said this, his lord the king of France arose from his seat to see those who wanted to grant him aid. Then arose Stephen Barbete, burgher of Paris, and spoke for the said town, and represented the townsfolk, saying that they were all ready to give him aid, each as he was able, and even according to possibility, to go where he would lead them, at their own expense, against the said Flemings. And so the king thanked them. And after the said Stephen, all the burghers who had come there for the communes, responded that they would willingly give him aid, and the king thanked them.

Celestine was put into custody, for fear that he might become the focal point of a papal schism. But he appears to have died of natural causes.

1 The chamberlain had access to the king's bedchamber and was thus among his most intimate courtiers.

MODES OF THOUGHT, FEELING, AND DEVOTION

7.19 Scholasticism: Thomas Aquinas, *Summa against the Gentiles* (1259-1264). Original in Latin.

THOMAS AQUINAS (1225-1274) WAS A Dominican, a university professor of theology at Paris, and perhaps the best known of the medieval scholastics—scholars who approached broad and significant topics systematically, using the tools of Aristotelian logic as their scaffolding. By his day, the entire corpus of Aristotle's works was available in Latin, and Thomas shows easy familiarity with all of it. He wrote the *Summa against the Gentiles* as a guide for missionaries working to convert the Muslims. For this reason, most of its arguments involved theological ideas that could be set forth through philosophy alone, without the aid of biblical revelation. Book 1 takes up the nature of God; Book 2 considers God's Creation and the nature of created creatures; Book 3 argues that the purpose of all creation, including human actions, institutions, and governments, is God; Book 4 takes up the topics that rely on revelation: the Trinity, the Incarnation, the sacraments, and so on. The excerpt below is from Book 3. Here Thomas discusses fornication and marriage. He begins, as always, with a proposition contrary to his own view: that "simple fornication is not a sin." He provides some arguments on its behalf, but in the main he refutes it. What developments in medieval logic do you see when considering the work of Avicenna, *Treatise on Logic*, above, p. 234; Abelard, *Glosses on Porphyry*, above, p. 313; and this work by Thomas? How does Thomas's view of the nature and obligations of sex and marriage accord with and differ from your own?

[Source: *Summa contra gentiles*, Book 3: *Providence*, Part II, trans. and ed. Vernon J. Bourke (Notre Dame: University of Notre Dame Press, 1956), pp. 142-47, 150-52 (slightly modified).]

Chapter 122: THE REASON WHY SIMPLE FORNICATION IS A SIN ACCORDING TO DIVINE LAW, AND THAT MATRIMONY IS NATURAL

[1] From the foregoing we can see the futility of the argument of certain people who say that simple fornication is not a sin. For they say: Suppose there is a woman who is not married, or under the control of any man, either her father or another man. Now, if a man performs the sexual act with her, and she is willing, he does not injure her, because she favors the action and she has control over her own body. Nor does he injure any other person, because she is understood to be under no other person's control. So, this does not seem to be a sin.

[2] Now, to say that he injures God would not seem to be an adequate answer. For we do not offend God except by doing something contrary to our own good, as has been said. But this does not appear contrary to man's good. Hence, on this basis, no injury seems to be done to God.

[3] Likewise, it also would seem an inadequate answer to say that some injury is done to one's neighbor by this action, inasmuch as he may be scandalized. Indeed, it is possible for him to be scandalized by something which is not in itself a sin. In this event, the act would be accidentally sinful. But our problem is not whether simple fornication is accidentally a sin, but whether it is so essentially.

[4] Hence, we must look for a solution in our earlier considerations. We have said that God exercises care over every person on the basis of what is good for him. Now, it is good for each person to attain his end, whereas it is bad for him to swerve away from his proper end. Now, this should be considered applicable to the parts, just as it is to the whole being; for instance, each and every part of man, and every one of his acts, should attain the proper end. Now,

though the male semen is superfluous in regard to the preservation of the individual, it is nevertheless necessary in regard to the propagation of the species. Other superfluous things, such as excrement, urine, sweat, and such things, are not at all necessary; hence, their emission contributes to man's good. Now, this is not what is sought in the case of semen, but, rather, to emit it for the purpose of generation, to which purpose the sexual act is directed. But man's generative process would be frustrated unless it were followed by proper nutrition, because the offspring would not survive if proper nutrition were withheld. Therefore, the emission of semen ought to be so ordered that it will result in both the production of the proper offspring and in the upbringing of this offspring.

[5] It is evident from this that every emission of semen in such a way that generation cannot follow, is contrary to the good for man. And if this be done deliberately, it must be a sin. Now, I am speaking of a way from which, *in itself*, generation could not result: such would be any emission of semen apart from the natural union of male and female. For which reason, sins of this type are called *contrary to nature*. But, if by accident generation cannot result from the emission of semen, then this is not a reason for it being against nature, or a sin; as for instance, if the woman happens to be sterile.

[6] Likewise, it must also be contrary to the good for man if the semen be emitted under conditions such that generation could result but the proper upbringing would be prevented. We should take into consideration the fact that, among some animals where the female is able to take care of the upbringing of offspring, male and female do not remain together for any time after the act of generation. This is obviously the case with dogs. But in the case of animals of which the female is not able to provide for the upbringing of offspring, the male and female do stay together after the act of generation as long as is necessary for the upbringing and instruction of the offspring. Examples are found among certain species of birds whose young are not able to seek out food for themselves immediately after hatching. In fact, since a bird does not nourish its young with milk, made available by nature as it were, as occurs in the case of quadrupeds, but

the bird must look elsewhere for food for its young, and since besides this it must protect them by sitting on them, the female is not able to do this by herself. So, as a result of divine providence, there is naturally implanted in the male of these animals a tendency to remain with the female in order to bring up the young. Now, it is abundantly evident that the female in the human species is not at all able to take care of the upbringing of offspring by herself, since the needs of human life demand many things which cannot be provided by one person alone. Therefore, it is appropriate to human nature that a man remain together with a woman after the generative act, and not leave her immediately to have such relations with another woman, as is the practice with fornicators.

[7] Nor, indeed, is the fact that a woman may be able by means of her own wealth to care for the child by herself an obstacle to this argument. For natural rectitude in human acts is not dependent on things accidentally possible in the case of one individual, but, rather, on those conditions which accompany the entire species.

[8] Again, we must consider that in the human species offspring require not only nourishment for the body, as in the case of other animals, but also education for the soul. For other animals naturally possess their own kinds of prudence whereby they are enabled to take care of themselves. But a man lives by reason, which he must develop by lengthy, temporal experience so that he may achieve prudence. Hence, children must be instructed by parents who are already experienced people. Nor are they able to receive such instruction as soon as they are born, but after a long time, and especially after they have reached the age of discretion. Moreover, a long time is needed for this instruction. Then, too, because of the impulsion of the passions, through which prudent judgment is vitiated,[1] they require not merely instruction but correction. Now, a woman alone is not adequate to this task; rather, this demands the work of a husband, in whom reason is more developed for giving instruction and strength is more available for giving punishment. Therefore, in the human species, it is not enough, as in the case of birds, to devote a small amount of time to bringing up offspring, for a long period of life is

---

1   Aristotle, *Nicomachean Ethics* 6. 5 (1140b 19). "Vitiated" = impaired.

required. Hence, since among all animals it is necessary for male and female to remain together as long as the work of the father is needed by the offspring, it is natural to the human being for the man to establish a lasting association with a designated woman, over no short period of time. Now, we call this society *matrimony*. Therefore, matrimony is natural for man, and promiscuous performance of the sexual act, outside matrimony, is contrary to man's good. For this reason, it must be a sin.

[9] Nor, in fact, should it be deemed a slight sin for a man to arrange for the emission of semen apart from the proper purpose of generating and bringing up children, on the argument that it is either a slight sin, or none at all, for a person to use a part of the body for a different use than that to which it is directed by nature (say, for instance, one chose to walk on his hands, or to use his feet for something usually done with the hands) because man's good is not much opposed by such inordinate use. However, the inordinate emission of semen is incompatible with the natural good; namely, the preservation of the species. Hence, after the sin of homicide whereby a human nature already in existence is destroyed, this type of sin appears to take next place, for by it the generation of human nature is precluded.

[10] Moreover, these views which have just been given have a solid basis in divine authority. That the emission of semen under conditions in which offspring cannot follow is illicit is quite clear. There is the text of Leviticus (18: 22–23): "thou shalt not lie with mankind as with womankind ... and thou shalt not copulate with any beast." And in I Corinthians (6: 10): "Nor the effeminate, nor liers with mankind ... shall possess the kingdom of God."

[11] Also, that fornication and every performance of the act of reproduction with a person other than one's wife are illicit is evident. For it is said: "There shall be no whore among the daughters of Israel, nor whoremonger among the sons of Israel" (Deut. 23: 17); and in Tobias (4: 13): "Take heed to keep thyself from all fornication, and beside thy wife never endure to know a crime"; and in I Corinthians (6:1 8): "Fly fornication."

[12] By this conclusion we refute the error of those who say that there is no more sin in the emission of

semen than in the emission of any other superfluous matter, and also of those who state that fornication is not a sin....

Chapter 124: THAT MATRIMONY SHOULD BE BE-TWEEN ONE MAN AND ONE WOMAN

[1] It seems, too, that we should consider how it is inborn in the minds of all animals accustomed to sexual reproduction to allow no promiscuity; hence, fights occur among animals over the matter of sexual reproduction. And, in fact, among all animals there is one common reason, for every animal desires to enjoy freely the pleasure of the sexual act, as he also does the pleasure of food; but this liberty is restricted by the fact that several males may have access to one female, or the converse. The same situation obtains in the freedom of enjoying food, for one animal is obstructed if the food which he desires to eat is taken over by another animal. And so, animals fight over food and sexual relations in the same way. But among men there is a special reason, for, as we said,[1] man naturally desires to know his offspring, and this knowledge would be completely destroyed if there were several males for one female. Therefore, that one female is for one male is a consequence of natural instinct.

[2] But a difference should be noted on this point. As far as the view that one woman should not have sexual relations with several men is concerned, both the aforementioned reasons apply. But, in regard to the conclusion that one man should not have relations with several females, the second argument does not work, since certainty as to offspring is not precluded if one male has relations with several women. But the first reason works against this practice, for, just as the freedom of associating with a woman at will is taken away from the husband, when the woman has another husband, so, too, the same freedom is taken away from a woman when her husband has several wives. Therefore, since certainty as to offspring is the principal good which is sought in matrimony, no law or human custom has permitted one woman to be a wife for several husbands. This was even deemed unfitting among the ancient Romans, of whom Maximus Valerius reports that they believed that the conjugal bond

---

1   In Chapter 123, where Thomas argued that matrimony should endure for an entire lifetime.

should not be broken even on account of sterility.[1]

[3] Again, in every species of animal in which the father has some concern for offspring, one male has only one female; this is the case with all birds that feed their young together, for one male would not be able to offer enough assistance to bring up the offspring of several females. But in the case of animals among whom there is no concern on the part of the males for their offspring, the male has promiscuous relations with several females and the female with plural males. This is so among dogs, chickens, and the like. But since, of all animals, the male in the human species has the greatest concern for offspring, it is obviously natural for man that one male should have but one wife, and conversely.

[4] Besides, friendship consists in an equality.[2] So, if it is not lawful for the wife to have several husbands, since this is contrary to certainty as to offspring, it would not be lawful, on the other hand, for a man to have several wives, for the friendship of wife for husband would not be free, but somewhat servile. And this argument is corroborated by experience, for among husbands having plural wives the wives have a status like that of servants.

[5] Furthermore, strong friendship is not possible in regard to many people, as is evident from the Philosopher in *Ethics*, ch. 8.[3] Therefore, if a wife has but one husband, but the husband has several wives, the friendship will not be equal on both sides. So, the friendship will not be free, but servile in some way.

[6] Moreover, as we said,[4] matrimony among humans should be ordered so as to be in keeping with good moral customs. Now, it is contrary to good behavior for one man to have several wives, for the result of this is discord in domestic society, as is evident from experience. So, it is not fitting for one man to have several wives.

[7] Hence it is said: "They shall be two in one flesh" (Gen. 2: 24).

[8] By this, the custom of those having several wives is set aside, and also the opinion of Plato who maintained that wives should be common.[5] And in the Christian period he was followed by Nicolaus, one of the seven deacons.[6]

7.20 Mysticism: Meister Eckhart, *Sermon 101* (1298-1305). Original in German.

MEISTER ECKHART (*c.*1260-*c.*1328), LIKE Thomas Aquinas, was a Dominican, a teacher at Paris, and a scholastic theologian. But above all, he was a mystic, and his most characteristic writings were sermons in his native German rather than Latin *summae*—all-inclusive treatises of the sort that scholastics like Thomas wrote. Throughout his career, Meister Eckhart walked a fine line between approbation and condemnation. He was made prior of Erfurt and vicar of Thuringia in 1298, provincial of the Dominican order in Saxony in 1303, and vicar of Bohemia in 1307. These were offices with major responsibilities, and there were others to come: professor at Paris (1311) and Strasbourg (1314), prior at Frankfort (1317), and professor at Cologne (1320). Yet at Strasbourg he was accused of reading the works of Beguines, who—despite the admiring biography of Mary of Oignies (see above, p. 405) and other such writings—by this time were no longer tolerated and were beset by charges of heresy. Near the time of his death he offered to retract any erroneous statements he had written, if such were found. He was condemned posthumously. How might you compare the mysticism of Eckhart with that of the Beguine Mary of Oignies?

---

1 Maximus Valerius, *Factorum et dictorum memorabilium* 2. 1. 4.
2 See Aristotle, *Nicomachean Ethics* 8. 5 (1157b 36).
3 Aristotle, *Nicomachean Ethics* 8. 6 (1158a 10).
4 In Chapter 123.
5 Plato, *Republic* 5. 449D ff; *Timaeus* 18C.
6 See St. Augustine, *De haeresibus* 5.

[Source: *Meister Eckhart: Sermons & Treatises*, vol. 1., trans. and ed. M O'C. Walshe (Longmead: Element Books, 1987), pp. 1-13 (slightly modified).]

"FOR WHILE ALL THINGS WERE IN QUIET SILENCE, AND THE NIGHT WAS IN THE MIDST OF HER COURSE, ETC."[1]

Here, in time, we are celebrating the eternal birth which God the Father bore and bears unceasingly in eternity,[2] because this same birth is now born in time, in human nature. St. Augustine says: "What does it avail me that this birth is always happening, if it does not happen in me? That it should happen in me is what matters."[3] We shall therefore speak of this birth, of how it may take place in us and be consummated in the virtuous soul, whenever God the Father speaks His eternal Word in the perfect soul. For what I say here is to be understood of the good and perfected man who has walked and is still walking in the ways of God; not of the natural, undisciplined man, for he is entirely remote from, and totally ignorant of this birth. There is a saying of the wise man: "When all things lay in the midst of silence, then there descended down into me from on high, from the royal throne, a secret word." This sermon is about that Word.[4]

Three things are to be noted here.[5] The first is, *where* in the soul God the Father speaks His Word, where this birth takes place and where she[6] is receptive of this act, for that can only be in the very purest, loftiest, subtlest part that the soul is capable of. In very truth, if God the Father in His omnipotence could endow the soul with anything more noble, and if the soul could have received from Him anything nobler, then the Father would have had to delay the birth for the coming of this greater excellence. Therefore the soul in which this birth is to take place must keep absolutely pure and must live in noble fashion, quite collected and turned entirely inward; not running out through the five senses into the multiplicity of creatures, but all inturned and collected and in the purest part—there is His place, He disdains anything less.

The second part of this sermon has to do with man's conduct in relation to this act, to God's speaking of this Word within, to this birth: whether it is more profitable for man to co-operate with it, so that it may come to pass in him through his own exertion and merit—by a man's creating in himself a mental image in his thoughts and disciplining himself that way by reflecting that God is wise, omnipotent, eternal, or whatever else he can imagine about God—whether this is more profitable and conducive to this birth from the Father; or whether one should shun and free oneself from all thoughts, words and deeds and from all images created by the understanding, maintaining a wholly God-receptive attitude, such that one's own self is idle, letting God work within one. Which conduct conduces best to this birth? The third point is the profit, and how great it is, which accrues from this birth.

Note in the first place that in what I am about to say I shall make use of natural proofs, so that you yourselves can grasp that it is so, for though I put more faith in the scriptures than in myself, yet it is easier and better for you to learn by means of arguments that can be verified.

First we will take the words: "In the midst of silence there was spoken within me a secret word."—"But sir, where is the silence and where is the place where the word is spoken?"[7]—As I said just now, it is in the

---

1   Wisd. of Sol. 18: 14.
2   A Christmas Day sermon. But the point is that Christ's birth is repeated unto all eternity.
3   Most of Eckhart's sources are quoted from memory and very hard to trace, as here.
4   The Word, or Logos, in St. John's Gospel is the Son in the trinity. Eckhart's theme is the birth of the Word in the soul.
5   The first point is the allegorical interpretation of the text, the second is the moral, and the third is the anagogical, which deals with eternal life. Eckhart omits the literal interpretation. Compare his exegetical method to that of Gregory the Great in his *Moralia in Job*, above, p. 26 and Gilbert of Poitiers, above, p. 316.
6   I.e., the soul.
7   This is a fictitious question from the audience.

purest thing that the soul is capable of, in the noblest part, the ground[1]—indeed in the very essence of the soul which is the soul's most secret part. There is the silent "middle," for no creature ever entered there and no image, nor has the soul there either activity or understanding, therefore she is not aware *there* of any image, whether of herself or of any other creature.

Whatever the soul effects, she effects with her powers.[2] What she understands, she understands with the intellect. What she remembers, she does with memory; if she would love, she does that with the will, and thus she works with her powers and not with her essence. Every external act is linked with some *means*. The power of sight works only through the eyes; otherwise it can neither employ nor bestow vision, and so it is with all the other senses. The soul's every external act is effected by some means. But in the soul's essence there is no activity, for the powers she works with emanate from the ground of being. Yet in that ground is the silent "middle": here nothing but rest and celebration for this birth, this act, that God the Father may speak His word there, for *this* part is by nature receptive to nothing save only the divine essence, without mediation. Here God enters the soul with His all, not merely with a part. God enters here the ground of the soul. None can touch the ground of the soul but God alone. No creature can enter the soul's ground, but must stop outside, in the "powers." Within, the soul sees clearly the image whereby the creature has been drawn in and taken lodging. For whenever the powers of the soul make contact with a creature, they set to work and make an image and likeness of the creature, which they absorb. That is how they know the creature. No creature can come closer to the soul than this, and the soul never approaches a creature without having first voluntarily taken an image of it into herself. Through this presented image, the soul approaches creatures—an image being something that the soul makes of (external) objects with her own powers. Whether it is a stone, a horse, a man or anything else that she wants to know, she gets out the image of it that she has already taken in, and is thus enabled to unite herself with it.

But for a man to receive an image in this way, it must of necessity enter from without through the senses. In consequence, there is nothing so unknown to the soul as herself. Accordingly, one master says that the soul can neither create nor obtain an image of herself. Therefore she has no way of knowing herself, for images all enter through the senses, and hence she can have no image of herself. And so she knows all other things, but not herself. Of nothing does she know so little as of herself, for want of mediation.

And you must know too that inwardly the soul is free and void of all means and all images—which is *why* God can freely unite with her without form or likeness. Whatever power you ascribe to any master, you cannot but ascribe that power to God without limit. The more skilled and powerful the master, the more immediately is his work effected, and the simpler it is. Man requires many means for his external works; much preparation of the material is needed before he can produce them as he has imagined them. But the sun in its sovereign mastery performs its task (which is to give light) very swiftly: the instant its radiance is poured forth, the ends of the earth are full of light. More exalted is the angel, who needs still less means for his work and has fewer images. The highest Seraph has but a single image: *he* seizes as a unity all that his inferiors regard as manifold. But God needs *no* image and has no image: without any means, likeness or image God operates in the soul—right in the ground where no image ever got in, but only He Himself with His own being. This no creature can do.

"How does God the Father give birth to His Son in the soul—like creatures, in images and likenesses?"

No, by my faith, but just as He gives birth to him in eternity—no more, no less.

"Well, but how *does* He give birth to him then?"

Now see: God the Father has a perfect insight into Himself, profound and thorough knowledge of Himself by Himself, and not through any image. And

---

1   For Eckhart, there are two parts to the soul. One—which Eckhart calls the "ground of the soul," the "ground of being," and "essence"—is where the birth takes place.

2   The second part of the soul consists of its powers. These are the agencies through which the soul operates. The higher powers are intellect, memory, and will—all the highest intuitive faculties—while the lower powers are the lower intellect, anger, desire, and the senses.

thus God the Father gives birth to His Son in the true unity of the divine nature. See, it is like this and in no other way that God the Father gives birth to the Son in the ground and essence of the soul, and thus unites Himself with her. For if any image were present there would be no real union, and in that real union lies the soul's whole beatitude.

Now, you might say, there is by nature nothing in the soul but images. Not at all! If that were so, the soul could never become blessed, for God cannot make any creature from which you can receive perfect blessedness—otherwise God would not be the highest blessing and the final goal, whereas it is His nature to be this, and it is His will to be the alpha and omega of all things. No creature can constitute your blessedness, nor can it be your perfection here on earth, for the perfection of *this* life—which is the sum of all the virtues—is followed by the perfection of the life to come. Therefore you have to be and dwell in the essence and in the ground, and *there* God will touch you with His simple essence without the intervention of any image. No image represents and signifies itself: it always aims and points to that of which it is the image. And, since you have no image but of what is outside yourself (which is drawn in through the senses and continually points to that of which it is the image), therefore it is impossible for you to be beatified by any image whatsoever. And *therefore* there must be a silence and a stillness, and the Father must speak in that, and give birth to His Son, and perform His works free from all images.

The second point is, what must a man contribute by his own actions, in order to procure and deserve the occurrence and the consummation of this birth in himself? Is it better to do something towards this, to imagine and think about God?—or should he keep still and silent in peace and quiet and let God speak and work in him, merely waiting for God to act? Now I say, as I said before, that these words and this act are only for the good and perfected people, who have so absorbed and assimilated the essence of all virtues that these virtues emanate from them naturally, without their seeking; and above all there must dwell in them

the worthy life and lofty teachings of our Lord Jesus Christ. They must know that the very best and noblest attainment in this life is to be silent and let God work and speak within. When the powers have been completely withdrawn from all their works and images, *then* the Word is spoken. Therefore he said: "In the midst of the silence the secret word was spoken unto me." And so, the more completely you are able to draw in your powers to a unity and forget all those things and their images which you have absorbed, and the further you can get from creatures and their images, the nearer you are to this and the readier to receive it. If only you could suddenly be unaware of all things, then you could pass into an oblivion of your own body as St. Paul did, when he said: "Whether in the body I cannot tell, or out of the body I cannot tell; God knows it."[1] In this case the spirit had so entirely absorbed the powers that it had forgotten the body: memory no longer functioned, nor understanding, nor the senses, nor the powers that should function so as to govern and grace the body, vital warmth and body-heat were suspended, so that the body did not waste during the three days when he neither ate nor drank. Thus too Moses fared, when he fasted for forty days on the mountain and was none the worse for it, for on the last day he was as strong as on the first. In this way a man should flee his senses, turn his powers inward and sink into an oblivion of all things and himself. Concerning this a master[2] addressed the soul thus: "Withdraw from the unrest of external activities, then flee away and hide from the turmoil of inward thoughts, for they but create discord." And so, if God is to speak His Word in the soul, she must be at rest and at peace, and *then* He will speak His Word, and Himself, in the soul—no image, but Himself!

Dionysius[3] says: "God has no image or likeness of Himself, for He is intrinsically all goodness, truth and being." God performs all His works, whether within Himself or outside of Himself, in a flash. Do not imagine that God, when He made heaven and earth and all things, made one thing one day and another the next. Moses describes it like that, but he really knew better: he did so for the sake of people

---

1   2 Cor. 12: 2.
2   Anselm of Canterbury.
3   A reference to Pseudo-Dionysius (*fl. c.*500). See above, p. 457, n. 6.

who could not conceive or grasp it any other way. All God did was this: He willed, He spoke, and they *were!* God works without means and without images, and the freer you are from images, the more receptive you are for His inward working, and the more introverted and self-forgetful, the nearer you are to this.

Dionysius exhorted his pupil Timothy in this sense saying: "Dear son Timothy, do you with untroubled mind soar above yourself and all your powers, above ratiocination [logic] and reasoning, above works, above all modes and existence, into the secret still darkness, that you may come to the knowledge of the unknown super-divine God." There must be a withdrawal from all things. God scorns to work through images.

Now you might say, "What does God do without images in the ground and essence?"

That I cannot know, because my soul-powers receive only in images; they have to know and lay hold of each thing in its appropriate image. They cannot recognize a horse when presented with the image of a man; and since all things enter from without, that knowledge is hidden from my soul—which is to her great advantage. This *not-knowing* makes her wonder and leads her to eager pursuit, for she perceives clearly *that* it is, but does not know *how* or *what* it is. Whenever a man knows the causes of things, then he at once tires of them and seeks to know something different. Always clamoring to know things, he is forever inconstant. And so this unknown-knowing keeps the soul constant and yet spurs her on to pursuit.

About this, the wise man said: "In the middle of the night when all things were in a quiet silence, there was spoken to me a hidden word. It came like a thief by stealth."[1] Why does he call it a word, when it was hidden? The nature of a word is to reveal what is hidden. It revealed itself to me and shone forth before me, declaring something to me and making God known to me, and therefore it is called a Word. Yet what it *was*, remained hidden from me. That was its stealthy coming in a whispering stillness to reveal itself. See,

just because it is hidden one must and should always pursue it. It shone forth and yet was hidden: we are meant to yearn and sigh for it. St. Paul exhorts us to pursue this until we espy it, and not to stop until we grasp it. After he had been caught up into the third heaven where God was made known to him and he beheld all things, when he returned he had forgotten nothing, but it was so deep down in his ground that his intellect could not reach it; it was veiled from him. He therefore had to pursue it and search for it in himself and not outside. It is all within, not outside, but wholly within. And knowing this full well, he said: "For I am persuaded that neither death nor any affliction can separate me from what I find within me."[2]

There is a fine saying of one pagan master to another about this. He said: "I am aware of something in me which shines in my understanding; I can clearly perceive that it is something, but what it may be I cannot grasp. Yet I think if I could only seize it I should know all truth." To which the other master replied: "Follow it boldly! for if you could seize it you would possess the sum-total of all good and have eternal life!" St. Augustine spoke in the same sense: "I am aware of something within me that gleams and flashes before my soul; were this perfected and fully established in me, that would surely be eternal life!" It hides, yet shows itself; it comes, but like a thief with intent to take and steal all things from the soul. But by emerging and showing itself a little it aims to lure the soul and draw her towards itself, to rob her and deprive her of herself. About this, the prophet says: "Lord, take from them their spirit and give them instead thy spirit."[3] This too was meant by the loving soul when she said: "My soul dissolved and melted away when Love spoke his word."[4] When he entered, I had to fall away. And Christ meant this by his words: "Whoever abandons anything for my sake shall be repaid a hundredfold, and whoever would possess me must deny himself and all things, and whoever will serve me must follow me and not go any more after his own."[5]

---

1   Wisd. of Sol. 18: 14,15.
2   Rom. 8: 38–39.
3   See Ps. 104: 29–30; Douay Ps. 103: 29–30.
4   Song of Sol. 5: 6.
5   See Mark 10: 29–30.

But now you might say, "But, good sir, you want to change the natural course of the soul and go against her nature! It is her nature to take things in through the senses in images. Would you upset this ordering?"

No! But how do you know what nobility God has bestowed on human nature, not yet fully described, and still unrevealed? For those who have written of the soul's nobility have gone no further than their natural intelligence could carry them; they had never entered her ground, so that much remained obscure and unknown to them. So the prophet said: "I will sit in silence and hearken to what God speaks within me"[1] Because it is so secret, this Word came in the night and in darkness. St. John says: "The light shone in the darkness, it came into its own, and as many as received it became in authority sons of God; to them was given power to become God's sons."[2]

Now observe the use and the fruit of this secret Word and this darkness. The Son of the heavenly Father is not born alone in this darkness, which is his own: you too can be born a child of the same heavenly Father and of none other, and to you too He will give power. Now observe how great the use is! For all the truth learnt by all the masters by their own intellect and understanding, or ever to be learnt till Doomsday, they never had the slightest inkling of this knowledge and this ground. Though it may be called a nescience, an unknowing, yet there is in it more than in all knowing and understanding without it, for this unknowing lures and attracts you from all understood things, and from yourself as well. This is what Christ meant when he said: "Whoever will not deny himself and will not leave his father and mother, and is not estranged from all these, is not worthy of me,"[3] as though he were to say: he who does not abandon creaturely externals can be neither conceived nor born in this divine birth. But divesting yourself of yourself and of everything external does truly give it to you. And in very truth I believe, nay I am sure, that the man who is established in this cannot in any way ever be separated from God. I say he can in no way lapse into mortal sin. He would rather suffer the most shameful death, as the saints have done before him, than commit the least of mortal sins. I say such people cannot willingly commit or consent to even a venial sin in themselves or in others if they can stop it. So strongly are they lured and drawn and accustomed to *that*, that they can never turn to any other way; to this way are directed all their senses, all their powers.

May the God who has been born again as man assist us to this birth, eternally helping us, weak men, to be born in him again as God. Amen.

7.21 Italian comes into its own: Dante, *Inferno,* Canto 5 (Paolo and Francesca); *Paradiso,* Canto 22 (Meeting with St. Benedict) (1313-1321). Original in Italian.

MUCH AS MEISTER ECKHART gave new luster to German, turning it into a language of philosophy, so Dante (1265-1321) turned his native Tuscan into the language of Italy through his vivid and compelling poetry. Born into a family that obtained noble status through mercantile activities (his father was a moneylender), his early aptitude for poetry was encouraged by teachers and literary figures. In his three-part poem *Divine Comedy*, Dante undertakes a metaphorical journey to hell, purgatory, and heaven, meeting famous—and infamous—people along the way, and using the experience to comment on all the issues of his day. The excerpts below, the first from the *Inferno* (Hell) and the second from *Paradiso* (Heaven), just begin to demonstrate the range of Dante's knowledge, interests, and imagination.

---

1 Source uncertain.
2 John 1: 5, 11–12.
3 Matt. 10: 37.

[Source: Dante Alighieri, *The Divine Comedy*, trans. and commentary, Charles S. Singleton, *Inferno* (Princeton, NJ: Princeton University Press, 1970), pp. 47, 49, 51, 53, 55, 57; *Paradiso* (Princeton, NJ: Princeton University Press, 1970), pp. 245, 247, 249, 251, 253 (notes added, adapted from the accompanying vols. of commentary by Singleton).]

Inferno CANTO V

Thus I descended from the first circle into the second, which girds less space, and so much greater woe that it goads to wailing. There stands Minos, horrible and snarling: upon the entrance he examines their offenses, and judges and dispatches them according as he entwines.[1] I mean that when the ill-begotten soul comes before him, it confesses all; and that discerner of sins sees which shall be its place in Hell, then girds himself with his tail as many times as the grades he wills that it be sent down. Always before him stands a crowd of them; they go, each in his turn, to the judgment; they tell, and hear,[2] and then are hurled below.

"O you who come to the abode of pain," said Minos to me, when he saw me, pausing in the act of that great office, "beware how you enter and in whom you trust; let not the breadth of the entrance deceive you!" And my leader[3] [said] to him, "Why do you too cry out? Do not hinder his fated going: thus is it willed there where that can be done which is willed; and ask no more."

Now the doleful notes begin to reach me; now I am come where much wailing smites me. I came into a place mute of all light, which bellows like the sea in tempest when it is assailed by warring winds.

The hellish hurricane, never resting, sweeps along the spirits with its rapine; whirling and smiting, it torments them. When they arrive before the ruin, there the shrieks, the moans, the lamentations; there they curse the divine power. I learned that to such torment are condemned the carnal sinners, who subject reason to desire.

And as their wings bear the starlings along in the cold season, in wide, dense flocks, so does that blast the sinful spirits; hither, thither, downward, upward, it drives them. No hope of less pain, not to say of rest, ever comforts them. And as the cranes go chanting their lays, making a long line of themselves in the air, so I saw shades come, uttering wails, borne by that strife; wherefore I said, "Master, who are these people that are so lashed by the black air?"

"The first of these of whom you wish to know," he said to me then, "was empress of many tongues. She was so given to lechery that she made lust licit in her law, to take away the blame she had incurred. She is Semiramis, of whom we read that she succeeded Ninus and had been his wife: she held the land the Sultan rules.[4] The next is she who slew herself for love and broke faith to the ashes of Sichaeus;[5] next is wanton Cleopatra.[6] See Helen, for whom so many years of ill revolved;[7] and see the great Achilles, who fought at

---

1   The first circle of the nine circles of Hell is Limbo, but it is still a bit outside Hell proper. That begins where Minos—in legend a king of Crete and in Virgil's *Aeneid* a judge of men's lives in Hell—stands snarling. Since Hell is funnel-shaped, each successive circle in the descent is smaller in circumference than the one above it. While the spirits in Limbo sigh, those in the next circle wail in pain.

2   The souls tell their sins and hear their judgment.

3   Dante's "leader," "Master," and "teacher" is Virgil, whose portrayal of Aeneas's visit to the underworld is echoed by Dante in many of the images in the *Inferno*. Hence Virgil is also sometimes called "the poet."

4   Semiramis is the Greek name of a queen of ancient Assyria. She was famous for her beauty and lust as well as for her prowess in war. Egypt, in Dante's time, was under the Sultan's rule. Apparently Dante confused Babylonia, a kingdom of the Assyrian empire, with Babylon (Old Cairo), a fortified city on the Nile.

5   "She who slew herself for love" was Dido, Queen of Carthage, who, after mourning her husband Sichaeus, fell in love with Aeneas despite her vow to remain faithful to the memory of her husband. When Aeneas left Dido to found Rome, she stabbed herself.

6   Cleopatra, queen of Egypt, was mistress of Julius Caesar and Mark Antony and was famous for her beauty and seductive ways.

7   Helen was the beautiful wife of the king of Sparta. Her abduction by Paris led to the long Trojan War.

the last with love.[1] See Paris, Tristan,"[2] and more than a thousand shades whom love had parted from our life he showed me, pointing them out and naming them.

When I heard my teacher name the ladies and the knights of old, pity overcame me and I was as one bewildered. "Poet," I began, "willingly would I speak with those two that go together and seem to be so light upon the wind."[3]

And he to me, "You shall see when they are nearer to us; and do you entreat them then by that love which leads them, and they will come."

As soon as the wind bends them to us, I raised my voice, "O wearied souls! come speak with us, if Another[4] forbid it not."

As doves called by desire, with wings raised and steady, come through the air, borne by their will to their sweet nest, so did these issue from the troop where Dido is, coming to us through the malignant air, such force had my compassionate cry.

"O living creature, gracious and benign, that go through the black air visiting us who stained the world with blood, if the King of the universe were friendly to us, we would pray Him for your peace, since you have pity on our perverse ill. Of that which it pleases you to hear and to speak, we will hear and speak with you, while the wind, as now, is silent for us.

"The city where I was born lies on that shore where the Po descends to be at peace with its followers.[5] Love, which is quickly kindled in a gentle heart, seized this one for the fair form that was taken from me—and the way of it afflicts me still. Love, which absolves no loved one from loving, seized me so strongly with delight in him,[6] that, as you see, it does not leave me even now. Love brought us to one death. Caina awaits him who quenched our life."[7]

These words were borne to us from them. And when I heard those afflicted souls I bowed my head and held it bowed until the poet said to me, "What are you thinking of?"

When I answered, I began, "Alas! How many sweet thoughts, what great desire, brought them to the woeful pass!"

Then I turned again to them, and I began, "Francesca, your torments make me weep for grief and pity; but tell me, in the time of the sweet sighs, by what and how did Love grant you to know the dubious desires?"

And she to me, "There is no greater sorrow than to recall, in wretchedness, the happy time; and this your teacher knows. But if you have such great desire to know the first root of our love, I will tell as one who weeps and tells. One day, for pastime, we read of Lancelot, how love constrained him; we were alone, suspecting nothing.[8] Several times that reading urged our eyes to meet and took the color from our faces, but one moment alone it was that overcame us. When we read how the longed-for smile was kissed by so great a lover, this one, who never shall be parted from me, kissed my mouth all trembling. A Gallehault was the book and he who wrote it;[9] that day we read no farther in it." While the one spirit said this, the other wept, so that for pity I swooned, as if in death, and fell as a dead body falls.

---

1   In medieval romances, Achilles, the hero of the Trojan War, was in love with Polyxena and was lured to his death by a sham rendezvous with her.

2   Tristan died for his love of Isolde.

3   "So light upon the wind": Dante sees two spirits that are more violently tossed by the wind than the others. According to the principle of just punishment, the heightened violence of the wind signifies that their love was particularly passionate.

4   The name of God is blasphemous in Hell. So Dante calls Him "Another."

5   The city is Ravenna and the speaker, who is not named until later, is Francesca, known as Francesca da Rimini. She was a real person, daughter of Guido da Polenta the elder, lord of Ravenna (d.1310) and the aunt of Guido Novello, Dante's host at Ravenna. She was married to Gianciotto Malatesta. No contemporary chronicle or document mentions the love between Francesca and Paolo or their death, but the story is told by Boccaccio as well as Dante.

6   This is Paolo Malatesta, who is never named here. He was the brother of Gianciotto, Francesca's husband.

7   Caina is a place in lower Hell.

8   This was the medieval romance *Lancelot of the Lake*. Lancelot was a knight at King Arthur's court and the lover of Arthur's Queen Guinevere.

9   "A Gallehault was the book": Gallehault brought Guinevere and Lancelot together for their first meeting and urged the two to kiss.

Overwhelmed with amazement, I turned to my guide,[1] like a little child who always runs back to where it has most confidence; and she, like a mother who quickly comforts her pale and gasping son with her voice which is wont to reassure him, said to me, "Do you not know that you are in heaven, do you not know that heaven is all holy, and that whatever is done here comes of righteous zeal? How the song, and I by smiling, would have transmuted you, you can now conceive, since this cry has so much moved you;[2] wherein, had you understood their prayers, already would be known to you the vengeance which you shall see before you die. The sword of here on high cuts not in haste nor tardily, save to his deeming who in longing or in fear awaits it. But turn now to the others, for you shall see many illustrious spirits, if you direct your sight as I say."

As was her pleasure, I turned my eyes, and I saw a hundred little spheres which together were making themselves beautiful with their mutual rays. I was standing as one who within himself represses the prick of his desire, who does not make bold to ask, he so fears to exceed. And the greatest and most shining of those pearls came forward to satisfy my desire concerning itself.[3] Then within it I heard, "If you could see, as I do, the charity which burns among us, you would have uttered your thoughts; but lest you, by waiting, be delayed in your lofty aim, I will make answer to the thought itself about which you are so circumspect.

"That mountain on whose slope Cassino lies was of old frequented on its summit by the folk deceived and perverse, and I am he who first bore up there His name who brought to earth that truth which so uplifts us; and such grace shone upon me that I drew away the surrounding towns from the impious worship that seduced the world. These other fires[4] were all contemplative men, kindled by that warmth which gives birth to holy flowers and fruits.

Here is Macarius, here is Romualdus, here are my brethren who stayed their feet within the cloisters and kept a steadfast heart."[5]

And I to him, "The affection you show in speaking with me, and the good semblance which I see and note in all your ardors, have expanded my confidence as the sun does the rose when it opens to its fullest bloom. Therefore I pray you—and do you, father, assure me if I am capable of receiving so great a grace, that I may behold you in your uncovered shape."

Whereon he, "Brother, your high desire shall be fulfilled up in the last sphere,[6] where are fulfilled all others and my own. There every desire is perfect, mature, and whole. In that alone is every part there where it always was, for it is not in space, nor has it poles; and our ladder reaches up to it, wherefore it steals itself from your sight. All the way thither the patriarch Jacob saw it stretch its upper part, when it appeared to him so laden with Angels.[7] But no one now lifts his foot from earth to ascend it, and my Rule remains for waste of paper. The walls, which used to be an abbey, have become dens, and the cowls are sacks full of foul meal. But heavy usury is not exacted so counter to God's pleasure as that fruit which makes the heart of monks so mad;[8] for whatsoever the Church has in

---

1   After many experiences in Hell and Purgatory, Dante is now in Paradise, and his guide is no longer Virgil but Beatrice. At the most literal level, Beatrice was a Florentine woman whom Dante loved; she was the wife of Simone de' Bardi and died in 1290. But in Dante's poetry, Beatrice took on numerous spiritual meanings as well.

2   "This cry": in Canto XXI, Dante heard a cry but did not understand its meaning.

3   "The greatest and most shining of those pearls" is the spirit of St. Benedict, founder of Monte Cassino, author of *The Benedictine Rule* (see above, p. 28), and here considered the father of monasticism.

4   The spirits in Paradise are portrayed as radiant fires or flames.

5   Macarius may refer to St. Macarius the Elder of Egypt or St. Macarius the Younger of Alexandria. Both were disciples of St. Antony, for whose *Life* by Athanasius see above, p. 36. Romualdus was St. Romuald (d.c.1027), whose monastery at Vallombrosa was strictly secluded from the world.

6   This is the Empyrean, the summit of Heaven.

7   In Gen. 28: 12, Jacob dreamed of a ladder reaching to heaven on which angels were ascending and descending. The ladder appears in *The Benedictine Rule* as the "steps of humility"; see above, p. 31.

8   In other words, even exorbitant usury, in which borrowers must pay high interest, is not so contrary to God's will as the Church taking money and making the monks avid for still more.

keeping is all for the folk that ask it in God's name, not for kindred, or for other filthier thing.[1] The flesh of mortals is so soft[2] that on earth a good beginning does not last from the springing of the oak to the bearing of the acorn. Peter began his fellowship without gold or silver, and I mine with prayer and with fasting, and Francis his with humility; and if you look at the beginning of each, and then look again whither it has strayed, you will see the white changed to dark.[3] Nevertheless, Jordan driven back, and the sea fleeing when God willed, were sights more wondrous than the succor here."[4]

Thus he spoke to me, then drew back to his company, and the company closed together; then like a whirlwind all were gathered upward. My sweet lady,[5] with only a sign, thrust me up after them by that ladder, so did her power overcome my nature; nor ever here below,[6] where we mount and descend by nature's law, was motion so swift as might match my flight. So may I return, reader, to that devout triumph for the sake of which I often bewail my sins and beat my breast,[7] you would not have drawn out and put your finger into the fire so quickly as I saw the sign which follows the Bull, and was within it.[8]

7.22 Romance: *Sir Gawain and the Green Knight* (last quarter of 14th c.). Original in Middle English.

The author of *Sir Gawain and the Green Knight* is anonymous; we know little more than that he (or she) wrote in a dialect characteristic of northwestern England in the last quarter of the fourteenth century. Chaucer (*c*.1340-1400), a much more famous writer, was working at the same time, but his language was the English of London, and more Frenchified than that of the *Gawain* poet. The poem begins, like many medieval romances, at the court of King Arthur. The green knight enters, a wondrous and frightful sight, and challenges the knights of the Round Table: he will allow one of them to behead him, but the next year that knight must find him at the Green Chapel and allow himself to be beheaded. Sir Gawain is chosen to answer the challenge. He lops off the Green Knight's head, but the victim picks it up and, reminding Gawain of his obligation on the following year, rides off. The next year Gawain dutifully begins his search for the Green Chapel. He comes upon a castle where his host, Bertilak, insists that he skip a hunt and spend time in bed. In fact, Bertilak intends to tempt him with his wife. Gawain passes the test, but he accepts two kisses and a belt from the lady. The kisses he returns to his host in a sort of bet, but he holds on to the belt. When he arrives at the Green Chapel, it turns out that the Green Knight is Bertilak, sent by Morgan le Fey (a fairy with magical powers) to test Gawain. On the whole, Gawain has passed the test, and Bertilak's first two blows stop before they hit Gawain's neck. But the last one cuts Gawain's flesh a bit—punishment for withholding the belt. The excerpt here begins with the day of the hunt at Bertilak's castle. How might you compare the themes of love and sex here with their counterparts in the troubadour poems above, pp. 389-91? How might you compare the nature and virtues of women in this romance with their counterparts in the epic poem *Raoul de Cambrai*, above, p. 384?

---

1   Benedict wants the money to go to the poor, not to the families of churchmen or worse—to bastards and concubines.
2   I.e., weak.
3   Peter is St. Peter: in Acts 3: 6, he says he has no silver or gold. Francis is St. Francis of Assisi, for whom see above, p. 408.
4   In other words, God rolled back the Jordan and parted the Red Sea, so do not despair.
5   Beatrice.
6   I.e., on earth.
7   Dante hopes to return to Paradise.
8   "The sign which follows the Bull," Taurus, is Gemini, the constellation under which Dante was born.

[Source: *Sir Gawain and the Green Knight*, ed. and trans. James Winny (Peterborough, ON: Broadview Press, 1992), pp. 67, 69, 71, 73, 75.]

Early before daybreak the household arose;
Guests who were leaving called for their grooms,
And they hurried quickly to saddle horses,
Make equipment ready and pack their bags.
1130 The noblest prepare themselves to ride finely dressed,
Leap nimbly into saddle, seize their bridles,
Each man taking the path that attracted him most.
The well-loved lord of the region was not the last
Prepared for riding, with a great many knights;
1135 Snatched a hasty breakfast after hearing mass,
And makes ready for the hunting-field with bugles
    blowing.
By the time the first glimmers of daylight appeared
He and his knights were mounted on horse.
Then experienced huntsmen coupled the hounds,
1140 Unlocked the kennel door and ordered them out,
Loudly blowing three long notes on their horns.
Hounds bayed at the sound and made a fierce noise;
And those who went straying were whipped in and
    turned back,
A hundred hunters, as I have been told,
1145   of the best.
        With keepers at their posts
        Huntsmen uncoupled hounds;
        Great clamor in the woods
        From mighty horn-blasts sounds.

At the first sound of the hunt the wild creatures
1150   trembled;
Deer fled from the valley, frantic with fear,
And rushed to the high ground, but were fiercely
    turned back
By the line of beaters, who yelled at them savagely.
They let the stags with their tall antlers pass,
1155 And the wonderful bucks with their broad horns;
For the noble lord had forbidden that in the close
    season
Anyone should interfere with the male deer.
The hinds were held back with shouts of hay! and
    war!
The does driven with great noise into the deep
    valleys.
1160 There you might see, as they ran, arrows flying—

At each turn in the wood a shaft shot through the
    air—
Deeply piercing the hide with their wide heads.
What! they cry out and bleed, on the slopes they are
    slaughtered,
And always swiftly pursued by the rushing hounds;
Hunters with screaming horns gallop behind   1165
With such an ear-splitting noise as if cliffs had
    collapsed.
Those beasts that escaped the men shooting at them
Were all pulled down and killed at the receiving
    points,
As they were driven from the high ground down to
    the streams.
The men at the lower stations were so skillful,   1170
And the greyhounds so large, that they seized them
    quickly
And tore them down as fast as men could number,
    right there.
        On horseback and on foot
        The lord, filled with delight,   1175
        Spent all that day in bliss
        Until the fall of night.

Thus this nobleman sports along the edges of woods,
And the good man Gawain lies in his fine bed,
Lying snug while the daylight gleamed on the walls,   1180
Under a splendid coverlet, shut in by curtains.
And as he lazily dozed, he heard slily made
A little noise at his door and it stealthily open;
And he raised up his head from the bedclothes,
Lifted a corner of the curtain a little,   1185
And takes a glimpse warily to see what it could be.
It was the lady, looking her loveliest,
Who shut the door after her carefully, not making a
    sound,
And came towards the bed. The knight felt confused,
And lay down again cautiously, pretending to sleep;   1190
And she approached silently, stealing to his bed,
Lifted the bed-curtain and crept within,
And seating herself softly on the bedside,
Waited there strangely long to see when he would
    wake.

The knight shammed sleep for a very long while,
Wondering what the matter could be leading to
Or portend. It seemed an astonishing thing,
Yet he told himself, "It would be more fitting
To discover straightway by talking just what she
   wants."
1200 Then he wakened and stretched and turned towards
   her,
Opened his eyes and pretended surprise,
And crossed himself as if protecting himself by prayer
   and this sign.
      With lovely chin and cheek
1205   Of blended color both,
      Charmingly she spoke
      From her small laughing mouth.

"Good morning, Sir Gawain," said that fair lady,
"You are an unwary sleeper, that one can steal in
   here:
Now you are caught in a moment! Unless we agree
1210   on a truce,
I shall imprison you in your bed, be certain of that!"
Laughing merrily the lady uttered this jest.
"Good morning, dear lady," said Gawain gaily,
"You shall do with me as you wish, and that pleases
   me much,
1215 For I surrender at once, and beg for your mercy,
And that is best, in my judgement, for I simply must,"
Thus he joked in return with a burst of laughter.
"But if, lovely lady, you would grant me leave
And release your captive, and ask him to rise,
1220 I would get out of this bed and put on proper dress,
And then take more pleasure in talking with you."
"No, indeed not, good sir," said that sweet one,
"You shall not leave your bed, I intend something
   better.
I shall tuck you in here on both sides of the bed,
1225 And then chat with my knight whom I have caught.
For I know well, in truth, that you are Sir Gawain,
Whom everyone reveres wherever you go;
Your good name and courtesy are honorably praised
By lords and by ladies and all folk alive.
And now indeed you are here, and we two quite
1230   alone,
My husband and his men have gone far away,
Other servants are in bed, and my women too,
The door shut and locked with a powerful hasp;

And since I have under my roof the man everyone
   loves,
I shall spend my time well, while it lasts,   1235
   with talk.
      You are welcome to me indeed,
      Take whatever you want;
      Circumstances force me
      To be your true servant."   1240

"Truly," replied Gawain, "I am greatly honored,
Though I am not in fact such a man as you speak of.
To deserve such respect as you have just described
I am completely unworthy, I know very well.
I should be happy indeed, if you thought it proper,   1245
That I might devote myself by words or by deed
To giving you pleasure: it would be a great joy."
"In all truth, Sir Gawain," replied the beautiful lady,
"If the excellence and gallantry everyone admires
Were I to slight or disparage, that would hardly be
   courteous;   1250
But a great many ladies would much rather now
Hold you, sir, in their power as I have you here,
To spend time amusingly with your charming talk,
Delighting themselves and forgetting their cares,
Than much of the treasure or wealth they possess.   1255
But I praise that same lord who holds up the heavens,
I have completely in my grasp the man everyone
   longs for,
      through God's grace."
      Radiant with loveliness
      Great favor she conferred;   1260
      The knight with virtuous speech
      Answered her every word.

"Lady," said the man pleasantly, "may Mary repay
   you,
For I have truly made proof of your great generosity,
And many other folk win credit for their deeds;   1265
But the respect shown to me is not at all my deserv-
   ing:
That honor is due to yourself, who know nothing but
   good."
"By Mary," said the noble lady, "to me it seems very
   different;
For if I were the worthiest of all women alive,
And held all the riches of the earth in my hand,   1270
And could bargain and pick a lord for myself,

For the virtues I have seen in you, sir knight, here,
Of good looks and courtesy and charming manner—
All that I have previously heard and now know to be
   true—
1275 No man on earth would be picked before you."
"Indeed, noble lady," said the man, "you have chosen
   much better,
But I am proud of the esteem that you hold me in,
And in all gravity your servant, my sovereign I
   consider you,
And declare myself your knight, and may Christ
   reward you."
1280 So they chatted of this and that until late morning,
And always the lady behaved as if loving him much.
The knight reacted cautiously, in the most courteous
   of ways,
Though she was the loveliest woman he could
   remember:
He felt small interest in love because of the ordeal he
1285   must face very soon—
      To stand a crushing blow,
      In helpless sufferance.
      Of leaving then she spoke,
      The knight agreed at once.

Then she bade him goodbye, glanced at him and
1290   laughed,
And as she stood astonished him with a forceful
   rebuke:
"May he who prospers each speech repay you this
   pleasure!
But that you should be Gawain I very much doubt."

"But why?" said the knight, quick with his question,
Fearing he had committed some breach of good
   manners;   1295
But the lady said "bless you" and replied, "For this
   cause;
So good a knight as Gawain is rightly reputed,
In whom courtesy is so completely embodied,
Could not easily have spent so much time with a lady
Without begging a kiss, to comply with politeness,   1300
By some hint or suggestion at the end of a remark."
Then Gawain said, "Indeed, let it be as you wish;
I will kiss at your bidding, as befits a knight,
And do more, rather than displease you, so urge it no
   further."
With that she approaches him and takes him in her
   arms,   1305
Stoops graciously over him and kisses the knight.
They politely commend each other to Christ's
   keeping:
She goes out of the room without one word more.
And he prepares to get up as quickly as he can,
Calls for his chamberlain, selects his clothes,   1310
Makes his way, when he was ready, contentedly to
   mass;
And then went to his meal that worthily awaited
   him,
And made merry all day until the moon rose
   with games.
      Never knight was entertained   1315
      By such a worthy pair,
      One old, the other young;
      Much pleasure did they share.

7.23 Medieval drama: *Directions for an Annunciation play* (14th c.). Original in Latin.

MEDIEVAL DRAMA GREW OUT OF church liturgy and the public hurly-burly of town life. By
the thirteenth century many churches were acting out the events of the Annunciation (when the
angel Gabriel announced to the Virgin Mary that she would "bring forth a son"). It was presented as an interlude during the mass, whether on the feast of the Annunciation itself (March 25) or
during Advent (beginning the fourth Sunday before Christmas). The play employed a relatively
small number of characters and some startling stagecraft. At Tournai (today in Belgium) a fake
dove—representing the Holy Spirit that impregnated Mary—descended from the cathedral vault;
at Parma (in Italy) the actor portraying Gabriel himself swung down. In the version printed here,
which was performed at Padua (also in Italy) in the fourteenth century, Gabriel handed the dove
to Mary, who "put it under her cloak."

[Source: *Medieval Popular Religion, 1000-1500: A Reader*, ed. John Shinners (Peterborough, ON: Broadview Press, 1997), pp. 128-29 (notes added). Translated by John Shinners.]

On the day of the feast of the Annunciation, after dinner, let the great bell be rung at the usual time, and meanwhile let the clergy gather at the church; they should prepare themselves in the main sacristy,[1] some of them wearing their copes[2] and other required things. In this sacristy Mary, Elizabeth, Joseph, and Joachim[3] should stand ready with a deacon and a subdeacon holding silver books. At the appointed time they should leave the sacristy in procession and make their way to the place prepared for them. Leaving them there, the procession should continue to the baptistery where a boy should be waiting seated on a chair dressed as Gabriel. Let him be lifted up on the chair and carried from the baptistery into the church along the side aisle and taken up the steps next to the choir. The clergy should stand in the middle of the church arranged like a chorus. Meanwhile the subdeacon should begin the prophetic epistle: "The Lord spoke again to Achaz."[4] After the prophecy is finished, the deacon should start the Gospel: "The angel Gabriel was sent"[5] and proceed up to the words "And when the angel had come to her, he said." At that point, Gabriel, kneeling with two fingers of his right hand upraised, should begin singing this antiphon in a loud voice: "Hail, Mary, full of grace, the Lord is with thee; blessed art thou among women." When this antiphon is finished, the deacon should continue reciting the Gospel up to the words "And the angel said to her." Then the Angel, again standing with his right hand completely open, should begin this antiphon: "Do not be afraid, Mary, for thou has found grace with God. Behold, thou shalt conceive in thy womb and shalt bring forth a son." When this antiphon is finished, the deacon should continue reciting up to the words "But Mary said to the angel." Then Mary should answer in a clear voice with this antiphon: "How shall this happen, angel of God, since I do not know man?" When this antiphon is finished, the deacon should continue reciting up to the words "And the angel answered and said to her"; and the Angel should again begin this verse: "Listen, Mary, virgin of Christ, the Holy Spirit shall come upon thee and the power of the Most High shall overshadow thee." But when he comes to the words "the Holy Spirit shall come upon thee," let him hold out a dove a little way from him. When this verse is finished, the deacon should continue reciting up to the words "But Mary said to the angel." When this is finished, Mary should stand up with her arms outstretched and begin saying in a loud voice, "Behold the handmaid of the Lord." Before the end of this antiphon, he should let go of the dove and Mary should take it and put it under her cloak. Antiphon: "Behold the handmaid of the Lord; be it done to me according to thy word."

When all this is ended, the deacon should continue on to the next verse, "Now in those days Mary arose and went with haste into the hill country" up to the words "And Elizabeth cried out with a loud voice, saying." Meanwhile, Mary should descend from her place and go over to where Elizabeth and Joachim are. Both of them should receive her according to the description in the Gospel. Having done this, Elizabeth should kneel, touch Mary's body with both hands, and begin this antiphon with a humble voice: "Blessed art thou among women and blessed is the fruit of thy womb!" When the antiphon is finished, Elizabeth should get up and, standing again, say this antiphon: "And how have I deserved that the mother of my Lord should come to me? For behold, the moment that the sound of thy greeting came to my ears, the babe in my womb leapt for joy. And blessed is she who has believed because the things promised her by the Lord shall be accomplished." When this is finished, the deacon should again continue up to "And Mary said." Then Mary should turn and face the people and in a loud voice sing at the eighth tone these three verses

---

1 The sacristy is the room in a church that houses the sacred vessels and vestments.
2 A cope is a long church vestment, a sort of cloak.
3 I.e., the actors portraying these characters in the drama. For the story of the Annunciation, see Luke 1: 26-38.
4 Isa. 7: 10.
5 Luke 1: 26.

[i.e., the Magnificat]: "My soul magnifies the Lord, and my spirit rejoices in God my Savior; because he has regarded the lowliness of his handmaid; for, behold, henceforth all generations shall call me blessed." When this is finished, the organ should answer with one verse, and the choir with the next, and so on until the end. When this is all done, let everyone return to the sacristy.

7.24 The feast of Corpus Christi: *The Life of Juliana of Mont-Cornillon* (1261–1264). Original in Latin.

MANY PEOPLE, PARTICULARLY WOMEN, were as devoted to the Eucharist as Juliana of Mont-Cornillon (1193–1258). Recall that when Mary of Oignies (above, p. 407) viewed the Host, she "saw between his hands the corporeal form of a beautiful boy." But Juliana, inspired by a vision, worked in addition to ensure that a special annual feast be declared for the Body of Christ (in Latin, "Corpus Christi"). Orphaned at the age of five, Juliana was raised at the house of Mont-Cornillon, a mixed institution for lepers as well as male and female religious founded by the citizens of near-by Liège. Eventually she became its prioress, was forced to leave for a time, was reinstated, and finally was forced out again. Her checkered career did not keep her from promoting Corpus Christi, and she was able to enlist the help of the canons of St. Martin of Liège, one of whom (though anonymous) very likely wrote the *Life* excerpted here. He wanted both to demonstrate Juliana's virtues and to give luster to her project. In this he may well have been successful: Jacques Pantaléon, a former archdeacon of Liège, established the feast of Corpus Christi in 1264, the last year of his pontificate as Urban IV. Taking into account the devotional life of St. Radegund (above, pp. 47–57), Queen Mathilda (above, p. 243), and Mary of Oignies (above, p. 405), what developments in female devotional practices can you trace? What evidence is there from the *Life of Juliana* that men, too, participated in the new Eucharistic devotion?

[Source: *The Life of Juliana of Mont-Cornillon*, trans. Barbara Newman (Toronto: Peregrina Publishing Co., [1988]), pp. 36–38, 80–84, 151.]

1.12. When she received the most holy Body of Christ, her only beloved and chosen—not only of a thousand but of all who dwell in heaven and earth[1]—then she was filled with such abundant dew of grace and devotion that her soul would melt like wax in the fire[2] and her spirit fail within her.[3] For then she would taste and see how good the Lord is[4] on receiving gifts of yet fuller grace. Indeed, in the feast of the sacred Body she experienced every delight and every savor of sweetness. For what the people of Israel received in a figure through the manna that rained down from heaven, Juliana received in reality when she partook of the living bread that came down from heaven, of which the manna was only a shadow.[5] Surely this bread tasted much sweeter and fresher, more delicious and more spiritual in Juliana's heart than the manna once did in the mouths of a carnal and stiff-necked people.

After receiving the Body of Christ our virgin liked to remain silent for at least a week. During that period she was upset by the approach of anyone whatsoever, except in the case of some great and urgent need or ad-

1 See Song of Sol. 5: 10.
2 See Song of Sol. 5: 6.
3 See Ps. 77: 3; Douay Ps. 76: 4.
4 See Ps. 34: 8; Douay Ps. 33: 9.
5 See John. 6: 48–51.

vantage. But you must not think that such an interval seemed long enough for her to celebrate the one she had received, for she would often tell the sisters who served her meals to give her no physical food at all for a month. Rather, they were not even to approach her, and they were to protect her from the approach of any visitors, whoever they might be. She felt certain there was such strength in the eating of that sacred bread that she did not doubt she could survive for so long, even physically, on the strength of such food. And she could easily have proved it, too, if the sisters who served her had not fallen short. But since Juliana was not given a period of rest and silence as long as she desired, she gave herself up yet again to the one she had received, the only one she loved. Utterly absorbed in spirit, the bride made way for her bridegroom. In overflowing intimate love and fervent fulfilment, she clung to him in a marvelous and ineffable union of spirit, and transformed by divine emotion, she could sense and savor nothing but God.

In short, to give you an idea of the singular privilege of grace that Christ bestowed on his handmaid when she received his Body and Blood, I need not conceal the fact that for many years before her death, whenever she received the Body of Christ (and she craved to do so often because of her boundless love), he revealed to her some new secret from his heavenly mysteries. But she concealed these secrets in such indiscreet humility (if it is right to say so) that she could justly appear to cry with the prophet, "My secret for myself! My secret for myself!"[1] Not only did she hide these secrets from strangers, but even to her closest and dearest friends she revealed them very rarely, except when she was drunk in the Spirit and could not be silent. From a tender age she was such a zealot for humility that, if anything she might say was likely to give her a reputation for saintliness, she would keep silent lest anyone think her better than she thought herself. Inwardly she despised herself, counting herself nothing in the privacy of her heart, and she did not want anyone else to prize her at a different value than she herself had decreed.

1.13. But behold! While the king was on his couch, his handmaid's nard [ointment] gave forth its fragrance.[2] From what follows, you can clearly understand how pleasing and acceptable a fragrance the sweet nard of Juliana's humility gave forth for Christ the King as he rested on his couch, that is, in the Father's bosom. He—the sublime Lord who looks upon the humble and beholds the proud from afar[3]—deigned to reveal his will to his handmaid above all mortals by means of a singular grace. To inaugurate a special feast in honor of the Sacrament of his most holy Body and Blood, a feast which Jesus Christ, the power of God and the wisdom of God, wished to be observed henceforth upon earth, he did not choose many of the noble and powerful of this world, of secular might or ecclesiastical rank. Rather, he who chose the weak of the world to confound the strong[4] wondrously chose the humble Juliana to accomplish this, having shown her a sign beforehand and divinely revealed its meaning. As for her, she prayed urgently to the Lord that such a lofty and difficult task might be imposed on someone else whose authority could achieve it more quickly. She received the reply that it should by all means begin with her, and even thereafter be promoted by humble people.

How this was revealed and accomplished, I will describe more fully at another time, if the Lord permits. But I have anticipated the subject here because in the preceding chapters I have mentioned the life-giving Sacrament of Christ's Body and Blood, for which Christ's virgin had a marvelous affection, and also to inform readers more clearly that Christ wished to distinguish her with a special gift of his love....

2.6. From her youth, whenever Christ's virgin gave herself to prayer, she saw a great and marvelous sign. There appeared to her the full moon in its splendor, yet with a little breach in its spherical body. When she had seen this sign for a long time she was astonished, not knowing what it might mean. But she could not marvel enough over the fact that, whenever she was intent on prayer, the sign constantly impressed itself

---

1 Isa. 24: 16.
2 See Song of Sol. 1: 11.
3 Ps. 138: 6; Douay Ps. 137: 6.
4 1 Cor. 1: 24–27.

on her vision. After she had tried with all her might to make it go away, as she wished, and could not succeed, she began to trouble herself unduly in fear and trembling, thinking that she was being tempted. So she prayed and asked people she trusted to pray that the Lord would rescue her from a temptation she was suffering, as she said. But when she could not drive the importunate sign away by any effort, nor by any prayer of her own or other Christians, she finally began to wonder if perhaps, instead of trying so hard to drive it away, she should seek to discover some mystery in it.

Then Christ revealed to her that the moon was the present Church, while the breach in the moon symbolised the absence of a feast which he still desired his faithful upon earth to celebrate. This was his will for the increase of faith at the end of a senescent age, and also for the growth and grace of the elect: that once every year, the institution of the Sacrament of his Body and Blood should be recollected more solemnly and specifically than it was at the Lord's Supper, when the Church was generally preoccupied with the washing of feet and the remembrance of his Passion. On this feast of the memorial of the Sacrament, what was passed over lightly or negligently on ordinary days should be celebrated with greater attention. Christ revealed these things to his virgin, therefore, and commanded her that she herself should inaugurate this feast and be the first to tell the world it should be instituted. But Juliana, considering the sublimity of the matter and observing her own lowliness and frailty, was more astonished than words can tell. She replied that she could not do what she had been commanded. Yet every time she prayed, Christ admonished her to accept the task for which he had chosen her above all mortals. And she always answered, "Lord, release me, and give the task you have assigned me to great scholars shining with the light of knowledge, who would know how to promote such a great affair. For how could I do it? I am not worthy, Lord, to tell the world about something so noble and exalted. I could not understand it, nor could I fulfill it." But he responded that by all means, she should be

the one to initiate this feast, and from then on it should be promoted by humble people. And once while she was praying, beseeching the Lord with all her heart to choose another for this task, she heard a voice saying, "I thank you, Father, Lord of heaven and earth, that you have hidden these things from the wise and understanding of this world, and revealed them to babes"[1] Even then she did not consent at once, but answered, "Rouse yourself, Lord, and raise up great scholars; and let me depart in peace, the least of your creatures"[2] And the voice came to her again, saying, "He has set in my mouth a new song, a song of praise to our God. I have not hidden your righteousness in my heart, I have told of your truth and your salvation: I have not hidden your mercy and your truth from the great congregation."[3]

2.7 Thus more than twenty years after this vision, when out of excessive humility Juliana had again prayed with unspeakable groaning[4] that Christ would give the task to someone else, but could not in the least obtain what she asked, she discerned that it was hard to kick against the goad of God's will[5] and submitted her will to his. For she had persisted in prayers and tears so long that she had no more tears to weep, and her eyes shed pure blood instead. Let no one be scandalized that Christ's virgin appeared to consent so belatedly to the divine admonition, for the cause did not lie in negligence or in any lack of devotion toward the Sacrament, but only in the most profound humility. For she always maintained that she was most unworthy in the sight of the Lord to proclaim so great a feast to the world, excusing herself as well on account of her lack of experience and power. But the more she reckoned herself unworthy, the more Christ, who loves and teaches humility, reckoned her worthy.

Consenting at last to the admonition she had so often received, therefore, she began by telling the whole story to a venerable man, Dom John of Lausanne,[6] a canon of St. Martin of Liège, of blessed memory—a man she loved dearly because of his excellent holiness. Since he knew many great scholars and religious who

---

1 Luke 10: 21.
2 Luke 2: 29.
3 Ps. 40: 3,9; Douay Ps. 39: 4,11.
4 See Rom. 8: 26.
5 See Acts 9: 5.
6 Dom is an honorific used before the names of churchmen.

came to him for his prayers, she asked him to set before them all she had told him, but without mentioning her name, in order to find out what great theologians might think of such a feast. See how a wise virgin behaves! She does nothing rashly, approaches nothing without counsel, but does everything in due time and with the utmost deliberation, discerning and wishing others to discern whether the spirits are from God.[1]

Let this be a lesson for men and women who are wise in their own eyes, believing in every spirit and thinking that whatever crosses their minds is a divine revelation. A sign is shown to Juliana, a mystery is revealed, a task is enjoined, or rather forced upon her, and all by him who can neither deceive nor be deceived. Even so, she submits everything to be reviewed by people who are learned in the divine law and possess the Spirit of God. But if the example of our virgin is not enough for them, let them hearken to Paul's behavior. Did he not decide to consult with others about his gospel, which he had received not from a human being but from Christ, lest somehow he should be running or had run in vain?[2] Where he is not secure, neither is Christ's handmaid. If anyone is, beware lest it be judged not security but rashness.

All these matters, then, were set before Dom Jacques of Troyes, then Archdeacon of Liège, a man extremely learned in the divine law and adorned with the merits of holiness, who, because he always showed himself faithful before the Lord in the little he received, was later found worthy to be set over much.[3] Afterward, in fact, he was made Bishop of Verdun, a post from which he was raised to Patriarch of Jerusalem. At last, as God wondrously advanced him, he was exalted to the papacy after Pope Alexander IV and took the name of Urban IV.[4] All these things were also set before Friar Hugh, then Prior Provincial of the Dominicans, who was later found worthy of promotion on his merits to Cardinal of the Roman Church;[5] and to the reverend father Dom Guiard, Bishop of Cambrai.[6] In those days these two men shone in the Church like the two great lights of heaven because of their life and learning. The matter was also related to the chancellor of Paris, an extremely erudite man,[7] and to the friars Gilles, John, and Gerard, lectors of the Dominicans in Liège,[8] along with many others who glistened like stars by virtue of their life and learning.

But when is the Holy Spirit ever divided against himself? When would he ever contradict himself? Certainly he did not say one thing by the mouth of his handmaid Juliana and another by the mouths of his faithful servants. No "yes and no" was found among them, but only "yes."[9] All these people, once they had carefully heard, understood, and considered the merits of this affair, pronounced with one mind that they could find no valid reason in divine law to preclude a special feast of the venerable Sacrament. It would be most fitting and right, it would increase both the honor of God and the growth and grace of the elect, if Mother Church were to celebrate every year a memorial of the institution of this Sacrament more specifically and solemnly than she had done before. When Christ's virgin learned of this unanimous opinion, she gave thanks to God that he had placed an answer in keeping with his will in the mouths of so many great dignitaries.

---

1 1 John 4: 1.

2 See Gal. 1: 12, 2: 2.

3 See Matt. 25: 21.

4 Jacques Pantaléon of Troyes, a shoemaker's son, was Archdeacon of Liège in the 1240s, Bishop of Verdun from 1252–1255, Patriarch of Jerusalem from 1255–1261, and Pope Urban IV from 1261–1264. A few months before his death, he issued the bull *Transiturus* which established Corpus Christi as a feast for the universal Church.

5 Hugh of St. Cher (d.1264), the famed theologian and exegete, was created Cardinal Presbyter of St. Sabina in 1244. In 1251–1252 he took an active role in promoting the feast of Corpus Christi in the diocese of Liège.

6 Guido or Guiard held this office from 1238–1247; he visited Juliana in August 1242. A famous preacher, he was influential in the spread of Eucharistic piety.

7 Philippe de Grèves (d.*c*.1236), also called Philip the Chancellor, was known for his elegant Latin hymns.

8 A Dominican house of studies had been opened in Liège in 1234.

9 See 2 Cor. 1: 19

TIMELINE FOR CHAPTER SEVEN

I200

——— 1st half 13th c. *Secret History of the Mongols*

1248-72 *Charters for a Hospital* ———   ——— 1246 Guyuk Khan, *Letter to Innocent IV*

1250 Béla IV, *Letter to Innocent IV* ———   I250 ——— 1250 *Ghibelline Annals of Piacenza*

1259-64 Thomas Aquinas, *Summa against the Gentiles* ———   ——— 1260-4 *Decrees of Hanseatic League*

1261-4 *The Life of Juliana of Mont-Cornillon* ———

1272 Joinville, *Life of St. Louis* ———

1275 *Statute of the Jewry* ———   ——— 1275 *Petition of the "Commonalty" of the Jews*

1295 *Summons to Parliament* ———   ——— 1296 Boniface VIII, *Clericis Laicos*

1300 Marco Polo, *Travels* ———   I300 ——— 14th c. *Annunciation Play*

1300 Meister Eckhart, *Sermon 101* ———   ——— 1302 Boniface VIII, *Unam Sanctam*

1303 William of Plaisians, *Charges of Heresy* ———   ——— 1306-7 Athanasius I, *Letter about Famine*

——— 1308 Mengu-Temir Khan, *Charter for Russian Church*

1313-21 Dante, *Divine Comedy* ———   ——— 1314 *Assembly of Estates General*

1318-25 Jacques Fournier, *Episcopal Register* ———

I350

1360s *Sarum manual* (Expulsion of a leper) ———

——— end of 14th c. *Sir Gawain and the Green Knight*

I400

EIGHT

CATASTROPHE AND CREATIVITY (*c*.1350-*c*.1500)

THE PLAGUE

8.1 A medical view: Nicephorus Gregoras, *Roman History* (*c*.1350). Original in Greek.

STRUCK BY THE PLAGUE IN 1347, Byzantium was badly hit, and its coastal cities, overrun by ship-borne rats, were depopulated. Militarily weakened by civil war, it was now more vulnerable to the Turks, whose territories were inland. Nicephorus Gregoras (1295-*c*.1361), a scholar, diplomat, theologian, and historian, wrote a highly objective report on the spread and medical effects of the plague in his *Roman*—that is "Byzantine"—*History*.

[Source: Christos S. Bartsocas, "Two Fourteenth Century Greek Descriptions of the 'Black Death,'" *Journal of the History of Medicine and Allied Sciences* 21 (1966): 395.]

During that time a serious and pestilential disease invaded humanity. Starting from Scythia and Maeotis and the mouth of the Tanais,[1] just as spring began, it lasted for that whole year, passing through and destroying, to be exact, only the continental coast, towns as well as country areas, ours and those that are adjacent to ours, up to Gadera and the columns of Hercules.[2]

During the second year it invaded the Aegean Islands. Then it affected the Rhodians, as well as the Cypriots and those colonizing the other islands. The calamity attacked men as well as women, rich and poor, old and young. To put matters simply, it did not spare those of any age or fortune. Several homes were emptied of all their inhabitants in one day or sometimes in two. No one could help anyone else, not even the neighbors, or the family, or blood relations.

The calamity did not destroy only men but also many animals living with and domesticated by men.

1 The Don River.
2 The Gibraltar Straits.

I speak of dogs and horses and all the species of birds, even the rats that happened to live within the walls of the houses. The prominent signs of this disease, signs indicating early death, were tumorous outgrowths at the roots of thighs and arms and simultaneously bleeding ulcerations, which, sometimes the same day, carried the infected rapidly out of this present life, sitting or walking. During that time, Andronicus, the youngest of the [emperor's] sons, died.

8.2 Processions at Damascus: Ibn Battuta, *Travels* (before 1368). Original in Arabic.

PILGRIM AND ADVENTURER, IBN BATTUTA (1304-1368) left his home in Tangiers in 1325 and had covered most of the Arab world by the end of his travels in 1354. He later dictated his story, a mixture of observations about culture, geography, and custom. Interspersed into his account were personal experiences, which he called "Anecdotes." The one recounted here recalled his trip to Damascus in July 1348, when he witnessed fasts, prayers, and processions meant to ward off the plague.

[Source: *The Travels of Ibn Battuta, A.D. 1325-1354*, trans. H.A.R. Gibb, vol. 1 (Cambridge: Cambridge University Press, 1958), pp. 142-44 (notes omitted).]

Among the sanctuaries of Damascus which are celebrated for their blessed power is the Mosque of the Footprints (Masjid al-Aqdam), which lies two miles to the south of Damascus, alongside the main highway which leads to the illustrious Hijaz, Jerusalem, and Egypt. It is a large mosque, abundant in blessing, and possessing many endowments, and the people of Damascus hold it in great veneration. The footprints from which it derives its name are certain footprints impressed upon a rock there, which are said to be the print of the foot of Moses (on him be peace). Within this mosque there is a small chamber containing a stone with the following inscription upon it: "A certain saintly man used to see the Chosen [i.e., Muhammad] (God bless and give him peace) in his sleep, and he would say to him 'Here is the grave of my brother Moses (on him be peace).'" On the road in the vicinity of this mosque is a place called the Red Sandhill; and near Jerusalem and Jericho there is a place which is also called the Red Sandhill and which is revered by the Jews.

Anecdote. I witnessed at the time of the Great Plague at Damascus in the latter part of the month of Second Rabi' of the year 49 [July 1348] a remarkable instance of the veneration of the people of Damascus for this mosque. Arghun-Shah, king of the emirs and the Sultan's viceroy, ordered a crier to proclaim through Damascus that the people should fast for three days and that no one should cook in the bazaar during the daytime anything to be eaten (for most of the people there eat no food but what has been prepared in the bazaar). So the people fasted for three successive days, the last of which was a Thursday. At the end of this period the emirs, sharifs, qadis, doctors of the Law, and all other classes of the people in their several degrees, assembled in the Great Mosque, until it was filled to overflowing with them, and spent the Thursday night there in prayers and liturgies and supplications. Then, after performing the dawn prayer [on the Friday morning], they all went out together on foot carrying Qur'ans in their hands—the emirs too barefooted. The entire population of the city joined in the exodus, male and female, small and large; the Jews went out with their book of the Law and the Christians with their Gospel, their women and children with them; the whole concourse of them in tears and humble supplications, imploring the favor of God through His Books and His Prophets. They made their way to the Mosque of the Footprints and remained there in supplication and invocation until near midday, then returned to the city and held the Friday service. God Most High lightened their affliction; the number of deaths in a single day reached a maximum of two thousand, whereas the number rose in Cairo and Old Cairo to twenty-four thousand in a day.

8.3 Prayers at York: Archbishop William, *Letter to His Official at York* (July 1348). Original in Latin.

DURING THE SAME MONTH as the Damascus processions, the English archbishop of York William de la Zouche (r.1342-1353), wrote from his residence at Cawood, a few miles southwest of York, to arrange for special processions, prayers, and masses to be held in his diocese to prevent the plague, which had already hit France. What commonalities and what differences were there in York's Christian and Damascus's Islamic religious responses to the plague?

[Source: *The Black Death*, ed. and trans. Rosemary Horrox (Manchester: Manchester University Press, 1994), pp. 111-12.]

Since the life of man on earth is a war, no wonder if those fighting amidst the miseries of this world are unsettled by the mutability of events: now favorable, now contrary. For Almighty God sometimes allows those he loves to be troubled while their strength is perfected in weakness by an outpouring of spiritual grace. There can be no one who does not know, since it is now public knowledge, how great a mortality, pestilence, and infection of the air are now threatening various parts of the world, and especially England; and this is surely caused by the sins of men who, while enjoying good times, forget that such things are the gifts of the most high giver. Thus, since the inevitable human fate, pitiless death, which spares no one, now threatens us, unless the holy clemency of the Savior is shown to his people from on high, the only hope is to hurry back to him alone, whose mercy outweighs justice and who, most generous in forgiving, rejoices heartily in the conversion of sinners; humbly urging him with orisons and prayers that he, the kind and merciful Almighty God, should turn away his anger and remove the pestilence and drive away the infection from the people whom he redeemed with his precious blood.

Therefore we command, and order you to let it be known with all possible haste, that devout processions are to be held every Wednesday and Friday in our cathedral church, in other collegiate and conventual churches, and in every parish church in our city and diocese, with a solemn chanting of the litany, and that a special prayer be said in mass every day for allaying the plague and pestilence, and likewise prayers for the lord king and for the good estate of the church, the realm and the whole people of England, so that the Savior, harkening to the constant entreaties, will pardon and come to the rescue of the creation which God fashioned in his own image.

And we, trusting in the mercy of Almighty God and the merits and prayers of his mother, the glorious Virgin Mary, and of the blessed apostles Peter and Paul, and of the most holy confessor William and of all the saints, have released 40 days of the penance enjoined by the gracious God on all our parishioners and on others whose diocesans have approved and accepted this our indulgence, for sins for which they are penitent, contrite, and have made confession, if they pray devoutly for these things, celebrate masses, undertake processions or are present at them, or perform other offices of pious devotion.[1] And you are to ensure that these things are speedily put into effect in every archdeaconry within our diocese by the archdeacons or their officials. Farewell.

---

1   The remission of penance was part of the theology of Purgatory. The archbishop here declares that certain pious acts carried out on earth were equivalent to 40 days of penance in Purgatory. Such a remission of days in Purgatory was called an indulgence.

8.4 Blaming the Jews: Heinrich von Diessenhoven, *On the Persecution of the Jews* (*c.*1350). Original in Latin.

IN THE THIRTEENTH CENTURY, JEWS WERE accused of having arcane and evil knowledge. In the fourteenth century this idea became lethal when the Black Death struck, as outcasts of every sort—lepers, beggars, and Jews—were accused of spreading poison. Soon the accusations focused on the Jews, who were killed (among other places) in parts of France, Germany, the Low Countries, and Italy. In the *Ecclesiastical History* of Heinrich von Diessenhoven (1299-1376), a canon lawyer close to the Hapsburgs, the burning of Jews in Germany was God's way to confound His enemies. Taking into account earlier persecutions and expulsions of Jews—R. Eliezer's poem (above, p. 286), the *Decrees of Lateran IV* (above, p. 395), Jocelin of Brakelond's *Chronicle* (above, p. 410), and the *Statute of the Jewry* in 1275 (above, p. 444)—consider how the plague added to and transformed their woes.

[Source: *The Black Death*, ed. and trans. Rosemary Horrox (Manchester: Manchester University Press, 1994), pp. 208-10 (some notes added).]

The persecution of the Jews began in November 1348, and the first outbreak in Germany was at Sölden, where all the Jews were burnt on the strength of a rumor that they had poisoned wells and rivers, as was afterwards confirmed by their own confessions and also by the confessions of Christians whom they had corrupted and who had been induced by the Jews to carry out the deed. And some of the Jews who were newly baptized said the same. Some of these remained in the faith but some others relapsed, and when these were placed upon the wheel[1] they confessed that they had themselves sprinkled poison or poisoned rivers. And thus no doubt remained of their deceitfulness which had now been revealed.

Within the revolution of one year, that is from All Saints [November 1] 1348 until Michaelmas [September 29] 1349 all the Jews between Cologne and Austria were burnt and killed for this crime, young men and maidens and the old along with the rest. And blessed be God who confounded the ungodly who were plotting the extinction of his church, not realizing that it is founded on a sure rock and who, in trying to overturn it, crushed themselves to death and were damned for ever.

But now let us follow the killings individually. First

Jews were killed or burnt in Sölden in November, then in Zofingen they were seized and some put on the wheel, then in Stuttgart they were all burnt. The same thing happened during November in Landsberg, a town in the diocese of Augsburg and in Bueron, Memmingen and Burgau in the same diocese. During December they were burnt and killed on the feast of St. Nicholas [December 6] in Lindau, on December 8 in Reutlingen, on December 13 in Haigerloch, and on December 20 in Horw they were burnt in a pit. And when the wood and straw had been consumed, some Jews, both young and old, still remained half alive. The stronger of them snatched up cudgels and stones and dashed out the brains of those trying to creep out of the fire, and thus compelled those who wanted to escape the fire to descend to hell. And the curse seemed to be fulfilled: "his blood be upon us and upon our children."[2]

On December 27 the Jews in Esslingen were burnt in their houses and in the synagogue. In Nagelten they were burnt. In the abovesaid town of Zofingen the city councillors, who were hunting for poison, found some in the house of a Jew called Trostli, and by experiment were satisfied that it was poison. As a result, two Jewish men and one woman were put

---

1 Breaking on the wheel was a form of torture.
2 Matt. 27: 24: the people's response to Pilate's statement, "I am innocent of the blood of this just man [Christ]. Look you to it."

on the wheel, but others were saved at the command of Duke Albrecht of Austria,[1] who ordered that they should be protected. But this made little difference, for in the course of the next year those he had under his protection were killed, and as many again in the diocese of Constance. But first those burnt in 1349 will be described in order.

Once started, the burning of the Jews went on increasing. When people discovered that the stories of poisoning were undoubtedly true they rose as one against the Jews. First, on January 2, 1349 the citizens of Ravensburg burnt the Jews in the castle, to which they had fled in search of protection from King Charles, whose servants were imprisoned by the citizens after the burning. On January 4th the people of Constance shut up the Jews in two of their own houses, and then burnt 330 of them in the fields at sunset on March 3rd. Some processed to the flames dancing, others singing and the rest weeping. They were burnt shut up in a house which had been specially built for the purpose. On January 12 in Buchen and on January 17 in Basel they were all burnt apart from their babies, who were taken from them by the citizens and baptized. They were burnt on January 21 in Messkirch and Waldkirch, on January 26 in Speyer, and on January 30 in Ulm, on February 11 in Überlingen, on February 14 in the city of Strasbourg (where it took six days to burn them because of the numbers involved), on February 16 in Mengen, on the 19th of the month in Sulgen, on the 21st in Schaffhausen and Zurich, on the 23rd in St. Gall and on March 3 in Constance, as described above, except for some who were kept back to be burnt on the third day after the Nativity of the Virgin [September 11].

They were killed and burnt in the town of Baden on March 18, and those in the castle below, who had been brought there from Rheinfelden for protection, were killed and then burnt. And on May 30 they were similarly wiped out in Radolfzell. In Mainz and Cologne they were burnt on August 23. On September 18, 330 Jews were burnt in the castle at Kyburg, where they had gathered from Winterthur and Diessenhoven and the other towns of their protector the Duke of Austria. But the imperial citizens did not want to go on supporting them any longer, and so they wrote to Duke Albrecht of Austria, who was protecting his Jewish subjects in the counties of Pfirt, Alsace and Kyburg, and told him that either he had them burnt by his own judges or they would burn them themselves. So the Duke ordered them to be burnt by his own judges, and they were finally burnt on September 18.

And thus, within one year, as I said, all the Jews between Cologne and Austria were burnt—and in Austria they await the same fate, for they are accursed of God. And I could believe that the end of the Hebrews had come, if the time prophesied by Elias and Enoch were now complete; but since it is not complete, it is necessary that some be reserved so that what has been written may be fulfilled: that the hearts of the sons shall be turned to their fathers, and of the fathers to the sons.[2] But in what parts of the world they may be reserved I do not know, although I think it more likely that the seed of Abraham will be reserved in lands across the sea than in these people. So let me make an end of the Jews here.[3]

---

1   Albert II (or Albrecht II), duke of Austria 1330–1358.

2   A reference to Mal. 4: 5–6: "Behold I will send you Elias the prophet, before the coming of the great and dreadful day of the lord. And he shall turn the heart of the fathers to the children and the hearts of the children to their fathers: lest I come and strike the earth with anathema." This text was taken to mean that after the coming of Antichrist the prophets Enoch and Elias would reconvert the apostates as a preliminary to the second coming of Christ and the Last Judgment. At the same time they would convert the Jews to Christianity. Heinrich's point is that because the second coming is not yet imminent, contemporary Jews could not be entirely wiped out or converted, because some had to survive to be converted by Enoch and Elias in the Last Days.

3   The sentence is ambiguous and, given the anti-semitism of the author, probably deliberately so. Its surface meaning is that he has come to the end of the two chapters devoted to the Jews and is now about to turn to other matters. But it could also be taken to mean that he hopes to see the extermination of the Jews in Europe, as there are likely to be enough elsewhere to meet the prophetic conditions laid down for Christ's second coming.

8.5 A legislative response: *Ordinances against the Spread of Plague at Pistoia* (1348). Original in Latin.

MANY CITY GOVERNMENTS RESPONDED TO THE plague by instituting new sanitation measures. They quickly recognized that the disease spread as infected people traveled from one place to another and as infected garments and corpses came into contact with the healthy. Although they had no germ theory, the idea that "bad air" and stench caused the plague led them to legislate particular slaughtering practices. At Pistoia the statutes promulgated in 1348 and printed below were revised less than a month later and then again a few weeks after that, illustrating how quickly the city responded to changing circumstances. How many statutes were concerned with travel in and out of Pistoia? How many with burial practices? How many with butchering? And how many—and why—with the consumption of luxury goods?

[Source: *The Black Death*, trans. Rosemary Horrox (Manchester: Manchester University Press, 1994), pp. 195-200 (some notes added).]

[2 May, 1348]

1. So that the sickness which is now threatening the region around Pistoia shall be prevented from taking hold of the citizens of Pistoia, no citizen or resident of Pistoia, wherever they are from or of what condition, status or standing they may be, shall dare or presume to go to Pisa or Lucca; and no one shall come to Pistoia from those places; penalty 500 pence. And no one from Pistoia shall receive or give hospitality to people who have come from those places; same penalty. And the guards who keep the gates of the city of Pistoia shall not permit anyone traveling to the city from Pisa or Lucca to enter; penalty 10 pence from each of the guards responsible for the gate through which such an entry has been made. But citizens of Pistoia now living within the city may go to Pisa and Lucca, and return again, if they first obtain permission from the common council—who will vote on the merits of the case presented to them. The licence is to be drawn up by the notary of the *anziani* and *gonfalonier* of the city.[1] And this ordinance is to be upheld and observed from

the day of its ratification until October 1st, or longer if the council sees fit.

2. No one, whether from Pistoia or elsewhere, shall dare or presume to bring or fetch to Pistoia, whether in person or by an agent, any old linen or woollen cloths, for male or female clothing or for bedspreads; penalty 200 pence, and the cloth is to be burnt in the public piazza of Pistoia by the official who discovered it.[2] However it shall be lawful for citizens of Pistoia traveling within Pistoia and its territories to take linen and woollen cloths with them for their own use or wear, provided that they are in a pack or fardle [bundle] weighing 30 lb or less. And this ordinance is to be upheld and observed from the day of its ratification until 1 January. And if such cloth has already been brought into Pistoia, the bringer must take it away within three days of the ordinance's ratification; same penalty.

3. The bodies of the dead shall not be removed from the place of death until they have been enclosed in a

---

1   Pistoia's government was dominated by the party of the *popolo*. Their chief administrators were twelve *anziani*, each elected for very short terms. The *popolo*'s chief military officers were the *capitano* and the *gonfalonier*. The other key figure in the city's government was the *podestà*, a single man holding administrative, judicial, and military powers. Almost always a "foreigner" from another city, this official was supposed to be above family and party loyalties. These men were expected to work together to enforce the sanitation ordinances of 1348.

2   Later outbreaks of plague in Italian cities were often associated with the movement of cloth, and this requirement suggests that the connection may already have been noted. Contemporaries—who were not aware of the role played by fleas in the transmission of the disease—explained the connection as due to the trapping of corrupt air within the folds of fabric.

wooden box, and the lid of planks nailed down[1] so that no stench can escape, and covered with no more than one pall, coverlet or cloth; penalty 50 pence to be paid by the heirs of the deceased or, if there are no heirs, by the nearest kinsmen in the male line. The goods of the deceased are to stand as surety for the payment of the penalty. Also the bodies are to be carried to burial in the same box; same penalty. So that the civic officials can keep a check on this, the rectors of the chapels in Pistoia must notify the *podestà* and *capitano* when a corpse is brought into their chapel, giving the dead man's name and the contrada [quarter] in which he was living when he died; same penalty. As soon as he has been notified, the *podestà* or *capitano* must send an official to the place, to find out whether this chapter of the ordinances is being observed, along with the other regulations governing funerals, and to punish those found guilty. And if the *podestà* or *capitano* is remiss in carrying out these orders he must be punished by those who appointed him; same penalty. But these regulations should not apply to the poor and destitute of the city, who are dealt with under another civic ordinance.

4. To avoid the foul stench which comes from dead bodies each grave shall be dug two and a half arms-length deep, as this is reckoned in Pistoia;[2] penalty 10 pence from anyone digging or ordering the digging of a grave which infringes the statute.

5. No one, of whatever condition, status, or standing, shall dare or presume to bring a corpse into the city, whether coffined or not; penalty 25 pence. And the guards at the gates shall not allow such bodies to be brought into the city; same penalty, to be paid by every guard responsible for the gate through which the body was brought.

6. Any person attending a funeral shall not accompany the corpse or its kinsmen further than the door of the church where the burial is to take place, or go back to the house where the deceased lived, or to any other house on that occasion; penalty 10 pence. Nor is he to go the week's mind of the deceased; same penalty.[3]

7. When someone dies, no one shall dare or presume to give or send any gift to the house of the deceased, or to any other place on that occasion, either before or after the funeral, or to visit the house, or eat there on that occasion; penalty 25 pence. This shall not apply to the sons and daughters of the deceased, his blood brothers and sisters and their children, or to his grandchildren. The *podestà* and *capitano*, when notified by the rector as in chapter 3, must send an official to enquire whether anything has been done to the contrary and to punish those responsible.

8. To avoid waste and unnecessary expense, no one shall dare or presume to wear new clothes during the mourning period or for the next eight days; penalty 25 pence. This shall not apply to the wife of the deceased, who may if she wishes wear a new garment of any fabric without penalty.

9. No crier, summoner, or drummer of Pistoia shall dare or presume to invite or summon any citizen of Pistoia, whether publicly or privately, to come to a funeral or visit the corpse; nor shall anyone send the same summoner, trumpeter, crier, or drummer; penalty 10 pence from each crier, trumpeter, summoner, or drummer, and from the people by whom they have been employed.

10. So that the sound of bells does not trouble or frighten the sick, the keepers of the campanile of the cathedral church of Pistoia shall not allow any of the bells to be rung during funerals, and no one else shall dare or presume to ring any of the bells on such occasions; penalty 10 pence, to be paid by the keepers who allowed the bells to be rung and by the heirs of the dead man, or his kinsmen should he have no heirs. When a parishioner is buried in his parish church, or a member of a fraternity within the fraternity church, the church bells may be rung, but only on one occasion and not excessively; same penalty.

---

1   The bodies of ordinary people were generally buried in shrouds, although they might be carried to church in a coffin. This ordinance probably implies that they were to be buried in a coffin.
2   A *bracchio* (armslength) in Pistoia measured between two and two and a half feet.
3   This last sentence refers to a ban on attendance at the commemorative mass one week after a death.

11. No one shall presume or dare to summon a gathering of people to escort a widow from the house of her dead husband, but only from the church to his burial place. But it shall be lawful for the widow's kinsmen to send up to four women to escort the widow from her husband's house at other times. No one shall dare to attend such a gathering; penalty 25 pence, paid by those invited and by those who issued the invitation.

12. No one shall dare or presume to raise a lament or crying for anyone who has died outside Pistoia, or summon a gathering of people other than the kinsfolk and spouse of the deceased, or have bells rung, or use criers or any other means to invite people throughout the city to such a gathering; penalty 25 pence from each person involved.

However it is to be understood that none of this applies to the burial of knights, doctors of law, judges, and doctors of physic, whose bodies can be honored by their heirs at their burial in any way they please.

13. So that the living are not made ill by rotten and corrupt food, no butcher or retailer of meat shall dare or presume to hang up meat, or keep and sell meat hung up in their storehouse or over their counter; penalty 10 pence. And that the rulers of the craft of butchery must investigate these matters on every day when slaughtering occurs, and immediately denounce any offenders to the lords, *podestà* or *capitano*, or to one of their officials; same penalty from the rulers of the craft if they fail to carry out these things in person or by deputy. The *podestà* and *capitano* must each send someone to look into these matters, and punish those found guilty, along with the rulers of the craft if they have failed to denounce them. The word of any official who finds an infringement of the regulations shall be taken as sufficient evidence.

14. Butchers and retailers of meat shall not stable horses or allow any mud or dung in the shop or other place where they sell meat, or in or near their storehouse, or on the roadway outside; nor shall they slaughter animals in a stable, or keep flayed [skinned] carcasses in a stable or in any other place where there is dung; penalty 10 pence. An official of the *podestà* or *capitano* is to enquire closely into such matters, and his word is to be taken on any infringement of these ordinances.

15. No butcher or retailer of meat shall dare or presume to keep on the counter where he sells meat, meat from more than one ox, calf, or cow at once, although he can keep the meat of an ox or cow alongside that of a calf, penalty 10 pence. The rulers of the craft must investigate the matter on every day on which animals are slaughtered and denounce any offenders to the *podestà* or *capitano* of the city; same penalty.

16. In May, June, July, and August butchers and retailers of meat shall slaughter meat on the days on which meat can be eaten, including Sundays and feast days, and sell it on the same day to those wishing to buy; the animals are to be vetted by the civic officials appointed for the purpose.[1]

17. No butcher or retailer shall dare or presume to kill any ox, cow or calf without first obtaining permission from officials of the *podestà* or *capitano*. As soon as the official's approval has been requested he shall go and see the animal, to decide whether it is healthy or not. When permission has been given the butcher himself must slaughter the animal properly in the official's presence; penalty 10 pence.

18. No butcher or any other retailer of meat shall kill any two- or three-year old boar or sow between March 1 and December 1; penalty 25 pence.

19. Butchers or retailers shall flay [skin] every two- or three-year old boar or sow killed between December 1 and March 1 before putting it on sale. If they wish to salt it down, that is permissible, but it must be flayed first; penalty 25 pence.

20. [Provisions for the election of officials to set the retail price of meat.]

---

1   In other words, the importance of ensuring a supply of fresh meat meant that slaughtering could take place on days when it was usually banned.

21. For the better preservation of health, there should be a ban on all kinds of poultry, calves, foodstuffs, and on all kinds of fat being taken out of Pistoia by anybody; penalty 100 pence and the confiscation of the things being carried contrary to the ban. And whoever can capture such carriers and the things carried and take them to the gaol [jail] of the commune of Pistoia shall have half of the fine and of the value of the goods, after the fine has been paid and the goods sold to the highest bidder.

22. To avoid harm to men by stink and corruption, there shall in future be no tanning of skins within the city walls of Pistoia; penalty 25 pence.

23. [Provisions for enforcement including the proviso that anyone can denounce an offender before the *podestà* or *capitano*, and receive a quarter of the fine if the accusation is upheld; the word of one man worthy of belief is to be sufficient evidence of guilt, or the statements of four men testifying to the common belief.]

8.6 A Turkish hero: Ashikpashazade, *Osman Comes to Power* (late 15th c.). Original in Turkish.

WRITING IN THE LATE FIFTEENTH CENTURY, the chronicler Ashikpashazade (1392–*c*.1481) based his account of the founder of the Ottoman Turks (Osman) on earlier sources and on his sense of the sort of heroic past such a leader needed to have. He depicted Osman creating a new empire through a combination of fate, "feigned friendships," religious fervor, force, and cunning. How might you compare Ashikpashazade's heroic image of Osman with ibn Shaddad's view of Saladin (above, p. 334)? How might you account for the differences?

[Source: *Die altosmanische Chronik des Asikpasazade*, ed. Friedrich Giese (Leipzig: Harrassowitz, 1929). Translated by Robert Dankoff.]

HOW OSMAN GHAZI BECAME SULTAN

Ertugrul Ghazi heard that Sultan 'Alaeddin[1] of the Seljuk dynasty had become King of Rum.[2] He said, "We have to determine the man's quality. We'll go to that country and perform the ghaza."[3] Ertugrul Ghazi had three sons, Osman, Gündüz, and Saruyati. Together they started out for Rum. While they were nomadizing in the province of Ghazi Hasan of Mosul, Ertugrul Ghazi sent his son Saruyati to 'Alaeddin, saying, "Provide us with a homeland and we will go and perform the ghaza." Sultan 'Alaeddin was extremely happy at their coming. The tekfur[4] of Sultan Önü and of Karaja Hisar was submissive, so Sultan 'Alaeddin provided them with Sögüt as their homeland, which was between Karaja Hisar and Bilejik. In addition, he gave them the ranges of Mount Domanich and Ermeni Beli. They passed directly through Ankara and settled in that province.

Several years later, Ertugrul Ghazi died. They preferred Osman Ghazi to succeed him in Sögüt. As soon as Osman Ghazi succeeded his father, he began a policy of "feigned friendship" with the neighboring infidels. Meanwhile, he began hostilities with the emir of Germiyan[5] because the latter was constantly harassing the populace of the surrounding countryside. Osman Ghazi also began to mount hunting expeditions far and wide.

HOW OSMAN GHAZI BEGAN FROM TIME TO TIME TO MAKE RAIDS AT NIGHTTIME AND IN THE DAY

At Inegöl there was an infidel named Aya Nikola. When Osman went to the summer pasture or to the winter pasture, Aya Nikola used to harass the migration. Osman Ghazi complained of this to the tekfur of Bilejik, and said, "What we would like from you is to let us deposit our baggage with you when we go to the summer pasture." He agreed. So whenever Osman Ghazi went to the summer pasture, he loaded his baggage on oxen and sent them along with some women to be deposited in Bilejik castle. And when they returned from the summer pasture, they sent cheese and knotted rugs and flatweaves and lambs in the way of gifts. Then they took back their belongings and went on their way. These infidels trusted them completely; but the infidels of Inegöl were wary of Osman, and he of them.

---

1 Apparently 'Ala' al-Din Kay Qubad III, who ruled intermittently between 1284 and 1302.
2 A reference to the Eastern Roman or Byzantine Empire, i.e., Anatolia.
3 Ghaza means conducting raids on the infidels. The warrior who gains fame in the ghaza gains the title of Ghazi.
4 Byzantine prince or governor. (The title "tekfur" is used for Christian emirs, or commanders.)
5 Turkish emirate (*beglik*) of western Anatolia with its capital at Kütahya (ancient Cotiaeum).

One day, Osman Ghazi came through Ermeni Beli with seventy men in order to set fire to Inegöl at night. A spy informed the infidels, who set up an ambush. The spy's name was Araton. Osman Ghazi had a Balkan sailor in his service. He came and informed them that the ambush was situated where the pass of Ermeni Beli emerged into the valley. The ghazis put their trust in God and marched straight toward the ambush. They were all on foot. There were many infidels. A great battle took place. Osman's brother Saruyati's son, whose name was Bay Hoca, was martyred. This occurred near the village of Hamza Beg, where the pass of Ermeni Beli emerges. Also, there is a ruined caravansary next to his shrine. From there, they turned back and Osman went to the summer pasture.

HOW OSMAN GHAZI HAD A DREAM, TO WHOM HE TOLD IT, AND WHAT ITS INTERPRETATION WAS

Osman Ghazi prayed, and for a moment he wept. He was overcome by drowsiness and he lay down and slept. Now in that vicinity there dwelt a certain holy sheikh named Edebali.[1] His many saintly qualities were evident, and he was believed by all the people. By name he was a dervish, but his dervishhood was concealed within;[2] he had an abundance of worldly goods and wealth, and he had torches and banners [signs of hospitality]. His guest-house was never empty, and Osman Ghazi also came sometimes and was the guest of this holy man.

As Osman Ghazi slept, he saw in his dream that a moon arose out of this holy man's breast and entered Osman Ghazi's breast. Then a tree sprouted out of Osman Ghazi's navel, and the shadow of the tree covered the entire world. In its shadow, there were mountains, with streams issuing from the foot of each mountain. And from these flowing streams some people drank, and some watered gardens, and some caused fountains to flow.

When he awoke, he came to the sheikh and told him the dream. The sheikh said, "Osman, my son! Sovereignty has been granted to you and your descen-

dants. And my daughter Malhun is to be your wife." He immediately gave his daughter to Osman Ghazi and married them.

This sheikh, Edebali, who interpreted Osman Ghazi's dream and gave tidings of sovereignty for himself and his descendants, had a disciple with him whose name was Kumral Dede, son of Dervish Durdi. That dervish now spoke, "O Osman! Since sovereignty has been given to you, it is proper for you to give us some token of gratitude." Osman replied, "At whatever time I become king, I will give you a city." The dervish said, "This little village is sufficient for us: we have renounced the city." Osman Ghazi accepted this. The dervish said, "Give us a document to that effect." Osman Ghazi replied, "Do you think that I write documents, that you want a document from me? Here is my sword. It was left to me by my father and my grandfather. I will give it to you. And I will also give you a goblet. Let them remain together in your hands, and let them preserve this stamp. And if God accepts me for this service, my descendants will recognize this sign, and will accept your claim." Now that sword is still in the hands of Kumral Dede's descendants. And whenever any of Osman Ghazi's descendants saw that sword, they bestowed favors upon those dervishes and they renewed the sword's scabbard. Every one of the House of Osman who has become king has made a pilgrimage to that sword....

HOW CERTAIN NEWS REACHED SULTAN 'ALAEDDIN, AND HOW THE INFIDELS WERE TREATING THE MUSLIMS

Now news reached Sultan 'Alaeddin that the infidels had fought against Osman Ghazi with large forces and had martyred his brother Saruyati. The sultan said, "It is well-known that the tekfur of Karaja Hisar is our enemy; also that the emir of Germiyan does not like those strangers [i.e., the Ottomans]. The greater part of the infidels' activities is due to his heedlessness, I know that myself. Now let our own army gather immediately! Shall we let those infidels get away with such actions? Is the zeal of Islam no longer in us?"

---

1   In this context, sheikh refers to a holy man or religious leader, in this case the head of a dervish order. See n. 2 below.
2   A dervish was an ascetic belonging to one of several Islamic orders. Some performed whirling dances and vigorous chants as part of their devotions.

With this command, a great army gathered to attack Karaja Hisar.

Osman Ghazi also came and joined the battle on one side. After the fighting had gone on for a day or two, word arrived that the Tatar Bayinjar[1] had taken Eregli, laid waste the houses and the people, and set fire to the city. Sultan 'Alaeddin summoned Osman Ghazi and handed over to him all the equipment which he had brought to take to Karaja Hisar. He said, "Osman Ghazi, my son! Upon you are many tokens of good fortune. There is no one in the world who will withstand you and your descendants. With you are my prayers, the favor of God, the aspiration of the saints, and the miracles of the Prophet." With that, he returned to his province. Osman pressed the battle for several more days. In the end, he captured the fortress, took the tekfur, let the ghazis plunder the city, distributed the houses to the ghazis and to others, and made it a Muslim city. This victory occurred in 1288....

HOW THE INFIDELS OF HARMAN KAYA BECAME ACQUAINTED WITH OSMAN GHAZI AND WHAT THEY DID

Whenever Osman Ghazi, who was now emir of the Banner, mounted for a raid, Köse Mihal was always with him. Most of the servants of these ghazis were infidels from Harman Kaya. One day Osman Ghazi said to Mihal, "We want to ride against Darakchi Yenijesi. What do you say?" Mihal replied, "My Khan![2] Let us pass to Sorgun by way of Saru Kaya and Besh Tash so that we can cross the Sakarya River. Then the ghazis on the other side will join us. It will also be easy to strike at the province of Mudurni, which is a prosperous place. Also, Samsa Chavush is settled near that province. We can keep him informed of our movements, and he can let us know when the time is right."

Following this advice, they marched out and camped at the dervish lodge at Besh Tash. They inquired of the sheikh, "Does the river afford a crossing?" "By the grace of God, there is a crossing for the ghazis!" the sheikh replied. They let their horses graze, then mounted and came to the river bank, where they found Samsa Chavush ready and waiting. He conducted the ghazis straight to Sorgun. The infidels of that province were well acquainted with Samsa Chavush. As soon as they saw him, and saw the army, they became submissive and obedient. The men and women came out to meet them. Among them was a rather distinguished infidel whom they summoned. He came and took a solemn oath with Osman Ghazi that they would accept whatever Samsa Chavush said....

HOW KÖSE MIHAL HAD A WEDDING PARTY, GIVING HIS DAUGHTER TO THE EMIR OF GÖL-FLANOZ

Köse Mihal made elaborate preparations, in order that the wedding party gain renown. When everything was ready, he sent people to summon the surrounding infidels and tekfurs. He also invited Osman Ghazi, and he informed the tekfurs, saying, "Come, get acquainted with this Turk so that you will be safe from his evil." They all came on the appointed day with elaborate gifts for the bride. Osman Ghazi arrived last. He brought good knotted carpets and flatweaves and herds of sheep. They were very pleased with Osman Ghazi's gifts. In short, the festivity went on for three days, and the tekfurs were astounded at Osman Ghazi's munificence. They found no opportunity to catch him up. As for Osman Ghazi, he showed great affection toward the tekfur of Bilejik. Previous to this, they had formed a friendship in absentia, as it were, since they had never met face to face; since Osman Ghazi used to deposit his goods in the Bilejik castle whenever he went to the summer pasture.

THE WEDDING PARTY OF THE TEKFUR OF BILEJIK

Now the tekfur of Bilejik also planned to have a wedding party, for he was to marry the daughter of the tekfur of Yar Hisar. First he summoned Mihal and consulted with him, arranging the plot against Osman. They completed all the arrangements for the wedding. Then he sent out messengers to invite the surrounding tekfurs. Even before the messenger got to Osman

---

1 Leader of the Chingizid Mongol forces in Anatolia.
2 Khan was the old Central Asian term for a ruler.

Ghazi, the latter sent a herd of sheep to the tekfur of Bilejik, saying, "Let my brother feed these to the servants at the wedding; and when I arrive, I shall bring my gifts for the bride, God willing, although I really have no gifts that befit my brother." The reason he sent these even before the messenger arrived was that at Mihal's wedding party certain arrangements had already been made, and the tekfur had sent Mihal to Osman Ghazi with the invitation. And he had also sent a number of gold and silver utensils. But when Mihal came, he informed Osman Ghazi what the intention of the tekfurs was, and he warned him to be on his guard. He also delivered the invitation. Osman Ghazi gave him the proper rewards for serving as the messenger, and said, "Emir Mihal, go, extend many greetings from me to my brother. Tell him that now is the time for us to migrate to the summer pasture. Also that my wife and mother-in-law wish to become acquainted with my brother's mother. Also my brother knows well how things are between the emir of Germiyan and myself. He has always borne our burden until now. May he be so gracious as to bear it once again this year, and allow us to deposit in the castle the baggage belonging to my mother and myself."

Mihal went and delivered Osman Ghazi's message to the tekfur, who received it with great pleasure, then sent Mihal back to arrange the day on which Osman Ghazi was to arrive. In addition to all this, Osman, in his message, had said, "Our women are accustomed to the wide plateau. Bilejik is too narrow to hold the wedding party there." The tekfur agreed to this as well, and they held it at Chakir Pinar.

On the appointed day, Osman Ghazi loaded the oxen and sent them in the company of the women who always brought them. They entered the castle in the dark of evening. As soon as one or two trains of oxen had entered, out of the bales of felt poured men with naked swords, who cut down the gatekeepers. There were few men in the castle itself, since most of them had gone to the wedding celebration. The castle was taken.

Now let us see what Osman Ghazi was doing in the meantime. He had dressed a number of his head-risking ghazis in women's clothes, and he sent word to the following effect: "Let them be housed in a place apart so that our women will not be ashamed to see the tekfurs there." The tekfur was very pleased at this as well,

thinking that the Turk's women as well as the men had fallen into his hands; so he housed them in a place apart. Osman Ghazi had also arranged with the oxen drivers to inform the tekfur that Osman himself would pay a visit at the time that they entered the castle. That very evening he did come, pretending that he did not wish his women to be left exposed. The tekfur received him cordially and put him up as a guest. But before the tekfur came to his own room, Osman Ghazi had mounted along with Mihal. The cry went up, "Hey! The Turk has escaped!" The tekfur also mounted, though he was rather tipsy, and pursued them as far as a nearby stream called Kadirayok, where he was caught. Osman Ghazi had the tekfur beheaded.

He continued riding and toward morning fell on Yar Hisar, captured its tekfur and the bride, and took most of the wedding guests captive. He then immediately sent Turgut Alp to Inegöl to prevent Aya Nikola from getting wind of events and escaping. Turgut Alp arrived in time and cordoned off Inegöl. Osman Ghazi brought all of the booty into Bilejik and saw to its disposition. Then they marched against Inegöl. As they approached, Osman Ghazi announced that the town would be open to plunder. When the ghazis heard the word "plunder," they raised a shout and poured into the castle. They cut up the tekfur, killed the men, and took the women captive, for this infidel had been the cause of many Muslims' being martyred.

TO WHOM THEY GAVE THE BRIDE WHOM THEY CAPTURED, SHE BEING THE DAUGHTER OF THE TEKFUR OF YAR HISAR

Osman Ghazi gave her to his son Orhan Ghazi. Her name was Lülüfer Khatun. At that time, Orhan was still a young man. He also had another son ['Alaeddin] whom he used to place in charge of the migration.

Once they had conquered these four castles [Karaja Hisar, Bilejik, Yar Hisar, and Inegöl] they established justice in their realm. All the surrounding villages prospered, even more than in the time of the infidels, and people began to come here from other provinces when they heard how well the infidels here were faring.

In short, Osman Ghazi made a wedding party and gave Lülüfer Khatun to his son Orhan Ghazi. This is the same Lülüfer Khatun who built a dervish lodge at the foot of the Bursa citadel near the Kapluja Gate. She is also the one who had the bridge constructed over the Lülüfer River, which is therefore known by her name. Murad Khan Ghazi and Süleyman Pasha were her sons, both by Orhan Ghazi.[1] When she died, she was buried with Orhan Ghazi in the Bursa citadel.

IN WHAT MANNER OSMAN GHAZI ESTABLISHED THE FRIDAY PRAYER, AND HOW THIS OCCURRED IN EVERY TOWN

When he took Karaja Hisar, the houses of the town were left empty, and quite a few people came from Germiyan and from other provinces asking Osman Ghazi for houses. Osman Ghazi gave them to them, and in a short time, the town was repopulated. He also gave them a number of churches which they made into mosques. They also set up a market.

Now these people decided that they wanted to perform the Friday congregational prayer, also that they wanted to have a qadi.[2] There was a holy man named Dursun Fakih who used to act as prayer-leader for those people. They explained their wish to him. He in turn came and spoke with Osman Ghazi's stepfather Edebali about it. While they were talking, Osman Ghazi came over and inquired into the matter. When he learned what they wanted, he said, "Do whatever seems correct to you." Dursun Fakih said, "My Khan! We must request permission from the sultan." Osman Ghazi replied, "I took this city by myself with my own sword. What does the sultan have to do with it that I should require his permission? God who bestowed the sultanate upon him also bestowed the office of khan on me by virtue of the ghaza. It is true that the sultan endowed me with this banner. But it is I who carried the banner into battle with the infidels! If he claims to be of the House of Seljuk, I claim to be the descendant of Gök Alp. And if he says that he came to this country before us, we say that my grandfather Süleyman Shah came before him."

This satisfied those people. They gave the offices of qadi and *khatib* [preacher] to Dursun Fakih. The Friday sermon was read first in Karaja Hisar. The festival sermon was read in Eskishehir, and they performed the festival prayer there.

The first sermon given in the name of Osman took place in 689 [1290].

OSMAN GHAZI'S LAWS AND REGULATIONS

The qadi was established, the military commander was in place, the market was in operation, and the sermon was being read. These people wanted a law. A man came from Germiyan and said, "Sell me the tax concession on this market." "Go to the Khan," said the people. So he went to the Khan and repeated his request. "What is a tax?" said Osman Ghazi. The man replied, "For whatever comes into the market I shall take a small amount of money." "Do you have a debt outstanding against the people of this market, that you wish to take money from them?" "My Khan," he answered, "this is a custom. The rulers of all countries do this." "Did God command this, or have the emirs themselves instituted it?" "It is a custom, my Khan, which has come down to us from the beginning of time." At this Osman Ghazi became very angry: "Should a man's earnings belong to another? It is his own property. What have I put into it that I should tell him to give me money? Out with you, scoundrel! Do not speak to me thus, or it will be to your own harm."

Afterwards, the people came and said, "My Khan, it is customary to give a little something to the market guards." Osman Ghazi said, "Now, since you say so, let everyone who sells one load give two *akçes*.[3] But whoever sells nothing should give nothing. Anyone who breaks this law of mine, may God cause his ruin in this world and the next. Furthermore, upon whomever I bestow a land grant, let it not be taken from his hands without reason; and when he dies, let it be given to his son, however young he may be. And at the time of campaign, his servants should accompany him so that he will be fit to fight. Whoever holds to this law, may God be pleased with him; but if one of my descendants is caused to establish a law other than this law, may God not be pleased with him who established it and with him who causes it to be established."

---

1 Orhan, the second Ottoman sultan, ruled *c*.1324–1360. His son Murad I ruled 1360–1389.
2 Qadi: a judge of religious law.
3 A silver coin.

8.7 Diplomacy: *Peace Agreement between the Ottoman Sultan Mehmed II and the Signoria of Venice* (January 25, 1478). Original in Greek.

MEHMED II'S SACK OF CONSTANTINOPLE was part of a larger plan to reconstitute the Roman Empire under his own rule. After 1453, Mehmed moved into the Balkans and the Aegean, coming up against the other major power in the region, Venice. Between 1463 and 1478, the Ottomans and Venetians waged war, although for much of that time Venice was looking for a way to make peace. This they finally arranged in 1478. Although all sides confirmed its provisions, the agreement has no signatures. Only the Venetian copy has survived, a scroll 23 inches long and 9½ inches wide, composed of pieces of Venetian paper pasted together. The top piece, with a scissors watermark, has Mehmed's gold *tugra*, or formal emblem, while the bottom piece has an eagle watermark and the text of the agreement. The first ten provisions repeat agreements previously made between the Ottomans and the Venetians. (They echo, as well, earlier agreements that the Venetians made with the Byzantines.) The remainder provides for Venice to surrender various territories and to pay the sultan large quantities of gold.

[Source: State Archives of Venice, ASV Documenti Turchi B1/2. Translated by Diana Gilliland Wright.]

I, the great lord and great emir, Sultan Mehmed-Bey,[1] son of the great and blessed lord Murad-Bey, do swear by the God of heaven and earth, and by our great prophet Mohammed, and by the seven *mushaf*[2] which we Moslems possess and confess, and by the 124 thousand prophets of God (more or less),[3] and by the faith which I believe and confess, and by my soul and by the soul of my father, and by the sword I wear:

Because my Lordship formerly had peace and friendship with the most illustrious and exalted Signoria of Venice, now again we desire to make a new peace and oath to confirm a true friendship and a new peace. For this purpose, the aforementioned illustrious Signoria sent the learned and wise Sir Giovanni Dario,[4] secretary, as emissary to my Lordship so we might make the said peace with the following old and new provisions. For this my Lordship swears by the above-written oaths that just as there was formerly peace and friendship between us, namely, with their lords and men and allies, I now profess good faith and an open peace by land and sea, within and without the Straits,[5] with the villages, fortresses, islands, and lands that raise the banner of San Marco,[6] and those who wish to raise the flag in the future, and all those places that are in their obedience and supervision,[7] and to the commerce which they have as of today and are going to have in the coming years.

---

1 Bey is a superior honorific in Turkish-related languages.

2 The seven *mushaf* were the seven accepted versions of the Qur'an: this emphasized Mehmed's Sunni allegiance.

3 The phrase "more or less" indicates that while they did not know the precise number of prophets, they did not wish to offend.

4 Giovanni Dario, the special Venetian emissary who brought the peace agreement to completion, was given a knighthood by Mehmed for his services. Dario's house, which Venice gave him in appreciation, can be seen in Venice: though small, it is one of the most conspicuous on the Grand Canal. See <http://www.campiello-venise.com/plan_interactif/b4_dario_3.htm>.

5 The Dardanelles, i.e., the strait that connects the Aegean Sea with the Sea of Marmara, the body of water that touches Constantinople's southern shore.

6 The banner of San Marco is red with a gold Venetian lion and a book that reads, "Pace tibi, Marce, evangelista meus [Peace unto you, St. Mark, my Evangelist]." See http://gallery.euroweb.hu/html/c/carpacci/5/06mark.html. The patron saint of Venice, Mark's body is believed to be buried in S. Marco.

7 This clause of the agreement refers to various other minor lords in the Aegean who gave nominal homage to Venice, including the Duke of Naxos (below, p. 498, n. 2).

[Confirmation of previous agreements.]

[1]¹ First, no man of my lordship will dare to inflict injury on or opposition to the Signoria of Venice or its men: if this happens, my Lordship is obligated to punish them according to the cause: similarly, the most illustrious Signoria is obligated toward us.

[2] Further, from this day forward, if either land or other goods of the most illustrious Signoria and its men is taken by the men of my Lordship, it will be returned: similarly, they are obligated to my Lordship.

[3] Their men and their merchandise may come by land and by sea to every land of my Lordship, and all the merchandise and the galleys and the ships will be secure and at ease: they are similarly obligated toward us in their lands.

[4] Similarly, the Duke of Naxos and his brothers and their lords and men with their ships and other boats are in the peace.² They will not owe my Lordship any service, but the Venetians will hold them just as it all used to be.

[5] Further, all ships and galleys, that is merchantmen and the fleet of my Lordship, wherever they may encounter the Venetians, will have good relations and peace with them. Corsairs and klefts, wherever they are taken, will be punished.³

[6] If any Venetian incurs a debt or commits other wrong in the lands of my Lordship, the other Venetians will bear no responsibility: similarly, the Signoria of Venice [vows the same] to our men.

[7] If any Venetian slave flees and comes into Turkish hands and becomes a Moslem, they will give his master 1000 *aspers*⁴; if he is a Christian he will be sent back.⁵

[8] If any Venetian boat is wrecked on the land of my Lordship, all the men will be freed and all the merchandise returned to their agent: they are similarly obligated to our men.

[9] If any Venetian man dies in the lands of my Lordship, without a will or heir, his goods are to be given to the Venetian *bailo*; if no *bailo* is found, they will be given into Venetian hands. Venice will write what to do.⁶

[10] Further, the most illustrious Signoria will have the right and authority specifically to send a *bailo* to Constantinople, with his household, according to custom, who will be able to dispense justice and administer Venetian affairs, according to their custom. The governor⁷ will be obligated to give him aid and cooperation.

[New provisions and conditions for peace.]

[11] If the said *bailo* wants to secure his position during this time, he is obligated to give my Lordship every year a gift of 10,000 Venetian florins⁸ from the commercial transactions.⁹

[12] Further, the most illustrious Signoria of Venice is obligated for every debt lying between us and for all debts whether common or private or of certain of their men, for all the past time before the war until today, to give to my Lordship 100,000 Venetian ducats within two years.¹⁰ Further, my Lordship cannot look for past debts, either from the most illustrious Signoria of Venice or from its men.¹¹

---

1 The numbers are not on the original document, but are found on the official Venetian Greek and Italian file copies.

2 Duke of Naxos: this refers to Jacopo III Crispo, who ruled the Cycladic islands 1463-1480. One of his brothers, Giovanni III, ruled 1480-1494.

3 Corsairs were pirates who were licensed by some official ruler, for example, a local Venetian or Ottoman governor. Klefts were bandits in Ottoman and Venetian territories in Greece.

4 One thousand aspers was then equal to about 22 ducats, a reasonable, if modest, price for a slave.

5 This matter of escaped slaves was a normal provision in treaties, frequently reiterated in correspondence.

6 As will be seen in Section 10, Venice was represented in Constantinople by a *bailo* who governed the large Venetian trading community and who acted as Venetian consul *vis à vis* the Turks.

7 The Ottoman governor of the city of Constantinople.

8 "Gift": the Greek means "little baskets," a Byzantine term for an obligatory gift from peasants to their landholder. The Ottomans used *florins* interchangeably with *ducats*.

9 Bayazid II, who succeeded his father Mehmed II in May 1481, reduced the annual 10,000 florins payment to 5,000.

10 It took two years to pay half the money. The 100,000 was money owed by two Venetian entrepreneurs for leases on Turkish alum mines.

11 The sultan here forgives the debts that were not specified in this agreement.

[13] Further, the most illustrious Signoria of Venice is obligated to hand over to my Lordship the fortress called Skodra[1] in Albania, except that it may remove the lord who is *rettor,* and the council, and all the other men[2] who wish to depart, specifically, with their merchandise, if they have any. The Signoria will take the equipment and all other military materiel or whatever is found in the fortress at present without any opposition.

[14] Further, the most illustrious Signoria of Venice is specifically obligated to transfer to my Lordship the island of Lemnos, except that they will take the *rettor* and the Venetian citizens. The other men who want to go will take whatever they have to go wherever they want. Those who want to remain on the island will be pardoned for what they did up to this point.[3]

[15] Further, the most illustrious Signoria of Venice will hand over to my Lordship the present fortresses and lands which were taken in the war from my Lordship, that is, the lands in the Morea,[4] except that the men in their authority may go wherever they want with whatever they have. If any want to remain in the present territories and fortresses they will have complete pardons, specifically, for every act, if they did anything up to now.

[16] Further, my Lordship is obligated to hand over to them the occupied lands, that is, to the former borders of their fortresses which abut the lands of my Lordship on all sides.[5]

The above-written provisions are confirmed and ratified and sworn.

The present writing was done in the year 6987, the 12th indiction, the 25th of the month of January, in Constantinople.[6]

---

1   The fortress of Skodra (Scutari, Skodar) had twice been under siege by Ottoman forces: the second had lasted since the previous May. Mehmed regarded the failure to take the fortress as a singular humiliation. It was handed over to him in March 1479 after the governor, Antonio de Leze, received a letter from Venice which began: "We don't doubt that you have already heard before this about the peace agreement."

2   "All the other men" was understood to include the soldiers, and all other (male) residents, their families, movable possessions, and trade goods. The *rettor* was the governor.

3   This is a blanket pardon for anyone who might have fought against Mehmed. Lemnos was captured by Mehmed in 1456, then taken, retaken, and ravaged by both sides for the next 20 years. Its strategic location at the approach to the Dardanelles made possession essential for the control of shipping.

4   The Morea was the usual name for southern Greece.

5   This became a major issue in settling Venetian-Ottoman boundaries in Greece and required a series of boundary commissions in which representatives and the oldest inhabitants from both sides worked out what should be the dividing line.

6   The Ottomans used Byzantine dating. The year 6987 was 5509 (from the Creation in September to the Incarnation) + 1478. As the Venetians counted their year from March 1, January was still 1478. While a number of Mehmed's letters and treaties use this dating, it is unclear whether this results from his secretaries following Byzantine precedents in dealing with the West, or whether it indicates his claim to rule the empire of the Romans. The peace agreement was not signed because in Ottoman tradition such documents, or ʿahd-names, were considered to be issued unilaterally by the sultan.

8.8 Before the fall: Patriarch Anthony, *Letter to the Russian Church* (1395). Original in Greek.

THIS IMPASSIONED LETTER TO Grand Prince Vasily I of Moscow from Patriarch Anthony IV (r.1389-1390 and again 1391-1397) evokes the imperial ideal that once held sway at Byzantium. At the end of the fourteenth century, the ruler of Moscow could boldly disparage the emperor, and the emperor, Manuel II Palaeologus (r.1391-1425), a weak vassal of the Ottoman sultan, could give no reply to their critiques. Byzantium had shrunk to include only a bit of Greece, a few islands, and the city of Constantinople, while the Turks were largely in control of vast regions that had once been Byzantine. Under these circumstances, the patriarch of Constantinople was the only man with enough standing to reply to Vasily.

[Source: Deno John Geanakoplos, *Byzantium: Church, Society, and Civilization Seen through Contemporary Eyes* (Chicago: University of Chicago Press, 1984), pp. 143-44.]

The holy emperor has a great place in the church, for he is not like other rulers or governors of other regions. This is so because from the beginning the emperors established and confirmed the [true] faith in all the inhabited world. They convoked the ecumenical councils and confirmed and decreed the acceptance of the pronouncements of the divine and holy canons regarding the correct doctrines and the government of Christians. They struggled boldly against heresies, and imperial decrees together with councils established the metropolitan sees of the archpriests and the divisions of their provinces and the delineation of their districts. For this reason the emperors enjoy great honor and position in the Church, for even if, by God's permission, the nations [primarily the Ottoman Turks] have constricted the authority and domain of the emperor, still to this day the emperor possesses the same charge from the church and the same rank and the same prayers [from the church]. The *basileus* [emperor] is anointed with the great myrrh and is appointed *basileus* and *autokrator* of the Romans, and indeed of all Christians. Everywhere the name of the emperor is commemorated by all patriarchs and metropolitans and bishops wherever men are called Christians, [a thing] which no other ruler or governor

ever received. Indeed he enjoys such great authority over all that even the Latins themselves, who are not in communion with our church, render him the same honor and submission which they did in the old days when they were united with us. So much more do Orthodox Christians owe such recognition to him....

Therefore, my son, you are wrong to affirm that we have the church without an emperor, for it is impossible for Christians to have a church and no empire. The *Basileia* [empire] and the church have a great unity and community—indeed they cannot be separated. Christians can repudiate only emperors who are heretics who attack the church, or who introduce doctrines irreconcilable with the teachings of the Apostles and the Fathers. But our very great and holy *autokrator*, by the grace of God, is most orthodox and faithful, a champion of the church, its defender and avenger, so that it is impossible for bishops not to mention his name in the liturgy. Of whom, then, do the Fathers, councils, and canons speak? Always and everywhere they speak loudly of the one rightful *basileus*, whose laws, decrees, and charters are in force throughout the world and who alone, only he, is mentioned in all places by Christians in the liturgy.

8.9 The fall bewailed: George Sphrantzes, *Chronicle* (before 1477). Original in Greek.

GEORGE SPHRANTZES (1401-1477), BORN INTO A noble and pious family, was brought up at the imperial court in Byzantium and personally knew the last three emperors. For much of his adult life, until the fall of the Byzantine Empire, he served Constantine XI (r.1449-1453) as diplomat, ambassador, and spy. His *Chronicle*, which uses the vernacular Greek of the time rather than the classicizing Greek of most Byzantine historians, is an unusually personal and often eyewitness account. With the fall of Constantinople, Sphrantzes was briefly enslaved, as was his wife, whom he ransomed. He continued to work for the remnants of the imperial house until, in 1456, he and his wife retired to monasteries.

[Source: *The Fall of the Byzantine Empire: A Chronicle by George Sphrantzes, 1401-1477*, trans. Marios Philippides (Amherst: The University of Massachusetts Press, 1980), pp. 21, 57-66, 69-72, 141-42 (notes modified).]

I am George Sphrantzes the pitiful First Lord of the Imperial Wardrobe, presently known by my monastic name Gregory. I wrote the following account of the events that occurred during my wretched life.

It would have been fine for me not to have been born or to have perished in childhood. Since this did not happen, let it be known that I was born on Tuesday, August 30, 6909 [1401]. The revered and holy Lady Thomais, as my godmother, sponsored my baptism....

28.7 On October 31, 6957 [1447], our emperor Lord John passed away. He was fifty-six years, ten months, and eleven days old. On November 1, he was buried in the Monastery of the Pantocrator. He had been emperor for twenty-three years, three months, and ten days.

29.1 On November 13 of the same year, Lord Thomas arrived by ship in the City [i.e., Constantinople]; he had heard of the emperor's death only as he was passing through Callipolis.[1]

2. His arrival put an end to the intrigues of his brother Lord Demetrius, or rather to those of his agents to declare him emperor. Demetrius was not a despot and had not been born in the purple; he had an older brother still alive, a man who excelled in all good activities and was free from misfortune. Proper claim and justice prevailed by command of the holy empress, her sons the despots, and by the opinion and will of the nobility.

3. On December 6, I set out with an embassy to inform the sultan that the empress, the brothers, right of birth, and the love and wisdom of nearly the whole population of the City chose Lord Constantine emperor. The sultan approved the choice and sent me away with honor and gifts.

4. In the same days lords from the City were sent to the Morea: Alexius Philanthropenus Lascaris, who had been dispatched to the City by my master together with Lord Thomas the despot, on the despot's business with the emperor, and Manuel Palaeologus Iagrus. Lord Constantine the despot was crowned emperor at Mistra on January 6 [1448].[2]

5. On March 12 of the same year [1448], he came to the City on board a Catalan vessel and was received with joy by all.

---

1   Later, Callipolis became Gallipoli. "Lord Thomas" was one of the brothers of "Lord John"—Emperor John VIII Palaeologus (r.1425-1448). So were Lord Demetrius and Lord Constantine, mentioned below. Constantine became emperor (with the approval of Sultan Mehmed II). Demetrius and Thomas vied for control over the Morea (southern Greece); both were despots there until 1460, when they had to surrender it to the Turks.

2   That the emperor of Constantinople was crowned at Mistra and not in the Church of Saint Sophia in Constantinople was thought by contemporary writers to be a serious break with tradition. Constantine is known to history as Constantine XI Palaeologus.

6. In August of the same year, the honored despot Lord Thomas, who was born in the purple, departed for the Morea.

7. On September 1, 6958 [1449], Lord Demetrius the despot also left for the Morea. Before their departure, a reconciliation took place in the presence of their lady mother, their brother the emperor, and ourselves, the chosen nobles: they took oaths which they violated, and were rewarded with misfortunes, as I saw later. How they were disposed toward each other is not essential to my narration, as I was absent from the City and do not have accurate knowledge.

30.1. On October 14 of the same year [1449], I was dispatched to the *mepes*—that is king—of Georgia, King George, and to the emperor of Trebizond, Lord John Comnenus, with remarkable gifts and a great, impressive retinue consisting of young nobles, soldiers, celibate priests, singers, physicians, and musicians with their instruments.[1] The Georgians knew the names of our instruments but had not seen them before and wished to inspect and hear them. For this reason many came from the furthest parts of Georgia to hear them.

2. My mission in those places was to arrange a marriage for my emperor [Constantine IX Palaeologus], whichever of the two families seemed suitable to me. He required me to submit my unbiased report on the advantages and disadvantages of each for his final decision. I sent messengers and letters by messengers, and my lord answered me by others. But his messengers' boat was wrecked in the Amisus area[2] and before my lord and emperor discovered what had passed and sent others, I spent two years minus thirty days in those parts.

3. While I was there, on March 23 of the same year [1450], our memorable holy empress, who had taken the veil under the name Patience and had become a nun, passed away and was buried next to her late husband, our memorable emperor, in the Monastery of the Pantocrator.

4. In February 6959 [1451], Sultan Murad died. I had not learned of his death while I was in Georgia,

but, when I reached Trebizond, the emperor Lord John Comnenus said to me: "Come, Mr. Ambassador, I have good news for you and you must congratulate me."

I rose, bowed, and responded: "May God grant Your Holy Majesty a long reign, as you have always been kind to us in many ways. Even now you are about to grace us, once more, with good news. I regret I have nothing worthy of Your Majesty to compensate for this favor."

He related the sultan's death and said that Murad's son [i.e., Mehmed II] was now in power, had bestowed many honors on him, and had even decided to continue the friendship which that house had enjoyed with his father.

5. Overcome by grief, as if I had been told of the death of those dearest to me, I stood speechless. Finally, with considerable loss of spirit, I said: "Lord, this news brings no joy; on the contrary, it is a cause for grief." "How so, my friend?" he asked. And I responded: "The late sultan was an old man, had given up the conquest of our City, and had no desire of attempting anything like it again; he only wished for friendship and peace. This man, who just became sultan, is young and an enemy of the Christians since childhood; he threatens with proud spirit that he will put in operation certain plans against the Christians.

6. "Our City has been in financial stress and is in great need of funds since the days of the illness of the emperor, your son-in-law; my lord, the newly crowned emperor, wants a period of peace in order to straighten out the City's affairs. If God should grant that the young sultan be overcome by his youth and evil nature and march against our City, I know not what will happen. Indeed God would have granted a joyous occasion if this man, Murad's son, had died instead. It would have been truly good news, since Murad had no other son, and he would have become weaker from grief and died soon after. In the meantime that house would have become stronger and, at his death, increased into great honor."

The emperor responded: "You are one of the more prudent and most honored advisors of his house. You

---

1　The empire of Trebizond was one of the Greek successor states that emerged in the aftermath of the Fourth Crusade, when, in 1204, crusader armies conquered Constantinople. For an account of this conquest, see above, p. 344.
2　The Amisus area is the southern coast of the Black Sea.

will know better about these matters. In any case, God has the power to bring about the best."

I said, "Indeed it is so, as you say." Our conversation was left at that.

31.1. After I heard this, and that the widow of the late sultan and daughter of the Serbian despot had returned to her parents with full honors, and as I was required to stay in Trebizond for many reasons, I sent by a boat leaving for the City some horses, two boys—whom the king of Georgia had taken as his booty in his expedition against Samahin and given to me as gifts—and some other things that had come into my possession as gifts or in other ways. I sat down and wrote a report to my lord the emperor concerning my mission in Georgia and my plans in Trebizond, as well as the reasons for my long stay.

2. Furthermore, I composed a second letter, the contents of which I will reveal presently, and gave one of the young nobles with me the letters. I sent him with the following instructions: "Present my first report to our lord the emperor when you pay your respects, and also give an oral, detailed version of our mission. Hand over my second letter on the following day."

3. The second letter ran as follows: "I was informed by the emperor of the sultan's death when I reached Trebizond. I also heard that the sultan's widow and cousin returned to her homeland and parents. So it seems to me better for many ends to propose marriage to her, should you agree to do it instead of my errand.

4. "I can discover only four arguments opposing this marriage: (1) Her family is inferior to yours; (2) the Church may object on the grounds of close kinship; (3) she has been married already; and (4) she is older and there is the factor that she may be in danger during childbirth, a common risk according to physicians.

5. "Against the first argument I suggest that it is not untoward, since she is not inferior to my lady, your memorable mother. Against the second, a marriage alliance with Trebizond will have to be pardoned by the Church if much money is donated to individual churches and to the poor. A pardon, on the other hand, will be more easily obtained if you marry in the Serbian House, in view of the fact that the Church, celibate priests, monks, nuns, and the poor are in the despot's debt and have respect for him.

6. "About the third argument I maintain that it is not against tradition; Lady Eudocia had been previously married to a Turkish chief of an insignificant and poor principality and had even given birth to his children before she married your grandfather. Your potential bride, by contrast, was the wife of a very powerful monarch, and she, it is generally believed, did not sleep with him. As for the fourth, it is up to God, and His will shall prevail.

7. "As the other advantages of this match have been demonstrated and her parents will gladly accept it, send one servant of your house, or a monk to test this proposal. Let there be no delay; do it."

8. When my messengers arrived in the City on May 28 [1451], the emperor was away, hunting wild boars. As soon as he was told of the return of the envoys from Georgia, he finished the hunt and came from the estate in high spirits. He rejoiced at the advice on the Serbian match, as my account will reveal later.

9. On the same night of May 28 I had a dream: it seemed to me that I was back in the City; as I made a motion to prostrate myself and kiss the emperor's feet, he stopped me, raised me, and kissed my eyes. Then I woke up and told those sleeping by me: "I just had this dream. Remember the date."[1]

10. When my lord and emperor realized that I had not returned, but that the envoys were members of my retinue, he read my first report, became sad, appeared depressed, and accused me of tardiness. On the following day he read my second report and regained his cheer, as if I had returned. Immediately, he dispatched to Serbia Manuel Palaeologus, the nephew of Lady Cantacouzena, our protostrator's wife, to test this proposal of marriage.[2] Her parents listened to it with delight and were ready to settle the final details.

11. Then it was discovered that the sultan's widow had made a vow to God and decided that if He freed her from the house of her late husband she would

---

1   The significance of this dream undoubtedly had something to do with the date of May 28, as it was early in the morning of May 29, 1453 that Constantinople fell to Mehmed and the emperor perished in the assault.

2   The protostrator was an important post at the imperial court.

not remarry for the rest of her life, but would remain in His service, as far as possible. Thus the proposed match failed.

12. In August of the same year [1451], our patriarch Lord Gregory [Mamas] fled the City and became an exile.[1]

32.1. On September 14, 6960 [1451], I arrived safely in the City on board the ship of Antonio Rizzo, the good man who later suffered martyrdom for his faith in Christ.[2] I had almost completed, or rather confirmed, a marriage with the House of Georgia, as I had come to the conclusion that a marriage with the House of Trebizond would be far less advantageous....

9. The document was prepared, signed, and sealed with gold. It specified that the daughter of the king would become the wife of the emperor and queen of Constantinople and that he would be her husband, according to the agreement reached by the king of Georgia and myself. We summoned the king's nobleman of the second rank, who had come with me in the City, and in his presence, my lord the emperor drew with his own hand three crosses in red ink on the upper part of the document, thus providing the confirmation demanded by Georgian tradition. He handed the document to the envoy and, pointing at me, he said: "With God's help, this man, in charge of three ships, shall arrive next spring in order to bring her to me." The envoy bowed and departed.

33.1. In the beginning of the same year [September 1451], rumors began circulating that the sultan intended to occupy the straits around the district Asomatos in order to build a castle.[3] The emperor decided to send an envoy to the Morea to escort one of his brothers to the City, if he accepted and remained faithful to the terms of the agreement, so that if the need arose to review their policy toward the sultan, one of the two might travel to the rulers of the West.

2. Once this had been decided, the emperor one day issued the following orders to me: "First Lord of the Imperial Wardrobe, as I have decided, I command you to travel to the Morea and, however you manage it, see whichever of my two brothers is willing to come here. Then you are to sail on to Cyprus and visit my niece, the queen. I will prepare the necessary provisions so that, when you return from Cyprus, you will proceed to Georgia and bring your future empress."

3. I responded: "My affection and loyal service demand a response to your command. I fear that my wife, your servant and mother of your godchildren, will be angry and leave me either to become a nun or to remarry. Only the other day I came back from Georgia and my twenty-three-month mission. If I am to depart again now, she will have good reason to pursue either course."

The emperor laughed and said: "Tell her to agree that you undertake just these missions. I will make her an oath that I shall burden you no more in this way.

4. "Indeed, you know better what we have in mind and have both agreed together and plan to do. This is certain and needs no sworn statement: the embassies under you will be discontinued." By this agreement he meant that we should send word to Loucas Notaras, our grand duke, that he could not hold the position of chief intermediary.

The emperor went on: "Because of his status, it is impossible to take the position from him; he must give it up himself. Let him have the first place of honor in the court and the senates as well as some income from a different source. I must appoint two nobles, as my brother, the emperor, had done; not as intermediaries, but as officials who will be with me from early in the day until late in the night, while I perform my duties." All this came to pass.

5. Word was sent to our grand duke by Neophytus, the spiritual brother and celibate priest, the godfather of his children and mine, who resided at the Kharsianites Monastery. Notaras obeyed, whether willingly

---

1 Gregory supported the provisions of the Council of Florence (1439), which declared the union of the Greek and Latin churches, recognized papal primacy, declared a form of the Creed congruent with the Catholic position, and recognized the existence of Purgatory. The whole package was extremely unpopular at Constantinople.

2 Although Sphrantzes does not refer to Rizzo again, we know his fate. After the construction of the Turkish fortress Rumeli Hisari, all vessels sailing south were ordered to stop and allow inspection of their cargo. Antonio Rizzo ignored these instructions and his vessel was sunk on November 26, 1452. Rizzo and his crew were captured and killed.

3 Mehmed built the fortress of Rumeli Hisari on the European side of the Bosporus (the Asomatos district).

or unwillingly, I cannot tell. At any rate, he made it known that it had been his wish also to do so in the hope that his sons would be honored. So it was decided but did not come to pass, as our common misfortune overwhelmed all of us.

6. The emperor commanded that I fill one of the positions, and he was considering Nicolaus Goudeles for the other.[1] He added that if we were to find each other's company agreeable, a match could be arranged between my son and Goudeles' daughter. This appointment would bring the end of my missions as ambassador.

7. Then the emperor said: "I really wished to dispatch to the Morea some older official. But I want to issue instructions written by my own hand, which will include five options: it will list the first possible compromise; then a second, third, fourth, or, if necessary, a fifth. But I believe that if anyone is sent other than you, they will promise to him a village with a silver-sealed confirmation, or a hereditary estate, and he will immediately consent to grant to them the fifth alternative, which would be difficult for us.

8. "Concerning Cyprus, do you know the monk I met a few days ago? He brought me a message from my niece that she is in need of something; she would have told me in her own voice what she wanted; had it been possible, she would have sent her message through a loyal, trusted courtier, but she has none. As she does not have one and cannot make the trip, I must send a man whom I consider appropriate to hear her message.

9. "Who is more qualified? To reach a conclusion, there is no need for argument: it is you, since you have acted and made decisions for me, know me personally, and have been informed. How could anyone else complete this mission?"

I gave my answer to the emperor: "Admittedly it is as you say. My wife, your servant, agrees, since the circumstances demand it and because she will enjoy, as you promised me, a position, honors, and fame above the other noblewomen. As for the rest, I really have no advice for you." As it was time for lunch, I went home....

35.1. On March 26 of the same year 6960 [1452], the sultan occupied the straits with the intention of constructing his castle. I kept postponing my mission from day to day, because a land route was now out of the question and would be dangerous; I had to locate a suitable ship.

2. In June of the same year the war was finally brought to our area; the Turkish army charged, captured all inhabitants found outside the walls, and blockaded the City. When the erection of the castle had been completed, the sultan left on August 31 and attacked the fortifications of the City.

3. On September 3, 6961 [1452], he departed for Adrianople; for two days he had been apparently securing his castle and its position.

4. In autumn of the same year Turahan, with his sons and a huge army, invaded the Morea.[2] At that time the inhabitants of the Morea captured one of his sons.

5. On January 17 of the same year [1453], Lord Andreas Palaeologus was born, the successor and heir of the Palaeologan Dynasty.

6. On April 4 of the same year [1453], the sultan returned and laid siege to the City with all sorts of engines and stratagems by land and sea. He surrounded the entire 18 miles of the City with 400 small and large vessels from the sea and with 200,000 men on the land side. In spite of the great size of our City, our defenders amounted to 4,773 Greeks, as well as just about 200 foreigners.

7. I was in a position to know the exact figure of our strength for the following reason: the emperor ordered the tribunes to take a census of their communities and to record the exact number of men—laity and clergy—able to defend the walls, and what weapons each man had for defense. All tribunes completed this task and brought the lists of their communities to the emperor.

8. The emperor said to me: "This task is for you and no one else, as you are skilled in arithmetic and also know how to guard and keep secrets. Take these lists and compute, in the privacy of your home, the exact figure of available defenders, weapons, shields, spears, and arrows." I completed my task and presented the

---

1 Goudeles was a powerful noble in Constantinople.
2 Turahan was a Turkish general.

master list to my lord and emperor in the greatest possible sadness and depression. The true figure remained a secret known only to the emperor and to myself.

9. On Tuesday May 29 [1453], early in the day, the sultan took possession of our City; in this time of capture my late master and emperor, Lord Constantine, was killed. I was not at his side at that hour but had been inspecting another part of the City, according to his orders. Alas for me; I did not know what times Providence had in store for me!

10. My late emperor, the martyr, lived for forty-nine years, three months, and twenty days. His reign lasted four years, four months, and twenty-four days. He had been the eighth emperor of the Palaeologan Dynasty. The first was Michael, the second Andronicus, the third Michael, the fourth Andronicus, the fifth John, the sixth Manuel, the seventh John, and the eighth was Constantine. The Palaeologan Dynasty ruled over the City for 194 years, ten months, and four days.

11. I was taken prisoner and suffered the evils of wretched slavery. Finally I was ransomed on September 1, 6962 [1453], and departed for Mistra. My wife and children had passed into the possession of some elderly Turks, who did not treat them badly. Then they were sold to the sultan's Mir Ahor (i.e., Master of the Horse), who amassed a great fortune by selling many other beautiful noble ladies.

12. My children's beauty and proper upbringing could not be concealed; thus, the sultan found out and bought my children from his Master of the Horse for many thousand aspers. Thus their wretched mother was left all alone in the company of a single nurse; the rest of her attendants had been dispersed.

36.1. Perhaps one would like to know the emperor's preparations before the siege, while the sultan was gathering his forces, and the aid that we received from the Christians abroad.

2. No aid whatsoever was dispatched by other Christians. On the contrary, an official of the sultan was sent to the Serbian despot Lord George in order to ask him to be the intermediary for the treaty with the Hungarians. Even though a Christian scribe in the retinue of the envoy had been instructed by certain members of the Turkish Council to inform the despot that the sultan intended to march against Constantinople once the treaty was signed and to delay the conclusion of this treaty, the despot paid no attention to him; the wretch of a despot did not consider the fact that once the head has been removed the limbs perish also.

3. An important meeting of the senate was held in Venice. The doge Francesco Foscari was opposed to dispatching aid not because he was inept (indeed, our emperor Lord John and others who had met him and talked to him maintained that they had not seen a wiser man in Italy), but because of spite and malice; for spite generally overlooks advantage. The reason for his attitude was the following: Foscari had sent Alvise Diedo as his intermediary to Lord Constantine—who was then the despot of the Morea—to propose marriage between his daughter and Lord Constantine, promising a handsome dowry. Lord Constantine agreed to this betrothal, not so much because of the dowry, but because his territories would be joined to those of Venice. I advised him to agree more forcefully than others, and he took my advice.

4. Once Constantine had become emperor and come to the City, this marriage was out of the question. What nobleman or noblewoman would ever receive the daughter of a Venetian—even though he might be the glorious doge—as queen and lady for more than a short time? Who would accept his other sons-in-law as the emperor's fellow sons-in-law, and his sons as the brothers-in-law of the emperor? The doge insisted on the marriage and, after our final rejection, this man became our enemy. Thus during this meeting of the senate, even though the noblemen Alvise Loredano and Antonio Diedo argued and demonstrated that Venetian interests would be hurt if the City fell, they were unable to prevail.

5. In Rome what measures were taken by the Church to prevent our downfall? The cardinal of Russia happened to be in the City and I argued, as his intermediary to my late lord, the emperor, that he should be appointed patriarch in the hope that various advantages would come from him and the then pope, or, at least, that the name of the pope should be commemorated in our services.[1]

---

1 Isidore, formerly the metropolitan of Kiev and later the cardinal of all Russias, arrived in Constantinople on October 26,

6. After many consultations and deliberations, my late master and emperor decided to abandon the first alternative altogether, since the appointed patriarch requires the obedience of all; otherwise riots and war ensue between him and those who are opposed to his appointment; especially at this time, when we were facing extreme war, what a misfortune to have a war inside the City as well! The emperor consented to have the pope's name commemorated in our services, by necessity, as we hoped to receive some aid. Whoever were willing would pronounce the commemoration in Saint Sophia; the rest would incur no blame and remain peaceful. These services took place on November 12.[1] Six months later we had received as much aid from Rome as had been sent to us by the sultan of Cairo.[2]

7. Although it was possible for the despot of Serbia to send money secretly from many places and, similarly, men, did anyone see a single penny? On the contrary, they provided huge financial aid and many men to the sultan who was besieging the City. Thus the Turks were able to boast in triumph that even Serbia was against us.[3]

8. Which of the Christians, the Trebizondian emperor, the lords of Walachia, or the Georgia king, contributed a single penny or a single soldier to our defense, openly or secretly?

8.10 After the fall: Archbishop Genady of Novgorod and Dmitry Gerasimov, *The Tale of the White Cowl* (end of the 15th c.). Original in Russian.

A COWL IS A HOOD. Drawing on the story in the *Donation of Constantine* (see above, p. 172) and predictions about the coming of the Kingdom of the Holy Spirit, Archbishop Genady of Novgorod and his co-writer, Dmitry Gerasimov, wrote of the fate of the White Cowl, symbol of Christ's Resurrection. First it was given by Emperor Constantine to the pope. Then, as the papacy fell into heresy (from the point of view of the Greek Church), it was given to Philotheus, the patriarch of Constantinople. He, in turn, gave it to Vasily, archbishop of Novgorod, where it was to remain, crown of the "Third Rome." The idea was one of transmission, from "old" Rome (the Rome of Italy) to the "second" Rome (Constantinople) to the "final" Rome (Novgorod). Written thirty or forty years after the fall of Constantinople in 1453, the "prediction" of the triumph of Islam in the story was a foregone conclusion. But the pre-eminence of Novgorod in the story was only a pipe dream: already in 1478 Ivan III (r.1462-1505), ruler of Muscovy, had conquered the Republic of Novgorod and made Moscow the center of the Russian Church.

[Source: *Medieval Russia's Epics, Chronicles, and Tales*, ed. and trans. Serge A. Zenkovsky (New York: E.P. Dutton, 1963), pp. 268-74 (notes slightly modified).]

1452 to enforce the decisions made at the Council of Florence. He was accompanied by a force of 200 archers. He remained in Constantinople during the siege, was taken captive during the sack, but managed to conceal his identity and escape to the West.

1 On December 12, 1452, the union of the two Churches was solemnly celebrated in the Church of Saint Sophia. The Greek monks and most of the Greek inhabitants of Constantinople were opposed to the union. Consequently, on the eve of the fall, Constantinople was a divided city. Two political parties were formed: the unionists, headed by the Palaeologi and other Greeks, and the antiunionists, headed by the grand duke Loucas Notaras, and by George Courtetsis Scholarius, who became the first patriarch under Mehmed's rule. It is no exaggeration to say that the situation in Constantinople was chaotic before—as during—the siege.

2 In fact, Isidore's 200 archers were paid by the pope, and preparations in the West were under way to aid Constantinople. Venetian ships had been equipped by means of financial aid from the pope and had reached Chios when news of the fall reached them; consequently, they returned to Venice.

3 The Serbian ruler was the vassal of the sultan.

At that time the Patriarch of Constantinople was Philotheus,[1] who was distinguished by his strict fasting and his virtuous ways. Once, he had a vision in the night of a youth from whom emanated light and who told him:

"Blessed teacher, in the olden times the Roman Emperor, Constantine, who, through the vision of the Holy Apostles Peter and Paul, was enlightened by God, decided to give Blessed Pope Sylvester the White Cowl to glorify the Holy Apostolic Church. Later, the unfaithful popes of the Latin heresies wanted to profane and destroy this cowl, but I appeared to the evil pope, and now this pope has sent this cowl to you. When the messengers arrive with it, you must accept it with all honors. Then send the White Cowl to the Russian land, to the city of Novgorod the Great with your written blessing. And there this cowl will be worn on the head of Vasily, Archbishop of Novgorod,[2] so that he may glorify the Holy Apostolic Cathedral of Holy Sophia and laud the Orthodox. There, in that land, the faith of Christ is truly glorified. And the popes, because of their shamelessness, will receive the vengeance of God." And having spoken these words, the youth became invisible.

The patriarch awoke filled with awe and joy and was unable to sleep throughout the remainder of the night. And he contemplated this vision. In the morning he ordered that the bells should sound the Matins, and when day came he summoned the Church council and revealed his vision. And all praised God, perceiving that a holy angel had appeared to the patriarch. Yet they did not fully understand the meaning of the message. When they were still in council and were filled with awe due to their great joy, there arrived a servant of the patriarch, and he announced to them that messengers had arrived from the Pope of Rome. The patriarch ordered that they be brought before him. The messengers came, bowed low to the patriarch, and gave him the message. The patriarch read the message and pondered it, praising God. He announced its contents to Emperor John who was reigning at that time and whose name was Cantacuzenus.[3] And then he went with the entire council to meet the bringers of the divine treasure which lay in an ark. He accepted it with all honors, broke the seal, and took from the ark the Holy White Cowl. He kissed it with reverence, and looked upon it with wonderment both for its creation and for the wonderful fragrance that emanated from it.

At that time the patriarch had diseased eyes and constant headaches, but when he placed the White Cowl upon his head, these afflictions immediately ceased to be. And he rejoiced with great joy and rendered glory to Christ, our Lord, to Constantine's blessed memory for his creating this wonderful cowl for Blessed Pope Sylvester. And he put the Holy Cowl on the golden salver [tray] that was also sent by the pope. He placed them in the great church in an honorable place until he could make a decision with the emperor's counseling.

After the White Cowl was sent from Rome, the evil pope, who was counseled by heretics, became angered against the Christian faith and was driven to a frenzy, extremely regretting his allowing the White Cowl to be sent to Constantinople. And he wrote an evil letter to the patriarch, in which he demanded the return of the White Cowl on the golden salver. The patriarch read this letter and, understanding the pope's evil and cunning design, sent him a letter in return that was based on Holy Scripture, and in it he called the pope both evil and godless, the apostate and precursor of the Antichrist. And the patriarch cursed the pope in the name of our Lord, Jesus Christ, the Holy Apostles, and the Church Fathers. And this letter came to the pope.

When the pope had read the letter and learned that the patriarch intended to send the White Cowl with great honor to the Russian land, to the city of Novgorod the Great, he uttered a roar. And his face changed and he fell ill, for he, the infidel, disliked the Russian land and could not even bear to hear of this land where the Christian faith was professed.

Patriarch Philotheus, having seen that the White Cowl was illumined with grace, began to ponder how he might keep it in Constantinople and wear it on his own head. He consulted with the emperor about

---

1 Philotheus was patriarch of Constantinople from 1353 to 1355, and from 1364 to 1376.
2 Vasily was archbishop of Novgorod from 1330 to 1342.
3 John VI Cantacuzenus was Emperor of Byzantium, 1347 to 1354.

the matter several times, and wanted to write to the other patriarchs and metropolitans to summon them to a council. After Matins one Sunday, the patriarch returned to his chambers and, after the usual prayers, lay down to rest. But he slept but lightly, and in this sleep he saw that two men, who were unknown to him, came through the door. And from them there emanated light. One of them was armed as a warrior and had an imperial crown upon his head. The other wore a bishop's vestments and was distinguished by his venerable white hair.

The latter spoke to the patriarch, saying: "Patriarch! Stop pondering your wearing of the White Cowl on your own head. If this were to be, our Lord, Jesus Christ, would have so predestined it from the founding of this city. And for a long time did divine enlightenment come from heaven, and then God's voice came to me and I learned that Rome had to betray God and embrace their Latin heresies. That is the reason I did not wish to wear this cowl upon my head, and thus I instructed other popes not to do so. And this imperial city of Constantinople will be taken by the sons of Hagar[1] because of its sins, and all holy shrines will be defiled and destroyed. Thus has it been predestined since the founding of this city.

"The ancient city of Rome will break away from the glory and faith of Christ because of its pride and ambition. In the new Rome, which will be the City of Constantinople, the Christian faith will also perish through the violence of the sons of Hagar. In the third Rome, which will be the land of Russia, the Grace of the Holy Spirit will be revealed. Know then, Philotheus, that all Christians will finally unite into one Russian nation because of its orthodoxy. Since ancient times and by the will of Constantine, Emperor of the Earth, the imperial crown of the imperial city is predestined to be given to the Russian tsar. But the White Cowl, by the will of the King of Heaven, Jesus Christ, will be given to the archbishop of Novgorod the Great. And this White Cowl is more honorable than the crown of the tsar, for it is an imperial crown of the archangelic spiritual order. Thus, you must send this Holy White Cowl to the Russian land, to the city of Novgorod the Great, as you were told to do in the vision of the angel. You should believe and trust in what I say: And when you send it to the Russian land, the Orthodox Faith will be glorified and the cowl will be safe from seizure by the infidel sons of Hagar and from the intended profanation by the Latin pope. And the grace, glory, and honor which were taken from Rome, as well as the Grace of the Holy Spirit, will be removed from the imperial city of Constantinople after its capture by the sons of Hagar. And all holy relics will be given to the Russian land in the predestined moment. And the Russian tsar will be elevated by God above other nations, and under his sway will be many heathen kings. And the power of the patriarch of this imperial ruling city will pass to the Russian land in the predestined hour. And that land will be called Radiant Russia, which, by the Grace of God, will be glorified with blessings. And its majesty will be strengthened by its orthodoxy, and it will become more honorable than the two Romes which preceded it."

And saying this, the man of the vision who was dressed in a bishop's vestment wished to leave, but the patriarch, seized by great awe, fell before the bishop and said: "Who are you, my lord? Your vision has seized me with great awe; my heart has been frightened by your words, and I tremble to my very bones."

The man in the bishop's vestments answered: "Don't you know who I am? I am Pope Sylvester, and I came to you because I was ordered by God to reveal to you the great mystery which will come to pass in the predestined time." Then, pointing to the other man in the vision, he added: "This is blessed Emperor Constantine of Rome to whom I gave rebirth in the holy font and whom I won over to the faith of our Lord, Jesus Christ. He was the first Christian emperor, my child in Christ, who created and gave me the White Cowl in place of the imperial crown." And saying this, he blessed the patriarch, and became invisible.

Waking up, the patriarch was seized with awe, remembering the words about the White Cowl and the conquest of Constantinople by the pagan sons of Hagar. And he wept for a long time. When the hour

---

1 Both the Byzantines and the Russians called all nomads, whether they were Turks, Mongols, or Arabs, the sons of Hagar. "Hagar" refers to the handmaid of the biblical patriarch Abraham. Here it refers to the Ottomans.

of the divine Mass arrived, the patriarch went to the church, fell before the icon of the Holy Mother of God, and remained lying there for some time. Then he arose, took the White Cowl with great reverence, kissed it piously, placed it upon his head, and then put it to his eyes and his heart. And his adoration for this cowl increased even more. And doing this, he wept. His clerics, who were around him and saw that he wept inconsolably, did not dare to inquire as to why he was weeping. Finally the patriarch ceased crying and told his clerics in detail of the vision of Pope Sylvester and Emperor Constantine. Having heard these words, the clerics wept sorrowfully, and exclaimed, "Thy will be done!"

The patriarch, mourning the forthcoming misfortunes of the city of Constantinople and fearing to trespass the divine will, told them that he must fulfill the will of the Lord and do with the White Cowl as he was commanded to do. After having deliberated with blessed Emperor John, he took the White Cowl and the golden salver, put them in the aforementioned ark, sealed it with his seal, and, as he was commanded by the holy angel and Blessed Pope Sylvester, put in his epistle with his blessings, and in it he commanded Archbishop Vasily and all other bishops who would follow Vasily to wear the White Cowl upon their heads. He added many other honorable and marvelous gifts from his clergy for the bishopric of Novgorod the Great. And he also sent vestments with their embroidered crosses for the glorification of the Holy Apostolic Church. And all this was placed in another ark. And he gave these arks to a bishop named Eumeny, and sent him forth with both joy and sorrow.

In the bishopric of the city of Novgorod the Great was Archbishop Vasily who distinguished himself by his fasting and virtuous ways. Once, in the night, he prayed to God and then lay down to rest, but he slept but lightly, and had a dream in which he saw the angel of God. This angel of God, who had a handsome appearance and radiant face, appeared before him in the garb of a monk and with the White Cowl upon his head. With his finger he pointed to his head and in a low voice announced: "Vasily! This White Cowl which you see on my head is from Rome. In olden times the Christian Emperor Constantine created it in honor of Sylvester, Pope of Rome. He gave it to this pope to wear upon his head. But God Almighty did

not permit the White Cowl to remain there because of their Latin heresies. Tomorrow morning you must go from the city with your clergymen and meet the bishop and messengers sent by the patriarch. And they will bring an ark, and in this ark you will find the White Cowl upon a golden salver. Accept it with all honors, for this White Cowl symbolizes the radiant Resurrection which came to pass on the third day. And from now on, you and all other archbishops of this city will wear it on your heads. And I have come to you to assure you before hand that all is as God wills it and to assuage any doubts you may have." And saying this, the angel became invisible.

Waking up, Archbishop Vasily was seized with awe and joy, pondering the meaning of the vision. The next morning he sent his clerics outside the city, to the crossroads, to see whether the messengers really would appear. In the vicinity of the city the servant of Archbishop Vasily met a Greek bishop who was unknown to him and who traveled to the city of Novgorod. They made a low obeisance [bow] and returned to the archbishop and told them all they had seen. The bishop then sent his messenger into the city to summon the clerics and the entire population. And he ordered the tolling of the bells, and both he and his clerics donned their vestments.

The procession had not gone far from the Cathedral of Holy Sophia when they met the aforementioned bishop, sent by the patriarch and bearing the ark that had been sealed by the patriarch, and which contained the venerable gifts, came to Archbishop Vasily, made a low obeisance before him, and gave him the epistles of the patriarch. They blessed and greeted each other in Christ's name. Archbishop Vasily accepted the epistles of the patriarch and the arks bearing the venerable gifts. And he went with them to the Cathedral of Holy Sophia, the Wisdom of God. There he put them in the middle of the church in an honorable place and ordered that the patriarchal epistles be read aloud. When the Orthodox people, who were in the cathedral, heard these writings read aloud, they rendered glory to God and rejoiced with great joy. Archbishop Vasily opened one of the arks and removed the cover. And a wonderful fragrance and miraculous radiance spread through the church. Archbishop Vasily and all present were in wonderment, witnessing these happenings. And Bishop Eumeny, who was sent by the patriarch, wondered about these blessed deeds of God that he had witnessed. And they all rendered glory to God, and celebrated the service of thanksgiving.

Archbishop Vasily took the White Cowl from the ark and saw that it appeared exactly like the one he had seen on the angel's head in his vision. And he kissed it with reverence. At that same moment there came a sonorous voice from the icon of the Lord, which was in the cupola of the church, saying, "Holy, holy." And after a moment of silence there came the same voice, which thrice announced, "Ispola eti despota."[1] And when the archbishop and all those present heard these voices, they were seized with awe and joy. And they said, "The Lord have mercy upon us!" And the archbishop then ordered that all present in the church be silent, and he revealed to them his vision of the angel and his words concerning the White Cowl. And he told of his vision as it had happened and in detail, even as it was told to him by the angel in the night.

Giving thanks to God for sending this cowl, the archbishop went forth from the church, preceded by the deacons in holy vestments carrying tapers and singing hymns. And they proceeded with serenity and piety. And the people crowded round, jostling each other and jumping so that they might see the White Cowl on the archbishop's head. And all were in wonderment. Thus, in this way, thanks to the Grace of our Lord, Jesus Christ, and to the blessing of his Holiness Philotheus, Patriarch of Constantinople, the White Cowl became a symbol upon the heads of the archbishops of Novgorod. And Archbishop Vasily was overcome with great joy, and for seven days he feasted all priests, deacons, and clerics of the city of Novgorod the Great. And he also offered food and drink to the poor, to monks, and to prisoners. And he asked that the prisoners be released. During the divine service he placed the holy and venerable gifts of the patriarch in the Cathedral of Holy Sophia and with the blessings of all clerics. And the golden salver, on which the White Cowl was placed, was also deposited in the Cathedral of Holy Sophia during the Mass.

The messengers of the patriarch who brought the Holy White Cowl were also shown great honor and they received many gifts. The archbishop sent gifts to the Emperor and Patriarch of Constantinople and sent the messengers forth with great honors. Thereafter, multitudes arrived from many cities and kingdoms to look upon, as if it were a miracle, the archbishop in the White Cowl. And they were in wonderment about it, and told of it in many lands. This Holy White Cowl was created by the first pious Christian Emperor, Constantine, for Blessed Pope Sylvester in the year 297 (5895). And this is the history of the Holy White Cowl up to this day.

---

1 *Ispola eti despota* is Greek for "Many years to the lord," or, more loosely translated, "Long live the bishop." The Russians used this expression during the Church service, and it was always pronounced in Greek.

8.11 Chivalric and non-chivalric models: Froissart, *Chronicles* (*c.*1400).
Original in French.

BORN IN VALENCIENNES, JUST OUTSIDE the kingdom of France, Jean Froissart (*c.*1337-*c.*1404)
served the rulers of Hainaut, especially Philippa of Hainaut, wife of the English king Edward III
(r.1327-1377). His most famous work was the *Chronicles*, a wide-ranging account of the first half
of The Hundred Years' War. Late in life, he began to revise this work thoroughly, although he
finished only a small section. Nevertheless, the result, parts of which are presented below, reflected his mature thinking on topics which Froissart had long written about: the glory of great feats
of arms and the nature and purposes of chivalric warfare. What forms of violence did Froissart
think knights were right to engage in? Were there limits to the violence that Froissart justified
and celebrated? In what ways were Osman's ambitions and sense of chivalry in Ashikpashazade's
Osman Comes to Power (above, p. 492) similar to and different from those of the Western knights
who populate the pages of Froissart?

[Source: Froissart, *Chroniques. Début du premier livre. Edition du manuscrit de Rome Reg. lat. 869*,
ed. George T. Diller (Geneva: Droz, 1972), pp. 303-07, 313-15, 633-39. Translated by Helen
Nicholson.]

CHAPTER 78: WALTER DE MANNY BEGINS THE
WAR [1339]

As soon as Lord Walter de Manny discovered and
realized that a formal declaration of war had been
made against the king of France and that the bishop
of Lincoln was on his way back [from delivering the
king of England's declaration of war to the king of
France], he gathered together 40 lances,[1] good companions from Hainaut and England, and left Brabant
and rode by night and day until he arrived in Hainaut.
He and his people rode undercover and no one knew
about them, except for themselves and a guide who
led them where they wanted to go. Then they hid in
the wood of Blaton. The noble knight had vowed in
England in the hearing of ladies and lords that, "If
war breaks out between my lord the king of England
and Philip of Valois who calls himself king of France,
I will be the first to arm himself and capture a castle
or town in the kingdom of France." And he did not
fail in this vow, for he came by night and hid in the

wood of Wiers [in modern Belgium], very close to
Mortagne [now in northern France]. When he had
arrived there, he told his companions what he wanted
to do and they agreed to his enterprise.

The town of Mortagne on the river Escaut—although it is very well protected—was in great danger
of being captured that day, for Lord Walter de Manny
and his band arrived at daybreak so close to the town
that they hid in ambush in the hedges and bushes
next to Mortagne. They had procured dresses and
women's clothes, which they had acquired in a village
on their road, and great flat baskets, in which women
who are going to market put butter, eggs and cheeses.
Four of their men dressed in the women's clothes
and wrapped lovely white head-wraps of white cloth
around their heads and they took the baskets, covered
with white cloths, and made out that they were coming to market to sell their butter and cheese. They
came to the gate at the hour of sunrise, and found it
closed and the wicket gate half open, and a man who
guarded it. He truly believed that these were women

---

1   The best guess of the meaning of "one lance" is that it was made up of two men, one the combatant and the other his ser-
     vant, and two horses.

from a village close by who were coming to market, and he opened the wicket gate wide open so that they could enter with their baskets. When these men in women's clothing were inside, they seized hold of the porter and drew long knives which they were carrying under their gowns and said to him, "If you say one word, you're dead." The man was absolutely terrified and feared death, so he remained silent and still in their midst.

Here comes Lord Walter de Manny and his companions, who were following them at a distance; and they had left their horses in the hedges and bushes, quite close to Mortagne, under the guard of their servants. When they saw that their companions had control of the gate, they hurried as fast as they could and entered in by the wicket gate at their ease. Then they went towards the tower and the castle keep, and expected to find it badly guarded; but they did not, for it was shut up. Then they stopped short, for they saw clearly that they had failed in their intentions and that it was worth nothing for them to hold the town without the castle. So they retraced their steps the way that they had come, and did not do any other damage to the town of Mortagne except that they set fire to two or three houses; and then they went out and mounted their horses and left without doing anything more. Many people from the town of Mortagne were still in their beds, and knew nothing about this adventure.

In order to accomplish his enterprise, Lord Walter de Manny and his companions rode and returned into Hainaut, and crossed the Escaut by a little bridge just below Condé. And that day they dined at the abbey of Vicoigne, and refreshed their horses there, and remained there until night. The country was not yet in a state of alarm. At sunset they mounted their horses and rode off, and passed through the Walers wood, and entered [the region of] Ostrevan. They had guides to lead them; and they came between Douai and Cambrai, passing the river of Sensee, which joins the Escaut at Bouchain. They rode until, at the hour of sunrise, they came to a castle, which is called Thun l'Evêque, sited on the river Escaut. They arrived at the very moment that the garrison of the castle were sending out the cattle to graze in the meadows that are close by, and the castellan[1] was still in his bed. So

they entered in through the gate, for they found it standing open, and made themselves lords and masters of the gate, and kicked out all the men and women whom they found inside. The said Lord Walter de Manny kept the castle for himself, and put it in order and gave it to a brother of his, a knight, who is known as Lord Giles de Manny. For the rest of that year, the latter gave the people of Cambrai plenty of trouble. When the said Lord Walter de Manny had completed these enterprises, he returned to his lord the king of England, whom he found at Maligne. The king of England had arrived there and was holding a council there....

CHAPTER 79: THE SACK OF SOUTHAMPTON [SEPT. 1338/9]

Just as, when the king of England and the king of France issued their challenges to each other, the English began to plot how they could harm and bring damage, so too all that season the French, the king of France, and his council thought about nothing except how to make their preparations by sea and land. Through the preparations that they saw and heard about they realized clearly enough that they would have war. They had established on the sea a number of Norman ships and a great crowd of Genoese and of mariners who are called "sea-going plunderers" [buccaneers]. Their leaders and commanders were Lord Charles Grimaldi, admiral of France, lord Hugh Quieret, [Nicholas] Behuchet and [Pietro] Barbavera; and they stationed themselves on the coast at Dieppe and Harfleur. As soon as the news of the king of England's challenge arrived at Paris, they were informed. Then these so-called plunderers left French waters and rode across the sea, and came, with the wind and the tide, to the harbor of Southampton [England], one Sunday when everybody was at mass. The town was taken so much by surprise that they had no opportunity to think about guarding their town and their harbor. All in all there were a good twenty thousand of these so-called plunderers, and for that day they were lords of Southampton. Those men, women and children who could escape fled to save themselves, and the raiders killed and captured many of them, and they carried

---

1 The man in command of the castle's garrison.

off all the wool and cloth that they could find in the town. When the tide came back in, they got into their ships, but first they set fire to the town in more than 60 places, and then they left the harbor and embarked on the sea; and they went back towards Normandy, taking with them many prisoners, whom they later ransomed.

The news spread throughout England of how the Normans had been at Southampton and how they had captured it and robbed and pillaged everything. Then the English certainly felt that the war between France and England had really begun....

CHAPTER 81: THE SIEGE OF CAMBRAI [1339]

You know, as my history stated above, that the city of Cambrai [today in northern France] had gone into the presence of King Philip [VI of France] to complain that they had heard that the king of England, as representative of Louis of Bavaria, king of Germany and emperor of Rome, was coming in strength to lay siege to their town. They had begged the king, as people who wanted to support him in everything, to send them men-at-arms, because they felt that they did not have sufficient forces. The king gave his consent to this plea and sent to garrison the city of Cambrai Lord Amé de Geneva, the Savoyard named "the Gaul of la Baume,"[1] Lord John [Guy] de Groullée, the lord of Vinai, Lord Louis de Chalon, Lord Tiebaut de Moruel, the lord [John] of Roye, the lord [John] of Fosseux, the lord of Biausaut, and a good 100 lances of good men-at-arms, knights and squires. He had all the castles of the Cambrai region equipped and resupplied with good men-at-arms so that no misfortune could take them by surprise. The lord [Enguerrand] of Coucy had sent around 40 lances of good comrades to Oisy in the Cambrai region, with [Robert] the lord of Clari at their head. The country was all prepared on the frontiers of Artois, Cambrai, and the Vermandois. As well as all this, King Philip issued a great summons throughout the whole of his kingdom and outside it, requesting his friends and commanding his subjects to come and fight the king of England, outside Cambrai or elsewhere. His intention was never to return to Paris until he had fought him; until then he would remain at Compiègne and send out his command.

When the king of England had lodged at Haspres for two days and many of his people had already crossed the sea and come to Naves, to Cagnoneles and the area around, he set out and approached Cambrai, halting at Iwuy in the Cambrai region. All the German lords crossed over in good order and came to set up siege before Cambrai. The second day after came the young count William of Hainaut and his uncle Lord John de Hainaut with a fine, large company of Hainauters. There were more than 500 lances, knights and squires, and they set up camp outside Cambrai. Six days later Duke John of Brabant arrived, with a good 900 helmets[2] in his company. Thus the English, German, Hainaut, and Teutonic men-at-arms surrounded the city of Cambrai.

Very soon after the duke of Brabant had joined the army outside Cambrai, the king of England begged and requested him to send a challenge to the king of France. The duke replied, saying that he would do so at once; but the king of France did not wish to do anything until such time as he saw that they were going to march on the kingdom of France. So the matter rested; but certainly the king of England intended never to withdraw until he had set fire to and burned the kingdom of France.

Those of the army had built a bridge across the River Escaut so that they could cross over to each other. Every day the English and the Germans raided across the Cambrai region as far as Bapaumes. The whole country had been warned before Cambrai went under siege, and most of the people had carried their possessions into the fortresses and driven their animals before them a long way into Artois or the Vermandois, because whatever was found on the flat countryside was lost. So while the city of Cambrai was under siege there were several assaults and skirmishes, but the fine body of knights who were within the city took such great care of it that they took and received neither blame nor damage. Lord John de Hainaut, the lord of Valkenburg and some knights from Gueldre and Juliers left the siege one day and rode so far that they reached Oisy in the Cambrai region. Some of

---

1 Master of the French king's crossbowmen.
2 A "helmet" in this context seems to mean a single armed warrior.

them dismounted at the barrier and there was a great skirmish, for the knights and the squires who were within the town on behalf of the lord of Coucy bore themselves valiantly and did not take any damage; and the Germans returned to the army without having achieved anything....

CHAPTER 186: NEGOTIATIONS BETWEEN JACQUES D'ARTEVELD AND EDWARD III [1340-1345]

At this time and at the same season Lord Godfrey de Harcourt, one of the greatest barons of Normandy, brother of the count of Harcourt and lord of Saint-Sauveur-le-Vicomte and of several towns in Normandy, incurred the great displeasure and hatred of the king of France. I am unable to explain the cause of this hatred to you, but it was so great that if the king of France could have laid hold of him in his anger he would have made him die a shameful death. The said Lord Godfrey had to hide, flee and leave the kingdom of France. He went to England to King Edward, offered him his service and placed himself under his command just as Lord Robert d'Artois had done formerly, and no one could ever make his peace with the king of France. The king of England received him and retained him at his side, and gave him sufficient means to maintain his position.

At this time that bourgeois of Ghent still reigned in the country of Flanders in great prosperity and power, Jacques d'Arteveld, who was a close ally of the king of England—so far as he could be, because he was always doubtful about the loyalty of the Flemings, whom he felt were unreliable. And he was right to be doubtful, as he came to such a miserable end, as I shall tell you. Above all he wished to disinherit the count of Flanders, Count Louis the Exile and his son Louis de Male; and he wished the king of England to inherit Flanders. This man Jacques d'Arteveld used to say that Flanders would become a duchy and the prince of Wales would be duke.

On this account at this time, he had the king of England, his close comrade, come to Sluys; but when the king arrived, he did not disembark from his ship. The good towns of Flanders—that is to say the consuls—came to see him and make him welcome at Sluys and laid the whole country open to him and his people, at his command, and begged him to agree to

come to Bruges and to Ghent, and said that everywhere he would be welcomed. The king, thanking them, replied very gently and said that at that moment he had not come to disembark on shore. That man Jacques d'Arteveld was present at all these discussions.

Soon afterwards, a conference was held on the king's ship, which was very large and beautiful, and was named the *Christofle*. All the consuls of the good towns of Flanders were present. Jacques d'Arteveld promised what was said above and demonstrated with various arguments, gilded with fine words, that it would be beneficial to accept the prince of Wales as their lord, and Flanders should be made into a duchy and the said duke and prince should stay in the country and govern the land and country of Flanders in all good customs, and maintain justice and reason for all people; and Jacques d'Arteveld begged the [consuls of the] good towns who were there to reply and give their opinion on this. At that they all exchanged glances and did not know what to say. In any case, they asked for permission to talk together, which was given to them. They all reached the same decision, and this was their reply: "Jacques, we have heard clearly what you said; and when we came here, we did not know that you were going to talk to us on this matter, and it came as news to us. And we cannot act on this by ourselves alone; it is necessary that all the land of Flanders agree; and when [representatives of the whole of the land are] assembled, it will be necessary to pick out and identify the rebels who do not wish to agree to this, and that they be publicly banished and lose what they now hold in the land of Flanders, without any hope of seeing it again or returning to it. In this way this inheritance can be secured, for, so far as we are concerned, we would very much like the prince of Wales as our lord, as has been proposed, saving and reserving the conditions aforesaid."

This reply greatly satisfied the king and his council, but the good towns of Flanders who had replied were asked when the king could expect their reply. They agreed on a month and a day; this was given to them. And they dined with the king in his own ship, and then departed and went back each to his place, some of them feeling abused and angered at this news they had heard, although they had replied to please the king and d'Arteveld. And it seemed to them a hard and strange thing to disinherit their lord, and if they did so they would be reputed to be infamous traitors for ever and ever. Nevertheless, d'Arteveld was so feared and dreaded in the land of Flanders that in fact none would have dared anger him or speak against his wishes. Jacques d'Arteveld remained with the king on his ships in Sluys after the rest had gone.

CHAPTER 187: JACQUES D'ARTEVELD IS ASSASSINATED AT GHENT [1345]

As the news spread that Jacques d'Arteveld was aiming for the prince of Wales to be lord of Flanders and to make it a duchy, great murmuring arose throughout the county of Flanders. Some, who supported the king of England, said, "This would be a good thing." Others said the opposite, that it would be shameful, blameworthy and great treason to disinherit their lord. The good people were very distressed at this, more for the sake of the son, Count Louis de Male, than they were for the father, because he had been cruel, violent, harsh and terrible to them, for which reason they had driven him out of Flanders. But they kept Louis, the young son, and said that they would bring him up in their own way, and he would be more familiar with Flemish customs than his father had been.

At that time Duke John of Brabant had a young daughter to marry off, and as a wise, skilful and astute man he had in mind that a marriage between his daughter and the son of the count of Flanders would be very advantageous. The count of Flanders was in sufficient agreement, but he was not lord or master of his son, because the Flemings held and guarded him and were bringing him up under good guards and did not allow him to leave the town of Ghent. The duke of Brabant carefully considered what was going to happen, and how Jacques d'Arteveld was at that time so powerful in Flanders that everything was done by him and without him nothing was done; and he was informed of the news that the king of England was at Sluys and lay there at anchor, and that he and Jacques d'Arteveld on his behalf were procuring that the king's son, the prince of Wales, should be duke of Flanders. The said duke of Brabant feared that all these things would come about, for they could too easily happen, and he decided that he would put a monkey-wrench in the works.

As for what happened in the town of Ghent: while the king of England was still in his ship before Sluys, and waited for the reply from those of the land of Flanders, a very great dispute arose in the town of Ghent between the weavers of cloth and Jacques d'Arteveld, and all at the instigation and through the advancement of their dean,[1] whose name was Thomas Denis. The duke of Brabant is said to have been the cause of these events. One day more than 400 of these weavers, on the instructions of their dean, assembled in front of d'Arteveld's lodging, and surrounded it from the front and rear, and showed that they wanted to enter by force. When the servants of this d'Arteveld saw them coming like this they wondered what they wanted, for this was not the custom of those of Ghent, nor had other people come in this way to speak to their master nor wishing to force their way into the house. So they began to speak roughly to them and tried to drive them out by force, but they could not; they were beaten and insulted and wounded first.

Jacques d'Arteveld was shut up in his bedchamber, and had heard much of the words and the fighting. So he went to a window that overlooked a road where all these people were assembled and asked them, "Good people, what do you want? Why are you so upset?" They replied, "We want to talk to you. Come out." Then Jacques replied: "And if I come out there, what do you want to say?" "We want you to give us an account of the great riches that you have taken from Flanders as you liked over the last seven years, and tell us what you have done with the money and where you have put it." Then Jacques d'Arteveld saw clearly that the situation was becoming ugly. This was an unprecedented state of affairs, and its outcome was unpredictable. Hoping to appease the crowd with gentle words, he said: "Good people, all of you go back to your own lodgings, and within three days I will summon you and I will be able to render you such a good account of the money that you will be quite content." They replied with one voice: "We don't want to wait so long, but come out of your lodging and give us account."

Jacques d'Arteveld then realized that things were looking bad, and that his life was in danger. So he said: "My lords, my lords, stay there, I will come at once and speak to you." At these words they all stood

---

1 The president of the guild of weavers at Ghent.

quietly, and he came out of his room and went to his stable and his horses, intending to mount and leave by the back gate and go on his way, but he could not. For the lodging was so surrounded on all sides that immediately what he intended to do was detected and noticed; and those who were guarding the door warned those who were at the front gate. Then a great tumult arose among them and they broke the doors by force and burst in, and came into the stable and found Jacques d'Arteveld who was getting ready to mount and go on his way. Immediately they attacked him and that man Thomas Denis, the dean of the weav-ers, gave him the first blow on the head with an axe, knocking him down. Jacques d'Arteveld had done him many good turns and had given him the posi-tion of dean of the weavers, and he was his comrade. Nevertheless all these things and affinities were for-gotten and put to one side. There Jacques d'Arteveld, who held such high rank, honour and prosperity in Flanders, was miserably slain. No man or judge who would take or levy compensation for this deed was ever to be found in Ghent. Thus go the fortunes of this world; wise persons cannot nor ever should place too much trust in worldly prosperity.

8.12 National feeling: Jeanne d'Arc, *Letter to the English* (1429). Original in French.

JEANNE D'ARC (*c*.1412-1431), BORN TO A PEASANT FAMILY in Lorraine, a region loyal to the French king during the Hundred Years' War, i.e., heir to the king of Franceheard voices telling her to defeat the English. She went to the court of Charles, the dauphin, i.e., heir to the King of France, to persuade him of her mission against the English on his behalf. Dictated in March 1429, this *Letter to the English* was written while Jeanne was undergoing "tests" ordered by Charles, to determine her orthodoxy and chastity. Female examiners attested to her virginity (this is why she called herself "the Maid"); while Jean Gerson (see below, p. 526), among other theologians, decided that her mission echoed those of biblical and classical heroines. In May 1429 the French army, accompanied by Jeanne riding with her own banner, defeated the English at Orléans. It was a psychological turning point of the Hundred Years' War. In July of the same year, Jeanne led Charles to Reims, where he was anointed king. But by the next year her fortunes had waned and, captured and sold to the English, she was tried in 1431 for witchcraft, heresy, and apostasy and, condemned for all, was burned at the stake. Her *Letter to the English*, copied by notaries working for the English side, was one of many letters she sent to recipients throughout Europe. It shows her radical identification of the divine plan with a particular king and kingdom. Comparing her ideas to those in crusading documents—especially Stephen of Blois's *Letter to His Wife, Adele* (above, p. 293), *The Conquest of Lisbon* (above, p. 300), and Helmold's *Chronicle* (above p. 342)—how might you argue that Jeanne's nationalistic vision was inspired by crusading ideals?

[Source: *Joan's Letter to the English*, trans. Nadia Margolis, in *Medieval Hagiography: An Anthology*, ed. Thomas Head (New York: Garland, 2000), pp. 821-22 (slightly modified).]

Jesus Mary,[1]
King of England and you, duke of Bedford,[2] who call yourself regent of the kingdom of France; you, Wil-liam Pole, earl of Suffolk; John, Lord Talbot; and you, Thomas, lord of Scales—who call yourselves lieuten-ants of the said duke of Bedford: set things aright with

---

1   Jeanne used this popular invocation on her standard and several of her letters. The words were also inscribed upon the ring she always wore, a gift from her mother. St. Catherine of Siena (*c*.1340–1387) began her letters with a similar phrase. (See below, p. 525).

2   When King Henry V died in 1422, his son—who immediately became King Henry VI (d.1471)—was only nine months old. Thus Duke John of Bedford (1389–1435) became regent. By the Treaty of Troyes (1420), and because he was also the principal architect of the Anglo-Burgundian alliance, Bedford ruled France as well as England. Controlling northern France including Paris and Rouen, he was thus Jeanne's most powerful adversary, both on the battlefield and at the Rouen trial.

the king of Heaven and render unto the Maid,[1] who has been sent here by God, the king of Heaven, the keys to all the good cities that you have pillaged and ravaged in France. The Maid has come on behalf of God to reclaim the blood royal. She is ready to make peace, if you are willing to settle with her by evacuating France and making restitution for whatever you have stolen. And all of you—archers, companions in arms, gentlemen, and others who are before the city of Orléans—go away, return to your country, by order of God. And if you do not do this, await news of the Maid, who will shortly pay you a visit, much to your disfavor, to inflict great damage upon you. King of England, if you do not do this, I am chief of the army[2] and am waiting to confront your men wherever they are in France; and I will make them leave, whether they wish to or not. And should they not obey, I will have them all killed. For I have been sent here by God, king of Heaven, to chase you completely out of France, body for body,[3] if necessary. Should they wish to obey me, then I shall take mercy upon them. May you have no other thought than this, since you do not

hold the kingdom of France by order of God, king of Heaven, son of Mary—but rather it is Charles who shall hold it as true heir. For God, king of Heaven, so wishes it, as revealed by the Maid unto Charles, who shall soon enter Paris in good company. If you do not believe this news sent on behalf of God via the Maid, then we shall strike you down, with such fury as has never been seen in France for a thousand years, wherever we might find you, if you do not comply with us. You may be sure that the king of Heaven will send more might to the Maid than you shall ever be able to muster against her and her good men, no matter how many times you attack; at the end of which we shall see on whose side God truly sits in Heaven. You, duke of Bedford, the Maid pleads and requests of you not to destroy yourself thus. If you comply with her, you may join her there where the French will achieve the greatest exploit ever for Christianity. Give us your answer whether you wish to make peace in the city of Orléans; and if you do not, much devastation will come to remind you.

8.13 The commons revolt: *Wat Tyler's Rebellion* (after 1381). Original in Anglo-French.

A PRESSING NEED FOR MORE REVENUE to fight the Hundred Years' War led the English Parliament to impose new poll taxes that hit the "commons" (*not* the House of Commons but rather peasants in the countryside and most people in the cities) very hard. Uncoordinated revolts in the countryside led eventually to coordinated ones, and two armies, one led by Wat Tyler, converged on London. Their chief demand was the end of serfdom. In the *Anonimal Chronicle of St. Mary's, York* an anonymous author who spelled Tyler "Teghler" or "Tighler" told the story in considerable detail, excerpted here. Although the rebels considered themselves loyal to the fourteen-year-old King Richard II (r.1377-1399), he and his counselors fled to the Tower of London. Later, when he met with the rebels at Mile End, Richard gave in to their demands, but the next day at Smithfield, the Mayor of London killed Tyler, and the insurrection largely fell apart. What does this account reveal about class prejudice and class mobility in fourteenth-century England?

[Source: Charles Oman, *The Great Revolt of 1381* (New York: Greenwood Press, 1969), pp. 186-93, 196-99, 201-03, 205 (language slightly updated; notes added).]

---

1   In her testimony on February 22, Jeanne said that she had originally said "Render to the king" here. Pro-English notaries may have changed her words to make her seem more vainglorious.
2   In her testimony on February 22, Jeanne affirmed that she never called herself "chief of the army." Her original words may have been changed to make her look more delusional.
3   In her testimony on February 22, Jeanne stated that she had never said this originally; it may have been added by detractors to make her seem more bloodthirsty.

Because in the year 1380 the subsidies [taxes] were over lightly granted at the Parliament of Northampton and because it seemed to various Lords and to the commons that the said subsidies were not honestly levied, but commonly exacted from the poor and not from the rich, to the great profit and advantage of the tax-collectors and to the deception of the King and the commons, the Council of the King ordained certain commissions to make inquiry in every township how the tax had been levied. Among these commissions, one for Essex was sent to one Thomas Bampton,[1] seneschal of a certain lord, who was regarded in that country as a king or great magnate for the state that he kept. And before Whitsuntide[2] he held a court at Brentwood in Essex to make inquisition, and [he] showed the commission that had been sent him to raise the money which was in default and to inquire how the collectors had levied the aforesaid subsidy. He had summoned before him the townships of a neighboring hundred and wished to have from them new contributions, commanding the people of those townships to make diligent inquiry, and give their answers, and pay their due. Among these townships was Fobbing, whose people made answer that they would not pay a penny more because they already had a receipt from himself for the said subsidy. On which the said Thomas threatened them angrily, and he had with him two sergeants-at-arms of our lord the king. And for fear of his malice the folks of Fobbing took counsel with the folks of Corringham, and the folks of these two places made levies and assemblies and sent messages to the men of Stanford to bid them rise with them for their common profit. Then the people of these three townships came together to the number of a hundred or more, and with one assent went to the said Thomas Bampton, and roundly gave him answer that they would have no traffic with him nor give him a penny. On which the said Thomas commanded his sergeants-at-arms to arrest these folks, and put them in prison. But the commons made insurrection against him, and would not be arrested, and went about to kill the said Thomas and the said sergeants. On this

Thomas fled towards London to the King's Council; but the commons took to the woods, for fear that they had of his malice, and they hid there some time, till they were almost famished, and afterwards they went from place to place to stir up other people to rise against the lords and great folk of the country. And because of these occurrences Sir Robert Belknap, Chief Justice of the King's Bench, was sent into the county with a commission of Trailbaston,[3] and indictments against various persons were laid before him, and the folks of the countryside were in such fear that they were proposing to abandon their homes. Wherefore the commons rose against him, and came before him, and told him that he was a traitor to the King, and that it was of pure malice that he would put them in default by means of false inquests made before him. And they took him and made him swear on the Bible that never again would he hold such a session, nor act as a justice in such inquests. And they made him give them a list of the names of all the jurors, and they took all the jurors they could catch, and cut off their heads, and cast their houses to the ground. So the said Sir Robert took his way home without delay. And afterwards the said commons assembled together, before Whitsunday, to the number of some 50,000, and they went to the manors and townships of those who would not rise with them, and cast their houses to the ground or set fire to them. At this time they caught three clerks of Thomas Bampton, and cut off their heads, and carried the heads about with them for several days stuck on poles as an example to others. For it was their purpose to slay all lawyers, and all jurors, and all the servants of the King whom they could find. Meanwhile the great lords of that country and other people of substance fled towards London, or to other counties where they might be safe. Then the commons sent various letters to Kent and Suffolk and Norfolk that they should rise with them, and when they were assembled they went about in many bands doing great mischief in all the countryside....

And they made chief over them Wat Teghler of Maidstone, to maintain them and be their councillor.

---

1 Thomas Bampton was a tax collector, one of many who had not obtained the full amount expected and now returned to the townships for more money.
2 That is, before the week of Pentecost, which is the seventh Sunday after Easter.
3 This was a commission, begun under Edward I (d.1307), for justices to consider both criminal and quasi-criminal cases.

And on the Monday next after Trinity Sunday[1] they came to Canterbury, before the hour of noon; and 4,000 of them entering into the Minster[2] at the time of High Mass, there made a reverence and cried with one voice to the monks to prepare to choose a monk for Archbishop of Canterbury, "for he who is Archbishop now is a traitor, and shall be decapitated for his iniquity." And so he was within five days after! And when they had done this, they went into the town to their fellows, and with one assent they summoned the Mayor, the bailiffs, and the commons of the said town, and examined them whether they would with good will swear to be faithful and loyal to King Richard and to the true commons of England or no. Then the mayor answered that they would do so willingly, and they made their oath to that effect. Then they [the rebels] asked them if they had any traitors among them, and the townsfolk said that there were three, and named their names. These three the commons dragged out of their houses and cut off their heads. And afterwards they took 500 men of the town with them to London, but left the rest to guard the town.

At this time the commons had as their councillor a chaplain of evil disposition named Sir John Ball, which Sir John advised them to get rid of all the lords, and of the archbishop and bishops, and abbots, and priors, and most of the monks and canons, saying that there should be no bishop in England save one archbishop only, and that he himself would be that prelate, and they would have no monks or canons in religious houses save two, and that their possessions should be distributed among the laity. For which sayings he was esteemed among the commons as a prophet, and labored with them day by day to strengthen them in their malice—and a fit reward he got, when he was hung, drawn, and quartered, and beheaded as a traitor. After this the said commons went to many places, and raised all the folk, some willingly and some unwillingly, till they were gathered together full 60,000. And in going towards London they met various men of law, and twelve knights of that country, and made

them swear to support them, or otherwise they should have been beheaded. They wrought much damage in Kent, and notably to Thomas Haselden, a servant of the Duke of Lancaster, because of the hate that they bore to the said duke. They cast his manors to the ground and all his houses, and sold his beasts—his horses, his good cows, his sheep, and his pigs—and all his store of corn, at a cheap price. And they desired every day to have his head, and the head of Sir Thomas Orgrave, Clerk of Receipt and sub-Treasurer of England.

When the King heard of their doings, he sent his messengers to them, on Tuesday after Trinity Sunday, asking why they were behaving in this fashion and for what cause they were making insurrection in his land. And they sent back by his messengers the answer that they had risen to deliver him and to destroy traitors to him and his kingdom. The King sent again to them bidding them cease their doings, in reverence for him, till he could speak with them, and he would make, according to their will, reasonable amendment of all that was ill-done in the realm. And the commons, out of good feeling to him, sent back word by his messengers that they wished to see him and speak with him at Blackheath. And the King sent again the third time to say that he would come willingly the next day, at the hour of Prime,[3] to hear their purpose. At this time the King was at Windsor, but he removed with all the haste he could to London, and the Mayor and the good folks of London came to meet him, and conducted him in safety to the Tower of London. There all the Council assembled and all the lords of the land round about, that is to say, the Archbishop of Canterbury, Chancellor of England; the Bishop of London; and the Master of the Hospital of St. John's, Clerkenwell, who was then Treasurer of England; and the Earls of Buckingham[4] and Kent, Arundel, Warwick, Suffolk, Oxford, and Salisbury, and others to the number of 600.

And on the vigil of Corpus Christi Day,[5] the commons of Kent came to Blackheath, three leagues from

---

1   Trinity Sunday is the first Sunday after Pentecost.
2   A minster is a monastery church.
3   The first hour of the day, around 6 a.m.
4   An error. Buckingham was in Wales.
5   The feast of Corpus Christi is celebrated on the first Thursday after Trinity Sunday, and the vigil is the day before: Wednesday.

London, to the number of 50,000, to wait for the King, and they displayed two banners of St. George and forty pennons.[1] And the commons of Essex came on the other side of the water to the number of 60,000 to aid them and to have their answer from the King. And on the Wednesday, the King being in the Tower of London, thinking to settle the business, had his barge got ready and took with him in his barge the Archbishop, and the Treasurer, and certain others of his Council, and four other barges for his train, and got him to Greenwich, which is three leagues from London. But there the Chancellor and the Treasurer said to the King that it would be too great folly to trust himself among the commons, for they were men without reason and had not the sense to behave properly. But the commons of Kent, since the King would not come to them because he was dissuaded by his Chancellor and Treasurer, sent him a petition requiring that he should grant them the head of the Duke of Lancaster and the heads of fifteen other lords, of whom three were bishops, who were present with him in the Tower of London. And these were their names: Sir Simon Sudbury, Archbishop of Canterbury, Chancellor of England; Sir Robert Hales, Prior of the Hospital of St. John's, Treasurer of England; the Bishop of London; Sir John Fordham, Bishop-elect of Durham and Clerk of the Privy Seal; Sir Robert Belknap, Chief Justice of the King's Bench; Sir Ralph Ferrers; Sir Robert Plessington, Chief Baron of the Exchequer; John Legge, Sergeant-at-arms of the King; and Thomas Bampton aforesaid. This the King would not grant them, wherefore they sent to him again a yeoman,[2] praying that he would come and speak with them: and he said that he would gladly do so, but the said Chancellor and Treasurer gave him contrary counsel, bidding him tell them that if they would come to Windsor on the next Monday they should there have a suitable answer.

And the said commons had among themselves a watchword in English, "With whome haldes you?"; and the answer was, "With kinge Richarde and the true comons"; and those who could not or would not so answer were beheaded and put to death.

And at this time there came a knight with all the haste that he could, crying to the King to wait; and the King, startled at this, awaited his approach to hear what he would say. And the said knight came to the King telling him that he had heard from his servant, who had been in the hands of the rebels on that day, that if he came to them all the land should be lost, for they would never let him loose, but would take him with them all round England, and that they would make him grant them all their demands, and that their purpose was to slay all the lords and ladies of great renown, and all the archbishops, bishops, abbots and priors, monks and canons, parsons and vicars, by the advice and counsel of the aforesaid Sir John Ball.

Therefore the King returned towards London as fast as he could and came to the Tower at the hour of Tierce.[3] And at this time the yeoman who has been mentioned above hastened to Blackheath, crying to his fellows that the King was departed and that it would be good for them to go on to London and carry out their purpose that same Wednesday. And before the hour of Vespers,[4] the commons of Kent came, to the number of 60,000, to Southwark, where was the Marshalsea.[5] And they broke and threw down all the houses in the Marshalsea and took out of prison all the prisoners who were imprisoned for debt or for felony. And they leveled to the ground a fine house belonging to John Imworth, then Marshal of the Marshalsea of the King's Bench and warden of the prisoners of the said place, and all the dwellings of the jurors and questmongers[6] belonging to the Marshalsea during that night. But at the same time, the commons of Essex came to Lambeth near London, a manor of the Archbishop of Canterbury, and entered into the buildings and destroyed many of the goods of the said Archbishop, and burnt all the books of register, and rules of remembrances belonging to the Chancellor, which they found there....

At this time the King was in a turret of the great

---

1 A pennon is a banner or streamer carried on a lance.
2 That is, one of their number; yeomen belonged to the class of farmers who owned their own plots of land.
3 The third hour of the day, around 9 a.m.
4 Vespers is at sunset.
5 The Marshalsea was a prison.
6 Questmongers were informers who then received a share of any fines they generated.

Tower of London, and could see the manor of the Savoy and the Hospital of Clerkenwell, and the house of Simon Hosteler near Newgate, and John Butterwick's place, all on fire at once. And he called all his lords about him to his chamber, and asked counsel what they should do in such necessity. And none of them could or would give him any counsel, wherefore the young King said that he would send to the Mayor of the City to bid him order the sheriffs and aldermen to have it cried round their wards that every man between the age of fifteen and sixty, on pain of life and members, should go next morning (which was Friday) to Mile End, and meet him there at seven o'clock. He did this in order that all the commons who were encamped around the Tower might be induced to abandon the siege and come to Mile End to see him and hear him, so that those who were in the Tower could get off safely whither they would and save themselves. But it came to nothing, for some of them did not get the good fortune to be preserved. And on that Thursday, the said feast of Corpus Christi, the King, being in the Tower very sad and sorry, mounted up into a little turret towards St. Catherine's, where were lying a great number of the commons, and had proclamation made to them that they all should go peaceably to their homes, and he would pardon them all manner of their trespasses. But all cried with one voice that they would not go before they had captured the traitors who lay in the Tower, nor until they had got charters to free them from all manner of serfdom, and had got certain other points which they wished to demand. And the King benevolently granted all and made a clerk write a bill in their presence in these terms: "Richard, King of England and France, gives great thanks to his good commons, for that they have so great a desire to see and to keep their king, and grants them pardon for all manner of trespasses and misprisions and felonies done up to this hour, and wills and commands that every one should now return to his own home, and wills and commands that each should put his grievances in writing and have them sent to him; and he will provide, with the aid of his loyal lords and his good council, such remedy as

shall be profitable both to him and to them, and to all the kingdom." On this document he sealed his signet in presence of them all, and sent out the said bill by the hands of two of his knights to the folks before St. Catherine's. And he caused it to be read to them, and the knight who read it stood up on an old chair before the others so that all could hear. All this time the King was in the Tower in great distress of mind. And when the commons had heard the Bill, they said that this was nothing but trifles and mockery. Therefore they returned to London and had it cried around the City that all lawyers, and all the clerks of the Chancery and the Exchequer and every man who could write a brief or a letter should be beheaded, whenever they could be found. At this time they burnt several more houses in the City, and the King himself ascended to a high garret of the Tower and watched the fires. Then he came down again and sent for the lords to have their counsel, but they did not know how they should counsel him, and all were very discouraged.

And next day, Friday, the commons of the countryside and the commons of London assembled in fearful strength, to the number of 100,000 or more, besides some four score who remained on Tower Hill to watch those who were in the Tower. And some went to Mile End, on the Brentwood Road, to wait for the coming of the King, because of the proclamation that he had made. But some came to Tower Hill, and when the King knew that they were there, he sent them orders by messenger to join their friends at Mile End, saying that he would come to them very soon. And at this hour of the morning he advised the Archbishop of Canterbury, and the others who were in the Tower, to go down to the Little Water-gate, and take a boat and save themselves. And the Archbishop did so, but a wicked woman raised a cry against him, and he had to turn back to the Tower, to his confusion.

And by seven o'clock the King came to Mile End, and with him his mother in a whirlecote,[1] and also the Earls of Buckingham,[2] Kent, Warwick, and Oxford, and Sir Thomas Percy, and Sir Robert Knolles, and the Mayor of London, and many knights and squires; and Sir Aubrey de Vere carried the sword of state.

---

1   A whirlecote was a wheeled carriage. But it is probably not true that the king's mother accompanied him, since all other accounts of the incident say that she remained in the Tower.
2   Again an error: Buckingham was still in Wales.

And when he was come the commons all knelt down to him, saying: "Welcome our Lord King Richard, if it pleases you, and we will not have any other king but you." And Wat Tighler, their leader and chief, asked in the name of the commons that he would allow them to take and deal with all the traitors against him and the law, and the King granted that they should have at their disposition all who were traitors, and could be proved to be traitors by process of law. The said Walter and the commons were carrying two banners and many pennons and pennoncels[1] while they made their petition to the King. And they required that for the future no man should be in serfdom, nor make any manner of homage or suit to any lord, but should give a rent of 4d.[2] an acre for his land. They asked also that no one should serve any man except by his own good will, and on terms of regular agreement.

And at this time the King made the commons draw themselves out in two lines, and proclaimed to them that he would confirm and grant it that they should be free, and generally should have their will, and that they might go through all the realm of England and catch all traitors and bring them to him in safety, and then he would deal with them as the law demanded.

Under color of this grant Wat Tighler and [some of] the commons took their way to the Tower to seize the Archbishop, while the rest remained at Mile End. During this time the Archbishop sang his mass devoutly in the Tower, and shrived[3] the Prior of the Hospitallers and others, and then he heard two masses or three, and chanted the *Commendacione*, and the *Placebo*, and the *Dirige*, and the Seven Psalms, and a Litany, and when he was at the words "Omnes sancti orate pro nobis," the commons burst in, and dragged him out of the chapel of the Tower, and struck and hustled him rudely, as they did also the others who were with him, and dragged them to Tower Hill. There they cut off the heads of Master Simon Sudbury, Archbishop of Canterbury, and of Sir Robert Hales, Prior of the Hospital of St. John's, Treasurer of England, and of Sir William Appleton, a great lawyer and surgeon, and later chief physician to the king, and the Duke of Lancaster. And some time later they beheaded John Legge, the King's Sergeant-at-arms, and with him a certain juror. And at the same time the commons made proclamation that whoever could catch any Fleming or other alien of any nation, might cut off his head, and so they did after this. Then they took the heads of the Archbishop and of the others and put them on wooden poles and carried them before them in procession as far as the shrine of Westminster Abbey, in despite of them and of God and Holy Church; and vengeance descended on them no long time after....

Then the King caused a proclamation to be made that all the commons of the country who were still in London should come to Smithfield, to meet him there; and so they did.

And when the King and his train had arrived there they turned into the Eastern meadow in front of St. Bartholomew's, which is a house of canons: and the commons arrayed themselves on the west side in great battalions. At this moment the Mayor of London, William Walworth, came up, and the King bade him go to the commons and make their chieftain come to him. And when he was summoned by the Mayor, by the name of Wat Tighler of Maidstone, he came to the King with great confidence, mounted on a little horse, that the commons might see him.... Presently Wat Tighler, in the presence of the King, sent for a flagon of water to rinse his mouth because of the great heat that he was in, and when it was brought he rinsed his mouth in a very rude and disgusting fashion before the King's face. And then he made them bring him a jug of beer and drank a great draught, and then, in the presence of the King, climbed on his horse again. At this time a certain valet from Kent, who was among the King's retinue, asked that the said Walter, the chief of the commons, might be pointed out to him. And when he saw him, he said aloud that he knew him for the greatest thief and robber in all Kent. Watt heard these words and bade him come out to him, wagging his head at him in sign of malice; but the valet refused to approach, for fear that he had of the mob. But at last the lords made him go out to him, to see what he [Wat] would do before the King. And

---

1 A pennoncel is a small pennon.
2 I.e., four pennies.
3 "To shrive" is to hear confession and give absolution to a penitent.

when Watt saw him he ordered one of his followers, who was riding behind him carrying his banner displayed, to dismount and behead the said valet. But the valet answered that he had done nothing worthy of death, for what he had said was true, and he would not deny it, but he could not lawfully make debate in the presence of his liege lord, without leave, except in his own defense: but that he could do without reproof; for if he was struck he would strike back again. And for these words Watt tried to strike him with his dagger and would have slain him in the King's presence; but because he strove so to do, the Mayor of London, William Walworth, reasoned with the said Watt for his violent behavior and spite, done in the King's presence, and arrested him. And because he arrested him, the said Watt stabbed the Mayor with his dagger in the stomach in great wrath. But, as it pleased God, the Mayor was wearing armor and took no harm, but like a hardy and vigorous man drew his cutlass and struck back at the said Watt and gave him a deep cut on the neck and then a great cut on the head. And during this scuffle one of the King's household drew his sword and ran Watt two or three times through the body, mortally wounding him. And he spurred his horse, crying to the commons to avenge him, and the horse carried him some four score paces, and then he fell to the ground half dead. And when the commons saw him fall, and knew not how for certain it was, they began to bend their bows and to shoot, wherefore the King himself spurred his horse, and rode out to them, commanding them that they should all come to him to Clerkenwell Fields....

[Tyler was beheaded by the Mayor.]

And when the commons saw that their chieftain, Watt Tyler, was dead in such a manner, they fell to the ground there among the wheat, like beaten men, imploring the King for mercy for their misdeeds. And the King benevolently granted them mercy, and most of them took to flight. But the King ordained two knights to conduct the rest of them, namely the Kentishmen, through London and over London Bridge without doing them harm, so that each of them could go to his own home. Then the King ordered the Mayor to put a helmet on his head because of what was to happen, and the Mayor asked for what reason he was to do so, and the King told him that he was much obliged to him, and that for this he was to receive the order of knighthood. And the Mayor answered that he was not worthy or able to have or to spend a knight's estate, for he was but a merchant and had to live by traffic: but finally the King made him put on the helmet and took a sword in both his hands and dubbed him knight with great good will. The same day he made three other knights from among the citizens of London on that same spot, and these are their names—John Philpott, and Nicholas Bramber, and [blank in the MS.]:[1] and the King gave Sir William Walworth £100 in land, and each of the others £40 in land, for them and their heirs. And after this the King took his way to London to the Wardrobe to ease him of his great toils....

Afterwards the King sent out his messengers into various regions to capture the malefactors and put them to death. And many were taken and hanged at London, and they set up many gallows around the City of London and in other cities and boroughs of the south country. At last, as it pleased God, the King, seeing that too many of his liege subjects would be undone and too much blood spilt, took pity in his heart and granted them all pardon, on condition that they should never rise again, under pain of losing life or members, and that each of them should get his charter of pardon and pay the King as fee for his seal twenty shillings, to make him rich. And so finished this wicked war.

---

1   From a later passage, we know that the third person was John Standwyche.

8.14 The humiliation of Avignon: St. Catherine of Siena, *Letter to Pope Gregory XI (1376).* Original in Latin.

A SAINT WITH A PUBLIC FACE, CATHERINE OF SIENA (1347-1380), a mystic and dedicated servant to the poor was also so committed to seeing the pope return to Rome that she herself went to Avignon to prod him. Her numerous letters, dictated in Italian but often translated into Latin, were sent to comfort, reform, upbraid, and encourage people in all walks of life, especially rulers, city magistrates, and the pope. In the letter below she shows no patience with those who were counseling Gregory XI to delay his decision to move to Rome. For Catherine, the pope's "proper throne" was Rome. Putting together Catherine's letter to the pope with Jeanne d'Arc's *Letter to the English* (above, p. 517) how would you characterize the attitude of women—or, at least, some exceptional ones—toward power and authority in this period?

[Source: *The Letters of Catherine of Siena,* trans. Suzanne Noffke, 2 vols. (Tempe, AZ: Arizona Center for Medieval and Renaissance Studies, 2001), pp. 215-17 (notes modified).]

In the name of Jesus Christ crucified and of gentle Mary.

Most holy father in Christ gentle Jesus,

Your poor unworthy daughter Caterina sends you greetings in the precious blood of the Lamb of God. I long to see you strong and firm as a rock in the good holy resolution you have already taken up, so that all the contrary winds beating against you won't hurt you.[1] They come from human enemies, rising up out of malice through the devil's ministry and satanic furies, who want to prevent all the good that will follow from your going [to Rome].

I understood from the note you sent me that you are being harassed by the enemies of all good, who never stop tempting you. And to persuade you the more convincingly of the evil they want, they are claiming that Pope Clement IV, whenever he had to do anything, never wanted to act without the advice of his brother cardinals. True, he usually preferred

their intentions and pronouncements to his own, even when he saw that his own were materially better, just as you yourself see what is right. Oimé![2] Most holy father, what malice and how much evil are arising because of the devil! These men cite Clement IV, plenty concerned about themselves and what is theirs, but much less concerned about the universal good to which everything else ought to be subordinate. Why don't these pious men also cite Pope Urban [V], who sought the cardinals' advice when he was in doubt as to whether or not to act, but who, when the matter was clear and obvious to him—as is your going [to Rome] to you, of which you are certain—didn't feel bound by their opinion even though they might all be against him. Let your enemies direct your attention to *him*[3]—but they can't, because they are your enemies.

What sane person doesn't see that the holiest thing is for the lord of all the world to be seated on his proper throne? Surely, unless they are blind, they will admit this easily. And this is what the counsel of the good will always tell you. It seems to me the advice of

---

1 See the parable of the house built on rock, Matt. 7: 24–25: "Anyone who hears my words and puts them into practice is like the wise man who built his house on rock. When the rainy season set in, the torrents came and the winds blew and buffeted the house. It did not collapse; it had been solidly set on rock."
2 "Woe is me."
3 That is, to Urban V.

good people is concerned only with God's honor, the salvation of souls, and the reform of holy Church, and not with their own selfish love for themselves. The advice of such people should be followed, I'm saying, but not the advice of those who love only their own life, honor, status, and pleasure—for their advice goes where their love is.

I beg you in the name of Christ crucified: let it please your holiness to hurry! Make use of a holy trick. I mean, let it look as if you are going to take a few more days, and then all of a sudden go! For the sooner you act, the sooner you will escape these tormenting anxieties. In fact, it seems to me their malice is becoming much more astute. Now they want to instruct you by giving you the example of the wild animals who, once they escape from a trap, never go back to it![1] But I am begging you to follow with complete commitment [my] sound advice. The blessed God freed you once from their wicked counsel when they interrupted your journey last year. The devil had in fact laid a trap on their tongues. You were caught, and holy counsel was taken captive. Evil and harm followed because of it—indeed the worst evil and harm we have suffered until now! So now that you're the wiser, with the Holy Spirit's guidance you *won't* fall back into it.

Let's go quickly, my dear *babbo*, and fearlessly! If God is for you, no one will be against you.[2] God himself will move you; God himself will be your guide, your helmsman, and your sailor. So God *is* with you. Go quickly to your bride, who is all pale, and is waiting for you to bring back her color.[3] And the moment you arrive she will be more beautiful than any other. I don't want to burden you with more words, for I would have much to say.

Keep living in God's holy and tender love. I am presumptuous: forgive me. I humbly ask your blessing.

Gentle Jesus! Jesus love!

8.15 The conciliarist movement: Jean Gerson, *Sermon at the Council of Constance* (1415). Original in Latin.

JEAN GERSON (1363-1429), CHANCELLOR OF THE University of Paris and a public intellectual of wide-ranging interests and influence, was called upon to address the Council of Constance (1414-1418) at a moment of crisis. Originally held under the auspices of John XXIII, the council seemed ready to depose him along with other popes, prompting John to flee in disguise in March 1415. His leaving—and calling on everyone else to follow him—threw the remaining prelates into a crisis of conscience: should they continue with the council without a papal sponsor? Gerson, a conservative who came to the conciliarist position only slowly, thought they could and must. His sermon, excerpted below, brought the logical vocabulary of scholasticism to bear on the meaning of a council. His speech was the turning point at Constance, leading the assembly to declare, about a month later in the decree known as *Haec sancta*, that "This holy synod … holds power directly from Christ; and … everyone of whatever estate or dignity he be, even papal, is obliged to obey it in those things which belong to the faith."[4] The Council deposed John and elected Martin V.

[Source: *Unity, Heresy and Reform, 1378-1460: The Conciliar Response to the Great Schism*, ed. C.M.D. Crowder (Kingston, ON: Limestone Press, 1986), pp. 76-82.]

---

1   The sense of the Latin seems to be that the cardinals are using the example of animals once trapped to convince the pope not to return to the "trap" of Rome.
2   See Rom. 8: 31. *Babbo* is equivalent to Daddy.
3   The "bride" is the Church.
4   *Haec sancta* in *Unity, Heresy and Reform, 1378-1460: The Conciliar Response to the Great Schism*, ed. C.M.D. Crowder (Kingston, ON: Limestone Press, 1986), p. 83.

… "Walk while ye have the light, lest darkness come upon you."[1] That light, most distinguished fathers, I repeat once more, that light is God, who is glorified in the council of the saints. As the psalmist says: "God is greatly to be feared in the assembly of the saints, and to be had in reverence of all them that are round about him."[2] We hold to this infallible promise of his: "Where two or three are gathered together in my name, there am I in the midst of them."[3] The psalmist saw this when he sang: "I will praise the Lord with my whole heart in the assembly of the upright, and in the congregation."[4] And we see in this assembly of the upright the unfolding of the mighty work of God, the freely given and scarcely hoped for way of resignation.

So when God has done all things to please himself and that he may be glorified, whose delight is to be with the sons of men, how may he obtain greater glory than in a council of the upright? For his praise is in the Church of the saints. You, fathers and lords, true believers and pleasing to God, are required to behave so as to constitute a council of saints and upright men. God has placed you in the world as so many true lights. "You are the light of the world," he says.[5] If ever it is your role to purge and illuminate others and to make them perfect, now is it especially so, when this holy convention is met, when the assembly is brought together in one place, when the Church is assembled; as it is written in Maccabees how they prayed and sought God's mercy:[6] that with his aid it might be decided what needed to be done. The spirit immediately rejoices, raising its eyes to take in what is happening, seeing all those who have assembled on your behalf, that is, for your benefit, O Christian people. My spirit observes and rejoices with you, and breaks out into this song of the Church. The citizens of the Apostles and the servants of God are here today, bearing a torch and bringing light to their fatherland to give peace to the peoples and to set the Lord's people free. How will they free them? By urging and crying out: "Walk while ye have the light, lest darkness come upon you;" the darkness of divisions and schism, the darkness of so many errors and heresies, in a word, the horrible darkness of so many vices that pour out of the Church's wretched body on a limitless tide. Walk, therefore, while you have light, that these aspects of the darkness do not come upon you....

The first problem is to keep the sequence of what is to be said clear and short. Because nothing is long if put together in orderly fashion. In the meantime, having broached the theme, let us turn our attention to what has been said: that God is he "who is greatly to be feared in the assembly of saints, and to be had in reverence of all them that are round about him."[7] Let us fix our mind on that text from the psalmist for fear we stray too far afield. If I am not mistaken, we see there the fourfold cause of this holy synod, that is its efficient, formal, final and material cause.[8]

If anyone wants to know the efficient cause, that is clear enough: God, greatly to be feared. It is by his impulse, mercy, inspiration and influence that the Church is now brought together, just as the psalmist, lifted up by the spirit, prophesied in song: It is God that "gathers together the outcasts of Israel";[9] and gathered his elect from the four winds "from the east and from the west, from the north and from the south."[10] Only let us pray that he who has begun the work perfects it. O sacred assembly "lift up your eyes round about you and see"; "all these are gathered together, they have come to you."[11] May it happen to you as was spoken by the prophet Isaiah: "Then thou shalt see, and flow together, and thine heart shall fear, and be enlarged."[12] And if it is enlarged, surely, will not God fill it with his spirit?

Next, the formal cause is this very bringing to-

---

1 John 12: 35.
2 Ps. 89: 7; Douay Ps. 88: 8.
3 Matt. 18: 20.
4 Ps. 111: 1; Douay Ps. 110: 1.
5 Matt. 5: 14.
6 See 1 Macc. 3: 44.
7 Ps. 89: 7; Douay Ps. 88: 8.
8 The idea of the four causes derives from Aristotle's logic.
9 Ps. 147: 2; Douay Ps. 146: 2.
10 Ps. 107: 3; Douay Ps. 106: 3.
11 Isa. 60: 5 and 49: 18.
12 Isa. 60: 5.

gether or association of the council of holy men formed and modeled in the Holy Spirit, the form and exemplar of our acts, who is the bond and connection linking separate members of the saints, making them one. The Church recognizes this when it asks in its own behalf that, gathered in the Holy Spirit, it may not be disturbed by the assault of any adversary.

If anyone goes further to ask for the final cause of this holy assembly, that, surely, is that God, greatly to be feared, should be glorified, as it is said in the words of the Apostle: "Do all to the glory of God."[1] This is the straight and effective path to obtaining all that we wish, so long as we first seek his glory. He gave this to be understood, when he said: "Seek ye first the Kingdom of God and his righteousness, and all these things will be added unto you."[2]

Finally, all those who are round about God can be taken as the material cause, of itself unformed. For just as men by falling into schism, as a result, deform in some way or other God's creation, since, according to Plato and Aristotle, man is the end of all things, so it is necessary that all things are modified according to the requirements of their end. Thus, by the contrary argument, everything should be reformed by this council of holy men, the Lord beginning and shaping the work and bringing it to its final conclusion. For thus does the Church sing about Christ's precious blood: "The earth, sea, stars and heavens are washed in that flood."[3] ...

[Thus] God, greatly to be feared, is glorified in this council of holy men, because he offers it sufficient and infallible authority as its efficient cause. That is the first foundation. Again for the second conclusion: God, greatly to be feared, guides and attracts all Christians in common to the unity of one true head, as the formative and model cause. That is the second foundation and the first basis of reform. Further, for the third conclusion: God, greatly to be feared, wills to be glorified thus in this council of holy men that all things may turn particularly to the honor and preservation of his law and faith, without which no one can please him. That is the third foundation and the

second basis of reform. Last of all, the fourth conclusion: God, greatly to be feared, is prepared to grant through this council of holy men to all creation, and especially to mankind, a measure of the beauty, glory, order and dignity of reform, with suitable provision against those who continue, not in upright behavior but on the treadmill of vice. And that is the fourth conclusion on the last foundation, and the third basis of reform.…

Twelve considerations are to be derived from the light of this teaching in the Creed and the Apostle,[4] like so many rays of the brilliant truth.

1 The unity of the Church consists in one head, Christ. It is bound fast together by the loving bond of the Holy Spirit by means of divine gifts, by qualities and attitudes, so to speak, which render the constitution of the mystical body harmonious, lively, and seemly, so as to undertake effectively the exercise of the spiritual aspects of life.

2 The unity of the Church consists in one secondary head, who is called supreme pontiff, vicar of Christ. And it is more creative, more various, more plentiful, and greater than the assembly of the synagogue was and than a civil assembly under one ruler, king, or emperor, is.

3 By the life-giving seed instilled into it by the Holy Spirit the Church has the power and capacity to be able to preserve itself in the integrity and unity of its parts, both essential or formal and material and changing.

4 The Church has in Christ a bridegroom who will not fail it. Thus, as the law stands, neither can Christ give the bride, his Church, a bill of divorce, nor the other way round.

5 The Church is not so bound by the bond of marriage to the vicar of her indefectible bridegroom

---

1 1 Cor. 10: 31.
2 Matt. 6: 33.
3 See Luke 21: 25.
4 The part of the Apostles' Creed that Gerson quotes is, "I believe in the Holy Spirit, the giver of life." The Apostle that he quotes is St. Paul in Eph. 4, where he speaks of the unity of the Church.

that they are unable to agree on a dissolution of the tie and give a bill of divorce.

6 The Church, or a general council representing it, is so regulated by the direction of the Holy Spirit under authority from Christ that everyone of whatsoever rank, even papal, is obliged to hearken to and obey it. If anyone does not, he is to be reckoned a gentile and a publican. That is clear from the unchanging law of God set out in Matt. 18 [at v. 17]. A general council can be described in this way: a general council is an assembly called under lawful authority at any place, drawn from every hierarchical rank of the whole catholic Church, none of the faithful who requires to be heard being excluded, for the wholesome discussion and ordering of those things which affect the proper regulation of the same Church in faith and morals.

7 When the Church or general council lays anything down concerning the regulation of the Church, the pope is not superior to those laws, even positive laws. So he is not able, at his choice, to dissolve such legislation of the Church contrary to the manner and sense in which it was laid down and agreed.

8 Although the Church and general council cannot take away the pope's plenitude of power, which has been granted by Christ supernaturally and of his mercy, it can, however, limit his use of it by known rules and laws for the edification of the Church. For it was on the Church's behalf that papal and other human authority was granted. And on this rests the sure foundation of the whole reform of the Church.

9 In many circumstances the Church or general council has been and is able to assemble without the explicit consent or mandate of a pope, even duly elected and alive. One instance among others is if a pope is accused and is summoned to hear, as a party to the dispute, the decision of the Church under the law of the Gospel, to which law he is subject, and he contumaciously[1] refuses to bring the Church together. Another case is where serious matters concerning the regulation of the Church fall to be decided by a general council and the pope contumaciously refuses to summon it. Another, if it has been laid down by a general council that it should be brought together from time to time. The other kind of situation is where there is reasonable doubt about the disputes of several claimants to the papacy.

10 If the Church or general council agrees on any way or lays down that one way is to be accepted by the pope to end schism, he is obliged to accept it. Thus he is obliged to resign, if that is the prevailing opinion, and when he goes further and offers resignation and anticipates the demand, more especially is he to be commended.

11 The Church or general council ought to be particularly dedicated to the prosecution of perfect unity, the eradication of errors, and the correction of the erring, without acceptance of persons.[2] Likewise to this: that the Church's hierarchical order of prelates and curates should be reformed from its seriously disturbed state to a likeness to God's heavenly hierarchy and in conformity to rules instituted in early times.

12 The Church has no more effective means to its own general reformation than to establish a continuous sequence of general councils, not forgetting the holding of provincial councils.

---

1 I.e., with obstinate disobedience.
2 "Acceptance of persons" means "partiality."

8.16 The Hussite program: *The Four Articles of Prague* (1420). Original in Czech.

INSPIRED BY THE ENGLISH PRIEST and scholar John Wyclif to call for a reformed church, the Bohemian Jan Hus (*c.*1370-1415) was burned at the stake by the Council of Constance. But in Bohemia his followers took up the cause, calling for a moral and less materialistic clergy and asking that even lay people be allowed full participation in both forms of the Eucharist—the bread *and* the wine. They were declared heretics, and the pope called a crusade against them. The first battles led the Hussites to articulate their views, which they summed up in four articles, frequently repeated in Hussite writings thereafter.

[Source: *The Crusade against Heretics in Bohemia, 1418-1437: Sources and Documents of the Hussite Crusades*, trans. and ed. Thomas A. Fudge (Aldershot: Ashgate, 2002), pp. 83-84.]

[First] … throughout the Kingdom of Bohemia the word of God shall be freely preached and proclaimed by Christian priests…. [Second] the holy sacrament of the body and blood of the Lord, in both kinds of bread and wine, shall be freely given to all true Christians who are not prohibited on account of some deadly sin just as our Savior did in the beginning and so commanded it…. [Third] numerous priests and monks, supported by temporal law possess worldly goods in opposition to the commandments of Christ. This is to the detriment of their office and is also harmful to the lords of the secular estates. These priests shall be deprived of such power, which is unlawful, and in keeping with the Scriptures shall live lives of good repute in accordance with the pattern of Christ and the apostles…. [Fourth] all serious sins, particularly those committed publicly, along with other offences against the Law of God shall be prohibited and punished regardless of their estate,[1] by those who possess the power to do so. [This is to be done] so that the evil and slanderous rumors about this country might be removed for the common good of the people and the Kingdom of Bohemia….

If anyone wishes to accuse us verbally or in writing with anything evil, heretical, shameful or unclean, we would ask that such an individual not be believed.

For such a one is speaking slander out of hatred and ill-will and is both malicious and a liar. We confess boldly before the Lord God and the entire world that with the help of God we have no other motive than to serve the Lord Jesus Christ with all of our hearts, power, strength and endurance and to be dedicated to the fulfilment of God's law and commandments which is appropriate for all good Christians. Any wicked enemy or anyone else who attempts to compel us away from this good we will withstand in keeping with the law and truth of God. On this position we shall defend the truth as well as ourselves against such violence through the use of secular weapons. Should something terrible happen through the zeal of one of our people, we assert that this is not our intention but we shall stand against all serious sins with God's help. And if someone comes to harm because of us it is because it was absolutely necessary or because that person is an enemy of God as well as of us. It is necessary to protect both ourselves and the law of God from such violence and cruelty. Beyond this, we declare with all solemnity that if it appears that we are incorrect in anything we are prepared to make amends and our hearts are open in all things to be instructed by enlightenment from the Holy Scriptures. Dated in the year of the Lord 1421.[2]

---

1   I.e., regardless of social status.
2   The date is 1420 by a modern calendar.

8.17 The Catholic rally against the Hussites: Emperor Sigismund, *Crusading Letter* (1421). Original in German.

SIGISMUND, HOLY ROMAN EMPEROR (r.1410-1436), MADE GOOD HIS claim to the Bohemian crown in 1420. He had been the power behind the Council of Constance (1414-1418), which ended the papal schism and burned Hus as a heretic. Once ruler of Bohemia, Sigismund began an energetic campaign against the Hussites. The letter printed below called upon officials in Lusatia (just north of Bohemia and west of Silesia) to recruit "all who are able" to "exterminate" the heretics. The general unity of Bohemians of every level against Sigismund meant, however, that the revolt ended not by stamping out the movement but by a negotiated settlement, achieved in 1437.

[Source: *The Crusade against Heretics in Bohemia, 1418-1437: Sources and Documents of the Hussite Crusades*, trans. and ed. Thomas A. Fudge (Aldershot: Ashgate, 2002), pp. 114-15.]

We, Sigismund, by the grace of God king of the Romans, for all time, commend to each and every lord, knight, vassal, mayor, councillor and citizen in general, as well as to the entire region and the common people of our land and the towns of Budyšin, Zhorjelc, Žitava, Lubán, Löbau and Kamentz, our dear and faithful ones.

We have no doubt that it has come to you what inhumanity the Wyclifites and the heretics in Bohemia have perpetrated in many towns: murder, arson, robbery, destruction and many other disastrous acts. In this way they have destroyed, burned and grievously put to death many pious Christians and they intend to do likewise wherever there are people who do not wish to join with their heretical faith. This business concerns souls, bodies, honor and possessions and it should rightly move all Christian people to resist them at this time.

All of the vassals, knights and towns of our princedom in Wrocław, Świdnica, Jawor, Śróda, Śląska and Namysłów have united on this. All who are able, young and old, wish to march towards them and against them and they plan to be in the field on the border with the noble Albrecht of Kolditz on the following Wednesday [May 21]. On this account we are also moved and we shall gather all of our force which we can assemble and will march through Moravia and we intend to join together with those from Silesia.

Therefore, we desire also to remind all of you of your honor that you are obliged to Almighty God, the Christian faith and to us, to take this matter to heart which concerns souls and that you would rise up and draw into the field with all of your might, all who are able to stand, young and old, on horse and on foot, together with the high-born Heinrich called Rumpold, duke of Glogów, our dear uncle and prince, as well as those aforementioned from Silesia, in order to resist and exterminate the aforementioned heretics. Make no delay in this. [By such action] you will win a reward from God, honor before the whole world, gratitude from the church, and we will never forget this goodness. Given in Trenčín on Trinity Sunday in the thirty-fifth year of our Hungarian reign, in the eleventh year of our Roman reign and in the first year of our Bohemian reign.[1]

---

1 Trenčín is in present-day Slovakia on the Váh River about halfway between Brno and Banská Bystrica.

8.18 Piety in the Low Countries: Salome Sticken, *Formula for Living* (c.1435). Original in Latin.

The *devotio moderna*—the "new devotion"—called for a lifestyle that was not quite mystical, not quite monastic, and not quite humanistic, borrowing from all of these in its quest for a voluntary life of virtue. Members of the *devotio moderna* agreed to pool their resources (following the model of the Apostles) and to live in common (men with "brothers," women with "sisters"). Their lives centered on prayer and labor and focused intensely on the imitation of Christ. Some lived in "houses," took no vows, and went about in the streets of cities to do their work. Others formed monasteries that followed the rule of St. Augustine—the rule long used by canons (priests who lived together). The document below is the *Formula for Living* that Salome Sticken (c.1369-1449) wrote as a guide to the devout life; she herself led the convent of Diepenveen (near Deventer) for 38 years. It describes the ardor, humility, and simplicity that the sisters were expected to feel and practice. How might you compare the lifestyle it proposes with that in *The Benedictine Rule*, above, p. 28. How might you compare it with the lifestyle of the Beguinages, as revealed, for example, in the *Life of Mary of Oignies*, above, p. 405?

[Source: *Devotio Moderna: Basic Writings*, trans. John van Engen (New York: Paulist Press, 1988), pp. 176-81.]

In the name of our most beloved Lord Jesus Christ, amen. Beloved sisters in Christ, when you hear the sound of the bell in the morning, rise quickly from your beds with so much fervor of devotion and gratitude as if you were in the very presence of our most beloved Lord Jesus Christ and his holy angels. Humbly prostrate yourselves in devout prayer before his feet and ask that he deign to give you a whole day to spend in his praise and glory, and that in the peace and quiet conducive to your own and your sisters' salvation. Then lift your heart ardently and affectionately to the Lord with meditation on some article of his passion, and beginning to read matins proffer them to the Lord with an alert heart and affectionate desire. You should imagine yourself standing in the presence of the Lord Savior and his holy angels, because the holy angels look with great interest to see how devoutly and ardently we read and offer our hours[1] to the Lord God, so they in turn may offer our prayers and pious desires to their and our most beloved Lord. But alas if we read the hours with vain, distracted, or lukewarm hearts, the demons quickly and joyously appear to offer them instead to their prince. When the hours are finished, you can begin your exterior labors in silence and with such desire and affection that some should inwardly wish, will, and say: "O Lord Jesus, would that I alone could finish everything to be done here because I am less suited to things spiritual, and the other sisters, freed from these matters, might then turn themselves to you more freely and devoutly." You also know, dearest sisters, that before prayer it is important to prepare ourselves with ardent desire if we wish to be found devout and affectionate in prayer before the Lord.

At the beginning of mass humbly prostrate yourselves before the face of our beloved Lord Jesus, and with affectionate sighs and desires confess to him all your faults, especially that vice which is your worst. During mass place before your eyes the dear passion of the Lord Jesus. Pour out to our most beloved Lord Jesus your every wish and whole heart in ardent desire and great gratitude, giving thanks to him with all your strength, for he, who is so incomprehensibly great, deigned to undergo and suffer such awful and repeated torment for you. With heartfelt desire, then, offer up to the heavenly Father the unspeakable and

---

1 "The hours" refers to the Divine Office, which is detailed in *The Benedictine Rule* (above, p. 28), but in the convents of the *devotio moderna* these periods of prayers were simplified.

dear passion of our sweet Lord Jesus as a most pleasing sacrifice, adding the superb and most worthy merits of the glorious Virgin Mary, the merits of all the saints, and the common prayer of the entire holy Catholic Church together with the humility, love, and pious desires of all good men as an acceptable and pleasing oblation [offering] to God for all your sins. With that oblation offer the Lord God as well the complete mortification and self-denial of your own hearts and souls, together with a sure and perfect will never to depart from his service. Moreover, beloved sisters, if we are fervent and diligent, we can by the grace of our Lord so unfold before us his dear passion, impress it on our minds, and affectionately unite ourselves to it that we are made ready to do and suffer all that he permits to come over us, be it chastisement, humiliation, temptation, or even the condemnation and rejection of all men. Unless we have undertaken to bear patiently such mortifying things, meditating upon the Lord's passion with only lukewarm hearts will be of little moment and bring us little good. But if through such mortification and self-denial you convert yourself to the Lord, he will flood your minds with his generous and overflowing grace, teaching and instructing you more in one moment than any mortal could ever accomplish in much writing or teaching.

When mealtime approaches, I wish that you would make your way to the refectory in silence and without clamor and there read the blessing on the meal with a devout mind. Those in the kitchen and serving the table should prepare the food in great reverence with piety and dignity, placing it before the sisters as if they were doing so before the most loving Lord Jesus, his beloved mother, and all the saints. And those who sit at table should similarly receive the food in great reverence with bowed heads as if they were being served by angels. I wish as well that while eating you would frequently lift your hearts up to the Lord. Those of you blessed with an affectionate heart and great yearning should seek out that in the dish which looks vilest and least appetizing. And if any food or drink should be served that is contrary to your nature or taste, call to mind that the king of all sweetness, the most loving Lord Jesus, drank hyssop and vinegar on the cross for you. While eating, take care to lower your eyes and carefully keep watch that you not try to learn what those sitting near you have or are eating. Instead, with

fervent desire convert your heart, and not just your ears, to what is being read, so that your souls may be nourished by the Word of God no less than your bodies by the food of the earth. I know that many of our sisters so turn themselves inward toward the Lord God and are so watchful over their eyes while eating that they hardly know who sits next to them or what has been placed before them. Nor is there any murmuring heard from our sisters over what is placed before them, but by the working of grace they humbly and simply eat what they are served. I heard from our confessor that during the time he has lived with us he has never heard any complaint about the food. But I have frequently heard our sisters complain that foods have been placed before them finer in quality and greater in quantity than necessary, even though what is served them is only crude and common. I also know some sisters who never know what they have before them because during mealtime they unite themselves totally and wholeheartedly with the Lord Jesus.

I write these things to your charity, dearest sisters, because I wish your hearts to be occupied with nothing other than affectionate meditation on the Lord. When you rise from the meal, read the grace with fervent gratitude, making request to the Lord God in behalf of your benefactors and for the remission of your sins in case you transgressed any way in gluttony or the like. I also ask that after the meal you maintain silence for at least one hour, though it is best to spend the whole day or what remains of it in silence and wholehearted devotion to the things of God, that is, [to meditate] on your sins of commission and omission, the uncertain day of your death, the awful day of judgment, the pains of hell and reward of the righteous which is eternal life, the benefits of the Lord, the life and passion of the Lord Jesus—all of which things, I suppose, you already practice and have written out in greater detail in your books. At all times and places, moreover, lift your hearts up frequently to our most loving Lord Jesus Christ in brief prayers poured out with groans and sighs; for instance, in the psalm "Create in me a clean heart, O God" or the hymn "Come Holy Spirit" or something similar. Each hour you should also look into yourself to examine your progress or decline, carefully reflecting on what gladdens or saddens you, what you love, what you hope in. Each evening as you sit before your bed, carefully scrutinize how you spent the preceding day, confessing to the Lord and humbly bemoaning your faults and failures and making a firm and strong resolution to make amends.

When it happens that you leave the convent for some work, I deeply desire that you devoutly pray to the Lord that he watch over your coming and going. So conduct yourself in all things, in your manners and deeds especially, that whoever sees or hears you will be improved and edified. I know some sisters so watchful over their eyes when they go out into public squares that they would have been run over if the Lord had not been watching over them, and on finishing their business they return so quickly to the house that it is as if they were gazing upon an earthly paradise. When people of the world come to you, I beg each of you to flee from them and avoid their conversation, always showing reluctance to accept them as guests. And even those assigned to talk with them, I exhort and admonish to be on your guard against asking about the rumors of this world or talking about vain and useless matters. If such people of the world begin to discuss vain and worldly stuff, interrupt their talk, if you can, with good matter concerning the Lord Jesus and his saints.

I heartily desire, dearest sisters, that you submit yourselves wholly to your [spiritual] mother and to those with charge over you. Do not do, do not even think, anything you know or suspect to be displeasing to them or contrary to their will. Be affectionate toward your mother; think nothing ill or malicious of what she orders. Try so to put off your own will and to put on your mother's that there comes between you a single will and complete agreement, with you doing whatever she wills. Those, too, who help the mother in keeping watch over the house should subject themselves to her so humbly that she can freely and confidently proceed with what she thinks best and most useful—just as I can with my helpers and sisters, though I am much too unworthy and useless for the office imposed on me. Indeed I bear the burden of office almost without burden when I consider the humble submission of the sisters, how they humbly yield and incline their wills, how they interject themselves into nothing and speak only on that which pertains to their care, how they are intent only upon preserving pure and unsullied consciences and pleasing the Lord alone. I see all this and more each day and I rejoice in them. For I know that some of the sisters are so obedient that if I ordered them to set fire to the house or to rip off the roof tiles they would do so without objection. Likewise if I charged them to make a journey of more than a hundred miles, they would be found ready to depart at once and without objection. Therefore I must often think things through in advance before I command, for I recognize that there have been among us a number of indiscretions owing to obedience. Moreover, I also freely afflict, exercise, and chastise them; the more I do so, the more they love me, opening their hearts and coming to me with even freer hearts. Indeed it requires effort for me to think out something whereby I can humble and lower them. But they would be sad if I did not do it, fearing that I was less content because I served up less than the usual dish. All that I impose and they suffer from my hand they seem to count as nothing; this only they hold for important, that I be content and free with them. I insert and write all this that you may know how much I desire you to humble and submit yourselves to your superiors....

I ask further that you vie with each other to be first in taking up humbling and vile work, competing with one another in this regard in a loving contest. Similarly when you gather for work, each should compete to grab the poorest tool. I heard once from a very devout priest that the grace of God is nowhere more plainly evident than in our humble and vile works, if they are done faithfully out of love for God and to counteract sensuality. This is the custom we have observed until now among our sisters. When we gather for work, each without regard for personal comfort fervently seizes work from the hands of others who often discover their work done by another before they have an opportunity to put a hand to it themselves. Often sisters come to me with weeping eyes such that I can hardly comfort them, and all they want is that I permit them to take up, as they wish, all the vile work themselves. There are others whose main complaint is that they are not able to join the rest in this vile work owing to the frailty of their natures. Our sisters go out to work dressed so poorly and commonly that when seen by some person of the world with little understanding of the things of God he usually mocks rather than honors them. I also know many in our house who care nothing about how they are dressed outwardly, but only that they please the Lord God inwardly. They are so inward in their ways and guarded with their eyes even at work that they do not know who is assisting or sitting near or passing them. This they observe not only at work but also in choir: Standing for two or three hours, they do not once open their eyes to look around, which I have observed with my own most careful scrutiny. O beloved sisters, to describe the virtues of all our sisters would take too long, and I am the least worthy to do it.

When the sisters gather with the mother, I greatly desire that their conversation be about our Lord Jesus Christ and the loving-kindness he showed us, the most loving passion he bore for us, and the life, virtue, and ways of his most holy mother as also over the life and teachings of the saints, so that by such pious discussions the sisters might be roused to mortify themselves in imitation. When they gather, they should also mutually admonish one another in love on faults they have observed. But each should be careful not to express something out of passion. When a sister feels herself provoked to say something out of passion, she should choose rather to keep silent or, if it is something worth saying, ask the mother and say, "I would like to say something to that sister, but I feel myself moved by passion and not by love." If the mother then orders her to say it, she should in all humility and modesty, "This or that seems to me true of that sister, and if such happened to me I would do thus and so, but perhaps there was another intention or another way to see it." Make every effort to see that this mutual admonition and correction proceeds with such goodwill and charity that it arouses mutual love and not mutual indignation. And if you see faults or infirmities in another, try always to excuse them in your own heart, reflecting in humble submission on your own infirmity and countless defects.

8.19 Re-evaluating antiquity: Cincius Romanus, *Letter to His Most Learned Teacher Franciscus de Fiana* (1416). Original in Latin.

SERVING POPE JOHN XXIII AT THE Council of Constance (1414-1418), Cincius Romanus (or de Rusticis) (d.1445) and his humanist friends Poggius Bracciolini and Bartholomeus Montepolitianus took advantage of the turmoil at the Council to hunt for old manuscripts and reminisce about the glories of ancient Rome. Although employed by the Roman curia, Cincius and his friends preferred ancient pagan art over the churches and art of Christian Rome. And although they no doubt heard Gerson (p. 526 above) give his speech in modern Latin, they considered that language barbaric compared to the Latin of Cicero and other ancient Romans. Their new valuation of antiquity—its monuments and its literature—were hallmarks of the Italian Renaissance mentality. What different symbolic meanings of Rome can you discover by comparing Cincius's evocation of it here with that in the letter of Catherine of Siena to Pope Gregory XI (above, p. 525) and that in turn with the *Tale of the White Cowl* (above, p. 507)? Account for the differences.

[Source: *Two Renaissance Book Hunters: The Letters of Poggius Bracciolini to Nicolaus de Niccolis*, trans. and ed. Phyllis Walter Goodhart Gordan (New York: Columbia University Press, 1974), pp. 187-90 (notes added).]

Let us break our silence occasionally, for it seems outrageous and contrary to the ties of friendship and against nature that those who are separated by a considerable distance, though they are bound by the strongest affection, should not take to writing letters back and forth, for simply thinking of an absent friend will not suffice when one is given the opportunity of writing to him. Since the chief pleasure in friendship derives from familiarity, people who receive letters, as symbols of their friends, find no small satisfaction in them. Therefore I urge you vigorously to be kind enough while you have the physical ability (for you have the mental ability all the time) to write me something. I promise to give my letters to be delivered to you to all the couriers leaving Constance for Rome. Take this letter as my assurance in the matter, like a hostage. But let us come to the point, which ought to make you very happy.

In Germany there are many monasteries with libraries full of Latin books. This aroused the hope in me that some of the works of Cicero, Varro, Livy, and other great men of learning, which seem to have completely vanished, might come to light, if a careful search were instituted.[1] A few days ago, Poggius and Bartholomeus Montepolitianus and I, attracted by the fame of the library, went by agreement to the town of St. Gall. As soon as we went into the library, we found *Jason's Argonauticon*, written by C. Valerius Flaccus in verse that is both splendid and dignified and not far removed from poetic majesty.[2] Then we found some discussions in prose of a number of Cicero's orations which make clearly comprehensible many legal practices and many modern equivalents of ancient institutions. We also found one book, a small volume but remarkable in the greatness of its eloquence and wisdom: Lactantius, *On Men of Both Sorts*, which plainly contradicts the statements of those who claim that the state of mankind is lower than that of beasts and more hopeless.[3] Among other books we found Vitruvius, *On Architecture* and Priscian the grammarian's com-

---

1 Cicero (106-43 B.C.E), Varro (116-27 B.C.E.), and Livy (c.59 B.C.E-17 C.E.) were all classical Roman writers.
2 C. Valerius Flaccus (*fl.*1st c. C.E.) was another classical Roman writer.
3 Lactantius (c.250-c.330 C.E.) was yet another Latin writer, but unlike the others mentioned here, he was a Christian.

ments on some of the poems of Virgil.[1] There was also in that library one book made of the bark of trees; some barks in the Latin language are called "libri," and from that, according to Jerome, books got their name.[2] Although this book was filled to overflowing with writings which were not exactly literature, still, because of its pure and holy antiquity I greeted it with the utmost devotion. In fact we have copies of all these books. But when we carefully inspected the nearby tower of the church of St. Gall in which countless books were kept like captives and the library neglected and infested with dust, worms, soot, and all the things associated with the destruction of books, we all burst into tears, thinking that this was the way in which the Latin language had lost its greatest glory and distinction. Truly, if this library could speak for itself, it would cry loudly: "You men who love the Latin tongue, let me not be utterly destroyed by this woeful neglect. Snatch me from this prison in whose gloom even the bright light of the books within cannot be seen." There were in that monastery an abbot and monks totally devoid of any knowledge of literature. What barbarous hostility to the Latin tongue! What damned dregs of humanity!

But why do I hate a tribe of barbarians for this kind of indifference to literature when the Romans, the parents of the Latin tongue, have inflicted a greater wound and heaped greater abuse on our native language, the prince over all the others? I call to mind innumerable libraries of Latin and Greek books in ruins in Rome which were carefully built by our ancestors, according to an inscription in Greek letters which was removed from the Porta Capena through one man's concern.[3] These libraries were destroyed partly through ignorance, partly through neglect, and partly so that the divine face of Veronica might be painted.[4] Anyway, I think that the perpetrators of this loathsome crime and those who did not stop them ought to suffer the severest punishment. Indeed if the laws say that he who has killed a man deserves capital punishment, what penalty and what suffering shall we require for those who deprive the public of culture, of the liberal arts, and actually of all nourishment of the human mind, without which men can hardly live at all or live like beasts? Two things used to stand out in Rome: the libraries and the monumental buildings which (and I shall omit the libraries) easily surpassed, in size and beauty, the pyramids of Egypt, the Basilica of Cyrus, and other wonders of the world which Herodotus mentions.[5] Every day you see citizens (if indeed a man should be called a citizen who is so degraded by abominable deeds) demolishing the Amphitheater or the Hippodrome or the Colosseum or statues or walls made with marvelous skill and marvelous stone and showing that old and almost divine power and dignity.[6] Truly I would prefer and would pay more for a small marble figure by Phidias or Praxiteles than for a living and breathing image of the man who turns the statues of those glorious men into dust or gravel.[7] But if anyone asks these men why they are led to destroy marble statues, they answer that they abominate the images of false gods. Oh voice of savages, who flee from one error to another! For it is not contrary to our religion if we contemplate a statue of Venus or of Hercules made with the greatest of skill and admire the almost divine art of the ancient sculptors.[8] But mistakes of this kind are to be blamed not only on those we have just mentioned but on the former governors of the city and on the popes, who have continually consented to this destructive

---

1 Vitruvius (*fl.* 1st c. C.E.) was a Roman architect. Priscian (*fl. c.*500 C.E.) wrote grammar books much in use during the Middle Ages. Virgil (70-19 B.C.E.) was a great classical Latin poet.
2 Jerome (*c.*347-*c.*420) was a Latin Church Father.
3 The Porta Capena was one of the gates of ancient Rome.
4 The "divine face of Veronica" is the image of Christ's face said to have been left on the cloth used to wipe his face (by Saint Veronica) as he carried his cross to Calvary.
5 Herodotus (5th c. B.C.E.) was a traveler and historian whose history of the Persian wars mentions (among many other things) the Egyptian and Persian monuments.
6 The Amphitheater, Hippodrome, and Colosseum were huge stadiums built by the ancient Romans. Some of the ruins remain today.
7 Phidias (*fl. c.*475-430 B.C.E.) and Praxiteles (*fl. c.*370-330 B.C.E.) were famous ancient Athenian sculptors.
8 Venus was a Roman goddess, Hercules a Greek and Roman god.

behavior which lowers the dignity of mankind.

It happens too that many books of Holy Scripture and many sacred structures have been lost through the carelessness of those who represented Christ on earth. We consider them the more despicable because the cure for all evil is expected from them. But I believe they follow the dictum of some wretch who, when he doubted that he could acquire for himself the name of virtue, burned the temple of Diana at Ephesus.[1]

So these priests of our religion, since they could not appreciate the excellence and beauty of the City and could accomplish nothing, strove for this kind of ruin and destruction. Let us pursue such inhuman, such savage stupidity with curses. And you, my teacher, gifted as you are in both poetry and prose, write something against these destroyers of our illustrious monuments. If you do so, you will assure yourself henceforth immortal glory and them perpetual shame. Farewell.

8.20 The search for a patron: George of Trebizond, *Prefatory letter to Mehmed II* (1465-1466). Original in Greek.

CALLING MEHMED THE "AUTOCRAT IMMINENTLY of the whole inhabited world" and thus happily predicting the sultan's world conquest, George of Trebizond (1395-1472/73) had a briefly heady career as a translator and commentator on ancient texts—until his work was brought under a cloud for inaccuracy. His importance is thus not his scholarship but his typically easy acceptance of Mehmed into the pantheon of his patrons—which included Pope Nicholas V (r.1447-1455) and the Hungarian King Matthias Corvinus (r.1458-1490). These men had in common the fostering of the Renaissance, even though Matthias and Mehmed fought one another on the battlefield, and Nicholas declared a crusade against the Sultan. The letter here served to preface George's Greek translation of his Latin introduction to Ptolemy's astronomical work, the *Great Synthesis* (best known by its Arabic title, *Almagest*). George hoped to convert the Sultan to Christianity, but in the end he never had an opportunity even to meet the ruler.

[Source: *Collectanea Trapezuntiana. Texts, Documents, and Bibliographies of George of Trebizond*, ed. John Monfasani (Binghamton, NY: Medieval and Renaissance Texts and Studies, 1984), pp. 281-82.]

To the Autocrat imminently of the whole inhabited world. Book I, An Introduction to the *Great Synthesis* of Ptolemy, and Book II, On that Autocrat's Eternal Glory, by George, of Trebizond by ancestry, but Cretan by birth and upbringing.

I arrived in Constantinople, O best king of kings and autocrat of autocrats, for no other reason than to talk with Your Highness and to demonstrate the zeal I have for the praise of your power, thinking that there is nothing better in the present life than to serve a wise king and one who philosophizes about the greatest matters. For in addition to your other manly virtues which befit a king, Your Mightiness is also said to study Aristotle even more than those who have a professional responsibility to study Aristotle. Your nature exceeds that of all other kings by so great a degree that you are able to unite with extraordinary perfection the two extreme opposite goods of human nature, I mean the loftiness of kingship and the profundity of philosophy, bringing together as one military leadership and scientific learning. I once wrote Your Highness a treatise in the Roman tongue on your military, indeed, your regal prowess in rul-

---

1 Plutarch (*c*.46-after 119 C.E.), an ancient Greek biographer avidly read by humanists such as Cincius, reported that Eratostratus burned down the much-admired temple of Diana at Ephesus in 356 B.C.E. in order to ensure eternal fame for himself.

ing and sent it from the City. However, now I write in Greek, encouraged to do so by that wise man of Trebizond, George Emiroutzes, even though I am not highly skilled in Greek.[1]

For when I talked with him (in truth, he is a friend), the conversation ranged over many different topics, but especially we talked of Ptolemy's *Great Synthesis*, to which as the supreme accomplishment all other learning looks. Because of the subtlety, difficulty, and importance [of these subjects] he asked me to write to Your Kingship on multiplication and division, not of wholes, but of fractions, and on other introductory material for the *Synthesis*, by which the difficulty and unapproachability of this summit of learning will be removed. Therefore, to discharge my promise to him, I had to use the Greek language. But let us thus begin:

The circle of the zodiac is divided into twelve sections, to wit, the zodia. Each of the zodia is further divided into 30 degrees so that there are 360 degrees in the circle, although the year is not 360 days, but 365 and a little more. The wise in these matters found it necessary to split each degree into 60 minutes (these they call the primary minutes) and not into any more or less than 60 because of the wondrous and, as it were, divine nature of the number sixty, as will be apparent from the matter. Since to have split up the whole circle completely, one would have had to carry the division into infinity, the wise, therefore, after the first splitting had resulted in divided wholes, or parts, such as the number of days in a year, then again split each of the first parts into 60 secondary parts, and then each of these into 60 tertiary parts, and so forth until they stopped the splitting at the sixth division of the minute—not because there remained nothing more to divide (for there is a remainder), but because it would be senseless to pursue the infinite, and because up to a point the remainder does not hinder such knowledge of the heavenly movements. For what does hinder is the magnitude [of the task] of ordering the data accumulated over a great expanse of time. The consequence is that, as if starting all over again, we have to establish the canons, to wit, the tables, of the motions.

This last work befits a king and an autocrat. For it brings to mankind a great aid for science, and, because of that, the greatest eternal glory to [the ruler] who has successfully directed it. Also, the successful direction of such a large-scale project would be otherwise impossible for a private individual. For it needs many men, and wise ones, whom only a king would be able to gather. It is for you to direct this work, along with your other manly accomplishments, and for us to contribute something towards that glory which is yours and, in memory of Your Mightiness, to have left behind in the Latin language, in which by God's grace we are supremely skilled, a record of your manly virtues for later generations.

But let God grant these things. If we, however, prove insufficient to the task, still no one will doubt that we have shown our zeal to Your Mightiness in these matters.

8.21 Old sources criticized: Lorenzo Valla, *Discourse on the Forgery of the Alleged Donation of Constantine* (1440). Original in Latin.

LORENZO VALLA (c.1407–1457) WAS AN ITALIAN humanist well known for his translations from the Greek, a Latin grammar textbook, and critical appraisals of legal documents, above all the *Donation of Constantine* (which is printed above, p. 172). Working in Naples for King Alfonso V of Aragon and Sicily, Valla no doubt hoped that his uncovering of the forgery would further Alfonso's ambitions in Italy against Pope Eugenius IV (r.1431–1447). He began his argument with a frank appraisal of princely desires and strategies, a far cry from pious "mirrors of princes" (see, for example, Photius, *Letter to the Bulgar Khan*, above, p. 143) and a precursor of Machiavelli's *The Prince*. He then turned to the very vocabulary of the *Donation*, showing that the words "satrap"

---

1 Although Greek was George's native language, he prided himself above all on his Latin writings.

and "nobles" (*optimates*, in Latin) for example, could not have been used in Constantine's day in the way that the *Donation* uses them. Valla's linguistic method helped to usher in modern historical criticism. In what ways did his critique of the *Donation of Constantine* complement the enthusiasm for the classics expressed by humanists such as Cincius Romanus (above, p. 536)?

[Source: *The Treatise of Lorenzo Valla on the Donation of Constantine: Text and Translation into English*, ed. and trans. Christopher B. Coleman (New Haven, CT: Yale University Press, 1922), pp. 21, 23, 25, 27, 29, 31, 33, 35, 83, 85, 87 (slightly modified).]

I have published many books, a great many, in almost every branch of learning. Inasmuch as there are those who are shocked that in these I disagree with certain great writers already approved by long usage, and charge me with rashness and sacrilege, what must we suppose some of them will do now! How they will rage against me, and if opportunity is afforded how eagerly and how quickly they will drag me to punishment! For I am writing against not only the dead, but the living also, not this man or that, but a host, not merely private individuals, but the authorities. And what authorities! Even the supreme pontiff, armed not only with the temporal sword as are kings and princes, but with the spiritual also, so that even under the very shield, so to speak, of any prince, you cannot protect yourself from him; from being struck down by excommunication, anathema, curse....

[But] the supreme pontiff may not bind nor loose any one contrary to law and justice. And to give one's life in defense of truth and justice is the path of the highest virtue, the highest honor, the highest reward. Have not many undergone the hazard of death for the defense of their terrestrial fatherland? In the attainment of the celestial fatherland (they attain it who please God, not men), shall I be deterred by the hazard of death? Away then with trepidation, let fears far remove, let doubts pass away. With a brave soul, with utter fidelity, with good hope, the cause of truth must be defended, the cause of justice, the cause of God....

I know that for a long time now men's ears are waiting to hear the offense with which I charge the Roman pontiffs. It is, indeed, an enormous one, due either to supine ignorance, or to gross avarice which is the slave of idols, or to pride of empire of which cruelty is ever the companion. For during some centuries now, either they have not known that the Donation of Constantine is spurious and forged, or else they themselves forged it, and their successors walking in the same way of deceit as their elders have defended as true what they knew to be false, dishonoring the majesty of the pontificate, dishonoring the memory of ancient pontiffs, dishonoring the Christian religion, confounding everything with murders, disasters and crimes. They say the city of Rome is theirs, theirs the kingdom of Sicily and of Naples,[1] the whole of Italy, the Gauls, the Spains, the Germans, the Britons, indeed the whole West; for all these are contained in the instrument of the Donation itself.[2] So all these are yours, supreme pontiff? And it is your purpose to recover them all? To despoil all kings and princes of the West of their cities or compel them to pay you a yearly tribute, is that your plan?

I, on the contrary, think it fairer to let the princes despoil you of all the empire you hold. For, as I shall show, that Donation whence the supreme pontiffs will have their right derived, was unknown equally to Sylvester and to Constantine.

But before I come to the refutation of the instrument of the Donation, which is their one defense, not only false but even stupid, the right order demands that I go further back. And first, I shall show that Constantine and Sylvester were not such men that the

---

1 Valla was in the service of the king of Sicily and Naples when he wrote this.
2 The phrase "Italy and the western provinces" in the *Donation of Constantine* meant to the forger of that document the Italian peninsula, including Lombardy, Venetia, Istria, and adjacent islands. Other countries probably did not occur to him as part of the Roman Empire. Valla, however, followed the current interpretation.

former would choose to give, would have the legal right to give, or would have it in his power to give those lands to another, or that the latter would be willing to accept them or could legally have done so. In the second place, if this were not so, though it is absolutely true and obvious, [I shall show that in fact] the latter did not receive nor the former give possession of what is said to have been granted, but that it always remained under the sway and empire of the Caesars. In the third place, [I shall show that] nothing was given to Sylvester by Constantine, but to an earlier Pope (and Constantine had received baptism even before that pontificate), and that the grants were inconsiderable, for the mere subsistence of the Pope. Fourth, that it is not true either that a copy of the Donation is found in the *Decretum* [of Gratian], or that it was taken from the History of Sylvester; for it is not found in it or in any history, and it is comprised of contradictions, impossibilities, stupidities, barbarisms and absurdities.[1] ...

It would not do to argue a public and quasi imperial case without more dignity of utterance than is usual in private cases. And so speaking as in an assembly of kings and princes, as I assuredly do, for this oration of mine will come into their hands, I choose to address an audience, as it were, face to face. I call upon you, kings and princes, for it is difficult for a private person to form a picture of a royal mind; I seek your thought, I search your heart, I ask your testimony. Is there any one of you who, had he been in Constantine's place, would have thought that he must set about giving to another out of pure generosity the city of Rome, his fatherland, the head of the world, the queen of states, the most powerful, the noblest and the most opulent of peoples, the victor of the nations, whose very form is sacred, and betaking himself thence to an humble little town, Byzantium; giving with Rome Italy, not a province but the mistress of provinces; giving the three Gauls; giving the two Spains; the Germans; the Britons; the whole West; depriving himself of one of the two eyes of his empire? That any one in possession of his senses would do this, I cannot be brought

to believe.

What ordinarily befalls you that is more looked forward to, more pleasing, more grateful, than for you to increase your empires and kingdoms, and to extend your authority as far and wide as possible? In this, as it seems to me, all your care, all your thought, all your labor, night and day is expended. From this comes your chief hope of glory, for this you renounce pleasures; for this you subject yourselves to a thousand dangers; for this your dearest pledges, for this your own flesh you sacrifice with serenity. Indeed, I have neither heard nor read of any of you having been deterred from an attempt to extend his empire by loss of an eye, a hand, a leg, or any other member. Nay, this very ardor and this thirst for wide dominion is such that whoever is most powerful, him it thus torments and stirs the most. Alexander, not content to have traversed on foot the deserts of Libya, to have conquered the Orient to the farthest ocean, to have mastered the North, amid so much bloodshed, so many perils, his soldiers already mutinous and crying out against such long, such hard campaigns, seemed to himself to have accomplished nothing unless either by force or by the power of his name he should have made the West also, and all nations, tributary to him. I put it too mildly; he had already determined to cross the ocean, and if there was any other world, to explore it and subject it to his will. He would have tried, I think, last of all to ascend the heavens. Some such wish all kings have, even though not all are so bold. I pass over the thought how many crimes, how many horrors have been committed to attain and extend power, for brothers do not restrain their wicked hands from the stain of brothers' blood, nor sons from the blood of parents, nor parents from the blood of sons. Indeed, nowhere is man's recklessness apt to run riot further nor more viciously. And to your astonishment, you see the minds of old men no less eager in this than the minds of young men, childless men no less eager than parents, kings than usurpers.

But if domination is usually sought with such great resolution, how much greater must be the resolution

---

1 The *Donation of Constantine*, a forgery of the 760s, grew out of various legends connected with the *Life of St. Silvester*. It was later incorporated into a ninth-century fusion of authentic and forged canon law called the *Pseudo-Isidorian Decretals*. Some of its chapters later got into Gratian's *Decretum*, and this is the version that Valla used and criticized.

to preserve it! For it is by no means so discreditable not to increase an empire as to impair it, nor is it so shameful not to annex another's kingdom to your own as for your own to be annexed to another's. And when we read of men being put in charge of a kingdom or of cities by some king or by the people, this is not done in the case of the chief or the greatest portion of the empire, but in the case of the last and least, as it were, and that with the understanding that the recipient should always recognize the donor as his sovereign and himself as an agent.

Now I ask, do they not seem of a base and most ignoble mind who suppose that Constantine gave away the better part of his empire? I say nothing of Rome, Italy, and the rest, but the Gauls where he had waged war in person, where for a long time he had been sole master, where he had laid the foundations of his glory and his empire! A man who through thirst for dominion had waged war against nations, and attacking friends and relatives in civil strife had taken the government from them, who had to deal with remnants of an opposing faction not yet completely mastered and overthrown; who waged war with many nations not only by inclination and in the hope of fame and empire but by very necessity, for he was harassed every day by the barbarians; who had many sons, relatives and associates; who knew that the Senate and the Roman people would oppose this act; who had experienced the instability of conquered nations and their rebellions at nearly every change of ruler at Rome; who remembered that after the manner of other Caesars he had come into power, not by the choice of the Senate and the consent of the populace, but by armed warfare; what incentive could there be so strong and urgent that he would ignore all this and choose to display such prodigality?

They say, it was because he had become a Christian. Would he therefore renounce the best part of his empire? I suppose it was a crime, an outrage, a felony, to reign after that, and that a kingdom was incompatible with the Christian religion! Those who live in adultery, those who have grown rich by usury, those who possess goods which belong to another, they after baptism are wont to restore the stolen wife, the stolen money, the stolen goods. If this be your idea, Constantine, you must restore your cities to liberty, not change their master. But that did not enter into the case; you were led to do as you did solely for the glory of your religion. As though it were more religious to lay down a kingdom than to administer it for the maintenance of religion! For so far as it concerns the recipients, that Donation will be neither honorable nor useful to them. But if you want to show yourself a Christian, to display your piety, to further the cause, I do not say of the Roman church, but of the Church of God, now of all times act the prince, so that you may fight for those who cannot and ought not to fight, so that by your authority you may safeguard those who are exposed to plots and injuries. To Nebuchadnezzar, to Cyrus, to Ahasuerus, and to many other princes, by the will of God, the mystery of the truth was revealed; but of none of them did God demand that he should resign his government, that he should give away part of his kingdom, but only that he should give the Hebrews their liberty and protect them from their aggressive neighbors. This was enough for the Jews; it will be enough for the Christians also. You have become a Christian, Constantine? Then it is most unseemly for you now as a Christian emperor to have less sovereignty than you had as an infidel. For sovereignty is an especial gift of God, to which even the gentile sovereigns are supposed to be chosen by God....

"The Emperor Constantine the fourth day after his baptism conferred this privilege on the pontiff of the Roman church, that in the whole Roman world priests should regard him as their head, as judges do the king." This sentence is part of the *[Life] of Sylvester....* But in the manner of those who fabricate lies, [the forger] begins with the truth for the purpose of winning confidence in his later statements, which are false, as Sinon says in Virgil:

"...Whate'er
My fate ordains, my words shall be sincere:
I neither can nor dare my birth disclaim;
Greece is my country, Sinon is my name."[1]

This first; then he put in his lies. So our Sinon does

---

1   Virgil, *Aeneid* 2.77–78. Dryden's translation. Sinon was known for first telling the truth—to get his audience off guard— and then telling lies.

here; for when he had begun with the truth, he adds:

> In this privilege, among other things, is this: "We—together with all our satraps and the whole Senate and the nobles also, and all the people subject to the government of the Roman church—considered it advisable that, as the blessed Peter is seen to have been constituted vicar of God on the earth, so the pontiffs who are the representatives of that same chief of the apostles, should obtain from us and our Empire the power of a supremacy greater than the clemency of our earthly imperial serenity is seen to have conceded to it."[1]

O thou scoundrel, thou villain! The same history [the *Life of Sylvester*] which you allege as your evidence, says that for a long time none of senatorial rank was willing to accept the Christian religion, and that Constantine solicited the poor with bribes to be baptized. And you say that within the first days, immediately, the Senate, the nobles, the satraps, as though already Christians, with the Caesar passed decrees for the honoring of the Roman church! What! How do you want to have satraps come in here? Numskull, blockhead! Do the Caesars speak thus; are Roman decrees usually drafted thus? Whoever heard of satraps being mentioned in the councils of the Romans?[2] I do not remember ever to have read of any Roman satrap being mentioned, or even of a satrap in any of the Roman provinces. But this fellow speaks of the Emperor's satraps, and puts them in before the Senate, though all honors, even those bestowed upon the ruling prince, are decreed by the Senate alone, or with the addition "and the Roman people." Thus we see carved on ancient stones or bronze tablets or coins two letters, "S. C.," that is "By decree of the Senate," or four, "S. P. Q. R.," that is, "The Senate and the Roman People." And according to Tertullian, when Pontius Pilate had written to Tiberius Caesar and not to the Senate concerning the wonderful deeds of Christ, inasmuch as magistrates were supposed to write concerning important matters to the Senate, the Senate gave way to spite and opposed Tiberius' proposal that Jesus be worshipped as a God, merely on account of its secret anger at the offense to senatorial dignity.[3] And, to show how weighty was the authority of the Senate, Jesus did not obtain divine worship.

What now! Why do you say "nobles" ["*optimates*"]? Are we to understand that these are leading men in the republic; then why should they be mentioned when the other magistrates are passed by in silence? Or are they the opposite of the "popular" party which curries favor with the people; the ones who seek and champion the welfare of every aristocrat and of the "better" elements, as Cicero shows in one of his orations? Thus we say that Caesar before the overthrow of the republic had been a member of the "popular" party, Cato of the "optimates." The difference between them Sallust explained. But the "optimates" are not spoken of as belonging to the [Emperor's] council, any more than the "popular" party, or other respectable men are....

8.22 Defending women: Christine de Pisan, *The Book of the City of Ladies* (1404-1407). Original in French.

BORN IN ITALY AND EDUCATED in France, Christine de Pisan (*c*.1365-*c*.1430) married at the age of 15 and was left a widow with two young children at age 25. Forced to support her family on her own, she turned to copying manuscripts and writing poetry and prose, both often commissioned by royal and other wealthy patrons. In *The Book of the City of Ladies* she defended the virtue, intelligence, and capabilities of women against the many men who disparaged the female sex. The book presents a dream or vision in which the author—with the help of three ladies

---

1 See *The Donation of Constantine*, § 11, above, p. 175; the key word "satraps" is there, but Valla quotes a somewhat different version.

2 The word *satrap* was in fact applied to higher officials at Rome only in the middle of the eighth century.

3 Tertullian tells this apocryphal story in his *Apology*, chaps. 5 and 21.

(Reason, Rectitude, and Justice, all "daughters of God")—populates a new city with the best women from the past and present. Those worthy of the city are named in the course of question-and-answer dialogues between Christine and the three ladies. In the passage below, Christine asks Lady Reason about women's ability to govern. In the course of their discussion Queen Fredegund, wife of King Chilperic and the nemesis of Gregory of Tours (see above, p. 65), comes up. Compare Christine's and Gregory's opinions of Fredegund and speculate on why they might be so different.

[Source: Christine de Pizan, *The Book of the City of Ladies*, trans. Earl Jeffrey Richards, rev. ed. (New York: Persea Books, 1992), pp. 30-34.]

CHRISTINE ASKS REASON WHY WOMEN ARE NOT IN THE SEATS OF LEGAL COUNSEL; AND REASON'S RESPONSE.

"Most high and honored lady, your fair words [about a different matter] amply satisfy my thinking. But tell me still, if you please, why women do not plead law cases in the courts of justice, are unfamiliar with legal disputes, and do not hand down judgments? For these men say that it is because of some woman (who I don't know) who governed unwisely from the seat of justice."

"My daughter, everything told about this woman is frivolous and contrived out of deception. But whoever would ask the causes and reasons of all things would have to answer for too much in this question, even though Aristotle in the *Problemata* takes account of many things and even though his *Categoriae* contains the essences of so many natural actions.[1] Now, as to this particular question, dear friend, one could just as well ask why God did not ordain that men fulfill the offices of women, and women the offices of men. So I must answer this question by saying that just as a wise and well ordered lord organizes his domain so that one servant accomplishes one task and another servant another task, and that what the one does the other does not do, God has similarly ordained man and woman to serve Him in different offices and also to aid, comfort, and accompany one another, each in their ordained task, and to each sex has given a fitting and appropriate nature and inclination to fulfill their offices. Inasmuch as the human species often errs in what it is supposed to do, God has given men strong and hardy bodies for coming and going as well as for speaking boldly. And for this reason, men with this nature learn the laws—and must do so—in order to keep the world under the rule of justice and, in case anyone does not wish to obey the statutes which have been established by reason of law, are required to make them obey with physical constraint and force of arms, a task which women could never accomplish. Nevertheless, though God has given women great understanding—there are many such women—because of the integrity to which women are inclined, it would not be at all appropriate for them to go and appear so brazenly in the courts like men, for there are enough men who do so. What would be accomplished by sending three men to lift a burden which two can carry easily?

But if anyone maintained that women do not possess enough understanding to learn the laws, the opposite is obvious from the proof afforded by experience, which is manifest and has been manifested in many women—just as I will soon tell—who have been very great philosophers and have mastered fields far more complicated, subtle, and lofty than written laws and man-made institutions. Moreover, in case anyone says that women do not have a natural sense for politics and government, I will give you examples of several great women rulers who have lived in past times. And so that you will better know my truth, I will remind you of some women of your own time who remained widows and whose skill governing—both past and present—in all their affairs following the deaths of their husbands provides obvious demonstration that a woman with a mind is fit for all tasks."

---

1 The point is that even Aristotle's books on *Problems* and *Categories* cannot explain everything.

HERE SHE TELLS OF NICAULA, EMPRESS OF ETHIO-
PIA, AND AFTERWARDS ABOUT SEVERAL QUEENS
AND PRINCESSES OF FRANCE.

"Please tell me where there was ever a king endowed
with greater skill in politics, government, and sovereign justice, and even with such lofty and magnificent
style as one can read about the most noble Empress
Nicaula.[1] For though there had been many kings of
great fame called pharaohs in the vast, wide, and varied lands which she governed, and from whom she
was descended, during her rule this lady was the first
to begin to live according to laws and coordinated
policies, and she destroyed and abolished the crude
customs found in the territories over which she was
lord and reformed the rude manners of the savage
Ethiopians. This lady accomplished even more praiseworthy deeds than reforming the rough manners of
others, according to the authors who speak of her. She
remained the heiress of these pharaohs, and not just
of a small land but of the kingdom of Arabia, Ethio-
pia, Egypt, and the island of Meroë (which is very
long and wide and filled with all kinds of goods and
is near to the Nile), which she governed with wonderful prudence. What more should I tell you about
this lady? She was so wise and so capable a ruler that
even the Holy Scriptures speak of her great virtue.
She herself instituted laws of far-reaching justice for
governing her people. She enjoyed great nobility and
vast wealth—almost as much as all the men who have
ever lived. She was profoundly learned in the Scriptures and all fields of knowledge, and she had so lofty
a heart that she did not deign to marry, nor did she
desire that any man be at her side."

HERE REASON SPEAKS OF A QUEEN OF FRANCE,
NAMED FREDEGUND.

"I could tell you a great deal about ladies who governed wisely in ancient times, just as what I will presently tell you will deal with this question. In France
there was once a queen, Fredegund, who was the wife
of King Chilperic. Although she was cruel, contrary
to the natural disposition of women, nevertheless, following her husband's death, with great skill this lady
governed the kingdom of France which found itself at
this time in very great unrest and danger, and she was
left with nothing else besides Chilperic's heir, a small
son named Clothar. There was great division among
the barons regarding the government, and already a
great civil war had broken out in the kingdom. Having assembled the barons in council, she addressed
them, all the while holding her child in her arms:
'My lords, here is your king. Do not forget the loyalty
which has always been present among the French, and
do not scorn him because he is a child, for with God's
help he will grow up, and when he comes of age he
will recognize his good friends and reward them according to their deserts, unless you desire to disinherit
him wrongfully and sinfully. As for me, I assure you
that I will reward those who act well and loyally with
such generosity that no other reward could be better.'
Thus did this queen satisfy the barons, and through
her wise government, she delivered her son from the
hands of his enemies. She herself nourished him until
he was grown, and he was invested by her with the
crown and honor of the kingdom, which never would
have happened if she had not been so prudent.

"Similarly, the same can be said of the most wise
and in every instance virtuous and noble Queen
Blanche [of Castile], mother of Saint Louis [King
Louis IX] who governed the kingdom of France while
her son was a minor so nobly and so prudently that it
was never better ruled by any man. Even when he was
grown, she was still the head of his council because of
her experience of wise government, nor was anything
done without her, and she even followed her son to
war."

---

1 The "Queen of Sheba" of the Bible.

8.23 Satirizing society: François Villon, *Testament* (1461). Original in French.

FRANÇOIS VILLON (1431-1463) WAS A FRENCH POET whose unorthodox and quasi-criminal life left him with very few patrons. As a result, he wrote little for the court and a lot about himself: his failed love-life, his run-ins with the law, his friendships and enmities. Excerpted here is his *Testament*, finished in 1461. It parodies a will with its bequests and legal formulae; it also includes some other pieces, such as a *Ballade* to his girlfriend and a lay (a song). How might you use Villon's poem to discuss the conditions of France just after the Hundred Years' War?

[Source: *The Complete Works of François Villon*, trans. and ed. Anthony Bonner (New York: David McKay, 1960), pp. 23, 25, 63, 65, 67, 71, 73, 75 (some notes used and modified).]

THE TESTAMENT

In this my thirtieth year,
having drunk my fill of shame,
being neither wholly wise nor foolish,
in spite of the many miseries
I've had, all of which have come
from the hands of Thibaud d'Auxigny …[1]
If he's a bishop, blessing streets,
thank God, at least, that he's not mine.

He's not my lord or bishop, I hold
no land from him unless it's fallow;
I owe him no faith, nor any hommage
—I'm not his serf or doe.[2]
He fed me on dry bread
and water one whole summer;
generous or stingy—to me he was
a miser; may God so be with him.

Should someone try to blame me
and say I bring a curse on him,
I don't—let's make that clear.
In no way do I slander him;
the only evil that I speak is this:
if he has shown me mercy,

may Jesus, King of Paradise,
do likewise to his soul and body.

And if he's been more harsh and cruel
than I now care to tell,
then may the Lord Eternal
do the same to him …
But the Church tells us that we
must pray for our enemies,
and so I say, "I am wrong and shamed:
whatever he has done, let God be judge."

Thus, willingly, I'll pray for him,
on the soul of good Cotart, now dead.[3]
But how then? It could only be by rote,
for I am lazy when it comes to reading.
I'll offer him a Picard's prayer,[4] and if
he doesn't know it, he must learn it,
if he trusts me, before it is too late,
at Lille or Douai in Flanders.

However, if he wants my prayer
for him, provided he not tell
a soul, I give my word
he won't be disappointed.
When I have a psalter near at hand,

---

1 Thibaud d'Auxigny was the hard, uncompromising bishop of Orléans who had Villon incarcerated in the dungeons of the episcopal palace of Meung. "Blessing streets" means blessing the people as he passes in a street procession.
2 This is a pun on *serf* ("serf") and *cerf* ("stag"); hence the "doe" following.
3 Cotart was Villon's lawyer.
4 The Picards were a heretical sect which rejected the use of prayer; hence, saying a Picard's prayer is equivalent to saying absolutely nothing. Although Lille and Douai are now in France, in those days, as part of the enormous domains of the Duke of Burgundy, they belonged to Flanders, and a branch of this sect seems to have established itself there.

one bound in neither cordovan nor leather,
I'll take the seventh verse
of the *Deus Laudem* psalm.[1]

So I pray to the blessed Son of God,
whom I invoke in all my needs,
that my poor prayer find favor
with Him, to whom I owe my soul and body,
and who has kept me from such misery
and delivered me from vile authority.
Let us praise Him, and Our Lady,
and France's good King Louis.[2]…

I feel my heart grow feeble
and can hardly speak.
Fremin, sit near my bed[3]
so people cannot spy on me.
Take pen and ink, and paper,
and write down quickly what I say,
then have it copied everywhere.
Here is the beginning:

In the name of God, eternal Father,
and of the Son, born of virgin,
God and Father coeternal
together with the Holy Ghost,
who saved what Adam lost
and adorns the heavens with the damned …
That man is worthy who believes
the dead are turned to saints.

They were dead in soul and body,
doomed forever to damnation,
their bodies rotten, their souls in flames,
no matter what had been their state before.
I make exception, though,
of all the patriarchs and prophets
who, as I see things,
never had their buttocks overheated.

Some, no doubt, will tell me: "How dare you,

who are no master of theology,
make such remarks as these.
Your presumption is a bit too much."
I would tell him this was Jesus'
parable about the rich man buried
in Hell's flames rather than a downy bed,
and Lazarus on high above him.[4]

Had he seen Lazarus' finger burning
he would not have asked to have it
cool him, nor to feel the water at its tip
refresh his burning throat.
Guzzlers who, since drinks are so expensive,
imbibe their coats and shirts
would not fare so well down there.
May God spare us this, all jokes aside.

In the name of God, as I have said,
and of His Glorious Mother,
may this work be finished without taint
of sin by me, who am more haggard than a ghost;
if I have had no cholera,
it's thanks to Heaven's clemency.
But of my other miseries and bitter loss
I now say nothing—and so begin.

First I give my poor soul
to the Blessed Trinity
and commend it to Our Lady,
chamber of Divinity,
praying that through the charity
of those nine worthy Orders
of Heaven, this gift be brought,
before the precious Throne.[5]

Item: my body I bequeath and give
to our great mother earth;
the worms won't find much fat,
for hunger's waged too rude a war on it.
Let it be delivered soon:
from earth it came and to earth returns.

---

1 Ps. 109; Douay, Ps. 108.
2 This is Louis XI, who had become king in 1461. On Louis's passage through Meung Villon had been freed from prison.
3 Fremin was not a real person, but in *The Testament* he has the role of the clerk who takes down Villon's bequest.
4 Luke 16: 19-31 gives the parable of Lazarus and the rich man.
5 The Nine Orders are the Nine Choirs of Angels.

All things, unless they wander too far off,
willingly come back to their own place.

Item: to my more than father
Master Guillaume de Villon,[1]
who to me has been more tender than a mother
with a child removed from swaddling clothes;
he got me out of many scrapes,
but is none too happy over this one,
so on my knees I beg him
to leave this foul affair to me.

I bequeath to him my library,
and the *Romance of the Devil's Fart*,[2]
which Master Guy Tabary,
a very honest fellow, copied:[3]
it's in notebooks beneath a table.
Even though it's not well written,
its subject is so notable
as to compensate for all defects.

Item: I bequeath to my poor mother,
who for me bore bitter pain,
God knows, and many sorrows,
a salutation to Our Mistress—
I have no other house or fortress
in which to rest my soul and body
when some grim distress comes over me—
neither has my mother, poor old woman! …

Item: to my love, my dearest Rose[4]
neither heart nor faith I give;
she might prefer some other thing,
although the cash she has is quite enough.
Hm? Perhaps a big, silk purse,
deep, wide, and full of coins.
But I hope they hang the man (and me
included) who gives her any money.

Even without me she's got enough,
but these things no longer bother me;
the worst of all my miseries are over
and my pants no longer hot.
I leave her to the heirs of that Michaud
they called the Fearless Fucker,
pray for him and jump for joy—
he lies at Saint-Satur below Sancerre.[5]

However, to acquit myself toward Love,
rather than toward her,
for never would she give me
even one small ray of hope
(I don't know—and this still bothers me—
if she was so recalcitrant with everyone;
but by Saint Mary's beauty,
I now can finally laugh at this),

to her I send this ballade
with all the rhymes in R.
Who'll take it to her? Let me see.
Why not Perrenet de la Barre,[6]
on condition that if he meets
my lady with the twisted nose,
he'll say to her, with no formalities:
"Where've you been, you filthy slut?"

BALLADE
(*To his Girlfriend*)

False beauty, for which I pay so great a price,
harsh behind a mask of sweetness and hypocrisy,
a love that's tougher on the teeth than steel
and surely harbinger of my undoing,
felon charm, death of my poor heart,
secret pride which sends men to their destruction,
eyes which have no pity, will not justice
help a poor man without crushing him?

---

1 Guillaume de Villon, chaplain at a church near the Sorbonne, raised and educated the young François, who adopted his name.
2 The *Romance of the Devil's Fart* was Villon's lost early work concerning a student escapade of 1451-1452.
3 Guy Tabary was involved in a robbery with Villon and others. Tabary confessed to the crime and named his accomplices. Villon, a wanted man, had to leave Paris.
4 Rose, here, is not a girl's name but rather an epithet for Villon's mistress.
5 If he ever really existed, Michaud, the Fearless Fucker, quickly passed into legend.
6 Among Villon's friends, the one most resembling the above-mentioned Michaud is Perrenet Marchand.

I would have done much better seeking help
some other place; my honor would have been
    unscathed
No other lure would then have tempted me,
but now I must retreat in shame,
Help me, help me, anyone!
But what? I'll die and not get in one blow?
Or will Pity, moved by these sad words
help a poor man without crushing him?

A time will come when your flower, now in bloom,
will dry up, wilt and turn yellow;
then I'll laugh, if I still can move my jaws;
but no, that would be madness:
I'll be old, you ugly and without color.
So drink deep before the stream runs dry;
don't bring down this misery on everyone—
help a poor man without crushing him.

Prince of lovers, greatest of them all,
I wouldn't like to bring on your disfavor,
but, by Our Lord, all noble hearts must
help a poor man without crushing him.

    Item: to Master Ythier Marchand[1]
to whom I left my sword before,
I now bequeath ten lines of verse
which he must set for voice,
and for the lute, a *De Profundis*
for his old loves, whose names
I will not mention, or otherwise
he would forever hate me.

LAY
(*Rondeau*)

Mort, j'appelle de ta rigueur,
Qui m'as ma maistresse ravie,
Et n'es pas encore assouvie
Se tu ne me tiens en langueur.

Oncques puis n'eus force, vigueur;
Mais que te nuysoit elle en vie?
Mort, j'appelle de ta rigueur,
Qui m'as ma maistresse ravie.

Deux estions et n'avions qu'ung cuer;
S'il est mort, force est que devie,
Voire, on que je vive sans vie
Comme les images, par cuer.

LAY
(*Rondeau*)

Death, I appeal against your harshness
which took away my mistress,
and still you'll not be satisfied
until you have me listless too.

Since then, I've had no strength or vigor.
But when alive, what harm did she do you?
Death, I appeal against your harshness
which took away my mistress.

We were two, but only had one heart;
if it is dead, I too must pass away—
yes, live entirely lifeless
like an image carved in stone.

---

1   Ythier Marchand was likely a boyhood friend of Villon. He didn't set to music the *De Profundis*, the Lay on Death, that
    follows, but someone else from the time did this. The music here is in modern notation. It should be performed by a voice
    (the top part) and two instruments.

Et n'est pas en - co - re as - - sou -

- - vi - - e Se tu ne me

tiens en lan - - - - gueur.

8.24 An Islamic Renaissance thinker: Ibn Khaldun, *Muqaddimah* (1377-1381). Original in Arabic.

IBN KHALDUN (1332-1406) WAS BORN IN Tunis and worked there and in Morocco for a time, but he spent most of his life at Cairo, where he served as a chief judge under the Mamluk rulers. A pioneer in the philosophy of history, ibn Khaldun wrote the *Muqaddimah*, excerpted here, as the prelude to his universal history. In it he analyzed the factors—economic, social, and above all psychological—that led to the evolution of civilizations. In his view "group feeling" was key to political strength. How might you compare ibn Khaldun's notions of human society with those of Augustine in the *City of God* (above, p. 21) and al-Farabi in *The Perfect State* (above, p. 231)?

[Source: Ibn Khaldun, *The Muqaddimah: An Introduction to History*, trans. Franz Rosenthal, 3 vols. (New York: Pantheon Books, 1958), 1:261-65, 344-45; 2: 235-37 (slightly modified).]

Ch 2. [7] *Only tribes held together by group feeling can live in the desert.*

It should be known that God put good and evil into the nature of man. Thus, He said in the Qur'an: "We led him along the two paths."[1] He further said: "And inspired the soul with its wickedness as well as its fear of God."[2]

Evil is the quality that is closest to man when he fails to improve his customs and when religion is not used as the model to improve him. The great mass of mankind is in that condition, with the exception of those to whom God gives success. Evil qualities in man are injustice and mutual aggression. He who casts his eye upon the property of his brother will lay his hand upon it to take it, unless there is a restraining influence to hold him back. The poet thus said:

Injustice is a human characteristic. If you find
A moral man, there is some reason why he is not
    unjust.

Mutual aggression of people in towns and cities is averted by the authorities and the government, which hold back the masses under their control from attacks and aggression upon each other. They are thus prevented by the influence of force and governmental authority from mutual injustice, save such injustice as comes from the ruler himself.

Aggression against a city from outside may be averted by walls, in the event of negligence, a surprise attack at night, or inability of the inhabitants to withstand the enemy during the day. Or, it may be averted with the help of a militia of government auxiliary troops, if the inhabitants are otherwise prepared and ready to offer resistance.

The restraining influence among Bedouin tribes comes from their sheikhs and leaders. It results from the great respect and veneration they generally enjoy among the people. The hamlets of the Bedouins are defended against outside enemies by a tribal militia composed of noble youths of the tribe who are known for their courage. Their defense and protection are successful only if they are a closely-knit group of common descent. This strengthens their stamina and makes them feared, since everybody's affection for his family and his group is more important than anything else. Compassion and affection for one's blood relations and relatives exist in human nature as something God put into the hearts of men. It makes for mutual support and aid, and increases the fear felt by the enemy.

This may be exemplified by the story in the Qur'an about Joseph's brothers. They said to their father: "If the wolf eats him, while we are a group, then, indeed, we have lost out."[3] This means that one cannot imag-

---

1 Sura 90: 10.
2 Sura 91: 8.
3 Sura 12: 14.

ine any hostile act being undertaken against anyone who has his group feeling to support him.

Those who have no one of their own lineage to care for rarely feel affection for their fellows. If danger is in the air on the day of battle, such a one slinks away and seeks to save himself, because he is afraid of being left without support and dreads that prospect. Such people, therefore, cannot live in the desert, because they would fall prey to any nation that might want to swallow them up.

If this is true with regard to the place where one lives, which is in constant need of defense and military protection, it is equally true with regard to every other human activity, such as prophecy, the establishment of royal authority, or propaganda for a cause. Nothing can be achieved in these matters without fighting for it, since man has the natural urge to offer resistance. And for fighting one cannot do without group feeling, as we mentioned at the beginning. This should be taken as the guiding principle of our later exposition.

God gives success.

[8] *Group feeling results only from (blood) relationship or something corresponding to it.*

Respect for blood ties is something natural among men, with the rarest exceptions. It leads to affection for one's relations and blood relatives, the feeling that no harm ought to befall them nor any destruction come upon them. One feels shame when one's relatives are treated unjustly or attacked, and one wishes to intervene between them and whatever peril or destruction threatens them. This is a natural urge in man, for as long as there have been human beings. If the direct relationship between persons who help each other is very close, so that it leads to close contact and unity, the ties are obvious and clearly require the existence of a feeling of solidarity without any outside prodding. If, however, the relationship is somewhat distant, it is often forgotten in part. However, some knowledge of it remains and this causes a person to help his relatives for the known motive, in order to escape the shame he would feel in his soul were a person to whom he is somehow related treated unjustly.

Clients and allies belong in the same category. The affection everybody has for his clients and allies results from the feeling of shame that comes to a person when one of his neighbors, relatives, or a blood relation in any degree of kinship is humiliated. The reason for it is that a client-master relationship leads to close contact exactly, or approximately in the same way, as does common descent. It is in that sense that one must understand Muhammad's remark, "Learn as much of your pedigrees as is necessary to establish your ties of blood relationship." It means that pedigrees are useful only in so far as they imply the close contact that is a consequence of blood ties and that eventually leads to mutual help and affection....

Ch. 3 [12] *Dynasties have a natural life span like individuals.*

... We have stated that the duration of the life of a dynasty does not as a rule extend beyond three generations. The first generation retains the desert qualities, desert toughness, and desert savagery. Its members are used to privation and to sharing their glory with each other; they are brave and rapacious. Therefore, the strength of group feeling continues to be preserved among them. They are sharp and greatly feared. People submit to them.

Under the influence of royal authority and a life of ease, the second generation changes from the desert attitude to sedentary culture, from privation to luxury and plenty, from a state in which everybody shared in the glory to one in which one man claims all the glory for himself while the others are too lazy to strive for glory, and from proud superiority to humble subservience. Thus, the vigor of group feeling is broken to some extent. People become used to lowliness and obedience. But many of the old virtues remain in them, because they had had direct personal contact with the first generation and its conditions, and had observed with their own eyes its prowess and striving for glory and its intention to protect and defend itself. They cannot give all of it up at once, although a good deal of it may go. They live in hope that the conditions that existed in the first generation may come back, or they live under the illusion that those conditions still exist.

The third generation, then, has completely forgotten the period of desert life and toughness, as if it had never existed. They have lost the taste for the sweetness of fame and for group feeling, because they are dominated by force. Luxury reaches its peak among them, because they are so much given to a life of prosperity and ease. They become dependent on the dynasty and are like women and children who need to be defended by someone else. Group feeling disappears completely. People forget to protect and defend themselves and to press their claims. With their emblems, apparel, horseback riding, and fighting skill, they deceive people and give them the wrong impression. For the most part, they are more cowardly than women upon their backs. When someone comes and demands something from them, they cannot repel him. The ruler, then, has need of other, brave people for his support. He takes many clients and followers. They help the dynasty to some degree, until God permits it to be destroyed, and it goes with everything it stands for....

Ch. 4 [1] *Dynasties are prior to towns and cities. Towns and cities are secondary products of royal authority.*

The explanation for this is that building and city planning are features of sedentary culture brought about by luxury and tranquillity, as we have mentioned before. Such features of sedentary culture come after Bedouin life and the features that go with it.

Furthermore, towns and cities with their monuments, vast constructions, and large buildings, are set up for the masses and not for the few. Therefore, united effort and much cooperation are needed for them. They are not among the things that are necessary matters of general concern to human beings, in the sense that all human beings desire them or feel compelled to have them. As a matter of fact, human beings must be forced and driven to build cities. The stick of royal authority is what compels them, or they may be stimulated by promise of reward and compensation. Such reward amounts to so large a sum that only royal authority and a dynasty can pay for it. Thus, dynasties and royal authority are absolutely necessary for the building of cities and the planning of towns.

Then, when the town has been built and is all finished, as the builder saw fit and as the climatic and geographical conditions required, the life of the dynasty is the life of the town. If the dynasty is of short duration, life in the town will stop at the end of the dynasty. Its civilization will recede, and the town will fall into ruins. On the other hand, if the dynasty is of long duration and lasts a long time, new constructions will always go up in the town, the number of large mansions will increase, and the walls of the town will extend farther and farther. Eventually, the layout of the town will cover a wide area, and the town will extend so far and so wide as to be almost beyond measurement. This happened in Baghdad and similar cities.

The Khatib mentioned in his *History* that in the time of al-Ma'mun, the number of public baths in Baghdad reached 65,000.[1] Baghdad included over forty of the adjacent neighboring towns and cities. It was not just one town surrounded by one wall. Its population was much too large for that. The same was the case with al-Qayrawan, Córdoba, and al-Mahdiyah in Islamic times. It is the case with Egypt and Cairo at this time, so we are told.

The dynasty that has built a certain town may be destroyed. Now, the mountainous and flat areas surrounding the city are a desert that constantly provides for an influx of population. This fact, then, will preserve the existence of the town, and the town will continue to live after the dynasty is dead. This situation can be observed in Fez and Bougie in the West, and in the non-Arab Iraq in the East, which get their population from the mountains. When the conditions of the inhabitants of the desert reach the utmost ease and become most profitable, the situation thus created causes the inhabitants of the desert to look for the tranquillity and quiet that human beings desire by nature. Therefore, they settle in towns and cities and form an urban population.

Or, it may happen that a town founded by a dynasty now destroyed has no opportunity to replenish its population by a constant influx of settlers from a desert near the town. In this case, the destruction of the dynasty will leave it unprotected. It cannot be maintained. Its civilization will gradually decay, until its population is dispersed and gone. This happened in

---

1   The reference seems to be to al-Khatib al-Baghdadi, *Ta'rikh Baghdad*, 1.117, but Ibn Khaldun probably quotes him indirectly.

Baghdad, Egypt, and al-Kufah in the East, and in al-Qayrawan, al-Mahdiyah, and Qal'at Bani Hammad in the West, as well as in other cities. This should be understood.

Frequently it happens that after the destruction of the original builders of a town, that town is used by another realm and dynasty as its capital and residence. This then makes it unnecessary for the new dynasty to build another town for itself as a settlement. In this case, the new dynasty will protect the town. Its buildings and constructions will increase in proportion to the improved circumstances and the luxury of the new dynasty. The life of the new dynasty gives the town another life. This has happened in contemporary Fez and Cairo.

This should be considered, and God's secret plans for His creation should be understood.

FINDING A NEW WORLD

Plate 8.1 A new kind of map: Gabriel de Valseca, *Portolan Chart* (1447).

BEGINNING *c.*1300 THE COASTLINE of the Mediterranean (and, by 1500, of Africa and other regions) was mapped on portolan charts with a precision hitherto unknown. Named after the Italian word *portolano*, meaning "written directions for sailing," portolan charts were practical navigational guides. Whether fancy—with flags, town names, and even a compass rose—or simple, all used a spider's web of "rhumb lines." These were carefully constructed as a series of 32 equidistant spokes radiating from a point, each spoke indicating a wind direction. One color was used for the eight primary directions—north, northeast, east, and so on—while other colors indicated the half- and quarter-winds. Above all, sailors used these directional signals to skirt headlands, which otherwise would ground them, and to find estuaries, where they could obtain fresh water and access to inland routes. The portolan chart shown here, drawn by the Majorcan Gabriel de Valseca, follows the coastlines from the Strait of Gibraltar to the eastern end of the Mediterranean and across to the Black Sea, paying particular attention to the islands.

[Source: Paris, Bibliothèque Nationale de France, Rés. Ge. C 4607.]

Taking Mexico: Hernán Cortés, *The Second Letter* (1520). Original in Spanish.

HERNÁN CORTÉS (1485-1547) CONFRONTED A "NEW WORLD," but he interpreted it with the mental categories of the old. Determined to secure the rulers of Mexico as "vassals" of Emperor Charles V (r.1500-1558), he struck out on his own, without the authorization of his commanding officer, to stage his version of the *reconquista* of the new land. Setting up a community—complete with officials whose titles echoed those known in Spanish cities—Cortés sent representatives of his "municipality" to Spain to plead his cause to the emperor. His *Second Letter*, following on this visit, depicts him as a loyal upholder of the realm, working to secure vassals for His Majesty and to conquer and win souls on God's behalf. How might you argue that this letter is part of the crusading tradition?

[Source: Hernan Cortes, *Letters from Mexico*, trans. and ed. Anthony Pagden (New Haven, CT: Yale University Press, 2001), pp. 54-60.]

Most Powerful Lord, I traveled for three days through the country and the kingdom of Cempoal, where I was very well received and accommodated by all the natives. On the fourth day I entered a province which is called Sienchimalen,[1] in which there is a town which is very strong and built in a defensible position on the side of a very steep mountain. There is only one entrance, up steep steps which can only be climbed on foot and that with considerable difficulty. In the plain there are many villages and hamlets of five or three or two hundred inhabitants, so that there are in all as many as five or six thousand warriors; and this land is in the kingdom of Mutezuma [Montezuma]. Here they received me very well and generously provided the provisions I needed for the journey. They told me that they knew I was going to visit their lord Mutezuma, and that I should be confident he was my friend and had sent word that they were to give me every facility, for they served him by so doing. I responded to their great kindness by saying that Your Majesty had received news of him and had sent me to see him, and that I was going for no other purpose. Then I went over a pass which is at the frontier of this province, and we called it Nombre de Dios, because it was the first we had crossed in these lands: it is so rough and steep that there is none in Spain so difficult. But I did cross it, safely and without adverse incident. On the slopes below the pass there are other villages and a fortress called Ceyxnacan,[2] which also belongs to Mutezuma; here we were no less well received than at Sienchimalen; also, they told us, because Mutezuma wished it. And I replied as before.

From there I continued for three days through desert country which is uninhabitable because of its infertility and lack of water and because of the extreme cold. God knows how much my people suffered from thirst and hunger, and especially from a hail- and rainstorm that hit us there, which I thought would cause the deaths of many people from cold; and indeed several Indians from the island of Fernandina who had not enough to wear did die from it. After three days we crossed another pass not so steep as the first. At the top of it there was a small tower, almost like a wayside shrine, in which they kept a number of idols, and around the tower were more than a thousand cartloads of firewood, all very well stacked; for this reason we called it the Firewood Pass.[3] On the descent from this pass, between some very steep mountains, there is a valley thickly inhabited with people who seemed to be very poor. After going two leagues through this region without learning anything about it, I reached a flatter place where the chief of that valley appeared to live; for he had the largest and the best-constructed buildings we had seen in that land so far. They were

---

1   Xicochimalco.
2   Ixhuacan.
3   Puerto de la Leña.

all of dressed stone and very well built and very new, and they had very large and beautiful halls in them and many rooms, also well built: this valley and town are called Caltanmí.[1] By the chief and the people I was very well received and lodged.

After I had spoken to him on behalf of Your Majesty and of the reason for my coming to these parts, I asked him if he was a vassal of Mutezuma or owed some other allegiance. And he showed surprise at my question, and asked who was not a vassal of Mutezuma, meaning that here he is king of the whole world. I replied by telling him of the great power of Your Majesty and of the many other princes, greater than Mutezuma, who were Your Highness's vassals and considered it no small favor to be so; Mutezuma also would become one; as would all the natives of these lands. I therefore asked him to become one, for if he did it would be greatly to his honor and advantage, but if, on the other hand, he refused to obey he would be punished. And to acknowledge that he had been received into Your Royal service, I begged him to give me some gold to send to Your Majesty. He replied that he had gold but would give me none unless Mutezuma commanded it, but that once this had been done he would surrender to me the gold and his own person and all that he had. So as not to offend him and for fear that some calamity might befall my endeavor and my journey, I dissembled as best I could and told him that very soon I would have Mutezuma order him to give the gold and all that he owned.

Here two other chieftains who held lands in that valley came to see me: one lived four leagues down the valley and the other two leagues up the valley, and they gave me several gold necklaces of little weight and value and seven or eight female slaves. After staying there four or five days, I left them all very pleased and went up the valley to the town of the other chief I spoke of, which is called Ystacmastitán.[2] His territory consists of some three or four leagues' extent of built-up land, lying in the valley floor beside a small river which runs through it. On a very high hill is this chief's house, with a better fortress than any to be found in the middle of Spain, and fortified with better walls and barbicans and earthworks. On top of this hill live some five or six thousand inhabitants with very good houses and somewhat richer than those living in the valley. Here likewise I was very well received, and this chief said that he was also a vassal of Mutezuma. I remained in this town three days, to allow my people to recover from the hardships they had suffered in the desert as well as to await the return of four native messengers from Cempoal who had come with me and whom I had sent from Catalmy to a very large province called Tascalteca,[3] which they told me was very close by, and so it seemed to be. They had also told me that the natives of this province were their friends and very hated enemies of Mutezuma, and they wished to be my allies for they were many and very strong. They shared a large frontier with Mutezuma and fought continual wars with him and would help me if Mutezuma wished to oppose me. But the whole time I was in that valley, which was eight days in all, the messengers did not return; so I asked those chieftains of Cempoal who traveled in my company why the messengers had not returned. They replied that the land must be far away and they could not return so quickly. When I saw how long they were in coming, and that the chieftains of Cempoal so assured me of the friendship and good faith of those of that province, I set out thither.

On leaving this valley I found a great barrier built of dry stone and as much as nine feet high, which ran right across the valley from one mountain range to the other. It was some twenty paces wide and all along the top was a battlement a foot and a half thick to provide an advantageous position for battle; it had only one entrance, some ten paces wide. At this entrance one wall doubled over the other, in the manner of a ravelin [a curved wall], within a space of forty paces, so that the entrance was not direct but had turns in it. When I asked the reason for this wall they replied that that was the frontier of the province of Tascalteca, whose inhabitants were Mutezuma's enemies and were always at war with him. The natives of the valley, because I was going to see Mutezuma their lord, begged me not to go through the territory

---

1 Most likely the modern Zautla.
2 Ixtacamaxtitlan (Puebla).
3 Tlaxcala.

of his enemies, for they might be hostile to me and do me some harm; they themselves would lead me to Mutezuma without leaving his territory, in which I would always be well received.

But those of Cempoal told me not to do this, but to go through Tascalteca, for what the others had said was only to prevent me from forming an alliance with that province. They said that all Mutezuma's people were wicked traitors and would lead me to a place whence I could not escape. As I held those of Cempoal in greater esteem than the others, I took their advice, leading my men with as much caution as possible. And I, with some six horsemen, rode half a league ahead, not in anticipation of what later befell me, but to explore the land, so that if anything should happen I might have time to gather and instruct my men.

After proceeding four leagues, we reached the brow of a hill, and the two horsemen who went in front of me saw some Indians dressed in the feathers they wear in battle, and bearing swords and bucklers, who when they saw the horses began to run away. I arrived soon after and I called out to them to return and not to be afraid; as we approached them (there must have been about fifteen Indians) they banded together and began to throw spears and to call to others of their people who were in a valley. They fought so fiercely with us that they killed two horses and wounded three others and two horsemen. At this point the others appeared who must have been four or five thousand. Some eight horsemen were now with me, not counting the dead, and we fought them making several charges while we waited for the other soldiers whom I had sent a horseman to fetch; and in the fighting we did them some damage, in that we killed fifty or sixty of them and ourselves suffered no harm, although they fought with great courage and ferocity. But as we were all mounted we attacked in safety and retreated likewise.

When they saw our men approaching, they withdrew, for they were few, and left us the field. After they had gone, several messengers arrived, who said they came from the chieftains of that province and with them two of the messengers I had sent, who said that the lords of the province knew nothing of what those others had done; for they were of an independent community and had done it without his permission. They regretted what had happened and would pay me for the horses which had been killed; they wanted to be my friends, wished me good fortune and said I would be welcomed by them. I replied that I was grateful to them and that I held them as friends and would go where they said. That night I was forced to sleep in a river bed one league beyond where this happened, for it was late and the men were tired.

There I took all the precautions I could, with watchmen and scouts both on foot and on horseback. When it was light I departed, keeping my vanguard and baggage in close formation and my scouts in front. When, at sunrise, I arrived at a very small village I found the other two messengers weeping, saying that they had been tied up to be killed, but had escaped that night. Only a stone's throw from them there appeared a large number of Indians, heavily armed, who with a great shout began to attack us with many javelins and arrows. I began to deliver the formal requerimiento [demand for peace] through the interpreters who were with me and before a notary, but the longer I spent in admonishing them and requesting peace, the more they pressed us and did us as much harm as they could. Seeing therefore that nothing was to be gained by the requerimiento or protestations we began to defend ourselves as best we could, and so drew us fighting into the midst of more than 100,000 warriors who surrounded us on all sides. We fought all day long until an hour before sunset, when they withdrew; with half a dozen guns and five or six harquebuses and forty crossbowmen and with the thirteen horsemen who remained, I had done them much harm without receiving any except from exhaustion and hunger. And it truly seemed that God was fighting for us, because from such a multitude, such fierce and able warriors and with so many kinds of weapons to harm us, we escaped so lightly.

That night I fortified a small tower on top of a hill, where they kept their idols. When it was day I left two hundred men and all the artillery behind and rode out to attack them with the horsemen, one hundred foot soldiers and four hundred Indians of those I brought from Cempoal, and three hundred from Yztaemesti-tan [sic]. Before they had time to rally, I burnt five or six small places of about a hundred inhabitants, and took prisoner about four hundred persons, both men and women; and returned to the camp having suffered no loss whatever. The following day at dawn, more than 149,000 men, who covered the entire ground, attacked the camp with such force that some of them broke in and fought the Spaniards hand to hand. We then went out and charged them, and so much did Our Lord help us that in four hours' fighting we had advanced so far that they could no longer harm us in the camp, although they still made some attacks. And so we fought until late, when they retired.

The following day I left before dawn by a different route, without being observed, with the horsemen, a hundred foot soldiers and my Indian allies. I burnt more than ten villages, in one of which there were more than three thousand houses, where the inhabitants fought with us, although there was no one there to help them. As we were carrying the banner of the Cross and were fighting for our Faith and in the service of Your Sacred Majesty in this Your Royal enterprise, God gave us such a victory that we killed many of them without ourselves receiving any hurt. Having gained our victory, we returned to camp a little after midday, for the enemy was gathering from all directions.

TIMELINE FOR CHAPTER EIGHT

1348 Archbishop William, *Letter to His Official*			1348 *Pistoia Ordinances*
1350 Gregoras, *Roman History*		**1350**	1350 Heinrich von Diessenhoven, *Persecution of the Jews*
bef. 1368 Ibn Battuta, *Travels*			
1377-81 Ibn Khaldun, *Muqaddimah*			1378 St. Catherine, *Letter*
aft. 1381 *Wat Tyler's Rebellion*			
1395 Anthony, *Letter to Russian church*			
1400 Froissart, *Chronicles*		**1400**	
1404-7 Christine de Pisan, *City of Ladies*			
1415 Gerson, *Sermon*			1416 Cincius Romanus, *Letter to Franciscus de Fiana*
1420 *Four Articles of Prague*			1421 King Sigismund, *Crusading Letter*
1429 Jeanne d'Arc, *Letter*			
1435 Salome Sticken, *Formula*			
1440 Valla, *Forgery of the Donation of Constantine*			
1447 Gabriel de Valseca, *Portolan Chart*			
		1450	
1461 Villon, *Testament*			
1465-6 George of Trebizond, *Letter to Mehmed*			
1477 Sphrantzes, *Chronicle*			1478 *Mehmed's and Venice's Peace Agreement*
late 15ᵗʰ c. *Tale of the White Cowl*			late 15ᵗʰ c. Ashikpashazade, *Osman*
		1500	
1520 Hernán Cortés, *Second Letter*			
		1550	

APPENDIX

A TOPICAL ARRANGEMENT OF READINGS

THIS ARRANGEMENT IS MEANT ONLY to be suggestive; the readings may be organized in a great variety of ways. For example, the excerpt from Bede is not only illustrative of historical thought (as here) but also of the papacy and its reputation in England, of kingship and its role in Christianization, of the development of the Church, and so on. In addition, many different topics might have been chosen. However, I deliberately avoided three obvious possibilities: "Islam," "Byzantium," and "women." In my view the main point of this reader is to allow students to see cross-cultural similarities and differences; and *every* document has implications for women.

Chronicles and Histories

Religion, the Church, and devotion (excluding papacy and crusades)

Commerce and town institutions

Law

Literature

Monasticism

Papacy

Rulers (kings, queens, emperors, the Prophet, caliphs, and sultans)

Saints and other holy men and women

SOURCES

Chapter 1

1.1] Christianity becomes official: *Edict of Milan* (313). *Church and State Through the Centuries: A Collection of Historic Documents with Commentaries*, trans. and ed. Sidney Z. Ehler and John B. Morrall. Copyright 1954, The Newman Press, Westminster, MD.

1.2] Christian History: Eusebius, *The History of the Church* (c.325). Selections from Eusebius, *The History of the Church from Christ to Constantine*, trans. G.A. Williamson. Copyright © 1965, Penguin Books. Reprinted by permission of the Penguin Group Ltd.

1.3] Imperial legislation: *The Theodosian Code* (438). *The Theodosian Code and Novels and the Sermondian Constitutions*, trans. Clyde Pharr. © 1952 in the name of the author, 1980 renewed in name of Roy Pharr, executor. Reprinted by permission of Princeton University Press.

1.4] The attraction of classical traditions: Procopius, *History of the Wars* (c.550). Procopius, *History of the Wars, Books I and II*, trans. H.B. Dewing, vol. I, Loeb Classical Library ® Volume 48. Harvard University Press, 1914. Reprinted by permission of the publishers and the Trustees of the Loeb Classical Library. The Loeb Classical Library ® is a registered trademark of the President and Fellows of Harvard College.

1.5] The Donatists: *A Donatist Sermon* (c.318). *Donatist Martyr Stories: The Church in Conflict in Roman North Africa*, trans. Maureen A. Tilley, Translated Texts for Historians, Volume 24. Liverpool University Press, 1996, ISBN 0-85323-931-2. Reprinted by permission of Liverpool University Press.

1.6] Orthodoxy's declaration: *The Nicaean Creed* (325). J.N.D. Kelly, *Early Christian Doctrines*. Harper & Row, 1958, 1960 (second edition). Reprinted by permission of Continuum International Publishing Group.

1.7] Relating this world to the next: Augustine, *The City of God* (413-426). Augustine, *Concerning the City of God Against the Pagans*, trans. Henry Bettenson. Penguin Books, copyright © 1972 (first published 1972 by Pelican Books), reprinted 1976, 1977. Reprinted by permission of the Penguin Group Ltd.

1.9] Monasticism: *The Benedictine Rule* (c.540). *The Rule of St. Benedict: In Latin and English with Notes*, ed. Timothy Fry. Copyright © 1981, The Liturgical Press, ISBN 0-8146-1211-3. Reprinted by permission of the Liturgical Press.

1.10] The eremitical life: Athanasius, *Life of St. Antony of Egypt* (356=372). Athanasius of Alexandria, *Medieval Hagiography: An Anthology*, ed. Thomas Head. Garland Publishing, 2000, ISBN 0-8153-2123-6. Reprinted by permission of Taylor and Francis Publishers.

1.11] The active life: Sulpicius Severus, *The Life of St. Martin of Tours* (396). *Medieval Saints: A Reader*, ed. Mary-Ann Stouck. Broadview Press, 1999. Reprinted by kind permission of the editor.

1.12] Radegund as ascetic: Venantus Fortunatus, *The Life of St. Radegund* (before c.600). "Venantius Fortunatus, the Life of St. Radegund" and "Baudonivia, The Life of St. Radegund," *Sainted Women of the Dark Ages*, ed. and trans. Ann McNamara, John E. Halborg, E. Gordon Whatley. Copyright 1992, Duke University Press. All rights reserved. Used by permission of the publisher.

1.13] St. Radegund as relic collector: Baudonivia, *The Life of St. Radegund* (c.600). "Venantius Fortunatus, the Life of St. Radegund" and "Baudonivia, The Life of St. Radegund," *Sainted Women of the Dark Ages*, ed. and trans. Ann McNamara, John E. Halborg, E. Gordon Whatley. Copyright 1992, Duke University Press. All rights reserved. Used by permission of the publisher.

1.14] The conversion of Clovis: Bishop Avitus of Vienne, *Letter to Clovis* (508?). *Avitus of Vienne: Letters and Selected Prose*, trans. Danuta Shanzer and Ian Wood, Translated Texts for Historians, Volume 38. Liverpool University Press, 2002, ISBN 0-85323-588-0. Reprinted by permission of Liverpool University Press.

1.15] Church legislation in Gaul: *The Council of Orléans* (511). *Christianity and Paganism, 350-750: The Conversion of Western Europe*, ed. J.N. Hillgarth. First published in 1969 by Prentice-Hall Inc. under the title "The Conversion of Western Europe," revised edition first published by University of Pennsylvania Press, 1986, ISBN 0-8122-7993-X. Reprinted by permission of the University of Pennsylvania Press.

1.17] Christian history/personal history: Gregory of Tours, *History* (576-594). *Gregory of Tours: The Merovingians*, trans. and ed. Alexander Callander Murray. Broadview Press, 2005. Reprinted by permission of the editor and translator.

Chapter 2

2.1] The culture of the small independent farmer: *The Farmer's Law* (8th c.?). Walter Ashburner, "The Farmer's Law, II," *The Journal of Hellenic Studies*, Volume 32. Macmillan and Co., 1912. Reprinted by permission of the Hellenic Society.

2.2] Byzantine village life and the education of a saint: *The Life of St. Theodore of Sykeon* (7th c.). "The Life of St. Theodore of Sykeon," *Three Byzantine Saints: Contemporary Biographies*, trans. Elizabeth Dawes and Norman H. Baynes. St. Vladimir's Seminary Press, first published 1948, reissued 1977, ISBN 0-913836-44-3. Reprinted by permission of St. Vladimir's Seminary Press, 575 Scarsdale Rd. Crestwood, NY 10707.

2.5] Vilifying the iconoclasts: *The Chronicle of Theophanes Confessor* (before 818). *The Chronicles of Theophanes Confessor: Byzantine and Near Eastern History, AD 284-813*, trans. Cyril Mango and Roger Scott. Clarendon Press (Oxford University Press), 1997. Copyright © 1997 by Cyril Mango and Roger Scott. Used by permission of Oxford University Press, Inc.

2.6] Pre-Islamic Arabic poetry: Al-A`sha, *Bid Hurayra Farewell* (before 625). "Bid Hurayra Farewell," *Desert Tracings*, trans. Michael A. Sells. © 1989 by Michael A. Sells and reprinted with permission by Wesleyan University Press.

2.7] The sacred text: *Qur'an Suras* I (c.610-622). *Approaching the Qur'an: The Early Revelations*, trans. Michael A. Sells. Copyright © 1999 by Michael A. Sells, White Cloud Press, Ashland, Oregon, USA. Reprinted by permission of publisher.

2.8] Umayyad diplomacy: *The Treaty of Tudmir* (713). *Medieval Iberia: Readings from Christian, Muslim and Jewish Sources*, ed. Olivia Remie Constable. University of Pennsylvania Press, 1997, ISBN 0-8122-1569-9. Reprinted by permission of the University of Pennsylvania Press.

2.9] Taxation: *A Tax Demand in Egypt* (710). *Islam: From the Prophet Muhammad to the Capture of Constantinople*, Vol. 2: *Religion and Society*, ed. and trans. Bernard Lewis. Copyright © 1987 by Bernard Lewis. Used by permission of Oxford University Press, Inc.

2.10] Civil servants: 'Abd al-Hamid, *Letter to the Secretaries* (before 750). Ibn Khaldun, *The Muqaddimah*, trans. Franz Rosenthal. © 1958, 1967 by PUP. Reprinted by permission of Princeton University Press.

2.11] Creating a Roman Catholic identity for England: Bede, *The Ecclesiastical History of the English People* (731). Bede, "The Greater Chronicle" and "Letter to Egbert," *The Ecclesiastical History of the English People*, ed. Judith McClure and Roger Collins, World's Classics. Oxford University Press, 1994. Text of *The Ecclesiastical History* copyright © 1968 Oxford University Press. Editorial matter and translation of "The Greater Chronicle" and "Letter to Egbert" © 1994 by Judith McClure and Roger Collins. Used by permission of Oxford University Press, Inc.

2.12] The private penitential tradition: *Penitential of Finnian* (late 6th c.). *The Irish Penitentials: Scriptores Latini Hiberniae*, ed. Ludwig Bieler, vol. V. The Dublin Institute for Advanced Studies, 1963. Reprinted by permission of The School of Celtic Studies at The Dublin Institute for Advanced Studies.

2.13] A modern martyr in Francia: *The Passion of Leudegar* (680s). *From Roman to Merovingian Gaul: A Reader*, ed. and trans. Alexander Callander Murray. Broadview Press, 2000. Reprinted by kind permission of the editor and translator.

2.14] The settlement of disputes: *Judgment of Childebert III* (709 or 710). *From Roman to Merovingian Gaul: A Reader*, ed. and trans. Alexander Callander Murray. Broadview Press, 2000. Reprinted by kind permission of the editor and translator.

2.16] The papacy: *The Life of Gregory II* in *The Book of the Pontiffs* (c.730). *The Lives of the Eighth-Century Popes (Liber Pontificalis): The Ancient Biographies of Nine Popes from AD 715 to AD 817*, trans. Raymond Davis, Translated Texts for Historians, Volume 13. Liverpool University Press, 1992, ISBN 0-85323-018-8. Reprinted by permission of Liverpool University Press.

Chapter 3

3.1] Manors in the West: *Polyptyque of the Church of Saint Mary of Marseille* (814-815). *Carolingian Civilization: A Reader*, 2nd edition, ed. Paul Edward Dutton. Broadview Press, 2004. Reprinted by permission of the editor.

3.2] Commerce in the Islamic world: Abu `Uthman Al-Jahiz, *Avarice and the Avaricious* (850s?). Abu `Uthman 'Amr ibn Bahr al-Jahiz, *Avarice and the Avaricious*, trans. Jim Colville. The Kegan Paul Arabia Library, Volume Five. Kegan Paul International, 1999, ISBN 0-7103-0645-8. Reprinted by permission of Kegan Paul International.

3.4] The sale of a slave in Italy: *A Contract of Sale* (724). *Medieval Trade in the Mediterranean World*, trans. and ed. Robert S. Lopez and Irving W. Raymond. Columbia University Press, copyright © 1955, 1990, 2001, ISBN 0-231-12357-4. Reprinted by permission of Access Copyright on behalf of Columbia University Press.

3.5] The post-iconoclastic church: Photius, *Letter to the Bulgar Khan* (864- 867?). *The Patriarch and the Prince: The Letter of Patriarch Photios of Constantinople to Khan Boris of Bulgaria*, trans. Despina Stratoudaki White and Joseph R. Berrigan, Jr. The Archbishop Iakovos Library of Ecclesiastical and Historical Sources, No. 6. Holy Cross Orthodox Press, 1982, ISBN 0-916-586-52-9.

3.6] The conversion of the Slavs: Constantine/Cyril, *Prologue to the Gospel* (863-867). Roman Jakobson, "St. Constantine's Prologue to the Gospel," *St. Vladimir's Seminary Quarterly* 7 (1963). Reprinted by permission of St. Vladimir's Seminary Press, 575 Scarsdale Rd., Crestwood, NY 10707.

3.7] An early view of the Prophet: Muhammad ibn Ishaq, *Life of Muhammad* (754-767). *The Life of Muhammad: A Translation of Ishaq's Sirat Rasul Allah*, trans. and ed. A. Guillaume. Oxford University Press, copyright 1955.

3.8] The "New poetry": Abu Nuwas, *Youth and I* (c.800). "Abu Nuwas, verse 29," *Translations of Eastern Poetry and Prose*, trans. Reynold A. Nicholson. Greenwood Press, 1969, ISBN 8371-2301-1. Reprinted by permission of Cambridge University.

3.9] Hadith: Al-Bukhari, *On Fasting* (9th c.). *A Reader on Islam: Passages from Standard Arabic Writings Illustrative of the Beliefs and Practices of Muslims*, ed. Arthur Jeffery. Mouton & Co, 1962.

3.10] Law: Abu Dawud al-Sijistani, *Compilation of the Jurisprudential Responses of Ahmad ibn Hanbal* (before 888). Chapters on Marriage and Divorce: Responses of Ibn Hanbal and Ibn Rahwayh, translated with introduction and notes by Susan A. Spectorsky. Copyright © 1993. Reprinted by permission of the University of Texas Press.

3.11] Fiction: *Sindbad the Sailor* (9th c.). *The Thousand and Once Nights: The Hunchback, Sindbad, And Other Tales*, trans. N.J. Dawood. Penguin Books, copyright © 1954. Reprinted by permission of The Penguin Group Ltd.

3.12] The minority–that is, Christian–view: *Chronicle of Albelda* (c.883). *Medieval Iberia: Readings from Christian, Muslim and Jewish Sources*, ed. Olivia Remie Constable. University of Pennsylvania Press, 1997. Reprinted by permission of the University of Pennsylvania Press.

3.13] An Islamic Andalusian voice: Ibn ʿAbd Rabbihi, *I Have Never Seen* (before 940). Ibn ʿAbd Rabbihi, "White Skin," *Poems of Arab Andalusia*, trans. Cola Franzen from the Spanish versions of Emilio García Gómez. City Lights Books, 1989, ISBN 0-87286-242-9. Reprinted by permission of the translator.

3.14] A Jewish poet in al-Andalus: Dunash ben Labrat, *There Came a Voice* (mid-10th c.). *Wine, Women and Death*, trans. and ed. Raymond Scheindlin. The Jewish Publication Society. © 1999 by Raymond Scheindlin. Reprinted by permission of the publisher.

3.15] The Imperial claims of the papacy: *The Donation of Constantine* (760s). *Carolingian Civilization: A Reader*, 2nd edition, ed. Paul Edward Dutton. Broadview Press, 2004. Reprinted by kind permission of the editor.

3.16] Charlemagne as the light of the world: Anonymous, *Once Again my Burdened Anchor* (early 9th c.). *Carolingian Civilization: A Reader*, 2nd edition, ed. Paul Edward Dutton. Broadview Press, 2004. Reprinted by kind permission of the editor.

3.17] Modeling the state on Old Testament Israel: *The Admonitio Generalis* (789). *Christianity Through the Thirteenth Century*, ed. Marshall W. Baldwin. Harper & Row Publishers, 1970.

3.18] Imperial administration: *Double Capitulary of Thionville for the missi* (805). *The Reign of Charlemagne: Documents on Carolingian Government and Administration*, ed. H.R. Loyn and John Percival. Copyright © 1975, St. Martin's Press. Reproduced with permission of Palgrave Macmillan.

3.19] Ideals of family and fidelity: Dhuoda, *Handbook for her Son* (841-843). Dhuoda, *Handbook for William: A Carolingian Woman's Counsel for Her Son*, translated and with an introduction by Carol Neel. Copyright © 1991 by the University of Nebraska Press. Reprinted by permission of the University of Nebraska Press.

Chapter 4

4.1] Fragmentation in the Islamic world: Al-Tabari, *The Defeat of the Zanj Revolt* (c.915). *The History of al-Tabari: The ʿAbbasid Recovery*, vol. 27, trans. Philip M. Fields. © 1987 State University of New York. Reprinted by permission. All rights reserved.

4.2] The powerful in the Byzantine countryside: Romanus Lecapenus, *Novel* (934). *The Land Legislation of the Macedonian Emperors*, trans. and ed. Eric McGeer. © 2000 by the Pontifical Institute of Mediaeval Studies, Toronto. Reprinted by permission of the publisher.

4.3] Donating to Cluny: Cluny's *Foundation Charter* (910) and various charters of donation (10th -11th c.). *Readings in Medieval History*, 3rd ed., ed. Patrick J. Geary. Broadview Press, 2003. Reprinted by kind permission of the editor.

4.5] The Peace of God at Bourges: Andrew of Fleury, *The Miracles of St. Benedict* (1040-1043). *The Peace of God: Social Violence and Religious Response in France Around the Year 1000*, ed. Thomas Head and Richard Landes. Copyright © 1992 by Cornell University. Reprinted by permission of the publisher.

4.6] A castellan's revenues and properties in Catalonia: *Charter* of *Guillem Guifred* (1041-1075). Pierre Bonnassie, *Debating the Middle Ages: Issues and Readings*, ed. Lester K. Little and Barbara H. Rosenwein. Blackwell Publishing, 1998, ISBN 1577-180007-0. Reprinted by permission of Blackwell Publishing.

4.7] Military life: Constantine VII Porphyrogenitus, *Military Advice to His Son* (950-958). *Constantine Porphyrogenitus: Three Treatises on Imperial Military Expeditions*, trans. John F. Haldon. From the Corpus Fontium Historiae Byzantinae Series. Vindobonensis, Österreichische Akademie der Wissenschaften und dem Institut für Byzantinistik und Neogräzistik der Universität Wien unter der Leitung von Herbert Hunger, 1997, ISBN 3-7001-1778-7. Reprinted by permission of the Österreichische Akademie der Wissenschaften.

4.8] Imperial rule: Michael Psellus, *Portrait of Basil II* (c.1063). *Fourteen Byzantine Rulers: The Chronographia of Michael Psellus*, translated with an introduction by E.R.A. Sewter. Penguin, 1966. Copyright © by the Estate of E.R.A. Sewter, 1966. Reprinted by permission of the publisher.

4.9] Political theory: Al-Farabi, *The Perfect State* (c.940-942). *Al-Farabi on the Perfect State: Abu Nasr Al-Farabi's Mabadi Ara Ahl Al-Madina Al-Fadila*, ed. and trans. Richard Walzer. Clarendon Press (Oxford University Press), copyright © 1985, ISBN 0-19-824505-X. Reprinted by permission of Oxford University Press.

4.10] Logic: Ibn Sina (Avicenna), *Treatise on Logic* (1020s or 1030s). *Avicenna's Treatise on Logic*: Part One of *Danesh-Name Alai* (*A concise Philosophical Encyclopedia and Autobiography*), ed. and trans. Farhang Zabeeh. Martinus Nijhoff, 1971, ISBN 90-247-5108-X. Reprinted with kind permission of Springer Science and Business Media.

4.11] Kievan Rus: *The Russian Primary Chronicle* (c.1113). *The Russian Primary Chronicle: Laurentian Text*, ed. and trans. Samuel Hazzard Cross and Olgerd P. Sherbowitz-Wetzor. Medieval Academy, 1953. Reprinted by permission of the Medieval Academy of America.

4.12] Hungary: King Stephen, *Laws* (1000-1038). *The Laws of the Medieval Kingdom of Hungary*, volume 1: *1000-1301*, trans. and ed. János M. Bak, György Bónis, and James Ross Sweeney. Charles Schlacks, Jr., Publisher, 1989.

4.13] An Ottonian queen: *The "Older Life" of Queen Mathilda* (973-974). *Queenship and Sanctity: The Lives of Mathilda and the Epitaph of Adelheid*, trans. Sean Gilsdorf. The Catholic University of America Press, 2004, ISBN 0-8132-1374-6. Used with permission: The Catholic University of America Press, Washington, D.C.

4.14] An Ottonian king: Thietmar of Merseberg, *The Accession of Henry II* (1013-1018). *Ottonian Germany: The Chronicon of Thietmar of Merseburg (975-1018)*, trans. David A. Warner. Manchester University Press, copyright © 2001. Reprinted by permission of Manchester University Press.

4.15] Literacy: King Alfred, Prefaces to Gregory the Great's *Pastoral Care* (c.890). *Alfred the Great: Asser's Life of King Alfred and Other Contemporary Sources*, trans. Simon Keynes and Michael Lapidge. Penguin Books, copyright © 1983. Reprinted by permission of the Penguin Group Ltd.

4.16] Literature: *Battle of Maldon* (not long after 991). *The Battle of Maldon and Other Old English Poems*, trans. Kevin Crossley-Holland, ed. Bruce Mitchell. Macmillan, London, and St. Martin's Press, New York, copyright © 1965 (reprinted 1966). Reprinted by permission of Palgrave Macmillan.

4.17] Law: King Æthelred, *Law Code* (1008). *English Historical Documents*: Vol. I: *c. 300-1042*, 2nd ed., ed. Dorothy Whitelock. Routledge, copyright © 1955 and 1979, re-issued by Routledge in 1996 and reprinted 2002 (first published in 1955 by Eyre and Spottiswoode Ltd.). Reproduced by permission of Routledge/Taylor & Francis Group, LLC.

Chapter 5

5.2] Local markets: Ibn Jubayr, *A Market near Aleppo* (1184). *Medieval Trade in the Mediterranean World*, trans. and ed. Robert S. Lopez and Irving W. Raymond. Columbia University Press, copyright © 1955, 1990, 2001, ISBN 0-231-12357-4. Reprinted by permission of Access Copyright on behalf of Columbia University Press.

5.3] The role of royal patronage: Henry I, *Privileges for the Citizens of London* (1130-1133). *English Historical Documents*: Vol. 2: *1042-1189*, 2nd ed., ed. David C. Douglas and George W. Greenaway. Routledge, copyright © 2001 (first edition, copyright 1953 by Eyre Methuen Ltd., published in the U.S.A. by Oxford University Press). Reproduced by permission of Routledge/Taylor & Francis Group, LLC.

5.4] The royal view: Henry IV, *Letter to Gregory VII* (1075). *Imperial Lives and Letters of the Eleventh Century*, trans. Theodor E. Mommsen, ed. Karl F. Morrison. Columbia University Press, copyright © 2000, ISBN 0-231-12121-0. Reprinted by permission of Access Copyright for Columbia University Press.

5.5] The papal view: Gregory VII, *Letter to Hermann of Metz* (1076). *The Register of Pope Gregory VII: 1073-1085*, trans. H.E.J. Cowdrey. Oxford University Press, copyright © 2002, ISBN 0-19-924980-6. Used by permission of Oxford University Press.

5.7] The Greek experience: Anna Comnena, *The Alexiad* (c.1148). *The Alexiad of Anna Comnenea*, trans. E.R.A. Sewter. Penguin Books, copyright © 1969. Used by permission of the Penguin Group Ltd.

5.8] A Westerner in the Holy Land: Stephen of Blois, *Letter to His Wife* (March 1098). *The Crusades: A Reader*, ed. S.J. Allen and Emilie Amt. Broadview Press, 2003. Reprinted by kind permission of the editors.

5.9] The Muslim reaction: Ibn al-Athir, *The First Crusade* (13th c.). *Arab Historians of the Crusades*, trans. Francesco Gabrieli and E.J. Costello. University of California Press, 1969. Copyright 1969, Routledge and Kegan Paul. Reprinted by permission of The Regents of the University of California.

5.10] The crusade in Spain and Portugal: *The Conquest of Lisbon* (1147-1148). *De expugnatione Lyxbonensi: The conquest of Lisbon*, trans. Charles Wendell David. Columbia University Press, copyright © 1936, 2001, ISBN 0-231-12122-9. Reprinted by permission of Access Copyright for Columbia University Press.

5.11] The pro-Norman position: William of Jumièges, *The Deeds of the Dukes of the Normans* (c.1070). *The Norman Conquest*, ed. and trans. R. Allen Brown. Edward Arnold Publishers, copyright © 1984, ISBN 0-7131-6406-9. Reprinted by permission of Boydell & Brewer Ltd.

5.12] The native position: "Florence of Worcester," *Chronicle of Chronicles* (early 12th c.). *English Historical Documents*: Vol. 2: *1042-1189*, 2nd edition, ed. David C. Douglas and George W. Greenaway. Copyright © 2001 (first edition, copyright 1953 by Eyre Methuen Ltd., published in the U.S.A. by Oxford University Press). Reproduced by permission of Routledge/Taylor & Francis Group, LLC.

5.13] Exploiting the Conquest: *Domesday Book* (1087). *Domesday Book: A Complete Translation*, ed. Ann Williams and G.H. Martin. Alecto Historical Editions (Domesday), copyright © 1992 (Penguin Books, 2002). Reprinted by permission of Alecto Historical Editions.

5.14] Logic: Abelard, *Glosses on Porphyry* (c.1100). *Basic Issues in Medieval Philosophy: Selected Readings Presenting the Interactive Discourses Among the Major Figures*, ed. Richard N. Bosley and Martin M. Tweedale. Broadview Press, 1997. Reprinted by kind permission of the editors.

5.16] Rethinking the religious life: Heloise, *Letter* (1130s). *The Letters of Abelard and Heloise*, trans. Betty Radice. Penguin Books, copyright © 1974 (reprinted 1975, 1976). Reprinted by permission of the Penguin Group Ltd.

5.17] Medicine: *The Trotula* (c.1250, based on 12th-c. sources). *The Trotula: A Medieval Compendium of Women's Medicine*, ed. and trans. Monica H. Green. University of Pennsylvania Press, copyright © 2001, ISBN 0-8122-3789-4. Reprinted by permission of the University of Pennsylvania Press.

5.18] The Cistercian view: St. Bernard, *Apologia* (1125). *The Cistercian World: Monastic Writings of the Twelfth Century*, trans. and ed. Pauline Matarasso. Penguin, copyright © 1993. Reprinted by permission of the Penguin Group Ltd.

5.19] The Cluniac view: Peter the Venerable, *Miracles* (mid 1130s-mid 1150s). Peter the Venerable, *De miraculis* I.9, ed. Denise Bouthillier, trans. Barbara H. Rosenwein. Brepols, copyright © 1988. Printed by permission of the translator.

Chapter 6

6.1] Saladin: Ibn Shaddad, *The Rare and Excellent History of Saladin* (1198-1216). Baha' al-Din Ibn Shaddad. *The Rare and Excellent History of Saladin or al-Nawadir al-Sultaniyya wa'l-Mahasin al-Yusufiyya*, trans. D.S. Richards. Ashgate Publishing, copyright © 2001, ISBN 07546-0143-9. Reprinted by kind permission of the translator and Ashgate Publishing Limited.

6.2] The lone Byzantine warrior: *Digenis Akritis* (12th c.). *Digenis Akritis: The Grottaferrata and Escorial versions*, ed. and trans. Elizabeth Jeffreys. Cambridge University Press, copyright © 1998. Reprinted with the permission of Cambridge University Press.

6.3] The Northern Crusade: Helmold, *The Chronicle of the Slavs* (1167-1168). Helmold, Priest of Bosau, *The Chronicle of the Slavs*, trans. Francis Joseph Tschan. Columbia University Press, copyright © 1935. Reprinted by permission of Access Copyright for the Columbia University Press.

6.4] The Fourth Crusade: Nicetas Choniates, *O City of Byzantium* (c.1215). *O City of Byzantium: Annals of Niketas Choniatēs*, trans. Harry J. Magoulias. © 1984, reprinted with the permission of the Wayne State University Press.

6.5] English common law: *The Assize of Clarendon* (1166). *English Historical Documents*: Vol. 2: *1042-1189*, 2nd ed., ed. David C. Douglas and George W. Greenaway. Routledge, copyright © 2001 (first edition, copyright 1953 by Eyre Methuen Ltd., published in the U.S.A. by Oxford University Press). Reproduced by permission of Routledge/Taylor & Francis Group, LLC.

6.6] English litigation on the ground: *The Costs of Richard of Anstey's Law Suit* (1158-1163). *English Historical Documents*: Vol. 2: *1042-1189*, 2nd ed., ed. David C. Douglas and George W. Greenaway. Routledge, copyright © 2001 (first edition, copyright 1953 by Eyre Methuen Ltd., published in the U.S.A. by Oxford University Press). Reproduced by permission of Routledge/Taylor & Francis Group, LLC.

6.7] The legislation of a Spanish king: *The Laws of Cuenca* (1189-1193). *The Code of Cuenca: Municipal Law on the Twelfth-Century Castilian Frontier*, trans. James F. Powers. University of Pennsylvania Press, 2000, ISBN 0-8122-3545-2. Reprinted by permission of the University of Pennsylvania Press.

6.9] Doing business: A Genoese *societas* (1253). *Medieval Trade in the Mediterranean World: Illustrative Documents*, trans. Robert S. Lopez and Irving W. Raymond. Columbia University Press, copyright © 1955, 1990, 2001. Reprinted by permission of Access Copyright on behalf of Columbia University Press.

6.10] Women's work: *Guild Regulations of the Parisian Silk Fabric Makers* (13th c.). *Women's Lives in Medieval Europe: A Sourcebook*, ed. Emilie Amt. Routledge, Chapman and Hall, 1993. Reproduced by permission of Routledge/Taylor & Francis Group, LLC.

6.11] Men's work: *Guild Regulations of the Shearers of Arras* (1236). *A Source Book for Medieval Economic History*, trans. R.C. Cave and H.H. Coulson. Milwaukee: The Bruce Publishing Co., 1936; New York: Biblio and Tannen, 1965.

6.12] The growth of papal business: Innocent III, *Letters* (1200-1202). *Selected Letters of Pope Innocent III concerning England (1198-1216)*, ed. C.R. Cheney and W.H. Semple. Thomas Nelson and Sons, 1953.

6.13] Petitioning the papacy: *Register of Thomas of Hereford* (1281). *English Historical Documents*: Vol. 3: *1189-1327*, ed. Harry Rothwell. Routledge, 1975 (first published in 1975 by Eyre and Spottiswoode Ltd., re-issued in 1996 by Routledge and reprinted in 2002). Reproduced by permission of Routledge/Taylor & Francis Group, LLC.

6.14] Mocking the papal bureaucracy: *The Gospel according to the Marks of Silver* (c.1200). *The Medieval Record: Sources of Medieval History*, ed. Alfred J. Andrea. Copyright © 1997 by Houghton Mifflin. Reprinted by permission of Houghton Mifflin Company.

6.15] Henry II and Becket: *Constitutions of Clarendon* (1164). *English Historical Documents*: Vol. 2: *1042-1189*, 2nd ed., ed. David C. Douglas and George W. Greenaway. Routledge, copyright © 2001 (first edition, copyright 1953 by Eyre Methuen Ltd., published in the U.S.A. by Oxford University Press). Reproduced by permission of Routledge/Taylor & Francis Group, LLC.

6.16] Emperor and pope: *Diet of Besançon* (1157). *The Deeds of Frederick Barbarossa. By Otto of Freising and His Continuator, Rahewin*, trans. Charles Christopher Mierow. W.W. Norton & Company, 1966 (original copyright 1953, Columbia University Press), ISBN 0-393-09697-0. Reprinted by permission of Access Copyright for the Columbia University Press.

6.17] King and nobles: *Magna Carta* (1215). *English Historical Documents*: Vol. 3: *1189-1327*, ed. Harry Rothwell. Routledge, 1975 (first published in 1975 by Eyre and Spottiswoode Ltd., re-issued in 1996 by Routledge and reprinted in 2002). Reprinted by permission of Routledge/Taylor & Francis Group, LLC.

6.18] Epic poetry: *Raoul de Cambrai* (1180-1223). *Raoul de Cambrai*, ed. and trans. Sarah Kay. Oxford University Press, 1992, ISBN 0-19-815868-8. Used by permission of Oxford University Press.

6.19] A troubadour poem of love: Jaufré Rudel, *When Days are Long in May* (c.1125-1150). *Lyrics of the Troubadours and Trouvères*, trans. Frederick Goldin. Copyright © 1973 by Frederick Goldin. Used by permission of Doubleday, a division of Random House, Inc.

6.20] A poem of war: Bertran de Born, *I Love the Joyful Time* (12th c.). *Lyrics of the Troubadours and Trouvères*, trans. Frederick Goldin. Copyright © 1973 by Frederick Goldin. Used by permission of Doubleday, a division of Random House, Inc.

6.21] Song of a *trobairitz*: Comtessa de Dia, *I've Been in Great Anguish* (c.1200?). *The Writings of Medieval Women*, trans. Marcelle Thiébaux, vol. 14, series B. Garland Library of Medieval Literature. Garland Publishing, 1987. Reproduced by permission of Routledge/Taylor & Francis Group, LLC.

6.22] Fabliaux: *Browny, the Priest's Cow* and *The Priest Who Peeked* (13th c.). *Cuckolds, Clerics & Countrymen: Medieval French Fabliaux*, trans. John Duval, ed. Raymond Eichmann. Reprinted by permission of the University of Arkansas Press.

6.23] Disciplining and purifying Christendom: *Decrees of Lateran IV* (1215). *Decrees of the Ecumenical Councils*: Vol. 1: *Nicaea I to Lateran V*, ed. Norman P. Tanner. Sheed & Ward and Georgetown University Press, 1990, ISBN 0-87840-490-2.

6.24] Art and architecture as religious devotion: Suger, *On What was Done under his Administration* (1148–1149). *Abbot Suger on the Abbey Church of St. Denis and its Art Treasures*, 2nd ed., ed. and trans. Erwin Panofsky. © 1946, Princeton University Press, 1974 renewed PUP. Reprinted by permission of Princeton University Press.

6.25] Devotion through poverty: *Peter Waldo in the Chronicle of Laon* (1173-1178). *The Birth of Popular Heresy*, ed. and trans. R.I. Moore. St. Martin's Press, copyright © 1975. Reproduced with permission of Palgrave Macmillan.

6.26] Devotion through mysticism: Jacques de Vitry, *The Life of Mary of Oignies* (1213). *Medieval Women's Visionary Literature*, ed. Elizabeth Alvilda Petroff, trans. Margot King. Oxford University Press, copyright © 1986. Reprinted by permission of Brepols publishers N.V., Turnhout, Belgium.

6.27] The mendicant movement: St. Francis, *The Canticle to Brother Sun* (1225). *Francis and Clare: The Complete Works*, trans. Regis J. Armstrong, O.F.M. CAP. and Ignatius C. Brady, O.F.M. The Classics of Western Spirituality, copyright © 1982 by Paulist Press, Inc., New York/ Mahwah, NJ. Used with permission of Paulist Press. <www.paulistpress.com>.

6.28] The expulsion of the Jews from Bury St. Edmunds: Jocelin of Brakelond, *Chronicle* (1190-1202). *The Chronicle of Jocelin of Brakelond: concerning the Acts of Samson, Abbot of the Monastery of St. Edmund*, trans. H.E. Butler. Thomas Nelson and Sons, 1949.

6.29] Burning heretics in Germany: *Chronicle of Trier* (1231). *Heresies of the High Middle Ages*, ed. and trans. Walter L. Wakefield and Austin P. Evans. Columbia University Press, copyright © 1969. Reprinted by permission of Access Copyright on behalf of Columbia University Press.

Chapter 7

7.1] The Mongols speak: *The Secret History of the Mongols* (first half of the 13th c.). *The Secret History of the Mongols: The Origin of Chinghis Khan*, trans. Francis Woodman Cleaves, adapted by Paul Kahn. North Point Press, 1984, ISBN 0-86547-138-X.

7.2] A Mongol reply to the pope: Guyuk Khan, *Letter to Pope Innocent IV* (1246). *The Mongol Mission: Narratives and Letters of the Franciscan Missionaries in Mongolia and China in the Thirteenth and Fourteenth Centuries*, ed. Christopher Dawson. Sheed & Ward, copyright © 1955. Copyright administered by The Continuum International Publishing Group Ltd. Used by permission.

7.3] Accommodations: Mengu-Temir Khan, *Charter to Protect the Russian Church* (1308). "A Mongol Charter...," *A Source Book for Russian History from Early Times to 1917*: Vol. 1: *Early Times to the Late Seventeenth Century*, ed. George Vernadsky. Yale University Press, copyright © 1972, selections from page 49. Reprinted by permission of Yale University Press.

7.5] Mongol trade routes: Marco Polo, *The Travels* (c.1300). *The Travels of Marco Polo*, trans. Ronald Latham. Penguin, copyright © 1958. Reprinted by permission of the Penguin Group Ltd.

7.6] The *popolo* gains power: *The Ghibelline Annals of Piacenza* (1250). *The Towns of Italy in the Later Middle Ages*, ed. and trans. Trevor Dean. Manchester University Press, copyright © 2000, ISBN 0-7190-5203-3. Reprinted by permission of Manchester University Press.

7.8] Hospitals: *Charters for Bury St. Edmunds* (1248-1272). *Charters of the Medieval Hospitals of Bury St Edmunds*, ed. Christopher Harper-Bill. The Boydell Press for the Suffolk Records Society, copyright © 1994. Reprinted by kind permission of the editor.

7.9] Famine at Constantinople: Athanasius I, Patriarch of Constantinople, *Letters* (1306-1307). *The Correspondence of Athanasius I Patriarch of Constantinople: Letters to the Emperor Andronicus II, Members of the Imperial Family and Officials*, ed. and trans. A. Maffry Talbot. Dumbarton Oaks Center for Byzantine Studies, 1975. Courtesy of Dumbarton Oaks Research Library and Collection, Trustees for Harvard University, Washington, D.C.

7.10] Inquisition: Jacques Fournier, *Episcopal Register* (1318-1325). "Witnesses against Guillaume Austatz of Ornolac...," *Medieval Popular Religion, 1000-1500: A Reader*, ed. John Shinners. Broadview Press, 1997. Reprinted by kind permission of the editor.

7.11] Procedures for isolating lepers: *Sarum manual* (based on materials from *c.*1360s). "Ceremony for the exclusion of a Leper," *Medieval Popular Religion, 1000-1500: A Reader*, ed. John Shinners. Broadview Press, 1997. Originally published in *The Medieval Hospitals of England*, trans. Rotha Mary Clay. Frank Cass, 1909. From A. Jefferies, *Manuale ad Usum Percelebris Ecclesie Sarisburiensis.*

Henry Bradshaw Society, 1960, v. 91, pp. 182-185. Reprinted by kind permission of the Henry Bradshaw Society.

7.12] Jews in England: *Statute of the Jewry* (1275) and *Petition of the "Commonalty" of the Jews* (shortly after 1275). *English Historical Documents*: Vol. 3: *1189-1327*, ed. Harry Rothwell. Routledge, 1975 (first published in 1975 by Eyre and Spottiswoode, re-issued in 1996 by Routledge and reprinted in 2002). Reproduced by permission of Routledge/Taylor & Francis Group, LLC.

7.13] A charismatic king: Joinville, *The Life of St. Louis* (1272). *Joinville and Villehardouin: Chronicles of the Crusades*, trans. Rene Hague. The Makers of Christendom series, ed. Christopher Dawson. Sheed & Ward (Penguin Group), copyright © 1955. Copyright administered by The Continuum International Publishing Group Ltd. Used by permission.

7.18] Assembly of the Estates General in Paris: *Grand Chronicles of France* (1314). *Medieval Representative Institutions: Their Origins and Nature*, ed. William M. Bowsky, trans. Thomas N. Bisson. The Dryden Press, copyright © 1973. Reprinted by kind permission of Thomas Bisson.

7.19] Scholasticism: Thomas Aquinas, *Summa against the Gentiles* (1259-1264). *Summa contra gentiles*: Book 3: *Providence*, trans. Vernon J. Bourke. Copyright © 1956 by Doubleday, a division of Random House, Inc. Used by permission of Doubleday, a division of Random House, Inc.

7.20] Mysticism: Meister Eckhart, *Sermon 101* (1298-1305). *Meister Eckhart: Sermons & Treatises*, vol. 1, trans. and ed. M O'C. Walshe. Element Books, 1987 (first published by Watkins Publishing, 1979).

7.21] Italian comes into its own: Dante, *Inferno*, Canto 5 (Paolo and Francesca); *Paradiso*, Canto 22 (Meeting with St. Benedict) (1313-1321). Dante Alighieri, *The Divine Comedy: Inferno*, 2 Vols. © 1970 Princeton University Press, 1998 renewed PUP. Reprinted by permission of Princeton University Press.

7.22] Romance: *Sir Gawain and the Green Knight* (last quarter of 14th c.). *Sir Gawain and the Green Knight*, ed. and trans. James Winny. Broadview Press, copyright © 1992, reprinted 1997. Reprinted by kind permission of the estate of James Winny.

7.23] Medieval drama: *Directions for an Annunciation play* (14th c.). "Directions for an Annunciation play," *Medieval Popular Religion, 1000-1500: A Reader*, ed. John Shinners. Broadview Press, copyright © 1997. Reprinted by kind permission of the editor.

7.24] The feast of Corpus Christi: *The Life of Juliana of Mont-Cornillon* (1261-1264). *The Life of Juliana of Mont-Cornillon*, trans. Barbara Newman. Peregrina Translations Series 13. Peregrina Publishing, copyright © 1988. Reprinted by permission of Brepols publishers N.V., Turnhout, Belgium.

Chapter 8

8.1] A medical view: Nicephorus Gregoras, *Roman History* (*c.*1350). Christos S. Bartsocas, "Two Fourteenth Century Greek Descriptions of the 'Black Death'," *Journal of the History of Medicine and Allied Sciences* 21. Oxford University Press, copyright © 1966. Reprinted by permission of Oxford University Press and Christos S. Bartsocas.

8.2] Processions at Damascus: Ibn Battuta, *Travels* (before 1368). *The Travels of Ibn Battuta: A.D. 1325-1354*, vol. 1, trans. H.A.R. Gibb, ed. C. Defremery and B.R. Sanguinetti. Cambridge University Press for the Hakluyt Society, copyright © 1958. Permission granted by the David Higham Associates on behalf of The Hakluyt Society.

8.3] Prayers at York: Archbishop William, *Letter to His Official at York* (July 1348). *The Black Death*, ed. and trans. Rosemary Horrox. Manchester University Press, copyright © 1994. Reprinted by permission of Manchester University Press.

8.4] Blaming the Jews: Heinrich von Diessenhoven, *On the Persecution of the Jews* (*c.*1350). *The Black Death*, ed. and trans. Rosemary Horrox. Manchester University Press, copyright © 1994. Reprinted by permission of Manchester University Press.

8.5] A legislative response: *Ordinances against the Spread of Plague at Pistoia* (1348). *The Black Death*, ed. and trans. Rosemary Horrox. Manchester University Press, copyright © 1994. Reprinted by permission of Manchester University Press.

8.6] A Turkish Hero: Ashikpashazade, *Osman Comes to Power* (late 15th c.). Printed by kind permission of Robert Dankoff.

8.8] Before the fall: Patriarch Anthony, *Letter to the Russian Church* (1395). Deno John Geanakoplos, *Byzantium: Church, Society, and Civilization Seen through Contemporary Eyes*. Copyright © 1984 by The University of Chicago. Reprinted by permission of the University of Chicago Press.

8.9] The fall bewailed: George Sphrantzes, *Chronicle* (before 1477). *The Fall of the Byzantine Empire: A Chronicle by George Sphrantzes, 1401-1477*, trans. Marios Philippides. The University of Massachusetts Press, copyright © 1980. Reprinted by permission of The University of Massachusetts Press.

8.10] After the fall: Archbishop Genady of Novgorod and Dmitry Gerasimov, *The Tale of the White Cowl* (end of the 15th c.). "The Tale of the White Cowl," *Medieval Russia's Epics, Chronicles, and Tales*, ed. and trans. Serge A. Zenkovsky. Copyrights © 1963, 1974 by Serge A. Zenkovsky; renewed © 1991 by Betty Jean Zenkovsky. Used by permission of Dutton, a division of Penguin Group (USA) Inc.

8.12] National feeling: Jeanne d'Arc, *Letter to the English* (1429). *Medieval Hagiography: An Anthology*, ed. Thomas Head. Garland

Publishing, copyright © 2000. Reprinted by permission of Taylor & Francis Publishing, U.S.A. Reproduced by permission of Routledge/Taylor & Francis Group, LLC.

8.14] The humiliation of Avignon: St. Catherine of Siena, *Letter to Pope Gregory XI* (1376). "Letters to Pope Gregory XI," *Letters of St. Catherine of Siena*, Vol. II, trans. Suzanne Noffke. MRTS Volume 203. Arizona Center for Medieval and Renaissance Studies, 2001. Copyright Arizona Board of Regents for Arizona State University. Reprinted with permission.

8.15] The Conciliarist movement: Jean Gerson, *Sermon at the Council of Constance* (1415). *Unity, Heresy and Reform, 1378-1460: The Conciliar Response to the Great Schism*, ed. C.M.D. Crowder. Limestone Press. Copyright © C.M.D. Crowder 1977, 1986. Reproduced by permission of Edward Arnold.

8.16] The Hussite program: *The Four Articles of Prague* (1420). *The Crusade against Heretics in Bohemia, 1418-1437: Sources and Documents for the Hussite Crusades*, trans. and ed. Thomas A. Fudge. Ashgate Publishing, copyright © 2002. Reprinted by permission of Ashgate Publishing.

8.17] The Catholic rally against the Hussites: Emperor Sigismund, *Crusading Letter* (1421). *The Crusade against Heretics in Bohemia, 1418-1437: Sources and Documents for the Hussite Crusades*, trans. and ed. Thomas A. Fudge. Ashgate Publishing, copyright © 2002. Reprinted by permission of Ashgate Publishing.

8.18] Piety in the Low Countries: Salome Sticken, *Formula for Living* (*c.*1435). *Devotio Moderna: Basic Writings*, trans. and introduced by John Van Engen. The Classics of Western Spirituality. Copyright © 1988 by John Van Engen, Paulist Press, Inc. New York/Mahwah, N.J. Used with permission of Paulist Press. <www.paulistpress.com>.

8.19] Re-evaluating antiquity: Cincius Romanus, *Letter to His Most Learned Teacher Franciscus de Fiana* (1416). *Two Renaissance Book Hunters: The Letters of Poggius Bracciolini to Nicolaus de Niccolis*, trans. and ed. Phyllis Walter Goodhart Gordan. Columbia University Press, 1974. Reprinted by permission of Access Copyright for Columbia University Press.

8.20] The search for a patron: George of Trebizond, *Prefatory letter to Mehmed II* (1465-1466). *Collectanea Trapezuntiana: Texts, Documents and Bibliographies of George of Trebizond*, Vol. 8, ed. John Monfasani. MRTS Volume 25. Medieval and Renaissance Texts and Studies, 1984. Copyright Arizona Board of Regents for Arizona State University. Reprinted with permission.

8.22] Defending women: Christine de Pisan, *The Book of the City of Ladies* (1404-1407). Christine de Pizan, *The Book of the City of Ladies*, trans. Earl Jeffrey Richards. Copyright © 1982. Reprinted by permission of Persea Books, Inc. (New York).

8.23] Satirizing society: François Villon, *Testament* (1461). *Complete*

Works of Francois Villon, trans. and ed. Anthony Bonner. Copyright © 1960 by Bantam Books, a division of Random House, Inc. Used by permission of Bantam Books, a division of Random House, Inc.

8.24] An Islamic Renaissance thinker: Ibn Khaldun, *Muqaddimah* (1377-1381). Ibn Khaldun, *The Muqaddimah*, trans. Franz Rosenthal. © 1958, 1967 by PUP. Reprinted by permission of Princeton University Press.

8.25] Taking Mexico: Hernán Cortés, *The Second Letter* (1520). Hernan Cortes, *Letters from Mexico*, trans. and ed. Anthony Pagden. Originally published by Grossman Publishers in 1971, first published in the US as a Yale Nota Bene book in 2001, revised edition copyright © Yale University, 1986. Reprinted by permission of Yale University Press.

Maps

Frontispiece map: *Important Places Frequently Mentioned in the Sources*

Map 3.1] Major European Slave Exports (700-900). Michael Mc-Cormick, "Map 25.1: Main European Slave Exports: A.D. 700-900," *Origins of the European Economy: Communications and Commerce A.D. 300-900.* Cambridge University Press, 2001. Reprinted with the permission of Cambridge University Press.

Plates

Plate 4.1] Christianity comes to Denmark: *The Jelling Monument* (960s). Image reprinted by permission of the Antikvarisk-Topografisk Arkiv, The National Museum, Copenhagen, Denmark.

Plate 5.1] The West: *T-O Map* (12th c.). Africa as the Largest Continent. From a twelfth-century manuscript of the De bello Jugurthino of Sallust, MS. lat. 5751, fol. 18r, diameter of the original: 4 cm. Image reprinted by permission of the Biliothèque Nationale de France, Paris.

Plate 5.2] The West: *The Image of the World* (late 12th c.). Parker Library, MS 66, p. 2, Corpus Christi College, Cambridge. Image reprinted by permission of Corpus Christi College, Cambridge.

Plate 5.3] The Islamic world: *Directions to Mecca* (12th c.). Oxford Bodleian Library, MS. Marsh 592 folio 88 verso. Image reprinted by permission of the Bodleian Library, University of Oxford.

Plate 5.4] Byzantium: *The Inhabited World* from a copy of Ptolemy's *Geography* (13th c.). Rome, Biblioteca Apostolica Vaticana Urbinas Graecus 82, fols. 60v-61r. Image reprinted by permission of the Biblioteca Apostolica Vaticana.

Plate 5.5] The Conquest depicted: *The Bayeux Tapestry* (end of the 11th c.). Musée de la Tapisserie de Bayeux (The Oath Scene 1, detail). Image reprinted by special permission of the City of Bayeux.

Plate 5.6] Gilbert of Poitiers, *Gloss on Psalm 101* (c.1117). Troyes, Bibliothèque Municipale 988 folio 157 verso. Photographie: P. Jacquinot. Image reprinted by permission of Médiathéque de l'agglomération troyenne (France).

Plate 5.7] The "standard gloss": *Glossa Ordinaria on Psalm 101* (1130s). Paris: Bibliothèque Mazarine MS. 89, fol. 136 and 136v. Image reprinted by permission of the Bibliothèque Mazarine.

Plate 8.1] A new kind of map: Gabriel de Valseca, *Portolan Chart* (1447). Paris, Bibliothèque Nationale de France, Rés. Ge. C 4607. Image reprinted by permission of the Bibliothèque Nationale de France.

Cover

Seated monk (detail), from MS on the 4th book of Gratian's Decretales. Lons-le-Saunier, Archives Departmentales du Jura, MS 22, Vol. 2. Reprinted by permission of the Archives Départementales du Jura.

The editor of the book and the publisher have made every attempt to locate the authors of copyrighted materials or their heirs and assigns, and would be grateful for information that would allow them to correct any errors or omissions in a subsequent edition of the work.

INDEX

Almundar, 168

Amarra, 133

Amasea, 9

Amaya, 167

Ambrose, Saint (339-397), 283-84, 302, 354

Amé de Geneva, 514

Amiens, 44

Amir Canal, 203

Amisus area, 502

Amul, 198

Anastasioupolis, 74

Anastasius, patriarch (d.754), 85

Anastasius I, emp. (r.491-518), 284

Anastasius II, pope (496-498), 284

Anastasius II Artemis, emp. (r.714-715), 125

Anatolia, 74, 144, 225n5, 294n1, 338, 432, 492n2. *See also* Asia Minor

Ancyra, 74

al-Andalus/Andalusia, 170, 296. *See also* Spain

Andrew, Saint, 54

Andrew of Fleury, 219

Andronicus II Palaeologus (r.1281-1328), 432

Anian II, bishop of St. Asaph, 367

Ankara, 492

Anna Comnena (1083-1148), 290, 344

Anonimal Chronicle of St. Mary's, York, 518

Ansedeus, 213

Anselm, archbishop and Saint (d.1109), 373n5, 450, 467n2

Anselm of Laon (d.1117), 318

Antony, Saint (d.356), 36-42, 47, 112, 328

Anthony IV, patriarch (r.1389-1390), 500

Antioch, 85, 144, 175, 293-99

Antiochus, king of Syria, 209

Antiochus, Praetorian Prefect, 13, 85

Apollinarios, patriarch of Alexandria, 144

Apologia [of St. Bernard] (1125), 327

Appleton, William, 523

Aquinas, Thomas, Saint (1225-1274), 461

Aquitaine/Aquitainia, 43, 126, 187n2

Arabia, 229, 294, 545

Aragon, 302

Arcadius, emp. (395-408), 12-13

Archelaus, Augustal Prefect, 13

Arghun-Shah, 484

Aribert II, king (r.701-712), 125

Aristotle (384-322 B.C.E.), 234, 235n1, 313, 323, 461, 462n1, 464n2, 528, 538, 544

Arius, Alexandrian priest, 19, 81-82

Armenia, 294

Arnulf, bishop, 253-54

'Arqua, 299

Arras, 363

Asaph, Saint, 368

Ascalon, 299, 337

al-A'sha, 86

Ashikpashazade (1392-1481), 492, 512

Ashtara, 335

Asia Minor, 290, 297. *See also* Anatolia

Askar Rayhan, 202-3

Assam, Turkish prince, 294

Assisi, 408

Assize of Clarendon (1166), 350-52, 380n8

Astorga, 167-68

Athanasius, bishop of Alexandria (d.373), 35n1, 36, 47

Athanasius I, patriarch (r.1289-1293 and 1303-1309), 432

Æthelred II the Unready (r.978-1016), 238, 262

Athies, 49, 54

Athulf, 255

Athyra, 290

Atsiz ibn Uwaq, 297

Attila, king of the Huns (d.453), 421n3

Augsburg, 486

Augustine, archbishop of Canterbury (d.c.605), 97-101, 104, 257

Augustine, St., Bishop of Hippo (354-430), 21, 28, 231, 316, 317n6, 320, 323, 443, 465, 468, 552

Aunemundus, bishop of Lyon (c.650-c.660), 106n9

Ausonia, 251

Austatz, Guillaume, 435-42, 458

Austrasia, 114

Austria, 486

Authié, Pierre, heretic, 439

Autun, 112-13, 115, 118, 211

Avarice and the Avaricious (850s?), 133

Avicenna. *See* Ibn Sina, known as Avicenna (980-1037)

Avignon, 435, 525

Avitus, bishop of Vienne, 58

Aya Nikola, 492, 495

Baden, 487

Baghdad, 133, 157, 162-63, 165, 198-99, 231, 299, 554-55

Baldwin, count of Flanders, 344

Baldwin of Boulogne (d.1118), 296, 298

Balgatia, 74

Balkaiz, 167

Ball, John, 520-21

Balthild, queen, 112-13

Bamberg, 253

Bampton, Thomas, 519, 521

Bar Musawir Canal, 200

Barbavera, Pietro, 513

Barbete, Stephen, 460

Basel, 487

Basil, duke, 126-27

Basil, Lord Chamberlain, 227-28

Basil I the Macedonian, emp. (r.867-886), 136n1, 225

Basil II the Bulgar-Slayer, emp. (r.963-1025), 227-30, 238n1, 252, 338

Basra, 133, 159-60, 163, 165, 198

Bassin, king, 48

Battle of Maldon, 258-61

Baudonivia, 53

Orihuela, 92
Orléans, 60, 517–18
Ornolac, 435–39
Orton Waterville, 310–11
Osimo, 127
Osman Ghazi, 492–95, 512
Ostrevan, region of, 513
Oswiu (d.670), 106
Otto, count palatine of Bavaria, 376
Otto (c.830/40-912), duke of Saxony, 244–45
Otto I, emp. (r.936-973), 246–48, 252
Otto II, emp. (r.961-983), 248, 250n5, 251–52
Otto III, emp. (r.983-1002), 253
Ouse River, 306
Ovid, 321n3
Oviedo, 167–68

Paderborn, 254
Padua, 476
Paglia, Orlando, 361-62
Palaeologus, Andreas, 505
Palaeologus, Manuel, 503
Palladius, Praetorian Prefect, 11
Pamiers, 435, 437–39, 441, 456
Pannonia, 43
Paris, 120–21, 318, 362, 458–59, 461, 513, 518
Parma, 428, 476
Passion of Leudegar (680s), 112
Pastoral Care, 256-57
Patak, 421
Patience, empress, 502
Paul, earl of Orkney, 306
Paul, Saint, 23n1, 40, 74, 107, 123, 174–75, 177, 179, 209, 211–12, 253, 282, 285, 468, 485, 528
Paul the patrician, 126–27
Paulinus, bishop of Tyre, 5–6
Paulinus, bishop of York and Rochester (d.644), 100, 106
Pavia, 43
Peace Agreement between the Ottoman Sultan Mehmed II and Signoria of Venice (1478), 497
Peace of God, 219
Pelekanum, 292
Peña Santa, 167
Penitential of Finnian, 109–12
Pentapolis, 127
Percy, Thomas, 522
Perfect State (c.940-942), 231
Périgord region, 390
Péronne, 50
Persia, 159
Persiceto, 127
Pertenhall, 311
Peter, bishop of Oporto, 300–301
Peter, bishop of Senlis, 402
Peter, duke of Rome, 127
Peter, Saint, 77, 107–8, 117, 122, 125–26, 172, 174–75, 177, 209,

211–13, 282–83, 285, 457, 473, 485
Peter de Fontaines, 453
Peter of Amiens, 346
Peter of Winchester, 378
Peter the Hermit, 290
Peter the Venerable (c.1093-1156), 331–32
Peter Waldo (d.bef.1218), 404–5, 408
Peterborough, 310–11
Petition of the "Commonality" of the Jews (shortly after 1275), 444, 446
Pevensey, 304, 307
Phidias (*fl. c.*475-430 B.C.E.), 537
Philea, 290, 344
Philip II Augustus, king of France (r.1180-1223), 362, 384
Philip IV The Fair, king of France (r.1285-1314), 448n1, 449, 455–56, 458–60
Philip VI, king of France (r.1328-1350), 514
Philip of Valois, 512
Philippa of Hainaut, 512
Philippe de Grèves (d.c.1236), also called Philip the Chancellor, 481n7
Philippicus Bardanes, emp. (r.711-713), 125
Philotheus, 507–11
Philpott, John, 524
Phocas, Bardas, 228n2
Phocas, emp. (r.602-610), 105
Photius (820-c.897), 143–44, 146, 539
Phrygia, 223–24
Piacenza, 428–29
Pibo, bishop, 284
Pippin III, king of Franks (d.768), 181n7, 402
Pisa, 488
Pistoia, 488–91
Plato, 313–14, 464, 528
Plato, archdeacon, 66–67
Plessington, Robert, 521
Plön, 343
Pöhlde, 255
Poitiers, 47, 51, 55–56, 69, 213, 218
Poitou, 451
Poland, 238n3
Polvorosa, 168
Polyainos (*fl.* 2nd c. C.E.), 224
Polyptyque of the Church of Saint Mary of Marseille (814-815), 130
Ponthieu, 304
Pontius Pilate, 144, 543
Porphyry (d.c.300), 313
Portolan Chart (1447), 556
Praxiteles (*fl. c.* 370-330 B.C.E.), 537
Pribislav, 342
Priest Who Peeked (13th c.), 391
Priscian, 536
Privileges for the Citizens of London (1130-1133), 279
Procopius (c.500-after 562), 15–16
Prologue to the Gospel (863-867), 146
Propontis (Sea of Marmara), 290, 292

Provence, 130
Psellus, Michael (1018–c.1092), 227, 237, 252, 338
Pseudo-Dionysius (*fl. c.*500), 79, 401, 457, 467–68
Ptolemy (*fl.* 2nd c. C.E.), 276, 538–39
Puerto de la Leña, 557n3
Puliti, Giovanni, 361-62

Qal'at Bani Hammad, 555
al-Qayrawan, 554–55
Quedlinburg, 247, 249, 252
"Queen of Sheba," 545n1
Quieret, Hugh, 513
Quilij Arslan II (r.1156–1192), 278n1
Qur'an Suras, 89
Quraysh, 148–49
Qurra ibn Sharik, 93

Raban, 296, 344
Raculf (Grossi family?), 211
Radegund, Saint, 47–57, 405, 442, 478
Radolfzell, 487
Raimodis, 213
Rainald of Dassel, 376
Ralph, prior of St. Oswald (Yorkshire) (r.1199-1208), 367n1
Ramla, 337
Ranieri of Verona, 361
Raoul, count, 292–93
Raoul de Cambrai (1180-1223), 213, 384–88, 473
Rare and Excellent History of Saladin (1198-1216), 334
Ratislav, 146
Ravenna, 126–27, 471n5
Ravensburg, 487
Raymond de la Côte, 436–40
Raymond of St. Gilles (d.1109), 295
Raymond Sabatié, 439
Reccesvinth, king (r.649-672), 64
Red Sandhill, 484
Register of Thomas of Hereford (1281), 367
Reims, 517
Remigius, 316
Remiremont, 284
Renaud de Trit, 454
Rerronianum, 127
Rethar of Paderborn (983-1009), 254
Reykjavik, 268
Reynald, prince, 336
Rhine valley, 286
Riccal, 306
Richard, prior, 431
Richard I the Lion-Heart (d.1199), 391n1
Richard II, king (r.1377-1399), 518, 520, 522–23
Richard of Anstey, 353
Richard of Lucé, 353
Riculf, priest, 66, 69
Riculf, subdeacon, 67–68
Ridwan of Aleppo, 294n4

Rigunth, queen, 68
Rikbert, 253
Ripon, 107
Rizzo, Antonio, 504
Robert d'Artois, 515
Robert de Sorbon, 448–50
Robert of Jumièges, 304
Roger de Rolveston (1195-1223), 366n1
Roger of Ledsham, 367
Roho, bishop of Angoulême (*c.*1020-*c.*1030), 214
Roland Bandinelli, later Pope Alexander III (1159-1181), 374, 376
Roman History [of Nicephorus Gregoras] (*c.*1350), 483
Romania, 294
Romanus I Lecapenus, emp. (r.920-944), 204, 227n1
Rome, 22, 85, 103, 105, 121, 125–27, 172, 176, 178n1, 251, 374,
    376–77, 411, 506, 509, 525, 536–37, 540–42
Romualdus, Saint, 472
Romulus, count of the Sacred Imperial Largesses, 13
Ronan, 106
Rotrudis, 212
Rouen, 304
Rufinianus, 100
Rufinus of Aquileia, 35n1
Rule of Arles, 52
Rule of St. Augustine, 367n1, 405, 532
Rule of St. Benedict, 28–35, 94, 186, 189n2, 208, 320, 321n7, 322,
    327n1, 427n7, 532
Rum. *See* Anatolia
Rumpold, duke of Glogów, 531
Runnymede, 378, 383
Rus, 237
Russia, 418, 420, 509
Russian Primary Chronicle (*c.*1113), 237
Rustichello, 422
Rusticus, Saint, 401

Sabaria, 43
Sabarthès, 440
Saffuriya, 337
Sage (Jesus son of Sirach), 328
Saint-Denis, church of, 400-03
Saint-Gilles, 298
Saix, 51, 54
Sakarya River, 494
Saladin (r.1171-1193), 334–38, 344, 447, 492
Salerno, 324
Salisbury, 353, 442
Sallust, 543
Salvius, bishop of Albi (*c.*571-584), 69
Samahin, 503
Samsa Chavush, 494
Samson, abbot (d.1211), 410
Sæmund the priest, 271
San Sisto, 429
Sanahuja, 221–22
Sandwich, 306